1999

Ethical Theory and Business

FIFTH EDITION

Edited by

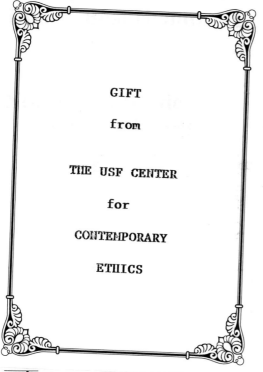

GIFT

from

THE USF CENTER

for

CONTEMPORARY

ETHICS

Prentice Hall
Upper Saddle River, New Jersey 07458

Library of Congress Cataloging-in-Publication Data

Ethical theory and business / edited by Tom L. Beauchamp, Norman E.
  Bowie.—5th ed.
      p.   cm.
  Includes bibliographical references.
  ISBN 0-13-398520-2
      1. Business ethics—United States.   2. Business ethics—United
States—Case studies.   3. Industries—Social aspects—United States.
4. Industries—Social aspects—United States—Case studies.
5. Commercial crimes—United States—Cases.   6. Consumer protection—
Law and legislation—United States—Cases.   I. Beauchamp, Tom L.
II. Bowie, Norman E.
HF5387.E82   1997
174′.4—dc20   97–8098
                                                                               CIP

Editorial/production supervision
   and interior design: *Bruce Hobart (Pine Tree Composition)*
Cover design: *Bruce Kenselaar*
Cover credit: Office buildings—blur effect.
               Photographer: *Pierre Yves Goavec*
               Photo courtesy of *The Image Bank*
Manufacturing buyer: *Nick Sklitsis*
Acquisitions editor: *Angela Stone*

© 1997, 1993, 1988, 1983, 1979 by Prentice-Hall, Inc.
Simon & Schuster/A Viacom Company
Upper Saddle River, New Jersey 07458

Printed in the United States of America

10   9   8   7   6

ISBN 0-13-398520-2

Prentice-Hall International (UK) Limited, *London*
Prentice-Hall of Australia Pty. Limited, *Sydney*
Prentice-Hall Canada Inc., *Toronto*
Prentice-Hall Hispanoamericana, S.A., *Mexico*
Prentice-Hall of India Private Limited, *New Delhi*
Prentice-Hall of Japan, Inc., *Tokyo*
Simon & Schuster Asia Pte. Ltd., *Singapore*
Editora Prentice-Hall do Brasil, Ltda., *Rio de Janeiro*

Contents

Chapter Six
HIRING, FIRING, AND DISCRIMINATING   361

AFFIRMATIVE ACTION AND REVERSE DISCRIMINATION

PAY EQUITY AND COMPARABLE WORTH

SEXUAL HARASSMENT

LEGAL PERSPECTIVES

CASES

Chapter Seven
GATHERING, CONCEALING, AND GILDING INFORMATION   443

DISCLOSING AND BLUFFING

Chapter Eight
ETHICAL ISSUES IN INTERNATIONAL BUSINESS   514

INTERNATIONAL NORMS

THE REGULATION OF INTERNATIONAL BUSINESS

LEGAL PERSPECTIVES

CASES

Preface

Ethical Theory and Business is now in its fifth edition and has been in print for two decades. The good fortune of this book has been made possible by the many comments and suggestions that loyal readers have given us for more than twenty years. We are very grateful for this help.

The changes in the fifth edition are not as radical as those in earlier editions. We have not added or jettisoned whole chapters, and our ordering of the chapters follows the fourth edition. Increased stability in the field is reflected in increased stability in the book. Nonetheless, each chapter does contain significant modifications to keep the book current and comprehensive. For example, we have added two articles on the Federal Sentencing Guidelines, an article on the ethical issues involved in doing business in Russia and Eastern Europe, and an article by a Japanese scholar that contrasts Japanese business ethics with American business ethics. Several of the chapters have also been reorganized to capture the current state of the literature.

In preparing this edition we have been ably assisted by several people who deserve recognition. Norman Bowie was assisted in bibliographical research and editorial matters by Jeffrey Smith. Tom Beauchamp was similarly assisted by Jeff Greene, Emily Wilson, Kier Olsen, and Moheba Hanif. Finally, we appreciate the anonymous reviewers arranged by the publisher as well as three thorough evaluations given directly to us by Thomas Carson, Dean E. Dowling, and J. David Newell. We also wish to recognize previous reviewers arranged by Prentice Hall who are now known to us: John R. Boatright, James E. Roper, Robert L. Cunningham, Jeffrey Barach, Robert Adler, Robert Ashmore, Michael A. Payne, and Michael S. Pritchard.

Tom L. Beauchamp
Norman E. Bowie

Chapter One

——— • ———

Ethical Theory and Business Practice

C AN LARGE BUSINESS organizations be just? Should the chief obligation of business be to look out for the bottom line? Is nonvoluntary employee drug testing immoral? How far should business go to protect and preserve the environment? These are some of the many questions that permeate discussions of the role of ethics in business.

The essays and cases in this book provide an opportunity to discuss these questions by reading and reflecting on influential arguments that have been made on these subjects. The goal of this first chapter is to provide a foundation in ethical theory sufficient for reading and critically evaluating the material in the ensuing chapters. The first part of this chapter introduces basic and recurring distinctions, definitions, and issues. The second part examines influential and relevant types of normative ethical theory. The third part discusses "the case method" as an exercise in moral reflection.

PART ONE: FUNDAMENTAL CONCEPTS AND PROBLEMS

Morality and Ethical Theory

Since the distinction between morality and ethical theory runs throughout this volume, it is important to distinguish them. This distinction is especially important in light of the fact that in classroom discussions of business ethics, the various participants insist on many different ways to make the distinction. The term *morality* refers to the principles or rules of moral conduct. Thus, the term *morality* has a broad meaning that extends beyond the rules in professional codes of conduct adopted by corporations and professional associations. *Morality* suggests a social institution, composed of a set of standards pervasively acknowledged by the members of a culture. In this understanding, morality is concerned with practices defining right and wrong. These practices, together with other kinds of customs, rules, and mores, are transmitted within cultures and institutions from generation to generation.

Morality, then, has an objective status as a body of guidelines for individual action. Similar to political constitutions and natural languages, morality exists prior to the acceptance (or rejection) of its standards by particular individuals. That is, individuals do not make their own rules; morality cannot be purely a personal policy or code.

The term *morality* fails to capture various aspects of moral reflection encountered in this volume. In contrast to morality, the terms *ethical theory* and *moral philosophy* suggest reflection on the nature and justification of right actions. These words refer to attempts to introduce clarity, substance, and precision of argument into the domain of morality. Many people go through life with an understanding of morality largely dictated by their culture. Other persons are not satisfied simply to conform to the morality of society. They want difficult questions answered: Is what our society forbids wrong? Are social values the best values? What is the purpose of morality? Does religion have anything to do with morality? Do the moral rules of society fit together in a unified whole? If there are conflicts and inconsistencies in our practices and beliefs, how should they be resolved? What should people do when facing a moral problem for which society has, as yet, provided no instruction?

Moral philosophers seek to answer such questions and to put moral beliefs and social practices of morality into a more unified and defensible package of guidelines and concepts. Sometimes this task involves challenging traditional moral beliefs by assessing the quality of moral arguments and suggesting modifications in existing beliefs. Morality, we might say, consists of what persons ought to do in order to conform to society's norms of behavior, whereas ethical theory concerns the philosophical reasons for or against the morality stipulated by society. Usually the latter effort centers on *justification:* Philosophers seek to justify a system of standards or some moral point of view on the basis of carefully analyzed and defended concepts and principles such as respect for autonomy, distributive justice, equal treatment, human rights, beneficence, and truthfulness.

Most moral principles are already embedded in public morality, but usually only in a vague and underanalyzed form. Justice is a good example. Recurrent topics in the pages of the *Wall Street Journal, Fortune, Business Week,* and other leading business journals often discuss the justice of the present system of corporate and individual taxation as well as the salaries paid to chief executive officers. However, an extended or detailed analysis of principles of justice is virtually never provided. Such matters are left at an intuitive level, where the correctness of a moral point of view is assumed, without argumentation. Yet the failure to provide anything more than superficial justification, in terms of intuitive principles learned from parents or peers, leaves people unable to defend their principles when challenged. In a society with many diverse views of morality, one can be fairly sure that one's principles will be challenged.

Thus the terms *ethical theory, philosophical ethics,* and even *moral philosophy* are reserved for philosophical theories that include reflection on and criticism of social morality.

What if the term *ethics* is used in contrast to *ethical theory?* Although many people distinguish *ethics* and *morality,* philosophers tend to use *ethics* as a general term referring to both moral beliefs and ethical theories. This philosophic practice is followed in this book.

Morality and Prudence

Many students do not encounter moral philosophy as a topic of study until college or graduate school. Morality, however, is learned by virtually every young child as part of the acculturation process. The first step in this process is learning to distinguish moral rules from rules of prudence (self-interest). This task can be difficult, because the two kinds of rules are taught simultaneously, without being distinguished by the children's teachers. For example, people are constantly reminded in their early years to observe rules such as, "Don't touch the hot stove," "Don't cross the street without looking both ways," "Brush your teeth after meals," and "Eat your vegetables." Most of these oughts and ought-nots are instructions in self-interest; that is, they are instructions in prudence. At the same time, however, people are given oughts or ought-nots of a moral kind. Parents, teachers, and peers teach that certain things *ought not* be done because they are "wrong" and that certain things *ought* to be done because they are "right." "Don't pull your sister's hair." "Don't take money from your mother's pocketbook." "Share your toys." "Write a thank-you note to Grandma." These moral instructions seek to control actions that affect the interests of other people. As people mature, they learn what society expects of them in terms of taking into account the interests of other people.

One of the most common observations in business is that self-interest and good ethics can coincide, because it is often in one's interest to act morally. This fact makes evaluating another's conduct difficult. A simple example of both moral and prudential reasoning at work in business is found in an executive decision at Procter and Gamble to take off the market its Rely brand tampons, which had been causally linked to toxic shock syndrome.[1] Procter and Gamble had invested twenty years of research and approximately $75 million in the product's preparation. At first, when scientific research offered some evidence that the material in the tampons did not encourage bacterial growth, Edward G. Harness, then chairman of the board and chief executive officer, said he was "determined to fight for a brand, to keep an important brand from being hurt by insufficient data in the hands of a bureaucracy."[2] However, Procter and Gamble later stopped production of the Rely tampon, in part because of negative publicity and also because of a report from the Center for Disease Control that statistically linked Rely to toxic shock syndrome, a report that Procter and Gamble's physicians, microbiologists, and epidemiologists were unable to refute.

"That was the turning point," Harness said. The company subsequently pledged its research expertise to the Center for Disease Control to investigate toxic shock syndrome and agreed to finance and direct a large educational program about the disease, as well as to issue a warning to women not to use Rely. Referring to the Rely case, Harness made the following public announcement:

> Company management must consistently demonstrate a superior talent for keeping profit and growth objectives as first priorities. However, it also must have enough breadth to recognize that enlightened self-interest requires the company to fill any reasonable expectation placed upon it by the community and the various concerned publics. Keeping priorities straight and maintaining the sense of civic responsibility will achieve important secondary objectives of the firm. Profitability and growth go hand in hand with fair treatment of employees, of direct customers, of consumers, and of the community.[3]

Here prudence and morality flow together, perhaps because an appeal to prudence persuades some in the audience, whereas an appeal to morality persuades others.

Such a mixture of moral language with the language of prudence is often harmless. Persons who are more concerned about the actions businesses take than about their motivations will be indifferent as to whether businesses use the language of prudence or the language of morality to justify what they do. The distinction is important to philosophers, though, because a business practice that might be prudential may nonetheless be morally wrong. History has shown how some actions that were long accepted or at least condoned in the business community have become condemned as immoral, for example, the discharge of pollution into the air and water, plant relocation purely for economic gain, and large political contributions to people of influence.

Because businesses exist within a larger social framework, businesspeople must reflect on the morality of their actions, not because it is prudent to do so but because it is right to do so. It is generally believed that acting morally is in the interest of business, and thus prudence seems to be a justifiable motive for acting ethically. However, throughout this text the reader will see that prudence often suggests a different business decision than does morality.

Morality and Law

Business ethics in the United States is currently involved in an entangled, complex, and mutually stimulating relationship with law as illustrated in the legal cases reprinted at the ends of the following chapters. Morality and law share concerns over matters of basic social importance and often have in common certain principles, obligations, and criteria of evidence. Law is the public's agency for translating morality into explicit social guidelines and practices and for stipulating punishments for offenses. Chapter selections mention both case law (judge-made law expressed in court decisions) and statutory law (federal and state statutes and their accompanying administrative regulations). In these forms law has forced vital issues before the public. Case law, in particular, has established influential precedents that provide material for reflection on both legal and moral questions.

Some have said that corporate concern about business ethics can be reduced or eliminated by turning problems over to the legal department. The operative phrase here is this: "Let the lawyers decide; if it's legal, it's moral." Although this tactic would simplify matters, moral evaluation needs to be distinguished from legal evaluation. Despite an intersection between morals and law, the law is not the repository of a society's moral standards and values, even when the law is directly concerned with moral problems. A law-abiding person is not necessarily morally sensitive or virtuous, and the fact that something is legally acceptable does not imply that it is morally acceptable. For example, the doctrine of employment at will permits employers to fire employees for unjust reasons and is (within certain limits) legal, yet such firings are often morally unacceptable. Again, questions are raised in later chapters about the morality of business actions, such as plant relocation and mergers that cause unemployment, even though such actions are not illegal.

A typical example is the following: It was perfectly legal when Houston financier Charles E. Hurwitz doubled the rate of tree cutting in the nation's largest privately owned virgin redwood forest. He did so to reduce the debt he incurred when his company, the Maxxam Group, borrowed money to complete successfully a hostile takeover of Pacific Lumber Company, which owned the redwoods. Before the takeover, Pacific Lumber had followed a conservative cutting policy but nonetheless had consistently operated at a profit. Despite the clear legality of the new clear-cutting policy, it has been criticized as immoral.[4]

A related problem involves the belief that a person found guilty under law is therefore morally guilty. Such judgments are not necessarily correct but rather depend on the moral acceptability of the law on which the judgment has been reached. For example, before the Foreign Corrupt Practices Act was signed into law by President Jimmy Carter, slush funds, bribes, and the like had not been illegal for U.S. corporations dealing with foreign governments. Ever since the new legislation was enacted, an intense and still ongoing debate has surrounded the act's implications. It served to frustrate many businesses whose now illegal practices were deemed not only acceptable but also necessary to the conduct of business in various foreign cultures. Many businesspeople believe that the act put U.S. business firms at a competitive disadvantage, because other industrialized countries have no such laws. Many people today still believe there is nothing unethical or morally corrupt in these now illegal acts. The real problem, they contend, is a shortsightedness in the legislation.

Furthermore, the courts have often been accused, with some justification, of causing moral inequities through court judgments rendered against corporations. Here are some examples:[5] (1) Monsanto Chemical was successfully sued for $200 million, although the presiding judge asserted that there was no credible evidence linking Monsanto's Agent Orange to the severe harms that had been described in the case. (2) Chevron Oil was successfully sued for mislabeling its cans of paraquat, although the offending label conformed exactly to federal regulations, which permitted no other form of label to be used. (3) Although whooping cough vaccine indisputably reduces the risk of this disease for children who receive the vaccine, almost no manufacturer will produce it for fear of costly suits brought under product liability laws. In each of these instances it is easy to understand why critics have considered as morally unjustified various regulations, legislation, and decisions in case law. Taken together, these considerations lead to the following conclusion: If something is legal, it is not necessarily moral; if something is illegal, it is not necessarily immoral.

The Rule of Conscience

"I cannot in good conscience continue my . . . association with Mellon Bank Corporation," said J. David Barnes, a member of the bank's advisory board of directors, upon tendering his resignation.[6] Mellon Bank had offered to lend $150 million to T. Boone Pickens of Mesa Petroleum in his attempt to obtain control of Phillips Petroleum. In effect, Barnes resigned because he could not in good moral conscience condone the bank's money going to a person he regarded as a morally unscrupulous operator.

The slogan "Let your conscience be your guide" has long been, for many, what morality is all about. Yet, despite their admiration for persons of conscience, philosophers have typically judged appeals to conscience alone as insufficient and untrustworthy for ethical judgment. Consciences vary radically from person to person and time to time; moreover, they are often altered by circumstance, religious belief, childhood, and training. For example, Stanley Kresge, the son of the founder of S. S. Kresge Company — now known as the K-Mart Corporation — is a teetotaler for religious reasons. When the company started selling beer and wine, Kresge sold all his stock. His conscience, he said, would not let him make a profit on alcohol. The company, though, dismissed his objection as "his own business" and said that it sees nothing wrong with earning profits on alcohol.[7]

The reliability of conscience, then, is not self-certifying. Moral justification must be based on a source external to conscience itself. This external source is often the common morality or ethical theory, as we shall see.

Approaches to the Study of Morality

Morality and ethical theory can be studied and developed by a variety of methods, but three general approaches have dominated the literature. Two of these approaches describe and analyze morality, presumably without taking moral positions. The other approach takes a moral position and appeals to morality or ethical theory to underwrite judgments. These three approaches can be outlined as follows:

Descriptive approaches
Conceptual approaches
Prescriptive (normative) approaches

These categories do not express rigid and always clearly distinguishable approaches. Nonetheless, when understood as broad, polar, and contrasting positions, they can serve as models of inquiry and as valuable distinctions.

Social scientists often refer to the *descriptive approach* as the *scientific study* of ethics. Factual description and explanation of moral behavior and beliefs, as performed by anthropologists, sociologists, and historians, are typical of this approach. Moral attitudes, codes, and beliefs are described, to include corporate policies on sexual harassment, codes of ethics in trade associations, and so forth. Examples of this approach can be found in *Harvard Business Review* articles and *Forbes* magazine polls that report what business executives believe is morally acceptable and unacceptable.

The second approach involves the *conceptual study* of ethics. Here, the meanings of central terms in ethics such as *right, obligation, justice, good, virtue,* and *responsibility* are analyzed. Crucial terms in business ethics such as *liability* and *deception* can be given this same kind of careful conceptual attention. The proper analysis of the term *morality* (as defined at the beginning of this chapter) and the distinction between the moral and the nonmoral are typical examples of these conceptual problems.

The third approach, *prescriptive or normative ethics,* is a prescriptive study attempting to formulate and defend basic moral norms. Normative moral philosophy aims at determining what *ought* to be done, which needs to be distinguished from what *is,* in fact, practiced. Ideally, an ethical theory provides reasons for adopting a whole system of moral principles or virtues. *Utilitarianism* and *Kantianism* are widely discussed theories, but they are not the only such theories. Utilitarians argue that there is but a single fundamental principle determining right action, which can be roughly stated as follows: "An action is morally right if and only if it produces at least as great a balance of value over disvalue as any available alternative action." Kantians, by contrast, have argued that one or more of these fundamental principles of ethics differ from the principle of utility, for instance, principles of obligation such as "Never treat another person merely as a means to your own goals." Both forms of these theories, together with other dimensions of ethical theory, are examined in Part Two of this chapter.

Principles of normative ethics are commonly used to treat specific moral problems such as abortion, famine, conflict of interest, mistreatment of animals, and racial and sexual discrimination. This use of ethical theory is often referred to, somewhat misleadingly, as *applied ethics.* Philosophical treatment of medical ethics, engineering ethics, journalistic ethics, jurisprudence, and business ethics involves distinct areas that employ general ethical principles to attempt to resolve moral problems that commonly arise in the professions.

Substantially the same general ethical principles apply to the problems across professional fields and in areas beyond professional ethics as well. One might appeal to principles of justice, for example, to illuminate and resolve issues of taxation, health care distribution, environmental responsibility, criminal punishment, and reverse discrimination. Similarly, principles of veracity (truthfulness) apply to debates about secrecy and deception in international politics, misleading advertisements in business ethics, balanced reporting in journalistic ethics, and disclosure of illness to a patient in medical ethics. Increased clarity about the general conditions under which truth must be told and when it may be withheld would presumably enhance understanding of moral requirements in each of these areas.

The exercise of sound judgment in business practice together with appeals to ethical theory are central in the essays and cases in this volume. Rarely is there a straightforward "application" of principles that mechanically resolves problems. Principles are more commonly *specified,* that is, made more concrete for the context, than applied. Much of the best work in contemporary business ethics involves arguments for how to specify principles to handle particular problems.

Justification in Ethics

Almost everyone interested in moral problems asks questions about whether certain views can be justified. What, then, counts as adequate justification? An easy answer to this question is that moral judgments are justified by giving reasons for them. However, not all reasons are good reasons, and not all good reasons are sufficient for justification. For example, a good reason for regulating various business practices, such as those of industries involved in the use of radioactive products, is that radioactivity presents a clear and present danger to others. Many believe that this reason is also sufficient to justify a broad set of regulatory practices, such as government protections against environmental contamination. But is it?

There is a good reason against government regulation: it involves a deprivation of liberty; it takes away the freedom to act in any way one wishes to act. To counter the contention that government regulation is undesirable because it involves a deprivation of liberty, there would have to be additional reasons given to justify the deprivation of liberty. Consider, for example, the dire consequences to the public interest if government fails to intervene or the importance of protecting against inadvertent tragedies, such as the near disaster at the Three Mile Island nuclear generating station. A set of reasons is then offered to defend this perspective on the issues. In the example about radioactive materials, the set of *good* reasons for regulation might or might not count as *sufficient* justification for regulation, depending on the quality of the argument.

Every human belief is subject to challenge and, therefore, stands in need of justification by reasoned argument. But just as there are good and bad reasons, there are good and bad arguments. One must know whether the premises upon which these arguments rest are acceptable in order to know whether an argument proves or justifies anything. Are there such person-neutral premises?

Relativism and Objectivity of Belief

Some writers on ethics have contended that moral views simply express how one feels or how a culture accommodates the desires of its people. These sentiments are informal expressions of an important challenge to ethical theories: relativism.

Individual relativists claim that what an individual person thinks is right or wrong *really is* right or wrong for that person. Cultural relativists, on the other hand, believe that whatever a culture thinks is right or wrong *really is* right or wrong for that culture. Thus if the Swedish tradition allows abortion, then abortion really is morally permissible in Sweden, and if the Irish tradition forbids abortion, then abortion really is wrong in Ireland. If cultural relativism is correct, then there is no criterion independent of one's culture for determining whether a practice really is right or wrong. Some who have accepted cultural relativism believe that proper conduct in a world with widely differing moral practices is exhibited in the adage "When in Rome do as the Romans do."

Relativism has been defended because moral standards certainly do vary from place to place. In the early part of the twentieth century, defenders of relativism used the discoveries of anthropologists in the South Sea Islands, Africa, and South America as evidence of how widely moral practices vary throughout the world. More recently some spokespersons in Asia have criticized what they perceive as the attempt of Westerners to impose standards of morality on Asian countries. For example, Kishore Mahbubani, Singapore's permanent secretary of foreign affairs, has said, "to have good government, you often need less, not more democracy."[8]

Despite the remarks of Secretary Mahbubani and others, there have been many recent attempts by both government agencies and multinational corporations to promulgate international codes of business conduct that surmount relativism. These efforts will be discussed more fully in Chapter 8.

Moreover, moral philosophers have tended to reject relativism, and it is important to understand why. First, what does the argument from the fact of cultural diversity reveal? When early anthropologists probed beneath surface disagreements, they often discovered agreement on deeper levels. For example, one anthropologist discovered a tribe in which parents, after raising their children and when still in a relatively healthy state, would climb a high tree. Their children would then shake the tree until the parents fell to the ground and died. This cultural practice seems vastly different from Western practices. The anthropologist discovered, however, that the tribe believed that people went into the afterlife in the same bodily state in which they left this life. Their children, who wanted them to enter the afterlife in a healthy state, were no less concerned about their parents than are children in Western cultures. Although cultural disagreement exists concerning the afterlife, there is no ultimate moral disagreement over the moral principles determining how children should treat their parents.

Thus, despite differing practices and beliefs, people often actually agree about ultimate moral standards. For example, personal payments for special services are common in some cultures and punishable as bribery in others; it is undeniable that these customs are different, but it does not follow that the underlying moral principles providing justification of the customs are different. The two cultures may agree about basic principles of morality, yet disagree about how to live by these principles in particular situations.

This analysis implies that a fundamental conflict between cultural values could occur only if cultural disagreements about proper principles or rules exist at

the deepest level of moral rules. It does not follow that the underlying moral standards differ even if beliefs, judgments, or actions do differ. People may differ because they have different factual beliefs rather than different normative standards.
For instance, individuals differ over appropriate actions to protect the environment, not because they have different sets of standards about environmental ethics
but because they hold different factual views about how certain discharges of
chemicals and airborne particles will or will not harm the environment. Identical
sets of normative standards might be invoked in their arguments about environmental protection, yet different policies and actions might be recommended.

It is necessary, then, to distinguish *relativism of judgments* from *relativism of
standards*. This distinction rests on the fact that many different particular judgments call upon the same general standards for their justification. Moreover, relativism of judgment is so pervasive in human social life that it would be foolish to
deny it. However, when people differ about whether to buy one brand of telephone over another, it does not follow that they have different standards for telephones. Perhaps one person has had success with AT&T products in the past,
whereas another person has not. Similarly in ethics, people may differ about
whether one policy for keeping hospital information confidential is more acceptable than another, but it does not follow that they have different moral standards
of confidentiality. The people may hold the same moral standard on protecting
confidentiality but differ over how to implement that standard.

However, these observations do not decide whether a relativism of standards
provides the most adequate account of morality. If moral conflict did turn out to
be fundamental, such conflict could not be removed even if there were perfect
agreement about the facts, concepts, and background beliefs of a case.

Suppose, then, that disagreement exists at the deepest level of moral thinking, that is, suppose that two cultures disagree on basic or fundamental norms. It
still does not follow from this relativity of standards that there is no ultimate norm
or set of norms in which everyone *ought* to believe. Consider the following analogy
to religious disagreement: from the fact that people have incompatible religious or
atheistic beliefs, it does not follow that there is no single correct set of religious or
atheistic propositions. Nothing more than skepticism seems justified by the facts
about religion that are adduced by anthropology; and nothing more than this
skepticism would be justified if fundamental conflicts of belief were discovered in
ethics.

Cultural Objectivity and Moral Stultification. People can evaluate various (but
not all) problems of relativism by focusing on (1) the objectivity of morals within
cultures and (2) the stultifying consequences of a serious commitment to moral
relativism. Because the first focus provides an argument against individual relativism and the second provides an argument against cultural relativism, each
should be considered independently.

It was noted previously that morality is concerned with practices of right and
wrong transmitted within cultures from one generation to another. The terms of
social life are set by these practices, whose rules are pervasively acknowledged and

shared in that culture. Within the culture, then, is a significant measure of moral objectivity, because morality by its nature does not exist through a person's individual preferences. Individuals cannot create morality by stipulation or correctly call a personal policy a morality. Such moral individualism is as dubious as anarchism in politics and law, and few readily accept a declaration that a person's political and legal beliefs are legitimately determined by that person alone. Nor can a corporation develop professional ethics alone. A hospital corporation like Humana cannot draw up a code brushing aside either the confidentiality of patient information or the requirement of obtaining adequate consents before surgery. Similarly, a brokerage house cannot simply define a conflict of interest according to its institutional preference. If these codes deviate significantly from standard or accepted rules, they must be rejected as subjective and mistaken.

Room for invention or alteration in morality is restricted by the broader understanding of morality in culture. Rules cannot be *moral* standards simply because an individual so labels them. Because individual relativism claims that they can be invented or labelled, this theory seems both *conceptually* and *factually* mistaken.

Our discussion now can shift to the second argument, which is directed at cultural relativism and which projects the pragmatic consequences of accepting cultural relativism, especially if it would prevent serious reflection on, and resolution of, moral problems. In circumstances of disagreement, moral reflection would be in order whether or not cultural relativism is true. When two parties argue about some serious, divisive, and contested moral issue — for example, conflicts of interest in business — people tend to think that some fair and justified compromise may be reached. People seldom infer from the mere fact of a conflict between beliefs that there is no way to judge one view as correct or as better argued than the other. The more absurd the position advanced by one party, the more convinced others become that some views are mistaken or require supplementation. People seldom conclude that there is no correct ethical perspective or reasonable negotiation.

Moreover, it seems that there is a set of basic moral principles that every culture must adopt. There would be no culture unless the members of the group adopted these moral principles. Consider an anthropologist who arrives on a populated island: how many tribes are on the island? To answer that question, the anthropologist tries to determine whether people on some parts of the island are permitted to kill, commit acts of violence against, or steal from persons on other parts of the island. If such behavior is not permitted, that prohibition counts as a reason for saying that there is only one tribe. The underlying assumption is that a set of moral principles exists that must be followed if there is to be a culture at all. With respect to those moral principles, adhering to them determines whether or not there is a culture.

However, what justifies these principles? A moral relativist would say that a culture justifies them, but there cannot be a culture unless the members of the culture follow the principles. Thus, it is reasonable to think that justification lies elsewhere.

Even if cultural relativism, interpreted as a relativism of standards, is not pragmatically acceptable, moral disagreement among cultures and individuals is common. Since moral philosophy is committed to reasoned debate and the resolution of moral conflict, what methods can be used to reduce moral disagreements? Ethical theories are examined in Part Two of this chapter, but because some methods for resolving moral disagreements are independent of specific moral theories, they will be presented now.

Moral Disagreements

In any pluralistic culture, dilemmas involving conflicts of value exist. In this volume a few of these dilemmas are examined, such as withholding pertinent information in business deals, whistle-blowing in industry, advertising on children's television, practicing preferential hiring policies, and the like. Although some disagreements seem overwhelming, there are ways to resolve them or at least to reduce the level of disagreement. The following sections discuss several methods that have been employed in the past to deal constructively with moral disagreements, each of which deserves recognition as a method of easing disagreement and conflict.

Obtaining Objective Information. Many moral disagreements can be at least partially resolved by obtaining additional factual information on which moral controversies turn. Earlier it was shown how useful such information can be in trying to ascertain whether cultural variations in belief are fundamental. Unfortunately, it has often been assumed that moral disputes are by definition produced solely by differences over moral principles or their application, and not by a lack of scientific or factual information. This assumption is misleading, inasmuch as moral disputes, that is, disputes over what morally ought or ought not to be done, often have nonmoral elements as their main ingredients. For example, debates over the allocation of tax dollars to prevent accidents or disease in the workplace often become bogged down in factual issues of whether particular measures such as the use of masks or lower levels of toxic chemicals actually function best to prevent death and disease.

In a publicized controversy over the morality of "exaggerated claims" in advertising, the Federal Trade Commission (FTC) alleged that the Standard Oil Company of California (SOCAL) was guilty of intentionally misleading the public with its commercials for Chevron gasoline containing the additive F-310. Among the most damaging of the FTC's charges was the claim that SOCAL was falsely representing its F-310 additive as a unique product, thereby deceiving and misleading the public. Preliminary conferences and investigations, however, substantiated the validity of SOCAL's claims regarding its product's uniqueness, and the FTC thereupon withdrew its demonstrably unfounded charges. Although the dispute regarding other aspects of the F-310 advertising campaign continued, the appeal to the facts narrowed and focused the ground of disagreement and advanced the moral and legal controversy toward a resolution.

Controversial issues such as the use of Nutrasweet in diet sodas; the presence of toxic substances in the workplace; the fluoridation of public waters; and the manufacture, dissemination, and advertisement of vaccines for medical use are laced with issues of both values and facts. The arguments used by disagreeing parties may turn on a dispute about liberty or justice and therefore may be primarily moral; but they may also rest on factual disagreements over, for example, the efficacy of a product. Information may thus have only a limited bearing on the resolution of some controversies, yet it may have a direct and almost overpowering influence in others.

Definitional Clarity. Sometimes controversies have been settled by reaching conceptual or definitional agreement over the language used by disputing parties. Controversies discussed in Chapter 6 over the morality of affirmative action, reverse discrimination, and comparable worth, for example, are often needlessly complicated because different senses of these expressions are employed, and yet disputing parties may have much invested in their particular definitions. If there is no common point of contention in such cases, parties will be addressing entirely separate issues through their conceptual assumptions. Often these parties will not have a bona fide moral disagreement.

Although conceptual agreement provides no guarantee that a dispute will be settled, it should at least facilitate direct discussion of the outstanding issues. For this reason, many essays in this volume dwell at some length on problems of conceptual clarity.

Example-Counterexample. Resolution of moral controversies can also be aided by posing examples and opposed counterexamples, that is, by bringing forward cases or examples that are favorable to one point of view and counterexamples that are in opposition. For instance, in a famous case against AT&T a dispute over discriminatory hiring and promotion between the company and the Equal Employment Opportunities Commission (EEOC) was handled through the citation of statistics and examples that (allegedly) documented the claims made by each side. AT&T showed, for example, that 55 percent of the employees on its payroll were women and that 33 percent of all management positions were held by women. To sharpen its allegation of discriminatory practices in the face of this evidence, the EEOC countered by citing a government study demonstrating that 99 percent of all telephone operators were female, whereas only 1 percent of craft workers were female. Such use of example and counterexample serves to weigh the strength of conflicting considerations.

Analysis of Arguments and Positions. Finally, a serviceable method of philosophical inquiry is that of exposing the inadequacies in and unexpected consequences of arguments and positions. A moral argument that leads to conclusions that a proponent is not prepared to defend and did not previously anticipate will have to be changed, and the distance between those who disagree will perhaps be reduced by this process. Inconsistencies not only in reasoning but also in organizational schemes or pronouncements can be uncovered. However, in a context of controversy, sharp attacks or critiques are unlikely to eventuate in an agreement unless a climate of reason prevails. A fundamental axiom of successful negotiation is "reason and be open to reason." The axiom holds for moral discussion as well as any other disagreement.

No contention is made here that moral disagreements can always be resolved or that every reasonable person must accept the same method for approaching such problems. Many moral disagreements may not be resolvable by any of the four methods that have been discussed. A single ethical theory or method may never be developed to resolve all disagreements adequately, and the pluralism of cultural beliefs often presents a considerable barrier to the resolution of issues. Given the possibility of continual disagreement, the resolution of crosscultural conflicts such as those faced by multinational corporations may prove especially elusive. However, if something is to be done about these problems, a resolution seems more likely to occur if the methods outlined in this section are used.

The Problem of Egoism

Attitudes in business have often been deemed fundamentally egoistic. Executives and corporations are said to act from prudence — that is, each business is out to promote solely its own interest. Some people say that the corporation has no other interest, because its goal is to be as successful in competition as possible.

The philosophical theory called *egoism* has familiar origins. Each person has been confronted, for example, with occasions on which a choice must be made between spending money on oneself or on some worthy charitable enterprise. When one elects to purchase new clothes for oneself rather than contribute to a university scholarship fund for poor students, self-interest is being given priority over the interests of others. Egoism generalizes beyond these occasions to all human choices. The egoist contends that all choices either involve or should involve self-promotion as their sole objective. Thus, a person's or a corporation's only goal and perhaps only obligation is self-promotion. No sacrifices or obligations are owed to others.

Psychological Egoism. There are two main varieties of egoism, psychological egoism and ethical egoism. Psychological egoism is the view that everyone is always motivated to act in his or her perceived self-interest. This factual theory regarding human motivation offers an explanation of human conduct, in contrast to a justification of human conduct. It claims that people always do what pleases them or what is in their interest. Popular ways of expressing this viewpoint include the following: "People are at heart selfish, even if they appear to be unselfish"; "People look out for Number One first"; "In the long run, everybody does what he or she wants to do"; and "No matter what a person says, he or she acts for the sake of personal satisfaction."

Psychological egoism presents a serious challenge to moral philosophy. If this theory is correct, there may be no purely altruistic moral motivation. Normative ethics (with the exception of ethical egoism) presupposes that people ought to behave in accordance with certain moral principles, whether or not such behavior promotes their own interests. If people *must act* in their own interest, to ask them to do otherwise would be absurd. Accordingly, if psychological egoism is true, the whole enterprise of normative ethics is futile.

Those who accept psychological egoism are convinced by their observation of themselves and others that people are entirely self-centered in their motivation. Conversely, those who reject the theory do so not only because they see many examples of altruistic behavior in the lives of friends, saints, heroes, and public servants but also because contemporary anthropology, psychology, and biology offer many compelling studies of sacrificial behavior. Even if it is conceded that people are basically selfish, critics of egoism say it seems undeniable that there are at least some outstanding examples of preeminently unselfish actions such as when corporations cut profits in order to provide public services (see Chapter 2) and when employees "blow the whistle" on unsafe or otherwise improper business practices even though they could lose their jobs and suffer social ostracism (see Chapter 5).

The defender of psychological egoism is not impressed by the exemplary lives of saints and heroes or by social practices of sacrifice. The psychological egoist maintains that all those persons who expend effort to help others, to promote fairness in competition, to promote the general welfare, or to risk their lives for the welfare of others are really acting to promote themselves; in loving others, they strengthen the love of others for themselves. By sacrificing for their children, parents receive satisfaction in their children's achievements. By following society's moral and legal codes, people avoid both the police and social ostracism.

Egoists maintain that no matter how self-sacrificing a person's behavior may at times seem, the desire behind the action is self-regarding. One is ultimately out for oneself, whether in the long or the short run, and whether one realizes it or not. Egoists view egoistic actions as perfectly compatible with behavior that others categorize as altruistic. For example, many corporations have adopted "enlightened self-interest" policies through which they are responsive to community needs and promote worker satisfaction to promote their corporate image and ultimately their earnings. The clever person or corporation can appear to be unselfish, but the action's true character depends on the *motivation* behind the appearance. Apparently altruistic agents may simply believe that an unselfish appearance best promotes their long-range interests. From the egoist's point of view, the fact that some (pseudo?) sacrifices may be necessary in the short run do not count against egoism.

Consider a typical example. In mid-1985 Illinois Bell argued before the Illinois Commerce Commission that its competitors should be allowed full access to markets and that there should be no regulation to protect Illinois Bell from its competitors. Illinois Bell had long been protected by such regulation, under which it had grown to be a successful $2.7 billion company. Why, then, was it now arguing that a complete free market would be the fairest business arrangement? *Forbes* magazine asked, "Is this 'altruism' or is it 'enlightened self-interest'?" *Forbes* editors answered that, despite the appearance of altruism, what Illinois Bell wanted was "to get the state regulators off their backs" so that the company would be able to compete more successfully with fewer constraints and to avoid losing business to large companies that could set up their own telephone systems. Self-interest, not fairness, was, according to *Forbes,* the proper explanation of Illinois Bell's behavior.[9]

Even if Illinois Bell's behavior is best explained as motivated by self-interest, it need not follow that all human behavior can best be explained as motivated by self-interest. The question remains, is psychological egoism correct? At one level this question can be answered only by empirical data — by looking at the facts. Significantly, there is a large body of evidence both from observations of daily practice and from experiments in psychological laboratories that counts against the universality of egoistic motivation.[10] The evidence from daily practice is not limited to heroic action but includes such mundane practices as voting and leaving tips in restaurants and hotels where a person does not expect to return and has nothing to gain.

When confronted with such conflicting empirical data, the dispute often is raised from the empirical level to the conceptual. It is tempting for the psychological egoist to make the theory necessarily true because of the difficulties in proving it to be empirically true. When confronted with what looks like altruistic acts, egoists may appeal to unconscious motives of self-interest or claim that every act is based on some desire of the person performing the act and that acting on that desire is what is meant by *self-interest.*

The latter explanation seems to be a conceptual or verbal trick: The egoist has changed the meaning of *self-interest.* At first, *self-interest* meant "acting exclusively on behalf of one's self-interest." Now the word has been redefined to mean "acting on any interest one has." Yet the central questions remain unresolved: Are there different kinds of human motives? Do people sometimes have an interest in acting for themselves and at other times on behalf of others, or do people act only for themselves? Philosophy and psychology have yet to establish that people never act contrary to perceived self-interest; for this reason psychological egoism remains a speculative hypothesis.

Ethical Egoism. Ethical egoism is a theory stating that the only valid standard of conduct is the obligation to promote one's well-being above everyone else's. Whereas psychological egoism is a descriptive, psychological theory about human motivation, ethical egoism is a normative theory about what people ought to do. According to psychological egoism, people always *do* act on the basis of perceived self-interest. According to ethical egoism, people always *ought* to act on the basis of perceived self-interest.

Ethical egoism is dramatically different from common morality. Consider maxims such as, "You're a sucker if you don't put yourself first and others second." This maxim is unacceptable by the norms of common morality, which requires that people return a lost wallet to a known owner and that they correct a bank loan officer's errors in their favor. Nevertheless, questions about why people should look out for the interests of others on such occasions have troubled many reflective persons. Some have concluded that acting against one's interest is contrary to reason. These thinkers, who regard conventional morality as tinged with irrational sentiment and indefensible constraints on the individual, are the supporters of ethical egoism. It is not their view that one should always ignore the interests of others but rather that one should consider the interests of others only when it suits one's own interests.

What would society be like if ethical egoism were the conventional, prevailing theory of proper conduct? Some philosophers and political theorists have argued that anarchism and chaos would result unless preventive measures were adopted. A classic statement of this position was made by the philosopher Thomas Hobbes. Imagine a world with limited resources, he says, where persons are approximately equal in their ability to harm one another and where everyone acts exclusively in his or her interest. Hobbes argued that in such a world everyone would be at everyone else's throat and society would be plagued by anxiety, violence, and constant danger. As Hobbes declared, life would be "solitary, poor, nasty, brutish, and short."[11] However, Hobbes also assumed that human beings are sufficiently rational to recognize their interests. To avoid the war of all against all, he urged his readers to form a powerful state to protect themselves.

Egoists accept Hobbes's view in the following form: Any clever person will realize that she or he has no moral obligations to others besides those obligations she or he voluntarily assumes. Each person should accept moral rules and assume specific obligations only when doing so promotes one's self-interest. Even if agreeing to live under a set of laws of the state that are binding on everyone, one should obey rules and laws only to protect oneself and to create a situation of communal living that is personally advantageous. One should also back out of an obligation whenever it becomes clear that it is to one's long-range disadvantage to fulfill the obligation. When confronted by a social revolution, the questionable trustworthiness of a colleague, or an incompetent administration at one's place of employment, no one is under an obligation to obey the law, fulfill contracts, or tell the truth. These obligations exist only because one assumes them, and one ought to assume them only as long as doing so promotes one's own interest.

In what ways can this form of ethical egoism be criticized? One criticism is that the theory gives incompatible directives in circumstances of moral conflict. If everyone were to act egoistically, it is likely that protracted conflicts would occur, just as many international conflicts now arise among nations primarily pursuing their own interests. According to ethical egoism, both parties in a circumstance of conflict ought to pursue their best interests exclusively, and it is morally right for both to do so. For example, it is in the interest of a consumer activist to stop production and distribution of an automobile of hazardous design; and at the same time, it is no less in the interest of the automobile manufacturer to prevent interruption of the production and distribution of the model. Egoism urges both parties to pursue their interests exclusively and holds both pursuits to be morally right.

The oddity of this situation can be highlighted by imagining that the consumer activist is an egoist. In order to be a consistent egoist, the activist must hold to a theory that the automobile manufacturer ought to pursue its interest, which would involve thwarting the activist's consumer objectives (all ought to pursue their interests and thwart others if necessary). In striving for theoretical consistency, the egoist supports a theory that works against his or her interest, and seems to fall into inconsistency. The egoist says that everyone ought to seek his or her maximal satisfaction, even if this pursuit would negatively affect the egoist's own pursuit of maximal satisfaction.

A plausible egoistic reply to this objection is that it springs from a misunderstanding of the rules and policies that an ethical egoist would promote. An arrangement whereby everyone acts on more or less fixed rules such as those found in conventional moral and legal systems would produce the most desirable state of affairs from an egoistic point of view. The reason is that such rules arbitrate conflicts and make social life more agreeable. These rules would include, for example, familiar moral and legal principles of justice that are intended to make everyone's situation more secure and stable.

Only an unduly narrow conception of self-interest, the egoist might argue, leads critics to conclude that the egoist would not willingly observe such rules of justice. If society can be structured to resolve personal conflicts through courts and other peaceful means, egoists will view it as in their interest to accept those binding social arrangements, just as they will perceive it as prudent to treat other individuals favorably in personal contacts. Notice that the egoist is not saying that his or her interests are served by promoting the good of others but rather is claiming that his or her personal interests are served by observing impartial rules irrespective of the outcome for others. Egoists do not care about the welfare of others unless it affects their welfare, and this desire for personal well-being alone motivates acceptance of the conventional rules of morality.

Egoistic Business Practices and Utilitarian Results. A different view from that of Hobbes, and one that has been extremely influential in the philosophy of the business community, is found in Adam Smith's economic and moral writings. Smith believed that the public good evolves out of a suitably restrained clash of competing individual interests. As individuals pursue their self-interest, the interactive process is guided by an "invisible hand," ensuring that the public interest is achieved. Ironically, according to Smith, egoism in commercial transactions leads not to the war of all against all but rather to a utilitarian outcome, that is, the largest number of benefits for the largest number of persons. The free market is, Smith thought, a better method of achieving the public good than the highly visible and authoritarian hand of Hobbes's all-powerful sovereign state.

Smith believed that government should be limited in order to protect individual freedom. At the same time, he recognized that concern with freedom and self-interest could get out of control. Hence, he proposed that minimal state regulatory activity is needed to provide and enforce the rules of the competitive game. Smith's picture of a restrained egoistic world has captivated many people in the business and economic community. They, like Smith, do not picture themselves as selfish and indifferent to the interests of others, and they recognize that a certain element of cooperation is essential if their interests are to flourish. These people recognize that when their interests conflict with the interests of others, they should pursue their interests within the established rules of the competitive game. Within the rules of business practice, they understand ethics as the maxims of a suitably restrained egoist. Their view is egoistic because it is based on the active pursuit of personal interest. It is restrained because self-interest is kept within the bounds of the prevailing rules of business for the sake of the common good.

Many people in the business community have actively supported the view that a restrained egoism leads to commendable utilitarian outcomes. This is one of the defenses of a free market economy; competition advances the good of corporations, and competition among individual firms advances the good of society as a whole. Hence, a popular view of business ethics might be captured by the phrase "Ethical egoism leads to utilitarian outcomes." As Smith said, corporations and individuals pursuing their individual interests also thereby promote the public good, so long as they abide by the rules that protect the public.

A controversial figure who defends his actions through this line of argument is the previously mentioned T. Boone Pickens, chairman of Mesa Petroleum Company. Pickens is a corporate "raider," who works to spot undervalued corporations and then threatens to take them over. Using speculative stock purchases and hostile tender offers, raiders such as Pickens strike fear in the hearts of corporate managers, who sometimes modify their growth plans to defend the corporation from the takeover attempt. Pickens believes that he is simply drawing attention to undervalued companies whose true value comes to light through his activities, benefiting the stockholders (the only owners of public corporations in his view), whose stock suddenly increases in monetary value. Pickens's immediate ambition is self-interest in gaining profit for himself and his company, but he claims that the public is a large benefactor of his efforts to improve his own financial position.

Many corporate managers vigorously disagree with Pickens, and many also disagree with the confident optimism underlying Adam Smith's more general perspective. Furthermore, they reject all forms of egoism. We can begin to understand their reservations by turning at this point to the study of ethical theory, and to utilitarian ethical theories in particular.

PART TWO: NORMATIVE ETHICAL THEORY

The central question discussed in Part Two is the following: What constitutes an acceptable ethical standard for business practice, and by what authority is the standard acceptable? One time-honored answer is that the acceptability of a moral standard is determined by prevailing practices in business or by authoritative, profession-generated documents such as codes. Many businesspersons find this viewpoint congenial and therefore do not see the need for revisions in practices that they find comfortable and adequate.

Professional standards, which do play a role in business ethics, will be discussed in some detail. Ultimately, however, these standards need to be justified in terms of independent ethical standards, just as the moral norms of a culture need to be justified. For this reason, the later parts in this section are devoted to a discussion of widely discussed theories and analyses of morality in the history of philosophy.

The Role of Professional Standards

The professional practice standard holds that obligations and other standards of moral conduct are determined by the customary practices of a professional community. Proponents of this standard argue that a businessperson is charged with various responsibilities — for example, avoiding harm, honoring warranties, removing conflicts of interest, and obeying legal requirements — and that they must use proper professional criteria for determining appropriate actions. Professional custom establishes the standards of obligatory conduct such as "due care." Any person without expert knowledge is unqualified to determine what should be done, and for this reason the professional community is the appropriate source. This rule is applied to determine the obligation of due care in a person's performance when wrong conduct is suspected. For example, the standard is used by courts to assess responsibility and liability for harm in negligence cases, usually because a client, patient, or customer seeks to punish the responsible party, to be compensated, or both. Professional malpractice is an instance of negligence in which professional standards of care have not been followed, as when an accountant fails to follow accepted accounting practices.

One area of uncertainty in contemporary business involves a failure by professionals, such as accountants, to probe deeply enough into an investigative report, thereby harming those who do not receive the information that the professional had some responsibility to uncover. For example, since a scandal at McKesson & Robbins in 1940, the Securities and Exchange Commission (SEC) has held that an accountant performing a corporate audit has an obligation to uncover gross management overstatements. Although accountants have long resisted the standard that they are guilty of negligence for overlooking management fraud, some recent legal cases have suggested that the courts expect accountants to uncover fraud when it is detectable. Auditors failing to notice red flags of suspicious conduct are held responsible for harms that result from their oversight, according to this stringent SEC standard.

Despite its popularity in business, the professional practice standard has shortcomings. This particular standard of duty (and negligence) would clearly be too high for some areas of practice. Even when the utmost care is exercised in some circumstances, a critical factor may have been omitted or distorted because of lack of access to sources or documents. Whether a customary standard of disclosure exists within the relevant fields of business is questionable, and it has not been decided how much consensus is required to establish such a standard, that is, how much consensus is needed for a norm to count as a standard prevalent in practice.

A further objection is that negligent care might be perpetuated if professionals in the same field offer the same inferior set of precautions, warranties, technology, and auditing strategies, whether through ignorance, as a genuine conviction, or for reasons of professional solidarity. If the elements of negligent behavior are to serve as a workable model for business decisions, the prevailing established obligations cannot be set at such a low level that virtually any conduct is acceptable.

Another objection centers on a basic assumption of the professional practice standard, that relevant professionals have sufficient expertise to recognize the proper precautions, information, warranties, auditing strategies, and so forth. This assumption is empirical, yet there are no reliable data on these issues, and current research on the effects of professional standards is both sketchy and inconclusive. It is also doubtful whether professional standards should be set by the professionals themselves when they do possess the relevant expertise. Customers, employees, and consumers generally desire more detailed disclosures or more extensive precautions, as standards of due care, than do professionals in practice. Decisions about due care are not even professional judgments, but rather ethical ones, and critics have a point in maintaining that they should not be made by the professional alone, or even primarily.

For example, drug use in the workplace has now become a serious national problem. What should a manager do to ensure a clean workplace unimpaired by drug use? Drug-use programs are becoming a commonly accepted business practice, but under what conditions are they morally acceptable? There are a number of relevant perspectives to consider. Some assessments focus on the consequences of implementing a drug-testing program. According to these assessments, the moral manager must compare the drug-testing program with other viable alternatives for dealing with drug abuse by employees. The good and bad consequences of each policy must then be determined in a way that enables the manager to choose the policy that provides the greatest balance of good over bad consequences. This choice is made irrespective of whether it conforms to standards of professional practice; indeed, the standards have merit only if they have the best consequences. Many people in the business community refer to this kind of reasoning as cost-benefit analysis. Ethical theorists who reason in this way are called utilitarians.

Utilitarian Theories

Utilitarian theories hold that the moral worth of actions or practices is determined solely by their consequences. An action or practice is right if it leads to the best possible balance of good consequences over bad consequences for all the parties affected. In taking this perspective, utilitarians believe that the purpose or function of morality is to promote human welfare by minimizing harms and maximizing benefits.

The first developed utilitarian philosophical writings were those of David Hume (1711–1776), Jeremy Bentham (1748–1832), and John Stuart Mill (1806–1873). Mill's *Utilitarianism* (1863) is still today considered the major theoretical exposition. Mill discusses two foundations or sources of utilitarian thinking: a *normative* foundation in the principle of utility and a *psychological* foundation in human nature. He proposes the principle of utility — the "greatest happiness principle" — as the foundation of normative ethical theory. Actions are right, Mill says, in proportion to their tendency to promote happiness or absence of pain, and wrong insofar as they tend to produce pain or displeasure. According to Mill, pleasure and freedom from pain are alone desirable as ends. All desirable things (which are numerous) are desirable either for the pleasure inherent in them or as means to promote pleasure and prevent pain.

Mill's second foundation derives from his belief that most persons, and perhaps all, have a basic desire for unity and harmony with their fellow human beings. Just as people feel horror at crimes, he says, they have a basic moral sensitivity to the needs of others. Mill sees the purpose of morality as tapping natural human sympathies to benefit others, while controlling unsympathetic attitudes that cause harm to others. The principle of utility is conceived as the best means to these basic human goals.

Essential Features of Utilitarianism. Several essential features of utilitarianism can be extracted from the reasoning of Mill and other utilitarians. First, utilitarianism is committed to the maximization of the good and the minimization of harm and evil. It asserts that society ought always to produce the greatest possible balance of positive value or the minimum balance of disvalue for all persons affected. The means to maximization is efficiency, a goal that persons in business find congenial, because it is highly prized throughout the economic sector. Efficiency is a means to higher profits and lower prices, and the struggle to be maximally profitable seeks to obtain maximum production from limited economic resources. The utilitarian commitment to the principle of optimal productivity through efficiency is an essential part of the traditional business conception of society and a standard part of business practice. In this respect the enterprise of business harbors a fundamentally utilitarian conception of the good society.

The need both to minimize harm and to balance risks against benefits has been a perennial concern of the business community. For example, executives in the petroleum industry know that oil and gas operations exist tenuously with wetlands areas, waterfowl, and fish. However, if the demands of U.S. consumers are to be met, corporate and public policies must balance possible environmental harms against the benefits of industrial productivity. Similarly, those in the nuclear power industry know that U.S. power plants are built with heavy containment structures to withstand internal failures; but they also recognize the possibility of a major disaster such as that at Chernobyl, then USSR, in 1986. Planning for such structures requires that the planners balance public benefits, probability of failure, and the magnitude of harm in the event of failure. The utilitarian believes that such examples from public policy exhibit a general truth about the moral life.

However, utilitarianism involves more than valuing efficiency, reducing evil, and maximizing positive outcomes in the tradeoff situation. A second essential feature of the utilitarian theory is *intrinsic value*. Efficiency itself is simply an instrumental good; that is, it is valuable strictly as a means to something else. In the corporation, efficiency is valuable as a means to growth and to profit maximization.

Within the free enterprise system of competing firms, efficiency is valuable as a means toward maximizing the production of goods and services. Within utilitarian ethical theory, efficiency is the means for maximizing human good.

But what is "good" according to the utilitarian? An answer to this question can be formed by considering the working of the New York stock market. Daily results on Wall Street are not intrinsically good. They are extrinsically good as a means to other ends, such as financial security and happiness. Utilitarians believe that people ought to seek certain experiences and conditions that are good in themselves without reference to further consequences, and that all values are ultimately to be gauged in terms of these intrinsic goods. Health, friendship, and freedom from pain are included among such values. An intrinsic value is simply a value in life that people wish to possess and enjoy just for its sake and not as a means to something else.

However, utilitarians disagree concerning what constitutes the complete range of things or states that are good. Bentham and Mill are hedonists. They believe that only pleasure or happiness (synonymous for the purposes of this discussion) can be intrinsically good. Everything besides pleasure is instrumentally good to the end of pleasure. *Hedonistic* utilitarians, then, believe that any act or practice that maximizes pleasure (when compared with any alternative act or practice) is right. Later utilitarian philosophers, however, have argued that other values besides pleasure possess intrinsic worth, for example, friendship, knowledge, courage, health, and beauty. Utilitarians who believe in multiple intrinsic values are referred to as *pluralistic* utilitarians.

In recent philosophy, economics, and psychology, neither the approach of the hedonists nor that of the pluralists has prevailed. Both approaches have seemed relatively useless for purposes of objectively aggregating widely different interests. Another approach appeals to individual preferences. From this perspective, the concept of utility is understood, not in terms of states of affairs such as happiness, but in terms of the satisfaction of individual preferences, as determined by a person's behavior. In the language of business, utility is measured by a person's purchases or pursuits. To maximize a person's utility is to provide that which he or she has chosen or would choose from among the available alternatives. To maximize the utility of all persons affected by an action or a policy is to maximize the utility of the aggregate group.

Although the preference-based utilitarian approach to value has been viewed by many as superior to its predecessors, it is not trouble-free as an ethical theory. A major problem arises over morally unacceptable preferences. For example, an airline pilot may prefer to have a few beers before going to work, or an employment officer may prefer to discriminate against women, yet such preferences are morally intolerable. Utilitarianism based purely on subjective preferences is satisfactory, then, only if a range of acceptable preferences can be formulated. This latter task has proved difficult in theory, and it may be inconsistent with a pure preference approach. Should products like cigarettes, fireworks, and semiautomatic rifles be legally prohibited because they cause such harm even though many people would prefer to purchase them? How could a preference utilitarian answer this question?

One possible utilitarian response is to ask whether society is better off as a whole when these preferences are prohibited and when the choices of those desiring them are frustrated. If these products work against the larger objectives of utilitarianism (maximal public welfare) by creating unhappiness, the utilitarian could argue that preferences for these products should not be counted in the calculus of preferences. Preferences that serve to frustrate the preferences of others would then be ruled out by the goal of utilitarianism. As Mill argued, the cultivation of certain kinds of desires and the exclusion of antithetical desires are built into the ideal of utilitarianism.

A third essential feature of utilitarianism is its commitment to the measurement and comparison of goods. With the hedonistic view, people must be able to measure pleasurable and painful states and be able to compare one person's pleasures with another's to decide which is greater. Bentham, for example, worked out a measurement device that he called the *hedonic calculus*. He thought he could add the quantitative units of individual happiness, subtract the units of individual unhappiness, and thereby arrive at a total measure of happiness. By the use of this system it is allegedly possible to determine the act or practice that will provide the greatest happiness to the greatest number of people.

Act and Rule Utilitarianism.   Utilitarian moral philosophers are conventionally divided into two types — act utilitarians and rule utilitarians. An *act utilitarian* argues that in all situations, one ought to perform that act which leads to the greatest good for the greatest number. The act utilitarian regards rules such as "You ought to tell the truth in making contracts" and "You ought not to manipulate persons through advertising" as useful guidelines, but also as expendable in business and other relationships. An act utilitarian would not hesitate to break a moral rule if breaking it would lead to the greatest good for the greatest number in a particular case. *Rule utilitarians,* however, reserve a more significant place for rules, which they do not regard as expendable on grounds that utility is maximized in the circumstances.

There are many applications of both types of utilitarianism in business ethics.[12] Consider the following case in which U.S. business practices and standards run up against the quite different practices of the Italian business community. The case involves the tax problems encountered by the Italian subsidiary of a major U.S. bank. In Italy the practices of corporate taxation typically involve elaborate negotiations among hired company representatives and the Italian tax service, and the tax statement initially submitted by a corporation is regarded as a dramatically understated bid intended only as a starting point for the negotiating process. In the case in question, the U.S. manager of the Italian banking subsidiary decided, against the advice of locally experienced lawyers and tax consultants, to ignore the native Italian practices and file a conventional U.S.–style tax statement (that is, one in which the subsidiary's profits for the year were not dramatically understated). His reasons for this decision included his belief that the local customs violated the moral rule of truth telling.[13]

An act utilitarian might well take exception to this conclusion. Admittedly, to file an Italian-style tax statement would be to violate a moral rule of truth telling; but the act utilitarian would argue that such a rule is only a rule of thumb and can justifiably be violated to produce the greatest good. In the present case, the greatest good would evidently be done by following the local consultants' advice and conforming to the Italian practices. Only by following those practices will the appropriate amount of tax be paid. This conclusion is strengthened by the ultimate outcome of the present case. The Italian authorities forced the bank to enter into the customary negotiations, a process in which the original, truthful tax statement was treated as an understated opening bid, and a dramatically excessive tax payment was consequently exacted.

In contrast to the position of act utilitarians, rule utilitarians hold that rules have a central position in morality that cannot be compromised by the demands of particular situations. Such compromises threaten the general effectiveness of the rules, the observance of which maximizes social utility. An example of rule utilitarian reasoning is found in a case involving John Zaccaro, the husband of 1984 vice-presidential candidate Geraldine A. Ferraro. In late 1982, Zaccaro was appointed the guardian of an elderly woman's estate. For his business purposes, Zaccaro borrowed $175,000 from the estate to be repaid at 12 percent interest. The propriety of Zacarro's actions was questioned in court, where it was determined that he had not acted dishonestly or with malicious intent and may well have earned larger dividends for the woman than she would have reaped through more conservative investing. In effect, the court found that Zaccaro may have maximized the utility of everyone who was directly affected.

Nonetheless, Zaccaro had placed himself in a position of conflict of interest, and the court found that "the rule is inflexible that a trustee shall not place himself in a position where his interest is or may be in conflict with his obligation." For his part, Zaccaro maintained that he acted in good faith and benefited the woman as best he could, but said, "I understand and accept the decision of the court that general principles of law must nevertheless be applied rigidly to guide the actions of other conservators."[14] In effect, both the judge and Zaccaro agreed that rule utilitarianism takes precedence over act utilitarianism. Even if Zaccaro had maximized everyone's utility in the circumstance, his act violated a basic, inflexible rule that had to take precedence.

For the rule utilitarian, then, actions are justified by appeal to abstract rules such as "Don't kill," "Don't bribe," and "Don't break promises." These rules, in turn, are justified by an appeal to the principle of utility. The rule utilitarian believes this position can escape the objections to act utilitarianism, because rules are not subject to change by the demands of individual circumstances. Utilitarian rules are in theory firm and protective of all classes of individuals, just as human rights are rigidly protective of all individuals regardless of social convenience and momentary need.

Act utilitarians, however, have a reply to these criticisms. They argue that there is a third option beyond ignoring rules and strictly obeying them, which is that the rules should be obeyed only sometimes. An example of this act utilitarian form of reasoning is found in the defense offered by A. Carl Kotchian, former president of Lockheed Corporation, of $12 million of "grease payments" made to high Japanese officials to facilitate sales of Lockheed's TriStar plane. Kotchian recognized that "extortion," as he called it, was involved and that U.S. rules of business ethics forbid such payments. Kotchian advanced these two arguments in defense of the payments: (1) "Such disbursements did not [at the time] violate American laws"; and (2) "the TriStar payments . . . would provide Lockheed workers with jobs and thus redounded to the benefit of their dependents, their communities, and stockholders of the corporation." Kotchian went on to argue that the financial consequences of "commercial success" and the public interest in both Japan and the United States were sufficient to override "a purely ethical and moral standpoint."[15] This is precisely the form of reasoning that rule utilitarians have generally rejected but act utilitarians have defended as at least meriting serious consideration. In the end, the act utilitarian view seems to invoke a prediction that society will be improved if people sometimes obey but sometimes disobey rules, because this kind of conduct will not fundamentally erode either moral rules or the general respect for morality.

However, it is appropriate to ask whether rule utilitarians can escape the very criticisms they level at act utilitarians. Rules often conflict. For example, rules of confidentiality conflict with rules protecting individual welfare. This issue surfaces in discussions of implementing genetic and drug-screening policies in the workplace. If the moral life were so ordered that everyone always knew which rules and rights should receive priority, there would be no serious problem for ethical theory. Yet such a ranking of rules seems impossible. Mill, who briefly considered this problem, held that the principle of utility should itself decide in any given circumstance which rule is to take priority. However, if this solution is accepted by rule utilitarians, their theory must, on some occasions, rely on the principle of utility to decide *directly* which actions are preferable to which alternatives in the absence of a governing rule. This view resembles those views associated with act reasoning rather than with rule reasoning.

Criticisms of Utilitarianism. A major problem for utilitarianism is whether units of happiness or some other utilitarian value can be measured and compared in order to determine the best action among the alternatives. In deciding whether to open a pristine national wildlife preserve to oil exploration and drilling, for example, how does one compare the combined value of an increase in the oil supply, jobs, and consumer purchasing power, with the value of wildlife preservation and environmental protection? How does a corporate public affairs officer decide how to distribute limited funds allocated for charitable contributions? If a corporate social audit (an evaluation of the company's acts of social responsibility) were attempted, how could the auditor measure and compare a corporation's ethical assets and liabilities?

Utilitarians have also encountered some problems with measurement. Economists, for example, either appropriated the word *utility* to denote the experience of satisfaction of preference or abandoned the word *utility* and talked about "preference ordering" instead. Many still doubt that construing utility in these ways resolves problems of measuring utilities. Suppose Jim prefers to spend his $0.97 on milk, and Sally prefers to spend her $0.97 on bread. Then suppose that Sally and Jim have only $1.30 to distribute between them. What can utilitarianism advise when utility is limited to preference ordering? It seems that no advice is possible unless some inferences are made that enable people to go from known preferences to other considerations of welfare and happiness.

The utilitarian reply to these criticisms is that the alleged problem is either a pseudoproblem or a problem that affects all ethical theories. People make crude, rough-and-ready comparisons of values every day, including those of pleasures and dislikes. For example, workers decide to go as a group to a bar rather than have an office party, because they think the bar function will satisfy more members of the group. Utilitarians acknowledge that accurate measurements of others' goods or preferences can seldom be provided because of limited knowledge and time. In everyday affairs such as purchasing supplies, administering business, or making legislative decisions, severely limited knowledge regarding the consequences of one's actions is often all that is available. It is crucial, from the utilitarian perspective, that a person conscientiously attempts to determine the most desirable action and then with equal seriousness attempts to perform that action.

Utilitarianism has also been criticized on the grounds that it ignores nonutilitarian factors that are needed to make moral decisions. Much of the remainder of this chapter considers these alleged sins of omission. The most prominent omission cited is a consideration of justice: The action that produces the greatest balance of value for the greatest number of people may bring about unjustified treatment of a minority. Suppose society decides that the public interest is served by denying health insurance of any sort to those testing positive for the AIDS virus. Moreover, in the interest of efficiency, suppose insurance companies are allowed to use as selective data lifestyle characteristics that are statistically associated with an enhanced risk of AIDS. Finally, suppose such policies would serve the larger public's financial interest. Utilitarianism seems to *require* that public law and insurance companies deny coverage to these AIDS victims. If so, would not this denial be unjust to those who have AIDS or are at high risk for contracting AIDS?

In the last opinion he wrote for the U.S. Supreme Court, former Chief Justice Warren Burger noted, "The fact that a given law or procedure is efficient, convenient and useful in facilitating functions of government, standing alone, will not save it if it is contrary to the Constitution. Convenience and efficiency are not the primary objectives, or the hallmarks, of democratic government."[16] Burger's criticism captures the essence of what many have argued against utilitarianism, that it fails to account for basic principles in documents such as the Bill of Rights in the U.S. Constitution that morally and legally cannot be modified in the name of efficiency, productivity, and convenience.

Utilitarians insist against such criticisms that all entailed costs and benefits of an action or practice must be weighed, including, for example, the costs that would occur from modifying a constitution or statement of basic rights. In a decision that affects employee and consumer safety, for example, the costs often include protests from labor and consumer groups, public criticism from the press, further alienation of employees from executives, the loss of customers to competitors, and the like. Also, rule utilitarians emphatically deny that narrow cost-benefit determinations are acceptable. Instead, they argue that general rules of justice (which are themselves justified by broad considerations of utility) ought to constrain particular actions or uses of cost-benefit calculations in all cases. Rule utilitarians maintain that the criticisms of utilitarianism previously noted are shortsighted because they focus on injustices that might be caused through a superficial or short-term application of the principle of utility. In a long-range view, utilitarians argue, promoting utility does not eventuate in overall unjust outcomes.

Kantian Ethics

Consider now a case involving the Plasma International Company.[17] After an earthquake in Nicaragua produced a sudden need for fresh blood, Plasma International supplied the blood from underdeveloped West African countries, paying the donors as little as 15 cents per pint. Because of the shortage in Nicaragua, Plasma sold the blood at a premium price. The transaction ultimately yielded the firm nearly a quarter of a million dollars in profits. What is it about Plasma International's conduct that provokes moral outrage?

Immanuel Kant's (1724–1804) ethical theory may help clarify the basis of this outrage. It is likely that Kant would argue that Plasma International treated human beings as though they were merely machines or capital and seemed to deny people the respect appropriate to their dignity as rational human beings. Kant's respect-for-persons principle says that persons should be treated as ends and never purely as means. Failure to respect persons is to treat them as a means in accordance with one's *own* ends, and thus as if they were not independent agents. To exhibit a lack of respect for a person is either to reject the person's considered judgments, to ignore the person's concerns and needs, or to deny the person the liberty to act on those judgments. For example, manipulative advertising that attempts to make sales by interfering with the potential buyer's reflective choice violates the principle of respect for persons.

In Kantian theories respect for the human being is said to be necessary — not just as an option or at one's discretion — because human beings possess a moral dignity and therefore should not be treated as if they had merely the conditional value possessed by machinery, industrial plants, robots, and capital. This idea of "respect for persons" has sometimes been expressed in corporate contexts as "respect for the individual." An example is found in Hewlett-Packard, a U.S. firm that has been praised for its employee relationships. Because Hewlett-Packard does not fire employees (instead, it uses partial-hour layoffs and similar strategies) and attempts to make the corporate setting as pleasant as possible for workers, its employees tend to be tenaciously loyal and highly productive. Hewlett-Packard has by gained a reputation as a corporation that respects rather than exploits the individual.

Some have interpreted Kant to hold categorically that people can never treat other persons as a means to their ends. This interpretation, however, is a misrepresentation. Kant did not categorically prohibit the use of persons as means to the ends of other people. He argued only that people must not treat other persons *exclusively* as means to ends. When employees are ordered to perform odious tasks, they are being treated as a means to an employer's or a supervisor's ends, but the employees are not exclusively used for others' purposes because they are not mere servants or objects. Kant's principle demands only that such persons be treated with the respect and moral dignity to which every person is entitled, including those times when they are used primarily as a means to the ends of others.

Kant's principle finds *motives* for actions morally important, in that it expects persons to make the right decisions *for the right reasons*. If persons are honest only because they believe that honesty pays, their "honesty" is cheapened. Indeed, it seems like no honesty at all, only an action that appears to be honest. For example, when corporate executives announce that the reason they made the morally correct decision was because it was good for their business, this reason seems to have nothing to do with morality. According to Kantian thinking, if a corporation does the right thing only when (and for the reason that) it is profitable or when it will enjoy good publicity, its decision is prudential, not moral.

Consider the following three examples of three people making personal sacrifices for a sick relative. Fred makes the sacrifices only because he fears the social criticism that would result if he failed to do so. He hates doing it and secretly resents being involved. Sam, by contrast, derives no personal satisfaction from taking care of his sick relative. He would rather be doing other things and makes the sacrifice purely from a sense of obligation. Bill, by contrast, is a kind-hearted person. He does not view his actions as a sacrifice and is motivated by the satisfaction that comes from helping others. Assume in these three cases that the consequences of all the sacrificial actions are equally good and that the sick relatives are adequately cared for, as each agent intends. The question to consider is which persons are behaving in a morally praiseworthy manner. If utilitarian theory is used, this question may be hard to answer, especially if act utilitarianism is the theory in question, because the good consequences in each case are identical. The Kantian believes, however, that motives — in particular, motives of moral obligation — count substantially in moral evaluation.

It appears that Fred's motives are not moral motives but motives of prudence that spring from fear, although his actions have good and intended consequences. Fred does not, however, deserve any moral credit for his acts because they are not morally motivated. To recognize the prudential basis of an action does not detract from its good consequences. Given the purpose or function of the business enterprise, a motive of self-interest may be the most appropriate motive to ensure good consequences. The point, however, is that a business executive derives no special moral credit for acting in the corporate self-interest, even if society is benefited by and pleased by the action.

If Fred's motive is not moral, what about Bill's and Sam's? Here moral philosophers disagree. Kant maintained that moral action must be motivated by obligation alone. From this perspective, Sam is the only individual whose actions may be appropriately described as moral. Bill deserves no more credit than Fred, because Bill is motivated by sympathy and compassion, not by obligation. Bill is naturally kindhearted and has been well socialized by his family, but this motivation merits no moral praise from a Kantian, who believes that actions motivated by self-interest alone or compassion alone cannot be morally praiseworthy. To be deserving of moral praise, a person must act from obligation.

Kant insisted that all persons must act not only *in accordance with* obligation, but for the *sake* of obligation; that is, the person's motive for action must be a recognition of the duty to act. Kant tried to establish the ultimate basis for the validity of rules of obligation in pure reason, not in intuition, conscience, utility, or compassion. Morality provides a rational framework of principles and rules that constrain and guide all people, independent of their personal goals and preferences. He believed that all considerations of utility and self-interest are secondary, because the moral worth of an agent's action depends exclusively on the moral acceptability of the rule according to which the person is acting, or, as Kant preferred to say, moral acceptability depends on the rule that determines the agent's will.

An action has moral worth only if performed by an agent who possesses what Kant called a "good will." A person has a good will only if the sole motive for action is moral obligation, as determined by a universal rule. Kant developed this notion into a fundamental moral law: "I ought never to act except in such a way that I can also will that my maxim should become a universal law." Kant called this principle the *categorical imperative*. It is categorical because it admits of no exceptions and is absolutely binding. It is imperative because it gives instruction about how one must act. He gave several controversial examples of imperative moral maxims: "Do not lie," "Help others in distress," "Do not commit suicide," and "Work to develop your abilities."

Kant's strategy was to show that the acceptance of certain kinds of action is self-defeating, because *universal* participation in such behavior undermines the action. Some of the clearest cases involve persons who make a unique exception for themselves for purely selfish reasons. Suppose a person considers breaking a promise that would be inconvenient to keep. According to Kant, the person must first formulate her or his reason as a universal rule. The rule would say, "Everyone should break a promise whenever keeping it is inconvenient." Such a rule is contradictory, Kant held, because if it were consistently recommended that all individuals should break their promises when it was convenient for them to do so, the practice of making promises would be senseless. Given the nature of a promise, a rule allowing people to break promises when it becomes convenient makes the institution of promise-making unintelligible. A rule that allows cheating on an exam similarly negates the purpose of testing. For Kant, one does not keep promises because it pays or because one has a natural disposition to do so, but rather from respect for moral law that requires the obligation of promise keeping.

Kant's belief is that the conduct stipulated in these rules could not be made universal without some form of contradiction emerging. If a corporation kites checks to reap a profit in the way E. F. Hutton Brokerage did in a scandal that led to the end of the firm, the corporation makes itself an exception to the system of monetary transfer, thereby cheating the system, which is established by certain rules. This conduct, if carried out consistently by other corporations, violates the rules presupposed by the system, thereby rendering the system inconsistent. Kant's view is that actions involving invasion of privacy, theft, line cutting, cheating, kickbacks, and bribes are contradictory in that they are not consistent with the institutions or practices they presuppose.

Despite Kant's contributions to moral philosophy, his various accounts have been criticized as narrow and inadequate to handle various problems in the moral life. He has no place for moral emotions or sentiments such as sympathy and caring. Neither does Kant have much to say about moral character and virtue other than his comments on the motive of obligation. John Stuart Mill even argued that Kant's theory does not successfully avoid an appeal to the utilitarian consequences of an action in determining its moral standing. On Mill's interpretation, the categorical imperative demands that an action should be morally prohibited if the consequences of adopting it would be disutilitarian. Kant fails in the extreme, Mill argued, to support moral rules by appealing to the idea of consistency.

Some people also think that Kant emphasized universal obligations (obligations common to all people) at the expense of particular obligations (obligations that fall only on those in particular relationships or who occupy certain roles such as those of a business manager). Whereas the obligation to keep a promise is a universal obligation, the obligation to grade students fairly falls only on teachers. Many managerial obligations result from special roles played in business. For example, businesspersons tend to treat each customer according to the history of their relationship. If a person is a regular customer and the merchandise being sold is in short supply, the regular customer will be given preferential treatment because a relationship of commitment and trust has already been established. Japanese business practice has extended this notion to relations with suppliers and employees. At many firms, after a trial period, the regular employee has a job for life. Also, the bidding system is used infrequently in Japan. Once a supplier has a history with a firm, the firm is loyal to its supplier, and each trusts the other not to exploit the relationship.

However, considerations of particular obligations and special relationships may not be inconsistent with Kantianism because they may be formulated as universal. For example, the rule "Quality control inspectors have special obligations for customer safety" can be made into a "universal" law for all quality control inspectors. Although Kant wrote little about such particular duties, he would no doubt agree that a complete explanation of moral agency in terms of duty requires an account of *both* universal *and* particular duties.

A related aspect of Kant's ethical theory that has been scrutinized by philosophers is his view that moral motivation involves *impartial* principles. Impartial motivation may be distinguished from the motivation that a person might have for treating a second person in a certain way because the first person has a particular interest in the well-being of the second person (a spouse or good friend, for example). A conventional interpretation of Kant's work suggests that if conflicts arise between one's obligation and other motivations — such as friendship, reciprocation, or love — the motive of obligation should always prevail. Arguing against this moral view, some critics maintain that persons appropriately show favoritism to their loved ones and that they are entitled to do so. This criticism suggests that Kantianism (and utilitarianism as well) does not adequately account for those parts of the moral life involving intimate and special relationships.

The moral value of this concern can be illustrated by the following example. Imagine that you are sick in bed and then a good friend comes to visit and cheer you up. Because it was inconvenient for her to make the trip, you thank her for coming. She tells you to think nothing of it. It is, she says, her obligation to visit all sick friends, and she acts only from obligation. She is completely sincere. How do you feel? Is there something missing from your friend's response? Critics of Kant argue that something is missing, namely, a concern for you as a particular individual, one with whom she has a special relationship. Acting from the motive of obligation in such situations seems to exclude a particular kind of moral value. Kantians fail to recognize this distinctive moral value, suggesting to many philosophers that there is something wrong with universal or impartialist ethical theories (again, including utilitarianism).

This notion of a special relationship with a unique history is often recognized in business. For instance, the Unocal Corporation sharply criticized its principal bank, Security Pacific Corporation, for knowingly making loans of $185 million to a group that intended to use the money to buy shares in Unocal for a hostile takeover. Fred Hartley, chairman and president of Unocal, argued that the banks and investment bankers were "playing both sides of the game." Hartley said that not only had Security Pacific promised him that it would not finance such takeover attempts three months before doing so but also it had acted under conditions "in which the bank [has] continually received [for the last 40 years] confidential financial, geological, and engineering information from the company."[18] A forty-year history in which the bank has stockpiled confidential information should not simply be cast aside for larger goals. Security Pacific had violated a special relationship it had with Unocal.

Nonetheless, impartiality seems at some level an irreplaceable moral concept, and ethical theory should recognize its centrality for many business relationships. For example, a major scandal occurred for some U.S. banks in 1991, because they were caught lending money to bank insiders.[19] The essence of federal rules is that banks can lend money to insiders if and only if insiders are treated exactly as outsiders are treated. Here the rule of impartiality is an essential moral constraint.

In concluding this section on Kantian ethics, it should be observed that almost no moral philosopher today finds Kant's system fully satisfactory. His defenders tend to say only that Kant provides the elements that are essential for a sound moral position. However, by using Kantian elements as a basis, some philosophers have attempted to construct a more encompassing theory. They use the Kantian notion of respect for persons as a ground for providing ethical theories of justice and rights. Considerable controversy persists as to whether Kantian theories are adequate to this task and whether they have been more successful than utilitarian theories.

Contemporary Challenges to the Dominant Theories

Thus far utilitarian and Kantian theories have been examined, both of which meld a wide variety of moral considerations into a surprisingly systematized framework, centered around a single major principle. There is much that is attractive in these theories, which have been the dominant models in ethical theory throughout much of the twentieth century. In fact, they have sometimes been presented as the only types of ethical theory, as if there were no available alternatives to choose from. However, much recent philosophical writing has focused on defects in these theories and on ways in which the two theories actually affirm a similar conception of the moral life oriented around universal principles and rules.

These critics promote alternatives to the utilitarian and Kantian models. They believe that the contrast between the two types of theory has been overestimated and that they do not merit the attention they have received and the lofty position they have occupied. Four popular replacements for, or perhaps supplements to, Kantian and utilitarian theories are (1) common morality theories (which are also obligation-based), (2) rights theories (which are based on human rights), (3) virtue theories (which are based on character traits), and (4) feminist theories and the ethics of care (which is disposition-based). These theories are the topics of the next four sections. Rights theories and feminist theories and the ethics of care will then be examined in more detail in Chapter 9.

Each of these four types of theory has treated some problems well and has supplied insights not found in utilitarian and Kantian theories. Although it may seem as if there is an endless array of disagreements across the theories, these theories are not in all respects competitive, and in many ways they are complementary. The convergent insights in these theories are valuable and we stand to learn from each.

Common Morality Theories

One set of theories builds on the idea that there is a common morality that all people share by virtue of communal life. A straightforward example of this type of theory is found in Alan Donagan's *The Theory of Morality,* in which he locates the "philosophical core" of the common morality in the Hebrew-Christian tradition, whose morality he interprets in secular rather than religious terms. His identification of the fundamental principle of this tradition is that "It is impermissible not to respect every human being, oneself or any other, as a rational creature."[20] Dona-gan believes that all other moral rules in the common morality are derivative from this fundamental rule.

There are many versions of a common morality approach, but W. D. Ross's theory has had a particularly imposing influence. He argues that there are several basic rules of moral obligation and that they do not derive from either the princi-ple of utility or Kant's categorical imperative. Some of Ross's basic rules are as fol-lows: "Promises create obligations of fidelity." "Wrongful actions create obligations of reparation." "The generous gifts of friends create obligations of gratitude." Ross defends several additional obligations, such as obligations of self-improvement, nonmaleficence, beneficence, and justice.

Unlike Kant's system and the utilitarian system, Ross's list of obligations is not based on a single overarching principle. Ross defends his principles on the grounds of their faithfulness to the ordinary moral beliefs and judgments. He ar-gues that to determine one's obligation, the greatest obligation in any given cir-cumstance must be found on the basis of the greatest balance of right over wrong in that particular context. To determine this balance, Ross introduces an influen-tial distinction between *prima facie* obligations and *actual* obligations. *Prima facie* refers to an obligation that must be acted upon unless it conflicts on a particular occasion with an equal or stronger obligation. Such an obligation is right and bind-ing, all other things being equal. A prima facie obligation becomes an obligation to be acted on in particular circumstances if it is not overridden or outweighed by some competing moral demand. One's actual obligation is determined by an ex-amination of the respective weights of the competing prima facie obligations. Al-though prima facie obligations are not absolute they are binding in a way that mere rules of thumb are not.

For example, Ross considers promise keeping a prima facie obligation. Does this consideration mean that a person must, under all circumstances, keep a promise, as if promise keeping were a categorical imperative? No, there are situa-tions in which breaking a promise is justified. To call promise breaking "prima facie wrong" means that promise breaking is always wrong *unless* some more weighty moral consideration in the circumstances is overriding. If the obligation to keep promises conflicts with the obligation to protect innocent persons, for exam-ple, then the actual obligation is to protect innocent persons (overriding the prima facie obligation of promise keeping).

The idea that moral principles are absolute has had a long but troubled his-tory. Both utilitarians and Kantians have defended their basic rule (the principle of utility and the categorical imperative) as absolute, but the claim that any rule or principle is absolute has been widely challenged. For Ross's reasons, among others, many moral philosophers have come to regard obligations and rights not as inflexi-ble standards but rather as strong prima facie moral demands that may be validly overridden in circumstances of competition with other moral claims. The idea of an exception-free hierarchy of rules and principles has vanished, as has the claim that moral principles can be arranged in a hierarchical order that avoids conflict.

This position also seems to entail that in cases of conflict there may not be a single right action, because two or more morally acceptable actions may be unavoidably in conflict and may prove to be of equal weight in the circumstances.

Rights Theories

Terms from moral discourse such as *value, goal,* and *obligation* have thus far in this chapter dominated the discussion. *Principles* and *rules* in Kantian, utilitarian, and common morality theories have been understood as statements of obligation. Yet many assertions that will be encountered throughout this volume are claims to have rights, and public policy issues often concern rights or attempts to secure rights. Many current controversies in professional ethics and public policy involve the rights to property, work, privacy, and the like. This section will show that rights have a distinctive character in ethical theory and yet are connected to the obligations that have previously been examined.

In the twentieth century, public discussion about moral protections for persons vulnerable to abuse, enslavement, or neglect have typically been stated in terms of human rights. Many believe these rights transcend national boundaries and particular governments. Unlike legal rights, human rights are held independently of membership in a state or other social organization. Historically, human rights evolved from the notion of natural rights. As formulated by Locke and others in early modern philosophy, natural rights are claims that individuals have against the state. If the state does not honor these rights, its legitimacy is in question. Natural rights were thought to consist primarily of rights to be free of interference, or liberty rights. Proclamations of rights to life, liberty, property, a speedy trial, and the pursuit of happiness subsequently formed the core of major Western political and legal documents. These rights came to be understood as powerful assertions demanding respect and status.

A number of influential philosophers have maintained that ethical theory or some part of it must be "rights-based."[21] They seek to ground ethical theory in an account of rights that is not reducible to a theory of obligations or virtues. Consider a theory to be discussed in Chapter 9 that insists liberty rights are basic. One representative of this theory, Robert Nozick, refers to his social philosophy as an "entitlement theory." The appropriateness of that description is apparent from this provocative line with which his book begins: "Individuals have rights, and there are things no person or group may do to them (without violating their rights)." Starting from this assumption, Nozick builds a political theory in which government action is justified only if it protects the fundamental rights of its citizens.

This political theory is also an ethical theory. Nozick takes the following moral rule to be basic: all persons have a right to be left free to do as they choose. The moral obligation not to interfere with a person follows from this right. That the obligation *follows* from the right is a clear indication of the priority of rights over obligations; that is, in this theory the obligation is derived from the right, not the other way around. A related rights-based conception uses *benefit* rights rather than *liberty* rights, as Alan Gewirth has proposed:

> Rights are to obligations as benefits are to burdens. For rights are justified claims to certain benefits, the support of certain interests of the subject or right-holder. Obligations, on the other hand, are justified burdens on the part of the respondent or obligation-bearer; they restrict his freedom by requiring that he conduct himself in ways that directly benefit not himself but rather the right-holder. But burdens are for the sake of benefits, and not vice versa. Hence obligations, which are burdens, are for the sake of rights, whose objects are benefits. . . .
> Respondents have correlative obligations *because* subjects have certain rights.[22]

These rights-based theories hold that rights form the justifying basis of obligations because they best express the purpose of morality, which is the securing of liberties or other benefits for a right-holder. Some might object that obligations are not necessarily burdens and that they may be welcomed as expressions of human rationality or as a basic form of human activity. However, rights theorists insist that obligations are essentially what Mill and Kant said they were — namely, moral constraints on autonomous choice — and, hence, burdens placed on autonomous action. Obligations restrict in a way that rights do not, and the purpose of morality is to benefit, not burden.

Theories of moral rights have not traditionally been a major focus of business ethics, but this situation seems at present to be changing. For example, employees traditionally could be fired for what superiors considered disloyal conduct, and employees have had no internal right to "blow the whistle" on corporate misconduct. When members of minority groups complain about discriminatory hiring practices that violate their human dignity and self-respect, one plausible interpretation of these complaints is that those who register them believe that their moral rights are being infringed. Current theories of employee, consumer, and stockholder rights all provide frameworks for contemporary debates within business ethics.

The language of moral rights is greeted by some with skepticism because of the apparently absurd proliferation of rights and the conflict among diverse claims to rights (especially in recent political debates). For example, some parties claim that a pregnant woman has a right to have an abortion, whereas others claim that fetuses have a right to life that precludes the right to have an abortion. As we shall see throughout this volume, rights language has been extended to include such controversial rights as the right to have financial privacy, rights of workers to obtain information, the right to work in a pollution-free environment, the right to hold a job, and the right to have health care.

Clashes between rights are often between what philosophers have distinguished as positive and negative rights. For instance, the right to well-being — that is, to receive goods and services when in need — is a positive right, whereas the right to liberty — the right not to be interfered with — is a negative right. The right to liberty is negative because no one has to act to honor it; presumably, all that must be done is to leave people alone. The same is not true regarding positive rights; in order to honor these rights, someone has to provide something. For example, if a starving person has a human right to well-being, someone has an obligation to provide that person with food.

The main difficulty is that positive rights place an obligation to provide something on others, who can respond that this requirement interferes with their property right to use their resources for their chosen ends. The distinction between positive and negative rights has often led those who would include various rights to well-being (to food, housing, health care, etc.) on the list of human rights to argue that the obligation to provide for positive rights falls on the political state. This distinction has intuitive appeal to many businesspersons, because they wish to limit both the responsibilities of their firms and the number of rights conflicts they must address.

However, this neat division of labor is suspicious. The government has already imposed some of the burden of positive rights on business. Employers contribute to retirement funds through contributions to social security, and firms are subject to the minimum wage laws. Moreover, many philosophers have doubts about the sharpness of the distinction between positive and negative rights. They argue that to protect a right to liberty, for example, society must do more than simply not interfere; society needs to protect individuals with police forces and courts.

The existence of apparently intractable conflicts among rights is one of the more troublesome aspects of contemporary rights theory. This conflict, however, is not simply between negative and positive rights. A conflict involving negative rights is illustrated by a strike at the Adolph Coors Brewery in Golden, Colorado, in which 1,400 workers at the brewery left their jobs in a situation that was to become a prolonged and bitter walkout.[23] At first the action appeared to turn on questions involving seniority, the nature of the work week, and the like; but more general issues of employee rights and employer obligations gradually emerged. Citing such practices as the use of lie detector tests in screening job applicants and the tendency of company interviewers to ask non–job-related questions, union spokespersons claimed that Coors's management was not fulfilling its moral obligation to respect employee rights to privacy. Such negative rights, the striking workers might say, carve out a sphere or zone of protected activity with which the employer is morally obligated not to interfere. Nevertheless, Coors's executives argued that they had the (negative) right to pursue business in ways they believe are most conducive to profit.

Many writers in ethics now agree that a person can legitimately exercise a right to something only if sufficient justification exists — that is, when a right has an overriding status. Rights such as a right to equal economic opportunity, a right to do with one's property as one wishes, and a right to be saved from starvation may have to compete with other rights. The fact that rights theorists have failed to provide a hierarchy for rights claims that has won even minimal acceptance may indicate that rights, like obligations, are prima facie claims, not absolute moral demands that cannot be overridden in particular circumstances by more stringent competing moral claims.

Virtue Ethics

The discussion of utilitarian, Kantian, common morality, and rights-based theories has looked chiefly at obligations and rights. These theories do not typically emphasize the agents or actors who perform actions, have motives, and follow principles. Yet people commonly make judgments about good and evil persons, their traits of character, and their willingness to perform actions. In recent years, several philosophers have proposed that ethics should redirect its preoccupation with principles of obligation, directive rules, and judgments of right and wrong and should look to decision making by persons of good character, that is, virtuous persons.

Virtue ethics, as it is called here, descends from the classical Hellenistic tradition represented by Plato and Aristotle, in which the cultivation of virtuous traits of character is viewed as morality's primary function. Aristotle held that virtue is neither a feeling nor an innate capacity but is rather a disposition bred from an innate capacity properly trained and exercised. People acquire virtues much as they do skills such as carpentry, playing a musical instrument, or cooking. They become just by performing just actions and become temperate by performing temperate actions. Virtuous character, says Aristotle, is neither natural nor unnatural; it is cultivated and made a part of the individual, much like a language or tradition.

But an ethics of virtue is more than habitual training. This approach relies even more than does Kant's theory on the importance of having a correct *motivational structure.* A just person, for example, has not only a disposition to act fairly but also a morally appropriate desire to do so. The person characteristically has a moral concern and reservation about acting in a way that would be unfair. Having only the motive to act in accordance with a rule of obligation, as Kant demands, is not morally sufficient for virtue. Imagine a Kantian who always performs his or her obligation because it is an obligation but who intensely dislikes having to allow the interests of others to be taken into account. Such a person does not cherish, feel congenial toward, or think fondly of others, and respects them only because obligation requires it. This person can nonetheless, on a theory of moral obligation such as Kant's or Mill's, perform a morally right action, have an ingrained disposition to perform that action, and act with obligation as the foremost motive. If the desire is not right, though, a necessary condition of virtue seems to be lacking, at least from the perspective of virtue ethics.

Consider an encounter with a tire salesperson. You tell the salesperson that safety is most important and that you want to be sure to get an all-weather tire. He listens carefully and then sells you exactly what you want, because he has been well trained by his manager to see his primary obligation as that of meeting the customer's needs. Apparently acting in this way is deeply ingrained in the salesperson. There is no more typical encounter in the world of retail sales than this one. However, going behind his behavior to his underlying motives and desires reveals that this man detests his job and hates having to spend time with every customer who comes through the door. He cares not at all about being of service to people or creating a better environment in the office. All he wants to do is watch the television set in the waiting area and pick up his paycheck. Although this man meets his role and moral obligations, something in his character is morally defective.

When people engage in business or take jobs simply for the profit or wages that will result, they may meet their obligations and yet not be engaged in a morally appropriate practice. On the other hand, if they start a business because they believe in a quality product — a new, healthier yogurt, for example — and deeply desire to sell that product, their business is on the road to being a morally appropriate practice. The practice of business is morally better if it is sustained by persons whose character manifests truthfulness, justice, compassion, respectfulness, and patience. These traits have greater moral depth than does a mere recognition of obligation. Some interesting discussions in business ethics now center on the appropriate virtues of managers, employees, and other participants in business activity, as will be seen many times in this book. These discussions have provided some much needed correctives to the approaches of traditional ethical theory.

There is a final reason why virtue ethics may be of constructive consequence for business ethics. A morally good person with the right desires or motivations is more likely to understand what should be done, more likely to be motivated to perform required acts, and more likely to form and act on moral ideals than would a morally bad person. A person who is ordinarily trusted is one who has an ingrained motivation and desire to perform right actions and who characteristically cares about morally appropriate responses. A person who simply follows rules of obligation and who otherwise exhibits no special moral character may not be trustworthy. It is not the rule follower, then, but the person disposed by *character* to be generous, caring, compassionate, sympathetic, and fair who should be the one recommended, admired, praised, and held up as a moral model. Many experienced businesspersons say that such trust is the moral cement of the business world.

Feminist Theories and the Ethics of Care

Related to virtue ethics in some respects is a body of moral reflection that has come to be known as the "ethics of care." This theory develops some of the themes found in virtue ethics about the centrality of character, but the ethics of care focuses on a set of character traits that are deeply valued in close personal relationships — sympathy, compassion, fidelity, love, friendship, and the like. Noticeably absent are universal moral rules and impartial utilitarian calculations such as those espoused by Kant and Mill.

The ideas behind an ethics of care have grown out of the eloquent work of a group of recent philosophers who have contributed to or are indebted to feminist theory. Feminist approaches to ethics may be characterized by at least two presuppositions. First, the subordination of women is as wrong as it is common. Second, the experiences of women are worthy of respect and should be taken seriously. Although these may seem entirely noncontroversial assumptions, feminists argue that if these suppositions were acted upon, the theory and practice of ethics in business and elsewhere would be radically transformed.[24] Feminist scholars are committed to pinpointing and excising male bias and to reformulating ethical theory in a manner that does not subordinate the interests of women. However, there is disagreement among feminists about how best to accomplish this task. The issues are complex, and feminists take different perspectives on matters such as equality, diversity, impartiality, community, autonomy, and the objectivity of moral knowledge.

Nonetheless, several central components of feminist ethical thinking may be delineated. Feminist philosophers point out that rationality in modern ethical theory, in particular in Kantian and utilitarian theories, has most often been understood in terms of the formulation and impartial application of universally binding moral principles. Many feminist philosophers now argue that universal principles are inadequate guides to action and that abstract formulations of hypothetical moral situations separate moral agents from the particularities of their individual lives and inappropriately separate moral problems from social and historical facts. Further, they have criticized the autonomous, unified, rational beings that typify both the Kantian and the utilitarian conception of the moral self. They also argue that moral decisions often require a sensitivity to the situation, as well as an awareness of the beliefs, feelings, attitudes, and concerns of each of the individuals involved and of the relationships of those individuals to one another.

Feminist philosophers generally agree that Kantian and utilitarian impartiality fails to recognize the moral importance of valuing the well-being of another for her or his own sake. Furthermore, they point out that although impartiality has historically been associated with respect for the individual, impartiality can actually undermine this very respect because it treats individuals impersonally, as anonymous and interchangeable moral agents without distinctive needs and abilities. In addition, impartial moral evaluations often pave over important differences in social, political, and economic power that are crucial to assessing the morally correct course of action in particular situations. For example, a statistical evaluation indicating that 40 percent of a telecommunication company's workforce consists of women would suggest that the company is morally praiseworthy in this respect. However, a different assessment may be appropriate if 90 percent of the women are employed as telephone operators and clerical staff. Similarly, in evaluating a waste disposal company's competitive contract bid, feminist philosophers would urge management to look beyond the bottom line if, for example, 80 percent of the company's toxic waste disposal sites are located in poor, minority neighborhoods.

Kantian and utilitarian theories have been widely criticized by contemporary feminist philosophers for advocating a conception of morality that leaves little room for virtues such as empathy, compassion, fidelity, love, and friendship. An understanding of the context of a situation is particularly important when taking into account the distinctive "voice" that many psychologists, philosophers, and management theorists have associated with women. This distinctive moral stance was first articulated by psychologist Carol Gilligan in her influential work *In a Different Voice.*[25] The voice is one of care and compassion, and although most feminist scholars do not associate this voice or perspective with women exclusively, they argue that it does represent an important contrast to the voice of rights and justice that Gilligan associated with men.

This distinct moral perspective is characterized by a concern with relationships, by responsiveness to the particular needs of others, and by a commitment to others' well-being. The ideas Gilligan advanced on the basis of her psychological studies have been developed by those who find the same "different voice" in contemporary philosophy. Contractarian models of ethics, with their emphasis on justice and rights, are firmly rejected because they omit integral virtues and place a premium on *autonomous choice* among *free* and *equal* agents. Here the ethics of care offers a fundamental rethinking of the moral universe: the terms of social cooperation, especially in families and in communal decision making, are *unchosen, intimate,* and among *unequals.* (See Annette Baier's article in Chapter 9 of this text.) The contractarian model fails to appreciate that parents and service-oriented professionals, for example, do not perceive their responsibilities to their children and customers in terms of contracts or universal rules but see them rather in terms of care, needs, and long-term attachment. Only if every form of human relation were modeled on an exchange could these forms of caring be reduced to contract or moral law.[26]

There are additional reasons for thinking that a morality centered on virtues of care and concern cannot be squeezed into a morality of rules. Both of their frameworks are fundamentally dissimilar. Human warmth, friendliness, and trust in responding to others cannot be brought under rules of behavior. For example, although a lawyer may follow all the rules of good legal practice in attending to the affairs of a bankrupt businessperson, the lawyer still does not display the sensitivity and warmth that this heartsick person needs; yet such virtues of a good lawyer may be the most important part of the encounter.

Crucial to the ethics of care is a willingness to listen to distinct and previously unacknowledged perspectives. For example, a manager considering the implementation of a mandatory drug testing program might come to an impasse because employers, employees, and customers have legitimate rights. Many feminists and management experts would urge the manager to help employees to feel concern for the customers while also striving to make the workplace experience one in which the worker is less alienated and hence less likely to take drugs. Employees must feel that they can trust their managers, and managers must be willing to listen and respond to their employees. The manager, in other words, must build solidarity among managers, employees, and customers.

This moral theory has the potential to transform business practice to exhibit more of the characteristics of a moral community. Traditional metaphors for business practice are often drawn from competitive arenas; they are war-oriented and sports-oriented. Family metaphors seem out of place, as does the language of cooperation and compassion. Yet such language is undeniably central to morality, and if some contemporary management theorists are correct, such language is central to success in business as well. Cooperation among managers and employers is no less important for success than product quality.

This aspect of business has traditionally been ignored as "soft" and less important than a strong bottom line. Perhaps business at the end of this century and the beginning of the next will be more open to the contributions of the ethics of care, resulting in an improvement in both corporate morality and corporate productivity.

A Prologue to Theories of Justice

Many rules and principles form the terms of cooperation in society. Society is laced with implicit and explicit arrangements and agreements under which individuals are obligated to cooperate or abstain from interfering with others. Philosophers are interested in the justice of these terms of cooperation. They pose questions such as these: "What gives one person or group of people the right to expect cooperation from another person or group of people in some societal interchange (especially an economic one) if the former benefit and the latter do not?" "Is it just for some citizens to have more property than others?" "Is it fair for one person to gain an economic advantage over another, if both abide strictly by existing societal rules?"

In their attempts to answer such questions, some philosophers believe that diverse human judgments and beliefs about justice can be brought into systematic unity through a general theory of justice. Justice has been analyzed differently, however, in rival and often incompatible theories. These general theories of justice are treated in Chapter 9. Here we need note only that in the literature on justice there exists a key distinction between just *procedures* and just *results*.

Ideally it is preferable to have both, but it is not always possible. For example, a person might achieve a just result in redistributing wealth but might use an unjust procedure to achieve that result, such as undeserved taxation of certain groups. By contrast, just procedures sometimes eventuate in unjust results, as when a fair trial finds an innocent person guilty. Some writers in business ethics are concerned with issues of procedural justice when they discuss such concerns as the use of ombudsmen, grievance procedures, peer review, and arbitration procedures.

Many problems of justice that a cooperative society must handle involve some system or set of procedures that foster, but do not ensure, just outcomes. Once there is agreement on appropriate procedures, the outcome must be accepted as just, even if it produces inequalities that seem unjust by other standards. If procedural justice is the best that can be attained — as, for example, is claimed in the criminal justice system — society should accept the results of its system with a certain amount of humility and perhaps make allowances for inevitable inequalities and even inequities and misfortunes.

PART THREE: ANALYSIS OF CASES

Every subsequent chapter of this volume contains judicial opinions ("case law") and cases involving business activities. Although these materials are not derived from ethical theory, they do merit moral analysis. The *case method,* as it is often called, has long been used in law and business for such purposes. However, only recently has philosophical ethics drawn attention to the importance of case studies and the case method, and their use is still controversial and unsettled.

The Case Method in Law

Case law establishes precedents of evidence and justification. The earliest developments in the law's use of the case method occurred around 1870, when Christopher Columbus Langdell revolutionized academic standards and teaching techniques by introducing this system at the Harvard Law School.[27] Langdell's textbooks contained cases selected and arranged to reveal the pervasive meaning of legal terms and the rules and principles of law. He envisioned a dialectical or Socratic manner of argument to show students how concepts, rules, and principles are found in the legal reasoning of the judges who wrote the opinions. A teacher or legal scholar was to extract fundamental principles, much in the way a skillful biographer might extract the principles of a person's reasoning by studying his or her considered judgments.

However, Langdell's "principles" did not prove to be as invariant or as consistently applied across courts, contexts, or times as Langdell had thought they would. It turned out that incompatible and rival theories or approaches by judges tended to control in many precedent cases. Nevertheless, the case method ultimately prevailed in U.S. law schools, and still today it offers teachers and students a powerful tool for generalizing from cases. Spanning the tangled web of details in particular situations are many generalizations embedded in legal reasoning. Fundamental doctrines can be both found in and applied to cases that came before courts. Moreover, training in the case method sharpens skills of legal reasoning. Someone can tear a case apart and then construct a better way of treating similar situations. In the thrust-and-parry classroom setting, teacher and student alike reach conclusions about a case's rights and wrongs.

The case method in law has come to be understood, then, as a way of learning to assemble facts and to judge the weight of evidence — enabling the transfer of that weight to new cases. This task is accomplished by generalizing and mastering the doctrines that control the transfer in the reasoning of judges.

The Case Method in Business

When the Harvard Business School was opened in 1908, its first dean, Edwin F. Gay, adopted the Law School curriculum as a prototype for courses on commercial law and eventually as a model throughout the business school. By 1919 the method had taken hold, and eventually it came to dominate business schools that emphasize deliberation and decision making, weighing competing considerations, and reaching a decision in complex and difficult circumstances.[28] Judgment, rather than doctrine, principle, or fact, was taught. Cases involving puzzles and dilemmas that have no definitive solution by reference to principles or precedents were preferred for instructional purposes over those failing to present a difficult dilemma.

Cases, in this method, are typically developed to recreate a managerial situation in which dilemmas are confronted. Cases are not primarily used to illustrate principles or rules, because the latter abstractions are invariably inadequate for final resolutions in real-world business situations. The objective is to develop a capacity to grasp problems and to find novel solutions that work in this context: *Knowing how* to think and act is more prized than *knowing that* something is the case or that a principle applies.

This use of the case method in business schools springs from an ideal of education that puts the student in the decision-making role after an initial immersion into the facts of a complex situation. Theories and generalizations are downplayed, and the skills of thinking and acting in complex and uncertain environments are upgraded. The essence of the case method is to present a situation replete with the facts, opinions, and prejudices an executive might encounter (often in an actual case) and to lead the student in making decisions in such an environment.

This method makes no assumption that there is a *right* answer to any problem but maintains only that there are more or less successful ways of handling problems. Understanding argument and analysis (as outlined in Part One of this chapter) is more important than understanding substantive theories (as presented in Part Two). These forms of understanding need not be antagonistic or competitive, but the case method in business schools has placed the premium on problem-based analysis rather than on analysis by appeal to theory. This method also avoids the authority-based method relied on in law schools, where judges and the body of law are overriding authorities. In a situation similar to the Protestant rejection of authority in the Roman Catholic Church, business education has rejected any overriding authority in its use of cases.

The Case Method in Ethics

The term *casuistry* is now commonly used in ethics to refer to a method of using cases to analyze and propose solutions for moral problems. Casuists see ethics as based on seasoned experience in resolving hard cases.[29] The casuistical method is to start with *paradigm* cases whose conclusions on ethical matters are settled and then to compare and contrast the central features in the paradigm (morally clear and settled) cases with the features of cases in need of a decision.

To illustrate this point, consider a comparison to case law and the doctrine of precedent, as previously discussed. Judicial decisions have the potential to become authoritative for other judges confronting similar cases in similar circumstances. Contemporary casuistry places a similar premium on case authority, together with a strong preference for analogical reasoning over ethical theory and abstract principles. It is analogical reasoning that links one case to the next. Moral reasoning occurs by appeal to analogies, models, classification schemes, and even immediate intuition and discerning insight about particulars.

Casuists also maintain that principles and rules are typically too indeterminate to yield specific moral judgments. It is therefore impossible, casuists insist, that there be a unidirectional movement of thought from principles to cases — what has often been called the "application" of a principle to a case. Moreover, from a casuist's perspective, principles are merely summaries of peoples' experience in reflecting on cases, not independent norms.

There is much in these casuistical arguments that is revealing and worth serious consideration, but casuists sometimes write as though cases lead to moral paradigms or judgments entirely by their facts alone. This thesis seems mistaken. The properties that people observe to be of moral importance in cases are selected by the values that they have already accepted as being morally important or have come to appreciate while examining the case. No matter how many salient facts are assembled, there will still need to be some *value* premises in order to reach a moral conclusion.

Appeals to "paradigm cases" can easily conceal this fact. These "cases" might just as well be called "cases that contain a norm." Paradigm cases gain status as paradigms because of some commitment to central values that are preserved from one case to the next case. For someone to move constructively from case to case, one or more values must connect the cases. Even to recognize a case as a paradigm case is to accept whatever principles or values allow the paradigms to be extended to other cases. Whatever can be learned from a case and then exported to another case cannot be entirely specific to the first case; only some form of general norm can lead to the next case.

In difficult cases, several morals emerge from analysis of a case, because maxims give conflicting advice. The casuist's job is to determine which maxim is to rule in the case and how powerfully the maxim is to rule. From this perspective, casuistry is a morality of cases that is complementary to the use of principles in ethics, though their exact relationship still needs to be worked out in moral philosophy.

Ethical Theory and Case Analysis

There are dangers in transferring the case methods in law and business to business ethics, and even casuistry needs careful restriction. Not much is drearier than a tedious and unrewarding exposure to the moral opinions of those ignorant of the kinds of material outlined in Part One and Part Two. Studying cases in business ethics is facilitated by a knowledge of the history of ethics and types of ethical theory. Theory and history, however, also should not remain isolated from modification by case study. Several reasons support this judgment.

First, it seems mistaken to say that ethical theory is not extracted from the examination of cases but only applied to or specified in cases. Cases not only provide data for theory but also act as the testing ground for theories as well. Illuminating cases lead to modification and refinements of theoretical commitments, especially by pointing to limitations of theories. In thinking through the possible role of case analysis in ethics, it is useful to consider John Rawls's celebrated account of "reflective equilibrium." In developing an ethical theory, he argues, it is appropriate to start with the broadest possible set of considered moral judgments and to erect a provisional set of principles that reflects them. Reflective equilibrium views ethics as a reflective testing of moral beliefs to make them as coherent as possible. Starting with paradigms of what is morally proper or morally improper, one then searches for principles that are consistent with these paradigms. Widely accepted principles of right action and considered judgments are taken, as Rawls puts it, "provisionally as fixed points" but also as "liable to revision."

Considered judgments is a technical term referring to "judgments in which our moral capacities are most likely to be displayed without distortion." Examples are judgments about the wrongness of racial discrimination, religious intolerance, and political conflict of interest. By contrast, judgments in which one's confidence level is low or in which one is influenced by the possibility of personal gain are excluded. The goal is to match and prune considered judgments and principles in an attempt to make them coherent.[30]

Traditional ethical theory, from this perspective, has as much to learn from practical decision-making contexts as the other way around. Ethical theory can profit from a close scrutiny of a wide variety of moral phenomena, and an understanding of right action could be constructed by generalizing from what is discovered. This strategy should prevent theoreticians from overly streamlining the complexity of the moral life. From this perspective, moral thinking is similar to other forms of theorizing: hypotheses must be tested, buried, or modified through experimental thinking. Principles can be justified, modified, or refuted, and new insights gained, by examination of cases that function as experimental data. Similarly, one's principles allow one to interpret cases and arrive at moral judgments in a reflective manner.

A complaint heard frequently among university administrators and teachers is that their students learn technical skills but never develop moral reasoning that can be carried into real-life situations. Derek Bok, former President of Harvard University, complained in *Beyond the Ivory Tower* that students learn too much about increasing profits and too little about "applied ethics" that could teach them how to confront moral dilemmas. Steven Muller, former president of Johns Hopkins, complained that the modern university teaches marvelous lessons learned from the scientific method but fails to teach that this method gives no insight into morality, which is at least as important. There is need for a university environment in which informed decision-making skills involving moral judgment are taught together with the technical skills and theoretical wisdom that dominate the curriculum. The case method has been cited as a promising entree, although not a complete solution, for teaching that meets these objectives.

In conclusion, we can now recall the previous discussions in Part One of relativism and moral disagreement. Often when discussing difficult cases, many points of view are bounced around the classroom, and the controversies may seem intractable and not subject to a persuasive form of analysis transcending personal opinion. Far from viewing their class as an environment of learning, students may perceive the class as a bulletin board upon which scores of opinions are tacked. It would be a mistake, however, to conclude that such discussion eventuates only in opinion and monologue. Many apparent dilemmas do turn out to be partially resolvable, and often a consensus position emerges through dialogue, even if no one entirely agrees on the best reasons for defending the position.

In case analysis, disagreements should not be avoided or minimized, but there should also be an attempt to surmount them. A study of cases to determine how management might avoid problems can be profitable, as can reflection on procedures that deflect or defuse problems. Cases should be examined in terms of alternative strategies and actions. Invariably many alternatives will be proposed, but just as invariably they will not all be equally good. Even if intractable disagreement does occur, learning how to spot problems and help alleviate or deflect them may turn out to be as important as the substantive issues themselves.

One temptation should be avoided, however. Those who study the facts of cases invariably desire more facts, viewing a solution as dependent on knowing more than is given in the write-up of the case. If additional data can be discovered, they think, the problems can be handled and the dilemmas disentangled. A related temptation is to doctor the known facts, thereby presenting a hypothetical case or a new case, rather than the actual cases. Both of these temptations should be avoided. Cases are interesting in part because only limited information is available. Discussants are called upon to treat problems under real-life conditions of information scarcity. Businesses function under such conditions day in and day out, and business people well know that a case must be addressed as it actually is and not as it might be in some possible world.

NOTES

1. Our discussion of this case is indebted to Richard Wokutch and also to Elizabeth Gatewood and Archie Carroll, "Anatomy of a Corporate Social Response: The Proctor and Gamble Rely Case," *Business Horizons,* September 1981.

2. Dean Rotbard and John A. Prestbo, "Killing a Product," *Wall Street Journal,* November 3, 1980.

3. Edward G. Harness, "Views on Corporate Responsibility," *Corporate Ethics Digest* 1 (September–October 1980).

4. Robert Lindsey, "Ancient Redwood Trees Fall to a Wall Street Takeover," *New York Times,* March 2, 1988, pp. A16–17.

5. Taken from Peter Huber, "The Press Gets Off Easy in Tort Law," *Wall Street Journal,* July 24, 1985, editorial page.

6. "Odds & Ends," *Wall Street Journal,* December 13, 1984, sec. 2, p. 1.

7. "Principle Sale," *Wall Street Journal,* May 22, 1985, p. 35.

8. Marcus W. Brauchli, "Asia, on the Ascent, Is Learning to Say No To 'Arrogant' West," *Wall Street Journal,* April 4, 1994.

9. "Bowing to the Inevitable," *Forbes,* August 12, 1985, p. 66.

10. See for example, Werner Guth, Rolf Schmittberger, and Bernd Schwarze, "An Experimental Analysis of Ultimatum Bargaining," *Journal of Economic Behavior and Organization* 3 (1982): 367–388.

11. Thomas Hobbes, *Leviathan,* Part I, chap. 13, par. 9.

12. For an act-utilitarian example in business ethics, see R. M. Hare, "Commentary on Beauchamp's Manipulative Advertising," *Business and Professional Ethics Journal* 3 (1984): 23–28; for a rule-utilitarian example, see Robert Almeder, "In Defense of Sharks: Moral Issues in Hostile Liquidating Takeovers," *Journal of Business Ethics* 10 (1991): 471–484.

13. Tom L. Beauchamp, ed., *Case Studies in Business, Society, and Ethics,* 4th ed. (Upper Saddle River, NJ: Prentice Hall, 1996), Chap. 6.

14. As quoted in Charles R. Babcock, "Zaccaro Ousted as Guardian of Elderly Woman's Estate," *Washington Post,* August 31, 1984, sec. A, pp. 1, 8.

15. A. Carl Kotchian, *Saturday Review,* July 9, 1977.

16. See Al Kamen, "Budget Law Rejected by High Court," *Washington Post,* July 8, 1986, p. 1.

17. T. W. Zimmerer and P. L. Preston, "Plasma International," in R. D. Hay, and others, *Business and Society* (Cincinnati, OH: South-Western publishing, 1976).

18. See Jennifer Hull, "Unocal Sues Bank," *Wall Street Journal,* March 13, 1985, p. 22; and Charles McCoy, "Mesa Petroleum Alleges Unocal Coerced Banks," *Wall Street Journal,* March 22, 1985, p. 6.

19. David S. Hilzenrath, "Taking Aim at Insider Bank Deals," *Washington Post,* September 30, 1991, Washington Business sec., p. 1.

20. See Alan Donagan, *The Theory of Morality* (Chicago: University of Chicago Press, 1977), p. 66.

21. Ronald Dworkin argues that *political* morality is rights-based in *Taking Rights Seriously* (London: Duckworth, 1977), p. 171. John Mackie has applied this thesis to *morality generally* in "Can There Be a Right-Based Moral Theory?" *Midwest Studies in Philosophy* 3 (1978): esp. p. 350.

22. Alan Gewirth, "Why Rights Are Indispensable," *Mind* 95 (1986): 333.

23. This case is taken from Vincent Barry, *Moral Issues in Business* (Belmont: CA: Wadsworth, 1979), p. 149.

24. For examples of the kind of transformation envisaged, see Ramona L. Paetzold and Bill Shaw, "A Postmodern Feminist View of 'Reasonableness' in Hostile Environment Sexual Harassment," *Journal of Business Ethics* 13 (September 1994): 681–691; Joan E. van Tol, "Eros Gone Awry: Liability Under Title VII for Workplace Sexual Favoritism," *Industrial Relations Law Journal* 13 (1991): 153–182; Liz Armstrong, "The Fight for Equality," *Canadian Insurance* 91 (December 1986): 24, 31.

25. Carol Gilligan, *In a Different Voice* (Cambridge, MA: Harvard University Press, 1982).

26. Annette Baier, *Moral Prejudices* (Cambridge, MA: Harvard University Press, 1994), Chapter 4; and *Postures of the Mind* (Minneapolis: University of Minnesota Press, 1985), pp. 210–219.

27. Christopher Columbus Langdell's first casebook on *Contracts* is treated in Lawrence M. Friedman, *A History of American Law* (New York: Simon and Schuster, 1973), pp. 531f. The general account of the case method in this section is in-

debted to this source, and also to G. Edward White, *Tort Law in America: An Intellectual History* (New York: Oxford University Press, 1980).

28. See M. P. McNair, ed., *The Case Method at the Harvard Business School* (New York: McGraw-Hill, 1954).

29. See Albert Jonsen and Stephen Toulmin, *Abuse of Casuistry* (Berkeley: University of California Press, 1988), pp. 11–19, 66–67, 251–254, 296–299; John Arras, "Principles and Particularity," *Indiana Law Journal* 69 (1994).

30. John Rawls, *A Theory of Justice* (Cambridge, MA: Harvard University Press, 1971), pp. 20ff, 46–48.

Chapter Two

———— • ————

Corporate Social Responsibility

THIS CHAPTER FOCUSES on corporate social responsibility. The socially responsible corporation is the good corporation. Over two thousand years ago the Greeks thought they could answer questions about the goodness of things by knowing about the purpose of things. These Greek philosophers provided a functional analysis of good. For example, if one determines what a good racehorse is by knowing the purpose of racehorses (to win races) and the characteristics — for instance, speed, agility, and discipline — horses must have to win races, then a good racehorse is speedy, agile, and disciplined. To adapt the Greeks' method of reasoning, one determines what a good (socially responsible) corporation is by investigating the purpose corporations should serve in society.

THE PURPOSE OF A CORPORATION IS TO MAKE A PROFIT

For many, the view that the purpose of the corporation is to make a profit for stockholders is beyond debate and is accepted as a matter of fact. The classical U.S. view that a corporation's primary and perhaps sole purpose is to maximize profits for stockholders is most often associated with the Nobel prize-winning economist Milton Friedman. This chapter presents arguments for and against the Friedmanite view that the purpose of a corporation is to maximize stockholder profits.

Friedman has two main arguments for his position. First, stockholders are the *owners* of the corporation, and hence corporate profits *belong* to the stockholders. Managers are agents of the stockholders and have a moral obligation to manage the firm in the interest of the stockholders, that is, to maximize shareholder wealth. If the management of a firm donates some of the firm's income to charitable organizations, it is seen as an illegitimate use of stockholders' money. If individual stockholders wish to donate their dividends to charity, they are free to do so since the money is theirs. But managers have no right to donate corporate funds to charity. If society decides that private charity is insufficient to meet the needs of the poor, to maintain art museums, and to finance research for curing diseases, it is the responsibility of government to raise the necessary money through taxation. It should not come from managers purportedly acting on behalf of the corporation.

Second, stockholders are entitled to their profits as a result of a contract among the corporate stakeholders. A product or service is the result of the productive efforts of a number of parties — employees, managers, customers, suppliers, the local community, and the stockholders. Each of these stakeholder groups has a contractual relationship with the firm. In return for their services, the managers and employees are paid in the form of wages; the local community is paid in the form of taxes; and suppliers, under the constraints of supply and demand, negotiate the return for their products directly with the firm. Funds remaining after these payments have been made represent profit, and by agreement the profit belongs to the stockholders. The stockholders bear the risk when they supply the capital, and profit is the contractual return they receive for risk taking. Thus each party in the manufacture and sale of a product receives the remuneration it has freely agreed to.

Friedman believes that these voluntary contractual arrangements maximize economic freedom and that economic freedom is a necessary condition for political freedom. Political rights gain efficacy in a capitalist system. For example, private employers are forced by competitive pressures to be concerned primarily with a prospective employee's ability to produce rather than with that person's political views. Opposing voices are heard in books, in the press, or on television so long as there is a profit to be made. Finally, the existence of capitalist markets limits the number of politically based decisions and thus increases freedom. Even political decisions reached democratically coerce the opposing minority. Once society votes on how much to spend for defense or for city streets, the minority must go along. In the market, each consumer can decide how much of a product or service he or she is willing to purchase. Thus Friedman entitled his book defending the classical view of the purpose of the firm *Capitalism and Freedom*.

The classical view that a corporation's primary responsibility is to maximize the stockholder profit is embodied in the legal opinion *Dodge v. Ford Motor Company* included in this chapter. The Court ruled that the benefits of higher salaries for Ford workers and the benefits of lower auto prices to consumers must not take priority over stockholder interests. According to *Dodge*, the interests of the stockholder are supreme.

It was not until 1953 in the case of *A. P. Smith Manufacturing Company v. Barlow et. al*, which permitted charitable contributions to Princeton University, that corporate officials had something approaching legal permission to undertake acts promoting the public good. In this appeal decision, which is reprinted in this chapter, Judge Jacobs recognized that corporations had public responsibilities as well as private ones.

What are these public responsibilities and how can they be justified? The justification for more public responsibilities has both a negative and a positive aspect. On the negative side, many have found Friedman's arguments for profit maximization to be inadequate. Limitations on the rights of ownership are already recognized as morally and legally legitimate. People cannot grow marijuana on their property or use their home for prostitution. Local ordinances place even more extreme restrictions on private property, and, of course, private property is taxed. Now most investment property is different from other kinds of personal property. Investment property is owned simply for its projected rate of return, and most stockholders are indifferent absentee owners who sell their stock whenever expedient. Consider the contrasting investment and care people take with personal property such as homes and cars. People seldom sell their homes just to make a quick financial killing. Since the owner of investment property has less incentive to take the same personal interest in managing, maintaining, and improving that property, there are even better arguments for regulating investment property for the public good.

As for the argument that profit-seeking firms maximize freedom, several things need pointing out. First, there are usually more people looking for work than there are jobs. Even a modest 5 percent unemployment rate means that one in twenty people is looking for work but cannot find it, and unemployment figures do not include those who have given up looking for work. Since the standard of living of most of the unemployed ranges from extremely modest to desperate, one is led to wonder how voluntary employment contracts really are. Second, many American firms operate under the employment-at-will doctrine where employees may be fired for many reasons unrelated to their contribution to the firm. In industries where the employment-at-will doctrine is practiced industrywide, employees with skills in those industries must accept employment at will if they want a job. Third, since the Bill of Rights does not apply in the corporate setting, many employees, in order to secure employment, are required to accept restrictions on their behavior on and off the job and are subject to honesty tests, drug tests, and other tests that many consider an invasion of privacy. (Employment at will and employee rights are considered at length in Chapter 5.) From this perspective, many employees hardly find the freedoms they want in the workplace.

Reasons independent of the criticisms of the Friedmanite view also indicate that corporations have purposes other than simply maximizing profits. In their essay contained here, John Simon, Charles Powers, and John Gunnemann maintain that all individuals and social institutions ought to adhere to certain moral standards which these authors refer to as the "moral minimum." If there is a genuine moral minimum to which all institutions, including businesses, must adhere, the pursuit of profit in violation of the moral minimum is morally irresponsible. In explaining the concept of the moral minimum, these authors draw on a distinction between negative injunctions and affirmative duties, a distinction that rests on the further distinction between not causing harm and doing everything one can to promote the good. They argue that although society cannot legitimately impose affirmative duties on corporations to promote the general welfare, society can legitimately impose negative injunctions on corporations. That is, society can legitimately insist that corporate activities not cause harm and that corporations therefore must take active steps to prevent potentially harmful activities. Thus it is morally acceptable for society to prevent companies from polluting our air but not to impose on companies an obligation to donate to charity.

When the moral minimum is taken into account, the classical Friedmanite view of the corporation may have to be revised. On this amended view the purpose of the corporation is to seek profits for stockholders while acting in conformity with the moral minimum. That is, corporations may strive for profits so long as they commit no harm.

Some argue that the obligation to avoid harm is too strong. The production and distribution of products and services almost always involve risks and tradeoffs among benefits and harms. For example, in the United States alone about 40,000 people die and over 200,000 are injured each year in automobile accidents. Such death and injury are avoidable, but surely this does not suggest that automobile companies should cease making automobiles.

This example points out the necessity of refining the avoidable harm criterion. It is a fundamental principle of ethics that "ought implies can." This expression means that one can be held accountable only for events that are within one's power. Now since the overwhelming majority of automobile deaths and injuries result from driver error and, to a lesser extent, from poor driving conditions due to inclement weather, the automobile manufacturer is not responsible for those deaths and injuries. It is responsible only for harms resulting from defective parts and design.

However, the preceding analysis lets the automobile manufacturer off the hook too easily. Simon, Powers, and Gunnemann understand that criteria for avoiding harm include both not causing harm and preventing harm. Thus an automobile manufacturer is obligated to decrease the incidence of death and injury due to driver error and bad weather by building safer cars.

Is a company obligated to build a car as safe as it knows how? Surely there must be some limitations on a corporation's obligation to prevent harm. Simon, Powers, and Gunnemann suggest four conditions — need, proximity, capability, and last resort — to assist corporations in determining their obligation to prevent harm.

Would the capability condition help an automobile manufacturer with the problem of auto safety? An auto executive might argue that the standards for safety must leave the car's cost within the price range of the consumer ("ought implies can" again). Comments about engineering and equipment capability are obvious enough. But for a business, capability is also a function of profitability. For a company to build a maximally safe car at a cost that makes it impossible to sell at a profit is beyond a company's capability. Whether tying capability to profitability is morally acceptable should be considered by the reader.

STAKEHOLDER THEORY

An alternative way to analyze the social responsibilities of business is to consider those affected by business decisions, referred to as *corporate stakeholders*. From the stakeholders' perspective, the classical view is problematic in that all emphasis is placed on one stakeholder — the stockholder. The interests of the other stakeholders are unfairly subordinated to the stockholders' interests. Although any person or group affected by corporate decisions is a stakeholder, most stakeholder analysis has focused on a special group of stakeholders: namely, members of groups whose existence was necessary for the firm's survival. Traditionally six stakeholder groups have been identified: stockholders, employees, customers, managers, suppliers, and the local community. Managers who manage from the stakeholder perspective see their task as harmonizing the legitimate interests of the primary corporate stakeholders. In describing stakeholder management, R. Edward Freeman proposes a set of principles that could make this kind of harmonizing possible.

Both in corporate and academic circles, stakeholder terminology has become very fashionable. However, many theoretical problems remain. Stakeholder theory is still in its early developmental stage. Much has been said of the obligations of managers to the other corporate stakeholders, but little has been said about the obligations of the other stakeholders, for instance, the community or employees, to the corporation. Do members of a community have an obligation to consider the moral reputation of a company when they make their purchasing decisions? Do employees have an obligation to stay with a company that has invested in their training even if they could get a slightly better salary by moving to another corporation?

Perhaps the most pressing problems for stakeholder theory is to specify in more detail the rights and responsibilities that each stakeholder group has and to suggest how the conflicting rights and responsibilities among the stakeholder groups can be resolved.

WHICH PERSPECTIVE IS BETTER?

Is the Friedmanite view that the purpose of the firm is to maximize profits or the stakeholder view that the firm is to be managed in the interests of the various stakeholders more adequate? In the three articles that conclude the chapter, Ken Goodpaster criticizes Freeman's stakeholder theory, while John Boatright presents additional difficulties for the Friedmanite position. Norman Bowie argues that as a practical matter there may not be a great difference between the two perspectives.

Ken Goodpaster's main complaint with Freeman's stakeholder analysis is that it seems to treat all stakeholder interests as equal. But that is a mistake, Goodpaster contends, because managers have special obligations to the stockholders that they do not have to any other stakeholder group. Managers have fiduciary duties to stockholders but only nonfiduciary duties to other stakeholders. These fiduciary duties are established in law and are characterized as the duties that agents have to principals. In a principal-agent relationship, the agent is to act in the best interest of the principal.

That an agent is always to act in the interest of the principal, implies that whenever the interests of the stockholders conflict with the interests of another stakeholder group, the manager is obligated to honor the interests of the stockholders. If this view is justifiable, isn't Goodpaster really defending the classical Friedmanite position? Goodpaster thinks not, because even in a fiduciary relationship the principal cannot demand that the agent do something in her or his behalf that violates the basic moral principles of the community. But Friedman himself states something similar to this view when he concludes his article by saying, "There is one and only one social responsibility of business — to use its resources and engage in activities designed to increase its profits so long as it stays within the rules of the game, which is to say, engages in open and free competition without deception or fraud." If free competition without deception or fraud represents the community's view of business morality, little difference seems to exist between the views of Friedman and Goodpaster. On the other hand, if Goodpaster has a broader notion of the "basic moral principles of the community," he must say more about resolving conflicts concerning fiduciary duties to stockholders and nonfiduciary duties to other stakeholders.

Whereas Goodpaster seeks to show that there is a special relationship between managers and stockholders, John Boatright asks provocatively, "What's so special about shareholders?" Boatright's point is that the rights of shareholders are sufficiently protected without an appeal to the special fiduciary duties Goodpaster supports. Moreover, he argues that Friedman and his followers are mistaken in their view that a firm is a nexus of contracts and that managers are mere agents of the stockholders. As Boatright points out, managers are denied some of the powers of genuine agents in the legal sense. Simultaneously, the managers are not significantly under the control of the stockholders — a view that has been argued for over fifty years and is often expressed by corporate raiders who desire to take over a firm. Boatright concludes by showing that stockholders have been given special attention because public policy believed it was in the public interest to do so.

But many critics have argued that it is no longer in the public interest to treat stockholders as special. These critics have argued that American managers are forced to manage to please Wall Street, which means they are forced to manage for the short term. Often these critics point to differences between the stockholder capitalism of America and the cooperative capitalism of Japan as evidence that the American approach is not the only successful one. More recently critics have argued that stockholders have received a disproportionate share of the productivity gains achieved by corporate mergers and corporate downsizing. Thus, from both academics and practitioners a central feature of American capitalism — the purpose of the firm is to increase stockholder profits — has become controversial.

In the concluding piece, Norman Bowie argues that, as a practical matter, a Friedmanite must consider the interests of all corporate stakeholders in order to make a profit. Even charitable giving and the attempt by corporations to solve social problems can be defended on Friedmanite grounds. In the twin cities of Minneapolis/St. Paul, it is believed that Target maintains a competitive advantage over WalMart because of the former's reputation for charitable activities. What distinguishes a Friedmanite from a stakeholder theorist is the motivation a manager has for considering stakeholder interests. The Friedmanite treats stakeholders well in order to make a profit, while the stakeholder theorist treats stakeholders well because it is the right thing to do. Bowie then argues that paradoxically treating stakeholders well because it is right may end up being more profitable. In 1987 the Dayton Hudson Corporation was able to avoid a hostile takeover by the Hafts because the Minnesota legislature intervened to protect a good corporate citizen.

The Social Responsibility of Business Is to Increase Its Profits

Milton Friedman

When I hear businessmen speak eloquently about the "social responsibilities of business in a free-enterprise system," I am reminded of the wonderful line about the Frenchman who discovered at the age of 70 that he had been speaking prose all his life. The businessmen believe that they are defending free enterprise when they declaim that business is not concerned "merely" with profit but also with promoting desirable "social" ends; that business has a "social conscience" and takes seriously its responsibilities for providing employment, eliminating discrimination, avoiding pollution and whatever else may be the catchwords of the contemporary crop of reformers. In fact they are — or would be if they or anyone else took them seriously — preaching pure and unadulterated socialism. Businessmen who talk this way are unwitting puppets of the intellectual forces that have been undermining the basis of a free society these past decades.

The discussions of the "social responsibilities of business" are notable for their analytical looseness and lack of rigor. What does it mean to say that "business" has responsibilities? Only people can have responsibilities. A corporation is an artificial person and in this sense may have artificial responsibilities, but "business" as a whole cannot be said to have responsibilities, even in this vague sense. The first step toward clarity in examining the doctrine of the social responsibility of business is to ask precisely what it implies for whom.

Presumably, the individuals who are to be responsible are businessmen, which means individual proprietors or corporate executives. Most of the discussion of social responsibility is directed at corporations, so in what follows I shall mostly neglect the individual proprietors and speak of corporate executives.

In a free-enterprise, private-property system, a corporate executive is an employee of the owners of the business. He has direct responsibility to his employers. That responsibility is to conduct the business in accordance with their desires, which generally will be to make as much money as possible while conforming to the basic rules of the society, both those embodied in law and those embodied in ethical custom. Of course, in some cases his employers may have a different objective. A group of persons might establish a corporation for an eleemosynary purpose — for example, a hospital or a school. The manager of such a corporation will not have money profit as his objective but the rendering of certain services.

In either case, the key point is that, in his capacity as a corporate executive, the manager is the agent of the individuals who own the corporation or establish the eleemosynary institution, and his primary responsibility is to them.

Needless to say, this does not mean that it is easy to judge how well he is performing his task. But at least the criterion of performance is straightforward, and the persons among whom a voluntary contractual arrangement exists are clearly defined.

Of course, the corporate executive is also a person in his own right. As a person, he may have many other responsibilities that he recognizes or assumes voluntarily — to his family, his conscience, his feelings of charity, his church, his clubs, his city, his country. He may feel impelled by these responsibilities to devote part of his income to causes he regards as worthy, to refuse to work for particular corporations, even to leave his job, for example, to join his country's armed forces. If we wish, we may refer to some of these responsibilities as "social responsibilities." But in these respects he is acting as a principal, not an agent; he is spending his own money or time or energy, not the money of his employers or the time or energy he has contracted to devote to their purposes. If these are "social responsibilities," they are the social responsibilities of individuals, not of business.

What does it mean to say that the corporate executive has a "social responsibility" in his capacity as businessman? If this statement is not pure rhetoric, it must mean that he is to act in some way that is not in the interest of his employers. For example, that he is to refrain from increasing the price of the product in order to contribute to the social objective of preventing inflation, even though a

price increase would be in the best interests of the corporation. Or that he is to make expenditures on reducing pollution beyond the amount that is in the best interests of the corporation or that is required by law in order to contribute to the social objective of improving the environment. Or that, at the expense of corporate profits, he is to hire "hardcore" unemployed instead of better qualified available workmen to contribute to the social objective of reducing poverty.

In each of these cases, the corporate executive would be spending someone else's money for a general social interest. Insofar as his actions in accord with his "social responsibility" reduce returns to stockholders, he is spending their money. Insofar as his actions raise the price to customers, he is spending the customers' money. Insofar as his actions lower the wages of some employees, he is spending their money.

The stockholders or the customers or the employees could separately spend their own money on the particular action if they wished to do so. The executive is exercising a distinct "social responsibility," rather than serving as an agent of the stockholders or the customers or the employees, only if he spends the money in a different way than they would have spent it.

But if he does this, he is in effect imposing taxes, on the one hand, and deciding how the tax proceeds shall be spent, on the other.

This process raises political questions on two levels: principle and consequences. On the level of political principle, the imposition of taxes and the expenditure of tax proceeds are governmental functions. We have established elaborate constitutional, parliamentary, and judicial provisions to control these functions, to assure that taxes are imposed so far as possible in accordance with the preferences and desires of the public — after all, "taxation without representation" was one of the battle cries of the American Revolution.

We have a system of checks and balances to separate the legislative function of imposing taxes and enacting expenditures from the executive function of collecting taxes and administering expenditure programs and from the judicial function of mediating disputes and interpreting the law.

Here the businessman — self-selected or appointed directly or indirectly by stockholders — is to be simultaneously legislator, executive, and jurist. He is to decide whom to tax by how much and for what purpose, and he is to spend the proceeds — all this guided only by general exhortations from on high to restrain inflation, improve the environment, fight poverty and so on and on.

The whole justification for permitting the corporate executive to be selected by the stockholders is that the executive is an agent serving the interests of his principal. This justification disappears when the corporate executive imposes taxes and spends the proceeds for "social" purposes. He becomes in effect a public employee, a civil servant, even though he remains in name an employee of a private enterprise. On grounds of political principle, it is intolerable that such civil servants — insofar as their actions in the name of social responsibility are real and not just window-dressing — should be selected as they are now. If they are to be civil servants, then they must be elected through a political process. If they are to impose taxes and make expenditures to foster "social" objectives, then political machinery must be set up to make the assessment of taxes and to determine through a political process the objectives to be served.

This is the basic reason why the doctrine of "social responsibility" involves the acceptance of the socialist view that political mechanisms, not market mechanisms, are the appropriate way to determine the allocation of scarce resources to alternative uses.

On the grounds of consequences, can the corporate executive in fact discharge his alleged "social responsibilities?" On the other hand, suppose he could get away with spending the stockholders' or customers' or employees' money. How is he to know how to spend it? He is told that he must contribute to fighting inflation. How is he to know what action of his will contribute to that end? He is presumably an expert in running his company — in producing a product or selling it or financing it. But nothing about his selection makes him an expert on inflation. Will his holding down the price of his product reduce inflationary pressure? Or, by leaving more spending power in the hands of his customers, simply divert it elsewhere? Or, by forcing him to produce less because of the lower price, will it simply contribute to shortages? Even if he could answer these questions, how much cost is he justified in imposing on his stockholders, customers, and employees for this social purpose? What is his appropriate share and what is the appropriate share of others?

And, whether he wants to or not, can he get away with spending his stockholders', customers' or employees' money? Will not the stockholders fire him? (Either the present ones or those who take over when his actions in the name of social responsibility have reduced the corporation's profits and the price of its stock.) His customers and his employees can desert him for other producers and employers less scrupulous in exercising their social responsibilities.

This facet of "social responsibility" doctrine is brought into sharp relief when the doctrine is used to justify wage restraint by trade unions. The conflict of interest is naked and clear when union officials are asked to subordinate the interest of their members to some more general purpose. If the union officials try to enforce wage restraint, the consequence is likely to be wildcat strikes, rank-and-file revolts, and the emergence of strong competitors for their jobs. We thus have the ironic phenomenon that union leaders — at least in the U.S. — have objected to Government interference with the market far more consistently and courageously than have business leaders.

The difficulty of exercising "social responsibility" illustrates, of course, the great virtue of private competitive enterprise — it forces people to be responsible for their own actions and makes it difficult for them to "exploit" other people for either selfish or unselfish purposes. They can do good — but only at their own expense.

Many a reader who has followed the argument this far may be tempted to remonstrate that it is all well and good to speak of Government's having the responsibility to impose taxes and determine expenditures for such "social" purposes as controlling pollution or training the hard-core unemployed, but that the problems are too urgent to wait on the slow course of political processes, that the exercise of social responsibility by businessmen is a quicker and surer way to solve pressing current problems.

Aside from the question of fact — I share Adam Smith's skepticism about the benefits that can be expected from "those who affected to trade for the public good" — this argument must be rejected on grounds of principle. What it amounts to is an assertion that those who favor the taxes and expenditures in question have failed to persuade a majority of their fellow citizens to be of like mind and that they are seeking to attain by undemocratic procedures what they cannot attain by democratic procedures. In a free society, it is hard for "evil" people to do "evil," especially since one man's good is another's evil.

I have, for simplicity, concentrated on the special case of the corporate executive, except only for the brief digression on trade unions. But precisely the same argument applies to the newer phenomenon of calling upon stockholders to require corporations to exercise social responsibility (the recent G.M. crusade for example). In most of these cases, what is in effect involved is some stockholders trying to get other stockholders (or customers or employees) to contribute against their will to "social" causes favored by the activists. Insofar as they succeed, they are again imposing taxes and spending the proceeds.

The situation of the individual proprietor is somewhat different. If he acts to reduce the returns of his enterprise in order to exercise his "social responsibility," he is spending his own money, not someone else's. If he wishes to spend his money on such purposes, that is his right, and I cannot see that there is any objection to his doing so. In the process, he, too, may impose costs on employees and customers. However, because he is far less likely than a large corporation or union to have monopolistic power, any such side effects will tend to be minor.

Of course, in practice, the doctrine of social responsibility is frequently a cloak for actions that are justified on other grounds rather than a reason for those actions.

To illustrate, it may well be in the long-run interest of a corporation that is a major employer in a small community to devote resources to providing amenities to that community or to improving its government. That may make it easier to attract desirable employees, it may reduce the wage bill or lessen losses from pilferage and sabotage or have other worthwhile effects. Or it may be that, given the laws about the deductibility of corporate charitable contributions, the stockholders can contribute more to charities they favor by having the corporation make the gift than by doing it themselves, since they can in that way contribute an amount that would otherwise have been paid as corporate taxes.

In each of these — and many similar — cases, there is a strong temptation to rationalize these actions as an exercise of "social responsibility." In the present climate of opinion, with its wide-spread aversion to "capitalism," "profits," the "soulless corporation," and so on, this is one way for a corporation to generate goodwill as a by-product of expenditures that are entirely justified in its own self-interest.

It would be inconsistent of me to call on corporate executives to refrain from this hypocritical window-dressing because it harms the foundations of a free society. That would be to call on them to exercise a "social responsibility"! If our institutions, and the attitudes of the public make it in their self-interest to cloak their actions in this way, I cannot summon much indignation to denounce them. At the same time, I can express admiration for those individual proprietors or owners of closely held corporations or stockholders of more broadly held corporations who disdain such tactics as approaching fraud.

Whether blameworthy or not, the use of the cloak of social responsibility, and the nonsense spoken in its name by influential and prestigious businessmen, does clearly harm the foundations of a free society. I have been impressed time and again by the schizophrenic character of many businessmen. They are capable of being extremely far-sighted and clear-headed in matters that are internal to their businesses. They are incredibly short-sighted and muddle-headed in matters that are outside their businesses but affect the possible survival of business in general. This short-sightedness is strikingly exemplified in the calls from many businessmen for wage and price guidelines or controls or income policies. There is nothing that could do more in a brief period to destroy a market system and replace it by a centrally controlled system than effective governmental control of prices and wages.

The short-sightedness is also exemplified in speeches by businessmen on social responsibility. This may gain them kudos in the short run. But it helps to strengthen the already too prevalent view that the pursuit of profits is wicked and immoral and must be curbed and controlled by external forces. Once this view is adopted, the external forces that curb the market will not be the social consciences, however highly developed, of the pontificating executives; it will be the iron fist of Government bureaucrats. Here, as with price and wage controls, businessmen seem to me to reveal a suicidal impulse.

The political principle that underlies the market mechanism is unanimity. In an ideal free market resting on private property, no individual can coerce any other, all cooperation is voluntary, all parties to such cooperation benefit or they need not participate. There are no values, no "social" responsibilities in any sense other than the shared values and responsibilities of individuals. Society is a collection of individuals and of the various groups they voluntarily form.

The political principle that underlies the political mechanism is conformity. The individual must serve a more general social interest — whether that be determined by a church or a dictator or a majority. The individual may have a vote and say in what is to be done, but if he is overruled, he must conform. It is appropriate for some to require others to contribute to a general social purpose whether they wish to or not.

Unfortunately, unanimity is not always feasible. There are some respects in which conformity appears unavoidable, so I do not see how one can avoid the use of the political mechanism altogether.

But the doctrine of "social responsibility" taken seriously would extend the scope of the political mechanism to every human activity. It does not differ in philosophy from the most explicitly collectivist doctrine. It differs only by professing to believe that collectivist ends can be attained without collectivist means. That is why, in my book *Capitalism and Freedom*, I have called it a "fundamentally subversive doctrine" in a free society, and have said that in such a society, "there is one and only one social responsibility of business — to use its resources and engage in activities designed to increase its profits so long as it stays within the rules of the game, which is to say, engages in open and free competition without deception or fraud."

The Responsibilities of Corporations and Their Owners

John G. Simon, Charles W. Powers, and Jon P. Gunnemann

... Our analysis of the controversies surrounding the notion of corporate responsibility — and the suggestion that the university as an investor should be concerned with corporate responsibility — proceeds in large part from our approach to certain issues in the area of social responsibility and public morals. In particular, we (1) make a distinction between negative injunctions and affirmative duties; (2) assert that all men have the "moral minimum" obligation not to impose social injury; (3) delineate those conditions under which one is held responsible for social injury, even where it is not clear that the injury was self-caused; and (4) take a position in the argument between those who strive for moral purity and those who strive for moral effectiveness.

NEGATIVE INJUNCTIONS AND AFFIRMATIVE DUTIES

A distinction which informs much of our discussion differentiates between injunctions against activities that injure others and duties which require the affirmative pursuit of some good. The failure to make this distinction in debate on public ethics often results in false dichotomies, a point illustrated by an article which appeared just over a decade ago in the *Harvard Business Review*. In that article, which provoked considerable debate in the business community, Theodore Levitt argued against corporate social responsibility both because it was dangerous for society and because it detracted from the primary goal of business, the making of profit. We deal with the merits of these arguments later; what is important for our immediate purpose, however, is Levitt's designation of those activities and concerns which constitute social responsibility. He notes that the corporation has become "more concerned about the needs of its employees, about schools, hospitals, welfare agencies and even aesthetics," and that it is "fashionable ... for the corporation to show that it is a great innovator; more specifically, a great public benefactor; and, very particularly, that it exists 'to serve the public.'"[1] Having so delimited the notion of corporate responsibility, Levitt presents the reader with a choice between, on the one hand, getting involved in the management of society, "creating munificence for one and all," and, on the other hand, fulfilling the profit-making function. But such a choice excludes another meaning of corporate responsibility: the making of profits in such a way as to minimize social in-jury. Levitt at no point considers the possibil-ity that business activity may at times injure others and that it may be necessary to regu-late the social consequences of one's business activities accordingly. . . .

Our public discourse abounds with similar failures to distinguish between positive and perhaps lofty ideals and minimal require-ments of social organization. During the elec-tion campaigns of the 1950s and the civil rights movement of the early 1960s, the slo-gan, "You can't legislate morality," was a pop-ular cry on many fronts. Obviously, we have not succeeded in devising laws that create within our citizens a predisposition to love and kindness; but we can devise laws which will minimize the injury that one citizen must suffer at the hands of another. Although the virtue of love may be the possession of a few, justice — in the minimal sense of not injur-ing others — can be required of all.

The distinction between negative injunc-tions and affirmative duties is old, having roots in common law and equity jurispru-dence.[2] Here it is based on the premise that it is easier to specify and enjoin a civil wrong than to state what should be done. In the Ten Commandments, affirmative duties are spelled out only for one's relations with God and parents; for the more public relation-ships, we are given only the negative injunc-tion: "Thou shalt not. . . ." Similarly, the Bill of Rights contains only negative injunctions.

AVOIDANCE AND CORRECTION OF SOCIAL INJURY AS A "MORAL MINIMUM"

We do not mean to distinguish between nega-tive injunctions and affirmative duties solely in the interests of analytical precision. The negative injunction to avoid and correct social injury threads its way through all morality. We

call it a "moral minimum," implying that how-ever one may choose to limit the concept of social responsibility, one cannot exclude this negative injunction. Although reasons may exist why certain persons or institutions can-not or should not be required to pursue moral or social good in all situations, there are many fewer reasons why one should be ex-cused from the injunction against injuring others. Any citizen, individual or institutional, may have competing obligations which could, under some circumstances, override this neg-ative injunction. But these special circum-stances do not wipe away the prima facie obligation to avoid harming others.

In emphasizing the central role of the neg-ative injunction, we do not suggest that affir-mative duties are never important. A society where citizens go well beyond the require-ment to avoid damage to others will surely be a better community. But we do recognize that individuals exhibit varying degrees of com-mitment to promote affirmatively the public welfare, whereas we expect everyone equally to refrain from injuring others.

The view that all citizens are equally oblig-ated to avoid or correct any social injury which is self-caused finds support in our legal as well as our moral tradition. H. L. A. Hart and A. M. Honoré have written:

> In the moral judgments of ordinary life, we have occasion to blame people because they have caused harm to others, and also, if less fre-quently, to insist that morally they are bound to compensate those to whom they have caused harm. These are the moral analogues of more precise legal conceptions: for, in all legal sys-tems liability to be punished or to make com-pensation frequently depends on whether ac-tions (or omissions) have caused harm. Moral blame is not of course confined to such cases of causing harm.[3]

We know of no societies, from the literature of anthropology or comparative ethics, whose moral codes do not contain some injunction against harming others. The specific notion of *harm* or *social injury* may vary, as well as the mode of correction and restitution, but the injunctions are present. . . .

We asserted earlier that it is easier to enjoin and correct a wrong than it is to prescribe affirmatively what is good for society and what ought to be done. Notions of the public good and the values that men actively seek to implement are subjects of intense disagreement. In this realm, pluralism is almost inevitable, and some would argue that it is healthy. Yet there can also be disagreement about what constitutes social injury or harm. What some people think are affirmative duties may be seen by others as correction of social injury. For example, the notion that business corporations should make special effort to train and employ members of minority groups could be understood by some to fulfill an affirmative duty on the part of corporations to meet society's problems; but it could be interpreted by others as the correction of a social injury caused by years of institutional racism. As a more extreme example, a Marxist would in all probability contend that *all* corporate activity is socially injurious and that therefore all social pursuits by corporations are corrective responses rather than affirmative actions.

Although the notion of *social injury* is imprecise and although many hard cases will be encountered in applying it, we think that it is a helpful designation and that cases can be decided on the basis of it. In the law, many notions (such as *negligence* in the law of torts or *consideration* in the law of contracts) are equally vague but have received content from repeated decision making over time. We would hope that under our proposed Guidelines similar "case law" would develop. Moreover, our Guidelines attempt to give some contents to the notion of *social injury* by referring to external norms: *social injury* is defined

as "particularly including activities which violate, or frustrate the enforcement of, rules of domestic or international law intended to protect individuals against deprivation of health, safety or basic freedoms."

In sum, we would affirm the prima facie obligation of all citizens, both individual and institutional, to avoid and correct self-caused social injury. Much more in the way of affirmative acts may be expected of certain kinds of citizens, but none is exempt from this "moral minimum."

In some cases it may not be true — or at least it may not be clear — that one has caused or helped to cause social injury, and yet one may bear responsibility for correcting or averting the injury. We consider next the circumstances under which this responsibility may arise.

NEED, PROXIMITY, CAPABILITY, AND LAST RESORT (THE KEW GARDENS PRINCIPLE)

Several years ago the public was shocked by the news accounts of the stabbing and agonizingly slow death of Kitty Genovese in the Kew Gardens section of New York City while thirty-eight people watched or heard and did nothing.[4] What so deeply disturbed the public's moral sensibility was that in the face of a critical human need, people who were close to that need and had the power to do something about it failed to act.

The public's reaction suggests that, no matter how narrowly one may conceive of social responsibility, there are some situations in which a combination of circumstances thrusts upon us an obligation to respond. Life is fraught with emergency situations in which a failure to respond is a special form of violation of the negative injunction against causing social injury: a sin of omission becomes a sin of commission.

Legal responsibility for aiding someone in cases of grave distress or injury, even when caused by another, is recognized by many European civil codes and by the criminal laws of one of our states:

(A) A person who knows that another is exposed to grave physical harm shall, to the extent that the same can be rendered without danger or peril to himself or without interference with important duties owed to others, give reasonable assistance to the exposed person unless that assistance or care is being provided by others. . . .

(C) A person who wilfully violates subsection (A) of this section shall be fined not more than $100.00.[5]

This Vermont statute recognizes that it is not reasonable in all cases to require a person to give assistance to someone who is endangered. If such aid imperils himself, or interferes with duties owed to others, or if there are others providing the aid, the person is excepted from the obligation. These conditions of responsibility give some shape to difficult cases and are in striking parallel with the conditions which existed at Kew Gardens. The salient features of the Kitty Genovese case are (1) critical need; (2) the proximity of the thirty-eight spectators; (3) the capability of the spectators to act helpfully (at least to telephone the police); and (4) the absence of other (including official) help; i.e., the thirty-eight were the last resort. There would, we believe, be widespread agreement that a moral obligation to aid another arises when these four features are present. What we have called the "moral minimum" (the duty to avoid and correct self-caused social injury) is an obvious and easy example of fulfillment of these criteria — so obvious that there is little need to go through step-by-step analysis of these factors. Where the injury is not clearly self-caused, the application of these criteria aids in deciding responsibility. We have

called this combination of features governing difficult cases the "Kew Gardens Principle." There follows a more detailed examination of each of the features:

Need. In cases where the other three criteria are constant, increased need increases responsibility. Just as there is no precise definition of social injury (one kind of need), there is no precise definition of need or way of measuring its extent.

Proximity. The thirty-eight witnesses of the Genovese slaying were geographically close to the deed. But proximity to a situation of need is not necessarily spatial. Proximity is largely a function of notice: we hold a person blameworthy if he knows of imperilment and does not do what he reasonably can do to remedy the situation. Thus, the thirty-eight at Kew Gardens were delinquent not because they were near but because nearness enabled them to know that someone was in need. A deaf person who could not hear the cries for help would not be considered blameworthy even if he were closer than those who could hear. So also, a man in Afghanistan is uniquely responsible for the serious illness of a man in Peoria, Illinois, if he has knowledge of the man's illness, if he can telephone a doctor about it, and if he alone has that notice. When we become aware of a wrongdoing or a social injury, we take on obligations that we did not have while ignorant.

Notice does not exhaust the meaning of proximity, however. It is reasonable to maintain that the sick man's neighbors in Peoria were to some extent blameworthy if they made no effort to inquire into the man's welfare. Ignorance cannot always be helped, but we do expect certain persons and perhaps institutions to look harder for information about critical need.[6] In this sense, proximity has to do with the network of social expectations that flow from notions of civic duty, duties to one's family, and so on. Thus, we expect a man to be more alert to the plight of his next-door neighbor than to the needs of a child in East Pakistan, just as we expect a man to be more alert to the situation of his own children than to the problems of the family down the block. The failure of the man to act in conformance with this expectation does not give him actual notice of need, but it creates what the law would call *constructive notice.* Both factors — actual notice and constructive notice growing out of social expectation — enter into the determination of responsibility and blame.

Capability. Even if there is a need to which a person has proximity, that person is not usually held responsible unless there is something he can reasonably be expected to do to meet the need. To follow Immanuel Kant, *ought* assumes *can.* What one is reasonably capable of doing, of course, admits to some variety of interpretation. In the Kew Gardens incident, it might not have been reasonable to expect someone to place his body between the girl and the knife. It was surely reasonable to expect someone to call the police. So also it would not seem to be within the canons of reasonability for a university to sacrifice education for charity. . . . But if the university is able, by non-self-sacrificial means, to mitigate injury caused by a company of which it is an owner, it would not seem unreasonable to ask it to do so.

Last Resort. In the emergency situations we have been describing, one becomes more responsible the less likely it is that someone else will be able to aid. Physical proximity is a factor here, as is time. If the knife is drawn, one cannot wait for the policeman. It is important to note here that determination of last resort becomes more difficult the more complex the social situation or organization. The man on the road to Jericho, in spite of the presence of a few other travelers, probably had a fairly good notion that he was the only person who could help the man attacked by thieves. But on a street in New York City, there is always the hope that someone else will step forward to give aid. Surely this rationalization entered into the silence of each of the thirty-eight: there were, after all, thirty-seven others. Similarly, within large corporations it is difficult to know not only whether one alone has notice of a wrongdoing, but also whether there is anyone else who is able to respond. Because of this diffusion of responsibility in complex organizations and societies, the notion of last resort is less useful than the other Kew Gardens criteria in determining whether one ought to act in aid of someone in need or to avert or correct social injury. Failure to act because one hopes someone else will act — or because one is trying to find out who is the last resort — may frequently lead to a situation in which no one acts at all. This fact, we think, places more weight on the first three features of the Kew Gardens Principle in determining responsibility, and it creates a presumption in favor of taking action when those three conditions are present.

NOTES

1. Theodore Levitt, "The Dangers of Social Responsibility," *Harvard Business Review* (Sept.–Oct. 1958): 41–50.
2. We are grateful to President Edward Bloustein of Rutgers University for suggesting this terminology and for inviting our attention to its historical antecedents. Further analysis of the distinction between *negative injunctions* and *affirmative duties* is given in the following sections of this chapter.
3. H. L. A. Hart and A. M. Honoré, *Causation in the Law* (Oxford, 1959), p. 59.
4. See A. M. Rosenthal, *Thirty-Eight Witnesses* (New York, 1964).

5. "Duty to Aid the Endangered Act," *Vt. Stat. Ann.*, Ch. 12, §519 (Supp. 1968). See G. Hughes, "Criminal Omissions," 67 *Yale L. J.* 590 (1958).

6. See, for example, Albert Speer's reflection on his role during the Hitler regime: "For being

in a position to know and nevertheless shunning knowledge creates direct responsibility for the consequences — from the very beginning." *Inside the Third Reich* (New York, 1970), p. 19.

A Stakeholder Theory of the Modern Corporation

R. Edward Freeman

INTRODUCTION

Corporations have ceased to be merely legal devices through which the private business transactions of individuals may be carried on. Though still much used for this purpose, the corporate form has acquired a larger significance. The corporation has, in fact, become both a method of property tenure and a means of organizing economic life. Grown to tremendous proportions, there may be said to have evolved a "corporate system" — which has attracted to itself a combination of attributes and powers, and has attained a degree of prominence entitling it to be dealt with as a major social institution.[1]

Despite these prophetic words of Berle and Means (1932), scholars and managers alike continue to hold sacred the view that managers bear a special relationship to the stockholders in the firm. Since stockholders own shares in the firm, they have certain rights and privileges, which must be granted to them by management, as well as by others. Sanctions, in the form of "the law of corporations," and other protective mechanisms in the form of social custom, accepted manage-

ment practice, myth, and ritual, are thought to reinforce the assumption of the primacy of the stockholder.

The purpose of this paper is to pose several challenges to this assumption, from within the framework of managerial capitalism, and to suggest the bare bones of an alternative theory, *a stakeholder theory of the modern corporation*. I do not seek the demise of the modern corporation, either intellectually or in fact. Rather, I seek its transformation. In the words of Neurath, we shall attempt to "rebuild the ship, plank by plank, while it remains afloat."[2]

My thesis is that I can revitalize the concept of managerial capitalism by replacing the notion that managers have a duty to stockholders with the concept that managers bear a fiduciary relationship to stakeholders. Stakeholders are those groups who have a stake in or claim on the firm. Specifically I include suppliers, customers, employees, stockholders, and the local community, as well as management in its role as agent for these groups. I argue that the legal, economic, political, and moral challenges to the currently

Portions of this essay are contained in William E. Evan and R. Edward Freeman, "A Stakeholder Theory of the Modern Corporation: Kantian Capitalism" published in the third (1988) and fourth (1993) edition of this anthology and in R. Edward Freeman, "The Politics of Stakeholder Theory," *Business Ethics Quarterly,* 4 (1994), pp. 409–21. I am grateful to the editors of this volume for their editing of these two works. Used by permission.

received theory of the firm, as a nexus of contracts among the owners of the factors of production and customers, require us to revise this concept. That is, each of these stakeholder groups has a right not to be treated as a means to some end, and therefore must participate in determining the future direction of the firm in which they have a stake.

The crux of my argument is that we must reconceptualize the firm around the following question: For whose benefit and at whose expense should the firm be managed? I shall set forth such a reconceptualization in the form of a *stakeholder theory of the firm*. I shall then critically examine the stakeholder view and its implications for the future of the capitalist system.

THE ATTACK ON MANAGERIAL CAPITALISM

The Legal Argument

The basic idea of managerial capitalism is that in return for controlling the firm, management vigorously pursues the interests of stockholders. Central to the managerial view of the firm is the idea that management can pursue market transactions with suppliers and customers in an unconstrained manner.

The law of corporations gives a less clearcut answer to the question: In whose interest and for whose benefit should the modern corporation be governed? While it says that the corporations should be run primarily in the interests of the stockholders in the firm, it says further that the corporation exists "in contemplation of the law" and has personality as a "legal person," limited liability for its actions, and immortality, since its existence transcends that of its members. Therefore, directors and other officers of the firm have a fiduciary obligation to stockholders in the sense that the "affairs of the corpo-

ration" must be conducted in the interest of the stockholders. And stockholders can theoretically bring suit against those directors and managers for doing otherwise. But since the corporation is a legal person, existing in contemplation of the law, managers of the corporation are constrained by law.

Until recently, this was no constraint at all. In this century, however, the law has evolved to effectively constrain the pursuit of stockholder interests at the expense of other claimants on the firm. It has, in effect, required that the claims of customers, suppliers, local communities, and employees be taken into consideration, though in general they are subordinated to the claims of stockholders.

For instance, the doctrine of "privity of contract," as articulated in *Winterbottom v. Wright* in 1842, has been eroded by recent developments in products liability law. Indeed, *Greenman v. Yuba Power* gives the manufacturer strict liability for damage caused by its products, even though the seller has exercised all possible care in the preparation and sale of the product and the consumer has not bought the product from nor entered into any contractual arrangement with the manufacturer. Caveat emptor has been replaced, in large part, with caveat venditor.[3] The Consumer Product Safety Commission has the power to enact product recalls, and in 1980 one U.S. automobile company recalled more cars than it built. Some industries are required to provide information to customers about a product's ingredients, whether or not the customers want and are willing to pay for this information.[4]

The same argument is applicable to management's dealings with employees. The National Labor Relations Act gave employees the right to unionize and to bargain in good faith. It set up the National Labor Relations Board to enforce these rights with management. The Equal Pay Act of 1963 and Title

VII of the Civil Rights Act of 1964 constrain management from discrimination in hiring practices; these have been followed with the Age Discrimination in Employment Act of 1967.[5] The emergence of a body of administrative case law arising from labor-management disputes and the historic settling of discrimination claims with large employers such as AT&T have caused the emergence of a body of practice in the corporation that is consistent with the legal guarantee of the rights of the employees. The law has protected the due process rights of those employees who enter into collective bargaining agreements with management. As of the present, however, only 30 percent of the labor force are participating in such agreements; this has prompted one labor law scholar to propose a statutory law prohibiting dismissals of the 70 percent of the work force not protected.[6]

The law has also protected the interests of local communities. The Clean Air Act and Clean Water Act have constrained management from "spoiling the commons." In an historic case, *Marsh v. Alabama,* the Supreme Court ruled that a company-owned town was subject to the provisions of the U.S. Constitution, thereby guaranteeing the rights of local citizens and negating the "property rights" of the firm. Some states and municipalities have gone further and passed laws preventing firms from moving plants or limiting when and how plants can be closed. In sum, there is much current legal activity in this area to constrain management's pursuit of stockholders' interests at the expense of the local communities in which the firm operates.

I have argued that the result of such changes in the legal system can be viewed as giving some rights to those groups that have a claim on the firm, for example, customers, suppliers, employees, local communities, stockholders, and management. It raises the question, at the core of a theory of the firm: In whose interest and for whose benefit should the firm be managed? The answer proposed by managerial capitalism is clearly "the stockholders," but I have argued that the law has been progressively circumscribing this answer.

The Economic Argument

In its pure ideological form managerial capitalism seeks to maximize the interests of stockholders. In its perennial criticism of government regulation, management espouses the "invisible hand" doctrine. It contends that it creates the greatest good for the greatest number, and therefore government need not intervene. However, we know that externalities, moral hazards, and monopoly power exist in fact, whether or not they exist in theory. Further, some of the legal apparatus mentioned above has evolved to deal with just these issues.

The problem of the "tragedy of the commons" or the free-rider problem pervades the concept of public goods such as water and air. No one has an incentive to incur the cost of clean-up or the cost of nonpollution, since the marginal gain of one firm's action is small. Every firm reasons this way, and the result is pollution of water and air. Since the industrial revolution, firms have sought to internalize the benefits and externalize the costs of their actions. The cost must be borne by all, through taxation and regulation; hence we have the emergence of the environmental regulations of the 1970s.

Similarly, moral hazards arise when the purchaser of a good or service can pass along the cost of that good. There is no incentive to economize, on the part of either the producer or the consumer, and there is excessive use of the resources involved. The institutionalized practice of third-party payment in health care is a prime example.

Finally, we see the avoidance of competitive behavior on the part of firms, each seeking to monopolize a small portion of the market and not compete with one another. In a number of industries, oligopolies have emerged, and while there is questionable evidence that oligopolies are not the most efficient corporate form in some industries, suffice it to say that the potential for abuse of market power has again led to regulation of managerial activity. In the classic case, AT&T, arguably one of the great technological and managerial achievements of the century, was broken up into eight separate companies to prevent its abuse of monopoly power.

Externalities, moral hazards, and monopoly power have led to more external control on managerial capitalism. There are de facto constraints, due to these economic facts of life, on the ability of management to act in the interests of stockholders.

A STAKEHOLDER THEORY OF THE FIRM

The Stakeholder Concept

Corporations have stakeholders, that is, groups and individuals who benefit from or are harmed by, and whose rights are violated or respected by, corporate actions. The concept of stakeholders is a generalization of the notion of stockholders, who themselves have some special claim on the firm. Just as stockholders have a right to demand certain actions by management, so do other stakeholders have a right to make claims. The exact nature of these claims is a difficult question that I shall address, but the logic is identical to that of the stockholder theory. Stakes require action of a certain sort, and conflicting stakes require methods of resolution.

Freeman and Reed (1983)[7] distinguish two senses of *stakeholder*. The "narrow definition" includes those groups who are vital to the survival and success of the corporation. The "wide-definition" includes any group or individual who can affect or is affected by the corporation. I shall begin with a modest aim: to articulate a stakeholder theory using the narrow definition.

Stakeholders in the Modern Corporation

Figure 1 depicts the stakeholders in a typical large corporation. The stakes of each are reciprocal, since each can affect the other in terms of harms and benefits as well as rights and duties. The stakes of each are not univocal and would vary by particular corporation. I merely set forth some general notions that seem to be common to many large firms.

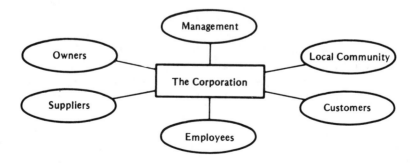

FIGURE 1.   A Stakeholder Model of the Corporation.

Owners have financial stake in the corporation in the form of stocks, bonds, and so on, and they expect some kind of financial return from them. Either they have given money directly to the firm, or they have some historical claim made through a series of morally justified exchanges. The firm affects their livelihood or, if a substantial portion of their retirement income is in stocks or bonds, their ability to care for themselves when they can no longer work. Of course, the stakes of owners will differ by type of owner, preferences for money, moral preferences, and so on, as well as by type of firm. The owners of AT&T are quite different from the owners of Ford Motor Company, with stock of the former company being widely dispersed among 3 million stockholders and that of the latter being held by a small family group as well as by a large group of public stockholders.

Employees have their jobs and usually their livelihood at stake; they often have specialized skills for which there is usually no perfectly elastic market. In return for their labor, they expect security, wages, benefits, and meaningful work. In return for their loyalty, the corporation is expected to provide for them and carry them through difficult times. Employees are expected to follow the instructions of management most of the time, to speak favorably about the company, and to be responsible citizens in the local communities in which the company operates. Where they are used as means to an end, they must participate in decisions affecting such use. The evidence that such policies and values as described here lead to productive company-employee relationships is compelling. It is equally compelling to realize that the opportunities for "bad faith" on the part of both management and employees are enormous. "Mock participation" in quality circles, singing the company song, and wearing the company uniform solely to please manage-

ment all lead to distrust and unproductive work.

Suppliers, interpreted in a stakeholder sense, are vital to the success of the firm, for raw materials will determine the final product's quality and price. In turn the firm is a customer of the supplier and is therefore vital to the success and survival of the supplier. When the firm treats the supplier as a valued member of the stakeholder network, rather than simply as a source of materials, the supplier will respond when the firm is in need. Chrysler traditionally had very close ties to its suppliers, even to the extent that led some to suspect the transfer of illegal payments. And when Chrysler was on the brink of disaster, the suppliers responded with price cuts, accepting late payments, financing, and so on. Supplier and company can rise and fall together. Of course, again, the particular supplier relationships will depend on a number of variables such as the number of suppliers and whether the supplies are finished goods or raw materials.

Customers exchange resources for the products of the firm and in return receive the benefits of the products. Customers provide the lifeblood of the firm in the form of revenue. Given the level of reinvestment of earnings in large corporations, customers indirectly pay for the development of new products and services. Peters and Waterman (1982)[8] have argued that being close to the customer leads to success with other stakeholders and that a distinguishing characteristic of some companies that have performed well is their emphasis on the customer. By paying attention to customers' needs, management automatically addresses the needs of suppliers and owners. Moreover, it seems that the ethic of customer service carries over to the community. Almost without fail the "excellent companies" in Peters and Waterman's study have good reputations in the community. I would argue that Peters and Waterman have found multiple applications of Kant's dictum, "Treat persons as ends unto themselves," and it should come as no surprise that persons respond to such respectful treatment, be they customers, suppliers, owners, employees, or members of the local community. The real surprise is the novelty of the application of Kant's rule in a theory of good management practice.

The local community grants the firm the right to build facilities and, in turn, it benefits from the tax base and economic and social contributions of the firm. In return for the provision of local services, the firm is expected to be a good citizen, as is any person, either "natural or artificial." The firm cannot expose the community to unreasonable hazards in the form of pollution, toxic waste, and so on. If for some reason the firm must leave a community, it is expected to work with local leaders to make the transition as smoothly as possible. Of course, the firm does not have perfect knowledge, but when it discovers some danger or runs afoul of new competition, it is expected to inform the local community and to work with the community to overcome any problem. When the firm mismanages its relationship with the local community, it is in the same position as a citizen who commits a crime. It has violated the implicit social contract with the community and should expect to be distrusted and ostracized. It should not be surprised when punitive measures are invoked.

I have not included "competitors" as stakeholders in the narrow sense, since strictly speaking they are not necessary for the survival and success of the firm; the stakeholder theory works equally well in monopoly contexts. However, competitors and government would be the first to be included in an extension of this basic theory. It is simply not true that the interests of competitors in an industry are always in conflict. There is no reason why trade associations and other multi-orga-nizational groups cannot band together to solve common problems that have little to do with how to restrain trade. Implementation of stakeholder management principles, in the long run, mitigates the need for industrial policy and an increasing role for government intervention and regulation.

The Role of Management

Management plays a special role, for it too has a stake in the modern corporation. On the one hand, management's stake is like that of employees, with some kind of explicit or implicit employment contract. But, on the other hand, management has a duty of safeguarding the welfare of the abstract entity that is the corporation. In short, management, especially top management, must look after the health of the corporation, and this involves balancing the multiple claims of conflicting stakeholders. Owners want higher financial returns, while customers want more money spent on research and development. Employees want higher wages and better benefits, while the local community wants better parks and day-care facilities.

The task of management in today's corporation is akin to that of King Solomon. The stakeholder theory does not give primacy to one stakeholder group over another, though there will surely be times when one group will benefit at the expense of others. In general, however, management must keep the relationships among stakeholders in balance. When these relationships become imbalanced, the survival of the firm is in jeopardy.

When wages are too high and product quality is too low, customers leave, suppliers suffer, and owners sell their stocks and bonds, depressing the stock price and making it difficult to raise new capital at favorable rates. Note, however, that the reason for paying returns to owners is not that they "own" the firm, but that their support is necessary for the survival of the firm, and that they have a legitimate claim on the firm. Similar reasoning applies in turn to each stakeholder group.

A stakeholder theory of the firm must redefine the purpose of the firm. The stockholder theory claims that the purpose of the firm is to maximize the welfare of the stockholders, perhaps subject to some moral or social constraints, either because such maximization leads to the greatest good or because of property rights. The purpose of the firm is quite different in my view.

"The stakeholder theory" can be unpacked into a number of stakeholder theories, each of which has a "normative core," inextricably linked to the way that corporations should be governed and the way that managers should act. So, attempts to more fully define, or more carefully define, a stakeholder theory are misguided. Following Donaldson and Preston, I want to insist that the normative, descriptive, instrumental, and metaphorical (my addition to their framework) uses of 'stakeholder' are tied together in particular political constructions to yield a number of possible "stakeholder theories." "Stakeholder theory" is thus a genre of stories about how we could live. Let me be more specific.

A "normative core" of a theory is a set of sentences that includes among others, sentences like:

(1) Corporations ought to be governed . . .
(2) Managers ought to act to . . .

where we need arguments or further narratives which include business and moral terms to fill in the blanks. This normative core is not always reducible to a fundamental ground like the theory of property, but certain normative cores are consistent with modern understandings of property. Certain elaborations of the theory of private property

plus the other institutions of political liberalism give rise to particular normative cores. But there are other institutions, other political conceptions of how society ought to be structured, so that there are different possible normative cores.

So, one normative core of a stakeholder theory might be a feminist standpoint one, rethinking how we would restructure "value-creating activity" along principles of caring and connection.[9] Another would be an ecological (or several ecological) normative cores. Mark Starik has argued that the very idea of a stakeholder theory of the *firm* ignores certain ecological necessities.[10] Exhibit 1 is suggestive of how these theories could be developed.

In the next section I shall sketch the normative core based on pragmatic liberalism. But, any normative core must address the questions in columns A or B, or explain why these questions may be irrelevant, as in the ecological view. In addition, each "theory," and I use the word hesitantly, must place the normative core within a more full-fledged account of how we could understand value-creating activity differently (column C). The only way to get on with this task is to see the stakeholder idea as a metaphor. The attempt to prescribe one and only one "normative core" and construct "a stakeholder theory" is at best a disguised attempt to smuggle a normative core past the unsophisticated noses of other unsuspecting academics who are just happy to see the end of the stockholder orthodoxy.

If we begin with the view that we can understand value-creation activity as a contractual process among those parties affected, and if for simplicity's sake we initially designate those parties as financiers, customers, suppliers, employees, and communities, then we can construct a normative core that reflects the liberal notions of autonomy, solidarity, and fairness as articulated by John

EXHIBIT 1:   A Reasonable Pluralism

	A. Corporations ought to be governed . . .	*B.* Managers ought to act . . .	*C.* The background disciplines of "value creation" are . . .
Doctrine of Fair Contracts	. . . in accordance with the six principles.	. . . in the interests of stakeholders.	—business theories —theories that explain stakeholder behavior
Feminist Standpoint Theory	. . . in accordance with the principles of caring/connection and relationships.	. . . to maintain and care for relationships and networks of stakeholders.	—business theories —feminist theory —social science understanding of networks
Ecological Principles	. . . in accordance with the principle of caring for the earth.	. . . to care for the earth.	—business theories —ecology —other

Rawls, Richard Rorty, and others.[11] Notice that building these moral notions into the foundations of how we understand value creation and contracting requires that we eschew separating the "business" part of the process from the "ethical" part, and that we start with the presumption of equality among the contractors, rather than the presumption in favor of financier rights.

The normative core for this redesigned contractual theory will capture the liberal idea of fairness if it ensures a basic equality among stakeholders in terms of their moral rights as these are realized in the firm, and if it recognizes that inequalities among stakeholders are justified if they raise the level of the least well-off stakeholder. The liberal ideal of autonomy is captured by the realization that each stakeholder must be free to enter agreements that create value for themselves, and solidarity is realized by the recognition of the mutuality of stakeholder interests.

One way to understand fairness in this context is to claim *a la* Rawls that a contract is fair if parties to the contract would agree to it in ignorance of their actual stakes. Thus, a

contract is like a fair bet, if each party is willing to turn the tables and accept the other side. What would a fair contract among corporate stakeholders look like? If we can articulate this ideal, a sort of corporate constitution, we could then ask whether actual corporations measure up to this standard, and we also begin to design corporate structures which are consistent with this Doctrine of Fair Contracts.

Imagine if you will, representative stakeholders trying to decide on "the rules of the game." Each is rational in a straightforward sense, looking out for its own self-interest. At least *ex ante,* stakeholders are the relevant parties since they will be materially affected. Stakeholders know how economic activity is organized and could be organized. They know general facts about the way the corporate world works. They know that in the real world there are or could be transaction costs, externalities, and positive costs of contracting. Suppose they are uncertain about what other social institutions exist, but they know the range of those institutions. They do not know if government exists to pick up the tab for any externalities, or if they will exist in the nightwatchman state of libertarian theory. They know success and failure stories of businesses around the world. In short, they are behind a Rawls-like veil of ignorance, and they do not know what stake each will have when the veil is lifted. What groundrules would they choose to guide them?

The first groundrule is "The Principle of Entry and Exit." Any contract that is the corporation must have clearly defined entry, exit, and renegotiation conditions, or at least it must have methods or processes for so defining these conditions. The logic is straightforward: each stakeholder must be able to determine when an agreement exists and has a chance of fulfillment. This is not to imply that contracts cannot contain contingent claims or other methods for resolving uncertainty, but rather that it must contain methods for determining whether or not it is valid.

The second groundrule I shall call "The Principle of Governance," and it says that the procedure for changing the rules of the game must be agreed upon by unanimous consent. Think about the consequences of a majority of stakeholders systematically "selling out" a minority. Each stakeholder, in ignorance of its actual role, would seek to avoid such a situation. In reality this principle translates into each stakeholder never giving up its right to participate in the governance of the corporation, or perhaps into the existence of stakeholder governing boards.

The third groundrule I shall call "The Principle of Externalities," and it says that if a contract between A and B imposes a cost on C, then C has the option to become a party to the contract, and the terms are renegotiated. Once again the rationality of this condition is clear. Each stakeholder will want insurance that it does not become C.

The fourth groundrule is "The Principle of Contracting Costs," and it says that all parties to the contract must share in the cost of

contracting. Once again the logic is straightforward. Any one stakeholder can get stuck.

A fifth groundrule is "The Agency Principle" that says that any agent must serve the interests of all stakeholders. It must adjudicate conflicts within the bounds of the other principals. Once again the logic is clear. Agents for any one group would have a privileged place.

A sixth and final groundrule we might call, "The Principle of Limited Immortality." The corporation shall be managed as if it can continue to serve the interests of stakeholders through time. Stakeholders are uncertain about the future but, subject to exit conditions, they realize that the continued existence of the corporation is in their interest. Therefore, it would be rational to hire managers who are fiduciaries to their interest and the interest of the collective. If it turns out the "collective interest" is the empty set, then this principle simply collapses into the Agency Principle.

Thus, the Doctrine of Fair Contracts consists of these six groundrules or principles:

(1) The Principle of Entry and Exit
(2) The Principle of Governance
(3) The Principle of Externalities
(4) The Principle of Contracting Costs
(5) The Agency Principle
(6) The Principle of Limited Immortality

Think of these groundrules as a doctrine which would guide actual stakeholders in devising a corporate constitution or charter. Think of management as having the duty to act in accordance with some specific constitution or charter.

Obviously, if the Doctrine of Fair Contracts and its accompanying background narratives are to effect real change, there must be requisite changes in the enabling laws of the land. I propose the following three principles to serve as constitutive elements of attempts to reform the law of corporations.

The Stakeholder Enabling Principle

Corporations shall be managed in the interests of its stakeholders, defined as employees, financiers, customers, employees, and communities.

The Principle of Director Responsibility

Directors of the corporation shall have a duty of care to use reasonable judgment to define and direct the affairs of the corporation in accordance with the Stakeholder Enabling Principle.

The Principle of Stakeholder Recourse

Stakeholders may bring an action against the directors for failure to perform the required duty of care.

Obviously, there is more work to be done to spell out these principles in terms of model legislation. As they stand, they try to capture the intuitions that drive the liberal ideals. It is equally plain that corporate constitutions which meet a test like the doctrine of fair contracts are meant to enable directors and executives to manage the corporation in conjunction with these same liberal ideals.[12]

NOTES

1. Cf. A. Berle and G. Means, *The Modern Corporation and Private Property* (New York: Commerce Clearing House, 1932), 1. For a reassessment of Berle and Means' argument after 50 years, see *Journal of Law and Economics* 26 (June 1983), especially G. Stigler and

C. Friedland, "The Literature of Economics: The Case of Berle and Means," 237–68; D. North, "Comment on Stigler and Friedland," 269–72; and G. Means, "Corporate Power in the Marketplace," 467–85.

2. The metaphor of rebuilding the ship while afloat is attributed to Neurath by W. Quine, *Word and Object* (Cambridge: Harvard University Press, 1960), and W. Quine and J. Ullian, *The Web of Belief* (New York: Random House, 1978). The point is that to keep the ship afloat during repairs we must replace a plank with one that will do a better job. Our argument is that stakeholder capitalism can so replace the current version of managerial capitalism.

3. See R. Charan and E. Freeman, "Planning for the Business Environment of the 1980s," *The Journal of Business Strategy* 1 (1980): 9–19, especially p. 15 for a brief account of the major developments in products liability law.

4. See S. Breyer, *Regulation and Its Reform* (Cambridge: Harvard University Press, 1983), 133, for an analysis of food additives.

5. See I. Millstein and S. Katsh, *The Limits of Corporate Power* (New York: Macmillan, 1981), Chapter 4.

6. Cf. C. Summers, "Protecting All Employees Against Unjust Dismissal," *Harvard Business Review* 58 (1980): 136, for a careful statement of the argument.

7. See E. Freeman and D. Reed, "Stockholders and Stakeholders: A New Perspective on Corporate Governance," in C. Huizinga, ed., *Corporate Governance: A Definitive Exploration of the Issues* (Los Angeles: UCLA Extension Press, 1983).

8. See T. Peters and R. Waterman, *In Search of Excellence* (New York: Harper and Row, 1982).

9. See, for instance, A. Wicks, D. Gilbert, and E. Freeman, "A Feminist Reinterpretation of the Stakeholder Concept," *Business Ethics Quarterly*, Vol. 4, No. 4, October 1994; and E. Freeman and J. Liedtka, "Corporate Social Responsibility: A Critical Approach," *Business Horizons*, Vol. 34, No. 4, July–August 1991, pp. 92–98.

10. At the Toronto workshop Mark Starik sketched how a theory would look if we took the environment to be a stakeholder. This fruitful line of work is one example of my main point about pluralism.

11. J. Rawls, *Political Liberalism,* New York: Columbia University Press, 1993; and R. Rorty, "The Priority of Democracy to Philosophy" in *Read-**ing Rorty: Critical Responses to Philosophy and the Mirror of Nature (and Beyond),* ed. Alan R. Malachowski, Cambridge, MA: Blackwell, 1990.

Business Ethics and Stakeholder Analysis

Kenneth E. Goodpaster

So we must think through what management should be accountable for; and how and through whom its accountability can be discharged. The stockholders' interest, both short- and long-term, is one of the areas. But it is only one.*

What is ethically responsible management? How can a corporation, given its economic mission, be managed with appropriate attention to ethical concerns? These are central questions in the field of business ethics. One approach to answering such questions that has become popular during the last two decades is loosely referred to as "stakeholder analysis." Ethically responsible management, it is often suggested, is management that includes careful attention not only to stockholders *but to stakeholders generally* in the decision-making process.

This suggestion about the ethical importance of stakeholder analysis contains an important kernel of truth, but it can also be misleading. Comparing the ethical relationship between managers and stockholders with their relationship to other stakeholders is, I will argue, almost as problematic as ignoring stakeholders (ethically) altogether — presenting us with something of a "stakeholder paradox."

---

*Peter Drucker, 1988. *Harvard Business Review.*

DEFINITION

The term "stakeholder" appears to have been invented in the early '60s as a deliberate play on the word "stockholder" to signify that there are other parties having a "stake" in the decision making of the modern, publicly held corporation in addition to those holding equity positions. Professor R. Edward Freeman, in his book *Strategic Management: A Stakeholder Approach* (Pitman, 1984), defines the term as follows:

> A stakeholder in an organization is (by definition) any group or individual who can affect or is affected by the achievement of the organization's objectives. (46)

Examples of stakeholder groups (beyond stockholders) are employees, suppliers, customers, creditors, competitors, governments, and communities. . . .

Another metaphor with which the term "stakeholder" is associated is that of a "player" in a game like poker. One with a "stake" in the game is one who plays and puts some economic value at risk.

Much of what makes responsible decision making difficult is understanding how there can be an ethical relationship between management and stakeholders that avoids being

---

From Kenneth E. Goodpaster, "Business Ethics and Stakeholder Analysis," *Business Ethics Quarterly,* 1 (January 1991), pp. 53–73. Reprinted by permission.

too weak (making stakeholders mere means to stockholders' ends) or too strong (making stakeholders quasistockholders in their own right). To give these issues life, a case example will help. So let us consider the case of General Motors and Poletown.

THE POLETOWN CASE

In 1980, GM was facing a net loss in income, the first since 1921, due to intense foreign competition. Management realized that major capital expenditures would be required for the company to regain its competitive position and profitability. A $40 billion five-year capital spending program was announced that included new, state-of-the-art assembly techniques aimed at smaller, fuel-efficient automobiles demanded by the market. Two aging assembly plants in Detroit were among the ones to be replaced. Their closure would eliminate 500 jobs. Detroit in 1980 was a city with a black majority, an unemployment rate of 18% overall and 30% for blacks, a rising public debt and a chronic budget deficit, despite high tax rates.

The site requirements for a new assembly plant included 500 acres, access to long-haul railroad and freeways, and proximity to suppliers for "just-in-time" inventory management. It needed to be ready to produce 1983 model year cars beginning in September 1982. The only site in Detroit meeting GM's requirements was heavily settled, covering a section of the Detroit neighborhood of Poletown. Of the 3,500 residents, half were black. The whites were mostly of Polish descent, retired or nearing retirement. An alternative "green field" site was available in another midwestern state.

Using the power of eminent domain, the Poletown area could be acquired and cleared for a new plant within the company's timetable, and the city government was eager

to cooperate. Because of job retention in Detroit, the leadership of the United Auto Workers was also in favor of the idea. The Poletown Neighborhood Council strongly opposed the plan, but was willing to work with the city and GM.

The new plant would employ 6,150 workers and would cost GM $500 million wherever it was built. Obtaining and preparing the Poletown site would cost an additional $200 million, whereas alternative sites in the midwest were available for $65 to $80 million.

The interested parties were many — stockholders, customers, employees, suppliers, the Detroit community, the midwestern alternative, the Poletown neighborhood. The decision was difficult. GM management needed to consider its competitive situation, the extra costs of remaining in Detroit, the consequences to the city of leaving for another part of the midwest, and the implications for the residents of choosing the Poletown site if the decision was made to stay. The decision about whom to talk to and *how* was as puzzling as the decision about *what* to do and *why*.

STAKEHOLDER ANALYSIS
AND STAKEHOLDER SYNTHESIS

Ethical values enter management decision making, it is often suggested, through the gate of stakeholder analysis. But the suggestion that introducing "stakeholder analysis" into business decisions is the same as introducing ethics into those decisions is questionable. To make this plain, let me first distinguish between two importantly different ideas: stakeholder analysis and stakeholder synthesis. I will then examine alternative kinds of stakeholder synthesis with attention to ethical content.

The decision-making process of an individual or a company can be seen in terms of a sequence of six steps to be followed after an issue or problem presents itself for resolution. For ease of reference and recall, I will name the sequence PASCAL, after the six letters in the name of the French philosopher-mathematician Blaise Pascal (1623–1662), who once remarked in reference to ethical decision making that "the heart has reasons the reason knows not of."

1. PERCEPTION or fact gathering about the options available and their short- and long-term implications;
2. ANALYSIS of these implications with specific attention to affected parties and to the decision-maker's goals, objectives, values, responsibilities, etc.;
3. SYNTHESIS of this structured information according to whatever fundamental priorities obtain in the mindset of the decision-maker;
4. CHOICE among the available options based on the synthesis;
5. ACTION or implementation of the chosen option through a series of specific requests to specific individuals or groups, resource allocation, incentives, controls, and feedback;
6. LEARNING from the outcome of the decision, resulting in either reinforcement or modification (for future decisions) of the way in which the above steps have been taken.

We might simplify this analysis, of course, to something like "input," "decision," and "output," but distinguishing interim steps can often be helpful. The main point is that the path from the presentation of a problem to its resolution must somehow involve gathering, processing, and acting on relevant information.

Now, by *stakeholder analysis* I simply mean a process that does not go beyond the first two steps mentioned above. That is, the affected parties caught up in each available option are identified and the positive and negative impacts on each stakeholder are determined. But questions having to do with processing this information into a decision and imple-

menting it are *left unanswered*. These steps are not part of the *analysis* but of the *synthesis, choice,* and *action*.

Stakeholder analysis may give the initial appearance of a decision-making process, but in fact it is only a *segment* of a decision-making process. It represents the preparatory or opening phase that awaits the crucial application of the moral (or nonmoral) values of the decision-maker. So, to be informed that an individual or an institution regularly makes stakeholder analysis part of decision making or takes a "stakeholder approach" to management is to learn little or nothing about the ethical character of that individual or institution. It is to learn only that stakeholders are regularly identified — *not why and for what purpose*. To be told that stakeholders are or must be "taken into account" is, so far, to be told very little. Stakeholder analysis is, as a practical matter, morally *neutral*. It is therefore a mistake to see it as a substitute for normative ethical thinking.

What I shall call "stakeholder synthesis" goes further into the sequence of decision-making steps mentioned above to include actual decision-making and implementation (S,C,A). The critical point is that stakeholder synthesis offers *a pattern or channel by which to move from stakeholder identification to a practical response or resolution*. Here we begin to join stakeholder analysis to questions of substance. But we must now ask: What kind of substance? And how does it relate to *ethics*? The stakeholder idea, remember, is typically offered as a way of integrating *ethical* values into management decision making. When and how does substance become *ethical* substance?

STRATEGIC STAKEHOLDER SYNTHESIS

We can imagine decision-makers doing "stakeholder analysis" for different underlying reasons, not always having to do with ethics. A management team, for example, might be careful to take positive and (especially) negative stakeholder effects into account for no other reason than that offended stakeholders might resist or retaliate (e.g., through political action or opposition to necessary regulatory clearances). It might not be *ethical* concern for the stakeholders that motivates and guides such analysis, so much as concern about potential impediments to the achievement of strategic objectives. Thus positive and negative effects on relatively powerless stakeholders may be ignored or discounted in the synthesis, choice, and action phases of the decision process.

In the Poletown case, General Motors might have done a stakeholder analysis using the following reasoning: our stockholders are the central stakeholders here, but other key stakeholders include our suppliers, old and new plant employees, the City of Detroit, and the residents of Poletown. These other stakeholders are not our direct concern as a corporation with an economic mission, but since they can influence our short- or long-term strategic interests, they must be taken into account. Public relation's costs and benefits, for example, or concerns about union contracts or litigation might well have influenced the choice between staying in Detroit and going elsewhere.

I refer to this kind of stakeholder synthesis as "strategic" since stakeholders outside the stockholder group are viewed instrumentally, as factors potentially affecting the overarching goal of optimizing stockholder interests. They are taken into account in the decision-making process, but as external environmental forces, as potential sources of either good will or retaliation. "We" are the economic principals and management; "they" are significant players whose attitudes and future actions might affect our short-term or long-term success. We must respect them in the way one "respects" the weather — as a set of forces to be reckoned with.

It should be emphasized that managers who adopt the strategic stakeholder approach are not necessarily *personally* indifferent to the plight of stakeholders who are "strategically unimportant." The point is that *in their role as managers,* with a fiduciary relationship that binds them as agents to principals, their basic outlook subordinates other stakeholder concerns to those of stockholders. . . . During the Poletown controversy, GM managers as individuals may have cared deeply about the potential lost jobs in Detroit, or about the potential dislocation of Poletown residents. But in their role as agents for the owners (stockholders) they could only allow such considerations to "count" if they served GM's strategic interests (or perhaps as legal constraints on the decision).

The essence of a strategic view of stakeholders is not that stakeholders are ignored, but that all but a special group (stockholders) are considered on the basis of their actual or potential influence on management's central mission. The basic normative principle is fiduciary responsibility (organizational prudence), supplemented by legal compliance.

IS THE SUBSTANCE ETHICAL?

The question we must ask in thinking about a strategic approach to stakeholder synthesis is this: Is it really an adequate rendering of the *ethical* component in managerial judgment? Unlike mere stakeholder *analysis,* this kind of synthesis does go beyond simply *identifying* stakeholders. It integrates the stakeholder information by using a single interest group (stockholders) as its basic normative touchstone. If this were formulated as an explicit rule or principle, it would have two parts and would read something like this: (1) Maximize the benefits and minimize the costs to the stockholder group, short- and long-term, and (2) Pay close attention to the interests of other stakeholder groups that might potentially influence the achievement of (1). But while expanding the list of stakeholders may be a way of "enlightening" self-interest for the organization, is it really a way of introducing ethical values into business decision making?

There are really two possible replies here. The first is that as an account of how ethics enters the managerial mind-set, the strategic stakeholder approach fails not because it is *im*moral; but because it is *non*moral. By most accounts of the nature of ethics, a strategic stakeholder synthesis would not qualify as an ethical synthesis, even though it does represent a substantive view. The point is simply that while there is nothing necessarily *wrong* with strategic reasoning about the consequences of one's actions for others, the kind of concern exhibited should not be confused with what most people regard as *moral* concern. Moral concern would avoid injury or unfairness to those affected by one's actions because it is wrong, regardless of the retaliatory potential of the aggrieved parties.

The second reply does question the morality (*vs.* immorality) of strategic reasoning as the ultimate principle behind stakeholder analysis. It acknowledges that strategy, when placed in a highly effective legal and regulatory environment and given a time-horizon that is relatively longterm, may well avoid significant forms of anti-social behavior. But it asserts that as an operating principle for managers under time pressure in an imperfect legal and regulatory environment, strategic analysis is insufficient. In the Poletown case, certain stakeholders (e.g., the citizens of Detroit or the residents of Poletown) may have merited more *ethical* consideration than the strategic approach would have allowed. Some critics charged that GM only considered these stakeholders *to the extent that* serving their interests also served GM's interests,

and that as a result, their interests were undermined.

Many, most notably Nobel Laureate Milton Friedman, believe that market and legal forces are adequate to translate or transmute ethical concerns into straightforward strategic concerns for management. He believes that in our economic and political system (democratic capitalism), direct concern for stakeholders (what Kant might have called "categorical" concern) is unnecessary, redundant, and inefficient, not to mention dishonest:

> In many cases, there is a strong temptation to rationalize actions as an exercise of "social responsibility." In the present climate of opinion, with its widespread aversion to "capitalism," "profits," the "soulless corporation" and so on, this is one way for a corporation to generate good will as a by-product of expenditures that are entirely justified in its own self-interest. If our institutions, and the attitudes of the public make it in their self-interest to cloak their actions in this way, I cannot summon much indignation to denounce them. At the same time, I can express admiration for those individual proprietors or owners of closely held corporations or stockholders of more broadly held corporations who disdain such tactics as approaching fraud.

Critics respond, however, that absent a pre-established harmony or linkage between organizational success and ethical success, some stakeholders, some of the time, will be affected a lot but will be able to affect in only a minor way the interests of the corporation. They add that in an increasingly global business environment, even the protections of law are fragmented by multiple jurisdictions.

At issue then is (1) defining ethical behavior partly in terms of the (nonstrategic) decision-making values *behind* it, (2) recognizing that too much optimism about the correlation between strategic success and virtue runs the risk of tailoring the latter to suit the former.

Thus the move toward substance (from analysis to synthesis) in discussions of the stakeholder concept is not necessarily a move toward ethics. And it is natural to think that the reason for this has to do with the instrumental status accorded to stakeholder groups other than stockholders. If we were to treat all stakeholders by strict analogy with stockholders, would we have arrived at a more ethically satisfactory form of stakeholder synthesis? Let us now look at this alternative, what I shall call a "multi-fiduciary" approach.

MULTI-FIDUCIARY STAKEHOLDER SYNTHESIS

In contrast to a strategic view of stakeholders, one can imagine a management team processing stakeholder information by giving the same care to the interests of, say, employees, customers, and local communities as to the economic interests of stockholders. This kind of substantive commitment to stakeholders might involve trading off the economic advantages of one group against those of another, e.g., in a plant closing decision. I shall refer to this way of integrating stakeholder analysis with decision making as "multi-fiduciary" since all stakeholders are treated by management as having equally important interests, deserving joint "maximization" (or what Herbert Simon might call "satisficing").

Professor Freeman, quoted earlier, contemplates what I am calling the multi-fiduciary view at the end of his 1984 book under the heading *The Manager As Fiduciary to Stakeholders:*

> Perhaps the most important area of future research is the issue of whether or not a theory of management can be constructed that uses the stakeholder concept to enrich "managerial cap-

italism," that is, can the notion that managers bear a fiduciary relationship to stockholders or the owners of the firm, be replaced by a concept of management whereby the manager *must* act in the interests of the stakeholders in the organization? (249)

As we have seen, the strategic approach pays attention to stakeholders as factors that might affect economic interests and as market forces to which companies must pay attention for competitive reasons. They become actual or potential legal challenges to the company's exercise of economic rationality. The multi-fiduciary approach, on the other hand, views stakeholders apart from their instrumental, economic, or legal clout. On this view, the word "stakeholder" carries with it, by the deliberate modification of a single phoneme, a dramatic shift in managerial outlook.

In 1954, famed management theorist Adolf Berle conceded a long-standing debate with Harvard law professor E. Merrick Dodd that looks in retrospect very much like a debate between what we are calling strategic and multi-fiduciary interpretations of stakeholder synthesis. Berle wrote:

> Twenty years ago, [I held] that corporate powers were powers in trust for shareholders while Professor Dodd argued that these powers were held in trust for the entire community. The argument has been settled (at least for the time being) squarely in favor of Professor Dodd's contention.

The intuitive idea behind Dodd's view, and behind more recent formulations of it in terms of "multiple constituencies" and "stakeholders, not just stockholders" is that by expanding the list of those in whose trust corporate management must manage, we thereby introduce ethical responsibility into business decision making.

In the context of the Poletown case, a multi-fiduciary approach by GM management might have identified the same stakeholders. But it would have considered the interests of employees, the city of Detroit, and the Poletown residents *alongside* stockholder interests, not solely in terms of how they might *influence* stockholder interests. This may or may not have entailed a different outcome. But it probably would have meant a different approach to the decision-making process in relation to the residents of Poletown (talking with them, for example).

We must now ask, as we did of the strategic approach: How satisfactory is multi-fiduciary stakeholder synthesis as a way of giving ethical substance to management decision making? On the face of it, and in stark contrast to the strategic approach, it may seem that we have at last arrived at a truly moral view. But we should be cautious. For no sooner do we think we have found the proper interpretation of ethics in management than a major objection presents itself. And, yes, it appears to be a *moral* objection!

It can be argued that multi-fiduciary stakeholder analysis is simply incompatible with widely-held moral convictions about the special fiduciary obligations owed by management to stockholders. At the center of the objection is the belief that the obligations of agents to principals are stronger or different in kind from those of agents to third parties.

THE STAKEHOLDER PARADOX

Managers who would pursue a multi-fiduciary stakeholder orientation for their companies must face resistance from those who believe that a strategic orientation is the only *legitimate* one for business to adopt, given the economic mission and legal constitution of the modern corporation. This may be disorienting since the word "illegitimate" has clear negative ethical connotations, and yet the multi-fiduciary approach is often defended on ethical grounds. I will refer to this anomalous situation as the *Stakeholder Paradox:*

> It seems essential, yet in some ways illegitimate, to orient corporate decisions by ethical values that go beyond strategic stakeholder considerations to multi-fiduciary ones.

I call this a paradox because it says there is an ethical problem whichever approach management takes. Ethics seems both to forbid and to demand a strategic, profit-maximizing mind-set. The argument behind the paradox focuses on management's *fiduciary* duty to the stockholder, essentially the duty to keep a profit-maximizing promise, and a concern that the "impartiality" of the multi-fiduciary approach simply cuts management loose from certain well-defined bonds of stockholder accountability. On this view, impartiality is thought to be a *betrayal of trust.*

TOWARD A NEW STAKEHOLDER SYNTHESIS

We all remember the story of the well-intentioned Doctor Frankenstein. He sought to improve the human condition by designing a powerful, intelligent force for good in the community. Alas, when he flipped the switch, his creation turned out to be a monster rather than a marvel! Is the concept of the ethical corporation like a Frankenstein monster?

Taking business ethics seriously need not mean that management bears *additional* fiduciary relationships to third parties (nonstockholder constituencies) as multi-fiduciary stakeholder synthesis suggests. It may mean that there are morally significant *nonfiduciary* obligations to third parties surrounding any fiduciary relationship (See *Figure 1.*) Such

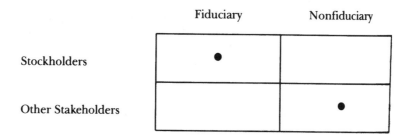

FIGURE 1.   Direct Managerial Obligations

moral obligations may be owed by private individuals as well as private-sector organizations to those whose freedom and well-being is affected by their economic behavior. It is these very obligations in fact (the duty not to harm or coerce and duties not to lie, cheat, or steal) that are cited in regulatory, legislative, and judicial arguments for constraining profit-driven business activities. These obligations are not "hypothetical" or contingent or indirect, as they would be on the strategic model, wherein they are only subject to the corporation's interests being met. They are "categorical" or direct. They are not rooted in the *fiduciary* relationship, but in other relationships at least as deep.

It must be admitted . . . that the jargon of "stakeholders" in discussions of business ethics can seem to threaten the notion of what corporate law refers to as the "undivided and unselfish loyalty" owed by managers and directors to stockholders. For this way of speaking can suggest a multiplication of management duties *of the same kind* as the duty to stockholders. What we must understand is that the responsibilities of management toward stockholders are of a piece with the obligations that *stockholders themselves* would be expected to honor in their own right. As an old Latin proverb has it, *nemo dat quod non habet,* which literally means "nobody gives what he doesn't have." Freely translating in this context we can say: No one can ex-

pect of an *agent* behavior that is ethically less responsible than what he would expect of himself. I cannot (ethically) *hire* to have done on my behalf something that I would not (ethically) *do* myself. We might refer to this as the "Nemo Dat Principle" (NDP) and consider it a formal requirement of consistency in business ethics (and professional ethics generally):

(NDP)   Investors cannot expect of managers (more generally, principals cannot expect of their agents) behavior that would be inconsistent with the reasonable ethical expectations of the community.

The NDP does not, of course, resolve in advance the many ethical challenges that managers must face. It only indicates that these challenges are of a piece with those that face us all. It offers a different kind of test (and so a different kind of stakeholder synthesis) that management (and institutional investors) might apply to policies and decisions.

The foundation of ethics in management — and the way out of the stakeholder paradox — lies in understanding that the conscience of the corporation is a logical and moral extension of the consciences of its principals. It is *not* an expansion of the *list* of principals, but a gloss on the principal-agent relationship itself. Whatever the structure of the principal-agent relationship, neither principal nor agent can ever claim that an agent has "moral immunity" from the basic obligations that would apply to any human being toward other members of the community.

Indeed, the introduction of moral reasoning (distinguished from multi-fiduciary stakeholder reasoning) into the framework of management thinking may *protect* rather than threaten private sector legitimacy. The conscientious corporation can maintain its private economic mission, but in the context of fundamental moral obligations owed by any member of society to others affected by that member's actions. Recognizing such obligations does *not* mean that an institution is a public institution. Private institutions, like private individuals, can be and are bound to respect moral obligations in the pursuit of private purposes.

Conceptually, then, we can make room for a moral posture toward stakeholders that is both *partial* (respecting the fiduciary relationship between managers and stockholders) and *impartial* (respecting the equally important nonfiduciary relationships between management and other stakeholders). . . .

Whether this conceptual room can be used *effectively* in the face of enormous pressures on contemporary managers and directors is another story, of course. For it is one thing to say that "giving standing to stakeholders" in managerial reasoning is conceptually coherent. It is something else to say that it is practically coherent.

Yet most of us, I submit, believe it. Most of us believe that management at General Motors *owed* it to the people of Detroit and to the people of Poletown to take their (nonfiduciary) interests very seriously, to seek creative solutions to the conflict, to do more than use or manipulate them in accordance with GM's needs only. We understand that managers and directors have a special obliga-

tion to provide a financial return to the stockholders, but we also understand that the word "special" in this context needs to be tempered by an appreciation of certain fundamental community norms that go beyond the demands of both laws and markets. There are certain class-action suits that stockholders ought not to win. For there is sometimes a moral defense.

CONCLUSION

The relationship between management and stockholders is ethically different in kind from the relationship between management and other parties (like employees, suppliers, customers, etc.), a fact that seems to go unnoticed by the multi-fiduciary approach. If it were not, the corporation would cease to be a private sector institution — and what is now called business ethics would become a more radical critique of our economic system than is typically thought. On this point, Milton Friedman must be given a fair and serious hearing.

This does not mean, however, that "stakeholders" lack a morally significant relationship to management, as the strategic approach implies. It means only that the relationship in question is different from a fiduciary one. Management may never have promised customers, employees, suppliers, etc. a "return on investment," but management is nevertheless obliged to take seriously its extra-legal obligations not to injure, lie to, or cheat these stakeholders *quite apart from* whether it is in the stockholders' interests.

As we think through the *proper* relationship of management to stakeholders, fundamental features of business life must undoubtedly be recognized: that corporations have a principally economic mission and competence; that fiduciary obligations to investors and general obligations to comply with the law cannot be set aside; and that abuses of economic power and disregard of corporate stewardship in the name of business ethics are possible.

But these things must be recognized as well: that corporations are not solely financial institutions; that fiduciary obligations go beyond short-term profit and are in any case subject to moral criteria in their execution; and that mere compliance with the law can be unduly limited and even unjust.

The *Stakeholder Paradox* can be avoided by a more thoughtful understanding of the nature of moral obligation and the limits it imposes on the principal-agent relationship. Once we understand that there is a practical "space" for identifying the ethical values shared by a corporation and its stockholders — a space that goes beyond strategic self-interest but stops short of impartiality — the hard work of filling that space can proceed.

Fiduciary Duties and the Shareholder-Management Relation: Or, What's So Special About Shareholders?

John R. Boatright

INTRODUCTION

It is well-established in law that officers and directors of corporations are fiduciaries. Much of the debate on corporate social responsibility from the 1930s to the present has focused on the questions: For whom are managers fiduciaries? And what are their specific fiduciary duties? The common-law view is that officers and directors are fiduciaries primarily for shareholders, who are legally the owners of a corporation, and their main fiduciary duty is to operate the corporation in the interests of the shareholders. As a result, the social responsibility of corporations is sharply restricted. In the words of Milton Friedman, "there is one and only one social responsibility of business," and that is to make as much money for the shareholders as possible.[1]

Those who argue for an expanded view of social responsibility offer a different answer to the question, for whom are managers fiduciaries? Merrick Dodd contended in 1932 that the powers of management are held in trust for the whole community. The modern corporation, he maintained, "has a social service as well as a profit-making function," and managers ought to take the interests of many different constituencies into account.[2] More recently, R. Edward Freeman has popularized the stakeholder approach, in which every group with a stake in a corporation has claims that rival those of stockholders.[3] Consequently, the fiduciary duties of management include serving the interests of employees, customers, suppliers, and the local community in addition to the traditional duties to shareholders.

From John R. Boatright, "Fiduciary Duties and the Shareholder Management Relation: Or, What's So Special About Shareholders?", *Business Ethics Quarterly,* 4 (1994). Reprinted by permission.

A prominent critic of both Dodd and Free-man is Kenneth E. Goodpaster, who cautions that a multi-fiduciary stakeholder approach overlooks an important point: that the "rela-tionship between management and stock-holders is ethically different in kind from the relationship between management and other parties (like employees, suppliers, customers, etc.)."[4] Goodpaster contends that managers have many *nonfiduciary* duties to various stakeholders, but the shareholder-manage-ment relation is unique in that managers have *fiduciary* duties to shareholders alone. Whether the relation between managers and shareholders is "ethically different," as Good-paster claims, is a question that requires some understanding of the ethical basis of the duties of management to different con-stituencies. The stakeholder approach fo-cuses largely on the basis of the duties of management to constituencies other than shareholders, which is to say, duties to em-ployees, suppliers, customers, and the like. Another procedure, however, is to look more closely at the ethical basis of the fiduciary du-ties of officers and directors of corporations to shareholders. Since the common-law view is that shareholders are special in that man-agers have a fiduciary duty to run the corpo-ration in their interests alone, we need to ask, what entitles them to this status? In short, what's so special about shareholders?

SHAREHOLDERS AS OWNERS

There is no question but that the fiduciary duties of management have been based, his-torically, on the assumption that sharehold-ers are the owners of a corporation. In *The Modern Corporation and Private Property,* Berle and Means observed that our thinking about the shareholder-management relation de-rives, in part, from the notion of equity in the

treatment of property owners, dating from the time when business ventures were under-taken by individuals with their own assets. About the origin of the fiduciary relation they wrote:

> Taking this doctrine back into the womb of eq-uity, whence it sprang, the foundation becomes plain. Wherever one man or a group of men entrusted another man or group with the man-agement of property, the second group became fiduciaries. As such they were obliged to act conscionably, which meant in fidelity to the in-terests of the persons whose wealth they had undertaken to handle.[5]

Ownership of a corporation is different, of course, from the ownership of personal as-sets. Most notably, shareholders do not have a right to possess and use corporate assets as they would their own; instead, they create a fictitious person to conduct business, with the shareholders as the beneficiaries. To the ex-tent that shareholders do not manage a cor-poration but leave control to others, there is a problem of ensuring that the hired man-agers run the corporation in the interests of the shareholders.

The law of corporate governance has ad-dressed this problem by creating a set of shareholder rights along with a set of legal duties for corporate officers and directors. The most important rights of shareholders are to elect the board of directors and to re-ceive the earnings of a corporation in the form of dividends. A main duty of officers and directors is to act as fiduciaries in the management of the corporation's assets. Since these various rights and duties are legally enforceable, they provide a relatively effective solution to the problem of account-ability.

Now, even if it is granted that shareholders are the owners of a corporation in the sense of possessing these rights, it does not follow that officers and directors have a fiduciary duty to run the corporation in the interests of shareholders. It is entirely consistent to hold that shareholders are the owners of a corporation and that the managers have a fiduciary duty to run the corporation in the interests of other constituencies. There is a logical gap, in other words, between the property rights of shareholders and the fiduciary duties of management. This does not mean that ownership is irrelevant to fiduciary duties. J. A. C. Hetherington has described ownership as "the formal legal substructure on which the fiduciary duty of management rests."[6] The point is, rather, that some further premises are needed for the argument to go through.

The most common argument for the fiduciary duties of officers and directors is that the property interests which holders have in a corporation can be protected only by a stringent set of duties to act in the interests of shareholders. Shareholders, as equity suppliers, are different from bondholders and others who provide debt — and they are different, as well, from suppliers, employees, customers, and others who have dealings with a corporation. The difference, as explained by Oliver E. Williamson, is: "The whole of their investment in the firm is potentially placed at hazard."[7] Bondholders, suppliers, and so on, are protected by contracts and other safeguards, leaving shareholders, as the owners of a corporation, to bear the preponderance of risk. The various rights of shareholders are thus important means for protecting the shareholders' investment.

Williamson observes that shareholders are unique in several other respects. He writes:

> They are the only voluntary constituency whose relation with the corporation does not come up for periodic renewal. . . . Labor, suppliers . . . debt-holders, and consumers all have opportunities to renegotiate terms when contracts are renewed. Stockholders, by contrast, invest for the life of the firm. . . . [8]

Shareholders are also unique in that "their investments are not associated with particular assets." This feature makes it more difficult to devise contracts and other safeguards like those which protect other constituencies, who can generally withdraw what they have provided. A shareholder, who has only a residual claim, can be protected only by assurance that the corporation will continue to prosper.

This argument — let us call it the equity argument — is an important justification for shareholder rights. Since shareholders are different in certain respects, and since their investment ought to be protected, it is necessary to create a governance structure which assigns them a significant role. The argument does not succeed, however, in supporting the strong claim that managers have fiduciary duties to shareholders and to shareholders alone.

First, if the only justification for fiduciary duties is the need to protect the shareholders' investment, then it is unclear why this end is not achieved by existing shareholder rights and, hence, why fiduciary duties are also necessary. That is, the rights of shareholders to elect the board of directors, vote on shareholder resolutions, and so on, constitute a kind of protection which other constituencies lack and which would seem to be adequate. Some of the fiduciary duties of management, especially those which prohibit self-dealing, may also be important safeguards, but the protection of shareholders can be achieved without a strong profit-maximizing imperative which imposes a fiduciary duty to act solely in the interests of shareholders. This more stringent fiduciary duty needs some further justification.

Second, shareholders have another important source of protection that is denied to other constituencies. Through the stock market, a shareholder can, with little effort or cost, dispose of a disappointing stock.[9] Banks, by contrast, are often stuck with bad loans; employees can change employers only with great difficulty; and communities must be content with the businesses located in their midst. The stock market also provides protection in the form of *ex ante* compensation, since stockholders have the opportunity to purchase stock that may increase in value. Investors are compensated for their risk by the opportunity to reap great rewards, and usually the greater the risk, the greater the potential rewards. Further, the stock market allows for diversification, so that a properly diversified investor should face little risk. Indeed, managers and employees of firms generally have far more at stake in the success of a corporation than do the shareholders.

For these reasons, then, the equity argument does not justify the view that officers and directors have a fiduciary duty to run a corporation in the interests of the shareholders. Insofar as shareholders are owners, they have property interests which ought to be protected, but doing so does fully account for the special status that common law gives to shareholders. Indeed, the argument treats shareholders as one class of investors among many, albeit an especially vulnerable class. Some observers have even suggested that shareholders are not properly the "owners" of the corporation at all. Just as bondholders own their bonds, so shareholders, they claim, are merely the owners of their stock.[10]

CONTRACTS AND AGENCY

Another possible basis for fiduciary duties is provided by the supposition of a contract between shareholders and management and, in particular, of an agency relation whereby the managers of a corporation agree specifically to act as agents of shareholders in the latter's pursuit of wealth. This basis is logically independent of ownership, but if we ask what enables shareholders to contract with management or act as a principal, one answer is their status as owners. Thus, the logical gap between ownership and fiduciary duties might be bridged by the idea that owners hire other persons by means of a contract to become the managers of their property.

In his rejection of a multi-fiduciary approach, Goodpaster clearly assumes that the shareholder-management relation is based on a contract or an agency relation. He writes:

> It can be argued that multi-fiduciary stakeholder analysis is simply incompatible with widely-held moral convictions about the special fiduciary obligations owed by management to stockholders. At the center of the objection is the belief that the obligations of agents to principals are stronger or different in kind from those of agents to third parties.[11]

In another passage Goodpaster explains how the duties of management to third parties can be "morally significant" yet different from the duties owed to shareholders by observing that "management may never have *promised* customers, employees, suppliers, etc. a 'return on investment,' but management is nevertheless obliged to take seriously its extra-legal obligations" to these stakeholders.[12] The suggestion is that management has made a promise to shareholders to act in their interests and that the obligation created by this promise is a legal obligation. The obligations to other constituencies, in contrast, are based on something other than a promise and are nonlegal in character.

Further, Goodpaster claims that what he calls the stakeholder paradox "can be avoided by a more thoughtful understanding of the nature of moral obligation and the limits it imposes on the principal-agent relationship."[13] The stakeholder paradox, according to Goodpaster, is that:

> It seems essential, yet in some ways illegitimate, to orient corporate decisions by ethical values that go beyond strategic stakeholder considerations to multi-fiduciary ones.[14]

The resolution of this paradox, in Goodpaster's view, lies in recognizing that just as shareholders themselves are constrained in the pursuit of their self-interest by the ethical expectations of society, managers are constrained by these same ethical expectations in their service as the agents of the shareholders. Goodpaster writes:

> The foundation of ethics in management — and the way out of the stakeholder paradox — lies in understanding that the conscience of the corporation is a logical and moral extension of the consciences of its principals. It is *not* an expansion of the list of principals, but a gloss on the principal-agent relationship itself. Whatever the structure of the principal-agent relationship, neither principal nor agent can ever claim that an agent has "moral immunity" from the basic obligations that would apply to any human being toward other members of the community.[15]

In order to base the fiduciary duties of management to shareholders on a contract between management and shareholders — and, in particular, to argue that the relation is a principal-agent relationship — it is necessary, obviously, to show that some kind of contract exists.[16] There is, of course, no *express* contract between the two parties that spells out in writing the terms of the relation, but a defender of the argument might contend that there is still an *implied* contract, which is a kind recognized in law. The courts have frequently found implied contracts to exist in the relations between buyers and sell-

ers and between employers and employees. Why not between shareholders and management?

The case for an implied contract is not very promising. In most cases, a shareholder buys shares of a corporation from previous owners, not from the corporation itself, and even in the case of original purchases of stock, there is no agreement beyond the prospectus. The available evidence suggests that shareholders buy stock with roughly the same expectations as those who make any other financial investment. The conclusion of one study is that "shareholders expect to be treated as 'investors,' much like bondholders, for example, and expect corporate managers to consider a wide constituency when making corporate decisions."[17] Moreover, the lack of any face-to-face dealings between the two parties and the lack of any specific representations by management to individual shareholders further mitigate against any presumption that an implied contract exists. In short, the standard legal conditions for an implied contract are absent in the shareholder-management relation.

Even if there is no legal contract, it is still possible to argue that the idea of a contract provides the best means for understanding the moral features of the shareholder-management relation. The classical social contract theories of Hobbes, Locke, and others provide a means for establishing political obligations, and recently some philosophers have made use of a social contract to provide a framework for the responsibility of corporations to society. Although social contract theory may be a useful normative model in some contexts, it is not easily applied to the shareholder-management relation.

First, the idea of a contract is most at home in situations in which two parties are able to negotiate a set of mutual obligations which governs specific interactions. In the case of shareholders and management, however, there is virtually no opportunity for the two parties to negotiate the terms of their relation. (As noted earlier, Williamson considers the fact that the relation never comes up for periodic renewal to be a reason for regarding shareholders as owners and not ordinary investors.) Also, the "terms" of any supposed contract are set largely by the laws of corporate governance, which have been created by legislatures and courts for reasons unrelated to any contract between shareholders and the management of a corporation. While employers and employees are free to negotiate on specific details, such as wages and working conditions, shareholders are offered shares of stock on a "take it or leave it" basis.

Second, and more important, there is relatively little interaction between shareholders and the managers with whom they are supposed to be related by means of a contract, and most of the obligations which are placed on managers are not related directly to shareholders, as the contractual model suggests. The fiduciary duties of management, for example, cover a wide variety of matters which make no reference to shareholders. . . .

THE AGENCY RELATION

Just as the shareholder-management relation does not meet the conditions for an implied contract, so too does it not fit the conditions for agency. As a matter of law, officers are agents, but they are agents of the corporation, not the shareholders; and directors, who in a sense are the corporation, are not agents at all. Furthermore, many of the fiduciary duties of management involve activities which are, for the most part, unrelated to shareholders, . . . Thus, the claim that managers are agents for shareholders, even if true, could not account for all of the fiduciary duties of management.

That corporate managers are not agents of the shareholders follows from the standard legal definition given by the second *Restatement of Agency*, Section 1 (1), which reads: "Agency is the fiduciary relation which results from the manifestation of consent by one person to another that the other shall act on his behalf and subject to his control, and consent by the other so to act." The crucial elements in this definition are: (1) consent to the relation, (2) the power to act on another's behalf, and (3) the element of control. None of these is present in the shareholder-management relation.

First, directors and officers, upon assuming their positions, agree to abide by a set of duties, which are largely those prescribed by the laws of a state concerning corporate governance. It is unrealistic to suppose that these managers do anything that can be described as "manifesting consent" to serve the shareholders' interests. Further, none of the fine distinctions used by the courts to decide when an agency relation has been created or terminated ("actual" versus "implied" agency, for example) or to distinguish among kinds of agency (such as "special" and "universal" agency) is usefully applied to the relation between shareholders and management.

Second, officers and directors have no power to act on behalf of the shareholders insofar as this is understood in the legal sense of changing a legal relation of the principal with regard to a third party. In fact, all decisions which change the legal relation of shareholders with regard to third parties (merging with another company, for example, or changing the bylaws of the corporation) must be approved by shareholders; management is barred by law from making decisions of this kind on its own authority. If managers were agents of the shareholders, they ought to have a right to make some decisions of this kind.

Third, management is in no significant sense under the control of the shareholders. Day-to-day operations of a corporation, along with long-term strategic planning, are the province of the officers and directors. Shareholders have no right to intervene, and even shareholder suits over mistaken decisions are generally blocked by the business judgment rule. As long as their fiduciary duties are met, management can enter into new lines of business and abandon old lines, undertake rapid expansion or cut back, and, in short, make virtually all ordinary business decisions without regard for the desires of shareholders. . . .

The inescapable conclusion is that officers and directors of corporations are not, legally, in a contractual or an agency relation with shareholders and that, moreover, there are no good ethical reasons for regarding them as being in such a relation. As a result, Goodpaster's claim — that the shareholder-management relation is fiduciary in character because of a contract or agency relation — is untenable. This cannot be the basis for the fiduciary duties of management and hence for the claim that such duties are owed to shareholders alone.

PUBLIC POLICY AS A BASIS

Even if Goodpaster is mistaken about the ethical basis for fiduciary duties, it is still possible for him to hold that the shareholder-management relation is "ethically different" because of its fiduciary character. There is an important distinction between fiduciary and nonfiduciary duties, which the stakeholder approach tends to disregard. Thus, Freeman argues for the stakeholder approach by citing the many legal obligations which management owes to various constituencies. Goodpaster willingly concedes that corporations

have these obligations and that they are "morally significant," but he insists that a crucial difference remains: the obligations of corporations to other constituencies are not fiduciary duties but duties of another kind. On this point Goodpaster is correct.

It is necessary, however, to find some basis for fiduciary duties, if they are to exist at all. And if fiduciary duties are confined to the shareholder-management relation, then a basis must be found which singles out shareholders as a special constituency. That is, there must be something special about shareholders which makes them, and no other constituency, the object of the fiduciary duties of management. . . . [It could be argued] that the value of maintaining the private, profit-making nature of the corporation comes from considerations of public policy. Put simply, the argument is that institutions in which management is accountable primarily to shareholders provides the most socially beneficial system of economic organization.

One exponent of this view was A. A. Berle, who conducted a debate with Merrick Dodd in the 1930s over a version of the stakeholder approach. Both Dodd and Berle recognized that the assumption that shareholders are the owners of a corporation no longer serves as a basis for the fiduciary duties of management. With the separation of ownership and control, the "traditional logic of property" became outmoded, with the result that shareholders lost any special status based on property rights. According to Berle and Means:

> . . . [T]he owners of passive property, by surrendering control and responsibility over the active property, have surrendered the right that the corporation should be operated in their sole interest, — they have released the community from the obligation to protect them to the full extent implied in the doctrine of strict property rights.[18]

But by taking control away from the owners, managers have not thereby conferred upon themselves the right to run the corporation for their benefit.

> The control groups have, rather, cleared the way for the claims of a group far wider than either the owners or the control. They have placed the community in a position to demand that the modern corporation serve not alone the owners or the control but all society.[19]

Dodd's position (and Freeman's, as well) is that the fiduciary duties of management should be extended now to include all other constituencies. Berle rejected this alternative, however, because he feared that extending the range of constituencies would result, not in benefits to these constituencies but in absolute power for management. In his response to Dodd, Berle wrote, "When the fiduciary obligation of the corporate management and 'control' to stockholders is weakened or eliminated, the management and 'control' become for all practical purposes absolute."[20] Thus, it would be dangerous to the community and harmful to business to remove the strong fiduciary duties which the law imposes on managers. He wrote:

> Unchecked by present legal balances, a social-economic absolutism of corporate administrators, even if benevolent, might be unsafe; and in any case it hardly affords the soundest base on which to construct the economic commonwealth which industrialism seems to require. Meanwhile . . . we had best be protecting the interests we know, being no less swift to provide for the new interests as they successively appear.[21]

Ultimately, Berle's argument is that corporations ought to be run for the benefit of shareholders, not because they "own" the corporation, or because of some contract or agency relation, but because all other con-stituencies are better off as a result. The underlying assumption is that the fiduciary duties of management are and ought to be determined by considerations of public policy. The present state of corporate governance is not ideal, but it is a workable arrangement that had been fashioned by historical forces. Any reform, therefore, should be incremental, so as to avoid unwanted disruptions.

Courts and legislatures in the United States have largely followed Berle's advice and have been very reluctant to weaken the strict profit-maximizing imperative that the law of fiduciary duties imposes on management. Managers, by law, must consider primarily the interests of shareholders in certain matters, and shareholders may bring suit against officers and directors for failing to do so.

The fiduciary duties of management have been weakened to some extent by so-called "other constituency" statutes, which permit (but do not require) officers and directors to consider the impact of their decisions on constituencies besides shareholders.[22] This is an exception that proves the rule, however, since these statutes have been enacted mainly to protect management from shareholder suits in the adoption of anti-takeover measures in the belief that the interests of the public are best served by allowing a wider range of considerations in defending against hostile takeovers. . . .

These considerations tend to support the Berle view that the basis for the fiduciary duties of management is public policy. If this is so, then the shareholder-management relation is not "ethically different" for any reason that is unique to that relation. Consequently, there is no reason in principle why the distinction between fiduciary and nonfiduciary duties and the distinction between shareholders and other constituencies should cut as neatly as Goodpaster suggests. And, indeed, we find that Goodpaster's identification of fiduciary duties with shareholders and non-fiduciary duties with other constituencies is not wholly accurate. Many of the fiduciary duties of officers and directors are owed not to shareholders but to the corporation as an entity with interests of its own, which can, on occasion, conflict with those of shareholders. Further, corporations have some fiduciary duties to other constituencies, such as creditors (to remain solvent so as to repay debts) and to employees (in the management of a pension fund, for example).

THE STAKEHOLDER PARADOX REVISITED

For Goodpaster, the distinction between fiduciary and nonfiduciary duties is at the heart of the stakeholder paradox. The reason why "[i]t seems essential to orient corporate decisions by ethical values that go beyond strategic stakeholder considerations to multi-fiduciary ones" is that other constituencies have interests which are the subject of many obligations that are nonfiduciary in character. The reason why orienting corporate decisions by multi-fiduciary ethical values seems illegitimate is that the fiduciary duties are concerned primarily with maintaining the profit-maximizing function of the corporation. It is the existence of both fiduciary and nonfiduciary duties, then, that makes what seems to be the same thing both "essential" and "illegitimate."

Goodpaster's solution to the paradox — that shareholders cannot expect managers as their agents to act in ways which are inconsistent with the ethical standards of the community — does not work, however, if managers are not agents of the shareholders. However, if public policy is accepted as the basis for fiduciary duties, then a rather different solution to the stakeholder paradox becomes possible.

In corporate law, a fairly sharp distinction is made between the fiduciary duties of officers and directors, for which they can be held personally liable, and their other obligations and responsibilities for which they are not personally liable. Traditionally, the fiduciary duties of management are those of obedience and diligence, which require that they act within the scope of their authority and exercise ordinary care and prudence. These duties constitute a minimal level of oversight for which managers are held to a high degree of personal accountability. As long as they fulfill these fiduciary duties and act in ways which they believe to be in the best interests of the corporation, officers and directors are shielded from personal liability for any losses that occur. Losses that occur because of honest mistakes of judgment are covered, instead, by the business judgment rule, which prevents the courts from "second-guessing" the judgment of management.

As a result of this distinction, the obligations of management to shareholders are themselves divisible into fiduciary and nonfiduciary. The shareholder-management relation is not a single relation that is fiduciary in character; rather, it is a manifold relation in which management has some obligations to shareholders which are fiduciary duties and other obligations which are nonfiduciary duties. The fiduciary duties of officers and directors in the corporation are limited, moreover, to the most general matters of organization and strategy, so that in the ordinary conduct of business, where the business judgment rule applies, the interests of other constituencies may be taken into account without the possibility of a successful shareholder suit for the breach of any fiduciary duty.

An alternative solution to the stakeholder paradox, then, is to distinguish between the decisions of management which bear on their fiduciary duties and those that do not.

A statement of the stakeholder paradox which includes this distinction might read as follows:

> It is illegitimate to orient corporate decisions that bear on the fiduciary duties of management by ethical values that go beyond strategic stakeholder considerations to include the interests of other constituencies, but it is essential to orient other corporate decisions by these values.

So stated, there is no longer any paradox, and we have an explanation of why "[e]thics seems both to forbid and to demand a strategic, profit-maximizing mind-set."[23]

The explanation is to be found, not in making the conscience of the corporation "a logical and moral extension of the consciences of its principals," as Goodpaster claims, but in the public policy considerations which have led to a distinction in law between fiduciary and nonfiduciary duties. On questions about the nature and structure of the corporation, with which fiduciary duties are largely concerned, courts and legislatures have held, for reasons of public policy, that the profit-making function of corporations and accountability to shareholders ought to be preserved. On questions of ordinary business operation, however, public policy dictates that corporations be allowed to take the interests of many constituencies besides shareholders into account.

CONCLUSION

This account of the relation between shareholders and management constitutes a third position, somewhere between Goodpaster's view and the stakeholder approach. On all three positions, fiduciary duties play a prominent but different role, and each involves a different ethical basis for the fiduciary duties of management. In the account presented here, shareholders are special to the extent that public policy considerations support the continuation of the corporation as a private, profit-making institution, with strong accountability to shareholders. . . .

Whether shareholders should continue to occupy the status that they do is also a matter to be decided by considerations of public policy. Since the 1930s, there has been a steady erosion in shareholder power, largely as a result of the increasing separation of ownership and control and the rise of large institutional investors. This has not occasioned much concern, since market forces and government regulation, along with a limited role for shareholders, have been regarded as sufficient checks on the power of management to ensure that corporate activity is generally beneficial. In recent years, there has been a movement to increase the influence of shareholders in major corporate decisions, but the main arguments have come from economists who believe that shareholder activism would force corporations to be more efficient.

The strongest force for change at the present time comes from once passive institutional investors who, in their role as fiduciaries for their own investors, have objected to anti-takeover measures, high executive compensation, and other matters that advance the interests of incumbent management over those of shareholders. Some of the largest pension funds have also taken an active role in major restructurings and the selection of CEOs. Pressure is also being placed on the SEC to change the interpretation of Rule 14a-8 to allow shareholder resolutions on a broader range of issues.

The current debate over the role of shareholders suggests that the delicate balance of shareholder power, market forces, and government regulation has not fully succeeded in achieving maximum efficiency or in preventing some management abuses. Whether the answer lies in increasing shareholder power, changing the conditions of competition, or imposing more government regulation — or in some combination of the three — remains to be decided. What is clear is that the current debate is being conducted, not on the basis of ownership or of a contract or an agency relation, but in terms of public policy. Thus, to answer the question posed in the title: except for the useful role they play in corporate governance, there is nothing special about shareholders.

NOTES

1. Milton Friedman, *Capitalism and Freedom* (Chicago: University of Chicago Press, 1962), 133; and "The Social Responsibility of Business Is to Increase Its Profits," *The New York Times Magazine*, September 13, 1970, p. 33.

2. E. Merrick Dodd, Jr., "For Whom Are Corporate Managers Trustees?" *Harvard Law Review*, 45 (1932), 1148.

3. R. Edward Freeman, *Strategic Management: A Stakeholder Approach* (Boston: Pitman, 1984). See also, R. Edward Freeman and Daniel R. Gilbert, Jr., *Corporate Strategy and the Search for Ethics* (Englewood Cliffs, NJ: Prentice Hall, 1988), and William M. Evan and R. Edward Freeman, "A Stakeholder Theory of the Modern Corporation: Kantian Capitalism," in Tom L. Beauchamp and Norman E. Bowie, eds., *Ethical Theory and Business*, 4th ed. (Englewood Cliffs, NJ: Prentice Hall, 1993), 75–84.

4. Kenneth E. Goodpaster, "Business Ethics and Stakeholder Analysis," *Business Ethics Quarterly*, 1 (1991), 69.

5. A. A. Berle, Jr., and Gardiner C. Means, *The Modern Corporation and Private Property* (New York: Macmillan, 1932), 336.

6. J. A. C. Hetherington, "Fact and Legal Theory: Shareholders, Managers, and Corporate Social Responsibility," *Stanford Law Review*, 21 (1969), 256.

7. Oliver E. Williamson, *The Economic Institutions of Capitalism* (New York: The Free Press, 1985), 304.

8. Williamson, *The Economic Institutions of Capitalism*, 304–5.

9. Williamson replies that although individual investors can protect themselves by selling stock, shareholders as a class cannot. Williamson, *The Economic Institutions of Capitalism*, 304.

10. See Bayless Manning, review of *The American Stockholder* by J. A. Livingston, *Yale Law Journal*, 67 (1958), 1492.

11. Goodpaster, "Business Ethics and Stakeholder Analysis," 63.

12. Goodpaster, "Business Ethics and Stakeholder Analysis," 69–70 (emphasis added).

13. Goodpaster, "Business Ethics and Stakeholder Analysis," 70.

14. Goodpaster, "Business Ethics and Stakeholder Analysis," 63. By "strategic stakeholder considerations" Goodpaster means considering the interests of stakeholders as a means to the end of serving the interests of the shareholders. A multi-fiduciary stakeholder approach makes the interests of all stakeholder groups the end of corporate activity.

15. Goodpaster, "Business Ethics and Stakeholder Analysis," 68.

16. The idea that corporations are a "nexus" of contracting relations among individuals is familiar from the work of agency theorists. See, for example, Michael C. Jensen and William H. Meckling. "Theory of the Firm: Managerial Behavior, Agency Costs and Ownership Structure," *Journal of Financial Economics*, 3 (1976), 310. Agency theory does not suppose that the relations in question are contracts that create obligations, however; it asks us, rather, to think of the relation involving shareholders, along with those of all other constituencies, *as though they were a multitude of contracts* for explanatory purposes only. On this point, see Robert C. Clark, "Agency Costs *versus* Fiduciary Duties," in John W. Pratt and Richard J. Zeckhauser, eds., *Principles and Agents: The Structure of Business* (Boston: Harvard Business School Press, 1985), 59–62.

17. Larry D. Sonderquist and Robert P. Vecchio, "Reconciling Shareholders' Rights and Corporate Responsibility: New Guidelines for Management," *Duke Law Journal*, 1978, p. 840.

18. Berle and Means, *The Modern Corporation and Private Property*, 355.

19. Berle and Means, *The Modern Corporation and Private Property*, 355–56.
20. A. A. Berle, Jr., "For Whom Corporate Managers Are Trustees: A Note," *Harvard Law Review*, 45 (1932), 1367.
21. Berle, "For Whom Corporate Managers Are Trustees," 1372.
22. At least 28 states have adopted other constituency statutes. In some states this has been accomplished by legislative enactments; in others, by court decisions interpreting state law. For an overview, see Charles Hansen, "Other Constituency Statutes: A Search for Perspective," *The Business Lawyer*, 46 (1991), 1355–75. A penetrating analysis that criticizes Hansen is Eric W. Orts, "Beyond Shareholders: Interpreting Corporate Constituency Statutes," *The George Washington Law Review*, 61 (1992), 14–135.
23. Goodpaster, "Business Ethics and Stakeholder Analysis," 63.

New Directions in Corporate Social Responsibility

Norman E. Bowie

Among philosophers writing in business ethics, something of a consensus has emerged in the past ten years regarding the social responsibility of business. Although these philosophers were critical of the classical view of Milton Friedman (the purpose of the corporation is to make profits for stockholders), the consensus view had much in common with Friedman, so much so that I referred to my own statement of this position as the neoclassical view of corporate responsibility (Bowie 1982). The heart of the neoclassical view was that the corporation was to make a profit while avoiding inflicting harm. In other formulations the corporation was to make a profit while (1) honoring the moral minimum or (2) respecting individual rights and justice. Tom Donaldson arrived at a similar neoclassical description of the purpose of the corporation by arguing that such a view is derived from the social contract that business has with society (1989).

The stakeholder theory made popular by Ed Freeman does seem to represent a major advance over the classical view (Freeman 1984; Evan and Freeman 1988). It might seem inappropriate to refer to the stakeholder position as neoclassical. Rather than argue that the job of the manager was to maximize profits for stockholders, Freeman argued that the manager's task was to protect and promote the rights of the various corporate stakeholders. Stakeholders were defined by Freeman as members of groups whose existence was necessary for the survival of the firm — stockholders, employees, customers, suppliers, the local community, and managers themselves.

Despite the vast increase in scope of managerial obligations, a Friedmanite might try to bring stakeholder theory under his or her umbrella. Of course, the managers must worry about the rights and interests of the other corporate stakeholders. If you don't look after them, these other stakeholders will not be as productive and profits will fall. A good manager is concerned with all stakeholders while increasing profits for stockholders. In the Friedmanite view, the stakeholder theorist does not give us an alternative theory of social responsibility; rather, he or she reminds us how an enlightened Friedmanite, as opposed to an unenlightened one, is supposed to manage. The unenlightened Friedmanite exploits stakeholders to increase profits. Although that strategy might succeed in the short run, the morale and hence the productivity of the other stakeholders plummets, and as a result long-run profits fall. To protect long-run profits, the enlightened manager is concerned with the health, safety, and family needs (day care) of employees, a no-question-asked return policy, stable long-term relations with suppliers, and civic activities in the local community. In this way, long-run profitability is protected or even enhanced. In the classical view, the debate between Milton Friedman and Ed Freeman is not a debate about corporate ends, but rather about corporate means to that end.

Moreover, some classicists argue, the neoclassical concern with avoiding harm or honoring the moral minimum does not add anything to Friedman's theory. In *Capitalism and Freedom* (1962) he argues that the manager must obey the law and moral custom. The quotation goes like this:

> In such an economy, there is one and only one social responsibility of business — to use its resources and engage in activities designed to increase its profits so long as it stays within the rules of the game, which is to say, engages in open and free competition, without deception or fraud.

If there really is a social contract that requires business to honor a moral minimum, then a business manager on the Friedmanite

model is duty-bound to obey it. To the extent that the moral minimum involves duties to not cause avoidable harm, or to honor individual stakeholder rights, or to adhere to the ordinary canons of justice, then the Friedmanite manager has these duties as well. Even if Friedman didn't emphasize the manager's duties to law and common morality, the existence of the duties are consistent with Friedman's position.

Unfortunately, the compatibility of the classical Friedmanite position with obedience to law and morality is undercut by some of Friedman's most well-known followers. The late Albert Carr (1968) substituted the morality of poker for ordinary morality. Indeed he argued that ordinary morality was inappropriate in business:

> Poker's own brand of ethics is different from the ethical ideals of civilized human relationships. The game calls for distrust of the other fellow. It ignores the claim of friendship. Cunning deception and concealment of one's strength and intentions, not kindness and openheartedness, are vital in poker. No one thinks any the worse of poker on that account. And no one should think the worse of the game of business because its standards of right and wrong differ from the prevailing traditions of morality in our society. . . .

Even more pervasive has been the influence of former *Harvard Business Review* editor Theodore Levitt. He defends various deceptive practices in advertising, which seem to be in violation of ordinary morality, as something consumers really like after all (1970):

> Rather than deny that distortion and exaggeration exist in advertising, in this article I shall argue that embellishment and distortion are among advertising's legitimate and socially desirable purpose; and that illegitimacy in advertising consists only of falsification with larcenous intent. . . . But the consumer suffers from an old dilemma. He wants "truth," but he also wants and needs the alleviating imagery and

tantalizing promise of the advertiser and designer.

The writings of these authors give Friedman's theory that "anything for profit" ring that its critics hear. But Friedman need not be interpreted in that way. Many profit-oriented business people do not espouse that interpretation; neither do some academic Friedmanites. What needs to be done is for the Friedmanite school to declare Carr and Levitt heretics and excommunicate them from the faith. The Friedmanites also need to include as part of their canon some statement of the moral minimum idea so the phrase "rules of the game" in *Capitalism and Freedom* has some flesh and bone.

On one important point the neoclassical theorists and the Friedmanites are already in explicit agreement. Both positions argue that it is *not* the purpose of business to do good. The neoclassicists agree with Levitt that providing for the general welfare is the responsibility of government. A business is not a charitable organization.

> Business will have a much better chance of surviving if there is no nonsense about its goals — that is, if long-run profit maximization is one dominant objective in practice as well as in theory. Business should recognize what government's functions are and let it go at that, stopping only to fight government where government directly intrudes itself into business. It should let government take care of the general welfare so that business can take care of the more material aspects of welfare. (Levitt 1958)

Both the classicists and the neoclassicists have elaborate arguments to support their views. The classicist arguments focus on legitimacy. Corporate boards and managers are not popularly elected. Politicians are. Hence, government officials have a legitimacy in spending tax dollars for public welfare that

corporate managers don't. Moreover, the corporate board and managers are agents of the stockholders. Unless the stockholders authorize charitable contributions, the corporate officers have no right to give the stockholders' money away and violate their fiduciary responsibility in doing so.

Levitt (1958) gives the legitimacy argument a final twist. It is the job of the government to provide for the general welfare; but if business starts doing the government's job, the government will take over business. As a result, business and government will coalesce into one powerful group at the expense of our democratic institutions.

Levitt seems to hold the traditional American view, adopted from Montesquieu, that the existence of a democracy requires a balance of competing powers among the main institutions of society. Levitt and Friedman both see the competing institutions as business, government, and labor, each with its distinct and competing interests. If business starts to take on the task of government, the balance of power is upset.

The neoclassical arguments are much more pragmatic. Corporations don't have the resources to solve social problems. Moreover, since the obligation to do good is an open-ended one, society cannot expect corporations to undertake it. A corporation that tries to solve social problems is an institutional Mother Teresa. What it does is good, but its actions, in the language of ethics, are supererogatory.

Some of the neoclassicists add a little sophistication to the argument by showing that competitive pressure will prevent corporations from doing good, even if the competitors all want to. If company X spends more of its money solving social problems than company Y, company Y gains a competitive advantage. Even if company Y wants to contribute to solving social problems, it will try to get company X to contribute even more. Company X has thought this all through; as a result it can't contribute (or contribute as much as it would like). The conclusion is that all competitive companies believe they can't focus on solving social problems even if they want to.

As a result of the arguments, a fairly orthodox position has developed both in theory and in practice. American corporations do not have an obligation to solve social problems. Whatever the notion of corporate responsibility means, it does not mean that. However, the orthodox position does have its critics, and these critics have arguments of their own.

Perhaps the three strongest arguments are based on the duties of gratitude and citizenship and the responsibilities of power. With respect to gratitude, defenders of a duty to help solve social problems argue that society provides tremendous resources to corporations. The local community provides public education that trains workers, a legal system complete with police and courts to enforce corporate contracts, and a huge infrastructure of highways, sewage and garbage disposal, and public health facilities. Corporate taxes are not sufficient payment for the corporations' share of these resources, therefore corporations have a duty out of gratitude to help solve social problems. Moreover, even if corporate taxes did cover their fair share, corporations are citizens morally similar to individual citizens; as a result, they have a similar obligation to help solve social problems. Thus, corporations have a duty based on citizenship to help solve social problems. Finally, the moral use of power requires that power be used responsibly. The term "stewardship" is often used to describe the responsibilities of those who have great power and resources. Individual corporate leaders make reference to the duties of stewardship when they establish private foundations. Carnegie and Rockefeller are two prominent examples. . . .

SOCIAL RESPONSIBILITY AND THE DUTY TO SOLVE SOCIAL PROBLEMS

I begin this section with an argument for a duty to solve social problems. This argument resembles one a Friedmanite could use to defend an obligation on the part of corporate managers to honor the needs and rights of corporate stakeholders. As you recall, a Friedmanite could argue that a concern with the needs and rights of corporate stakeholders is required for long-term profits. Treating one's customers, employees, and suppliers well is a means to profit.

That theme provides a rationale for an instrumental duty of business to solve social problems. The argument I shall make rests on a number of complicated and controversial empirical claims, and I have neither the expertise nor the space to argue for these empirical claims here. However, these empirical claims constitute something of a conventional wisdom on this subject.

Among the social problems the U.S. faces, most of the more important ones have a severe impact on the quality of the work force. The problem of drug use and other forms of substance abuse, the abysmal quality of public education, the decline in work ethic values, the instability of the family, and the short-term orientation of all corporate stakeholders all affect the firm negatively. The impact is especially acute on employees and suppliers. If the work force is poorly educated, affected with substance abuse, poorly motivated, and short-term oriented, productivity suffers both in quantity and quality.

In future international competition, the quality of the work force is the most important asset a company can have. If capital markets are open, the cost of capital will even out, so any advantage a country might gain through lower costs of capital is short-term. If a country gains an advantage through a technological discovery, highly developed technological competitors will reverse engineer the discovery so the advantage is short-term as well. The one advantage that is relatively long lasting is the quality of one's work force.

In that respect America is at a disadvantage. All the problems pointed out earlier have affected the quality of our work force more severely than in other countries. In addition, racial, religious, and ethnic tensions in our pluralistic work force affect productivity, putting us at a disadvantage against industrial societies with a more homogeneous work force. Thus, if America is to remain competitive, social problems that affect workforce productivity must be addressed.

However, the traditional institutional source for resolving social problems — government — seems to have neither the will nor the power to do so. After all, the costs are high and Americans — as events in the past decade have demonstrated — don't like taxes. In addition to being high, the costs are also immediate. However, the benefits, though higher, are very distant. Politicians have difficulty with a time frame beyond the next election. Therefore, there is little incentive for a politician to pay the costs now. A well worked-out statement of this view can be found in Alan Binder's *Hard Heads Soft Hearts* (1987).

To make matters worse, our high national debt, . . . the S&L debacle, and our aging infrastructure will only drain resources from social problems. If international competition requires that such problems be solved, but government is unwilling and perhaps unable to do so, it would seem that business has no choice but to become involved. The long-term competitiveness and hence long-term profitability of business is at stake. If the sce-

nario I have painted is at all accurate, then even a Friedmanite could argue that business should help solve social problems. Business initiative in that area is justified on the grounds that such action is necessary to increase profits.

There certainly is nothing inconsistent with a Friedmanite arguing that business should help solve social problems to increase profit, so long as the dangers from not doing so outweigh the dangers discussed earlier. But I doubt that people like Levitt would ever agree that the increase in profitability would be worth the cost of lost independence now enjoyed by the business community. Even though Friedmanites in theory could support a view of corporate responsibility that included a corporate duty to help solve social problems, in all probability they would not.

On the chance some Friedmanite might support such an expanded concept of social responsibility, let me argue why a Friedmanite approach to an obligation to help solve social problems would probably fail. My argument here is tied up with issues of motivation and intentionality.

Consider what philosophers call "the hedonic paradox": the more people consciously seek happiness the less likely they are to achieve it. The reader is invited to test this assertion by getting up tomorrow and framing his or her activities with a conscious goal of happiness. In other words, do everything to be happy. If you do, almost certainly you will fail to achieve happiness.

To understand the paradox, we must distinguish between the intended end of an action and the feelings we get when we succeed (achieve the goal). If you are thirsty, you seek a glass of water to extinguish the thirst. When you quench your thirst you feel pleasure or contentment. But you didn't get the glass of water to get the contentment that goes with quenching your thirst. And you generally don't act to be happy. You are happy when you succeed in obtaining the goals that constitute the basis of your actions. Happiness is not one of those goals; it is a state one achieves when one successfully gains one's other goals.

What does this have to do with profit? Should profit be a conscious goal of the firm, or the result of achieving other corporate goals? For simplicity's sake let us say there is some relation between providing meaningful work for employees, quality products for customers, and corporate profits. What is the nature of that relationship? Do you achieve meaningful work for employees and quality products for customers by aiming at profits (by making profits your goal), or do you aim at providing meaningful work for employees and quality products for customers (make them your goal) and achieve profits as a result? A Friedmanite is committed to making profits the goal. As we saw in the discussion of stakeholder theory, a Friedmanite will respect the needs and rights of the other stakeholders to increase profits for the stockholders. But for a genuine stakeholder theorist, the needs and rights of the various stakeholders take priority. Management acts in response to those needs; profits are often the happy result.

Both Friedmanites and non-Friedmanites can posit a relationship between profits and meeting stakeholder needs. What divides them is the strength of the casual arrow, a difference over which one should be the conscious objective of management. A Friedmanite argues for profit. A stakeholder theorist argues for the needs and rights of stakeholders. A Friedmanite argues that you treat employees and customers well to make a profit; good treatment is a means to an end. A stakeholder theorist argues that a manager should treat employees and customers well because it is the right thing to do; the needs and rights of the corporate stakeholders are the ends the manager should aim at. Profits are

the happy results that usually accompany these ends.

American corporations have thought like Friedmanites even when they speak the language of stakeholder theorists. They introduce quality circles or ESOPs to increase profits. Some of our international competitors have thought like stakeholder theorists even though they have achieved Friedman-like results.

With respect to the duty to help solve social problems, should that duty be taken on because by doing so profits may be increased, or because it is a moral responsibility to do so? To answer that question, I suggest we visit the work of Cornell economist Robert Frank (1988) and consider the spotty success of the introduction of quality circles and other forms of "enlightened" labor management in the U.S.

Frank's point, buttressed by a large amount of empirical evidence from psychology, sociology, and biology, is that an altruistic person (a person who will not behave opportunistically even when he or she can get away with it) is the most desirable person to make a deal with. After all, if you have a contractual relationship with someone, the best person you can deal with is someone you know will honor the terms of the contract even if he or she could get away with not honoring them. An employer wants employees who won't steal or cheat even if they could. A marriage partner wants a spouse who won't cheat even if he or she could. Altruists rather than profit maximizers make the best business partners.

Frank then goes on to make the point Immanuel Kant would make. You can't adopt altruism as a strategy like "honesty is the best policy" and gain the advantages of altruism. After all, if I knew you were being an altruist because it paid, I would conclude that in any case where altruism didn't pay, you would revert to opportunism. My ideal business partner is someone who doesn't merely adopt altruism because it pays but adopts it because he or she is committed to it. She or he is not an opportunist because opportunism is wrong. As Frank says:

> For the model to work, satisfaction from doing the right thing must not be premised on the fact that material gains may later follow; rather it must be *intrinsic* to the act itself. Otherwise a person will lack the necessary motivation to make self-sacrificing choices, and once others sense that, material gains will not, in fact, follow. Under the commitment model, moral sentiments do not lead to material advantage unless they are heartfelt.

Frank's theoretical account of the advantages of committed altruism over reciprocal altruism as the best payoff strategy helps explain the spotty record of "enlightened" employee management techniques. Techniques like quality circles that work very well in Japan and Sweden don't work as well in the U.S. Why? Cultural difference is not a sufficiently specific answer. What cultural differences make the transfer difficult? I hypothesize that since labor/management relations in the U.S. are opportunistically based, labor assumes — probably correctly — that such reforms are motivated not by employer concern for employees but by profit. If that is the motivation, labor reasons, why should labor embrace the reforms? The elements of trust created by genuine concern for employees are missing in the American context. Indeed, both labor and management assume the other will behave opportunistically. Academics assume that too, and agency theory provides a model for the opportunistic framework. Given that cultural and intellectual context, it is no surprise that labor would distrust an employer whose concern with an improved working environment was not genuinely altruistic.

This discussion affects the duty to help solve social problems. If the resolution of these problems would improve America's human capital, that result would be most likely to occur if the investment in human capital were altruistically motivated. The one good thing about corporate efforts to solve social problems is that it is easy to show that with respect to the individual firm, such efforts must be altruistic. After all, an improved labor force is a classic case of a public good. There is no guarantee that the money spent by an individual firm will benefit that firm. If a firm adopts an inner city elementary school and pours resources into it, there is no reason to think that firm will get its investment back. The reason need not be that many of the students of that elementary school won't work for the supporting firm. After all, it might gain employees from other schools supported by other firms. Rather, the reason is that some firms will ride free off the expenditures of the moral firms. Thus, employees who understand these considerations can be sure that the employers who give money to solve social problems are altruistic.

If this analysis is correct the following conclusions can be drawn:

1. It is in the interest of business to adopt an extended view of corporate social responsibility that includes a duty to help solve social problems.
2. If business adopts that duty because it thinks it will benefit, its actions will be viewed cynically.
3. Moreover, because an improved labor force is a public good for business, the only real reason for an individual firm to help solve social problems is altruistic.
4. Thus, employees and other corporate stakeholders have a good reason to believe that corporate attempts to solve social problems are altruistic.

OBLIGATIONS OF VARIOUS STAKEHOLDERS IN A SOCIALLY RESPONSIBLE CORPORATION

In the previous section I gave an argument to show that everyone has good reason to believe that corporate attempts to solve social problems are genuinely altruistic. What are the implications of this for the various corporate stakeholders, especially customers?

Our ordinary way of speaking is to say the corporation ought to respect stakeholder needs and rights. Thus, we say that the corporation should produce quality products for customers, or that the corporation should not subject its employees to lie detector tests. We speak of the obligation of the firm (firm's management) to employees, customers, and local community. However, this way of speaking tends to give a one-sided emphasis to the moral obligations of the corporation.

My concern is that within the firm conceived of as a moral community, we speak as if all the obligations fall on the firm, or its managers and stockholders. In a previous article, "The Firm as a Moral Community" (Bowie 1991), I argued that Kant's third formulation of the categorical imperative best captures the moral relations that exist among corporate stakeholders. Kant would view a corporation as a moral community in which all of the stakeholders would both create the rules that govern them and be bound to one another by these same rules.

Moral relations are reciprocal. In addition to the obligations of managers, what of the obligations of the employees, customers, or local community to the firm (firm's management)? For example, business ethicists are critical of the so-called employment-at-will doctrine under which employees can be let go for "any reason, no reason, or reason immoral." Such a doctrine is unresponsive to the needs and rights of employees; it permits a manager to ignore both the quality of an employee's work performance and the number of years he or she has been with the firm.

Similarly, business ethicists are critical of the noneconomic layoffs that often accompany a hostile takeover. An example of noneconomic layoffs is when people are fired just because they worked for the old company. The new managers simply want their people in those positions — an understandable view, but one that does not take into account the interests of the employees let go. Those people might have served the target company for 20 years with great loyalty and distinction. Now they find themselves out of work through no fault of their own.

However, these business ethicists seldom criticize employees who leave a corporation on short notice simply to get a better job. Business firms argue that they invest huge amounts of money in training new employees, and losses from turnover are very high. Sometimes the employee might have been given educational benefits or even paid leave to resolve personal problems such as alcohol and drug abuse. Others may have received company financial support for further education — perhaps even an M.B.A. Yet these employees think nothing of leaving the proven loyal employer for a better job elsewhere. As managers often remind us, loyalty is not a one-way street. . . .

Let us apply this analysis to a triadic stakeholder relationship — the firm's management, its customers, and the local community. One of the moral problems facing any community is environmental pollution. As with the employment-at-will doctrine, most business ethicists focus on the obligations of the firm. But what of the obligations of the consumers who buy and use the firm's products?

Consider the following instances reported by Alicia Swasy in a recent *Wall Street Journal* article (1988). Wendy's tried to replace foam plates and cups with paper, but customers in the test markets balked.

Procter and Gamble offered Downy fabric softener in a concentrated form that requires less packaging than ready-to-use products. However, the concentrate version is less convenient because it has to be mixed with water. Sales have been poor. Procter and Gamble also manufactures Vizir and Lenor brands of detergents in concentrate form. Europeans will take the trouble; Americans will not.

Kodak tried to eliminate its yellow film boxes but met customer resistance. McDonald's has been testing mini-incinerators that convert trash into energy but often meets opposition from community groups that fear the incinerators will pollute the air. A McDonald's spokesperson points out that the emissions are mostly carbon dioxide and water vapor and are "less offensive than a barbecue."

And Jerry Alder reports in *Newsweek* (1989) that Exxon spent approximately $40,000 each to "save" 230 otters. Otters in captivity cost $800. Fishermen in Alaska are permitted to shoot otters as pests.

Recently environmentalists have pointed out the environmental damage caused by the widespread use of disposable diapers. However, are Americans ready to give up Pampers and go back to cloth diapers and the diaper pail? Most observers think not.

If environmentalists want business to produce products that are more friendly to the environment, they must convince Americans to purchase them. Business will respond to the market. It is the consuming public that has the obligation to make the trade-off between cost and environmental integrity.

Yet another example involves corporate giving. . . . The Twin Cities, Minnesota business community provides an example of a local community where many of the firms gave either 2 percent or 5 percent of their

pretax profits back to the community. I have never heard anyone argue that on the principle of reciprocity, citizens of the Twin Cities have obligations to these firms. Yet I would argue that these citizens have an obligation to support socially responsible firms over firms that are either socially irresponsible or indifferent to social responsibility. The relation of a local citizen to the companies that do business locally is again not simply economic. Citizens who consider only price in choosing between two department stores are behaving in a socially irresponsible way. If one department store contributes to the local community and the other doesn't, that factor should be taken into account when citizens in that community decide on where to shop. It's more than a matter of price.

The Target department store chain is a branch of the Dayton Hudson Company. It has a special program for hiring the disabled, and even assists these people with up to one-third of their rent. At Christmas it closes its stores to the general public and opens them to the elderly and disabled. These people receive an additional 10 percent discount and free gift wrapping. In many stores 75 percent of the trash generated is recycled. Target is a member of the 5 percent club. The list of its activities that support the community goes on and on. Target's competitors, WalMart and K mart, have nothing comparable. I maintain that Target's superior social performance creates an obligation for members of the community to shop at Target.

All these examples lead to a general point. For too long corporate responsibility has been analyzed simply in terms of the responsibilities of the firm (firm's management) to all other corporate stakeholders except stockholders. I exclude stockholders because the cost of honoring stakeholder obligations comes almost exclusively from their profits. If we are to have a truly comprehensive theory of corporate social responsibility, we must develop a theory for determining the appropriate *reciprocal* duties that exist among corporate stakeholders. If the managers and stockholders have a duty to customers, suppliers, employees, and the local community, then the local community, employees, suppliers, and customers have a duty to managers and stockholders. What these duties are has barely been discussed.

THE COMPLICATIONS OF MORAL PLURALISM

A great complication that exists for any attempt to determine reciprocal stakeholder duties occurs when the existence of moral pluralism is taken into account. For purposes of this paper, moral pluralism is a descriptive term that applies to the widespread disagreement about moral matters that exists among the American people. People disagree as to what is right and wrong. Some consider drug testing to be right. Others think it's wrong. People also disagree about the priorities given to various rights and responsibilities. For example, does the firm's obligation to protect its customers override its obligation to protect the privacy of its employees? And suppose it is decided that the safety of the customers does take priority? Is testing all employees or random testing more fair? The general point is this: If people cannot agree as to what is right and wrong and how to set priorities when our duties conflict, what advice can be given to managers and other corporate stakeholders regarding what their duties are?

The unhappy situation that befell Dayton Hudson in late 1990 illustrates the point exactly. Dayton Hudson has long been a member of the Twin Cities 5 percent club. The funds are distributed through the Dayton Hudson Foundation. For many years Planned Parenthood has been the recipient of rela-

tively small grants of a few thousand dollars. Abortion opponents have charged Planned Parenthood with various degrees of complicity in abortion activities.

In 1990 Dayton Hudson announced that to avoid becoming embroiled in the abortion debate, it would no longer support Planned Parenthood. No decision could have gotten it more embroiled in the debate. Pro-choice forces announced an immediate boycott of Dayton Hudson and its Target stores; hundreds of people cut up their Dayton Hudson credit cards and mailed them back to the company. In a few days Dayton Hudson relented and agreed to provide a grant to Planned Parenthood as it had done in the past. Now the anti-abortion forces were enraged. They organized boycotts and demonstrations that continued into the holiday season.

Dayton Hudson officials were both embarrassed and angry, but they indicated they would not retreat from their position to give 5 percent of their pretax income to charity. Although little was said publicly, the Dayton Hudson public relations disaster gave many executives pause. Perhaps the Friedmanites were right. They were giving away stockholder money for causes deemed inappropriate. Obviously some stockholders would not approve of the company's choices, just as some of Dayton's customers and citizens of the local community didn't.

In addition, some executives were rumored to have taken the following position:

1. The money is ours;
2. If people don't like how we spend our money, then we won't spend it on charity at all.

These corporate officials saw Dayton Hudson's protesting customers and citizens in the Twin Cities as ungrateful and unappreciative of the largesse Dayton Hudson had given over the years. These ingrates did not deserve corporate support. Whether corporate support for charities in the Twin Cities will fall off over the next few years remains to be seen.

Should the Dayton Hudson problem become more widespread, a serious impediment toward any corporation's decision to help solve social problems will have arisen. How should such difficulties be resolved? To answer that question we need to return to our model of the firm as a nexus of moral relationships among stakeholders. From that perspective I might suggest some principles that can be used to help resolve the problems created by moral pluralism.

First, if a corporation really has a duty to help solve social problems, we can ask whether the corporation, through its managers, should have sole say as to how the money is to be spent. I think the answer to that question must be "no." A firm as constituted by its stakeholders is not narrowly defined. To let the managers have the sole say is to allow one stakeholder to make the decisions on behalf of all. How can that be justified?

Some argue that legal ownership justifies the decision. On this view the decision should be made by the stockholders, because they are the legal owners. To my knowledge, no corporation decides either the amount of charity or determines those organizations that receive charity by taking a vote of the stockholders. Of course, the matter could be settled in this way, but I have argued elsewhere (Bowie 1990) that the limited short-term view of most stockholders undercuts any moral claim that ownership might have to make the sole decision here.

These arguments, if valid, also count against any view that would justify the manager making this decision as the agent of the stockholder. If the stockholders have no right to make the sole determination in these matters, neither do the stockholders' agents. If

no one stakeholder should settle these issues, it seems reasonable to think that all stakeholders should have a voice. How this voice is exercised can be decided in a number of ways.

Some corporations might focus on providing funds to groups that have broad public support, such as the United Way. Agencies like the United Way reflect community decisions concerning which charities are considered worthwhile. Undoubtedly some people in the community will object to the list, and agencies like the United Way have been criticized for leaving out controversial nonprofits that really fight social problems while keeping "middle class" charities such as the Boy Scouts. Despite these objections, deferring to local agencies recognizes the voice of the local community in decisions that are made. Alternatively, a corporation might put community people on its foundation board or community affairs council. I would recommend the first approach. The latter approach runs the risk of filling a board or council with individuals who speak only to narrow interests. Moreover, in line with my argument that moral duties fall on all corporate stakeholders, I would argue that it is the moral responsibility of the community to structure the United Way and other social agencies to meet genuine social needs. It is up to the local community to find a place for unpopular but socially concerned and effective nonprofits. It is up to the local community to solve the problems of representation.

Many corporations have given voice to their employees by matching employee contributions to charity. If an employee gives $100 to his or her college alma mater, the company will kick in $100 as well. Corporations also support charitable organizations in cities and towns where they have plants. They might extend this to cities and towns where their suppliers are located as well. These strategies should be adopted as policy by other corporations unless other defensible ways of giving voice to employees and suppliers can be found.

As for customers, they are part of the local community; unless there are some special circumstances that should be taken into account. I think our analysis will suffice. Customers are given voice the same way the local community is — by supporting local agencies through the United Way or some other similar organization.

Finally, I turn to stockholders. Although I have argued that the amount and type of corporate support given to help solve social problems should not be decided by the stockholders alone, they certainly should have some say in the decisions. Management might poll stockholders to determine their interests or get them to specifically approve the company's program in this area when they cast their annual proxy vote for the election of the board and other matters.

As the tenor of these remarks suggest, we are further along than might have been suspected with regard to giving all stakeholders a voice in corporate decisions. However, we have a way to go, and I have made some suggestions as to the directions we might take.

Let me close by making a point that will seem obvious to philosophers but less obvious to others. In essence, I have approached the issues raised by ethical pluralism by process rather than substance. I have not tried to argue that one position on these matters is morally correct and the others morally flawed. Rather, I have tried to elucidate a just process so the various stakeholder voices in these matters can be heard and have some influence on the decision. To put my perspective in Rawls's language (1971), I think the issues presented by ethical pluralism can only be handled by just procedures rather than aiming at just results. In Rawls's language, I am suggesting a system of imperfect procedural justice to address this issue.

REFERENCES

Jerry Alder, "Alaska After Exxon," *Newsweek*, September 18, 1989, pp. 50–62.

Alan S. Blinder, *Hard Heads Soft Hearts* (Reading, Mass.: Addison Wesley, 1987).

Norman Bowie, *Business Ethics* (Englewood Cliffs, N.J.: Prentice Hall Inc., 1982).

Norman Bowie with Ronald Duska, *Business Ethics*, 2nd ed. (Englewood Cliffs, N.J.: Prentice Hall Inc., 1990).

Norman Bowie, "The Firm as a Moral Community," in Richard M. Coughlin, ed., *Perspectives on Socio-Economics* (White Plains, N.Y.: M.E. Sharpe, Inc., 1991).

Albert Carr, "Is Business Bluffing Ethical?" *Harvard Business Review*, January–February 1968, pp. 143–146.

Thomas Donaldson, *The Ethics of International Business* (New York: Oxford University Press, 1989).

William E. Evan and R. Edward Freeman, "A Stakeholder Theory of the Modern Corporation: Kantian Capitalism," in Tom L. Beauchamp and Norman E. Bowie, eds., *Ethical Theory and Business*, 3rd ed. (Englewood Cliffs, N.J.: Prentice Hall, 1988).

Robert Frank, *Passions Within Reason* (New York: W.W. Norton & Co., 1988).

R. Edward Freeman, *Strategic Management: A Stakeholder Approach* (Marshfield, Mass.: Pitman, 1984).

Milton Friedman, *Capitalism & Freedom* (Chicago: University of Chicago Press, 1962).

Milton Friedman, "The Social Responsibility of Business Is to Increase Its Profits," *New York Times Magazine*, September 13, 1970, pp. 32–34, 122–126.

Immanuel Kant, *Foundations of the Metaphysics of Morals* (Lewis White Beck, trans.) (Indianapolis: Bobbs Merrill, 1969).

Theodore Levitt, "The Dangers of Social Responsibility," *Harvard Business Review*, September–October 1958, pp. 41–50.

Theodore Levitt, "The Morality(?) of Advertising," *Harvard Business Review*, July–August 1970, pp. 84–92.

John Rawls, *A Theory of Justice* (Cambridge, Mass.: Harvard University Press, 1971).

Alicia Swasy, "For Consumers, Ecology Comes Second," *Wall Street Journal*, August 23, 1988, p. B1.

Dodge v. Ford Motor Co.

Michigan Supreme Court

. . . When plaintiffs made their complaint and demand for further dividends, the Ford Motor Company had concluded its most prosperous year of business. The demand for its cars at the price of the preceding year continued. It could make and could market in the year beginning August 1, 1916, more than 500,000 cars. Sales of parts and repairs would necessarily increase. The cost of materials was likely to advance, and perhaps the price of labor; but it reasonably might have expected a profit for the year of upwards of $60,000,000. . . . Considering only these facts, a refusal to declare and pay further dividends appears to be not an exercise of discretion on the part of the directors, but an arbitrary refusal to do what the circumstances required to be done. These facts and others call upon the directors to justify their action, or failure or refusal to act. In justification, the defendants have offered testimony tending to prove and which does prove, the following facts: It had been the policy of the corporation for a considerable time to annually reduce the selling price of cars, while keeping up, or improving, their quality. As early as in June, 1915, a general plan for the expansion of the productive capacity of the concern by a practical duplication of its plant had been talked over by the executive officers and directors and agreed upon; not all of the details having been settled, and no formal action of directors having been taken. The erection of a smelter was considered, and engineering and other data in connection therewith secured. In consequence, it was determined not to reduce the selling price of cars for the year beginning August 1, 1915, but to maintain the price to accumulate a large surplus to pay for the proposed expansion of plant and equipment, and perhaps to build a plant for smelting ore. It is hoped, by Mr. Ford, that eventually 1,000,000 cars will be annually produced. The contemplated changes will permit the increased output.

The plan, as affecting the profits of the business for the year beginning August 1, 1916, and thereafter, calls for a reduction in the selling price of the cars. . . . In short, the plan does not call for and is not intended to produce immediately a more profitable business, but a less profitable one; not only less profitable than formerly, but less profitable than it is admitted it might be made. The apparent immediate effect will be to diminish the value of shares and the returns to shareholders.

It is the contention of plaintiffs that the apparent effect of the plan is intended to be the continued and continuing effect of it, and that it is deliberately proposed, not of record and not by official corporate declaration, but nevertheless proposed, to continue the corporation henceforth as a semi-eleemosynary institution and not as a business institution. In support of this contention, they point to the attitude and to the expressions of Mr. Henry Ford. . . .

"My ambition," said Mr. Ford, "is to employ still more men, to spread the benefits of this industrial system to the greatest possible number, to help them build up their lives and their homes. To do this we are putting the greatest share of our profits back in the business."

204 Mich. 459, 170 N.W. 668, 3 A.L.R. 413 (1919). Majority opinion by Justice J. Ostrander.

"With regard to dividends, the company paid sixty per cent, on its capitalization of two million dollars, or $1,200,000, leaving $58,000,000 to reinvest for the growth of the company. This is Mr. Ford's policy at present, and it is understood that the other stockholders cheerfully accede to this plan."

He had made up his mind in the summer of 1916 that no dividends other than the regular dividends should be paid, "for the present."

"Q. For how long? Had you fixed in your mind any time in the future, when you were going to pay — A. No."
"Q. That was indefinite in the future? A. That was indefinite; yes, sir."

The record, and especially the testimony of Mr. Ford, convinces that he has to some extent the attitude towards shareholders of one who has dispensed and distributed to them large gains and that they should be content to take what he chooses to give. His testimony creates the impression, also, that he thinks the Ford Motor Company has made too much money, has had too large profits, and that, although large profits might be still earned, a sharing of them with the public, by reducing the price of the output of the company, ought to be undertaken. We have no doubt that certain sentiments, philanthropic and altruistic, creditable to Mr. Ford, had large influence in determining the policy to be pursued by the Ford Motor Company — the policy which has been herein referred to.

It is said by his counsel that —

"Although a manufacturing corporation cannot engage in humanitarian works as its principal business, the fact that it is organized for profit does not prevent the existence of implied powers to carry on with humanitarian motives such charitable works as are incidental to the main business of the corporation." . . .

In discussing this proposition counsel have referred to decisions [citations omitted]. These cases, after all, like all others in which the subject is treated, turn finally upon the point, the question, whether it appears that the directors were not acting for the best interests of the corporation. We do not draw in question, nor do counsel for the plaintiffs do so, the validity of the general proposition stated by counsel nor the soundness of the opinions delivered in the cases cited. The case presented here is not like any of them. The difference between an incidental humanitarian expenditure of corporate funds for the benefit of the employees, like the building of a hospital for their use and the employment of agencies for the betterment of their condition, and a general purpose and plan to benefit mankind at the expense of others, is obvious. There should be no confusion (of which there is evidence) of the duties which Mr. Ford conceives that he and the stockholders owe to the general public and the duties which in law he and his codirectors owe to protesting, minority stockholders. A business corporation is organized and carried on primarily for the profit of the stockholders. The powers of the directors are to be employed for that end. The discretion of directors is to be exercised in the choice of means to attain that end, and does not extend to a change in the end itself, to the reduction of profits, or to the nondistribution of profits among stockholders in order to devote them to other purposes. . . . As we have pointed out, and the proposition does not require argument to sustain it, it is not within the lawful powers of a board of directors to shape and conduct the affairs of a corporation for the merely incidental benefit of shareholders and for the primary purpose of benefiting others, and no one will contend that, if the avowed purpose of the defendant directors was to sacrifice the interests of shareholders, it would not be the duty of the courts to interfere. . . . It is obvious that an annual dividend of 60 per cent, upon $2,000,000, or $1,200,000, is the equivalent of a very small dividend upon $100,000,000, or more.

The decree of the court below fixing and determining the specific amount to be distributed to stockholders is affirmed. . . .

A. P. Smith Manufacturing Co. v. Barlow

Supreme Court of New Jersey

The Chancery Division, in a well-reasoned opinion by Judge Stein, determined that a donation by the plaintiff The A. P. Smith Manufacturing Company to Princeton University was *intra vires*. Because of the public importance of the issues presented, the appeal duly taken to the Appellate Division has been certified directly to this court under Rule 1:5–1(a).

The company was incorporated in 1896 and is engaged in the manufacture and sale of valves, fire hydrants, and special equipment, mainly for water and gas industries. Its plant is located in East Orange and Bloomfield and it has approximately 300 employees. Over the years the company has contributed regularly to the local community chest and on occasions to Upsala College in East Orange and Newark University, now part of Rutgers, the State University. On July 24, 1951 the board of directors adopted a resolution which set forth that it was in the corporation's best interests to join with others in the 1951 Annual Giving to Princeton University, and appropriated the sum of $1,500 to be transferred by the corporation's treasurer to the university as a contribution towards its maintenance. When this action was questioned by stockholders the corporation instituted a declaratory judgment action in the

Chancery Division and trial was had in due course.

Mr. Hubert F. O'Brien, the president of the company, testified that he considered the contribution to be a sound investment, that the public expects corporations to aid philanthropic and benevolent institutions, that they obtain good will in the community by so doing, and that their charitable donations create favorable environment for their business operations. In addition, he expressed the thought that in contributing to liberal arts institutions, corporations were furthering their self-interest in assuring the free flow of properly trained personnel for administrative and other corporate employment. Mr. Frank W. Abrams, chairman of the board of the Standard Oil Company of New Jersey, testified that corporations are expected to acknowledge their public responsibilities in support of the essential elements of our free enterprise system. He indicated that it was not "good business" to disappoint "this reasonable and justified public expectation," nor was it good business for corporations "to take substantial benefits from their membership in the economic community while avoiding the normally accepted obligations of citizenship in the social community." Mr. Irving S. Olds, former chairman of the board of the

98 A 2d 581 (1953). Opinion by Judge J. Jacobs.

United States Steel Corporation, pointed out that corporations have a self-interest in the maintenance of liberal education as the bulwark of good government. He stated that "Capitalism and free enterprise owe their survival in no small degree to the existence of our private, independent universities" and that if American business does not aid in their maintenance it is not "properly protecting the long-range interest of its stockholders, its employees, and its customers." Similarly, Dr. Harold W. Dodds, President of Princeton University, suggested that if private institutions of higher learning were replaced by governmental institutions our society would be vastly different and private enterprise in other fields would fade out rather promptly. Further on he stated that "democratic society will not long endure if it does not nourish within itself strong centers of non-governmental fountains of knowledge, opinions of all sorts not governmentally or politically originated. If the time comes when all these centers are absorbed into government, then freedom as we know it, I submit, is at an end." . . .

When the wealth of the nation was primarily in the hands of individuals they discharged their responsibilities as citizens by donating freely for charitable purposes. With the transfer of most of the wealth to corporate hands and the imposition of heavy burdens of individual taxation, they have been unable to keep pace with increased philanthropic needs. They have therefore, with justification, turned to corporations to assume the modern obligations of good citizenship in the same manner as humans do. Congress and state legislatures have enacted laws which encourage corporate contributions, and much has recently been written to indicate the crying need and adequate legal basis therefor[e]. . . .

During the first world war corporations loaned their personnel and contributed sub-

stantial corporate funds in order to insure survival; during the depression of the '30s they made contributions to alleviate the desperate hardships of the millions of unemployed; and during the second world war they again contributed to insure survival. They now recognize that we are faced with other, though nonetheless vicious, threats from abroad which must be withstood without impairing the vigor of our democratic institutions at home and that otherwise victory will be pyrrhic indeed. More and more they have come to recognize that their salvation rests upon sound economic and social environment which in turn rests in no insignificant part upon free and vigorous nongovernmental institutions of learning. It seems to us that just as the conditions prevailing when corporations were originally created required that they serve public as well as private interests, modern conditions require that corporations acknowledge and discharge social as well as private responsibilities as members of the communities within which they operate. Within this broad concept there is no difficulty in sustaining, as incidental to their proper objects and in aid of the public welfare, the power of corporations to contribute corporate funds within reasonable limits in support of academic institutions. But even if we confine ourselves to the terms of the common-law rule in its application to current conditions, such expenditures may likewise readily be justified as being for the benefit of the corporation; indeed, if need be the matter may be viewed strictly in terms of actual survival of the corporation in a free enterprise system. The genius of our common law has been its capacity for growth and its adaptability to the needs of the times. Generally courts have accomplished the desired result indirectly through the molding of old forms. Occasionally they have done it directly through frank rejection of the old and recognition of the new. But whichever path the common law has taken it has not been found wanting as the proper tool for the advancement of the general good. . . .

In the light of all of the foregoing we have no hesitancy in sustaining the validity of the donation by the plaintiff. There is no suggestion that it was made indiscriminately or to a pet charity of the corporate directors in furtherance of personal rather than corporate ends. On the contrary, it was made to a preeminent institution of higher learning, was modest in amount and well within the limitations imposed by the statutory enactments, and was voluntarily made in the reasonable belief that it would aid the public welfare and advance the interests of the plaintiff as a private corporation and as part of the community in which it operates. We find that it was a lawful exercise of the corporation's implied and incidental powers under common-law principles and that it came within the express authority of the pertinent state legislation. As has been indicated, there is now widespread belief throughout the nation that free and

vigorous non-governmental institutions of learning are vital to our democracy and the system of free enterprise and that withdrawal of corporate authority to make such contributions within reasonable limits would seriously threaten their continuance. Corporations have come to recognize this and with their enlightenment have sought in varying measures, as has the plaintiff by its contribution, to insure and strengthen the society which gives them existence and the means of aiding themselves and their fellow citizens. Clearly then, the appellants, as individual stockholders whose private interests rest entirely upon the well-being of the plaintiff corporation, ought not be permitted to close their eyes to present-day realities and thwart the long-visioned corporate action in recognizing and voluntarily discharging its high obligations as a constituent of our modern social structure.

The judgment entered in the Chancery Division is in all respects Affirmed.

CASE 1.   *Shutdown at Eastland*

When Speedy Motors Company closed its assembly plant in Eastland, Michigan, lobbyists for organized labor cited the case as one more reason why the Federal government should pass a law regulating plant closings. With less than a month's notice, the company laid off nearly 2,000 workers and permanently shut down the facility, which had been in operation more than 20 years. The local union president called the action "a callous and heartless treatment of the workers and of the community."

Company executives defended the decision as inevitable in view of the harsh competitive realities of the automotive industry. "Purchases of the Speedy model produced at Eastland have fallen to almost nothing and there is nothing we can do about changes in consumer preferences," a company spokesman said.

Labor lobbyists insist that instances such as this show the need for a Federal law which would require companies to give as much as two years' notice before closing a major fac-

---

Adapted from a case by John P. Kavanagh, Emeritus Assistant Professor of Philosophy, Center for the Study of Values, University of Delaware. Reprinted by permission.

tory, unless they can demonstrate that an emergency exists. The proposed legislation would also require the employer to provide special benefits to workers and the community affected by the shutdown.

"Closing plants needlessly and without warning is an antisocial, criminal act," a union leader said. "Giant corporations don't give a thought to the hardships they are imposing on long-time employees and communities that depend on their jobs. The only thing they consider is their profit."

Opponents of the legislation maintain that the proposed law would strike at the heart of the free enterprise system. "Companies must be free to do business wherever they choose without being penalized," a corporate spokesman argued. "Plant closing legislation

would constitute unjustified interference in private decision making. Laws which restrict the ability of management to operate a business in the most efficient manner are counterproductive and in direct conflict with the theory of free enterprise."

Questions

1. Does the closing of a plant when it ceases to be profitable violate the "moral minimum"?
2. Who are the affected stakeholders, and how should their interests be considered?
3. Who should take primary responsibility for those laid off or terminated because of a plant closing?

CASE 2.   *The NYSEG Corporate Responsibility Program*

We are responsible to the communities in which we live and work and to the world community as well. We must be good citizens and support good works and charities. . . . We must encourage civic improvements and better health and education.[1]

Many large corporations currently operate consumer responsibility or social responsibility programs, which aim to return something to the consumer or to the community in which the company does business. New York State Electric and Gas (NYSEG) is one company that has created a program to discharge

what its officers consider to be the company's responsibility to its public.

NYSEG is a New York Stock Exchange-traded public utility with approximately 60,500 shareholders. It supplies gas and electricity to New York State. NYSEG currently earns 89 percent of its revenues from electricity and 11 percent from gas sales. The company is generally ranked as having solid but not excellent financial strength. Earnings per share have declined in recent years because of the regulatory climate and the company's write-offs for its Nine Mile Point #2 nuclear unit. In order to finance the unit, the company at one point had to absorb delay costs of several million dollars per month. The setback reduced shareholders' dividends for the

---

[1]"The Johnson and Johnson Way" (from the Johnson and Johnson Company credo), 1986, p. 26.

first time in many years. NYSEG's financial base is now less secure than in the past because of the lowered earnings per share and the increased plant costs.

The company's corporate responsibility program has been in effect throughout this period of financial reversal. NYSEG designed the program to aid customers who are unable to pay their utility bills for various reasons. The program does not simply help customers pay their bills to the company. Rather, NYSEG hopes the program will find people in the community in unfortunate or desperate circumstances and alleviate their predicament. The two objectives often coincide.

NYSEG has created a system of consumer representatives, social workers trained to deal with customers and their problems. Since the program's 1978 inception, NYSEG has maintained a staff of 13 consumer representatives. Each handles approximately 40 cases a month, over half of which result in successful financial assistance. The remaining cases are referred to other organizations for further assistance.[2]

The process works as follows: When the company's credit department believes a special investigation should be made into a customer's situation, the employee refers the case to the consumer representative. Referrals also come from human service agencies and from customers directly. Examples of appropriate referrals include unemployed household heads; paying customers who suffer serious injury, lengthy illness, or death;

and low-income senior citizens or those on fixed incomes who cannot deal with rising costs of living. To qualify for assistance, NYSEG requires only that the customers must be suffering from hardships they are willing to work to resolve.

Consumer representatives are primarily concerned with preventing the shutoff of service to these customers. They employ an assortment of resources to put them back on their feet, including programs offered by the New York State Department of Social Services and the federal Home Energy Assistance Program (HEAP), which awards annual grants of varying amounts to qualified families. In addition the consumer representatives provide financial counseling and help customers with their medical bills and education planning. They arrange assistance from churches and social services, provide food stamps, and help arrange VA benefits.

NYSEG also created a direct financial assistance program called Project Share, which enables paying customers who are not in financial difficulty to make charitable donations through their bills. They are asked voluntarily to add to their bill each month one, two, or five extra dollars, which are placed in a special fund overseen by the American Red Cross. This special Fuel Fund is intended to help those 60 years and older on fixed incomes who have no other means of paying their bills. Help is also provided for the handicapped and blind who likewise have few sources of funds. Many Project Share recipients do not qualify for government-funded assistance programs but nonetheless face energy problems. Through December 1990 Project Share had raised over $1.5 million and had successfully assisted more than 8,000 people.

The rationale or justification of this corporate responsibility program is rooted in the history of public utilities and rising energy

[2]Consumer representatives are viewed as liaisons between NYSEG and human services agencies. All of these representatives have extensive training and experience in human services, including four to six years of college with a degree in social work or social science. They must also have a minimum of four years of work experience in human services so that they are adequately qualified to deal with the problems facing customers.

costs in North America. Originally public utilities provided a relatively inexpensive product. NYSEG and the entire industry considered its public responsibility limited to the business function of providing energy at the lowest possible costs and returning dividends to investors. NYSEG did not concern itself with its customers' financial troubles. The customer or the social welfare system handled all problems of unpaid bills.

However, the skyrocketing energy costs in the 1970s changed customer resources and NYSEG's perspective. The energy crisis caused many long-term customers to encounter difficulty in paying their bills, and the likelihood of power shutoffs increased as a result. NYSEG then accepted a responsibility to assist these valued customers by creating the Consumer Representative system.

NYSEG believes its contribution is especially important now because recent reductions in federal assistance programs have shifted the burden of addressing these problems to the private sector. Project Share is viewed as "a logical extension of the President's call for increased volunteerism at the local level."[3] NYSEG chose the American Red Cross to cosponsor Project Share because of its experience in providing emergency assistance.

The costs of NYSEG's involvement in the program are regarded by company officers as low. NYSEG has few additional costs beyond the consumer representatives' salaries and benefits, which total $462,625 annually and are treated as operating expenses. To augment Project Share's financial support, NYSEG shareholders give the program an annual, need-based grant. In the past, shareholder grants have ranged from $40,000 to $100,000. NYSEG also pays for some personnel and printing costs through consumer rate increases, despite a recent ruling by the New York State Supreme Court that forbids utilities from raising consumer rates to obtain funds for charitable contributions (*Cahill v. Public Service Commission*). The company has also strongly supported Project Share by giving $490,000 over a seven-year period. The company's annual revenues are in the range of $1.5 billion, and the company's total debt also runs to approximately $1.5 billion.

The company views some of the money expended for the corporate responsibility program as recovered because of customers retained and bills paid through the program. NYSEG assumes that these charges would, under normal circumstances, have remained unpaid and would eventually have been written off as a loss. NYSEG's bad-debt level is 20 percent lower than that of the average U.S. utility company. The company believes that its corporate responsibility policy is *both* altruistic *and* good business, despite the program's maintenance costs, which seem to slightly exceed recovered revenue.

Questions

1. Do you agree that NYSEG's Project Share is both altruistic and good business? Why or why not?
2. Would Ken Goodpaster believe that Project Share is consistent with NYSEG's fiduciary responsibility to its shareholders?
3. To what extent, if any, is Project Share an example of stakeholder management principles?
4. Could adherents to a stockholder theory of corporate responsibility and adherents to a stakeholder theory both endorse Project Share as socially responsible? Why or why not?

[3]NYSEG, Project Share Procedures Manual, 1988, p. 2.

Suggested Supplementary Readings

CARSON, THOMAS. "Friedman's Theory of Corporate Social Responsibility." *Business and Professional Ethics Journal* 12 (Spring 1993): 3–32.

CLARKSON, MAX B. E. "A Stakeholder Framework for Analyzing and Evaluating Corporate Social Performance." *The Academy of Management Review* 20 (January 1995): 92–117.

DONALDSON, THOMAS. *Corporations and Morality.* Englewood Cliffs, NJ: Prentice Hall, 1982.

DONALDSON, THOMAS, and LEE E. PRESTON. "The Stakeholder Theory of the Corporation: Concepts, Evidence, and Implications." *Academy of Management Review* 20 (January 1995): 65–91.

EPSTEIN, EDWIN M. "The Corporate Social Policy Process, Beyond Business Ethics, Corporate Social Responsibility, and Corporate Social Responsiveness." *California Management Review* 29 (Spring 1987): 99–114.

FREDERICK, WILLIAM C. "Toward CSR3: Why Ethical Analysis Is Indispensable and Unavoidable in Corporate Affairs." *California Management Review* 28 (Winter 1986): 126–41.

FREEMAN, R. EDWARD. *Strategic Management: A Stakeholder Approach.* Boston: Pitman, 1984.

FREEMAN, R. EDWARD, and DANIEL R. GILBERT, JR. *Corporate Strategy and the Search for Ethics.* Englewood Cliffs, NJ: Prentice Hall, 1988.

FRIEDMAN, MILTON. *Capitalism and Freedom.* Chicago University Press, 1962.

GOODPASTER, KENNETH E., and THOMAS R. HOLLORAN. "In Defense of a Paradox." *Business Ethics Quarterly* 4 (October 1994): 423–29.

JONES, THOMAS M. "Instrumental Stakeholder Theory: A Synthesis of Ethics and Economics." *The Academy of Management Review* 20 (April 1995): 404–37.

LANGTRY, BRUCE. "Stakeholders and the Moral Responsibilities of Business." *Business Ethics Quarterly* 4 (October 1994): 431–43.

LEVITT, THEODORE. "The Dangers of Social Responsibility." *Harvard Business Review* 36 (September–October 1958): 41–50.

MAITLAND, IAN. "The Morality of the Corporation: An Empirical or Normative Disagreement?" *Business Ethics Quarterly* 4 (October 1994): 445–58.

MINTZBERG, HENRY. "The Case for Corporate Social Responsibility." *Journal of Business Strategy* 4 (Fall 1983): 3–15.

SCHLOSSBERGER, EUGENE. "A New Model of Business: Dual Investor Theory." *Business Ethics Quarterly* 4 (October 1994): 459–74.

WALTON, CLARENCE C. *The Moral Manager.* Cambridge, MA: Ballinger Publishing Company, 1988.

WICKS, ANDREW C., DANIEL R. GILBERT, JR., and R. EDWARD FREEMAN. "A Feminist Reinterpretation of the Stakeholder Concept." *Business Ethics Quarterly* 4 (October 1994) 475–97.

Chapter Three

———— • ————

The Regulation of Business

C HAPTER TWO ADDRESSED the general problem of corporate responsibility. This chapter explores the important subject of mechanisms for achieving corporate responsibility. We focus on how corporate performance is to be monitored, by whom may business be legitimately regulated, and how and by whom should the norms of corporate responsibility be enforced. In many respects irresponsible corporations are analogous to individuals who know what is right but who yield to temptation and do what they know is morally wrong. Such individuals are said to suffer from weakness of will. There are two fundamental strategies for overcoming weakness of will. One relies on voluntary internal mechanisms of self-control and the other on coercive or manipulative external constraints on behavior. In business, codes of ethics are an example of voluntary internal mechanisms of self-regulation, whereas government regulation is the most common external constraint. The strengths and weaknesses of self-regulation and government regulation are the central concerns of this chapter.

SELF-REGULATION

In the vast majority of cases business leaders prefer self-regulation to government regulation to overcome weakness of will. When pressed to argue for this preference, many business leaders invoke three arguments on behalf of the greater efficacy of self-regulation. First, businesspersons know their business and their roles and commitments better than any outsiders could. Hence, the duties of business seem best established by a knowledgeable community of practitioners. Second, businesspersons are best situated to bring pressures to bear on their members when they fail to perform their duties or when they abuse the public trust. A professional organization of businesspersons with the proper resources can run education programs about ethics, produce codes to conduct, monitor members' practices, and discipline and punish misconduct. Third, self-regulation is cheaper, more efficient, and more respectful of the autonomy of individual businesspersons and business firms than is government regulation. In other words, government regulation is expensive and coercive.

If this case for self-regulation is sound, it is reasonable to consider the methods and means by which self-regulation can be made to function in practice. Most businesspersons agree that society can expect a high level of ethical conduct on the part of businesspersons only if the practices and reward-and-punishment structures of business reinforce that behavior — inculcating appropriate senses of pride, shame, and responsibility. Many strategies exist for institutionalizing ethics, some of which require changes in the way corporations are managed.

On some occasions all that is needed to ensure moral behavior is a suitable procedure. Substantive requirements are not needed. For example, a number of advertising companies have a routine procedure of making surprise visits to television stations and checking their records as to whether they in fact broadcast commercials that they contracted to broadcast. Gary Pranzo, director of local broadcasting at Young & Rubicam, considers it "our fiduciary responsibility to our employees to do surprise audits."[1] These checks, then, serve a double moral purpose: They keep broadcasters honest, and they fulfill an advertising agency's fiduciary responsibility to its clients. This same monitoring practice was previously performed by the Federal Communications Commission, which stopped investigating stations' commercial logs as part of its massive effort at deregulation.

Other strategies for institutionalizing ethics require changes in the way information is processed. In ascertaining the cause of the 1979 crash of Air New Zealand TE-901 into Mt. Erebus, the Royal Commission investigating the crash identified the essential cause of the crash as the failure of the airline to inform Captain Collins of the change of the coordinates in the aircraft's internal computer system. Further investigation indicated that this communications failure was not simply the oversight of one individual. Rather, the communications gap resulted from general flaws in management procedure. To avoid another disaster, the management needed to improve the means of communication so that pilots were given complete information concerning the coordinates placed into the aircraft's computer. The lesson learned from these cases is that successful self-regulation in business requires persons who are responsible for ethical issues and sound management procedures for effecting ethical results. These procedures include adequate lines of communication, designations of responsibility, and clear opportunities for the ethical ramifications of corporate decisions to be discussed.

Codes of Ethics

Among the most common means to this end of self-regulation is the code of ethics directed at the amelioration of specific professional problems, as, for example, those used by physicians, nurses, bankers, advertising agents, chemical engineers, or lawyers. There are several advantages to such codes: First, they provide guidance in ethically ambiguous situations. This process is done in a number of ways. Codes provide more stable guides to right or wrong than do human personalities or continual ad hoc decisions. Codes of ethics are particularly important in dealing with supervisors since they can act as at least some check on autocratic power. In theory, at least, a business code of ethics can provide an independent ground of appeal when one is urged by a supervisor to commit an unethical act. "I'm sorry, but company policy strictly forbids it" is a gracious and relatively safe way of ending a conversation about a "shady" deal. Finally, codes of conduct help specify the social responsibilities of business itself by defining policy concerning such issues as conflict of interest, receipt of gift and gratuities, and comprehension of questionable payment.

For example, with respect to insider information, IBM gives the following directives to its employees.[2]

> If IBM is about to announce a new product or make a purchasing decision and the news could affect the stock of a competitor or supplier, you must not trade in the stock of those companies.
> If IBM is about to make an announcement that could affect the price of its stock, you must not trade in IBM stock.
> If IBM is about to build a new facility, you must not invest in land or business near the new site.

And with respect to tips, gifts, and entertainment, IBM says,

> No IBM employee, or any member of his or her immediate family, can accept gratuities or gifts of money from a supplier, customer, or anyone in a business relationship. Nor can they accept a gift or consideration that could be perceived as having been offered because of the business relationship. "Perceived" simply means this: If you read about it in the local newspaper, would you wonder whether the gift just might have had something to do with a business relationship.
> No IBM employee can give money or a gift of significant value to a customer, supplier, or anyone if it could reasonably be viewed as being done to gain a business advantage.

A second advantage of a code of ethics is that it enables a company to do the morally responsible act that it wants to do but, because of competitive pressures, would otherwise be unable to do. In other words, sometimes the competitive nature of business makes it impossible for an individual corporation to do the morally appropriate act and survive. Suppose, for example, that textile company A is polluting a river and that expensive technology is now available to enable company A to reduce pollution. On the basis of the harm analysis provided by Simon, Powers, and Gunnemann (see Chapter Two), it seems that company A ought to install the pollution control device. However, suppose that company A can show that all other textile companies are similarly polluting rivers. If company A installs the pollution control devices and the other textile companies do not, company A's product will rise in price and hence will run the risk of becoming noncompetitive.

Eventually company A may be forced out of business. The competitive situation thus makes it unfair and, from an economic perspective, impossible for company A to do the morally appropriate thing. Only a rule that requires all textile companies to install pollution control devices will be fair and effective. It is often maintained that in situations paralleling this textile pollution case, government regulation is the only viable answer.

Kenneth Arrow argues that the textile pollution case can potentially be adequately handled by an industry-wide code of ethics and that at least some evidence exists that industry-wide codes can work. Not all moral problems of personal conflict in society need to be resolved in courts by law or by regulatory agencies. Some are suitably handled by society's general moral codes or even by formal committee decisions. Indeed, if moral codes and practices were not widely efficacious, the courts and the regulatory systems would be overwhelmed.

The most serious theoretical challenge to Arrow's analysis of codes of ethics and indeed to most forms of self-regulation is presented by Ian Maitland. Maitland believes that most forms of self-regulation are unable to solve the assurance problem. From Maitland's perspective, Arrow's defense of an industry-wide code of ethics solves only half the problem. If a firm is not to be at a competitive disadvantage by doing the right thing, the firm must be assured that competing firms will also agree to do the right thing and will keep their agreements. An industry-wide code of ethics solves the first problem but not the second. The code provides the agreement, but obviously no code can provide the assurance that parties to the agreement will in fact honor it. Although government regulation is one possible answer, Maitland suggests that associations (peak organizations) that are more complex than industry-wide associations should be a societal form of self-regulation.

Less theoretical objections to codes of ethics include the (1) worry that industry agreement would violate antitrust laws, (2) fact that they are often both vague and ambiguous, and (3) fact that they are not enforced. To some extent the force of all three objections can be lessened. With the advent of international competition, the antitrust laws have played a decreasing role in the life of business. The likelihood that industry standards on genuine ethical issues would fall victim to antitrust laws is remote. As for lack of enforcement, the solution is simple. Enforce them.

Perhaps the most serious objection of the three is the charge that codes of ethics are often both vague and ambiguous. Part of the problem is in the nature of language itself, and it is certainly true that codes of ethics need interpretation. However, when codes of ethics are written to provide guidance rather than window dressing for public relations, the problems of vagueness and ambiguity are no more serious than with other policy guides both within and outside business. And after all, even our Constitution needs a Supreme Court to interpret it.

Thus there are both strengths and weaknesses in business codes of conduct. Nevertheless, they are an increasing feature of business, not only in the United States but also in other parts of the world as well.

Values and Responsibility: Individual Versus Organizational

An especially difficult problem in regulation occurs when there is disagreement in an organization over whether an organization is behaving morally. The problem is especially acute when professionals within an organization believe that organizational decisions are compromising professional norms. This problem takes on added complexity if a corporate decision ends in disaster and society demands to know who should be held responsible. To what extent should the individuals who were opposed to the decision be held responsible? Many believe that determining the extent of responsibility of those who were opposed depends on how they behaved. Did they keep their opinions to themselves? Should they have gone to a higher authority, refused to sign off, or even resigned and blown the whistle? These issues are addressed in two articles that focus on two notoriously disastrous decisions by U.S. business firms — the decision by Ford regarding the placement of the gas tank in the Ford Pinto and the decision by Morton Thiokol to sign off on the launch of the space shuttle *Challenger*.

Richard T. De George defends the view that engineers are not morally responsible for general management decisions. Their responsibility is limited to bringing the relevant facts to the attention of management. In the Ford Pinto case, the engineers behaved responsibly because they informed management that a $6.65 modification would make the gas tank safer. Of course, management received many other suggestions for improving the Pinto — some safety-related, some convenience-related. The task of management is to examine the total package of suggested improvements and their implication for the total cost of the car and finally to decide what improvements should be made and which should not be made so that the cost of the car can be competitive. That decision is a management decision and not an engineering decision. Thus even if the decision not to modify the gas tank in a Ford Pinto was an immoral one, the engineers who worked on the Ford Pinto are not morally responsible for that decision.

But do professionals have more responsibility than just informing management of the risks? In the case of the explosion of the *Challenger,* the senior scientist and other scientists had informed management over and over again of the dangers and probability of failure of the O-rings, especially during a launch in cold temperatures. Although Morton Thiokol appointed a Seal Erosion Task Team to investigate the problem, the team received little organizational support, much to the frustration of Roger Boisjoly and his colleagues. On January 27, 1986, Morton Thiokol's vice-president of engineering recommended against the next day's scheduled launch on the grounds that the predicted low temperature of 18 degrees could compromise the O-rings. NASA went directly to Joe Kilminster, vice-president of Space Booster Programs. At first Kilminster backed his engineers, but after continued pressure he held a caucus among five managers to make a "management decision." The managers overruled the engineers and approved the launch. Boisjoly noted his disapproval in his diary, but no public action was taken by any of the engineers. Should they have done more, and what responsibility, if any, do they bear for the *Challenger* disaster?

Russell J. Boisjoly, Ellen F. Curtis, and Eugene Mellican argue, in their essay included in this book, that there are two targets for assigning responsibility: individuals and organizations. Organizational responsibility is determined by examining organizational processes to see if the organization's rules for decision making were followed. If a decision has bad results but the organization followed proper procedure, then no individuals within the organization are responsible for the unfortunate results. Although Russell Boisjoly, Curtis, and Mellican decry the notion of organizational responsibility, one must ask what the alternative should be. If the focus is one of individual responsibility, how should it be exercised? Should, contrary to De George, engineers be allowed to veto management decisions? One of the more difficult tasks that faces an organization is permitting a maximum degree of individual authority while avoiding anarchy and paralysis within the organization.

GOVERNMENT REGULATION — THE FEDERAL SENTENCING GUIDELINES

The obvious alternative to self-regulation is government regulation. Until the 1980s, the government regulation of business in the United States had increased steadily. In many respects that history of increased regulation is understandable. Just before and after the beginning of the twentieth century, regulation was aimed at controlling large corporations and thus at protecting competition. This was the era of monopoly-busting legislation. The next wave of regulation in the 1930s, which occurred during the Great Depression, was designed to protect stockholders, employees, and customers from the failures of capitalism. Protection was given to employees who formed unions, but protection from fraud was also given to consumers and stockholders. In the 1960s the regulation of business was expanded to achieve social goals, especially to end discrimination in the workplace and to protect the environment.

But government regulation brought burdens as well as benefits. Among the most common criticisms is that government regulation is expensive, inflexible, and unfair. As an example of unfairness, property owners are held responsible for cleaning up discovered environmentally hazardous material even if they were not responsible for its being there and even if they were not the owners of the property at the time the damage occurred. A recent *Newsweek* op. ed. piece described a daughter's lament as her elderly mother nearly lost everything as a result of hazardous waste being discovered on her property.[3] In 1952 her mother, a widow at thirty-eight with two small children to raise, used $1500 from death benefits to construct a small commercial building. One of the inhabitants was a small dry cleaner. The dry cleaner had disposed of chemicals according to the standard practice of the time. However, in 1995 the chemicals deposited on the property twenty years earlier were judged to be the likely cause of the contamination of city park well water. The State of Oregon was holding her responsible for the cleanup conservatively estimated to cost $200,000. Her mother's financial security, the small building, was worth $70,000. To bankrupt her mother for contamination caused by another and caused by following standard practice seemed unfair.

During the 1980s these objections began to turn the tide toward less regulation. As we enter the last half of the 1990s, the attack on regulation continues. Yet, ironically, the federal government adopted in 1991 the Federal Sentencing Guidelines. These guidelines apply to both individual and corporate misconduct. Selections from the section applying to the sentencing of corporations appears in the Legal Perspectives section of the chapter. In an era of deregulation, these guidelines have the potential for greatly increasing the regulatory burden of businesses, large and small.

These regulations are additionally significant because they virtually force business firms to adopt comprehensive systems of self-regulation. Should a business firm fail to have what are called "compliance systems" in place and should a firm commit a federal tort, the fines that might be levied could put any corporation out of business. This chapter concludes with two articles that focus on the Federal Sentencing Guidelines. The first, by Robert Rafalko, describes the Guidelines and considers three objections that are commonly raised against them. The second, by Jennifer Moore, provides the philosophical justification for the notion of corporate culpability upon which the guidelines depend. In her article, Moore defends a conception referred to as "corporate character theory" as the best grounding for a theory of corporate culpability. Moore then shows how the Guidelines are consistent with the theory of corporate character and are thus able "to pursue a wider range of sentencing aims than is traditional in the sentencing of corporations."

As this edition goes to press, there are relatively few cases where corporations have been sentenced strictly in accordance with the Guidelines. However the potential for a vast increase in the number of cases is certainly present. Should the Guidelines be strictly enforced, the self-regulatory burden on corporations to institute elaborate compliance procedures will increase. Indeed for many corporations that have adopted such procedures the burdens have already been shouldered.

NOTES

1. As quoted in Ronald Alsop, "Efficacy of Global Ad Projects Is Questioned in Firm's Survey," *Wall Street Journal*, September 13, 1984, p. 31.
2. IBM Business Code of Conduct Guidelines (internal document), pp. 11–12.
3. Carolyn Scott Kortge, "Taken to The Cleaners." *Newsweek*, October 23, 1995, p. 16.

Business Codes and Economic Efficiency

Kenneth J. Arrow

This paper makes some observations on the widespread notion that the individual has some responsibility to others in the conduct of his economic affairs. It is held that there are a number of circumstances under which the economic agent should forgo profit or other benefits to himself in order to achieve some social goal, especially to avoid a disservice to other individuals. For the purpose of keeping the discussion within bounds, I shall confine my attention to the obligations that might be imposed on business firms. . . . Is it reasonable to expect that ethical codes will arise or be created? . . . This may seem to be a strange possibility for an economist to raise. But when there is a wide difference in knowledge between the two sides of the market, recognized ethical codes can be, as has already been suggested, a great contribution to economic efficiency. Actually we do have examples of this in our everyday lives, but in very limited areas. The case of medical ethics is the most striking. By its very nature there is a very large difference in knowledge between the buyer and the seller. One is, in fact, buying precisely the service of someone with much more knowledge than you have. To make this relationship a viable one, ethical codes have grown up over the centuries, both to avoid the possibility of exploitation by the physician and to assure the buyer of medical services that he is not being exploited. I am not suggesting that these are universally obeyed, but there is a strong presumption that the doctor is going to perform to a large extent with your welfare in mind. Unneces-

sary medical expenses or other abuses are perceived as violations of ethics. There is a powerful ethical background against which we make this judgment. Behavior that we would regard as highly reprehensible in a physician is judged less harshly when found among businesspersons. The medical profession is typical of professions in general. All professions involve a situation in which knowledge is unequal on two sides of the market by the very definition of the profession, and therefore there have grown up ethical principles that afford some protection to the client. Notice there is a mutual benefit in this. The fact is that if you had sufficient distrust of a doctor's services, you wouldn't buy them. Therefore the physician wants an ethical code to act as assurance to the buyer, and he certainly wants his competitors to obey this same code, partly because any violation may put him at a disadvantage but more especially because the violation will reflect on him, since the buyer of the medical services may not be able to distinguish one doctor from another. A close look reveals that a great deal of economic life depends for its viability on a certain limited degree of ethical commitment. Purely selfish behavior of individuals is really incompatible with any kind of settled economic life. There is almost invariably some element of trust and confidence. Much business is done on the basis of verbal assurance. It would be too elaborate to try to get written commitments on every possible point. Every contract depends for its observance on a mass of unspecified conditions

---

which suggest that the performance will be carried out in good faith without insistence on sticking literally to its wording. To put the matter in its simplest form, in almost every economic transaction, in any exchange of goods for money, somebody gives up his valuable asset before he gets the other's; either the goods are given before the money or the money is given before the goods. Moreover there is a general confidence that there won't be any violation of the implicit agreement. Another example in daily life of this kind of ethics is the observance of queue discipline. People line up; there are people who try to break in ahead of you, but there is an ethic which holds that this is bad. It is clearly an ethic which is in everybody's interest to preserve; one waits at the end of the line this time, and one is protected against somebody's coming in ahead of him.

In the context of product safety, efficiency would be greatly enhanced by accepted ethical rules. Sometimes it may be enough to have an ethical compulsion to reveal all the information available and let the buyer choose. This is not necessarily always the best. It can be argued that under some circumstances setting minimum safety standards and simply not putting out products that do not meet them would be desirable and should be felt by the businessperson to be an obligation.

Now I've said that ethical codes are desirable. It doesn't follow from that that they will come about. An ethical code is useful only if it is widely accepted. Its implications for specific behavior must be moderately clear, and above all it must be clearly perceived that the acceptance of these ethical obligations by everybody does involve mutual gain. Ethical codes that lack the latter property are unlikely to be viable. How do such codes develop? They may develop as a consensus out of lengthy public discussion of obligations, discussion which will take place in legisla-

tures, lecture halls, business journals, and other public forums. The codes are communicated by the very process of coming to an agreement. A more formal alternative would be to have some highly prestigious group discuss ethical codes for safety standards. In either case to become and to remain a part of the economic environment, the codes have to be accepted by the significant operating institutions and transmitted from one generation of executives to the next through standard operating procedures, through education in business schools, and through indoctrination of one kind or another. If we seriously expect such codes to develop and to be maintained, we might ask how the agreements develop and above all, how the codes remain stable. After all, an ethical code, however much it may be in the interest of all, is, as we remarked earlier, not in the interest of any one firm. The code may be of value to the running of the system as a whole, it may be of value to all firms if all firms maintain it, and yet it will be to the advantage of any one firm to cheat — in fact the more so, the more other firms are sticking to it. But there are some reasons for thinking that ethical codes can develop and be stable. These codes will not develop completely without institutional support. That is to say, there will be need for focal organizations, such as government agencies, trade associations, and consumer defense groups, or all combined to make the codes explicit, to iterate their doctrine and to make their presence felt. Given that help, I think the emergence of ethical codes on matters such as safety, at least, is possible. One positive factor here is something that is a negative factor in other contexts, namely that our economic organization is to such a large extent composed of large firms. The corporation is no longer a single individual; it is a social organization with internal social ties and internal pressures for acceptability and esteem. The individual members of the corporation are not only parts of the corporation but also members of a larger society whose esteem is desired. Power in a large corporation is necessarily diffused; not many individuals in such organizations feel so thoroughly identified with the corporation that other kinds of social pressures become irrelevant. Furthermore, in a large, complex firm where many people have to participate in any decision, there are likely to be some who are motivated to call attention to violations of the code. This kind of check has been conspicuous in government in recent years. The Pentagon Papers are an outstanding illustration of the fact that within the organization there are those who recognize moral guilt and take occasion to blow the whistle. I expect the same sort of behavior to occur in any large organization when there are well-defined ethical rules whose violation can be observed.

One can still ask if the codes are likely to be stable. Since it may well be possible and profitable for a minority to cheat, will it not be true that the whole system may break down? In fact, however, some of the pressures work in the other direction. It is clearly in the interest of those who are obeying the codes to enforce them, to call attention to violations, to use the ethical and social pressures of the society at large against their less scrupulous rivals. At the same time the value of maintaining the system may well be apparent to all, and no doubt ways will be found to use the assurance of quality generated by the system as a positive asset in attracting consumers and workers.

One must not expect miraculous transformations in human behavior. Ethical codes, if they are to be viable, should be limited in their scope. They are not a universal substitute for the weapons mentioned earlier, the institutions, taxes, regulations, and legal remedies. Further, we should expect the codes to apply in situations where the firm has superior knowledge of the situation. I would not want the firm to act in accordance with some ethical principles in regard to matters of which it has little knowledge. For example, with quality standards which consumers can observe, it may not be desirable that the firm decide for itself, at least on ethical grounds, because it is depriving the consumer of the freedom of choice between high-quality, high-cost and low-quality, low-cost products. It is in areas where someone is typically misinformed or imperfectly informed that ethical codes can contribute to economic efficiency.

The Limits of Business Self-Regulation

Ian Maitland

In a liberal democracy, there are limits to the extent to which socially responsible behavior can be ordered by law. Beyond a certain point, the costs of expanding the apparatus of state control become prohibitive — in terms of abridged liberties, bureaucratic hypertrophy, and sheer inefficiency. This fact probably accounts for the lasting appeal of the concept of self-regulation — the idea that we would be better off if we could rely on the

From Ian Maitland, "The Limits of Business Self-Regulation," *California Management Review* 27:3 (1985), © 1985 by the Regents of the University of California. By permission of the Regents.

promptings of a corporate "conscience" to regulate corporate behavior instead of the heavy hand of government regulation.

To its advocates, the virtues of self-regulation — or "corporate social responsibility" — seem self-evident. It promises simultaneously to allay business fears of further government encroachment and to restore the public's faith in business. What is more, it asks of business only that it behave in its own enlightened self-interest. While this entails a radical break with the way managers have conceived of their role in the past, it does not make any impossible or self-contradictory demands that an imaginative manager cannot adapt to. In any case, such things as the new awareness of the fragility of the physical environment, the quantum leap in the power of large corporations, and a New American Ideology, all demand no less.

The period from the mid-1950s to the mid-1970s saw a stream of proposals for the moral reconstruction of the corporation. The principal obstacle to self-regulation was diagnosed as managers' single-minded preoccupation with profits maximization. This, in turn, was attributed to intellectual short-comings — managers' insularity, their failure to keep up with changing values, their inability to see their role in a system-wide perspective, and their attachment to an outmoded ideology which defined the public interest as the unintended outcome of the pursuit of selfish interests. Also implicated were the organizational structure and culture of the modern corporation which supposedly embodied and perpetuated this orientation to profit. The advocates of self-regulation saw their task as being the proselytizing and scolding of managers into a broader definition of their role and the drawing up of blueprints for the socially responsible corporation.

This most recent wave of enthusiasm for self-regulation has largely receded, leaving behind it few enduring achievements. By and large, the exhortations appear to have fallen on deaf ears, or at best to have had only a marginal impact on corporate conduct. The primacy of profit maximization remains unchallenged and we continue to rely — and will do so for the foreseeable future — on legal compulsion administered by the state to regulate the undesirable consequences of economic activity.

If the marriage between the corporation and self-regulation was made in heaven, why has it not been consummated? The failure of self-regulation to live up to its promise is attributable to factors that have, for the most part, been overlooked by its advocates. In their attempts to make over managers' value systems and restructure the modern corporation, they have largely neglected the very real limits on managers' discretion that result from the operation of a market economy. As a consequence of these limits, managers are largely *unable* to consider their firms' impact on society or to subordinate profit-maximization to social objectives, no matter how well-intentioned they are.

A GAME THEORETIC ANALYSIS OF SELF-REGULATION

The crux of this argument is the recognition that an individual firm's interests as a competitor in the marketplace often diverge from its interests as a part of the wider society (or, for that matter, as a part of the business community). In this latter role, the firm is likely to welcome a cleaner environment, but as a competitor in the marketplace it has an interest in minimizing its own pollution abatement costs. It may philosophically favor a free market, but it will probably lobby in favor of protection for itself. This observation is a commonplace one, but its implications are rarely fully explored.

The firm's interests as part of a broader group typically take the form of collective or public goods. Using a rational choice model of behavior, Mancur Olson has demonstrated that it is not in the interest of a group member (let us say, the firm) to contribute to the costs of providing such goods.[1] Public goods (e.g., a cleaner environment or the free market) are goods that are available to all firms irrespective of whether or not they have contributed to their upkeep or refrained from abusing them. Since their availability is not contingent on a firm having contributed, each firm has a rational incentive to free-ride, i.e., to leave the costs of providing them to other firms. However, if each firm succumbs to this temptation, as it must if it acts in its own rational self-interest, then the public good will not be provided at all. Thus, even when they are in agreement, "rational, self-interested individuals will not act to achieve their common or group interests."[2] In a rational world, Olson concludes, "it is certain that a collective good will *not* be provided unless there is coercion or some outside inducement."[3]

The typical objectives of business self-regulation and responsible corporate behavior — such as a cleaner environment — are public goods. Olson's theory therefore provides a basis for explaining why business self-regulation appears so hard to achieve.

Russell Hardin has pointed out that the logic underlying Olson's theory of collective action is identical to that of an n-person prisoner's dilemma (PD).[4] The strategy of not contributing toward the cost of a public good dominates the strategy of paying for it, in the sense that no matter what other firms do, any particular firm will be better off if it does not contribute.

. . . Ford Runge (following A. K. Sen) has argued that what appears to be a prisoner's dilemma proves, on closer inspection, to be an "assurance problem" (AP).[5] According to this theory, the group member (i.e., firm) does not withhold its contribution to a public good based on a rational calculation of the costs and benefits involved (as with the PD) but rather does so because it is unable to obtain the necessary assurance that other firms will contribute their fair share. In other words, the AP substitutes the more lenient assumption that firms prefer equal or fair shares for the PD's assumption that they invariably try to maximize their individual net gain. Under the AP, we can expect firms to regulate their own behavior in some larger interest so long as they are confident that other firms are doing the same.

But in a market economy, where decision making is highly dispersed, the prediction of other firms' behavior becomes problematic. As a consequence, no individual firm can be sure that it is not placing itself at a competitive disadvantage by unwittingly interpreting its own obligations more strictly than its competitors do theirs. In these circumstances, all firms are likely to undertake less self-regulation than they would in principle be willing (indeed, eager) to accept.

In spite of their differences, both the PD and the AP involve problems of collective action. In the case of the PD, the problem is that it is always in the rational interest of each firm to put its own individual interests ahead of its collective interests. In the case of the AP, the problem is that of coordinating firms' expectations regarding fair shares.

The sub-optimal supply of business self-regulation can be explained largely in terms of the barriers to collective action by firms. There are three levels of self-regulation: the firm level (corporate social responsibility); the industry level (industry self-regulation); and the level of the economy (business-wide self-regulation). It is only at the third level that the necessary collective action is likely to be of a socially benign variety.

THREE LEVELS OF SELF-REGULATION

Corporate Social Responsibility. Contemporary advocates of corporate social responsibility acknowledge the difficulties of implementing it, but they go on to proclaim its inevitability anyway. In their view, it has to work because nothing else will; at best, the law elicits grudging and literal compliance with certain minimal standards when what is needed is corporations' spontaneous and whole-hearted identification with the *goals* of the law.[6] As Christopher Stone says, there are clear advantages to "encouraging people to act in socially responsible ways because they believe it the 'right thing' to do, rather than because (and thus, perhaps, only to the extent that) they are ordered to do so."[7]

Advocates of social responsibility have offered a number of prescriptions for curing firms' fixation on profit maximization. The weakness of these proposals lies in their assumption that social responsibility can be produced by manipulating the corporation. They overlook the extent to which the firm's behavior is a function of market imperatives rather than of managers' values or corporate structure. . . .

This point is . . . illustrated by cases where competitive pressures have prevented firms from acting responsibly even where it would be in their economic interest to do so. Robert Leone has described how aerosol spray manufacturers were reluctant to abandon the use of fluorocarbon propellants (which were suspected of depleting the ozone layer in the stratosphere) even though the alternative technology was cheaper. The problem was that "any individual company that voluntarily abandoned the use of such propellants ran the risk of a sizeable loss of market share as long as competitors still offered aerosol versions of their products [which the public values for their convenience]."[8] In situations of this kind it is not unusual for responsible firms, aware of their own helplessness, to solicit regulation in order to prevent themselves being taken advantage of by competitors who do not share their scruples about despoiling the environment or injuring the industry's reputation. Thus aerosol manufacturers did not oppose the ban on fluorocarbons in spite of the tenuous scientific evidence of their dangers. Similarly, following the Tylenol poisonings, the pharmaceutical industry sought and obtained from the FDA a uniform national rule on tamper-resistant packaging, because no individual firm had wanted to unilaterally incur the expense of such packaging.[9] The list of examples is endless.

In a market economy, firms are usually *unable* to act in their own collective interests because "responsible" conduct risks placing the firms that practice it at a competitive disadvantage unless other firms follow suit. Where there is no well-defined standard that enjoys general acceptance, it will take some sort of tacit or overt coordination by firms to supply one. Even if that coordination survives the attentions of the Antitrust Division and the FTC, compliance will still be problematic because of the free-rider problem. Arrow has pointed out that a "code [of behavior] may be of value to . . . all firms if all firms maintain it, and yet it will be to the advantage of any one firm to cheat — in fact the more so, the more other firms are sticking to it."[10] We are therefore faced with the paradox that the voluntary compliance of the majority of firms may depend on the coercive imposition of the code of behavior on the minority of free riders. Thus, although it is fashionable to view voluntarism and coercion as opposites — and to prefer the former for being more humane and, ultimately, effective — they are more properly seen as interdependent.[11]

Industry Self-Regulation. If responsible corporate conduct must ultimately be backed by coercion, there remains the question of who is to administer the coercion. Is self-regulation by a trade association or other industry body a practical alternative to government regulation? The classic solution to the public goods dilemma is "mutual coercion, mutually agreed upon."[12] The possibility of "permitting businesses to coerce themselves" has been raised by Thomas Schelling who adds that such an approach "could appeal to firms which are prepared to incur costs but only on condition that their competitors do also."[13]

The record of industry self-regulation in the United States suggests that it does indeed commonly arise in response to the public goods problem. David A. Garvin explains the development of self-regulation in the advertising industry in this way.[14] Michael Porter has noted that self-regulation may be of particular importance to an emerging industry which is trying to secure consumer acceptance of its products. At this stage of its life cycle, an industry's reputation could be irretrievably injured by the actions of a single producer.[15] Thus the intense self-regulation in the microwave industry is understandable in terms of the industry's need to "overcome the inherent suspicion with which many people view 'new' technology like microwave ovens."[16] Nevertheless, industry self-regulation remains the exception in the United States. This is so because it is a two-edged sword: the powers to prevent trade abuses are the same powers that would be needed to restrain trade.

Because of the potential anti-competitive implications of industry self-regulation, its scope has been strictly limited. Anti-trust laws have significantly circumscribed the powers of trade associations. Legal decisions have proscribed industry-wide attempts to eliminate inferior products or impose ethical codes of conduct. Major oil firms were frustrated by the anti-trust statutes when they tried to establish an information system to rate the quality of oil tankers in an attempt to reduce the incidence of oil spills from substandard vessels.[17] Airlines have had to petition the Civil Aeronautics Board for antitrust immunity so that they could discuss ways of coordinating their schedules in order to reduce peak-hour overcrowding at major airports.[18]

In short, industry or trade associations appear to hold out little promise of being transformed into vehicles for industry self-regulation. The fear is too entrenched that industry self-regulation, however plausible its initial rationale, will eventually degenerate into industry protectionism.

Business Self-Regulation. If self-regulation at the level of the individual firm is of limited usefulness because of the free-rider problem, and if industry self-regulation is ruled out by anti-trust considerations, we are left with self-regulation on a business-wide basis, presumably administered by a confederation or peak organization. An "encompassing" business organization of this sort would be less vulnerable to the anti-trust objections that can be levelled at industry associations. This is so because the diversity of its membership would inhibit such an organization from aligning itself with the sectional interests of particular firms or industries. Because it would embrace, for example, both producers and consumers of steel, it would be unable to support policies specifically favoring the steel industry (such as a cartel or tariffs) without antagonizing other parts of its membership that would be injured by such policies. A business peak organization would thus be constrained to adopt a pro-competitive posture.[19]

How might a peak organization contribute to resolving the assurance problem and the prisoner's dilemma? In the case of the AP, we saw that the principal impediment to cooperation is the difficulty of predicting others' behavior — without which coordination is impossible. By defining a code of responsible corporate conduct — and/or making authoritative rulings in particular cases — a peak organization might substantially remove this difficulty. In particular, if it is equipped to *monitor* compliance with the code, it could provide cooperating firms with the necessary assurance that they were not shouldering an unfair burden.

The point here is not that a peak organization would necessarily be more competent to make ethical judgments or that its code would be ethically superior; it is that the code would be a *common* one that would enable firms to coordinate their behavior. As we have seen, where there is a multiplicity of standards, there is effectively no standard at all, because no firm can be confident that its competitors are playing by the same rules.

A common external code would also help defuse two contentious issues in top management's relations with the firm's stockholders. First managers would be at least partly relieved of the task of making subjective (and often thankless) judgments about the firm's obligations to various stakeholders — a task for which they are generally not equipped by training, by aptitude, or by inclination. Second, such a code would permit them to heed society's demands that the firm behave responsibly while at the same time protecting them from the charge that their generosity at the stockholders' expense was jeopardizing the firm's competitive position.[20]

So far we have assumed that each firm *wants* to cooperate (i.e., to contribute to the realization of the public good, in this case by acting responsibly) provided other firms do the same. As long as there is some means of coordinating their behavior, then firms can be counted on to cooperate. What happens if we allow for the likelihood that, while most firms may be disposed to comply with the code, some number of opportunistic firms will choose to defect?

A code of conduct — even if only morally binding — can be expected to exert a powerful constraining influence on the behavior of would-be defectors. Such a code would embody "good practice" and so would serve as a standard against which corporate behavior could be judged in individual cases. Consequently, firms which violated the code would be isolated and the spotlight of public indignation would be turned on them. In the cases where moral suasion failed, the code would still offer certain advantages (at least from business's standpoint). First, an adverse ruling by the peak organization would serve to distance the business community as a whole from the actions of a deviant firm and so would counter the impression that business was winking at corporate abuses.[21] Second, the standards defined by the peak organization might become the basis for subsequent legislation or regulatory rulemaking. By setting the agenda in this fashion, the peak organization might forestall more extreme or onerous proposals.

However, the defection of even a handful of firms (if it involved repeated or gross violation of the code) would undermine the social contract on which the consent of the majority was based. Their continued compliance would likely be conditional on the code being effectively policed. Therefore, it seems inconceivable that business self-regulation could be based on moral suasion alone. . . .

Thus, if we modify the AP to reflect the real-world probability that some number of opportunistic firms will disregard the code, the case for investing the peak organization with some powers of compulsion becomes unanswerable. The case is stronger still if we accept the axiom of the PD that firms will invariably defect when it is in their narrow self-interest to do so. Some form of sovereign to enforce the terms of the social contract then becomes indispensable. . . .

THE CONSEQUENCES
OF PEAK ORGANIZATION

Peak (or "encompassing") organizations are not merely larger special interest organizations. By virtue of the breadth and heterogeneity of their membership, they are transformed into a qualitatively different phenomenon. Indeed, peak organizations are likely to exert pressure on the behavior of their members in the direction of the public interest.

In the interests of its own stability, any organization must resist efforts by parts of its membership to obtain private benefits at the expense of other parts. It follows that the more inclusive or encompassing the organization, the larger the fraction of society it represents, and so the higher the probability that it will oppose self-serving behavior (by sections of its membership) that inflicts external costs on the rest of society. . . .

The officers of business peak organizations in Germany, Japan, and Sweden have a quasi-public conception of their role that is far removed from the American interest group model. According to Andrew Shonfield, Germany's two business *Spitzenverbände* "have typically seen themselves as performing an important public role, as guardians of the long-term interests of the nation's industries."[22] The same finding is reported by an American scholar who evidently has difficulty in taking at face value the claims made by leaders of the BDI (Confederation of German Industry): "To avoid giving an impression that it is an interest group with base, selfish and narrow aims, the BDI constantly identifies its own goals with those of the entire nation."[23] Finally, David Bresnick recently studied the role of the national confederation of employers and trade unions of six countries in the formation and implementation of youth employment policies. In Germany, these policies were largely made and administered by the confederations themselves. In Bresnick's words, "The system in Germany has evolved with minimal government regulation and maximum protection of the interests of the young, while promoting the interests of the corporations, trade unions and the society in general. It has reduced the government role to one of occasional intervenor. It has taken the government out of the business of tax collector and achieved a degree of social compliance that is extraordinary."[24]

A similar account is given by Ezra Vogel of the role of the Japanese business peak organization, *Keidanren*.[25] Keidanren concentrates on issues of interest to the business community as a whole and "cannot be partial to any single group or any industrial sector." Vogel reports that Japanese business leaders are surprised at "the extent to which American businessmen thought only of their own company and were unprepared to consider business problems from a broader perspective." In Japan, this "higher level of aggregation of interests within the business community tends to ensure that the highest level politicians also think in comparably broad terms."[26] . . .

While the data on . . . German and Japanese peak organizations are too unsystematic to constitute a strict test concerning the consequences of peak organizations, they do shed a revealing light on the role such an organization might play in the U.S. In particular, in administering a system of self-regulation, a peak organization would be in a position to take into account a broader range of interests than is catered for by our present structures of interest representation. Also, a peak organization might promote more harmonious business-government relations without entailing the cooptation or capture of either one by the other.

PROSPECTS

What are the prospects of [a] system of business self-regulation administered by a peak organization taking root in the U.S.? What incentives would an American peak organization be able to rely on to secure firms' compliance with its standards and rulings? We have seen that, by itself, recognition of the mutuality of gains to be had from a peak organization cannot guarantee such compliance. In order to overcome the free-rider problem, the would-be peak organization must be able to offer firms private benefits or "selective incentives" that are unavailable outside the organization but that are sufficiently attractive to induce firms to comply.[27]

Students of organizations have identified an array of incentives — both positive and negative — that have been used to attract and hold members. These include: selective access to information (e.g., about government actions, technical developments, and commercial practices) under the organization's control; regulation of jurisdictional disputes between members; predatory price-cutting; boycotts; withdrawal of credit; public disparagement; fines; social status; and conviviality.... Finally, purposive incentives — "intangible rewards that derive from the sense of satisfaction of having contributed to the attainment of a worthwhile cause" — have provided at least a transient basis for organization....

The difficulties encountered by trade associations that try to influence their members' behavior are compounded in the case of a would-be peak organization. A peak organization has access to fewer selective benefits with which to maintain members' allegiance, and its goals are even further removed from the immediate concerns of most firms. Moreover, these goals tend to be public goods (e.g., maintaining the private enterprise system or

avoiding higher taxes). Wilson notes that "no single businessman has an incentive to contribute to the attainment of what all would receive if the organized political efforts are successful." In these circumstances, "the creation and maintenance of an association such as the [U.S.] Chamber, which seeks to represent all business in general and no business in particular has been a considerable achievement."[28]

The Chamber, of course, seeks only to speak for business's collective interests. It is not difficult to imagine how much more precarious its existence would be if it also tried to set and enforce standards of conduct. It follows that if trade associations have generally been ineffective except when their powers have been underwritten by the government, a peak organization is *a fortiori* likely to be dependent on government support. And, in fact, in Western Europe, it appears that "many of the peak associations ... reached their hegemonic status with major contributions from the more or less official recognition of key government agencies."[29]

What form would such public support have to take in the U.S.? It might involve waiving anti-trust laws in the case of the peak organization, e.g., by permitting it to punish free-riding behavior by imposing fines or administering boycotts. Government might grant it certain prerogatives — e.g., privileged access to key policy deliberations or agency rule-making, which it might in turn use to obtain leverage over recalcitrant firms. The government might require — as in Japan[30] — that every firm be a registered member of the peak organization. All these actions would serve to strengthen the peak organization vis-á-vis its members.

However, the chances are slight that actions of this kind could be taken in the U.S. In the first place, as Salisbury says, "American political culture is so rooted in individualist assumptions that [interest] groups have no integral place."[31] In contrast with Europe, associations have not been officially incorporated into the process of policy formation; bureaucrats in the U.S. deal directly with constituent units (individual firms, hospitals, universities, etc.) not with associations.[32] Given the dubious legitimacy of interest organizations in general, it seems improbable that semi-official status or privileged access would be granted to a peak organization.

A second obstacle is the structure of American government. The fragmentation of power in the American system — federalism, separation of powers, legislators nominated and elected from single-member districts — has created multiple points of access for interests that want to influence the policy process. Wilson has persuasively argued that a country's interest group structure is largely a reflection of its political structure. Thus a centralized, executive-led government is likely to generate strong national interest associations and, conversely, "the greater decentralization and dispersion of political authority in the United States helps explain the greater variety of politically active American voluntary associations."[33] In the American context, then, it is virtually inconceivable that a peak organization could secure a monopolistic or privileged role in public policymaking in even a few key areas; but without superior access of this sort it is deprived of one of the few resources available to influence its members' behavior. . . .

CONCLUSION

. . . This article has examined the ways it might be possible for firms to coordinate their behavior (both in their own larger interests and the public interest) while at the same time minimizing the risk that this coordination would be exploited for anti-social purposes. Such a benign outcome could be obtained by permitting collective action to be administered by a business-wide peak organization. At this level of coordination, a competitive market economy could coexist with effective self-regulation. However, the United States — given its distinctive political institutions — is not likely to provide a congenial soil for such an organization to take root.

NOTES

1. Mancur Olson, *The Logic of Collective Action* (Cambridge, MA: Harvard University Press, 1965).

2. Ibid., p. 2.

3. Ibid., p. 44.

4. Russell Hardin, "Collective Action as an Agreeable n-Prisoner's Dilemma," *Behavioral Science,* vol. 16 (1971), pp. 472–79.

5. C. Ford Runge, "Institutions and the Free Rider: The Assurance Problem in Collective Action," *Journal of Politics,* vol. 46 (1984), pp. 154–81.

6. Cf. Henry Mintzberg, "The Case for Corporate Social Responsibility," *Journal of Business Strategy,* vol. 14 (1983), pp. 3–15.

7. Christopher Stone, *Where the Law Ends* (New York, NY: Harper Torchbooks, 1975), p. 112.

8. Robert A. Leone, "Competition and the Regulatory Boom," in Dorothy Tella, ed., *Government Regulation of Business: Its Growth, Impact, and Future* (Washington, D.C.: Chamber of Commerce of the United States, 1979), p. 34.

9. Susan Bartlett Foote, "Corporate Responsibility in a Changing Legal Environment," *California Management Review,* vol. 26 (1984), pp. 217–28.

10. Kenneth J. Arrow, "Social Responsibility and Economic Efficiency," *Public Policy,* vol. 21 (1973), p. 315.

11. See Thomas Schelling on "the false dichotomy of voluntarism and coercion," in "Command and Control," in James W. McKie, ed., *Social Responsibility and the Business Predicament* (Washington, D.C.: Brookings, 1974), p. 103.

12. The phrase is from Garrett Hardin's "The Tragedy of the Commons," *Science,* vol. 162 (1968), p. 1247.

13. Schelling, op. cit., p. 103.

14. David Garvin, "Can Industry Self-Regulation Work?" *California Management Review,* vol. 25 (1983), p. 42.

15. Michael Porter, *Competitive Strategy* (New York, NY: Free Press, 1980), p. 230.

16. Thomas P. Grumbly, "Self-Regulation: Private Vice and Public Virtue Revisited," in Eugene Bardach and Robert Kagan, eds., *Social Regulation: Strategies for Reform* (San Francisco, CA: Institute for Contemporary Studies, 1982), p. 97.

17. Garvin, op. cit., pp. 155, 156.

18. Christopher Conte, "Transport Agency's Dole Vows to Restrict Traffic at 6 Busy Airports if Carriers Don't," *Wall Street Journal,* August 16, 1984, p. 10.

19. Mancur Olson, *The Rise and Decline of Nations* (New Haven, CT: Yale University Press, 1982), pp. 47–48.

20. These objections lie at the heart of the complaint that the doctrine of corporate social responsibility provides no operational guidelines to assist managers in making responsible choices. The most sophisticated (but, I think, ultimately unsuccessful) attempt to supply an objective, external standard (located in what they call the public policy process) is Lee Preston and James Post, *Private Management and Public Policy* (Englewood Cliffs, NJ: Prentice-Hall, 1975).

21. See on this point the remarks of Walter A. Haas, Jr., of Levi Strauss quoted in Leonard Silk and David Vogel, *Ethics and Profits* (New York, NY: Simon & Schuster, 1976), pp. 25–27.

22. Andrew Shonfield, *Modern Capitalism* (New York and London: Oxford University Press, 1965), p. 245.

23. Gerard Baunthal, *The Federation of German Industries in Politics* (Ithaca, NY: Cornell University Press, 1965), pp. 56–57.

24. David Bresnick, "The Youth Employment Policy Dance: Interest Groups in the Formulation and Implementation of Public Policy," paper presented at the American Political Science Association meetings in Denver, September 2–5, 1982, p. 33.

25. Ezra Vogel, *Japan as Number 1* (New York, NY: Harper Colophon, 1979), chapter 5.

26. Ibid.

27. This is, of course, the essence of the argument in Olson's *Logic,* op. cit. This section draws heavily on James Q. Wilson, *Political Organizations,* op. cit.; Robert H. Salisbury, "Why No Corporatism in America?," in Philippe Schmitter and Gerhard Lehmbruch, *Trends Toward Corporatist Intermediation* (Beverly Hills: Sage, 1979); and Philippe Schmitter and Donald Brand, "Organizing Capitalists in the United States: The Advantages and Disadvantages of Exceptionalism," presented at a workshop at the International Institute of Management, Berlin, November 14–16, 1979.

28. James Q. Wilson, *Political Organizations* (New York, NY: Basic Books, 1973), pp. 153, 161.

29. Salisbury, op. cit., p. 215. See also Wilson, op. cit., p. 82.

30. Vogel, *Japan as Number 1,* op. cit., p. 112.

31. Salisbury, op. cit. p. 222.

32. Schmitter and Brand, op. cit., p. 71.

33. Wilson, op. cit., p. 83; see generally chapter 5.

Ethical Responsibilities of Engineers in Large Organizations: The Pinto Case

Richard T. De George

The myth that ethics has no place in engineering has been attacked, and at least in some corners of the engineering profession has been put to rest.[1] Another myth, however, is emerging to take its place — the myth of the engineer as moral hero. A litany of engineering saints is slowly taking form. The saints of the field are whistle blowers, especially those who have sacrificed all for their moral convictions. The zeal of some preachers, however, has gone too far, piling moral responsibility upon moral responsibility on the shoulders of the engineer. This emphasis, I believe, is misplaced. Though engineers are members of a profession that holds public safety paramount,[2] we cannot reasonably expect engineers to be willing to sacrifice their jobs each day for principle and to have a whistle ever by their sides ready to blow if their firm strays from what they perceive to be the morally right course of action. If this is too much to ask, however, what then is the actual ethical responsibility of engineers in a large organization?

I shall approach this question through a discussion of what has become known as the Pinto case, i.e., the trial that took place in Winamac, Indiana, and that was decided by a jury on March 16, 1980.

In August 1978 near Goshen, Indiana, three girls died of burns in a 1973 Pinto that was rammed in traffic by a van. The rear-end collapsed "like an accordian,"[3] and the gas tank erupted in flames. It was not the first such accident with the Pinto. The Pinto was introduced in 1971 and its gas tank housing was not changed until the 1977 model. Between 1971 and 1978 about fifty suits were brought against Ford in connection with rear-end accidents in the Pinto.

What made the Winamac case different from the fifty others was the fact that the State prosecutor charged Ford with three (originally four, but one was dropped) counts of reckless homicide, a *criminal* offense, under a 1977 Indiana law that made it possible to bring such criminal charges against a corporation. The penalty, if found guilty, was a maximum fine of $10,000 for each count, for a total of $30,000. The case was closely watched, since it was the first time in recent history that a corporation was charged with this criminal offense. Ford spent almost a million dollars in its defense.

With the advantage of hindsight I believe the case raised the right issue at the wrong time.

The prosecution had to show that Ford was reckless in placing the gas tank where and how it did. In order to show this the prosecution had to prove that Ford consciously disregarded harm it might cause and the disregard, according to the statutory definition of "reckless," had to involve "substantial deviation from acceptable standards of conduct."[4]

The prosecution produced seven witnesses who testified that the Pinto was moving at speeds judged to be between 15 and 35 mph when it was hit. Harly Copp, once a high-ranking Ford engineer, claimed that the Pinto did not have a balanced design and that for cost reasons the gas tank could withstand only a 20 mph impact without leaking and exploding. The prosecutor, Michael Cosentino, tried to introduce evidence that Ford knew the defects of the gas tank, that its executives knew that a $6.65 part would have made the car considerably safer, and that they decided against the change in order to increase their profits.

Federal safety standards for gas tanks were not introduced until 1977. Once introduced, the National Highway Traffic Safety Administration (NHTSA) claimed a safety defect existed in the gas tanks of Pintos produced from 1971 to 1976. It ordered that Ford recall 1.9 million Pintos. Ford contested the order. Then, without ever admitting that the fuel tank was unsafe, it "voluntarily" ordered a recall. It claimed the recall was not for safety but for "reputational" reasons.[5] Agreeing to a recall in June, its first proposed modifications failed the safety standard tests, and it added a second protective shield to meet safety standards. It did not send out recall notices until August 22. The accident in question took place on August 10. The prosecutor claimed that Ford knew its fuel tank was dangerous as early as 1971 and that it did not make any changes until the 1977 model. It also knew in June of 1978 that its fuel tank did not meet federal safety standards; yet it did nothing to warn owners of this fact. Hence, the prosecution contended, Ford was guilty of reckless homicide.

The defense was led by James F. Neal who had achieved national prominence in the Watergate hearings. He produced testimony from two witnesses who were crucial to the case. They were hospital attendants who had spoken with the driver of the Pinto at the hospital before she died. They claimed she had stated that she had just had her car filled with gas. She had been in a hurry and had left the gas station without replacing the cap on her gas tank. It fell off the top of her car as she drove down the highway. She noticed this and stopped to turn around to pick it up. While stopped, her car was hit by the van. The testimony indicated that the car was stopped. If the car was hit by a van going 50 mph, then the rupture of the gas tank was to be expected. If the cap was off the fuel tank, leakage would be more than otherwise. No small vehicle was made to withstand such impact. Hence, Ford claimed, there was no recklessness involved. Neal went on to produce films of tests that indicated that the amount of damage the Pinto suffered meant that the impact must have been caused by the van's going at least 50 mph. He further argued that the Pinto gas tank was at least as safe as the gas tanks on the 1973 American Motors Gremlin, the Chevrolet Vega, the Dodge Colt, and the Toyota Corolla, all of which suffered comparable damage when hit from the rear at 50 mph. Since no federal safety standards were in effect in 1973, Ford was not reckless if its safety standards were comparable to those of similar cars made by competitors; that standard represented the state of the art at that time, and it would be inappropriate to apply 1977 standards to a 1973 car.[6]

The jury deliberated for four days and finally came up with a verdict of not guilty. When the verdict was announced at a meeting of the Ford Board of Directors then taking place, the members broke out in a cheer.[7]

These are the facts of the case. I do not wish to second-guess the jury. Based on my reading of the case, I think they arrived at a proper decision, given the evidence. Nor do I wish to comment adversely on the judge's ruling that prevented the prosecution from introducing about 40% of his case because the evidence referred to 1971 and 1972 models of the Pinto and not the 1973 model.[8]

The issue of Ford's being guilty of acting recklessly can, I think, be made plausible, as I shall indicate shortly. But the successful strategy argued by the defense in this case hinged on the Pinto in question being hit by a van at 50 mph. At that speed, the defense successfully argued, the gas tank of any subcompact would rupture. Hence that accident did not show that the Pinto was less safe than other subcompacts or that Ford acted recklessly. To show that would require an accident that took place at no more than 20 mph.

The contents of the Ford documents that Prosecutor Cosentino was not allowed to present in court were published in the *Chicago Tribune* on October 13, 1979. If they are accurate, they tend to show grounds for the charge of recklessness.

Ford had produced a safe gas tank mounted over the rear axle in its 1969 Capri in Europe. It tested that tank in the Capri. In its over-the-axle position, it withstood impacts of up to 30 mph. Mounted behind the axle, it was punctured by projecting bolts when hit from the rear at 20 mph. A $6.65 part would help make the tank safer. In its 1971 Pinto, Ford chose to place the gas tank behind the rear axle without the extra part. A Ford memo indicates that in this position the Pinto has more trunk space, and that production costs would be less than in the over-the-axle position. These considerations won out.[9]

The Pinto was first tested it seems in 1971, after the 1971 model was produced, for rear-end crash tolerance. It was found that the tank ruptured when hit from the rear at 20 mph. This should have been no surprise, since the Capri tank in that position had ruptured at 20 mph. A memo recommends that rather than making any changes Ford should wait until 1976 when the government was expected to introduce fuel tank standards. By delaying making any change, Ford could save $20.9 million, since the change would average about $10 per car.[10]

In the Winamac case Ford claimed correctly that there were no federal safety standards in 1973. But it defended itself against recklessness by claiming its car was comparable to other subcompacts at that time. All the defense showed, however, was that all the subcompacts were unsafe when hit at 50 mph. Since the other subcompacts were not forced to recall their cars in 1973, there is *prima facie* evidence that Ford's Pinto gas tank mounting was substandard. The Ford documents tend to show Ford knew the danger it was inflicting on Ford owners; yet it did nothing, for profit reasons. How short-sighted those reasons were is demonstrated by the fact that the Pinto thus far in litigation and recalls alone has cost Ford $50 million. Some forty suits are still to be settled. And these figures do not take into account the loss of sales due to bad publicity.

Given these facts, what are we to say about the Ford engineers? Where were they when all this was going on, and what is their responsibility for the Pinto? The answer, I suggest, is that they were where they were supposed to be, doing what they were supposed to be doing. They were performing tests, designing the Pinto, making reports. But do they have no moral responsibility for the products they design? What after all is the moral responsibility of engineers in a large corporation? By way of reply, let me emphasize that no engineer can morally do what is immoral. If commanded to do what he should not morally do, he must resist and refuse. But in the Ford Pinto situation no engineer was told to produce a gas tank that would explode and kill people. The engineers were not instructed to make an unsafe car. They were morally responsible for knowing the state of the art, including that connected with placing and mounting gas tanks. We can assume that the Ford engineers were cognizant of the state of the art in producing the model they did. When tests were made in

1970 and 1971, and a memo was written stating that a $6.65 modification could make the gas tank safer,[11] that was an engineering assessment. Whichever engineer proposed the modification and initiated the memo acted ethically in doing so. The next step, the administrative decision not to make the modification was, with hindsight, a poor one in almost every way. It ended up costing Ford a great deal more not to put in the part than it would have cost to put it in. Ford still claims today that its gas tank was as safe as the accepted standards of the industry at that time.[12] It must say so, otherwise the suits pending against it will skyrocket. That it was not as safe seems borne out by the fact that only the Pinto of all the subcompacts failed to pass the 30 mph rear impact NHTSA test.

But the question of wrongdoing or of malicious intent or of recklessness is not so easily solved. Suppose the ordinary person were told when buying a Pinto that if he paid an extra $6.65 he could increase the safety of the vehicle so that it could withstand a 30 mph rear-end impact rather than a 20 mph impact, and that the odds of suffering a rear-end impact of between 20 and 30 mph was 1 in 250,000. Would we call him or her reckless if he or she declined to pay the extra $6.65? I am not sure how to answer that question. Was it reckless of Ford to wish to save the $6.65 per car and increase the risk for the consumer? Here I am inclined to be clearer in my own mind. If I choose to take a risk to save $6.65, it is my risk and my $6.65. But if Ford saves the $6.65 and I take the risk, then I clearly lose. Does Ford have the right to do that without informing me, if the going standard of safety of subcompacts is safety in a rear-end collision up to 30 mph? I think not. I admit, however, that the case is not clear-cut, even if we add that during 1976 and 1977 Pintos suffered 13 firey fatal rear-end collisions, more than double that of other U.S.

comparable cars. The VW Rabbit and Toyota Corolla suffered none.[13]

Yet, if we are to morally fault anyone for the decision not to add the part, we would censure not the Ford engineers but the Ford executives, because it was not an engineering but an executive decision.

My reason for taking this view is that an engineer cannot be expected and cannot have the responsibility to second-guess managerial decisions. He is responsible for bringing the facts to the attention of those who need them to make decisions. But the input of engineers is only one of many factors that go to make up managerial decisions. During the trial, the defense called as a witness Francis Olsen, the assistant chief engineer in charge of design at Ford, who testified that he bought a 1973 Pinto for his eighteen-year-old daughter, kept it a year, and then traded it in for a 1974 Pinto which he kept two years.[14] His testimony and his actions were presented as an indication that the Ford engineers had confidence in the Pinto's safety. At least this one had enough confidence in it to give it to his daughter. Some engineers at Ford may have felt that the car could have been safer. But this is true of almost every automobile. Engineers in large firms have an ethical responsibility to do their jobs as best they can, to report their observations about safety and improvement of safety to management. But they do not have the obligation to insist that their perceptions or their standards be accepted. They are not paid to do that, they are not expected to do that, and they have no moral or ethical obligation to do that.

In addition to doing their jobs, engineers can plausibly be said to have an obligation of loyalty to their employers, and firms have a right to a certain amount of confidentiality concerning their internal operations. At the same time engineers are required by their professional ethical codes to hold the safety of the public paramount. Where these obligations conflict, the need for and justification of whistle blowing arises. If we admit the obligations on both sides, I would suggest as a rule of thumb that engineers and other workers in a large corporation are morally *permitted* to go public with information about the safety of a product if the following conditions are met:

1. if the harm that will be done by the product to the public is serious and considerable;
2. if they make their concerns known to their superiors; and
3. if, getting no satisfaction from their immediate superiors, they exhaust the channels available within the corporation, including going to the board of directors.

If they still get no action, I believe they are morally *permitted* to make public their views; but they are not morally *obliged* to do so. Harly Copp, a former Ford executive and engineer, in fact did criticize the Pinto from the start and testified for the prosecution against Ford at the Winamac trial.[15] He left the company and voiced his criticism. The criticism was taken up by Ralph Nader and others. In the long run it led to the Winamac trial and probably helped in a number of other suits filed against Ford. Though I admire Mr. Copp for his actions, assuming they were done from moral motives, I do not think such action was morally required, nor do I think the other engineers at Ford were morally deficient in not doing likewise.

For an engineer to have a moral *obligation* to bring his case for safety to the public, I think two other conditions have to be fulfilled, in addition to the three mentioned above.[16]

4. He must have documented evidence that would convince a reasonable, impartial observer that his view of the situation is correct and the company policy wrong.

Such evidence is obviously very difficult to obtain and produce. Such evidence, however, takes an engineer's concern out of the realm of the subjective and precludes that concern from being simply one person's opinion based on a limited point of view. Unless such evidence is available, there is little likelihood that the concerned engineer's view will win the day simply by public exposure. If the testimony of Francis Olsen is accurate, then even among the engineers at Ford there was disagreement about the safety of the Pinto.

5. There must be strong evidence that making the information public will in fact prevent the threatened serious harm.

This means both that before going public the engineer should know what source (government, newspaper, columnist, TV reporter) will make use of his evidence and how it will be handled. He should also have good reason to believe that it will result in the kind of change or result that he believes is morally appropriate. None of this was the case in the Pinto situation. After such public discussion, five model years, and failure to pass national safety standards tests, Ford plausibly defends its original claim that the gas tank was acceptably safe. If there is little likelihood of his success, there is no moral obligation for the engineer to go public. For the harm he or she personally incurs is not offset by the good such action achieves.[17]

My first substantive conclusion is that Ford engineers had no moral *obligation* to do more than they did in this case.

My second claim is that though engineers in large organizations should have a say in setting safety standards and producing cost-benefit analyses, they need not have the last word. My reasons are two. First, while the degree of risk, e.g., in a car, is an engineering problem, the acceptability of risk is not. Second, an engineering cost-benefit analysis does not include all the factors appropriate in making a policy decision, either on the corporate or the social level. Safety is one factor in an engineering design. Yet clearly it is only one factor. A Mercedes-Benz 280 is presumably safer than a Ford Pinto. But the difference in price is considerable. To make a Pinto as safe as a Mercedes it would probably have to cost a comparable amount. In making cars as in making many other objects some balance has to be reached between safety and cost. The final decision on where to draw the balance is not only an engineering decision. It is also a managerial decision, and probably even more appropriately a social decision. . . .

Engineers in large corporations have an important role to play. That role, however, is not usually to set policy or to decide on the acceptability of risk. Their knowledge and expertise are important both to the companies for which they work and to the public. But they are not morally responsible for policies and decisions beyond their competence and control. Does this view, however, let engineers off the moral hook too easily?

To return briefly to the Pinto story once more, Ford wanted a subcompact to fend off the competition of Japanese imports. The order came down to produce a car of 2,000 pounds or less that would cost $2000 or less in time for the 1971 model. This allowed only 25 months instead of the usual 43 months for design and production of a new car.[18] The engineers were squeezed from the start. Perhaps this is why they did not test the gas tank for rear-end collision impact until the car was produced.

Should the engineers have refused the order to produce the car in 25 months? Should they have resigned, or leaked the story to the newspapers? Should they have refused to speed up their usual routine? Should they have complained to their professional society that they were being asked to do the impossible — if it were to be done right? I am not in a position to say what they should have done. But with the advantage of hindsight, I suggest we should ask not only what they should have done. We should especially ask what changes can be made to prevent engineers from being squeezed in this way in the future.

Engineering ethics should not take as its goal the producing of moral heroes. Rather it should consider what forces operate to encourage engineers to act as they feel they should not; what structural or other features of a large corporation squeeze them until their consciences hurt? Those features should then be examined, evaluated, and changes proposed and made. Lobbying by engineering organizations would be appropriate, and legislation should be passed if necessary. In general I tend to favor voluntary means where possible. But where that is utopian, then legislation is a necessary alternative. . . .

The means by which engineers with ethical concerns can get a fair hearing without endangering their jobs or blowing the whistle must be made part of a corporation's organizational structure. An outside board member with primary responsibility for investigating and responding to such ethical concerns might be legally required. . . . Another way of achieving a similar end is by providing an inspector general for all corporations with an annual net income of over $1 billion. An independent committee of an engineering association might be formed to investigate charges made by engineers concerning the safety of a product on which they are working[19]; a company that did not allow an appropriate investigation of employee charges would become subject to cover-up proceedings. Those in the engineering industry can suggest and work to implement other ideas. I have elsewhere outlined a set of ten such changes for the ethical corporation.[20] . . .

Many of the issues of engineering ethics within a corporate setting concern the ethics of organizational structure, questions of public policy, and so questions that frequently are amenable to solutions only on a scale larger than the individual — on the scale of organization and law. The ethical responsibilities of the engineer in a large organization have as much to do with the organization as with the engineer. They can be most fruitfully approached by considering from a moral point of view not only the individual engineer but the framework within which he or she works. We not only need moral people. Even more importantly we need moral structures and organizations. Only by paying more attention to these can we adequately resolve the questions of the ethical responsibility of engineers in large organizations.

NOTES

1. The body of literature on engineering ethics is now substantive and impressive. See, *A Selected Annotated Bibliography of Professional Ethics and Social Responsibility in Engineering,* compiled by Robert F. Ladenson, James Choromokos, Ernest d'Anjou, Martin Pimsler, and Howard Rosen (Chicago: Center for the Study of Ethics in the Professions, Illinois Institute of Technology, 1980). A useful two-volume collection of readings and cases is also available: Robert J. Baum and Albert Flores, *Ethical Problems in Engineering,* 2nd edition (Troy, N.Y.: Rensselaer Polytechnic Institute, Center for the Study of the Human Dimensions of Science and Technology, 1980. See also Robert J. Baum's *Ethics and Engineering Curricula* (Hastings-on-Hudson, N.Y.: Hastings Center, 1980).

2. See, for example, the first canon of the 1974 Engineers Council for Professional Development Code, the first canon of the National Council of Engineering Examiners Code, and the draft (by A. Oldenquist and E. Slowter) of a "Code of Ethics for the Engineering Profession" (all reprinted in Baum and Flores, *Ethical Problems in Engineering.*

3. Details of the incident presented in this paper are based on testimony at the trial. Accounts of the trial as well as background reports were carried by both the *New York Times* and the *Chicago Tribune.*

4. *New York Times,* February 17, 1980, IV, p. 9.

5. *New York Times,* February 21, 1980, p. A6; *Fortune,* September 11, 1978, p. 42.

6. *New York Times,* March 14, 1980, p. 1.

7. *Time,* March 24, 1980, p. 24.

8. *New York Times,* January 16, 1980, p. 16; February 7, 1980, p. 16.

9. *Chicago Tribune,* October 13, 1979, p. 1. and Section 2, p. 12.

10. *Chicago Tribune,* October 13, 1979, p. 1; *New York Times,* October 14, 1979, p. 26.

11. *New York Times,* February 4, 1980, p. 12.

12. *New York Times,* June 10, 1978, p. 1; *Chicago Tribune,* October 13, 1979, p. 1, and Section 2, p. 12. The continuous claim has been that the Pinto poses "no serious hazards."

13. *New York Times,* October 26, 1978, p. 103.

14. *New York Times,* February 20, 1980, p. A16.

15. *New York Times,* February 4, 1980, p. 12.

16. The position I present here is developed more fully in my book *Business Ethics* (New York: Macmillan, 1981). It differs somewhat from the dominant view expressed in the existing literature in that I consider whistle blowing an extreme measure that is morally obligatory only if the stringent conditions set forth are satisfied. Cf. Kenneth D. Walters, "Your Employees' Right to Blow the Whistle," *Harvard Business Review,* July–August, 1975.

17. On the dangers incurred by whistle blowers, see Gene James, "Whistle Blowing: Its Nature and Justification," *Philosophy in Context,* 10 (1980), pp. 99–117, which examines the legal context of whistle blowing; Peter Raven-Hansen, "Dos and Don'ts for Whistleblowers: Planning for Trouble," *Technology Review,* May 1980, pp. 34–44, which suggests how to blow the whistle; Helen Dudar, "The Price of Blowing the Whistle," *The New York Times Magazine,* 30 October, 1977, which examines the results for whistleblowers; David W. Ewing, "Canning Directions," *Harpers,* August 1979, pp. 17–22, which indicates "how the government rids itself of troublemakers" and how legislation protecting whistleblowers can be circumvented; and Report by the U.S. General Ac-

counting Office, "The Office of the Special Counsel Can Improve Its Management of Whistleblower Cases," December 30, 1980 (FPCD-81–10).

18. *Chicago Tribune,* October 13, 1979, Section 2, p. 12.

19. A number of engineers have been arguing for a more active role by engineering societies in backing up individual engineers in their attempts to act responsibly. See, Edwin Layton, *Revolt of the Engineers* (Cleveland: Case Western Reserve, 1971); Stephen H. Unger, "Engineering Societies and the Responsible Engineer," *Annals of the New York Academy of Sciences,* 196 (1973), pp. 433–37 (reprinted in Baum and Flores, *Ethical Problems in Engineering,* pp. 56–59; and Robert Perrucci and Joel Gerstl, *Profession Without Community: Engineers in American Society* (New York: Random House, 1969).

20. Richard T. De George, "Responding to the Mandate for Social Responsibility," *Guidelines for Business When Societal Demands Conflict* (Washington, D.C.: Council for Better Business Bureaus, 1978), pp. 60–80.

Roger Boisjoly and the *Challenger* Disaster: The Ethical Dimensions

Russell P. Boisjoly
Ellen Foster Curtis
Eugene Mellican

INTRODUCTION

On January 28, 1986, the space shuttle *Challenger* exploded 73 seconds into its flight, killing the seven astronauts aboard. As the nation mourned the tragic loss of the crew members, the Rogers Commission was formed to investigate the causes of the disaster. The Commission concluded that the explosion occurred due to seal failure in one of the solid rocket booster joints. Testimony given by Roger Boisjoly, Senior Scientist and acknowledged rocket seal expert, indicated that top management at NASA and Morton Thiokol had been aware of problems with the O-ring seals, but agreed to launch against the recommendation of Boisjoly and other engineers. Boisjoly had alerted management to problems with the O-rings as early as January 1985, yet several shuttle launches prior to the *Challenger* had been approved without correcting the hazards. This suggests that the management practice of NASA and Morton Thiokol had created an environment which altered the framework for decision making, leading to a breakdown in communication between technical experts and their supervisors, and top level management, and to the acceptance of risks that both organizations had historically viewed as unacceptable. With human lives and the national interest at stake, serious ethical concerns are embedded in this dramatic change in management practice.

In fact, one of the most important aspects of the *Challenger* disaster — both in terms of

From Russell P. Boisjoly, Ellen Foster Curtis, and Eugene Mellican, "Roger Boisjoly and the *Challenger* Disaster: The Ethical Dimensions," *Journal of Business Ethics* 8 (April 1989). Copyright © 1989 by Kluwer Academic Publishers. Reprinted by permission of Kluwer Academic Publishers.

the causal sequence that led to it and the lessons to be learned from it — is its ethical dimension. Ethical issues are woven throughout the tangled web of decisions, events, practices, and organizational structures that resulted in the loss of the *Challenger* and its seven astronauts. Therefore, an ethical analysis of this tragedy is essential for a full understanding of the event itself and for the implications it has for any endeavor where public policy, corporate practice, and individual decisions intersect.

The significance of an ethical analysis of the *Challenger* disaster is indicated by the fact that it immediately presents one of the most urgent, but difficult, issues in the examination of corporate and individual behavior today, i.e., whether existing ethical theories adequately address the problems posed by new technologies, new forms of organization, and evolving social systems. At the heart of this issue is the concept of responsibility. No ethical concept has been more affected by the impact of these changing realities. Modern technology has so transformed the context and scale of human action that not only do the traditional parameters of responsibility seem inadequate to contain the full range of human acts and their consequences, but even more fundamentally, it is no longer the individual that is the primary locus of power and responsibility, but public and private institutions. Thus, it would seem, it is no longer the character and virtues of individuals that determine the standards of moral conduct, it is the policies and structures of the institutional settings within which they live and work.

Many moral conflicts facing individuals within institutional settings do arise from matters pertaining to organizational structures or questions of public policy. As such, they are resolvable only at a level above the responsibilities of the individual. Therefore, some writers argue that the ethical responsi-bilities of the engineer or manager in a large corporation have as much to do with the organization as with the individual. Instead of expecting individual engineers or managers to be moral heroes, emphasis should be on the creation of organizational structures conducive to ethical behavior among all agents under their aegis. It would be futile to attempt to establish a sense of ethical responsibility in engineers and management personnel and ignore the fact that such persons work within a sociotechnical environment which increasingly undermines the notion of individual, responsible moral agency (Boling and Dempsey, 1981; De George, 1981).

Yet, others argue that precisely because of these organizational realities individual accountability must be re-emphasized to counteract the diffusion of responsibility within large organizations and to prevent its evasion under the rubric of collective responsibility. Undoubtedly institutions do take on a kind of collective life of their own, but they do not exist, or act, independently of the individuals that constitute them, whatever the theoretical and practical complexities of delineating the precise relationships involved. Far from diminishing individuals' obligations, the reality of organizational life increases them because the consequences of decisions and acts are extended and amplified through the reach and power of that reality. Since there are pervasive and inexorable connections between ethical standards and behavior of individuals within an organization and its structure and operation, "the sensitizing of professionals to ethical considerations should be increased so that institutional structures will reflect enhanced ethical sensitivities as trained professionals move up the organizational ladder to positions of leadership" (Mankin, 1981, p. 17).

By reason of the courageous activities and testimony of individuals like Roger Boisjoly, the *Challenger* disaster provides a fascinating illustration of the dynamic tension between organizational and individual responsibility. By focusing on this central issue, this article seeks to accomplish two objectives: first, to demonstrate the extent to which the *Challenger* disaster not only gives concrete expression to the ethical ambiguity that permeates the relationship between organizational and individual responsibility, but also, in fact, is a result of it; second, to reclaim the meaning and importance of individual responsibility within the diluting context of large organizations.

In meeting these objectives, the article is divided into two parts: a case study of Roger Boisjoly's efforts to galvanize management support for effectively correcting the high risk O-ring problems, his attempt to prevent the launch, the scenario which resulted in the launch decision, and Boisjoly's quest to set the record straight despite enormous personal and professional consequences; and an ethical analysis of these events.

PREVIEW FOR DISASTER

On January 24, 1985, Roger Boisjoly, Senior Scientist at Morton Thiokol, watched the launch of Flight 51-C of the space shuttle program. He was at Cape Canaveral to inspect the solid rocket boosters from Flight 51-C following their recovery in the Atlantic Ocean and to conduct a training session at Kennedy Space Center (KSC) on the proper methods of inspecting the booster joints. While watching the launch, he noted that the temperature that day was much cooler than recorded at other launches, but was still much warmer than the 18 degree temperature encountered three days earlier when he arrived in Orlando. The unseasonably cold weather of the past several days had produced the worst citrus crop failures in Florida history.

When he inspected the solid rocket boosters several days later, Boisjoly discovered evidence that the primary O-ring seals on two field joints had been compromised by hot combustion gases (i.e., hot gas blow-by had occurred) which had also eroded part of the primary O-ring. This was the first time that a primary seal on a field joint had been penetrated. When he discovered the large amount of blackened grease between the primary and secondary seals, his concern heightened. The blackened grease was discovered over 80 degree and 110 degree arcs, respectively, on two of the seals, with the larger arc indicating greater hot gas blow-by. Post-flight calculations indicated that the ambient temperature of the field joints at launch time was 53 degrees. This evidence, coupled with his recollection of the low temperature the day of the launch and the citrus crop damage caused by the cold spell, led to his conclusion that the severe hot gas blow-by may have been caused by, and related to, low temperature. After reporting these findings to his superiors. Boisjoly presented them to engineers and management at NASA's Marshall Space Flight Center (MSFC). As a result of his presentation at MSFC, Roger Boisjoly was asked to participate in the Flight Readiness Review (FRR) on February 12, 1985 for Flight 51-E which was scheduled for launch in April, 1985. This FRR represents the first association of low temperature with blow-by on a field joint, a condition that was considered an "acceptable risk" by Larry Mulloy, NASA's Manager for the Booster Project, and other NASA officials.

Roger Boisjoly had twenty-five years of experience as an engineer in the aerospace industry. Among his many notable assignments were the performance of stress and deflection analysis on the flight control equipment of the Advanced Minuteman Missile at Autonetics, and serving as a lead engineer on the lunar module of Apollo at Hamilton Standard. He moved to Utah in 1980 to take a position in the Applied Mechanics Department as a Staff Engineer at the Wasatch Division of Morton Thiokol. He was considered the leading expert in the United States on O-rings and rocket joint seals and received plaudits for his work on the joint seal problems from Joe C. Kilminster, Vice President of Space Booster Programs, Morton Thiokol (Kilminster, July, 1985). His commitment to the company and the community was further demonstrated by his service as Mayor of Willard, Utah from 1982 to 1983.

The tough questioning he received at the February 12th FRR convinced Boisjoly of the need for further evidence linking low temperature and hot gas blow-by. He worked closely with Arnie Thompson, Supervisor of Rocket Motor Cases, who conducted subscale laboratory tests in March, 1985, to further test the effects of temperature on O-ring resiliency. The bench tests that were performed provided powerful evidence to support Boisjoly's and Thompson's theory: Low temperatures greatly and adversely affected the ability of O-rings to create a seal on solid rocket booster joints. If the temperature was too low (and they did not know what the threshold temperature would be), it was possible that neither the primary or secondary O-rings would seal!

One month later the post-flight inspection of Flight 51-B revealed that the primary seal of a booster nozzle joint did not make contact during its two minute flight. If this damage had occurred in a field joint, the secondary O-ring may have failed to seal, causing the loss of the flight. As a result, Boisjoly and his colleagues became increasingly concerned about shuttle safety. This evidence from the inspection of Flight 51-B was presented at the FRR for Flight 51-F on July 1, 1985; the key engineers and managers at NASA and Morton Thiokol were now aware of the critical O-ring problems and the influ-

ence of low temperature on the performance of the joint seals.

During July, 1985, Boisjoly and his associates voiced their desire to devote more effort and resources to solving the problems of O-ring erosion. In his activity reports dated July 22 and 29, 1985, Boisjoly expressed considerable frustration with the lack of progress in this area, despite the fact that a Seal Erosion Task Force had been informally appointed on July 19th. Finally, Boisjoly wrote the following memo, labelled "Company Private," to R. K. (Bob) Lund, Vice President of Engineering for Morton Thiokol, to express the extreme urgency of his concerns. Here are some excerpts from that memo:

> This letter is written to insure that management is fully aware of the seriousness of the current O-ring erosion problem. . . . The mistakenly accepted position on the joint problem was to fly without fear of failure . . . is now drastically changed as a result of the SRM 16A nozzle joint erosion which eroded a secondary O-ring with the primary O-ring never sealing. If the same scenario should occur in a field joint (and it could), then it is a jump ball as to the success or failure of the joint. . . . The result would be a catastrophe of the highest order — loss of human life. . . .
>
> It is my honest and real fear that if we do not take immediate action to dedicate a team to solve the problem, with the field joint having the number one priority, then we stand in jeopardy of losing a flight along with all the launch pad facilities (Boisjoly, July, 1985a).

On August 20, 1985, R. K. Lund formally announced the formation of the Seal Erosion Task Team. The team consisted of only five full-time engineers from the 2500 employed by Morton Thiokol on the Space Shuttle Program. The events of the next five months would demonstrate that management had not provided the resources necessary to carry out the enormous task of solving the seal erosion problem.

On October 3, 1985, the Seal Erosion Task Force met with Joe Kilminster to discuss the problems they were having in gaining organizational support necessary to solve the O-ring problems. Boisjoly later stated that Kilminster summarized the meeting as a "good bullshit session." Once again frustrated by bureaucratic inertia, Boisjoly wrote in his activity report dated October 4th:

> . . . NASA is sending an engineering representative to stay with us starting Oct. 14th. We feel that this is a direct result of their feeling that we (MTI) are not responding quickly enough to the seal problem . . . upper management apparently feels that the SRM program is ours for sure and the customer be damned (Boisjoly, October, 1985b).

Boisjoly was not alone in his expression of frustration. Bob Ebeling, Department Manager, Solid Rocket Motor Igniter and Final Assembly, and a member of the Seal Erosion Task Force, wrote in a memo to Allan McDonald, Manager of the Solid Rocket Motor Project, "HELP! The seal task force is constantly being delayed by every possible means. . . . We wish we could get action by verbal request, but such is not the case. This is a red flag" (McConnell, 1987).

At the Society of Automotive Engineers (SAE) conference on October 7, 1985, Boisjoly presented a six-page overview of the joints and the seal configuration to approximately 130 technical experts in hope of soliciting suggestions for remedying the O-ring problems. Although MSFC had requested the presentation, NASA gave strict instructions not to express the critical urgency of fixing the joints, but merely to ask for suggestions for improvement. Although no help was forthcoming, the conference was a milestone in that it was the first time that NASA allowed information on the O-ring difficulties to be expressed in a public forum. That NASA also recognized that the O-ring problems were not receiving appropriate attention and manpower considerations from Morton Thiokol management is further evidenced by Boisjoly's October 24 log entry, ". . . Jerry Peoples (NASA) has informed his people that our group needs more authority and people to do the job. Jim Smith (NASA) will corner Al McDonald today to attempt to implement this direction."

The October 30 launch of Flight 61-A of the *Challenger* provided the most convincing, and yet to some the most contestable, evidence to date that low temperature was directly related to hot gas blow-by. The left booster experienced hot gas blow-by in the center and aft field joints without any seal erosion. The ambient temperature of the field joints was estimated to be 75 degrees at launch time based on post-flight calculations. Inspection of the booster joints revealed that the blow-by was less severe than that found on Flight 51-C because the seal grease was a grayish black color, rather than the jet black hue of Flight 51-C. The evidence was now consistent with the bench tests for joint resiliency conducted in March. That is, at 75 degrees the O-ring lost contact with its sealing surface for 2.4 seconds, whereas at 50 degrees the O-ring lost contact for 10 minutes. The actual flight data revealed greater hot gas blow-by for the O-rings on Flight 51-C which had an ambient temperature of 53 degrees than for Flight 61-A which had an ambient temperature of 75 degrees. Those who rejected this line of reasoning concluded that temperature must be irrelevant since hot gas blow-by had occurred even at room temperature (75 degrees). This difference in interpretation would receive further attention on January 27, 1986.

During the next two and one-half months, little progress was made in obtaining a solution to the O-ring problems. Roger Boisjoly made the following entry into his log on January 13, 1986, "O-ring resiliency tests that were requested on September 24, 1985 are now scheduled for January 15, 1986."

THE DAY BEFORE THE DISASTER

At 10 a.m. on January 27, 1986, Arnie Thompson received a phone call from Boyd Brinton, Thiokol's Manager of Project Engineering at MSFC, relaying the concerns of NASA's Larry Wear, also at MSFC, about the 18 degree temperature forecast for the launch of flight 51-L, the *Challenger*, scheduled for the next day. This phone call precipitated a series of meetings within Morton Thiokol, at the Marshall Space Flight Center; and at the Kennedy Space Center that culminated in a three-way telecon involving three teams of engineers and managers, that began at 8:15 p.m. E.S.T.

Joe Kilminster, Vice President, Space Booster Programs, of Morton Thiokol began the telecon by turning the presentation of the engineering charts over to Roger Boisjoly and Arnie Thompson. They presented thirteen charts which resulted in a recommendation against the launch of the *Challenger*. Boisjoly demonstrated their concerns with the performance of the O-rings in the field joints during the initial phases of *Challenger's* flight with charts showing the effects of primary O-ring erosion, and its timing, on the ability to maintain a reliable secondary seal. The tremendous pressure and release of power from the rocket boosters create rotation in the joint such that the metal moves away from the O-rings so that they cannot maintain contact with the metal surfaces. If, at the same time, erosion occurs in the primary O-ring for any reason, then there is a reduced probability of maintaining a secondary seal. It is highly probable that as the ambient temperature drops, the primary O-ring will not seat that there will be hot gas blow-by and erosion of the primary O-ring; and that a

catastrophe will occur when the secondary O-ring fails to seal.

Bob Lund presented the final chart that included the Morton Thiokol recommendations that the ambient temperature including wind must be such that the seal temperature would be greater than 53 degrees to proceed with the launch. Since the overnight low was predicted to be 18 degrees, Bob Lund recommended against launch on January 28, 1986, or until the seal temperature exceeded 53 degrees.

NASA's Larry Mulloy bypassed Bob Lund and directly asked Joe Kilminster for his reaction. Kilminster stated that he supported the position of his engineers and he would not recommend launch below 53 degrees.

George Hardy, Deputy Director of Science and Engineering at MSFC, said he was "appalled at that recommendation," according to Allan McDonald's testimony before the Rogers Commission. Nevertheless, Hardy would not recommend to launch if the contractor was against it. After Hardy's reaction, Stanley Reinartz, Manager of Shuttle Project Office at MSFC, objected by pointing out that the solid rocket motors were qualified to operate between 40 and 90 degrees Fahrenheit.

Larry Mulloy, citing the data from Flight 61-A which indicated to him that temperature was not a factor, strenuously objected to Morton Thiokol's recommendation. He suggested that Thiokol was attempting to establish new Launch Commit Criteria at 53 degrees and that they couldn't do that the night before a launch. In exasperation Mulloy asked, "My God, Thiokol, when do you want me to launch? Next April?" (McConnell, 1987). Although other NASA officials also objected to the association of temperature with O-ring erosion and hot gas blow-by, Roger Boisjoly was able to hold his ground and demonstrate with the use of his charts and pictures that there was indeed a relationship: The lower the temperature the higher the probability of erosion and blow-by and the greater the likelihood of an accident. Finally, Joe Kilminster asked for a five-minute caucus off-net.

According to Boisjoly's testimony before the Rogers Commission, Jerry Mason, Senior Vice President of Wasatch Operations, began the caucus by saying that "a management decision was necessary." Sensing that an attempt would be made to overturn the no-launch decision, Boisjoly and Thompson attempted to re-review the material previously presented to NASA for the executives in the room. Thompson took a pad of paper and tried to sketch out the problem with the joint, while Boisjoly laid out the photos of the compromised joints from Flights 51-C and 61-A. When they became convinced that no one was listening, they ceased their efforts. As Boisjoly would later testify, "There was not one positive pro-launch statement ever made by anybody" (Report of the Presidential Commission, 1986, IV, p. 792, hereafter abbreviated as R.C.).

According to Boisjoly, after he and Thompson made their last attempts to stop the launch, Jerry Mason asked rhetorically, "Am I the only one who wants to fly?" Mason turned to Bob Lund and asked him to "take off his engineering hat and put on his management hat." The four managers held a brief discussion and voted unanimously to recommend *Challenger's* launch.

Exhibit I shows the revised recommendations that were presented that evening by Joe Kilminster after the caucus to support management's decision to launch. Only one of the rationales presented that evening supported the launch (demonstrated erosion sealing threshold is three times greater than 0.038" erosion experienced on SRM-15). Even so, the issue at hand was sealability at low temperature, not erosion. While one other rationale could be considered a neutral statement of engineering fact (O-ring pressure leak check places secondary seal in outboard position which minimizes sealing time), the other seven rationales are negative, anti-launch, statements. After hearing Kilminster's presentation, which was accepted without a single probing question, George Hardy asked him to sign the chart

EXHIBIT 1.   MTI Assessment Of Temperature Concern on SRM-25 (51L) Launch

- CALCULATIONS SHOW THAT SRM-25 O-RINGS WILL BE 20° COLDER THAN SRM-15 O-RINGS
- TEMPERATURE DATA NOT CONCLUSIVE ON PREDICTING PRIMARY O-RING BLOW-BY
- ENGINEERING ASSESSMENT IS THAT:
  - COLDER O-RINGS WILL HAVE INCREASED EFFECTIVE DUROMETER ("HARDER")
  - "HARDER" O-RINGS WILL TAKE LONGER TO "SEAT"
  - MORE GAS MAY PASS PRIMARY O-RING BEFORE THE PRIMARY SEAL SEATS (RELATIVE TO SRM-15)
  - DEMONSTRATED SEALING THRESHOLD IS 3 TIMES GREATER THAN 0.038" EROSION EXPERIENCED ON SRM-15
  - IF THE PRIMARY SEAL DOES NOT SEAT, THE SECONDARY SEAL WILL SEAT
  - PRESSURE WILL GET TO SECONDARY SEAL BEFORE THE METAL PARTS ROTATE
  - O-RING PRESSURE LEAK CHECK PLACES SECONDARY SEAL IN OUTBOARD POSITION WHICH MINIMIZES SEALING TIME
- MTI RECOMMENDS STS-51L LAUNCH PROCEED ON 28 JANUARY 1986
  - SRM-25 WILL NOT BE SIGNIFICANTLY DIFFERENT FROM SRM-15

Joe C. Kilminster, Vice President Space Booster Programs.

and telefax it to Kennedy Space Center and Marshall Space Flight Center. At 11 p.m. E.S.T. the teleconference ended.

Aside from the four senior Morton Thiokol executives present at the teleconference, all others were excluded from the final decision. The process represented a radical shift from previous NASA policy. Until that moment, the burden of proof had always been on the engineers to prove beyond a doubt that it was safe to launch. NASA, with their objections to the original Thiokol recommendation against the launch, and Mason, with his request for a "management decision," shifted the burden of proof in the opposite direction. Morton Thiokol was expected to prove that launching *Challenger* would not be safe (R.C., IV, p. 793).

The change in the decision so deeply upset Boisjoly that he returned to his office and made the following journal entry:

I sincerely hope this launch does not result in a catastrophe. I personally do not agree with some of the statements made by Joe Kilminster's written summary stating that SRM-25 is okay to fly (Boisjoly, 1987).

THE DISASTER AND ITS AFTERMATH

On January 28, 1986, a reluctant Roger Boisjoly watched the launch of the *Challenger*. As the vehicle cleared the tower, Bob Ebeling whispered, "We've just dodged a bullet." (The engineers who opposed the launch assumed that O-ring failure would result in an explosion almost immediately after engine ignition.) To continue in Boisjoly's words, "At approximately T+60 seconds Bob told me he had just completed a prayer of thanks to the Lord for a successful launch. Just thirteen seconds later we both saw the horror of the destruction as the vehicle exploded" (Boisjoly, 1987).

Morton Thiokol formed a failure investigation team on January 31, 1986, to study the *Challenger* explosion. Roger Boisjoly and Arnie Thompson were part of the team that was sent to MSFC in Huntsville, Alabama. Boisjoly's first inkling of a division between himself and management came on February 13 when he was informed at the last minute that he was to testify before the Rogers Commission the next day. He had very little time to prepare for his testimony. Five days later, two Commission members held a closed session with Kilminster, Boisjoly, and Thompson. During the interview Boisjoly gave his memos and activity reports to the Commissioners. After that meeting, Kilminster chastised Thompson and Boisjoly for correcting his interpretation of the technical data. Their response was that they would continue to correct his version if it was technically incorrect.

Boisjoly's February 25th testimony before the Commission, rebutting the general manager's statement that the initial decision against the launch was not unanimous, drove a wedge further between him and Morton Thiokol management. Boisjoly was flown to MSFC before he could hear the NASA testimony about the pre-flight telecon. The next day, he was removed from the failure investigation team and returned to Utah.

Beginning in April, Boisjoly began to believe that for the previous month he had been used solely for public relations purposes. Although given the title of Seal Coordinator for the redesign effort, he was isolated from NASA and the seal redesign effort. His design information had been changed without his knowledge and presented without his feedback. On May 1, 1986, in a briefing preceding closed sessions before the Rogers Commission, Ed Garrison, President of Aerospace Operations for Morton Thiokol, chastised Boisjoly for "airing the company's dirty laundry" with the memos he had given the Commission. The next day, Boisjoly testified about the change in his job assignment. Commission Chairman Rogers criticized Thiokol management, ". . . if it appears that you're punishing the two people or at least two of the people who are right about the decision and objected to the launch which ultimately resulted in criticism of Thiokol and then they're demoted or feel that they are being retaliated against, that is a very serious matter. It would seem to me, just speaking for myself, they should be promoted, not demoted or pushed aside" (R.C., V, p. 1586).

Boisjoly now sensed a major rift developing within the corporation. Some co-workers perceived that his testimony was damaging the company image. In an effort to clear the air, he and McDonald requested a private meeting with the company's three top executives, which was held on May 16, 1986. According to Boisjoly, management was unreceptive throughout the meeting. The CEO told McDonald and Boisjoly that the company "was doing just fine until Al and I testified about our job reassignments" (Boisjoly, 1987). McDonald and Boisjoly were nominally restored to their former assignments, but Boisjoly's position became untenable as time passed. On July 21, 1986, Roger Boisjoly requested an extended sick leave from Morton Thiokol.

ETHICAL ANALYSIS

It is clear from this case study that Roger Boisjoly's experiences before and after the *Challenger* disaster raise numerous ethical questions that are integral to any explanation of the disaster and applicable to other management situations, especially those involving highly complex technologies. The difficulties and uncertainties involved in the management of these technologies exacerbate the kind of bureaucratic syndromes that generate ethical conflicts in the first place. In fact,

Boisjoly's experiences could well serve as a paradigmatic case study for such ethical problems, ranging from accountability to corporate loyalty and whistle blowing. Underlying all these issues, however, is the problematic relationship between individual and organizational responsibility. Boisjoly's experiences graphically portray the tensions inherent in this relationship in a manner that discloses its importance in the causal sequence leading to the *Challenger* disaster. The following analysis explicates this and the implications it has for other organizational settings.

By focusing on the problematic relationship between individual and organizational responsibility, this analysis reveals that the organizational structure governing the space shuttle program became the locus of responsibility in such a way that not only did it undermine the responsibilities of individual decision makers within the process, but it also became a means of avoiding real, effective responsibility throughout the entire management system. The first clue to this was clearly articulated as early as 1973 by the board of inquiry that was formed to investigate the accident which occurred during the launch of *Skylab 1*:

> The management system developed by NASA for manned space flight places large emphasis on rigor, detail, and thoroughness. In hand with this emphasis comes formalism, extensive documentation, and visibility in detail to senior management. While nearly perfect, such a system can submerge the concerned individual and depress the role of the intuitive engineer or analyst. It may not allow full play for the intuitive judgment or past experience of the individual. An emphasis on management systems can, in itself, serve to separate the people engaged in the program from the real world of hardware (Quoted in Christiansen, 1987, p. 23).

To examine this prescient statement in ethical terms is to see at another level the serious consequences inherent in the situation it describes. For example, it points to a dual meaning of responsibility. One meaning emphasizes carrying out an authoritatively prescribed review process, while the second stresses the cognitive independence and input of every individual down the entire chain of authority. The first sense of responsibility shifts the ethical center of gravity precipitously away from individual moral agency onto the review process in such a way that what was originally set up to guarantee flight readiness with the professional and personal integrity of the responsible individuals, instead becomes a means of evading personal responsibility for decisions made in the review process.

A crucial, and telling, example of this involves the important question asked by the Rogers Commission as to why the concerns raised by the Morton Thiokol engineers about the effects of cold weather on the O-rings during the teleconference the night before the launch were not passed up from Level III to Levels II or I in the preflight review process. The NASA launch procedure clearly demands that decisions and objections methodically follow a prescribed path up all levels. Yet, Lawrence Mulloy, operating at Level III as the Solid Rocket Booster Project Manager at MSFC, did not transmit the Morton Thiokol concerns upward (through his immediate superior, Stanley Reinartz) to Level II. When asked by Chairman Rogers to explain why, Mr. Mulloy testified:

> At that time, and I still consider today, that was a Level III issue, Level III being a SRB element or an external tank element or Space Shuttle main engine element or an Orbiter. There was no violation of Launch Commit Criteria. There was no waiver required in my judgment at that time and still today (R.C., I, p. 98).

In examining this response in terms of shifting responsibility onto the review process

itself, there are two things that are particularly striking in Mr. Mulloy's statement. The first is his emphasis that this was a "Level III issue." In a formal sense, Mr. Mulloy is correct. However, those on Level III also had the authority — and, one would think, especially in this instance given the heated discussion on the effects of cold on the O-rings, the motivation — to pass objections and concerns on to Levels II and I. But here the second important point in Mr. Mulloy's testimony comes into play when he states, "there was no violation of Launch Commit Criteria." In other words, since there was no Launch Commit Criteria for joint temperature, concerns about joint temperature did not officially fall under the purview of the review process. Therefore, the ultimate justification for Mr. Mulloy's position rests on the formal process itself. He was just following the rules by staying within the already established scope of the review process.

This underscores the moral imperative executives must exercise by creating and maintaining organizational systems that do not separate the authority of decision makers from the responsibility they bear for decisions, or insulate them from the consequences of their actions or omissions.

Certainly, there can be no more vivid example than the shuttle program to verify that, in fact, "an emphasis on management systems can, in itself, serve to separate the people engaged in the program from the real world of hardware." Time and time again the lack of communication that lay at the heart of the Rogers Commission finding that "there was a serious flaw in the decision making process leading up to the launch of flight 51-L" (R.C., I, p. 104) was explained by the NASA officials or managers at Morton Thiokol with such statements as, "that is not my reporting channel," or "he is not in the launch decision chain," or "I didn't meet with Mr. Boisjoly, I met with Don Ketner, who is the task team leader" (R.C., IV, p. 821, testimony of Mr. Lund). Even those managers who had direct responsibility for line engineers and workmen depended on formalized memo writing procedures for communication to the point that some "never talked to them directly" (Feynman, 1988, p. 33).

Within the atmosphere of such an ambiguity of responsibility, when a life threatening conflict arose within the management system and individuals (such as Roger Boisjoly and his engineering associates at Morton Thiokol) tried to reassert the full weight of their individual judgments and attendant responsibilities, the very purpose of the flight readiness review process, i.e., to arrive at the "technical" truth of the situation, which includes the recognition of the uncertainties involved as much as the findings, became subverted into an adversary confrontation in which "adversary" truth, with its suppression of uncertainties, became operative (Wilmotte, 1970).

What is particularly significant in this radical transformation of the review process, in which the Morton Thiokol engineers were forced into "the position of having to prove that it was unsafe instead of the other way around" (R.C., IV, p. 822; see also p. 793), is that what made the suppression of technical uncertainties possible is precisely that mode of thinking which, in being challenged by independent professional judgments, gave rise to the adversarial setting in the first place: groupthink. No more accurate description for what transpired the night before the launch of the *Challenger* can be given than the definition of groupthink as:

> . . . a mode of thinking that people engage in when they are deeply involved in a cohesive in-group, when the members' strivings for unanimity override their motivation to realistically appraise alternative courses of action. . . . Groupthink refers to the deterioration of mental efficiency, reality testing, and moral judg-

ment that results from in-group pressures (Janis, 1972, p. 9).

From this perspective, the full import of Mr. Mason's telling Mr. Lund to "take off his engineering hat and put on his management hat" is revealed. He did not want another technical, reality-based judgment of an independent professional engineer. As he had already implied when he opened the caucus by stating "a management decision was necessary," he wanted a group decision, specifically one that would, in the words of the Rogers Commission, "accommodate a major customer" (R.C., I, p. 104). With a group decision the objections of the engineers could be mitigated, the risks shared, fears allayed, and the attendant responsibility diffused.

This analysis is not meant to imply that groupthink was a pervasive or continuous mode of thinking at either NASA or Morton Thiokol. What is suggested is a causal relationship between this instance of groupthink and the ambiguity of responsibility found within the space shuttle program. Whenever a management system such as NASA's generates "a mindset of 'collective responsibility'" by leading "individuals to defer to the anonymity of the process and not focus closely enough on their individual responsibilities in the decision chain," (N.R.C. Report, 1988, p. 68) and there is a confluence of the kind of pressures that came to bear on the decision making process the night before the launch, the conditions are in place for groupthink to prevail.

A disturbing feature of so many of the analyses and commentaries on the *Challenger* disaster is the reinforcement, and implicit acceptance, of this shift away from individual moral agency with an almost exclusive focus on the flaws in the management system, organizational structures and/or decision making process. Beginning with the findings of the Rogers Commission investigation, one could practically conclude that no one had any responsibility whatsoever for the disaster. The Commission concluded that "there was a serious flaw in the decision making process leading up to the launch of flight 51-L. A well structured and managed system emphasizing safety would have flagged the rising doubts about the Solid Rocket Booster joint seal." Then the Commission report immediately states, "Had these matters been clearly stated and emphasized in the flight readiness process in terms reflecting the views of most of the Thiokol engineers and at least some of the Marshall engineers, it seems likely that the launch of 51-L might not have occurred when it did" (R.C., I, p. 104). But the gathering and passing on of such information was the responsibility of specifically designated individuals, known by name and position in the highly structured review process. Throughout this process there had been required "a series of formal, legally binding certifications, the equivalent of airworthiness inspections in the aviation industry. In effect the myriad contractor and NASA personnel involved were guaranteeing *Challenger's* flight readiness with their professional and personal integrity" (McConnell, 1987, p. 17).

When the Commission states in its next finding that "waiving of launch constraints appears to have been at the expense of flight safety," the immediate and obvious question would seem to be: Who approved the waivers and assumed this enormous risk? And why? This is a serious matter! A launch constraint is only issued because there is a safety problem serious enough to justify a decision not to launch. However, the Commission again deflects the problem onto the system by stating, "There was no system which made it imperative that launch constraints and waivers of launch constraints be considered by all levels of management" (R.C., 1986, I, p. 104).

There are two puzzling aspects to this Commission finding. First, the formal system

already contained the requirement that project offices inform at least Level II of launch constraints. The Commission addressed the explicit violation of this requirement in the case of a July 1985 launch constraint that had been imposed on the Solid Rocket Booster because of O-ring erosion on the nozzle:

> NASA Levels I and II apparently did not realize Marshall had assigned a launch constraint within the Problem Assessment System. This communication failure was contrary to the requirement, contained in the NASA Problem Reporting and Corrective Action Requirements System, that launch constraints were to be taken to Level II (R.C., 1986, I, pp. 138–139; see also p. 159).

Second, the Commission clearly established that the individual at Marshall who both imposed and waived the launch constraint was Lawrence Mulloy, SRB Project Manager. Then why blame the management system, especially in such a crucial area as that of launch constraints, when procedures of that system were not followed? Is that approach going to increase the accountability of individuals within the system for future flights?

Even such an independent minded and probing Commission member as Richard Feynman, in an interview a year after the disaster, agreed with the avoidance of determining individual accountability for specific actions and decisions. He is quoted as saying, "I don't think it's correct to try to find out which particular guy happened to do what particular thing. It's the question of how the atmosphere could get to such a circumstance that such things were possible without anybody catching on." Yet, at the same time Feynman admitted that he was not confident that any restructuring of the management system will ensure that the kinds of problems that resulted in the *Challenger* disaster — "danger signs not seen and warnings not heeded" — do not recur. He said, "I'm really not sure that any kind of simple mechanism can cure stupidity and dullness. You can make up all the rules about how things should be, and they'll go wrong if the spirit is different, if the attitudes are different over time and as personnel change" (Chandler, 1987, p. 50).

The approach of the Rogers Commission and that of most of the analyses of the *Challenger* disaster is consistent with the growing tendency to deny any specific responsibility to individual persons within corporate or other institutional settings when things go wrong. Although there are obviously many social changes in modern life that justify the shift in focus from individuals to organizational structures as bearers of responsibility, this shift is reinforced and exaggerated by the way people think about and accept those changes. One of the most pernicious problems of modern times is the almost universally held belief that the individual is powerless, especially within the context of large organizations where one may perceive oneself, and be viewed, as a very small, and replaceable, cog. It is in the very nature of this situation that responsibility may seem to become so diffused that no one person IS responsible. As the National Research Council committee, in following up on the Rogers Commission, concluded about the space shuttle program:

> Given the pervasive reliance on teams and boards to consider the key questions affecting safety, 'group democracy' can easily prevail . . . in the end all decisions become collective ones . . . (N.R.C. Report, pp. 68 and 70).

The problem with this emphasis on management systems and collective responsibility is that it fosters a vicious circle that further and further erodes and obscures individual responsibility. This leads to a paradoxical — and untenable — situation (such as in the space shuttle program) in which decisions are made and actions are performed by individuals or groups of individuals but not attributed to them. It thus reinforces the tendency to avoid accountability for what anyone does by attributing the consequences to the organization or decision making process. Again, shared, rather than individual, risktaking and responsibility became operative. The end result can be a cancerous attitude that so permeates an organization or management system that it metastasizes into decisions and acts of life-threatening irresponsibility.

In sharp contrast to this prevalent emphasis on organizational structures, one of the most fascinating aspects of the extensive and exhaustive investigations into the *Challenger* disaster is that they provide a rare opportunity to re-affirm the sense and importance of individual responsibility. With the inside look into the space shuttle program these investigations detail, one can identify many instances where personal responsibility, carefully interpreted, can properly be imputed to NASA officials and to its contractors. By so doing, one can preserve, if only in a fragmentary way, the essentials of the traditional concept of individual responsibility within the diluting context of organizational life. This effort is intended to make explicit the kind of causal links that are operative between the actions of individuals and the structures of organizations.

The criteria commonly employed for holding individuals responsible for an outcome are two: (1) their acts or omissions are in some way a cause of it; and (2) these acts or omissions are not done in ignorance or under coercion (Thompson, 1987, p. 47). Although there are difficult theoretical and practical questions associated with both criteria, especially within organizational settings, nevertheless, even a general application of them to the sequence of events leading up to the *Challenger* disaster reveals those places where the principle of individual responsibility must be factored in if our understanding of it is to be complete, its lessons learned, and its repetition avoided.

The Rogers Commission has been criticized — and rightly so — for looking at the disaster "from the bottom up but not from the top down," with the result that it gives a clearer picture of what transpired at the lower levels of the *Challenger's* flight review process than at its upper levels (Cook, 1986). Nevertheless, in doing so, the Commission report provides powerful testimony that however elaborately structured and far reaching an undertaking such as the space shuttle program may be, individuals at the bottom of the organizational structure can still play a crucial, if not deciding, role in the outcome. For in the final analysis, whatever the defects in the *Challenger's* launch decision chain were that kept the upper levels from being duly informed about the objections of the engineers at Morton Thiokol, the fact remains that the strenuous objections of these engineers so forced the decision process at their level that the four middle managers at Morton Thiokol had the full responsibility for the launch in their hands. This is made clear in the startling testimony of Mr. Mason, when Chairman Rogers asked him: "Did you realize, and particularly in view of Mr. Hardy's (Deputy Director of Science and Engineering at MSFC) point that they wouldn't launch unless you agreed, did you fully realize that in effect, you were making a decision to launch, you and your colleagues?" Mr. Mason replied, "Yes, sir" (R.C., 1986, IV, p. 770).

If these four men had just said no, the launch of the *Challenger* would not have taken place the next day. . . .

Although fragmentary and tentative in its formulation, this set of considerations points toward the conclusion that however complex and sophisticated an organization may be,

and no matter how large and remote the institutional network needed to manage it may be, an active and creative tension of responsibility must be maintained at every level of the operation. Given the size and complexity of such endeavors, the only way to ensure that tension of attentive and effective responsibility is to give the primacy of responsibility to that ultimate principle of all moral conduct: the human individual — even if this does necessitate, in too many instances under present circumstances, that individuals such as Roger Boisjoly, when they attempt to exercise their responsibility, must step forward as moral heroes. In so doing, these individuals do not just bear witness to the desperate need for a system of full accountability in the face of the immense power and reach of modern technology and institutions. They also give expression to the very essence of what constitutes the moral life. As Roger Boisjoly has stated in reflecting on his own experience, "I have been asked by some if I would testify again if I knew in advance of the potential consequences to me and my career. My answer is always an immediate 'yes'. I couldn't live with any self-respect if I tailored my actions based upon the personal consequences . . ." (Boisjoly, 1987).

REFERENCES

Boisjoly, Roger M.: 1985a, Applied Mechanics Memorandum to Robert K. Lund, Vice President, Engineering, Wasatch Division, Morton Thiokol, Inc., July 31.

Boisjoly, Roger M.: 1985b, Activity Report, SRM Seal Erosion Task Team Status, October 4.

Boisjoly, Roger M.: 1987, Ethical Decisions: Morton Thiokol and the Shuttle Disaster. Speech given at Massachusetts Institute of Technology, January 7.

Boling, T. Edwin and Dempsey, John: 1981, "Ethical dilemmas in government: Designing an organizational response," *Public Personnel Management Journal* 10, 11–18.

Chandler, David: 1987. "Astronauts gain clout in 'revitalized' NASA," *Boston Globe* 1 (January 26):50.

Christiansen, Donald: 1987, "A system gone awry," *IEEE Spectrum* 24(3):23.

Cook, Richard C.: 1986, "The Rogers commission failed," *The Washington Monthly* 18 (9), 13–21.

De George, Richard T.: 1981, "Ethical responsibilities of engineers in large organizations: The Pinto Case," *Business and Professional Ethics Journal* 1, 1–14.

Feynman, Richard P.: 1988, "An outsider's view of the Challenger inquiry," *Physics Today* 41 (2):26–37.

Janis, Irving L.: 1972, *Victims of Groupthink*, Boston, MA: Houghton Mifflin Company.

Kilminster, J. C.: 1985, Memorandum (E000-FY86–003) to Robert Lund, Vice President, Engineering, Wasatch Division, Morton Thiokol, Inc., July 5.

Mankin, Hart T.: 1981, "Commentary on 'Ethical responsibilities of engineers in large organizations: The Pinto Case,'" *Business and Professional Ethics Journal* 1, 15–17.

McConnell, Malcolm: 1987, *Challenger, A Major Malfunction: A True Story of Politics, Greed, and the Wrong Stuff*, Garden City, N.J.: Doubleday and Company, Inc.

National Research Council: 1988, *Post-Challenger Evaluation of Space Shuttle Risk Assessment and Management*, Washington, D.C.: National Academy Press.

Report of the Presidential Commission on the Space Shuttle Challenger Accident: 1986, Washington, D.C.: U.S. Government Printing Office.

Thompson, Dennis F.: 1987, *Political Ethics and Public Office*, Cambridge, MA: Harvard University Press.

Wilmotte, Raymond M.: 1970, "Engineering truth in competitive environments," *IEEE Spectrum* 7 (5):45–49.

Remaking the Corporation: The 1991 U.S. Sentencing Guidelines

Robert J. Rafalko

I. OBSTACLES TO EFFECTIVE PUNISHMENT

Some corporations sometimes engage in criminal conduct. Sometimes the crime committed is the result of the actions of a single errant employee for which the corporation nevertheless must bear some measure of legal liability. At other times, the criminal conduct may well be the result of deliberate high-level policy in the corporation and represent a pattern of abuse condoned or even promoted over the years by the company's management.

The Exxon Valdez affair is a spectacular case because of unprecedented environmental damage. The captain of the vessel was not at his post and let an improperly qualified subordinate steer the oil tanker through treacherous waters. This resulted in the massive Prince William Sound oil spill. The captain of the vessel was negligent, but the company could have taken numerous steps to prevent such an accident from occurring and

From Robert J. Rafalko, "Remaking the Corporation: The 1991 U.S. Sentencing Guidelines," *Journal of Business Ethics*, 13 (1994), Copyright © 1994 by Kluwer Academic Publishers. Reprinted by permission of Kluwer Academic Publishers.

in that respect joined the ship's captain in some measure of his negligence.

One clear case of the second class of corporate law-breaking, a company long displaying disregard for the law, is the repeated history of chemical dumping by Hooker Chemical Company. The notorious "Love Canal" incident is but one instance of such dumping by the company from a period that stretched from 1942 through 1979. The Hooker Chemical Company case shows how a corporation can write off fines for detected violations and governmental enforcement actions as "just the cost of doing business."

Cases such as these have repeatedly caused jurists and politicians to remark that the penalties for such behavior — which traditionally have taken the forms of monetary fines — have been too lenient. Having reached that conclusion, many of the same people found themselves stymied in proposing an alternative form of penalty. The reason for their difficulty is that the modern corporation is an exceedingly "odd duck" in the metaphysics of legal studies. It is not an individual; it is an organization. Nevertheless, the corporation has the status of "personhood" as a legal fiction under some aspects of the law.

Furthermore, the corporation is best defined as a liability-limiting mechanism. The reason for its existence throughout its history is the immunity from legal liability it provides to its investors. The problem is this: How do we make such a liability-immunizing mechanism as the modern corporation socially and ethically responsible for its actions? Or falling short of attaining that kind of responsibility, how do we deter the corporation from such activity in the future?

The problem is that truly ponderous fines, if imposed on the corporation convicted of criminal activity, have a ripple effect on innocent parties. . . . Such fines may cause the corporation to significantly scale down its investment. Heavy fines may put a company out of business thereby putting its employees out of work. Fines may cause a company to close down a plant, depriving a community of a tax base and an important source of employment. Furthermore, such fines may have the effect of withdrawing an important product or service from the market, or eliminating an important source of competition which keeps down prices for such products or services.

For this reason, judges, who previously had a great deal of discretion in their sentencing powers, have been slow to impose such fines. What fines they did impose were little more than a slap on the wrist. In a study, the U.S. Sentencing Commission found that the median fine to corporation has been only 20% of the loss caused by the offending corporation. Between 1984 and 1987, the average fine was $48,000 and 67 percent of all such fines amounted to less than $10,000.[1]

Perhaps, in some cases, legal censure alone was sufficient to cause many otherwise responsible corporations to initiate reforms so that such conduct would not recur, but many other companies simply went right on doing what they were doing that brought on the enforcement actions in the first place.

The problem might be phrased in this way: some corporations may be *criminally liable,* but we exact mainly *civil penalties* against them. Such civil penalties have been ineffectual. Some have proposed that what is needed is something analogous to *corporeal* punishment for corporations. This would be a "critically explorative" use of the metaphor of corporations as "persons," a metaphor which I have argued is taken too literally by many philosophers and legal scholars.

The way the courts deal with repeat criminal offenders is to restrain or confine them, thereby effectively separating them from society. Can an analogous solution be found for organizations such as corporations? Interestingly enough, some attempts have been made to find a way to incarcerate corporations for criminal behavior. In one such case, *U.S. v. Mitsubishi International Corp.*, the courts attempted to find an analogue to probation for the corporation by requiring the chief executive to donate services to a charity over the course of one year. Even more notable was the case of *U.S. v. Allgheny Bottling Co.* (1988) in which the court actually sentenced the corporation to one year in prison! The presiding judge presumably intended "imprisoning" the corporation by means of some sort of restraint on doing business. However, the judge put the corporation on suspended sentence and required probation in the form of community service for four of the company's highest executives. The sentence of probation was later overturned by an appeals court — presumably because the individual executives remain shielded by the corporate veil of legal liability immunity — so the effect of this amusing and highly imaginative solution may never be fully tested.

The upshot of these considerations is that the courts needed to find some new ideas on how to deal with organizations that have grievously broken the law. Judges have found themselves holding the horns of a dilemma: whether to fine offending corporations with sufficient severity to deter future wrongdoing and thereby risk harm to innocent individuals, or to repeat the old stuck-in-a-rut solutions and fine the organizations so leniently that the company writes off the fine as the cost of doing business. When new options are explored, they are often wildly implausible and devoid of common sense — such as when a judge places an offending corporation under "house arrest" or sentences the company to a term in prison. What was needed was a whole new approach that is both effective and commonsensical. In its November, 1991 Sentencing Guidelines, the U.S. Sentencing Commission may well have accomplished both objectives.

II. THE 1991 SENTENCING GUIDELINES

In November 1991, new sentencing guidelines went into effect for federal court cases. A large part of the guidelines have been revised where organizations are concerned. According to an article by Tracy Thompson in the *Washington Post* these guidelines impose fines on offending corporations in the following ways:

> . . . under the current guidelines, a judge would look at a table in which various crimes are assigned "offense levels," which in turn correspond to a graduated table of fines. The formula then calls for that figure — or the loss to the government, whichever is higher — to then be enhanced by various "aggravating factors," such as the degree of knowledge about the scheme on the part of the senior management. Mitigating factors also can be taken into account, such as steps taken by management to prevent wrongdoing from recurring.[2]

Suppose, for example, that XYZ Corporation defrauds the government of $100,000 in padded expense accounts for government contracts. Suppose further that senior management at XYZ, Inc. were aware of the fraud and made no effort to stop it, and XYZ, Inc. was convicted of fraud. Under the old sentencing guidelines, the fine that XYZ, Inc. would receive, based on the average fine to American corporations convicted of crimes between 1984 and 1987, might be only $48,000. Yet, that would mean that the taxpayers of America *lost* $52,000, not including court cost. Under the new guidelines, however, the judge would be able to fine the company two-to-three times the amount of money that XYZ Corporation cost the American taxpayer.

Stiffer fines are hardly a new idea. More importantly, it may be hard for us to see how they solve the related problem of a ripple effect on innocent or non-company connected individuals such as those in the surrounding community who might be harmed by cutbacks, slowdowns or plant closings resultant upon the imposition of harsh fines. However, the 1991 Sentencing Guidelines actually do offer some new ideas — and effective ones at that.

Writing about the new Guidelines in an issue of a recent legal journal, John Levitski, Jr. points out the "mitigating circumstances" which the guidelines define and which can result in far less severe penalties:

> Under the . . . Guidelines, a substantial probability exists that some socially-responsible companies will be forced to pay for the criminal conduct of errant employees. However, the . . . Guidelines do consider four mitigating factors in setting fines: (1) lack of knowledge of the offense by corporate management; (2) a meaningful compliance program in effect at the time of the offense; (3) prompt reporting of the offense or cooperation in the criminal investigation; and (4) steps taken by the corporation to remedy the harm, discipline individuals, and prevent a recurrence.[3]

The new ideas contained in the Sentencing Guidelines are roughly analogous to the difference between cure and prevention. Whereas in the past medicine had been confined mainly to the search for medical cures, recent advances in medical care have come to stress *prevention* (or, as the popular jargon has termed it, *"wellness."*) The terms of that ethical or legal preventative medicine for business can be summed up by incentives offered by the federal government to the corporation in terms of the creation of a comprehensive ethics compliance program within the company. Those are indeed negative incentives — hence, there should be a deterrent effect. But it is important to emphasize that those provisions for mitigating factors are designed to work in a constructive and positive avenue of reform rather than in a negative atmosphere of strict deterrence.

The idea is this: make the penalties harsh for lack of compliance with the Guidelines in order to compel the corporation to implement the Guidelines, but once a comprehensive ethics program is in place in the corporation, it will have an automatic and self-correcting effect on how morally business is conducted.

Thus, in a commentary in *Business Week* entitled, "What's Behind Business' Sudden Fervor for Ethics," Bruce Hager noting the doubling or tripling of fines for lawbreaking corporations, writes:

> However, companies with tough ethics policies will receive much more lenient treatment as long as they cooperate with prosecutors and their policies meet the guidelines' standards. For instance, a fine of $1 million to $2 million could be knocked down to as low as $50,000 for a company with a comprehensive program including a code of conduct, an ombudsman, a hotline, and mandatory training seminars for executives. Explains Judge William W. Wilkins Jr., chairman of the U.S. Sentencing Commission: "Even the best efforts to prevent crime may not be successful in every case. But we have to reward the corporation that was trying to be a good corporate citizen."[4]

Interestingly, Chairman Wilkins describes his commission's guidelines for sentencing not in terms of penalties, but in terms of *rewards* for good behavior. The rewards come in the form of dramatic reductions in fines provided that the company had the good sense and foresight to put in place an ethics program of the kind suggested here. This is certainly a new idea — possibly even a major breakthrough in the concept of punishment.

Let us look in some detail about precisely how the program is to be implemented. The key paragraph which describes the program is paragraph (k) of Section 8A1.2 of the November, 1991 U.S. Sentencing Guidelines:

(k) An "effective program to prevent and detect violations of law" means a program that has been reasonably designed, implemented, and enforced so that it generally will be effective in preventing and detecting criminal conduct. Failure to prevent or detect the instant offense, by itself, does not mean that the program was not effective. The hallmark of an effective program to prevent and detect violations of law is that the organization exercised due diligence in seeking to prevent and detect criminal conduct by its employees and other agents.[5]

The concept of "due diligence" is specified in seven steps:

(1) The organization must have established compliance standards and procedures to be followed by its employees and other agents that are reasonably capable of reducing the prospect of criminal conduct.

(2) Specific individual(s) within high-level personnel of the organization must have been assigned overall responsibility to oversee compliance with such standards and procedures.

(3) The organization must have used due care not to delegate substantial discretionary authority to individuals whom the organization knew, or should have known through the exercise of due diligence, had a propensity to engage in illegal activities.

(4) The organization must have taken steps to communicate effectively its standards and procedures to all employees and other agents, *e.g.,* by requiring participation in training programs or by disseminating publications that explain in a practical manner what is required.

(5) The organization must have taken reasonable steps to achieve compliance with its standards, *e.g.,* by utilizing monitoring and auditing systems reasonably designed to detect criminal conduct by its employees and other agents and by having in place and publicizing a reporting system whereby employees and other agents could report criminal conduct by others within the organization without fear of retribution.

(6) The standards must have been consistently enforced through appropriate disciplinary mechanisms, including, as appropriate, discipline of individuals responsible for the failure to detect an offense. Adequate discipline of individuals responsible for an offense is a necessary component of enforcement; however, the form of discipline that will be appropriate will be case specific.

(7) After an offense has been detected, the organization must have taken all reasonable steps to respond appropriately to the offense and to prevent further similar offenses — including any necessary modifications to its program to prevent and detect violations of law.

Each of these seven steps (with the exception of the second) allows for a large measure of latitude in interpretation on how the steps may be satisfied. For example, the comprehensive ethics program that Bruce Hager describes, consisting of a code of conduct, an ombudsman, a hotline, and mandatory training seminars for executives, would very probably be more than sufficient for most corporations in terms of satisfying the guidelines. However, there are three relevant factors to consider when assessing how much a company needs to do to be in compliance: (1) the size of the organization; (2) the nature of the business; and (3) the prior history of the company in terms of enforcement actions against it.

Notice that a very small corporation, perhaps a company which employs 50 people, might need to do less than what Hager suggests in order for the company to come into compliance. It might be enough for the CEO of such a company to convene a meeting of his executives and staff, read aloud the corporate code of conduct, warn employees that violations of the code would result in dismissal and full cooperation with the prosecution against them, and then call for the statements to be entered into the written minutes of the meeting for annual review.

Larger companies, however, clearly need to do more. And very large companies, with past histories of violations of the law in a business heavily reliant on federal contracts (such as the defense industry) might well need to do everything that Hager suggests and more. Indeed, they might need to "go the extra mile" in assuring everyone concerned that the company is making every effort to comply with the guidelines not only to the letter but also to the very spirit of the law.

Let us consider each of the seven steps which constitute "due diligence" in turn.

Step 1

Provision (k)(1) may be understood to be the "minimum threshold requirement" of the Sentencing Guidelines' conditions for leniency. Without some sort of "Corporate Code of Conduct" in place (such as the model proposed by the American Society for Public Administrators), i.e., a detailed set of "standards and procedures" specific to the company which will keep the corporate members within the provisions of the law, then any other effort the company may make in behalf of compliance with the law might go for naught when the judge considers conditions for leniency in sentencing. For example, in all sincerity a company might bring in an outside speaker to address its middle-level managers on the importance of ethics in their business dealings but without a detailed code of conduct in place, that company would be in danger of non-compliance with the Guidelines and unable to avail itself of conditions of leniency as specified here. This interpretation is especially true if the company is a large one, or if it has a prior history of violations or is in an especially sensitive

area of production (for example, a company which produces environmentally toxic substances).

That interpretation might be surprising to some unless we realize that the steps from (1) through (7) are listed in approximate order of importance. Provision (k)(1) is therefore the provision selected by the U.S. Sentencing commission as the most important of them all.[6] However, from a strictly practical point of view, we might argue that Provision (k)(2) is even more important than (k)(1).

Step 2

Provision (k)(2) requires that a specific individual (or individuals) "within high-level personnel of the organization must have been assigned overall responsibility to oversee compliance with such standards and procedures."

This provision is the one exception to the rule that permits each of the other steps to be more-or-less open to a variety of interpretations. This provision is extremely specific, even to the extent of carefully defining who is to count as "high-level personnel of the organization." According to Section 8A1.3 (b), high-level personnel of the organization "means individuals who have substantial control over the organization or who have a substantial role in the making of policy within the organization. The term includes: a director; an executive officer; an individual in charge of a major business or functional unit of the organization, such as sales, administration, or finance; and an individual with a substantial ownership interest."

One of the practical reasons that (k)(2) may be the most important of the seven steps is that without a high-level individual charged with the responsibility of overseeing the ethics compliance program, not even the creation of a code of conduct can get off the ground. One real difficulty in implementing the ethics compliance program in most corporations is that the responsibility to create one presently rests on no existing officer inside the corporation. Most large companies have a "Human Resource Director," and it might seem as that individual would be most likely charged with the responsibility of overseeing compliance programs, but in fact such officers of the corporation often have their duties restricted to personnel hiring and public relations work. Internal Audit is usually even more narrowly charged with duties relating to little more than accounting work, and company legal departments tend to be reactive rather than anticipatory. Outside of perhaps the CEO or Board of Directors, then, most companies have no high-level officer who has the responsibility to oversee ethics programs. Unless the directive to create such a program comes from the very top, then there is no way to get a program started. . . .

Step 3

Section (k)(3) largely speaks for itself in cautioning against "substantial discretionary authority" being delegated to individuals in the company who have (or had) "a propensity to engage in illegal activities." If a bank vice president has had prior convictions for insider trading, then permitting him access to sensitive merger information clearly puts the bank in jeopardy of violating this condition. However, the same condition arguably may put a company in an impossible position of gathering prior knowledge of larcenous behavior of an employee when that employee has no prior record of criminal activity. "You should have known better" is a delicious bit of second guessing and too facile a posture for an overly ambitious prosecutor to take. Furthermore, given this provision, a company

may be less inclined to give a second chance to someone who has sincerely reformed after having "paid his debt to society," so one would hope the courts would demonstrate some common sense when taking (k)(3) into consideration.

Step 4

Section (k)(4) is open to a wide range of interpretations and therefore is most in need of discussion at length. It is a directive to a company not only to have standards of ethics compliance but to communicate them effectively to *every* employee and concerned party in ways that are relevant to their jobs. Obviously, if a company has a written code of conduct but employees are not aware of its existence or of the details of the code of conduct, then that company is in almost certain violation of this condition. We might well regard (k)(4) as the directive which insures that a company doesn't merely pay lip service to its standards of ethics. The compliance standards must have a substantial impact on the conduct of the company and its employees.

However, the same section merely lists some suggestions on how to accomplish the communication of the company's standards. One way is to disseminate the published code of conduct throughout the company, but if the code doesn't make its way past departmental managers to the workers under their charge, then *de facto* compliance is in doubt. Likewise, if employees are merely directed to routinely "sign off" on a sheet of paper that they read and understand the code of conduct, the courts may question the effectiveness of its methods of communication or the sincerity of the commitment of the company to its code of conduct.

For this reason, training programs for the company's code of conduct is a surer method of compliance with (k)(4). However, this is a time-consuming and an expensive method, one that is probably prohibitive to all but the largest and most successful companies or to companies that have a history of enforcement actions taken against them. Yet, training programs are the best way to fill important gaps in the way a company code of conduct is drawn up and in the way that the code is communicated. . . .

Step 5

Section (k)(5) sanctions "whistle-blowing" for violations of law within the company and requires the company to have in place an effective mechanism "whereby employees and other agents could report criminal conduct by others within the organization without fear of retribution." For example, the company may designate "ombudsmen" or establish a company-wide telephone "hotline" to allow employees to report such violations. The code of conduct should specifically guarantee protection to the careers of any employee who sincerely and non-frivolously reports a suspected violation of law or ethics within the company and a grievance or appeals procedure should be in place to allow an employee redress in the event that he believes he has been unfairly treated for a sincere and non-frivolous whistle-blowing incident.

Step 6

Such a grievance procedure has an important role in Step 6 as well which directs the company to enforce its standards "through appropriate disciplinary mechanisms . . . ," section (k)(6). Such disciplinary actions may be "case specific," but adequate to deter others in the company from participating in illegal or relevantly unethical behavior. For example, a corporation may have some discretion about whether to fire an employee who is accused of sexual harassment, or, if it is a first offense, a venial one or one [of] questionable veracity, transfer the offender to another position in the company with sufficiently stern warnings to prevent the offense from happening again. But, whatever the discipline the company deems appropriate, the employee must surely have his rights of due process secured — a protection best accomplished by creating an independent grievance board or by hiring an independent arbitrator to hear the evidence and decide on the appropriateness or justice of the company's actions.

Step 7

Section (k)(7) looks to be sweepingly general, requiring the company to take "all reasonable steps to respond appropriately to the offense and to prevent further offenses. . . ." However, we can probably make out its intent to include three factors: first, that the company sincerely and thoroughly cooperate in the investigation and prosecution of violations of law within its purview; second, that the company make "any necessary modifications to its program to prevent and detect violations of law" — for example, if the code of conduct does not explicitly prohibit sexual harassment, it must be modified to do so in the future; third, section (k)(7) spells out the conditions of thoroughness, a given company must take regarding the training and communication and enforcement of its compliance standards with regard to all members of the organization and its agents. Those conditions, we have already mentioned, are three in number and explicitly specified in section (k)(7):

(i) Size of the organization.
(ii) Likelihood that certain offenses may occur because of the nature of its business.

(iii) Prior history of the organization concerning past infractions of the law.

We previously raised the question a number of times about how far a company needs to go in the creation of an ethics program to be in full compliance with these conditions. Section (k)(7), articles (i) — (iii) help us to find an answer to that question. Does a company need to have a telephone hotline in order to facilitate reports of violations? Does the company need to establish regular and comprehensive training seminars in its code of conduct? Should a company prohibit gifts to its employees or agents or limit the acceptance of those gifts to a specific dollar amount of value? The answers depend on how large the company is, the nature of its business and the history of prior legal violations within the company. When concerns arise about the company under any of these classifications, the rule is that "more" is safer: the more expansive the program, the more likely the company is under compliance.

III. THE GUIDELINES AND CORPORATE SOCIAL RESPONSIBILITY

How effective will the 1991 U.S. Sentencing Guidelines be in deterring future corporate crime and creating an ethical environment within the corporation? Let's consider some of the possible objections.

Objection 1. *The program will fail because it will create a competitive disadvantage for the companies which comply.*

This objection may take many different forms in many different directions, but in one clear sense it is false. In the past, it may have been true that some companies which instituted strict ethics compliance programs suffered some competitive disadvantage (we'll concede this for sake of argument.) However, where those competitive disadvantages occurred, let us suggest that the problem arose because of the difficulties reformers faced in instituting the standards industry-wide.

Many of the so-called "professions" (law, medicine, etc.) have recognized the need for "industry-wide" voluntary regulation within their ranks and constructed codes of conduct with varying degrees of success. The problems they faced are instructive. We may point to one example in particular.

In the 1950's and '60's in the United States, a morally repugnant practice was widely adopted by many in the real estate profession that came to be known as "blockbusting." This was the practice of some real estate agents (both white and black) of introducing newly middle-class blacks to exclusively white neighborhoods and then frightening white homeowners into panic-selling by warning them that their property values would decline now that blacks were living next door. Blockbusting not only exploited racial fears for profit, it intensified them, and a good measure of the racial tension that exists in the United States today can be traced to this practice. The financial conditions of black and white homeowners alike were detrimentally affected by blockbusting; only the real estate agents who practiced it came out ahead.

At first, voluntary local associations of realtors and citizens were formed to stave off the practice by unscrupulous realtors. Eventually, their outcry was heard by the National Association of Real Estate Brokers which amended its nationally distributed "Code of Ethics and Standards of Practice" to prevent blockbusting. This in turn led to the passage of Title VIII of the 1968 Civil Rights Act which outlawed the practice once and for all, but it took more than twenty years to ban blockbusting and it ended only when federal legislation was introduced.

More relevant (and more successful) are the 1988 Defense Industry Initiatives. The U.S. Sentencing Guidelines are similar in many respects to this voluntary agreement among twenty-six signatories of the defense industry to create ethics improvement programs. The initiatives were prompted, in part, as a result of the defense procurement scandals of the Eighties. Despite obvious pressure from the Federal government at the time, the point should be stressed that these were indeed voluntary agreements and the defense contractors involved created programs so original that they have served as a source (among others) that the U.S. Sentencing Commission considered in drafting the Guidelines. However, the Sentencing Guidelines apply to all corporations (and not just the defense contractors).

The Defense Industry Initiatives, as admirable as they are, face many of the shortcomings of other attempts at industry-wide self-regulation, viz., they tend to be conservative, looking for short-term or stopgap reforms, and they do not specify means of enforcement. But the U.S. Sentencing Guidelines are visionary in their commitment to making ethical conduct an internality of American business, they certainly do specify means of enforcement, and they are universally applicable to organizations in the United States (including the defense industry).

Objection 2. *The program will fail because it will create an international competitive disadvantage for the companies which comply.*

This objection is far more worrisome. While American companies are bound by the strictures of their corporate codes of conduct, no such requirements are uniformly imposed on our competitors in, say, Japan or Korea or Italy. For example, bribery is routine in many countries. Without a recogni-

tion of that reality, American corporations may suffer severe disadvantages if they are held to compliance with *American* prohibitions against bribery overseas.

It should be noted that the customary practice of bribing foreign officials in return for lucrative contracts is now not only regarded as unethical in the United States, it is for the most part illegal as well. The Foreign Corrupt Practices Act (1979) has made payments to foreign government officials in order to promote or retain business a federal crime. That, of course, does not by itself solve our problem, for two reasons. First, the Act together with the even stiffer penalties encouraged by the Sentencing Guidelines may actually intensify the U.S. competitive disadvantage since most other nations do not have similar legislation. And, second, the Foreign Corrupt Practices Act, as Mark Pastin and Michael Hooker have pointed out, doesn't rule out 'grease' payments to certain employees in clerical or ministerial positions in order to persuade them to carry out their normal duties, so an ethical problem is still posed here for American corporations in how to deal with such people.[7]

A direct answer to our question requires the concession that ethical practice in these dealings may well post at least a short-term disadvantage to American corporations. Yet, the effects of such practices are not easily quantified in the longer run. George C. Dillon, the Director of Manville Corporation, tells a story about how his company was faced with an apparent ethical dilemma in dealing with the market in Japan. U.S. regulations required that Manville label an ingredient in one of its products as a recognized carcinogen, but no such regulations prevailed in Japan. Faced with the question of whether Manville should include its warning in Japanese, the company decided to go ahead anyway, despite the fact that its customers in Japan had warned that, if Manville did so, they would cancel the sale (which they did). Yet, Dillon reports that Manville was rewarded with lucrative contracts from Japan for the same product some years later because many Japanese companies declared that they came to respect Manville for its ethical integrity in the handling of this matter. In a speech on the subject, Dillon suggests:

> If we are merely complying with today's regulations we aren't taking advantage of an opportunity to create competitive advantage. We may, in fact, be failing to represent the best interests of our investors, the long-term best interest of our companies, and the interests of the communities in which we exist. . . . Ultimately, business is accountable for *tomorrow's* law. An organization that really wants to get ahead of the pack must look at the evolving trends and philosophy of society as they emerge in the form of public opinion. This will make tomorrow's law.[8]

Dillon's point is that complying with such ethical standards in an international market may be a competitive trade off in the long run. Concern about the short-term competitive disadvantage may make one blind to the possibility of *creating* future competitive advantages. Furthermore, complying with ethical standards internationally is legally prudent since the laws both here and abroad are changing to be in conformity with such standards. . . .

Objection 3. *While it may be true that the Guidelines will coerce ethical compliance, that won't make corporations genuinely socially responsible. The Guidelines are not promoting ethics in the true spirit of free volition on the part of corporations. Therefore, corporate compliance is of dubious moral worth.*

This objection trades on an equivocation of the word 'responsible.' We can make a corporation "responsible" in the sense of requiring it to be responsive to social needs, but in doing so we do not make the corporation a "responsible" citizen or person. We don't need to.

Motives, free will, volitions, intentions, responsibility, ideals and so forth are the collective paraphernalia of moral theory. But these do not adapt well to the situation of the modern corporation, however much we press the analogy of the corporation of the person. The fact is that corporations, despite their legal characterization as "fictional persons," are not persons. As Thomas Donaldson has pointed out, persons are intentional beings, but a corporation cannot be shown to have an intention which belongs to the corporation itself because that corporation's course of action may have been determined by a collective of individuals, each with widely different intentions.[9]

Rather, it is clear that corporations are social instruments. They live, die or prosper according to the needs of society. When they serve those needs well, they prosper. When they do so poorly, we change them, regulate them and restrict them in order to serve those needs better.

Sometimes those social needs include protection of property rights — the rights of owners or investors, for example. Sometimes those needs are political and ethical. Some property rights however are also moral rights and sometimes moral property rights come into conflict with other moral concerns of society. This is why the subject of business ethics is so riddled with cases of apparent moral dilemmas. However those cases are to be resolved, the corporation *per se* has no authentic claim to personhood, "responsibility," moral worth, or the natural rights of persons, and to suppose they do only serves to confuse the issue.

Two things are at issue. First, a set of guidelines is needed to insure that the corporate system serves the generally recognized needs of society to safeguard its environment, to produce needed products and services, to generate returns capital and investment and to adequately and safely employ and compensate the workers of the nation. The Sentencing Guidelines go a long way in promoting these ends.

Second, a set of guidelines is needed to insure that employees and other agents of the corporation can maintain their own ethical integrity while serving the needs of the corporation. A sales force must not be instructed, at the cost of their jobs, that they must meet a sales quota, "whatever it takes," while the company turns a blind eye to their practices. A manager or high-level executive must feel free to steer his company in ethical and socially responsible directions without fear of being held accountable for diminished profit margins as a result. Since the Sentencing Guidelines make the code of conduct an internality of the company's operation, these goals are largely assured, at least on the level which concerns possible transgressions of federal statutes. In time, perhaps the Guidelines will serve as models for sentencing in state and local ordinances as well. In any case, compelling corporations to have codes of conduct and to faithfully adhere to their dictates will doubtlessly produce profound and welcome changes in the way America does business.

NOTES

1. Tracy Thompson, "Corporations Face Stiffer Sentencing," *The Washington Post,* November 8, 1989, p. B4.

2. *Ibid.*

3. John Levitske, Jr., "Will the U.S. Sentencing Commission's New Proposed Guidelines for Crimes by Organizations Provide an Effective Deterrent for Crimes Attributed to Corporations (Or Will the New Proposed Guidelines Put an Exclamation Point in the Sentence for Corporate Crime)?" *Duquesne Law Review,* Vol. 29, 783, p. 793.

4. Bruce Hager, "What's Behind Business' Sudden Fervor for Ethics?," *Business Week,* September 23, 1991, p. 65.

5. *United States Sentencing Commission Guidelines Manual,* November 1, 1991, S8A1.3, p. 352.

6. Win Swenson, Deputy General Counsel, the U.S. Sentencing Commission (in conversation).

7. Mark Pastin and Michael Hooker, "Ethics and the Foreign Corrupt Practices Act," *Business Horizons,* December, 1980, p. 44. . . .

8. George C. Dillon, Director, Manville Corporation, "The Prospect of Competitive Ethics: Good Ethics Is Good Business," Speech Delivered at the Racing for a Competitive Edge Conference, New York, March 20, 1991, *Vital Speeches of the Day, June, 1991.*

9. Thomas Donaldson, *Corporations and Morality,* Englewood Cliffs, N.J.: Prentice-Hall, Inc., 1982, pp. 21–22. . . .

Corporate Culpability Under the Federal Sentencing Guidelines

Jennifer Moore

INTRODUCTION

In 1984, Congress created the United States Sentencing Commission to promulgate criminal sentencing guidelines for the federal courts. The first task of the Commission was the development of sentencing guidelines for individuals. When these were completed in 1987, the Commission began to formulate guidelines for organizations. The fourth and final draft of the organizational guidelines became law on November 1, 1991.

The new organizational guidelines take an explicitly "carrot and stick" approach to sentencing. Under section 8C2, calculating the appropriate fine for an organizational offender begins with the determination of a "base fine" chosen to reflect the seriousness of the offense. The base fine is then adjusted according to a series of aggravating and mitigating factors: the participation of authority personnel, the history of the organization, cooperation with law enforcement authorities, and the presence or absence of a program to prevent and detect crime. In part, these factors are intended to provide an incentive for organizations to "strengthen internal mechanisms for deterring, detecting and reporting criminal conduct by their agents and employees." But an additional result of the Guidelines is to make corporate punishment proportional to what would, in an individual, be called "culpability": the deliberateness of the offense, the extent of the offender's involvement, and the offender's "character." Indeed, the Guidelines explicitly use the term "culpability" and refer to the list of aggravating and mitigating factors as the organization's "culpability score."

Although the Guidelines are applicable to all "organizations," they were designed with corporations in mind, and it is on corporations that they are expected to have their greatest impact. Yet the Guidelines' use of organizational culpability represents a departure from the traditional principles of substantive corporate criminal law. The dominant aim of corporate criminal law has been deterrence rather than retribution, rehabilitation, or incapacitation. This has meant that culpability has played a relatively minor role. To be sure, courts have had to develop theories of corporate mens rea in order to hold corporations liable for crimes requiring intent. But these theories are the products of necessity rather than careful analysis or conceptual rigor; they stem less from a belief in the importance of corporate culpability than from the perceived need to extend criminal liability to corporations. The Guidelines, in contrast, employ a well-considered, theoretically satisfying conception of corporate culpability that is driven by the purposes of sentencing set out in 18 U.S.C. § 3553(a)(2): just punishment, adequate deterrence, protection of the public, rehabilitation of the offender, proportionality with the seri-

From Jennifer Moore, "Corporate Culpability Under the Federal Sentencing Guidelines," *Arizona Law Review* 34 (1992). Reprinted with the permission of the author and the *Arizona Law Review* and from *The United States Law Week*, Vol. 59, pp. 4226–29 (March 26, 1991). Published by The Bureau of National Affairs, Inc. (800–372–1033).

ousness of the offense, and the need to promote respect for the law.

This article examines the use of corporate culpability in the Federal Sentencing Guidelines and addresses three major questions: In light of the traditional unimportance of culpability in corporate criminal law, is corporate culpability an appropriate concern of the Guidelines? If so, how is corporate culpability best conceptualized? Finally, how do the Guidelines understand corporate culpability, and how close do they come to embodying this most satisfying theory? Part I of the Article discusses the principal reasons why culpability has been important at the trial and sentencing of individual criminals, and argues that similar reasons justify concern with culpability in the sentencing of corporate offenders. Although culpability is not the only important factor in corporate sentencing, Part I concludes, it is a legitimate concern of the Guidelines. Part II sets out three alternative conceptions of corporate culpability, those implicit in the two prevailing theories of corporate criminal liability — the doctrine of respondeat superior and the doctrine of Section 2.07 of the *Model Penal Code* — and a third conception that has received considerable support from scholars of corporate crime. Part II argues that it is this third conception, termed the "corporate character theory," that provides the most adequate understanding of corporate culpability, and that this theory is particularly well-suited for use in the sentencing of organizational criminals. Finally, Part III explores the use of culpability by the organizational guidelines themselves, and contends that they employ a conception of corporate culpability that is closely related to the corporate character theory. In addition, it attempts to show how the adoption of the corporate character theory allows the Guidelines to pursue a wider range of sentencing aims than is traditional in the sentencing of corporations. . . .

I. CULPABILITY AND THE CRIMINAL LAW

* * *

C. Corporate Culpability

. . . There are several reasons why one might believe that corporate culpability is not an appropriate concern. Corporations are artificial entities, not biological persons, and thus may seem unsuitable objects of moral blame and accompanying "stigma." Even if there is a sense in which corporations can be "culpable," they are likely to have weaker claims to the fair treatment, liberty, and reduction of anxiety emphasized by Hart than individuals do. Finally, the high number of strict liability offenses for which corporations can be liable suggests a lack of legislative concern with the issue of corporate culpability. These arguments are ultimately unpersuasive, however. I will argue that, although corporations cannot be blameworthy in the literal sense in which individuals can, corporations cause and direct the acts of their agents in a way that makes it natural to call them "culpable." Once this is conceded, corporate culpability merits attention in the criminal law for the same reasons that individual culpability does.

Although corporations always act through individual agents, and it is always an individual agent or group of agents who breaks the law, it is fair to say that corporations frequently *cause* their agents to violate the law. The behavior of individuals in corporations is not merely the product of individual choice; it is stimulated and shaped by goals, rules, policies, and procedures that are features of the corporation as an entity. How to design these features to ensure that agents act predictably and in the interest of the organization — that is, how to control the behavior of corporate agents — is the central question of organizational theory. Establishing a chain of command, delegating to each member a sphere of authority, setting up standard operating procedures, training members, and controlling the flow of information are all part of this task. Ultimately, organizational theorist Herbert Simon explains, the goal is for the organization to "take[] from the individual some of his decisional autonomy, and substitute[] for it an organization decision-making process."[1] Where this process is likely to result in violations on behalf of the corporation on the part of its agents, it seems natural to say that the corporation is "culpable" or "at fault."

It is important to distinguish this argument from the claim that it is sometimes difficult to locate the specific corporate agents responsible for a criminal act. Although this claim is true, it is an evidentiary point rather than a philosophical one. My argument is somewhat different: Because of the diffusion of responsibility in organizations and the ways in which individual decisions are channelled by corporate rules, policies and structures, there may in fact *be* no individual or group of individuals that is "justly to blame" for the crime. Individuals in corporations frequently operate in a kind of "twilight zone" of autonomy; they may simply exert insufficient choice or control to be suitable recipients of blame. In this situation, the "overflow" blame is properly attributed to the corporation.

Scholars of corporate crime recognize that characteristics of the corporation can cause criminal behavior on the part of its agents. Martin and Carolyn Needleman, for example, argue that "at least some criminal behavior usefully may be viewed not as personal deviance, but rather as a predictable product of the individual's membership in or contact with certain organizational systems."[2] Many theorists have identified a corporate character or "corporate culture"[3] which endures over time and transcends the character of the corporation's members. Christopher Stone has found that corporations, like political ad-

ministrations, have distinct and characteristic attitudes toward the demands of law and morality.[4] "In [the corporate] setting," Stone writes, "each man's own wants, ideas — even his perceptions and emotions — are swayed and directed by an institutional structure so pervasive that it might be construed as having a set of goals and constraints (if not a mind and purpose) of *its* own."[5] . . . There appear to be "good" and "bad" corporations, law-abiding corporations and recidivists, and there is a remarkable consensus as to which corporations are which. The ability of theorists to identify corporate characters is evidence that it is not inappropriate to speak of corporate culpability.

The idea of corporate culpability is not merely a product of organizational theory and research on corporate crime; it is part of ordinary moral discourse. People behave in ways that suggest they blame corporations and feel retributive sentiments toward them. They frequently voice moral judgments about corporations, such as "Union Carbide is indifferent to safety" or "Johns-Manville took advantage of its employees." Such statements may be merely shorthand ways of blaming corporate executives whose identities are unknown to the speaker. But they can also be read as judgments passed on the character or policies of the corporation. This interpretation is strengthened when the judgments apply to the corporation over a substantial period of time, or are accompanied by acts directed at the corporation as an entity, such as picketing or boycotts. Moreover, there is evidence that the stigma of moral blameworthiness that accompanies these judgments is capable of seriously injuring not merely individuals, but the corporation as a whole. The effect of such stigma is so strong that several commentators have suggested the use of court-ordered adverse publicity as a criminal sanction against corporate offenders. . . .

II. CONCEPTUALIZING CORPORATE CULPABILITY

* * *

C. The Corporate Character Theory

Neither of the theories of corporate culpability currently employed at the trial stage, then, is completely satisfactory. The respondeat superior theory, [which essentially inputs any crime committed by an employee within the scope of employment,] assigns culpability to the corporation even when the agent's crime was the work of a "rogue employee," with no link to corporate character or policy. Moreover, without substantial gerrymandering, the theory is unable to find corporations culpable for acts that cannot be attributed to an identifiable agent or group of agents. These problems plague the theory of respondeat superior because it does not provide a genuine theory of corporate entity culpability, but rather works by borrowing the culpability of a corporate agent. The *Model Penal Code,* in contrast, does contain a theory of corporate entity culpability, but its conception is too narrow. . . . [It makes corporate culpability dependent on the direct participation, authorization or tolerance of high managerial officials, and fails to take account of the fact that corporations may be "justly to blame" even when such officials are not involved.] What is needed is a concept of corporate culpability capable of assigning fault not only when high managerial officials are involved, but also when corporate rules, policies, structures or procedures encourage criminal acts in less direct, more subtle, ways.

For such a concept, we must turn to a theory of corporate culpability that has received considerable attention from academics, but has not been explicitly adopted by the courts. This theory builds on the findings of organizational research by recognizing that corporations shape and control the behavior of their agents not only through direct supervision by high managerial officials, but also through the use of such devices as standard operating procedures, hierarchical structures, decision rules and disciplinary sanctions. As noted in Part I, rules, structures, policies and procedures are appropriate loci of corporate fault because they are intended to replace agents' decisional autonomy with an organizational decision-making process. Their effect is to create a corporate "culture" or "character" which endures over time and which channels behavior in ways that are in the interest of the corporation. Because this third theory of corporate culpability makes fault depend upon the character of the corporation, it will be termed the "corporate character theory." Under the corporate character theory, a corporation is culpable when its policies, structures, or procedures — features of the corporate character — cause its agents to commit illegal acts on its behalf. Generally, the corporate character theory is advanced as an alternative to the two theories of corporate criminal liability presently in use at the trial stage. However, it can also be used to assess the degree of a corporate offender's liability at sentencing. Indeed, in Part II.C.3., I will contend that the corporate character theory is *more* suitable for use at sentencing than at trial. In Part III, I will argue that a version of this theory has been adopted by the Federal Sentencing Guidelines for organizations.

1. Contours of the Corporate Character Theory. There are many proponents of the corporate character theory, and each has articulated the theory in a slightly different way. Nevertheless, it is possible to discern from the literature three distinct sets of circumstances under which most corporate character theorists would find the corporation at fault. First, and most straightforwardly, a corporation is culpable under the corporate character theory if it has adopted a policy that is illegal, and an agent of the corporation carries out that policy. In such a case, it is clear that the resulting illegal act is a product of the corporate character, rather than the act of a rogue employee, and that the corporation is "justly to blame." . . .

Second, like the *Model Penal Code,* most versions of the corporate character theory find the corporation culpable when an illegal act is committed, authorized, ordered or endorsed by a high managerial official in the corporation. As the drafters of the *Model Penal Code* recognized, some corporate officials are so closely identified with the organization and have so much authority within it, that their acts per se count as "corporate policy." The participation of a high managerial official in an illegal act makes it extremely likely that the act will be carried out. It is difficult to imagine an organization with a "good" character whose officials tolerate or participate in criminal activity. Of course, the question of who counts as a high managerial official is a difficult one, heavily dependent on the circumstances in each case. Generally, the higher an official, the more likely it is that he or she does represent corporate policy; but lower officials may also represent corporate policy if they have been delegated sufficient discretion.

Third, several corporate character theorists argue that a corporation should be found culpable of an employees' illegal act if it implicitly ratifies or endorses the violation. There are at least two ways in which such ratification can take place. First, the organization may fail to correct a particular violation once it is discovered. Even if an act is initially committed by a rogue employee, failure to correct it suggests that the violation is consistent with corporate policy. Second, the organization may have a history of similar violations. Such a history suggests that the crimes are not mere anomalies, but are the result of

some feature of the corporation; failure to correct the circumstances leading to the violation endorses it by implication. In both cases, there is strong evidence that the bad act is a product of the corporate character. Similar assumptions are commonly made in making judgments about the culpability of individuals. While a first offender can plausibly repudiate his crime by arguing that the crime does not genuinely reflect his character, this argument is not persuasive for a recidivist. Repetition of a crime, and failure to respond appropriately to the harms it caused, suggests that the crime was not a mistake, but a genuine outgrowth of the character of the offender. . . .

III. THE CORPORATE CHARACTER THEORY AND THE FEDERAL SENTENCING GUIDELINES

. . . Under the corporate character theory, a corporation is culpable when a corporate policy or custom causes an agent of the corporation to violate the law on the corporation's behalf. Although use of the corporate character theory at the trial stage presents several difficulties, the theory is well-suited for use at sentencing, where judges have traditionally engaged in a broad-based assessment of the character of offenders. In this section of the paper, I explain the ways in which the Federal Sentencing Guidelines are informed by the corporate character theory.

Given the traditional unimportance of culpability in corporate criminal law, one would expect the Guidelines to ignore culpability altogether. At most, the Guidelines would be expected to employ a concept of imputed culpability, consistent with the doctrine of respondeat superior used at the trial stage in the federal courts. Instead, Part III shows, the Guidelines adopt a genuine theory of organizational entity culpability, and give it concrete content through the device of the "culpability score." The argument of Part III is threefold: Section A describes the evolution of the Guidelines and the decision of the Sentencing Commission to make culpability a significant part of the sentencing process. Section B analyzes the "culpability score" and concludes that the Guidelines require an assessment of the organization's character strikingly similar to that prescribed by the corporate character theory. Section C shows how the adoption of a version of the corporate character theory enables the Guidelines to pursue a wider range of sentencing aims than is traditional in the sentencing of organizations.

A. The Use of Culpability in the Organizational Sentencing Guidelines

. . . The new Guidelines are complex and reflect a broad range of sentencing principles. Section 8B requires offenders to remedy any harm resulting from an offense and to compensate victims. It also provides for restitution orders, remedial orders, community service, and notice to victims. Section 8C1 subjects "criminal purpose organizations" to the organizational equivalent of the death penalty — a fine large enough to divest them of all their assets. Criminal purpose organizations are defined as organizations operating "primarily for criminal purposes or primarily for criminal means." Section 8C2.9 provides for the disgorgement of any gain from an offense that is not removed by fine or restitution order. The central portions of the Guidelines, however, are the provisions for fines for non-criminal purpose organizations and the provisions for probation. In both portions, culpability plays a substantial role.

The principle underlying section 8C2 (fines for non-criminal purpose organiza-

tions) is that "the fine range . . . should be based on the seriousness of the offense and the culpability of the organization." The seriousness of an offense is represented by its appropriate "base fine." An organization's culpability depends on its "culpability score." A sentencing judge is directed to start with the base fine, and multiply it by a set of numbers derived from its culpability score to arrive at the "guideline fine range." Adjustments within the range and, in special cases, departures from the range, determine the final fine. . . .

Once the court has determined the base fine, it calculates the organization's culpability score. Convicted organizations begin the sentencing process with a culpability score of five. The score can be raised to as high as ten or reduced to as little as zero by the presence of one or more aggravating or mitigating factors. The four aggravating factors are 1) the involvement in or tolerance of criminal activity by "high level" or "substantial authority" personnel; 2) a recent history of similar misconduct on the part of the organization; 3) violation of a judicial order or condition of probation; and 4) obstruction of justice. The two mitigating factors are 1) the presence of "an effective program to prevent and detect violations of law" on the part of corporate agents and 2) cooperation with law enforcement officials. . . .

The court is entitled to consider both offense seriousness and culpability again once the Guideline fine range is determined. The organization's role in the offense, any prior criminal or civil misconduct that was not taken into account in determining the culpability score, an unusually high or low culpability score, or the presence of any aggravating or mitigating factor may warrant adjustments within the range. . . .

Culpability also plays a major role in section 8D, on probation. The "culpability score" is not referred to explicitly in this section, but several of the aggravating and miti-gating factors from the score re-appear. For organizations with over fifty employees, for example, a court is required to order a term of probation if the organization does not have an effective program to prevent and detect violations of law. Where the organization or a high-level official within the organization recently engaged in similar misconduct, probation is likewise required. . . . But the most significant feature of the probation section is its authorization of intrusion into the organizational decision-making process to change features of the organization that lead to crime. Development of a program to prevent and detect violations of the law, for example, may be made a condition of probation. This "incapacitation" and "rehabilitation" of the organization is predicated on the possibility of organizational culpability.

B. The Organizational Guidelines and the Corporate Character Theory

The Guidelines not only make organizational culpability a central feature of their provisions on fines and probation, they give concrete content to the notion of organizational culpability through the device of the organization's "culpability score." Significantly, the aggravating and mitigating factors in the score include the same features of the organization which serve as the locus for organizational culpability under the corporate character theory: the conduct of high managerial officials, prior history, and corporate policies, customs, and procedures. The Guidelines never explicitly adopt any theory of corporate culpability, and they are not consistent with the corporate character theory in every respect. Nevertheless, the determination of an organization's culpability score under the Guidelines is best understood as an assessment of the character of the organization.

1. Participation of High Managerial Officials. As noted in Part II, corporate character theorists generally agree that some organizational officials are so closely identified with the organization that their acts can be said to represent corporate policy. Where such an official authorizes, participates in, or knowingly tolerates a criminal act on the part of an employee of the organization, the organization is therefore culpable. The Guidelines adopt a similar principle, stating that "an organization is more culpable when individuals who manage the organization or who have substantial discretion in acting for the organization participate in, condone, or are willfully ignorant of criminal conduct." In keeping with this principle, the Guidelines make the participation of high managerial officials an aggravating factor in an organizational offender's culpability score. Depending on the size of the organization, the Guidelines add as many as five points to the score when "an individual within high-level personnel of the organization [or the unit of the organization within which the offense was committed] participated in, condoned, or was willfully ignorant of the offense." The additional five points result in a 100–200% increase in the organization's base fine. "High-level personnel" are defined as

individuals who have substantial control over the organization or who have a substantial role in the making of policy within the organization. The term includes: a director; an executive officer; an individual in charge of a major business or functional unit of the organization . . . an individual with substantial ownership interest.

"High level personnel" are not the only officials whose actions can result in organizational culpability, however. As noted in Part II, even the participation of agents who do not have official authority to make policy may have sufficient de facto authority to "send a message" to other members of the organization that illegal acts "will be countenanced." Whether a given individual has such de facto authority is a difficult, fact-dependent question; nevertheless, an attempt to avoid the issue by adopting a formalistic definition of persons with policy-making authority is likely to result in culpable organizations being judged not at fault. The Guidelines avoid this temptation. Instead, they add as many as five points to an organization's culpability score where "tolerance by substantial authority personnel was pervasive throughout the organization." "Substantial authority personnel" are "individuals who within the scope of their authority exercise a measure of discretion in acting on behalf of the organization.... Whether an individual falls within this category must be determined on a case-by-case basis." "Pervasiveness" depends upon

> the number, and degree of responsibility, of individuals within substantial authority personnel who participated in, condoned, or were willfully ignorant of the offense. Fewer individuals need to be involved for a finding of pervasiveness if those individuals exercised a relatively high degree of authority.

The requirement that tolerance by substantial authority personnel must be "pervasive" before points are added to the culpability score represents an oversimplification, and may result in underestimating the culpability of some organizations. Nevertheless, the Guidelines' approach is consistent with the corporate character theory. When a practice is pervasive, it becomes a way of doing business, part of the organizational decision-making process. It has an influence that it would not have if only a single employee with "substantial authority" had engaged in it. The more "pervasive" tolerance of illegal activity is, in other words, the more likely it is that the activity represents an organizational custom or policy, and the more likely it is that the organization is culpable. . . .

2. Prior History. The question of whether a defendant is a first-time or repeat offender has long been central to the sentencing of individual criminals. Before the advent of the "just deserts" school, information about an offender's prior conduct was considered essential because it enabled the court to determine the need for incapacitation and the offender's susceptibility to rehabilitation. As Andrew von Hirsch points out, however, an offender's past conduct is also relevant to his or her culpability and "desert." A first offender can plausibly argue that an offense was an anomaly, a lone departure from past standards of behavior. The act should not really be attributed to him, the offender can argue, because it was not "in character." After the first offense, however, this claim lacks credibility. Repetition has the effect of "endorsing" the earlier offense. It becomes safe to conclude that subsequent offenses are genuinely a product of the offender's character.

A similar argument can be made in the organizational context. Repeat offenses by an organization suggest that the offenses are not mere anomalies, but were caused by some feature of the organizational entity. Moreover, the fact that the organization has not changed this feature to prevent further offenses indicates that the offenses are consistent with the organization's policy or character. The corporate character theory builds on this insight by holding that repeated misconduct on the part of an organization constitutes a "ratification" or "endorsement" of its agent's criminal acts. Where the organization is a recidivist, its crimes cannot be dismissed as the acts of a "rogue employee."

Consistent with the corporate character theory, the Guidelines take account or prior history by adding one point to the culpability score of an organizational offender if it "committed any part of the instant offense" within ten years after either a "criminal adjudication based on similar misconduct" or a "civil or administrative adjudication based on two or more separate instances of similar misconduct." Two points are added if the instant offense took place within five years of the criminal or civil adjudication. "Similar misconduct" is defined as "prior conduct that is similar in nature to the instant offense, without regard to whether or not such conduct violated the same statutory provision." For example, the Guidelines explain that prior Medicare fraud would constitute misconduct similar to an offense involving another type of fraud. Additional points are added to the culpability score if the offense violated a judicial order, injunction, or condition of probation. . . .

3. Obstruction of Justice and Cooperation with Authorities.

The Guidelines add three points to the organization's culpability score if the organization willfully obstructed justice, attempted to obstruct justice, or failed to prevent obstruction of justice during the investigation, prosecution or sentencing of the organization's offense. This aggravating factor is best understood in conjunction with a mitigating factor of "self-reporting, cooperation, and acceptance of responsibility." An organization that cooperates with prosecutors not only avoids the addition of three points to its culpability score; it may subtract five points from its score if "prior to an imminent threat of disclosure" and "within a reasonably prompt time after becoming aware of the offense, [it] reported the offense to appropriate governmental authorities, fully cooperated in the investigation, and clearly demonstrated recognition and affirmative acceptance of responsibility for its criminal conduct." If the organization did not report the offense, but fully cooperated and demonstrated acceptance of responsibility, it is entitled to subtract two points from its culpability score. Acceptance of responsibility alone entitles the organization to subtract one point from its score.

At first glance, ex-post obstruction of justice and cooperation with authorities seem to have little to do with culpability. The corporate character theory makes no mention of such post-offense behavior. The twin aggravating/mitigating factors seem primarily a way to lower law enforcement costs and increase the likelihood of conviction. By making entry of a guilty plea and admission of involvement in the offense "significant evidence of affirmative acceptance of responsibility," the Guidelines encourage organizations to plead guilty. In addition, self-reporting must be "thorough" in order for the organization to qualify for the mitigation credit, and the Guidelines state that "[a] prime test of whether the organization has disclosed all pertinent information is whether the information is sufficient for law enforcement personnel to identify the nature and extent of the offense and the individual(s) responsible for the criminal conduct." These provisions encourage organizations to uncover violations by their agents and to turn in the individuals responsible.

Nevertheless, cooperation with authorities and acceptance of responsibility are not irrelevant to culpability. They have long been important in the sentencing of individuals. Although cooperation and acceptance of responsibility can involve an admission of guilt, they also express remorse, contrition, and renunciation of the crime. They are thus relevant to the broad-based character assessment of the offender that has traditionally taken place at the sentencing stage. Like the first offender who plausibly argues that his crime is not "in character," the genuinely remorseful criminal distances himself from the commission of the crime and expresses an intent to reform. Obstruction of justice, in contrast, represents a continued identification with and continuation of the crime.

Obstruction of justice and cooperation with authorities are also capable of revealing organizational character. When an organization attempts to conceal a crime, it ratifies it, endorses it, and accepts it as its own. The protection of an employee who has violated the law implies that it is the corporation's policy to support such violations; an organization with a "good" character would likely have disciplined or fired the offending employee. Eliminating a criminal employee from the organizational decision-making process improves the corporate character and represents an important first step in the reform of the organization. . . .

4. Program to Prevent and Detect Violations of the Law. The corporate character theory holds that an organization is at fault, even when there is no involvement by policy-making officials, if an organizational policy or custom causes an agent of the organization to commit a violation on the organization's behalf. The policy or custom need not have been formally adopted, nor is it necessary for the policy itself to be illegal. Rather, a corporation is justly to blame for the illegal act of an agent whenever it was reasonably foreseeable that a corporate policy or practice would lead to the crime. The Guidelines provide no aggravating factor for offenses that are caused by organizational policy or custom. Instead, they appear to assume a causal link between policy and offense, and offer the organization the opportunity to rebut this assumption. To do so, the organization must show that the offense occurred, "despite an effective program to prevent and detect violations of law." If it is successful, three points are subtracted from its culpability score. . . .

CONCLUSION

Although corporations cannot be culpable in the same way that individuals can, this Article has argued that there is a sense in which they may be "justly held to blame" for the acts of their agents. Corporate crime is not always the result of individual choice. Often, it is the product of goals, rules, policies and procedures that are features of the organization as an entity. By substituting an organizational decision-making process for its agents' individual autonomy, the corporation shapes and controls their behavior. When this process is likely to result in violations on behalf of the corporation on the part of its agents, the corporate entity may be said to be at fault.

Corporate criminal law has generally failed to take adequate account of the culpability of the corporate entity. The principal doctrine of corporate criminal liability, that of respondeat superior, works by imputing to the corporation the culpability of the agent who committed the crime. The *Model Penal Code's* location of corporate culpability in the participation of high managerial officials is more promising, but ultimately too narrow. The lack of a coherent theory of corporate culpability at the trial stage results in the risk that some corporations will be held liable even when they are not culpable, and, conversely, that some culpable corporations will succeed in evading liability. At the sentencing stage, failure to recognize corporate culpability has led to an impoverished vision of the range of sentencing options and of the purposes of corporate sentencing.

The Federal Sentencing Guidelines for organizations represent a significant advance over the current treatment of corporate culpability in the criminal law. In a marked departure from tradition, the Guidelines give culpability an explicit and important role in organizational sentencing. They flesh out the concept of organizational culpability concretely through the device of the culpability score. The Guidelines employ a version of the most theoretically satisfying of three competing theories of corporate culpability, the "corporate character theory." The theory builds on the insights of organizational scholars by holding that an organization is culpable when its policies, customs and procedures — features of the organizational character — cause its agents to violate the law on its behalf. Adopting the corporate character theory, I have argued, makes it possible for the Guidelines to employ innovative organizational sentencing strategies and to pursue the full range of sentencing aims. . . .

NOTES

1. Herbert A. Simon, *Administrative Behavior* 8 (3d ed. 1976).
2. Martin Needleman & Carolyn Needleman, *Organizational Crime: Two Models of Criminogenesis*, 20 Soc. Q. 517 (1979). *See also* Marshall B. Clinard & Peter C. Yeager, Corporate Crime 58–60, 63–67 (1980) (cultural norms of the corporation can encourage criminal behavior); Laura S. Schrager & James R. Short, Jr., *Toward a Sociology of Organizational Crime*, 25 Soc. Probs. 407, 410 (1978) (criminal behavior is caused more by roles assigned to members of the corporation than by personalities of the members); Note, *Increasing Community Control over Corporate Crime — A Problem in the Law of Sanctions*, 71 Yale L.J. 280, 282 (1961)

(goal of criminal acts by members of corporations is frequently enrichment of the corporation rather than of individuals).
3. *See, e.g.,* Terence E. Deal & Allen A. Kennedy, Corporate Cultures (1982); Thomas J. Peters & Robert H. Waterman, Jr., In Search of Excellence (1982); Christopher D. Stone, Where the Law Ends, 228–48 (1975). Although the corporate culture is strongly influenced by top management, it is independent of it. Clinard and Yeager argue that corporate executives "are subject . . . to the same kinds of indoctrination into the corporate mind as are employees at lower levels." Clinard & Yeager, *supra* note 58, at 66.
4. Stone, *supra* note 59, at 237. Stone discusses a study finding that coal mines owned by steel firms have significantly better worker safety records than coal mines owned by coal mining companies. One of the most commonly given explanations for the discrepancy, he reports, is simply a difference in attitude between steel companies and coal companies: "[t]he steel companies have just not evolved what was called 'a "coal mentality"' that accepts a great loss of life and limb as the price of digging coal." *Id.* at 238 (citing *Coal-Mines Study Shows Record Can Be Improved When Firms Really Try*, Wall St. J., Jan. 18, 1973, at p. 1, col. 6).
5. Stone, *supra* note 59, at 7.

Licensee Responsibility to Review Records Before Their Broadcast

A number of complaints received by the Commission concerning the lyrics of records played on broadcasting stations relate to a subject of current and pressing concern: the use of language tending to promote or glorify the use of illegal drugs as marijuana, LSD, "speed," etc. This Notice points up the

licensee's long-established responsibilities in this area.

Whether a particular record depicts the dangers of drug abuse, or, to the contrary, promotes such illegal drug usage is a question for the judgment of the licensee. The thrust of this Notice is simply that the li-

Public Notice of March 5, 1971, 28 F.C.C. 2d 409. Commission decision with statements by Robert E. Lee and H. Rex Lee, Federal Communications Commission.

censee must make that judgment and cannot properly follow a policy of playing such records without someone in a responsible position (i.e., a management level executive at the station) knowing the content of the lyrics. Such a pattern of operation is clearly a violation of the basic principle of the licensee's responsibility for, and duty to exercise adequate control over, the broadcast material presented over his station. It raises serious questions as to whether continued operation of the station is in the public interest, just as in the case of a failure to exercise adequate control over foreign-language programs.

In short, we expect broadcast licensees to ascertain, before broadcast, the words or lyrics of recorded musical or spoken selections played on their stations. Just as in the case of the foreign-language broadcasts, this may also entail reasonable efforts to ascertain the meaning of words or phrases used in the lyrics. While this duty may be delegated by licensees to responsible employees, the licensee remains fully responsible for its fulfillment.

Thus, here as in so many other areas, it is a question of responsible, good faith action by the public trustee to whom the frequency has been licensed. No more, but certainly no less, is called for.

Action by the Commission February 24, 1971. Commissioners Burch (Chairman), Wells and Robert E. Lee with Commissioner Lee issuing a statement, Commissioners H. Rex Lee and Houser concurring and issuing statements, Commissioner Johnson dissenting and issuing a statement, and Commissioner Bartley abstaining from voting.

STATEMENT OF COMMISSIONER ROBERT E. LEE

I sincerely hope that the action of the Commission today in releasing a "Public Notice" with respect to *Licensee Responsibility to Review Records Before Their Broadcast* will discourage, if not eliminate, the playing of records which tend to promote and/or glorify the use of illegal drugs.

We are all aware of the deep concern in our local communities with respect to the use of illegal drugs particularly among the younger segment of our population. Public officials, at all levels of government, as well as all interested citizens are attempting to cope with this problem.

It is in this context that I expect the Broadcast Industry to meet its responsibilities of reviewing records before they are played. Obviously, if such records promote the use of illegal drugs, the licensee will exercise appropriate judgment in determining whether the broadcasting of such records is in the public interest.

CONCURRING STATEMENT OF COMMISSIONER H. REX LEE

While the title of the notice seemingly applies to the licensee's responsibility to review all records before they are broadcast, the notice itself is directed solely at records which allegedly use "language tending to promote or glorify the use of illegal drugs. . . ."

Although I am concurring, I would have preferred it if the Commission had not decided to restrict today's notice to so-called "drug lyrics." The Commission may appear to many young people as not being so concerned with other pressing broadcasting problem areas. And to many of these young people (and not just to that segment who use illegal drugs) the Commission may appear as "an ominous government agency" merely out to clamp down on *their* music.

A preferable approach would have been to repeat, with an additional reference to drug abuse of all kinds, our 1960 *Program Policy Statement* wherein we stated:

Broadcast licensees must assure responsibility for all material which is broadcast through their facilities. *This includes all programs and advertising material which they present to the public. . . .* This duty is personal to the licensee and may not be delegated. He is obligated to bring his positive responsibility affirmatively to bear upon all who have a hand in providing broadcast material for transmission through his facilities so as to assure the discharge of his duty to provide acceptable program schedule consonant with operating in the public interest in his community.[1] [Emphasis added.]

Because of the Commission's expressed concern with the drug problem, I would hope that we could initiate action with other appropriate Federal agencies to require a reassessment by pharmaceutical manufacturers, advertisers, and the media, looking toward the reform of advertising practices in the non-prescription drug industry. *Advertising Age* expressed its concern with the increased use of drugs — both the legal and illegal types — when it stated in an editorial:

With an estimated $289,000,000 being spent annually on TV advertising of medicines, this serious question is being raised: Is the flood of advertising for such medicines so pervasive that it is convincing viewers that there is a medical panacea for any and all of their problems, medical and otherwise? Are we being so consistently bombarded with pills for this and pills for that and pills for the other thing that we have developed a sort of Pavlovian reaction which makes us reach for a pill everytime we are faced with

an anxious moment, be it of physical or psychic origin?[2]

Drug abuse *is* a serious problem in the United States. It is found in every sector of the population, not merely among the young who listen to hard rock music.

I believe the broadcasting industry has made a good start in helping to discourage illegal drug abuse. Many local radio and television stations and the four networks have broadcast documentaries and specials, carried spot announcements, helped to raise funds for local drug abuse clinics and information centers, and have helped to establish "tie-lines" and "switchboards" where all people can call for free medical and psychological help and guidance. These activities represent "communicating" in the best sense of the word.

My concurrence in this notice, therefore, should not be regarded as a reflection on the good start that I think that most broadcasters have made in dealing with this problem. They must continue with even more determination and support from everyone.

NOTES

1. *Report and Statement of Policy re: Commission En Banc Programming Inquiry,* FCC 60–970, 20 R.R. 1901, 1912–1913 (July 27, 1960).
2. *Advertising Age* (May 11, 1970), p. 24.

product, it must have established standards and procedures designed to prevent fraud.

(iii) Prior history of the organization — An organization's prior history may indicate types of offenses that it should have taken actions to prevent. Recurrence of misconduct similar to that which an organization has previously committed casts doubt on whether it took all reasonable steps to prevent such misconduct.

An organization's failure to incorporate and follow applicable industry practice or the standards called for by any applicable governmental regulation weighs against a finding of an effective program to prevent and detect violations of law.

PART B — REMEDYING HARM FROM CRIMINAL CONDUCT

Introductory Commentary

As a general principle, the court should require that the organization take all appropriate steps to provide compensation to victims and otherwise remedy the harm caused or threatened by the offense. A restitution order or an order of probation requiring restitution can be used to compensate identifiable victims of the offense. A remedial order or an order of probation requiring community service can be used to reduce or eliminate the harm threatened, or to repair the harm caused by the offense, when that harm or threatened harm would otherwise not be remedied. An order of notice to victims can be used to notify unidentified victims of the offense. . . .

* * *

2. Determining the Fine — Other Organizations

* * *

§8C2.4. Base Fine

(a) The base fine is the greatest of:
   (1) the amount from the table in subsection (d) below corresponding to the offense

level determined under §8C2.3 (Offense Level); or
(2) the pecuniary gain to the organization from the offense; or
(3) the pecuniary loss from the offense caused by the organization, to the extent the loss was caused intentionally, knowingly, or recklessly.

(b) *Provided,* that if the applicable offense guideline in Chapter Two includes a special instruction for organizational fines, that special instruction shall be applied, as appropriate.

(c) *Provided, further,* that to the extent the calculation of either pecuniary gain or pecuniary loss would unduly complicate or prolong the sentencing process, that amount, *i.e.,* gain or loss as appropriate, shall not be used for the determination of the base fine.

(d)

Offense Level Fine Table

Offense Level	Amount
6 or less	$5,000
7	$7,500
8	$10,000
9	$15,000
10	$20,000
11	$30,000
12	$40,000
13	$60,000
14	$85,000
15	$125,000
16	$175,000
17	$250,000
18	$350,000
19	$500,000
20	$650,000
21	$910,000
22	$1,200,000
23	$1,600,000
24	$2,100,000
25	$2,800,000
26	$3,700,000
27	$4,800,000
28	$6,300,000
29	$8,100,000
30	$10,500,000
31	$13,500,000
32	$17,500,000
33	$22,000,000
34	$28,500,000

35	$36,000,000
36	$45,500,000
37	$57,500,000
38 or more	$72,500,000

* * *

§8C2.5. Culpability Score

(a) Start with 5 points and apply subsections (b) through (g) below.

(b) Involvement in or Tolerance of Criminal Activity

If more than one applies, use the greatest:

(1) If —
(A) the organization had 5,000 or more employees and
(i) an individual within high-level personnel of the organization participated in, condoned, or was willfully ignorant of the offense; or
(ii) tolerance of the offense by substantial authority personnel was pervasive throughout the organization; or
(B) the unit of the organization within which the offense was committed had 5,000 or more employees and
(i) an individual within high-level personnel of the unit participated in, condoned, or was willfully ignorant of the offense; or
(ii) tolerance of the offense by substantial authority personnel was pervasive throughout such unit,
add 5 points; or

(2) If —
(A) the organization had 1,000 or more employees and
(i) an individual within high-level personnel of the organization participated in, condoned, or was willfully ignorant of the offense; or
(ii) tolerance of the offense by substantial authority personnel was pervasive throughout the organization; or
(B) the unit of the organization within which the offense was committed had 1,000 or more employees and
(i) an individual within high-level personnel of the unit partici-

pated in, condoned, or was willfully ignorant of the offense; or
(ii) tolerance of the offense by substantial authority personnel was pervasive throughout such unit,
add 4 points; or

(3) If —
(A) the organization had 200 or more employees and
(i) an individual within high-level personnel of the organization participated in, condoned, or was willfully ignorant of the offense; or
(ii) tolerance of the offense by substantial authority personnel was pervasive throughout the organization; or
(B) the unit of the organization within which the offense was committed had 200 or more employees and
(i) an individual within high-level personnel of the unit participated in, condoned, or was willfully ignorant of the offense; or
(ii) tolerance of the offense by substantial authority personnel was pervasive throughout such unit,
add 3 points; or

(4) If the organization had 50 or more employees and an individual within substantial authority personnel participated in, condoned, or was willfully ignorant of the offense, add 2 points; or

(5) If the organization had 10 or more employees and an individual within substantial authority personnel participated in, condoned, or was willfully ignorant of the offense, add 1 point.

(c) Prior History

If more than one applies, use the greater:

(1) If the organization (or separately managed line of business) committed any part of the instant offense less than 10 years after (A) a criminal adjudication based on similar misconduct; or (B) civil or administrative adjudication(s) based on two or more separate instances of similar misconduct, add 1 point; or

(2) If the organization (or separately managed line of business) committed any part of the instant offense

less than 5 years after (A) a criminal adjudication based on similar misconduct; or (B) civil or administrative adjudication(s) based on two or more separate instances of similar misconduct, add 2 points.

(d) Violation of an Order

If more than one applies, use the greater:

(1) (A) If the commission of the instant offense violated a judicial order or injunction, other than a violation of a condition of probation; or (B) if the organization (or separately managed line of business) violated a condition of probation by engaging in similar misconduct, *i.e.,* misconduct similar to that for which it was placed on probation, add 2 points; or

(2) If the commission of the instant offense violated a condition of probation, add 1 point.

(e) Obstruction of Justice

If the organization willfully obstructed or impeded, attempted to obstruct or impede, or aided, abetted, or encouraged obstruction of justice during the investigation, prosecution, or sentencing of the instant offense, or, with knowledge thereof, failed to take reasonable steps to prevent such obstruction or impedance or attempted obstruction or impedance, add 3 points.

(f) Effective Program to Prevent and Detect Violations of Law

If the offense occurred despite an effective program to prevent and detect violations of law, subtract 3 points.

Provided, that this subsection does not apply if an individual within high-level personnel of the organization, a person within high-level personnel of the unit of the organization within which the offense was committed where the unit had 200 or more employees, or an individual responsible for the administration or enforcement of a program to prevent and detect violations of law participated in, condoned, or was willfully ignorant of the offense. Participation of an individual within substantial authority personnel in an offense results in a rebuttable presumption that the organization did not have an effective program to prevent and detect violations of law.

Provided, further, that this subsection does not apply if, after becoming aware of an offense,

the organization unreasonably delayed reporting the offense to appropriate governmental authorities.

(g) Self-Reporting, Cooperation, and Acceptance of Responsibility

If more than one applies, use the greatest:

(1) If the organization (A) prior to an imminent threat of disclosure or government investigation; and (B) within a reasonably prompt time after becoming aware of the offense, reported the offense to appropriate governmental authorities, fully cooperated in the investigation, and clearly demonstrated recognition and affirmative acceptance of responsibility for its criminal conduct, subtract 5 points; or

(2) If the organization fully cooperated in the investigated and clearly demonstrated recognition and affirmative acceptance of responsibility for its criminal conduct, subtract 2 points; or

(3) If the organization clearly demonstrated recognition and affirmative acceptance of responsibility for its criminal conduct, subtract 1 point. . . .

§8C.2.6. Minimum and Maximum Multipliers

Using the culpability score from §8C2.5 (Culpability Score) and applying any applicable special instruction for fines in Chapter Two, determine the applicable minimum and maximum fine multipliers from the table below.

Culpability Score	Minimum Multiplier	Maximum Multiplier
10 or more	2.00	4.00
9	1.80	3.60
8	1.60	3.20
7	1.40	2.80
6	1.20	2.40
5	1.00	2.00
4	0.80	1.60
3	0.60	1.20
2	0.40	0.80
1	0.20	0.40
0 or less	0.05	0.20

* * *

§8C2.8. Determining the Fine Within the Range (Policy Statement)

(a) In determining the amount of the fine within the applicable guideline range, the court should consider:

(1) the need for the sentence to reflect the seriousness of the offense, promote respect for the law, provide just punishment, afford adequate deterrence, and protect the public from further crimes of the organization;

(2) the organization's role in the offense;

(3) any collateral consequences of conviction, including civil obligations arising from the organization's conduct;

(4) any nonpecuniary loss caused or threatened by the offense;

(5) whether the offense involved a vulnerable victim;

(6) any prior criminal record of an individual within high-level personnel of the organization or high-level personnel of a unit of the organization who participated in, condoned, or was willfully ignorant of the criminal conduct;

(7) any prior civil or criminal misconduct by the organization other than that counted under §8C2.5(c);

(8) any culpability score under §8C2.5 (Culpability Score) higher than 10 or lower than 0;

(9) partial but incomplete satisfaction of the conditions for one or more of the mitigating or aggravating factors set forth in §8C2.5 (Culpability Score); and

(10) any factor listed in 18 U.S.C. § 3572(a).

(b) In addition, the court may consider the relative importance of any factor used to determine the range, including the pecuniary loss caused by the offense, the pecuniary gain from the offense, any specific offense characteristic used to determine the offense level, and any aggravating or mitigating factor used to determine the culpability score.

CASE 1. *The Advertising Code Case*

The Advertising Code of American Business was part of a program of industry self-regulation announced 28, September, 1971. This program arose in response to mounting public criticism of the advertising industry, to more aggressive action by federal regulatory agencies, and to fear of even greater government control in the future.

In announcing the new program of self-regulation, enforcement was emphasized. Complaints are received or initiated by the National Advertising Division (NAD) of the Council of Better Business Bureaus. During the first year, 337 complaints were placed on the table. Of these 337, investigations were completed on 184. Seventy-two of those complaints were upheld. In every case, the advertiser either agreed to withdraw the objectionable ad or to modify it. Six of the cases which were dismissed were appealed to a higher body, the National Advertising Review Board. Of the six cases, the NARB accepted the decision of the NAD in four cases, but agreed with two complaints. In these two cases, the challenged ads were withdrawn. All complaints were settled within several months. Supporters of the NAD applaud their time record for handling complaints as compared with frequent delays of several years in federal suits.*

---

*These figures may be found in Howard H. Bell's "Self-Regulation by the Advertising Industry," in *The Unstable Ground: Corporate Social Policy in a Dynamic Society,* ed. S. Prakash Sethi (Los Angeles: Melville Publishing Company, 1974).

Adapted from "Advertising Code of American Business," 1971. Reprinted by permission of the American Advertising Federation and the author, Norman E. Bowie.

The Advertising Code of American Business reads as follows:

1. *Truth.* Advertising shall tell the truth, and shall reveal significant facts, the concealment of which would mislead the public.
2. *Responsibility.* Advertising agencies and advertisers shall be willing to provide substantiation of claims made.
3. *Taste and Decency.* Advertising shall be free of statements, illustrations or implications which are offensive to good taste or public decency.
4. *Bait Advertising.* Advertising shall offer only merchandise or services which are readily available for purchase at the advertised price.
5. *Guarantees and Warranties.* Advertising of guarantees and warranties shall be explicit. Advertising of any guarantee or warranty shall clearly and conspicuously disclose its nature and extent, the manner in which the guarantor or warrantor will perform, and the identity of the guarantor or warrantor.
6. *Price Claims.* Advertising shall avoid price or savings claims which are false or misleading, or which do not offer provable bargains or savings.
7. *Unprovable Claims.* Advertising shall avoid the use of exaggerated or unprovable claims.
8. *Testimonials.* Advertising containing testimonials shall be limited to those of competent witnesses who are reflecting a real and honest choice.

Questions

1. How should rule 7 which forbids exaggerated claims be interpreted?
2. Is the set of rules comprehensive enough to forbid deceptive advertising?
3. Evaluate the described enforcement mechanism. Suggest improvements if you think any are needed.
4. Is the rule on "taste and decency" too broad and amorphous?

CASE 2.   *Beech-Nut Corporation*

Beech-Nut Corporation was the second-largest baby food company in the United States. It was founded in 1891 and was incorporated in the state of Pennsylvania. The company primarily produced and distributed baby food and dietetic specialty products. Over the years, Beech-Nut had built a reputation on purity, high-quality products, and natural ingredients. Because of competition and other difficulties, however, Beech-Nut was eventually forced to reduce its product line to a single product, which was baby food. This product line, unfortunately, had almost never turned a profit.[1] Its market share in 1977 was only 15 percent compared with a 70 percent market share attained by the Gerber company, its major competitor. By 1978, Beech-Nut, burdened with losses, owed millions of dollars to suppliers and was under great financial pressure.[2]

To cope with the threat of insolvency, Beech-Nut executives switched to a supplier that offered apple juice concentrate at a price 20 percent below market. At that time, rumors of apple juice adulteration had already spread in the industry, and therefore the purchase of concentrate at 20 percent below market raised suspicions among the employees in Beech-Nut's Research and Development Department.[3] In 1977, tests by a

This case was prepared by Rogene Buchholz of Loyola University, New Orleans, and reprinted from *Business Environment and Public Policy,* Prentice Hall, 1992.

company-hired laboratory suggested that the cheap apple concentrate that Beech-Nut bought from Universal Juice Company might be adulterated. The company, however, continued to claim that its products contained no artificial ingredients.

In 1981, Jerome J. LiCari, director of research and development at Beech-Nut, mounted a major drive to improve adulteration testing. He found that the apple juice concentrate Beech-Nut was buying to use in its juice and other products was a blend of beet sugar, cane syrup, and other synthetic ingredients. With this fresh evidence, LiCari informed Niels Hoyvald and John Lavery, then president and vice-president of Beech-Nut, respectively, that the concentrate was bogus, and he suggested getting another concentrate supplier. He believed that continuing to deal with Universal could jeopardize the productline restructuring that Beech-Nut was planning, which would emphasize nutritional values and the absence of artificial ingredients in its products.[4] Despite LiCari's efforts, Hoyvald and Lavery took no action, and the company continued to produce and distribute adulterated apple juice under the label "100% fruit juice."

In 1982, federal and state agencies started investigations and established that Universal's concentrate was bogus. Beech-Nut immediately canceled its apple concentrate contracts, but it continued to distribute millions of bottles of "fake" apple juice at deep discounts in the U.S. market as well as other parts of the world. Despite warnings from the Food and Drug Administration and the New York State Agriculture Department, Beech-Nut did not issue a national apple juice recall until late October of the year and continued to unload its $3.5 million of inventory of adulterated apple juice. This behavior gave the prosecutors reason to believe that the company's main concern was making money even if it meant selling a phony product.[5]

NOTES

1. Chris Welles, "What Led Beech-Nut Down the Road to Disgrace." *Business Week,* February 22, 1988, p. 125.
2. Ibid.
3. Ibid.
4. Ibid., p. 125.
5. Leonard Burder, "Two Former Executives of Beech-Nut Guilty in Phony Juice Case," *Wall Street Journal,* February 18, 1988, p. D-3.

Questions

1. After reporting his findings to Hoyvald and Lavery, did LiCari have any additional moral responsibility to expose the distribution of the adulterated apple juice?
2. In what ways is LiCari's position as director of research and development at Beech-Nut similar to Boisjoly's at Morton Thiokol? To the engineers in charge of the Ford Pinto?
3. Who is responsible for distribution of the adulterated apple juice in 1977? In 1981?
4. Evaluate the options available to LiCari after he reported his findings to Beech-Nut's senior management.

Suggested Supplementary Readings

ACQUAAH, KWAMENA. *International Regulation of Transnational Corporations.* New York: Praeger, 1986.

ARTHUR, E. EUGENE. "The Ethics of Corporate Governance." *Journal of Business Ethics* 6 (January 1987): 59–70.

BARAM, MICHAEL S. *Alternatives to Regulation.* Lexington, MA: Lexington Books, 1981.

BROOKS, LEONARD, J. "Ethical Codes of Conduct: Deficient in Guidance for Canadian Accounting Profession." *Journal of Business Ethics* 8 (May 1989): 325–35.

————. "Corporate Codes of Conduct." *Journal of Business Ethics* 8 (February–March 1989): 117–29.

CORLETT, J. ANGELO. "Corporate Responsibility and Punishment." *Public Affairs Quarterly* 2 (January 1988): 1–16.

DAVIS, MICHAEL. "Technical Decisions: Time to Rethink the Engineer's Responsibilities?" 11 (Fall–Winter 1992): 41–55.

DE GEORGE, RICHARD T. "GM and Corporate Responsibility." *Journal of Business Ethics* 5 (June 1986): 177–79.

GARRETT, JAN EDWARD. "Unredistributable Corporate Moral Responsibility." *Journal of Business Ethics* 8 (July 1989): 535–45.

GETZ, KATHLEEN A. International Codes of Conduct: An Analysis of Ethical Reasoning." *Journal of Business Ethics* 9 (July 1990): 567–77.

GRUNDER, RICHARD S. "Just Punishment and Adequate Deterrence for Organizational Misconduct: Scaling Economic Penalties Under the New Corporate Sentencing Guidelines." *Southern California Law Review* 66 (1993): 225–88.

HILL, IVAN. *The Ethical Basis of Economic Freedom.* Chapel Hill, NC: American Viewpoint Inc., 1975.

HOFFMAN, W. MICHAEL, JENNIFER MILLS MOORE, and DAVID FEDO, eds. *Corporate Governance and Institutionalizing Ethics.* Lexington, MA: Lexington Books, 1984.

JAMAL, KARIM, and NORMAN E. BOWIE. "Theoretical Considerations for a Meaningful Code of Professional Ethics." *Journal of Business Ethics* 14 (September 1995): 703–14.

MATHEWS, M. C. "Codes of Ethics: Organizational Behaviour and Misbehaviour." *Research in Corporate Social Performance* 9 (1987): 107–30.

MITNICK, BARRY M. *The Political Economy of Regulation.* New York: Columbia University Press, 1980.

MURPHY, PATRICK M. "Corporate Ethics Statements: Current Status and Future Prospects." *Journal of Business Ethics* 14 (September 1995): 727–40.

NAGEL, ILENE H., and WINTHROP W. SWENSON. "The Federal Sentencing Guidelines For Corporations: Their Development, Theoretical Underpinnings, and Some Thoughts About Their Future." *Washington University Law Quarterly* 71 (1993): 205–59.

NIELSEN, RICHARD P. "What Can Managers Do About Unethical Management?" *Journal of Business Ethics* 6 (May 1987): 309–20.

PHILLIPS, MICHAEL J. "Corporate Moral Responsibility." *Business Ethics Quarterly* 5 (July 1995): 555–76.

STONE, CHRISTOPHER D. *Where the Law Ends: The Social Control of Corporate Behavior.* New York: Harper and Row, 1975.

WEIDENBAUM, MURRAY L. *The Future of Business Regulation.* New York: AMACON, 1979.

WERHANE, PATRICIA H. "Engineers and Management: The Challenge of the *Challenger* Incident." *Journal of Business Ethics* 10 (August 1991): 605–16.

Chapter Four

———— • ————

Acceptable Risk

GOVERNMENT IS CONSTITUTED to protect citizens from risk to the environment, risk from external invasion, risk to health, risk from crime, risk from fire, risk of highway accidents, and similar risks. A natural extension of this idea is that the social contract obligates government to protect citizens against risks to health, bodily safety, financial security, and the environment. However, society has not yet decided on the extent to which government should restrain business activities in order to protect health, safety, financial security, and environmental interests.

Corporate activities present several types of risk of harm. This chapter concentrates on judgments of acceptable risk for consumers, workers, investors, and the environment. We focus more on the responsibilities of business and methods for reducing risk and less on the nature and types of harm caused. These risk-reduction methods include disclosure of information about risks as well as risk-reduction techniques.

NATURE AND TYPES OF RISK

The Nature of Harm

Competing conceptions of harm exist, but Joel Feinberg has supplied this useful working definition:

> [Interests] can be blocked or defeated by events in impersonal nature or by plain bad luck. But they can only be "invaded" by human beings, . . . singly, or in groups and organizations. . . . One person harms another in the present sense, then, by invading, and thereby thwarting or setting back, his interest. The test . . . of whether such an invasion has in fact set back an interest is whether that interest is in a worse condition than it would otherwise have been in had the invasion not occurred at all. . . . Not all invasions of interest are wrongs, since some actions invade another's interests excusably or justifiably, or invade interests that the other has no right to have respected.[1]

Causing a setback to interests in health, financial goals, or the environment can constitute a harm without necessarily being an unjustifiable harm. Almost everyone would agree that harming another person's interests is blameworthy if the harm results in little compensating benefit and if the damage could easily be avoided. But people rarely, if ever, experience such a clear and uncomplicated scenario. Benefits that offset risk usually exist, and the risk of harm is often expensive to eliminate or control. Some heated debates over products that appeared to be harmful — for example, presweetened children's cereals — have shown that they also create benefits. In the workplace it has become increasingly difficult simply to banish dangerous chemicals that provide major social benefits. In each case their risks must be weighed against their benefits.

Kinds of Risk

Different kinds of risk raise distinct issues. For example, risks of psychological harm, physical harm, legal harm, and economic harm require different analyses and different remedies. Some representative risks pertinent to the material in this chapter are the following:

Risks to Consumers (and Their Families)

Prepared foods (increased fat and sugar)
Drugs (side effects such as gastrointestinal bleeding)
Cigarettes (lung cancer)

Risks to Workers (and Their Families)

Benzene (leukemia)
Asbestos (asbestosis)
Lead (impairment of reproductive capacities)

Risks to the Public and the Environment

Coal-dust emissions (respiratory complications)
Carbon and other fuel emissions (respiratory complications)
Toxic chemicals (genetic defects)

Risks to Investors

Savings accounts (decline in the rate of return)
Stocks (decline of principal)
Real estate (loss of liquidity)

Problems of Risk Assessment

Society has not yet adequately grasped the extent of the risks inherent in thousands of toxic chemicals, foods, drugs, energy sources, machines, and environmental emissions. Some elements have serious, irreversible consequences; others do not. Moreover, the *probability* of exposure to a risk may be known with some precision, whereas virtually nothing may be known about the harm's *magnitude;* or the magnitude may be precisely expressible, whereas the probability remains too indefinite to be calculated accurately. "Wild guess" sometimes best describes the accuracy with which physical and chemical risks may be determined, for example, for a worker who constantly changes locations, who works with multiple toxic substances, and whose physical problems can be attributed in part to factors independent of the workplace, such as smoking.

PRODUCT SAFETY AND RISK TO CONSUMERS

We all consume products that carry minor, significant, or unknown risks. No household is complete without several dozen potentially hazardous products, including ovens, electrical lines, furniture cleaners, spray paints, insecticides, medicines, and video display terminals. Millions of people in North America are the victims of household and office accidents involving these products every year, and more of our young people die from failures and accidents involving products than from disease. Thousands of lawsuits are filed by businesses against other businesses each year because of product failure, hazard, and harm, and there are related problems about deceptive marketing practices and inadequate warranties.

Some responsibility for the occurrence of these harms rests primarily on the consumer, who may carelessly use products or fail to read clearly written instructions. However, some risks can be described as inherent in the product: A cautious and reasonable judgment of acceptable risk has been made that the product cannot be made less risky without unduly increasing cost or limiting use. Still other problems of risk derive from use of cheap materials, careless design, poor construction, or new discovery about risk in an already marketed product.

Disclosure of Risk Information

A consumer presumably controls what to purchase, because the seller must satisfy consumers or fail to sell the product and be driven from the market; yet serious questions exist about whether the information supplied to the consumer is adequate for making an informed and free choice. For example, is a customer told how a kerosene heater should be cleaned and stored and how often new filters should be installed? Are the side effects of a drug disclosed when a prescription is filled? Sellers may list only a minimal set of facts about known hazards, especially regarding technologically advanced products, because a seller attempts to sell in the most cost-effective manner. Disclosure of risk information costs money and adversely affects sales. Thus, the seller has an economic incentive to keep disclosure to a selective minimum.

These topics of disclosure and understanding have been under intense discussion in recent years. By the late 1970s a major right-to-know movement had taken hold in consumer affairs and in the U.S. workplace. Numerous laws were passed, notably the Consumer Product Safety Act of 1972, to protect consumers by setting safety standards, examining consumer product marketing, providing more adequate risk information, and upgrading the quality of warranty statements.

Product Safety and Quality Control

Quality control supplements disclosure of risk information as a strategy to protect consumers. Corporations such as Johns Manville (asbestos) and A. H. Robins (the Dalkon Shield) have faced massive product liability judgments. Although higher standards of quality control would also protect manufacturers, both theoretical and practical problems exist in establishing and enforcing such standards. Consumer protection methods incur significant costs that increase product price and frequently force companies to abandon the market. For example, some lawn mower prices almost doubled after the introduction of new safety requirements, with the result that several companies floundered. Liberty issues are also at stake. For instance, the freedom to put a new "junk food" on the market might be jeopardized (in theory, the freedom to produce junk foods would be eliminated), and the freedom to buy cheap, substandard products would be lost (because they could not be marketed).

These quality control controversies raise questions about liability and manufacturer warranties, discussed in this chapter in *Henningsen v. Bloomfield Motors and Chrysler Corporation*. In this case, the court held both Chrysler and the car dealer liable for an injury caused by a defective steering gear, without finding any evidence of negligence. The court argued that an implied warranty of suitability for use is owed the purchaser and contended that a major assumption behind free-market "contracting" — bargaining among equals — can be questioned when products prove to be defective. Because the *Henningsen* case cast doubt on the efficacy of disclaimers by manufacturers, it quickly came to be applied to many products, including glass doors, guns, and stoves.

Manuel G. Velasquez considers in his essay how to differentiate between the obligations of consumers to themselves and the obligations of manufacturers to consumers. He distinguishes three theories of business obligations, showing that each strikes a different balance between consumer and manufacturer obligations. The first theory rests on an account of the social contract between consumers and business (under which Velasquez cites *Henningsen* as a classic example), and the second theory provides a theory of due care. The third theory presents an account of strict liability, a discussion of which follows.

Liability for Harm

Two tests affecting liability are that professionals should conform to the minimally acceptable professional standards and that they should perform any actions that a reasonably prudent person would perform in the circumstances. Sometimes even when the utmost care has been exercised, an accident, lack of information, or lack of documents might still cause harm. However, if due care has been exercised to make a product safe (and affected parties have been apprised of known risks), it would appear that a business is not at fault for any harm caused, even if the business helped bring about the harm.

This rule suggests that a manufacturer can be held liable for unsafe or ineffi-cacious products or unsafe workplaces only if the manufacturer knew or *should have known* about the risks involved. However, difficulties arise regarding what an employer or manufacturer "should have known." A product or technique may be so thoroughly researched and thus delayed that the time involved will ensure a manufacturer's loss rather than profit. Should businesses be held to this kind of economic risk? If so, how can it be determined that enough research and develop-ment had been carried out? Can the problem be handled through adequate insur-ance? Or is a modified conception of liability needed?

Some argue that manufacturers should be held liable not only to a standard of prudent behavior but also to a stronger standard: liability for injuries caused to parties by defects in the manufacturing process, even if the manufacturer exer-cised due diligence and still could not have reasonably foreseen the problem. This principle is referred to as *strict product liability*, that is, liability without fault. Here questions of good faith, negligence, and absence of knowledge are not pertinent to a determination of liability. The advocates of this no-fault principle use primarily utilitarian arguments. They maintain that manufacturers are in the best position to pay and recover the costs of injury because they can pass the costs on through the product's price and, moreover, will have the added benefit of increasing manufac-turers' objectivity, diligence, and prudence before marketing a product. This argu-ment constitutes a shift from the traditional doctrine of "let the buyer beware" (*caveat emptor*) to "let the seller beware."

This utilitarian justification is controversial and is assessed in this chapter by George G. Brenkert, who thinks it more important to ask whether strict liability conforms to principles of justice, and in particular, whether it is just to ask manu-facturers to bear the cost of injury merely because they are in the best position to do so. Brenkert maintains that in a free market society it is just to use strict liability because it is essential to maintain a consumer's equal opportunity to function.

PROTECTING INVESTORS AGAINST FINANCIAL RISK

Many of the problems regarding risk of economic harm to consumers apply equally well to investors. At issue is a complex set of relationships encompassing problems of conflict of interest as well as problems of deception and manipulation through improper disclosures. Brokerages houses, money managers, and investment counselors demand as much freedom as possible to deal with their clients. The time spent making disclosures to customers is uncompensated and restricted by business requirements. Brokers with a large client base often do not adequately grasp the risk attached to the financial instruments they sell. Monitoring systems are usually loose, and direct supervisors do not closely track how investments are sold or which, if any, disclosures are made to clients. For example, Paine Webber, Inc., was fined $900,000 by the New York Stock Exchange in early 1992 for ignoring these problems and allowing its brokers to make hundreds of overly risky recommendations to customers.

Small investors who use brokerage houses and banks usually do not have the same access to relevant information that is available to professional investors. Amateur investors, not having such inside information, can only hope that their brokers are well informed or that the market price already reflects the relevant information. Even if brokers are sufficiently informed, the house policy may be more aggressive and thus may introduce more risk than the average customer wishes. For example, the firm may be primarily interested in limited partnerships in real estate, fully margined common stock, futures and commodities, and oil and gas drilling partnerships, rather than the more mundane unit investment trusts, certificates of deposit, and municipal bonds that a particular customer needs.

A broker has little incentive to match client needs with investments aside from the desire to maintain a business relationship. Although brokerage firms often advertise a full range of products and free financial planning by experts, brokers dislike financial planning per se, because it requires much time and carries no commission. They also dislike pedestrian forms of investing such as certificates of deposit and no-load mutual funds. Riskier investments generally carry higher commissions, and brokerage houses typically give brokers complete discretion to recommend a range of investments to their clients. At the same time, brokers are skillfully taught to be salespersons, to avoid lengthy phone calls, and to flatter clients who pride themselves on making their own decisions. In some firms brokers are taught to make recommendations to clients based primarily on the commission. Consequently, brokers are motivated to sell risky and complicated forms of investment to unsuspecting clients.

An inherent conflict of interest troubles many industry critics. The broker has a fiduciary responsibility to make recommendations based on the client's financial best interest, but the broker is also a salesperson who makes a living by selling securities and who is obligated to maximize profits for the brokerage house. The more trades that are made, the better it is for the broker, but this rule seldom works to the client's advantage. Commissions are an ever-present temptation influencing a recommendation, and the structure of incentives drives up the risk for the client.

The law requires securities firms to disclose commissions to clients. However, statistics on the full range of fees involved in many instruments are rarely mentioned to clients. When available, the figures are usually buried beneath a pile of information in a thick prospectus that clients do not read prior to a purchase. Most clients do not obtain the prospectus until after the purchase, which often places no dollar figure on the commission. Brokers are not required to disclose commissions in advance of a sale to clients, nor are they required to disclose that they are given additional, expensive free vacations for selling large numbers of certain mutual funds. Moreover, clients rarely ask about the commission amount or the range of fees, not because of lack of interest, but because they fear that the inquiry might harm their relationship with the broker.

The U.S. Securities and Exchange Commission (SEC) was created by the Securities Exchange Act of 1933 to regulate a wide variety of manipulative stock practices. Although sensitive to issues such as insider trading, the SEC does not set ceilings on commissions and does not require brokers to receive written consent from clients prior to purchase. The SEC occasionally determines that a brokerage house's markup is so high that the commission amounts to fraud, but these cases are rare.

In recent years ethical brokerage houses have increasingly realized that tighter SEC control and a more developed sense of moral responsibility may serve their best interest. Ethical lapses are so common to the financial markets that the whole industry has been tarred with the brush of greed. Many reformers who lack an adequate understanding of the industry have introduced new legislation in order to control the industry more tightly. Although significant reforms are beginning to emerge, their outline is not yet clear.

One proposal for protecting investors, which is seriously considered in this chapter's essay by Robert E. Frederick and W. Michael Hoffman, is that the at-risk investor be denied access to securities markets to safeguard the investor from financial harm. The authors argue that restricting access to markets is justified only in cases in which the right not to be harmed by exposure to excessive risk is being protected. In a second article, Robert F. Bruner and Lynn Sharp Paine argue that the managers' fiduciary obligations to shareholders are jeopardized in a circumstance of management buyouts. These managers have an obligation to maximize the shareholders' interest by keeping the price high, but they have a strong incentive to negotiate a low price on their own behalf, thereby minimizing shareholders' interests. Buyouts place investors at the risk of having managers taking advantage of shareholders through their superior knowledge and control over information and by their intentionally understating the stock's value. The authors note that the management buyout functions to undermine shareholder trust in corporate leadership, and yet buyouts often present shareholders with a rich opportunity to protect their investments and sell at the highest possible price. Bruner and Paine argue for standards whereby a buyout offer should at least equal the value shareholders could achieve on their own. Such standards, they maintain, protect the at-risk investor and satisfy management's fiduciary obligations to shareholders.

WORKER SAFETY, OCCUPATIONAL RISK, AND THE RIGHT TO KNOW

Critics of business and government have long contended that uninformed workers are routinely, and often knowingly, exposed to dangerous conditions. For example, employers did not tell asbestos workers for many years of the known dangers of contracting asbestosis. Although little is currently understood about the knowledge and comprehension of workers, evidence from at least some industries shows that ignorance is a causal factor in occupational illness or injury. The simplest solution is to ban hazardous products from use, but to do so would be to shut down a large segment of industrial manufacturing. Hundreds of products still contain asbestos because no functional substitute is available.

The implications of worker ignorance are chillingly present in the following worker's testimony before an Occupational Safety and Health Administration (OSHA) hearing on the toxic agent DBCP:

> We had no warning that DBCP exposure might cause sterility, testicular atrophy, and perhaps cancer. If we had known that these fumes could possibly cause the damage that we have found out it probably does cause, we would have worn equipment to protect ourselves. As it was, we didn't have enough knowledge to give us the proper respect for DBCP.[2]

The regulation of workplace risks has consistently sought to determine an objective level of acceptable risk and then to ban or limit exposure above that level. However, the goal of safety is not the primary justification for disclosures of risk. Individuals need the information upon which the objective standard is based to determine whether the risk it declares acceptable is *to them*. Here a subjective standard of acceptable risk seems more appropriate than an objective standard established by "experts." Choosing to risk testicular atrophy seems rightly a worker's personal choice, one not fully decidable by health and safety standards established for groups of workers. Even given objective standards, substantial ambiguity prevails when the experts are uncertain about the risks and dangerous dose levels cannot be established.

Problems also surface about both the strategy of information disclosure and the strategy of protective schemes if either is used in isolation. Often there are no meaningful figures to define the relationship between acceptable risk and the ease with which the risk can be eliminated or controlled. There also may be no consensus about which levels of probability of serious harm, such as death, constitute risks sufficiently high to require that steps be taken to reduce or eliminate the risk or to provide information to those affected.

Both the employer's responsibility to inform employees and the employee's right to refuse hazardous job assignments are the concern of the essay by Ruth Faden and Tom L. Beauchamp. They support a standard of information disclosure and consider three possible standards for determining the justifiability of a refusal to work or of a safety walkout. Also included in the legal perspectives section of this chapter is the case of *Automobile Workers v. Johnson Controls, Inc.*, which determined that employers cannot legally adopt "fetal protection policies" that exclude women of childbearing age from a hazardous workplace, because such policies involve illegal sex discrimination. However, the Supreme Court decision was, in some respects, narrow; it left U.S. corporations in uncertainty over an acceptable policy for protecting fetuses from reproductive hazards.

RISK TO HEALTH AND THE ENVIRONMENT

Controversy over protecting the environment and preventing the depletion of natural resources has mushroomed in the last three decades, a period that has caught business, government, and the general public unprepared to handle environmental problems. In the 1960s and 1970s, the government instituted regulatory programs, and ever since then the public has become increasingly concerned about the environmental impact of chemical dumping, supersonic transport, burning coal, nuclear power, the Alaska pipeline, and the like. In this debate, environmental deterioration is often linked to corporate actions, and thus corporate responsibility has become a major issue.

Environmental issues have traditionally been conceived in free-market terms: Natural resources are available to entrepreneurs who are free to purchase and use them. Markets transfer resources, and rules of private property and free choice allow use of the environment to maximize profits. Conflicts were handled by relatively simple procedures that balanced conflicting interests. Those who polluted, for example, could be prosecuted and fined. People assumed that the environment, once properly tended to, was sufficiently resilient to return to its former state.

Recently this optimistic outlook has been vigorously challenged. First, it became apparent that a market conception of resource use did not fit the environment, because air, water, and much of the land environment is owned in common, and their value is not determined by prices in the market. Also, new technology and increased production now appear to have damaged the environment to a point at which unrectifiable and uncontrollable global imbalances may emerge. Yet, corporations still "externalize" rather than internalize costs by passing on the costs of pollution to the public. Attempts to bring market "externalities" such as pollution into standard pricing mechanisms — by, for instance, taxing effluents — have proved inadequate in handling environmental problems.

Some writers depict the environment as analogous to a common rangeland where competing cattle ranchers graze so many cattle in search of profits (as it is economically rational for each cattle rancher to do) that eventually the common land is overgrazed and can no longer support animal life. As businesspersons pursue their economic interests, collectively they work toward the ruin of all humanity. This analysis has been disputed by those who see environmental problems as involving tradeoffs that need not do irreversible damage to "the commons." However, society acknowledges that some tradeoffs will require additional tradeoffs that may only mortgage the future. For example, air-pollution scrubbers used in industry to remove sulfur dioxide from flue gas produce three to six tons of sludge for every ton of sulfur dioxide they remove. The sludge is then buried in landfills, creating a risk of water pollution. Efforts to clean the air thereby risk polluting the water.

Classic conflicts between public and private interests have emerged in these environmental debates. For example, there have been attempts to show that fluorocarbons in aerosol spray cans so badly damage the earth's ozone shield that serious repercussions may occur from continued use — for example, melting the polar ice caps, flooding the cities along the world's coasts, and producing radioactive contamination. Critics have charged that the food industry rapes the land by its failure to balance high-level methods of food production with the land's lower-level production capacity. Environmentalists have accused the timber industry of deforestation without replenishment. Responsibility for various forms of pollution has been attributed to bottle and can industries, plastics industries, smelters, chemical industries, and the oil industry. In recent years industrial disposal of hazardous wastes, including mercury, benzene, and dioxin, has been condemned because of the contamination of groundwater, landfills, and even waste recovery plants.

Those who promote a new environmental ethic argue that Western culture has a special problem because of entrenched attitudes about the use of nature for human enjoyment and betterment. Within this conception, humans live not as part of the ecosystem but as external dwellers. Others argue, however, that people should view the environment in a different way only to the extent that doing so would improve the quality of life and continued existence. They maintain that environmental concerns are valid only if they improve the human situation and not because animals, plants, or ecosystems have rights. This approach emphasizes the freedom of businesses to use the environment unless their activities harm other individuals in society.

Many now believe that only severe curbs on industry and severe judicial penalties will protect the environment, whereas others believe that environmental impact statements and various now-standard practices are sufficient. The core of the environmental problem is how to balance the liberty rights of those who want to use the environment in typical free-market style with the rights of those who want safe workplaces, safe products, and the right to a contamination-free environment.

Three readings in this chapter examine these problems of environmental risk and protection. The Supreme Court of New Jersey held, in the case of *State Department of Environmental Protection v. Ventron Corporation,* that corporations which create problems of mercury pollution for state waterways are liable for all resultant damages of their actions under common-law principles. The court found that toxic wastes are "abnormally dangerous" discharges that assess *strict liability* for harm, including liability for all clean-up costs. The court's conclusion that "even if they did not intend to pollute or adhered to the standards of the time, all [corporate] parties remain liable" is of far-reaching significance.

The article by Jang B. Singh and V. C. Lakhan demonstrates the extent of the annual production of hazardous wastes and its increase since the 1940s. They are particularly concerned with a diverse set of moral problems in the thriving international trade in hazardous substances. Finally, W. Michael Hoffman explores the relationship between business activities and the current interest in a broad environmental ethics. He argues that corporations have moral obligations to protect the environment that exceed the standards of environmental law and that corporations should be eager to cooperate with the government in protecting and cleaning up the environment. However, he denies that the slogans "good ethics is good business" or "protect the environment in order to protect human health" should be used as the moral basis of corporate environmental programs. He argues for a deeper moral perspective that focuses on the value of the environment itself.

NOTES

1. Joel Feinberg, *Harm to Others* (New York: Oxford University Press, 1984) 34–35.
2. Occupational Safety and Health Administration, "Access to Employee Exposure and Medical Records — Final Rules," *Federal Register,* May 23, 1980, p. 35222.

The Ethics of Consumer Production

Manuel G. Velasquez

Where . . . does the consumer's duties to protect his or her own interests end, and where does the manufacturer's duty to protect consumers' interests begin? Three different theories on the ethical duties of manufacturers have been developed, each one of which strikes a different balance between the consumer's duty to himself or herself and the manufacturer's duty to the consumer: the contract view, the "due care" view, and the social costs view. The contract view would place the greater responsibility on the consumer, while the "due care" and social costs views place the larger measure of responsibility on the manufacturer. We will examine each of these views.

THE CONTRACT VIEW
OF BUSINESS'S DUTIES
TO CONSUMERS

According to the contract view of the business firm's duties to its customers, the relationship between a business firm and its customers is essentially a contractual relationship, and the firm's moral duties to the customer are those created by this contractual relationship.[1] When a consumer buys a product, this view holds, the consumer voluntarily enters into a "sales contract" with the business firm. The firm freely and knowingly agrees to give the consumer a product with certain characteristics and the consumer in turn freely and knowingly agrees to pay a certain sum of money to the firm for the product. In virtue of having voluntarily entered this agreement, the firm then has a duty to provide a product with those characteristics, and the consumer has a correlative right to get a product with those characteristics. . . .

Traditional moralists have argued that the act of entering into a contract is subject to several secondary moral constraints:

1. Both of the parties to the contract must have full knowledge of the nature of the agreement they are entering.
2. Neither party to a contract must intentionally misrepresent the facts of the contractual situation to the other party.

From Manuel G. Velasquez, *Business Ethics: Concepts and Cases,* 3rd ed., pp. 277–92. © 1992 Prentice Hall, Inc. Reprinted by permission of Prentice Hall, Upper Saddle River, New Jersey.

3. Neither party to a contract must be forced to enter the contract under duress or undue influence.

These secondary constraints can be justified by the same sorts of arguments that Kant and Rawls use to justify the basic duty to perform one's contracts. Kant, for example, easily shows that misrepresentation in the making of a contract cannot be universalized, and Rawls argues that if misrepresentation were not prohibited, fear of deception would make members of a society feel less free to enter contracts. But these secondary constraints can also be justified on the grounds that a contract cannot exist unless these constraints are fulfilled. For a contract is essentially a *free agreement* stuck between two parties. Since an agreement cannot exist unless both parties know what they are agreeing to, contracts require full knowledge and the absence of misrepresentation. And since freedom implies the absence of coercion, contracts must be made without duress or undue influence.

The contractual theory of business's duties to consumers, then, claims that a business has four main moral duties: The basic duty of (1) complying with the terms of the sales contract, and the secondary duties of (2) disclosing the nature of the product, (3) avoiding misrepresentation, and (4) avoiding the use of duress and undue influence. By acting in accordance with these duties, a business respects the right of consumers to be treated as free and equal persons, that is, in accordance with their right to be treated only as they have freely consented to be treated.

The Duty to Comply

The most basic moral duty that a business firm owes its customers, according to the contract view, is the duty to provide consumers with a product that lives up to those claims that the firm expressly made about the product, which led the customer to enter the contract freely, and which formed the customer's understanding concerning what he or she was agreeing to buy. In the early 1970s, for example, Winthrop Laboratories marketed a pain-killer that the firm advertised as "nonaddictive." Subsequently, a patient using the painkiller became addicted to it and shortly thereafter died from an overdose. A court in 1974 found Winthrop Laboratories liable for the patient's death because, although it had expressly stated that the drug was nonaddictive, Winthrop Laboratories had failed to live up to its duty to comply with this express contractual claim.[2]

As the above example suggests, our legal system has incorporated the moral view that firms have a duty to live up to the express claims they make about their products. The Uniform Commercial Code, for example, states in Section 2-314:

> Any affirmation of fact or promise made by the seller to the buyer that related to the goods and becomes part of the basis of the bargain creates an express warranty that the goods shall conform to the affirmation or promise.

In addition to the duties that result from the *express* claim a seller makes about the product, the contract view also holds that the seller has a duty to carry through on any *implied* claims he or she knowingly makes about the product. The seller, for example, has the moral duty to provide a product that can be used safely for the ordinary and special purposes for which the customer, relying on the seller's judgment, has been led to believe it can be used. . . .

The express or implied claims that a seller might make about the qualities possessed by the product range over a variety of areas and are affected by a number of factors. Frederick

Sturdivant classifies these areas in terms of four variables: "The definition of product quality used here is: the degree to which product performance meets predetermined expectation with respect to (1) reliability, (2) service life, (3) maintainability, and (4) safety."[3]

Reliability. Claims of reliability refer to the probability that a product will function as the consumer is led to expect that it will function. If a product incorporates a number of interdependent components, then the probability that it will function properly is equal to the result of multiplying together each component's probability of proper functioning.[4] As the number of components in a product multiplies, therefore, the manufacturer has a corresponding duty to ensure that each component functions in such a manner that the total product is as reliable as he or she implicitly or expressly claims it will be. This is especially the case when malfunction poses health or safety hazards. The U.S. Consumer Product Safety Commission lists hundreds of examples of hazards from product malfunctions in its yearly report.[5]

Service Life. Claims concerning the life of a product refer to the period of time during which the product will function as effectively as the consumer is led to expect it to function. Generally, the consumer implicitly understands that service life will depend on the amount of wear and tear to which one subjects the product. In addition, consumers also base some of their expectations of service life on the explicit guarantees the manufacturer attaches to the product.

A more subtle factor that influences service life is the factor of obsolescence.[6] Technological advances may render some products obsolete when a new product appears that carries out the same functions more efficiently. Or purely stylistic changes may make last year's product appear dated and less desirable. The contract view implies that a seller who knows that a certain product will become obsolete has a duty to correct any mistaken beliefs he or she knows buyers will form concerning the service life they may expect from the product.

Maintainability. Claims of maintainability are claims concerning the ease with which the product can be repaired and kept in operating condition. Claims of maintainability are often made in the form of an express warranty. Whirlpool Corporation, for example, appended this express warranty on one of its products:

> During your first year of ownership, all parts of the appliance (except the light bulbs) that we find are defective in materials or workmanship will be repaired or replaced by Whirlpool free of charge, and we will pay all labor charges. During the second year, we will continue to assume the same responsibility as stated above except you pay any labor charges.[7]

But sellers often also imply that a product may be easily repaired even after the expiration date of an express warranty. In fact, however, product repairs may be costly, or even impossible, due to the unavailability of parts.

Product Safety. Implied and express claims of product safety refer to the degree of risk associated with using a product. Since the use of virtually any product involves some degree of risk, questions of safety are essentially questions of *acceptable known levels* of risk. That is, a product is safe if its attendant risks are known and judged to be "acceptable" or "reasonable" by the *buyer* in view of the benefits the buyer expects to derive from using the product. This implies that the seller complies with his or her part of a free agreement if the seller provides a product that involves only those risks he or she says it involves, and the buyer purchases it with that understanding. The National Commission on Product Safety, for example, characterized "reasonable risk" in these terms:

> Risks of bodily harm to users are not unreasonable when consumers understand that risks exist, can appraise their probability and severity, know how to cope with them, and voluntarily accept them to get benefits they could not obtain in less risky ways. When there is a risk of this character, consumers have reasonable opportunity to protect themselves; and public authorities should hesitate to substitute their value judgments about the desirability of the risk for those of the consumers who choose to incur it. But preventable risk is not reasonable (a) when consumers do not know that it exists; or (b) when, though aware of it, consumers are unable to estimate its frequency and severity; or (c) when consumers do not know how to cope with it, and hence are likely to incur harm unnecessarily; or (d) when risk is unnecessary in that it could be reduced or eliminated at a cost in money or in the performance of the product that consumers would willingly incur if they knew the facts and were given the choice.[8]

Thus the seller of a product (according to the contractual theory) has a moral duty to provide a product whose use involves *no greater risks* than those the seller *expressly* communicates to the buyer or those the seller *implicitly* communicates by the implicit claims made when marketing the product for a use whose normal risk level is well known. . . .

The Duty of Disclosure

An agreement cannot bind unless both parties to the agreement know what they are doing and freely choose to do it. This implies that the seller who intends to enter a contract with a customer has a duty to disclose exactly what the customer is buying and what the terms of the sale are. At a minimum, this means the seller has a duty to inform the

buyer of any facts about the product that would affect the customer's decision to purchase the product. For example, if the product the consumer is buying possesses a defect that poses a risk to the user's health or safety, the consumer should be so informed. Some have argued that sellers should also disclose a product's components or ingredients, its performance characteristics, costs of operation, product ratings, and any other applicable standards.[9]

Behind the claim that entry into a sales contract requires full disclosure is the idea that an agreement is free only to the extent that one knows what alternatives are available: Freedom depends on knowledge. The more the buyer knows about the various products available on the market and the more comparisons the buyer is able to make among them, the more one can say that the buyer's agreement is voluntary. . . .[10]

Since entry into a contract requires *freely* given consent, the seller has a duty to refrain from exploiting emotional states that may induce the buyer to act irrationally against his or her own best interests. For similar reasons, the seller also has the duty not to take advantage of gullibility, immaturity, ignorance, or any other factors that reduce or eliminate the buyer's ability to make free rational choices.

Problems with the Contractual Theory

The main objections to the contract theory focus on the unreality of the assumptions on which the theory is based. First, critics argue, the theory unrealistically assumes that manufacturers make direct agreements with consumers. Nothing could be farther from the truth. Normally, a series of wholesalers and retailers stand between the manufacturer and the ultimate consumer. The manufacturer sells the product to the wholesaler, who sells it to the retailer, who finally sells it to the consumer. The manufacturer never enters into any direct contract with the consumer. How then can one say that manufacturers have contractual duties to the consumer?

Advocates of the contract view of manufacturers' duties have tried to respond to this criticism by arguing that manufacturers enter into "indirect" agreements with consumers. Manufacturers promote their products through their own advertising campaigns. These advertisements supply the promises that lead people to purchase products from retailers who merely function as "conduits" for the manufacturer's product. Consequently, through these advertisements, the manufacturer forges an indirect contractual relationship not only with the immediate retailers who purchase the manufacturer's product but also with the ultimate consumers of the product. The most famous application of this doctrine of broadened indirect contractual relationships is to be found in a 1960 court opinion, *Henningsen v. Bloomfield Motors.*[11] . . . .

A second objection to the contract theory focuses on the fact that a contract is a double-edged sword. If a consumer can freely agree to buy a product *with* certain qualities, the consumer can also freely agree to buy a product *without* those qualities. That is, freedom of contract allows a manufacturer to be released from his or her contractual obligations by explicitly *disclaiming* that the product is reliable, serviceable, safe, etc. Many manufacturers fix such disclaimers on their products. . . . The contract view, then, implies that if the consumer has ample opportunity to examine the product and the disclaimers and voluntarily consents to buy it anyway, he or she assumes the responsibility for the defects disclaimed by the manufacturer, as well as for any defects the customer may carelessly have overlooked. Disclaimers can effectively

nullify all contractual duties of the manufacturer.

A third objection to the contract theory criticizes the assumption that buyer and seller meet each other as equals in the sales agreement. The contractual theory assumes that buyers and sellers are equally skilled at evaluating the quality of a product and that buyers are able to adequately protect their interests against the seller. . . . In practice, this laissez faire ideology gave birth to the doctrine of "caveat emptor": let the buyer take care of himself.

In fact, sellers and buyers do not exhibit the equality these doctrines assume. A consumer who must purchase hundreds of different kinds of commodities cannot hope to be as knowledgeable as a manufacturer who specializes in producing a single product. Consumers have neither the expertise nor the time to acquire and process the information on which they must base their purchase decisions. Consumers, as a consequence, must usually rely on the judgment of the seller in making their purchase decisions, and are particularly vulnerable to being harmed by the seller. Equality, far from being the rule, as the contract theory assumes, is usually the exception.

THE DUE CARE THEORY

The "due care" theory of the manufacturer's duties to consumers is based on the idea that consumers and sellers do not meet as equals and that the consumer's interests are particularly vulnerable to being harmed by the manufacturer who has a knowledge and an expertise that the consumer does not have. Because manufacturers are in a more advantaged position, they have a duty to take special "care" to ensure that consumers' interests are not harmed by the products that they offer them.

The doctrine of "caveat emptor" is here replaced with a weak version of the doctrine of "caveat vendor": let the seller take care. . . .

The "due care" view holds, then, that because consumers must depend upon the greater expertise of the manufacturer, the manufacturer not only has a duty to deliver a product that lives up to the express and implied claims about it, but in addition the manufacturer has a duty to exercise due care to prevent others from being injured by the product, *even if the manufacturer explicitly disclaims such responsibility and the buyer agrees to the disclaimer.* The manufacturer violates this duty and is "negligent" when there is a failure to exercise the care that a reasonable person could have foreseen would be necessary to prevent others from being harmed by use of the product. Due care must enter into the design of the product, into the choice of reliable materials for constructing the product, into the manufacturing processes involved in putting the product together, into the quality control used to test and monitor production, and into the warnings, labels, and instructions attached to the product. In each of these areas, according to the due care view, the manufacturer, in virtue of a greater expertise and knowledge, has a positive duty to take whatever steps are necessary to ensure that when the product leaves the plant it is as safe as possible, and the customer has a right to such assurance. Failure to take such steps is a breach of the moral duty to exercise due care and a violation of the injured person's right to expect such care, a right that rests on the consumer's need to rely on the manufacturer's expertise. . . .

The Duty to Exercise Due Care

According to the due care theory, manufacturers exercise sufficient care when they take adequate steps to prevent whatever injurious

effects they can foresee that the use of their product may have on consumers after having conducted inquiries into the way the product will be used and after having attempted to anticipate any possible misuses of the product. A manufacturer, then, is *not* morally negligent when others are harmed by a product and the harm was not one that the manufacturer could possibly have foreseen or prevented. Nor is a manufacturer morally negligent after having taken all reasonable steps to protect the consumer and to ensure that the consumer is informed of any irremovable risks that might still attend the use of the product. A car manufacturer, for example, cannot be said to be negligent from a moral point of view when people carelessly misuse the cars the manufacturer produces. A car manufacturer would be morally negligent only if the manufacturer had allowed unreasonable dangers to remain in the design of the car that consumers cannot be expected to know about or that they cannot guard against by taking their own precautionary measures.

What specific responsibilities does the duty to exercise due care impose on the producer? In general, the producer's responsibilities would extend to three areas:

Design. The manufacturer should ascertain whether the design of an article conceals any dangers, whether it incorporates all feasible safety devices, and whether it uses materials that are adequate for the purposes the product is intended to serve. The manufacturer is responsible for being thoroughly acquainted with the design of the item, and to conduct research and tests extensive enough to uncover any risks that may be involved in employing the article under various conditions of use. . . .

Production. The production manager should control the manufacturing processes to eliminate any defective items, to identify any weaknesses that become apparent during production, and to ensure that short-cuts, substitution of weaker materials, or other economizing measures are not taken during manufacture that would compromise the safety of the final product. To ensure this, there should be adequate quality controls over materials that are to be used in the manufacture of the product and over the various stages of manufacture.

Information. The manufacturer should fix labels, notices, or instructions on the product that will warn the user of all dangers involved in using or misusing the item and that will enable the user to adequately guard himself or herself against harm or injury. These instructions should be clear and simple, and warnings of any hazards involved in using or misusing the product should also be clear, simple, and prominent. . . .

Problems with "Due Care"

The basic difficulty raised by the "due care" theory is that there is no clear method for determining when one has exercised enough "due care." That is, there is no hard and fast rule for determining how far a firm must go to ensure the safety of its product. Some authors have proposed the general utilitarian rule that the greater the probability of harm and the larger the population that might be harmed, the more the firm is obligated to do. But this fails to resolve some important issues. Every product involves at least some small risk of injury. If the manufacturer should try to eliminate even low-level risks, this would require that the manufacturer invest so much in each product that the product would be priced out of the reach of most consumers. Moreover, even *attempting* to bal-

ance higher risks against added costs involves measurement problems: How does one quantify risks to health and life?

A second difficulty raised by the "due care" theory is that it assumes that the manufacturer can discover the risks that attend the use of a product before the consumer buys and uses it. In fact, in a technologically innovative society new products whose defects cannot emerge until years or decades have passed will continually be introduced into the market. Only years after thousands of people were using and being exposed to asbestos, for example, did a correlation emerge between the incidence of cancer and exposure to asbestos. Although manufacturers may have greater expertise than consumers, their expertise does not make them omniscient. Who, then, is to bear the costs of injuries sustained from products whose defects neither the manufacturer nor the consumer could have uncovered beforehand?

Thirdly, the due care view appears to some to be paternalistic for it assumes that the *manufacturer* should be the one who makes the important decisions for the consumer, at least with respect to the levels of risks that are proper for consumers to bear. But one may wonder whether such decisions should not be left up to the free choice of consumers who can decide for themselves whether or not they want to pay for additional risk reduction.

THE SOCIAL COSTS VIEW OF THE MANUFACTURER'S DUTIES

A third theory on the duties of the manufacturer would extend the manufacturer's duties beyond those imposed by contractual relationships and beyond those imposed by the duty to exercise due care in preventing injury or harm. This third theory holds that a manufacturer should pay the costs of any injuries sustained through any defects in the product, *even when the manufacturer exercised all due care in the design and manufacture of the product and has taken all reasonable precautions to warn users of every foreseen danger.* According to this third theory a manufacturer has a duty to assume the risks of even those injuries that arise out of defects in the product that no one could reasonably have foreseen or eliminated. The theory is a very strong version of the doctrine of "caveat vendor": let the seller take care.

This third theory, which has formed the basis of the legal doctrine of "strict liability," is founded on utilitarian arguments. The utilitarian arguments for this third theory hold that the "external" costs of injuries resulting from unavoidable defects in the design of an artifact constitute part of the costs society must pay for producing and using an artifact. By having the manufacturer bear the external costs that result from these injuries as well as the ordinary internal costs of design and manufacture, all costs will be internalized and added on as part of the price of the product. Internalizing all costs in this way, according to proponents of this theory, will lead to a more efficient use of society's resources. First, since the price will reflect *all* the costs of producing and using the artifact, market forces will ensure that the product is not overproduced, and that resources are not wasted on it. (Whereas if some costs were not included in the price, then manufacturers would tend to produce more than is needed.) Second, since manufacturers have to pay the costs of injuries, they will be motivated to exercise greater care and to thereby reduce the number of accidents. Manufacturers will therefore strive to cut down the social costs of injuries, and this means a more efficient care for our human resources. In order to produce the maximum benefits possible from our limited resources, therefore, the social costs of injuries from defective products should be internalized by passing them on to the manufacturer, even when the manufac-

turer has done all that could be done to eliminate such defects. And third, internalizing the costs of injury in this way enables the manufacturer to distribute losses among all the users of a product instead of allowing losses to fall on individuals who may not be able to sustain the loss by themselves.

Underlying this third theory on the duties of the manufacturer are the standard utilitarian assumptions about the values of efficiency. The theory assumes that an efficient use of resources is so important for society that social costs should be allocated in whatever way will lead to a more efficient use and care of our resources. On this basis, the theory argues that a manufacturer should bear the social costs for injuries caused by defects in a product, even when no negligence was involved and no contractual relationship existed between the manufacturer and the user.

Problems with the Social Costs View

The major criticism of the social costs view of the manufacturer's duties is that it is unfair.[12] It is unfair, the critics charge, because it violates the basic canons of compensatory justice. Compensatory justice implies that a person should be forced to compensate an injured party only if the person could foresee and could have prevented the injury. By forcing manufacturers to pay for injuries that they could neither foresee nor prevent, the social costs theory (and the legal theory of 'strict liability' that flows from it) treats manufacturers unfairly. Moreover, insofar as the social costs theory encourages passing the costs of injuries on to all consumers (in the form of higher prices), consumers are also being treated unfairly.

A second criticism of the social costs theory attacks the assumption that passing the costs of all injuries on to manufacturers will reduce the number of accidents.[13] On the contrary, critics claim, by relieving consumers of the responsibility of paying for their own injuries, the social costs theory will encourage carelessness in consumers. And an increase in consumer carelessness will lead to an increase in consumer injuries.

A third argument against the social costs theory focuses on the financial burdens the theory imposes on manufacturers and insurance carriers. Critics claim that a growing number of consumers successfully sue manufacturers for compensation for any injuries sustained while using a product, even when the manufacturer took all due care to ensure that the product was safe.[14] Not only have the number of "strict liability" suits increased, critics claim, but the amounts awarded to injured consumers have also escalated. Moreover, they continue, the rising costs of the many liability suits that the theory of "strict liability" has created have precipitated a crisis in the insurance industry because insurance companies end up paying the liability suits brought against manufacturers. . . .

The arguments for and against the social costs theory deserve much more discussion than we can give them here. The theory is essentially an attempt to come to grips with the problem of allocating the costs of injuries between two morally innocent parties: The manufacturer who could not foresee or prevent a product-related injury, and the consumer who could not guard himself or herself against the injury because the hazard was unknown. This allocation problem will arise in any society that, like ours, has come to rely upon a technology whose effects do not become evident until years after the technology is introduced. Unfortunately, it is also a problem that may have no "fair" solution.

NOTES

1. See Thomas Garrett and Richard J. Klonoski, *Business Ethics*, 2nd ed. (Englewood Cliffs, NJ: Prentice Hall, 1986), p. 88.
2. *Crocker v. Winthrop Laboratories, Division of Sterling Drug, Inc.*, 514 Southwestern 2d 429 (1974).
3. Frederick D. Sturdivant, *Business and Society*, 3rd ed. (Homewood, IL: Richard D. Irwin, Inc., 1985), p. 392.
4. Ibid., p. 393.
5. U.S. Consumer Products Safety Commission, *1979 Annual Report* (Washington, DC: U.S. Government Printing Office, 1979), pp. 81–101.
6. A somewhat dated but still incisive discussion of this issue is found in Vance Packard, *The Wastemakers* (New York: David McKay Co., Inc., 1960).
7. Quoted in address by S. E. Upton (vice-president of Whirlpool Corporation) to the American Marketing Association in Cleveland, OH: 11 December 1969.
8. National Commission on Product Safety, *Final Report,* quoted in William W. Lowrance, *Of Acceptable Risk* (Los Altos, CA: William Kaufmann, Inc., 1976), p. 80.
9. See Louis Stern, "Consumer Protection via Increased Information," *Journal of Marketing*, 31, no. 2 (April 1967).
10. Lawrence E. Hicks, *Coping with Packaging Laws* (New York: AMACOM, 1972), p. 17.
11. *Henningsen v. Bloomfield Motors, Inc.*, 32 New Jersey 358, 161 Atlantic 2d 69 (1960). [See this text, pp. 236–40.]
12. George P. Fletcher, "Fairness and Utility in Tort Theory," *Harvard Law Review*, 85, no. 3 (January 1972): 537–73.
13. Posner, *Economic Analysis of Law*, 2nd ed. (Boston: Little, Brown and Co., 1977), pp. 139–42.
14. See "Unsafe Products: The Great Debate Over Blame and Punishment," *Business Week*, 30 April 1984; Stuart Taylor, "Product Liability: the New Morass," *New York Times*, 10 March 1985; "The Product Liability Debate," *Newsweek*, 10 September 1984.

Strict Products Liability and Compensatory Justice

George G. Brenkert

I

Strict products liability is the doctrine that the seller of a product has legal responsibilities to compensate the user of that product for injuries suffered because of a defective aspect of the product, even when the seller has not been negligent in permitting that defect to occur.[1] Thus, even though a manufacturer, for example, has reasonably applied the existing techniques of manufacture and has anticipated and cared for nonintended uses of the product, he may still be held liable for injuries a product user suffers if it can be shown that the product was defective when it left the manufacturer's hands.

To say that there is a crisis today concerning this doctrine would be to utter a commonplace which few in the business community would deny. The development of the doctrine of strict products liability, according to most business people, threatens many businesses financially. Furthermore, strict products liability is said to be a morally questionable doctrine, since the manufacturer or seller has not been negligent in permitting the injury-causing defect to occur. On the other hand, victims of defective products complain that they deserve full compensation for injuries sustained in using a defective product whether or not the seller is at fault. Medical expenses and time lost from one's job are costs no individual should have to bear by himself. It is only fair that the seller share such burdens.

In general, discussions of this crisis focus on the limits to which a business ought to be held responsible. Much less frequently, discussions of strict products liability consider the underlying question of whether the doctrine of strict products liability is rationally justifiable. But unless this question is answered it would seem premature to seek to determine the limits to which businesses ought to be held liable in such cases. In the following paper I discuss this underlying philosophical question and argue that there is a rational justification for strict products liability which links it to the very nature of the free enterprise system.

II

. . . To begin with, it is crucial to remember that what we have to consider is the relationship between an entity doing business and an individual. The strict liability attributed to business would not be attributed to an individual who happened to sell some product he had made to his neighbor or a stranger. If Peter sold an article he had made to Paul and Paul hurt himself because the article had a defect which occurred through no negligence of Peter's, we would not normally hold Peter morally responsible to pay for Paul's injuries. . . .

It is different for businesses. They have been held to be legally and morally obliged to pay the victim for his injuries. Why? What is the difference? The difference is that when Paul is hurt by a defective product from corporation X, he is hurt by something produced in a socioeconomic system purportedly embodying free enterprise. In other words, among other things:

1. Each business and/or corporation produces articles or services it sells for profit.
2. Each member of this system competes with other members of the system in trying to do as well as it can for itself not simply in each exchange, but through each exchange for its other values and desires.
3. Competition is to be "open and free, without deception or fraud."
4. Exchanges are voluntary and undertaken when each party believes it can benefit thereby. One party provides the means for another party's ends if the other party will provide the first party the means to its ends.
5. The acquisition and disposition of ownership rights — that is, of private property — is permitted in such exchanges.
6. No market or series of markets constitutes the whole of a society.
7. Law, morality, and government play a role in setting acceptable limits to the nature and kinds of exchange in which people may engage.

What is it about such a system which would justify claims of strict products liability against businesses? . . . In the free enterprise system, each person and/or business is obligated to follow the rules and understandings which define this socioeconomic system. Following the rules is expected to channel competition among individuals and businesses to socially positive results. In providing the means to fulfill the ends of others, one's own ends also get fulfilled.

Though this does not happen in every case, it is supposed to happen most of the time. Those who fail in their competition with others may be the object of charity, but not of other duties. Those who succeed, qua members of this socioeconomic system, do not have moral duties to aid those who fail. Analogously, the team which loses the game may receive our sympathy but the winning team is not obligated to help it to win the next game or even to play it better. Those who violate the rules, however, may be punished or penalized, whether or not the violation was intentional and whether or not it redounded to the benefit of the violator. Thus, a team may be assessed a penalty for something that a team member did unintentionally to a member of the other team but which injured the other team's chances of competition in the game by violating the rules.

This point may be emphasized by another instance involving a game that brings us close to strict products liability. Imagine that you are playing table tennis with another person in his newly constructed table tennis room. You are both avid table tennis players and the game means a lot to both of you. Suppose that after play has begun, you are suddenly and quite obviously blinded by the light over the table — the light shade has a hole in it which, when it turned in your direction, sent a shaft of light unexpectedly into your eyes. You lose a crucial point as a result. Surely it would be unfair of your opponent to seek to maintain his point because he was faultless — after all, he had not intended to blind you when he installed that light shade. You would correctly object that he had gained the point unfairly, that you should not have to give up the point lost, and that the light shade should be modified so that the game can continue on a fair basis. It is only fair that the point be played over.

Businesses and their customers in a free enterprise system are also engaged in competition with each other. The competition here, however, is multifaceted as each tries to gain the best agreement he can from the other with regard to the buying and selling of raw materials, products, services, and labor. Such agreements must be voluntary. The competition which leads to them cannot involve coercion. In addition, such competition must be fair and ultimately result in the benefit of the entire society through the operation of the proverbial invisible hand.

Crucial to the notion of fairness of competition are not simply the demands that the competition be open, free, and honest, but also that each person in a society be given an equal opportunity to participate in the system in order to fulfill his or her own particular ends. . . .

. . . Equality of opportunity requires that one not be prevented by arbitrary obstacles from participating (by engaging in a productive role of some kind or other) in the system of free enterprise, competition, and so on in order to fulfill one's own ends ("reap the benefits"). Accordingly, monopolies are restricted, discriminatory hiring policies have been condemned, and price collusion is forbidden.

However, each person participates in the system of free enterprise *both* as a worker/producer *and* as a consumer. The two roles interact; if the person could not consume he would not be able to work, and if there were no consumers there would be no work to be done. Even if a particular individual is only (what is ordinarily considered) a consumer, he or she plays a theoretically significant role in the competitive free enterprise system. The fairness of the system depends upon what access he or she has to information about goods and services on the market, the lack of coercion imposed on that person to buy goods, and the lack of arbitrary restrictions imposed by the market and/or government on his or her behavior.

In short, equality of opportunity is a doctrine with two sides which applies both to producers and to consumers. If, then, a person as a consumer or a producer is injured by a defective product — which is one way his

activities might arbitrarily be restricted by the action of (one of the members of) the market system — surely his free and voluntary participation in the system of free enterprise will be seriously affected. Specifically, his equal opportunity to participate in the system in order to fulfill his own ends will be diminished.

Here is where strict products liability enters the picture. In cases of strict liability the manufacturer does not intend for a certain aspect of his product to injure someone. Nevertheless, the person is injured. As a result, he is at a disadvantage both as a consumer and as a producer. He cannot continue to play either role as he might wish. Therefore, he is denied that equality of opportunity which is basic to the economic system in question just as surely as he would be if he were excluded from employment by various unintended consequences of the economic system which nevertheless had racially or sexually prejudicial implications. Accordingly, it is fair for the manufacturer to compensate the person for his losses before proceeding with business as usual. That is, the user of a manufacturer's product may justifiably demand compensation from the manufacturer when its product can be shown to be defective and has injured him and harmed his chances of participation in the system of free enterprise.

Hence, strict liability finds a basis in the notion of equality of opportunity which plays a central role in the notion of a free enterprise system. That is why a business which does *not* have to pay for the injuries an individual suffers in the use of a defective article made by that business is felt to be unfair to its customers. Its situation is analogous to that of a player's unintentional violation of a game rule which is intended to foster equality of competitive opportunity.

A soccer player, for example, may unintentionally trip an opposing player. He did not mean to do it; perhaps he himself had stumbled. Still, he has to be penalized. If the referee looked the other way, the tripped player would rightfully object that he had been treated unfairly. Similarly, the manufacturer of a product may be held strictly liable for a product of his which injures a person who uses that product. Even if he is faultless, a consequence of his activities is to render the user of his product less capable of equal participation in the socioeconomic system. The manufacturer should be penalized by way of compensating the victim. Thus, the basis upon which manufacturers are held strictly liable is compensatory justice.

In a society which refuses to resort to paternalism or to central direction of the economy and which turns, instead, to competition in order to allocate scarce positions and resources, compensatory justice requires that the competition be fair and losers be protected.[2] Specifically, no one who loses should be left so destitute that he cannot reenter the competition. Furthermore, those who suffer injuries traceable to defective merchandise or services which restrict their participation in the competitive system should also be compensated.

Compensatory justice does not presuppose negligence or evil intentions on the part of those to whom the injuries might ultimately be traced. It is not perplexed or incapacitated by the relative innocence of all parties involved. Rather, it is concerned with correcting the disadvantaged situation an individual experiences due to accidents or failures which occur in the normal working of that competitive system. It is on this basis that other compensatory programs which alleviate the disabilities of various minority groups are founded. Strict products liability is also founded on compensatory justice.

An implication of the preceding argument is that business is not morally obliged to pay, as such, for the physical injury a person suffers. Rather, it must pay for the loss of equal competitive opportunity — even though it usually is the case that it is because of a (physical) injury that there is a loss of equal opportunity. Actual legal cases in which the injury which prevents a person from going about his or her daily activities is emotional or mental, as well as physical, support this thesis. If a person were neither mentally nor physically harmed, but still rendered less capable of participating competitively because of a defective aspect of a product, there would still be grounds for holding the company liable.

For example, suppose I purchased and used a cosmetic product guaranteed to last a month. When used by most people it is odorless. On me, however, it has a terrible smell. I can stand the smell, but my co-workers and most other people find it intolerable. My employer sends me home from work until it wears off. The product has not harmed me physically or mentally. Still, on the above argument, I would have reason to hold the manufacturer liable. Any cosmetic product with this result is defective. As a consequence my opportunity to participate in the socioeconomic system is curbed. I should be compensated.

III

There is another way of arriving at the same conclusion about the basis of strict products liability. To speak of business or the free enterprise system, it was noted above, is to speak of the voluntary exchanges between producer and customer which take place when each party believes he has an opportunity to benefit. Surely customers and producers may miscalculate their benefits; something they voluntarily agreed to buy or sell may turn out not to be to their benefit. The successful person does not have any moral responsibilities to the unsuccessful person — at least as a member of this economic system. If, however, fraud is the reason one person does not benefit, the system is, in principle, undermined. If such fraud were universalized, the system would collapse. Accordingly, the person committing the fraud does have a responsibility to make reparations to the one mistreated.

Consider once again the instance of a person who is harmed by a product he bought or used, a product that can reasonably be said to be defective. Has the nature of the free enterprise system also been undermined or corrupted in this instance? Producer and consumer have exchanged the product but it has not been to their mutual benefit; the manufacturer may have benefited, but the customer has suffered because of the defect. Furthermore, if such exchanges were universalized, the system would also be undone.

Suppose that whenever people bought products from manufacturers the products turned out to be defective and the customers were always injured, even though the manufacturers could not be held negligent. Though one party to such exchanges might benefit, the other party always suffered. If the rationale for this economic system — the reason it was adopted and is defended — were that in the end both parties share the equal opportunity to gain, surely it would collapse with the above consequences. Consequently, as with fraud, an economic system of free enterprise requires that injuries which result from defective products be compensated. The question is: Who is to pay for the compensation?

There are three possibilities. The injured party could pay for his own injuries. However, this is implausible since what is called for is compensation and not merely payment for injuries. If the injured party had simply injured himself, if he had been negligent or careless, then it is plausible that he should pay for his own injuries. No compensation is at stake here. But in the present case the injury stems from the actions of a particular manufacturer who, albeit unwittingly, placed the defective product on the market and stands to gain through its sale.

The rationale of the free enterprise system would be undermined, we have seen, if such actions were universalized, for then the product user's equal opportunity to benefit from the system would be denied. Accordingly, since the rationale and motivation for an individual to be part of this socioeconomic system is his opportunity to gain from participation in it, justice requires that the injured product user receive compensation for his injuries. Since the individual can hardly compensate himself, he must receive compensation from some other source.

Second, some third party — such as government — could compensate the injured person. This is not wholly implausible if one is prepared to modify the structure of the free enterprise system. And, indeed, in the long run this may be the most plausible course of action. However, if one accepts the structure of the free enterprise system, this alternative must be rejected because it permits the interference of government into individual affairs.

Third, we are left with the manufacturer. Suppose a manufacturer's product, even though the manufacturer wasn't negligent, always turned out to be defective and injured those using his products. We might sympathize with his plight, but he would either have to stop manufacturing altogether (no one would buy such products) or else compensate the victims for their losses. (Some people might buy and use his products under these conditions.) If he forced people to buy and use his products he would corrupt the free enterprise system. If he did not compensate the injured users, they would not buy and he would not be able to sell his products. Hence, he could partake of the free enterprise system — that is, sell his products —

only if he compensated his user/victims. Accordingly, the sale of this hypothetical line of defective products would be voluntarily accepted as just or fair only if compensation were paid the user/victims of such products by the manufacturer.

The same conclusion follows even if we consider a single defective product. The manufacturer put the defective product on the market. Because of his actions others who seek the opportunity to participate on an equal basis in this system in order to benefit therefrom are unable to do so. Thus, a result of his actions, even though unintended, is to undermine the system's character and integrity. Accordingly, when a person is injured in his attempt to participate in this system, he is owed compensation by the manufacturer. The seller of the defective article must not jeopardize the equal opportunity of the product user to benefit from the system. The seller need not guarantee that the buyer/user will benefit from the purchase of the product; after all, the buyer may miscalculate or be careless in the use of a nondefective product. But if he is not careless or has not miscalculated, his opportunity to benefit from the system is illegitimately harmed if he is injured in its use because of the product's defectiveness. He deserves compensation.

It follows from the arguments in this and the preceding section that strict products liability is not only compatible with the system of free enterprise but that if it were not attributed to the manufacturer the system itself would be morally defective. And the justification for requiring manufacturers to pay compensation when people are injured by defective products is that the demands of compensatory justice are met.[3]

NOTES

1. This characterization of strict products liability is adapted from Alvin S. Weinstein et al., *Products Liability and the Reasonably Safe Product* (New York: John Wiley & Sons, 1978), ch. 1. I understand the seller to include the manufacturer, the retailer, distributors, and wholesalers. For the sake of convenience, I will generally refer simply to the manufacturer.
2. I have drawn heavily, in this paragraph, on the fine article by Bernard Boxhill, "The Morality of Reparation," reprinted in *Reverse Discrimination*, ed. Barry R. Gross (Buffalo, New York: Prometheus Books, 1977), pp. 270–278.
3. I would like to thank the following for providing helpful comments on earlier versions of this paper: Betsy Postow, Jerry Phillips, Bruce Fisher, John Hardwig, and Sheldon Cohen.

The Right to Risk Information and the Right to Refuse Workplace Hazards

Ruth R. Faden
and Tom L. Beauchamp

In recent years, the right of employees to be informed about health hazards in the workplace has become a major issue in occupational health policy. We focus on several philosophical and policy-oriented problems concerning the right to know and correlative obligations to disclose relevant information. Related rights are also addressed, including the right to refuse hazardous work and the right of workers to contribute to workplace safety standards.

I

A government and industry consensus has gradually evolved that workers have a right to know about occupational risks, and correlatively that there is a moral and a legal obligation to disclose relevant information to workers.[1] The National Institute for Occupational Safety and Health (NIOSH) and other U.S. federal agencies informed the U.S. Senate as early as July, 1977 that "workers have the right to know whether or not they are exposed to hazardous chemical and physical agents regulated by the Federal Government."[2] The Occupational Safety and Health Administration (OSHA) implemented regulations in 1980 guaranteeing workers access to medical and exposure records,[3] and then developed regulations in 1983, 1986, and 1988 regarding the right to know about hazardous chemicals and requiring right-to-know training programs in many industries.[4] Numerous states and municipalities have passed additional legislation.[5]

Although some form of right to risk information is now well established in law and ethics, no consensus exists about the nature and extent of an employer's obligation to disclose such information. Considerable ambiguity also attends the nature and scope of the right — that is, which protections and actions the right entails, to whom these rights apply, and when notification should occur. For example, corporations and workers usually do not distinguish between the obligation to disclose currently available information, to seek information through literature searches, to generate information through new research, and to communicate hazards through educational or other training programs. The relevant literature also does not discuss whether corporations owe workers information that exceeds federal and state requirements.

II

A diverse set of recent U.S. laws and federal regulations reflect the belief that citizens in general, and workers in particular, have a right to learn about significant risks. These

Copyright 1982, 1987, 1992, 1996, Ruth R. Faden and Tom L. Beauchamp. This article includes parts of an earlier article that appeared in the *Canadian Journal of Philosophy*, Supplementary Volume, 1982. We are indebted to John Cuddihy and Ilise Feitshans for helpful comments and criticisms on later revisions.

include The Freedom of Information Act, The Federal Insecticide, Fungicide, and Rodenticide Amendments and Regulations, The Motor Vehicle and School Bus Safety Amendments, The Truth-in-Lending Act, The Pension Reform Act, The Real Estate Settlement Procedures Act, The Federal Food, Drug, and Cosmetic Act, The Consumer Product Safety Act, and The Toxic Substances Control Act. Taken together, this legislation communicates the message that manufacturers and other businesses have a moral (and often a legal) obligation to disclose information needed by individuals to decide about their participation, employment, or enrollment.

Recent developments in the right to know in the workplace have consistently held to this general trend towards disclosure and have included an expanded notion of corporate responsibility to provide adequate information to workers. These developments could revolutionize corporate workplace practices. Until the 1983 OSHA Hazard Communication Standard (HCS) went into effect in 1986 for the manufacturing sector and in 1988 for the non-manufacturing sector,[6] workers did not routinely receive extensive information from many employers.

Today, by contrast, some corporations have established model programs. For example, the Monsanto Company has a right-to-know program in which it distributes information on hazardous chemicals to its employees, and both notifies and monitors past and current employees exposed to carcinogenic and toxic chemicals. Hercules Inc. has videotape training sessions that incorporate frank discussions of workers' anxieties. The tapes depict workplace dangers and on-the-job accidents. Those employees who have seen the Hercules film are then taught how to read safety data and how to protect themselves.[7]

Job-training programs, safety data sheets, proper labels, and a written program are all now HCS-mandated. According to the present standards, all employers must "establish hazard-communication programs to transmit information on the hazards of chemicals to their employees." The training of new employees must occur before they are exposed to hazardous substances, and each time a new hazard is introduced. Each employee must sign a written acknowledgment of training, and OSHA inspectors may interview employees to check on the effectiveness of the training sessions.[8]

The sobering statistics on worker exposure and injury and on dangerous chemicals in the workplace make such corporate programs essential. The annual Registry of Toxic Effects of Chemical Substances lists over 25,000 hazardous chemicals, at least 8,000 of which are present in the workplace. As OSHA mentioned in the preamble to its Hazard Communication Standard, an estimated 25 million largely uninformed workers in North America (1 in 4 workers) are exposed to toxic substances regulated by the federal government. Approximately 6,000 U.S. workers die from workplace injuries each year, and perhaps as many as 100,000 deaths annually are caused to some degree by workplace exposure and consequent disease. One percent of the labor force is exposed to known carcinogens, and over 44,000 U.S. workers are exposed full time to OSHA-regulated carcinogens.[9]

Despite OSHA's HCS regulations, compliance problems persist. By March, 1989, OSHA had recorded over 49,000 HCS violations in the workplace. The agency described the non-compliance rate as "incredible."[10] Part of the problem stems from ignorance both about the dangers and current OSHA requirements.

III

The most developed models of general disclosure obligations and the right to know are presently found in the extensive literature on informed consent, which also deals with informed refusal. Physicians have broadly recognized moral and legal obligations to disclose known risks (and benefits) that are associated with a proposed treatment or form of research. No parallel obligation has traditionally been recognized in relationships between management and workers. Workmen's compensation laws originally designed for problems of accident in instances of immediately assessable damage handled risks in this environment. Obligations to warn or to disclose were irrelevant under the "no-fault" conception in workmen's compensation.

However, needs for information in the workplace have gradually become associated with occupational disease. In particular, knowledge is needed about the serious long-term risks of injury, disease, and death from exposure to toxic substances. These risks to health carry increased need for information on the basis of which a person may wish to take various actions, including choosing to forgo employment completely, to refuse certain work environments within a place of employment, to request improved protective devices, and to request lowered levels of exposure. Notification of workers should provide benefits of early disease diagnosis and prevention and promote needed lifestyle as well as occupational changes. Information should also improve workers' opportunities for appropriate compensation.[11]

Employee-employer relationships — unlike physician-patient relationships — are often confrontational and present to workers a constant danger of undisclosed or underdisclosed risk. This danger and the relative powerlessness of employees may not be sufficient to justify employer disclosure obligations in all circumstances, but placing relevant information in the workers' hands seems morally required in all hazardous conditions.

By what criteria, then, shall such disclosure obligations be determined?

One plausible argument is the following: Because large employers, unions, and government agencies must deal with multiple employees and complicated causal conditions, no standard should be more demanding than the so-called reasonable person standard. This standard is what a fair and informed member of the relevant community believes is needed. Under this standard, no employer, union, or other party should be held responsible for disclosing information beyond that needed to make an informed choice about the adequacy of safety precautions, industrial hygiene, long-term hazards, and the like, as determined by what the reasonable person in the community would judge to be the worker's need for information material to a decision about employment or working conditions.

However, this reasonable person standard of disclosure is not adequate for all disclosures. In the case of serious hazards — such as those involved in short-term, concentrated doses of radiation — a standard tied to individual persons may be more appropriate. When disclosures to individual workers may be expected to have a subjective impact that varies with each individual, the reasonable person standard should be supplemented by a standard that addresses each worker's personal informational needs.

Perhaps the best solution to the problem of a general standard is a compromise between a reasonable-person and a subjective standard: Whatever a reasonable person would judge material to the decision-making process should be disclosed, and in addition any remaining information that is material to an individual worker should be provided through a process of asking whether he or she has any additional or special concerns. This standard should avoid a narrow focus on the employer's obligation to disclose information and should seek to ensure the quality of a worker's understanding and consent. These problems center on communication rather than on legal standards of disclosure. The key to effective communication is to invite participation by workers in a dialogue. Asking questions, eliciting concerns, and establishing a climate that encourages questions may be more meaningful than the full corpus of disclosed information. Different levels of education, linguistic ability, and sophistication about the issues need to be accommodated.

We need also to consider which groups of workers will be included. The majority of the nation's workplaces are presently exempted from OSHA regulations, leaving these workers largely uninformed. Even in workplaces that are covered, former workers often have as much of a need for the information as do presently employed workers. The federal government has the names of approximately 250,000 former workers whose risk of cancer, heart disease, and lung disease has been increased by exposure to asbestos, polyvinyl chloride, benzene, arsenic, beta-naphthalamine, and dozens of other chemicals. Employers have the names of several million such workers.

The U.S. Congress has passed a bill to notify those workers at greatest risk, so that checkups and diagnosis of disease can be made before a disease's advanced stage.[12] But at this writing, neither industry nor the government has developed a systematic program. They claim that the expense of notifications would be prohibitive, that many workers would be unduly alarmed, and that existing screening and surveillance programs should prove adequate in monitoring and treating disease. Critics rightly charge, however, that existing programs are inadequate and that workers have a right to know in order to investigate potential problems at their initiative.[13]

IV

Despite the apparent consensus on the desirability of having some form of right to know in the workplace, hurdles exist that will make it difficult to implement this right. Complicated questions arise about the kinds of information to be disclosed, by whom, to whom, under what conditions, and with what warrant in ambiguous or uncertain circumstances. Trade secrets have also been a long-standing thorn in the side of progress,[14] because companies resist disclosing information about an ingredient or process claimed as a trade secret. They insist that they should never be required to reveal their substances or processes if their competitors could then obtain the information. For this reason, OSHA has been required to balance the protection of workers through disclosure against the protection of corporate interests in nondisclosure. Also, economic and related social constraints sometimes inhibit workers from exercising their full range of workplace options. For example, in industries in which ten people apply for every available position, bargaining for increased protection is an unlikely event.

However, we must set these problems aside in order to consider perhaps the most perplexing difficulty about the right to know in the workplace: the right to refuse hazardous work assignments and to have effective mechanisms for workers to reduce the risks they face. Shortly after the Hazard Communication Standard went into effect, labor saw that the right to know was often of little practical use unless some parallel method were in place to modify hazardous working conditions. U.S. law has generally made unsafe working conditions a publishable offense, and the United States Occupational Safety and Health Act of 1970 (OSH Act)[15] limited rights to refuse to work when there is good evidence of life-threatening conditions. Specifically, the OSH Act grants workers the right to request an OSHA inspection if they believe an OSHA standard has been violated or an imminent hazard exists. Under the Act, employees also have the right to "walk-around," i.e. to participate in OSHA inspections of the worksite and to consult freely with the inspection officer. Most importantly, the OSH Act expressly protects employees who request an inspection or otherwise exercise their rights under the OSH Act from discharge or any discriminatory treatment in retaliation for legitimate safety and health complaints.[16]

While these worker rights under the OSH Act are essential, they are not sufficiently strong to assure that all workers have effective mechanisms for initiating inspections of suspected health hazards. The OSH Act does not cover small businesses (those employing fewer than ten workers) or federal, state, and municipal employees. Questions also remain about OSHA's ability to enforce these provisions of the OSH Act. But if workers are to effectively use disclosed information on health hazards, they must have access to a workable and efficient regulatory system. The OSH Act is also written to protect the rights of individuals, not groups. It has no provisions for collective action by workers and does not mandate workplace health and safety committees, as does legislation in some countries.

Workers still need an adequately protected right to refuse unsafe work and a right to refuse an employer's request that they sign OSHA-mandated forms acknowledging that they have been trained about hazardous chemicals. One cannot easily determine the current extent to which these rights are protected.[17] Although the OSH Act does not grant a general right to refuse unsafe work, provisions to this effect exist in some state occupational safety laws. In addition, former Secretary of Labor Ray Marshall issued a regulation that interprets the OSH Act as including a limited right to refuse unsafe work, a right upheld by the U.S. Supreme Court in 1980.[18] The Labor-Management Relations Act (LMRA) also provides a limited right of refusal, which is also included implicitly in the National Labor Relations Act (NLRA).[19]

These statutory protections have not established uniform conditions granting to workers a right to refuse. For example, OSHA regulations allow workers to walk off the job if there is a "real danger of death or serious injury," while the LMRA permits refusals only under "abnormally dangerous conditions."[20] Under the LMRA, the nature of the occupation determines the extent of danger justifying refusal, while under OSHA the character of the threat, or so-called "imminent danger," determines worker action. By contrast, under the NLRA a walk-out by two or more workers may be justified for even minimal safety problems, so long as the action can be construed as a "concerted activity" for mutual aid and protection and a no-strike clause does not exist in any collective bargaining agreements. While the NLRA appears to provide the broadest protection to workers, employees refusing to work under the NLRA can lose the right to be reinstated in their positions if permanent replacements can be hired.

The relative merits of the different statutes are further confused by questions of overlapping authority, called "preemption." It is not always clear (1) whether a worker is eligible to claim protection under a given law, (2) which law affords a worker maximum protections or remedies in a particular circumstance, and (3) whether or under what conditions a worker can seek relief under another law or through the courts, once a claim under a given law has been rejected or invalidated.

The current legal situation concerning the right to refuse hazardous work also fails to resolve other questions. Consider, for example, whether a meaningful right to refuse hazardous work entails an obligation to continue to pay nonworking employees, or to award the employees back-pay if the issue is resolved in their favor. On the one hand, workers without union strike benefits or other income protections would be unable to exercise their right to refuse unsafe work due to economic pressures. On the other hand, to permit such workers to draw a paycheck is to legitimize strike with pay, a practice traditionally considered unacceptable by management and by Congress.

The situation does not resolve whether the right to refuse unsafe work should be restricted to cases of obvious, imminent, and serious risks to health or life (the current OSHA and LMRA position) or should be expanded to include lesser risks and uncertain risks — for example, exposure to suspected toxic or carcinogenic substances that although not immediate threats, may prove more dangerous over time. In order for "the right to know" to lead to meaningful worker action, workers must be able to remove themselves from exposure to suspected hazards, as well as obvious or known hazards.

The question of the proper standard for determining whether a safety walkout is justified is connected to this issue. At least three different standards have been applied in the past: a good-faith subjective standard, which requires only that the worker honestly believe that a health hazard exists; a reasonable person standard, which requires that the belief be reasonable under the circumstances as well as sincerely held; and an objective standard, which requires evidence — commonly established by expert witnesses — that the threat exists. Although the possibility of worker abuse of the right to refuse has been a major factor in a current trend to reject the good faith standard, recent commentary has argued that this trend raises serious equity issues in the proper balancing of this concern with the needs of workers confronted with basic self-preservation issues.[21]

No less important is whether the right to refuse hazardous work should be protected only until a formal review of the situation is initiated (at which time the worker must return to the job) or whether the walk-out should be permitted until the alleged hazard is at least temporarily removed. Requirements that workers continue to be exposed while OSHA or the NLRB conduct investigations is certain to prove unacceptable to workers when the magnitude of potential harm is significant. However, compelling employers to remove suspected hazards during the evaluation period may also result in intolerable economic burdens. This situation is worsened by the fact that workers are often not in a position to act on information about health hazards by seeking alternative employment elsewhere.

We need, then, to delineate the conditions under which workers may be compelled to return to work during an alleged hazard investigation and the conditions that can compel employers to remove alleged hazards.

V

Legal rights will prove useless if workers remain ignorant of their options. Despite recent requirements that employers initiate training programs, it remains doubtful that many workers, particularly nonunion workers and those in small businesses, are aware that they have a legally protected right to refuse hazardous work, let alone that at least three statutory provisions protect that right. Even if workers were to learn of such a right, they could probably not weave their way through the maze of legal options unaided. OSHA officials have acknowledged that both employers and workers are puzzled about proper strategies of education and compliance.[22] But if the workplace is to have a meaningful right to know, workers must have an adequate program to educate them not only about hazards but about their rights and how to exercise them. In general, they attempt to regulate the workplace rather than to empower workers in the workplace — two very different strategies.

Although the interests in health and safety of business are sometimes in sharp conflict with the interests of workers and society, employers and managers have an obligation to explain the right to notification and the right (at least temporarily) to refuse work under unduly hazardous conditions. Such programs of information and training in hazards are as important for employers and managers as for workers. In several recent court cases corporate executives have been tried — and in some cases convicted — for murder and manslaughter, because they negligently caused worker deaths by failing to notify of hazards. In Los Angeles and Chicago occupational deaths are investigated as possible homicides.[23] An improved system of corporate disclosures of risk and the rights of workers will therefore benefit everyone.

NOTES

1. See, for example, International Commission on Occupational Health, "Occupational Health Code of Ethics," *Bulletin of Medical Ethics,* No. 82 (October 1992): 7–11.
2. NIOSH, et al., "The Right to Know: Practical Problems and Policy Issues Arising from Exposures to Hazardous Chemical and Physical Agents in the Workplace," (Washington, D.C.: July 1977), pp. 1 and 5; see also Ilise L. Feitshans, "Hazardous Substances in the Workplace: How Much Does the Employee Have the Right to Know?" *Detroit Law Review* 3 (1985).
3. Occupational Safety and Health Administration, "Access to Employee Exposure and Medical Records — Final Rules," *Federal Register,* May 23, 1980, pp. 35212–77.
4. OSHA, Regulations 29 CFR 1910.1200 et seq; printed in 48 FR 53, 278 (1983) and (1986). See also *United Steelworkers v. Auchter,* No. 83–3554 et al; 763 F.2d 728 (3rd Cir., 1985).
5. See Deborah Shalowitz, "OSHA to Ease State Right-to-Know Burdens," *Business Insurance* 22 (Jan. 11, 1988), p. 17.
6. 29 CFR 1910.1200; 48 FR 53, 280 (1983); and see Linda D. McGill, "OSHA's Hazard Communication Standards: Guidelines for Compliance," *Employment Relations Today* 16 (Autumn 1989): 181–87.
7. Laurie Hays, "New Rules on Workplace Hazards Prompt Intensified On the Job Training Programs," *The Wall Street Journal,* July 8, 1986, p. 31; Cathy Trost, "Plans to Alert Workers," *The Wall Street Journal,* March 28, 1986, p. 15.
8. "Hazard Communication," *Federal Register,* August 24, 1987; and see William J. Rothwell, "Complying with OSHA," *Training & Development Journal* 43 (May 1989): 53–54; McGill, "OSHA's Hazard Communication Standards: Guidelines for Compliance," p. 184.
9. See 48 CFR 53, 282 (1983); Office of Technology Assessment, *Preventing Illness and Injury in the Workplace* (Washington: U.S. Government Printing Office, 1985). See also Sheldon W. Samuels, "The Ethics of Choice in the Struggle against Industrial Disease," *American Journal of Industrial Medicine* 23 (1993): 43–52, and David Rosner and Gerald E. Markowitz, eds. *Dying for Work: Workers' Safety and Health in Twentieth-Century America.* Bloomington: University of Indiana Press, 1987.
10. Current Reports, *O.S.H. Reporter* (March 15, 1989), p. 1747, as quoted in McGill, "OSHA's Hazard Communication Standard," p. 181.
11. See the articles by Gregory Bond, Leon Gordis, John Higgenson and Flora Chu, Albert Jonsen, and Paul A. Schulte in *Industrial Epidemiology Forum's Conference on Ethics in Epidemiology,* ed. William E. Fayerweather, John Higgenson, and Tom L. Beauchamp. New York: Pergamon Press, 1991.
12. High Risk Occupational Disease Notification and Prevention Act, HR 1309.
13. See Cathy Trost, "Plans to Alert Workers to Health Risks Stir Fears of Lawsuits and High Costs," *The Wall Street Journal,* March 28, 1986, p. 15; Peter Perl, "Workers Unwarned," *The Washington Post,* January 14, 1985, pp. A1, A6.
14. Under current standards, an employer is not required to disclose the name or any information about a hazardous chemical that would require disclosure of a bona fide trade secret; but in a medical emergency the company

must disclose this information to physicians or nurses as long as confidentiality is assured.

15. 29 U.S.C. §651–658 (1970).

16. OSH Act 29 U.S.C. 661(c). If the health or safety complaint is not determined to be legitimate, there are no worker protections.

17. The right to refuse an employer's request to sign a training acknowledgment form is upheld in *Beam Distilling Co. v. Distillery and Allied Workers' International,* 90 Lab. Arb. 740 (1988). See also Ronald Bayer, ed. *The Health and Safety of Workers.* New York: Oxford University Press, 1988; James C. Robinson, *Toil and Toxics: Workplace Struggles and Political Strategies for Occupational Health.* Berkeley: University of California Press, 1991.

18. *Whirlpool v. Marshall* 445 US 1 (1980).

19. See the exposition in Susan Preston, "A Right Under OSHA to Refuse Unsafe Work or A Hobson's Choice of Safety or Job?," *University*

of Baltimore Law Review 8 (Spring 1979), pp. 519–550.

20. 29 U.S.C. §143 (1976), and 29 CFR §1977.12 (1979).

21. James C. Robinson, "Labor Union Involvement in Occupational Safety and Health, 1957–1987," *Journal of Health Politics, Policy, and Law* 13 (Fall 1988), p. 463; Nancy K. Frank, "A Question of Equity: Workers' Right to Refuse Under OSHA Compared to the Criminal Necessity Defense," *Labor Law Journal* 31 (October 1980), pp. 617–626.

22. McGill, "OSHA's Hazard Communication Standard," p. 181.

23. See *Illinois v. Chicago Magnet Wire Corporation,* No. 86–114, *Amicus Curiae* for The American Federation of Labor and Congress of Industrial Organizations; R. Henry Moore, "OSHA: What's Ahead for the 1990s," *Personnel* 67 (June 1990), p. 69.

Business Ethics and the International Trade in Hazardous Wastes

Jang B. Singh and V. C. Lakhan

The export of hazardous wastes by the more developed countries to the lesser developed nations is escalating beyond control. The ethical implications and environmental consequences of this trade in hazardous wastes highlight the need for international controls and regulations in the conduct of business by corporations in the more developed countries. In the late 1970s, the Love Canal environmental tragedy awakened the world to the effects of ill conceived and irresponsible disposal of hazardous by-products of industries.

Today, the media focuses its attention on the alleged illegal dumping of hazardous wastes in the lesser developed countries (see Barthos, 1988, and Harden, 1988). The most recent dramatic case so far is that of Koko, Nigeria where more than eight thousand drums of hazardous wastes were dumped, some of which contained polychlorinated biphenyl (PCB), a highly carcinogenic compound and one of the world's most toxic wastes (Tifft, 1988)....

Journal of Business Ethics 8 (1989): 889–99. © 1989 Kluwer Academic Publishers. Reprinted by permission of Kluwer Academic Publishers.

THE INTERNATIONAL TRADE IN HAZARDOUS WASTES AND ATTENDANT PROBLEMS

Miller (1988) defined hazardous waste as any material that may pose a substantial threat or potential hazard to human health or the environment when managed improperly. These wastes may be in solid, liquid or gaseous form and include a variety of toxic, ignitable, corrosive, or dangerously reactive substances. Examples include acids, cyanides, pesticides, solvents, compounds of lead, mercury, arsenic, cadmium, and zinc, PCB's and dioxins, fly ash from power plants, infectious waste from hospitals, and research laboratories, obsolete explosives, herbicides, nerve gas, radioactive materials, sewage sludge, and other materials which contain toxic and carcinogenic organic compounds.

Since World War II, the amount of toxic byproducts created by the manufacturers of pharmaceuticals, petroleum, nuclear devices, pesticides, chemicals, and other allied products has increased almost exponentially. From an annual production of less than 10 million metric tons in the 1940's, the world now produces more than 320 million metric tons of extremely hazardous wastes per year. The United States is by far the biggest producer, with "over 275 million metric tons of hazardous waste produced each year" (Goldfarb, 1987). The total is well over one ton per person. But the United States is not alone. European countries also produce millions of tons of hazardous wastes each year (Chiras, 1988). Recent figures reported by Tifft (1988) indicate that the twelve countries of the European Community produce about 35 million tons of hazardous wastes annually. . . .

The United States and certain European countries are now turning to areas in Africa, Latin America, and the Caribbean to dump their wastes. Historically, the trade in wastes has been conducted among the industrialized nations. A major route involving industrialized nations is that between Canada and the United States. The movement of wastes from the United States into Canada is governed by the Canada–U.S.A. Agreement on the Trans-boundary Movement of Hazardous Waste which came into effect on November 8, 1986 (Environment Canada). In 1988, the United States exported 145,000 tons. Of this amount, only one third was recyclable, leaving approximately 96,667 tons of hazardous organic and inorganic wastes such as petroleum by-products, pesticides, heavy metals, and organic solvents and residues for disposal in the Canadian environment. Of interest is the fact that Canada restricts the import of nuclear waste, but not toxic, flammable, corrosive, reactive, and medical wastes from the United States.

Most of the United States' hazardous wastes are shipped from the New England states, New York and Michigan and enter Ontario and Quebec which in 1988 received approximately 81,899 and 62,200 tons respectively. The neutralization and disposal of the imported hazardous wastes are done by several Canadian companies, with the two largest being Tricil and Stablex Canada, Inc. Tricil, with several locations in Ontario, imports wastes from more than 85 known American companies which it incinerates and treats in lagoons and landfill sites. Stablex Canada imports a wide variety of hazardous wastes from more than 300 U.S. companies. It uses various disposal methods, including landfills and cement kilns which burn not only the components needed for cement but also hazardous waste products. With the established Canada–U.S. Agreement on the Transboundary Movement of Hazardous Waste, companies like Tricil and Stablex may increase their importation of hazardous wastes generated in the United States. As it stands, the United States Environmental Protection Agency estimates that over 75% of the wastes exported from the U.S. is disposed of in Canada (Vallette, 1989). This estimate will likely have to be raised in the near future. Canada–United States trade in hazardous wastes is not a one-way route. It is believed that all of the hazardous wastes imported by the United States (estimated at 65,000 tons in 1988) is generated in Canada (Ibid).

An especially controversial trend in the international trade in hazardous wastes is the development of routes between industrialized and "lesser developed countries." For example, according to the United States Environmental Protection Agency there have been more proposals to ship hazardous wastes from the United States to Africa during 1988, than in the previous four years (Klatte et al., 1988).

African nations have recently joined together to try to completely ban the dumping of toxic wastes on their continent. They have referred to the practice as "toxic terrorism" performed by Western "merchants of death." Some African government officials are so disturbed by the newly exposed practices that they have threatened to execute guilty individuals by firing squad. Recently, Lagos officials seized an Italian and a Danish ship along with fifteen people who were associated with transporting toxic wastes in the swampy Niger River delta into Nigeria. This occurred shortly after the discovery of 3,800 tons of hazardous toxic wastes, which had originated in Italy. Local residents immediately became ill from inhaling the fumes from the leaking drums and containers which were filled with the highly carcinogenic compound PCB, and also radioactive material.

Companies in the United States have been responsible for sending large quantities of hazardous wastes to Mexico. Although Mexico only accepts hazardous wastes for recycling, which is referred to as "sham re-cy-

cling," there are numerous reports of illegal dumping incidents. . . .

Given the fact that hazardous wastes are:

1. Toxic
2. Highly reactive when exposed to air, water, or other substances that they can cause explosions and generate toxic fumes
3. Ignitable that they can undergo spontaneous combustion at relatively low temperatures
4. Highly corrosive that they can eat away materials and living tissues
5. Infectious
6. Radioactive

Miller (1988) has, therefore, emphasized correctly that the proper transportation, disposal, deactivation, or storage of hazardous wastes is a grave environmental problem which is second only to nuclear war.

The practice of transporting and dumping hazardous wastes in lesser developed nations, where knowledge of environmental issues is limited, is causing, and will pose, major problems to both human health and the environment. Several comprehensive studies have outlined the detrimental impacts which hazardous waste can have on humans and natural ecosystems. Epstein et al., (1982) have provided a thorough and dramatic coverage of the impacts of hazardous wastes, while Regenstein (1982), in his book *America the Poisoned*, gives a good overview of the implications of hazardous wastes. Essentially, hazardous wastes not only contaminate ground water, destroy habitats, cause human disease, contaminate the soil; but also enter the food chain at all levels, and eventually damage genetic material of all living things. . . .

The hazardous wastes can also directly threaten human health through seeping into the ground and causing the direct pollution of aquifers, which supply "pure" drinking water. Today, in the United States, a long list of health related problems are caused by hazardous chemicals from "leaking underground storage tanks" (LUST). Investigations now show that human exposure to hazardous wastes from dumpsites, water bodies, and processing and storage areas can cause the disposed synthetic compounds to interact with particular enzymes or other chemicals in the body, and result in altered functions. Altered functions have been shown to include mutagenic (mutation-causing), carcinogenic (cancer-causing), and teratogenic (birth defect-causing) effects. In addition, they may cause serious liver and kidney dysfunction, sterility, and numerous lesser physiological and neurological problems (see Nebel, 1987). . . .

THE ETHICAL IMPLICATIONS

The international trade in hazardous wastes raises a number of ethical issues. The rest of this paper examines some of these.

The Right to a Livable Environment

The desire for a clean, safe and ecologically balanced environment is an often expressed sentiment. This is especially so in industrialized countries where an awareness of environmental issues is relatively high — a fact that is gaining recognition in political campaigns. However, expression of the desire for a clean, safe environment is not the same as stating that a clean, safe environment is the right of every human being. But the right of an individual to a livable environment is easily established at the theoretical level. Blackstone (1983) examines the right to a livable environment from two angles — as a human right and as a legal right. The right to a clean, safe environment is seen as a human right since the absence of such a condition

would prevent one from fulfilling one's human capacities.

> Each person has this right qua being human and because a livable environment is essential for one to fulfill his human capacities. And given the danger to our environment today and hence the danger to the very possibility of human existence, access to a livable environment must be conceived as a right which imposes upon everyone a correlative moral obligation to respect. (Blackstone, 1983, p. 413)

Guerrette (1986) illustrates this argument by reference to the Constitution of the United States. He proposes that people cannot live in a chemically toxic area, they cannot experience freedom in an industrially polluted environment and they cannot be happy worrying about the quality of air they breathe or the carcinogenic effects of the water they drink (Guerrette, 1986, p. 409). Some even argue (e.g., Feinberg, 1983) that the right to a livable environment extends to future generations and that it is the duty of the present generation to pass on a clean, safe environment to them.

Establishing the right to a livable environment as a human right is not the same as establishing it as a legal right. This requires the passing of appropriate legislation and the provision of a legal framework that may be used to seek a remedy if necessary. Such provisions are more prevalent in the industrialized countries and this is one of the push factors in the export of hazardous wastes to the lesser developed countries. This points to the need for a provision in international law of the right to a decent environment which with accompanying policies to save and preserve our environmental resources would be an even more effective tool than such a framework at the national level (Blackstone, 1983, p. 414). As ecologists suggest, serious harm done to one element in an ecosystem will invariably lead to the damage or even destruction of other elements in that and other ecosystems (Law Reform Commission of Canada, 1987, p. 262) and ecosystems transcend national boundaries. . . .

A more direct harmful effect of the international trade in hazardous wastes is the damage to the health of workers involved in the transportation and disposal of these toxic substances. For example, prolonged exposure to wastes originating in Italy and transported by a ship called Zanoobia is suspected of causing the death of a crew person and the hospitalization of nine others (Klatte et al., 1983, p. 12). Whereas worker rights in workplace health and safety are gaining wider recognition in many industrialized nations, this is not so in the "less developed" countries which are increasingly becoming the recipients of hazardous wastes. Widespread violation of workers' rights to a clean, safe work environment should therefore be expected to be a feature of the international trade in hazardous wastes.

Racist Implications

The recent trend of sending more shipments of hazardous wastes to Third World countries has led to charges of racism. *West Africa,* a weekly magazine, referred to the dumping of toxic wastes as the latest in a series of historical traumas for Africa. . . . Charges of racism in the disposal of wastes have been made before at the national level in the United States. A study of waste disposal sites found that race was the most significant among variables tested in association with the location of commercial hazardous wastes facilities. The findings of this national study which were found to be statistically significant at the 0.0001 level showed that communities with the greatest number of commercial hazardous wastes facilities had the highest concentration of racial minorities (Lee, 1987, pp. 45–46). The

study found that although socioeconomic status appeared to play a role in the location of commercial hazardous wastes facilities, race was a more significant factor.

In the United States, one of the arguments often advanced for locating commercial waste facilities in lower income areas is that these facilities create jobs. This is also one of the arguments being advanced for sending wastes to poor, lesser developed countries. . . . Nearly all the countries receiving hazardous wastes have predominantly coloured populations. This is the reason why charges of racism are being made against exporters of wastes. However, it must be noted that even though the trend of sending wastes to other countries . . . has recently gained strength, the bulk of the international trade in hazardous wastes is still within industrialized Europe and North America which have predominantly non-coloured populations.

For example, the United States Environmental Protection Agency estimates that as much as 75% of the wastes exported from the United States is disposed of in Canada (Klatte et al., 1988, p. 9). Another striking example is that a dump outside Schonberg, East Germany, is the home of well over 500,000 tons of waste a year from Western Europe (Rubbish Between Germans, March 1, 1986, p. 46). Thus, while charges of racism in the export of hazardous wastes are being made by some Third World leaders, figures on the international trade in such substances do not substantiate these claims.

Corporate Responsibility

The international trade in hazardous wastes basically involves three types of corporations — the generators of wastes, the exporters of wastes, and the importers of wastes. These entities, if they are to act in a responsible manner, should be accountable to the public for their behaviour.

> Having a corporate conscience means that a company takes responsibility for its actions, just as any conscientious individual would be expected to do. In corporate terms, this means that a company is accountable to the public for its behaviour not only in the complex organizational environment but in the natural physical environment as well. A company is thus responsible for its product and for its effects on the public. (Guerrette, 1986, p. 410)

Using Guerrette's definition of corporate responsibility, it seems clear that a corporation involved in the international trade in hazardous wastes is not likely to be a responsible firm. The importer of hazardous wastes is clearly engaged in activities that will damage the environment while the exporter being aware that this is a possibility, nevertheless, sends these wastes to the importer. However, it is the generator of hazardous wastes that is the most culpable in this matter. If the wastes are not produced then obviously their disposal would not be necessary. Therefore, in view of the fact that virtually no safe method of disposing hazardous wastes exists, a case of corporate irresponsibility could easily be formulated against any corporation involved in the international trade in these substances.

Government Responsibility

Why do countries export wastes? A major reason is that many of them are finding it difficult to build disposal facilities in their own countries because of the NIMBY syndrome mentioned earlier. Other reasons are that better technologies may be available in another country, facilities of a neighboring country may be closer to a generator of waste than a site on national territory and economies of scale may also be a factor. However, to these reasons must be added the fact

that corporations may be motivated to dispose of waste in another country where less stringent regulations apply (Transfrontier Movements, March 1984, p. 40). It is the responsibility of governments to establish regulations governing the disposal of wastes. In some countries these regulations are stringent while in others they are lax or non-existent. Moreover, some countries have regulations governing disposal of wastes within national boundaries as well as regulations relating to the export of hazardous wastes. For example, companies in the United States that intend to export hazardous wastes are requested to submit notices to the Environmental Protection Agency (EPA) and to demonstrate that they have the permission of the receiving country (Porterfield and Weir, 1987, p. 341). However, the effectiveness of these controls is in question. The General Accounting Office has found that "the E.P.A. does not know whether it is controlling 90 percent of the existing waste or 10 percent. Likewise it does not know if it is controlling the wastes that are most hazardous" (Ibid.). Moreover, there is evidence indicating that other U.S. government agencies are encouraging the export of hazardous wastes. The Navy, the Army, the Defense Department, the Agriculture Department and the Treasury Department are some government agencies that have provided hazardous wastes to known exporters. Also, major U.S. cities, sometimes with the approval of the State Department, have been suppliers to the international trade in hazardous wastes (Porterfield and Weir, 1987, p. 342).

While more stringent regulations, higher disposal costs, and heightened environmental awareness are pushing many companies in industrial countries to export hazardous wastes, it must be, nevertheless, realized that the governments of lesser developed countries are allowing such imports into their countries because of the need for foreign exchange.

These governments are willing to damage the environment in return for hard currency or the creation of jobs. One must assume that on the basis of cost-benefit analysis these governments foresee more benefits than harm resulting from the importation of hazardous wastes. However, these benefits go mainly to a few waste brokers while the health of large numbers of people is put at risk. In some cases decisions to import wastes are made by governments which hold power by force and fraud. For example, Haiti which has imported wastes is ruled by a military dictatorship and Guyana which is actively considering the importation of industrial oil wastes and paint sludge is ruled by a minority party which has rigged all elections held in that country since 1964. The ethical dilemma posed by this situation is that of whether or not an unrepresentative government of a country could be trusted to make decisions affecting the life and health of its citizens. In fact, a larger question is whether or not any government has the right to permit business activity that poses a high risk to human life and health.

Generally, governments of waste generating countries, in reaction to political pressure, have imposed stringent regulations on domestic disposal and some restrictions on the export of hazardous wastes; however, as the examples above illustrate, the latter restrictions are not strictly enforced, hence, indicating a duplicitous stance on the part of the generating countries. The governments of importing countries, in allowing into their countries wastes that will disrupt ecosystems and damage human health, deny their citizens the right to a livable environment.

CONCLUSION

Hazardous wastes are, in the main, by-products of industrial processes that have contributed significantly to the economic development of many countries. Economic development, in turn, has led to lifestyles which also generate hazardous wastes. To export these wastes to countries which do not benefit from waste-generating industrial processes or whose citizens do not have lifestyles that generate such wastes is unethical. It is especially unjust to send hazardous wastes to lesser developed countries which lack the technology to minimize the deleterious effects of these substances. Nevertheless, these countries are increasingly becoming recipients of such cargoes. The need for stringent international regulation to govern the trade in hazardous wastes is now stronger than ever before. However, this alone will not significantly curb the international trade in hazardous wastes. International regulation must be coupled with a revolutionary reorganization of waste-generating processes and change in consumption patterns. Until this is achieved the international trade in hazardous wastes will continue and with it a plethora of unethical activities.

BIBLIOGRAPHY

Barthos, G.: 1988, "Third World Outraged at Receiving Toxic Trash," *Toronto Star,* June 26, pp. 1, 4.

Blackstone, W. T.: 1983, "Ethics and Ecology," in Beauchamp, T. L. and Bowie, N. E. (Eds), *Ethical Theory and Business,* 2nd. edition (Prentice Hall, Englewood Cliffs, New Jersey), pp. 411–424.

Brooke, J.: 1988, "Africa Fights Tide of Western Wastes," *Globe and Mail,* July 18, p. A10.

Chiras, D. D.: 1988, *Environmental Science* (Benjamin Commings Publishing Co. Inc., Denver).

Environment Canada: 1986, *Canada–U.S.A. Agreement on the Transboundary Movement of Hazardous Waste* (Environment Canada, Ottawa).

Epstein, S. S., Brown, L. O., and Pope, C.: 1982, *Hazardous Waste in America* (Sierra Club Books, San Francisco).

Feinberg, J.: 1983, "The Rights of Animals and Unborn Generation," in Beauchamp, T. L., and Bowie, N. E., (Eds), *Ethical Theory and Business,* 2nd. edition. (Prentice Hall, Englewood Cliffs, New Jersey) pp. 428–436.

Goldfarb, T. D.: 1987, *Taking Sides: Clashing Views on Controversial Environmental Issues* (Dushkin Publishing Co., Inc., CT).

Guerrette, R. H.: 1986, "Environmental Integrity and Corporate Responsibility," *Journal of Business Ethics,* Vol. 5. pp. 409–415.

Harden, B.: 1988, "Africa Refuses to Become Waste Dump for the West," *Windsor Star,* July 9, p. A-6.

Klatte, E., Palacio, F., Rapaport, D., and Vallette, J.: 1988, *International Trade in Toxic Wastes: Policy and Data Analysis* (Greenpeace International, Washington, D.C.).

Law Reform Commission of Canada: 1987, "Crimes Against the Environment" in Poff, D. and Waluchow, W., *Business Ethics in Canada* (Prentice Hall, Canada Inc., Scarborough), pp. 261–264.

Lee, C.: Summer 1987, "The Racist Disposal of Toxic Wastes," *Business and Society Review,* Vol. 62, pp. 43–46.

Miller, T.: 1988, *Living in the Environment* (Wadsworth Publishing Co., California).

Montreal Gazette: April 27, 1987, "Mexico Sends Back U.S. Barge Filled With Tonnes of Garbage," p. F9.

Morrison, A.: 1988, "Dead Flowers to U.S. Firms that Plan to Send Waste to Guyana," *Catholic Standard,* Sunday, May 8.

Nobel, B. J.: 1987, *Environmental Science* (Prentice Hall, New Jersey).

OECD Observer: March 1984, "Transfrontier Movements of Hazardous Wastes: Getting to Grips with the Problem," pp. 39–41.

Porterfield, A. and Weir, D.: 1987, "The Export of U.S. Toxic Wastes," *The Nation,* Vol. 245, Iss. 10 (Oct. 3), pp. 341–344.

Regenstein, L.: 1982, *America the Poisoned* (Acropolis Books, Washington, D.C.).

The Economist: March 1, 1986, "Rubbish Between Germans," p. 46.

Tifft, S.: 1988, "Who Gets the Garbage," *Time,* July 4, pp. 42–43.

Vallette, J.: 1989, *The International Trade in Wastes: A Greenpeace Inventory,* 4th edition. (Greenpeace International, Luxembourg).

Business and Environmental Ethics

W. Michael Hoffman

... Concern over the environment is not new. Warnings came out of the 1960s in the form of burning rivers, dying lakes, and oil-fouled oceans. Radioactivity was found in our food, DDT in mother's milk, lead and mercury in our water. Every breath of air in the North American hemisphere was reported as contaminated. Some said these were truly warnings from Planet Earth of eco-catastrophe, unless we could find limits to our growth and changes in our lifestyle.

Over the past few years Planet Earth began to speak to us even more loudly than before, and we began to listen more than before. The message was ominous, somewhat akin to God warning Noah. It spoke through droughts, heat waves, and forest fires, raising fears of global warming due to the buildup of carbon dioxide and other gases in the atmosphere. It warned us by raw sewage and medical wastes washing up on our beaches, and by devastating oil spills — one despoiling

From W. Michael Hoffman, "Business and Environmental Ethics," *Business Ethics Quarterly* 1 (2): 169–84, 1991. Reprinted by permission.

Prince William Sound and its wildlife to such an extent that it made us weep. It spoke to us through increased skin cancers and discoveries of holes in the ozone layer caused by our use of chlorofluorocarbons. It drove its message home through the rapid and dangerous cutting and burning of our primitive forests at the rate of one football field a second, leaving us even more vulnerable to greenhouse gases like carbon dioxide and eliminating scores of irreplaceable species daily. It rained down on us in the form of acid, defoliating our forests and poisoning our lakes and streams. Its warnings were found on barges roaming the seas for places to dump tons of toxic incinerator ash. And its message exploded in our faces at Chernobyl and Bhopal, reminding us of past warnings at Three Mile Island and Love Canal. . . .

I

In a 1989 keynote address before the "Business, Ethics and the Environment" conference at the Center for Business Ethics, Norman Bowie offered some answers to the first two questions.

> Business does not have an obligation to protect the environment over and above what is required by law; however, it does have a moral obligation to avoid intervening in the political arena in order to defeat or weaken environmental legislation.[1]

I disagree with Bowie on both counts.

Bowie's first point is very Friedmanesque.[2] The social responsibility of business is to produce goods and services and to make profit for its shareholders, while playing within the rules of the market game. These rules, including those to protect the environment, are set by the government and the courts. To do more than is required by these rules is, ac-

cording to this position, unfair to business. In order to perform its proper function, every business must respond to the market and operate in the same arena as its competitors. As Bowie puts this:

> An injunction to assist in solving societal problems [including depletion of natural resources and pollution] makes impossible demands on a corporation because, at the practical level, it ignores the impact that such activities have on profit.[3]

If, as Bowie claims, consumers are not willing to respond to the cost and use of environmentally friendly products and actions, then it is not the responsibility of business to respond or correct such market failure.

Bowie's second point is a radical departure from this classical position in contending that business should not lobby against the government's process to set environmental regulations. To quote Bowie:

> Far too many corporations try to have their cake and eat it too. They argue that it is the job of government to correct for market failure and then they use their influence and money to defeat or water down regulations designed to conserve and protect the environment.[4]

Bowie only recommends this abstinence of corporate lobbying in the case of environmental regulations. He is particularly concerned that politicians, ever mindful of their reelection status, are already reluctant to pass environmental legislation which has huge immediate costs and in most cases very long-term benefits. This makes the obligations of business to refrain from opposing such legislation a justified special case.

I can understand why Bowie argues these points. He seems to be responding to two extreme approaches, both of which are inappropriate. Let me illustrate these extremes by the following two stories.

At the Center's First National Conference on Business Ethics, Harvard Business School Professor George Cabot Lodge told of a friend who owned a paper company on the banks of a New England stream. On the first Earth Day in 1970, his friend was converted to the cause of environmental protection. He became determined to stop his company's pollution of the stream, and marched off to put his new-found religion into action. Later, Lodge learned his friend went broke, so he went to investigate. Radiating a kind of ethical purity, the friend told Lodge that he spent millions to stop the pollution and thus could no longer compete with other firms that did not follow his example. So the company went under, 500 people lost their jobs, and the stream remained polluted.

When Lodge asked why his friend hadn't sought help from the state or federal government for stricter standards for everyone, the man replied that was not the American way, that government should not interfere with business activity, and that private enterprise could do the job alone. In fact, he felt it was the social responsibility of business to solve environmental problems, so he was proud that he had set an example for others to follow.

The second story portrays another extreme. A few years ago "Sixty Minutes" interviewed a manager of a chemical company that was discharging effluent into a river in upstate New York. At the time, the dumping was legal, though a bill to prevent it was pending in Congress. The manager remarked that he hoped the bill would pass, and that he certainly would support it as a responsible citizen. However, he also said he approved of his company's efforts to defeat the bill and of the firm's policy of dumping wastes in the meantime. After all, isn't the proper role of business to make as much profit as possible within the bounds of law? Making the laws — setting the rules of the

game — is the role of government, not business. While wearing his business hat the manager had a job to do, even if it meant doing something that he strongly opposed as a private citizen.

Both stories reveal incorrect answers to the questions posed earlier, the proof of which is found in the fact that neither the New England stream nor the New York river was made any cleaner. Bowie's points are intended to block these two extremes. But to avoid these extremes, as Bowie does, misses the real managerial and ethical failure of the stories. Although the paper company owner and the chemical company manager had radically different views of the ethical responsibilities of business, both saw business and government performing separate roles, and neither felt that business ought to cooperate with government to solve environmental problems.[5]

If the business ethics movement has led us anywhere in the past fifteen years, it is to the position that business has an ethical responsibility to become a more active partner in dealing with social concerns. Business must creatively find ways to become a part of solutions, rather than being a part of problems. Corporations can and must develop a conscience, as Ken Goodpaster and others have argued — and this includes an environmental conscience.[6] Corporations should not isolate themselves from participation in solving our environmental problems, leaving it up to others to find the answers and to tell them what not to do.

Corporations have special knowledge, expertise, and resources which are invaluable in dealing with the environmental crisis. Society needs the ethical vision and cooperation of all its players to solve its most urgent problems, especially one that involves the very survival of the planet itself. Business must work with government to find appropriate solutions. It should lobby for good environmental legislation and lobby against bad legislation, rather than isolating itself from the legislative process as Bowie suggests. It should not be ethically quixotic and try to go it alone, as our paper company owner tried to do, nor should it be ethically inauthentic and fight against what it believes to be environmentally sound policy, as our chemical company manager tried to do. Instead business must develop and demonstrate moral leadership.

There are examples of corporations demonstrating such leadership, even when this has been a risk to their self-interest. In the area of environmental moral leadership one might cite DuPont's discontinuing its Freon products, a $750-million-a-year business, because of their possible negative effects on the ozone layer, and Proctor and Gamble's manufacture of concentrated fabric softener and detergents which require less packaging. But some might argue, as Bowie does, that the real burden for environmental change lies with consumers, not with corporations. If we as consumers are willing to accept the harm done to the environment by favoring environmentally unfriendly products, corporations have no moral obligation to change so long as they obey environmental law. This is even more the case, so the argument goes, if corporations must take risks or sacrifice profits to do so. . . .

Even Bowie admits that perhaps business has a responsibility to educate the public and promote environmentally responsible behavior. But I am suggesting that corporate moral leadership goes far beyond public educational campaigns. It requires moral vision, commitment, and courage, and involves risk and sacrifice. I think business is capable of such a challenge. Some are even engaging in such a challenge. Certainly the business ethics movement should do nothing short of encouraging such leadership. I feel morality demands such leadership.

II

If business has an ethical responsibility to the environment which goes beyond obeying environmental law, what criterion should be used to guide and justify such action? Many corporations are making environmentally friendly decisions where they see there are profits to be made by doing so. They are wrapping themselves in green where they see a green bottom line as a consequence. . . .

The frequent strategy of the new environmentalists is to get business to help solve environmental problems by finding profitable or virtually costless ways for them to participate. They feel that compromise, not confrontation, is the only way to save the earth. By using the tools of the free enterprise system, they are in search of win-win solutions, believing that such solutions are necessary to take us beyond what we have so far been able to achieve.

I am not opposed to these efforts; in most cases I think they should be encouraged. There is certainly nothing wrong with making money while protecting the environment, just as there is nothing wrong with feeling good about doing one's duty. But if business is adopting or being encouraged to adopt the view that good environmentalism is good business, then I think this poses a danger for the environmental ethics movement — a danger which has an analogy in the business ethics movement.

As we all know, the position that good ethics is good business is being used more and more by corporate executives to justify the building of ethics into their companies and by business ethics consultants to gain new clients. . . .

Is the rationale that good ethics is good business a proper one for business ethics? I think not. One thing that the study of ethics has taught us over the past 2,500 years is that being ethical may on occasion require that we place the interests of others ahead of or at least on par with our own interests. And this implies that the ethical thing to do, the morally right thing to do, may not be in our own self-interest. What happens when the right thing is not the best thing for the business?

Although in most cases good ethics may be good business, it should not be advanced as the only or even the main reason for doing business ethically. When the crunch comes, when ethics conflicts with the firm's interests, any ethics program that has not already faced up to this possibility is doomed to fail because it will undercut the rationale of the program itself. We should promote business ethics, not because good ethics is good business, but because we are morally required to adopt the moral point of view in all our dealings — and business is no exception. In business, as in all other human endeavors, we must be prepared to pay the costs of ethical behavior.

There is a similar danger in the environmental movement with corporations choosing or being wooed to be environmentally friendly on the grounds that it will be in their self-interest. There is the risk of participating in the movement for the wrong reasons. But what does it matter if business cooperates for reasons other than the right reasons, as long as it cooperates? It matters if business believes or is led to believe that it only has a duty to be environmentally conscientious in those cases where such actions either require no sacrifice or actually make a profit. And I am afraid this is exactly what is happening. . . .

I am not saying we should abandon attempts to entice corporations into being ethical, both environmentally and in other ways, by pointing out and providing opportunities where good ethics is good business. And there are many places where such attempts fit well in both the business and environmental

ethics movements. But we must be careful not to cast this as the proper guideline for business's ethical responsibility. Because when it is discovered that many ethical actions are not necessarily good for business, at least in the short run, then the rationale based on self-interest will come up morally short, and both ethical movements will be seen as deceptive and shallow.

III

What is the proper rationale for responsible business action toward the environment? A minimalist principle is to refrain from causing or prevent the causing of unwarranted harm, because failure to do so would violate certain moral rights not to be harmed. There is, of course, much debate over what harms are indeed unwarranted due to conflict of rights and questions about whether some harms are offset by certain benefits. . . .

Some naturalistic environmentalists only include other sentient animals in the framework of being deserving of moral consideration; others include all things which are alive or which are an integral part of an ecosystem. This latter view is sometimes called a biocentric environmental ethic as opposed to the homocentric view which sees all moral claims in terms of human beings and their interests. Some characterize these two views as deep *versus* shallow ecology.

The literature on these two positions is vast and the debate is ongoing. The conflict between them goes to the heart of environmental ethics and is crucial to our making of environmental policy and to our perception of moral duties to the environment, including business's. I strongly favor the biocentric view. And although this is not the place to try to adequately argue for it, let me unfurl its banner for just a moment.

A version of R. Routley's "last man" example[7] might go something like this: Suppose you were the last surviving human being and were soon to die from nuclear poisoning, as all other human and sentient animals have died before you. Suppose also that it is within your power to destroy all remaining life, or to make it simpler, the last tree which could continue to flourish and propagate if left alone. Furthermore you will not suffer if you do not destroy it. Would you do anything wrong by cutting it down? The deeper ecological view would say yes because you would be destroying something that has value in and of itself, thus making the world a poorer place.

It might be argued that the only reason we may find the tree valuable is because human beings generally find trees of value either practically or aesthetically, rather than the atoms or molecules they might turn into if changed from their present form. The issue is whether the tree has value only in its relation to human beings or whether it has a value deserving of moral consideration inherent in itself in its present form. The biocentric position holds that when we find something wrong with destroying the tree, as we should, we do so because we are responding to an intrinsic value in the natural object, not to a value we give to it. This is a view which argues against a humanistic environmental ethic and which urges us to channel our moral obligations accordingly.

Why should one believe that nonhuman living things or natural objects forming integral parts of ecosystems have intrinsic value? . . . I suspect Arne Naess gives as good an answer as can be given.

Faced with the ever returning question of "Why?," we have to stop somewhere. Here is a place where we well might stop. We shall admit that the value in itself is something shown in intuition. We attribute intrinsic value to ourselves and our nearest, and the validity of further identification can be contested, and is contested by many. The negation may, however, also be attacked through a series of "whys?" Ultimately, we are in the same human predicament of having to start somewhere, at least for the moment. We must stop somewhere and treat where we then stand as a foundation.[8]

In the final analysis, environmental biocentrism is adopted or not depending on whether it is seen to provide a deeper, richer, and more ethically compelling view of the nature of things.

If this deeper ecological position is correct, then it ought to be reflected in the environmental movement. Unfortunately, for the most part, I do not think this is being done, and there is a price to be paid for not doing so. . . .

Furthermore, there are many cases where what is in human interest is not in the interest of other natural things. Examples range from killing leopards for stylish coats to destroying a forest to build a golf course. I am not convinced that homocentric arguments, even those based on long-term human interests, have much force in protecting the interests of such natural things. Attempts to make these interests coincide might be made, but the point is that from a homocentric point of view the leopard and the forest have no morally relevant interests to consider. It is simply fortuitous if nonhuman natural interests coincide with human interests, and are thereby valued and protected. Let us take an example from the work of Christopher Stone. Suppose a stream has been polluted by a business. From a homocentric point of view, which serves as the basis for our legal system, we can only correct the problem through finding some harm done to human beings who use the stream. Reparation for such harm might involve cessation of the pollution and restoration of the stream, but it is also possible that the business might settle with the people by paying them for their damages and continue to pollute the stream. Homocentrism provides no way for the stream to be made whole again unless it is in the interests of human beings to do so. In short it is possible for human beings to sell out the stream.[9]. . .

At the heart of the business ethics movement is its reaction to the mistaken belief that business only has responsibilities to a narrow set of its stakeholders, namely its stockholders. Crucial to the environmental ethics movement is its reaction to the mistaken belief that only human beings and human interests are deserving of our moral consideration. I suspect that the beginnings of both movements can be traced to these respective moral insights.

NOTES

1. Norman Bowie, "Morality, Money, and Motor Cars," *Business, Ethics, and the Environment: The Public Policy Debate*, eds., W. Michael Hoffman, Robert Frederick, and Edward S. Petry, Jr. (New York: Quorum Books, 1990), p. 89.
2. See Milton Friedman, "The Social Responsibility of Business Is to Increase Its Profits," *The New York Times Magazine* (September 13, 1970).
3. Bowie, p. 91.
4. Bowie, p. 94.
5. Robert Frederick, Assistant Director of the Center for Business Ethics, and I have developed and written these points together. Frederick has also provided me with invaluable assistance on other points in this paper.
6. Kenneth E. Goodpaster, "Can a Corporation Have an Environmental Conscience?" *The Corporation, Ethics, and the Environment*, eds., W. Michael Hoffman, Robert Frederick, and Edward S. Petry, Jr. (New York: Quorum Books, 1990).
7. Richard Routley and Val Routley, "Human Chauvinism and Environmental Ethics," *Environmental Philosophy*, Monograph Series, No. 2, eds., Don Mannison, Michael McRobbie, and Richard Routley (Australian National University, 1980), pp. 121ff.
8. Arne Naess, "Identification as a Source of Deep Ecological Attitudes," *Deep Ecology*, ed., Michael Tobias (San Marcos, CA: Avant Books, 1988), p. 266.
9. Christopher D. Stone, "Should Trees Have Standing? — Toward Legal Rights for Natural Objects," in *People, Penguins, and Plastic Trees*, pp. 86–87.

The Individual Investor in Securities Markets: An Ethical Analysis

Robert E. Frederick and W. Michael Hoffman

Securities markets are full of pitfalls for individual investors. Examples of fraud and regulatory violations in the markets are common. For instance, a recent *Business Week* cover story reports that investors are being duped out of hundreds of millions a year in penny stock scams in spite of SEC regulations.[1] A report in the *Wall Street Journal* on the Chicago futures trading fraud highlights the "danger of being ripped off in futures markets" by un-

Journal of Business Ethics 9 (1990): 579–89. © 1990 Kluwer Academic Publishers. Reprinted by permission of Kluwer Academic Publishers.

scrupulous floor brokers filling customers' "market orders" — a type of order that "individual investors should avoid using."[2]

But securities markets present risks to individual investors that go beyond clear violations of regulations and fraud. The above *Wall Street Journal* story, for example, also issued a more general warning to investors:

> Futures are fast moving, risky investment vehicles that are unsuitable for anyone who can't afford to lose and who doesn't have time to pay close attention to trading positions?[3]

Furthermore, it is not only the high risk futures and commodities markets that are perilous for investors. For example, the North American Securities Administration reports that "the securities industry isn't responding well to the problems of small investors in the wake of the stock market crash," problems such as poor execution of trades and being misled by brokers.[4] Even the bond markets, which in the past at least gave the outside appearance of stability, are in increasing turmoil. For instance, the SEC is now investigating the possibility that securities firms dumped billions of dollars of risky municipal bonds on individual investors because they were unable to sell them to institutions.[5] And MetLife is suing RJR-Nabisco on the grounds that individual investors were unjustifiably harmed when the A rated corporate bonds they purchased lost millions in value due to the junk bond financing of the RJR-Nabisco leveraged buyout.[6]

In light of these and many other examples that could be given, suppose the SEC announced that individual investors, for their own protection, no longer have access to securities markets. They are no longer permitted to buy stocks, bonds, or commodities or futures options. If this were to happen there surely would be a public outcry of protest, even moral outrage. The reasons for such

outrage probably would revolve around the belief that some fundamental right had been violated, perhaps the presumed right that markets should be free and open so that everyone has an opportunity to better his or her position and enjoy the goods and services of society.

A quick look, however, reveals that not all markets have unrestricted access. Nor is there a generally accepted belief that any rights are being unjustifiably violated in such cases. In consumer markets, for example, individuals under a certain age are prohibited from voting, buying alcoholic beverages, and seeing certain movies. Regardless of age, not just anyone can buy a fully automatic rifle or order a few dozen hand grenades. In fact, not just anyone can drive a car; one must pass a test and be licensed to do that. Furthermore, even after being allowed to drive, this privilege can be revoked if it is abused. And, of course, none of our citizens is legally permitted to participate in certain drug markets, such as cocaine.

But it will be argued that there is good reason for these and other such restrictions. We are attempting to prevent people, the argument goes, from harming themselves or causing harm to others. This is what makes it morally permissible, or even obligatory, to restrict access to certain kinds of consumer products. The ethical principle here is that, when possible, persons ought to be protected from undue harm. Hence, the restrictions in question are justified.

Yet might not this be exactly the rationale behind a possible SEC ban against individual investors entering securities markets? Just as unrestricted access to some drugs is thought to present unacceptable risks to consumers, trading in today's securities markets may present unacceptable risks to many investors, resulting in great financial rather than physical harm. And since we feel justified in prohibiting consumers from buying what we take to be highly dangerous drugs or other consumer products, shouldn't we, by analogy, be justified in prohibiting certain investors from buying highly risky financial instruments? . . .

EXACTLY WHAT KIND OF INVESTOR ARE WE TALKING ABOUT?

The type of investor we will be concerned with, and the type we take to be the most likely candidate for the SEC prohibition mentioned earlier, is one that (a) is at relatively *high risk*, where risk is a function of the probability of a certain market event occurring and the degree of harm the investor would suffer were the event to occur, and (b) an investor who is relatively *unsophisticated* about the functioning of the market and hence unappreciative of the degree of risk he or she faces. For example, suppose Jones invests his life savings in high yield bonds issued to finance an LBO, and suppose a few months later the company that issued the bonds suddenly announces that it is going into Chapter 11 bankruptcy. The value of the bonds drops precipitously and, for all practical purposes, in a matter of hours Jones' savings are wiped out. If Jones did not realize that the high return he was initially receiving was a reflection of the risky nature of the bonds, then he would fall within the category of investors with which we are concerned even assuming he had several million dollars invested. . . .

DO AT RISK INVESTORS HAVE A RIGHT TO PARTICIPATE IN SECURITIES MARKETS?

Obviously at risk investors are legally permitted to invest in securities markets, but do they have a right to do so? And if they do, what kind of right is it? These questions are important since how they are answered will determine in large part what kind of justification will be required to restrict or suspend investments by at risk investors, or whether a justification is possible at all.

Since the word "right" is used in many different senses, we will give rough definitions of the sense in which we will use "right" and associated terms. A "claim right," as we will understand it, is a right established within a system of rules. To have such a right is to have a valid or justified claim for action or forbearance against some person or institution. The notion of a "liberty" is weaker than that of a right. To have a liberty is not to have a duty or obligation to act toward a person or institution in a certain way. Rights imply liberties, but one may have a liberty without an associated right. A still weaker notion is that of a "privilege." To have a privilege is to have revocable permission to act in a certain way.[7]

Claim rights, liberties, and privileges can be either legal or moral depending on whether the rules in question are established by legislative action or follow from a system of morality. It is important to see that legal rights and moral rights need not be the same. A moral right may not be recognized by law, and one may have a legal right to engage in an immoral action.

If at risk investors have claim rights to invest in the market, then the government has a corresponding duty not to interfere with their activity. On the other hand, if they have a liberty to invest, they have no duty not to invest. If they have a privilege, then they are permitted to invest but such permission can be withdrawn. Now, if at risk investors have a claim right to invest, as opposed to a weaker liberty or an even weaker privilege to invest, then the justification required for infringing on that right will be very different from that required if they have a liberty or privilege. Hence, it is important to decide, as best we can, exactly which they have.

We believe a strong case can be made that at risk investors have a moral claim right to invest in the market, and that this right follows from the classic "right to freedom" that is so much a part of the American tradition. . . .

It follows from the right to freedom that it is morally permissible for persons to choose to invest in any way they deem appropriate within the bounds of law and a proper regard for the wrongful effects their actions may have on the lives of others.

If this is correct, then any interference with this right, whether by some individual or government agency, is prima facie unjustified. There are, however, several objections that could be raised. One of them is that persons simply have no such moral right because they have no rights at all other than those granted by law. Thus, no moral right is violated if the legal right to invest is altered or eliminated. Another is that although persons have moral rights, they do not have the right to freedom that we have attributed to them. . . .

There is one other objection to the right of freedom that we proposed. It is that even if all competent persons have an equal right to freedom, it still does not follow that they have the right to make any choice within the sphere of choices that do not wrongfully harm others. It does not follow, for example, that they have the right to make choices that seriously harm themselves. Intervention in such cases may be justified to prevent harm.

But is it? In order to decide, we must consider the possible justifications for interfering with the choices of others.

WHAT SORT OF JUSTIFICATION MIGHT BE OFFERED FOR RESTRICTING THE INVESTMENTS OF AT RISK INVESTORS?

One kind of justification that might be proposed is paternalistic. By paternalism we roughly mean interfering with a person's actions or preferences by restricting their freedom of action or the range of choices normally available to them for the reason that such a restriction promotes or preserves their good, welfare, happiness, or interests. A paternalistic justification for restricting at risk investors would be that exposure to risk for many investors is too great to permit them to continue without some sort of protection that reduces the risk to an acceptable degree. For certain investors an acceptable degree may be no risk at all. For others some risk may be permissible. In either case, the argument goes, as long as the intent of intervention is to protect or promote the good of at risk investors, and as long as it does not wrong other persons, then intervention is at least permissible and may be obligatory. It is only in this way that harm to many investors can be prevented.

The standard objection to paternalistic justifications is something like this: If people choose to run the risk to gain what they believe will be the rewards, who are we to interfere? From where do we derive a special dispensation to overrule their choices and interfere with their lives?

Although there is a kernel of truth in this objection, it is much too facile. Some paternalistic acts are clearly justified. Paternalistic reasoning is commonly used to justify restricting the choices of children and people judged incompetent or otherwise unable rationally to consider the consequences of their acts. Moreover, paternalistic justifications are not obviously unreasonable even in cases where the competence of the person is not in question. It is at least initially credible that some consumer products, such as prescription drugs, are not in unrestricted circulation precisely because of paternalistic reasons.

Let us confine our discussion to those persons ordinarily taken to be competent and rational. We still do not believe that paternalism *per se* justifies restricting at risk investors that fall within this category. One reason is that it may be impossible to find out just what the good or welfare of an individual investor is. Not only is there the thorny problem of trying to reach a common and precise understanding of the vague idea of the "good" of a person, there are immense practical difficulties in discovering whether a certain individual's good is served by restricting his or her access to the market. There may be situations where an individual's good is not served, and intervention in those cases would be a wrongful violation of his or her rights.

But suppose regulators do know the good of some individuals. Would paternalism then justify intervening to preserve or promote their good? We believe not in cases where regulators and the person in question have differing conceptions of that person's good. Even if regulators happen to know a person's "true" good better than he or she does themselves, imposing on that person a conception of his or her good they do not accept is not justified. Regulators may attempt to persuade at risk investors to take a different course or provide them with information that they need to make an informed decision, but it is not permissible to deny them the right to direct their lives. . . .

Although paternalism as characterized thus far does not justify interference with the choices of at risk investors, there are circumstances in which intervention is justified. This can best be explained by using an example not related to investing. Suppose Jones mistakenly believes the food he is about to eat is wholesome but we have good reason to think it is contaminated with botulism. As he raises the fork to his mouth we only have time to strike it away. At first he is angry, but after we explain the reason for our action he is grateful. The act of striking the fork away is an example of paternalistic intervention since it is done for Jones' good but against his wishes. It seems obvious, however, that we acted prop-

erly. Intervention in this case is justified since if Jones were fully aware of the circumstances he would act differently or would agree to have us intervene on his behalf. He would consent to our action. Hence, intervention here respects his right to freedom since it is compatible with his goals and does not force upon him some version of his good he would not accept.

Note that it is not merely our superior knowledge of the situation that justifies interference, but also our judgment that Jones would agree that our actions preserve or promote his good. The case would be different were Jones attempting suicide instead of trying to have a decent meal. Paternalistic intervention may not be justified when a person voluntarily undertakes an action harmful to him- or herself, provided that person has a reasonably complete understanding of his or her circumstances and the consequences of the action. But it is at least prima facie justified, we suggest, when an action is based on incomplete information and thus is, in one sense, less than fully voluntary.

Now suppose there are compelling grounds to believe that some otherwise competent investors are unappreciative of the high degree of risk they face, and that if they were presented with information about those risks they would act either to reduce or eliminate them, or would consent to having restrictions placed on the kinds of investments they could make. Since they would consent to intervention or act differently were they fully aware of the circumstances, intervention on their behalf is justified just as it was justified for Jones. Their rights are not violated since nothing is imposed on them that they would not consent to were they fully aware of the dangers they faced.

A major difference between the Jones case and at risk investors is that we dealt with Jones as an individual, but a regulatory or legislative body would have to deal with at risk investors as a group. There simply is no way to reach them all individually. Furthermore, although such bodies may be able to make reasonable assumptions about the kinds of risks acceptable to most at risk investors, and about the kinds of restrictions to which most of them would agree, it seems inevitable that there will be some investors that would not consent to restrictions because, for example, they have an unusual conception of their good or welfare, or because they find the restrictions highly offensive. For these people restrictions on investing will impose a foreign conception of their good on them and thus is not compatible with their right to direct their lives. . . .

If the *reason* given for intervening is promoting the good of at risk investors as a group, then, as we have tried to argue, it is not justified. Suppose, however, the reason is not only that the good of some investors is promoted, but that there is a duty to intervene to protect certain *rights,* in particular, the right of investors not to be harmed. The argument would go something like this: There is good reason to believe that some at risk investors would consent to having restrictions placed on them to protect their financial position and prevent them from suffering financial harm. Since it is a basic function of government to protect its citizens from harm, there is a duty to protect these investors. Hence, placing restrictions on their investment activities is justified even though such restrictions may violate the right of other investors to direct their lives as they see fit.

If this argument is plausible, then there is a conflict of rights between two groups of at risk investors. This is a genuine moral dilemma that can only be resolved by deciding whose rights are to prevail. We believe it should be the right not to be harmed. An analogy with prescription drugs may be helpful here. One reason there are restrictions on access to drugs is to prevent harm to persons who do not know how to use them correctly. These restrictions are justified, in our view, even supposing there are some individuals willing to take the risk. The right to freedom of this latter group should be and should remain a serious consideration in devising restrictions on drugs, but it does not override the right of others not to be exposed to excessive risk and possible serious harm.

The same holds true of at risk investors. The right of some of them not to be exposed to excessive risk and possible serious financial harm overrides the right of others to invest without restrictions. We emphasize, however, that the right to freedom cannot be lightly dismissed, and must be given due consideration when formulating policies and regulations governing the markets. . . .

IF SOME INVESTORS ARE RESTRICTED, HOW SHOULD IT BE DONE?

Since we are not experts in the regulation of securities markets, the best we can do here is make a few suggestions that seem to us worthy of additional investigation. It is a basic premise, essential for any just system of regulation and law, that relevantly different classes of persons be treated in relevantly different ways. Hence, it clearly would be unjust to restrict the activities of all investors to protect some of them. It also follows from this basic premise that distinctions must be drawn within the class of at risk investors. It may turn out in the end that there is no workable method of protecting some at risk investors while preserving the rights of all of them, but it would be a mistake to begin with this assumption.

In light of this it might be suggested that the only plausible course of action is to make sure that at risk investors have all the information they need to make investment decisions. This has at least three advantages. The first is that providing information does not seriously infringe any rights. And establishing stringent policies to ensure that the information is received also may be reasonable. For example, suppose that to demonstrate a minimum level of competence persons must pass an examination before investing, just as they have to pass a driving exam before driving. Different kinds of exams could be given for different kinds of investments. Would such a procedure violate any rights? It certainly would be costly and inconvenient, but we doubt that it is an inordinate restriction on the right to freedom.

A second advantage is that providing information is already one function of the Securities and Exchange Commission. According to the Commission's pamphlet "Consumers' Financial Guide" the three main responsibilities of the Commission are:

1. To require that companies that offer their securities for sale in "interstate commerce" register with the Commission and make available to investors complete and accurate information.
2. To protect investors against misrepresentation and fraud in the issuance and sale of securities.
3. To oversee the securities markets to ensure they operate in a fair and orderly manner.

Although the pamphlet goes on to advise investors that "whatever the choice of investment, make sure that you have complete and accurate information before investing to ensure that you use your funds wisely," it also emphasizes that the SEC does not see itself as the guarantor of investments:

> Registration . . . does not insure investors against loss of their investments, but serves rather to provide information upon which investors may base an informed and realistic evaluation of the worth of a security.

Thus providing information to at risk investors is consistent with the mission of the SEC and would not require massive restructuring of the Commission.

The third advantage is that providing information would be the most direct way to discover whether investors would consent to restrictions. Earlier we argued that restrictions on some at risk investors are justified because they would consent to intervention if they were fully aware of the risk they faced. But instead of imposing regulations based on what investors *would* do were they to have all the relevant information, it is preferable to give them the information whenever possible and see what they *actually* do. This would avoid the danger of imposing on them a conception of their good that they do not accept.

We agree that providing information to at risk investors is a good idea, and propose that methods be initiated that ensure that investors receive the information, rather than just having it available for those that seek it out. However, this may not be enough to eliminate unacceptable risks for at risk investors. Consider the prescription drug market again, and assume that the FDA made strenuous efforts to provide consumers with complete information about drugs. Supposing for a moment that it is legally permissible for consumers to buy drugs, as it is in some countries, this might be enough to eliminate unacceptable risk of harm from drugs for the few that had the time, energy, and expertise to use the information. But for most people it would be an overwhelming blizzard of paper that would be of no real use. As Steven Kelman has argued, the cost of organizing and understanding the information may be so high that the most sensible course of action for most people would be to assign their right to select drugs to some individual or institution with special expertise, provided the choice was made with their best interests in mind.[8] Merely providing information about drugs does not protect persons from harm unless the information is understood. When it appears unlikely that a large class of people will devote the time needed to understand it, then it is appropriate, we believe, to place legal restrictions on their choices. This protects them from harm, but is not an intolerable limitation of freedom.

The same reasoning applies in the securities markets. So much information is available and it is so complex that for many investors beyond a certain point it would be too costly to make the investment in time required to assimilate it all. Having "complete and accurate information," as the SEC suggests, is not enough. Leaving aside the issue of how one determines whether it is complete and accurate (note that not even the SEC does that), there remains the problem of understanding it well enough to make a wise investment decision. Perhaps it could be done, but would it be done by most at risk investors? We are inclined to think not. So we suggest that, just as with prescription drugs, at risk investors be required by law to engage the services of an expert. This would go a long way toward eliminating unacceptable risks for them, and given the significant possibility of harm many investors face, we do not feel it would be an excessive restriction on their freedom. Exceptions would have to be made for those investors willing to become

expert in the markets (since they would no longer meet the definition of an at risk investor), and some system of qualifications would need to be established to identify investment counselors capable of advising the other investors. . . .

NOTES

1. "The Penny Stock Scandal," *Business Week*, 23 Jan. 1989, pp. 74–82.
2. "Investors Can Take a Bite Out of Fraud," *Wall Street Journal*, 24 Jan. 1989, p. C1.
3. *Wall Street Journal*, 24 Jan. 1989, p. C1.
4. "Many Crash Complaints Unresolved," *Wall Street Journal*, 10 Oct. 1988, p. C1. For additional information on problems faced by individual investors, see John L. Casey, *Ethics in the Financial Marketplace*, (Scudder, Stevens & Clark, New York, 1988).
5. "SEC Studies Municipals in Trusts," *Wall Street Journal*, 11 Oct. 1988, p. C1.
6. "Bondholders Are Mad as Hell — And No Wonder," *Business Week*, 5 Dec. 1988, p. 28.
7. Joel Feinberg, *Social Philosophy* (Prentice Hall, Englewood Cliffs, NJ, 1973), pp. 55–56. These definitions are based on the ones given by Feinberg.
8. Steven Kelman, "Regulation and Paternalism," in *Ethical Theory and Business*, eds. T. L. Beauchamp and N. E. Bowie (Prentice Hall, Englewood Cliffs, NJ, 1988), p. 153.

Management Buyouts and Managerial Ethics

Robert F. Bruner and Lynn Sharp Paine

Because of their unusual terms, size, and number, management buyouts (MBOs) have emerged as one of the more arresting features in the corporate landscape. W. T. Grimm and Company estimated that in 1979 the value of firms going private was $636 million.[1] By 1986, Mergers and Acquisitions estimated the value of firms going private to be $40.9 billion.[2] As the volume of management buyouts rises, so does the volume of criticism. There are several avenues of attack. For instance, many critics doubt the social value of these transactions. They argue that MBOs threaten the financial stability of the American economy and are only financial rearrangements having no effect on the utilization of real assets.[3]

The attack most interesting from the standpoints of directors, senior managers, and shareholders rests on the claim that buyouts are unethical because of management's conflict of interest. In a buyout, managers' personal interests are pitted against their fiduciary duties to shareholders. Critics ask whether stockholders are getting the managerial loyalty to which they are entitled.[4] . . .

THE PROBLEM WITH BUYOUTS

In recent years, management buyouts have offered shareholders attractive returns. The cash flow gains from increased leverage and depreciation have permitted buyers to pay a premium over market price and at the same time to earn supernormal rates of return. On average, it appears that sellers receive almost a 30 percent premium for their equity claim. On the buyers' side, detailed case analyses suggest substantial internal rates of return on investment ranging from 25 to 50 percent. Superficially at least, it appears that both sides of the transaction win. Why, then, has management's role in buyouts been so heavily criticized?

The criticism is about fairness for the public shareholders. Management's position on both sides of the bargaining table may make buyout prices suspect even when shareholders are bought out at premiums. Critics find it difficult to see how management members of the buyout team can serve effectively as fiduciaries of selling shareholders and at the same time negotiate on their own behalf as buyers. As fiduciary, management's objective should be to obtain the highest price possible. As members of the buyout team, however, it would be natural for management to try to push the price as low as possible. A low price makes the purchase more attractive and enhances the potential future gains from going public again.

The risk is that management may take advantage of shareholders; but even if the buyout team offers shareholders a fair deal — one that satisfies its fiduciary obligations — the deal may not be perceived as fair by those who are aware of management's conflict of interest. The bevy of shareholder derivative lawsuits that have followed recent buyouts, even those at premium prices, and the criticisms produced by academics and policy makers indicate that shareholders lack confidence in the fairness of the prices they are offered.

Management's conflicting objectives are one source of concern about buyouts, but other issues are also involved. Management's superior knowledge exacerbates the problem of conflicting objectives. As insiders, managers have privileged access to information, sometimes secret, about the firm's prospects, and they have a unique feel for the company's value which comes from experience in handling its day-to-day affairs. Their knowledge of the firm and their special appreciation for its value give managers a decided advantage vis-à-vis shareholders and potential competitors when proposing a buyout price. A price which appears fair in light of publicly available information may be unfair when undisclosed plans, discoveries, and inventions are taken into account.

Management also has the ability to affect the company's stock price by controlling the flow of information, by its choice of accounting procedures, and by timing its strategic decisions. Opportunities to manipulate share price in conjunction with a buyout bid are significant. Quite apart from any deliberate efforts to manipulate stock prices, however, management has a unique ability to choose the most opportune time to propose a buyout.

Presumably, management proposes or participates in a buyout only if it is advantageous to management to do so. If management believes the share price is significantly below what could be obtained by releveraging or liquidating the company, it makes sense for management to buy the company and take steps to redeploy its assets. Under these circumstances shareholders may justifiably wonder whether management is taking for itself some opportunity that properly belongs to the corporation. Traditionally, under the corporate opportunity doctrine, the law has prohibited officers, directors, and senior managers from taking personal advantage of opportunities that come to them in their official capacities and are of potential benefit to the corporation.[5] If corporate leaders exploit corporate opportunities for themselves, the law permits shareholders to impose a trust on the profits earned. Couldn't management relever or liquidate directly to benefit shareholders rather than first taking the company private? On the face of it, the MBO appears to be a mechanism for transferring value from shareholders to management.

MANAGEMENT'S FIDUCIARY OBLIGATIONS

The concerns about conflicting interests, insider advantages, and misappropriation of corporate opportunities reflect management's special obligations to the corporation and its shareholders. In contrast to the arm's-length relationship that normally obtains between buyers and sellers in the marketplace, managers have a fiduciary responsibility toward the corporation and shareholders for whom they work.

According to the orthodox theory of the corporation, shareholders own — or at least invest in — the firm, while management runs it. In order for this arrangement to work, shareholders must be able to trust that the management will devote adequate attention to corporate business and run the business competently in a way that promotes the shareholders' interests. This trust is in part promoted through the board of directors, whose job it is to monitor management's performance on behalf of shareholders. But it depends more fundamentally on the continuing good faith performance by men and women in management positions.

The classic legal statement of the responsibility of corporate fiduciaries is found in the well-known case of *Guth v. Luft* decided by the Supreme Court of Delaware in 1939:

> A public policy, existing through the years, and derived from a profound knowledge of human characteristics and motives ... demands of a corporate officer or director ... the most scrupulous observance of his duty, not only affirmatively to protect the interests of the corporation committed to his charge, but also to refrain from doing anything that would work injury to the corporation, or to deprive it of profit or advantage which his skill and ability might properly bring to it, or to enable it to make in the reasonable and lawful exercise of its powers.[6]

The central element of this ideal is that management be dedicated to advancing the interests of the corporation, but most especially that management should not advance its own interests at the expense of the corporation.

The separation of ownership and control which underlies the modern public corporation is possible only if shareholders trust corporate leadership. In the absence of trust, monitoring management's performance becomes very costly. Without some fundamental assurance that their interests will be protected, equity investors would have little incentive to put their capital in the hands of professional managers. The benefits of corporate enterprise that flow to consumers, employees, suppliers, communities, and the general public — as well as to shareholders — are in jeopardy if management loses sight of its fiduciary obligations.

AN ETHICAL PERSPECTIVE ON MANAGEMENT BUYOUTS

Management buyouts threaten to undermine shareholder trust in corporate leadership if they are seen as or used as techniques for shrewd managers to benefit at shareholders' expense. Management's personal interest in buyouts, coupled with the absence of any generally accepted standard of fairness for evaluating buyout bids, make them especially potent threats to investor confidence. If there were no potential benefits for shareholders in these arrangements, there would be every reason to prohibit them. But, as noted earlier, buyouts sometimes offer shareholders the best alternative for protecting their investment or realizing its value. For example, management may be able, because of its position and superior knowledge, to see potential where outsiders do not, and thus be willing to take a seemingly moribund company private and rejuvenate it.[7] Management may, because of its position, be able to take a company private to ward off a hostile takeover bid offering a lower price.[8] Even in the absence of threatening conditions, a buyout may offer shareholders the best opportunity to realize the value of their investment because of the tax advantages and leveraging opportunities available as a result of going private. Any discussion of buyouts must recognize that sometimes they may be in shareholders' best interests.

From the perspective of managerial ethics, the practical challenge, then, is both to specify the conditions under which going private is consistent with management's fiduciary obligations and to motivate managers to propose only buyouts which satisfy those conditions.

MANAGEMENT'S CONFLICT OF INTEREST

Some observers consider buyouts inherently inconsistent with management's fiduciary obligations because of management's conflicting personal interests. These observers and many others apparently take the position that it is unethical to place oneself in a position in which personal interest may conflict with obligation. The appeal of such a position is obvious. In conflict of interest situations, there is always the possibility that personal interest will overwhelm obligation, that an abuse of trust will occur. However, the principle may be criticized on two grounds.

First, it is based on a misconception of conflicts of interest, one which sees potential conflict as characteristic of discrete, identifiable situations — which can be easily marked off from the normal state of affairs.

In fact, whenever a person is charged to act for the benefit of another — as corporate fiduciary, as parent, as employee — a conflict between personal interest and obligation to promote the interests of the other can erupt. The conflict may arise in connection with almost any type of decision or activity. An employee's decision not to search more widely for a competitive supplier, for example, may involve such a conflict. Potential conflict is not limited to exchanges between the agent and principal. Recognition that the potential for conflict exists continuously in every agency relationship renders the principle requiring avoidance of potential conflict totally unworkable. It is impossible to eliminate all potential conflicts without eliminating the relationships that give rise to them, and that would be too great a price to pay. Practical judgment is required to identify situations in which the potential gain to the agent or loss to the principle is great enough to warrant steps to monitor or restrain the agent's behavior.

The principle requiring avoidance of all potential conflict situations may also be criticized because it sometimes penalizes the very party it is meant to protect. If, for example, corporate directors were flatly prohibited from doing business with the corporations they serve, some opportunities advantageous to the corporation would have to be foregone. Courts and state legislatures have long recognized the possibility that a flat prohibition on dealing between a corporation and its directors can in some circumstances work to the detriment of the corporation.

Conflicts of interest are problematic not because they are themselves unethical, but because they may lead to conduct that is unethical. It may be difficult to do what obligation requires when important personal interests seem to point in a different direction. More commonly, personal interest may threaten the objectivity or integrity of professional judgment. When personal interests loom large, the decision maker may have difficulty determining where his firm's interests lie. There is a very natural tendency to want to see the interests of the firm and self-interest as aligned, even if, from a more objective perspective, they are not.

While there is little reason to recommend avoiding all situations in which personal interest may conflict with fiduciary obligation, there is good reason for looking more closely at situations in which a conflict creates a risk of significant losses to the principal or benefits to the agent. A buyout is just such a situation. . . .

FAIR PRICE

Who is entitled to the gains from management buyouts? Selling shareholders may believe that the gains from the buyout should be theirs. The value created derives from unused debt capacity and a depreciable asset base. Shareholders own both of these before the transaction. Buyers, no doubt, believe that their ability to leverage the company beyond the level normally available to a public corporation entitles them to the gains. In a normal arm's-length transaction, buyers and sellers negotiate from these different perceptions to reach a mutually acceptable price.

Should the situation be any different in a management buyout? Should the normal arm's-length standard for fair price apply in the buyout context? Sometimes it is assumed that if buyouts give shareholders a premium over market price, then there should be no complaints. Shareholders should gladly accept the premium and be grateful to management for having taken the initiative to unlock some added value. This position, however, fails to take into account management's fiduciary obligation and the foundation upon which it rests.

A buyout proposal is, in effect, a proposal to convert a fiduciary relationship into an arm's-length relationship. Whether the buyout group should be held to a fiduciary standard under these circumstances is central to the analysis of fair price. Our discussion of disclosure and review was based on the view that management's fiduciary obligations continue even after a buyout is proposed. Permitting management unilaterally to divest itself of its responsibilities to the firm by making a buyout proposal and then permitting the buyout group to negotiate on the basis of information and resources management acquired in its capacity as fiduciary would seriously undermine shareholder confidence. From the time a buyout is proposed until it is consummated or the proposal dropped, management should be held to a fiduciary standard. Unlike the approach which says that anything over market price is fair, our approach to fair price takes management's fiduciary responsibility into account.

As stated earlier, at the heart of management's fiduciary responsibility is the obligation to promote the corporation's interests. But most especially, management must not benefit at the expense of shareholders. Sometimes it is easy to see when corporate fiduciaries are benefiting at the expense of shareholders. When they misappropriate corporate assets for themselves, for example, the

harm to shareholders and the corresponding benefit to the fiduciaries is simply measured by the value of the assets taken. Determining the harm to shareholders in a buyout case is more difficult. While shareholders may benefit to the extent that the price exceeds market value, they may be harmed to the extent that the price is less than it ought to be by some other standard. For example, a buyout bid might be higher than market price, but still not as high as the price the shares would bring if management took certain initiatives such as relevering the company to improve share price.

Moreover, when a fiduciary steals from the corporation, there is no uncertainty about entitlements: The assets belong to the corporation and no reasonable person can claim to have any entitlement to them by virtue of his status in the corporation. However, where the question is the appropriate division of newly created wealth, particularly wealth created through the combined efforts of many people, entitlements are ambiguous. In order to determine whether one party is benefiting at the expense of another, there must be some benchmark or standard for the appropriate division of the gains. In the buyout situation, if shareholders get too little, then the buyout group benefits at their expense. Part of the problem of identifying buyouts which satisfy managements' fiduciary obligations is to specify a standard for determining whether the price is appropriate or fair.

Perhaps the most obvious standard is the firm's stock price before the buyout. Under the theory of capital market efficiency, the firm's value in the open market is fair in the sense that it reflects all public information about the company. One defect of this standard for evaluating buyout bids is that it is vulnerable to the asymmetry of information between insiders (i.e., managers) and outsiders (i.e., public shareholders). Asymmetries can arise because of differences in technical expertise between managers and the public, the possibly high cost of information gathering, and the size and complexity of the firm. A second defect of this standard is that it fails to distinguish between management's existing policies and those that might prevail if the firm were restructured or the management incentive scheme changed. To the extent that stock price before a buyout reflects managers' failure to utilize all their skills and abilities to maximize shareholder wealth, using it as a standard of fair price endorses managerial inefficiency.

A second standard is the price the firm would fetch if sold in an open auction. This standard explicitly controls for the fact that the buyout bid is not derived from arm's-length bidding. Certainly any bid lower than what an open market auction would bring is too low and may indicate that management is seeking to take advantage of shareholders. But the open market rule has the limitation that competing arm's-length bids are rarely available unless solicited, and even then may not be forthcoming. Nevertheless, this is an important standard because competing open market bidders have been known to intervene in instances of apparently low management bids.[9] Some commentators advocate a rule of open bidding once a management buyout is proposed. Such a rule has much to be said for it, but in the absence of actual interested bidders, it fails to give much guidance for assessing buyout bids.

A third and more useful standard of comparison is the value shareholders could obtain if they synthesized the buyout on their own: borrowed heavily, repurchased a large percentage of shares, and increased the shareholdings of managers (by sale or outright gift). Even the value created by depreci-

ation tax shields can be synthesized by selling plant and equipment and then leasing them back. This standard is not only more useful, since it does not depend on the presence of competing bidders, but it is also more consistent with management's duty of loyalty to shareholders. Management's fiduciary duty requires that it put forth its best efforts on shareholders' behalf. . . .

NOTES

1. News release, Doremus & Company, Chicago, January 12, 1984, p. 2.
2. "1987 Profile," *Mergers & Acquisitions* (May/ June 1986): 71.
3. Louis Lowenstein, "No More Cozy Management Buyouts," *Harvard Business Review* (January/February 1986): 147–156.
4. Benjamin J. Stein, "Going Private Is Unethical," *Fortune,* November 11, 1985, p. 169.
5. For instance, *Durfee v. Durfee & Canning, Inc.,* 323 Mass. 187 (1948). See generally, Victor Brudney and Robert Charles Clark, "A New Look at Corporate Opportunities," *Harvard Law Review,* 94 (1981): 997–1062.
6. *Guth v. Loft,* 5A.2d 503, 510 (Del. Supr. 1939).
7. For instance, employees at Weirton Steel saved it from imminent closing, then took a 19 percent pay cut, and raised $300 million to buy the assets in 1983. Since then, Weirton has embarked on a significant modernization program.
8. For instance, in April 1987, Dart Group, Inc., made an unsolicited takeover bid for Supermarkets General Corporation for $1.75 billion. Two weeks later, management offered to take the company private for $1.8 billion.
9. For example, competitive bidders intervened in response to J. B. Fuqua's 1981 attempt to buy out Fuqua Industries and in response to Chairman David Mahoney's 1983 proposal to take Norton Simon, Inc., private.

Henningsen v. Bloomfield Motors, Inc. and Chrysler Corporation

Supreme Court of New Jersey

Claus H. Henningsen purchased a Plymouth automobile, manufactured by defendant Chrysler Corporation, from defendant Bloomfield Motors, Inc. His wife, plaintiff Helen Henningsen, was injured while driving it and instituted suit against both defendants to recover damages on account of her injuries. Her husband joined in the action seeking compensation for his consequential losses. The complaint was predicated upon breach of express and implied warranties and upon negligence. At the trial the negligence counts were dismissed by the court and the case was submitted to the jury for determination solely on the issues of implied warranty of merchantability.* Verdicts were returned against both defendants and in favor of the plaintiffs. Defendants appealed and plaintiffs cross-appealed from the dismissal of their negligence claim. . . .

. . . The particular car selected was described as a 1955 Plymouth, Plaza "6," Club Sedan. The type used in the printed parts of the [purchase order] form became smaller in size, different in style, and less readable toward the bottom where the line for the purchaser's signature was placed. The smallest type on the page appears in the two paragraphs, one of two and one-quarter lines and the second of one and one-half lines, on which great stress is laid by the defense in the case. These two paragraphs are the least legi-

*["Merchantability": The articles shall be of the kind described and be fit for the purpose for which they were sold. Fitness is impliedly warranted if an item is merchantable. Ed.]

ble and the most difficult to read in the instrument, but they are most important in the evaluation of the rights of the contesting parties. They do not attract attention and there is nothing about the format which would draw the reader's eye to them. In fact, a studied and concentrated effort would have to be made to read them. De-emphasis seems the motive rather than emphasis. . . . The two paragraphs are:

"The front and back of this Order comprise the entire agreement affecting this purchase and no other agreement or understanding of any nature concerning same has been made or entered into, or will be recognized. I hereby certify that no credit has been extended to me for the purchase of this motor vehicle except as appears in writing on the face of this agreement.

"I have read the matter printed on the back hereof and agree to it as a part of this order the same as if it were printed above my signature. . . ."

The testimony of Claus Henningsen justifies the conclusion that he did not read the two fine print paragraphs referring to the back of the purchase contract. And it is uncontradicted that no one made any reference to them, or called them to his attention. With respect to the matter appearing on the back, it is likewise uncontradicted that he did not read it and that no one called it to his attention.

. . . The warranty, which is the focal point of the case, is set forth [on the reverse side of the page]. It is as follows:

Atlantic Reporter 161 A2d 69, pp. 73–75, 78–81, 83–87, 93–96, 102. This opinion was written by Justice John J. Francis.

"7. It is expressly agreed that there are no warranties, express or implied, *made* by either the dealer or the manufacturer on the motor vehicle, chassis, or parts furnished hereunder except as follows.

"The manufacturer warrants each new motor vehicle (including original equipment placed thereon by the manufacturer except tires), chassis or parts manufactured by it to be free from defects in material or workmanship under normal use and service. Its obligation under this warranty being limited to making good at its factory any part or parts thereof which shall, within ninety (90) days after delivery of such vehicle *to the original purchaser* or before such vehicle has been driven 4,000 miles, whichever event shall first occur, be returned to it with transportation charges prepaid and which its examination shall disclose to its satisfaction to have been thus defective: *This warranty being expressly in lieu of all other warranties expressed or implied, and all other obligations or liabilities on its part,* and it neither assumes nor authorizes any other person to assume for it any other liability in connection with the sale of its vehicles. . . ." [Emphasis added] . . .

The new Plymouth was turned over to the Henningsens on May 9, 1955. No proof was adduced by the dealer to show precisely what was done in the way of mechanical or road testing beyond testimony that the manufacturer's instructions were probably followed. Mr. Henningsen drove it from the dealer's place of business in Bloomfield to their home in Keansburg. On the trip nothing unusual appeared in the way in which it operated. Thereafter, it was used for short trips on paved streets about the town. It had no servicing and no mishaps of any kind before the event of May 19. That day, Mrs. Henningsen drove to Asbury Park [New Jersey]. On the way down and in returning the car performed in normal fashion until the accident occurred. She was proceeding north on Route 36 in Highlands, New Jersey, at 20–22 miles per hour. The highway was paved and smooth, and contained two lanes for northbound travel. She was riding in the right-hand lane. Suddenly she heard a loud noise "from the bottom, by the hood." It "felt as if something cracked." The steering wheel spun in her hands; the car veered sharply to the right and crashed into a highway sign and a brick wall. No other vehicle was in any way involved. A bus operator driving in the left-hand lane testified that he observed plaintiff's car approaching in normal fashion in the opposite direction; "all of a sudden [it] veered at 90 degrees . . . and right into this wall." As a result of the impact, the front of the car was so badly damaged that it was impossible to determine if any of the parts of the steering wheel mechanism or workmanship or assembly were defective or improper prior to the accident. The condition was such that the collision insurance carrier, after inspection, declared the vehicle a total loss. It had 468 miles on the speedometer at the time. . . .

The terms of the warranty are a sad commentary upon the automobile manufacturers' marketing practices. Warranties developed in the law in the interest of and to protect the ordinary consumer who cannot be expected to have the knowledge or capacity or even the opportunity to make adequate inspection of mechanical instrumentalities, like automobiles, and to decide for himself whether they are reasonably fit for the designed purpose. . . . But the ingenuity of the Automobile Manufacturers Association, by means of its standardized form, has metamorphosed the warranty into a device to limit the maker's liability. To call it an "equivocal" agreement, as the Minnesota Supreme Court did, is the least that can be said in criticism of it.

The manufacturer agrees to replace defective parts for 90 days after the sale or until the car has been driven 4,000 miles, whichever is first to occur, *if the part is sent to the factory, transportation charges prepaid, and if examination discloses to its satisfaction that the part is defective.* . . .

Chrysler points out that an implied warranty of merchantability is an incident of a contract of sale. It concedes, of course, the making of the original sale to Bloomfield Motors, Inc., but maintains that this transaction marked the terminal point of its contractual connection with the car. Then Chrysler urges that since it was not a party to the sale by the dealer to Henningsen, there is no privity of contract* between it and the plaintiffs, and the absence of this privity eliminates any such implied warranty.

There is no doubt that under early common-law concepts of contractual liability only those persons who were parties to the bargain could sue for a breach of it. In more recent times a noticeable disposition has appeared in a number of jurisdictions to break through the narrow barrier of privity when dealing with sales of goods in order to give realistic recognition to a universally accepted fact. The fact is that the dealer and the ordinary buyer do not, and are not expected to, buy goods, whether they be foodstuffs or automobiles, exclusively for their own consumption or use. Makers and manufacturers know this and advertise and market their products on that assumption; witness the "family" car, the baby foods, etc. The limitations of privity in contracts for the sale of goods developed their place in the law when marketing conditions were simple, when maker and buyer frequently met face to face on an equal bargaining plane and when many of the products were relatively uncomplicated and conducive to inspection by a buyer competent to evaluate their quality. With the advent of mass marketing, the manufacturer became remote from the purchaser, sales were accomplished through intermediaries, and the demand for the product was created by advertising media. In such an economy it became obvious that the consumer was the person being cultivated. Manifestly, the connotation of "consumer" was broader than that of "buyer." He signified such a person who, in the reasonable contemplation of the parties to the sale, might be expected to use the product. Thus, where the commodities sold are such that if defectively manufactured they will be dangerous to life or limb, then society's interests can only be protected by eliminating the requirement of privity between the maker and his dealers and the reasonably expected ultimate consumer. In that way the burden of losses consequent upon use of defective articles is borne by those who are in a position to either control the danger or make an equitable distribution of the losses when they do occur. . . .

Under modern conditions the ordinary layman, on responding to the importuning of colorful advertising, has neither the opportunity nor the capacity to inspect or to determine the fitness of an automobile for use; he must rely on the manufacturer who has control of its construction, and to some degree on the dealer who, to the limited extent called for by the manufacturer's instructions, inspects and services it before delivery. In such a marketing milieu his remedies and those of persons who properly claim through him should not depend "upon the intricacies of the law of sales. The obligation of the manufacturer should not be based alone on privity of contract. It should rest, as was once said, upon 'the demands of social justice.'" . . .

In a society such as ours, where the automobile is a common and necessary adjunct of daily life, and where its use is so fraught with

---

*["Privity of contract": A contractual relation existing between parties that is sufficiently close to confer a legal claim or right. Ed.]

danger to the driver, passengers, and the public, the manufacturer is under a special obligation in connection with the construction, promotion, and sale of his cars. Consequently, the courts must examine purchase agreements closely to see if consumer and public interests are treated fairly. . . .

What influence should these circumstances have on the restrictive effect of Chrysler's express warranty in the framework of the purchase contract? As we have said, warranties originated in the law to safeguard the buyer and not to limit the liability of the seller or manufacturer. It seems obvious in this instance that the motive was to avoid the warranty obligations which are normally incidental to such sales. The language gave little and withdrew much. In return for the delusive remedy of replacement of defective parts at the factory, the buyer is said to have accepted the exclusion of the maker's liability for personal injuries arising from the breach of the warranty, and to have agreed to the elimination of any other express or implied warranty. An instinctively felt sense of justice cries out against such a sharp bargain. But does the doctrine that a person is bound by his signed agreement, in the absence of fraud, stand in the way of any relief? . . .

The warranty before us is a standardized form designed for mass use. It is imposed upon the automobile consumer. He takes it or leaves it, and he must take it to buy an automobile. No bargaining is engaged in with respect to it. In fact, the dealer through whom it comes to the buyer is without authority to alter it; his function is ministerial — simply to deliver it. The form warranty is not only standard with Chrysler but, as mentioned above, it is the uniform warranty of the Automobile Manufacturers Association. . . . Of these companies, the "Big Three" (General Motors, Ford, and Chrysler) represented 93.5% of the passenger-car production for 1958 and the independents 6.5%.[1]

And for the same year the "Big Three" had 86.72% of the total passenger vehicle registrations. . . .

In the context of this warranty, only the abandonment of all sense of justice would permit us to hold that, as a matter of law, the phrase "its obligation under this warranty being limited to making good at its factory any part or parts thereof" signifies to an ordinary reasonable person that he is relinquishing any personal injury claim that might flow from the use of a defective automobile. Such claims are nowhere mentioned. . . .

In the matter of warranties on the sale of their products, the Automobile Manufacturers Association has enabled them to present a united front. From the standpoint of the purchaser, there can be no arm's-length negotiating on the subject. Because his capacity for bargaining is so grossly unequal, the inexorable conclusion which follows is that he is not permitted to bargain at all. He must take or leave the automobile on the warranty terms dictated by the maker. He cannot turn to a competitor for better security.

Public policy is a term not easily defined. Its significance varies as the habits and needs of a people may vary. It is not static and the field of application is an ever increasing one. A contract, or a particular provision therein, valid in one era may be wholly opposed to the public policy of another. Courts keep in mind the principle that the best interests of society demand that persons should not be unnecessarily restricted in their freedom to contract. But they do not hesitate to declare void as against public policy contractual provisions which clearly tend to the injury of the public in some way. . . .

In the framework of this case, illuminated as it is by the facts and the many decisions noted, we are of the opinion that Chrysler's attempted disclaimer of an implied warranty of the merchantability and of the obligations arising therefrom is so inimical to the public good as to compel an adjudication of its invalidity. . . .

The principles that have been expounded as to the obligation of the manufacturer apply with equal force to the separate express warranty of the dealer. This is so, irrespective of the absence of the relationship of principle and agent between these defendants, because the manufacturer and the Association establish the warranty policy for the industry. The bargaining position of the dealer is inextricably bound by practice to that of the maker and the purchaser must take or leave the automobile, accompanied and encumbered as it is by the uniform warranty. . . .

Under all of the circumstances outlined above, the judgments in favor of the plaintiffs and against the defendants are affirmed.

NOTES

1. Standard and Poor (Industrial Surveys, Autos, Basic Analysis, June 25, 1959), p. 4109.

Automobile Workers v. Johnson Controls, Inc.

Supreme Court of the United States

In this case we are concerned with an employer's gender-based fetal-protection policy. May an employer exclude a fertile female employee from certain jobs because of its concern for the health of the fetus the woman might conceive?

I

Respondent Johnson Controls, Inc., manufactures batteries. In the manufacturing process, the element lead is a primary ingredient. Occupational exposure to lead entails health risks, including the risk of harm to any fetus carried by a female employee.

Before the Civil Rights Act of 1964, 78 Stat. 241, became law, Johnson Controls did not employ any woman in a battery-manufacturing job. In June 1977, however, it announced its first official policy concerning its employment of women in lead-exposure work. . . .

Johnson Controls "stopped short of excluding women capable of bearing children from lead exposure," *id.*, at 138, but emphasized that a woman who expected to have a child should not choose a job in which she would have such exposure. The company also required a woman who wished to be considered for employment to sign a statement that she had been advised of the risk of having a child while she was exposed to lead. . . .

Five years later, in 1982, Johnson Controls shifted from a policy of warning to a policy of exclusion. Between 1979 and 1983, eight employees became pregnant while maintaining blood lead levels in excess of 30 micrograms per deciliter. Tr. of Oral Arg. 25, 34. This appeared to be the critical level noted by the Occupational Health and Safety Administra-

---

89 U.S. 1215 (1991). Opinion delivered by Justice Blackmun.

tion (OSHA) for a worker who was planning to have a family. See 29 CFR § 1910.1025 (1989). The company responded by announcing a broad exclusion of woman from jobs that exposed them to lead:

"... [I]t is [Johnson Controls'] policy that women who are pregnant or who are capable of bearing children will not be placed into jobs involving lead exposure or which could expose them to lead through the exercise of job bidding, bumping, transfer or promotion rights." App. 85–86.

The policy defined "women . . . capable of bearing children" as [a]ll women except those whose inability to bear children is medically documented." *Id.*, at 81. It further stated that an unacceptable work station was one where, "over the past year," an employee had recorded a blood lead level of more than 30 micrograms per deciliter or the work site had yielded an air sample containing a lead level in excess of 30 micrograms per cubic meter. *Ibid.*

II

In April 1984, petitioners filed in the United States District Court for the Eastern District of Wisconsin a class action challenging Johnson Controls' fetal-protection policy as sex discrimination that violated Title VII of the Civil Rights Act of 1964, as amended, 42 U.S. C. §2000e *et seq.* Among the individual plaintiffs were petitioners [such as] Mary Craig, who had chosen to be sterilized in order to avoid losing her job. . . .

III

The bias in Johnson Controls' policy is obvious. Fertile men, but not fertile women, are given a choice as to whether they wish to risk their reproductive health for a particular job. Section 703(a) of the Civil Rights Act of 1964, 78 Stat. 255, as amended, 42 U.S.C. §2000e-2(a), prohibits sex-based classifications in terms and conditions of employment, in hiring and discharging decisions, and in other employment decisions that adversely affect an employee's status. Respondent's fetal-protection policy explicitly discriminates against women on the basis of their sex. The policy excludes women with childbearing capacity from lead-exposed jobs and so creates a facial classification based on gender. Respondent assumes as much in its brief before this Court. Brief for Respondent 17, n. 24.

Nevertheless, the Court of Appeals assumed, as did the two appellate courts who already had confronted the issue, that sex-specific fetal-protection policies do not involve facial discrimination. . . . The court assumed that because the asserted reason for the sex-based exclusion (protecting women's unconceived offspring) was ostensibly benign, the policy was not sex-based discrimination. That assumption, however, was incorrect.

First, Johnson Controls' policy classifies on the basis of gender and childbearing capacity, rather than fertility alone. Respondent does not seek to protect the unconceived children of all its employees. Despite evidence in the record about the debilitating effect of lead exposure on the male reproductive system, Johnson Controls is concerned only with the harms that may befall the unborn offspring of its female employees. . . . Johnson Controls' policy is facially discriminatory because it requires only a female employee to produce proof that she is not capable of reproducing.

Our conclusion is bolstered by the Pregnancy Discrimination Act of 1978 (PDA), 92 Stat. 2076, 42 U.S.C. §2000e(k), in which Congress explicitly provided that, for purposes of Title VII, discrimination "on the basis of sex" includes discrimination "because of or on the basis of pregnancy, childbirth, or related medical conditions." "The Pregnancy Discrimination Act has now made clear that, for all Title VII purposes, discrimination based on a woman's pregnancy is, on its face, discrimination because of her sex." *Newport News Shipbuilding & Dry Dock Co. v. EEOC*, 462 U.S. 669, 684 (1983). In its use of the words "capable of bearing children" in the 1982 policy statement as the criterion for exclusion, Johnson Controls explicitly classifies on the basis of potential for pregnancy. Under the PDA, such a classification must be regarded, for Title VII purposes, in the same light as explicit sex discrimination. Respondent has chosen to treat all its female employees as potentially pregnant; that choice evinces discrimination on the basis of sex. . . .

The beneficence of an employer's purpose does not undermine the conclusion that an explicit gender-based policy is sex discrimination under § 703(a) and thus may be defended only as a BFOQ [bona fide occupational qualification].

The enforcement policy of the Equal Employment Opportunity Commission accords with this conclusion. On January 24, 1990, the EEOC issued a Policy Guidance in the light of the Seventh Circuit's decision in the present case. . . .

In sum, Johnson Controls' policy "does not pass the simple test of whether the evidence shows 'treatment of a person in a manner which but for that person's sex would be different.'" . . .

IV

Under § 703(e)(1) of Title VII, an employer may discriminate on the basis of "religion, sex, or national origin in those certain instances where religion, sex, or national origin is a bona fide occupational qualification rea-

sonably necessary to the normal operation of that particular business or enterprise." 42 U.S. C. §2000e-2(e)(1). We therefore turn to the question whether Johnson Controls' fetal-protection policy is one of those "certain instances" that come within the BFOQ exception. . . .

The PDA's amendment to Title VII contains a BFOQ standard of its own: Unless pregnancy employees differ from others "in their ability or inability to work," they must be "treated the same" as other employees "for all employment-related purposes." 42 U.S. C. §2000e(k). This language clearly sets forth Congress' remedy for discrimination on the basis of pregnancy and potential pregnancy. Women who are either pregnant or potentially pregnant must be treated like others "similar in their ability . . . to work." *Ibid.* In other words, women as capable of doing their jobs as their male counterparts may not be forced to choose between having a child and having a job. . . .

V

We have no difficulty concluding that Johnson Controls cannot establish a BFOQ. Fertile women, as far as appears in the record, participate in the manufacture of batteries as efficiently as anyone else. Johnson Controls' professed moral and ethical concerns about the welfare of the next generation do not suffice to establish a BFOQ of female sterility. Decisions about the welfare of future children must be left to the parents who conceive, bear, support, and raise them rather than to the employers who hire those parents. Congress has mandated this choice through Title VII, as amended by the Pregnancy Discrimination Act. Johnson Controls has attempted to exclude women because of their reproductive capacity. Title VII and the PDA simply do not allow a woman's dismissal because of her failure to submit to sterilization.

Nor can concerns about the welfare of the next generation be considered a part of the "essence" of Johnson Controls' business. . . .

Johnson Controls argues that it must exclude all fertile women because it is impossible to tell which women will become pregnant while working with lead. This argument is somewhat academic in light of our conclusion that the company may not exclude fertile women at all; it perhaps is worth noting, however, that Johnson Controls has shown no "factual basis for believing that all or substantially all women would be unable to perform safely and efficiently the duties of the job involved." *Weeks v. Southern Bell Tel. & Tel. Co.*, 408 F. 2d 228, 235 (CA5 1969), quoted with approval in *Dothard*, 433 U.S., at 333. Even on this sparse record, it is apparent that Johnson Controls is concerned about only a small minority of women. Of the eight pregnancies reported among the female employees, it has not been shown that any of the babies have birth defects or other abnormalities. The record does not reveal the birth rate for Johnson Controls' female workers but national statistics show that approximately nine percent of all fertile women become pregnant each year. The birthrate drops to two percent for blue collar workers over age 30. See Becker, 53 U. Chi. L. Rev., at 1233. Johnson Controls' fear of prenatal injury, no matter how sincere, does not begin to show that substantially all of its fertile women employees are incapable of doing their jobs. . . .

It is no more appropriate for the courts than it is for individual employers to decide whether a woman's reproductive role is more important to herself and her family than her economic role. Congress has left this choice to the woman as hers to make.

The judgment of the Court of Appeals is reversed and the case is remanded for further proceedings consistent with this opinion.

State Department of Environmental Protection v. Ventron Corporation

Supreme Court of New Jersey

This appeal concerns the responsibility of various corporations for the cost of the cleanup and removal of mercury pollution seeping from a forty-acre tract of land into Berry's Creek, a tidal estuary of the Hackensack River that flows through the Meadowlands. The plaintiff is the State of New Jersey, Department of Environmental Protection (DEP); the primary defendants are Velsicol Chemical Corporation (Velsicol), its former subsidiary, Wood Ridge Chemical Corporation (Wood Ridge), and Ventron Corporation (Ventron), into which Wood Ridge was merged. . . .

Beneath its surface, the tract is saturated by an estimated 268 tons of toxic waste, primarily mercury. For a stretch of several thousand feet, the concentration of mercury in

Berry's Creek is the highest found in fresh water sediments in the world. The waters of the creek are contaminated by the compound methyl mercury, which continues to be released as the mercury interacts with other elements. Due to depleted oxygen levels, fish no longer inhabit Berry's Creek, but are present only when swept in by the tide and, thus, irreversibly toxified.

The contamination at Berry's Creek results from mercury processing operations carried on at the site for almost fifty years. In March, 1976, DEP filed a complaint against Ventron, Wood Ridge, Velsicol, Berk, and the Wolfs, charging them with violating the "New Jersey Water Quality Improvement Act of 1971," *N.J.S.A.* 58:10–23.1 to – 23.10, and *N.J.S.A.* 23:5–28, and further, with creating or maintaining a nuisance. . . .

After a fifty-five-day trial, the trial court determined that Berk and Wood Ridge were jointly liable for the cleanup and removal of the mercury; [and] that Velsicol and Ventron were severally liable for half of the costs. . . .

The Appellate Division substantially affirmed the judgment, but modified it in several respects, including the imposition of joint and several liability on Ventron and Velsicol for all costs incurred in the cleanup and removal of the mercury pollution in Berry's Creek. . . . We modify and affirm the judgment of the Appellate Division.

I

From 1929 to 1960, first as lessee and then as owner of the entire forty-acre tract, Berk operated a mercury processing plant, dumping untreated waste material and allowing mercury-laden effluent to drain on the tract. Berk continued uninterrupted operations until 1960, at which time it sold its assets to Wood Ridge and ceased its corporate existence.

In 1960, Velsicol formed Wood Ridge as a wholly-owned subsidiary for the sole purpose of purchasing Berk's assets and operating the mercury processing plant. . . . Wood Ridge continued to operate the processing plant on the 7.1-acre tract from 1960 to 1968, when Velsicol sold Wood Ridge to Ventron. . . .

In 1968, Velsicol sold 100% of the Wood Ridge stock to Ventron, which began to consider a course of treatment for plant wastes. Until this time, the waste had been allowed to course over the land through open drainage ditches. In March 1968, Ventron engaged the firm of Metcalf & Eddy to study the effects of mercury on the land, and three months later, Ventron constructed a weir to aid in monitoring the effluent. . . .

In 1970, the contamination at Berry's Creek came to the attention of the United States Environmental Protection Agency (EPA), which conducted a test of Wood Ridge's waste water. The tests indicated that the effluent carried two to four pounds of mercury into Berry's Creek each day. . . .

On February 5, 1974, Wood Ridge granted to Robert Wolf, a commercial real estate developer, an option to purchase the 7.1-acre tract on which the plant was located, and on May 20, 1974, Ventron conveyed the tract to the Wolfs. The Wolfs planned to demolish the plant and construct a warehousing facility. In the course of the demolition, mercury-contaminated water was used to wet down the structures and allowed to run into the creek. The problem came to the attention of DEP, which ordered a halt to the demolition, pending adequate removal or containment of the contamination. DEP proposed a containment plan, but the Wolfs implemented another plan and proceeded with their project. DEP then instituted this action. . . .

The trial court concluded that the entire tract and Berry's Creek are polluted and that additional mercury from the tract has reached, and may continue to reach, the creek via ground and surface waters. Every operator of the mercury processing plant contributed to the pollution; while the plant was in operation, the discharge of effluent resulted in a dangerous and hazardous mercurial content in Berry's Creek. The trial court found that from 1960–74 the dangers of mercury were becoming better known and that Berk, Wood Ridge, Velsicol, and Ventron knew of those dangers. . . .

II

The lower courts imposed strict liability on Wood Ridge under common-law principles for causing a public nuisance and for "unleashing a dangerous substance during non-natural use of the land." . . .

Twenty-one years ago, without referring to either *Marshall v. Welwood* or *Rylands v. Fletcher*, this Court adopted the proposition that "an ultrahazardous activity which introduces an unusual danger into the community . . . should pay its own way in the event it actually causes damage to others." *Berg v. Reaction Motors Div., Thiokol Chem. Corp.*, 37 N.J. 396, 410 (1962). . . .

We believe it is time to recognize expressly that the law of liability has evolved so that a landowner is strictly liable to others for harm caused by toxic wastes that are stored on his property and flow onto the property of others. Therefore, we . . . adopt the principle of liability originally declared in *Rylands v. Fletcher*. The net result is that those who use, or permit others to use, land for the conduct of abnormally dangerous activities are strictly liable for resultant damages. . . .

Under the *Restatement [(Second) of Torts]* analysis, whether an activity is abnormally dangerous is to be determined on a case-by-case basis, taking all relevant circumstances into consideration. As set forth in the *Restatement:*

In determining whether an activity is abnormally dangerous, the following factors are to be considered:
a. existence of a high degree of risk of some harm to the person, land or chattels of others;
b. likelihood that the harm that results from it will be great;
c. inability to eliminate the risk by the exercise of reasonable care;
d. extent to which the activity is not a matter of common usage;
e. inappropriateness of the activity to the place where it is carried on; and
f. extent to which its value to the community is outweighed by its dangerous attributes. [*Restatement (Second) of Torts* § 520 (1977)].

Pollution from toxic wastes that seeps onto the land of others and into streams necessarily harms the environment. . . . The lower courts found that each of those hazards was present as a result of the contamination of the entire tract. . . . With respect to the ability to eliminate the risks involved in disposing of hazardous wastes by the exercise of reasonable care, no safe way exists to dispose of mercury by simply dumping it onto land or into water. . . .

Even if they did not intend to pollute or adhered to the standards of the time, all of these parties remain liable. Those who poison the land must pay for its cure.

We approve the trial court's finding that Berk, Wood Ridge, Velsicol, and Ventron are liable under common-law principles for the abatement of the resulting nuisance and damage. . . .

III

We agree with the trial court's finding that both Berk and Wood Ridge violated the statute by intentionally permitting mercury-laden effluent to escape onto the land surrounding Berry's Creek. . . .

In an appropriate exercise of its original jurisdiction under R. 2:10–5, the Appellate Division found that the record overwhelmingly supported the conclusion that the mercury pollution in Berry's Creek and the surrounding area presented a substantial and imminent threat to the environment, thus satisfying the requirement for a retroactive application of the act. Our independent analysis leads us to the same conclusion. Thus, we find Berk, Wood Ridge, and Velsicol liable under the Spill Act. Ventron is liable because it expressly assumed the liabilities of Wood Ridge in their merger. . . .

As amended, the Spill Act provides: "Any person who has discharged a hazardous substance *or is in any way responsible* for any hazardous substance . . . shall be strictly liable, jointly and severally, without regard to fault, for all clean up and removal costs." *N.J.S.A.* 58:10–23.11g(c) (emphasis added). . . .

From 1967 to 1974, and thereafter, Velsicol could have controlled the dumping of mercury onto its own thirty-three-acre tract. By permitting Wood Ridge, even after it became a Ventron subsidiary in 1968, to use that tract as a mercury dump, Velsicol made possible the seepage of hazardous wastes into Berry's Creek. Furthermore, from 1960 to 1968, Velsicol was the sole shareholder of Wood Ridge and all members of the Wood Ridge Board of Directors were Velsicol employees. Velsicol personnel, officers, and directors were involved in the day-to-day operation of Wood Ridge. In addition to constant involvement in Wood Ridge's activities, Velsicol permitted the dumping of waste material on the thirty-three-acre tract. When viewed together, those facts compel a finding that Velsicol was "responsible" within the meaning of the Spill Act for the pollution that occurred from 1960 to 1968. . . .

Through the merger of Wood Ridge into Ventron, the latter corporation assumed all of Wood Ridge's liabilities, including those arising out of the pollution of Berry's Creek. See *N.J.S.A.* 14A:10–6(c). Ventron, however, did not assume Velsicol's liability.

Pursuant to the mandate of the Spill Act, see *N.J.S.A.* 58:10–23.11g(c), Berk, Wood Ridge, Velsicol, and Ventron are jointly and severally liable without regard to fault. Only Ventron and Velsicol remain in existence, and we affirm that portion of the Appellate Division judgment that holds them jointly and severally liable for the cleanup and removal of mercury from the Berry's Creek area.

IV

. . . As modified, the judgment of the Appellate Division is affirmed.

CASE 1.   *Protecting Consumers Against Tobacco*

The dangers of smoking cigarettes are now generally conceded by almost everyone except the tobacco companies. Far less clear is how to protect the consumer and the potential consumer of cigarettes. A major source of marketing is newspaper advertising. At the same time, newspapers are a major source of information transmitted to the public about the dangers of smoking cigarettes. Thus newspapers have not only an interest in revenue from cigarette advertising but also an interest in informing the public about the dangers of what they advertise. No one needs to be reminded that most newspapers are businesses interested in making a profit but are also interested in customer satisfaction.

The American Newspaper Publishers Association and the Magazine Publishers Association have appealed to First Amendment protections of the right to advertise and to present the facts as newspapers see fit in order to justify their view that this matter should be left up to each individual newspaper.

The New Republic commissioned reporter David Owen to write an article on cancer and the cigarette lobby. He wrote a piece so blunt in stating the issues and laying blame that *The New Republic*'s editors killed it. According to *USA Today*, "In the candid (and no doubt regretted) words of Leon Wieseltier, the editor who assigned it, the threat of 'massive losses of advertising revenue' did it in." Although the editors of *The New Republic* had been will-

ing to report on the dangers of smoking and on the pressures brought by lobbyists, they were not willing to support the forcefulness with which Owen stated his case. Owen later published his piece in the *Washington Monthly*, where he wrote that "The transcendent achievement of the cigarette lobby has been to establish the cancer issue as a 'controversy' or a 'debate' rather than as the clear-cut scientific case that it is." Owen portrayed an industry that intentionally uses newspapers and magazines to enhance its appeal by depicting the young smoker as healthy and sexy.

According to research by Kenneth E. Warner, rejection of Owens's article is one of many cases in which the American news media refused to report on smoking hazards for fear of loss of advertising revenue. This general problem prompted *Washington Post* ombudsman Sam Zagoria to chide newspapers for a failure to see the issues as moral rather than legal:

> Couldn't the newspapers of the country agree — voluntarily and collectively — to refuse cigarette advertising? Couldn't they do what is right rather than only what is not prohibited by law? Most papers take great pride in the service they render to their communities, not only in providing information but also in philanthropic activities that provide scholarships and underwrite athletic tournaments. Is not helping some youngster avert the tortures of life-shortening lung cancer even a greater gift? . . . Is there any media group for social responsibility?

This case was prepared by Tom L. Beauchamp. The case is based on the following sources: Charles Trueheart, "The Tobacco Industry's Advertising Smoke Screen," *USA Today,* March 15, 1985, p. 3D; Kenneth E. Warner, "Cigarette Advertising and Media Coverage of Smoking and Health," *New England Journal of Medicine,* Vol. 312, No. 6, February 7, 1985, pp. 384–88; Sam Zagoria, "Smoking and the Media's Responsibility," *Washington Post,* December 18, 1985, p. A26; Elizabeth Whelan, "Second Thoughts on a Cigarette-Ad Ban," *Wall Street Journal,* December 18, 1985, p. 28; Sam Zagoria, "Consumer Watchdogs," *Washington Post,* April 24, 1985, p. A24; Robert J. Samuelson, "Pacifying Media Hype," *Washington Post,* October 9, 1985, pp. F1, F12.

Only 6 out of 1,700 daily American newspapers, Zagoria noted (using statistics taken from the *New York State Journal of Medicine*), attempt wholeheartedly to report on the dangers of smoking.

During National Consumer Week in 1985, Zagoria wrote another column in which he took the position that the press has a "watchdog" role to play not only in government but in consumer safety as well. Few journalists disagree with Zagoria's judgment that this role is legitimate or that a newspaper can validly choose to emphasize reporting on the risks of smoking without introducing a bias. However, Zagoria's contentions that the press has an *obligation* to promote the interests of consumers has met a hostile reaction in newspaper front offices.

Questions

1. Has Zagoria confused the industry's responsibility and the government's responsibility to protect the public with that of the media's responsibilities, as many managers at newspapers believe?

2. Does anyone's obligation to protect consumers stretch as far as Zagoria suggests?

3. Are stiff warnings on packages of cigarettes adequate to protect consumers? Potential consumers?

CASE 2. *Do Apple Computer Shareholders Need Protection?*

In 1982 Apple Computer, Inc., announced its new disk drive "Twiggy." The drive was introduced to the market in the spring of 1983 but was discontinued the following September. The price of Apple's stock dropped 25% ($8.00 a share) the day after the drive was scrapped. Apple stockholders brought suit against the company and some of its officers, charging them with making materially misleading statements about the product in 1982 news releases. The case worked its way to the courts in May 1991.

The disk drive had a failure rate as high as 40% when it was released on the market. As a result, Apple had to recall the product. Since Apple technicians and executives knew there were problems with the disk, stockholders argued that the company's officers should be held morally and legally responsible not only for the quality of the product but also for the decline in the stock price. The stockholders argued that they were due compensation for the money they had lost.

Stockholders noted that more is at stake than a conflict of interest between management's responsibility to the stockholders and their profit objective. Stockholders rely on having materially correct information about developments they cannot confirm or disconfirm first hand. Because they had been given incomplete information about the market risks of the product, stockholders believed management failed to make honest disclosures and thereby failed in its fiduciary obligations.

Questions

1. Should management put profitability above responsibilities to disclose full information to shareholders?

This case was prepared by Tom L. Beauchamp.

2. Do managers have a responsibility to pay the stockholders all or some of the money they lost?

3. Were the officers deliberately misleading investors in failing to make a full disclosure?

4. Does management's duty to the stockholders require reports of the risks of a new technology, even when so doing might jeopardize future sales of the product?

CASE 3. *Virazole and Investor Risk*

On October 7, 1991, the U.S. Securities and Exchange Commission (SEC) filed suit against two pharmaceutical firms in a District of Columbia federal District Court, charging that the companies had falsely and misleadingly presented to investors a product's promise for combating the AIDS virus. The suit grew out of a four-year SEC investigation of ICN Pharmaceuticals and its Costa Mesa, California-based subsidiary, Viratek, Inc. The U.S. Food and Drug Administration (FDA) had approved the companies to market the drug ribavirin under the trade name Virazole, for hospital use in treating respiratory syncytial virus. In a January 1987 press conference, the companies announced that ribavirin had, in addition, proved effective in delaying the onset of AIDS symptoms in HIV-infected patients. Shortly after this announcement Viratek stock climbed from $14.00 a share to $70.00 a share. On the date the SEC filed suit, the stock declined to $5.12 a share.

The company provided a summary of its scientific findings, but AIDS advocacy groups maintained that ICN and Viratek had supplied few hard facts and test results to substantiate the conclusions announced. The SEC lawsuit alleged that corporate officials in 1987 deliberately made untrue claims regarding virazole's effectiveness. According to SEC

officials, in the placebo-controlled clinical trials, the patients who received placebos had exhibited severely weakened immune systems before the trial and so were certain to fare worse than the patients receiving the drug being tested. The placebo patients also showed an unusually rapid progression toward acute AIDS symptoms. Consequently, the ribavirin patients appeared to benefit from treatment only because their AIDS symptoms developed more slowly in comparison with their placebo counterparts. In April 1987, the FDA declined to approve ribavirin for AIDS treatment, based on its analysis of the clinical trials. When ICN and Viratek subsequently neglected to inform investors of the results of clinical trials, the SEC launched its investigation.

After the SEC filed its lawsuit, ICN and Viratek officials signed a consent order that did not address corporate culpability but that did stipulate that the corporations involved would take precautions not to make potentially "misleading statements to investors" in the future. At the same time, company spokespersons denied any wrongdoing in the ribavirin controversy. They held that the consent order was signed only because it was the fastest way to resolve the affair. According to Viratek's CEO, "We have always operated our business with integrity, and as good citizens

---

This case was prepared by John Cuddihy, based in part on a report by Tracy Thompson in *The Washington Post,* "Drug Maker Settles SEC Suit over Notification of Investors," October 8, 1991, D3.

we will continue to do so." The company claimed that it had a different view of the scientific evidence than the SEC did and that it had no moral or legal obligation to make disclosures to investors of the sort proposed by the SEC. Investors did not file suit in the case.

Questions

1. What should Viratek have told stockholders and potential stockholders? Should

any information disclosure include a full, conservatively stated estimate of the scientific evidence?
2. Did Viratek officials manipulate potential investors into buying the stock through an incomplete disclosure?
3. Assuming trade secrets are involved, is the scientific evidence proprietary to the company and also confidential? If so, could hard facts and test results be disclosed without damage to the company?

CASE 4.   *OSHA Noncompliance and Security*

TMW Corporation produces three-quarters of the world's micro-synchronizers, an integral part of apartment vacuum systems. This corporation has plants mostly in the Midwest, although a few are scattered on both the East and West Coasts. The plants in the Midwest employ Electronic Worker's Union members under a contract that became effective last August and is in force for three years. This union is strong and the employees will do anything to preserve and maintain the strong union benefits that have been won.

Last year an OSHA official visited the St. Louis plant and discovered several discrepancies with the standards established by the OSH Act, including the absence of safety goggles on employees who weld tiny wires together, and also an automatic shutoff switch on the wire-splicing machine. OSHA issued warnings to TMW for the noncompliance and informed company officials that it would impose drastic fines if they did not correct them.

The company immediately proceeded to correct the problems. They had to shut parts of the Midwest plants down on a rotating

basis to alter the wire-splicing machines. These measures upset the union members, because the employer laid off older employees, not the new trainees on the machines. They threatened a walkout.

The safety goggles presented the company with another OSHA compliance hurdle. When told of the need to wear their goggles, the welders refused, saying they could not see as well. The welders said they would take responsibility for not wearing the goggles. The unions backed the welders in their refusal.

Questions

1. Was the TMW Corporation wrong in laying off the senior employees?
2. Should the company force the welders to comply with the safety goggle requirements? Since the welders refused to comply and assumed responsibility, is the company released of all responsibility in the event of an accident?
3. Should OSHA intervene and fine those responsible for any violations of OSHA

This case was prepared by Professor Kenneth A. Kovach. Printed with permission.

standards? Is this case too minor for such intervention?

Suggested Supplementary Readings

Consumer Protection

BROBECK, STEPHEN. *The Modern Consumer Movement.* Boston, MA: G.K. Hall & Co., 1990.

CAVANILLAS MUGICA, SANTIAGO. "Protection of the Weak Consumer Under Product Liability Rules." *Journal of Consumer Policy* 13 (1990).

OWEN, DAVID G. "Rethinking the Policies of Strict Products Liability." *Vanderbilt Law Review* 33 (1980).

PROSSER, WILLIAM L. "The Assault Upon the Citadel (Strict Liability to the Consumer)." *Yale Law Journal* 69 (1960).

SAXE, DIANNE. "The Fiduciary Duty of Corporate Directors to Protect the Environment for Future Generations." *Environmental Values* 1 (Autumn 1992): 243–252.

SORELL, TOM. "The Customer Is Not Always Right." *Journal of Business Ethics* 13 (November 1994): 913–18.

VISCUSI, W. KIP. "Toward a Proper Role for Hazard Warnings in Products Liability Cases." *Journal of Products Liability* 13 (1991).

WARNE, COLSTON E. *The Consumer Movement,* edited by Richard L. D. Morse. Manhattan, KS: Family Economics Trust Press, 1993.

Worker Protection

BEAUCHAMP, TOM L. *Case Studies in Business, Society, and Ethics.* 3rd ed. Englewood Cliffs, NJ: Prentice Hall, 1997. Chaps. 1, 5.

BERITIC, T. "Workers at High Risk: The Right to Know." *Lancet* 341 (April 10, 1993): 933–34.

BRUENING, JOHN. "Risk Communication." *Occupational Hazards* 52 (October 1990).

EZORSKY, GERTRUDE, ed. *Moral Rights in the Workplace.* Albany: State University of New York Press, 1987.

GIBSON, MARY. *Workers Rights.* Totowa, NJ: Rowman and Littlefield, 1983.

GOLDSMITH, WILLIS. "The Expanding Scope of Employers' Duties Under the Hazard Communication Standard and State and Local Right-to-Know Laws." *Employee Relations Law Journal* 12 (Spring 1987).

HIMMELSTEIN, JAY S., and HOWARD FRUMKIN. "The Right to Know About Toxic Exposures: Implications for Physicians." *New England Journal of Medicine* 312 (March 14, 1985): 687–90.

LURIE, SUE GENA. "Ethical Dilemmas and Professional Roles in Occupational Medicine." *Social Science and Medicine* 38 (May 1994): 1367–74.

SASS, ROBERT. "The Worker's Right to Know, Participate, and Refuse Hazardous Work: A Manifesto Right." *Journal of Business Ethics* 5 (April 1986).

U.S. Congress. Office of Technology Assessment. *Reproductive Hazards in the Workplace. Contractor Documents, Volume 1: Selected Ethical Issues in the Management of Reproductive Health Hazards in the Workplace.* [Set of six papers]. Washington: U.S. Office of Technology Assessment, January 1986.

WALTERS, VIVIENNE, and MARGARET DENTON. "Workers' Knowledge of Their Legal Rights and Resistance to Hazardous Work." *Industrial Relations* 45 (Summer 1990).

WOKUTCH, RICHARD E. *Worker Protection, Japanese Style.* Ithaca, NY: ILR Press, 1992.

Environmental Protection

ATTFIELD, ROBIN. *The Ethics of Environmental Concern.* New York: Columbia University Press, 1983.

BLACKSTONE, WILLIAM T., ed. *Philosophy and Environmental Crisis.* Athens: University of Georgia Press, 1974.

ENGEL, J. RONALD, and JOAN GIBB ENGEL, eds. *Ethics of Environment and Development.* Tucson: University of Arizona Press, 1991.

Environmental Ethics. "An Interdisciplinary Journal Dedicated to the Philosophical Aspects of Environmental Problems." 1979 to present.

GIBSON, MARY. *To Breathe Freely: Risk, Consent, and Air.* Totowa, NJ: Rowman and Littlefield, 1985.

GOODIN, ROBERT E. "Property Rights and Preservationist Duties." *Inquiry* 33 (1991).

HARRIS, CHRISTOPHER, and others. "Criminal Liability of Federal Hazardous Waste Law: The 'Knowledge' of Corporations and their Executives." *Wake Forest Law Review* 23 (1988).

HOCH, DAVID, and ROBERT A. GIACALONE. "On the Lumber Industry: Ethical Concerns as the Other Side of Profits." *Journal of Business Ethics* 13 (May 1994): 357–67.

HOFFMAN, W. MICHAEL, and others, eds. *Business, Ethics, and the Environment: The Public Policy Debate.* New York: Quorum Books, 1990.

———, eds. *The Corporation, Ethics and the Environment.* New York: Quorum Books, 1990.

LUDWIG, DEAN C., and JUDITH A. LUDWIG. "The Regulation of Green Marketing: Learning Lessons from the Regulation of Health and Nutrition Claims." *Business and Professional Ethics Journal* 11 (Fall–Winter 1992): 73–91.

MILLER, ALAN S. *Gaia Connections: An Introduction to Ecology, Ecoethics, and Economics.* Totowa, NJ: Rowman and Littlefield, 1991.

NAESS, ARNE. *Ecology, Community, and Lifestyle,* trans. by D. Rothenberg. New York: Cambridge University Press, 1990.

NEWTON, LISA H. "The Chainsaws of Greed: The Case of Pacific Lumber." *Business and Professional Ethics Journal* 8 (Fall 1989): 29–61.

REGAN, TOM, ed. *Earthbound: New Introductory Essays in Environmental Ethics.* New York: Random House, 1984.

ROLSTON, HOLMES, III. *Environmental Ethics: Duties to and Values in The Natural World.* Philadelphia: Temple University Press, 1988.

———. *Philosophy Gone Wild: Environmental Ethics.* Buffalo, NY: Prometheus Books, 1991.

———. "Just Environmental Business." In *Just Business,* edited by Tom Regan. Philadelphia: Temple University Press, 1983.

SAGOFF, MARK. *The Economy of the Earth.* New York: Cambridge University Press, 1990.

SAXE, DIANNE. "The Fiduciary Duty of Corporate Directors to Protect the Environment for Future Generations." *Environmental Values* 1 (Fall 1992): 243–52.

SKORPEN, ERLING. "Images of the Environment in Corporate America." *Journal of Business Ethics* 10 (1991).

SMITH, DENIS, ed. *Business and The Environment: Implications of the New Environmentalism.* New York: St. Martin's Press, 1993.

STARIK, MARK. "Should Trees Have Managerial Standing? Toward Stakeholder Status for Non-Human Nature." *Journal of Business Ethics* 14 (March 1995): 207–17.

VANDEVEER, DONALD, and CHRISTINE PIERCE. *Environmental Ethics and Policy Book: Philosophy, Ecology and Economics.* Belmont, CA: Wadsworth Publishing Co., 1994.

Investor Protection

ALMEDER, ROBERT F., and MILTON SNOEYENBOS. "Churning: Ethical and Legal Issues." *Business and Professional Ethics Journal* 6 (Spring 1987).

ALMEDER, ROBERT F., and DAVID CAREY. "In Defense of Sharks: Moral Issues in Hostile Liquidating Takeovers." *Journal of Business Ethics* 10 (1991): 471–84.

BROWN, DONNA. "Environmental Investing: Let the Buyer Beware." *Management Review* 79 (June 1990).

DAMM, RICHARD E. "A Question of Bias." *Best's Review* 86 (December 1985).

EASTERWOOD, JOHN C., RONALD F. SINGER, and ANJU SETH. "Controlling the Conflict of Interest in Management Buyouts." *The Review of Economics and Statistics* 76 (August 1994): 512–22.

FRANKS, JULIAN, and COLIN MAYER. *Risk, Regulation, and Investor Protection: The Case of Investment Management.* Oxford: Clarendon Press, 1989.

HEACOCK, MARIAN, and others. "Churning: An Ethical Issue in Finance." *Business and Professional Ethics Journal* 6 (Spring 1987).

HOFFMAN, W. MICHAEL, and RALPH J. MCQUADE. "A Matter of Ethics." *Financial Strategies and Concepts* 4 (1986).

JONES, THOMAS M., and REED O. HUNT. "The Ethics of Leveraged Management Buyouts Revisited." *Journal of Business Ethics* 10 (November 1991): 833–40.

KESTER, W. C., and T. A. LUEHRMAN. "Rehabilitating the Leveraged Buyout." *Harvard Business Review* 73 (May–June 1995): 119–30.

MOORE, JENNIFER. "What Is Really Unethical About Insider Trading?" *Journal of Business Ethics* 9 (March 1990).

"Note: Recent Trends in the Organization and Regulation of Securities Markets." *Financial Market Trends* 46 (May 1990).

SCHADLER, F. P., and J. E. KARNS. "The Unethical Exploitation of Shareholders in Management Buyout Transactions." *Journal of Business Ethics* 9 (July 1990): 595–602.

SCHIFRIN, MATTHEW. "Sellers Beware (lack of regulation and information in the defaulted junk market)." *Forbes* 147 (January 21, 1991): 36–38.

WILLIAMS, OLIVER, and others. *Ethics and the Investment Industry*. Savage, MD: Rowman and Littlefield, 1989.

Chapter Five

——— • ———

Rights and Obligations of Employers and Employees

TRADITIONALLY, BUSINESS FIRMS are organized hierarchically, with production line employees at the bottom and the CEO at the top. Also the interests of the stockholders are given priority over the interests of the other stakeholders. However, much recent literature presents a challenge to these arrangements, especially to underlying classical economic assumptions whereby labor is treated as analogous to land, capital, and machinery, that is, as replaceable and as a means to profit. Employees primarily want to be treated as persons who are genuine partners in the business enterprise. They want decent salaries and job security, as well as appreciation from supervisors, a sense of accomplishment, and fair opportunities to display their talents. Many employees are also interested in participating in planning the future directions of the company, defining the public responsibilities of the corporation, evaluating the role and quality of management, and — most especially — helping to set the tasks assigned to their jobs.[1] These new developments in labor relations are all to the good, but they must be understood in light of a very different tradition whereby an employee is clearly subordinate to the employer, is legally obligated to obey the employer's orders, and has few rights except the right to quit.

STATUS AND SCOPE OF EMPLOYEE RIGHTS

In the traditional view, the freedom of the employee to quit, the freedom of the employer to fire, and the right of the employer to order the employee to do his or her bidding define the essence of the employment contract. The legal principle behind the traditional view is called the *employment-at-will principle*. This principle says that in the absence of a specific contract or law, an employer may hire, fire, demote, or promote an employee whenever the employer wishes. Moreover, the employer may act with justification, with inadequate justification, or with no justification at all. In the selection that opens this chapter, Patricia Werhane and Tara Radin consider several arguments for the employment-at-will doctrine and find them wanting.

Over the years this master-servant relationship, which is at the core of the employment-at-will doctrine, has been legally constrained. Once unions were given legal protection, collective bargaining produced contracts that constrained the right of employers to fire at will. Employees who were protected by union contracts usually could be fired only for cause and then only after a lengthy grievance process. During the height of the union movement, the chief protection against an unjust firing was the union-negotiated contract. However, during the 1980s and early 1990s the percentage of the U.S. workforce belonging to unions fell into the teens, and as a result the protection offered by the union-negotiated contract covers millions fewer workers.

Some might argue that the decline in the number of U.S. workers who belong to unions has not significantly increased the number of employees who are at risk of an unjust dismissal. These people argue that a large number of enlightened companies have adopted policies that provide the same type of protection against unjust dismissal as was previously found in union-negotiated contracts. Moreover, where such policies exist they have the force of law. For example, on May 9, 1985, the New Jersey Supreme Court held that Hoffman-LaRoche Inc. was bound by job security assurances that were implied in an employee manual. The manual seemed to pledge that employees could be fired only for just cause and then only if certain procedures were followed. Hoffman-LaRoche argued that although the company manual gave company policy, adherence to it was voluntary and not legally enforceable. The court, however, said employers cannot have it both ways without acting unfairly and so illegally. Hoffman-LaRoche had to reinstate an employee who had been fired on grounds that his supervisor had lost confidence in his work.

In response to this and similar rulings, a number of corporations have taken steps to make it more difficult for employees to use company manuals and policy statements to protect their jobs. Some are simply eliminating the manuals and dismantling their grievance procedure apparatus. Sears Roebuck and other employers have their employees sign a form declaring that they can be fired "with or without just cause." Finally, several companies have developed internal procedures that examine every dismissal case as though it were a specific contract with a just-cause-for-firing provision in it.[2]

Others point out that during the 1980s and early 1990s, certain grounds for firing employees have been made illegal by federal or state law. Antidiscrimination statutes protect workers from being fired because of their race or sex, because they are handicapped, or because of age. Federal law also protects workers from being fired because they resist sexual advances from their bosses or refuse to date them. The protection given employees from this and other forms of sexual harassment is discussed in Chapter 6.

Although such laws are needed to curb past abuses, they are not always clear nor always effective. In the recession of 1991 and the subsequent downsizing that has occurred, many highly qualified white collar middle management employees who were over forty and laid off found it virtually impossible to find similar employment elsewhere. Rightly or wrongly, many of these people thought their age was a factor in their inability to obtain similar employment.

Yet another important development is the evolution of a common law protection to one's job if an employee disobeys an employer on the grounds that the employer ordered him or her to do something illegal or immoral. The notion that employees should not lose their jobs because they refuse to behave illegally or immorally might seem obvious, but as the two recent New Jersey cases included in this chapter show, the situation is more complex than it might appear. On some issues there is near unanimity that a course of action is right or wrong. But on other matters there is considerable difference of opinion. As we saw in the discussions of the Ford Pinto and the *Challenger* in Chapter 2, conflicts concerning what is morally appropriate often occur between managers and engineers. As a practical matter, a large corporation cannot allow employees to refuse to abide by a corporate decision whenever it conflicts with a personal moral position. On the other hand, the public must support employees who refuse to obey an order or accept a decision that threatens the public with serious harm. *Potter v. Village Bank of New Jersey* and *Warthen v. Toms River Community Memorial Hospital* illustrate how the courts try to balance the public interest and legitimate business concerns on this issue.

Even more important, these laws do not provide sufficient protection for what many employees consider their most important workplace right — the right to a job. From the perspective of most employees, the most important contribution of capitalism is providing work. Job security is often ranked higher than increased pay in terms of what employees most want from employers. The desire for job security is captured in employee demands that workers have a right to a job and that this right deserves protection. The claim that a person has a right to a job has two components. First, workers believe they have a right to a job in the first place. Second, as employees continue to work at a job, they believe they have a right to retain that job. Provision of the right to a job in the first place is usually considered to be the responsibility of government and is not discussed here. However, the notion that employees gain rights to a job that they have been holding is a new idea. In an era in which downsizing has destroyed even the traditional social contract, the idea that a person can come to hold a right to one's job is not widely held.

Indeed some scholars, especially from the law and economics school, have continued to support the traditional employment at will doctrine. For example, Richard A. Epstein has argued, in the article reprinted in this chapter, that employment at will is both fair and efficient. Spokespersons from the law and economics school take efficiency concerns very seriously, and Epstein spends considerable time developing some of these concerns.

DRUG TESTING AND THE RIGHT TO PRIVACY

Although a right to one's job may be the workplace right that employees most value and want honored, they believe they have other rights that should be honored as well. Many people believe that the rights guaranteed by the Bill of Rights in the Constitution are rights that each U.S. citizen has in all aspects of his or her life.

But this is not the case. Americans are protected against government infringements of the Bill of Rights, but they are not protected against corporate infringement of these rights. The Bill of Rights does not apply within the corporation. Thus there is no right to free speech within the corporation. Many believe that such a gap in the protection of the Constitution for individual citizens seems unjustified. They argue that since business activity takes place within U.S. society, business activity should be conducted consistent with the Bill of Rights. Others argue, however, that applying the Bill of Rights in the corporate setting would create great inefficiencies because discipline would break down. Besides, there are many companies in the United States for which a person can work, but there is only one U.S. government. Therefore, it is more important to have a Bill of Rights to protect individuals from government than to have a Bill of Rights to protect individuals from their boss.

Debates regarding the extent and scope of employee rights are commonplace in U.S. business. Theft by employees and customers is a huge problem, accounting for billions of dollars in losses every year. Until recently a common technique for deterring theft was to subject employees to polygraph (lie detector) tests. However, doubts about their accuracy and arguments that the tests invaded the privacy of employees led to a legal prohibition of their use, enacted initially by some states and then by the federal government. Now employers are turning to honesty tests that are based on statistical correlations between the answers to certain questions on the honesty test and the likelihood that an employee will commit theft.[3] The same issues of accuracy and invasion of privacy that confronted the use of polygraphs confront the use of honesty tests. However, the American Psychological Association has certified the validity of some tests, and the tests have escaped serious legal challenge up to the present time.[4]

Another serious problem facing corporate America is the rising cost of health insurance. In order to reduce their insurance premiums, many corporations are taking a great interest in the personal habits of their employees. Some will not hire people who smoke.[5] Others will insist that employees lose weight, exercise, and abstain from risky activities off the job.[6]

Rules that prohibit an employee from smoking tobacco violate both an employee's right to liberty and an employee's right to privacy. Employers argue that such violations are necessary with respect to tobacco in order to keep the cost of health insurance under control. To illustrate the ethical issues that could arise as technology improves, a selection by Joseph Kupfer has been included that considers the ethical issues which could be raised if business employed genetic testing in its hiring decisions. Genetic testing already makes it possible to identify people who are at risk for certain diseases. Given the high cost of treating those diseases, businesses could lower their insurance costs if they simply did not hire people who were at risk. But would such a policy be fair? Would genetic testing of this sort constitute an unjustified invasion of a person's privacy?

These attempts to regulate individual employee behavior off the job are extremely controversial, and perhaps the most controversial is the attempt by corporations to prevent employees from using drugs.

Many corporations now give drug tests to prospective employees. If they fail, they are not hired. An increasing number of companies are giving drug tests to persons they already employ. If any of these employees fail, companies take different actions. Some fire the employee outright; some retest the employee after a period of supposed abstinence and fire the employee if he or she tests positive again; still others insist that employees enroll in a drug treatment program. However, there is a common thread to all these approaches: the use of drugs even off the job will not be tolerated.

In most matters the authority of the boss ends at the company gate. What employees do on their own time is the employees' business. However, some conduct off the job may affect the employees' performance on the job or interfere with the employer's right to make a living by damaging the perception of the company and driving away customers. Even recreational use of relatively harmless drugs like marijuana are alleged to have these effects. In his article, Mark A. Rothstein documents how drugs can cause economic harm to employers, how drug testing works, what it measures, and how accurate it is. He then assesses the legal arguments against drug testing and concludes that drug testing is legal so long as it is reasonable. Rothstein ends by describing the elements of a legal, ethical, and effective drug-testing program.

Despite the fact that the vast majority of companies do some drug testing and the fact that well-constructed drug-testing programs are legal, a few companies still do not test for drugs. One of the most remarkable is the Drexelbrook Engineering Company, a 300-employee company in Horsham, Pennsylvania, that designs and manufactures electronic systems that measure and control levels of hazardous chemicals. Drexelbrook's vice president and general counsel, Lewis Maltby, admits that one of its employees on drugs could cause a disaster as tragic as the one that occurred in Bhopal, India, but despite the huge potential legal liability, they still won't test their employees for drugs. According to Maltby, the fundamental flaw with drug testing is that it tests the wrong thing. "A realistic program to detect workers whose condition puts the company or other people at risk would test for the condition that actually creates the danger. . . . A serious program would recognize that the real problem is worker's impairment and test for that."[7] A philosophical defense of Maltby's position is provided by the article by Joseph DesJardins and Ronald Duska.

Although the notion of testing for job impairment rather than drug use is appealing from the ethical point of view, there are certainly some occupations — teaching and law, for example — in which tests for impairment would be difficult to devise. In other situations testing for job impairment might be inordinately expensive. How much would it cost a school district to test its school bus drivers every school day? Thus the outlook for employee rights is mixed. Current trends indicate that a larger number of employee rights will be recognized and that some that are currently recognized will be expanded. On the other hand, the pressure on corporations to control cost will continue and, as a result, so will the pressures to avoid expenditures for honoring rights.

WHISTLE-BLOWING AND THE DUTY OF LOYALTY

To suggest that the moral problems in employee-employer relationships are all about employee rights would, of course, be one-sided. No less important are employee obligations. Employees have moral obligations to respect the property of the corporation, to abide by employment contracts, and to operate within the bounds of the company's procedural rules. Indeed it is legally established that an employer has a right to loyalty. This right is captured in the so-called law of agency. For example, Section 387 of the Restatement of Agency (1958) expresses the general principle that "an agent is subject to his principal to act solely for the benefit of the principal in all matters connected with his agency."[8] Specifically, the "agent is also under a duty not to act or speak disloyally," and the agent is to keep confidential any information acquired by him as an employee that might damage the agent or his business.[9]

Even if an employer is legally entitled to loyalty, is she or he morally entitled to loyalty? Ronald Duska has argued that loyalty can apply only in a relationship that transcends self-interest and must be based on a stable relationship of trust and confidence. The relationship of an employee to the corporation is not that kind of relationship, in his view, because it is a relationship of mutual self-interest. In this form of relationship, the employee does not have an obligation of loyalty to the employer.

If a corporation takes the position advocated by Milton Friedman in Chapter 2, then Duska's argument seems persuasive and indeed Friedman himself would probably accept it. In Friedman's view the only concern of the firm is to manage its assets in order to obtain profits for the stockholders, and the only concern of the workers is to get the best working conditions they can. Loyalty simply isn't in the picture. But if a broader stakeholder theory like R. Edward Freeman's is adopted, the corporation does have genuine obligations to employees. In a stakeholder-managed firm, the relationship between the employer and the employee is more likely to be characterized as a relationship of trust and confidence that transcends self-interest. If Duska accepted this characterization of the stakeholder account, these firms would be morally entitled to loyalty.

However, the duty of loyalty is not absolute. That an employee should be loyal is a *prima facie* duty. The object of the employee's duty must be deserving if the duty is genuine and overriding rather than *prima facie*. The virtue of loyalty does not require that the employee accept blindly the boss or corporate cause to which he or she is loyal. Nor does it require that when loyalty to the employer conflicts with other duties — such as protecting the public from harm — the duty to the employer is always overriding. Indeed, when a corporation is engaged in activity that is seriously wrong, employees may have a higher obligation to be disloyal to their employer and blow the whistle.

In her article, Sissela Bok attempts to define whistle-blowing and to indicate the conditions under which it is justified. Since from the business organization's standpoint, whistle-blowing is an accusation against the hierarchy and hence disloyal, Bok argues that the evil being exposed should be immediate and specific and should be done from a moral motive. Whistle-blowing should benefit the public; should be done only after internal channels within the business firm have been exhausted; should treat the one accused fairly; and usually should be done openly, rather than anonymously.

Well-publicized cases of whistle-blowing bring public acclaim to the whistle-blower but little else. The whistle-blower finds it nearly impossible to get an equivalent job in the same industry and difficult enough to get another job at all. Many corporate executives share the sentiments of the former president of General Motors James M. Roche.

> Some of the enemies of business now encourage an employee to be disloyal to the enterprise. They want to create suspicion and disharmony, and pry into the proprietary interests of the business. However this is labelled — industrial espionage, whistleblowing, or professional responsibility — it is another tactic for spreading disunity and creating conflict.[10]

Although Roche illegitimately confuses industrial espionage and whistle-blowing, the attitude expressed by his remarks explains why it is so difficult for the whistle-blower to find another job.

In conclusion, many of the moral grounds for employee loyalty have been destroyed. Commentators refer to the collapse of the social contract between a company and its employees. Each day seems to bring another announcement of a corporate downsizing. Yet there are some minimum requirements of loyalty based in law. Even today the most disgruntled employees usually treat others who whistle-blow negatively; for them whistle-blowing seems to violate a moral obligation to loyalty. Thus it is important pragmatically as well as ethically that whistle-blowing be justifiable.

NOTES

1. Brian Dumaine, "Who Needs a Boss?" *Fortune,* May 7, 1990, pp. 52–60.
2. See "Fear of Firing," *Forbes* December 2, 1985, p. 90; and John Hoerr, and others, "Beyond Unions: A Revolution in Employee Rights in the Making," *Business Week,* July 8, 1985, p. 72.
3. Peggy Schmidt, "Lie-Detector Tests in a New Guise," *New York Times,* October 1, 1989, pp. 29, 31.
4. Gilbert Fuchsberg, "Prominent Psychologists Group Gives Qualified Support to Integrity Tests," *Wall Street Journal,* March 2, 1991.
5. "If You Light Up on Sunday, Don't Come in on Monday," *Business Week,* August 26, 1991, pp. 68–72.
6. "Privacy," *Business Week,* March 28, 1988, pp. 61–68.
7. Lewis Maltby, "Why Drug Testing Is a Bad Idea," *Inc.,* June 1987, p. 153.
8. Quoted from Phillip I. Blumberg, "Corporate Responsibility and the Employee's Duty of Loyalty and Obedience," in *Ethical Theory and Business,* edited by Thomas

Beauchamp and Norman E. Bowie (Englewood Cliffs, N.J.: Prentice Hall, 1979), 307.

9. Ibid., pp. 308, 307.
10. James M. Roche, "The Competitive System, to Work, to Preserve, and to Protect," *Vital Speeches of the Day* (May 1971), p. 445.

Employment at Will and Due Process

Patricia H. Werhane and Tara J. Radin

In 1980, Howard Smith III was hired by the American Greetings Corporation as a materials handler at the plant in Osceola, Arkansas. He was promoted to forklift driver and held that job until 1989, when he became involved in a dispute with his shift leader. According to Smith, he had a dispute with his shift leader at work. After work he tried to discuss the matter, but according to Smith, the shift leader hit him. The next day Smith was fired.

Smith was an "at will" employee. He did not belong to, nor was he protected by, any union or union agreement. He did not have any special legal protection, for there was no apparent question of age, gender, race, or handicap discrimination. And he was not alleging any type of problem with worker safety on the job. The American Greetings Employee Handbook stated that "We believe in working and thinking and planning to provide a stable and growing business, to give such service to our customers that we may provide maximum job security for our employees." It did not state that employees could not be fired without due process or reasonable cause. According to the common law principle of Employment at Will (EAW), Smith's job at American Greetings could, therefore, legitimately be terminated at any time without cause, by either Smith or his employer, as long as that termination did not violate any law, agreement, or public policy.

Smith challenged his firing in the Arkansas court system as a "tort of outrage." A "tort of outrage" occurs when employer engages in "extreme or outrageous conduct" or intentionally inflicts terrible emotional stress. If such a tort is found to have occurred, the action, in this case, the dismissal, can be overturned.

Smith's case went to the Supreme Court of Arkansas in 1991. In court the management of American Greetings argued that Smith was fired for provoking management into a fight. The Court held that the firing was not in violation of law or a public policy, that the employee handbook did not specify restrictions on at will terminations, and that the alleged altercation between Smith and his shift leader "did not come close to meeting" criteria for a tort of outrage. Howard Smith lost his case and his job.[1]

The principle of EAW is a common-law doctrine that states that, in the absence of law or contract, employers have the right to hire, promote, demote, and fire whomever and whenever they please. In 1887, the principle was stated explicitly in a document by H. G. Wood entitled *Master and Servant*. According to Wood, "A general or indefinite hiring is prima facie a hiring at will."[2] Although the term "master-servant," a medieval expression, was once used to characterize employment relationships, it has been dropped from most of the recent literature on employment.[3]

In the United States, EAW has been interpreted as the rule that, when employees are not specifically covered by union agreement, legal statute, public policy, or contract, em-

ployers "may dismiss their employees at will
. . . for good cause, for no cause, *or even for
causes morally wrong*, without being thereby
guilty of legal wrong."[4] At the same time, "at
will" employees enjoy rights parallel to employer prerogatives, because employees may
quit their jobs for any reason whatsoever (or
no reason) without having to give any notice
to their employers. "At will" employees range
from part-time contract workers to CEOs, including all those workers and managers in
the private sector of the economy not covered by agreements, statutes, or contracts.
Today at least 60% of all employees in the
private sector in the United States are "at
will" employees. These employees have no
rights to due process or to appeal employment decisions, and the employer does not
have any obligation to give reasons for demo-
tions, transfers, or dismissals. Interestingly,
while employees in the *private* sector of the
economy tend to be regarded as "at will" employees, *public*-sector employees have guaranteed rights, including due process, and are
protected from demotion, transfer, or firing
without cause.

Due process is a means by which a person
can appeal a decision in order to get an explanation of that action and an opportunity
to argue against it. Procedural due process is
the right to a hearing, trial, grievance procedure, or appeal when a decision is made concerning oneself. Due process is also substantive. It is the demand for rationality and
fairness: for good reasons for decisions. EAW
has been widely interpreted as allowing employees to be demoted, transferred or dismissed without due process, that is, without
having a hearing and without requirement of
good reasons or "cause" for the employment
decision. This is not to say that employers do
not have reasons, usually good reasons, for
their decisions. But there is no moral or legal
obligation to state or defend them. EAW thus
sidesteps the requirement of procedural and

substantive due process in the workplace, but
it does not preclude the institution of such
procedures or the existence of good reasons
for employment decisions.

EAW is still upheld in the state and federal
courts of this country, as the Howard Smith
case illustrates, although exceptions are
made when violations of public policy and
law are at issue. According to the *Wall Street
Journal*, the court has decided in favor of the
employees in 67% of the wrongful discharge
suits that have taken place during the past
three years. These suits were won not on the
basis of a rejection of the principle of EAW
but, rather, on the basis of breach of contract, lack of just cause for dismissal when a
company policy was in place, or violations of
public policy. The court has carved out the
"public policy" exception so as not to encourage fraudulent or wrongful behavior on the
part of employers, such as in cases where employees are asked to break a law or to violate
state public policies, and in cases where employees are not allowed to exercise fundamental rights, such as the rights to vote, to
serve on a jury, and to collect worker compensation. For example, in one case, the
court reinstated an employee who was fired
for reporting theft at his plant on the
grounds that criminal conduct requires such
reporting.[5] In another case, the court reinstated a physician who was fired from the
Ortho Pharmaceutical Corporation for refusing to seek approval to test a certain drug on
human subjects. The court held that safety
clearly lies in the interest of public welfare,
and employees are not to be fired for refusing to jeopardize public safety.[6]

During the last ten years, a number of positive trends have become apparent in employment practices and in state and federal court
adjudications of employment disputes. Shortages of skilled managers, fear of legal repercussions, and a more genuine interest in
employee rights claims and reciprocal obliga-

tions have resulted in a more careful spelling out of employment contracts, the development of elaborate grievance procedures, and in general less arbitrariness in employee treatment.[7] While there has not been a universal revolution in thinking about employee rights, an increasing number of companies have qualified their EAW prerogatives with restrictions in firing without cause. Many companies have developed grievance procedures and other means for employee complaint and redress.

Interestingly, substantive due process, the notion that employers should give good reasons for their employment actions, previously dismissed as legal and philosophical nonsense, has also recently developed positive advocates. Some courts have found that it is a breach of contract to fire a long-term employee when there is not sufficient cause — under normal economic conditions even when the implied contract is only a verbal one. In California, for example, 50% of the implied contract cases (and there have been over 200) during the last five years have been decided in favor of the employee, again, without challenging EAW.[8] In light of this recognition of implicit contractual obligations between employees and employers, in some unprecedented court cases *employees* have been held liable for good faith breaches of contract, particularly in cases of quitting without notice in the middle of a project and/or taking technology or other ideas to another job.[9]

These are all positive developments. At the same time, there has been neither an across-the-board institution of due process procedures in all corporations nor any direct challenges to the *principle* (although there have been challenges to the practice) of EAW as a justifiable and legitimate approach to employment practices. Moreover, as a result of mergers, downsizing, and restructuring, hundreds of thousands of employees have been laid off summarily without being able to appeal those decisions.

"At will" employees, then, have no rights to demand an appeal to such employment decisions except through the court system. In addition, no form of due process is a requirement preceding any of these actions. Moreover, unless public policy is violated, the law has traditionally protected employers from employee retaliation in such actions. It is true that the scope of what is defined as "public policy" has been enlarged so that "at will" dismissals without good reason are greatly reduced. It is also true that many companies have grievance procedures in place for "at will" employees. But such procedures are voluntary, procedural due process is not *required,* and companies need not give any reasons for their employment decisions.

In what follows we shall present a series of arguments defending the claim that the right to procedural and substantive due process should be extended to all employees in the private sector of the economy. We will defend the claim partly on the basis of human rights. We shall also argue that the public/private distinction that precludes the application of constitutional guarantees in the private sector has sufficiently broken down so that the absence of a due process requirement in the workplace is an anomaly.

EMPLOYMENT AT WILL

EAW is often justified for one or more of the following reasons:

1. The proprietary rights of employers guarantee that they may employ or dismiss whomever and whenever they wish.
2. EAW defends employee and employer rights equally, in particular the right to freedom of contract, because an employee voluntarily contracts to be hired and can quit at any time.

3. In choosing to take a job, an employee voluntarily commits herself to certain responsibilities and company loyalty, including the knowledge that she is an "at will" employee.

4. Extending due process rights in the workplace often interferes with the efficiency and productivity of the business organization.

5. Legislation and/or regulation of employment relationships further undermine an already overregulated economy.

Let us examine each of these arguments in more detail. The principle of EAW is sometimes maintained purely on the basis of proprietary rights of employers and corporations. In dismissing or demoting employees, the employer is not denying rights to *persons*. Rather, the employer is simply excluding that person's *labor* from the organization.

This is not a bad argument. Nevertheless, accepting it necessitates consideration of the proprietary rights of employees as well. To understand what is meant by "proprietary rights of employees" it is useful to consider first what is meant by the term "labor." "Labor" is sometimes used collectively to refer to the workforce as a whole. It also refers to the activity of working. Other times it refers to the productivity or "fruits" of that activity. Productivity, labor in the third sense, might be thought of as a form of property or at least as something convertible into property, because the productivity of working is what is traded for remuneration in employee-employer work agreements. For example, suppose an advertising agency hires an expert known for her creativity in developing new commercials. This person trades her ideas, the product of her work (thinking), for pay. The ideas are not literally property, but they are tradable items because, when presented on paper or on television, they are sellable by their creator and generate income. But the activity of working (thinking in this case) cannot be sold or transferred.

Caution is necessary, though, in relating productivity to tangible property, because there is an obvious difference between productivity and material property. Productivity requires the past or present activity of working, and thus the presence of the person performing this activity. Person, property, labor, and productivity are all different in this important sense. A person can be distinguished from his possessions, a distinction that allows for the creation of legally fictional persons such as corporations or trusts that can "own" property. Persons cannot, however, be distinguished from their working, and this activity is necessary for creating productivity, a tradable product of one's working.

In dismissing an employee, a well-intentioned employer aims to rid the corporation of the costs of generating that employee's work products. In ordinary employment situations, however, terminating that cost entails terminating that employee. In those cases the justification for the "at will" firing is presumably proprietary. But treating an employee "at will" is analogous to considering her a piece of property at the disposal of the employer or corporation. Arbitrary firings treat people as things. When I "fire" a robot, I do not have to give reasons, because a robot is not a rational being. It has no use for reasons. On the other hand, if I fire a person arbitrarily, I am making the assumption that she does not need reasons either. If I have hired people, then, in firing them, I should treat them as such, with respect, throughout the termination process. This does not preclude firing. It merely asks employers to give reasons for their actions, because reasons are appropriate when people are dealing with other people.

This reasoning leads to a second defense and critique of EAW. It is contended that EAW defends employee and employer rights equally. An employer's right to hire and fire "at will" is balanced by a worker's right to accept or reject employment. The institution of any employee right that restricts "at will" hiring and firing would be unfair unless this restriction were balanced by a similar restriction controlling employee job choice in the workplace. Either program would do irreparable damage by preventing both employees and employers from continuing in voluntary employment arrangements. These arrangements are guaranteed by "freedom of contract," the right of persons or organizations to enter into any voluntary agreement with which all parties of the agreement are in accord.[10] Limiting EAW practices or requiring due process would negatively affect freedom of contract. Both are thus clearly coercive, because in either case persons and organizations are forced to accept behavioral restraints that place unnecessary constraints on voluntary employment agreements.[11]

This second line of reasoning defending EAW, like the first, presents some solid arguments. A basic presupposition upon which EAW is grounded is that of protecting equal freedoms of both employees and employers. The purpose of EAW is to provide a guaranteed balance of these freedoms. But arbitrary treatment of employees extends prerogatives to managers that are not equally available to employees, and such treatment may unduly interfere with a fired employee's prospects for future employment if that employee has no avenue for defense or appeal. This is also sometimes true when an employee quits without notice or good reason. Arbitrary treatment of employees *or* employers therefore violates the spirit of EAW — that of protecting the freedoms of both the employees and employers.

The third justification of EAW defends the voluntariness of employment contracts. If these are agreements between moral agents, however, such agreements imply reciprocal obligations between the parties in question for which both are accountable. It is obvious

that, in an employment contract, people are rewarded for their performance. What is seldom noticed is that, if part of the employment contract is an expectation of loyalty, trust, and respect on the part of an employee, the employer must, in return, treat the employee with respect as well. The obligations required by employment agreements, if these are free and noncoercive agreements, must be equally obligatory and mutually restrictive on both parties. Otherwise one party cannot expect — morally expect — loyalty, trust, or respect from the other.

EAW is most often defended on practical grounds. From a utilitarian perspective, hiring and firing "at will" is deemed necessary in productive organizations to ensure maximum efficiency and productivity, the goals of such organizations. In the absence of EAW unproductive employees, workers who are no longer needed, and even troublemakers, would be able to keep their jobs. Even if a business *could* rid itself of undesirable employees, the lengthy procedure of due process required by an extension of employee rights would be costly and time-consuming, and would likely prove distracting to other employees. This would likely slow production and, more likely than not, prove harmful to the morale of other employees.

This argument is defended by Ian Maitland, who contends,

[I]f employers were generally to heed business ethicists and institute workplace due process in cases of dismissals and take the increased costs or reduced efficiency out of workers' paychecks — then they would expose themselves to the pirating of their workers by other employers who would give workers what they wanted instead of respecting their rights in the workplace. . . . In short, there is good reason for concluding that the prevalence of EAW does accurately reflect workers' preferences for wages over contractually guaranteed protections against unfair dismissal.[12]

Such an argument assumes (a) that due process increases costs and reduces efficiency, a contention that is not documented by the many corporations that have grievance procedures, and (b) that workers will generally give up some basic rights for other benefits, such as money. The latter is certainly sometimes true, but not always so, particularly when there are questions of unfair dismissals or job security. Maitland also assumes that an employee is on the same level and possesses the same power as her manager, so that an employee can choose her benefit package in which grievance procedures, whistleblowing protections, or other rights are included. Maitland implies that employers might include in that package of benefits their rights to practice the policy of unfair dismissals in return for increased pay. He also at least implicitly suggests that due process precludes dismissals and layoffs. But this is not true. Procedural due process demands a means of appeal, and substantive due process demands good reasons, both of which are requirements for other managerial decisions and judgments. Neither demands benevolence, lifetime employment, or prevents dismissals. In fact, having good reasons gives an employer a justification for getting rid of poor employees.

In summary, arbitrariness, although not prohibited by EAW, violates the managerial ideal of rationality and consistency. These are independent grounds for not abusing EAW. Even if EAW itself is justifiable, the practice of EAW, when interpreted as condoning arbitrary employment decisions, is not justifiable. Both procedural and substantive due process are consistent with, and a moral requirement of, EAW. The former is part of recognizing obligations implied by freedom of contract, and the latter, substantive due process, conforms with the ideal of managerial rationality that is implied by a consistent application of this common law principle.

EMPLOYMENT AT WILL, DUE PROCESS AND THE PUBLIC/PRIVATE DISTINCTION

The strongest reasons for allowing abuses of EAW and for not instituting a full set of employee rights in the workplace, at least in the private sector of the economy, have to do with the nature of business in a free society. Businesses are privately owned voluntary organizations of all sizes from small entrepreneurships to large corporations. As such, they are not subject to the restrictions governing public and political institutions. Political procedures such as due process, needed to safeguard the public against the arbitrary exercise of power by the state, do not apply to private organizations. Guaranteeing such rights in the workplace would require restrictive legislation and regulation. Voluntary market arrangements, so vital to free enterprise and guaranteed by freedom of contract, would be sacrificed for the alleged public interest of employee claims.

In the law, courts traditionally have recognized the right of corporations to due process, although they have not required due process for employees in the private sector of the economy. The justification put forward for this is that since corporations are public entities acting in the public interest, they, like people, should be afforded the right to due process.

Due process is also guaranteed for permanent full-time workers in the public sector of the economy, that is, for workers in local, state and national government positions. The Fifth and Fourteenth Amendments protect liberty and property rights such that any alleged violations or deprivation of those rights may be challenged by some form of due process. According to recent Supreme Court decisions, when a state worker is a permanent employee, he has a property interest in his employment. Because a person's productivity contributes to the place of employment, a public worker is entitled to his job unless there is good reason to question it, such as poor work habits, habitual absences, and the like. Moreover, if a discharge would prevent him from obtaining other employment, which often is the case with state employees who, if fired, cannot find further government employment, that employee has a right to due process before being terminated.[13]

This justification for extending due process protections to public employees is grounded in the public employee's proprietary interest in his job. If that argument makes sense, it is curious that private employees do not have similar rights. The basis for this distinction stems from a tradition in Western thinking that distinguishes between the public and private spheres of life. The public sphere contains that part of a person's life that lies within the bounds of government regulation, whereas the private sphere contains that part of a person's life that lies outside those bounds. The argument is that the portion of a person's life that influences only that person should remain private and outside the purview of law and regulation, while the portion that influences the public welfare should be subject to the authority of the law.

Although interpersonal relationships on any level — personal, family, social, or employee-employer — are protected by statutes and common law, they are not constitutionally protected unless there is a violation of some citizen claim against the state. Because entrepreneurships and corporations are privately owned, and since employees are free to make or break employment contracts of their choice, employee-employer relationships, like family relationships, are treated as "private." In a family, even if there are no due process procedures, the state does not interfere, except when there is obvious harm or abuse. Similarly, employment relationships are considered private relationships contracted between free adults, and so long as no gross violations occur, positive constitutional guarantees such as due process are not enforceable.

The public/private distinction was originally developed to distinguish individuals from the state and to protect individuals and private property from public — i.e., governmental — intrusion. The distinction, however, has been extended to distinguish not merely between the individual or the family and the state, but also between universal rights claims and national sovereignty, public and private ownership, free enterprise and public policy, publicly and privately held corporations, and even between public and private employees. Indeed, this distinction plays a role in national and international affairs. Boutros Boutros-Ghali, the head of the United Nations, recently confronted a dilemma in deciding whether to go into Somalia without an invitation. His initial reaction was to stay out and to respect Somalia's right to "private" national sovereignty. It was only when he decided that Somalia had fallen apart as an independent state that he approved U.N. intervention. His dilemma parallels that of a state, which must decide whether to intervene in a family quarrel, the alleged abuse of a spouse or child, the inoculation of a Christian Scientist, or the blood transfusion for a Seventh-Day Adventist.

There are some questions, however, with the justification of the absence of due process with regard to the public/private distinction. Our economic system is allegedly based on private property, but it is unclear where "private" property and ownership end and "public" property and ownership begin. In the workplace, ownership and control is often divided. Corporate assets are held by an ever-changing group of individual and institutional shareholders. It is no longer true that owners exercise any real sense of control over their property and its management. Some do, but many do not. Moreover, such complex property relationships are spelled out and guaranteed by the state. This has prompted at least one thinker to argue that "private property" should be defined as "certain patterns of human interaction underwritten by public power."[14]

This fuzziness about the "privacy" of property becomes exacerbated by the way we use the term "public" in analyzing the status of businesses and in particular corporations. For example, we distinguish between privately owned business corporations and government-owned or -controlled public institutions. Among those companies that are not government owned, we distinguish between regulated "public" utilities whose stock is owned by private individuals and institutions; "publicly held" corporations whose stock is traded publicly, who are governed by special SEC regulations, and whose financial statements are public knowledge; and privately held corporations and entrepreneurships, companies and smaller businesses that are owned by an individual or group of individuals and not available for public stock purchase.

There are similarities between government-owned, public institutions and privately owned organizations. When the air controllers went on strike in the 1980s, Ronald Reagan fired them, and declared that, as public employees, they could not strike because it jeopardized the public safety. Nevertheless, both private and public institutions run transportation, control banks, and own property. While the goals of private and public institutions differ in that public institutions are allegedly supposed to place the public good ahead of profitability, the simultaneous call for businesses to become socially responsible and the demand for governmental organizations to become efficient and accountable further question the dichotomy between "public" and "private."

Many business situations reinforce the view that the traditional public/private di-

chotomy has been eroded, if not entirely, at least in large part. For example, in 1981, General Motors (GM) wanted to expand by building a plant in what is called the "Poletown" area of Detroit. Poletown is an old Detroit Polish neighborhood. The site was favorable because it was near transportation facilities and there was a good supply of labor. To build the plant, however, GM had to displace residents in a nine-block area. The Poletown Neighborhood Council objected, but the Supreme Court of Michigan decided in favor of GM and held that the state could condemn property for private use, with proper compensation to owners, when it was in the public good. What is particularly interesting about this case is that GM is not a government-owned corporation; its primary goal is *profitability*, not the common good. The Supreme Court nevertheless decided that it was in the *public* interest for Detroit to use its authority to allow a company to take over property despite the protesting of the property owners. In this case the public/private distinction was thoroughly scrambled.

The overlap between private enterprise and public interests is such that at least one legal scholar argues that "developments in the twentieth century have significantly undermined the 'privateness' of the modern business corporations, with the result that the traditional bases for distinguishing them from public corporations have largely disappeared."[15] Nevertheless, despite the blurring of the public and private in terms of property rights and the status and functions of corporations, the subject of employee rights appears to remain immune from conflation.

The expansion of employee protections to what we would consider just claims to due process gives to the state and the courts more opportunity to interfere with the private economy and might thus further skew what is seen by some as a precarious but delicate balance between the private economic sector and public policy. We agree. But if the distinction between public and private institutions is no longer clear-cut, and the traditional separation of the public and private spheres is no longer in place, might it not then be better to recognize and extend constitutional guarantees so as to protect all citizens equally? If due process is crucial to political relationships between the individual and the state, why is it not central in relationships between employees and corporations since at least some of the companies in question are as large and powerful as small nations? Is it not in fact inconsistent with our democratic tradition *not* to mandate such rights?

The philosopher T. M. Scanlon summarizes our institutions about due process. Scanlon says,

> The requirement of due process is one of the conditions of the moral acceptability of those institutions that give some people power to control or intervene in the lives of others.[16]

The institution of due process in the workplace is a moral requirement consistent with rationality and consistency expected in management decision-making. It is not precluded by EAW, and it is compatible with the overlap between the public and private sectors of the economy. Convincing business of the moral necessity of due process, however, is a task yet to be completed.

NOTES

1. *Howard Smith III* v. *American Greetings Corporation*, 304 Ark. 596; 804 S.W.2d 683.

2. H. G. Wood, *A Treatise on the Law of Master and Servant* (Albany, N.Y.: John D. Parsons, Jr., 1877), p. 134.

3. Until the end of 1980 the *Index of Legal Periodicals* indexed employee-employer relationships under this rubric.

4. Lawrence E. Blades, "Employment at Will versus Individual Freedom: On Limiting the Abusive Exercise of Employer Power," *Columbia Law Review,* 67 (1967), p. 1405, quoted from *Payne* v. *Western,* 81 Tenn. 507 (1884), and *Hutton* v. *Watters,* 132 Tenn. 527, S.W. 134 (1915).

5. *Palmateer* v. *International Harvester Corporation,* 85 Ill. App. 2d 124 (1981).

6. *Pierce* v. *Ortho Pharmaceutical Corporation* 845 NJ 58 (NJ 1980), 417 A.2d 505. See also Brian Heshizer, "The New Common Law of Employment: Changes in the Concept of Employment at Will," *Labor Law Journal,* 36 (1985), pp. 95–107.

7. See David Ewing, *Justice on the Job: Resolving Grievances in the Nonunion Workplace* (Boston: Harvard Business School Press, 1989).

8. See R. M. Bastress, "A Synthesis and a Proposal for Reform of the Employment at Will Doctrine," *West Virginia Law Review,* 90 (1988), pp. 319–51.

9. See "Employees' Good Faith Duties," *Hastings Law Journal,* 39 (198). See also *Hudson* v. *Moore Business Forms,* 609 Supp. 467 (N.D. Cal. 1985).

10. See *Lockner* v. *New York,* 198 U.S. (1905), and Adina Schwartz, "Autonomy in the Workplace," in Tom Regan, ed., *Just Business* (New York: Random House, 1984), pp. 129–40.

11. Eric Mack, "Natural and Contractual Rights," *Ethics,* 87 (1977), pp. 153–59.

12. Ian Maitland, "Rights in the Workplace: A Nozickian Argument," in Lisa Newton and Maureen Ford, eds., *Taking Sides* (Guilford, CT: Dushkin Publishing Group), 1990, pp. 34–35.

13. Richard Wallace, "Union Waiver of Public Employees' Due Process Rights," *Industrial Relations Law Journal,* 8 (1986), pp. 583–87.

14. Morris Cohen, "Dialogue on Private Property," *Rutgers Law Review* 9 (1954), pp. 357. See also *Law and the Social Order* (1933) and Robert Hale, "Coercion and Distribution in a Supposedly Non-Coercive State," *Political Science Quarterly,* 38 (1923), pp. 470; John Brest, "State Action and Liberal Theory," *University of Pennsylvania Law Review* (1982), 1296–1329.

15. Gerald Frug, "The City As a Legal Concept," *Harvard Law Review,* 93 (1980), p. 1129.

16. T. M. Scanlon, "Due Process," in J. Roland Pennock and John W. Chapman, eds., *Nomos XVIII: Due Process* (New York: New York University Press, 1977), p. 94.

In Defense of the Contract at Will

Richard A. Epstein

The persistent tension between private ordering and government regulation exists in virtually every area known to the law, and in none has that tension been more pronounced than in the law of employer and employee relations. During the last fifty years, the balance of power has shifted heavily in favor of direct public regulation, which has been thought strictly necessary to redress the perceived imbalance between the individual and the firm. In particular the employment relationship has been the subject of at least two major statutory revolutions. The first, which culminated in the passage of the National Labor Relations Act in 1935, set the basic structure for collective bargaining that persists to the current time. The second, which is embodied in Title VII of the Civil Rights Act of 1964, offers extensive protection to all individuals against discrimination on the basis of race, sex, religion, or national origin. The effect of these two statutes is so pervasive that it is easy to forget that, even after their passage, large portions of the employment relation remain subject to the traditional common law rules, which when all was said and done set their face in support of freedom of contract and the system of voluntary exchange. One manifestation of that position was the prominent place that the common law, especially as it developed in the nineteenth century, gave to the contract at will. The basic position was sell set out in an oft-quoted passage from *Payne v. Western & Atlantic Railroad*:

> [M]en must be left, without interference to buy and sell where they please, and to discharge or retain employees at will for good cause or for no cause, or even for bad cause without thereby being guilty of an unlawful act *per se*. It is a right which an employee may exercise in the same way, to the same extent, for the same cause or want of cause as the employer.[1]

. . .

In the remainder of this paper, I examine the arguments that can be made for and against the contract at will. I hope to show that it is adopted not because it allows the employer to exploit the employee, but rather because over a very broad range of circumstances it works to the mutual benefit of both parties, where the benefits are measured, as ever, at the time of the contract's formation and not at the time of dispute. To justify this result, I examine the contract in light of the three dominant standards that have emerged as the test of the soundness of any legal doctrine: intrinsic fairness, effects upon utility or wealth, and distributional consequences. I conclude that the first two tests point strongly to the maintenance of the at-will rule, while the third, if it offers any guidance at all, points in the same direction.

I. THE FAIRNESS OF THE CONTRACT AT WILL

The first way to argue for the contract at will is to insist upon the importance of freedom of contract as an end in itself. Freedom of contract is an aspect of individual liberty, every bit as much as freedom of speech, or freedom in the selection of marriage partners

From: Richard A. Epstein, "In Defense of the Contract at Will", *University of Chicago Law Review* 34 (1984). Reprinted by permission of the University of Chicago Law Review.

or in the adoption of religious beliefs or affiliations. Just as it is regarded as prima facie unjust to abridge these liberties, so too is it presumptively unjust to abridge the economic liberties of individuals. The desire to make one's own choices about employment may be as strong as it is with respect to marriage or participation in religious activities, and it is doubtless more pervasive than the desire to participate in political activity. Indeed for most people, their own health and comfort, and that of their families, depend critically upon their ability to earn a living by entering the employment market. If government regulation is inappropriate for personal, religious, or political activities, then what makes it intrinsically desirable for employment relations?

It is one thing to set aside the occasional transaction that reflects only the momentary aberrations of particular parties who are overwhelmed by major personal and social dislocations. It is quite another to announce that a rule to which vast numbers of individuals adhere is so fundamentally corrupt that it does not deserve the minimum respect of the law. With employment contracts we are not dealing with the widow who has sold her inheritance for a song to a man with a thin mustache. Instead we are dealing with the routine stuff of ordinary life; people who are competent enough to marry, vote, and pray are not unable to protect themselves in their day-to-day business transactions.

Courts and legislatures have intervened so often in private contractual relations that it may seem almost quixotic to insist that they bear a heavy burden of justification every time they wish to substitute their own judgment for that of the immediate parties to the transactions. Yet it is hardly likely that remote public bodies have better information about individual preferences than the parties who hold them. This basic principle of autonomy, moreover, is not limited to some areas of in-

dividual conduct and wholly inapplicable to others. It covers all these activities as a piece and admits no ad hoc exceptions, but only principled limitations.

This general proposition applies to the particular contract term in question. Any attack on the contract at will in the name of individual freedom is fundamentally misguided. As the Tennessee Supreme Court rightly stressed in *Payne,* the contract at will is sought by both persons.[2] Any limitation upon the freedom to enter into such contracts limits the power of workers as well as employers and must therefore be justified before it can be accepted. In this context the appeal is often to an image of employer coercion. To be sure, freedom of contract is not an absolute in the employment context, any more than it is elsewhere. Thus the principle must be understood against a backdrop that prohibits the use of private contracts to trench upon third-party rights, including uses that interfere with some clear mandate of public policy, as in cases of contracts to commit murder or perjury.

In addition, the principle of freedom of contract also rules out the use of force or fraud in obtaining advantages during contractual negotiations; and it limits taking advantage of the young, the feeble-minded, and the insane. But the recent wrongful discharge cases do not purport to deal with the delicate situations where contracts have been formed by improper means or where individual defects of capacity or will are involved. Fraud is not a frequent occurrence in employment contracts, especially where workers and employers engage in repeat transactions. Nor is there any reason to believe that such contracts are marred by misapprehensions, since employers and employees know the footing on which they have contracted: the phrase "at will" is two words long and has the convenient virtue of meaning just what it says, no more and no less.

An employee who knows that he can quit at will understands what it means to be fired at will, even though he may not like it after the fact. So long as it is accepted that the employer is the full owner of his capital and the employee is the full owner of his labor, the two are free to exchange on whatever terms and conditions they see fit, within the limited constraints just noted. If the arrangement turns out to be disastrous to one side, that is his problem; and once cautioned, he probably will not make the same mistake a second time. More to the point, employers and employees are unlikely to make the same mistake once. It is hardly plausible that contracts at will could be so pervasive in all businesses and at all levels if they did not serve the interests of employees as well as employers. The argument from fairness then is very simple, but not for that reason unpersuasive.

II. THE UTILITY OF THE CONTRACT AT WILL

The strong fairness argument in favor of freedom of contract makes short work of the various for-cause and good-faith restrictions upon private contracts. Yet the argument is incomplete in several respects. In particular, it does not explain why the presumption in the case of silence should be in favor of the contract at will. Nor does it give a descriptive account of *why* the contract at will is so commonly found in all trades and professions. Nor does the argument meet on their own terms the concerns voiced most frequently by the critics of the contract at will. Thus, the commonplace belief today (at least outside the actual world of business) is that the contract at will is so unfair and one-sided that it cannot be the outcome of a rational set of bargaining processes any more than, to take the extreme case, a contract for total slavery. While we may not, the criticism continues, be

able to observe them, defects in capacity at contract formation nonetheless must be present: the ban upon the contract at will is an effective way to reach abuses that are pervasive but difficult to detect, so that modest government interference only strengthens the operation of market forces.

In order to rebut this charge, it is necessary to do more than insist that individuals as a general matter know how to govern their own lives. It is also necessary to display the structural strengths of the contract at will that explain why rational people would enter into such a contract, if not all the time, then at least most of it. The implicit assumption in this argument is that contracts are typically for the mutual benefit of both parties. Yet it is hard to see what other assumption makes any sense in analyzing institutional arrangements (arguably in contradistinction to idiosyncratic, nonrepetitive transactions). To be sure, there are occasional cases of regret after the fact, especially after an infrequent, but costly, contingency comes to pass. There will be cases in which parties are naive, befuddled, or worse. Yet in framing either a rule of policy or a rule of construction, the focus cannot be on that biased set of cases in which the contract aborts and litigation ensues. Instead, attention must be directed to standard repetitive transactions, where the centralizing tendency powerfully promotes expected mutual gain. It is simply incredible to postulate that either employers or employees, motivated as they are by self-interest, would enter routinely into a transaction that leaves them worse off than they were before, or even worse off than their next best alternative.

From this perspective, then, the task is to explain how and why the at-will contracting arrangement (in sharp contrast to slavery) typically works to the mutual advantage of the parties. Here, as is common in economic matters, it does not matter that the parties themselves often cannot articulate the reasons that render their judgment sound and breathe life into legal arrangements that are fragile in form but durable in practice. The inquiry into mutual benefit in turn requires an examination of the full range of costs and benefits that arise from collaborative ventures. It is just at this point that the nineteenth-century view is superior to the emerging modern conception. The modern view tends to lay heavy emphasis on the need to control employer abuse. Yet, as the passage from *Payne* indicates, the rights under the contract at will are fully bilateral, so that the employee can use the contract as a means to control the firm, just as the firm uses it to control the worker.

The issue for the parties, properly framed, is not how to minimize employer abuse, but rather how to maximize the gain from the relationship, which in part depends upon minimizing the sum of employer and employee abuse. Viewed in this way the private-contracting problem is far more complex. How does each party create incentives for the proper behavior of the other? How does each side insure against certain risks? How do both sides minimize the administrative costs of their contracting practices? . . .

1. *Monitoring Behavior.* The shift in the internal structure of the firm from a partnership to an employment relation eliminates neither bilateral opportunism nor the conflicts of interest between employer and employee. Begin for the moment with the fears of the firm, for it is the firm's right to maintain at-will power that is now being called into question. In all too many cases, the firm must contend with the recurrent problem of employee theft and with the related problems of unauthorized use of firm equipment and employee kickback arrangements. . . . [The] proper concerns of the firm are not limited to obvious forms of criminal misconduct. The employee on a fixed wage can, at the margin, capture only a portion of the gain from his labor, and therefore has a tendency to reduce output. The employee who receives a commission equal to half the firm's profit attributable to his labor may work hard, but probably not quite as hard as he would if he received the entire profit from the completed sale, an arrangement that would solve the agency-cost problem only by undoing the firm. . . .

The problem of management then is to identify the forms of social control that are best able to minimize these agency costs. . . . One obvious form of control is the force of law. The state can be brought in to punish cases of embezzlement or fraud. But this mode of control requires extensive cooperation with public officials and may well be frustrated by the need to prove the criminal offense (including mens rea) beyond a reasonable doubt, so that vast amounts of abuse will go unchecked. Private litigation instituted by the firm may well be used in cases of major grievances, either to recover the property that has been misappropriated or to prevent the individual employee from further diverting firm business to his own account. But private litigation, like public prosecution, is too blunt an instrument to counter employee shirking or the minor but persistent use of firm assets for private business. . . .

Internal auditors may help control some forms of abuse, and simple observation by coworkers may well monitor employee activities. (There are some very subtle tradeoffs to be considered when the firm decides whether to use partitions or separate offices for its employees.) Promotions, bonuses, and wages are also critical in shaping the level of employee performance. But the carrot cannot be used to the exclusion of the stick. In order to maintain internal discipline, the firm may have to resort to sanctions against individual employees. It is far easier to use those powers that can be unilaterally exercised: to fire, to demote, to withhold wages, or to reprimand.

These devices can visit very powerful losses upon individual employees without the need to resort to legal action, and they permit the firm to monitor employee performance continually in order to identify both strong and weak workers and to compensate them accordingly. The principles here are constant, whether we speak of senior officials or lowly subordinates, and it is for just this reason that the contract at will is found at all levels in private markets. . . .

In addition, within the employment context firing does not require a disruption of firm operations, much less an expensive division of its assets. It is instead a clean break with consequences that are immediately clear to both sides. The lower cost of both firing and quitting, therefore, helps account for the very widespread popularity of employment-at-will contracts. There is no need to resort to any theory of economic domination or inequality of bargaining power to explain at-will contracting, which appears with the same tenacity in relations between economic equals and subordinates and is found in many complex commercial arrangements, including franchise agreements, except where limited by statutes.

Thus far, the analysis generally has focused on the position of the employer. Yet for the contract at will to be adopted ex ante, it must work for the benefit of workers as well. And indeed it does, for the contract at will also contains powerful limitations on employers' abuses of power. To see the importance of the contract at will to the employee, it is useful to distinguish between two cases. In the first, the employer pays a fixed sum of money to the worker and is then free to demand of the employee whatever services he wants for some fixed period of time. In the second case, there is no fixed period of employment. The employer is free to demand whatever he wants of the employee, who in turn is free to withdraw for good reason, bad reason, or no reason at all.

The first arrangement invites abuse by the employer, who can now make enormous demands upon the worker without having to take into account either the worker's disutility during the period of service or the value of the worker's labor at contract termination. A fixed-period contract that leaves the worker's obligations unspecified thereby creates a sharp tension between the parties, since the employer receives all the marginal benefits and the employee bears all the marginal costs.

Matters are very different where the employer makes increased demands under a contract at will. Now the worker can quit whenever the net value of the employment contract turns negative. As with the employer's power to fire or demote, the threat to quit (or at a lower level to come late or leave early) is one that can be exercised without resort to litigation. Furthermore, that threat turns out to be most effective when the employer's opportunistic behavior is the greatest because the situation is one in which the worker has least to lose. To be sure, the worker will not necessarily make a threat whenever the employer insists that the worker accept a less favorable set of contractual terms, for sometimes the changes may be accepted as an uneventful adjustment in the total compensation level attributable to a change in the market price of labor. This point counts, however, only as an additional strength of the contract at will, which allows for small adjustments *in both directions* in ongoing contractual arrangements with a minimum of bother and confusion. . . .

2. *Reputational Losses.* Another reason why employees are often willing to enter into at-will employment contracts stems from the asymmetry of reputational losses. Any party who cheats may well obtain a bad reputation

that will induce others to avoid dealing with him. The size of these losses tends to differ systematically between employers and employees — to the advantage of the employee. Thus in the usual situation there are many workers and a single employer. The disparity in number is apt to be greatest in large industrial concerns, where the at-will contract is commonly, if mistakenly, thought to be most unsatisfactory because of the supposed inequality of bargaining power. The employer who decides to act for bad reason or no reason at all may not face any legal liability under the classical common law rule. But he faces very powerful adverse economic consequences. If coworkers perceive the dismissal as arbitrary, they will take fresh stock of their own prospects, for they can no longer be certain that their faithful performance will ensure their security and advancement. The uncertain prospects created by arbitrary employer behavior is functionally indistinguishable from a reduction in wages unilaterally imposed by the employer. At the margin some workers will look elsewhere, and typically the best workers will have the greatest opportunities. By the same token the large employer has more to gain if he dismisses undesirable employees, for this ordinarily acts as an implicit increase in wages to the other employees, who are no longer burdened with uncooperative or obtuse coworkers.

The existence of both positive and negative reputational effects is thus brought back to bear on the employer. The law may tolerate arbitrary behavior, but private pressures effectively limit its scope. Inferior employers will be at a perpetual competitive disadvantage with enlightened ones and will continue to lose in market share and hence in relative social importance. The lack of legal protection to the employees is therefore in part explained by the increased informal protections that they obtain by working in large concerns.

3. *Risk Diversification and Imperfect Information.* The contract at will also helps workers deal with the problem of risk diversification. . . . Ordinarily, employees cannot work more than one, or perhaps two, jobs at the same time. Thereafter the level of performance falls dramatically, so that diversification brings in its wake a low return on labor. The contract at will is designed in part to offset the concentration of individual investment in a single job by allowing diversification among employers *over time*. The employee is not locked into an unfortunate contract if he finds better opportunities elsewhere or if he detects some weakness in the internal structure of the firm. A similar analysis applies on the employer's side where he is a sole proprietor, though ordinary diversification is possible when ownership of the firm is widely held in publicly traded shares.

The contract at will is also a sensible private adaptation to the problem of imperfect information over time. In sharp contrast to the purchase of standard goods, an inspection of the job before acceptance is far less likely to guarantee its quality thereafter. The future is not clearly known. More important, employees, like employers, *know what they do not know*. They are not faced with a bolt from the blue, with an "unknown unknown." Rather they face a known unknown for which they can plan. The at-will contract is an essential part of that planning because it allows both sides to take a wait-and-see attitude to their relationship so that new and more accurate choices can be made on the strength of improved information. ("You can start Tuesday and we'll see how the job works out" is a highly intelligent response to uncertainty.) To be sure, employment relationships are more personal and hence often stormier than those that exist in financial markets, but that is no warrant for replacing the contract at will with a for-cause contract provision. The proper question is: will the shift in methods of control work a change for the benefit of both parties, or will it only make a difficult situation worse?

4. *Administrative Costs.* There is one last way in which the contract at will has an enormous advantage over its rivals. It is very cheap to administer. Any effort to use a for-cause rule will in principle allow all, or at least a substantial fraction of, dismissals to generate litigation. Because motive will be a critical element in these cases, the chances of either side obtaining summary judgment will be negligible. Similarly, the broad modern rules of discovery will allow exploration into every aspect of the employment relation. Indeed, a little imagination will allow the plaintiff's lawyer to delve into the general employment policies of the firm, the treatment of similar cases, and a review of the individual file. The employer for his part will be able to examine every aspect of the employee's performance and personal life in order to bolster the case for dismissal. . . .

III. DISTRIBUTIONAL CONCERNS

Enough has been said to show that there is no principled reason of fairness or utility to disturb the common law's longstanding presumption in favor of the contract at will. It remains to be asked whether there are some hitherto unmentioned distributional consequences sufficient to throw that conclusion into doubt. . . .

The proposed reforms in the at-will doctrine cannot hope to transfer wealth systematically from rich to poor on the model of comprehensive systems of taxation or welfare benefits. Indeed it is very difficult to identify in advance any deserving group of recipients that stands to gain unambiguously from the universal abrogation of the at-will contract. The proposed rules cover the whole range from senior executives to manual labor. At every wage level, there is presumably some differential in workers' output. Those who tend to slack off seem on balance to be most vulnerable to dismissal under the at-will rule; yet it is very hard to imagine why some special concession should be made in their favor at the expense of their more diligent fellow workers.

The distributional issues, moreover, become further clouded once it is recognized that any individual employee will have interests on both sides of the employment relation. Individual workers participate heavily in pension plans, where the value of the holdings depends in part upon the efficiency of the legal rules that govern the companies in which they own shares. If the regulation of the contract at will diminishes the overall level of wealth, the losses are apt to be spread far and wide, which makes it doubtful that there are any gains to the worst off in society that justify somewhat greater losses to those who are better off. The usual concern with maldistribution gives us situations in which one person has one hundred while each of one hundred has one and asks us to compare that distribution with an even distribution of, say, two per person. But the stark form of the numerical example does not explain how the skewed distribution is tied to the concrete choice between different rules governing employment relations. Set in this concrete context, the choices about the proposed new regulation of the employment contract do not set the one against the many but set the many against each other, all in the context of a shrinking overall pie. The possible gains from redistribution, even on the most favorable of assumptions about the diminishing marginal utility of money, are simply not present.

If this is the case, one puzzle still remains: who should be in favor of the proposed legislation? One possibility is that support for the change in common law rules rests largely on ideological and political grounds, so that the legislation has the public support of persons who may well be hurt by it in their private capacities. Another possible explanation could identify the hand of interest-group politics in some subtle form. For example, the lawyers and government officials called upon to administer the new legislation may expect to obtain increased income and power, although this explanation seems insufficient to account for the current pressure. A more uncertain line of inquiry could ask whether labor unions stand to benefit from the creation of a cause of action for wrongful discharge. Unions, after all, have some skill in working with for-cause contracts under the labor statutes that prohibit firing for union activities, and they might be able to promote their own growth by selling their services to the presently nonunionized sector. In addition, the for-cause rule might give employers one less reason to resist unionization, since they would be unable to retain the absolute power to hire and fire in any event. Yet, by the same token, it is possible that workers would be less inclined to pay the costs of union membership if they received some purported benefit by the force of law without unionization. The ultimate weight of these considerations is an empirical question to which no easy answers appear. What is clear, however, is that even if one could show that the shift in the rule either benefits or hurts unions and their members, the answer would not justify the rule, for it would not explain why the legal system should try to skew the balance one way or the other. The bottom line therefore remains unchanged. The case for a legal requirement that renders employment contracts terminable only for cause is as

weak after distributional considerations are taken into account as before. . . .

CONCLUSION

The recent trend toward expanding the legal remedies for wrongful discharge has been greeted with wide approval in judicial, academic, and popular circles. In this paper, I have argued that the modern trend rests in large measure upon a misunderstanding of the contractual processes and the ends served by the contract at will. No system of regulation can hope to match the benefits that the contract at will affords in employment relations. The flexibility afforded by the contract at will permits the ceaseless marginal adjustments that are necessary in any ongoing productive activity conducted, as all activities are, in conditions of technological and business change. The strength of the contract at will should not be judged by the occasional cases in which it is said to produce unfortunate results, but rather by the vast run of cases where it provides a sensible private response to the many and varied problems in labor contracting. All too often the case for a wrongful discharge doctrine rests upon the identification of possible employer abuses, as if they were all that mattered. But the proper goal is to find the set of comprehensive arrangements that will minimize the frequency and severity of abuses by employers and employees alike. Any effort to drive employer abuses to zero can only increase the difficulties inherent in the employment relation. Here, a full analysis of the relevant costs and benefits shows why the constant minor imperfections of the market, far from being a reason to oust private agreements, offer the most powerful reason for respecting them. The doctrine of wrongful discharge is the problem and not the solution. This is one of the many situations in which courts and legislatures should leave well enough alone.

NOTES

1. Payne v. Western & Atl. R.R., 81 Tenn. 507, 518–19 (1884), *overruled on other grounds*, Hut-

ton v. Watters, 132 Tenn. 527, 544, 179 S.W. 134, 138 (1915). . . .

2. Payne v. Western & Atl. R.R., 81 Tenn. 507, 518–19 (1884). . . .

Drug Testing in the Workplace:
The Challenge to Employment Relations
and Employment Law

Mark A. Rothstein

THE PROBLEM OF DRUG ABUSE

Drug abuse is one of America's most pervasive, serious, tragic, and seemingly intractable social problems. According to the National Institute on Drug Abuse (NIDA), over seventy million Americans have experimented with illegal drugs and twenty-three million Americans are currently using some type of illegal substance.[1] Over twenty-two million Americans have experimented with cocaine and ten million are cocaine-dependent. In the last ten years there has been a 200% increase in cocaine-related deaths and a 500% increase in admissions to drug abuse treatment programs.[2]

The abuse of legal drugs, especially alcohol, also is a source for great concern. Over 100 million Americans use alcohol and there may be as many as eighteen million adult alcoholics in the United States. Alcohol is involved in nearly half of all automobile accidents and homicides, one-fourth of all

suicides, and four-fifths of all family court cases. . . . [3]

With regard to illicit drug use, more educated and affluent people had a significant decline in drug use, while less educated and poor people had little or no decline in drug use. With the exception of heroin and crack (a smokable form of cocaine) used by the poor, the use of illegal drugs, although still high, seems to have peaked. . . .

Drug abuse exacts a heavy toll from society: from the health care system, from the criminal justice system, and from drug abusers and their families. Drug abuse is also very costly to employers. According to one estimate, ninety percent of drug and alcohol abusers work and a significant number of employees use drugs on the job.

Different occupations often tend to have a particular type of drug problem. For instance, marijuana use on the job is most prevalent in the entertainment/recreation industry (17%), construction industry (13%),

From Mark A. Rothstein, "Drug Testing in the Workplace: The Challenge to Employment Relations and Employment Law," *Chicago-Kent Law Review* 63:3 (1987). Reprinted by permission of ITT Chicago-Kent College of Law.

personal services (11%), and manufacturing of durable goods (10%).[4] On the other hand, alcohol abuse is most prevalent among "blue collar" workers.[5] Undoubtedly, age, education, income, and other characteristics of the work force are responsible for these trends.

Regardless of the drug involved, it is clear that employee drug abuse is very costly to employers. The costs of employee drug abuse borne by employers can be divided into six categories: (1) lost productivity; (2) accidents and injuries; (3) insurance; (4) theft and other crimes; (5) employee relations; and (6) legal liability.

Lost Productivity

Several studies have attempted to measure whether the use of drugs by employees adversely affects their performance on the job. Using verbal, written, physiological, and physical testing, the studies concluded that drug abusers were functioning at only 50% to 67% capacity.[6] Specifically, drug abusers demonstrated poor work quality, failure to follow up or complete assignments, inadequate preparation, impaired memory, lethargy, reduced coordination, carelessness, mistakes, and slowdowns.[7]

A second measure of lost productivity attributed to drug abuse is absenteeism. Drug-abusing employees have a higher rate of absenteeism, with estimates ranging from 2.5 to 16 times higher than employees who do not use drugs.[8] Thus, employers are faced with increased costs for additional sick leave and medical insurance.

Finally, drug abusers have a higher turnover rate.[9] According to one study, illicit drug users (particularly marijuana users who also use alcohol or other drugs) had average termination dates ten months earlier for males and sixteen months earlier for females.[10]

Estimates of the total financial impact of lost productivity from drugs borne by American business vary widely. The most frequently cited estimates are those of the Research Triangle Institute, which estimates that lost productivity totals $99 billion annually, with two-thirds attributable to alcohol.[11]

Accidents and Injuries

In 1984 American business lost an estimated $81 billion due to accidents, and many people believe that drug abuse is responsible for a significant share of the losses.[12] In the last ten years there have been a number of highly publicized accidents where employee drug abuse was a factor, including thirty-seven deaths in the railroad industry. Overall, it has been reported that drug users have three to four times as many accidents as nonusers.[13]

There has been little scientific study, however, of the relationship between drugs and accidents. In a study by the National Institute for Occupational Safety and Health (NIOSH), out of 2,979 workplace injuries in the chemical industry in 1984 and 1985, drugs were a primary factor in only two injuries and a partial factor in only six more.[14] Similarly, a study by the Mine Safety and Health Administration (MSHA), found only ten accidents in four years involved drugs.[15]

Despite any doubts raised by these contradictory studies, there is a perception that many workplace accidents are caused by drugs, and there is certainly the potential for drug-related accidents. Thus, many policies appear to be based on the assumption of a causal relationship between drugs and accidents.

Insurance

Drug and alcohol abuse may increase insurance costs by as much as $50 billion annually.[16] Employers that provide employees with insurance coverage as a part of the employee benefits package pay a substantial part of these increased costs. For example, employees with drug problems are more likely to use medical insurance and file workers' compensation claims.

Theft and Other Crimes

A common concern about the employment of people who use drugs is that to support their drug habit they are likely to steal from their employer, embezzle money, sell company products or trade secrets without authorization, steal from coworkers or customers, and sell drugs on company premises. Although these concerns have not been proven empirically, there is anecdotal evidence, and many employer policies appear to be based on the assumption that these concerns are valid.

Employee Relations

Another cost associated with drug abuse that is difficult to quantify is the negative impact of drugs on employee relations. Lost productivity, safety risks, and "work shifting" (nonusers being forced to do more than their share of work) can lower employee morale. Employees who use drugs also may try to sell drugs to coworkers or to spread the use of drugs to coworkers. Consequently, management must resolve intraemployee frictions and disputes. Meanwhile, management energies also must be committed to drug detection, crime prevention, drug education, quality control, accident prevention, and rehabilitation — all without invading employee privacy or undermining labor-management relations.

Legal Liability

Employer policies dealing with drugs in the workplace also must consider the issue of legal liability. Every injured person, damaged piece of property, defective product, breached contract, or other wrongful act attributable to employee drug usage has the potential for substantial employer liability. On the other hand, overzealous efforts to combat drug abuse in the workplace also have the potential for liability. Thus, employers must navigate a careful course between insouciance and overreaction to the threat of drugs in the workplace.

DRUG TESTING — HOW IT WORKS AND WHAT IT MEASURES

Drug Testing Technology

In the last decade, technological advances in drug testing and the commercial exploitation of these advances have made workplace drug testing commonplace. Despite the frequency of drug testing, however, there remains widespread misunderstanding about how the tests work, what they measure, and how their accuracy is determined.

Drug tests analyze a body specimen for the presence of drugs or their by-products, metabolites. The most commonly used specimen for workplace testing is urine, although blood, breath, saliva, hair, and other specimens have been used in settings other than the workplace. Blood testing by employers is mostly limited to retrospective testing after the occurrence of an accident.

Scientifically valid drug testing is a two-step process. In the initial step, a "screening" test eliminates from further testing those specimens with negative results, indicating either the absence of targeted substances or the presence of levels below a designated threshold or "cut-off" point. A result which reveals substance levels at or above the cut-off is considered positive. All positive specimens are then retested using a "confirmatory" test. According to the Toxicology Section of the American Academy of Forensic Sciences, the confirmatory test must be "based upon different chemical or physical principles than the initial analysis method(s)."[17] Confirmatory testing is essential to establish both the identity and quantity of the substances in the specimen.

There are three main types of initial screening tests: color or spot tests, thin layer chromatography and immunoassays. The most widely used are the immunoassays, which are of three types, enzyme, radio, and fluorescence. All of these latter tests are based on immunological principles. A known quantity of the tested-for drug is bound to an enzyme or radioactive iodine and is added to the urine. If the urine contains the drug, the added, "labeled" drug competes with the drug in the specimen and cannot bind to the antibodies. As a result, the enzyme or radioactive iodine remains active. By measuring enzyme activity or radioactivity, the presence and amount of the drug can be determined.

The most commonly used immunoassay is the enzyme multiplied immunoassay technique or EMIT. An advantage of EMIT is that it tests for a broad spectrum of drugs and their metabolites, including opiates, barbiturates, amphetamines, cocaine and its metabolite, benzodiazepines, methaqualone, methadone, phencyclidine, and cannabinoids. It is also fast and cheap. A single test may cost about five dollars. In addition, portable kits starting at $300 are sold for on-site use by individuals with minimal training.

The radioimmunoassay (RIA) can measure only one drug at a time, but has broad-spectrum detection capabilities similar to

EMIT. RIA is more expensive than EMIT, however, and requires a more highly trained technician. The fluorescence polarization immunoassay (FPIA) is a relatively new technique and, as yet, not widely used.

The most widely used confirmatory test is gas chromatography/mass spectrometry (GC/MS). In GC the sample is pretreated to extract drugs from the urine. The drugs are converted to a gaseous form and transported through a long glass column of helium gas. By application of varying temperatures to the column the compounds are separated according to their unique properties, such as molecular weight and rate of reaction. These particular properties are used to identify the compound. Although GC can be used alone, the superior method combines it with a mass spectrometer (MS), which breaks down the compound molecules into electrically charged ion fragments. Each drug or metabolite produces a unique fragment pattern, which can be detected by comparison with known fragment patterns. GC/MS requires expensive equipment and highly trained technicians to prepare the sample and interpret test results. The process is also time-consuming because only one sample and one drug per sample may be tested at a time. High performance liquid chromatography (HPLC) is also used as a confirmatory test, but GC/MS has become the standard confirmatory test.

The pricing structures for drug tests vary widely. Some laboratories charge customers a flat fee per specimen tested; others divide the fee so that those samples requiring a confirmatory test incur an additional charge. Other factors affecting price are the type of analysis used, the number of specimens tested, and the types of drugs tested for. In general, laboratory charges for single-procedure methods range from $5 to $20; GC/MS confirmation costs from $30 to $100.[18]

What the Tests Measure

It is essential to understand that a positive result on a drug test does not indicate impairment of the subject. Drug metabolites detected in urine are the inert, inactive by-products of drugs and cannot be used to determine impairment. Although a blood test can reveal the presence of drugs in the blood in their active state, with the exception of ethanol, there is no known correlation between the detection of metabolites in urine and blood concentrations. Moreover, there is no agreement among experts on what level of drug indicates impairment.

Many variables influence how a drug will affect an individual user, including the type of drug, dose, time lapse from administration, duration of effect and use, the interactions with other drugs. The individual's age, weight, sex, general health state, emotional state, and drug tolerance also are important factors. Consequently, the wide individual variations make generalizing extremely speculative. According to one expert:

> Testing does only one thing. It detects what is being tested. It does not tell us anything about the recency of use. It does not tell us anything about how the person was exposed to the drug. It doesn't even tell us whether it affected performance.[19]

A final factor that complicates interpretation of a positive result is the often-considerable duration of detectability of drugs in urine. As indicated in the following table [Table 1], drug metabolites can be detected in urine from one day to several weeks following exposure. The usual *effects* of most drugs persist for only a few hours after use. Therefore, drugs are detectable long after their effects have subsided and any correlations between a positive test and impairment are impossible.

TABLE 1. Approximate Duration of Detectability of Selected Drugs in Urine[20]

Drugs	Approximate Duration of Detectability
Amphetamines	2 days
Barbiturates	1–7 days
Benzodiazepines	3 days
Cocaine metabolites	2–3 days
Methadone	3 days
Codeine	2 days
PCP	8 days
Cannabinoids	
Single use	3 days
Moderate smoker	
(4 times/week)	5 days
Heavy smoker (daily)	10 days
Chronic heavy smoker	21 days

How Accurate Are the Tests?

Before discussing the accuracy of drug tests, it is important to review how accuracy in medical tests is measured. The key concepts are "sensitivity" and "specificity." The sensitivity of a test is a measure of its ability to identify persons with the tested-for condition. It is the percentage of persons with the condition who register a positive test result:

$$\frac{\text{True positive test results}}{\substack{\text{Persons with condition} \\ \text{(True positives + False negatives)}}} \times 100 \text{ percent}$$

Therefore, if 100 persons have a condition and the test is able to identify 90 of them, the test would be 90% sensitive.

The specificity of a test is a measure of its ability to identify persons who do not have a condition. It is the percentage of persons free of the condition who register a negative test result:

$$\frac{\text{True negative test results}}{\begin{array}{c}\text{Persons free of conditions}\\\text{(True negatives + False positives)}\end{array}} \times 100 \text{ percent}$$

Therefore, if 100 persons are free of a condition and the test is able to identify 90 of them, the test would be 90% specific.

The "positive predictive value" of a test refers to the value of a positive test result in identifying the presence of a condition. It is the percentage of persons whose test results are positive who actually have the condition:

$$\frac{\begin{array}{c}\text{Persons with condition}\\\text{(True positives)}\end{array}}{\begin{array}{c}\text{Positive test results}\\\text{(True positives + False positives)}\end{array}} \times 100 \text{ percent}$$

According to independent studies,[21] the EMIT test has a sensitivity of about 99% and a specificity of about 90%.[22] The positive predictive value of the test, however, varies greatly depending on the prevalence of drug usage in the tested population. The following tables illustrate how important prevalence is to the predictive value of a test.

Table 2 assumes a 50% prevalence — perhaps individuals in a drug treatment program or, in a workplace setting, individuals selected for testing based upon reasonable suspicion. The test correctly identifies 4950 of the 5000 true positives, with 50 false negatives. It correctly identifies 4500 of the 5000

true negatives, with 500 false positives. Therefore, of the 5450 positives, 4950 are true positives. The positive predictive value of the test is 4950/5450 or 90.8%.

Table 3 assumes a 5% prevalence — a reasonable estimate of the prevalence of recent drug users among job applicants. The test correctly identifies 495 of the 500 true positives, with 5 false negatives. It correctly identifies 8550 of the 9500 true negatives, with 950 false positives. Therefore, of the 1445 positives, 495 are true positives. The positive predictive value of the test is 495/1445 or 34.3%.

Table 3 demonstrates why it is essential to use confirmatory tests. Two out of three positives identified by the test will be false positives. Unfortunately, pre-employment drug tests, where the prevalence and predictive values are low, are also the tests least likely to be confirmed due to cost considerations.

Because drug tests detect metabolites of drugs rather than the drugs themselves, commonly used screening tests (and to a lesser extent confirmatory tests as well) sometimes incorrectly identify as metabolites of illicit drugs the metabolites of other substances or normal human enzymes such as lysozyme and malate dehydrogenase. Table 4 indicates some of the substances for which this effect, cross-reactivity, has been documented.

The problem of cross-reactivity is one important reason why it is important to use pretest questionnaires inquiring about medications and other cross-reactants and to give

TABLE 2. Predictive Value of EMIT Test with 99% Sensitivity, 90% Specificity, 50% Prevalence, and 10,000 Subjects

Subjects	True Positives	False Negatives
5000+	4950	50
	False Positives	*True Negatives*
5000−	500	4500

TABLE 3. Predictive Value of EMIT Test with 99% Sensitivity, 90% Specificity, 5% Prevalence, and 10,000 Subjects

Subjects	True Positives	False Negatives
500+	495	5
	False Positives	*True Negatives*
9500−	950	8550

TABLE 4.   Some Commonly Available Substances That Cross-React with Widely Tested-For Drugs

Type of Drug	Cross-Reactants
Amphetamines	1. over-the-counter cold medications (decongestants)
	2. over-the-counter and prescription dietary aids
	3. asthma medications
	4. anti-inflammatory agents
Barbiturates	1. anti-inflammatory agents
	2. phenobarbital (used to treat epilepsy)
Cocaine	1. herbal teas (made from coca leaves)
Marijuana (cannabinoids)	1. nonsteroidal anti-inflammatory agents
	2. Ibuprofen (Advil, Motrin, Nuprin)
Morphine, opiates	1. codeine
	2. prescription analgesics and antitussives
	3. poppy seeds
	4. over-the-counter cough remedies
Phencyclidine (PCP)	1. prescription cough medicines
	2. Valium

individuals an opportunity to explain a positive result. A related concern is that a drug test will be positive because of "passive inhalation." There is disputed evidence about whether a marijuana test using a cutoff of 20 nanograms per milliliter of urine will test positive if the subject was exposed to the marijuana smoke of other people. Using a higher cutoff, however, such as 100 nanograms per milliliter of urine, will eliminate this problem.

The accuracy of drug tests also may be affected by several other factors. Alteration of the specimen, such as by substitution or dilution, improper calibration of equipment or cleaning of equipment (the so-called carry-over effect), mislabeling, contamination, or technician error all may undermine test accuracy. Indeed, even the best methodologies will yield valid results only to the extent that the testing laboratory adheres to rigid standards of quality control. Laboratory proficiency criteria, however, have been extremely inadequate. . . .

PRIVATE EMPLOYERS AS DRUG TESTERS

Although drug testing began in the private sector, it was not until public employers began testing that private sector drug testing became so widespread. For the most part, it is the large companies that have embraced drug testing. Among *Fortune* 500 corporations, only ten percent performed urinalysis in 1982; by 1985 the figure had reached twenty-five percent;[23] and by 1987 nearly fifty percent of the largest corporations performed drug testing.[24]

As the size of the company declines, so too does the prevalence of drug testing. In a 1987 survey of companies with more than 500 employees, seventeen percent of the companies tested current workers for drugs and twenty-three percent tested applicants.[25] Smaller companies reported less testing. Transportation and manufacturing companies were most likely to test, electronics/communications and insurance/finance companies were least likely to test. The specifics of drug testing also vary by size of the company, geography, industry, and other factors. Larger companies are more likely to use confirmatory testing and refer those testing positive to an employee assistance program; smaller companies are more likely to use only screening tests and to respond to a positive test with summary dismissal.

According to one study, almost all of the companies (94.5%) that perform urinalysis test job applicants and nearly three-fourths of the companies (73%) test current employees on a "for cause" basis.[26] Only fourteen percent conducted random tests and those companies tended to be smaller, with a significant number of them testing people in jobs of a "sensitive or high risk nature."[27] The most widely cited reason for testing (37%) was health and safety.[28] Other reasons for testing were the identification of a workplace substance abuse problem (21%), the awareness of drugs as a national problem (11%), and the high-risk nature of the job (9%).[29]

It is also valuable to consider why the companies without drug testing programs have declined to engage in testing. According to the American Management Association, the most common reasons for not performing drug testing are as follows: moral issues or privacy (68%); inaccuracy of tests (63%); negative impact on morale (53%); tests show use, not abuse (43%); employee opposition (16%); and union opposition (7%).[30] Interestingly, fear of litigation was not mentioned, but it certainly may be an increasingly significant consideration.

LEGAL ISSUES

A number of constitutional arguments have been raised to challenge the legality of employee drug testing. Because of the governmental action requirement, federal constitutional protections are limited to public employees and private employees where drug testing is mandated by federal, state, or local governments.

The most frequently raised argument is that drug testing constitutes an unreasonable search and seizure in violation of the fourth amendment. In *Schmerber v. California*, the Supreme Court held that taking a blood sample from a criminal defendant to determine whether he was intoxicated was a search within the meaning of the fourth amendment. Lower court decisions after *Schmerber* have recognized that requiring a urine sample is far less intrusive than extracting blood, but have nonetheless concluded that a mandatory urine screen also is a search for purposes of the fourth amendment. The limited nature of the intrusion, however, may be important in determining the validity of the search.

The fourth amendment does not bar all searches, only unreasonable ones. Therefore, it must be determined whether the drug test is unreasonable. This in turn often depends on the nature of the search: who is searched, when the search is made, how it is made, and what is done with the results. Courts balance the degree of intrusion of the search on the person's fourth amendment right of privacy against the need for the search to promote some legitimate governmental interest.

One essential factor is whether the individual has a reasonable expectation of privacy relative to the circumstances of the search. Government employees have a reasonable expectation of privacy at work and "do not surrender their fourth amendment rights merely because they go to work for the government."[31] Yet, government employers maintain rights in conducting warrantless searches "for the proprietary purpose of preventing future damage to the agency's ability to discharge effectively its statutory responsibilities."[32]

Three distinct privacy interests have been identified in urinalysis. First is the expectation of privacy as to the urine itself. According to one court, "[a]n individual cannot retain a privacy interest in a waste product that, once released, is flushed down the drain."[33] Another court, however, has observed that "[t]he urine excreted for a drug test ... is not expected to be a waste product, flushed down a toilet. Indeed, precautions are taken in the test procedure to prevent the sample from being thus disposed of."[34] Second is the expectation of privacy in the information contained in the urine. "Obviously, one does not expect that he will be made to discharge urine so that it can be analyzed in order to discover the personal physiological secrets it may hold. Thus, as with blood, there is an expectation of privacy concerning the 'information' body fluids may hold."[35] Third is the expectation of privacy in the process of urination. "[T]he act of urination is a private one and, if interfered with, protected by the Fourth Amendment."[36] Therefore, policies requiring direct observation of an individual urinating would be more difficult to sustain.

An interesting issue is whether the fourth amendment protects an individual's refusal to submit to a mandatory urinalysis. In *Everett v. Napper,* the Atlanta Bureau of Fire Services was conducting an investigation into drug trafficking by fire fighters and one of the subjects of the investigation listed the plaintiff as one of the fire fighters who had purchased drugs from him. The plaintiff denied the allegation and refused to submit to a urinalysis. After his discharge for refusal to cooperate with the investigation, he sued claiming, among other things, a violation of his fourth amendment rights. The Eleventh Circuit, in upholding the discharge, held that "since Everett did not submit to the urinalysis, there was no 'search' and therefore no possible fourth amendment violation."[37]

The court's reasoning in *Everett* is disturbing. Although the court could have sustained the discharge on the ground that the intended search was reasonable, it is questionable whether the court could flatly state that because he refused to take the drug test there was no search and therefore no fourth amendment violation. It is unlikely that the court would want to embrace the notion that one must acquiesce in an illegal search in

order to have standing to challenge the search when negative consequences already have attached to the refusal. At the least, it would seem to violate substantive due process to discharge a public employee for refusal to consent to an unlawful act.

Other courts to consider this issue, unlike the *Everett* court, have not focused on whether the refusal negated the search, but whether it was lawful for the government to require consent to the search. For example, in *McDonell v. Hunter,* the Eighth Circuit stated: "If a search is unreasonable, a government employer cannot require that its employees consent to that search as a condition of employment."[38]

A related but distinct constitutional protection has been established to protect the "right of privacy." Although this right is not explicit in the Constitution, the Supreme Court has found that it includes the individual's interest in avoiding disclosure of personal matters and independence in making certain kinds of important decisions, such as marriage, procreation, and family relationships. This privacy interest, however, is not absolute and must be balanced against legitimate governmental interests in disclosure.

In the context of drug testing, the courts have been reluctant to apply privacy principles distinct from those recognized under the fourth amendment.

> The "privacy" rights of the public employees have been vindicated under the Fourth Amendment by this court's determination that [the transit agency's] random program is unreasonable. To find that the testing procedure implicates a further, separate protection would require an expansive reading of the Fourteenth Amendment that this court is unwilling to undertake.[39]

Another constitutional argument often raised in drug testing cases is procedural due process. The argument has been used to challenge both test procedures and employee termination procedures. As to the former, it has been held that termination of employment on the basis of an unconfirmed EMIT test violated due process and that it violated due process when voluntarily-submitted urine samples were destroyed before they could be sent out for independent testing. Even the addition of confirmatory testing may not satisfy due process concerns about the proper handling of the specimen and cleaning and calibration of test equipment. As to the latter, employee termination procedures, the termination of an individual's employment must be preceded by notice and opportunity for a hearing appropriate to the nature of the case, although a full, predischarge hearing is not required. . . .

Although the specific legal criteria vary with the source of the legal protection, essentially the courts seek to determine whether a challenged drug testing program is reasonable under the circumstances. One way of looking at the issue is to see whether reasonable grounds exist to suspect that the testing will turn up evidence of work-related drug use and whether the measures adopted are not excessively intrusive. Another way is to focus upon the following four factors: who is tested, when is the testing performed, how is the testing performed, and what is done with test results.

Who Is Tested?

The starting point for determining whether any particular drug testing is reasonable is to look at the individual being tested. In other words, the job description and responsibilities of the person tested are very important. The courts have been more willing to sanction the use of drug testing where employees and co-workers may be endangered by drug impairment. Drug testing in other job classifications is less likely to be upheld.

When Is the Testing Performed?

Drug testing may be conducted at a variety of stages during the employment relationship, including pre-employment, periodic, upon return to work following a leave of absence, after an accident, based on suspicion of drug use, and randomly. The timing or circumstances of the test often affect the legality of the test.

Pre-employment testing is the most prevalent form of drug testing. It is also the most likely to be upheld. Applicants do not have any vested rights in their jobs and if they are denied a job because of a drug test they have only lost an expectancy as opposed to current employees whose loss probably would be considered more tangible.

Periodic testing, especially when used as part of an overall medical evaluation of fitness, also is likely to be upheld. For other types of testing, without a particularized or individualized need for testing, the courts are more inclined to find that testing is unnecessary and therefore unreasonable. Random testing, particularly unsystematic random testing, where the individuals to be tested are selected subjectively, has been looked upon with distrust by the courts who are fearful of abuses in selection. Similarly, surprise, mass testing has been held to be unlawful.

With specific evidence of the need to test, the courts are more inclined to uphold the testing. Drug testing of certain employees who were identified in reports as drug users has been upheld. Post-accident testing also has been upheld. In *Division 241, Amalgamated Transit Union v. Suscy,* the Seventh Circuit upheld the Chicago Transit Authority's rule mandating drug testing for bus drivers involved in a serious accident or suspected of being intoxicated.

The courts have not required "probable cause" before upholding an individual drug test. "Reasonable suspicion," a lesser standard, has been widely adopted. "The 'reasonable suspicion' test requires that to justify this intrusion, officials must point to specific, objective facts and rational inferences that they are entitled to draw from these facts in the light of their experience."[40]

Reasonable suspicion goes to individual drug testing. An unresolved issue is whether evidence of widespread drug abuse in the community or a problem within a group of workers is needed to justify wider testing. In *Lovvorn v. City of Chattanooga,* the drug testing of fire fighters was struck down because of a lack of reasonable suspicion of the need to test:

> The City has not pointed to any objective facts concerning deficient job performance or physical or mental deficiencies on the part of its fire fighters, either in general or with respect to specific personnel, which might lead to a reasonable suspicion upon which tests could be based.[41]

How Is the Testing Performed?

The testing procedures used may affect the legality of the testing. In *Jones v. McKenzie,* the court held that the use of an unconfirmed EMIT test, which violated a specific regulation mandating confirmation, was arbitrary and capricious. Confirmatory testing, such as the use of gas chromatography/mass spectrometry to confirm an initial immunoassay, will increase the accuracy of the test and the likelihood of legality. In *National Treasury Employees Union v. Von Raab,* the Fifth Circuit upheld drug testing by the Customs Service in large part because of specific measures to ensure the reliability of test results. These measures included confirmatory testing, chain-of-custody procedures, allowing the employee to choose a laboratory for re-testing, and a quality assurance program.[42]

Safeguarding the chain-of-custody of the specimen is necessary to eliminate the possibility of confusion, mishandling, or sabotage. In addition, it may be necessary to retain the sample to allow for independent confirmation of the results. In *Banks v. FAA,* the discharges of air traffic controllers were set aside because the urine samples had been destroyed before they could be re-tested by an independent laboratory.

A final issue relates to sample collection. The courts have recognized a substantial privacy interest in urination.

> There are few activities in our society more personal or private than the passing of urine. Most people describe it by euphemisms if they talk about it at all. It is a function traditionally performed without public observation; indeed, its performance in public is generally prohibited by law as well as social custom.[43]

Consequently, direct observation of urination is unlikely to be upheld. In *Caruso v. Ward,* police officers were required to urinate in the presence of a superior officer of the same sex to ensure the regularity of the sample. The court found this process especially troublesome. "[T]he subject officer would be required to perform before another person what is an otherwise very private bodily function which necessarily includes exposing one's private parts, an experience which even if courteously supervised can be humiliating and degrading. . . ."[44]

What Is Done with Test Results

Workplace drug-testing programs are more likely to be upheld if individuals who test positively are rehabilitated rather than discharged. This often relates closely with the duty to make reasonable accommodation to handicapped workers. For example, in *Hazlett v. Martin Chevrolet, Inc.,* an employer was found to have violated Ohio's handicap discrimination law by discharging an employee suffering from drug and alcohol addiction and refusing to grant a one month disability or sick leave so that the employee could obtain treatment. Employees with other illnesses previously had been given leaves.

THE ELEMENTS OF A LEGAL, ETHICAL, AND EFFECTIVE DRUG TESTING PROGRAM

If there is one general criticism that can be leveled at managers in the public and private sectors regarding drug testing, it is that they have too eagerly embraced drug testing as *the* solution to the problem of workplace drug abuse. Before drug testing is implemented there must be a detailed and thoughtful consideration of whether there is a workplace drug abuse problem, whether drug testing is essential to combat the problem, whether the benefits of drug testing outweigh the costs to employers and employees, and whether drug testing can be undertaken in a way that will ensure accuracy, fairness, and privacy.

While some people have recommended unrestricted drug testing or no drug testing at all, there is a growing consensus — from the AFL-CIO to the AMA — that limited drug testing is permissible. For example, the AMA's Council on Scientific Affairs recommended:

> That the AMA take the position that urine drug and alcohol testing of employees should be limited to: (a) preemployment examinations of those persons whose jobs affect the health and safety of others, (b) situations in which there is reasonable suspicion that an employee's job performance is impaired by drug and alcohol use, and (c) monitoring as part of a comprehensive program of treatment and rehabilitation of alcohol and drug abuse or dependence.[45]

Placing careful controls on drug testing is an attempt to accommodate the legitimate concerns about test accuracy and privacy with legitimate concerns about public health and safety. It is even more difficult to move beyond generalities to concrete guidelines on workplace drug testing. A legal, ethical, and effective drug testing program should satisfy each of the following requirements.

1. *Reasonable suspicion exists to believe that there is at least some class-wide problem of drug abuse among the relevant group of employees.*

Drug testing is an extreme measure and it should not be undertaken lightly. The only compelling reason to test is to protect employee and public safety. Although drug testing should not be started only *after* a tragic accident, there are sound reasons why it should not be initiated unless there is at least some evidence of a drug abuse problem in the locality, in a particular profession or job classification, or at a particular employer. One way of determining whether there is a drug abuse problem at a particular workplace is for all employees to take a drug test anonymously. The results will indicate whether there is a problem and, if so, its nature and scope. This information also is valuable in designing education and rehabilitation programs.

2. *There are no feasible alternatives to detecting impairment, including supervision and simulation.*

The primary concern underlying drug testing is that drug-impaired employees will be impaired on the job. Drug testing, however, does not measure impairment. It measures prior exposure, which is used as a surrogate for impairment based on one of the two following theories. First, employees who use drugs off the job are more likely to use drugs on the job or to report to work under the influence of drugs. Second, prior drug use may impede performance even though no impairment is noticeable. If impairment or the effects of impairment are detectable, then there is no need for drug testing. One way to detect impairment is through regular, close supervision. Another way is for the employee to demonstrate fitness via simulation.

3. *The drug testing program is limited to workers who, if working while impaired, would pose a substantial danger to themselves, other persons, or property.*

Among the numerous asserted justifications for employee drug testing are the following: (1) drug use is illegal and therefore employers have a responsibility to discover employees who may be breaking the law; (2) drug abusing employees often need substantial sums of money to buy drugs and these employees are likely to steal from their employer or to accept bribes on the job; (3) employees using drugs are likely to have a reduction in their productivity; (4) maintaining a drug-free workplace is essential to an employer's public image; and (5) drug testing is essential to protect safety and health.

First, as to illegality, it is clear that employers are not concerned about illegality per se. If they were concerned simply about lawbreaking, measures other than drug testing are likely to be much more effective in detecting wrongdoing. For example, an employee (and management) federal income tax return screening every April 15th would undoubtedly be quite revealing. Of course, it is the province of the Internal Revenue Service and not the employer to detect tax irregularities. Similarly, it is the responsibility of law enforcement agencies and not employers to prevent illegal drug use.

Second, as to theft and bribery, the sudden need for more money to support a drug habit is only one reason why an employee might become dishonest. To be thorough, employers would need to know if an employee were gambling, suffering losses in the stock market, or even having an extra-marital affair. Pre-employment background and reference checks and post-hiring supervision

and auditing are much more effective in preventing theft and bribery than urinalysis.

Third, productivity is a legitimate concern of an employer. Productivity, however, is directly measurable and is done so on a continual basis by employers. A decline in productivity is an end point and it is irrelevant whether the decline is caused by boredom, personal problems, or drug abuse. Lack of productivity is a better measure of lack of productivity than urinalysis.

Fourth, from a legal and policy standpoint, public image is a deeply troubling rationale for employment policies. Historically, many forms of employment discrimination have been defended on grounds such as "customer preference." The law has correctly rejected such asserted defenses. Public image is not only so vague as to justify nearly any action, but in the case of drug testing, it is a two-edged sword. Drug abuse in the United States is a pervasive, intractable social problem and the fact that an employer has, among its employees, one or more individuals with a substance abuse problem is unlikely to generate public disdain. The way in which the employer deals with the problem, however, may directly affect a public image. Indiscriminate and heedless drug testing without regard for employee rights can influence the way in which the employer is regarded by current employees, potential employees, customers, and shareholders.

Fifth, safety is the only justifiable reason for employee drug testing. It is true that current drug tests do not measure impairment and only measure prior exposure. Nevertheless, there is ample evidence that individuals who use drugs often take them at work or report to work impaired. For employees in safety-sensitive positions, prudence demands that public safety considerations outweigh even the legitimate concerns of employees. For employees not in safety-sensitive positions, such as retail or clerical workers, there is no justification for drug testing. Reasonable supervision will ensure that satisfactory performance is not impeded for any reason, including drugs.

If safety is the only compelling reason for drug testing, the nature of this exception needs to be further defined. The danger posed by an impaired worker must be *substantial.* This is based on the severity of the consequences, the likelihood of danger, and the immediacy of the harm. To justify drug testing, the risk of harm from an impaired worker also must be otherwise unpreventable (as by supervision, quality control, and work review) and the consequences irreparable. Nuclear power, chemical plant, and transportation workers are the best examples. Even as to these employees, however, the other elements still need to be satisfied.

4. *Testing not based on individualized, reasonable suspicion is limited to pre-employment and periodic testing.*

Pre-employment and periodic testing (especially as part of a pre-employment or annual medical examination) are the least objectionable forms of testing. They permit the discovery of individuals who have a substance abuse problem within the context of a medical examination. There is no stigma attached to supplying a urine sample in this context. The medical setting also helps to encourage truthful disclosure by a substance-abusing employee, protects confidentiality, and facilitates treatment.

The other acceptable time for testing is when there is reasonable suspicion of impairment. This is a closer case. If an employee in a safety-sensitive job is observed to be drowsy, dizzy, disoriented, or otherwise is suspected of being impaired, regardless of the results of a drug test, the employee should not be permitted to continue work and should be referred to a physician. Thus, the need for a drug test under these circumstances may be questioned because the behavior establishing reasonable

cause also demands action immediately and cannot await the results of a drug test. The other issue raised by reasonable cause testing is that clear guidelines must be established for determining reasonable cause. Without such guidelines there is a danger of arbitrariness in selecting the employee for testing.

Despite the drawbacks of reasonable cause testing, employers should be provided with some basis for a periodic or unprogrammed testing. Recreational as well as compulsive drug users may be able to forego the use of drugs for a short period of time each year to test negatively. In those job categories where drug testing is acceptable, it ought to be effective. Reasonable cause testing, including post-accident testing, should be permissible.

Some people have suggested (and some statutes have used the approach) that the *only* permissible drug testing is for reasonable cause. For employees working alone (such as truck drivers), it is hard to imagine that there ever would be reasonable cause until after a tragic accident occurred. Thus, reasonable cause testing should not be the only basis for drug testing.

Random testing and surprise, round-up testing are unacceptable. As noted earlier, these tests have been struck down in several public sector cases on constitutional grounds.

5. *State of the art screening and confirmatory test procedures are performed by trained professionals, off-site, under laboratory conditions.*

Employers that use "do-it-yourself" drug testing kits and unconfirmed screening tests are engaged in a false economy. Unless the best technology is used, drug test results are unreliable and likely to be challenged in court. Even the best analytical techniques are only as good as the people performing the tests. Careful laboratory selection and ongoing quality review are essential.

6. *Specimen collection is not observed.*

With the growth of employee drug testing there have been numerous reports of employees attempting to substitute "clean urine" or otherwise tampering with specimens. Some employers, in response, have taken to observing employees in the act of urination. For many employees, this aspect of drug testing is the most objectionable, degrading, and insensitive element. It is highly unlikely that the benefits of observation (preventing tampering by a few individuals whose drug problems were not otherwise detectable) outweigh the human relations, employment relations, and public relations costs of observation.

7. *Testing is performed for the presence of prescription drugs and alcohol as well as illicit drugs.*

If the underlying purpose of drug testing is safety, there is no reason why drug testing should be limited to illicit drugs. In terms of the number of people who abuse them and the fatalities, injuries, and property damage caused by their effects in the workplace, alcohol and prescription drugs (often in combination) pose a much greater threat than illicit drugs.

8. *There is valid employee consent before the testing and an opportunity to explain a positive test result.*

An argument could be made that consent to drug testing is never voluntary (or valid) when employees are likely to be discharged or applicants not hired if they refuse. Nevertheless, if drug testing is essential to protect public safety in the face of a drug abuse problem by certain employees, and if the other criteria for testing are met, an employer ought to be able to make consent to drug testing a condition of employment. Employers, however, should not perform drug testing surreptitiously, such as by simply testing all urine samples obtained as part of a pre-employment or periodic medical examination.

A related issue is whether applicants and employees should be given advance notice that a pre-employment or periodic drug test will be performed. Some federal and state laws specifically mandate advance notice, but there is generally no such legal requirement. The obvious drawback to notice is that it permits individuals to abstain before being tested and then to resume drug use after the test. This drawback, however, may be outweighed by the following considerations. First, providing employees with notice improves employee acceptability of the program. It indicates that the purpose of the testing is to promote public safety and not to "catch" employees. Second, as to applicants, company resources will be saved because habitual drug users will not proceed further with their application. Third, individuals genuinely interested in obtaining or retaining employment may cease using drugs before the test, and surveillance, supervision, and retesting may ensure that they do not resume drug use.

Finally, individuals should be given an opportunity to explain a positive test result. As noted earlier, even state of the art confirmatory testing may produce false positive results due to laboratory error or cross-reactivity with some medicines and foods.

9. *Test results are kept confidential.*

Drug test results should be regarded in the same way as other medical records. Specifically, the data should be stored in the medical department (assuming there is one) and access should be limited to medical personnel. Supervisory and managerial employees should only be notified of the consequences of the results (e.g., employee A is medically unfit for work), but not the specific results. Other information essential to personnel actions should be provided only on a "need-to-know" basis. When an initial drug screen is positive and a confirmatory test is scheduled, no results should be released until after the confirmatory test. The failure to maintain confidentiality may lead to liability based on invasion of privacy, defamation, intentional infliction of emotional distress, or other torts.

10. *The test procedures or resulting personnel actions do not violate applicable legal rights of applicants and employees.*

As discussed previously, a wide range of constitutional, statutory, and common law doctrines may be implicated by drug testing. Both the testing itself and any personnel actions based on the testing must be in accordance with these legal requirements.

11. *Drug testing is only part of an overall drug abuse program, including education and rehabilitation.*

Drug testing should be only one part, and indeed should be the least important part, of a comprehensive drug abuse program. The other two components of the program should be drug awareness and employee assistance.

Drug awareness programs are educational activities aimed at supervisors and employees. Supervisors need to be trained to recognize some of the "suspect changes in employee job performance and behavior that may portend a drug abuse problem."[46] They also need to be trained in how to respond to employees suspected of having a drug abuse problem.

Employees also should be involved in a separate drug education program. Although there are several different models of programs, all programs teach employees to recognize the signs of drug abuse in themselves, family, friends, and co-workers. All programs also discuss the dangers of drug abuse and describe company and community services available for dealing with drug abuse.

The other essential part of a drug abuse program is an employee assistance program (EAP). There are 8,000[47] to 10,000[48] EAPs today, giving about twenty percent of the work force access to such a program.[49] Most of the EAPs are in large companies. Some of the programs are run in-house, others are run on a contract basis. Both types of EAPs work the same way. An employee may voluntarily enter the program or may be referred by a supervisor. The employee contacts the EAP and works out an individual treatment program. Participation in an EAP is kept confidential. In some instances, employer discipline is waived on the condition that the employee complete the EAP.

CONCLUSION

Drug abuse in America and drug abuse in American workplaces are complicated problems. Drug abuse will not be eliminated or even brought under control simply through law enforcement, military action, public relations campaigns, rehabilitation, legalization of certain drugs, or prohibiting any current drug user from obtaining private or public employment. Similarly, a facile solution to the problem of workplace drug abuse will not be found in a specimen jar or a million specimen jars.

At best, drug testing is a sometimes-necessary evil that is part of a comprehensive program to insure the public health and safety. At worst, it is an unholy alliance of politics, profiteering, unrestrained technology, and heedless personnel policies.

The efficacy and desirability of drug testing in the workplace will continue to be weighed by judges, legislators, and policy makers in the public and private sectors. In making these decisions, it is essential to consider the limits of technology, the inability of drug testing to resolve the underlying problem of drug abuse, and the human and organizational costs of implementing drug testing programs. Drug testing must be considered in the light of established employment law principles, such as equal opportunity, job-related decisionmaking, and reasonable accommodation. Drug testing also must be viewed in the larger context of a society that is built on values of autonomy, privacy, and dignity.

NOTES

1. Press Office, National Institute on Drug Abuse, "Highlights of the 1985 National Household Survey on Drug Abuse," *NIDA Capsules* (Nov. 1986 rev.) [hereinafter NIDA Highlights].

2. Smith, Deborah W., and Andrew S. Silberman, "Treatment Resources for Chemical Dependency," 1 *Seminars in Occup. Med.* 265 (1986) (citing the National Institute on Alcohol Abuse and Alcoholism (NIAAA), "Fifth Special Report to Congress on Alcohol and Health" (1984)) .

3. Ross, Robert N., and Diana Chapman Walsh, "Treatment for Chemical Dependency and Mental Illness: The Payer's Perspective," 1 *Seminars in Occup. Med.* 277 (1986).

4. Walsh, J. Michael, and Steven W. Gust, "Drug Abuse in the Workplace: Issues, Policy Decisions, and Corporate Response," 1 *Seminars in Occup. Med.* (1986) (citing C.R. Shuster, Testimony Before the House Select Committee on Narcotics Abuse and Control (May 7 1986)), 237–38.

5. Ross and Walsh, Note 3, at 285.

6. Dogoloff, Lee I., "Drug Abuse in the Workplace," 1 *Occup. Med.: State of the Art Rev's* 643 (1986) (67%); Imwinkelried, Edward J., "Some Preliminary Thoughts on the Wisdom of Governmental Prohibition or Regulation of Employee Urinalysis Testing," 11 *Nova L. Rev.* 563, 565 (1987) (65%); *Alcohol, Drug Factor in Accidents Discussed, Disputed at Montreal Session,* 17 O.S.H. Rep. (BNA) 93 (1987) (50–65%) [hereinafter Montreal Session].

7. P. Bensinger, *Drugs in the Workplace: Employers' Rights and Responsibilities* 1 (1984), at 1.

8. Dogoloff, Note 6, at 645 (2.5 times); Imwinkelreid, Note 6, at 565 (16 times).

9. Walsh & Gust, Note 4, at 237.

10. *Id.* (citing study by Kandel, D., and Yamaguchi, K.).

11. BNA Special Report, "Alcohol & Drugs in the Workplace: Costs, Controls, and Controversies," 7 (1986), at 7.

12. *Id.* at 7 (quoting P. Bensinger).

13. P. Bensinger, Note 7, at 1 (3.5 times); "BNA Special Report," Note 11, at 8 (3 to 4 times) (quoting P. Bensinger); Dogoloff, Note 6, at 645 (3.6 times); "Montreal Session," Note 6, at 93 (4 times) (quoting an industrial hygienist for the Department of Agriculture).

14. "Montreal Session," Note 6, at 93–94.

15. *Id.* See also *Few Sound Studies Link Drug, Alcohol Abuse with Workplace Accident Rates, Physician Says,* 17 O.S.H. Rep. (BNA) 825 (1987) (quoting Dr. Bob Brewer of the Rush Occupational Health Network).

16. "Study: $50 Billion Wasted Annually from Abuse of Drugs and Alcohol," 1 *Employee Rel. Weekly* (BNA) 1554 (1986) (citing a study by the Comprehensive Care Corp.).

17. Dubowski, Kurt M., "Drug-Use Testing: Scientific Perspectives," 11 *Nova L. Review* (1987), at 437.

18. Hoyt, David W., Robert E. Finnigan, Thomas Nee, Theodore F. Shults, and Thorne J. Butler, "Drug Testing in the Workplace — Are Methods Legally Defensible?," 258 *J.A.M.A.* 504, 508 (1987). See also Hudner, Edward J., "Urine Testing for Drugs," 11 Nova L. Rev. 553, 555 (1987); McBay, Arthur J., "Efficient Drug Testing: Addressing the Basic Issues," 11 Nova L. Rev. 647, 648 (1987); Morikawa, Dennis J., Peter J. Hurtgen, Terence G. Connor and Joseph J. Costello, "Implementation of Drug and Alcohol Testing in the Unionized Workplace," 11 *Nova L. Rev.* 653, 656 (1987); Schroeder, Patricia, and Andrea L. Nelson, "Drug Testing in the Federal Government," 11 *Nova L. Rev.* 685, 688–89 (1987).

19. Professor Ronald K. Seigel of UCLA Medical School, forensic psychopharmacologist, quoted in Denenberg, Tia Schneider, and Richard V. Denenberg, "Drug Testing from the Arbiter's Perspective," 11 *Nova L. Rev.* (1987), at 399.

20. Council on Scientific Affairs, American Medical Association, "Scientific Issues in Drug Testing," 257 *J.A.M.A.* (1987), at 3112.

21. Fenton, John, Michael Schaffer, Nancy W. Chen, and E. W. Bermes, Jr., "A Comparison of Enzyme Immunoassay and Gas Chromatography/Mass Spectrometry in Forensic Toxicology," 25 *J. Forensic Sci.* 314 (1980).

22. False positive rates vary based on the substance tested for and the test procedure used. The EMIT test false positive rates are: cocaine — 10%; opiates — 5.6%; barbiturates — 5.1%; amphetamines — 12.5%; and marijuana — 19%. *Id.* The average is about 10%, for a specificity of 90%.

23. Chapman, "The Ruckus Over Medical Testing," *Fortune*, Aug. 19, 1985, at 57, 58.

24. Boyer, "ABC to Conduct Drug-Use Tests on Applicants for Full-Time Jobs," *N.Y. Times*, July 10, 1987, at Y 44; "Labor Letter: Drug Tests Spread," *Wall St. J.*, April 7, 1987, at 1.

25. "Drug Testing Popular," *Occup. Health & Safety*, Aug. 1987, at 12 (based on survey by Business and Legal Reports).

26. "Survey Shows Little Use of Random Test Programs," 1 *Nat'l Rep. on Substance Abuse* (BNA), Sept. 16, 1987, at 2 (citing study at Executive Knowledgeworks).

27. *Id.*

28. *Id.*

29. *Id.*

30. Teleconference on Drug Testing, *U.S.A. Today*, Feb. 5, 1987, at 1.

31. *Allen v. City of Marietta*, 601 F. Supp. 482, 491 (N.D. Ga. 1985).

32. *Id.*

33. *Turner v. Fraternal Order of Police*, 500 A.2d 1005, 1011 (D.C. 1985).

34. *National Treasury Employees Union v. Von Raab*, 816 F. 2d 170, 175 (5th Cir. 1987).

35. *Caruso v. Ward*, 133 Misc. 2d 544, 547, 506 N.Y.S.2d 789, 792 (Sup. Ct. 1986).

36. *Turner*, 500 A.2d at 1011.

37. 825 F.2d 341 (11th Cir. 1987), at 345.

38. 809 F.2d 1302 (8th Cir. 1987), at 1310. *Accord National Fed'n of Fed. Employees*, 818 F.2d at 943.

39. *Amalgamated Transit Union, Local 1277, AFL-CIO v. Sunline Transit Agency*, 663 F. Supp. 1560, 1572 (C.D. Cal. 1987). See also *Shoemaker v. Handel*, 795 F.2d 1136 (3d Cir. 1986).

40. *City of Palm Bay*, 475 So. 2d at 1326.

41. 647 F. Supp. 875 (E.D. Tenn. 1986), at 882.

42. 816 F.2d 170 (5th Cir. 1987), at 181–82.

43. *National Treasury Employees Union*, 816 F.2d at 175.

44. 133 Misc. 2d 544, 506 N.Y.S. 2d 789 (Sup. Ct. 1986), at 548, 506 N.Y.S.2d at 793.

45. Council on Scientific Affairs, American Medical Association, "Issues in Employee Drug Testing," 258 *J.A.M.A.* 2089 (1987), at 2095. In the interest of disclosure, it should be noted that the author was the legal consultant to the American Medical Association in the drafting of this recommendation.

46. Jack E. Nelson, "Drug Abusers on the Job," 23 *J. Occup. Med.* 403 (1981).

47. Masi, Dale A., "Employee Assistance Programs," 1 *Occup. Med.: State of the Art Rev's* 653 (1986).

48. Bureau of National Affairs, "Alcohol and Drugs in the Workplace" 15 (1986) at 39.

49. *Id.* at 40.

Drug Testing in Employment

Joseph DesJardins
and Ronald Duska

According to one survey, nearly one-half of all *Fortune* 500 companies were planning to administer drug tests to employees and prospective employees by the end of 1987.[1] Counter to what seems to be the current trend in favor of drug testing, we will argue that it is rarely legitimate to override an employee's or applicant's right to privacy by using such tests or procedures.

From Joseph DesJardins and Ronald Duska, "Drug Testing in Employment," *Business & Professional Ethics Journal* 6 (1987). Reprinted by permission of the authors.

OPENING STIPULATIONS

We take privacy to be an "employee right" by which we mean a presumptive moral entitlement to receive certain goods or be protected from certain harms in the workplace.[2] Such a right creates a *prima facie* obligation on the part of the employer to provide the relevant goods or, as in this case, refrain from the relevant harmful treatment. These rights prevent employees from being placed in the fundamentally coercive position where they must choose between their job and other basic human goods.

Further, we view the employer-employee relationship as essentially contractual. The employer-employee relationship is an economic one and, unlike relationships such as those between a government and its citizens or a parent and a child, exists primarily as a means for satisfying the economic interests of the contracting parties. The obligations that each party incurs are only those that it voluntarily takes on. Given such a contractual relationship, certain areas of the employee's life remain their own private concern and no employer has a right to invade them. On these presumptions we maintain that certain information about an employee is rightfully private, i.e., the employee has a right to privacy.

THE RIGHT TO PRIVACY

According to George Brenkert, a right to privacy involves a three-place relation between a person A, some information X, and another person B. The right to privacy is violated only when B deliberately comes to possess information X about A, and no relationship between A and B exists which would justify B's coming to know X about A.[3] Thus, for example, the relationship one has with a mortgage company would justify that company's coming to know about one's salary, but the relationship one has with a neighbor does not

justify the neighbor's coming to know that information. Hence, an employee's right to privacy is violated whenever personal information is requested, collected and/or used by an employer in a way or for any purpose that is *irrelevant to* or *in violation of* the contractual relationship that exists between *employer and employee.*

Since drug testing is a means for obtaining information, the information sought must be relevant to the contract in order for the drug testing not to violate privacy. Hence, we must first decide if knowledge of drug use obtained by drug testing is job-relevant. In cases where the knowledge of drug use is *not* relevant, there appears to be no justification for subjecting employees to drug tests. In cases where information of drug use is job-relevant, we need to consider if, when, and under what conditions using a means such as drug testing to obtain that knowledge is justified.

IS KNOWLEDGE OF DRUG USE JOB RELEVANT INFORMATION?

There seem to be two arguments used to establish that knowledge of drug use is job relevant information. The first argument claims that drug use adversely affects job performance thereby leading to lower productivity, higher costs, and consequently lower profits. Drug testing is seen as a way of avoiding these adverse effects. According to some estimates $25 billion ($25,000,000,000) are lost each year in the United States because of drug use.[4] This occurs because of loss in productivity, increase in costs due to theft, increased rates in health and liability insurance, and such. Since employers are contracting with an employee for the performance of specific tasks, employers seem to have a legitimate claim upon whatever personal information is relevant to an employee's ability to do the job.

The second argument claims that drug use has been and can be responsible for considerable harm to the employee him or herself, fellow employees, the employer, and/or third parties, including consumers. In this case drug testing is defended because it is seen as a way of preventing possible harm. Further, since employers can be held liable for harms done both to third parties, e.g., customers, and to the employee or his or her fellow employees, knowledge of employee drug use will allow employers to gain information that can protect themselves from risks such as liability. But how good are these arguments? We turn to examine the arguments more closely.

THE FIRST ARGUMENT: JOB PERFORMANCE AND KNOWLEDGE OF DRUG USE

The first argument holds that drug use leads to lower productivity and consequently implies that a knowledge of drug use obtained through drug testing will allow an employer to increase productivity. It is generally assumed that people using certain drugs have their performances affected by such use. Since enhancing productivity is something any employer desires, any use of drugs that reduces productivity affects the employer in an undesirable way, and that use is, then, job-relevant. If such production losses can be eliminated by knowledge of the drug use, then knowledge of that drug use is job-relevant information. On the surface this argument seems reasonable. Obviously some drug use in lowering the level of performance can decrease productivity. Since the employer is entitled to a certain level of performance and drug use adversely affects performance, knowledge of that use seems job-relevant.

But this formulation of the argument leaves an important question unanswered. To what level of performance are employers entitled? Optimal performance, or some lower level? If some lower level, what? Employers have a valid claim upon some *certain level* of performance, such that a failure to perform up to this level would give the employer a justification for disciplining, firing or at least finding fault with the employee. But that does not necessarily mean that the employer has a right to a maximum or optimal level of performance, a level above and beyond a certain level of acceptability. It might be nice if the employee gives an employer a maximum effort or optimal performance, but that is above and beyond the call of the employee's duty and the employer can hardly claim a right at all times to the highest level of performance of which an employee is capable.

That there are limits on required levels of performance and productivity becomes clear if we recognize that job performance is person related. It is person-related because one person's best efforts at a particular task might produce results well below the norm, while another person's minimal efforts might produce results abnormally high when compared to the norm. For example a professional baseball player's performance on a ball field will be much higher than the average person's since the average person is unskilled at baseball. We have all encountered people who work hard with little or no results, as well as people who work little with phenomenal results. Drug use by very talented people might diminish their performance or productivity, but that performance would still be better than the performance of the average person or someone totally lacking in the skills required. That being said, the important question now is whether the employer is entitled to an employee's maximum effort and best results, or merely to an effort sufficient to perform the task expected.

If the relevant consideration is whether the employee is producing as expected (according to the normal demands of the position and contract) not whether he or she is producing as much as possible, then knowledge of drug use is irrelevant or unnecessary. Let's see why.

If the person is producing what is expected, knowledge of drug use on the grounds of production is irrelevant since, *ex hypothesi* the production is satisfactory. If, on the other hand, the performance suffers, then, to the extent that it slips below the level justifiably expected, the employer has *prima facie* grounds for warning, disciplining or releasing the employee. But the justification for this is the person's unsatisfactory performance, not the person's use of drugs. Accordingly, drug use information is either unnecessary or irrelevant and consequently there are not sufficient grounds to override the right of privacy. Thus, unless we can argue that an employer is entitled to optimal performance, the argument fails.

This counter-argument should make it clear that the information which is job-relevant, and consequently which is not rightfully private, is information about an employee's level of performance and not information about the underlying causes of that level. The fallacy of the argument which promotes drug testing in the name of increased productivity is the assumption that each employee is obliged to perform at an optimal, or at least quite high, level. But this is required under few, if any, contracts. What is required contractually is meeting the normally expected levels of production or performing the tasks in the job-description adequately (not optimally). If one can do that under the influence of drugs, then on the grounds of job-performance at least, drug use is rightfully private. If one cannot perform the task adequately, then the employee is not fulfilling the contract, and knowledge of the cause of the failure to perform is irrelevant on the contractual model.

Of course, if the employer suspects drug use or abuse as the cause of the unsatisfactory performance, then she might choose to help the person with counseling or rehabilitation. However, this does not seem to be something morally required of the employer. Rather, in the case of unsatisfactory performance, the employer has a *prima facie* justification for dismissing or disciplining the employee.

Before turning to the second argument which attempts to justify drug testing, we should mention a factor about drug use that is usually ignored in talk of productivity. The entire productivity argument is irrelevant for those cases in which employees use performance enhancing drugs. Amphetamines and steroids, for example, can actually enhance some performances. This points to the need for care when tying drug testing to job-performance. In the case of some drugs used by athletes, for example, drug testing is done because the drug-influenced performance is too good and therefore unfair, not because it leads to inadequate job-performance. In such a case, where the testing is done to ensure fair competition, the testing may be justified. But drug testing in sports is an entirely different matter than drug testing in business.

To summarize our argument so far. Drug use may affect performances, but as long as the performance is at an acceptable level, the knowledge of drug use is irrelevant. If the performance is unacceptable, then that is sufficient cause for action to be taken. In this case an employee's failure to fulfill his or her end of a contract makes knowledge of the drug use unnecessary.

THE SECOND ARGUMENT: HARM AND THE KNOWLEDGE OF DRUG USE TO PREVENT HARM

Even though the performance argument is inadequate, there is an argument that seems somewhat stronger. This is an argument based on the potential for drug use to cause harm. . . . One could argue that drug testing might be justified if such testing led to knowledge that would enable an employer to prevent harm. Drug use certainly can lead to harming others. Consequently, if knowledge of such drug use can prevent harm, then, knowing whether or not one's employee uses drugs might be a legitimate concern of an employer in certain circumstances. This second argument claims that knowledge of the employee's drug use is job-relevant because employees who are under the influence of drugs can pose a threat to the health and safety of themselves and others, and an employer who knows of that drug use and the harm it can cause has a responsibility to prevent it. Employers have both a general duty to prevent harm and the specific responsibility for harms done by their employees. Such responsibilities are sufficient reason for an employer to claim that information about an employee's drug use is relevant if that knowledge can prevent harm by giving the employer grounds for dismissing the employee or not allowing him/her to perform potentially harmful tasks. Employers might even claim a right to reduce unreasonable risks, in this case the risks involving legal and economic liability for harms caused by employees under the influence of drugs, as further justification for knowing about employee drug use.

This second argument differs from the first in which only a lowered job performance was relevant information. In this case, even to allow the performance is problematic, for the performance itself, more than being inadequate, can hurt people. We cannot be as sanguine about the prevention of harm as we can about inadequate production. Where drug use can cause serious harms, knowledge of that use becomes relevant if the knowledge of such use can lead to the prevention of harm and drug testing becomes justified as a means for obtaining that knowledge.

As we noted, we will begin initially by accepting this argument . . . where restrictions on liberty are allowed in order to prevent harm to others. . . . In such a case an employer's obligation to prevent harm may override the obligation to respect an employee's privacy.

But let us examine this more closely. Upon examination, certain problems arise, so that even if there is a possibility of justifying drug testing to prevent harm, some caveats have to be observed and some limits set out.

JOBS WITH POTENTIAL TO CAUSE HARM

To say that employers can use drug-testing where that can prevent harm is not to say that every employer has the right to know about the drug use of every employee. Not every job poses a serious enough threat to justify an employer coming to know this information.

In deciding which jobs pose serious enough threats certain guidelines should be followed. First the potential for harm should be *clear* and *present*. Perhaps all jobs in some extended way pose potential threats to human well-being. We suppose an accountant's error could pose a threat of harm to someone somewhere. But some jobs like those of airline pilots, school bus drivers, public transit drivers and surgeons, are jobs in which unsatisfactory performance poses a clear and present danger to others. It would be much harder to make an argument that job performances by auditors, secretaries, executive vice-presidents for public relations, college teachers, professional athletes, and the like, could cause harm if those performances were carried on under the influence of drugs. They would cause harm only in exceptional cases.

NOT EVERY PERSON IS
TO BE TESTED

But, even if we can make a case that a particular job involves a clear and present danger for causing harm if performed under the influence of drugs, it is not appropriate to treat everyone holding such a job the same. Not every job-holder is equally threatening. There is less reason to investigate an airline pilot for drug use if that pilot has a twenty-year record of exceptional service than there is to investigate a pilot whose behavior has become erratic and unreliable recently, or than one who reports to work smelling of alcohol and slurring his words. Presuming that every airline pilot is equally threatening is to deny individuals the respect that they deserve as autonomous, rational agents. It is to ignore previous history and significant differences. It is also probably inefficient and leads to the lowering of morale. It is the likelihood of causing harm, and not the fact of being an airline pilot *per se,* that is relevant in deciding which employees in critical jobs to test.

So, even if knowledge of drug use is justifiable to prevent harm, we must be careful to limit this justification to a range of jobs and people where the potential for harm is clear and present. The jobs must be jobs that clearly can cause harm, and the specific employee should not be someone who is reliable with a history of such reliability. Finally, the drugs being tested should be those drugs, the use of which in those jobs is really potentially harmful.

LIMITATIONS ON DRUG
TESTING POLICIES

Even when we identify those jobs and individuals where knowledge of drug use would be job relevant information, we still need to examine whether some procedural limitations

should not be placed upon the employer's testing for drugs. We have said that in cases where a real threat of harm exists and where evidence exists suggesting that a particular employee poses such a threat, an employer could be justified in knowing about drug use in order to prevent the potential harm. But we need to recognize that as long as the employer has the discretion for deciding when the potential for harm is clear and present, and for deciding which employees pose the threat of harm, the possibility of abuse is great. Thus, some policy limiting the employer's power is called for.

Just as criminal law places numerous restrictions protecting individual dignity and liberty on the state's pursuit of its goals, so we should expect that some restrictions be placed on an employer in order to protect innocent employees from harm (including loss of job and damage to one's personal and professional reputation). Thus, some system of checks upon an employer's discretion in these matters seems advisable. Workers covered by collective bargaining agreements or individual contracts might be protected by clauses in those agreements that specify which jobs pose a real threat of harm (e.g., pilots but not cabin attendants) and what constitutes a just cause for investigating drug use. Local, state, and federal legislatures might do the same for workers not covered by employment contracts. What needs to be set up is a just employment relationship — one in which an employee's expectations and responsibilities are specified in advance and in which an employer's discretionary authority to discipline or dismiss an employee is limited.

Beyond that, any policy should accord with the nature of the employment relationship. Since that relationship is a contractual one, it should meet the condition of a morally valid contract, which is informed consent. Thus, in general, we would argue that only methods that have received the informed consent of employees can be used in acquiring information about drug use.[5]

A drug-testing policy that requires all employees to submit to a drug test or to jeopardize their job would seem coercive and therefore unacceptable. Being placed in such a fundamentally coercive position of having to choose between one's job and one's privacy does not provide the conditions for a truly free consent. Policies that are unilaterally established by employers would likewise be unacceptable. Working with employees to develop company policy seems the only way to insure that the policy will be fair to both parties. Prior notice of testing would also be required in order to give employees the option of freely refraining from drug use. It is morally preferable to prevent drug use than to punish users after the fact, since this approach treats employees as capable of making rational and informed decisions.

Further procedural limitations seem advisable as well. Employees should be notified of the results of the test, they should be entitled to appeal the results (perhaps through further tests by an independent laboratory) and the information obtained through tests ought to be kept confidential. In summary, limitations upon employer discretion for administering drug tests can be derived from the nature of the employment contract and from the recognition that drug testing is justified by the desire to prevent harm, not the desire to punish wrong doing.

EFFECTIVENESS OF DRUG TESTING

Having declared that the employer might have a right to test for drug use in order to prevent harm, we still need to examine the second argument a little more closely. One must keep in mind that the justification of drug testing is the justification of a means to

an end, the end of preventing harm, and that the means are a means which intrude into one's privacy. In this case, before one allows drug testing as a means, one should be clear that there are not more effective means available.

If the employer has a legitimate right, perhaps duty, to ascertain knowledge of drug use to prevent harm, it is important to examine exactly how effectively, and in what situations, the *knowledge* of the drug use will prevent the harm. So far we have just assumed that the *knowledge* will prevent the harm. But how?

Let us take an example to pinpoint the difficulty. Suppose a transit driver, shortly before work, took some cocaine which, in giving him a feeling of invulnerability, leads him to take undue risks in his driving. How exactly is drug-testing going to contribute to the knowledge which will prevent the potential accident?

It is important to keep in mind that; (1) if the knowledge doesn't help prevent the harm, the testing is not justified on prevention grounds; (2) if the testing doesn't provide the relevant knowledge it is not justified either; and finally, (3) even if it was justified, it would be undesirable if a more effective means for preventing harm were discovered.

Upon examination, the links between drug testing, knowledge of drug use, and prevention of harm are not as clear as they are presumed to be. As we investigate, it begins to seem that the knowledge of the drug use even though relevant in some instances is not the most effective means to prevent harm.

Let us turn to this last consideration first. Is drug testing the most effective means for preventing harm caused by drug use?

Consider. If someone exhibits obviously drugged or drunken behavior, then this behavior itself is grounds for preventing the person from continuing in the job. Administering urine or blood tests, sending the specimens out for testing and waiting for a response, will not prevent harm in this instance. Such drug testing because of the time lapse involved, is equally superfluous in those cases where an employee is in fact under the influence of drugs, but exhibits no or only subtley impaired behavior.

Thus, even if one grants that drug testing somehow prevents harm an argument can be made that there might be much more effective methods of preventing potential harm such as administering dexterity tests of the type employed by police in possible drunk-driving cases, or requiring suspect pilots to pass flight simulator tests.[6] Eye-hand coordination, balance, reflexes, and reasoning ability can all be tested with less intrusive, more easily administered, reliable technologies which give instant results. Certainly if an employer has just cause for believing that a specific employee presently poses a real threat of causing harm, such methods are just more effective in all ways than are urinalysis and blood testing.

Even were it possible to refine drug tests so that accurate results were immediately available, that knowledge would only be job relevant if the drug use was clearly the cause of impaired job performance that could harm people. Hence, testing behavior still seems more direct and effective in preventing harm than testing for the presence of drugs *per se*.

In some cases, drug use might be connected with potential harms not by being causally connected to motor-function impairment, but by causing personality disorders (e.g., paranoia, delusions, etc.) that affect judgmental ability. Even though in such cases a *prima facie* justification for urinalysis or blood testing might exist, the same problems of effectiveness persist. How is the knowledge of the drug use attained by urinalysis and/or blood testing supposed to prevent the harm? Only if there is a causal link between the use and the potentially harmful behavior, would

such knowledge be relevant. Even if we get the results of the test immediately, there is the necessity to have an established causal link between specific drug use and anticipated harmful personality disorders in specific people.

But it cannot be the task of an employer to determine that a specific drug is causally related to harm-causing personality disorders. Not every controlled substance is equally likely to cause personality changes in every person in every case. The establishment of the causal link between the use of certain drugs and harm-causing personality disorders is not the province of the employer, but the province of experts studying the effects of drugs. The burden of proof is on the employer to establish that the substance being investigated has been independently connected with the relevant psychological impairment and then, predict on that basis that the specific employee's psychological judgment has been or will soon be impaired in such a way as to cause harm.

But even when this link is established, it would seem that less intrusive means could be used to detect the potential problems, rather than relying upon the assumption of a causal link. Psychological tests of judgment, perception and memory, for example, would be a less intrusive and more direct means for acquiring the relevant information which is, after all, the likelihood of causing harm and not the presence of drugs *per se*. In short, drug testing even in these cases doesn't seem to be very effective in preventing harm on the spot.

Still, this does not mean it is not effective at all. Where it is most effective in preventing harm is in its getting people to stop using drugs or in identifying serious drug addiction. Or to put it another way, urinalysis and blood tests for drug use are more effective in preventing potential harm when they serve as a deterrent to drug use *before* it occurs, since it is very difficult to prevent harm by diagnosing drug use *after* it has occurred but before the potentially harmful behavior takes place.

Drug testing can be an effective deterrent when there is regular or random testing of all employees. This will prevent harm by inhibiting (because of the fear of detection) drug use by those who are occasional users and those who do not wish to be detected.

It will probably not inhibit or stop the use by the chronic addicted user, but it will allow an employer to discover the chronic user or addict, assuming that the tests are accurately administered and reliably evaluated. If the chronic user's addiction would probably lead to harmful behavior of others, the harm is prevented by taking that user off the job. Thus regular or random testing will prevent harms done by deterring the occasional user and by detecting the chronic user.

There are six possibilities for such testing:

1. Regularly scheduled testing of all employees
2. Regularly scheduled testing of randomly selected employees
3. Randomly scheduled testing of all employees
4. Randomly scheduled testing of randomly selected employees
5. Regularly scheduled testing of employees selected for probable cause
6. Randomly scheduled testing of employees selected for probable cause

Only the last two seem morally acceptable as well as effective.

Obviously, randomly scheduled testing will be more effective than regularly scheduled testing in detecting the occasional user, because the occasional users can control their use to pass the tests, unless of course tests were given so often (a practice economically unfeasible) that they needed to stop altogether. Regular scheduling probably will detect the habitual or addicted user. Randomly selecting people to test is probably cheaper,

as is random scheduling, but it is not nearly as effective as testing all. Besides, the random might miss some of the addicted altogether, and will not deter the risk takers as much as the risk aversive persons. It is, ironically, the former who are probably potentially more harmful.

But these are merely considerations of efficiency. We have said that testing without probable cause is unacceptable. Any type of regular testing of all employees is unacceptable. We have argued that testing employees without first establishing probable cause is an unjustifiable violation of employee privacy. Given this, and given the expense of general and regular testing of all employees (especially if this is done by responsible laboratories), it is more likely that random testing will be employed as the means of deterrence. But surely testing of randomly selected innocent employees is as intrusive to those tested as is regular testing. The argument that there will be fewer tests is correct on quantitative grounds, but qualitatively the intrusion and unacceptability are the same. The claim that employers should be allowed to sacrifice the well-being of (some few) innocent employees to deter (some equally few) potentially harmful employees seems, on the face of it, unfair. Just as we do not allow the state randomly to tap the telephones of just any citizen in order to prevent crime, so we ought not allow employers to drug test all employees randomly to prevent harm. To do so is again to treat innocent employees solely as a means to the end of preventing potential harm.

This leaves only the use of regular or random drug-testing as a deterrent in those cases where probable cause exists for believing that a particular employee poses a threat of harm. It would seem that in this case, the drug testing is acceptable. In such cases only the question of effectiveness remains: Are the standard techniques of urinalysis and blood-testing more effective means for preventing harms than alternatives such as dexterity tests? It seems they are effective in different ways. The dexterity tests show immediately if someone is incapable of performing a task, or will perform one in such a way as to cause harm to others. The urinalysis and blood-testing will prevent harm indirectly by getting the occasional user to curtail their use, and by detecting the habitual or addictive user, which will allow the employer to either give treatment to the addictive personality or remove them from the job. Thus we can conclude that drug testing is effective in a limited way, but aside from inhibiting occasional users because of fear of detection, and discovering habitual users, it seems problematic that it does much to prevent harm that couldn't be achieved by other means.

Consider one final issue in the case of the occasional user. They are the drug users who do weigh the risks and benefits and who are physically and psychologically free to decide. The question in their case is not simply "will the likelihood of getting caught by urinalysis or blood-testing deter this individual from using drugs?" Given the benefits of psychological tests and dexterity tests described above, the question is "will the rational user be more deterred by urinalysis or blood testing than by random psychological or dexterity tests?" And, if this is so, is this increase in the effectiveness of a deterrent sufficient to offset the increased expense and time required by drug tests? We see no reason to believe that behavioral or judgment tests are not, or cannot be made to be, as effective in determining what an employer needs to know (i.e., that a particular employee may presently be a potential cause of harm). If the behavioral, dexterity and judgment tests can be as effective in determining a potential for harm, we see no reason to believe that they cannot be as effective a deterrent as drug tests. Finally, even if a case can be made for an increase in deterrent effect of drug test-

ing, we are skeptical that this increased effectiveness will outweigh the increased inefficiencies.

In summary, we have seen that deterrence is effective at times and under certain conditions allows the sacrificing of the privacy rights of innocent employees to the future and speculative good of preventing harms to others. However, there are many ways to deter drug use when that deterrence is legitimate and desirable to prevent harm. But random testing, which seems the only practicable means which has an impact in preventing harm is the one which most offends workers rights to privacy and which is most intrusive of the rights of the innocent. Even when effective, drug testing as a deterrent must be checked by the rights of employees. . . .

DRUG TESTING FOR PROSPECTIVE EMPLOYEES

Let's turn finally to drug testing during a pre-employment interview. Assuming the job description and responsibilities have been made clear, we can say that an employer is entitled to expect from a prospective employee whatever performance is agreed to in the employment contract. Of course, this will always involve risks, since the employer must make a judgment about future performances. To lower this risk, employers have a legitimate claim to some information about the employee. Previous work experience, training, education, and the like are obvious candidates since they indicate the person's ability to do the job. Except in rare circumstances drug use itself is irrelevant for determining an employee's ability to perform. (Besides, most people who are interviewing know enough to get their systems clean if the prospective employer is going to test them.)

We suggest that an employer can claim to have an interest in knowing (a) whether or not the prospective employee *can* do the job and (b) whether there is reason to believe that once hired the employee *will* do the job. The first can be determined in fairly straightforward ways: past work experience, training, education, etc. Presumably past drug use is thought more relevant to the second question. But there are straightforward and less intrusive means than drug testing for resolving this issue. Asking the employee "Is there anything that might prevent you from doing this job?" comes first to mind. Hiring the employee on a probationary period is another way. But to inquire about drug use here is to claim a right to know too much. It is to claim a right to know not only information about what an employee *can* do, but also a right to inquire into whatever background information *might* be (but not necessarily *is*) causally related to what an employee *will* do. But the range of factors that could be relevant here, from medical history to psychological dispositions to family plans, is surely too open-ended for an employer to claim as a *right* to know.

It might be responded that what an employer is entitled to expect is not a certain level of output, but a certain level of effort. The claim here would be that while drug use is only contingently related to what an employee *can* do, it is directly related to an employee's *motivation* to do the job. Drug use then is *de facto* relevant to the personal information that an employee is *entitled* to know.

But this involves an assumption mentioned above. The discussion so far has assumed that drugs will adversely affect job performance. However, some drugs are performance *enhancing* whether they are concerned with actual *output* or *effort*. The widespread use of steroids, pain-killers, and dexadrine among professional athletes are perhaps only the most publicized instances of performance enhancing drugs. (A teacher's use of caffeine before an early-morning class is perhaps a more common example.) More

to the point, knowledge of drug use tells little about motivation. There are too many other variables to be considered. Some users are motivated and some are not. Thus the motivational argument is faulty.

We can conclude, then, that whether the relevant consideration for prospective employees is output or effort, knowledge of drug use will be largely irrelevant for predicting. Employers ought to be positivistic in their approach. They should restrict their information gathering to measurable behavior and valid predictions (What has the prospect done? What can the prospect do? What has the prospect promised to do?) and not speculate about the underlying *causes* of this behavior. With a probationary work period always an option, there are sufficient non-intrusive means for limiting risks available to employers without having to rely on investigations into drug use.

In summary, we believe that drug use is information that is rightfully private and that only in exceptional cases can an employer claim a right to know about such use. Typically, these are cases in which knowledge of drug use could be used to prevent harm. However, even in those cases we believe that there are less intrusive and more effective means available than drug testing for gaining the information that would be necessary to prevent the harm. Thus, we conclude that drug testing of employees is rarely justified, and mostly inefficacious.

NOTES

1. *The New Republic,* March 31, 1986.
2. "A Defense of Employee Rights," Joseph DesJardins and John McCall, *Journal of Business Ethics* 4, (1985). We should emphasize that our concern is with the *moral* rights of privacy for employees and not with any specific or prospective *legal* rights. Readers interested in pursuing the legal aspects of employee drug

testing should consult: "Workplace Privacy Issues and Employee Screening Policies" by Richard Lehe and David Middlebrooks in *Employee Relations Law Journal* (Vol. 11, no. 3) pp. 407–21; and "Screening Workers for Drugs: A Legal and Ethical Framework" by Mark Rothstein, in *Employee Relations Law Journal* (vol. 11, no. 3) pp. 422–36.

3. "Privacy, Polygraphs, and Work," George Brenkert, *Business and Professional Ethics Journal* Vol. 1, no. 1 (Fall 1981). For a more general discussion of privacy in the workplace see "Privacy in Employment" by Joseph DesJardins, in *Moral Rights in the Workplace* edited by Gertrude Ezorsky (SUNY Press, 1987). A good resource for philosophical work on privacy can be found in "Recent Work on the Concept of Privacy" by W. A. Parent, in *American Philosophical Quarterly* (Vol. 20, Oct. 1983) pp. 341–56.

4. *U.S. News and World Report,* Aug. 1983; *Newsweek,* May 1983.

5. The philosophical literature on informed consent is often concerned with "informed consent" in a medical context. For an interesting discussion of informed consent in the workplace, see Mary Gibson, *Worker's Rights* (Rowman and Allanheld, 1983), especially pp. 13–14 and 74–75.

6. For a reiteration of this point and a concise argument against drug testing, see Lewis L. Maltby, "Why Drug Testing Is a Bad Idea," *Inc.* June 1987, pp. 152–53. "But the fundamental flaw with drug testing is that it tests for the wrong thing. A realistic program to detect workers whose condition puts the company or other people at risk would test for the condition that actually creates the danger. The reason drunk or stoned airline pilots and truck drivers are dangerous is their reflexes, coordination, and timing are deficient. This impairment could come from many situations — drugs, alcohol, emotional problems — the list is almost endless. A serious program would recognize that the real problem is workers' impairment, and test for that. Pilots can be tested in flight simulators. People in other jobs can be tested by a trained technician in about 20 minutes — at the job site," p. 152.

The Ethics of Genetic Screening in the Workplace

Joseph Kupfer

Today we are witnessing the onslaught of "testing" in the workplace. We test for personality, aptitude, competence, "truthfulness," drugs, and now genetic make-up. Clearly, some of this testing may well be warranted, but genetic "screening" as it's called raises some peculiar questions of its own — questions of meaning and questions of morality. In what follows, I shall spell out the nature of genetic screening, its possible purposes or values, and then raise some moral questions about it.

THE ISSUE AND ITS BACKGROUND

Genetic research is one of those areas of science which has clear practical benefits. If we know that we are carrying a gene for an inheritable illness, such as Huntington's dis-

From Joseph Kupfer, "The Ethics of Genetic Screening in the Workplace," *Business Ethics Quarterly* 3:1 (1993). Reprinted with permission.

ease, we can make a more informed choice about procreation. Knowledge of our genetic disposition toward heart disease or high blood pressure can prompt us to change our patterns of eating and exercise. And once informed of our genetically-based vulnerability to lung disease, we are able to avoid threatening work conditions. Indeed, this was the first goal of genetic screening in the workplace: to enable the employee to steer clear of work situations which were liable to call forth a disabling condition or disease (henceforth, simply "disorder").

Obviously, businesses also had an interest in this goal. Fewer disabled workers means reduction in costs caused by illness, absenteeism, health insurance, workers' compensation, and turnover. In addition, the first workplace screening was a response by business to 1970's legislation making business responsible for health in the workplace. DuPont, Dow Chemical, and Johnson and Johnson were among the first companies to implement genetic screening.[1] The tests were voluntary and there was no threat of job loss, rather, "warning" and "relocating" to less hazardous conditions or functions were the procedure. Indeed, DuPont's testing for sickle cell trait was requested by its own black workers! So, at its inception, genetic screening of workers seemed to be a mutually agreed upon practice aimed at mutual benefits — workers and owners cooperating for the good of all.

If this were all there was to genetic screening in the workplace, obviously, there would be little need for moral discussion. But, corporations have an interest in extending the purpose of screening beyond its original scope — to deny people work. What began as a benign program can be modified to serve only the interests of business. After all, relocating workers or modifying existing conditions so that they will be less hazardous takes time, effort, and money. It's just plain

cheaper to fire or not hire a worker who is at "genetic risk." The facts of the matter, however, make the whole issue more complicated. They also point to moral difficulties with the use of genetic screening to exclude workers from jobs, what we shall consider "discriminatory genetic screening."

Before investigating the moral issues involved, we must get clear on the scientific ones concerning *how* genetic screening, in fact, works. There are serious limitations to what we can learn from genetic screening and they have moral implications. The limitations on the knowledge afforded by genetic screening are of two sorts — technical and causal. Technical limitations are determined by the level of sophistication of our techno-scientific understanding. Causal constraints depend upon how genes actually bring about disorders.

Each kind of limitation itself involves two sets of variables. Technical restrictions on genetic knowledge turn on (1) whether the gene itself has been located or simply correlated with other DNA material, and (2) whether knowledge of other family members is necessary to determine the presence of the affecting gene. Causal restrictions on genetic knowledge involve (1) whether the affecting gene requires other genes to produce the disorder, and (2) whether the gene causes the disorder with inevitability or just creates a vulnerability to it. We shall consider the two sorts of limitations on genetic knowledge by examining in order these sets of variables for their significance for the practice of genetic screening.

TECHNICAL LIMITATIONS

First is the question of whether the gene itself has been located. Hemophilia, Duchenne muscular dystrophy, and cystic fibrosis are among the few exceptions where the genetic test actually identifies the gene in question. What is more typical are DNA "probes" or "markers" which indicate the likelihood of the gene's presence. "Most of today's probes aren't capable of pinpointing a bad gene. They can only detect sequences of healthy genes called markers, that are usually found near a bad one."[2] When "restriction" enzymes are introduced into the chromosome material, DNA fragments are generated: specifically, strips of genetic material called restriction fragment length polymorphisms (RFLPs), whose patterns can be statistically associated with the occurrence of a particular disorder.[3] In the case of Huntington's disease, for example, the probe detects "a piece of DNA that is so close to the as yet unidentified Huntington's gene that it is inherited along with the gene."[4]

This technical limitation — inability to locate the particular gene in question — means that we are usually dealing with statistical correlations. The marker can be inherited without the defective gene; therefore, uncovering the marker must be treated with caution. Conversely, as Marc Lappe warns,[5] failure to turn up the marker does not guarantee the gene's absence!

In order to establish the correlation between the marker and the disorder, collateral data may be needed. One kind, "linkage analysis," points to our second set of variables — whether or not reference to family members is needed. Linkage analysis is comparing a given individual's DNA pattern with both affected and unaffected family members. The marker for Huntington's disease, for example, is useless if there are no living family members *with* the disease. This is because what is needed is to identify the piece of DNA material *as* a marker for Huntington's disease. Its association with the disease must be ascertained by comparison with DNA fragments of surviving relatives.

This is obviously very time consuming and expensive, prohibitively so for workplace application. It also requires the consent of family members who may not be employed by the company (over whom the company can exert little leverage). In contrast, "direct markers" indicate a genetic connection with a disorder without linkage analysis. The marking of the genes for hemophilia, cystic fibrosis, and adult polycystic kidney disease can be ascertained directly. These are more feasible for workplace screening.

Another sort of collateral data that is frequently needed involves the use of "flanking probes" in order to ascertain the presence of "modifier" genes. This leads us to consideration of the causal limitations of the knowledge gleaned from genetic screening.

CAUSAL LIMITATIONS

Our third set of variables concerns how the genetic material generates the disorder: whether the disorder is caused by one or several genes. When a disorder is coded for by more than a single gene, the gene in question must interact with these other genes in order to be expressed (as a disorder). For screening to have predictive value it must indicate the presence (or absence) of these auxiliary, "modifier" genes. For instance, in the case of Gaucher's disease, the gene marked by the DNA probe is associated with three forms of the disease. While one of the varieties of this neurological disorder is severe, the other two are fairly mild.[6] Without corroboration from modifier genes, which form of Gaucher's disease the individual will develop can't be determined.

One interesting combination of variables occurs in Huntington's disease. It is caused by a single gene; however, that gene has not yet been located. Therefore, it is identified by means of other DNA material, *and* correlation of the material with the disease requires linkage analysis. Because it is caused by a single gene, if that gene can be identified, then linkage analysis won't be needed. In addition, it will be known with virtual certainty that the individual will be afflicted. As with adult polycystic kidney disease, all carriers of the gene for Huntington's disease develop the disorder. The causal tie between the gene and the disorder is virtually absolute.

But this is the rare exception. The great majority of genes do not lead inevitably to the disorder. They create a susceptibility or vulnerability, not a certainty of expression. Our last set of variables concerns this — the nature of the gene's causal efficacy. Conditions such as high cholesterol levels and high blood pressure, and diseases such as Alzheimer's disease and diabetes, are determined by "contingency" genes. Certain contingencies must be met before these genes bring about their respective disorders.

One of these contingencies is the presence of other genes, as we have just noted. In addition, the expression of most genetically based disorders requires the influence of biological, social, or psychological factors. It is already common knowledge that diet and exercise (biological and social influences) can affect the onset of coronary artery disease and high blood pressure. The same also holds for diabetes and back arthritis.

What does it *mean* to say that the gene produces a disposition or susceptibility to a disorder? One fourth of the people with the genetic marker for "ankylosing spondylitis" develop this debilitating back arthritis. Put another way, someone with the marker is between forty and one hundred times more likely to develop ankylosing spondylitis than is someone without this genetic material.[7] Even in such "high odds" cases like this one, however, seventy-five percent of the people

with the genetic marker do *not* develop the arthritis. Work and work conditions, for instance, contribute greatly to its onset. For many genetically determined disorders, the individual may have considerable control over whether and how severely the disorder occurs. Knowledge of our genetic constitution can be helpful in making practical decisions rather than simply forecasting our fate.

CONSIDERATIONS OF PRIVACY

We come now to the moral questions of whether and to what extent genetic screening in the workplace is justified. Recall that we are talking about discriminatory screening which is designed to exclude workers from jobs, rather than to "warn and relocate." I shall argue that considerations of privacy and justice mitigate against screening or at least its untrammeled deployment.

Let's begin with considerations of privacy. When information is gathered about us our privacy may be infringed upon in varying degrees. Whether our privacy is violated depends on such things as whether we consent to the gathering of the information, the nature of the information, and what happens as a result of its gathering. What I would like to focus on here is the issue of control and autonomy. Many different sorts of information can be obtained, most of it valuable to the company. Some information concerns such things as credit ratings or religious affiliations, other involves ascertaining physical facts by monitoring drug use. Is genetic screening any different in principle from drug screening, polygraph tests, or surveillance? In at least one regard it seems to be. Although in most cases, we have some control over whether a gene is expressed as a disorder, we cannot control whether we *have* the gene in the first place. Whether we have the disposition, the vulnerability to the disorder, is out of our hands.

We have some say over our work, religion, credit rating, and most of us can choose to use drugs or not. But not so with genes. They are in and of us, forever. This lack of control is especially compounded in the workplace because of related lack of power in this context. First, most workers are not in a position to refuse to cooperate with demands for screening. When this is the case, they have no control over the gathering of information about which they also lack control. This lack of power is magnified by workers' overall status in the workplace. In spite of unionization, most workers have little say over working conditions, product manufacture, wages, promotions, and firing.

We need to see testing in general, and genetic screening in particular, within the context of the employer-employee relationship. Testing workers gives employers and managers still greater control over workers' lives. Screening of all sorts would be different, and experienced differently, in a context in which power were more equitably distributed in the workplace. This seems especially important in the area of testing for genetically-based disorders, precisely because we have no control over our genetic makeup.

This sense of powerlessness is critical to the special type of stigmatization associated with genetic defects. When screening uncovers a genetic abnormality, the individual can feel morally defective — cursed or damned. This could and has happened simply from acquiring genetic information under the most benign circumstances. Thus, Madeleine and Lenn Goodman found considerable stigmatization among Jewish people identified as carriers of Tay-Sachs disease even though no obvious disadvantages followed from such identification.[8] But when the information is used prejudicially, as in the workplace discrimination we are here considering, the like-lihood and intensity of stigmatization increases. As Thomas Murray notes, diagnosing an illness as genetically caused may *label* the person as *constitutionally* weak, making finding another job difficult.[9]

All of these aspects of the situation help explain why the loss of privacy suffered in genetic screening in the workplace is serious. The screening is for properties over which the worker has no control and is not responsible; it occurs in a context of relative powerlessness; and it is likely to result in stigmatization with profound costs to his or her life-chances. The genetic screening as described here involves loss of privacy, but the stigmatization and its repercussions, as we shall see, are a matter of *injustice*. Loss or forfeiture of privacy is less defendable the less just the situation under which it occurs and the less just the purposes for which it is used.

The invasion of privacy is greater when the genetic screening is "across the board" rather than selective. When businesses screen for *any* potential disease or debilitating condition, it is like having the police come and search your house just to see what they'll turn up. In both cases, there is clearly an "interest" in uncovering the relevant danger. The state and employer reduce their respective risks. But such interests are not overriding, not in a society which claims to value the individual's autonomy and privacy. The employer has no more right to a total genetic profile than he has to information about one's sexual habits, recreational activities, or religious and political beliefs — even though knowledge of these and other details of our lives might well be of use to him.

Testing for job-specific susceptibilities is more warranted since directly connected to the work context and the employer's role in bringing about the disorder. It is more like searching someone's home for specific items, such as guns or counterfeit money. Presumably, there is a good reason for looking in both sorts of case. Since screening for just a *few,* job-related genetic dispositions, less of the self is being "searched." Therefore, there is probably less sense of being violated or stigmatized. The individual is told that she is unfit to do this particular job, for example, heavy lifting because of the disposition to back arthritis. She is not labelled as constitutionally weak due to some general condition, such as vulnerability to heart disease.

Even here, however, another threat looms. It is all too likely that employers will tend to use such information to fire employees rather than improve workplace conditions. It's cheaper. But perhaps it's the employer's responsibility to make the workplace safe, even for those with susceptibilities to environmentally-triggered disorders. People who have a disposition to lung disease, for example, might be able to work in this particular factory at no increased risk *if* the employer provided better air ventilation and circulation. This issue seems to be a matter of justice: who should bear the burden of workplace danger.

CONSIDERATIONS OF JUSTICE

We turn now directly to considerations of justice. The first sort of consideration focuses on the individual and the nature of genetic causation. The second concerns these individuals as members of a paying public.

In the great majority of cases, genetic markers indicate merely a predisposition for a disorder, not the inevitability of its onset. (Even when inevitable, in many cases the degree of severity remains unpredictable.) It seems unjust to penalize an individual for something that has not yet come to pass and which may well be prevented by him. It is unjust to act as if the individual is already diseased or disabled, especially when he may run a *lower* risk than others without the

marker because of healthful life-choices made on the basis of this information.

It is like treating someone as though guilty until proven innocent. In the case of genetically caused susceptibility to a disorder, it is worse because carrying the gene is beyond the person's control. Considerations of justice suggest that there is something wrong in penalizing people for conditions which are beyond their control. Of course, sometimes people are justly denied benefits or privileges on account of uncontrollable conditions. Thus, we don't allow blind people to drive or people who have slow reaction times to be air-traffic controllers. But this is not penalizing someone so much as finding them unqualified for performance of a task. Public safety certainly does and should operate as a constraint on opportunity. However, this kind of consideration is rare in the case of genetically based disorders; moreover, it should come into play only with the onset of the disabling condition, not with the mere discovery of a genetic propensity toward it. In a society proclaiming commitment to egalitarian principles, we shouldn't further handicap people who may become disabled by depriving them of work while they are still able to do the job.

The question of the justness of discriminatory genetic screening can also be posed from the larger, social perspective. It arises from the social nature and purpose of genetic research. Genetic research, including testing individuals and groups, was developed to help people. By diagnosing genetic predispositions, testing could enable people to make beneficial decisions concerning themselves, family members, and potential offspring. When individuals already manifested certain disorders, voluntary genetic counselling was designed to help provide diagnosis, prognosis, and information for vital decisions.

This is analogous to diagnostic reading tests conducted in the public schools. These are designed to help students get remedial help when needed. Instead, imagine a situation where such tests were used to "weed out" the weakest students so that they didn't clutter up the classroom and drain teaching resources. Surely we would find such a policy unjust, if not outrageous! This would be similar to the discriminatory use of genetic screening. Like individuals with contingency markers, slow readers often can *alter* their futures. In both cases, the diagnostic tests can be used to assist the individual to deal with his problem and make life-enhancing choices. On the other hand, the tests can be used to exclude the individual from certain beneficial opportunities: jobs in the case of genetic screening, and instruction to improve reading skills in the case of the reading tests.

Each use of the diagnostic test can be viewed as part of a larger model. The "diagnostic-therapeutic" model takes as primary the interests of the individuals being tested. The "competition" model, however, takes as primary the interests of some other group or institution: the business in the case of genetic testing, the school or superior students in the case of reading diagnosis. On the competition model, the "defective" worker or student is displaced in favor of the competing interests.

My analogy between the school reading test and genetic screening being used against the diagnosed individuals faces the following objection. In the case of the reading test, public education is paid for by public monies; therefore, everybody has an equal right to instruction, including those with reading disabilities. But in the case of genetic screening, the employer is operating privately. She is under no obligation to serve the interests of the employee (or prospective employee). The parallel between people with reading disabilities and those genetically marked for disorders would then break down on the basis of the public/private distinction.

My reply is that genetic research and the procedures employed in genetic screening were developed with public monies. They were carried out by means of government grants and publicly financed facilities such as state universities. Even private universities and research institutes rely greatly on government monies for equipment and salaries, as well as the findings generated by the public institutions. Moreover, these public funds were allocated for the expressed purposes of increasing scientific knowledge and helping society's members. Promotion of these social goods was used to legitimate if not justify investing society's taxes in genetic research. For private businesses to use the knowledge and technology developed through this research in order to deny some of its members employment seems unjust. This is so even if private companies market instruments and procedures for the genetic screening; the technologies *these* private companies are selling could only have been developed on the shoulders of publicly financed (and publicly available) research.

This brings us to the importance of health. Health is unlike most other goods because it is a prerequisite for so many things we value. Without it, we are cut off from the joys of recreation, travel, the arts, work, socializing, sometimes even life itself. Depending on the degree of infirmity, even such simple, apparently available delights as reading, talking, or walking may be denied the individual. The economic benefits of work are usually needed for people to receive adequate long-term health care, so that depriving them of work is likely to be condemning people to lack of health.

Denying a person work on the basis of the *disposition* to develop a disorder may, ironically, increase its likelihood of occurrence. Prevention of its occurrence might require repeated diagnostic tests, treatment, or therapy; it might require the economic wherewithal for a particular health regimen, such as exercise. Even if the lack of work doesn't contribute to the onset of the genetically marked disorder through economic deprivation, it compounds the individual's plight. He not only suffers from the potential to develop this particular disorder, but is now unemployed (and probably uninsured) to boot. He is now economically unprotected against *other* misfortunes and subjected to the psychological stress which could foster other disorders.

What should we conclude from all this? It seems to me that these considerations of privacy and justice argue strongly against general, discriminatory genetic screening in the workplace. Thomas Murray has a list of requirements that a morally defensible exclusion policy must meet. Among them are two that especially turn on considerations of justice.[10] The policy must exclude workers from but a few jobs so that those affected stand a good chance of finding other employment. Otherwise, we'd be treating them unjustly by virtually denying them the opportunity to work at all. In addition, the exclusion shouldn't single out groups that have already been unjustly treated. This is important since genetic dispositions are often inherited along racial and ethnic lines such as the high black incidence of sickle cell anemia and the high Jewish incidence of Tay-Sachs. This, too, is a matter of justice. We shouldn't compound prior injustices with present ones.

I would qualify Murray's conditions with the following restrictions. Corporate screening should be confined to work-specific disorders, rather than probe for a general genetic profile. Moreover, the company should make it a policy to try to relocate the employee to a less hazardous work site or activity, just as the first companies engaged in screening did. This degree of constraint seems minimal in light of the importance of privacy and justice.

NOTES

1. William Pat Patterson, "Genetic Screening: How Much Should We Test Employees?," *Industry Week,* June 1, 1987, pp. 47–48.

2. Kathleen McAuliffe, "Predicting Diseases," *U.S. News and World Report,* May 25, 1987, p. 65.

3. Kathleen Nolan and Sara Swenson, "New Tools, New Dilemmas: Genetic Frontiers," *The Hastings Center Report,* October/November, 1988, p. 65.

4. Gina Kolati, "Genetic Screening Raises Questions For Employers and Insurers," *Research News,* April 18, 1986, p. 317.

5. Marc Lappe, "The Limits of Genetic Inquiry," *The Hastings Center Report,* August, 1987, p. 7.

6. *Ibid.,* p. 8.

7. Marc Lappe, *Genetic Politics* (New York: Simon and Schuster, 1979), p. 61.

8. Madeleine and Lenn Goodman, "The Overselling of Genetic Anxiety," *The Hastings Center Report,* October, 1982, p. 249. There was, however, fear of loss of marriage eligibility among many of the people tested. The Goodmans also cite a study of sickle cell trait in Greece, where "possession of sickle cell trait had become a socially stigmatized status, introducing new anxieties into this rural community," p. 26.

9. Thomas Murray, "Warning: Screening Workers for Genetic Risk," *The Hastings Center Report,* February, 1983.

10. *Ibid.,* p. 8. Murray also includes the following: sound scientific basis linking anomaly to exposure to disease; risk should be very large and the disease should be severe and irreversible; and that the number of people excluded should be very small. This last stricture doesn't strike me as all that convincing. It isn't the number of people affected that *makes* a policy unjust. Although many suffering an injustice is worse than few suffering it, injustice done even to few is still injustice and weighs against the policy.

Whistleblowing and Professional Responsibility

Sissela Bok

"Whistleblowing" is a new label generated by our increased awareness of the ethical conflicts encountered at work. Whistleblowers sound an alarm from within the very organization in which they work, aiming to spotlight neglect or abuses that threaten the public interest.

The stakes in whistleblowing are high. Take the nurse who alleges that physicians enrich themselves in her hospital through unnecessary surgery; the engineer who discloses safety defects in the braking systems of a fleet of new rapid-transit vehicles; the Defense Department official who alerts Congress to military graft and overspending: all know that they pose a threat to those whom they denounce and that their own careers may be at risk.

MORAL CONFLICTS

Moral conflicts on several levels confront anyone who is wondering whether to speak out about abuses or risks or serious neglect. In the first place, he must try to decide whether, other things being equal, speaking out is in fact in the public interest. This choice is often made more complicated by factual uncertainties: Who is responsible for the abuse or neglect? How great is the threat? And how likely is it that speaking out will precipitate changes for the better?

In the second place, a would-be whistleblower must weigh his responsibility to serve the public interest against the responsibility he owes to his colleagues and the institution in which he works. While the professional ethic requires collegial loyalty, the codes of ethics often stress responsibility to the public over and above duties to colleagues and clients. Thus the United States Code of Ethics for Government Servants asks them to "expose corruption wherever uncovered" and to "put loyalty to the highest moral principles and to country above loyalty to persons, party, or government."[1] Similarly, the largest professional engineering association requires members to speak out against abuses threatening the safety, health, and welfare of the public.[2]

A third conflict for would-be whistleblowers is personal in nature and cuts across the first two: even in cases where they have concluded that the facts warrant speaking out, and that their duty to do so overrides loyalties to colleagues and institutions, they often have reason to fear the results of carrying out such a duty. However strong this duty may seem in theory, they know that, in practice, retaliation is likely. As a result, their careers and their ability to support themselves and their families may be unjustly impaired.[3] A government handbook issued during the Nixon era recommends reassigning "undesirables" to places so remote that they would prefer to resign. Whistleblowers may also be downgraded or given work without responsibility or work for which they are not qualified; or else they may be given many more tasks than they can pos-

From Sissela Bok, "Whistleblowing and Professional Responsibility," *New York University Education Quarterly,* 11 (Summer 1980): 2–7. Reprinted with permission.

sibly perform. Another risk is that an outspoken civil servant may be ordered to undergo a psychiatric fitness-for-duty examination,[4] declared unfit for service, and "separated" as well as discredited from the point of view of any allegations he may be making. Outright firing, finally, is the most direct institutional response to whistleblowers.

Add to the conflicts confronting individual whistleblowers the claim to self-policing that many professions make, and professional responsibility is at issue in still another way. For an appeal to the public goes against everything that "self-policing" stands for. The question for the different professions, then, is how to resolve, insofar as it is possible, the conflict between professional loyalty and professional responsibility toward the outside world. The same conflicts arise to some extent in all groups, but professional groups often have special cohesion and claim special dignity and privileges.

The plight of whistleblowers has come to be documented by the press and described in a number of books. Evidence of the hardships imposed on those who chose to act in the public interest has combined with a heightened awareness of professional malfeasance and corruption to produce a shift toward greater public support of whistleblowers. Public service law firms and consumer groups have taken up their cause; institutional reforms and legislation have been proposed to combat illegitimate reprisals.[5]

Given the indispensable services performed by so many whistleblowers, strong public support is often merited. But the new climate of acceptance makes it easy to overlook the dangers of whistleblowing: of uses in error or in malice; of work and reputations unjustly lost for those falsely accused; of privacy invaded and trust undermined. There comes a level of internal prying and mutual suspicion at which no institution can function. And it is a fact that the disappointed, the incompetent, the malicious, and the paranoid all too often leap to accusations in public. Worst of all, ideological persecution throughout the world traditionally relies on insiders willing to inform on their colleagues or even on their family members, often through staged public denunciations or press campaigns.

No society can count itself immune from such dangers. But neither can it risk silencing those with a legitimate reason to blow the whistle. How then can we distinguish between different instances of whistleblowing? A society that fails to protect the right to speak out even on the part of those whose warnings turn out to be spurious obviously opens the door to political repression. But from the moral point of view there are important differences between the aims, messages, and methods of dissenters from within.

NATURE OF WHISTLEBLOWING

Three elements, each jarring, and triply jarring when conjoined, lend acts of whistleblowing special urgency and bitterness: dissent, breach of loyalty, and accusation.

Like all dissent, whistleblowing makes public a disagreement with an authority or a majority view. But whereas dissent can concern all forms of disagreement with, for instance, religious dogma or government policy or court decisions, whistleblowing has the narrower aim of shedding light on negligence or abuse, or alerting to a risk, and of assigning responsibility for this risk.

Would-be whistleblowers confront the conflict inherent in all dissent: between conforming and sticking their necks out. The more repressive the authority they challenge, the greater the personal risk they take in speaking out. At exceptional times, as in times of war, even ordinarily tolerant authorities may come to regard dissent as unacceptable and even disloyal.[6]

Furthermore, the whistleblower hopes to stop the game; but since he is neither referee nor coach, and since he blows the whistle on his own team, his act is seen as a violation of loyalty. In holding his position, he has assumed certain obligations to his colleagues and clients. He may even have subscribed to a loyalty oath or a promise of confidentiality. Loyalty to colleagues and to clients comes to be pitted against loyalty to the public interest, to those who may be injured unless the revelation is made.

Not only is loyalty violated in whistleblowing, hierarchy as well is often opposed, since the whistleblower is not only a colleague but a subordinate. Though aware of the risks inherent in such disobedience, he often hopes to keep his job.[7] At times, however, he plans his alarm to coincide with leaving the institution. If he is highly placed, or joined by others, resigning in protest may effectively direct public attention to the wrongdoing at issue.[8] Still another alternative, often chosen by those who wish to be safe from retaliation, is to leave the institution quietly, to secure another post, and then to blow the whistle. In this way, it is possible to speak with the authority and knowledge of an insider without having the vulnerability of that position.

It is the element of accusation, of calling a "foul," that arouses the strongest reactions on the part of the hierarchy. The accusation may be of neglect, of willfully concealed dangers, or of outright abuse on the part of colleagues or superiors. It singles out specific persons or groups as responsible for threats to the public interest. If no one could be held responsible — as in the case of an impending avalanche — the warning would not constitute whistleblowing.

The accusation of the whistleblower, moreover, concerns a present or an imminent threat. Past errors or misdeeds occasion such an alarm only if they still affect current practices. And risks far in the future lack the immediacy needed to make the alarm a compelling one, as well as the close connection to particular individuals that would justify actual accusations. Thus an alarm can be sounded about safety defects in a rapid-transit system that threaten or will shortly threaten passengers, but the revelation of safety defects in a system no longer in use, while of historical interest, would not constitute whistleblowing. Nor would the revelation of potential problems in a system not yet fully designed and far from implemented.[9]

Not only immediacy, but also specificity, is needed for there to be an alarm capable of pinpointing responsibility. A concrete risk must be at issue rather than a vague foreboding or a somber prediction. The act of whistleblowing differs in this respect from the lamentation or the dire prophecy. An immediate and specific threat would normally be acted upon by those at risk. The whistleblower assumes that his message will alert listeners to something they do not know, or whose significance they have not grasped because it has been kept secret.

The desire for openness inheres in the temptation to reveal any secret, sometimes joined to an urge for self-aggrandizement and publicity and the hope for revenge for past slights or injustices. There can be pleasure, too — righteous or malicious — in laying bare the secrets of co-workers and in setting the record straight at last. Colleagues of the whistleblower often suspect his motives: they may regard him as a crank, as publicity-hungry, wrong about the facts, eager for scandal and discord, and driven to indiscretion by his personal biases and shortcomings.

For whistleblowing to be effective, it must arouse its audience. Inarticulate whistleblowers are likely to fail from the outset. When they are greeted by apathy, their message dissipates. When they are greeted by disbelief, they elicit no response at all. And when the audience is not free to receive or to act on the information — when censorship or fear of retribution stifles response — then the message rebounds to injure the whistleblower. Whistleblowing also requires the possibility of concerted public response: the idea of whistleblowing in an anarchy is therefore merely quixotic.

Such characteristics of whistleblowing and strategic considerations for achieving an impact are common to the noblest warnings, the most vicious personal attacks, and the delusions of the paranoid. How can one distinguish the many acts of sounding an alarm that are genuinely in the public interest from all the petty, biased, or lurid revelations that pervade our querulous and gossip-ridden society? Can we draw distinctions between different whistleblowers, different messages, different methods?

We clearly can, in a number of cases. Whistleblowing may be starkly inappropriate when in malice or error, or when it lays bare legitimately private matters having to do, for instance, with political belief or sexual life. It can, just as clearly, be the only way to shed light on an ongoing unjust practice such as drugging political prisoners or subjecting them to electroshock treatment. It can be the last resort for alerting the public to an impending disaster. Taking such clearcut cases as benchmarks, and reflecting on what it is about them that weighs so heavily for or against speaking out, we can work our way toward the admittedly more complex cases in which whistleblowing is not so clearly the right or wrong choice, or where different points of view exist regarding its legitimacy — cases where there are moral reasons both for concealment and for disclosure and where judgments conflict. Consider the following cases:[10]

A. As a construction inspector for a federal agency, John Samuels (not his real name) had personal knowledge of shoddy and deficient construction practices by private contractors.

He knew his superiors received free vacations and entertainment, had their homes remodeled and found jobs for their relatives — all courtesy of a private contractor. These superiors later approved a multimillion no-bid contract with the same "generous" firm.

Samuels also had evidence that other firms were hiring nonunion laborers at a low wage while receiving substantially higher payments from the government for labor costs. A former superior, unaware of an office dictaphone, had incautiously instructed Samuels on how to accept bribes for overlooking sub-par performance.

As he prepared to volunteer this information to various members of Congress, he became tense and uneasy. His family was scared and the fears were valid. It might cost Samuels thousands of dollars to protect his job. Those who had freely provided Samuels with information would probably recant or withdraw their friendship. A number of people might object to his using a dictaphone to gather information. His agency would start covering up and vent its collective wrath upon him. As for reporters and writers, they would gather for a few days, then move on to the next story. He would be left without a job, with fewer friends, with massive battles looming, and without the financial means of fighting them. Samuels decided to remain silent.

B. Engineers of Company "A" prepared plans and specifications for machinery to be used in a manufacturing process and Company "A" turned them over to Company "B" for production. The engineers of Company "B," in reviewing the plans and specifications, came to the conclusion that they included certain miscalculations and technical deficiencies of a nature that the final product might be unsuitable for the purposes of the ultimate users, and that the equipment, if built according to the original plans and specifications, might endanger the lives of persons in proximity to it. The engineers of Company "B" called the matter to the attention of appropriate officials of their employer who, in turn, advised Company "A." Company "A" replied that its engineers felt that the design and specifications for the equipment were adequate and safe and that Company "B" should proceed to build the equipment as designed and specified. The officials of Company "B" instructed its engineers to proceed with the work.

C. A recently hired assistant director of admissions in a state university begins to wonder whether transcripts of some applicants accurately reflect their accomplishments. He knows that it matters to many in the university community, including alumni, that the football team continue its winning tradition. He has heard rumors that surrogates may be available to take tests for a fee, signing the names of designated applicants for admission, and that some of the transcripts may have been altered. But he has no hard facts. When he brings the question up with the director of admissions, he is told that the rumors are unfounded and asked not to inquire further into the matter.

INDIVIDUAL MORAL CHOICE

What questions might those who consider sounding an alarm in public ask themselves? How might they articulate the problem they see and weigh its injustice before deciding whether or not to reveal it? How can they best try to make sure their choice is the right one? In thinking about these questions it helps to keep in mind the three elements mentioned earlier: dissent, breach of loyalty, and accusation. They impose certain requirements — of accuracy and judgment in dissent; of exploring alternative ways to cope with improprieties that minimize the breach of loyalty; and of fairness in accusation. For each, careful articulation and testing of arguments are needed to limit error and bias.

Dissent by whistleblowers, first of all, is expressly claimed to be intended to benefit the public. It carries with it, as a result, an obligation to consider the nature of this benefit and to consider also the possible harm that may come from speaking out: harm to persons or institutions and, ultimately, to the public interest itself. Whistleblowers must, therefore, begin by making every effort to consider the effects of speaking out versus those of remaining silent. They must assure themselves of the accuracy of their reports, checking and rechecking the facts before speaking out; specify the degree to which there is genuine impropriety; consider how

imminent is the threat they see, how serious, and how closely linked to those accused of neglect and abuse.

If the facts warrant whistleblowing, how can the second element — breach of loyalty — be minimized? The most important question here is whether the existing avenues for change within the organization have been explored. It is a waste of time for the public as well as harmful to the institution to sound the loudest alarm first. Whistleblowing has to remain a last alternative because of its destructive side effects: it must be chosen only when other alternatives have been considered and rejected. They may be rejected if they simply do not apply to the problem at hand, or when there is not time to go through routine channels or when the institution is so corrupt or coercive that steps will be taken to silence the whistleblower should he try the regular channels first.

What weight should an oath or a promise of silence have in the conflict of loyalties? One sworn to silence is doubtless under a stronger obligation because of the oath he has taken. He has bound himself, assumed specific obligations beyond those assumed in merely taking a new position. But even such promises can be overridden when the public interest at issue is strong enough. They can be overridden if they were obtained under duress or through deceit. They can be overridden, too, if they promise something that is in itself wrong or unlawful. The fact that one has promised silence is no excuse for complicity in covering up a crime or a violation of the public's trust.

The third element in whistleblowing — accusation — raises equally serious ethical concerns. They are concerns of fairness to the persons accused of impropriety. Is the message one to which the public is entitled in the first place? Or does it infringe on personal and private matters that one has no right to invade? Here, the very notion of what is in the public's best "interest" is at issue: "accusations" regarding an official's unusual sexual or religious experiences may well appeal to the public's interest without being information relevant to "the public interest."

Great conflicts arise here. We have witnessed excessive claims to executive privilege and to secrecy by government officials during the Watergate scandal in order to cover up for abuses the public had every right to discover. Conversely, those hoping to profit from prying into private matters have become adept at invoking "the public's right to know." Some even regard such private matters as threats to the public: they voice their own religious and political prejudices in the language of accusation. Such a danger is never stronger than when the accusation is delivered surreptitiously. The anonymous accusations made during the McCarthy period regarding political beliefs and associations often injured persons who did not even know their accusers or the exact nature of the accusations.

From the public's point of view, accusations that are openly made by identifiable individuals are more likely to be taken seriously. And in fairness to those criticized, openly accepted responsibility for blowing the whistle should be preferred to the denunciation or the leaked rumor. What is openly stated can more easily be checked, its source's motives challenged, and the underlying information examined. Those under attack may otherwise be hard put to defend themselves against nameless adversaries. Often they do not even know that they are threatened until it is too late to respond. The anonymous denunciation, moreover, common to so many regimes, places the burden of investigation on government agencies that may thereby gain the power of a secret police.

From the point of view of the whistleblower, on the other hand, the anonymous message is safer in situations where retaliation is likely. But it is also often less likely to be taken seriously. Unless the message is accompanied by indications of how the evidence can be checked, its anonymity, however safe for the source, speaks against it.

During the process of weighing the legitimacy of speaking out, the method used, and the degree of fairness needed, whistleblowers must try to compensate for the strong possibility of bias on their part. They should be scrupulously aware of any motive that might skew their message: a desire for self-defense in a difficult bureaucratic situation, perhaps, or the urge to seek revenge, or inflated expectations regarding the effect their message will have on the situation. (Needless to say, bias affects the silent as well as the outspoken. The motive for holding back important information about abuses and injustice ought to give similar cause for soulsearching.)

Likewise, the possibility of personal gain from sounding the alarm ought to give pause. Once again there is then greater risk of a biased message. Even if the whistleblower regards himself as incorruptible, his profiting from revelations of neglect or abuse will lead others to question his motives and to put less credence in his charges. If, for example, a government employee stands to make large profits from a book exposing the iniquities in his agency, there is danger that he will, perhaps even unconsciously, slant his report in order to cause more of a sensation.

A special problem arises when there is a high risk that the civil servant who speaks out will have to go through costly litigation. Might he not justifiably try to make enough money on his public revelations — say, through books or public speaking — to offset his losses? In so doing he will not strictly speaking have *profited* from his revelations: he merely avoids being financially crushed by their sequels. He will nevertheless still be suspected at the time of revelation, and his message will therefore seem more questionable.

Reducing bias and error in moral choice often requires consultation, even open debate:[11] methods that force articulation of the moral arguments at stake and challenge privately held assumptions. But acts of whistle-blowing present special problems when it comes to open consultation. On the one hand, once the whistleblower sounds his alarm publicly, his arguments will be subjected to open scrutiny; he will have to articulate his reasons for speaking out and substantiate his charges. On the other hand, it will then be too late to retract the alarm or to combat its harmful effects, should his choice to speak out have been ill-advised.

For this reason, the whistleblower owes it to all involved to make sure of two things: that he has sought as much and as objective advice regarding his choice as he can *before* going public; and that he is aware of the arguments for and against the practice of whistleblowing in general, so that he can see his own choice against as richly detailed and coherently structured a background as possible. Satisfying these two requirements once again has special problems because of the very nature of whistleblowing: the more corrupt the circumstances, the more dangerous it may be to seek consultation before speaking out. And yet, since the whistleblower himself may have a biased view of the state of affairs, he may choose not to consult others when in fact it would be not only safe but advantageous to do so; he may see corruption and conspiracy where none exists.

NOTES

1. Code of Ethics for Government Service passed by the U.S. House of Representatives in the 85th Congress (1958) and applying to all government employees and office holders.

2. Code of Ethics of the Institute of Electrical and Electronics Engineers, Article IV.

3. For case histories and descriptions of what befalls whistleblowers, see Rosemary Chalk and Frank von Hippel, "Due Process for Dissenting Whistle-Blowers," *Technology Review* 81 (June–July 1979): 48–55; Alan S. Westin and Stephen Salisbury, eds., *Individual Rights in the Corporation* (New York: Pantheon, 1980); Helen Dudar, "The Price of Blowing the Whistle," *New York Times Magazine*, 30 October 1979, pp. 41–54; John Edsall, *Scientific Freedom and Responsibility* (Washington, D.C.: American Association for the Advancement of Science, 1975), p. 5; David Ewing, *Freedom Inside the Organization* (New York: Dutton, 1977); Ralph Nader, Peter Petkas, and Kate Blackwell, *Whistle Blowing* (New York: Grossman, 1972); Charles Peter and Taylor Branch, *Blowing the Whistle* (New York: Praeger, 1972).

4. Congressional hearings uncovered a growing resort to mandatory psychiatric examinations.

5. For an account of strategies and proposals to support government whistleblowers, see Government Accountability Project, *A Whistleblower's Guide to the Federal Bureaucracy* (Washington, D.C.: Institute for Policy Studies, 1977).

6. See, e.g., Samuel Eliot Morison, Frederick Merk, and Frank Friedel, *Dissent in Three American Wars* (Cambridge: Harvard University Press, 1970).

7. In the scheme worked out by Albert Hirschman in *Exit, Voice and Loyalty* (Cambridge: Harvard University Press, 1970), whistleblowing represents "voice" accompanied by a preference not to "exit," though forced "exit" is clearly a possibility and "voice" after or during "exit" may be chosen for strategic reasons.

8. Edward Weisband and Thomas N. Franck, *Resignation in Protest* (New York: Grossman, 1975).

9. Future developments can, however, be the cause for whistleblowing if they are seen as resulting from steps being taken or about to be taken that render them inevitable.

10. Case A is adapted from Louis Clark, "The Sound of Professional Suicide," *Barrister*, Summer 1978, p. 10; Case B is Case 5 in Robert J. Baum and Albert Flores, eds., *Ethical Problems of Engineering* (Troy, N.Y.: Rensselaer Polytechnic Institute, 1978), p. 186.

11. I discuss these questions of consultation and publicity with respect to moral choice in chapter 7 of Sissela Bok, *Lying* (New York: Pantheon, 1978); and in *Secrets* (New York: Pantheon Books, 1982), Ch. IX and XV.

Whistleblowing and Employee Loyalty

Ronald Duska

There are proponents on both sides of the issue — those who praise whistleblowers as civic heroes and those who condemn them as "finks." Maxwell Glen and Cody Shearer, who wrote about the whistleblowers at Three Mile Island say, "Without the *courageous* breed of assorted company insiders known as whistleblowers — workers who often risk their livelihoods to disclose information about construction and design flaws — the Nuclear Regulatory Commission itself would be nearly as idle as Three Mile Island. . . . That whistleblowers deserve both gratitude and protection is beyond disagreement."[1]

Still, while Glen and Shearer praise whistleblowers, others vociferously condemn them. For example, in a now infamous quote, James Roche, the former president of General Motors said:

> Some critics are now busy eroding another support of free enterprise — the loyalty of a management team, with its unifying values and cooperative work. Some of the enemies of business now encourage an employee to be *disloyal* to the enterprise. They want to create suspicion and disharmony, and pry into the proprietary interests of the business. However this is labeled — industrial espionage, whistle blowing, or professional responsibility — it is another tactic for spreading disunity and creating conflict.[2]

From Roche's point of view, not only is whistleblowing not "courageous" and not deserving of "gratitude and protection" as Glen and Shearer would have it, it is corrosive and impermissible.

Discussions of whistleblowing generally revolve around three topics: (1) attempts to define whistleblowing more precisely, (2) debates about whether and when whistleblowing is permissible, and (3) debates about whether and when one has an obligation to blow the whistle.

In this paper I want to focus on the second problem, because I find it somewhat disconcerting that there is a problem at all. When I first looked into the ethics of whistleblowing it seemed to me that whistleblowing was a good thing, and yet I found in the literature claim after claim that it was in need of defense, that there was something wrong with it, namely that it was an act of disloyalty.

If whistleblowing is a disloyal act, it deserves disapproval, and ultimately any action of whistleblowing needs justification. This disturbs me. It is as if the act of a good Samaritan is being condemned as an act of interference, as if the prevention of a suicide needs to be justified.

In his book *Business Ethics,* Norman Bowie claims that "whistleblowing . . . violate(s) a *prima facie* duty of loyalty to one's employer." According to Bowie, there is a duty of loyalty that prohibits one from reporting his employer or company. Bowie, of course, recognizes that this is only a *prima facie* duty, that is, one that can be overridden by a higher duty to the public good. Nevertheless, the axiom that whistleblowing is disloyal is Bowie's starting point.[3]

Bowie is not alone. Sissela Bok sees "whistleblowing" as an instance of disloyalty:

> The whistleblower hopes to stop the game; but since he is neither referee nor coach, and since he blows the whistle on his own team, his act is

seen as a *violation of loyalty*. In holding his position, he has assumed certain obligations to his colleagues and clients. He may even have subscribed to a loyalty oath or a promise of confidentiality.... Loyalty to colleagues and to clients comes to be pitted against loyalty to the public interest, to those who may be injured unless the revelation is made.[4]

Bowie and Bok end up defending whistleblowing in certain contexts, so I don't necessarily disagree with their conclusions. However, I fail to see how one has an obligation of loyalty to one's company, so I disagree with their perception of the problem and their starting point. I want to argue that one does not have an obligation of loyalty to a company, even a *prima facie* one, because companies are not the kind of things that are properly objects of loyalty. To make them objects of loyalty gives them a moral status they do not deserve and in raising their status, one lowers the status of the individuals who work for the companies. Thus, the difference in perception is important because those who think employees have an obligation of loyalty to a company fail to take into account a relevant moral difference between persons and corporations.

But why aren't companies the kind of things that can be objects of loyalty? To answer that we have to ask what are proper objects of loyalty. John Ladd states the problem this way, "Granted that loyalty is the wholehearted devotion to an object of some kind, what kind of thing is the object? Is it an abstract entity, such as an idea or a collective being? Or is it a person or group of persons?"[5] Philosophers fall into three camps on the question. On one side are the idealists who hold that loyalty is devotion to something more than persons, to some cause or abstract entity. On the other side are what Ladd calls "social atomists," and these include empiricists and utilitarians, who think that at most one can only be loyal to individu-

als and that loyalty can ultimately be explained away as some other obligation that holds between two people. Finally, there is a moderate position that holds that although idealists go too far in postulating some superpersonal entity as an object of loyalty, loyalty is still an important and real relation that holds between people, one that cannot be dismissed by reducing it to some other relation.

There does seem to be a view of loyalty that is not extreme. According to Ladd, "'loyalty' is taken to refer to a relationship between persons — for instance, between a lord and his vassal, between a parent and his children, or between friends. Thus the object of loyalty is ordinarily taken to be a person or a group of persons."[6]

But this raises a problem that Ladd glosses over. There is a difference between a person or a group of persons, and aside from instances of loyalty that relate two people such as lord/vassal, parent/child, or friend/friend, there are instances of loyalty relating a person to a group, such as a person to his family, a person to this team, and a person to his country. Families, countries, and teams are presumably groups of persons. They are certainly ordinarily construed as objects of loyalty.

But to what am I loyal in such a group? In being loyal to the group am I being loyal to the whole group or to its members? It is easy to see the object of loyalty in the case of an individual person. It is simply the individual. But to whom am I loyal in a group? To whom am I loyal in a family? Am I loyal to each and every individual or to something larger, and if to something larger, what is it? We are tempted to think of a group as an entity of its own, an individual in its own right, having an identity of its own.

To avoid the problem of individuals existing for the sake of the group, the atomists insist that a group is nothing more than the individuals who comprise it, nothing other than a mental fiction by which we refer to a group of individuals. It is certainly not a reality or entity over and above the sum of its parts, and consequently is not a proper object of loyalty. Under such a position, of course, no loyalty would be owed to a company because a company is a mere mental fiction, since it is a group. One would have obligations to the individual members of the company, but one could never be justified in overriding those obligations for the sake of the "group" taken collectively. A company has no moral status except in terms of the individual members who comprise it. It is not a proper object of loyalty. But the atomists go too far. Some groups, such as a family, do have a reality of their own, whereas groups of people walking down the street do not. From Ladd's point of view the social atomist is wrong because he fails to recognize the kinds of groups that are held together by "the ties that bind." The atomist tries to reduce these groups to simple sets of individuals bound together by some externally imposed criteria. This seems wrong.

There do seem to be groups in which the relationships and interactions create a new force or entity. A group takes on an identity and a reality of its own that is determined by its purpose, and this purpose defines the various relationships and roles set up within the group. There is a division of labor into roles necessary for the fulfillment of the purposes of the group. The membership, then, is not of individuals who are the same but of individuals who have specific relationships to one another determined by the aim of the group. Thus we get specific relationships like parent/child, coach/player, and so on, that don't occur in other groups. It seems then that an atomist account of loyalty that restricts loyalty merely to individuals and does not include loyalty to groups might be inadequate.

But once I have admitted that we can have loyalty to a group, do I not open myself up to criticism from the proponent of loyalty to the company? Might not the proponent of loyalty to business say: "Very well. I agree with you. The atomists are short-sighted. Groups have some sort of reality and they can be proper objects of loyalty. But companies are groups. Therefore companies are proper objects of loyalty."

The point seems well taken, except for the fact that the kinds of relationships that loyalty requires are just the kind that one does not find in business. As Ladd says, "The ties that bind the persons together provide the basis of loyalty." But all sorts of ties bind people together. I am a member of a group of fans if I go to a ball game. I am a member of a group if I merely walk down the street. What binds people together in a business is not sufficient to require loyalty.

A business or corporation does two things in the free enterprise system: It produces a good or service and it makes a profit. The making of a profit, however, is the primary function of a business as a business, for if the production of the good or service is not profitable, the business would be out of business. Thus nonprofitable goods or services are a means to an end. People bound together in a business are bound together not for mutual fulfillment and support, but to divide labor or make a profit. Thus, while we can jokingly refer to a family as a place where "they have to take you in no matter what," we cannot refer to a company in that way. If a worker does not produce in a company or if cheaper laborers are available, the company — in order to fulfill its purpose — should get rid of the worker. A company feels no obligation of loyalty. The saying "You can't buy loyalty" is true. Loyalty depends on ties that demand self-sacrifice with no expectation of reward. Business functions on the basis of enlightened self-interest. I am devoted to a company not because it is like a parent to me; it is not. Attempts of some companies to create "one big happy family" ought to be looked on with suspicion. I am not devoted to it at all, nor should I be. I work for it because it pays me. I am not in a family to get paid, I am in a company to get paid.

The cold hard truth is that the goal of profit is what gives birth to a company and forms that particular group. Money is what ties the group together. But in such a commercialized venture, with such a goal, there is no loyalty, or at least none need be expected. An employer will release an employee and an employee will walk away from an employer when it is profitable for either one to do so.

Not only is loyalty to a corporation not required, it more than likely is misguided. There is nothing as pathetic as the story of the loyal employee who, having given above and beyond the call of duty, is let go in the restructuring of the company. He feels betrayed because he mistakenly viewed the company as an object of his loyalty. Getting rid of such foolish romanticism and coming to grips with this hard but accurate assessment should ultimately benefit everyone.

To think we owe a company or corporation loyalty requires us to think of that company as a person or as a group with a goal of human fulfillment. If we think of it in this way we can be loyal. But this is the wrong way to think. A company is not a person. A company is an instrument, and an instrument with a specific purpose, the making of profit. To treat an instrument as an end in itself, like a person, may not be as bad as treating an end as an instrument, but it does give the instrument a moral status it does not deserve; and by elevating the instrument we lower the end. All things, instruments and ends, become alike.

Remember that Roche refers to the "management team" and Bok sees the name "whistleblowing" coming from the instance of a referee blowing a whistle in the presence of a foul. What is perceived as bad about whistleblowing in business from this perspective is that one blows the whistle on one's own team, thereby violating team loyalty. If the company can get its employees to view it as a team they belong to, it is easier to demand loyalty. Then the rules governing teamwork and team loyalty will apply. One reason the appeal to a team and team loyalty works so well in business is that businesses are in competition with one another. Effective motivation turns business practices into a game and instills teamwork.

But businesses differ from teams in very important respects, which makes the analogy between business and a team dangerous. Loyalty to a team is loyalty within the context of sport or a competition. Teamwork and team loyalty require that in the circumscribed activity of the game I cooperate with my fellow players, so that pulling all together, we may win. The object of (most) sports is victory. But winning in sports is a social convention, divorced from the usual goings on of society. Such a winning is most times a harmless, morally neutral diversion.

But the fact that this victory in sports, within the rules enforced by a referee (whistleblower), is a socially developed convention taking place within a larger social context makes it quite different from competition in business, which, rather than being defined by a context, permeates the whole of society in its influence. Competition leads not only to victory but to losers. One can lose at sport with precious few consequences. The consequences of losing at business are much larger. Further, the losers in business can be those who are not in the game voluntarily (we are all forced to participate) but who are still affected by business decisions. People cannot choose to participate in business. It permeates everyone's lives.

The team model, then, fits very well with the model of the free market system, because there competition is said to be the name of the game. Rival companies compete and their object is to win. To call a foul on one's own teammate is to jeopardize one's chances of winning and is viewed as disloyalty.

But isn't it time to stop viewing corporate machinations as games? These games are not controlled and are not ended after a specific time. The activities of business affect the lives of everyone, not just the game players. The analogy of the corporation to a team and the consequent appeal to team loyalty, although understandable, is seriously misleading, at least in the moral sphere where competition is not the prevailing virtue.

If my analysis is correct, the issue of the permissibility of whistleblowing is not a real issue since there is no obligation of loyalty to a company. Whistleblowing is not only permissible but expected when a company is harming society. The issue is not one of disloyalty to the company, but of whether the whistleblower has an obligation to society if blowing the whistle will bring him retaliation.

NOTES

1. Maxwell Glen and Cody Shearer, "Going After the Whistle-blowers," *Philadelphia Inquirer,* Tuesday, August 2, 1983, Op-ed page, p. 11A.
2. James M. Roche, "The Competitive System, to Work, to Preserve, and to Protect," *Vital Speeches of the Day* (May 1971): 445.
3. Norman Bowie, *Business Ethics* (Englewood Cliffs, N.J.: Prentice Hall, 1982), pp. 140–143.
4. Sissela Bok, "Whistleblowing and Professional Responsibilities," *New York University Education Quarterly* 2 (1980): 3, and here p. 330.
5. John Ladd, "Loyalty," *The Encyclopedia of Philosophy* 5: 97.
6. Ibid.

Warthen v. Toms River Community Memorial Hospital

Superior Court of New Jersey

Plaintiff Corrine Warthen appeals from a summary judgment of the Law Division dismissing her action against defendant Toms River Community Memorial Hospital (Hospital). Plaintiff sought to recover damages for her allegedly wrongful discharge in violation of public policy following her refusal to dialyze a terminally ill double amputee patient because of her "moral, medical and philosophical objections" to performing the procedure.

The facts giving rise to this appeal are not in dispute and may be summarized as follows.

The Hospital, where plaintiff had been employed for eleven years as a registered nurse, terminated plaintiff from its employment on August 6, 1982. For the three years just prior to her discharge, plaintiff had worked in the Hospital's kidney dialysis unit. It is undisputed that plaintiff was an at-will employee.

Plaintiff alleges that during the summer of 1982 her supervisor periodically assigned her to dialyze a double amputee patient who suffered from a number of maladies. On two occasions plaintiff claims that she had to cease treatment because the patient suffered cardiac arrest and severe internal hemorrhaging during the dialysis procedure. During the first week of 1982 plaintiff again was scheduled to dialyze this patient. She approached her head nurse and informed her that "she had moral, medical, and philosophical objections" to performing this procedure on the patient because the patient was terminally ill and, she contended, the procedure was causing the patient additional complications. At that time the head nurse granted plaintiff's request for reassignment.

On August 6, 1982, the head nurse again assigned plaintiff to dialyze the same patient. Plaintiff once again objected, apparently stating that she thought she had reached agreement with the head nurse not to be assigned to this particular patient. She also requested the opportunity to meet with the treating physician, Dr. DiBello. Dr. DiBello informed plaintiff that the patient's family wished him kept alive through dialysis and that he would not survive without it. However, plaintiff continued to refuse to dialyze the patient, and the head nurse informed her that if she did not agree to perform the treatment, the Hospital would dismiss her. Plaintiff refused to change her mind, and the Hospital terminated her.

Plaintiff subsequently instituted this action alleging that she was wrongfully discharged by the Hospital without justification and in violation of public policy. The Hospital denied liability to plaintiff and alleged, by way of a separate defense, that plaintiff's termination was appropriate because she had the status of an at-will employee. Following completion of pretrial discovery, the Hospital moved for summary judgment, which the trial court denied because it perceived "that there [was] . . . a question of fact as to whether or not there is a public policy as articulated in the nurses' code of ethics that would permit somebody in the nursing profession to refuse to participate in a course of treatment which

is against her principles in good faith." However, upon reconsideration, the trial court granted the motion, concluding that "the nurses' code of ethics is a personal moral judgment and permits the nurse to have a personal moral judgment, but it does not rise to a public policy in the face of the general public policies that patients must be cared for in hospitals and patients must be treated basically by doctors and doctors' orders must be carried out." This appeal followed.

Plaintiff contends that the trial court erred in granting summary judgment because her refusal to dialyze the terminally-ill patient was justified as a matter of law by her adherence to the *Code for Nurses,* a code of ethics promulgated by the American Nurses Association, and that determining whether adherence to the *Code* "constitutes a public policy question" is a question of fact which should be resolved by a jury, not by the trial court. We disagree. . . .

Plaintiff relies on the "public policy" exception to the "at-will employment" doctrine to justify her claim that defendant wrongfully discharged her. As has often been stated at common law, "in the absence of an employment contract, employers or employees have been free to terminate the employment relationship with or without cause." . . . Recently, in *Pierce v. Ortho Pharmaceutical Corp., supra,* the Supreme Court recognized a developing exception to the traditional "at-will employment" doctrine, holding that "an employee has a cause of action for wrongful discharge when the discharge is contrary to a clear mandate of public policy." . . .

As a preliminary matter plaintiff contends that identifying the "clear mandate of public policy" constitutes a genuine issue of material fact for the jury rather than, as occurred in the instant case, a threshold question for the trial judge. To support her contention plaintiff cites *Kalman v. Grand Union Co.,* . . . in which we said:

It is the employee's burden to identify "a specific expression" or "a clear mandate" of public policy which might bar his discharge. [Citation omitted]. What constitutes a qualifying mandate is a fact question. . . .

However, quoting the following explanatory language from *Ortho Pharmaceutical*, we went on to emphasize that "the judiciary must define the cause of action in case-by-case determinations." . . .

In *Ortho Pharmaceutical* plaintiff, a physician and research scientist, was dismissed because of her opposition to continued laboratory research, development and testing of the drug loperamide, which Ortho intended to market for the treatment of diarrhea. The plaintiff was opposed to the drug because it contained saccharin and because she believed that by continuing work on loperamide she would violate her interpretation of the Hippocratic oath. The Court held, *as a matter of law*, that where plaintiff merely contended saccharin was controversial, not dangerous, and the FDA had not yet approved human testing of loperamide, the Hippocratic oath did not contain a clear mandate of public policy preventing the physician from continuing research. Then, not finding any issue of material fact, the Supreme Court remanded the case to the trial court for the entry of summary judgment.

Thus, identifying the mandate of public policy is a question of law, analogous to interpreting a statute or defining a duty in a negligence case. . . . As the Chancery Court said in *Schaffer v. Federal Trust Co.,* . . .

"Public policy has been defined as that principle of law which holds that no person can lawfully do that which has a tendency to be injurious to the public, or against the public good." . . . The term admits of no exact definition. . . . The source of public policy is the statutes enacted by the legislature and in the decisions of the courts; there we find what acts are consid-

ered harmful to the public and therefore unlawful.

Public policy is not concerned with minutiae, but with principles. Seldom does a single clause of a statute establish public policy; policy is discovered from study of the whole statute, or even a group of statutes *in pari materia*. . . .

Based on the foregoing, we hold that where a discharged at-will employee asserts wrongful discharge on public policy grounds, the trial court must, as a matter of law, determine whether public policy justified the alleged conduct. Then, assuming the pleadings raise a genuine issue of material fact, it is for the jury to determine the truth of the employee's allegations. Here, therefore, the issue of whether the *Code for Nurses* represented a clear expression of public policy did not present a genuine issue of material fact precluding the entry of summary judgment.

Plaintiff next contends that, as a matter of law, the *Code for Nurses* constitutes an authoritative statement of public policy which justified her conduct and that the trial court therefore improperly granted defendant's motion for summary judgment. In *Ortho Pharmaceutical* the Supreme Court discussed the role of professional codes of ethics as sources of public policy in "at-will employment" cases:

In certain instances, a professional code of ethics may contain an expression of public policy. However, not all such sources express a clear mandate of public policy. For example, a code of ethics designed to serve only the interests of a profession or an administrative regulation concerned with technical matters probably would not be sufficient. Absent legislation, the judiciary must define the cause of action in case-by-case determinations. An employer's right to discharge an employee at will carries a correlative duty not to discharge an employee who declines to perform an act that would require a violation of a clear mandate of public policy. However, unless an employee at will identifies a specific expression of public policy, he may be discharged with or without cause. . . .

The Court carefully warned against confusing reliance on professional ethics with reliance on personal morals:

> Employees who are professionals owe a special duty to abide not only by federal and state law, but also by the recognized codes of ethics of their professions. That duty may oblige them to decline to perform acts required by their employers. However, an employee should not have the right to prevent his or her employer from pursuing its business because the employee perceives that a particular business decision violates the employee's personal morals, as distinguished from the recognized code of ethics of the employee's profession. . . .

The burden is on the professional to identify "a specific expression" or "a clear mandate" of public policy which might bar his or her dismissal. . . .

Here, plaintiff cites the *Code for Nurses* to justify her refusal to dialyze the terminally ill patient. She refers specifically to the following provisions and interpretive statement:

> THE NURSE PROVIDES SERVICES WITH RESPECT FOR HUMAN DIGNITY AND THE UNIQUENESS OF THE CLIENT UNRESTRICTED BY CONSIDERATIONS OF SOCIAL OR ECONOMIC STATUS, PERSONAL ATTRIBUTES, OR THE NATURE OF HEALTH PROBLEMS.
>
> 1.4 THE NATURE OF HEALTH PROBLEMS
> The nurse's concern for human dignity and the provision of quality nursing care is not limited by personal attitudes or beliefs. If personally opposed to the delivery of care in a particular case because of the nature of the health problem or the procedures to be used, the nurse is justified in refusing to participate. Such refusal should be made known in advance and in time for other appropriate arrangements to be made for the client's nursing care. If the nurse must knowingly enter such a case under emergency circumstances or enters unknowingly, the obligation to provide the best possible care

is observed. The nurse withdraws from this type of situation only when assured that alternative sources of nursing care are available to the client. If a client requests information or counsel in an area that is legally sanctioned but contrary to the nurse's personal beliefs, the nurse may refuse to provide these services but must advise the client of sources where such service is available. [American Nurses Association, *Code for Nurses with Interpretive Statements*. . . .

Plaintiff contends that these provisions constitute a clear mandate of public policy justifying her conduct. . . .

It is our view that as applied to the circumstances of this case the passage cited by plaintiff defines a standard of conduct beneficial only to the individual nurse and not to the public at large. The overall purpose of the language cited by plaintiff is to preserve human dignity; however, it should not be at the expense of the patient's life or contrary to the family's wishes. The record before us shows that the family had requested that dialysis be continued on the patient, and there is nothing to suggest that the patient had, or would have, indicated otherwise. . . .

Recently, in *In re Conroy, supra,* our Supreme Court confirmed this State's basic interest in the preservation of life, . . . and our recognition, embraced in the right to self-determination, that all patients have a fundamental right to expect that medical treatment will not be terminated against their will. . . . This basic policy mandate clearly outweighs any policy favoring the right of a nurse to refuse to participate in treatments which he or she personally believes threatens human dignity. Indeed, the following passage from the *Code for Nurses* echoes the policy cited by *Conroy* and severely constrains the ethical right of nurses to refuse participation in medical procedures:

> 1.4 THE NATURE OF HEALTH PROBLEMS
> The nurse's respect for the worth and dignity of the individual human being applies irrespec-

tive of the nature of the health problem. It is reflected in the care given the person who is disabled as well as the normal; the patient with the long-term illness as well as the one with the acute illness, or the recovering patient as well as the one who is terminally ill or dying. It extends to all who require the services of the nurse for the promotion of health, the prevention of illness, the restoration of health, and the alleviation of suffering. [American Nurses Association, *Code for Nurses with Interpretive Statements*. . . .

The position asserted by plaintiff serves only the individual and the nurses' profession while leaving the public to wonder when and whether they will receive nursing care. . . . Moreover, as the Hospital argues, "[i]t would be a virtual impossibility to administer a hospital if each nurse or member of the administration staff refused to carry out his or her duties based upon a personal private belief concerning the right to live. . . ."

Concededly, plaintiff had to make a difficult decision. Viewing the facts in a light most beneficial to plaintiff, she had dialyzed the particular patient on several occasions in the past, and on two of those occasions plaintiff says the patient had suffered cardiac arrest and severe internal hemorrhaging during the dialysis procedure. The first time plaintiff objected to performing the procedure her head nurse agreed to reassign her, and at that time plaintiff apparently believed she had an agreement with the head nurse not to be assigned to this particular patient. She also believed she had fulfilled her ethical obligation by making her refusal to participate in the procedure "known in advance and in time for other appropriate arrangements to be made for the client's nursing care."

Nonetheless, we conclude as a matter of law that even under the circumstances of this case the ethical considerations cited by plaintiff do not rise to the level of a public policy mandate permitting a registered nursing professional to refuse to provide medical treatment to a terminally ill patient, even where that nursing professional gives his or her superiors advance warning. Beyond this, even if we were to make the dubious assumption that the *Code for Nurses* represents a clear expression of public policy, we have no hesitancy in concluding on this record that plaintiff was motivated by her own personal morals, precluding application of the "public policy" exception to the "at-will employment" doctrine. Plaintiff alleged that each time she refused to dialyze the patient she told the head nurse that she had "moral, medical and philosophical objections" to performing the procedure. She makes no assertion that she ever referred to her obligations and entitlements pursuant to her code of ethics. In addition, the very basis for plaintiff's reliance on the *Code for Nurses* is that she was personally opposed to the dialysis procedure. By refusing to perform the procedure she may have eased her own conscience, but she neither benefited the society-at-large, the patient, nor the patient's family.

Accordingly, the judgment under review is affirmed.

Potter v. Village Bank of New Jersey

Superior Court of New Jersey

The crucial question raised in this appeal is whether a bank president and chief executive officer who blows the whistle on suspected laundering of Panamanian drug money is protected from retaliatory discharge by the public policy of this State. We answer in the affirmative. We also hold that the retaliatory discharge in this case constituted an intentional tort which exposed defendants to compensatory and punitive damages. We affirm the judgment.

A

Plaintiff Dale G. Potter became the president and chief executive officer of the Village Bank of New Jersey (Village Bank) on November 15, 1982. His employment was terminated in May or June 1984. On June 13, 1984 plaintiff filed a complaint in the Chancery Division against Village Bank alleging that his job had been wrongfully terminated. Plaintiff sought reinstatement to his position as chief executive officer and president of the bank. . . .

After the matter was transferred to the Law Division, plaintiff filed an amended complaint. . . . In the four-count amended complaint plaintiff sought compensatory and punitive damages based on (1) fraudulent inducement, (2) breach of contract, (3) tortious interference with the employment relationship and (4) wrongful termination.

The case was tried to a jury over a four-day period. . . . At the end of plaintiff's case, the trial judge granted defendants' motion for involuntary dismissal of plaintiff's claims of

fraudulent inducement, breach of contract and wrongful interference with the employment relationship. The only remaining claim was for wrongful discharge. . . .

The claim of wrongful discharge was submitted to the jury as to the remaining defendants, Village Bank and Em Kay. The jury answered the following special interrogatories:

Q1. Did the Defendants wrongfully discharge the plaintiff?

A. Yes.

Q2. Was the plaintiff damaged by such wrongful discharge?

A. Yes.

Q3. What amount of compensatory damages, if any, should the plaintiff be awarded for such wrongful discharge?

A. $50,000.

Q4. What amount of punitive damages, if any, should the plaintiff be awarded for such wrongful discharge?

A. $100,000.

After the trial judge denied defendants' motion for judgment notwithstanding the verdict, final judgment was entered in the sum of $162,575.40, which consisted of $100,000 in punitive damages, $50,000 in compensatory damages plus $12,575.40 in prejudgment interest on the compensatory damages.

Village Bank and Em Kay Holding Corporation have appealed from the entire judgment. Plaintiff has cross-appealed from the involuntary dismissals at the end of plaintiff's evidence.

543 A.2d 80 (1985). Opinion by Judge J. H. Coleman.

The pivotal issue presented to the jury was whether plaintiff resigned or was discharged in violation of a clear mandate of public policy. Based on the evidence presented, the jury concluded he was fired contrary to a clear mandate of public policy. The following evidence supports that finding. Em Kay Holding Corporation (Em Kay) owns 93% of the stock of Village Bank. The remaining 7% is distributed among other shareholders. Em Kay is owned by the Em Kay Group which has its headquarters in Panama City, Panama. Em Kay Group is owned by Mory Kraselnick and Moises Kroitoro.

Bart and Kraselnick negotiated with plaintiff for employment at Village Bank. In September 1982 when the president of Village Bank suffered a heart attack, plaintiff was offered and accepted a position with the bank as a "holding company consultant." Plaintiff became president and chief executive officer of Village Bank two months later. Between then and January 1983, Kraselnick frequently telephoned plaintiff to request that Village Bank make large loans to companies that did business with Kraselnick and companies owned by Kraselnick. With few exceptions, plaintiff refused these requests.

After a January 21, 1983 meeting Kraselnick told plaintiff: "[I]f I ever ask you to do anything wrong, I'll stand up in front of you." At the time, plaintiff did not understand the meaning of the statement. Over the next couple of months, however, many cash deposits of between $8,000 and $9,300 were made into the accounts of Kraselnick, Bart, Noel Kinkella (office manager of Em Kay Equities whose president was Bart) and several of the companies in the Em Kay Group.

On March 24, 1983 plaintiff learned that Village Bank was advertising his job in the *Wall Street Journal.* When plaintiff confronted Kraselnick about this, he was told "You're not as outspoken and enthusiastic as I want you to be when you meet me." After plaintiff defended his position, the two temporarily reconciled.

On March 31, 1983 Kinkella went to Village Bank with a shopping bag filled with money. She made seven $9,000 deposits to accounts held by Kraselnick, Bart, Kinkella and four Em Kay related companies. Plaintiff became suspicious that drug money was being laundered so he called the New Jersey Commissioner of Banking and reported the transactions and requested advice. Before plaintiff could meet with the Commissioner, Kinkella deposited another package of about $50,000 in cash. When plaintiff asked Bart about the money, Bart told him that it was for lease payments between two related aeronautical companies in the Em Kay Group. Plaintiff became more suspicious that the large cash deposits were related to laundering of Panamanian drug money. When the Commissioner eventually met with plaintiff, he told plaintiff to maintain anonymity and that a full investigation would be undertaken. The jury was not informed about the details of plaintiff's suspicions.

Audits of the bank were conducted starting around the end of April or the beginning of May 1983. On June 28, 1983 plaintiff advised Village Bank's board of directors of the examination, but not of his meeting with the Commissioner. In July 1983 plaintiff filed currency transaction reports with the Department of the Treasury reporting the cash deposits.

In September 1983 Village Bank's board of directors raised plaintiff's salary from $65,000 to $75,000. Kraselnick also offered plaintiff a $10,000 bonus in cash so he "wouldn't pay income taxes" on it. When plaintiff refused to accept the bonus in cash, the bonus was not paid. In December 1983 the United States Attorney's Office for New Jersey issued subpoenas to the bank for the production of documents "on a list of accounts" related to the Em Kay Group. Plaintiff was also interviewed by representatives from that office.

On January 6, 1984 plaintiff executed his first written employment contract with Village Bank. The term was for one year beginning November 15, 1983. The contract provided for a base salary of $75,000, with a bonus at the discretion of the board of directors.

At some time between July and December 1983, plaintiff told Steven S. Radin, secretary to the Village Bank board of directors, that he "had gone to the Commissioner and reported the [cash] transactions." In January 1984 Radin informed Bart and Kraselnick of what plaintiff had told him. This angered Kraselnick. At the next scheduled board meeting, the directors were informed.

Immediately after the board meeting, Kraselnick asked plaintiff why he went to the Commissioner of Banking. When plaintiff responded "I thought that it was drug money," Kraselnick stated "you're probably right." From that point on, plaintiff contended that he was isolated from running the bank effectively since his subordinates in the bank were ordered not to talk to him. Further, there were several instances where Kraselnick questioned plaintiff's judgment and accused him of doing things incorrectly.

Plaintiff testified that Radin and at least two of Village Bank's directors advised him that he was about to be fired before plaintiff wrote a letter on May 22, 1984. The letter was written to Kraselnick which stated in pertinent part:

I wanted to be able to communicate directly with you and since my requests for a face to face meeting with you have been rejected, I am using this as my only recourse. At this point in time, I am considering myself "de facto" fired since Allan Bart has told several directors and John Bjerke, among others, that "Potter's gone" and in turn at least one director has communicated the same to several customers who have even discussed it with people in the Bank including myself. Needless to say, the lack

of discretion in discussing this situation in this way can only serve to hurt the Bank and the people in it. However, it has been done and the effect of it, in my opinion, has been that I consider myself at this point in time essentially to be terminated only without the pre-requisite action of the Board of Directors.

Shortly after the letter was written, plaintiff told members attending a board meeting that the letter was not intended as a letter of resignation. He reiterated this point in a May 31, 1984 letter to Radin.

By letter dated June 1, 1984, Radin notified plaintiff that

. . . it was the consensus of the Board that the Bank pay you full salary until the termination (November 15, 1984) of your present contract. During that period of time you would have the use of a car, office and secretarial assistance. Also you would receive all ordinary employee benefits. In consideration of these severance terms the Board requested a general release from you for the Bank, its directors and officers. The Board gave you until June 1, 1984 to accept or reject this offer. From May 24, 1984 until June 1, 1984 you were placed on leave of absence with pay.

Plaintiff rejected the proposal made by the board. When plaintiff attempted to attend a June 11 board meeting with his attorney, the board asked him to leave the bank. . . .

B

Subsequent to the trial in this matter Kraselnick, Bart, Bjerke and Village Bank were indicted by a federal grand jury for the District of New Jersey for allegedly conspiring to defraud the United States and making fraudulent statements in violation of 31 *U.S.C.* § 5311 *et seq.*, 31 *C.F.R.* § 103.22 *et seq.*, and 18 *U.S.C.* §§ 371, 1001 and 1002. The alleged criminal violations are based on their failure to report large cash transactions at Village

Bank during the time Potter was president and chief executive officer.

31 *U.S.C.* § 5313(a) provides, in pertinent part:

> (a) When a domestic financial institution is involved in a transaction for the . . . receipt . . . of United States coins or currency (or other monetary instruments the Secretary of the Treasury prescribes), in an amount, denomination, or amount and denomination, or under circumstances the Secretary prescribes by regulation, the institution and any other participant in the transaction the Secretary may prescribe shall file a report on the transaction at the time and in the way the Secretary prescribes. A participant acting for another person shall make the report as the agent or bailee of the person and identify the person for whom the transaction is being made.

Pursuant to this authority, the Secretary of the Treasury promulgated regulations which mandate the reporting of transactions in currency of more than $10,000.

Because the deposits in this case were slightly less than $10,000, plaintiff was not required by the strict wording of the statute and regulations to report the cash transactions. However, there is existing authority holding that a bank officer may not structure a single transaction in currency as multiple transactions to avoid the reporting requirements. A financial institution must aggregate all transactions by one customer in one day.

. . . Potter did much more than "protest [] [the] directors' improprieties" relating to a regulatory scheme. He blew the whistle on suspected criminal conduct involving one or more directors. Hence, Potter's termination relates to the public policy designed to encourage citizens to report suspected criminal violations to the proper authorities in order to ensure proper enforcement of both state and federal penal laws. . . . Nowhere in our society is the need for protection greater than in protecting well motivated citizens

who blow the whistle on suspected white collar and street level criminal activities. If "no person can lawfully do that which has a tendency to be injurious to the public or against the public good" because of public policy, *Allen v. Commercial Casualty Insurance Co.,* . . . surely whistle blowers of suspected criminal violations must be protected from retaliatory discharge. It stands to reason that few people would cooperate with law enforcement officials if the price they must pay is retaliatory discharge from employment. Clearly, that would have a chilling effect on criminal investigations and law enforcement in general.

Additionally, after the plaintiff's employment was terminated, the Legislature enacted the Conscientious Employee Protection Act, . . . effective September 5, 1986. Under the act, an employee who has been terminated because of reporting suspected criminal violations, has the right to file a retaliatory tort claim in addition to other remedies. We read this legislative enactment as a codification of public policy established through judicial decisions. . . .

We hold that the public policy of the State of New Jersey should protect at will employees — including bank presidents — who in good faith blow the whistle on one or more bank directors suspected of laundering money from illegal activities. . . .

C

We hold that an at will employee who has sustained a retaliatory discharge in violation of a clear mandate of public policy is entitled to recover economic and noneconomic losses. Such an employee may recover (1) the amount he or she would have earned from the time of wrongful discharge for a reasonable time until he or she finds new employment, including bonuses and vacation pay, less any unemployment compensation received in the interim, . . . (2) expenses associated with finding new employment and mental anguish or emotional distress damages proximately related to the retaliatory discharge, . . . and (3) the replacement value of fringe benefits such as an automobile and insurance for a reasonable time until new employment is obtained. . . .

The jury awarded $50,000 in compensatory damages. In addition, the jury awarded $100,000 in punitive damages. We are completely satisfied that both the compensatory and punitive damages awarded are supported by sufficient credible evidence and were consonant with the law. . . .

Luedtke v. Nabors Alaska Drilling, Inc.

Superior Court of Alaska

This case addresses one aspect of drug testing by employers. A private employer, Nabors Alaska Drilling, Inc. (Nabors), established a drug testing program for its employees. Two Nabors employees, Clarence Luedtke and Paul Luedtke, both of whom worked on drilling rigs on the North Slope, refused to submit to urinalysis screening for drug use as required by Nabors. As a result they were fired by Nabors. The Luedtkes challenge their discharge on the following grounds:

1. Nabors' drug testing program violates the Luedtkes' right to privacy guaranteed by article I, section 22 of the Alaska Constitution;
2. Nabors' demands violate the covenant of good faith and fair dealing implicit in all employment contracts;
3. Nabors' urinalysis requirement violates the public interest in personal privacy, giving the Luedtkes a cause of action for wrongful discharge; and
4. Nabors' actions give rise to a cause of action under the common law tort of invasion of privacy.

Nabors argues that the Luedtkes were "at will" employees whose employment relationship could be terminated at any time for any

reason. Alternatively, even if termination had to be based on "just cause," such cause existed because the Luedtkes violated established company policy relating to employee safety by refusing to take the scheduled tests.

This case raises issues of first impression in Alaska law including: whether the constitutional right of privacy applies to private parties; some parameters of the tort of wrongful discharge; and the extent to which certain employee drug testing by private employers can be controlled by courts.

FACTUAL AND PROCEDURAL BACKGROUND

The Luedtkes' cases proceeded separately to judgment. Because they raised common legal issues, on Nabors' motion they were consolidated on appeal.

Paul's Case

Factual Background. Paul began working for Nabors, which operates drilling rigs on Alaska's North Slope, in February 1978. He

---

768 P. 2d 1123 (1989). Opinion by Judge Compton.

began as a temporary employee, replacing a permanent employee on vacation for two weeks. During his two weeks of temporary work, a permanent position opened up on the rig on which he was working and he was hired to fill it. Paul began as a "floorman" and was eventually promoted to "driller." A driller oversees the work of an entire drilling crew.

Paul started work with Nabors as a union member, initially being hired from the union hall. During his tenure, however, Nabors "broke" the union. Paul continued to work without a union contract. Paul had no written contract with Nabors at the time of his discharge.

During his employment with Nabors, Paul was accused twice of violating the company's drug and alcohol policies. Once he was suspended for 90 days for taking alcohol to the North Slope. The other incident involved a search of the rig on which Paul worked. Aided by dogs trained to sniff out marijuana, the searchers found traces of marijuana on Paul's suitcase. Paul was allowed to continue working on the rig only after assuring his supervisors he did not use marijuana.

In October 1982, Paul scheduled a two-week vacation. Because his normal work schedule was two weeks of work on the North Slope followed by a week off, a two-week vacation amounted to 28 consecutive days away from work. Just prior to his vacation, Paul was instructed to arrange for a physical examination in Anchorage. He arranged for it to take place on October 19, during his vacation. It was at this examination that Nabors first tested Paul's urine for signs of drug use. The purpose of the physical, as understood by Paul, was to enable him to work on off-shore rigs should Nabors receive such contracts. Although Paul was told it would be a comprehensive physical he had no idea that a urinalysis screening test for drug use would be performed. He did voluntarily give a urine sample but assumed it would be tested only for "blood sugar, any kind of kidney failure [and] problems with bleeding." Nabors' policy of testing for drug use was not announced until November 1, 1982, almost two weeks after Paul's examination.

In early November 1982, Paul contacted Nabors regarding his flight to the North Slope to return to work. He was told at that time to report to the Nabors office in Anchorage. On November 5, Paul reported to the office where a Nabors representative informed him that he was suspended for "the use of alcohol or other illicit substances." No other information was forthcoming from Nabors until November 16 when Paul received a letter informing him that his urine had tested positive for cannabinoids. The letter informed him that he would be required to pass two subsequent urinalysis tests, one on November 30 and the other on December 30, before he would be allowed to return to work. In response Paul hand delivered a letter drafted by his attorney to the Manager of Employee Relations for Nabors, explaining why he felt the testing and suspension were unfair. Paul did not take the urinalysis test on November 30 as requested by Nabors. On December 14, Nabors sent Paul a letter informing him he was discharged for refusing to take the November 30 test.

Procedural Background. Following his discharge, Paul applied for unemployment compensation benefits with the Alaska State Department of Labor (DOL). DOL initially denied Paul benefits for the period of December 12, 1982 through January 22, 1983 on the ground that his refusal to take the urinalysis test was misconduct under AS 23.30.379(a). Paul appealed that decision and on January 27, 1983, the DOL hearing officer concluded that the drug re-test requirement was unreasonable. On that basis, the hearing officer held that Paul's dismissal was not for misconduct. Nabors appealed to the Commissioner of Labor, who sustained the decision of the appeals tribunal.

Paul initiated this civil action in November 1983. He asserted claims for wrongful dismissal, breach of contract, invasion of privacy, and defamation. Nabors moved for and was granted summary judgment on the invasion of privacy claim, on both the constitutional and common law tort theories. Prior to trial Paul voluntarily dismissed his defamation claim. The trial court, in a non-jury trial, held for Nabors on Paul's wrongful dismissal and breach of contract claims.

Paul appeals the trial court's rulings with regard to his wrongful dismissal, breach of contract, and invasion of privacy claims.

Clarence's Case

Factual Background. Clarence has had seasonal employment with Nabors, working on drilling rigs, since the winter of 1977–78. Prior to beginning his first period of employment, he completed an employment application which provided for a probationary period.

In November 1982 Clarence became subject to the Nabors drug use and testing policy. In mid-November a list of persons scheduled for drug screening was posted at Clarence's rig. His name was on the list. The people listed were required to complete the test during their next "R & R" period. During that next "R & R" period Clarence decided he would not submit to the testing and informed Nabors of his decision.

Nabors offered to allow Clarence time to "clean up" but Clarence refused, insisting that he thought he could pass the test, but was refusing as "a matter of principle." At that point Nabors fired Clarence. The drug test that would have been performed on Clarence was the same as that performed on Paul.

Procedural Background. Following his discharge Clarence also sought unemployment compensation benefits with the DOL. Nabors objected because it believed his refusal to submit to the drug test was misconduct under AS 23.20.379(a). After a factual hearing and two appeals, the Commissioner of Labor found that "Nabors has not shown that there is any connection between off-the-job drug use and on-the-job performance." Thus, there was no showing that Nabors' test policy was related to job misconduct. Furthermore, the Commissioner adopted factual findings that 1) no evidence had been submitted by Nabors linking off-duty drug use with on-the-job accidents, and 2) Nabors was not alleging any drug use by Clarence.

Clarence filed his complaint in this case in November 1984. He alleged invasion of privacy, both at common law and under the Alaska Constitution, wrongful termination, breach of contract, and violation of the implied covenant of good faith and fair dealing. The trial court granted summary judgment in favor of Nabors on all of Clarence's claims. No opinion, findings of fact or conclusions of law were entered.

Clarence appeals the award of summary judgment on all counts.

DISCUSSION

The Right to Privacy

The right to privacy is a recent creation of American law. The inception of this right is generally credited to a law review article published in 1890 by Louis Brandeis and his law partner, Samuel Warren. Brandeis & Warren, *The Right to Privacy,* 4 Harv.L.Rev. 193 (1890). Brandeis and Warren observed that in a modern world with increasing population density and advancing technology, the number and types of matters theretofore easily concealed from public purview were rapidly decreasing. They wrote:

> Recent inventions and business methods call attention to the next step which must be taken for the protection of the person, and for securing to the individual what Judge Cooley calls the right "to be let alone." Instantaneous photographs and newspaper enterprise have invaded the sacred precincts of private and domestic life; and numerous mechanical devices threaten to make good the prediction that "what is whispered in the closet shall be proclaimed from the housetops."

Id. at 195 (footnotes omitted). Discussing the few precedential cases in tort law in which courts had afforded remedies for the publication of private letters or unauthorized photographs, Brandeis and Warren drew a common thread they called "privacy." They defined this right as the principle of "inviolate personality." *Id.* at 205.

While the legal grounds of this right were somewhat tenuous in the 1890's, American jurists found the logic of Brandeis and Warren's arguments compelling. The reporters of the first Restatement of Torts included a tort entitled "Interference with Privacy." By 1960, Professor Prosser could write that "the right of privacy, in one form or another, is declared to exist by the overwhelming majority of the American courts." . . . He cited cases in which private parties had been held liable in tort for eavesdropping on private conversations by means of wiretapping and microphones, or for peering into the windows of homes. In addition, while Brandeis and Warren were mainly concerned with the publication of private facts, Professor Prosser identified four different manifestations of the right to privacy: intrusion upon the plaintiff's seclusion; public disclosure of embarrassing private facts; publicity which places the plaintiff in a false light; and appropriation, for the defendant's pecuniary advantage of the plaintiff's name or likeness. Professor Prosser's categories form the framework of the expanded tort of invasion of privacy found in the Restatement (Second) of Torts.

Eventually the right to privacy attained sufficient recognition to be incorporated in several state constitutions. Alaska (adopted 1972); Cal. (adopted 1972); Haw. (adopted 1978); Mont. (adopted 1972).

Interpreting the Constitution of the United States, the United States Supreme Court in 1965 held that a Connecticut statute banning the use of birth control devices by married couples was "repulsive to the notions of privacy surrounding the marriage relationship." . . . The Supreme Court wrote that "specific guarantees in the Bill of Rights have penumbras, formed by emanations from those guarantees that help give them life and substance. Various guarantees create zones of privacy." . . . Justice Goldberg's concurrence suggested that the right of marital privacy was fundamental to the concept of liberty. . . . Since *Griswold* the Supreme Court has found the federal constitutional right of privacy to apply to a number of other situations. . . .

In this case the plaintiffs seek to fit their cases within at least one of four legal frameworks in which the right to privacy has found expression: constitutional law, contract law, tort law, and the emerging mixture of theories known as the public policy exception to the at-will doctrine of employment law.

The Right to Privacy Under the Alaska Constitution

The Alaska Constitution was amended in 1972 to add the following section:

Right of Privacy. The right of the people to privacy is recognized and shall not be infringed. The legislature shall implement this section.

We observe initially that this provision, powerful as a constitutional statement of citizens' rights, contains no guidelines for its application. Nor does it appear that the legislature has exercised its power to apply the provision; the parties did not bring to our attention any statutes which "implement this section."

The Luedtkes argue that this court has never clearly answered the question of whether article I, section 22 applies only to state action or whether it also governs private action. The Luedtkes urge this court to hold that section 22 governs private action. This question was broached in *Allred v. State*. In *Allred* this court was faced with the question of whether a psychotherapist-patient privilege exists in Alaska. We found the privilege in the common law rather than under the constitutional right to privacy:

> Since it is apparent that [the psychotherapist] was not a police agent, we do not perceive any state action that would trigger the constitutional privacy guarantees. . . .

Our dictum in *Allred* comports with traditional constitutional analysis holding that the constitution serves as a check on the power of government: "That all lawful power derives from the people and must be held in check to preserve their freedom is the oldest and most central tenet of American constitutionalism." L. Tribe, *American Constitutional Law.* In the same vein, we have written in regard to Alaska's constitutional right to privacy: "[T]he primary purpose of these constitutional provisions is the protection of 'personal privacy and dignity against unwarranted intrusions by the State.'" . . .

[1] The parties in the case at bar have failed to produce evidence that Alaska's constitutional right to privacy was intended to operate as a bar to private action, here Nabors' drug testing program. Absent a history demonstrating that the amendment was intended to proscribe private action, or a proscription of private action in the language of the amendment itself, we decline to extend the constitutional right to privacy to the actions of private parties.

Wrongful Termination

[2] In *Mitford v. de LaSala*, this court held that at-will employment contracts in Alaska contain an implied covenant of good faith and fair dealing. In *Knight v. American Guard & Alert, Inc.* (Alaska 1986), we acknowledged that violation of a public policy could constitute a breach of that implied covenant. We wrote:

> The [plaintiff's] claim, concerning alleged termination in violation of public policy, is in accord with a theory of recovery accepted in many states. We have never rejected the public policy theory. Indeed, it seems that the public policy approach is largely encompassed within the implied covenant of good faith and fair dealing which we accepted in *Mitford.*

We conclude that there is a public policy supporting the protection of employee privacy. Violation of that policy by an employer may rise to the level of a breach of the implied covenant of good faith and fair dealing. However, the competing public concern for employee safety present in the case at bar leads us to hold that Nabors' actions did not breach the implied covenant.

The Luedtkes Were At-Will Employees. [3, 4] First, we address the Luedtkes' arguments that they were not at-will employees, but rather that they could be fired only for good cause. The key difference between these two types of employment is whether the employment contract is for a determinable length of time. Employees hired on an at-will basis can be fired for any reason that does not violate the implied covenant of good faith and fair dealing. However, employees hired for a specific term may not be discharged before the expiration of the term except for good cause. Neither of the Luedtkes had any formal agreements for a specified term, so any such term, if it existed, must be implied.

In *Eales v. Tanana Valley Medical-Surgical Group, Inc.*, 663 P.2d 958 (Alaska 1983), we held that where an employer promised employment that would last until the employee's retirement age, and that age was readily determinable, a contract for a definite duration would be implied. We also held that no additional consideration need be given the employee to create a contract for a definite term.

The Luedtkes' cases are distinguishable from that of the plaintiff in *Eales*. The Luedtkes received benefits, such as medical insurance and participation in a pension or profit sharing plan, which continued as long as they were employed. However, Nabors never gave an indication of a definite duration for their employment, nor a definite endpoint to their employment. Instead, Nabors merely provided benefits consistent with modern employer/employee relations.

There Is a Public Policy Supporting Employee Privacy. The next question we address is whether a public policy exists protecting an employee's right to withhold certain "private" information from his employer. We believe such a policy does exist, and is evidenced in the common law, statutes and constitution of this state. . . .

Alaska law clearly evidences strong support for the public interest in employee privacy.

First, state statutes support the policy that there are private sectors of employee's lives not subject to direct scrutiny by their employers. For example, employers may not require employees to take polygraph tests as a condition of employment. AS 23.10.037. In addition, AS 18.80.200(a) provides:

> It is determined and declared as a matter of legislative finding that discrimination against an inhabitant of the state because of race, religion, color, national origin, age, sex, marital status, changes in marital status, pregnancy, or parenthood is a matter of public concern and that this discrimination not only threatens the rights and privileges of the inhabitants of the state but also menaces the institutions of the state and threatens peace, order, health, safety and general welfare of the state and its inhabitants.

This policy is implemented by AS 18.80.220, which makes it unlawful for employers to inquire into such topics in connection with prospective employment. This statute demonstrates that in Alaska certain subjects are placed outside the consideration of employers in their relations with employees. The protections of AS 18.80.220 are extensive. This statute has been construed to be broader than federal anti-discrimination law. . . . We believe it evidences the legislature's intent to liberally protect employee rights.

Second, as previously noted, Alaska's constitution contains a right to privacy clause. While we have held, *supra*, that this clause does not proscribe the private action at issue, it can be viewed by this court as evidence of a public policy supporting privacy. . . .

Third, there exists a common law right to privacy. The Restatement (Second) of Torts § 652B provides:

> *Intrusion upon Seclusion* One who intentionally intrudes, physically or otherwise, upon the solitude or seclusion of another or his private af-

fairs or concerns, is subject to liability to the other for invasion of his privacy, if the intrusion would be highly offensive to a reasonable person.

While we have not expressly considered the application of this tort in Alaska, we have recognized its existence.

Thus, the citizens' right to be protected against unwarranted intrusions into their private lives has been recognized in the law of Alaska. The constitution protects against governmental intrusion, statutes protect against employer intrusion, and the common law protects against intrusions by other private persons. As a result, there is sufficient evidence to support the conclusion that there exists a public policy protecting spheres of employee conduct into which employers may not intrude. The question then becomes whether employer monitoring of employee drug use outside the work place is such a prohibited intrusion.

The Public Policy Supporting Employee Privacy Must Be Balanced Against the Public Policy Supporting Health and Safety. Since the recent advent of inexpensive urine tests for illicit drugs, most litigation regarding the use of these tests in the employment context has concerned government employees. The testing has been challenged under the proscriptions of federal fourth amendment search and seizure law. This body of law regulates only governmental activity, and as a result is of limited value to the case at bar, which involves private activity. However, the reasoning of the federal courts regarding the intrusiveness of urine testing can illuminate this court's consideration of the extent to which personal privacy is violated by these tests.

In *Capua v. City of Plainfield,* 643 F. Supp. city firefighters sued to enjoin random urinalysis tests conducted by the fire department. The court wrote:

Urine testing involves one of the most private of functions, a function traditionally performed in private, and indeed, usually prohibited in public. The proposed test, in order to ensure its reliability, requires the presence of another when the specimen is created and frequently reveals information about one's health unrelated to the use of drugs. If the tests are positive, it may affect one's employment status and even result in criminal prosecution.

We would be appalled at the spectre of the police spying on employees during their free time and then reporting their activities to their employers. Drug testing is a form of surveillance, albeit a technological one. Nonetheless, it reports on a person's off-duty activities just as surely as someone had been present and watching. It is George Orwell's "Big Brother" Society come to life.

While there is a certain amount of hyperbole in this statement, it does portray the *potential* invasion that the technology of urinalysis makes possible. It is against this potential that the law must guard. Not all courts view urine testing with such skepticism, believing the intrusion justified in contemporary society.

Judge Patrick Higginbotham assumed a more cynical stance in *National Treasury Employees Union v. Von Raab,* observing that there is little difference between the intrusiveness of urine testing and the intrusiveness of other affronts to privacy regularly accepted by individuals today. He wrote:

The precise privacy interest asserted is elusive, and the plaintiffs are, at best, inexact as to just what that privacy interest is. Finding an objectively reasonable expectation of privacy in urine, a waste product, contains inherent contradictions. The district court found such a right of privacy, but, in fairness, plaintiffs do not rest there. Rather, it appears from the plaintiffs' brief that it is the manner of taking the samples that is said to invade privacy, because outer garments in which a false sample might be hidden must be removed and a person of the same sex remains outside a stall while the applicant urinates. Yet, apart from the partial disrobing (apparently not independently challenged) persons using public toilet facilities experience a similar lack of privacy. The right must then be a perceived indignity in the whole process, a perceived affront to personal identity by the presence in the same room of another while engaging in a private body function.

It is suggested that the testing program rests on a generalized lack of trust and not on a developed suspicion of an individual applicant. Necessarily there is a plain implication that an applicant is part of a group that, given the demands of the job, cannot be trusted to be truthful about drug use. The difficulty is that just such distrust, or equally accurate, care, is behind every background check and every security check; indeed the information gained in tests of urine is not different from that disclosed in medical records, for which consent to examine is a routine part of applications for many sensitive government posts. In short, given the practice of testing and background checks required for so many government jobs, whether any expectations of privacy by these job applicants were objectively reasonable is dubious at best. Certainly, to ride with the cops one ought to expect inquiry, and by the surest means, into whether he is a robber.

. . . As Judge Higginbotham observes, society often tolerates intrusions into an individual's privacy under circumstances similar to those present in urinalysis. We find this persuasive. It appears, then, that it is the reason the urinalyis is conducted, and not the conduct of the test, that deserves analysis.

This court discussed, on the one hand, the reasons society protects privacy, and, on the other hand, the reasons society rightfully intrudes on personal privacy in *Ravin v. State*. *Ravin* addressed the issue of whether the state could prohibit the use of marijuana in the home. We held that it could not. We observed that "the right to privacy amendment to the Alaska Constitution cannot be read so as to make the possession or ingestion of marijuana itself a fundamental right." Rather, we "recognized the distinctive nature of the home as a place where the individual's pri-

vacy receives special protection." However, we recognized also that this "fundamental right" was limited to activity which remained in the home. We acknowledged that when an individual leaves his home and interacts with others, competing rights of others collectively and as individuals may take precedence:

> Privacy in the home is a fundamental right, under both the federal and Alaska constitutions. We do not mean by this that a person may do anything at anytime as long as the activity takes place within a person's home. There are two important limitations on this facet of the right to privacy. First, we agree with the Supreme Court of the United States, which has strictly limited the *Stanley* guarantee to possession for purely private, noncommercial use in the home. And secondly, we think this right must yield when it interferes in a serious manner with the health, safety, rights and privileges of others or with the public welfare. No one has an absolute right to do things in the privacy of his own home which will affect himself or others adversely. Indeed, one aspect of a private matter is that it is private, that is, that it does not adversely affect persons beyond the actor, and hence is none of their business. When a matter does affect the public, directly or indirectly, it loses its wholly private character, and can be made to yield when an appropriate public need is demonstrated.

The *Ravin* analysis is analogous to the analysis that should be followed in cases construing the public policy exception to the at-will employment doctrine. That is, there is a sphere of activity in every person's life that is closed to scrutiny by others. The boundaries of that sphere are determined by balancing a person's right to privacy against other public policies, such as "the health, safety, rights and privileges of others." . . .

The Luedtkes claim that whether or not they use marijuana is information within that protected sphere into which their employer, Nabors, may not intrude. We disagree. As we have previously observed, marijuana can impair a person's ability to function normally:

> The short-term physiological effects are relatively undisputed. An immediate slight increase in the pulse, decrease in salivation, and a slight reddening of the eyes are usually noted. There is also impairment of psychomotor control. . . .

We also observe that work on an oil rig can be very dangerous. We have determined numerous cases involving serious injury or death resulting from accidents on oil drilling rigs. In addition, in Paul's case the trial court expressly considered the dangers of work on oil rigs. It found:

> 13. It is extremely important that the driller be drug free in the performance of his tasks in order to insure the immediate safety of the other personnel on the particular drill rig.
> 14. It is extremely important that the driller be drug free in the performance of his tasks in order to insure the safety and protection of the oil field itself and the oil resource contained within it.

[5] Where the public policy supporting the Luedtkes privacy in off-duty activities conflicts with the public policy supporting the protection of the health and safety of other workers, and even the Luedtkes themselves, the health and safety concerns are paramount. As a result, Nabors is justified in determining whether the Luedtkes are possibly impaired on the job by drug usage off the job.

We observe, however, that the employer's prerogative does have limitations.

First, the drug test must be conducted at a time reasonably contemporaneous with the employee's work time. The employer's interest is in monitoring drug use that may directly affect employee performance. The employer's interest is not in the broader police function of discovering and controlling the use of illicit drugs in general society. In the context of this case, Nabors could have tested the Luedtkes immediately prior to their departure for the North Slope, or immediately upon their return from the North Slope when the test could be reasonably certain of detecting drugs consumed there. Further, given Nabors' need to control the oil rig community, Nabors could have tested the Luedtkes at any time they were on the North Slope.

Second, an employee must receive notice of the adoption of a drug testing program. By requiring a test, an employer introduces an additional term of employment. An employee should have notice of the additional term so that he may contest it, refuse to accept it and quit, seek to negotiate its conditions, or prepare for the test so that he will not fail it and thereby suffer sanctions.

[6, 7] These considerations do not apply with regard to the tests both Paul and Clarence refused to take. Paul was given notice of the future tests. He did not take the November 30 test. As a result, Nabors was justified in discharging Paul. Clarence had notice and the opportunity to schedule his test at a reasonable time. However, he refused to take any test. As a result, Nabors was justified in discharging Clarence. Neither discharge violated the implied covenant of good faith and fair dealing. . . .

Common Law Right to Privacy Claims

We recognize that "[t]he [common law] right to be free from harassment and constant intrusion into one's daily affairs is enjoyed by all persons." *Siggelkow v. State*,. . . . As previously discussed, that law is delineated in the Restatement (Second) of Torts § 652B, entitled Intrusion upon Seclusion. That section provides: "One who intentionally intrudes . . . upon the solitude or seclusion of another or his private affairs or concerns, is subject to liability ... if the intrusion would be highly offensive to a reasonable person."

[8, 9] It is true, as the Luedtkes contend, that publication of the facts obtained is not necessary. Instead, the liability is for the offensive intrusion.... However, courts have construed "offensive intrusion" to require either an unreasonable manner of intrusion, or intrusion for an unwarranted purpose.... Paul has failed to show either that the manner or reason for testing his urine was unreasonable. During his physical, he voluntarily gave a urine sample for the purpose of testing. Therefore, he cannot complain that urine testing is "highly offensive." ... Paul can only complain about the purpose of the urine test, that is, to detect drug usage. However, we have held, *supra,* that Nabors was en-

titled to test its employees for drug usage. As a result, the intrusion was not unwarranted. Paul complains additionally that he was not aware his urine would be tested for drug usage. In this regard we observe that Paul was not aware of any of the tests being performed on his urine sample. Nor did he know the ramifications of those tests. But he did know that whatever the results were they would be reported to Nabors. Therefore, his complaint about a particular test is without merit. We conclude that for these reasons Paul could not maintain an action for invasion of privacy with regard to the urinalysis conducted October 19.

As to the urinalyses Paul and Clarence refused to take, we hold that no cause of action for invasion of privacy arises where the intrusion is prevented from taking place....

CASE 1. *A Matter of Principle*

Nancy Smith was hired May 1, 1988, as the associate director of Medical Research at a major pharmaceutical company. The terms of Ms. Smith's employment were not fixed by contract, and as a result she is considered to be an "at-will" employee. Two years later Ms. Smith was promoted to Director of Medical Research Therapeutics, a section that studied nonreproductive drugs.

One of the company's research projects involved the development of loperamide — a liquid treatment for acute and chronic diarrhea to be used by infants, children, and older persons who were unable to take solid medication. The formula contained saccharin in an amount that was 44 times higher than that the Food and Drug Administration

permitted in 12 ounces of an artificially sweetened soft drink. There are, however, no promulgated standards for the use of saccharin in drugs.

The research project team responsible for the development of loperamide unanimously agreed that because of the high saccharin content, the existing formula loperamide was unsuitable for distribution in the United States (apparently the formula was already being distributed in Europe). The team estimated that the development of an alternative formula would take at least three months.

The pharmaceutical's management pressured the team to proceed with the existing formula, and the research project team finally agreed. Nancy Smith maintained her

This case was prepared by Norman E. Bowie on the basis of the appeal decision in *Pierre v. Ortho Pharmaceutical Corporation,* Superior Court of New Jersey, 1979.

opposition to the high saccharin formula and indicated that the Hippocratic Oath prevented her from giving the formula to old people and children. Nancy Smith was the only medical person on the team, and the grounds for her decision was that saccharin was a possible carcinogen. Therefore Nancy Smith was unable to participate in the clinical testing.

Upon learning that she was unwilling to participate in the clinical testing, the management removed her from the project and gave her a demotion. Her demotion was posted, and she was told that management considered her unpromotable. She was charged specifically with being irresponsible, lacking in good judgment, unproductive, and uncooperative with marketing. Nancy Smith had never been criticized by supervisors before. Nancy Smith resigned because she believed she was being punished for refusing to pursue a task she thought unethical.

Questions

1. Was Nancy Smith terminated, or did she resign voluntarily?
2. Should the pharmaceutical's management have the right to terminate Nancy Smith if she refused to participate in the clinical testing?
3. Under the circumstances of her "resignation," should she have the right to sue for reinstatement to her position as Director of Medical Research Therapeutics?
4. If you were the judge in such a court case, how would you rule and on what grounds?

CASE 2.   *Catching a Thief by Honesty Exams*

Employee theft is a serious problem. The American Management Association estimates that as many as 20 percent of the firms that go out of business do so because of employee theft. Since the polygraph or lie detector has been restricted, a number of firms have turned to honesty tests. As described in the *Wall Street Journal,* the tests are given in the employer's office, take about an hour, and are relatively cheap, at $6 to $14 a test. Among the questions on the test are the following: What's your favorite alcoholic drink? Which drugs have you tried? Did you ever make a false insurance claim? Do you blush often? Have you ever gotten really angry at someone for being unfair to you?[1] Let us assume that the questions are statistically correlated with employee theft, that the tests are administered by the test manufacturer, and that persons failing the test are given an opportunity to establish their innocence on other grounds.

Many employees answer the questions openly, and many provide damaging information. As one corporate spokesperson said, "You become amazed at how many people believe it is acceptable conduct to steal just a little bit, maybe 50 cents, maybe a dollar a day."

Nonetheless, the tests have come under severe criticism from some unions, some lawyers, and the American Civil Liberties Union. They criticize many of the questions as non-job-related and as violations of rights of privacy. Others find the use of the tests intimidating.

Case prepared by Norman Bowie. Reprinted by permission.

NOTES

1. Wall Street Journal, August 3, 1981.

Questions

1. Does the honesty test violate an employee's right to privacy? Could a test be devised that didn't?

2. Is the use of honesty tests to curtail theft morally justifiable? Explain.

3. Would your answer to question 2 be any different if the management of the firm used one-way mirrors or "plants" instead of honesty tests to deter employee theft?

4. How would you deter employee theft, and what arguments would you give for the moral acceptability of your plan?

Suggested Supplementary Readings

ARVEY, RICHARD D., and GARY L. RENZ. "Fairness in the Selection of Employees." *Journal of Business Ethics* 11 (May, 1992): 331–40.

BRENKERT, GEORGE. "Freedom, Participation and Corporations: The Issue of Corporate (Economic) Democracy." *Business Ethics Quarterly* 2 (July 1992): 251–69.

BRENKERT, GEORGE. "Privacy, Polygraphs, and Work." *Business and Professional Ethics Journal* 1 (Fall 1981): 19–34.

CASTE, NICHOLAS J. "Drug Testing and Productivity." *Journal of Business Ethics* 11 (April 1992): 301–06.

DALTON, DAN R., and MICHAEL B. METZGER. "'Integrity Testing' for Personnel Selection: An Unsparing Perspective." *Journal of Business Ethics* 12 (February 1993): 147–56.

DANDEKAR, NATALIE. "Can Whistleblowing Be FULLY Legitimated?" *Business and Professional Ethics Journal* 10 (Spring 1991): 89–108.

DE GEORGE, RICHARD. "The Right to Work: Law and Ideology." *Valparaiso University Law Review* 19 (Fall 1984): 15–35.

DESJARDINS, JOSEPH R., and JOHN J. McCALL. "A Defense of Employee Rights." *Journal of Business Ethics* 4 (October 1985): 367–76.

EWIN, R. E. "Corporate Loyalty: Its Objects and Its Grounds." *Journal of Business Ethics* 12 (May 1993): 387–96.

EWING, DAVID W. *Freedom Inside the Organization: Bringing Civil Liberties to the Workplace.* New York: E. P. Dutton, 1977.

EXTEJT, MARIAN M., and WILLIAM N. BOCKANIC. "Issues Surrounding the Theories of Negligent Hiring and Failure to Fire." *Business and Professional Ethics Journal* 8 (Winter 1989): 21–34.

EZORSKY, GERTRUDE, ed. *Moral Rights in the Workplace.* Albany, N.Y.: State University of New York Press, 1987.

FIELDER, JOHN H. "Organizational Loyalty." *Business and Professional Ethics Journal* 11 (Spring 1992): 71–90.

GLAZER, M. P., and P. M. GLAZER. *The Whistle Blowers: Exposing Corruption in Government and Industry.* New York: Basic Books, 1989.

GREENBERGER, DAVID, MARCIA MICELI, and DEBRA COHEN. "Oppositionists and Group Norms: The Reciprocal Influence of Whistleblowers and Co-workers." *Journal of Business Ethics* 6 (October 1987): 527–42.

HANSON, KAREN. "The Demands of Loyalty." *Idealistic Studies* 16 (April 1986): 195–204.

HAUGHEY, JOHN C. "Does Loyalty In the Workplace Have a Future?" *Journal of Business Ethics* 3 (January 1993): 1–16.

HIRSCHMAN, ALBERT. *Exit, Voice and Loyalty.* Cambridge, MA: Harvard University Press, 1970.

KEELEY, MICHAEL, and JILL W. GRAHAM. "Exit, Voice and Ethics." *Journal of Business Ethics* 10 (May 1991): 349–55.

KUPFER, JOSEPH. "Privacy, Autonomy, and Self-Concept." *American Philosophical Quarterly* 24 (January 1987): 81–89.

LEE, BARBARA A. "Something Akin to a Property Right: Protections for Job Security." *Business and Professional Ethics Journal* 8 (Fall 1989): 63–81.

LIPPKE, RICHARD L. "Work, Privacy, and Autonomy." *Public Affairs Quarterly* 3 (April 1989): 41–53.

MAITLAND, IAN. "Rights in the Workplace: A Nozickian Argument." *Journal of Business Ethics* 8 (December 1989): 951–54.

MOORE, JENNIFER. "Drug Testing and Corporate Responsibility: The 'Ought Implies Can' Argument." *Journal of Business Ethics* 8 (April 1989): 279–87.

NADER, RALPH, PETER J. PETKAS, and KATE BLACK-WELL, eds. *Whistle Blowing: The Report of the Conference on Professional Responsibility.* New York: Grossman, 1972.

NEAR, JANEY P., and MARCIA P. MICELI. "Whistle-Blowers in Organizations: Dissidents or Reformers?" *Research in Organizational Behavior* 9 (1987): 321–68.

NIXON, JUDY L., and JUDY F. WEST. "The Ethics of Smoking Policies." *Journal of Business Ethics* 8 (December 1989): 409–14.

PETTIT, PHILIP. "The Paradox of Loyalty." *American Philosophical Quarterly* 25 (April 1988): 163–71.

PFEIFFER, RAYMOND S. "Owing Loyalty to One's Employer", *Journal of Business Ethics* 11 (July 1992): 535–43.

PHILLIPS, MICHAEL J. "Should We Let Employees Contract Away Their Rights Against Arbitrary Discharge?" *Journal of Business Ethics* 13 (April 1994): 233–42.

RUST, MARK. "Drug Testing." *ABA Journal* 1 (November 1986): 51–54.

STIEBER, JACK, and MICHAEL MURRAY. "Protection Against Unjust Discharge: The Need for a Federal Statute." *Journal of Law Review* 16 (Winter 1983): 319–41.

WESTIN, ALAN F., and STEVEN SALISBURY. *Individual Rights in the Corporation: A Reader on Employee Rights.* New York: Pantheon, 1980.

WINSTON, MORTON, E. "Aids, Confidentiality, and the Right to Know." *Public Affairs Quarterly* 2 (April 1988): 91–104.

Chapter Six

————— • —————

Hiring, Firing, and Discriminating

For decades women and minorities were barred from some of the most desirable institutions in North America. Even when declared unconstitutional, discrimination often persisted. This discrimination has led to a widespread demand for effective policies to produce justice for those previously and presently discriminated against. However, policies that establish goals, timetables, and quotas that are intended to ensure more equitable opportunities have provoked controversy. Recent controversy has centered on whether *affirmative action* programs, *reverse discrimination*, and criteria of *comparable worth* are appropriate forms of remedy.

The term *affirmative action* refers to positive steps taken to hire persons from groups previously and presently discriminated against. This term has been used to refer to everything from open advertisement of positions to employment quotas. For over two decades U.S. federal laws have encouraged or required corporations to advertise jobs fairly and to promote the hiring of members of formerly abused groups. As a result, corporate planning has often used employment goals or targeted employment outcomes to eliminate the vestiges of discrimination.

The term *preferential hiring* refers to hiring that gives preference in recruitment and ranking to groups previously and presently affected by discrimination. This preference can be in the form of goals or quotas or in the act of choosing minorities over other candidates having equal credentials.

A powerful symbolic difference exists between a *goal* and a *quota*, although both can be expressed in percentages. Goals are mandated or negotiated targets and timetables, whereas quotas have come to symbolize policies that can result in reverse discrimination, primarily against white males.

THE BASIS OF PREFERENTIAL POLICIES

Affirmative action programs have affected U.S. businesses in profound ways. Consider, for example, the impact of these policies on the Monsanto Chemical Company. In 1971, Monsanto found itself with few black and few female employees. In that same year, the Department of Labor announced that affirmative action would be enforced. In complying, Monsanto tripled the number of minority employees in the next fourteen years, aggressively promoted women and blacks into middle management positions, and eliminated racial hiring patterns in technical and craft positions. Monsanto reported that it achieved these goals without diluting the quality of its employees. The firm has also said that it has no intention of abandoning its affirmative action programs. The program's focus has, however, shifted from *hiring* minorities to *promoting* them within the company.[1]

Such preferential policies are often said to have their foundations in the principle of compensatory justice, which requires that if an injustice has been committed, just compensation or reparation is owed to the injured person(s). Everyone agrees that if an individual has been injured by past discrimination, he or she should be compensated for past injustice. However, controversy has arisen over whether past discrimination against *groups* such as women and minorities justifies compensation for current group members. Critics of group preferential policies hold that only identifiable discrimination against individuals calls for compensation.

Ronald Reagan was the first U.S. President to oppose preferential hiring. He and his successor, George Bush, campaigned against quotas and then sought to roll them back. The Department of Justice was the administration's vanguard, but other government agencies were intimately involved. In 1985, Chairman of the U.S. Civil Rights Commission, Clarence Pendleton, reported to the President his conviction that the Commission had succeeded in making racial and group quotas a "dead issue." He maintained that public controversy over preferential treatment had been replaced with a vision of a color-blind society that is an "opportunity society" rather than a "preference society."[2]

Although the conclusion that quotas are a dead issue is questionable, given current civil rights law and business practice, Pendleton's comment illustrates the split that now exists between two primary, competing positions in U.S. society: (1) that the only means to the end of a color-blind, sex-blind society is preferential treatment and (2) that a color-blind, sex-blind society can be achieved by guaranteeing equal opportunities to all citizens. According to the second position, employers must never use criteria favoring color, sex, or any such irrelevant consideration when hiring or promoting personnel. The goal is to eradicate discrimination, not to perpetuate it through reverse discrimination. These two competing positions agree that compensation is justified for particular victims of discrimination, but they disagree about whether compensation is owed to individuals as members of groups.

The articles in this chapter by Louis Pojman and by philosopher Thomas Nagel address the ethical issues that have emerged from congressional, executive, and judicial conclusions about the moral and legal responsibilities of businesses to eradicate discrimination. A major moral issue is whether preferential policies requiring that preference be given to minority candidates over otherwise better qualified white males is a justified instance of compensatory justice or a form of unjust discrimination. The dispute centers on whether such practices of preferential treatment are either (1) just, (2) unjust, or (3) not just, but still permissible.

1. Those who claim that such compensatory measures are just, or are required by justice, argue that past discrimination persists in the present. Blacks who were victims of past discrimination are still handicapped or discriminated against, whereas the families of past slave owners are still being unduly enriched by inheritance laws. Those who have inherited wealth accumulated by iniquitous practices have no more right to their wealth than the sons of slaves, who have some claim to it as a matter of compensation. In the case of women, the argument is that our culture is structured to equip them with a lack of self-confidence, that it prejudicially excludes them from much of the workforce, and that it treats them as a low-paid auxiliary labor unit. Consequently, only highly independent women can be expected to compete with males on initially fair terms. A slightly stronger argument is that compensation is fair because it is owed to those who have suffered unjust treatment. For example, if veterans are owed preferential treatment because of their service and sacrifice to country, blacks and women are owed preferential treatment because of their economic sacrifices, systematic incapacitation, and consequent family and group losses.

2. Those who claim that group compensatory measures are unjust argue that no criteria exist for measuring just compensation, that employment discrimination in society is presently minor and controllable, and that those harmed by past discrimination are no longer alive to be compensated. Instead of providing compensation, they argue, strict equality as well as merit hiring and promotion should be enforced, while attacking the roots of discrimination. Also, some now successful but once underprivileged minority groups argue that their long struggle for equality is being jeopardized by programs of "favoritism" to blacks and women.

3. The third view is that some compensatory measures are not just because they violate principles of justice, but are still justifiable by moral principles other than justice. Nagel, a proponent of this view, argues that "there is an element of individual unfairness" in strong affirmative action plans, but these plans are justified as a means to the end of eradicating an intolerable social situation. Tom L. Beauchamp argues that even some forms of reverse discrimination can be justified as a means to the end of a nondiscriminatory society.

THE PROBLEM OF REVERSE DISCRIMINATION

The U.S. Supreme Court has held that federal law permits private employers to create plans that favor groups traditionally discriminated against. The moral justification, if any, for such plans and the acceptability of any reverse discrimination created by the plans, however, remain controversial.

Among writers who support policies even when they permit reverse discrimination, a mainline approach has been to argue that under certain conditions compensation owed for past wrongs justifies present policies that produce reverse discrimination. Beauchamp does not employ this argument that compensation is owed to classes for *past* wrongs; instead, he maintains that reverse discrimination is permissible to eliminate or alleviate *present* discriminatory practices that affect whole classes of persons (especially practices of minority exclusion). He introduces factual evidence for his claim that invidious discrimination is pervasive in society. Because discrimination now prevails, Beauchamp contends that policies that may eventuate in reverse discrimination are unavoidable in reaching the end of eliminating ongoing discrimination.

Opponents of this position argue that reverse discrimination violates fundamental, overriding principles of justice and cannot be justified. As Pojman points out in his essay, there exist quite a variety of arguments in opposition to both affirmative action and reverse discrimination. Arguments that have received widespread attention include the following: (1) Some persons who are not responsible for the past discrimination (for example, qualified young white males) pay the price; preferential treatment is invidiously discriminatory because innocent persons are penalized solely on the basis of their race or sex. (2) Male members of minority groups such as Polish, Irish, Arabic, Chinese, and Italian members of society — who were previously discriminated against — inevitably will bear a heavy and unfair burden of compensating women and other minority groups. (3) Many individual members of any class selected for preferential treatment never have been unjustly treated and therefore do not deserve preferential policies. (4) Compensation can be provided to individuals who were previously treated unfairly without resorting to reverse discrimination.

As the court cases in this chapter indicate, the problems associated with preferential and discriminatory hiring are surprisingly complicated. In three cases decided in the late 1980s, the Supreme Court supported the permissibility of specific numerical goals in affirmative action plans that are intended to combat a manifest imbalance in traditionally segregated job categories (even if the particular workers drawn from minorities were not victims of past discrimination). In *Local 28 v. Equal Employment Opportunity Commission,* otherwise known as *Sheet Metal Workers,* a specific minority hiring goal of 29.23 percent had been established. The Court held that quotas involved in the 29 percent goal are justified when dealing with persistent or egregious discrimination. The Supreme Court held that the history of Local 28 was one of complete "foot-dragging resistance" to the idea of hiring without discrimination in their apprenticeship training programs from minority groups. The Court argued that

> even where the employer or union formally ceases to engage in discrimination, informal mechanisms may obstruct equal employment opportunities. An employer's reputation for discrimination may discourage minorities from seeking available employment. In these circumstances, affirmative race-conscious relief may be the only means available to assure equality of employment opportunities and to eliminate those discriminatory practices and devices which have fostered racially stratified job environments to the disadvantage of minority citizens.

However, in a 1989 opinion also included in this chapter, the Supreme Court held in *City of Richmond v. J. A. Croson* that Richmond, Virginia, officials could not require contractors to set aside 30 percent of their budget for subcontractors who owned "minority business enterprises." The Court held that this plan did not exhibit sufficient government interest to justify the plan and that the plan was not written to remedy the effects of prior discrimination. The Court found that this way of fixing a percentage based on race, in the absence of evidence of identified past discrimination, denied citizens an equal opportunity to compete for the subcontracts. Parts of the reasoning in *Croson* were affirmed in the 1995 case of *Adarand Constructors Inc. v. Pena.* Two concurring opinions by Justices Scalia and Thomas, both firmly opposed to reverse discrimination, are also reprinted in this chapter.

Some writers have interpreted *Croson, Adarand,* and other recent cases as the dismantling of affirmative action, specifically all affirmative action plans that contain specific numerical goals. Other readers of these cases, however, find a continuation of the Supreme Court's long line of vigorous defenses of minority rights and the protection of those rights, including the implementation of the rights in corporate policies. As important as these cases are, no comprehensive criteria have yet been established for legally valid affirmative action plans.

COMPARABLE WORTH

The slogan "equal pay for equal work" has been at the center of discussions about workplace discrimination, and the gap between men's and women's pay has been the major issue. *Comparable worth* refers to comparable pay for work of comparable value. This notion is used to refer to several principles that persons should be paid on an identical scale for jobs requiring the same competence, education, effort, stress, and responsibility. Laurie Shrage, Jennifer M. Quinn, and Robert Simon discuss these principles in this chapter as attempts to grasp the justice and implications of the idea of "comparable pay for comparable worth." They link the issues to gender discrimination, class interests, and liberal and conservative philosophies, with a particular emphasis on whether there is a need to reorganize society to achieve a more equitable wage structure. (See Chapter 9 for issues of social justice and fair wages.)

The term *comparable worth* continues to be unpopular in the corporate environment, because adjusting pay scales to eliminate discrimination undercuts setting pay scales according to free market values. In the corporate world, rating scales and employment practices modeled on the idea of comparable pay are typically referred to as schemes of "pay equity" or "internal equity," rather than comparable worth.

Federal law in the United States holds that workers in the same job cannot be paid differently merely because of race or sex. The Equal Pay Act of 1963 specifies that employers must pay employees the same wages for equal work in jobs requiring equal skill, effort, and responsibility. However, a pay differential may be permissible if based on merit, seniority, or the quality or quantity of production. Few would dispute these premises, but the principle of comparable worth extends beyond the notions of "same job" and "equal work" to "jobs of the same value." For example, San Francisco's Amfac Corp. hired a consultant to ensure that their "french-fry cooker in Portland is paid the same as [their] sugar-cane worker in Hawaii,"[3] under the assumption that their jobs are of the same value to the corporation.

Comparable worth is based on the idea that traditionally male positions, such as miner and truck driver, can be rated comparably to traditionally female positions, such as secretary or nurse. Any unjustified differential in pay can be reduced or eliminated. The goal is to pay women and others who may have been discriminated against according to their responsibilities, experience, contributions, and training. Jobs that are equal in value with respect to these characteristics are to be considered identical in value, despite the fact that women and minorities in these positions have typically been paid less than men. Comparable-worth advocates believe that a system that values such work less is discriminatory.

In the mid-1980s, the U.S. Civil Rights Commission adopted a report that urged federal agencies to reject the principle of comparable worth. The Commission's chairman once called the principle of comparable worth "the looniest idea since 'Looney Tunes' came on the screen." The Commission held that employers should be held accountable for individual discriminatory acts and policies but be required to combat social attitudes or to alter industry-preferred forms of evaluating the worth of jobs. Two months later the Equal Employment Opportunity Commission unanimously adopted the principle that federal law does not require comparable worth and that factual differences in pay scales are no grounds for asserting discrimination. Shortly thereafter, the Justice Department filed its first "friend-of-the-court" brief in a comparable-worth case and sided with the state of Illinois in a case in which nurses were seeking higher pay on comparable-worth grounds. In this context, the Justice Department argued that the comparable-worth theory made "a mockery of the ideal of pay equity" and would necessarily depend on "subjective evaluations" by those who made judgments of comparability.[4]

Part of this dispute is conceptual. As the authors in this chapter note, there are different meanings attached to "comparable worth" and to the principles that implement it. The Reagan administration defined *comparable worth* as requiring that all jobs of the same value to society be paid equally. This interpretation required a wholesale restructuring of wage scales and was therefore judged extremely difficult to implement. However, many who favor comparable worth and believe it can be implemented use a different definition based on the idea of pay equity, as specified in the Equal Pay Act of 1963: All differentials in wages must be justified by nondiscriminatory and relevant considerations such as seniority, merit pay, skills, and stress.

Corporate America has typically taken a negative view of comparable worth in its public statements, as have the *Wall Street Journal's* editors, the U.S. Chamber of Commerce, and the National Association of Manufacturers, among others. This skepticism may, in part, stem from the conceptual confusion over the definition of *comparable worth*. But there are other problems as well. Opponents of comparable worth argue that it cannot be implemented because it is beyond the experts' capacity to determine objective values for different jobs. They claim that its enforcement would require massive federal intervention, even if it could be implemented. In addition, comparable worth invites exorbitant contract disputes and unending litigation, disturbs the flexibility and diversity in hiring and promotion that is essential to a free market, and neglects the facts that women have less work experience, less seniority, and a lower rate of unionization.

Proponents of comparable worth believe the principle itself is an essential tool needed to eliminate the systematic undervaluation of women's contributions. Proponents additionally argue that policies of comparable worth are essential to fairness. Policies can be implemented and structured along the lines of models already being used in traditional job-analysis and job-evaluation processes. Proponents point out that corporations have tried to implement "equal value to the company" by using ratings, pay scales, job-evaluation systems, and so forth. Management has furthered this attempt by using market-wage survey techniques. From this perspective, comparable worth expresses the need for a unified system of job evaluation that measures the relative value of all positions in the corporation. It also introduces a broader element of fairness into employment practices and reduces or possibly eliminates institutionalized systems of injustice. Proponents often admit that unfairness cannot be completely eliminated, but they insist that unfairnesses can be carefully monitored.

Implementation of comparable-worth criteria has been particularly controversial. Presumably implementation can proceed by (1) negotiation at the bargaining table, (2) internal development at corporations, and (3) external imposition by governments. All three means are currently under discussion and experiment. The first approach to comparable worth has been heavily promoted by the American Federation of State, County, and Municipal Employees (AFSCME), which won impressive precedential comparable-worth pay adjustments in Chicago, Los Angeles, Iowa, Minnesota, Wisconsin, New York, and Connecticut. These changes were achieved by labor negotiation, not court battles.

Some corporations have begun to develop programs of comparable worth. For example, major corporations such as AT&T, BankAmerica, Chase Manhattan, IBM, Motorola, and Tektronix have introduced systems of job comparisons that will allow the cross-job evaluations essential for comparable worth. In these systems, factors that express a job's "worth" — years of education, degree of responsibility, necessary skill, amount of noise in the work environment, and physical labor — are rated on a point scale. Jobs with equal points are to be compensated equally. For example, AT&T worked with its unions to devise a plan in which fourteen measurements were adopted to evaluate by point ratings such factors as keyboard skills, job stress, and abilities to communicate.[5]

A similar set of potentially revolutionary changes that would be externally imposed on corporations are under scrutiny in several state legislatures, but these developments have slowed in recent years. Minnesota was the first to adopt such a plan for state employees. The U.S. federal government has been largely uninterested. Meanwhile, other countries have been more aggressive. Canada enacted a comparable-worth law that covers all workers under federal jurisdiction, and in

Great Britain a similar law was imposed on an unwilling Prime Minister. A comparison between Canada (Ontario), the United States, and Great Britain is found in this chapter in the essay by Quinn.

THE PROBLEM OF SEXUAL HARASSMENT

Among the oldest forms of discrimination in the workplace, but one of the newest in business ethics and U.S. courts, is sexual harassment. Statistics on its prevalence are somewhat unreliable, but studies and surveys suggest that between 15 percent and 65 percent of working women encounter some form of sexual harassment, depending on type of job, workforce, location, and the like. Studies also indicate an increase of sexual harassment complaints during the past decade. The landmark U.S. Supreme Court case of *Meritor Savings Bank v. Vinson* (reprinted in this chapter) was decided in 1986. This case cited a wide range of activities in the workplace as constituting sexual harassment under Title VII of the Civil Rights Act of 1964. The case has significantly impacted discussions of workplace discrimination and the development of corporate policies to police it.

The most widespread form of sexual harassment now seems to be offensive sexual innuendo and suggestion that generate embarrassment and anger, rather than coercive threats demanding sexual favors or physical abuse. Some studies suggest that sexual harassment has recently become less overt but not less commonplace. Forms of sexual harassment that condition a job or promotion on sexual favors have declined, but an increase has occurred in unwanted sexual advances such as straightforward propositions, offensive posters, degrading comments, kisses and caresses, improper joking and teasing, and the like.

Men and women often have different views of what constitutes an unwelcome sexual advance, comment, or environment. However, in *Meritor,* the Supreme Court extended protections against sexual harassment beyond circumstances of asking for sexual favors to any form of offensive remark and sexual conduct that creates a hostile working environment.

Establishing precise definition of *sexual harassment* has proved difficult. The centerpiece of many definitions has been how to take account of persistent behavior involving unwelcome sexual remarks, advances, or requests that negatively affects working conditions and put these behaviors in the form of a definition. The conduct need not involve making a sexual favor a condition of employment or promotion, and it need not be imposed on persons who are in no position to resist the conduct. Even someone who is in a strong position to resist the approach can be sexually harassed. Derogatory gestures, offensive touching, and leering can affect workers' performance and create a sense that the workplace is inhospitable, irrespective of their ability to resist. The conduct need not be "sexual" in a narrow sense or even sexually motivated. For example, the conduct can be gender-specific, involving demeaning remarks about, for example, how women underperform in their job assignments.

Before *Meritor,* sexual harassment was often thought to involve attempted coercion: a threat the person approached could not reasonably resist. In the typical case, a person's job or promotion was conditioned on performing a sexual favor. However, after *Meritor,* it has been widely agreed that many forms of sexual harassment do not involve an irresistible threat and are not coercive. In this chapter, Edmund Wall and Vaughana Feary discuss the broad array of meanings and types of sexual harassment. They take an especially careful look at the complicated questions that surround the problems of defining the term and of limiting its scope so that it is neither too narrow nor too broad. Wall argues that sexual harassment cannot be understood in terms of types of behavior, because everyone must understand how a form of communication violates a person's privacy rights. Significant parts of his definition are challenged in Feary's wide-ranging article.

The notion of causing or allowing a "hostile working environment" has been at the forefront of recent attempts in government and law to define "sexual harassment," but it has proved difficult to define both terms so that they are not overly broad. What makes for a hostile or intimidating workplace? Do teasing and denigrating remarks count? What is it to denigrate? Which forms of conduct overstep the bounds of being friendly and humorous? Employees in some corporations have complained that corporate policies are written so that asking someone out for a drink after work or expressing sexual humor can easily be construed as unwelcome conduct that creates a hostile working environment.

Standards of offensive or unwelcome sexual behavior have been as difficult to formulate as definitions. The "reasonable person" standard of what counts as offensive or unwelcome has been replaced in some courts with a "reasonable woman" standard that tries to determine whether a male's comments or advances directed toward a woman would be considered offensive by taking the reasonable woman's point of view rather than the reasonable person's point of view. This shift from a gender-neutral standard should make it easier for women to file lawsuits successfully, because men might not find offensive what a woman would. However, if one takes the view, as many now do, that harassment is in large measure a matter of how the individual feels when approached by another person, then the standard of the reasonable woman will be too weak. The standard would have to be whether *this person* finds conduct offensive, not whether *the reasonable woman* so finds it. Although the law is not likely to move in the direction of a subjective standard, ethics literature is increasingly moving in that direction.

Efforts to remove sexual harassment from the corporate workplace appear to have increased since the 1986 *Meritor* decision and the well-known testimony by Anita Hill, although there is controversy about how seriously to take the increased interest. Many major corporations now have some form of training and grievance policies. Corporations with sexual harassment policies for all management levels report that unwelcome comments and touching have declined significantly after initiating the policies. One reason for increased corporate interest is that corporations have been held legally liable for the behavior of their supervisors, even when corporate officials above the supervisors were unaware of the behavior. Although these lawsuits and corporate policies have made corporations more sensitive to the issues, little evidence exists that top executives have given urgent priority to the improvement and enforcement of sexual harassment policies.

NOTES

1. Aric Press, and others, "The New Rights War," *Newsweek,* December 30, 1985, pp. 66–69.
2. Juan Williams, "Quotas Are a 'Dead Issue,' Rights Panel Chairman Says," *Washington Post,* January 30, 1985, p. A2.
3. "Labor Letter," *Wall Street Journal,* April 16, 1985, p. 1, col. 5.
4. Brief filed with the 7th U.S. Circuit Court of Appeals in Chicago. See Los Angeles Times Service, "U.S. Court Brief Assails 'Comparable Worth' Pay," *International Herald Tribune,* August 19, 1985, p. 3.
5. Cathy Trost, "Pay Equity, Born in Public Sector, Emerges as an Issue in Private Firms," *Wall Street Journal,* July 8, 1985, p. 15.

A Defense of Affirmative Action

Thomas Nagel

The term "affirmative action" has changed in meaning since it was first introduced. Originally it referred only to special efforts to ensure equal opportunity for members of groups that had been subject to discrimination. These efforts included public advertisement of positions to be filled, active recruitment of qualified applicants from the formerly excluded groups, and special training programs to help them meet the standards for admission or appointment. There was also close attention to procedures of appointment, and sometimes to the results, with a view to detecting continued discrimination, conscious or unconscious.

More recently the term has come to refer also to some degree of definite preference for members of these groups in determining access to positions from which they were formerly excluded. Such preference might be allowed to influence decisions only between candidates who are otherwise equally qualified, but usually it involves the selection of women or minority members over other candidates who are better qualified for the position.

Let me call the first sort of policy "weak affirmative action" and the second "strong affirmative action." It is important to distinguish them, because the distinction is sometimes blurred in practice. It is strong affirmative action — the policy of preference — that arouses controversy. Most people would agree that weak or precautionary affirmative action is a good thing, and worth its cost in time and energy. But this does not imply that strong affirmative action is also justified.

I shall claim that in the present state of things it is justified, most clearly with respect

---

Testimony before the Subcommittee on the Constitution of the Senate Judiciary Committee, June 18, 1981. Reprinted by permission of Professor Nagel.

to blacks. But I also believe that a defender of the practice must acknowledge that there are serious arguments against it, and that it is defensible only because the arguments for it have great weight. Moral opinion in this country is sharply divided over the issue because significant values are involved on both sides. My own view is that while strong affirmative action is intrinsically undesirable, it is a legitimate and perhaps indispensable method of pursuing a goal so important to the national welfare that it can be justified as a temporary, though not short-term, policy for both public and private institutions. In this respect it is like other policies that impose burdens on some for the public good.

THREE OBJECTIONS

I shall begin with the argument against. There are three objections to strong affirmative action: that it is inefficient; that it is unfair; and that it damages self-esteem.

The degree of inefficiency depends on how strong a role racial or sexual preference plays in the process of selection. Among candidates meeting the basic qualifications for a position, those better qualified will on the average perform better, whether they are doctors, policemen, teachers, or electricians. There may be some cases, as in preferential college admissions, where the immediate usefulness of making educational resources available to an individual is thought to be greater because of the use to which the education will be put or because of the internal effects on the institution itself. But by and large, policies of strong affirmative action must reckon with the costs of some lowering in performance level: the stronger the preference, the larger the cost to be justified. Since both the costs and the value of the results will vary from case to case, this suggests that no one policy of affirmative action is likely to be

correct in all cases, and that the cost in performance level should be taken into account in the design of a legitimate policy.

The charge of unfairness arouses the deepest disagreements. To be passed over because of membership in a group one was born into, where this has nothing to do with one's individual qualifications for a position, can arouse strong feelings of resentment. It is a departure from the ideal — one of the values finally recognized in our society — that people should be judged so far as possible on the basis of individual characteristics rather than involuntary group membership.

This does not mean that strong affirmative action is morally repugnant in the manner of racial or sexual discrimination. It is nothing like those practices, for though like them it employs race and sex as criteria of selection, it does so for entirely different reasons. Racial and sexual discrimination are based on contempt or even loathing for the excluded group, a feeling that certain contacts with them are degrading to members of the dominant group, that they are fit only for subordinate positions or menial work. Strong affirmative action involves none of this: it is simply a means of increasing the social and economic strength of formerly victimized groups, and does not stigmatize others.

There is an element of individual unfairness here, but it is more like the unfairness of conscription in wartime, or of property condemnation under the right of eminent domain. Those who benefit or lose out because of their race or sex cannot be said to deserve their good or bad fortune.

It might be said on the other side that the beneficiaries of affirmative action deserve it as compensation for past discrimination, and that compensation is rightly exacted from the group that has benefited from discrimination in the past. But this is a bad argument, because as the practice usually works, no effort is made to give preference to those who have suffered most from discrimination, or to prefer them especially to those who have benefited most from it, or been guilty of it. Only candidates who in other qualifications fall on one or other side of the margin of decision will directly benefit or lose from the policy, and these are not necessarily, or even probably, the ones who especially deserve it. Women or blacks who don't have the qualifications even to be considered are likely to have been handicapped more by the effects of discrimination than those who receive preference. And the marginal white male candidate who is turned down can evoke our sympathy if he asks, "Why me?" (A policy of explicitly *compensatory* preference, which took into account each individual's background of poverty and discrimination, would escape some of these objections, and it has its defenders, but it is not the policy I want to defend. Whatever its merits, it will not serve the same purpose as direct affirmative action.)

The third objection concerns self-esteem, and is particularly serious. While strong affirmative action is in effect, and generally known to be so, no one in an affirmative action category who gets a desirable job or is admitted to a selective university can be sure that he or she has not benefited from the policy. Even those who would have made it anyway fall under suspicion, from themselves and from others: it comes to be widely felt that success does not mean the same thing for women and minorities. This painful damage to esteem cannot be avoided. It should make any defender of strong affirmative action want the practice to end as soon as it has achieved its basic purpose.

JUSTIFYING AFFIRMATIVE ACTION

I have examined these three objections and tried to assess their weight, in order to decide how strong a countervailing reason is needed to justify such a policy. In my view, taken together they imply that strong affirmative action involving significant preference should be undertaken only if it will substantially further a social goal of the first importance. While this condition is not met by all programs of affirmative action now in effect, it is met by those which address the most deep-seated, stubborn, and radically unhealthy divisions in the society, divisions whose removal is a condition of basic justice and social cohesion.

The situation of black people in our country is unique in this respect. For almost a century after the abolition of slavery we had a rigid racial caste system of the ugliest kind, and it only began to break up twenty-five years ago. In the South it was enforced by law, and in the North, in a somewhat less severe form, by social convention. Whites were thought to be defiled by social or residential proximity to blacks, intermarriage was taboo, blacks were denied the same level of public goods — education and legal protection — as whites, were restricted to the most menial occupations, and were barred from any positions of authority over whites. The visceral feeling of black inferiority and untouchability that this system expressed were deeply ingrained in the members of both races, and they continue, not surprisingly, to have their effect. Blacks still form, to a considerable extent, a hereditary social and economic community characterized by widespread poverty, unemployment, and social alienation.

When this society finally got around to moving against the caste system, it might have done no more than to enforce straight equality of opportunity, perhaps with the help of weak affirmative action, and then wait a few hundred years while things gradually got better. Fortunately it decided instead to accelerate the process by both public and private institutional action, because there was wide recognition of the intractable character of the problem posed by this insular minority and its place in the nation's history and collective consciousness. This has not been going on very long, but the results are already impressive, especially in speeding the advancement of blacks into the middle class. Affirmative action has not done much to improve the position of poor and unskilled blacks. That is the most serious part of the problem, and it requires a more direct economic attack. But increased access to higher education and upper-level jobs is an essential part of what must be achieved to break the structure of drastic separation that was left largely undisturbed by the legal abolition of the caste system.

Changes of this kind require a generation or two. My guess is that strong affirmative action for blacks will continue to be justified into the early decades of the next century, but that by then it will have accomplished what it can and will no longer be worth the costs. One point deserves special emphasis. The goal to be pursued is the reduction of a great social injustice, not proportional representation of the races in all institutions and professions. Proportional racial representation is of no value in itself. It is not a legitimate social goal, and it should certainly not be the aim of strong affirmative action, whose drawbacks make it worth adopting only against a serious and intractable social evil.

This implies that the justification for strong affirmative action is much weaker in the case of other racial and ethnic groups, and in the case of women. At least, the practice will be justified in a narrower range of circumstances and for a shorter span of time than it is for blacks. No other group has been treated quite like this, and no other group is in a comparable status. Hispanic-Americans occupy an intermediate position, but it seems to me frankly absurd to include persons of oriental descent as beneficiaries of affirmative action, strong or weak. They are not a se-

verely deprived and excluded minority, and their eligibility serves only to swell the numbers that can be included on affirmative action reports. It also suggests that there is a drift in the policy toward adopting the goal of racial proportional representation for its own sake. This is a foolish mistake, and should be resisted. The only legitimate goal of the policy is to reduce egregious racial stratification.

With respect to women, I believe that except over the short term, and in professions or institutions from which their absence is particularly marked, strong affirmative action is not warranted and weak affirmative action is enough. This is based simply on the expectation that the social and economic situation of women will improve quite rapidly under conditions of full equality of opportunity. Recent progress provides some evidence for this. Women do not form a separate hereditary community, characteristically poor and uneducated, and their position is not likely to be self-perpetuating in the same way as that of an outcast race. The process requires less artificial acceleration, and any need for strong affirmative action for women can be expected to end sooner than it ends for blacks.

I said at the outset that there was a tendency to blur the distinction between weak and strong affirmative action. This occurs especially in the use of numerical quotas, a topic on which I want to comment briefly.

A quota may be a method of either weak or strong affirmative action, depending on the circumstances. It amounts to weak affirmative action — a safeguard against discrimination — if, and only if, there is independent evidence that average qualifications for the positions being filled are no lower in the group to which a minimum quota is being assigned than in the applicant group as a whole. This can be presumed true of unskilled jobs that most people can do, but it becomes less likely, and harder to establish, the greater the skill and education required for the position. At these levels, a quota proportional to population, or even to representation of the group in the applicant pool, is almost certain to amount to strong affirmative action. Moreover it is strong affirmative action of a particularly crude and indiscriminate kind, because it permits no variation in the degree of preference on the basis of costs in efficiency, depending on the qualification gap. For this reason I should defend quotas only where they serve the purpose of weak affirmative action. On the whole, strong affirmative action is better implemented by including group preference as one factor in appointment or admission decisions, and let-

ting the results depend on its interaction with other factors.

I have tried to show that the arguments against strong affirmative action are clearly outweighed at present by the need for exceptional measures to remove the stubborn residues of racial caste. But advocates of the policy should acknowledge the reasons against it, which will ensure its termination when it is no longer necessary. Affirmative action is not an end in itself, but a means of dealing with a social situation that should be intolerable to us all.

The Moral Status of Affirmative Action

Louis P. Pojman

Hardly a week goes by but that the subject of Affirmative Action does not come up. Whether in the guise of reverse discrimination, preferential hiring, non-traditional casting, quotas, goals and time tables, minority scholarships, or race-norming, the issue confronts us as a terribly perplexing problem. . . .

There is something salutary as well as terribly tragic inherent in this problem. The salutary aspect is the fact that our society has shown itself committed to eliminating unjust discrimination. Even in the heart of Dixie there is a recognition of the injustice of racial discrimination. Both sides of the affirmative action debate have good will and appeal to moral principles. Both sides are attempting to bring about a better society, one which is color blind, but they differ profoundly on the morally proper means to accomplish that goal.

And this is just the tragedy of the situation: good people on both sides of the issue are ready to tear each other to pieces over a problem that has no easy or obvious solution. And so the voices become shrill and the rhetoric hyperbolic. The same spirit which divides the pro-choice movement from the right to life movement on abortion divides liberal pro–Affirmative Action advocates from liberal anti–Affirmative Action advocates. This problem, more than any other, threatens to destroy the traditional liberal consensus in our society. I have seen family members and close friends who until recently fought on the same side of the barricades against racial injustice divide in enmity over this issue. The anti-affirmative liberals ("liberals who've been mugged") have tended towards a form of neo-conservatism and the pro-affirmative liberals have tended to side

From Louis P. Pojman, "The Moral Status of Affirmative Action," *Public Affairs Quarterly* 6, 2, April 1992.

with the radical left to form the "politically correct ideology" movement.

In this paper I will confine myself primarily to Affirmative Action policies with regard to race, but much of what I say can be applied to the areas of gender and ethnic minorities.

DEFINITIONS

First let me define my terms:

Discrimination is simply judging one thing to differ from another on the basis of some criterion. "Discrimination" is essentially a good quality, having reference to our ability to make distinctions. As rational and moral agents we need to make proper distinctions. To be rational is to discriminate between good and bad arguments, and to think morally is to discriminate between reasons based on valid principles and those based on invalid ones. What needs to be distinguished is the difference between rational and moral discrimination, on the one hand, and irrational and immoral discrimination, on the other hand.

Prejudice is a discrimination based on irrelevant grounds. It may simply be an attitude which never surfaces in action, or it may cause prejudicial actions. A prejudicial discrimination in action is immoral if it denies someone a fair deal. . . .

Equal Opportunity is offering everyone a fair chance at the best positions that society has at its disposal. Only native aptitude and effort should be decisive in the outcome, not factors of race, sex or special favors.

Affirmative Action is the effort to rectify the injustice of the past by special policies. Put this way, it is Janus-faced or ambiguous, having both a backward-looking and a forward-looking feature. The backward-looking feature is its attempt to correct and compensate for past injustice. This aspect of Affirmative

Action is strictly deontological. The forward-looking feature is its implicit ideal of a society free from prejudice; this is both deontological and utilitarian. . . .

It is also useful to distinguish two versions of Affirmative Action. *Weak Affirmative Action* involves such measures as the elimination of segregation(namely the idea of "separate but equal"), widespread advertisement to groups not previously represented in certain privileged positions, special scholarships for the disadvantaged classes (e.g., all the poor), using underrepresentation or a history of past discrimination as a tie breaker when candidates are relatively equal, and the like.

Strong Affirmative Action involves more positive steps to eliminate past injustice, such as reverse discrimination, hiring candidates on the basis of race and gender in order to reach equal or near equal results, proportionate representation in each area of society. . . . [1]

ARGUMENTS AGAINST AFFIRMATIVE ACTION

1. Affirmative Action Requires Discrimination Against a Different Group

Weak Affirmative Action weakly discriminates against new minorities, mostly innocent young white males, and Strong Affirmative Action strongly discriminates against these new minorities. . . . This discrimination is unwarranted, since, even if some compensation to blacks were indicated, it would be unfair to make innocent white males bear the whole brunt of the payments. In fact, it is poor white youth who become the new pariahs on the job market. The children of the wealthy have no trouble getting into the best private grammar schools and, on the basis of superior early education, into the best universities, graduate schools, managerial and professional positions. Affirmative Action simply shifts injustice, setting blacks and women against young white males, especially ethnic and poor white males. It does little to rectify the goal of providing equal opportunity to all. If the goal is a society where everyone has a fair chance, then it would be better to concentrate on support for families and early education and decide the matter of university admissions and job hiring on the basis of traditional standards of competence.

2. Affirmative Action Perpetuates the Victimization Syndrome

Shelby Steele admits that Affirmative Action may seem "the meagerest recompense for centuries of unrelieved oppression" and that it helps promote diversity. At the same time, though, notes Steele, Affirmative Action reinforces the spirit of victimization by telling blacks that they can gain more by emphasizing their suffering, degradation and helplessness than by discipline and work. This message holds the danger of blacks becoming permanently handicapped by a need for special treatment. It also sends to society at large the message that blacks cannot make it on their own. . . .

3. Affirmative Action Encourages Mediocrity and Incompetence

Last Spring Jesse Jackson joined protesters at Harvard Law School in demanding that the Law School faculty hire black women. Jackson dismissed Dean of the Law School, Robert C. Clark's standard of choosing the best qualified person for the job as "Cultural anemia." "We cannot just define who is qualified in the most narrow vertical academic terms," he said. "Most people in the world are yellow, brown, black, poor, non-Christian and don't speak English, and they can't wait for some White males with archaic rules to ap-

praise them."[2] It might be noted that if Jackson is correct about the depth of cultural decadence at Harvard, blacks might be well advised to form and support their own more vital law schools and leave places like Harvard to their archaism.

At several universities, the administration has forced departments to hire members of minorities even when far superior candidates were available. Shortly after obtaining my Ph.D. in the late 70's I was mistakenly identified as a black philosopher (I had a civil rights record and was once a black studies major) and was flown to a major university, only to be rejected for a more qualified candidate when it discovered that I was white.

Stories of the bad effects of Affirmative Action abound. The philosopher Sidney Hook writes that "At one Ivy League university, representatives of the Regional HEW demanded an explanation of why there were no women or minority students in the Graduate Department of Religious Studies. They were told that a reading knowledge of Hebrew and Greek was presupposed. Whereupon the representatives of HEW advised orally: 'Then end those old fashioned programs that require irrelevant languages. And start up programs on relevant things which minority group students can study without learning languages.'"[3] . . .

Government programs of enforced preferential treatment tend to appeal to the lowest possible common denominator. Witness the 1974 HEW Revised Order No. 14 on Affirmative Action expectations for preferential hiring: "Neither minorities nor female employees should be required to possess higher qualifications than those of the lowest qualified incumbents."

Furthermore, no tests may be given to candidates unless it is *proved* to be relevant to the job.

No standard or criteria which have, by intent or effect, worked to exclude women or minorities as a class can be utilized, unless the institution can demonstrate the necessity of such standard to the performance of the job in question.

Whenever a validity study is called for . . . the user should include . . . an investigation of suitable alternative selection procedures and suitable alternative methods of using the selection procedure which have as little adverse impact as possible. . . . Whenever the user is shown an alternative selection procedure with evidence of less adverse impact and substantial evidence of validity for the same job in similar circumstances, the user should investigate it to determine the appropriateness of using or validating it in accord with these guidelines.[4]

At the same time Americans are wondering why standards in our country are falling and the Japanese are getting ahead. Affirmative Action with its twin idols, Sufficiency and Diversity, is the enemy of excellence. . . .

4. Affirmative Action Policies Unjustly Shift the Burden of Proof

Affirmative Action legislation tends to place the burden of proof on the employer who does not have an "adequate" representation of "underutilized" groups in his work force. He is guilty until proven innocent. I have already recounted how in the mid-eighties the Supreme Court shifted the burden of proof back onto the plaintiff, while Congress is now attempting to shift the burden back to the employer. Those in favor of deeming disproportional representation "guilty until proven innocent" argue that it is easy for employers to discriminate against minorities by various subterfuges, and I agree that steps should be taken to monitor against prejudicial treatment. But being prejudiced against employers is not the way to attain a just solution to discrimination. The principle: innocent until proven guilty, applies to employers as well as criminals. Indeed, it is clearly special pleading to reject this basic principle of Anglo-American law in this case of discrimination while adhering to it everywhere else.

5. An Argument from Merit

Traditionally, we have believed that the highest positions in society should be awarded to those who are best qualified. . . . Rewarding excellence both seems just to the individuals in the competition and makes for efficiency. Note that one of the most successful acts of integration, the recruitment of Jackie Robinson in the late 40's, was done in just this way, according to merit. If Robinson had been brought into the major league as a mediocre player or had batted .200 he would have been scorned and sent back to the minors where he belonged.

Merit is not an absolute value. There are times when it may be overridden for social goals, but there is a strong prima facie reason for awarding positions on its basis, and it should enjoy a weighty presumption in our social practices. . . .

We generally want the best to have the best positions, the best qualified candidate to win the political office, the most brilliant and competent scientist to be chosen for the most challenging research project, the best qualified pilots to become commercial pilots, only the best soldiers to become generals. Only when little is at stake do we weaken the standards and content ourselves with sufficiency (rather than excellence) — there are plenty of jobs where "sufficiency" rather than excellence is required. . . .

But note, no one is calling for quotas or proportional representation of *underutilized* groups in the National Basketball Association where blacks make up 80% of the players. But if merit and merit alone reigns in sports, should it not be valued at least as much in education and industry?

6. The Slippery Slope

Even if Strong AA or Reverse Discrimination could meet the other objections, it would face a tough question: once you embark on this project, how do you limit it? Who should be excluded from reverse discrimination? Asians and Jews are over-represented, so if we give blacks positive quotas, should we place negative quotas to these other groups? Since white males, "WMs," are a minority which is suffering from reverse discrimination, will we need a New Affirmative Action policy in the 21st century to compensate for the discrimination against WMs in the late 20th century?

Furthermore, Affirmative Action has stigmatized the *young* white male. Assuming that we accept reverse discrimination, the fair way to make sacrifices would be to retire *older* white males who are more likely to have benefited from a favored status. Probably the least guilty of any harm to minority groups is the young white male — usually a liberal who has been required to bear the brunt of ages of past injustice. Justice Brennan's announcement that the Civil Rights Act did not apply to discrimination against whites shows how the clearest language can be bent to serve the idealogy of the moment.

7. The Mounting Evidence Against the Success of Affirmative Action

Thomas Sowell of the Hoover Institute has shown in his book *Preferential Policies: An International Perspective* that preferential hiring almost never solves social problems. It generally builds in mediocrity or incompetence and causes deep resentment. It is a short term solution which lacks serious grounding in social realities. . . .

Often it is claimed that a cultural bias is the cause of the poor performance of blacks

on SAT (or IQ tests), but Sowell shows that these test scores are actually a better predictor of college performance for blacks than for Asians and whites. He also shows the harmfulness of the effect on blacks of preferential acceptance. At the University of California, Berkeley, where the freshman class closely reflects the actual ethnic distribution of California high school students, more than 70% of blacks fail to graduate. All 312 black students entering Berkeley in 1987 were admitted under "Affirmative Action" criteria rather than by meeting standard academic criteria. So were 480 out of 507 Hispanic students. In 1986 the median SAT score for blacks at Berkeley was 952, for Mexican Americans 1014, for American Indians 1082 and for Asian Americans 1254. (The average SAT for all students was 1181.)

The result of this mismatching is that blacks who might do well if they went to a second tier or third tier school where their test scores would indicate they belong, actually are harmed by preferential treatment. They cannot compete in the institutions where high abilities are necessary. . . .

The tendency has been to focus at the high level end of education and employment rather than on the lower level of family structure and early education. But if we really want to help the worst off improve, we need to concentrate on the family and early education. It is foolish to expect equal results when we begin with grossly unequal starting points — and discriminating against young white males is no more just than discriminating against women, blacks or anyone else.

CONCLUSION

Let me sum up. The goal of the Civil Rights movement and of moral people everywhere has been equal opportunity. The question is: how best to get there. Civil Rights legislation removed the legal barriers to equal opportunity, but did not tackle the deeper causes that produced differential results. Weak Affirmative Action aims at encouraging minorities in striving for the highest positions without unduly jeopardizing the rights of majorities, but the problem of Weak Affirmative Action is that it easily slides into Strong Affirmative Action where quotas, "goals," and equal results are forced into groups, thus promoting mediocrity, inefficiency, and resentment. Furthermore, Affirmative Action aims at the higher levels of society — universities and skilled jobs — yet if we want to improve our society, the best way to do it is to concentrate on families, children, early education, and the like. Affirmative Action is, on the one hand, too much, too soon and on the other hand, too little, too late.

Martin Luther said that humanity is like a man mounting a horse who always tends to fall off on the other side of the horse. This seems to be the case with Affirmative Action.

Attempting to redress the discriminatory iniquities of our history, our well-intentioned social engineers engage in new forms of discriminatory iniquity and thereby think that they have successfully mounted the horse of racial harmony. They have only fallen off on the other side of the issue.[5]

NOTES

1. Editor's Note: A section has been deleted in which arguments in favor of affirmative action were given by Professor Pojman.
2. *New York Times,* May 10, 1990 issue.
3. Nicholas Capaldi, *Out of Order* (Buffalo, N.Y., 1985), p. 85.
4. *Ibid.*
5. I am indebted to Jim Landesman, Michael Levin, and Abigail Rosenthal for comments on a previous draft of this paper. I am also indebted to Nicholas Capaldi's *Out of Order* for first making me aware of the extent of the problem of Affirmative Action.

Goals and Quotas in Hiring and Promotion

Tom L. Beauchamp

Since the 1960s, government and corporate policies that set goals for hiring women and minorities have been sharply criticized. Their opponents maintain that many policies establish indefensible quotas and discriminate in reverse against sometimes more qualified white males. In 1991, President George Bush referred to the word "quota" as the "dreaded q-word." Quotas, he said, had "finally" been eliminated from government policies. Such

opposition is understandable. No worker wants to lose a job to a less qualified person, and no employer wants to be restricted in its hiring and promotion by a quota.

Although some policies that set target goals and adopt quotas sometimes violate rules of fair and equal treatment, such policies can be justified. My objective in this paper is to defend policies that set goals and quotas. I argue that goals and quotas, rightly conceived, are congenial to management — not hostile as they are often depicted. Both the long-range interest of corporations and the public interest are served by carefully selected preferential policies.

I. TWO POLAR POSITIONS

In 1965, President Lyndon Johnson issued an executive order that announced a toughened federal initiative requiring goals and timetables for equal employment opportunity.[1] This initiative was the prevailing regulatory approach for many years. But recently two competing schools of thought on the justifiability of preferential programs have come into sharp conflict, one mirroring the views of Bush, and the other mirroring those of Johnson.

The first school, like Bush, stands in opposition to quotas, accepting the view that all persons are entitled to an equal opportunity and to constitutional guarantees of equal protection in a color-blind, nonsexist society. Civil rights laws, in this approach, should offer protection only to individuals who have been victimized by forms of discrimination, not groups. Hiring goals, timetables, and quotas only work to create new victims of discrimination.

The second school, like Johnson, supports strong affirmative action policies. The justification of affirmative action programs is viewed as the correction of discriminatory employment practices, not group compensation for prior injustice. This second school views the first school as construing "equal opportunity" and "civil rights" so narrowly that persons affected by discrimination do not receive adequate aid in overcoming the effects of prejudice. This second school believes that mandated hiring protects minorities and erodes discrimination, whereas the identification of individual victims of discrimination

would be, as the editors of *The New York Times* once put it, the "project of a century and [would] leave most victims of discrimination with only empty legal rights."[2]

These two schools may not be as far apart morally as they first appear. If legal enforcement of civil rights law could efficiently and comprehensively identify discriminatory treatment and could protect its victims, both schools would agree that the legal-enforcement strategy is preferable. But there are at least two reasons why this solution will not be accepted by the second school. First, there is the unresolved issue of whether those in contemporary society who have been advantaged by *past* discrimination (for example, wealthy owners of family businesses) deserve their advantages. Second, there is the issue of whether *present,* ongoing discrimination can be successfully, comprehensively, and fairly combatted by identifying and prosecuting violators without resorting to quotas. This second issue is the more pivotal and is closely related to the justification of quotas.

A "quota," as used here, does not mean that fixed numbers of employees should be hired regardless of an individual's qualification for a position. Quotas are simply target employment percentages. In some cases a less qualified person may be hired or promoted; but it has never been a part of affirmative action to hire below the threshold of "basically qualified,"[3] and often significant questions exist in the employment situation about the exact qualifications needed for positions.[4] Quotas, then, are numerically expressible goals that one is obligated to pursue with good faith and due diligence. If it is impossible to hire the basically qualified persons called for by the goals in a given time frame, the schedule can be relaxed, as long as the target goals, the due diligence, and the good faith continue. The word *quota* does not mean "fixed number" in any stronger sense.

II. DATA ON DISCRIMINATION

Discrimination affecting hiring and promotion is not present everywhere in our society, but it is pervasive. An impressive body of statistics constituting prima facie evidence of discrimination has been assembled in recent years. It indicates that: (1) women with identical credentials are promoted at approximately one-half the rate of their male counterparts; (2) 69% or more of the white-collar positions in the United States are held by women, but only approximately 10% of the management positions are held by women; (3) 87% of all professionals in the private business sector are of oriental origin, but they constitute only 1.3% of the management positions; (4) in the total U.S. population, 3 out of 7 employees hold white-collar positions, whereas the ratio is only 1 of 7 for blacks; (5) blacks occupy over 50% of the nation's jobs as garbage collectors and maids, but only 4% of the nation's management positions.[5]

Such statistics are not decisive indicators of discrimination, but additional facts also support the conclusion that racist and sexist biases powerfully influence the marketplace. Consider prevailing biases in real estate rentals and sales. Studies have shown that there is an 85% probability that blacks will encounter discrimination in rental housing and a 50% probability that blacks will suffer discrimination in purchasing a house and in applying for a mortgage; that blacks suffer more discrimination than other economically comparable minority groups; and that there may be as many as two million instances of discrimination in the U.S. housing market each year in the United States. One study indicates that approximately 80% of American residential neighborhoods in the largest 29 metropolitan areas remained entirely segregated from 1960 to 1980. Not socioeconomic status, but race, is the difference in real estate sales and loans.[6]

If we shift from housing to jobs, a similar pattern is found, especially for black males, for whom employment has become steadily more difficult in almost every sector from the mid-1970s through the early 1990s.[7] In 1985 the Grier Partnership and the Urban League produced independent studies that reveal striking disparities in the employment levels of college-trained blacks and whites in Washington, D.C., one of the best markets for blacks. Both studies found that college-trained blacks have much more difficulty than their white counterparts in securing employment. Both cite discrimination as the major underlying factor.[8]

A 1991 study by the Urban Institute is a powerful illustration of the problem. This study examined employment practices in Washington, D.C. and Chicago. Equally qualified, identically dressed white and black applicants for jobs were used to test for bias in the job market, as presented by newspaper-advertised positions. Whites and blacks were matched identically for speech patterns, age, work experience, personal characteristics, and physical build. Investigators found repeated discrimination against black male applicants. The higher the position, the higher they found the level of discrimination to be. The white men received job offers three times more often than the equally qualified blacks who interviewed for the same position. The authors of the study concluded both that discrimination against black men is "widespread and entrenched" and that fears of reverse discrimination by white males are unfounded because the effects of discrimination more than offset any effects of reverse discrimination.[9]

These statistics help frame the significance of racial discrimination in the United States. Although much is now known about patterns of discrimination, much remains to be discovered, in part because it is hidden and subtle.

III. PROBLEMS OF PROOF AND INTENTION

We typically conceive racism and sexism as an intentional form of favoritism or exclusion, but major problems confronting American business and government arise from *unintended* institutional practices. Employees are frequently hired through a network that, without design, excludes women or minority groups. For example, hiring may occur through personal connections or by word of mouth, and layoffs may be entirely controlled by a seniority system. The actual hiring policies themselves may be racially and sexually neutral. Nonetheless, they can have an adverse effect on the ability of minorities in securing positions. There may be no intention to discriminate against anyone; nonetheless, the system has discriminatory consequences. In some cases, past discrimination that led to unfair hiring practices and an imbalanced work force is perpetuated even when there is no desire to perpetuate them.

In 1985 the U.S. Supreme Court unanimously held that persons may be guilty of discriminating against the handicapped when there is no "invidious animus, but rather [a discriminatory effect] of thoughtlessness and indifference — of benign neglect." The Court held that discrimination would be difficult and perhaps impossible to prevent if *intentional* discrimination alone qualified as discrimination.[10] Discrimination is still invisible to many who discriminate. This, in my judgment, is the main reason quotas are an indispensable government and management tool: They are the only way to break down old patterns of discrimination and thereby change the configuration of the workplace.

Courts in the United States have on a few occasions resorted to quotas because an employer had an intractable history and a bull-headed resistance to change that necessitated strong measures. The Supreme Court has never directly supported quotas using the term "quota,"[11] but it has upheld affirmative action programs that contain numerically expressed hiring formulas that are intended to reverse the patterns of both intentional and unintentional discrimination.[12] At the same time, the Supreme Court has suggested that some programs using these formulas have gone too far.[13] Whether the formulas are excessive depends on the facts in the individual case. From this perspective, there is no inconsistency between *Fullilove v. Klutznick* (1980), which allowed percentage set-asides for minority contractors, and *City of Richmond v. J. A. Croson Co.* (1989), which disallowed certain set-asides. The later case of *Adarand Constructors Inc. v. Pena* (1995) defended a standard requiring that there be a compelling governmental interest for race-based preferences in construction contracts for minority-owned companies; it continued the long line of cases that weigh and balance different interests.

I believe the Supreme Court has consistently adhered to this balancing strategy and that it is the right moral perspective as well as the proper framework for American law.[14] Numerical goals or quotas should be implemented only when necessary to overcome the discriminatory impact of insensitive institutional policies and irrelevant criteria used for employment. Proposed formulas can be excessive here just as they can elsewhere.

Although I have distinguished between intentional practices and unintentional practices that have discriminatory impact, the two often work together. For example, the practices and framework of policies in a corporation may be nondiscriminatory, but those implementing the practices and policies may have discriminatory attitudes. Fair rules can easily be exploited or evaded by both personnel officers and unions, who often use criteria for hiring and promotion such as "self-confidence," "fitting in," "collegiality," and "personal appearance," among other superficial characteristics.[15]

Issues about the breadth and depth of discrimination may divide us as a society more than any other issue about affirmative action. If one believes there is but a narrow slice of surface discrimination, one is likely to agree with what I have called the first school. But if one believes discrimination is deeply, almost invisibly entrenched in our society, one is apt to agree with the second school. I have been arguing for the perspective taken by the second school, but this perspective needs to be specified to prevent it from assuming the same bullheaded insensitivity that it pretends to locate elsewhere. Discriminatory attitudes and practices are likely to be deep-seated in some institutions, while shallow or absent in others. Society is not monolithic in the depth and breadth of discrimination. In some cases affirmative action programs are not needed, in other cases only modest good faith programs are in order, and in still others enforced quotas are necessary to break down discriminatory patterns.

Because we deeply disagree about the depth, breadth, and embeddedness of discrimination, we disagree further over the social policies that will rid us of the problem. Those who believe discrimination is relatively shallow and detectable look for formulas and remedies that center on *equal opportunity*. Those who believe discrimination is deep, camouflaged, and embedded in society look for formulas that center on *measurable outcomes*.[16]

IV. WHY CORPORATIONS SHOULD WELCOME GOALS AND QUOTAS

Little has been said to this point about corporate policy. I shall discuss only so-called *voluntary* programs that use target goals and quotas. They stand in sharp contrast to legally enforced goals and quotas, and there are at least three reasons why it is in the interest of responsible businesses to use aggressive plans that incorporate goals and quotas: (1) an improved workforce, (2) maintenance of a bias-free corporate environment, and (3) congeniality to managerial planning.

(1) First, corporations that discriminate will fail to look at the full range of qualified persons in the market and, as a result, will employ a higher percentage of second-best employees. The U.S. workforce is projected to be 80% women, minorities, and immigrants by the year 2000, and corporations are already reporting both that they are finding fewer qualified workers for available positions and that they have profited from vigorous, internally-generated rules of nonracial, nonsexist hiring.[17] Hal Johnson, a senior vice-president at Travelers Cos., noted the benefits in adopting goals and quotas: "In [the 1990s] more of the work force is going to be minorities — Hispanics, blacks — and women. The companies that started building bridges back in the 1970s will be all right. Those that didn't won't."[18]

Goals and quotas that are properly conceived should yield superior, not inferior employees. No one would argue, for example, that baseball has poorer talent for dropping its color barrier. To find the best baseball talent, bridges had to be built that extended, for example, into the population of Puerto Rico. Businesses will be analogously improved if they extend their boundaries and provide proper training and diversity programs. Bill McEwen of the Monsanto Corporation and spokesperson for the National Association of Manufacturers (NAM) notes that this extension has long been happening at NAM companies:

We have been utilizing affirmative action plans for over 20 years. We were brought into it kicking and screaming. But over the past 20 years we've learned that there's a reservoir of talent out there, of minorities and women that we hadn't been using before. We found that [affirmative action] works.[19]

Maintaining a high quality workforce is consistent with the management style already implemented in many companies. For example, James R. Houghton, Chairman of Corning Glass, has established voluntary quotas to increase the quality of employees, not merely the number of women and black employees. Corning established the following increased-percentage targets for the total employment population to be met between 1988 and 1991: women professionals to increase from 17.4% to 23.2%, black professionals to increase from 5.1% to 7.4%, the number of black senior managers to increase from 1 to 5, and the number of women senior managers to increase from 4 to 10. Corning management interpreted the targets as follows: "Those numbers were not commandments set in stone. We won't hire people just to meet a number. It will be tough to meet some of [our targets]." Corning found that it could successfully recruit in accordance with these targets, but also found severe difficulty in maintaining the desired target numbers in the workforce because of an attrition problem. The company continues to take the view that in an age in which the percentage of white males in the employment pool is constantly declining, a "total quality company" must vigorously recruit women and minorities using target goals.[20]

A diverse work force can, additionally, create a more positive employment environment and better serve its customers. An internal U S West study found that white males were ten times more likely to be promoted than minority women (black, Hispanic, and Asian). As a result, the company designed a plan to promote its female employees and to prepare employees for more demanding positions. U S West adopted the view that a diverse group of employees is better suited to develop new and creative ideas than a homogeneous group that approaches problems from a similar perspective and that racial and sexual patterns of discrimination in hiring have to be combatted by target-driven hiring programs. They therefore targeted "Women of Color" for training and promotion.[21]

Many corporations have found that vigorous affirmative action has economic and not only social benefits. Diversity in the workforce produces diversity of ideas, different perspectives on strategic planning, and improved, more open personnel policies. As a result, as the director of personnel at Dow Chemical puts it, "If anything there is [in the corporate world] a new push on affirmative action plans because of the increasing numbers of women and minorities entering the work force."[22]

(2) Second, pulling the foundations from beneath affirmative-action hiring would open old wounds in many municipalities and corporations that have been developing target goals and quotas through either a consent-decree process with courts or direct negotiations with representatives of minority groups and unions. These programs have, in some cases, been agonizingly difficult to develop and would disintegrate if goals and timetables were ruled impermissible. The P. Q. Corporation, for example, reports that it has invested years of training in breaking down managerial biases and stereotypes while getting managers to hire in accordance with affirmative action guidelines. The corporation is concerned that without the pressure of affirmative action programs, managers will fail to recognize their own biases and use of stereotypes. Removal of voluntary programs might additionally stigmatize a business by signalling to minorities that a return to older patterns of discrimination is permissible.

Such stigmatization is a serious blow in today's competitive market.[23]

(3) Third, affirmative action programs involving quotas have been successful for the corporations that have adopted them, and there is no need to try to fix what is not broken. As the editors of *Business Week* maintained, "Over the years business and regulators have worked out rules and procedures for affirmative action, including numerical yardsticks for sizing up progress, that both sides understand. It has worked and should be left alone."[24] It has worked because of the abovementioned improved workforce and because of a businesslike approach typical of managerial planning: Managers set goals and timetables for almost everything — from profits to salary bonuses. From a manager's point of view, setting goals and timetables is simply a basic way of measuring progress.

One survey of 200 major American corporations found that the same approach has often been taken to the management of affirmative action: Over 75% of these corporations already use "voluntary internal numerical objectives to assess [equal employment opportunity] performance." Another survey of 300 top corporate executives reported that 72% believe that minority hiring improves rather than hampers productivity, while 64% said there is a need for the government to help bring women and minorities into the mainstream of the workforce. Many corporations have used their records in promotion and recruitment to present a positive image of corporate life in public reports and recruiting brochures. Such reports and brochures have been published, for example, by Schering-Plough, Philip Morris, Exxon, AT&T, IBM, Westinghouse, and Chemical Bank.[25]

Affirmative action has also worked to increase productivity and improved consumer relationships. Corporations in consumer goods and services industries report in-

creased respect and increased sales after achieving affirmative action results. They report that they are able to target some customers they otherwise could not reach, enjoy increased competitiveness, and better understand consumer complaints as a result of a more diverse workforce. Corporations with aggressive affirmative action programs have also been shown to outperform their competitors.[26]

CONCLUSION

If the social circumstances of discrimination were to be substantially altered, my conclusions in this paper would be modified. I agree with critics that the introduction of preferential treatment on a large scale runs the risk of producing economic advantages to individuals who do not deserve them, protracted court battles, congressional lobbying by power groups, a lowering of admission and work standards, reduced social and economic efficiency, increased racial and minority hostility, and the continued suspicion that well-placed minorities received their positions purely on the basis of quotas. These reasons constitute a strong case against affirmative action policies that use numerical goals and quotas. However, this powerful case is not sufficient to overcome the still stronger counterarguments.

NOTES

1. Executive Order 11,246. C.F.R. 339 (1964–65). This order required all federal contractors to develop affirmative action policies.
2. "Their Right to Remedy, Affirmed," *The New York Times,* July 3, 1986, p. A30.
3. This standard has been recognized at least since *EEOC v. AT&T,* No. 73-149 (E.D. Pa. 1973). See also U.S. Department of Labor,

Employment Standards Administration, Office of Federal Contract Compliance Programs," "OFCCP: Making EEO and Affirmative Action Work," January 1987 OFCCP-28.

4. See Laura Purdy, "Why Do We Need Affirmative Action?" *Journal of Social Philosophy* 25 (1994): 133–143.

5. See Bron Taylor, *Affirmative Action at Work: Law, Politics, and Ethics* (Pittsburgh: University of Pittsburgh Press, 1991); National Center for Education Statistics, *Faculty in Higher Education Institutions, 1988, Contractor Survey Report,* compiled Susan H. Russell, et al (Washington: U.S. Dept. of Education, March 1990), pp. 5–13; Herman Schwartz, "Affirmative Action," *Minority Report,* ed. L. W. Dunbar (New York: Pantheon Books, 1984), pp. 61–62; Betty M. Vetter, ed., *Professional Women and Minorities: A Manpower Data Resource Service,* 8th edn. (Washington: Commission on Science and Technology, 1989); Irene Pave, "A Woman's Place Is at GE, Federal Express, P&G. . . ." *Business Week,* June 23, 1986, pp. 75–76.

6. See *A Common Destiny: Blacks and American Society,* ed. Gerald D. Jaynes and Robin M. Williams, Jr., Committee on the Status of Black Americans, Commission on Behavioral and Social Sciences and Education, National Research Council (Washington: NAS Press, 1989), pp. 12–13, 138–48; Glenn B. Canner and Wayne Passmore, "Home Purchase Lending in Low-Income Neighborhoods and to Low-Income Borrowers," *Federal Reserve Bulletin* 81 (Feb. 1995): 71–103; Yi-Hsin Chang, "Mortgage Denial Rate for Blacks in '93 Was Double the Level for Whites, Asians," July 29, 1994, p. A2; "Business Bulletin," *The Wall Street Journal,* February 28, 1985, p. 1; Constance L. Hays, "Study Says Prejudice in Suburbs Is Aimed Mostly at Blacks," *The New York Times,* November 23, 1988, p. A16.

7. Paul Burstein, *Discrimination, Jobs, and Politics* (Chicago: University of Chicago Press, 1985). Bureau of Labor Statistics, *Employment and Earnings* (Washington: U.S. Dept. of Labor, Jan. 1989). *A Common Destiny,* op. cit., pp. 16–18, 84–88.

8. As reported by Rudolf A. Pyatt, Jr., "Significant Job Studies," *The Washington Post,* April 30,1985, pp. D1–D2.

9. See Margery Austin Turner, Michael Fix, and Raymond Struyk, *Opportunities Denied, Opportunities Diminished: Discrimination in Hiring* (Washington, D.C.: The Urban Institute, 1991).

10. *Alexander v. Choate,* 469 U.S. 287, at 295.

11. But the Court comes very close in *Local 28 of the Sheet Metal Workers' International Association v. Equal Employment Opportunity Commission,* 106 S.Ct. 3019 — commonly known as *Sheet Metal Workers.*

12. *Fullilove v. Klutznick,* 448 U.S. 448 (1980); *United Steelworkers v. Weber,* 443 U.S. 193 (1979); *United States v. Paradise,* 480 U.S. 149 (1987); *Johnson v. Transportation Agency,* 480 U.S. 616 (1987).

13. *Firefighters v. Stotts,* 467 U.S. 561 (1984); *City of Richmond v. J. A. Croson Co.,* 109 S.Ct. 706 (1989); *Adarand Constructors Inc. v. Federico Pena,* 63 LW 4523 (1995); *Wygant v. Jackson Bd. of Education,* 476 U.S. 267 (1986); *Wards Cove Packing v. Atonio,* 490 U.S. 642.

14. For a very different view, stressing inconsistency, see Yong S. Lee, "Affirmative Action and Judicial Standards of Review: A Search for the Elusive Consensus." *Review of Public Personnel Administration* 12 (Sept.–Dec. 1991): 47–69.

15. See the argument to this effect in Gertrude Ezorsky, *Racism & Justice: The Case for Affirmative Action* (Ithaca, N.Y.: Cornell University Press, 1991), Chap. 1.

16. For a balanced article on this topic, see Robert K. Fullinwider, "Affirmative Action and Fairness," *Report from the Institute for Philosophy & Public Policy* 11 (University of Maryland, Winter 1991), pp. 10–13.

17. See L. Joseph Semien, "Opening the Utility Door for Women and Minorities," *Public Utilities Fortnightly,* July 5, 1990, pp. 29–31; Irene Pave, "A Woman's Place," p. 76.

18. As quoted in Walter Kiechel, "Living with Human Resources," *Fortune,* August 18, 1986, p. 100.

19. As quoted in Peter Perl, "Rulings Provide Hiring Direction: Employers Welcome Move," *The Washington Post,* July 3, 1986, pp. A1, A11.

20. Tim Loughran, "Corning Tries to Break the Glass Ceiling," *Business & Society Review* 76 (Winter 1991), pp. 52–55.

21. Richard Remington, "Go West, Young Woman!" in *Telephony* 215 (Nov. 1988), pp. 30–32; Diane Feldman, "Women of Color Build a Rainbow of Opportunity," *Management Review* 78 (Aug. 1989), pp. 18–21.

22. Loughran, op. cit., p. 54.

23. See Jeanne C. Poole and E. Theodore Kautz, "An EEO/AA Program that Exceeds Quotas — It Targets Biases," *Personnel Journal* 66 (Jan. 1987), pp. 103–105. Mary Thornton, "Justice Dept. Stance on Hiring Goals Resisted," *The Washington Post*, May 25, 1985, p. A2; Pyatt, "The Basis of Job Bias," p. D2; Linda Williams, "Minorities Find Pacts with Corporations Are Hard to Come By and Enforce," *The Wall Street Journal*, August 23, 1985, p. 13.

24. Editorial, "Don't Scuttle Affirmative Action," *Business Week*, April 5, 1985, p. 174.

25. "Rethinking *Weber*: The Business Response to Affirmative Action," *Harvard Law Review* 102 (Jan. 1989), p. 661, note 18; Robertson, "Why Bosses Like to Be Told," p. 2.

26. See "Rethinking *Weber*," esp. pp. 668–70; Joseph Michael Pace and Zachary Smith, "Understanding Affirmative Action: From the Practitioner's Perspective," *Public Personnel Management* 24 (Summer 1995): 139–147.

Some Implications of Comparable Worth

Laurie Shrage

INTRODUCTION

The passage of the Equal Pay Act in 1963 established the principle of "equal pay for equal work" in the American legal system. Workers who perform identical work must be paid equivalent wages, regardless of a worker's sex or race. However, due to historic occupational segregation, the vast majority of men and women do not perform work that is essentially similar in content. Moreover, occupational categories in which the incumbents are predominantly women (nurse, clerical worker, nursery school teacher, and the like) provide, on average, lower wages than those awarded to jobs predominantly performed by men.

The persistent gap in wages between male and female dominated professions involving similar training, experience, and working conditions, indicates *prima facie* that wage differentials are affected by gender discrimination. For the past decade, feminist civil rights organizations have affirmed the existence of gender-based wage discrimination, and the need to compensate women more equitably for their work. The remedy they commonly advocate appeals to the principle of comparable worth: jobs which are dissimilar in content, but comparable in terms of their value to an employer, should be rewarded equally. While the idea of "equal pay for jobs of comparable worth" is widely accepted among feminists, it is established neither in the law nor in the academy.

Despite its narrow base of support, the comparable worth movement has made considerable progress. Several labor unions have successfully negotiated wage adjustments based on comparable worth studies, and many states have passed or rewritten legislation which will facilitate the litigation of comparable worth complaints.[1] In response to these gains, conservative political economists have criticized the doctrine of comparable worth for promoting regulations that

From Laurie Shrage, "Some Implications of Comparable Worth," copyright © 1987 by *Social Theory and Practice*, Vol. 13, No. 1: 77–87 (Spring 1987).

threaten to disrupt our free market economy.[2] Business and management experts too have begun to question the validity of job evaluation techniques that have served management in the past, but which now form the basis of comparable worth demands.

Recently, comparable worth has attracted criticism not only from conservatives but from progressives as well. Critics on the left argue that comparable worth primarily serves the class interests of middle-class white women, and fails to address the needs of minorities, the poor, and working class people.[3] Because the principle of comparable worth ties compensation to job merit — rather than, for example, to employee need — its enforcement, these critics allege, will primarily benefit those in our society whose work carries high social status (in other words, white-collar, managerial and professional workers over blue-collar, skilled or unskilled manual laborers).

Although proponents of comparable worth have frequently addressed the concerns of conservative critics, they have not similarly confronted the issues raised by social progressives.[4] Since comparable worth is motivated by a concern for equality, its proponents should be especially sensitive to the charge that their goals reflect some degree of middle-class elitism. This paper will examine the theoretical assumptions behind the demand for comparable worth, in order to see if it can be maintained in light of the criticisms raised by progressive theorists.

THE THEORY OF COMPARABLE WORTH AND ITS JUSTIFICATION

The demand for comparable worth contains five distinct components:

1) Work which is dissimilar in content, but which requires similar levels of training, expe-

rience, and responsibility, and is performed under similar conditions, is of comparable value to employers. Workers whose work is of comparable value should receive equal compensation from employers, regardless of race or sex.

2) The occurrence of systemic economic discrimination against women and minorities in our society can be inferred from a pervasive pattern of salary differentials — a pattern in which wages paid for work performed predominantly by women and minorities average approximately 60–75 percent of wages paid to white men for work of comparable value.

3) The job evaluation systems developed by business and management experts, and which have a long history of use by employers, are helpful for comparing jobs in terms of their value to an employer.

4) However, job evaluation techniques that are currently in use must be reexamined to eliminate sex and ethnic bias both in their form (for example, how job factors are weighted, which factors are chosen, how jobs are described, and so forth) and in their application (for example, whether women and minorities participate in administering them).[5]

5) Public and private employers must conduct their own bias-free job evaluation studies to determine the extent to which wage differentials in their institutions have been affected by race or gender, and must then make appropriate adjustments to their wage structure if inequities are found to exist.[6] If employers do not voluntarily undertake these actions, then such studies and adjustments should be brought about by union negotiations, or by state or federal law.

Parts (1), (4) and (5) summarize the prescriptive components of the demand for comparable worth: that adjustments to wages should be made in accordance with the principle of equal pay for work of comparable value, using the findings of gender and ethnic neutral job evaluation techniques. Parts (2) and (3) summarize the empirical presuppositions of comparable worth theory: that statistical data on existing wage differentials, together with the findings of unbiased job evaluation studies, strongly imply the existence of systemic race and sex discrimination in our society in the setting of compensation levels. Components (2) and (3) provide some justification for (1), (4) and (5) in that if discrimination against women and minorities in the form of wage suppression exists, and if we believe the wage structure should be equitable, it follows that some steps to remedy this situation should be taken. However, what does not follow from these claims is that the remedy morally and practically required is the one proposed in (1), (4) and (5). Hence, to justify the prescriptive components of the theory, additional considerations and principles which indicate their unique remedial potential must be brought forth. In this section I will explore and develop some of these considerations.

Economists report that "women who work full time all year earn about 60 percent of what full-time men earn."[7] Despite the entrance of women in past years into jobs traditionally held by men, and despite a dramatic increase in the number of women in the work force, the gap in earnings between women and men has remained constant, or has even slightly increased, since 1955. Conversely, workers in male-dominated occupations earn 30–50% more than those in integrated or female-dominated occupations, and "the more an occupation is dominated by women, the less it pays."[8]

Some of the differences in earnings between men and women can be explained by the amount of labor supplied, in other words, the number of hours worked. This is one example of a so-called "human capital" or "productivity-related job content" variable that economists and sociologists attempt to isolate and hold constant, in order to explain some portion of the wage gap. By identifying relevant variables, social scientists attempt to determine whether factors which are independent of employer bias (such as an employee's

years of training, previous experience, or the level of responsibility a job demands) can account for salary differentials between male- and female-dominated occupations. While some portion of the earnings gap can be predicted by observing variation in "human capital" characteristics other than gender or race, even conservative critics find that these correlations leave a significant portion of the gap in wages (perhaps 60 percent) unexplained.[9]

Some social scientists maintain that the unpredicted portion of the wage gap merely reflects the degree of difficulty involved in measuring certain "human capital" variables. By contrast, other scholars claim that the "unexplained" portion of the wage gap is predictable when wage differentials are correlated with human capital features, such as race and sex. However, such correlations imply the occurrence of sex and race discrimination in the evolution of the wage structure; thus, they raise controversial issues. Nevertheless, according to civil rights attorney Winn Newman, the occurrence of discrimination can be inferred from "a consistent pattern of underpayment of women's jobs . . . in virtually every work place, public and private, in this country."[10] . . .

The theories of liberal economists generally make little use of the notion of discrimination because discrimination — as liberals conceive of it — is difficult to observe and measure. For them "discrimination in hiring and promotion" refers to the extent to which individual employers make decisions based upon their own biases or prejudices against particular segments of the population. To determine the extent of this phenomenon, one must measure the number of intentionally discriminatory acts of individuals. . . . To assume common intentional action on the part of employers is to postulate a conspiracy, which is not only unlikely, but the product of paranoid thinking.

Some explanations of social phenomena employ a conception of discrimination that differs from the liberal model. By "discrimination in hiring and promotion," some theorists are referring to implicit principles of social organization which have adverse consequences for certain social groups, but which are generally not recognized by individuals because they are subsumed or entailed by the accepted, unquestioned values of their society. On this model, sex discrimination is implicit in a society which is organized so that all Jills are paid less than all Jacks for comparable work. Employers may promote and perpetuate discrimination of this sort even if their individual actions happen to be relatively free of personal bias or the intention to discriminate. Indeed, they perpetuate economic discrimination against women and minorities when their actions are merely consistent with dominant cultural beliefs and stereotypes. In short, one need not be aware of the principles which organize our social institutions in order to behave "normally," just as one need not be aware of the syntactical rules of one's native language in order to speak grammatically. Nevertheless, as social theorists, we can recognize the existence of rules which structure our social interaction, and which reproduce a social hierarchy that places women and minorities in the weakest economic positions. Because this type of discrimination focuses on structural features of cultural systems or institutions, it is variously referred to as "structural," "systemic" or "institutional discrimination."

Given the statistical data on earnings, few would dispute that discrimination against women and minorities, as our second model defines it, exists in our society. What remains at issue, however, is how to reorganize our society in order to achieve a more equitable wage structure. In other words, even if components (2) and (3) are valid, do they justify the prescriptive claims in (1), (4) and (5)?

Comparable worth proponents are skeptical of the proposition that free market competition will in its course bring about an equitable wage structure. For instance, according to some liberal economists, discriminatory practices based on race and sex should prove unprofitable to an employer. However, even if this is true — even if reserving well paid work for white males is economically harmful — the disappearance of this custom once it has been established may disrupt the lives of those who have, or simply feel they have, benefited from it. According to economists Ray Marshall and Beth Paulin, "to suggest that the elimination of discrimination in internal labor markets is optimal for the profit-maximizing firm is to misunderstand the importance of order (and security) in the efficient operation of the production process in these markets."[11] Clearly, the economic utility of a practice cannot be assessed without regard to its historical context, which means that in some settings a segregated, hierarchical work force may boost an employer's profits.

Some liberal economists argue that if employers pay low wages to women and minorities for certain types of work, the labor supply for these jobs will decrease, forcing a rise in wage levels. However, this cycle will be interrupted, allowing wages to remain low, when the reserve of unemployed and unskilled workers — homemakers, immigrants, and so on — is larger than the number of jobs. Where shortages do occur, employers have other options besides raising wages. They can demand more overtime from fewer employees, hire temporary workers, cut back in service or production, or look for cheaper labor markets. Such actions by employers, have been common for example, in response to recurring shortages of nurses.[12]

Proponents of comparable worth also doubt that the current level of regulation on the market is high enough to bring about an equitable wage structure. In other words, they believe the achievement of equal pay for substantively equal work, together with the

Title VII prohibitions against sex and race discrimination in hiring, are not sufficient to correct historical wage suppression. Women and minorities who work in occupations which have been traditionally dominated by their sex or race will continue to feel the effect of past discrimination on their wages: their wages are and will remain lower than they would be if these jobs were, or had been, performed predominantly by white men.[13] The great majority of women and minority men work in segregated occupations. Moreover, efforts to integrate the work force have primarily benefited younger, college-educated persons,[14] leaving most of the work force untouched. Therefore, policies which raise the wages of traditionally undervalued occupations are necessary, both to compensate equitably those unaffected by new opportunities for mobility into jobs traditionally held by white males, and to attract white males into occupations from which they have been historically absent.

Since progressive political theorists doubt the therapeutic effects of the forces of supply and demand, they should be sympathetic to the demand for regulations that are designed to correct existing inequities. Moreover, since discrimination against certain economic classes in society and the underpayment of labor similarly reflect implicit structures of discrimination, theorists on the left should have little difficulty recognizing systemic economic discrimination based on race and sex. Despite these areas of compatibility between radical political philosophy and comparable worth theory, some radical theorists argue that comparable worth wrongly implies that once the market is corrected for sex and race discrimination and other imperfections through regulation, the wage structure in our society will be fair. Comparable worth theorists assume, according to these critics, that all white males in our society (including working class men), are equitably compensated for their work, and once women and minorities receive equal rates of compensation for comparable work, their wages too will be equitable. In other words, the doctrine uncritically assumes that wide differentials in pay are fair as long as they are correlated with features other than race or gender. For this reason they charge the doctrine of comparable worth with legitimating an elitist system of compensation, and with overlooking the injustices of our society's class system.[15] . . .

3. EQUALITY AND WORTH

The theory of comparable worth is based on the fundamental assumption that the wages workers receive should not reflect their race or sex. Such attributes are irrelevant to the value of the work performed, and thus, to equitable rates of compensation. In other words, the theory presupposes a fundamental equality of ability, talent and intelligence between persons of different gender and color. One consequence of the assumption of equality is the desire to have compensation levels set with consistency and impartiality. This means that whatever standards are employed to establish pay rates, they should be applied without regard to an employee's gender or race.

The theory's use of the concept of "worth" may be misleading. The crucial assumption underlying the theory's claims about worth is *not* that wages should be proportionate to worth, but that the labor of women and minorities is of equal worth to the labor of white men. If salary levels among white males were roughly equivalent — in other words, if large disparities in pay did not exist — then comparable worth would entail comparable salary levels and differentials for women and minorities. Moreover, it is consistent with the doctrine of comparable worth to acknowledge that some white male workers are compensated unfairly under the present system. At most, comparable worth assumes, as I have already stated, that the wages white male workers receive are, on average, less exploitative than the wages received by women and minorities.

I am not claiming that comparable worth is inconsistent with liberal, meritocratic principles. Instead, I am arguing these principles are neither entailed, nor presupposed, by the doctrine of comparable worth. Indeed, the idea of comparable worth is even consistent with tying wage levels to workers' needs, as long as the needs of women and minorities are not underrated in this process. If such principles of compensation were the norm, the supporters of comparable worth might modify their demand to one for equal pay for workers with comparable needs. The demand to pay women and minorities what their jobs are worth is made simply to ensure that women and minorities are not treated differently than white males in relation to the distribution of income.

Although the doctrine of comparable worth is not inconsistent with liberal theory, liberals are likely to find less justification for it. The reason for this is that liberals have difficulty recognizing systemic discrimination, a point I raised earlier. Since the model of discrimination they invoke involves decisions individuals make on the basis of personal biases, discrimination will be difficult to identify and measure. . . .

NOTES

1. The most significant case so far is *AFSCME* (American Federation of State, County and Municipal Employees) v. *State of Washington.*

2. For an apocalypse-threatening diatribe in this vein, see Jeremy Rabkin, "Comparable Worth as Civil Rights Policy: Potentials for Disaster,"

in *Comparable Worth: Issue for the 80's* (Washington, D.C.: U.S. Commission on Civil Rights, 1984), Vol. 1, pp. 187–95.

3. Drew Christie, "Comparable Worth and Distributive Justice," a paper presented on April 25, 1985 in Chicago to a meeting of the Radical Philosophy Association held in conjunction with the American Philosophical Association Western Division meetings.

4. For an excellent rebuttal of the claim that current wage differentials reflect the free play of neutral forces existing in a free market, see Donald Treiman and Heidi Hartmann, eds., *Women, Work, and Wages: Equal Pay for Jobs of Equal Value* (Washington, D.C.: National Academy Press, 1981).

5. For a summary of how sex bias can enter job evaluation systems, see Helen Remick, "Major Issues in *a priori* Applications," in *Comparable Worth and Wage Discrimination*, pp. 106–108.

6. Remick, p. 99.

7. Paula England, "Explanations of Job Segregation and the Sex Gap in Pay," in *Comparable Worth: Issue for the 80's*, Vol. 1, p. 54.

8. Andrea Beller, "Occupational Segregation and the Earnings Gap," in *Comparable Worth: Issue for the 80's*, Vol. 1, p. 23.

9. England, "Explanation of Job Segregation and the Sex Gap in Pay," p. 60.

10. Winn Newman, Statement to the U.S. Commission on Civil Rights at their Consultation on Comparable Worth, June 7, 1984, in *Comparable Worth: Issue for the 80's*, Vol. 2, p. 87.

11. Ray Marshall and Beth Paulin, "The Employment and Earnings of Women: The Comparable Worth Debate," in *Comparable Worth: Issue for the 80's*, Vol. 1, p. 202.

12. See Joy Ann Grune, "Pay Equity Is a Necessary Remedy for Wage Discrimination," in *Comparable Worth: Issue for the 80's*, Vol. 1, p. 169.

13. See Ronnie Steinberg, "Identifying Wage Discrimination and Implementing Pay Equity Adjustments," in *Comparable Worth: Issue for the 80's*, Vol. 1, p. 99.

14. England, "Explanations of Job Segregation and the Sex Gap in Pay," p. 55. Also see Beller, "Occupational Segregation and the Earnings Gap," p. 32.

15. Christie, "Comparable Worth and Distributive Justice."

Visibility and Value: The Role of Job Evaluation in Assuring Equal Pay for Women

Jennifer M. Quinn

INTRODUCTION

In the 1970s, feminist and labor advocates won substantial victories around the world by obtaining legislation that guaranteed women the right to earn pay equal to that of their male counterparts. During this initial phase of the pay equity movement, employers, prompted by the threat of lawsuits, sought to ensure that women and men performing essentially the same jobs or "like work" were receiving the same wages. By the mid 1980s, several factors, including the persistence of the gap between male and female earnings, created pressure to adopt a concept of pay equity known as "comparable worth," prompting litigation in several countries to broaden the scope of employer liability for gendered pay inequities. Although several years have passed, judicial and legislative involvement in the pay equity area shows no signs of abating, leaving employers' obligations under pay equity laws around the world in a state of considerable flux.

As a result, multinational corporations find themselves subject to widely divergent and occasionally incomprehensible sets of obligations that they must resolve to comply with the pay equity laws of the countries in which they operate. The purpose of this Note is to describe and analyze practical examples of the types of legal pay equity regimes currently in force. In particular, this Note has chosen to focus on the pay equity regimes of Ontario, Great Britain, and the United States. Although employers in each of these regions are prohibited from discriminating on the basis of gender in the wages paid to their employees, the principle of pay equity varies greatly among the three legal systems, creating substantial compliance burdens for multinational corporations.

Specifically, this Note focuses on the role of job evaluation in determining whether pay equity has been achieved under each of these regimes. From the perspective of the employer as well as the pay equity advocate, the role of job evaluation in a pay equity regime is extremely important for two reasons. First, job evaluation is the primary mechanism for comparing the values of jobs with different work requirements. Therefore, to the extent that a legal system permits women to claim pay equity with men who are not performing identical jobs, job evaluation is the mechanism for comparing the relative worth of these jobs and whether they deserve equal compensation. Second, job evaluation has great potential for reducing the wage gap between women and men precisely because the inequity is so pervasive. Throughout Ontario, Great Britain, and the United States, job evaluation is one of the principal tools used by employers and unions to provide the raw data upon which wage determinations are based. As a result, job evaluation has become

Source: *Law & Policy in International Business*, Vol. 25 (1994): 1403–1444. Reprinted by permission of the author.

a central issue in both the delineation of female employees' rights to pay equity as well as employer defenses to liability. . . .

Pervasive patterns of gender segregation in the work forces of Ontario, Great Britain, and the United States ensure that unless a comparable worth approach to pay equity allowing comparisons of unlike jobs is permitted, many women will be left without any viable pay equity remedies. . . . [Also] gender stereotypes permeate traditional methods of job evaluation used to compare unlike jobs, which results in the undervaluation and undercompensation of work performed predominantly by women. . . .

THE ROLE OF JOB EVALUATION IN ACHIEVING PAY EQUITY

A. The Gender Gap

It is well-documented that women as a whole in Ontario, Great Britain, and the United States earn substantially less than men. According to the most recent statistics, the female to male earnings ratios in these three states were as follows:

Ontario, 1989: 67.4%[1]
Great Britain, 1989: 76%[2]
United States, 1992: 74.2%[3]

This gender gap in earnings exists not only for women overall, but also across all levels of the labor market. Women are disproportionately represented in certain low paying occupations. In Ontario, for example, one-third of the female work force holds clerical jobs. Similarly, British women represent only forty-eight percent of the work force, yet, eighty-two percent of those women hold jobs in the service industry.[4] U.S. women are also highly concentrated in clerical and service jobs.[5]

"[E]ven within finely defined occupations . . . jobs are frequently segregated by sex."[6]

Moreover, studies suggest that the nature of the segregated jobs that women perform does not explain the entire gender wage gap. According to one U.S. study, each one percent increase in the number of female employees in an occupation results in an average decline of $42 in annual income.[7] On average, an employee in a female dominated occupation can expect to receive $4000 less in income per year.[8] This same effect has been documented in Great Britain.[9] Indeed, these figures are consistent with experience: when previously male dominated fields have opened up to women, the relative wages paid for those jobs have tended to decrease.[10] Therefore, in addition to the nature of the work itself, there is something about a job being associated with women that makes it less valuable: women's lower social status as compared to that of men within our society.[11] . . .

In opposition to pay equity advocates, proponents of human capital theory, which argues that the market accurately rewards personal characteristics related to productivity, contend that important differences between women and men, such as education, experience, and job commitment, account for the wage gap.[12] It is true that there are some important overall differences in the job qualifications of men and women that are potentially related to earnings. Women, many of whom are new to the work force, have less job experience than men.[13] Women tend to have higher turnover rates than men, which makes them statistically less likely to receive the benefits of on-the-job training and the upward mobility that comes with longer tenure at one job.[14]

Although human capital theory provides some insight into explaining the wage gap, it has two principal limitations. First and most importantly, human capital theory "does not resolve the key issue of cause and effect: that is, the extent to which low wages and discrimination discourage women from investing in human capital,"[15] the education, experience, and long-term commitment that would result in higher wages. Second, at all educational levels, women earn less than men with comparable credentials.[16] . . .

Therefore, gender segregation among and within occupations has important consequences in any attempt to close the wage gap through equal pay legislation. The depth of commitment embodied in a pay equity regime should be measured by its ability to overcome occupational segregation as a bar to women's claims for equality. Given the high degree of occupational segregation present in Ontario, Great Britain, and the United States, any pay equity regime that guarantees a woman merely the same pay as her male coworkers doing the same job, is a very narrow remedy indeed. Moreover, this "like work" approach to pay equity does nothing to remedy the cycle whereby women's low social status contributes to their earning low wages, which in turn reinforces their low social status. Only a comparable worth approach to pay equity, providing equal pay for work of equal value, can overcome the obstacle of gender segregation and help to break the cycle of women's social and economic subordination.

B. Job Evaluation: How It Works

Within a pay equity regime, job evaluation is potentially important because it is the primary mechanism for comparing the value of jobs with different content. Without some form of job evaluation, it would be virtually impossible for women to claim pay equity with any men other than those employed in identical jobs. Given the high levels of gender segregation in the work place, any regulatory regime which prescribed such a limited set of male comparators would leave many women without a viable pay equity remedy.

Job evaluation is the process of gathering information about the content of jobs within an organization and arranging them into a hierarchy for the purposes of wage-setting. Originally, job evaluation was developed by management, not as a tool for change, but as a means of entrenching the status quo. In fact, many job evaluation systems were intended to do nothing more than to describe existing pay structures, identifying various job characteristics that impacted compensation and using them to justify wage differentials within the hierarchy.

There are two broad categories of job evaluation, the "whole jobs" approach and point factor systems. Essentially, the whole jobs approach arranges jobs into a hierarchy according to what "feels fair." Since it is so unspecific, the whole jobs approach creates problems in uniform application and is particularly prone to subjectivity and the problem of gender bias. Therefore, the whole jobs evaluation method holds little positive value in pay equity determinations and is only mentioned in order to point out what kinds of job evaluation should not, probably under any circumstances, be accorded any judicial deference.

In contrast, point factor systems are analytical. Management designates factors that it thinks are indicative of job value and worthy of compensation, such as skill, effort, and responsibility. Additionally, management assigns these factors' weights, in terms of maximum point values, based upon what it decides is their relative importance. Job evaluation teams, which often consist of both management and employee representatives, collect data about various jobs, either through observation, or commonly, an employee questionnaire. The jobs are then arranged into a hierarchy based upon the total number of points awarded. Several "benchmark" jobs are selected and their compensation rates are adjusted so as to be competitive with other companies either in the industry or geographic area. The benchmark jobs are then used to set the compensation for other positions in the firm.

C. Job Evaluation: Problems of Gender Bias

As currently used, point factor job evaluation systems have several limitations as a means of comparing different jobs in order to claim pay equity for work of equal value. First, the point factors typically used reflect skills predominantly associated with men's jobs. Point factor job evaluation developed after World War II, when there were few women in the work force, and service industries were not nearly as important in large economies as they are today. . . .

Moreover, traditional methods of gathering information about job content may be ill-suited to predominantly female jobs. . . . [A] time-allotment method fails to capture the primary difficulty associated with many women's jobs: having to deal with constant interruptions (phones, bosses, doctors, customers) while performing an ongoing task such as typing or providing care. . . .

In contrast to the institutionalized recognition of the demands of predominantly male jobs, many skills associated with the types of jobs held by women, such as nursing, teaching, and the like, seem to go unrecognized precisely because they mirror traditional duties within the home. . . . So while men, for example, typically receive points for dirt and grease that they encounter on the job under a factor designated "working conditions," nurses, who deal with vomit, blood, and excrement on a daily basis, receive no such points.[17] Similarly, men typically receive

points for noise attributed to machinery in factories, but clerical workers rarely get credit for concentrating amidst the sounds of phones and typewriters.

Similarly, clerical jobs are predominantly held by women and require a relatively high degree of training but are not highly valued. In contrast to many manufacturing and trade jobs which require a great deal of visible on the job training, skills such as typing and stenography are prerequisites for a job, and must be learned outside of the employer's presence. . . . Thus, women do not receive the points and therefore the compensation that their skills seem to merit.

Finally, the use of benchmark jobs by employers to make internal pay scales competitive with prevailing market rates is inconsistent with the notion of pay equity, broadly defined, because it incorporates the pervasive undervaluation of women's work in the marketplace and ensures that it will merely be replicated.

Therefore, the uncritical use of job evaluation as a means of achieving pay equity poses substantial risks for women. Currently, most job evaluation systems embody gender stereotypes that result in the undervaluation of women's work in the labor marketplace. Unless pay equity advocates can eradicate these stereotypes and create job evaluation systems that recognize the value of work done predominantly by women, providing the basis of increased wages, this strategy risks legitimating the status quo. . . .

Of the three paradigms discussed in this Note, Ontario's model makes the greatest use of job evaluation and possesses the most potential for promoting pay equity, given the high levels of gender segregation both within and among occupations. Unlike the U.S. and British models, which encourage employers to conduct voluntary job evaluation as a means of avoiding or defending against liability in litigation, Ontario's pay equity regime places a mandatory duty upon employers to conduct job evaluation.

Even using traditional methods, mandatory job evaluation would likely substantially increase the wages of women in predominantly female occupations. Yet Ontario's model for pay equity goes even further, permitting broad challenges to employer job evaluation schemes as discriminatory for their failure to capture and to compensate the skills, effort and responsibility associated with predominantly female occupations. Not only the factors used to identify job worth are open to challenge, but also their relative weight. Under Ontario's model, the Hearings Tribunal will substitute the employer's and the market's evaluation with its own assessment of job value to ensure that jobs of equal value are compensated equally. Therefore, the Ontarian model is extremely capable of overcoming the problem of occupational segregation in comparing and achieving pay equity among jobs of comparable worth that are predominantly segregated by gender.

Admittedly, Ontario's model involves a substantial amount of government regulation and interference in the employer/employee relationship. Moreover, there have been serious problems implementing Ontario's model that have undermined its efficacy in promoting pay equity.

Even if Ontario's model is not ultimately adopted elsewhere, however, its central principle: that the skills, effort, and responsibilities required by predominantly female jobs should be made visible, recognized, and adequately compensated, can and should be applied within other pay equity models. Certainly, this principle can be applied to broaden the concepts of indirect gender discrimination in traditional job evaluation recognized by both "like work" and more limited comparable worth models.

Perhaps more importantly, gender neutrality in job evaluation can become both a political issue as well as a focus of negotiation between employers and employees, particularly in predominantly female occupations. The collaboration of employers and employees in developing gender-neutral pay equity plans mandated under Ontario's model has its own inherent value. By calling into question the discriminatory notions of skill and job value embodied in traditional job evaluation systems, this process has the potential to improve popular, as well as women's own perceptions about the value of women's work. Where this gender-conscious reassessment of job value for the purpose of promoting pay equity is not legally required, female employees should mobilize, through organized labor where it is available, to claim this right for themselves.

As the discussion of traditional job evaluation illustrates, cultural attitudes are not inconsequential but have pervasive impact. Increased awareness of the previously unrecognized value of predominantly female jobs will elevate the status of the women who perform them. Only a serious reassessment of traditional, gender-biased notions of job value has the potential to break the cycle by which women's low social status and depressed wages are mutually reinforced.

NOTES

1. Ellen E. Hodgson, *Equal Pay for Work of Equal Value in Ontario and Great Britain: A Comparison,* 30 Alberta L. Rev. 926, 928 (1992).

2. Fiona Neathey, *Job Assessment, Job Evaluation and Equal Value, in* Equal Value / Comparable Worth in the UK and the USA, 65, 66 (Peggy Kahn & Elizabeth Meehan eds., 1992).

3. *Weekly Earnings, Earnings Increased 3.3 Percent for Wage, Salary Workers in 1991,* 21 Daily Lab. Rep. (BNA) No. 21, at B.4 (Feb. 5,1992).

4. Neathey, *supra* note 8, at 66.

5. Committee on Occupational Classification and Analysis, National Research Council,

Women, Work, and Wages: Equal Pay for Jobs of Equal Value 25 (Donald J. Treiman & Heidi I. Hartmann eds., 1981) [hereinafter Women, Work, and Wages].

6. *Id.* at 24.
7. *Women, Work, and Wages, supra* note 13, at 28.
8. *Id.*
9. Michael Rubenstein, *Equal Pay for Work of Equal Value: The New Regulations and Their Implications* 19 (1984).
10. *Id.*
11. Townsend-Smith, *supra* note 5, at 15.
12. *See* Rubenstein, *supra* note 20, at 13–14.

13. *Id.* at 15 (citing many studies which conclude that factors such as education and job responsibilities, standing alone, contribute very little to the gender wage gap).
14. *Id.*
15. *Id.* at 16.
16. *Id.* at 14.
17. *See* Ronnie Steinberg & Lois Haignere, *Equitable Compensation: Methodological Criteria for Comparable Worth, in Ingredients for Women's Employment Policy* 157, 168 (Christine Bose & Glenna Spitze eds., 1987) (discussing frequently ignored female working conditions).

Comparable Pay for Comparable Work?

Robert L. Simon

"Equal pay for equal work" is one of the most defensible and most widely accepted principles to have been implemented in this country in the name of equal opportunity. However, implementation of the principle of equal pay for equal work has not significantly closed the gap between the pay men receive and the pay women receive in the marketplace. Thus, in 1955, women's earnings were about 60 percent of the earnings of men, and today women continue to make only about 60 cents for every dollar men make in the workplace.[1]

One fact that helps explain a significant portion of this gap between men's and women's earnings is the concentration of women in low-paying job categories. Roughly four-fifths of all women work in 25 of the 420 job categories listed by the Department of Labor.[2] Clearly, implementation of the principle of equal pay for equal work will not close the gap between the earnings of males

and earnings of females as long as, on the average, men and women are not doing the *same* work.

Accordingly, the support of many advocates of pay equity has shifted from the principle of equal pay for equal work to a new principle: the principle of *comparable pay for work of comparable worth* (PCW). Proponents of PCW argue that if the jobs in which women are concentrated are equal in worth to traditionally male jobs but pay less, then unequal pay across these jobs categories is inequitable and unjust.

Such an approach is not entirely new. For example, systems of job evaluation have been employed by the federal government and by many private employees to assess comparative pay of different job categories.[3] On a more intuitive level, who has not wondered whether some highly paid job category is really more important than a lower paid one? Is the work done by police officers of less worth

Reprinted by permission of the author, who gratefully acknowledges the National Endowment for the Humanities for summer stipend that supported the work on this paper.

than that performed by better paid corporate vice presidents in charge of advertising? Isn't the work of teachers equal in value to that of many lawyers, professional athletes, or entertainers?

Advocates of comparable worth want to generate a social policy from the sentiments that lie behind such questions. However, implementation of some version of PCW should take place only after extensive debate and consideration. If the difficulties PCW generates are not understood and faced, this principle is all too likely to become a purely political weapon that, while capable of generating intense feelings of discontent, is unlikely to result in more equity in the workplace. In the following pages we will explain and examine some of these difficulties in an effort to evaluate comparable worth as a social policy.

THE MEANING OF COMPARABLE WORTH

As we will see, many questions can be raised about the justice and fairness of various versions of PCW. However, before turning to such fundamental *moral* concerns, we must be clear about the notion of comparable worth itself. In particular, what does it *mean* to say that two jobs are of comparable worth? How are we to tell when two jobs are comparable? These questions, sometimes blurred together under the heading "the measurement problem," are of fundamental importance. Principles such as PCW can guide conduct only if they are clear enough so that those to whom they apply can understand what is being required of them.

As suggested above, the measurement problem really has two distinct parts. The first is to explain what is meant by "comparable worth." The second is to formulate a criterion for measuring comparable worth, as so defined. Without solutions to these prob-

lems, enforcement of PCW would be arbitrary and inequitable. Jobs judged comparable by one conception of comparable worth would not be so judged by another. Even if there were agreement on a conception of comparable worth, different criteria of measurement would yield different rankings of job categories. But justice and equity cannot vary arbitrarily; they require consistent application of defensible principles so that similar cases are treated alike.

We can begin with the question of meaning. What does it mean to say that two jobs are of comparable worth? Unfortunately, comparable worth can be understood in a variety of ways, many of which are irrelevant to understanding what advocates have in mind. For example, if we take the worth of a job to refer to its *intrinsic moral worth,* jobs would be comparable only when their intrinsic moral worth was equivalent. To the extent that this notion is intelligible at all (for it is far from clear that jobs even have intrinsic moral worth, let alone different degrees of it), it might rest on intuitions that some jobs — for example modeling for pornographic pictures — seem less worthy than others — for example that of a dedicated physician.

However, this clearly is not what advocates of comparable worth have in mind, and for good reason. It is difficult to see how an overall ranking of the intrinsic moral worth of different jobs is to be derived, or what would make it defensible. Moreover, it is doubtful if any one such ranking, even if it could be shown to be defensible, should be implemented in a pluralistic society in which the intuitions of many individuals and groups are likely to differ significantly.

If advocates of comparable worth do not mean to refer to the moral value of jobs, what do they mean? Perhaps the best clue is the reliance by advocates on job evaluation studies as measuring devices. These studies assess such factors as the degree of responsibility a job requires, the quality of working conditions, the training needed to do the work, the degree of skill required, and so forth. This list suggests that advocates of comparable worth conceive of the worth of a job as its "level of demand," where the demand a job makes on a worker is a function of the application of a variety of demand-making criteria. Different jobs are comparable when they make equivalent demands on the worker, as measured by a variety of demand-making factors. "Level of demand" here is being used as a technical term to refer to the aggregate of factors held to be criteria of what the job requires. So, in this view, secretaries are underpaid relative to truck drivers if and only if truck drivers make more than secretaries but their jobs are no more demanding.

The problem with this view is that there does not appear to be any one favored set of demand-making criteria specifying the "level of demand" of particular jobs. On the contrary, job evaluations themselves rest on controversial value judgments. For example, should enhanced responsibility be viewed as a burden that makes a job more difficult or as an asset that makes a job more stimulating? Is outdoor work more demanding than indoor work since workers may have to be on the job in inclement weather, or is it less demanding since workers get fresh air and are not chained to a desk? Even if we could arrive at uncontroversial answers to questions regarding criteria for the level of demand, how would we *weigh* such criteria in case of conflict? If librarians require more training than city bus drivers, but the bus drivers work under greater stress, which job is of greater worth? Clearly, each of these questions calls for complex evaluations which raise normative issues rather than ones that can be settled by straightforward observation of the *"facts."*

Conceptions of comparable worth can vary, then, according to the criteria for the level of demand that are employed and the weight assigned to each. Therefore, we should think of comparable worth not as one principle but as a related family of principles that differ from one another, often in significant respects. Thus, in any debate about comparable worth, it is important to make sure that all parties involved are considering the same conception.

Perhaps more importantly, if there is no way of showing that one conception of comparable worth is more defensible than others, application of any one conception rather than another seems arbitrary. Even if there is a defensible conception, if we can't tell what it is, implementation of comparable worth will be open to charges of inequity and unfairness. Jobs will be rated as comparable or non-comparable without a justified basis for doing so.

So far we have been talking only about the meaning of comparable worth. However, even if we could agree on the nature and weight of the criteria of comparable worth, application of such criteria also involves normative issues. For example, even if we agree that, all else being equal, greater responsibility entails a greater level of demand, how are we to measure responsibility? Is responsibility related to the number of people one supervises, the level of decision making one holds within a firm, the costs of misjudgment, or what? Thus, an airline mechanic may supervise few people but has a great deal of responsibility for people's lives. Is the mechanic's responsibility greater than that of top executives in the airline's office? How are we to tell?

The problems of meaning and measurement often are claimed to undermine completely the case for comparable worth. How can comparable worth be an instrument for securing social justice if there are no defensible criteria of comparability, no defensible assignments of weight to conflicting criteria, and no clear way to measure application of the criteria in controversial cases?

At this point advocates of comparable worth may agree that comparison of jobs does rest on arguable value judgments. It does not follow, they will point out, that such judgments must be entirely arbitrary or indefensible. For one thing, even though many judgments about comparability will be controversial, many more may not. For example, most of us would agree that normally a person who has the responsibility for evaluating the work of many employees has more responsibility than an employee who performs routine clerical tasks. Moreover, even if it is arguable in theory that a routine job should receive greater compensation than one that involves stimulating responsibilities, which presumably are their own reward, that is not the way the market traditionally has worked. Males with responsible jobs generally have received greater compensation than those performing routine tasks. Accordingly, proponents of comparable worth can argue that there are widely shared intuitions and inherited practices that can form a core of standards for evaluating conceptions of comparable worth. Although the core will have to be expanded in controversial ways to deal with difficult cases, advocates claim that it is equally controversial to rely on the market alone.

In other words, advocates of comparable worth can argue that starting with relatively uncontested judgments and practices, society, through debate, can work toward a *reflective equilibrium* on job comparability.[4] Such a reflective equilibrium will have been reached when the jobs we intuitively feel are comparable are shown to be so by principles we are willing to accept and which yield no conflicting or counterintuitive decisions in other cases. The process of reaching such a reflective equilibrium involves the mutual adjustment and readjustment of judgments and principles until they fit together in harmony. While a reflective equilibrium is reached, if at all, only after an extended process of consideration and debate, the process itself is likely to move us closer to consensus. In any case, advocates would argue that the results are likely to be less unjust and unfair than the way the market currently treats women.

Such an approach does at least show that problems of meaning and measurement are not necessarily unresolvable. Since the process of achieving reflective equilibrium takes considerable time, it will be unclear at any given point in the process whether particular job comparisons are warranted. This would count substantially against attempts to impose standards of comparable worth in one giant leap; for example, through congressional action or Supreme Court decision. Without actually going through the process, we would have no reason to place confidence in the defensibility of the imposed standards.

Moreover, even if this problem could be avoided, perhaps by having individual firms autonomously adopt their own standards of comparable worth, greater problems remain. For one thing, there is no guarantee that a social consensus about comparability will emerge. Individuals may arrive at their own personal reflective equilibriums, but why should those individual systematizations be in agreement with one another? Perhaps even more importantly, even if such a social agreement were to emerge from individual reflection, what moral weight would it have? Why should it be equated with the dictates of equity and justice rather than being regarded as a socially determined political consensus reflecting persuasion and political tradeoffs? How are we to distinguish a mere consensus from rational convergence on a common and defensible point of view?[5]

While such objections surely have force, they may not be decisive. After all, while there is no guarantee that a defensible equilibrium will be reached, there is no guarantee in other areas of social policy either. To the extent that the process of open discussion and democratic decision making is itself justifiable, it is as defensible in the area of comparable worth as in other areas of policy making. At the very least, by encouraging free discussion and criticism of prevailing views, biases are likely to be detected and criteria of comparability are likely to be gradually improved by exposure to the light of rational examination.

Our discussion suggests, then, that although questions of meaning are fundamental, they may not be so severe as to entirely undermine the case for comparable worth. Of course, if there is no clear account of how comparable worth is to be understood, it is likely to become a political football employed simply to advance the interests of groups that would benefit by its implementation. That may or may not be good policy, but it should not be confused with social justice. Nevertheless, it is at least arguable that defensible standards of comparability, initially based on considered judgments and existing practice, will emerge from the democratic decision-making process. Surely the burden of proof may still be on advocates to show that a given conception of comparable worth is defensible. Nevertheless, there may exist a procedure that would enable them to meet the task. Although healthy scepticism about that procedure may be warranted, it has not been established by the arguments we have considered that comparable worth is a necessarily unintelligible notion to be thrown out on grounds of incomprehensibility alone.

COMPARABLE WORTH AND SOCIAL JUSTICE

As we have seen, women tend to work in only a few of the occupations listed by the Labor Department, and there tend to be very few males in these occupations. For example, 97 percent of registered nurses are female, 99 percent of secretaries are female, and 84 percent of elementary school teachers are female. Moreover, as the number of males in a job category increases, so does the pay.[6] For example, household workers, 95 percent of which are female, make about half the average salary of janitors, 85 percent of which are males. Secretaries make only about three-fourths the average salary of truck drivers, virtually all of whom are male.[7] As stated earlier, overall women's earnings tend to be about 60 percent of the earnings of men in the marketplace.

This suggests a rationale for comparable worth. Most advocates of some version of PCW do not view it as a principle of ideal social justice, which any society must implement if it is to be fully just. . . . However, they argue that when differences in wages reflect sex discrimination, then the market has not operated properly, and corrective application of PCW is called for. . . . The point of instituting comparable worth is to correct for a breakdown in the market involving discrimination against women. Hence, comparable worth need not be instituted across the board, but only in those areas where women have been victimized by unfair treatment.

What is the evidence that women have been discriminated against? The wage gap itself often is cited as evidence of overt discrimination against women by employers. But while it cannot be doubted that such overt discrimination exists, there is considerable disagreement over whether it explains a significant proportion of the wage gap. Broad generalizations of the form, "Women make only X percent of what men make," tend not to be helpful, since it is the significance of such statistical claims that is at issue.

Many labor economists cite such pre-market factors as the greater tendency of women to interrupt their careers, sex differences in educational background, and the greater willingness of women to sacrifice career goals for family responsibilities as explanations for a significant part of the wage gap.[8] Thus, according to one recent study of a corporation, even when offered promotions and responsibilities commensurate with those of men, women tend to turn them down more often.[9] Many labor economists argue further that when women make the same market choices as men, they are similarly rewarded, as comparisons of the earnings of never-married working men and women suggest.[10] One typical statement by a labor economist asserts that "perhaps half of the overall 40 percent differential between the earnings of men and women is due to premarket factors."[11]

Statistics by themselves will not show whether the wage gap, as well as the disproportionate representation of women in certain job categories, results from discrimination, the choices women make, or some complex interaction between the two. According to the theory of rational choice, women make rational decisions, based on their own values, to subordinate career to family responsibilities to a greater extent than men. According to critics of such a view, women make such decisions only because their expected return on the market is much less than men because of discrimination, and hence they have less incentive to pursue careers.[12]

We cannot decide between these two views here, but several points can be made. First, even if overt discrimination does play some role in contributing to the wage gap, it is far from clear that comparable worth is an appropriate or necessary response. Existing equal opportunity legislation prohibits the kind of on-the-job discrimination by employers that is at issue. Second, even if on-the-job discrimination were eliminated, the wage gap would persist so long as women remain concentrated in lower-paying job categories. Such concentration does not seem to be caused primarily by employer discrimination,

since it occurs when women first enter the job market and overt discrimination would take place after women were actually on the job.

However, advocates of comparable worth might plausibly distinguish overt on-the-job discrimination from the more systematic and covert discrimination that limits women's choices in the market. For example, until very recently, not only were many jobs held largely by males (such as that of bartender) deemed unsuitable for females, but such prejudices were upheld by the courts.[13] Since women saw that their opportunities in the job market were limited, it became rational for them to devote more time to family than to their careers. Women, in other words, are caught in a vicious circle. "Women stay home because of low wages; women earn low wages because they stay at home."[14] It is widespread social and economic barriers, ranging from guidance counselors who steer women into "acceptable" career paths to socially enforced stereotypes about unsuitable jobs for women, that keep women concentrated in low-paying job categories.

Such theories of covert discrimination seem more relevant to the case for comparable worth than appeals to overt discrimination by employers, since they call into question the legitimacy of the initial situation within which women first make economic choices. However, such approaches are not free from difficulty. For one thing, they run the risk of degenerating into the kind of feminist theories about socialization and conditioning that deny that women function as autonomous agents in the first place. It seems far too self-serving to dismiss the traditional preferences of many women as simply the products of conditioning while always assuming that preferences more to one's liking are the truly autonomous ones. Such a claim might sometimes be true, but it makes it all too easy, as one writer sympathetic to feminism points out, "to slide into the convenient idea that *whenever* women make choices which feminists think they ought not to make, they must be conditioned, so giving feminists an excuse to discount those opinions. . . . The attempt to free women turns into a different way of coercing them."[15] Indeed, the picture of women as brainwashed puppets is unacceptable — and in fact is contradicted by the recent behavior of women in the work force who have integrated many predominantly male job categories.

However, advocates of the theory of covert discrimination need not dismiss the claim that women make autonomous choices. Indeed, the fact that women are moving into predominantly male job categories suggests that when given the same opportunities and the same expected return, many women will make market choices that are similar to those of men. In this view, the concentration of women in low-paying job categories does reflect women's choices, but their choices frequently don't reflect the values women would express in a fair and equal context for decision making. Rather, they are rational responses to the illegitimately confining set of incentives that women face.

This argument is not implausible, especially when it is shown to be compatible with some aspects of rational choice theory. However, its connection with comparable worth is not clear. Advocates assume that if covert discrimination is a principal factor underlying the wage gap, comparable worth is justified. But is that assumption correct?

For one thing, comparable worth does not seem to be a form of compensation for individual victims of discrimination. Comparable worth affects everyone in a benefited job category, whether or not they have individually suffered from discrimination. Indeed, not only does comparable worth ignore the important principle that compensation should be proportional to injury; it virtually stands it on its head. Older women, who have fewer years left to work but who presumably are most likely to have been victims of discrimination, will receive the fewest benefits. Younger women, particularly those just entering the job market, who are least likely to have been victims of discrimination, will work the greatest number of years under comparable worth and hence will receive the greatest benefits.

Advocates of comparable worth rightly will reply that their goal is not to compensate individuals for discrimination. But what then is the connection between comparable worth and alleged discrimination in the market? Perhaps it is that since the market wage scale is heavily influenced by sex discrimination, comparable worth provides an untainted and therefore fairer standard of compensation. It is not that market wages, set by supply and demand, are *inherently* unfair. Rather, it is that since women in our society have not been in a fair market, comparable worth should replace the wage standards set by a tainted pseudomarket procedure.

Before adopting such a procedure, however, we should be sure that adoption of some form of comparable worth does promote overall fairness. If the adoption of comparable worth would itself generate serious problems of justice and fairness, we would need to consider whether overall gains, in terms of social justice, outweigh losses before recommending adoption.

Consider, first, the problems that would arise if a single standard of comparable worth were promulgated through legislation or as the result of a major court decision. How would such a single standard be arrived at? On what basis would it be selected? What would justify the standard employed? If, as suggested earlier, judgments of comparability are all too likely to rest upon highly controversial and contestable value judgments, why should the new pay scale be any more equitable than the old one? If the standard cannot be justified, those who are disadvantaged by it will have no reason to accept the resulting wage scale as fair. Thus, even without considering the kinds of complications to be discussed below, it is doubtful whether clear gains in equity would be achieved by implementation of a single standard of comparable worth, at least so long as judgments of comparability lack a substantial basis.

Perhaps this difficulty can be avoided by implementing comparable worth on a piece-meal basis, in a long-term effort to reach a reflective equilibrium on comparability. In this view, individual firms, or perhaps individual localities, adopt their own internal comparable worth plans, and these need not be identical.

But this piece-meal approach also raises problems of justice and fairness. One such problem is that workers doing the same job in different firms might have their jobs evaluated totally differently. In Firm X security guards and secretaries might be regarded as comparable while in Firm Y they might not be regarded as comparable. Suppose that as a result of comparability rankings, secretaries in X were paid more than secretaries in Y, even though all the secretaries do the same work. Of course, secretaries in different firms are presently paid differently, just as assistant professors at Harvard may receive higher compensation than assistant professors at a less highly rated institution; but this would not be a result of a purely internal job evaluation scheme that might later be found to be in sharp conflict with our considered judgments.

Perhaps some initial arbitrariness must be expected as the price to be paid as we move toward a less arbitrary reflective equilibrium. After all, as advocates of comparable worth would claim, the market itself reflects inequity in the treatment of women. The temporary unfairness generated by piece-meal approaches to comparable worth may be less than the unfairness that would persist if the status quo were simply allowed to stand.

Even though such a rejoinder has force, other serious problems of equity remain. Some of these are not problems of pure theory, but may become particularly acute when some form of comparable worth is applied in the real world. For example, the piece-meal approach to comparable worth generates economic incentives for firms to select those evaluators whose conceptions of comparable worth create the least economic disadvantage. Each employer reasons that if other employers adopt comparable worth plans without regard to market advantage, she can do better by adopting a less disadvantageous plan. Indeed, even employers with some genuine commitment to comparable worth may have to act in such fashion as a defensive measure against other firms that use comparable worth to secure market gains. In either case, it is rational for the employer to select the conception of comparable worth that departs least from the wage structure the market would have dictated. We are left with the inequitable result that employers most seriously committed to comparable worth are most open to exploitation by less-committed competitors. Indeed, without a defensible standard of comparable worth, how are employers who take unfair advantage of the system even to be identified?

The evaluation of equity becomes even more complicated when other costs of comparable worth are considered. It is extremely likely, for instance, that implementation of some form of comparable worth will lead to an overall rise in wages. Thus, if the work of a firm's clerical staff is found to be comparable to that of higher-paid truckers, it is unlikely that pay cuts can be forced on the truckers. Instead, the salaries of the clerical workers will be raised to a comparable level. This means that the firm's overall costs of production will rise. These costs are generally passed on to consumers, but firms in weak positions may be unable to do this and in some cases may even be forced out of business.

Suppose that costs are passed on to consumers in the form of higher prices. It is by no means clear that such costs will be passed on equitably. If the firm produces necessities, the poor will pay a disproportionate share of the cost, since they spend a higher percentage of their income on necessities than do the more affluent. When the employer in question is the federal, state, or local government, services may be cut in an effort to avoid tax hikes that pay increases would otherwise require. Again these cuts in services may disproportionately affect the relatively poor and powerless.

Perhaps most importantly, many economists argue that comparable worth may not help (and may even harm) the very group it is designed to benefit.[16] If comparable worth raises the employer's costs of doing business, it creates an incentive to reduce the number of employees whose salaries are above the market price. In other words, if comparable worth makes the cost of employing people in certain job categories excessive, employers will have an incentive to reduce the number of people holding such jobs. Since the jobs in question are those held predominantly by women, comparable worth may ultimately create fewer employment opportunities for women than would otherwise have existed.[17]

Of course, it is possible that such dire empirical consequences will not come about, or that negative consequences will be outweighed by gains. The issues here are in part empirical as well as conceptual and moral. The moral point, however, is that harmful or inequitable consequences must be given adequate weight in the evaluation of comparable worth and must not be ignored because of perhaps justified indignation about the economic situation of women in the market.

Finally, when considering questions of equity and fairness, we need to consider how much *weight* comparable worth should be given when it is in conflict with other values, such as efficiency. Suppose, for example, that a state's job evaluation plan finds that electrical engineers and city planners do comparable work but that the state is faced with a shortage of electrical engineers and a surplus of city planners. One way of luring talented engineers to the area, or of inducing students to study electrical engineering, is to raise the wages of the electrical engineers. But if in order to do so the state must also raise the wages of all workers in comparable jobs, not only may the costs be prohibitive but the incentive effects of higher wages would be lost. In spite of social needs, individuals would find it just as desirable to become city planners as electrical engineers. Comparable worth, then, is inefficient insofar as it limits our ability to use higher compensation to attract people to positions where they are needed.

Of course, some losses in efficiency may be warranted by gains in the overall justice of the system. Indeed, it is plausible to think that small gains in justice and fairness outweigh larger losses in overall efficiency, since it is normally wrong to make some people better off by treating others unjustly. On the other hand, losses in efficiency may become so great as to outweigh minor gains in justice or equity, or may themselves constitute an injustice if sufficiently great and distributed in unfair or questionable ways. Clearly, enormous losses in efficiency normally are not justified by small gains in the overall justice or fairness of a system. We have already seen that the costs of comparable worth may be borne disproportionately by the relatively poor and powerless or perhaps even by some of those women the policy was designed to help. But even if these costs are ignored, the inefficiencies generated by departure from the pricing system have to be balanced against whatever gains comparable worth may promote. Thus, before implementing any particular conception of comparable worth, we must decide *the degree to which implementation will be restricted in case of conflict with other values.* In other words, if comparable worth is not to be an absolute to be applied regardless of other costs, what tradeoffs should we be prepared to make?

It will be well to remember here that the line between such values as efficiency, on one hand, and equity and justice, on the other, is not always a sharp one. If the costs of inefficiency are borne disproportionately by the least advantaged and the least powerful, questions of equity and social justice are raised. Our discussion suggests that this may actually be the case with comparable worth. At the very least, we need good reason to think the costs will be fairly distributed before we hop aboard the comparable worth bandwagon.

Finally, before concluding our discussion of equity and fairness, we need to consider in what sense comparable worth might be a "remedy" for the concentration of women in low-paying job categories. It is unlikely that it will eliminate such concentration; in fact, it may perpetuate it. Since institution of comparable worth would remove much of the economic incentive for women to follow the same career paths as men, by compensating "women's" work comparably to "men's" work, it could be argued that women would have less reason to leave traditional female career paths than under the present system.[18] As a matter of empirical fact, in recent years, there has been significant movement of women into some previously male-dominated jobs. In 1960, for example, only 9 percent of insurance adjusters were female, while in 1981, 58 percent were female. Similarly, recent figures reveal that 47 percent of bartenders now are women — a significant change from times when the courts refused even to allow women to be bartenders on the paternalistic grounds that women were too pure to be sullied by such work.[19] Gains in female representation also have been made in law, medicine, and business, although many other job categories tend to remain almost exclusively male. Would comparable worth remove financial incentives for even more sexual integration in the workplace?

We need to be careful of trying to have it both ways on this point. It is surely possible that higher pay for traditionally female jobs will draw more male candidates, contributing to sexual integration through the back door. In turn, increased competition may require more and more women to try for employment in traditionally male job categories. The empirical issues here are difficult, and no prediction is likely to be uncontroversial. But it is at least possible that comparable worth will result in a reduction of jobs in traditionally female employment categories, the consequent forcing out of women who are unprepared for or who prefer not to engage in traditionally male work, and only minimal male interest in traditionally female jobs. While this is undoubtedly a "worst possible case" scenario, is it any less probable than more favorable alternatives? On the other hand, if we don't promulgate a version of comparable worth, will more women in the work force be worse off than if we did? What kind of evidence do we need before we decide? Morally, what is the fairest way of distributing benefits and burdens? What should public policy be under conditions of uncertainty and even radical disagreement on such fundamental points?

CONCLUSIONS

What does our discussion suggest about the overall case for comparable worth? For one thing, it suggests that simplistic approaches and political analysis by slogan are to be rejected. Clarence Pendleton, Chair of the U.S. Civil Rights Commission in 1985, who referred to comparable worth as "looney tunes," surely is mistaken. On the other hand, unquestioning adherence to comparable worth simply because the intent of the policy is to benefit women, or because of support by some feminists, may also be unwarranted.

Just because the situation is complex, it does not follow that nothing sensible can be said about it. One thing rational analysis can do, even when no entirely satisfactory alternative is available, is to set out the costs of holding different positions. This not only puts each of us in a better position to see what objections need to be answered and to see which policy best coheres with our other moral judgments, it may also promote reasonable choice under conditions of uncertainty.

In particular, proponents of comparable worth face serious difficulties. For one thing, it is at best unclear whether jobs can be compared in the way required. Imposition of a single nationwide standard of comparability seems unjustified, given the difficulties of justification that we have explored. Alternatively, even if we might eventually achieve a societal reflective equilibrium on comparability through the piece-meal approach, we do not have one now. Hence, promulgation of some form of comparable worth will not necessarily promote more equity in the workplace, particularly at the start. Moreover, it also is unclear whether comparable worth will help women as a class, or whether it will only help some women perhaps at significant expense to others. Finally, comparable worth may assign costs to those least able to bear them and may encourage gerrymandering of individual comparable worth plans to secure market advantages.

Proponents of comparable worth may acknowledge these difficulties, but they reply that the overall costs, including any possible inequities, are less serious than those generated by present reliance on the market. Be that as it may, such a reply seems insufficient to justify adoption of comparable worth, at least at the present time. For one thing, as we have seen, the degree to which the wage gap is explained by discrimination, even of the covert variety, is controversial. But even leaving that point aside, is it sensible to adopt a new broad-scale social formula for setting wages without any guarantee, or even reasonable assurances, that gains in equity and social justice will result? Without such reasonable assurances, comparable worth looks more and more like a social policy that will benefit some groups at the expense of others rather than a requirement of social justice.

In short, we started out with the claim that comparable worth is needed to remedy the unjust treatment of women in the workplace. Our discussion suggests, however, that the burden of proof remains on advocates of comparable worth. That is, while the evidence we have considered warrants neither total rejection nor total acceptance of comparable worth, it does support a healthy skepticism. Unless there is good reason to believe that comparisons of jobs will be supportable, that the costs of implementation will be distributed fairly, and that some mechanism will be instituted to balance comparable worth against other values in case of conflict, adoption of comparable worth seems premature at best. Perhaps these problems can be resolved, but adoption of this policy in advance of a resolution would be unwarranted.

This does not mean that the plight of women in the job market should be ignored. Greater enforcement of equal opportunity legislation surely is needed. Where possible, work options such as "flex-time" and the institution of regulated day-care centers can help all workers, male or female, to reconcile responsibilities to both family and career.

Greater sensitivity among educators and guidance personnel can contribute to even greater sexual integration in the work force. Finally, the economic contribution that women make to their families can receive greater recognition and protection by law.

Accordingly, before we implement some version of comparable worth, we need to resolve the problems it presents. In view of the real difficulties facing it, we should not just assume that it is a clear requirement of justice and fairness in the workplace. Rather, we need to consider whether comparable worth really is a defensible remedy for social injustice rather than a device that will simply replace old problems with new ones while moving us no closer to the goals of fairness and justice that we all should seek.

NOTES

1. Ronald G. Ehrenberg and Robert S. Smith, *Modern Labor Economics* (Glenview, Ill.: Scott, Foresman and Company, 1982), 396. If a different base year is selected, different results are obtained. Thus, if 1964 is taken as the base, one finds a slight decrease in the gap by 1979. Clearly, great care must be taken in the use of statistics in this area.
2. "Paying Women What They're Worth," *Report from the Center for Philosophy & Public Policy* 3 (1983): 1–2.
3. For discussion, see Sharon P. Smith, *Equal Pay in the Public Sector: Fact or Fantasy.* (Princeton, N.J.: Princeton University Press, 1977).
4. The idea of reflective equilibrium is developed and applied to the justification of a theory of justice by John Rawls, in his *A Theory of Justice* (Cambridge: Harvard University Press, 1971), especially pp. 46–48, 577–579.
5. R. M. Hare argues that appeal to reflective equilibrium amounts to little more than appeal to accepted beliefs in his "Rawls' Theory

of Justice," *The Philosophical Quarterly,* 23 (1973): 144–155, 241–251.
6. Bureau of Labor Statistics, 1981, reprinted in "Paying Women What They're Worth."
7. Bureau of Labor Statistics, 1982, reprinted in "Paying Women What They're Worth."
8. For discussion, see Michael Evan Gold, *A Dialogue on Comparable Worth* (Ithaca: Cornell University Press, 1983), and Ehrenberg and Smith, *Modern Labor Economics*, 395–397.
9. See Carl Hoffmann and John Shelton Reed, "Sex Discrimination? — the XYZ Affair," *The Public Interest* 62 (1980): 21–39.
10. U.S. Bureau of Labor Statistics, *Handbook of Labor Statistics,* Table 60. However, other figures show that some significant inequality of results persists even when never married men and women are compared; see Ehrenberg and Smith, *Modern Labor Economics,* pp. 397–398.
11. Ehrenberg and Smith, *Modern Labor Economics,* p. 39.
12. For discussion, see Gold, *A Dialogue on Comparable Worth,* pp. 14–16.
13. See, for example, *Goesaert v. Cleary,* 335 U.S. 464 (1948), upholding a Michigan law which provided that no woman (unless she was the wife or daughter of the male owner) could obtain a bartender's license.
14. Gold, *A Dialogue on Comparable Worth,* p. 14.
15. Janet Radcliffe Richards, *The Sceptical Feminist* (Boston: Routledge and Kegan Paul, 1980).
16. For discussion, see George Hildebrand, "The Market System," in *Comparative Worth,* ed. Robert Libernash (Washington, D.C.: Equal Treatment Advisory Council, 1980), especially p. 106.
17. This point is debated throughout Gold, *A Dialogue on Comparable Worth.*
18. Conversely, higher salaries for traditionally female jobs may attract males to compete for such positions. However, this incentive effect may be less than expected if there is a stigma attached to men doing "women's work."
19. "More Women Work at Traditional Male Jobs," *New York Times,* No. 15, 1982, p. C26.

The Definition of Sexual Harassment

Edmund Wall

As important as current managerial, legal and philosophical definitions of sexual harassment are, many of them omit the interpersonal features which define the concept. Indeed, the mental states of the perpetrator and the victim are the essential defining elements. In this essay arguments are presented against mere behavior descriptions of sexual harassment, definitions formulated in terms of the alleged discriminatory and coercive effects of a sexual advance, and the federal legal definition which omits reference to relevant mental states. It is argued that sexual harassment is essentially a form of invasive communication that violates a victim's privacy rights. A set of jointly necessary and sufficient conditions of sexual harassment are defended which purport to capture the more subtle instances of sexual harassment while circumventing those sexual advances that are not sexually harassive. . . .

Probably any behavior which constitutes sexual harassment . . . constitute[s] sexual abuse — whether physical or verbal. When an individual is maliciously or negligently responsible for unjustified harm to someone, it would seem that he has abused that person. Abuse can be subtle. It may include various ways of inflicting psychological harm. In fact, there is a more subtle form of sexual harassment accomplished through stares, gestures, innuendo, etc. For example, a manager may sexually harass his employee by staring at her and "undressing her with his eyes." *In light of this and the other limitations of behavior descriptions we need a set of jointly necessary and sufficient conditions of sexual harassment capable of capturing all subtle instances of sexual harassment while filtering out (even overt) sexual behavior which is not harassive.*

Wherein X is the sexual harasser and Y the victim, the following are offered as jointly necessary and sufficient conditions of sexual harassment:

(1) X does not attempt to obtain Y's consent to communicate to Y, X's or someone else's purported sexual interest in Y.

(2) X communicates to Y, X's or someone else's purported sexual interest in Y. X's motive for communicating this is some perceived benefit that he expects to obtain through the communication.

(3) Y does not consent to discuss with X, X's or someone else's purported sexual interest in Y.

(4) Y feels emotionally distressed because X did not attempt to obtain Y's consent to this discussion and/or because Y objects to the content of X's sexual comments.

The first condition refers to X's failure to attempt to obtain Y's consent to discuss someone's sexual interest in Y. X's involvement in the sexual harassment is not defined by the sexual proposition that X may make to Y. If the first condition was formulated in terms of the content of X's sexual proposition, then the proposed definition would circumvent some of the more subtle cases of sexual harassment. After all, Y may actually agree to a sexual proposition made to her by X and still be sexually harassed by X's attempting to discuss it with her. In some cases Y might not feel that it is the proper time or place to discuss such matters. In any event *sexual harassment primarily involves wrongful communication.* Whether or not X attempts to obtain Y's con-

Source: *Public Affairs Quarterly*, Vol. 5 (1991): 371–381. Reprinted by permission.

sent to a certain type of communication is crucial. What is inherently repulsive about sexual harassment is not the possible vulgarity of *X*'s sexual comment or proposal, but his failure to show respect for *Y*'s rights. It is the obligation that stems from privacy rights that is ignored. . . . If *X* does not attempt to obtain *Y*'s approval to discuss such private matters, then he has not shown *Y* adequate respect.

X's lack of respect for *Y*'s rights is not a sufficient condition of sexual harassment. *X*'s conduct must constitute a rights violation. Essentially, the second condition refers to the fact that *X* has acted without concern for *Y*'s right to consent to the communication of sexual matters involving her. Here *X* "communicates" to *Y* that *X* or someone else is sexually interested in *Y*. This term includes not only verbal remarks made by *X*, but any purposeful conveyance such as gestures, noises, stares, etc. that violate its recipient's privacy rights. Such behavior can be every bit as intrusive as verbal remarks.

We need to acknowledge that *X* can refer to some third party's purported sexual interest in *Y* and still sexually harass *Y*. When he tells her, without her consent, that some third party believes she is physically desirable, this may be a form of sexual harassment. *Y* may not approve of *X* telling her this — even if *Y* and the third party happen to share a mutual sexual interest in each other. This is because *X*'s impropriety lies in his invasive approach to *Y*. It does not hinge upon the content of what he says to *Y*. *X* may, for example, have absolutely no sexual interest in *Y*, but believes that such remarks would upset *Y*, thereby affording him perverse enjoyment. Likewise, his report that some third party is sexually interested in *Y* may be inaccurate but this does not absolve him from his duty to respect *Y*'s privacy.

X's specific motive for communicating what he does to *Y* may vary, but it always includes some benefit *X* may obtain from this illegitimate communication. *X* might or might not plan to have sexual relations with *Y*. Indeed, as we have seen, he might not a have a sexual interest in *Y* at all and still obtain what he perceives to be beneficial to himself, perhaps the satisfaction of disturbing *Y*. . . . The point is that, whatever the perceived benefit, it is the utility of the approach as perceived by *X*, and not necessarily the content of his message, that is important to the harasser. Furthermore, the "benefit" that moves him to action might not be obtainable or might not be a genuine benefit, but, nevertheless, in his attempt to obtain it, he violates his victim's rights.

The third condition refers to *Y*'s not consenting to discuss with *X*, *X*'s or someone else's purported sexual interest in *Y*. Someone might argue that the first condition is now unnecessary, that *X*'s failure to obtain *Y*'s consent to the type of discussion outlined in the third condition will suffice; the provision concerning *X*'s failure to *attempt* to obtain *Y*'s consent is, therefore, unnecessary. This objection would be misguided, however. The first condition insures that some sexual comments will not be unjustly labelled as "harassive." Consider the possibility that the second and third conditions are satisfied. For example, *X* makes a sexual remark about *Y* to *Y* without her consent. Now suppose that the first condition is not satisfied, that is, suppose that *X* *did attempt* to obtain *Y*'s consent to make such remarks. Furthermore, suppose that somewhere the communication between *X* and *Y* breaks down and *X* honestly believes he has obtained *Y*'s consent to this discussion when, in fact, he has not. In this case, *X*'s intentions being what they are, he does not sexually harass *Y*. *X* has shown respect for *Y*'s privacy. *Y* may certainly *feel* harassed in this case, but there is no offender here. However, after *X* sees *Y*'s displeasure at his remarks, it is now his duty to refrain from such remarks, unless, of course, *Y* later consents to such a discussion.

The case of the ignorant but well-intentioned X demonstrates the importance of distinguishing between accidents (and merely unfortunate circumstances) and sexual harassment. The remedy for avoiding the former is the encouragement of clear communication between people. Emphasis on clear communication would also facilitate the identification of some offenders, for some offenders would not refrain from making sexual remarks after their targets clearly expressed their objections to those remarks. The above case also reveals that the alleged victim needs to clearly express her wishes to others. For example, when she wishes not to discuss an individual's sexual interest in her, it would be foolish for her to make flirting glances at this individual. Such gestures may mislead him to conclude that she consents to this communication.

The first three conditions are not jointly sufficient descriptions of sexual harassment. What is missing is a description of Y's mental state. In sexual harassment cases the maligned communication must distress Y for a certain reason. Let us say that X has expressed interest in Y without any attempt to obtain her consent. She, in fact, does not consent to it. However, perhaps she has decided against the discussion because she finds X too refined and anticipates that his sexual advances will not interest her. Perhaps she welcomes crass discussions about sexual matters. In this case she might not be sexually harassed by X's remarks. As the fourth condition indicates, Y must be distressed because X did not attempt to insure that it was permissible to make sexual comments to Y which involve her, or because the content of X's sexual comments are objectionable to Y. Yet another possibility is that both the invasiveness of X's approach and the content of what X says causes Y emotional distress. In this case, however, it would appear that Y would neither object to the content of X's sexual remarks nor to the fact that X did not attempt to obtain Y's consent to make these remarks to her. Due to Y's views concerning sexual privacy this case is similar to one in which X does not attempt to obtain Y's consent to discuss with Y how well she plays tennis, or some other mundane discussion about Y. . . .

The fact that male employers and managers represent the bulk of the reported offenders has caused some legal theorists and philosophers to conclude that sexual harassment necessarily involves discrimination against women as a class. This approach is unacceptable. The proposed description of sexual harassment in terms of interpersonal relations is incompatible with this account. . . .

For a given sexual harassment case, gender may not be a consideration at all. Picture the bisexual employer who is not in control of his sexual desires. He might indiscriminately threaten or proposition his employees without giving consideration to the gender of his victims. . . . Indeed, since, as argued above, sexual harassment is primarily a matter of communication which infringes on basic privacy rights, there is no presumption of gender. . . .

Sexual Harassment: Why the Corporate World Still Doesn't "Get It"

Vaughana Macy Feary

With the widely publicized charges of sexual harassment brought by neurosurgeon Dr. Frances Conley against Stanford Medical School, the electrifying allegations of Professor Anita Hill against Judge Clarence Thomas, and the sordid Tailhook scandal involving sexual misconduct in the military, the problem of sexual harassment finally exploded into the headlines. As yesterday's silent victims began joining a swelling chorus of protest from today's working women, corporate America suddenly began admitting that sexual harassment is an explosive communication problem. Yet despite all the recent ballyhoo over sexual harassment in the workplace, corporate America still doesn't really "get it" much less understand how to put an end to it.

If sexual harassment in the workplace is to be understood and eliminated, then not only corporate America, but the entire international business community must recognize and discard some old myths about the nature of ethics, and about the relationship between ethics, law and business, as well as some newer myths about sexual harassment, itself. . . .

SEXUAL HARASSMENT AS A WIDESPREAD MORAL PROBLEM

Why has the business community taken so long to admit that sexual harassment in the workplace is a serious problem? The reason seems to be that it still believes Myth Number One — the tired old joke that business ethics is an oxymoron; business should not really take ethics seriously.

There are numerous statistical studies which show that sexual harassment is an old problem. One of the earliest surveys, conducted by *Redbook* magazine in 1976, found that nine out of ten women responding to the survey had encountered sexual harassment on the job.[1] . . . *A Working Woman* survey published in June, 1992 found that 60% of the respondents had been victimized; it attributed this still higher percentage to the fact that the women polled held positions as executives, for "women in managerial and professional positions, as well as those working in male dominated companies are more likely to experience harassment."[2] . . .

One tenth of sexual harassment complaints are now being filed by men.[3] Studies also show that workers may be victimized by supervisors or peers, individuals or groups. . . .

Despite all the evidence indicating that sexual harassment was a major problem in the workplace, the business community remained largely indifferent. . . . A few companies such as Corning, which began its attempts to combat sexual harassment as early as the 1970s, and DuPont which has long held workshops designed to sensitize managers to the problem, were responsive.[4] Few other companies followed their leadership. It took the Thomas hearings to finally galvanize the business community into recognizing that sexual harassment was rapidly becoming the communication problem of the '90s. . . .

SEXUAL HARASSMENT IN THE WORKPLACE — AN HISTORICAL OVERVIEW

It was not until *Meritor Savings Bank* v. *Vinson* 447 U.S. 57 (1986), a case in which the plaintiff alleged that she had been harassed, raped, threatened, and forced to acquiesce to further sexual contacts for fear of losing her job, that the Supreme Court, relying heavily upon the 1980 EEOC guidelines, affirmed that "quid pro quo sexual harassment" AND "environmental harassment" ("unwelcome" sexual conduct that "unreasonably interferes with an individual's job performance" or sustains an "intimidating, hostile or offensive working environment") both constitute violations of Title VII. . . .

Still more legal problems are emerging because now even alleged perpetrators are suing on the grounds of wrongful discharge. Corporations who have faced, or are facing, such suits include: Polaroid, Newsday, General Motors, AT & T, DuPont, Boeing, and Rockwell International.[5] According to the most recent 1992 *Working Woman* survey, it may cost corporate America more than $1 billion over the next five years to settle existing lawsuits. The business community has paid a high price for its allegiance to outworn myths, not only in punitive damages, but also in marred corporate images. Any lessons learned, have been learned at too high a cost.

WHY CORPORATIONS STILL DON'T GET IT

. . . Corporations STILL don't get it, but they are trying. Most corporations have adopted the recommendations of the United States Merit Systems Protections Board, enunciated in 1988. . . . One management consultant in the field estimates that 90% of Fortune 500 companies will offer . . . programs within the year — despite the fact that her package can cost as much as $100,000.[6] Ironically, sexual harassment has now become a thriving business.

Unfortunately, it is doubtful that most of the existing types of sexual harassment education currently being offered by human resource consultants are likely to be very effective because such programs overlook the role of power in organizations and the potential for the abuse of organizational power in today's job market. An effective educational program should result in the reduction and eventual elimination of harassing behaviors without inflicting further damage upon the groups most likely to be victimized, but it is doubtful that even where there is a clearly defined corporate policy about sexual harassment, a formal grievance procedure, and strictly enforced sanctions for non-compliance that incidents of sexual harassment will be fully reported or greatly reduced. . . .

It is very difficult for employees in subordinate positions to insist upon their rights. Sexual harassment is often subtle and difficult to prove. Even if victims do prove their case, they have every reason to fear subtle forms of retaliation in their current positions and subtle forms of discrimination if they attempt to secure other positions. Claims about unfair hiring and promotion decisions are difficult to substantiate, especially in a climate where there are too many equally-well qualified applicants for the few positions available. . . .

The kinds of sexual harassment education currently being offered in most corporations are not likely to deter potential victimizers because they are still based on old myths . . . — [e.g.] the belief that most moral problems result from ignorance about facts, explains why corporations are hiring consultants to deluge employees with facts about sexual harassment. Of course we need to know the facts, but a lot of this information is old news, and educating people about facts is simply not enough. Moral problems occur not only when there is ignorance or disagreement about facts, but also when there is disagreement about values. There is no logical inconsistency between acknowledging legal and statistical facts about sexual harassment and refusing to take a moral stand. Only moral education can bridge the gap by providing reasons for giving up deeply entrenched ideas that, at best, the issue of sexual harassment is "much ado about nothing" or, at worst, a "legal menace" to which many managers may deeply resent being subjected. . . .

THE DEFINITION OF SEXUAL HARASSMENT

Undoubtedly one of the biggest obstacles to "getting" sexual harassment is . . . the belief that the concept of sexual harassment (like most moral concepts) is "murky." Some people worry that there are such deep cultural and gender based differences about the topic that no satisfactory definition can ever be provided. . . . A great deal of this popular wisdom, however, seems to stem from ignorance about the sophistication of EEOC guidelines, or from deliberate attempts on the part of some members of the political, business, or legal communities to prey on such ignorance and to create a backlash. . . .

[Edmund] Wall . . . believes that the mental states of both the perpetrator and the victim are essential defining elements of sexual harassment.[7] He believes that subjective features are essential in defining sexual harassment because, although a range of behaviors can, on occasion, be identified as sexual harassment, almost any of the behaviors, given different mental states of alleged victimizers

and victims, may not qualify as sexual harassment at all. Perhaps a quid pro quo offer was only "banter" or perhaps the alleged victim really welcomed the offer as a "career opportunity."[8] Wall seems very concerned with preventing the much popularized innocent man/paranoid woman scenario.[9] Certainly, his inclusion of the perpetrator's mental states differs from EEOC guidelines which focus on the mental states of a victim, or more accurately, a reasonable victimized person. . . .

Some theorists, such as Larry May and John C. Huges, as well as EEOC guidelines, hold that sexual harassment always constitutes discrimination.[10] . . . Wall disagree[s] because, . . . [he] argues, a bisexual might sexually harass both sexes without the action being discriminatory. This line of argument seems rather silly as an objection to EEOC guidelines and does nothing to establish that sexual harassment is not discriminatory. The whole purpose of Title VII was to prevent invidious discrimination against any employee in the work place, not merely women. . . .

Wall . . . [is] also in agreement that the presence of coercion and/or negative consequences resulting from harassment, are not necessary conditions for the existence of sexual harassment because the victim's personality and values contribute to the effect that a sexual offer will have upon that person. . . . [He is] no doubt correct, but . . . [he] fails to appreciate that the revised EEOC guidelines are compatible with their position. EEOC guidelines do not define sexual harassment in terms of coercion. EEOC guidelines hold that for behavior to constitute sexual harassment, it must be "unwelcome," and decisions about whether a victim found conduct to be unwelcome are to be based upon facts about her conduct. Furthermore, where the victim has submitted to the sexual conduct, the pivotal issue in determining whether the conduct was harassment is whether the conduct was unwelcome; the issue of whether the conduct was voluntary has been ruled to have "no materiality" whatever. . . .

Wall believes that distress on the part of the actual victim is one of the necessary conditions for sexual harassment. Wall simply seems to be wrong here. Women have been conditioned to stoically accept a great deal of sexual behavior which may harm them professionally. Nevertheless, a reasonable person who had not been so conditioned, might be quite justifiably distressed. It is the issue of whether it would be rational to be distressed, rather than the issue of actual distress which seems central to defining sexual harassment, and this issue is already accommodated within EEOC guidelines.

If we examine the definitions finally proposed by . . . Wall, we will see that neither definition is any improvement over the definition already proposed by the EEOC. . . .

There seem to be a number of difficulties with Wall's definition. The worst difficulty is that it is too narrow. It excludes sexist harassment (e.g., demeaning remarks about women in general) and a great deal of environmental harassment (e.g., the display of objectionable sexual objects, discussions of sexual matters unrelated to work, etc.) which most people would want to include. Certainly excluding those elements requires considerably more argument than the perfunctory claim that "girlie" posters probably are better classified as bad taste rather than sexual harassment.[11] Wall's definition does not seem to accord with our basic intuitions. If indeed Judge Thomas did discuss the kinds of topics (e.g., his sexual endowments and prowess, pornographic movies, and the coke can incident) with Professor Hill that she alleges he did, most people would agree that she was certainly being subjected to a hostile work environment, even if he never said that he had an interest in engaging in sex with her or suggested that anyone else had such an interest.

This seems to contradict Wall's belief that the content of what is communicated is immaterial.

There could also be cases of even quid pro quo sexual harassment in which few of the four conditions Wall specifies obtain. Wall simply fails to recognize that, in the case of sexual harassment, communication fails, not merely because the message is not communicated in an appropriate manner, but because, given the inequalities in status and income between employees, many employees (most of them women) do not feel at liberty to communicate honestly; few can afford to pay the price of honest communication.

If . . . Wall's definitions won't do, how should sexual harassment be defined? Don't their difficulties provide still more justification for all the current ballyhoo about the "murkiness" of sexual harassment and the new dangers perfectly well intentioned men and employers may face now that the problem of sexual harassment is being publicly acknowledged? Quite the contrary, defining sexual harassment for the purposes of business ethics is NOT a major philosophical problem. Although, given the difficulty of honest communication, one can hope that the courts will ultimately employ the reasonable person standards in deciding whether conduct is "welcome," the meaning of sexual harassment is reasonably well defined in EEOC guidelines.

Sexual harassment seems to be one of those concepts like the concept "game," to use Wittgenstein's famous example, which form a family. Family members have family resemblances, but there is no shared feature all members of a family necessarily have in common. As a consequence, trying to set out necessary and sufficient conditions for sexual harassment is a thoroughly futile enterprise. The futility of that enterprise, however, does nothing to support the myth that the concept of sexual harassment is hopelessly murky. We are clear enough in paradigm cases about what people mean when they claim they are being sexually harassed. . . .

Of course, in addition to paradigmatic cases of sexual harassment identified by law, there are also borderline cases about which corporations, and in some cases the courts, will have to make decisions. As sexual harassment is a quasi-moral term, legal decisions about borderline cases will almost certainly be based upon whether the questionable behavior is sufficiently morally objectionable to count as sexual harassment in the legal sense. All of this suggests that, for the purpose of business ethics, corporations would be well advised not only to educate their employees about EEOC guidelines, but also to educate them about the moral reasons which justify the belief that sexual harassment is genuinely immoral and ought to be legally prohibited. . . .

WHY SEXUAL HARASSMENT IN THE WORKPLACE IS MORALLY WRONG AND WHY IT OUGHT TO BE LEGALLY PROHIBITED

. . . What follows is a very brief outline of some good moral reasons for taking the problem of sexual harassment in the workplace seriously, for regarding it as morally objectionable, and for believing that it should be illegal.

First, sexual harassment is morally wrong because it physically and psychologically harms victims, and because environments which permit sexual harassment seem to encourage such harms. Even the most liberal moral theories acknowledge that harm to others is our strongest moral reason for restricting liberty. As the majority of victims in the past have been women, most of the evidence in support of the claim that sexual harassment is harmful is based upon evidence

about women, but presumably any group which was habitually so victimized would suffer similar effects.

Some sexual harassment cases associated with "intimidating, hostile, or offensive working environment" involve rape or physical assault. Furthermore, both quid pro quo harassment and environmental harassment can cause sexual harassment trauma syndrome. This syndrome involves both physical and psychological symptoms. . . .

Some sexual touching which qualifies as sexual harassment under EEOC guidelines (even when it is confined to a single severe incident) may not inflict any direct physical harm on women, but permitting unwanted touching may encourage physical violence against women. . . .

EEOC guidelines also hold that nonphysical conduct (e.g., sexual jokes, sexual conversation, the display of pornographic materials, etc.) in cases whether it forms a repeated pattern does qualify as sexual harassment. The courts have been divided about this matter.[12] The 1986 Attorney General's Commission on Pornography did conclude that, although there is no general connection between pornography and violence, exposure to sexually degrading and violent materials does contribute to sexual violence against women.[13] The EEOC guidelines can be justified, in part, on the grounds of preventing physical harm to women.

Second, Wall is quite correct in emphasizing that sexual harassment violates privacy rights. Privacy, like pornography is a controversial subject. . . . Presumably unwanted sexual touching would violate zones of privacy emanating from the Third and Fourth Amendments; if our homes cannot be invaded, presumably our bodies should be doubly sacrosanct. There are also moral rights to specific types of privacy in the workplace.[14] . . . Given that sexual matters are irrelevant in assessing an individual's ability to perform a job, privacy rights seem to preclude any inquiries by managers about the sexual lives of their employees outside of the workplace, and to provide a clear moral justification for discouraging sexual conversations within it.

Third, there are certainly historical and causal correlations between sexual harassment and discrimination. . . . Recent studies verify that women, and especially women of color, are still the group most likely to be victimized by sexual harassment, and that they are usually harassed by men occupying positions of superior authority. Given the complicated connections between discrimination, violence, inequalities in power, and sexual misconduct, corporations have a duty to insist upon sexual propriety in the workplace in order to protect any employee from becoming a victim of further discrimination.

Fourth, sexual harassment violates liberty rights. . . . Sexual harassment restricts liberty. A 1979 Working Women's Institute study found that 24% of sexual harassment victims were fired for complaining, while another 42% left their jobs. . . . To suggest that women should leave their jobs and deviate from their career tracks when confronted with sexual harassment is only to add injury to injury. Worse yet, it plays into vicious stereotypes that victims of sexual abuse "ask for it."

Fifth, sexual harassment violates rights to fair equality of opportunity. . . . There is a wealth of evidence to suggest that women do not enjoy fair equality in the workplace and that sexual harassment is part of the problem. Sexual harassment stress syndrome, resulting from quid pro quo and environmental harassment, impairs job performance. A hostile work environment undermines respect for women making it difficult for them to exercise authority and command respect. Pornography, sexual conversation, sexual and sexist jokes, girlie posters, and the like, are morally objectionable because they vio-

late women's rights to enjoy fair equality of opportunity. . . .

CONCLUSION

. . . Sexual harassment is a serious moral problem. To get to the root of the problem, the corporate world must begin to reason critically, to relinquish old myths, to take a strong moral stand, and to provide moral education for employees. It must then assess the effectiveness of that education by conducting anonymous surveys of those groups with the least powerful positions or with the most complaints in the past to determine whether there is a reduction of complaints among those respondents. Until then, sexual harassment will be a potentially explosive communication problem.

NOTES

1. Conte, Alba. *Sexual Harassment in the Workplace: Law and Practice.* New York: Wiley Law Publications, John Wiley and Sons, Inc., 1990, p. 2.
2. Sandoff, Ronni. 'Sexual Harassment: The Inside Story', (Working Woman Survey). *Working Woman,* June 1992.
3. Templin, Neal. 'As Women Assume More Power, Charges Filed by Men May Rise', *The Wall Street Journal* (October 18, 1991): B3.
4. Segal, Troy and Zachary Schiller. 'Six Experts Suggest Ways to Negotiate the Minefield', *BusinessWeek* (October 12, 1991): 33.
5. Lublin, JoAnn. 'As Harassment Charges Rise, More Men Fight Back', *The Wall Street Journal* (October 18, 1991; B4).
6. Lublin, JoAnn. "Sexual Harassment Is Topping Agenda in Many Executive Education Programs', *The Wall Street Journal* (December 2, 1991): B1.
7. Wall, Edmund. 'The Definition of Sexual Harassment', *Public Affairs Quarterly* Vol. 5, No. 4 (October 1991): 371–385.

8. *Ibid.*, pp. 380–1.
9. *Ibid.*, pp. 376–378.
10. Hughes, Larry and May, John C, 'Is Sexual Harassment Coercive?', in Gertrude Ezorsky, Ed., *Moral Rights in the Workplace*. New York: State of New York Press, 1982, pp. 115–22.
11. Wall, p. 383.
12. Siegel, Larry J. *Criminology*. 4th ed. St. Paul, Minnesota: West Publishing Co., 1989, pp. 491–493.
13. Siegel, p. 406.
14. Brenkert, George G. 'Privacy, Polygraphs and Work', *Contemporary Issues in Business Ethics.* ed. Joseph R. DesJardins and John J. McCall. Belmont, California: Wadsworth Publishing Co., 1985, 227–237.

Local 28 of the Sheet Metal Workers' International Association v. Equal Employment Opportunity Commission

Supreme Court of the United States

In 1975, petitioners were found guilty of engaging in a pattern and practice of discrimination against black and Hispanic individuals (nonwhites) in violation of Title VII of the Civil Rights Act of 1964, 42 U.S.C. § 2000e *et seq.*, and ordered to end their discriminatory practices, and to admit a certain percentage of nonwhites to union membership by July 1981. In 1982 and again in 1983, petitioners were found guilty of civil contempt for disobeying the District Court's earlier orders. They now challenge the District Court's contempt finding, and also the remedies the court ordered both for the Title VII violation and for contempt. Principally, the issue presented is whether the remedial provision of Title VII, see 42 U.S.C. § 2000e-5(g), empowers a district court to order race-conscious relief that may benefit individuals who are not identified victims of unlawful discrimination.

Petitioner Local 28 of the Sheet Metal Workers' International Association (Local 28) represents sheet metal workers employed by contractors in the New York City metropolitan area. Petitioner Local 28 Joint Apprenticeship Committee (JAC) is a management-labor committee which operates a 4-year apprenticeship training program designed to teach sheet metal skills. . . .

Petitioners, joined by the EEOC, argue that the membership goal, the [Employment, Training, Education and Recruitment Fund ("the Fund")] order, and other orders which require petitioners to grant membership preferences to nonwhites are expressly prohibited by § 706(g), 42 U.S.C. § 2000e-5(g), which defines the remedies available under Title VII. Petitioners and the EEOC maintain that § 706(g) authorizes a district court to award preferential relief only to the actual victims of unlawful discrimination. They maintain that the membership goal and the Fund violate this provision, since they require petitioners to admit to membership, and otherwise to extend benefits to, black and Hispanic individuals who are not the identified victims of unlawful discrimination. We reject this argument, and hold that § 706(g) does not prohibit a court from ordering, in appropriate circumstances, affirmative race-conscious relief as a remedy for past discrimination. Specifically, we hold that such relief may be appropriate where an employer or a labor union has engaged in persistent or egregious discrimination, or where necessary to dissipate the lingering effects of pervasive discrimination.

Section 706(g) states: "If the court finds that the respondent has intentionally engaged in or is intentionally engaging in an unlawful employment practice . . . , the court may enjoin the respondent from engaging in such unlawful employment practice, and order such affirmative action as may be appropriate, which may include, but is not limited to, reinstatement or hiring of employees, with or without back pay . . . , or any other equitable relief as the court deems appropriate. . . . No order of the court shall require the admission or reinstatement of an individual as a member of a union, or the hiring, reinstatement, or promotion of an individual as an employee, or the payment to him of any back pay, if such individual was refused admission, suspended, or expelled, or was refused employment or advancement or was suspended or discharged for any reason other than discrimination on account of race, color, religion, sex, or national origin in violation of . . . this title." 78 Stat. 261, as amended and as set forth in 42 U.S.C. § 2000e-5(g).

The language of § 706(g) plainly expresses Congress' intent to vest district courts with broad discretion to award "appropriate" equitable relief to remedy unlawful discrimination. . . . Nevertheless, petitioners and the EEOC argue that the last sentence of § 706(g) prohibits a court from ordering an

employer or labor union to take affirmative steps to eliminate discrimination which might incidentally benefit individuals who are not the actual victims of discrimination. This reading twists the plain language of the statute.

The last sentence of § 706(g) prohibits a court from ordering a union to admit an individual who was "refused admission . . . for any reason other than discrimination." It does not, as petitioners and the EEOC suggest, say that a court may order relief only for the actual victims of past discrimination. The sentence on its face addresses only the situation where a plaintiff demonstrates that a union (or an employer) has engaged in unlawful discrimination, but the union can show that a particular individual would have been refused admission even in the absence of discrimination, for example, because that individual was unqualified. In these circumstances, § 706(g) confirms that a court could not order the union to admit the unqualified individual. . . . In this case, neither the membership goal nor the Fund order required petitioners to admit to membership individuals who had been refused admission for reasons unrelated to discrimination. Thus, we do not read § 706(g) to prohibit a court from ordering the kind of affirmative relief the District Court awarded in this case.

The availability of race-conscious affirmative relief under § 706(g) as a remedy for a violation of Title VII also furthers the broad purposes underlying the statute. Congress enacted Title VII based on its determination that racial minorities were subject to pervasive and systematic discrimination in employment. . . . Title VII was designed "to achieve equality of employment opportunities and remove barriers that have operated in the past to favor an identifiable group of white employees over other employees. . . . In order to foster equal employment opportunities, Congress gave the lower courts broad power under § 706(g) to fashion "the most complete relief possible" to remedy past discrimination. . . .

In most cases, the court need only order the employer or union to cease engaging in discriminatory practices, and award make-whole relief to the individuals victimized by those practices. In some instances, however, it may be necessary to require the employer or union to take affirmative steps to end discrimination effectively to enforce Title VII. Where an employer or union has engaged in particularly longstanding or egregious discrimination, an injunction simply reiterating Title VII's prohibition against discrimination will often prove useless and will only result in endless enforcement litigation. In such cases, requiring recalcitrant employers or unions to hire and to admit qualified minorities roughly in proportion to the number of qualified minorities in the work force may be the only effective way to ensure the full enjoyment of the rights protected by Title VII. . . .

Affirmative race-conscious relief may be the only means available "to assure equality of employment opportunities and to eliminate those discriminatory practices and devices which have fostered racially stratified job environments to the disadvantage of minority citizens." . . .

Finally, a district court may find it necessary to order interim hiring or promotional goals pending the development of nondiscriminatory hiring or promotion procedures. In these cases, the use of numerical goals provides a compromise between two unacceptable alternatives: an outright ban on hiring or promotions, or continued use of a discriminatory selection procedure. . . .

Many opponents of Title VII argued that an employer could be found guilty of discrimination under the statute simply because of a racial imbalance in his work force, and would be compelled to implement racial "quotas" to avoid being charged with liability.

Weber, 443 U.S., at 205, 99 S.Ct., at 2728. At the same time, supporters of the bill insisted that employers would not violate Title VII simply because of racial imbalance, and emphasized that neither the Commission nor the courts could compel employers to adopt quotas solely to facilitate racial balancing. *Id.,* at 207, n. 7, 99 S.Ct., at 2729, n. 7. The debate concerning what Title VII did and did not require culminated in the adoption of § 703(j), which stated expressly that the statute did not require an employer or labor union to adopt quotas or preferences simply because of a racial imbalance. However, while Congress strongly opposed the use of quotas or preferences merely to maintain racial balance, it gave no intimation as to whether such measures should be acceptable as *remedies* for Title VII violations. . . .

The purpose of affirmative action is not to make identified victims whole, but rather to dismantle prior patterns of employment discrimination and to prevent discrimination in the future. Such relief is provided to the class as a whole rather than to individual members; no individual is entitled to relief, and beneficiaries need not show that they were themselves victims of discrimination. In this case, neither the membership goal nor the Fund order required petitioners to indenture or train particular individuals, and neither required them to admit to membership individuals who were refused admission for reasons unrelated to discrimination. . . .

The court should exercise its discretion with an eye towards Congress' concern that race-conscious affirmative measures not be invoked simply to create a racially balanced work force. In the majority of Title VII cases, the court will not have to impose affirmative action as a remedy for past discrimination, but need only order the employer or union to cease engaging in discriminatory practices and award make-whole relief to the individuals victimized by those practices. However, in some cases, affirmative action may be necessary in order effectively to enforce Title VII. As we noted before, a court may have to resort to race-conscious affirmative action when confronted with an employer or labor union that has engaged in persistent or egregious discrimination. Or such relief may be necessary to dissipate the lingering effects of pervasive discrimination. Whether there might be other circumstances that justify the use of court-ordered affirmative action is a matter that we need not decide here. We note only that a court should consider whether affirmative action is necessary to remedy past discrimination in a particular case before imposing such measures, and that the court should also take care to tailor its orders to fit the nature of the violation it seeks to correct. In this case, several factors lead us to conclude that the relief ordered by the District Court was proper.

First, both the District Court and the Court of Appeals agreed that the membership goal and Fund order were necessary to remedy petitioners' pervasive and egregious discrimination. The District Court set the original 29% membership goal upon observing that "[t]he record in both state and federal courts against [petitioners] is replete with instances of their bad faith attempts to prevent or delay affirmative action." 401 F.Supp., at 488. The court extended the goal after finding petitioners in contempt for refusing to end their discriminatory practices and failing to comply with various provisions of RAAPO. In affirming the revised membership goal, the Court of Appeals observed that "[t]his court has twice recognized Local 28's long continued and egregious racial discrimination . . . and Local 28 has presented no facts to indicate that our earlier observations are no longer apposite." 753 F.2d, at 1186. In light of petitioners' long history of "foot-dragging resistance" to court orders, simply enjoining them from once again engaging in

discriminatory practices would clearly have been futile. Rather, the District Court properly determined that affirmative race-conscious measures were necessary to put an end to petitioners' discriminatory ways.

Both the membership goal and Fund order were similarly necessary to combat the lingering effects of past discrimination. In light of the District Court's determination that the union's reputation for discrimination operated to discourage nonwhites from even applying for membership, it is unlikely that an injunction would have been sufficient to extend to nonwhites equal opportunities for employment. Rather, because access to admission, membership, training, and employment in the industry had traditionally been obtained through informal contacts with union members, it was necessary for a substantial number of nonwhite workers to become members of the union in order for the effects of discrimination to cease. The Fund, in particular, was designed to insure that non-whites would receive the kind of assistance that white apprentices and applicants had traditionally received through informal sources. On the facts of this case, the District Court properly determined that affirmative, race-conscious measures were necessary to assure the equal employment opportunities guaranteed by Title VII.

Second, the District Court's flexible application of the membership goal gives strong indication that it is not being used simply to achieve and maintain racial balance, but rather as a benchmark against which the court could gauge petitioners' efforts to remedy past discrimination. The court has twice adjusted the deadline for achieving the goal, and has continually approved of changes in the size of the apprenticeship classes to account for the fact that economic conditions prevented petitioners from meeting their membership targets; there is every reason to believe that both the court and the administrator will continue to accommodate *legiti-mate* explanations for petitioners' failure to comply with the court's orders. Moreover, the District Court expressly disavowed any reliance on petitioners' failure to meet the goal as a basis for the contempt finding, but instead viewed this failure as symptomatic of petitioners' refusal to comply with various subsidiary provisions of RAAPO. In sum, the District Court has implemented the membership goal as a means by which it can measure petitioners' compliance with its orders, rather than as a strict racial quota.

Third, both the membership goal and the Fund order are temporary measures. Under AAAPO "[p]referential selection of [union members] will end as soon as the percentage of [minority union members] approximates the percentage of [minorities] in the local labor force." *Weber,* 443 U.S., at 208–209, 99 S.Ct., at 2730; see *United States v. City of Alexandria,* 614 F.2d, at 1366. Similarly, the Fund is scheduled to terminate when petitioners achieve the membership goal, and the court determines that it is no longer needed to remedy past discrimination. The District Court's orders thus operate "as a temporary tool for remedying past discrimination without attempting to 'maintain' a previously achieved balance." *Weber,* 443 U.S., at 216, 99 S.Ct., at 2734 (Blackmun, J., concurring).

Finally, we think it significant that neither the membership goal nor the Fund order "unnecessarily trammel[s] the interests of white employees." *Id.* 443 U.S., at 208, 99 S.Ct., at 2730; *Teamsters,* 431 U.S., at 352–353, 97 S.Ct., at 1863–1864. Petitioners concede that the District Court's orders did not require any member of the union to be laid off, and did not discriminate against existing union members. See *Weber, supra,* 443 U.S., at 208, 99 S.Ct., at 2729–2730; see also 30 St. Louis U.L.J., at 264. While whites seeking admission into the union may be denied bene-

fits extended to their nonwhite counterparts, the court's orders do not stand as an absolute bar to such individuals; indeed, a majority of new union members have been white. See *City of Alexandria, supra,* at 1366. Many provisions of the court's orders are race-neutral (for example, the requirement that the [Joint Apprenticeship Committee (JAC)] assign one apprentice for every four journeyman workers), and petitioners remain free to adopt the provisions of AAAPO and the Fund order for the benefit of white members and applicants.

Petitioners also allege that the membership goal and Fund order contravene the equal protection component of the Due Process Clause of the Fifth Amendment because they deny benefits to white individuals based on race. We have consistently recognized that government bodies constitutionally may adopt racial classifications as a remedy for past discrimination.... We conclude that the relief ordered in this case passes even the most rigorous test — it is narrowly tailored to further the Government's compelling interest in remedying past discrimination.

In this case, there is no problem ... with a proper showing of prior discrimination that would justify the use of remedial racial classifications. Both the District Court and Court of Appeals have repeatedly found petitioners guilty of egregious violations of Title VII, and have determined that affirmative measures were necessary to remedy their racially discriminatory practices. More importantly, the District Court's orders were properly tailored to accomplish this objective. First, the District Court considered the efficacy of alternative remedies, and concluded that, in light of petitioners' long record of resistance to official efforts to end their discriminatory practices, stronger measures were necessary.... Again, petitioners concede that the District Court's orders did not disadvantage *existing* union members. While white applicants for union membership may be denied certain benefits available to their nonwhite counterparts, the court's orders do not stand as an absolute bar to the admission of such individuals; again, a majority of those entering the union after entry of the court's orders have been white. We therefore conclude that the District Court's orders do not violate the equal protection safeguards of the Constitution.

Finally, Local 28 challenges the District Court's appointment of an administrator with broad powers to supervise its compliance with the court's orders as an unjustifiable interference with its statutory right to self-governance. See 29 USC § 401(a). Preliminarily, we note that while AAAPO gives the administrator broad powers to oversee petitioners' membership practices, Local 28 retains complete control over its other affairs. Even with respect to membership, the administrator's job is to insure that petitioners comply with the court's orders and admit sufficient numbers of nonwhites; the administrator does not select the particular individuals that will be admitted, that task is left to union officials. In any event, in light of the difficulties inherent in monitoring compliance with the court's orders, and especially petitioners' established record of resistance to prior state and federal court orders designed to end their discriminatory membership practices, appointment of an administrator was well within the District Court's discretion. . . .

To summarize our holding today, six members of the Court agree that a district court may, in appropriate circumstances, order preferential relief benefiting individuals who are not the actual victims of discrimination as a remedy for violations of Title VII, . . . that the District Court did not use incorrect statistical evidence in establishing petitioners' nonwhite membership goal, that the contempt fines and Fund order were proper remedies for civil contempt, and that the District Court properly appointed an administrator to supervise petitioners' compliance with the court's orders. Five members of the Court agree that in this case, the District Court did not err in evaluating petitioners' utilization of the apprenticeship program, and that the membership goal and the Fund order are not violative of either Title VII or the Constitution. The judgment of the Court of Appeals is hereby *Affirmed*. . . .

City of Richmond v. J. A. Croson Company

Supreme Court of the United States

In this case, we confront once again the tension between the Fourteenth Amendment's guarantee of equal treatment to all citizens, and the use of race-based measures to ameliorate the effects of past discrimination on the opportunities enjoyed by members of minority groups in our society. . . .

I

On April 11, 1983, the Richmond City Council adopted the Minority Business Utilization Plan (the Plan). The Plan required prime contractors to whom the city awarded construction contracts to subcontract at least 30% of the dollar amount of the contract to one or more Minority Business Enterprises (MBEs). Ordinance No. 83-69-59, codified in Richmond, Va., City Code, § 12-156(a) (1985). The 30% set-aside did not apply to city contracts awarded to minority-owned prime contractors. *Ibid.*

The Plan defined an MBE as "[a] business at least fifty-one (51) percent of which is owned and controlled . . . by minority group members." § 12-23, p. 941. "Minority group members" were defined as "[c]itizens of the United States who are Blacks, Spanish-speaking, Orientals, Indians, Eskimos, or Aleuts." *Ibid.* There was no geographic limit to the Plan; an otherwise qualified MBE from anywhere in the United States could avail itself of the 30% set-aside. The Plan declared that it was "remedial" in nature, and enacted "for the purpose of promoting wider participation by minority business enterprises in the construction of public projects." § 12-158(a). The Plan expired on June 30, 1988, and was in effect for approximately five years. *Ibid.*

The Plan authorized the Director of the Department of General Services to promulgate rules which "shall allow waivers in those individual situations where a contractor can prove to the satisfaction of the director that the requirements herein cannot be achieved." § 12-157. To this end, the Director promulgated Contract Clauses, Minority Business Utilization Plan (Contract Clauses). Section D of these rules provided: "No partial or complete waiver of the foregoing [30% set-aside] requirement shall be granted by the city other than in exceptional circumstances. To justify a waiver, it must be shown that every feasible attempt has been made to comply, and it must be demonstrated that sufficient, relevant, qualified Minority Business Enterprises . . . are unavailable or unwilling to participate in the contract to enable meeting the 30% MBE goal." . . .

The Plan was adopted by the Richmond City Council after a public hearing. App. 9–50. Seven members of the public spoke to the merits of the ordinance: five were in opposition, two in favor. Proponents of the set-aside provision relied on a study which indicated that, while the general population of Richmond was 50% black, only .67% of the city's prime construction contracts had been awarded to minority businesses in the 5-year period from 1978 to 1983. . . .

There was no direct evidence of race discrimination on the part of the city in letting contracts or any evidence that the city's prime contractors had discriminated against minority-owned subcontractors. . . .

. . . On September 6, 1983, the city of Richmond issued an invitation to bid on a project for the provision and installation of certain plumbing fixtures at the city jail. On September 30, 1983, Eugene Bonn, the regional manager of J.A. Croson Company (Croson), a mechanical plumbing and heating contractor, received the bid forms. The project involved the installations of stainless steel urinals and water closets in the city jail. Products of either of two manufacturers were specified, Acorn Engineering Company (Acorn) or Bradley Manufacturing Company (Bradley). Bonn determined that to meet the 30% set-aside requirement, a minority contractor would have to supply the fixtures. The provision of the fixtures amounted to 75% of the total contract price. . . .

Bonn subsequently began a search for potential MBE suppliers. The only potential MBE fixture supplier was Melvin Brown, president of Continental Metal Hose, hereafter referred to as "Continental." However, because of Continental's inability to obtain credit approval, Continental was unable to submit a bid by the due date of October 13, 1983. Shortly thereafter and as a direct result, Croson submitted a request for a waiver of the 30% set-aside. Croson's waiver request indicated that Continental was "unqualified" and that the other MBEs contacted had been unresponsive or unable to quote. Upon learning of Croson's waiver request, Brown contacted an agent of Acorn, the other fixture manufacturer specified by the city. Based upon his discussions with Acorn, Brown subsequently submitted a bid on the fixtures to Croson. Continental's bid was $6,183.29 higher than the price Croson had included for the fixtures in its bid to the city. This constituted a 7% increase over the market price for the fixtures. With added bonding and insurance, using Continental would have raised the cost of the project by $7,663.16. On the same day that Brown contacted Acorn, he also called city procurement officials and told them that Continental, an MBE, could supply the fixtures specified in the city jail contract. On November 2, 1983, the city denied Croson's waiver request, indicating that Croson had 10 days to submit an MBE Utilization Commitment Form, and warned that failure to do so could result in its bid being considered unresponsive.

Croson wrote the city on November 8, 1983. In the letter, Bonn indicated that Continental was not an authorized supplier for either Acorn or Bradley fixtures. He also noted that Acorn's quotation to Brown was subject to credit approval and in any case was substantially higher than any other quotation Croson had received. Finally, Bonn noted that Continental's bid had been submitted some 21 days after the prime bids were due. In a second letter, Croson laid out the additional costs that using Continental to supply the fixtures would entail, and asked that it be allowed to raise the overall contract price accordingly. The city denied both Croson's request for a waiver and its suggestion that the contract price be raised. The city informed Croson that it had decided to rebid the project. On December 9, 1983, counsel for Croson wrote the city asking for a review of the waiver denial. The city's attorney responded that the city had elected to rebid the project, and that there is no appeal of such a decision. Shortly thereafter Croson brought this action under 42 U.S.C. § 1983 in the Federal District Court for the Eastern District of Virginia, arguing that the Richmond ordinance was unconstitutional on its face and as applied in this case.

The District Court upheld the Plan in all respects ... [and held that] the 30% figure was "reasonable in light of the undisputed fact that minorities constitute 50% of the population of Richmond." *Ibid.*

Croson sought certiorari from this Court. We granted the writ, vacated the opinion of the Court of Appeals, and remanded the case for further consideration in light of our intervening decision in *Wygant v. Jackson Board of Education,* 476 U.S. 267, 106 S.Ct. 1842, 90 L.Ed.2d 260 (1986)....

On remand, a divided panel of the Court of Appeals struck down the Richmond set-aside program as violating both prongs of strict scrutiny under the Equal Protection Clause of the Fourteenth Amendment. *J.A. Croson Co. v. Richmond,* 822 F.2d 1355 (CA4 1987) (*Croson II*)....

In this case, the debate at the city council meeting "revealed no record of prior discrimination by the city in awarding public contracts...." *Croson II, supra,* at 1358. Moreover, the statistics comparing the minority population of Richmond to the percentage of *prime* contracts awarded to minority firms had little or no probative value in establishing prior discrimination in the relevant market, and actually suggested "more of a political than a remedial basis for the racial preference." 822 F.2d, at 1359. The court concluded that, "[i]f this plan is supported by a compelling governmental interest, so is every other plan that has been enacted in the past or that will be enacted in the future." *Id.*, at 1360.

The Court of Appeals went on to hold that even if the city had demonstrated a compelling interest in the use of a race-based quota, the 30% set-aside was not narrowly tailored to accomplish a remedial purpose. The court found that the 30% figure was "chosen arbitrarily" and was not tied to the number of minority subcontractors in Richmond or to any other relevant number. *Ibid.* The dissenting judge argued that the majority had "misconstrue[d] and misapplie[d]" our decision in Wygant. 822 F.2d, at 1362. We noted probable jurisdiction of the city's appeal, . . . and we now affirm the judgment.

II

. . . Congress, unlike any State or political subdivision, has a specific constitutional mandate to enforce the dictates of the Fourteenth Amendment. The power to "enforce" may at times also include the power to define situations which *Congress* determines threaten principles of equality and to adopt prophylactic rules to deal with those situations. . . .

That Congress may identify and redress the effects of society-wide discrimination does not mean that, *a fortiori*, the States and their political subdivisions are free to decide that such remedies are appropriate. Section 1 of the Fourteenth Amendment is an explicit *constraint* on state power, and the States must undertake any remedial efforts in accordance with that provision. To hold otherwise would be to cede control over the content of the Equal Protection Clause to the 50 state legislatures and their myriad political subdivisions. The mere recitation of a benign or compensatory purpose for the use of a racial classification would essentially entitle the States to exercise the full power of Congress under § 5 of the Fourteenth Amendment and insulate any racial classification from judicial scrutiny under § 1. We believe that such a result would be contrary to the intentions of the Framers of the Fourteenth Amendment, who desired to place clear limits on the States' use of race as a criterion for legislative action, and to have the federal courts enforce those limitations. . . .

It would seem equally clear, however, that a state or local subdivision (if delegated the authority from the State) has the authority to eradicate the effects of private discrimination within its own legislative jurisdiction. This authority must, of course, be exercised within the constraints of § 1 of the Fourteenth Amendment. . . . As a matter of state law, the city of Richmond has legislative authority over its procurement policies, and can use its spending powers to remedy private discrimination, if it identifies that discrimination with the particularity required by the Fourteenth Amendment. . . .

Thus, if the city could show that it had essentially become a "passive participant" in a system of racial exclusion practiced by elements of the local construction industry, we think it clear that the city could take affirmative steps to dismantle such a system. It is beyond dispute that any public entity, state or federal, has a compelling interest in assuring that public dollars, drawn from the tax contributions of all citizens, do not serve to finance the evil of private prejudice. . . .

III.A

The Equal Protection Clause of the Fourteenth Amendment provides that "[N]o State shall . . . deny to *any person* within its jurisdiction the equal protection of the laws" (emphasis added). As this Court has noted in the past, the "rights created by the first section of the Fourteenth Amendment are, by its terms, guaranteed to the individual. The rights established are personal rights." *Shelley v. Kraemer,* 334 U.S. 1, 22, 68 S.Ct. 836, 846, 92 L.Ed. 1161 (1948). The Richmond Plan denies certain citizens the opportunity to compete for a fixed percentage of public contracts based solely upon their race. To whatever racial group these citizens belong, their "personal rights" to be treated with equal dignity and respect are implicated by a rigid rule erecting race as the sole criterion in an aspect of public decision making. . . .

Classifications based on race carry a danger of stigmatic harm. Unless they are strictly reserved for remedial settings, they may in fact promote notions of racial inferiority and lead to a politics of racial hostility. . . .

III.B

The District Court found the city council's "findings sufficient to ensure that, in adopting the Plan, it was remedying the present effects of past discrimination in the *construction industry.*" Supp.App. 163 (emphasis added). Like the "role model" theory employed in *Wygant,* a generalized assertion that there has been past discrimination in an entire industry provides no guidance for a legislative body to determine the precise scope of the injury it seeks to remedy. It "has no logical stopping point." *Wygant, supra,* at 275, 106 S.Ct., at 1847 (plurality opinion). "Relief" for such an ill-defined wrong could extend until the percentage of public contracts awarded to MBEs in Richmond mirrored the percentage of minorities in the population as a whole.

Appellant argues that it is attempting to remedy various forms of past discrimination that are alleged to be responsible for the small number of minority businesses in the local contracting industry. Among these the city cites the exclusion of blacks from skilled construction trade unions and training programs. This past discrimination has prevented them "from following the traditional path from laborer to entrepreneur." Brief for Appellant 23–24. The city also lists a host of nonracial factors which would seem to face a member of any racial group attempting to establish a new business enterprise, such as deficiencies in working capital, inability to meet bonding requirements, unfamiliarity with bidding procedures, and disability caused by an inadequate track record. *Id.,* at 25–26, and n. 41.

While there is no doubt that the sorry history of both private and public discrimination in this country has contributed to a lack of opportunities for black entrepreneurs, this observation, standing alone, cannot justify a rigid racial quota in the awarding of public contracts in Richmond, Virginia. Like the claim that discrimination in primary and secondary schooling justifies a rigid racial preference in medical school admissions, an amorphous claim that there has been past discrimination in a particular industry cannot justify the use of an unyielding racial quota.

It is sheer speculation how many minority firms there would be in Richmond absent past societal discrimination, just as it was sheer speculation how many minority medical students would have been admitted to the medical school at Davis absent past discrimination in educational opportunities. Defining these sorts of injuries as "identified discrimination" would give local governments license to create a patchwork of racial preferences based on statistical generalizations about any particular field of endeavor.

These defects are readily apparent in this case. The 30% quota cannot in any realistic sense be tied to any injury suffered by anyone. . . .

There is nothing approaching a prima facie case of a constitutional or statutory violation by *anyone* in the Richmond construction industry. . . .

The District Court accorded great weight to the fact that the city council designated the Plan as "remedial." But the mere recitation of a "benign" or legitimate purpose for a racial classification, is entitled to little or no weight. . . . Racial classifications are suspect, and that means that simple legislative assurances of good intention cannot suffice. . . .

In this case, the city does not even know how many MBEs in the relevant market are qualified to undertake prime or subcontracting work in public construction projects. . . . Nor does the city know what percentage of total city construction dollars minority firms now receive as subcontractors on prime contracts let by the city.

To a large extent, the set-aside of sub-contracting dollars seems to rest on the unsupported assumption that white prime contractors simply will not hire minority firms. . . . Without any information on minority participation in subcontracting, it is quite simply impossible to evaluate overall minority representation in the city's construction expenditures.

The city and the District Court also relied on evidence that MBE membership in local contractors' associations was extremely low. Again, standing alone this evidence is not probative of any discrimination in the local construction industry. There are numerous explanations for this dearth of minority participation, including past societal discrimination in education and economic opportunities as well as both black and white career and entrepreneurial choices. Blacks may be disproportionately attracted to industries other than construction. . . . The mere fact that black membership in these trade organizations is low, standing alone, cannot establish a prima facie case of discrimination. . . .

While the States and their subdivisions may take remedial action when they possess evidence that their own spending practices are exacerbating a pattern of prior discrimination, they must identify that discrimination, public or private, with some specificity before they may use race-conscious relief. . . .

In sum, none of the evidence presented by the city points to any identified discrimination in the Richmond construction industry. We, therefore, hold that the city has failed to demonstrate a compelling interest in apportioning public contracting opportunities on the basis of race. To accept Richmond's claim that past societal discrimination alone can serve as the basis for rigid racial preferences would be to open the door to competing claims for "remedial relief" for every disadvantaged group. The dream of a Nation of equal citizens in a society where race is irrelevant to personal opportunity and achievement would be lost in a mosaic of shifting preferences based on inherently unmeasurable claims of past wrongs. . . .

IV

Since the city must already consider bids and waivers on a case-by-case basis, it is difficult to see the need for a rigid numerical quota. . . .

Given the existence of an individualized procedure, the city's only interest in maintaining a quota system rather than investigating the need for remedial action in particular cases would seem to be simple administrative convenience. But the interest in avoiding the bureaucratic effort necessary to tailor remedial relief to those who truly have suffered the effects of prior discrimination cannot justify a rigid line drawn on the basis of a suspect classification. . . . Under Richmond's scheme, a successful black, Hispanic, or Oriental entrepreneur from anywhere in the country enjoys an absolute preference over other citizens based solely on their race. We think it obvious that such a program is not narrowly tailored to remedy the effects of prior discrimination.

V

. . . Because the city of Richmond has failed to identify the need for remedial action in

the awarding of its public construction contracts, its treatment of its citizens on a racial basis violates the dictates of the Equal Protection Clause. Accordingly, the judgment of the Court of Appeals for the Fourth Circuit is Affirmed.

Two Concurring Opinions
in *Adarand Constructors Inc. v. Pena*

Supreme Court of the United States

JUSTICE SCALIA, concurring in part and concurring in the judgment.

In my view, government can never have a "compelling interest" in discriminating on the basis of race in order to "make up" for past racial discrimination in the opposite direction. See *Richmond* v. *J. A. Croson Co.*, 488 U.S. 469, 520 (1989) (SCALIA, J., concurring in judgment). Individuals who have been wronged by unlawful racial discrimination should be made whole; but under our Constitution there can be no such thing as either a creditor or a debtor race. That concept is alien to the Constitution's focus upon the individual, see Amdt. 14, §1 ("[N]or shall any State . . . deny *to any person*" the equal protection of the laws) (emphasis added), and its rejection of dispositions based on race, see Amdt. 15, §1 (prohibiting abridgment of the right to vote "on account of race") or based on blood, see Art. III, §3 ("[N]o Attainder of Treason shall work Corruption of Blood");

Art. I, §9 ("No Title of Nobility shall be granted by the United States"). To pursue the concept of racial entitlement — even for the most admirable and benign of purposes — is to reinforce and preserve for future mischief the way of thinking that produced race slavery, race privilege and race hatred. In the eyes of government, we are just one race here. It is American.

JUSTICE THOMAS, concurring in part and concurring in the judgment.

I agree with the majority's conclusion that strict scrutiny applies to *all* government classifications based on race. I write separately, however, to express my disagreement with the premise underlying JUSTICE STEVENS' and JUSTICE GINSBURG's dissents: that there is a racial paternalism exception to the principle of equal protection. I believe that there is a "moral [and] constitutional equivalence," *post,* at 3, (STEVENS, J., dissenting), between laws designed to subjugate a race and those that distribute benefits on the basis of race in order to foster some current notion of equality. Government cannot make us equal; it can only recognize, respect, and protect us as equal before the law.

That these programs may have been motivated, in part, by good intentions cannot provide refuge from the principle that under our Constitution, the government may not make distinctions on the basis of race. As far as the Constitution is concerned, it is irrelevant whether a government's racial classifications are drawn by those who wish to oppress a race or by those who have a sincere desire to help those thought to be disadvantaged. There can be no doubt that the paternalism that appears to lie at the heart of this program is at war with the principle of inherent equality that underlies and infuses our Constitution. See Declaration of Independence ("We hold these truths to be self-evident, that all men are created equal, that they are endowed by their Creator with certain unalienable Rights, that among these are Life, Liberty, and the pursuit of Happiness").

These programs not only raise grave constitutional questions, they also undermine the moral basis of the equal protection principle. Purchased at the price of immeasurable human suffering, the equal protection principle reflects our Nation's understanding that such classifications ultimately have a destructive impact on the individual and our society. Unquestionably, "[i]nvidious [racial] discrimination is an engine of oppression," *post,* at 3. It is also true that "[r]emedial" racial preferences may reflect "a desire to foster equality in society," *ibid.* But there can be no doubt that racial paternalism and its unintended consequences can be as poisonous and pernicious as any other form of discrimination. So-called "benign" discrimination teaches many that because of chronic and apparently immutable handicaps, minorities cannot compete with them without their patronizing indulgence. Inevitably, such programs engender attitudes of superiority or, alternatively, provoke resentment among those who believe that they have been wronged by the government's use of race. These programs stamp minorities with a badge of inferiority and may cause them to develop dependencies or to adopt an attitude that they are "entitled" to preferences. Indeed, JUSTICE STEVENS once recognized the real harms stemming from seemingly "benign" discrimination. See *Fullilove* v. *Klutznick,* 448 U.S. 448, 545 (1980) (STEVENS, J., dissenting) (noting that "remedial" race legislation "is perceived by many as resting on an assumption that those who are granted this special preference are less qualified in some respect that is identified purely by their race").

In my mind, government-sponsored racial discrimination based on benign prejudice is just as noxious as discrimination inspired by malicious prejudice. In each instance, it is racial discrimination, plain and simple.

Meritor Savings Bank, FSB v. Vinson, et al.

Supreme Court of the United States

This case presents important questions concerning claims of workplace "sexual harassment" brought under Title VII of the Civil Rights Act of 1964, 78 Stat. 253, as amended, 42 U.S.C. § 2000e *et seq.*

I

In 1974, respondent Mechelle Vinson . . . started as a teller-trainee, and thereafter was promoted to teller, head teller, and assistant branch manager. She worked at the same branch for four years, and it is undisputed that her advancement there was based on merit alone. In September 1978, respondent notified her supervisor, Sidney Taylor that she was taking sick leave for an indefinite period. On November 1, 1978, the bank discharged her for excessive use of that leave.

Respondent brought this action against Taylor and the bank, claiming that during her four years at the bank she had "constantly been subjected to sexual harassment" by Taylor in violation of Title VII. She sought injunctive relief, compensatory and punitive damages against Taylor and the bank, and attorney's fees.

At the 11-day bench trial, the parties presented conflicting testimony about Taylor's behavior during respondent's employment.*

---

*Like the Court of Appeals, this Court was not provided a complete transcript of the trial. We therefore rely largely on the District Court's opinion for the summary of the relevant testimony.

Respondent testified that during her probationary period as a teller-trainee, Taylor treated her in a fatherly way and made no sexual advances. Shortly thereafter, however, he invited her out to dinner and, during the course of the meal, suggested that they go to a motel to have sexual relations. At first she refused, but out of what she described as fear of losing her job she eventually agreed. According to respondent, Taylor thereafter made repeated demands upon her for sexual favors, usually at the branch, both during and after business hours; she estimated that over the next several years she had intercourse with him some 40 or 50 times. In addition, respondent testified that Taylor fondled her in front of other employees, followed her into the women's restroom when she went there alone, exposed himself to her, and even forcibly raped her on several occasions. These activities ceased after 1977, respondent stated, when she started going with a steady boyfriend.

Respondent also testified that Taylor touched and fondled other women employees of the bank, and she attempted to call witnesses to support this charge. But while some supporting testimony apparently was admitted without objection, the District Court did not allow her "to present wholesale evidence of a pattern and practice relating to sexual advances to other female employees in her case in chief, but advised her that she might well be able to present such evidence in rebuttal to the defendants' cases." *Vinson v. Taylor,* 22 EPD ¶30, 708, p. 14,693, n. 1, 23

FEP Cases 37, 38–39, n. 1 (DC 1980). Respondent did not offer such evidence in rebuttal. Finally, respondent testified that because she was afraid of Taylor she never reported his harassment to any of his supervisors and never attempted to use the bank's complaint procedure.

Taylor denied respondent's allegations of sexual activity, testifying that he never fondled her, never made suggestive remarks to her, never engaged in sexual intercourse with her, and never asked her to do so. He contended instead that respondent made her accusations in response to a business-related dispute. The bank also denied respondent's allegations and asserted that any sexual harassment by Taylor was unknown to the bank and engaged in without its consent or approval.

The District Court denied relief and . . . ultimately found that respondent "was not the victim of sexual harassment and was not the victim of sexual discrimination" while employed at the bank.

Although it concluded that respondent had not proved a violation of Title VII, the District Court nevertheless went on to address the bank's liability. After noting the bank's express policy against discrimination, and finding that neither respondent nor any other employee had ever lodged a complaint about sexual harassment by Taylor, the court ultimately concluded that "the bank was without notice and cannot be held liable for the alleged actions of Taylor."

The Court of Appeals for the District of Columbia Circuit reversed. . . . The court stated that a violation of Title VII may be predicated on either of two types of sexual harassment: harassment that involves the conditioning of concrete employment benefits on sexual favors, and harassment that, while not affecting economic benefits, creates a hostile or offensive working environment. . . . Believing that "Vinson's grievance

was clearly of the [hostile environment] type," and that the District Court had not considered whether a violation of this type had occurred, the court concluded that a remand was necessary.

The court further concluded that the District Court's findings that any sexual relationship between respondent and Taylor "was a voluntary one" did not obviate the need for a remand. . . .

As to the bank's liability, the Court of Appeals held that an employer is absolutely liable for sexual harassment practiced by supervisory personnel, whether or not the employer knew or should have known about the misconduct. The court relied chiefly on Title VII's definition of "employer" to include "any agent of such a person," 42 U.S.C. §2000e(b), as well as on the EEOC Guidelines. The court held that a supervisor is an "agent" of his employer for Title VII purposes, even if he lacks authority to hire, fire, or promote, since "the mere existence — or even the appearance — of a significant degree of influence in vital job decisions gives any supervisor the opportunity to impose on employees." . . .

In accordance with the foregoing, the Court of Appeals reversed the judgment of the District Court and remanded the case for further proceedings. . . .

II

Title VII of the Civil Rights Act of 1964 makes it "an unlawful employment practice for an employer . . . to discriminate against any individual with respect to his compensation, terms, conditions, or privileges for employment, because of such individual's race, color, religion, sex, or national origin." . . .

Respondent argues, and the Court of Appeals held, that unwelcome sexual advances that create an offensive or hostile working environment violate Title VII. Without question, when a supervisor sexually harasses a subordinate because of the subordinate's sex, that supervisor "discriminate[s]" on the basis of sex. . . .

First, the language of Title VII is not limited to "economic" or "tangible" discrimination. The phrase "terms, conditions, or privileges of employment" evinces a congressional intent "'to strike at the entire spectrum of disparate treatment of men and women'" in employment. . . .

Second, in 1980 the EEOC issued Guidelines specifying that "sexual harassment," as there defined, is a form of sex discrimination prohibited by Title VII. . . .

In defining "sexual harassment," the Guidelines first describe the kinds of workplace conduct that may be actionable under Title VII. These include "[u]nwelcome sexual advances, requests for sexual favors, and other verbal or physical conduct of a sexual nature." 29 CFR § 1604.11(a) (1985). Relevant to the charges at issue in this case, the Guidelines provide that such sexual misconduct constitutes prohibited "sexual harassment," whether or not it is directly linked to the grant or denial of an economic *quid pro quo,* where "such conduct has the purpose or effect of unreasonably interfering with an individual's work performance or creating an intimidating, hostile, or offensive working environment." . . .

In concluding that so-called "hostile environment" (*i.e.,* non *quid pro quo*) harassment violates Title VII, the EEOC drew upon a substantial body of judicial decisions and EEOC precedent holding that Title VII affords employees the right to work in an environment free from discriminatory intimidation, ridicule, and insult. . . .

Since the Guidelines were issued, courts have uniformly held, and we agree, that a plaintiff may establish a violation of Title VII by proving that discrimination based on sex has created a hostile or abusive work environment. . . .

For sexual harassment to be actionable, it must be sufficiently severe or pervasive "to alter the conditions of [the victim's] employment and create an abusive working environment." *Ibid.* Respondent's allegations in this case — which include not only pervasive harassment but also criminal conduct of the most serious nature — are plainly sufficient to state a claim for "hostile environment" sexual harassment. . . .

The fact that sex-related conduct was "voluntary," in the sense that the complainant was not forced to participate against her will, is not a defense to a sexual harassment suit brought under Title VII. The gravamen of any sexual harassment claim is that the alleged sexual advances were "unwelcome." 29 CFR § 1604.11(a) (1985). While the question whether particular conduct was indeed unwelcome presents difficult problems of proof and turns largely on credibility determinations committed to the trier of fact, the District Court in this case erroneously focused on the "voluntariness" of respondent's participation in the claimed sexual episodes. The correct inquiry is whether respondent by her conduct indicated that the alleged sexual advances were unwelcome, not whether her actual participation in sexual intercourse was voluntary. . . .

III

Although the District Court concluded that respondent had not proved a violation of Title VII, it nevertheless went on to consider the question of the bank's liability. Finding that "the bank was without notice" of Taylor's alleged conduct, and that notice to Taylor was not the equivalent of notice to the bank, the court concluded that the bank therefore could not be held liable for Taylor's alleged actions. The Court of Appeals took the opposite view, holding that an employer is strictly liable for a hostile environment created by a supervisor's sexual advances, even though the employer neither knew nor reasonably could have known of the alleged misconduct. The court held that a supervisor, whether or not he possesses the authority to hire, fire, or promote, is necessarily an "agent" of his employer for all Title VII purposes, since "even the appearance" of such authority may enable him to impose himself on his subordinates. . . .

The EEOC, in its brief as *amicus curiae*, contends that courts formulating employer liability rules should draw from traditional agency principles. Examination of those principles has led the EEOC to the view that where a supervisor exercises the authority actually delegated to him by his employer, by making or threatening to make decisions affecting the employment status of his subordinates, such actions are properly imputed to the employer whose delegation of authority empowered the supervisor to undertake them. . . . Thus, the courts have consistently held employers liable for the discriminatory discharges of employees by supervisory personnel, whether or not the employer knew, should have known, or approved of the supervisor's actions. . . .

The EEOC suggests that when a sexual harassment claim rests exclusively on a "hostile environment" theory, however, the usual basis for a finding of agency will often disappear. In that case, the EEOC believes, agency principles lead to

> "a rule that asks whether a victim of sexual harassment had reasonably available an avenue of complaint regarding such harassment, and, if available and utilized, whether that procedure was reasonably responsive to the employee's complaint. If the employer has an expressed policy against sexual harassment and has implemented a procedure specifically designed to re-

solve sexual harassment claims, and if the victim does not take advantage of that procedure, the employer should be shielded from liability absent actual knowledge of the sexually hostile environment (obtained, *e.g.*, by the filing of a charge with the EEOC or a comparable state agency). In all other cases, the employer will be liable if it has actual knowledge of the harassment or if, considering all the facts of the case, the victim in question had no reasonably available avenue for making his or her complaint known to appropriate management officials." Brief for United States and EEOC as *Amici Curiae* 26.

As respondent points out, this suggested rule is in some tension with the EEOC Guidelines, which hold an employer liable for the acts of its agents without regard to notice. 29 CFR § 1604.11(c) (1985). The Guidelines do require, however, an "examin[ation of] the circumstances of the particular employment relationship and the job [f]unctions performed by the individual in determining whether an individual acts in either a supervisory or agency capacity."

We hold that the Court of Appeals erred in concluding that employers are always automatically liable for sexual harassment by their supervisors. For the same reason, absence of notice to an employer does not necessarily insulate that employer from liability. *Ibid.*

Finally, we reject petitioner's view that the mere existence of a grievance procedure and a policy against discrimination, coupled with respondent's failure to invoke that procedure, must insulate petitioner from liability. While those facts are plainly relevant, the situation before us demonstrates why they are not necessarily dispositive. Petitioner's general nondiscrimination policy did not address sexual harassment in particular, and thus did not alert employees to their employer's interest in correcting that form of discrimination. App. 25. Moreover, the bank's grievance procedure apparently required an employee to complain first to her supervisor, in this case

Taylor. Since Taylor was the alleged perpetrator, it is not altogether surprising that respondent failed to invoke the procedure and report her grievance to him. Petitioner's contention that respondent's failure should insulate it from liability might be substantially stronger if its procedures were better calculated to encourage victims of harassment to come forward.

IV

In sum, we hold that a claim of "hostile environment" sex discrimination is actionable under Title VII, that the District Court's findings were insufficient to dispose of respondent's hostile environment claim, and that the District Court did not err in admitting testimony about respondent's sexually provocative speech and dress. As to employer liability, we conclude that the Court of Appeals was wrong to entirely disregard agency principles and impose absolute liability on employers for the acts of their supervisors, regardless of the circumstances of a particular case.

Accordingly, the judgment of the Court of Appeals reversing the judgment of the District Court is affirmed, and the case is remanded for further proceedings consistent with this opinion.

CASE 1.   *"Harassment" at Brademore Electric*

Maura Donovan is a recent graduate of UCLA who now works as a low-level administrative assistant for Keith Sturdivant at the Brademore Electric Corporation, a large Los Angeles electrical contractor. Keith interviewed and hired Maura to work directly under him.

Maura had been employed at Brademore only three weeks when Keith approached her to go out on the weekend. Maura was taken somewhat by surprise and declined, thinking it best not to mix business and pleasure. But two days later Keith persisted, saying that Maura owed him something in return for his "getting" her the job. Maura was offended by this comment, knowing that she was well qualified for the position, but Keith seemed lonely, almost desperate, and she agreed to go with him to the Annual Renaissance Fair on Saturday afternoon. As it turned out, she did not have an enjoyable time. She liked the fair, but found Keith a bit crude and at times

almost uncivil in the way he treated employees at the Fair. She hoped he would not ask her out again.

But Monday morning he came back with the idea that they go on an overnight sailboat trip with some of his friends the next weekend. Maura politely declined. But Keith persisted, insisting that she owed her job to him. Maura found herself dreading the times she saw Keith coming down the corridor. What had been a very nice work environment for her had turned into a place of frequent dread. She spent a lot of time working to avoid Keith.

For four straight weeks, Keith came up with a different idea for how they might spend the weekend — always involving an overnight trip. Maura always declined. After the second week, she lied and told him that she was dating a number of other men. She said she was quite interested in two of these men and that she did not see any future with

---

This case was prepared by Tom L. Beauchamp.

Keith. Keith's reaction was to become even more insistent that they had a future together and to continue to ask her out.

Keith had become quite infatuated with Maura. He watched her every movement, whenever he had the opportunity. Sometimes he openly stared at her as she walked from one office to another. He began to have sexual fantasies about her, which he disclosed to two male supervisors. However, he never mentioned to Maura that he had in mind any form of sexual relationship.

Keith's direct supervisor, Vice President B. K. Singh, became aware of Keith's interest in Maura from two sources. First, he was told about the sexual fantasies by one of Keith's two male friends to whom Keith made the disclosures. Second, Maura had that same day come to his office to complain about what she considered sexual harassment. Mr. Singh became concerned about a possible contaminated work environment, but he did not think that he or Maura could make any form of harassment charge stick. The company had no corporate policy on harassment. Mr. Singh considered the situation to be just another case of one employee asking another out and being overly persistent. Mr. Singh decided not to do anything right away, not even to discuss the problem with Keith. He was worried that if he did take up the matter with Keith at such an early stage, he would himself be creating a hostile work environment. He believed Keith's advances would have to worsen before he should intervene or take the problem to the President.

Questions

1. Is Keith's conduct a case of sexual harassment? Is it a clear case, a borderline case, or no case at all?

2. Is it justifiable for Mr. Singh to adopt a position of nonintervention? Should he speak with Keith? What would you do if you were in his position?

3. Does the fact that Maura agreed once to go out with Keith mean that she has encouraged him to make further requests? If so, was she sufficiently discouraging at a later point?

CASE 2. *Sing's Chinese Restaurant*

The Bali Hai Corporation started as a small Chinese restaurant in Boston, Massachusetts, in 1959. The restaurant was an exact replica of a Chinese pagoda. Over the years, the restaurant, owned and managed by Arnold Sing, became known for its food and atmosphere. Customers were made to feel as if they were actually in China. In the last few years, Sing decided to incorporate and open other similar restaurants throughout the country. Sing, who had come to the United States from China in the early 1940s, was very strict in keeping up his reputation for good food and atmosphere. He had a policy of hiring only waiters of Oriental descent. He felt this added to his customers' dining pleasure and made for a more authentic environment. For kitchen positions, though, Sing hired any qualified applicants.

About a year ago at Sing's Bali Hai in Washington, D.C., there was a shortage of waiters. An advertisement was placed in the newspaper for waiters, and the manager of the store was instructed by Sing to hire only

Orientals. The manager was also reminded of Bali Hai's commitment to a reputation for good food and atmosphere. Two young men, one black and one white, both with considerable restaurant experience, applied for the waiter's jobs. The manager explained the policy of hiring only Orientals to the young men, and he also told them he could get them work in his kitchen. The two men declined the positions and instead went directly to the area Equal Employment Office and filed a complaint. Sing's defense was that the policy was only to preserve the atmosphere of the restaurant. He said the Oriental waiters were

needed to make it more authentic. Sing also added that he hired blacks, whites, and other races for his kitchen help.

Questions

1. Is Sing's defense a good one under the law? Why or why not?
2. Is Sing's defense a good one under the standards of morality? Why or why not?
3. Is this a case of "preferential hiring"? Of "reverse discrimination"?

CASE 3.   *USAir's Hiring Channel*

In June 1991 USAir agreed to abandon an informal hiring practice it had long used: USAir employees and influential friends of the company would no longer be invited to recommend pilots who were their acquaintances or relatives directly to the two vice presidents of Flying, thereby skirting the usual company screens for minimum qualifications. Under this former policy, a vice president could pursue or otherwise act on these recommendations as he or she saw fit. All other pilot applicants were first screened in the front office. Only white pilots had ever been hired through the alternative hiring channel.

Two black pilots who became employed by USAir — one through a standard system of application and the other through a corporate merger — complained that they would have been hired earlier if USAir's backdoor policy had not been in place. They claimed the policy was a preferential hiring system for friends and relatives of employees and that it

discriminated against blacks. These two pilots claimed rights to back pay and seniority. They sued for both.

A federal judge held that they were entitled to immediate back pay and seniority, dating to the time they likely would have been hired but were not because of the preferential policy. The court found that several white pilots who had been hired instead of the two black pilots did not meet minimum objective criteria used in standard front-office screens. Conversely, many black applicants who did meet these criteria had never been hired. The court also found that the alternative hiring channel lacked access to black applicants and, therefore, was a segregated system that advantaged whites and intentionally discriminated against blacks on the basis of race. In the final settlement, USAir agreed both to discontinue all existing special channels of recommendation and hiring *and* to establish a new special channel for recruiting black employees for the next thirty months.

This case was prepared by Tom L. Beauchamp on the basis of *Garland v. USAir, Inc.,* 767 F. Supp. 715 (April 25, 1991), and 56 Fair Empl. Prac. Cas. (BNA) 377 (June 10, 1991).

Questions

1. Does the new "special channel for recruiting black employees" unjustifiably discriminate against new white applicants? Is this special channel an instance of affirmative action?
2. Was USAir guilty of intentional discrimination? Did the corporate policy create a segregated system?

3. Is it justifiable for businesses to use any form of hiring that bypasses screens in employment offices? For example, in small family businesses, can family members legitimately bypass normal screens?

CASE 4.   *Weber and the Kaiser Aluminum Steelworkers Plan*

In 1974 the United Steelworkers of America and Kaiser Aluminum & Chemical Corp. established an employment agreement that addressed an overwhelming racial imbalance in employment in Kaiser plants. Of primary concern was the lack of skilled black craftworkers. This concern arose because of an ongoing exclusion of black craftsworkers. In an attempt to remove the disparity and create a fair employment policy, an affirmative action plan ("the plan") was agreed to, whereby

> black craft-hiring goals were set for each Kaiser plant equal to the percentage of blacks in the respective local labor forces . . . [and] to enable plants to meet these goals, on-the-job training programs were established to teach unskilled workers — black and white — the skills necessary to become craftsworkers (443 U.S. 198 [1979]).

Under the guidelines of the plan, 50 percent of those selected for the newly instituted training program were to be black employees *until* the goals of the plan were accomplished, after which the 50 percent provision would be discontinued.

Such a plan was instituted at the Gramercy, Louisiana, plant from which the major problems had arisen and where blacks constituted less than 2 percent of the skilled craftsworkers, although they were approximately 39 percent of the Gramercy labor force. Subsequently, thirteen trainees, of which seven were black, were selected in accordance with the guidelines of the plan. The black trainees had less seniority than many white production workers who were denied training status. Brian Weber, one such production worker, argued that he and others had been unduly discriminated against. He thought the plan was a violation of Title VII of the Civil Rights Act of 1964. A District Court and a Court of Appeals held that Title VII had been violated. The U.S. Supreme Court then addressed the issue of whether employers were forbidden from enacting such affirmative action plans to alleviate racial imbalances.

The Supreme Court held that forbidding such affirmative action plans under Title VII would be in direct contradiction to its purpose, because the statutory words call upon "employers and unions to self-examine and to self-evaluate their employment practices and to endeavor to eliminate, so far as possible, the vast vestiges of an unfortunate and ignominious page in this country's history" (433 U.S. 204 [1978]). The Supreme Court

This case was abstracted from Supreme Court materials by Katie Marshall and Tom L. Beauchamp.

concluded that the Kaiser plan purposes "mirror[ed] those of the statute," because both the plan and the statute "were designed to break down old patterns of racial segregation [and] both were structured to open employment opportunities for Negroes in occupations which have been traditionally closed to them." The Supreme Court reversed the opinions of the lower courts (433 U.S. 208 [1978]).

Questions

1. Are the percentage figures in this case "quotas"? Are they justified under the circumstances?
2. Does Kaiser have a fair employment policy? If not, how should it be revised?
3. Is there reverse discrimination against Weber? If so, is it justified?

CASE 5.   *Comparable Worth in the Female Section?*

During the early 1970s, the County of Washington, Oregon, established salary scales for its guards in the county jail. Female guards in the female section were paid one-third to one-eighth less than male guards of the comparable rank and experience in the male section.

The female guards complained that they were paid unequal wages for work substantially equal to that performed by male guards and that the underlying reason was sex discrimination. The pay scale for males had been determined by the county's survey of outside markets for guards, but the pay scale for females was not similarly set. The survey indicated that the average outside pay standard is that female correctional officials are paid about 95 percent as much as male correctional officials. Nonetheless, the County of Washington decided to pay women only 70 percent of the salary paid to men. The county thus had scaled down the female guards' work below the outside market level. However, the county had not had difficulty hiring women in the local region at its pay scales.

The county said there were two major differences in the jobs for men and women: The

male guards supervised more than ten times as many prisoners per guard as did the female guards, and the females, unlike the males, were required to spend part of their time on clerical jobs (considered less valuable by the county). The county therefore held that the females' jobs were not substantially equal to those of the male guards and merited less than equal pay. The county objected to the idea that any outside authority such as the courts could evaluate its pay scales without placing virtually every employer at risk of scrutiny by the courts for not paying comparable wages.

Questions

1. Is this a "comparable worth" case, or a case involving sex discrimination, or a simple case of fair salaries? Is it all of these?
2. Are there relevant differences between the male jobs and the female jobs that would justify a lower scale for women?

This case was prepared by Tom L. Beauchamp.

Suggested Supplementary Readings

AALBERTS, ROBERT J., and LORNE H. SEIDMAN. "Sexual Harassment by Clients, Customers, and Suppliers: How Employers Should Handle an Emerging Legal Problem." *Employee Relations Law Journal* 20 (Summer 1994): 85–100.

BLOCH, FARRELL. *Antidiscrimination Law and Minority Employment: Recruitment Practices and Regulatory Constraints.* Chicago, IL: The University of Chicago Press, 1994.

BLUM, LINDA M. *Between Feminism and Labor: The Significance of the Comparable Worth Movement.* Berkeley, CA: University of California Press, 1991.

BLUMROSEN, ALFRED W. *Modern Law: The Law Transmission System and Equal Employment Opportunity.* Madison, WI: The University of Wisconsin Press, 1993.

BOXILL, BERNARD. *Blacks and Social Justice.* Totowa, NJ: Rowman and Littlefield, 1992.

BROWNE, M. NEIL, and ANDREA M. GIAMPETRO. "The Socially Responsible Firm and Comparable Worth." *American Business Law Journal* 25 (Fall 1987).

COHEN, MARSHALL, THOMAS NAGEL, and THOMAS SCANLON, eds. *Equality and Preferential Treatment.* Princeton, N.J.: Princeton University Press, 1977.

CRAIN, KAREN, A., and KENNETH A. HEISCHMIDT. "Implementing Business Ethics: Sexual Harassment." *Journal of Business Ethics* 14 (April 1995): 299–308.

DANDEKER, NATALIE. "Contrasting Consequences: Bringing Charges of Sexual Harassment Compared with Other Cases of Whistleblowing." *Journal of Business Ethics* 9 (1990).

EGLER, THERESA DONAHUE. "Five Myths About Sexual Harassment." *HR Magazine* 40 (January 1995): 27–30.

ENGLAND, PAULA. *Comparable Worth: Theories and Evidence.* New York: Aldine De Gruyter, 1992.

EZORSKY, GERTRUDE. *Racism and Justice.* Ithaca, N.Y.: Cornell University Press, 1991.

FINE, LESLIE M., C. DAVID SHEPHERD, and SUSAN L. JOSEPHS. "Sexual Harassment in the Sales Force: The Customer Is NOT Always Right." *Journal of Personal Selling & Sales Management* 14 (Fall 1994): 15–30.

FISCHEL, DANIEL, and EDWARD LAZEAR. "Comparable Worth and Discrimination in Labor Markets." *University of Chicago Law Review* 53 (Summer 1986).

FULLINWIDER, ROBERT. *The Reverse Discrimination Controversy.* Totowa, N.J.: Rowman and Allanheld, 1980.

GUNDERSON, MORLEY. "Male-Female Wage Differentials and Policy Responses." *Journal of Economic Literature* 27 (March 1989).

GUNDERSON, MORLEY. "Pay and Employment Equity in the United States and Canada." *International Journal of Manpower* 15 (1994): 26–43.

HORNE, GERALD. *Reversing Discrimination: The Case for Affirmative Action.* New York: International Publishers, 1992.

KALANTARI, BEHROOZ. "Dynamics of Job Evaluation and the Dilemma of Wage Disparity in the United States." *Journal of Business Ethics* 14 (1995): 397–403.

KILLINGSWORTH, MARK R. *The Economics of Comparable Worth.* Kalamazoo, MI: W.E. Upjohn Institute for Employment Research, 1990.

LEAP, TERRY L., and LARRY R. SMELTZER. "Racial Remarks in the Workplace: Humor or Harassment?" *Harvard Business Review* 62 (1984).

LYNCH, F. R. *Invisible Victims: White Males and the Crisis of Affirmative Action.* Westport, CT: Greenwood Press, 1989.

MICELI, MARCIA P., and Others. "Employers' Pay Practices and Potential Responses to 'Comparable Worth' Litigation." *Journal of Business Ethics* 7 (May 1988).

MORRIS, CELIA. *Bearing Witness: Sexual Harassment and Beyond — Everywoman's Story.* Boston, MA: Little, Brown & Company, 1994.

OLNEY, PETER B., JR. "Meeting the Challenge of Comparable Worth." *Compensation and Benefits Review* 19 (March–April 1987).

ORAZEM, PETER F., and J. PETER MATTILA. "The Implementation Process of Comparable Worth." *Journal of Political Economy* 98 (February 1990).

PACE, JOSEPH MICHAEL, and ZACHARY SMITH. "Understanding Affirmative Action: From the Practitioner's Perspective." *Public Personnel Management* 24 (Summer 1995): 139–147.

PAETZOLD, RAMONA L., and BILL SHAW. "A Postmodern Feminist View of "Reasonableness" in Hostile Environment Sexual Harassment." *Jour-*

nal of Business Ethics 13 (September 1994): 681–692.

PAUL, ELLEN FRANKEL. *Equity and Gender: The Comparable Worth Debate.* New Brunswick, NJ: Transaction Publishers, 1989.

PETERSEN, DONALD J. and DOUGLAS P. MASSENGILL. "Sexual Harassment Cases Five Years After Meritor Savings Bank v. Vinson." *Employee Relations Law Journal* 18 (Winter 1992–93): 489–515.

PHILIPS, MICHAEL. "Preferential Hiring and the Question of Competence." *Journal of Business Ethics* 10 (1991).

POSNER, RICHARD. "An Economic Analysis of Sex Discrimination Laws." *University of Chicago Law Review* 56 (Fall 1989).

PURDY, LAURA. "Why Do We Need Affirmative Action?" *Journal of Social Philosophy* 25 (Spring 1994): 133–143.

QUINN, JENNIFER M. "Visibility and Value: The Role of Job Evaluation in Assuring Equal Pay for Women." *Law & Policy in International Business* 25 (Summer 1994): 1403–1444.

RAISIAN, JOHN, and others. "Pay Equity and Comparable Worth." *Contemporary Policy Issues* 4 (1986).

REMICK, HELEN. *Comparable Worth and Wage Discrimination.* Philadelphia: Temple University Press, 1984.

RHOADS, STEVEN F. *Incomparable Worth: Pay Equity Meets the Market.* Cambridge, England: Cambridge University Press, 1993.

ROSENFELD, MICHEL. *Affirmative Action and Justice: A Philosophical and Constitutional Inquiry.* New Haven: Yale Univ Press, 1991.

SEGRAVE, KERRY, *The Sexual Harassment of Women in Workplace, 1600 to 1993.* Jefferson, NC: McFarland & Company, Inc., Publisher, 1994.

SHANEY, MARY JO. "Perceptions of Harm: The Consent Defense in Sexual Harassment Cases." *Iowa Law Review* 71 (1986).

SINGER, M. S., and A. E. SINGER. "Justice in Preferential Hiring." *Journal of Business Ethics* 10 (1991).

SUNSTEIN, CASS R. "The Limits of Compensatory Justice." *Nomos* 33 (1991): 281–310.

THOMAS, LAURENCE. "On Sexual Offers and Threats." In *Moral Rights in the Workplace,* edited by Gertrude Ezorsky. Albany, NY: State University of New York Press, 1987.

U.S. Supreme Court. *Burwell v. Eastern Air Lines, Inc.* 450 U.S. 965 (1981).

——. *Firefighters v. Stotts,* 467 U.S. 561 (1984).

——. *Johnson v. Transportation Agency,* 480 U.S. 616 (1987).

——. *McDonnell Douglas Corp. v. Green,* 411 U.S. 792 (1973).

——. *Price Waterhouse v. Hopkins,* 490 U.S. ___ , 104 L.Ed. 268 (1989).

——. *United Steelworkers v. Weber,* 443 U.S. 193 (1979).

——. *United States v. Paradise,* 480 U.S. 149.

——. *Watson v. Fort Worth Bank & Trust,* 487 U.S. 977 (1988).

——. *Wygant v. Jackson Bd. of Education,* 476 U.S. 267 (1986).

WAGNER, ELLEN J. *Sexual Harassment in the Workplace: How to Prevent, Investigate, and Resolve Problems in Your Organization.* New York: Amacom [American Management Association], 1992.

WALL, EDMUND, ed. *Sexual Harassment: Confrontations and Decisions.* Buffalo, NY: Prometheus Books, 1992.

WELLS, DEBORAH L., and BEVERLY J. KRACHER. "Justice, Sexual Harassment, and the Reasonable Victim Standard." *Journal of Business Ethics* 12 (June 1993): 423–431.

YORK, KENNETH M. "Defining Sexual Harassment in Workplaces: A Policy-Capturing Approach." *Academy of Management Journal* 32 (1989).

Chapter Seven

———— • ————

Gathering, Concealing, and Gilding Information

ADVERTISING IS THE MOST visible way businesses present information to the public, but it is not the only way in which information is communicated in business, nor even the most important. Sales information, annual reports containing financial audits, public relations presentations, warranties, trade secrets, and public education and public health campaigns are other vital means by which corporations manage, communicate, and limit information.

A wide array of moral problems confront these activities. Some problems are commonplace — for example, withholding vital information, distortion of data, and bluffing. Other problems of information control are more subtle. These include using information to attract customers, using annual reports as public relations devices, giving calculated "news releases" to the press, avoiding disclosures to workers that directly affect their health and welfare, and industrial spying.

Rights of autonomy and free choice are at the center of these discussions. In some forms, withholding information and manipulating advertising messages threaten to undermine the free choice of consumers, clients, stockholders, and even colleagues. Deceptive and misleading statements limit freedom by restricting the range of choice and causing a person to do what he or she otherwise might not do.

Aside from these *autonomy*-based problems, there are *harm*-based problems that may have little to do with making a choice. For example, when the Nestlé corporation was pressured to suspend infant formula advertising and aggressive marketing tactics in developing countries, the controversy focused less on the freedom-based issue of the right to the dissemination of information than on preventing a population from harming itself through inadequate breastfeeding and inadequate appreciation of the risks of the use of infant formula. Harm-based issues are mentioned in this chapter, but restrictions of free choice by manipulative influence is the central issue.

FREE CHOICE OR UNFAIR INFLUENCE?

A classic defense of American business practice is that business provides the public with what it wants; the consumer is king in the free enterprise system, and the market responds to consumer demands. This response is often said to represent the chief strength of a market economy over a collectivist system: freedom of consumer choice is unaffected by government and corporate controls.

But consider the following controversy about freedom of choice. The Federal Trade Commission (FTC) in late 1984 and early 1985 "reconsidered" its rule prohibiting supermarket advertising of items when they did not have those items in stock. The rule had been enacted in 1971 to combat frustration among shoppers who found empty shelves in place of advertised goods and often wound up substituting more expensive items. FTC officials suggested that the rule may have been unduly burdensome for the supermarket industry and that "market forces" would eliminate or curtail those who dishonestly advertise. Consumer groups argued that relaxing the rule would permit more expensive stores to lure shoppers by advertising low prices, leading many shoppers to spend more overall than they would have spent in a low-budget store. Mark Silbergeld of the Consumers Union argued that the Commission was acting in ignorance of the *real purpose* of supermarket advertising, which is to present a "come-on to get people into their stores."[1]

On the one hand, if advertisements succeed in manipulating persons to buy products through false or empty advertising, these purchase decisions may not be as free as consumers think or as supermarket companies suggest. On the other hand, shoppers can refuse to buy substitutes for the missing goods or can return later for the unavailable items. Does such advertising represent a deprivation of free choice, or is it rather an example of how free choice determines market forces? Can it function as both for certain populations of persons?

Control over a person is exerted through various kinds of influence, but not all influences actually control. Some forms of influence are desired and accepted by those who are influenced, whereas others are unwelcome. Many influences can easily be resisted by most persons; others can prove irresistible. Human reactions to influences such as corporate-sponsored information and advertising presentations cannot in many cases be determined or easily studied. Frank Dandrea, vice president of marketing for Schiefflin & Co., the importer of Hennessy's Cognac, once said that in their advertisements "the idea is to show a little skin, a little sex appeal, a little tension."[2] This effect is accomplished by showing a scantily clad woman holding a brandy snifter and staring provocatively in response to a man's interested glance. Hennessy tries to use a mixture of sex and humor. Other companies use rebates and coupons. All these methods are attempts to influence, and it is well known that they are at least partially successful. However, the influence of these strategies and the moral acceptability of these influences have been less carefully examined.

There is a continuum of controlling influence in our daily lives, running from coercion, at the controlling end of the continuum, to persuasion and education, both noncontrolling influences. Coercion requires an intentional and successful influence through an irresistible threat of harm. A coercive action negates freedom because it entirely controls the person's action. Persuasion, by contrast, involves a successful appeal to reason in order to convince a person to accept freely what is advocated by the persuader. Like informing, persuading is entirely compatible with free choice.

Manipulation covers the great gray area of influence. It is a catchall category that suggests the act of getting people to do what is advocated without resorting to coercion and without appealing to reasoned argument. In the case of *informational* manipulation, on which several selections in this chapter concentrate, information is managed so that the manipulated person will do what the manipulator intends. Whether such uses of information necessarily compromise or restrict free choice is an unresolved issue. One plausible view is that some manipulations — for instance, the use of rewards such as free trips or lottery coupons in direct mail advertising — are compatible with free choice, whereas others — such as deceptive offers or tantalizing ads aimed at young children — are not compatible with free choice. Beer and wine advertising aimed at teenagers and young adults has been under particularly harsh criticism in recent years, on grounds that in the advertising sex, youth, fun, and beauty are directly linked to dangerous products, with noticeable success. As Tom Beauchamp and George Brenkert point out in their essays, these issues raise complex questions of both individual moral responsibility and collective moral responsibility in marketing products.

Many problems with advertising fall somewhere between acceptable and unacceptable manipulation. Consider these two examples: Anheuser-Busch ran a television commercial for its Budweiser Beer showing some working men heading for a brew at day's end. The commercial began with a shot of the Statue of Liberty in the background, included close-up shots of a construction crew working to restore the Statue, and ended with the words, "This Bud's for you, you know America takes pride in what you do." This statement may seem innocent, but the Liberty–Ellis Island Foundation accused Anheuser-Busch of a "blatant attempt to dupe [i.e., manipulate] consumers" by implying that Budweiser was among the sponsors helping to repair the Statue. The Foundation was particularly irritated because Anheuser-Busch had refused such as sponsorship when invited by the Foundation, whereas its rival, Stroh Brewing Company, had subsequently accepted an exclusive brewery sponsorship.[3]

A second case comes from Kellogg's advertising for its All-Bran product. The company ran a campaign linking its product to the prevention of cancer, apparently causing an immediate increase in sales of 41 percent for All-Bran. Although many food manufacturers advertise the low-salt, low-fat, low-calorie, or high-fiber content of their products, Kellogg went further, citing a specific product as a way to combat a specific disease. It is illegal to make claims about the health benefits of a specific food product without FDA approval, and Kellogg did not have this approval. Yet officials at both the National Cancer Institute and the FDA were not altogether critical of the ads. On the one hand, officials at these agencies agree that a high-fiber, low-fat diet containing some of the ingredients in All-bran does help prevent cancer. On the other hand, no direct association exists between eating a given product and preventing cancer, and certainly no single food product can function like a drug as a preventative or remedy for such a disease.

The Kellogg ad strongly suggested that eating All-Bran was everything one needed to do to prevent cancer. Such a claim is potentially misleading in several respects. The ad did not suggest how much fiber people should eat, nor did it note that people can consume too much fiber while neglecting other essential minerals. Further, no direct scientific evidence linked the consumption of this product with the prevention of cancer, and this product could not be expected to affect all types of cancer. Is the Kellogg promise manipulative, or is the ad, as Kellogg claims, basically a truthful, health-promotion campaign? Does it contain elements of both?

These examples help illustrate the broad categories on the continuum of controlling influences that are under examination in this chapter. Other forms of influence such as *indoctrination* and *seduction* might be mentioned, but, in the end, especially for advertising, the difference between *manipulation* and *persuasion* is the key matter.

DECEPTION, BLUFFING, AND STRATEGIC DISCLOSURE

Manipulation can take many forms: offering rewards, threatening punishments, instilling fear, and so forth. The principal form discussed in this chapter is the manipulation of information. Here the manipulator modifies a person's sense of options by affecting the person's understanding of the situation. Deception, bluffing, and the like are used by the manipulator to change not the person's *actual* options but only the person's *perception* of the options. The more a person is deprived of a relevant understanding in the circumstances, the greater the effect on the person's free choice.

One does not need extensive experience in business to know that many deceptive practices, like bluffing and slick sales techniques, are widely practiced and widely accepted. It is common knowledge that automobile dealers do not expect people to pay the sticker price for automobiles; but it is a closely guarded secret as to how much can be knocked off that price. A certain amount of quoting of competitors, bargaining, moving "extras" under the basic price, and going to managers for approval is part of the game. A similar situation prevails in real estate transactions, in which the asking price for a house is seldom the anticipated selling price, as well as at bargaining sessions, in which labor leaders overstate wage demands and management understates the wage increases it is willing to grant.

The intent is to manipulate, however gently. In his article "Is Business Bluffing Ethical?" Albert Z. Carr recognizes that such practices are characteristic of business and maintains that they are analogous to the game of poker. According to Carr, just as conscious misstatement, concealment of pertinent facts, exaggeration, and bluffing are morally acceptable in poker, they are acceptable in business. What makes such practices acceptable, Carr says, is that all parties understand the rules of the game. In advertising, for example, exaggeration and bluffing are understood to be part of the selling game. Only an extraordinarily naive person would believe advertisements without casting a skeptical eye on the images and words issuing from a television set.

Yet there are moral limits to the game, even if the rules of the game are grasped by all. Suppose that Pamela is willing to sell her home for $60,000, if that is the best price she can get. She puts the home on the market at $70,000. A potential buyer's initial offer is $60,000. Pamela turns the offer down, telling him that $65,000 is her rock-bottom price. He then purchases the home for $65,000. Many people would characterize her behavior as shrewd bluffing and certainly not an immoral lie. Many people would think more of her, rather than less. However, suppose she manufactured the claim that another party was writing up a contract to buy the house for $65,000 and that she would sell it to him for the same $65,000 price because both she and he were Baptists. In this case many people would maintain that she had told at least one lie, probably two; but are the lies unjustified or merely part of the game? Would it make any moral difference if she were to have her brother pretend to make her an offer and draw up a fake contract so that the prospective buyer would be pressured to buy?

The sophistication of the audience, standard practice in the business, and intention of the informer all need to be considered to decide whether gilded information is unacceptable. Manipulation and deception can result as much from what is not said as from what is said. For example, true information can be presented out of context and thereby be misleading. The reasoning of Chief Justice Earl Warren in *FTC v. Colgate-Palmolive Co.* demonstrates how the omission of certain facts can be misleading, whereas the omission of other facts is not misleading. At issue is a television commercial depicting someone shaving sandpaper that had been generously lathered with Rapid Shave. The FTC found that Rapid Shave could soften and shave sandpaper, but the sandpaper needed to soak in Rapid Shave for approximately eighty minutes before it could be shaved. On this basis, the FTC declared the ad a deceptive trade practice because the television viewer was not informed about the eighty-minute period in which the sandpaper had to soak. This omission constituted a misrepresentation of the product's moisturizing power.

Colgate-Palmolive disagreed. It compared its "experiment" to the use of mashed potatoes substituted for ice cream in television ice-cream ads. Just as the hot television lights made the use of ice cream impossible — a fact ice-cream ads do not disclose — so the eighty-minute duration made showing an actual experiment with Rapid Shave impossible. The court rejected this analogy, on grounds that the mashed potatoes prop was not used for proof of the quality of the product, whereas the Rapid Shave commercial was attempting to provide such proof. The decision could be generalized as follows: whether undisclosed information is an example of deception and manipulation depends on whether the information relates to claims about the quality of the product.

Another problem about disclosure of information appears in *Backman v. Polaroid Corporation*. In this case investors alleged that Polaroid had obtained negative information about its product Polavision but had failed to disclose to investors unfavorable facts that were known about the product. In effect, the claim is that Polaroid manipulated investors into purchasing the stock at a higher value than its actual worth. A similar charge led to accusations against Salomon, Inc., in late 1991 for both moral and legal failures to disclose properly to shareholders a stock option plan and cash bonus plan that benefited top corporate executives. Investors charged that the level of compensation diluted the value of the stock. Salomon responded that it had "followed the rules" of disclosure in its mailings to stockholders.[4]

Despite such examples, Carr maintains that it is morally permissible to deceive others in these ways as long as everyone knows that such actions are accepted in the business world as standard practice. Carr would presumably say that neither Polaroid nor Salomon did anything wrong so long as it is accepted that unfavorable facts about a product or compensation scheme do not have to be disclosed. However, this perception raises many problems. For example, bluffing, active deception, and lack of disclosure interfere with the way markets work when good information is available and may also create instability in markets and may hurt productivity and stifle competition.

Carr's criteria are either rejected or restated in a more guarded form in the next article by Thomas Carson. Carson argues that people commonly misstate their bargaining positions in the course of business negotiations, but that these misstatements often do not involve lying. He maintains that bluffing and other forms of negotiation are legitimate when one has good reason to believe that the other party understands the rules and is engaging in the same form of activity. However, it is impermissible to misstate one's negotiating or bargaining position whenever one does not have good reason to believe that the other party is engaging in a similar form of misstatement. Thus, by contrast to Carr, Carson argues that bluffing is often immoral when the attempt to lie or bluff is unilateral. To follow out the game metaphor, Carson is insisting not only that the rules of the game be understood but that the game be on a level playing surface for all players.

DISCLOSING AND CONCEALING INFORMATION IN SALES

These issues about disclosure, deception, and manipulation are as prominent in sales as in advertising. As the marketplace for products has grown more complex and sophisticated, buyers have become more dependent upon salespersons to know their products and to tell the truth about them. The implicit assumption in some sales contexts is that bargaining and deception about a selling price are parts of the game, just as they are in real estate and labor negotiations. Nevertheless, this "flea market" and "horse-trader" model of sales is unsuited to other contemporary markets. The salesperson is expected to have superior knowledge and is treated as an expert on the product, or at least as one who obtains needed information about a product. In this climate, it seems unethical for salespersons to take advantage of a buyer's implicit trust by using deceptive or manipulative techniques. Yet, if it is unethical to disclose too little, does it follow that the ethical salesperson has an obligation to disclose everything that might be of interest to the customer? For example, must the salesperson disclose that his or her company charges more than a competitor? What principles rightly govern the transfer of information during sales?

James M. Ebejer and Michael J. Morden point out in their article in this chapter that some salespersons view their relationship to the customer under the model of *caveat emptor* (let the buyer beware), whereas, at the other extreme, some salespersons see their role as that of paternalistic protector of the customer's interests. These authors argue for a professional sales ethic that they describe as "limited paternalism," which they propose as a regulative standard. Using this standard, a salesperson should be his or her "buyers' keeper" by identifying the needs of customers and disclosing information essential to meeting those needs. The salesperson is obligated to use this approach even if customers do not understand what their best interests are. Ebejer and Morden believe this approach maximizes mutual exchange and mutual advantage, evidently a utilitarian criterion for proper sales disclosures.

In a second article on sales practices, Kerry S. Walters argues against Ebejer and Morden. He urges that, however appealing their standard, its application can and will produce a counterproductive moral dilemma that he calls "the Pontius Pilate Plight." The dilemma occurs in the assumption that moral agents' hands are clean when they live up to limited paternalism even when they have done something that they themselves condemn as immoral to their personal morality. For example, if a shop owner has deep moral reservations about selling cigarettes in her or his store, limited paternalism suggests that the owner's hands are clean as long as she or he discloses the dangers of cigarettes when making the sales. Limited paternalism may be a necessary condition for ethical sales, Walters argues, but it is not a sufficient condition. He goes on to conclude with the suggestion that two additional criteria, when complemented by the limited paternalism principle, will prove to be jointly sufficient conditions of ethical sales.

INFORMATION GATHERING

Proprietary information was introduced in Chapter 5 as an issue of intellectual property rights and trade secrets. The present chapter treats a related issue: how corporations should gather information about competitors and their products. Because competitor intelligence that is acquired to help managers understand their competitors is highly valued, thousands of firms have adopted some form of systematic approach to acquiring intelligence about their competitors. Some form of intelligence gathering is practiced by almost all corporations that are the size of those in the Fortune 500 and is generally considered by managers to be essential to compete adequately. Paradoxically, although firms approve gaining such information, they condemn what they see as unethical intelligence-gathering methods used by others. Despite these ready condemnations, few corporations have a policy on the ethics of intelligence gathering in their codes of conduct.

It is commercial stealing to use proprietary information without permission, and using espionage, bribery, and trespass to obtain information is clearly unethical. However, many gray areas remain between theft and legitimate collection of information about competitors. Not surprisingly, litigation over property rights and criminal charges of pirated materials has increased in recent years. Management surveys suggest that a wide range of questionable activities in the pursuit of intelligence gathering now exists. Attempts to obtain research data and newly developed technologies through employee piracy, industrial espionage, and sensitive listening devices are typical problems. Deceit, bribery, raiding of employees, invading confidential data banks, and covert surveillance have all been used by U.S. corporations.

These activities are rarely discussed in corporations as ethically questionable activities and are almost never included in corporate codes of conduct. However, some significant changes have taken place in defense-related industries as a result of some accusations and resignations involving secret procurement of Pentagon documents by Navy contractors such as Bath Iron Works, Martin Marietta, United Technologies, and Unisys.

In her article in this chapter, Lynn Sharp Paine identifies ways in which intelligence gathering takes place, concentrating on circumstances in which corporations use misrepresentation, improper influence, and various strategies that undermine relationships of trust and confidence. Many of the techniques she discusses involve manipulation not of customers or competitors but of employees, potential employees, or trusted associates of competitors. Paine identifies some ethical principles that can help managers draw the line between legitimate and illegitimate methods of intelligence gathering. She also points to the costs that corporations and the public will incur if they fail to pay closer attention to these problems than they have in the past and suggests methods managers can use to introduce moral leadership in this area.

Paine's arguments are not intended to suggest that intelligence gathering per se is unwelcome or immoral. Market success may require some forms of intelligence gathering about development efforts, plans for expansion, reasons for price reductions, sales strategy, customer base, pricing, and the like. Some consulting firms and societies specialize in acquiring and then rapidly disseminating information about a wide range of products in some part of the industry. Successful competition has proved difficult in some parts of business unless a data base is maintained on competitors' products and plans.

Sometimes when the transfer of information occurs that a company might hope to have prevented, the transfer is not necessarily an invalid discovery or disclosure of information. If the company's carelessness in using the information is the source of the problem, it would be expected that the company will take reasonable precautions to protect itself against discovery by industrial spies. When the Kellogg Company stopped its once-famous plant tours, the primary reason was a fear that the tours created a legitimate opportunity for industrial sleuths to discover state-of-the-art manufacturing secrets.[5]

Accordingly, discussion of intelligence gathering suggests a need to distinguish between legitimate methods of acquiring information and illegitimate methods. The line is often difficult to draw, so that borderline cases are inevitable. Only a slight shade of difference sometimes exists between what one is inclined to think appropriate and what one judges inappropriate. It is essential, however, to try to draw that line not only to meet one's moral responsibility but to stop the tide of litigation.

NOTES

1. Sari Horwitz, "FTC Considers Letting Food Stores Advertise Out-of-Stock Items," *Washington Post,* December 27, 1984, p. E1.

2. As quoted in Amy Dunkin and others, "Liquor Makers Try the Hard Sell in a Softening Market," *Business Week,* May 13, 1985, p. 56.

3. "Anheuser-Busch Sued on Ad Showing Statue of Liberty," *Wall Street Journal,* November 28, 1984, p. 43.

4. Robert J. McCartney, "Investors Hit Salomon on Bonuses," *Washington Post,* October 23, 1991, pp. C1, C5.

5. Damon Darlin, "Kellogg Is Snapping Its 80-Year Tradition of Cereal Tours," *Wall Street Journal,* April 10, 1986, p. 1.

Is Business Bluffing Ethical?

Albert Z. Carr

A respected businessman with whom I discussed the theme of this article remarked with some heat, "You mean to say you're going to encourage men to bluff? Why, bluffing is nothing more than a form of lying! You're advising them to lie!"

I agreed that the basis of private morality is a respect for truth and that the closer a businessman comes to the truth, the more he deserves respect. At the same time, I suggested that most bluffing in business might be regarded simply as game strategy — much like bluffing in poker, which does not reflect on the morality of the bluffer.

I quoted Henry Taylor, the British statesman who pointed out that "falsehood ceases to be falsehood when it is understood on all sides that the truth is not expected to be spoken" — an exact description of bluffing in poker, diplomacy, and business. I cited the analogy of the criminal court, where the criminal is not expected to tell the truth when he pleads "not guilty." Everyone from the judge down takes it for granted that the job the of the defendant's attorney is to get his client off, not to reveal the truth; and this is considered ethical practice. I mentioned Representative Omar Burleson, the Democrat from Texas, who was quoted as saying, in regard to the ethics of Congress, "Ethics is a barrel of worms"[1] — a pungent summing up of the problem of deciding who is ethical in politics.

I reminded my friend that millions of businessmen feel constrained every day to say *yes* to their bosses when they secretly believe *no* and that this is generally accepted as permissible strategy when the alternative might be the loss of a job. The essential point, I said, is that the ethics of business are game ethics, different from the ethics of religion.

He remained unconvinced. Referring to the company of which he is president, he declared: "Maybe that's good enough for some businessmen, but I can tell you that we pride ourselves on our ethics. In 30 years not one customer has ever questioned my word or asked to check our figures. We're loyal to our customers and fair to our suppliers. I regard my handshake on a deal as a contract. I've never entered into price-fixing schemes with my competitors. I've never allowed my salesmen to spread injurious rumors about other companies. Our union contract is the best in our industry. And, if I do say so myself, our ethical standards are of the highest!"

He really was saying, without realizing it, that he was living up to the ethical standards of the business game — which are a far cry from those of private life. Like a gentlemanly poker player, he did not play in cahoots with others at the table, try to smear their reputations, or hold back chips he owed them.

But this same fine man, at that very time, was allowing one of his products to be advertised in a way that made it sound a great deal better than it actually was. Another item in his product line was notorious among dealers for its "built-in obsolescence." He was holding back from the market a much-improved product because he did not want to interfere with sales of the inferior item it would have replaced. He had joined with certain of his competitors in hiring a lobbyist to push a state legislature, by methods that he preferred not to know too much about, into amending a bill then being enacted.

In his view these things had nothing to do with ethics; they were merely normal business practice. He himself undoubtedly avoided outright falsehoods — never lied in so many words. But the entire organization that he ruled was deeply involved in numerous strategies of deception.

PRESSURE TO DECEIVE

Most executives from time to time are almost compelled, in the interests of their companies or themselves, to practice some form of deception when negotiating with customers, dealers, labor unions, government officials, or even other departments of their companies. By conscious misstatements, concealment of pertinent facts, or exaggeration — in short, by bluffing — they seek to persuade others to agree with them. I think it is fair to say that if the individual executive refuses to bluff from time to time — if he feels obligated to tell the truth, the whole truth, and nothing but the truth — he is ignoring opportunities permitted under the rules and is at a heavy disadvantage in his business dealings.

But here and there a businessman is unable to reconcile himself to the bluff in which he plays a part. His conscience, perhaps spurred by religious idealism, troubles him. He feels guilty; he may develop an ulcer or a nervous tic. Before any executive can make profitable use of the strategy of the bluff, he needs to make sure that in bluffing he will not lose self-respect or become emotionally disturbed. If he is to reconcile personal integrity and high standards of honesty with the practical requirements of business, he must feel that his bluffs are ethically justified. The justification rests on the fact that business, as practiced by individuals as well as by corporations, has the impersonal character of a game — a game that demands both special strategy and an understanding of its special ethics.

The game is played at all levels of corporate life, from the highest to the lowest. At the very instant that a man decides to enter business, he may be forced into a game situation, as is shown by the recent experience of a Cornell honor graduate who applied for a job with a large company. This applicant was given a psychological test which included the statement, "Of the following magazines, check any that you have read either regularly or from time to time, and double-check those which interest you most. *Reader's Digest, Time, Fortune, Saturday Evening Post, The New Republic, Life, Look, Ramparts, Newsweek, Business Week, U.S. News & World Report, The Nation, Playboy, Esquire, Harper's, Sports Illustrated.*"

His tastes in reading were broad, and at one time or another he had read almost all of these magazines. He was a subscriber to The New Republic, an enthusiast for Ramparts, and an avid student of the pictures in Playboy. He was not sure whether his interest in Playboy would be held against him, but he had a shrewd suspicion that if he confessed to an interest in Ramparts and The New Republic, he would be thought a liberal, a radical, or at least an intellectual, and his chances of getting the job, which he needed, would greatly diminish. He therefore checked five of the more conservative magazines. Apparently it was a sound decision, for he got the job.

He had made a game player's decision, consistent with business ethics.

A similar case is that of a magazine space salesman who, owing to a merger, suddenly found himself out of a job:

This man was 58, and, in spite of a good record, his chance of getting a job elsewhere in a business where youth is favored in hiring practice was not good. He was a vigorous, healthy man, and only a considerable amount of gray in his hair suggested his age. Before beginning his job search he touched up his hair with a black dye to confine the gray to his temples. He knew that the truth about his age might well come out in time, but he calculated that he could deal with that situation when it arose. He and his wife decided that he could easily pass for 45, and he so stated his age on his résumé.

This was a lie: yet within the accepted rules of the business game, no moral culpability attaches to it.

THE POKER ANALOGY

We can learn a good deal about the nature of business by comparing it with poker. While both have a large element of chance, in the long run the winner is the man who plays with steady skill. In both games ultimate victory requires intimate knowledge of the rules, insight into the psychology of the other players, a bold front, a considerable amount of self-discipline, and the ability to respond swiftly and effectively to opportunities provided by chance.

No one expects poker to be played on the ethical principles preached in churches. In poker it is right and proper to bluff a friend out of the rewards of being dealt a good hand. A player feels no more than a slight twinge of sympathy, if that, when — with nothing better than a single ace in his hand — he strips a heavy loser, who holds a pair, of the rest of his chips. It was up to the other fellow to protect himself. In the words of an excellent poker player, former President Harry Truman, "If you can't stand the heat, stay out of the kitchen." If one shows mercy to a loser in poker, it is a personal gesture, divorced from the rules of the game.

Poker has its special ethics, and here I am not referring to rules against cheating. The man who keeps an ace up his sleeve or who marks the cards is more than unethical; he is a crook, and can be punished as such — kicked out of the game or, in the Old West, shot.

In contrast to the cheat, the unethical poker player is one who, while abiding by the letter of the rules, finds ways to put the other players at an unfair disadvantage. Perhaps he unnerves them with loud talk. Or he tries to get them drunk. Or he plays in cahoots with someone else at the table. Ethical poker players frown on such tactics.

Poker's own brand of ethics is different from the ethical ideals of civilized human relationships. The game calls for distrust of the other fellow. It ignores the claim of friendship. Cunning deception and concealment of one's strength and intentions, not kindness and openheartedness, are vital in poker. No one thinks any the worse of poker on that account. And no one should think any the worse of the game of business because its standards of right and wrong differ from the prevailing traditions of morality in our society. . . .

'WE DON'T MAKE THE LAWS'

Wherever we turn in business, we can perceive the sharp distinction between its ethical standards and those of the churches. Newspapers abound with sensational stories growing out of this distinction:

We read one day that Senator Philip A. Hart of Michigan has attacked food processors for deceptive packaging of numerous products.[2]

The next day there is a Congressional to-do over Ralph Nader's book, *Unsafe At Any Speed,* which demonstrates that automobile companies for years have neglected the safety of car-owning families.[3]

Then another Senator, Lee Metcalf of Montana, and journalist Vic Reinemer show in their book, *Overcharge,* the methods by which utility companies elude regulating government bodies to extract unduly large payments from users of electricity.[4]

These are merely dramatic instances of a prevailing condition; there is hardly a major industry at which a similar attack could not be aimed. Critics of business regard such behavior as unethical, but the companies concerned know that they are merely playing the business game.

Among the most respected of our business institutions are the insurance companies. A group of insurance executives meeting recently in New England was startled when their guest speaker, social critic Daniel Patrick Moynihan, roundly berated them for "unethical" practices. They had been guilty, Moynihan alleged, of using outdated actuarial tables to obtain unfairly high premiums. They habitually delayed the hearings of lawsuits against them in order to tire out the plaintiffs and win cheap settlements. In their employment policies they use ingenious devices to discriminate against certain minority groups.[5]

It was difficult for the audience to deny the validity of these charges. But these men were business game players. Their reaction to Moynihan's attack was much the same as that of the automobile manufacturers to Nader, of the utilities to Senator Metcalf, and of the food processors to Senator Hart. If the laws governing their businesses change, or if public opinion becomes clamorous, they will make the necessary adjustments. But morally they have in their view done nothing wrong. As long as they comply with the letter of the law, they are within their rights to operate their businesses as they see fit.

The small business is in the same position as the great corporation in this respect. For example:

In 1967 a key manufacturer was accused of providing master keys for automobiles to mail-order customers, although it was obvious that some of the purchasers might be automobile thieves. His defense was plain and straightforward. If there was nothing in the law to prevent him from selling his keys to anyone who ordered them, it was not up to him to inquire as to his customers' motives. Why was it any worse, he insisted, for him to sell car keys by mail, than for mail-order houses to sell guns that might be used for murder? Until the law was changed, the key manufacturer could regard himself as being just as ethical as any other businessman by the rules of the business game.[6]

Violations of the ethical ideals of society are common in business, but they are not necessarily violations of business principles. Each year the Federal Trade Commission orders hundreds of companies, many of them of the first magnitude, to "cease and desist" from practices which, judged by ordinary standards, are of questionable morality but which are stoutly defended by the companies concerned.

In one case, a firm manufacturing a well-known mouthwash was accused of using a cheap form of alcohol possibly deleterious to health. The company's chief executive, after testifying in Washington, made this comment privately:

"We broke no law. We're in a highly competitive industry. If we're going to stay in business, we have to look for profit wherever the law permits. We don't make the laws. We obey them. Then why do we have to put up with this 'holier than thou' talk about ethics? It's sheer hypocrisy. We're not in business to promote ethics. Look at the cigarette companies, for God's sake! If the ethics aren't embodied in the laws by the men who made them, you can't expect businessmen to fill the lack. Why, a sudden submission to Christian ethics by businessmen would bring about the greatest economic upheaval in history!" It may be noted that the government failed to prove its case against him.

CAST ILLUSIONS ASIDE

Talk about ethics by businessmen is often a thin decorative coating over the hard realities of the game. . . .

The illusion that business can afford to be guided by ethics as conceived in private life is often fostered by speeches and articles containing such phrases as, "It pays to be ethical," or, "Sound ethics is good business." Actually, this is not an ethical position at all; it is a self-serving calculation in disguise. The speaker is really saying that in the long run a company can make more money if it does not antagonize competitors, suppliers, employees, and customers by squeezing them too hard. He is saying that oversharp policies reduce ultimate gains. That is true, but it has nothing to do with ethics. The underlying attitude is much like that in the familiar story of the shopkeeper who finds an extra $20 bill in the cash register, debates with himself the ethical problem — should he tell his partner? — and finally decides to share the money because the gesture will give him an edge over the s.o.b. the next time they quarrel.

I think it is fair to sum up the prevailing attitude of businessmen on ethics as follows:

We live in what is probably the most competitive of the world's civilized societies. Our customs encourage a high degree of aggression in the individual's striving for success. Business is our main area of competition, and it has been ritualized into a game of strategy. The basic rules of the game have been set by the government, which attempts to detect and punish business frauds. But as long as a company does not transgress the rules of the game set by law, it has the legal right to shape its strategy without reference to anything but its profits. If it takes a long-term view of its profits, it will preserve amicable relations, so far as possible, with those with whom it deals. A wise businessman will not seek advantage to the point where he generates dangerous hostility among employees, competitors, customers, government, or the public at large. But decisions in this area are, in the final test, decisions of strategy, not of ethics.

. . . If a man plans to make a seat in the business game, he owes it to himself to master the principles by which the game is played, including its special ethical outlook. He can then hardly fail to recognize that an occasional bluff may well be justified in terms of the game's ethics and warranted in terms of economic necessity. Once he clears his mind on this point, he is in a good position to match his strategy against that of the other players. He can then determine objectively whether a bluff in a given situation has a good chance of succeeding and can decide when and how to bluff, without a feeling of ethical transgression.

To be a winner, a man must play to win. This does not mean that he must be ruthless, cruel, harsh, or treacherous. On the contrary, the better his reputation for integrity, honesty, and decency, the better his chances of victory will be in the long run. But from time to time every businessman, like every poker player, is offered a choice between certain loss or bluffing within the legal rules of the game. If he is not resigned to losing, if he wants to rise in his company and industry, then in such a crisis he will bluff — and bluff hard. . . .

In the last third of the twentieth century even children are aware that if a man has become prosperous in business, he has sometimes departed from the strict truth in order to overcome obstacles or has practiced the more subtle deceptions of the half-truth or the misleading omission. Whatever the form of the bluff, it is an integral part of the game, and the executive who does not master its techniques is not likely to accumulate much money or power.

NOTES

1. *The New York Times,* March 9, 1967.
2. *The New York Times,* November 21, 1966.
3. New York, Grossman Publishers, Inc., 1965.
4. New York, David McKay Company, Inc., 1967.
5. *The New York Times,* January 17, 1967.
6. Cited by Ralph Nader in "Business Crime," *The New Republic,* July 1, 1967, p. 7.

Second Thoughts About Bluffing

Thomas Carson

INTRODUCTION

In the United States it is common, perhaps even a matter of course, for people to misstate their bargaining positions during business negotiations. I have in mind the following kinds of cases, all of which involve deliberate false statements about one's bargaining position, intentions, or preferences in a negotiation: 1. I am selling a house and tell a prospective buyer that $90,000 is absolutely the lowest price that I will accept, when I know that I would be willing to accept as little as $80,000 for the house. 2. A union negotiator says that $13.00 an hour is the very lowest wage that his union is willing to consider when, in fact, he has been authorized by the union to accept a wage as low as $12.00 an hour. 3) I tell a prospective buyer that I am in no hurry to sell my house when, in fact, I am desperate to sell it within a few days.[1] Such statements would seem to constitute lies — they are deliberate false statements made with the intent to deceive others about the nature of one's own bargaining position. 1) and 2) clearly constitute lies according to standard dictionary definitions of lying. The *Oxford English Dictionary* defines the word "lie" as follows: "a false statement made with the intent to deceive." Also see *Webster's International Dictionary of the English Language* (1929), "to utter a falsehood with the intent to deceive."

The cases described above should be contrasted with instances of bluffing which do not involve making false statements. An example of the latter case would be saying "I want more" in response to an offer which I am willing to accept rather than not reach an agreement at all. This paper will focus on cases of bluffing which involve deliberate false statements about one's bargaining position or one's "settlement preferences."

I will defend the following two theses:

a. Appearances to the contrary, this kind of bluffing typically does not constitute lying. (I will argue that standard dictionary definitions of lying are untenable and defend an alternative definition hinted at, but never clearly formulated, by W. D. Ross. On my definition, deliberate false statements about one's negotiating position usually do not constitute lies *in this society*.)

b. It is usually permissible to misstate one's bargaining position or settlement preferences when one has good reason to think that one's negotiating partner is doing the same and it is usually impermissible to misstate one's negotiating position if one does not have good reason to think that the other party is misstating her position (preferences).

There are significant puzzles and uncertainties involved in applying my definition of lying to cases of misstating one's bargaining position. Because of this, I intend to make my argument for b) independent of my argument for a). My arguments for b) are compatible with (but do not presuppose) the view that misstating one's position is lying and that lying is *prima facie* wrong. I will conclude the paper with a brief examination of other related deceptive stratagems in negotiations.

THE ECONOMIC SIGNIFICANCE OF BLUFFING

In a business negotiation there is typically a range of possible agreements that each party would be willing to accept rather than reach no agreement at all. For instance, I might be willing to sell my home for as little as $80,000. (I would prefer to sell the house for $80,000 *today*, rather than continue to try to sell the house.) My range of acceptable agreements extends upward without limit — I would be willing to accept any price in excess of $80,000 rather than fail to make the sale today. Suppose that a prospective buyer is willing to spend as much as $85,000 for the house. (She prefers to buy the house for $85,000 today rather than not buy it at all today.) The buyer's range of acceptable agreements presumably extends downward without limit — she would be willing to purchase the house for any price below $85,000. In this case the two bargaining positions overlap and an agreement is possible (today). Unless there is some overlap between the minimum bargaining positions of the two parties, no agreement is possible. For example, if the seller's lowest acceptable price is $80,000 and the buyer's highest acceptable price is $70,000 no sale will be possible unless at least one of the parties alters her position.

If there is an overlap between the bargaining positions of the negotiators, then the actual outcome will depend on the negotiations. Consider again our example of the negotiation over the sale of the house. The owner is willing to sell the house for as little as $80,000 and the prospective buyer is willing to pay as much as $85,000. Whether the house sells for $80,000, $85,000, somewhere between $80,000 and $85,000, or even whether it sells at will be determined by the negotiations. In this case, it would be very advantageous for either party to know the other person's minimum acceptable position and disadvantageous for either to reveal her position to the other. For example, if the buyer knows that the lowest price that the seller is willing to accept is $80,000, she can drive him towards the limit of his range of acceptable offers. She knows that he will accept an offer of $80,000 rather than have her break off the negotiations. In negotiations both buyer and seller will ordinarily have reason to keep their own bargaining positions and intentions secret.

It can sometimes be to one's advantage to mislead others about one's own minimum bargaining position. In the present case, it would be to the seller's advantage to cause the buyer to think that $85,000 is the lowest price that he (the seller) will accept. For in this case the buyer would offer $85,000 for the house — the best possible agreement from the seller's point of view. (It would also be easy to imagine cases in which it would be to the buyer's advantage to mislead the seller about her bargaining position.) There are various ways in which the seller might attempt to bluff the buyer in order to mislead her about his position. 1. He might set a very high "asking price," for example, $100,000. 2. He might initially refuse an offer and threaten to cut off the negotiations unless a higher offer is made while at the same time being prepared to accept the offer before the other person breaks off the negotiations. (I have in mind some-

thing like the following. The prospective buyer offers $80,000 and the seller replies: "I want more than that; I'm not happy with $80,000 why don't you think about it and give me a call tomorrow.") 3. He might misrepresent his own bargaining position.

The kind of deception involved in 1) and 2) does not (or need not) involve lying or making false statements. 3) involves a deliberate false statement intended to deceive the other party and thus constitutes lying according to the standard definition of lying.

Attempting to mislead the other person about one's bargaining position can backfire and prevent a negotiation from reaching a mutually acceptable settlement which both parties would have preferred to no agreement at all. For example, suppose that the seller tells the buyer that he won't accept anything less than $95,000 for the house. If the buyer believes him she will break off the negotiations, since, by hypothesis, she is not willing to pay $95,000 for the house. Unless he knows the other person's bargaining position, a person who misrepresents his own position risks losing the opportunity to reach an acceptable agreement. By misstating one's position one also risks angering the other party and thereby causing him to modify his position or even break off the negotiations. (Truthful statements about one's own position might be perceived as lies and thus also risk alienating one's counterpart.)

THE CONCEPT OF LYING

* * *

A New Definition of Lying

. . . My definition of lying is inspired by Ross's claim that the duty not to lie is a special case of the duty to keep promises. Ross holds that (at least in ordinary contexts) we make an implicit promise to be truthful when we use language to communicate with others. To lie is to break an implicit promise to be truthful.[2]

Ross's view that making a statement (ordinarily) involves making an implicit promise that what one says is true suggests the following provisional definition of "lying" (Ross himself never attempts to define "lying"):

> A lie is a false statement which the "speaker" does not believe to be true made in a context in which the speaker warrants the truth of what he says.

This definition handles the earlier counterexample. Not only is the implicit warranty of truthfulness in force in the case of the witness's testimony in court, the witness explicitly warrants the truth of what he says by swearing an oath. Another virtue of the present analysis is that it makes sense of the common view that lying involves a violation of trust. To lie, on my view, is to invite trust and encourage others to believe what one says by warranting the truth of what one says and at the same time to betray that trust by making false statements which one does not believe to be true. . . .

Lying and Bluffing

What are the implications of my analysis of lying for the issue of bluffing? Negotiations between experienced and "hardened" negotiators in our society (e.g, horse traders and realtors) are akin to a game of "Risk." It is understood that any statements one makes about one's role or intentions as a player during a game of "Risk" are not warranted to be true. In negotiations between hardened and cynical negotiators statements about one's intentions or settlement preferences are not warranted to be true. But it would be too strong to hold that nothing that one says in

negotiations is warranted to be true. Convention dictates that other kinds of statements concerning the transaction being contemplated, e.g., statements to the effect that one has another offer, are warranted as true. So, for example, on my view, it would be a lie if I (the seller) were to falsely claim that someone else has offered me $85,000 for my house.

I am strongly inclined to believe that statements about one's minimum negotiating position are not warranted to be true in negotiations between "hardened negotiators" who recognize each other as such. I cannot here propose general criteria for determining when one may be said to warrant the truth of what one says. Therefore, what follows is somewhat conjectural. A cynical negotiator typically does not expect (predict) that her counterpart will speak truthfully about his minimum negotiating position. This alone is not enough to remove the implicit warranty of truth. A pathological liar who denies his every misdeed warrants the truth of what he says, even if those he addresses do not *expect* (predict) that what he says is true. The crucial feature of a negotiation which distinguishes it from the foregoing case is that in ordinary negotiations each party *consents* to renouncing the ordinary warranty of truth. There are various ways in which people consent to removing the default warranty of truth. Business negotiations are ritualized activities to which certain unstated rules and expectations (both in the sense of predictions and demands) apply. It is not expected that one will speak truthfully about one's negotiating position. Those who understand this and who enter into negotiations with other parties who are known to share this understanding implicitly consent to the rules and expectations of the negotiating ritual. In so doing, they consent to remove the warranty of truth for statements about one's minimum negotiating position. . . .

Before moving on to other issues, I would again like to stress the following two points: 1) my application of my definition of lying to this case is tentative and conjectural, and 2) my arguments concerning the moral status of bluffing do not depend on the assumption that misstating one's bargaining position or intentions is (typically) not a case of lying (my arguments are compatible with the view that misstating one's position or intentions is lying).

THE MORAL STATUS OF BLUFFING (PRELIMINARY CONSIDERATIONS)

* * *

Carr's Defense of Bluffing

In a well-known paper Albert Carr argues that misstating one's negotiating position is morally permissible.[3] Business, he argues, is a game like poker — a game in which special norms apply. The moral norms appropriate to the game of business or a game of poker are different from those appropriate to ordinary contexts.

> No one expects poker to be played on the ethical principles preached in churches. In poker it is right and proper to bluff a friend out of the rewards of being dealt a good hand. . . . Poker's own brand of ethics is different from the ethical ideals of civilized human relationships. The game calls for distrust of the other fellow. It ignores the claim of friendship. Cunning, deception, and concealment of one's strength and intentions, not kindness and openheartedness, are vital in poker. No one thinks any the worse of poker on that account. And no one should think any the worse of business because its standards of right and wrong differ from the prevailing traditions of morality in our society. . . . [4]

Carr claims that just as bluffing is permissible according to the special rules of poker, so it is permissible according to the rules of business.

What are the rules of the business game? How can we determine whether or not a particular rule or practice is part of the business game? Carr's position is confused on this point. At a number of points he suggests that the "rules of the business game" are simply our society's conventional moral standards for business, i.e., those standards which are thought by most people to govern the conduct of businesspeople. Carr defends a number of questionable business practices and argues that they are all morally justifiable, *because* they are standard practice and are regarded as permissible by conventional morality.

> In his view these things had nothing to do with ethics; they were merely normal business practice.[5]
> This was a lie; yet within the accepted rules of the business game, no moral culpability attaches to it.[6]

In other passages Carr seems to assume that the appropriate rules for business are those set by the law.

> If the laws governing their business change, or if public opinion becomes clamorous, they will make the necessary adjustments. But morally they have in their view done nothing wrong. As long as they comply with the letter of the law, they are within their rights to operate their businesses as they see fit.[7]

There are three possible ways to interpret the principle to which Carr appeals in trying to justify bluffing and other questionable business practices.

a. Any action or practice engaged in by businesspeople in a given society is morally permissible provided that it is consistent with the ethical rules or principles which are generally accepted in that society.

b. Any action or practice engaged in by business-people in a given society is morally permissible provided that it is consistent with the laws of that society.

c. Any action or practice engaged in by business-people in a given society is morally permissible provided that it is consistent with *both* i) the society's conventional ethical rules or principles governing those actions and practices, *and* ii) the laws of that society.

On any of these readings, Carr's argument is most implausible. One can't justify an act or practice *simply because* it is consistent with conventional morality. Similarly, the fact that an action or practice is permitted by the law does not suffice to establish its moral permissibility. Conventional morality and the law are not infallible moral guidelines. In the past, many immoral practices, most notably slavery, were condoned by the conventional morality and legal codes of our own and many other societies. . . .

VARIATIONS ON THE EXAMPLE

1) Is *lying worse than mere deception?* Consider the following case. Suppose that I want the other party to hold false beliefs about my minimum bargaining position. I want him to think that $90,000 is the lowest price that I'm willing to accept for my house when, in fact, I'm willing to sell it for as little as $80,000. However, I am very much averse to lying about this and I believe that misstating my own position would be a lie. I am willing to try to deceive or mislead him about my intentions, but I am not willing to lie about them. Here, as in many cases, it is possible to think of true but equally misleading things to say so as to avoid lying. Suppose that our lowest acceptable selling price is $80,000, but I want you to think that it is actually around $85,000. Instead of lying, I could say "my wife told me to tell you that $85,000 is absolutely

the lowest price that we are willing to accept." The trick here would be to have my wife utter the words "tell the buyer that $85,000 is absolutely the lowest price that we will accept." In saying this she would not be stating our minimum position, but rather helping to create the ruse to fool the buyer. It is very doubtful that this is morally preferable to lying. Intuitively, it strikes me as worse. Many people (perhaps most) seem to believe that making true but deceptive statements is preferable to lying. This is demonstrated by the fact that many (most?) of us will, on occasion, go through verbal contortions or give very careful thought to exactly what we say in order to mislead others without lying. In this kind of case lying does not seem to be morally preferable to "mere deception."

Consider another example in which the difference between lying and mere deception does not seem to be morally significant. Suppose that two parents go out of town for the weekend leaving their two adolescent children home alone. The parents give their son strict orders that under no circumstances is he permitted to entertain his girlfriend in the house while they are away. The parents call during the weekend to "check up" on the children. They speak with their daughter. "What's going on there? What is your brother up to? He doesn't have Nora [his girlfriend] there does he?" The son is entertaining Nora in the house at the time that they call. The daughter does not want to get her brother in trouble, but, on the other hand, she doesn't want to lie. She does not answer the last question directly, but replies with the following true, but misleading, statement. "He's fine; he's watching the ball game with Bob." (Bob is a male friend who *is* there but is about to leave.)

2) *Claiming to have another offer.* On my view, the fact that misstating one's position is a very common practice can often help justify misstating one's own position. Because misstat-

ing one's bargaining position is such a wide-spread practice in our society, one is often justified in assuming that one's negotiating partner is misrepresenting her position. If the other person states a minimum bargaining position, then one is justified in thinking that she is misrepresenting that position, in the absence of reasons for thinking that she is not.

There are other ways of deceiving others about one's bargaining position which are not common practice. The following two cases are among the kinds that I have in mind here:

Case #1. I (the seller) say to a prospective buyer "I have another offer for $80,000, but I'll let you have it if you can beat the offer" when, in fact, I don't have another offer.

Case #2. I (the seller) want you to think that I have another offer. I have my brother come over and in your presence pretend to offer me $80,000 for the condo. (You don't know that he is my brother.) I say to may brother "the other person was here first. I'll have to let him/her see if he/she wants to meet the offer." I turn to the seller and say "It's yours for $80,000."

What I say in the first case is clearly a lie. It is a deliberate false statement which is warranted to be true and is intended to deceive others. My action in this case is *prima facie* very wrong. I am putting extreme pressure on the other person and may panic her into a rash decision. Falsely claiming to have another offer could, in principle, be justified by appeal to SD [the principle of self-defense].

If the buyer was falsely representing the possibility of another comparable deal, then a Rossian theory might conceivably justify me in doing the same. This is very unlikely in the ordinary course of things. This means that it is unlikely that one could defend lying in such a case by appeal to the need to defend one's own interests. My actions in case #2 seem intuitively even worse than those in #1. Case #2 does not involve lying but it does involve an elaborate scheme of deception and is potentially very harmful to the buyer. The same general things that I said about case #1 apply here. My actions in this case are *prima facie* very wrong. In principle, a Rossian theory could justify those actions, but that is very unlikely. . . .

NOTES

1. This example is taken from "Shrewd Bargaining on the Moral Frontier: Towards a Theory of Morality in Practice," J. Gregory Dees and Peter C. Crampton, *Business Ethics Quarterly,* Vol. 1, No. 2, April 1991, p. 143.

2. W. D. Ross, *The Right and the Good,* (Oxford, 1930), p. 21.

3. Albert Carr, "Is Business Bluffing Ethical?" in *Ethical Issues in Business,* third edition, Thomas Donaldson and Patricia Werhane, eds., (Prentice Hall, 1988).

4. Carr, pp. 72–73; see also pp. 69 and 70.

5. Carr, p. 70.

6. Carr, p. 72.

7. Carr, p. 73; also see p. 75.

Paternalism in the Marketplace: Should a Salesman Be His Buyer's Keeper?

James M. Ebejer
and Michael J. Morden

The moral relationship between salespersons and their customers can range from *caveat emptor* to paternalism. We propose that between these extremes is a realistic professional ethic for sales that we will refer to as "limited paternalism."

At one extreme is *caveat emptor* — "let the buyer beware." We do not claim there is anything inherently immoral about such a position, only that it is no longer appropriate in our society. Games can be played by various rules, as long as all participants know those rules. When two old horse-traders tried to strike a bargain, it was understood that the seller could be assumed to misrepresent the condition of the animal and the buyer was warned to be on his guard. Perhaps this situation was not unfair since both participants knew the rules, entered into the agreement voluntarily, and had the opportunity to examine the merchandise. However, the contemporary consumer frequently purchases goods or services which he cannot be expected to judge for himself. The workings of an insurance policy are as mysterious to us as those of a VCR. A salesperson, with her superior understanding, is in such a position to exploit our ignorance, that few of us would want to play the game if the rule of the market-place were understood to be strictly "let the buyer beware."

At the other extreme is the practice of paternalism. A standard definition of paternalism is "the interference with a person's liberty of action justified by reasons referring exclusively to the welfare, good, happiness, needs, interests, or values of the person being coerced" (Dworkin, 1971). In other words, paternalism occurs when an individual, presumably in a position of superior knowledge, makes a decision for another person to protect this other from some type of harm. Paternalism implies that the first person deprives the second of liberty of autonomy. This infraction on liberty is thought justified because, in the mind of the first person, it is "for his own good." Recently, a merchant refused to sell tropical fish to a patron because she felt he was not changing the water in his tank often enough. Although the merchant was infringing on the customer's liberty based on her superior knowledge, the interference was for his own good (and presumably the good of the fish). The merchant was being paternalistic.

Most of us expect paternalism in certain situations. If the service we are purchasing is an appendectomy, we typically allow the salesman (in this case the surgeon) a major role in deciding whether we need the service. We rely on the ethics of the profession to protect us from the possible exploitation. The old-fashioned physician considered such paternalism part of his role, but modern medicine emphasizes the patient's informed consent. The professionals use their superior knowledge to make the medical diagnosis, but they are expected to explain treatment options

Journal of Business Ethics 7 (1988) 337–339. © 1988 by Kluwer Academic Publishers. Reprinted by permission of Kluwer Academic Publishers.

available to the patient so the latter can make the moral decision. Thus even in the most paternalistic of contexts we find that professionalism justifies only a limited paternalism.

This limited paternalism, which is typically an element in professionalism, applies when an individual in a position of superior knowledge has an active duty to explain the consequences of a decision. Here the "father-like" individual does not make the decision for the other. The only liberty that is violated is the freedom to be ignorant: the consumer is protected from an uninformed decision that could be detrimental to him.

To claim that a salesperson is professionally required to inform customers fully about a product or service, to disclose fully all relevant information without hiding crucial stipulations in small print, to ascertain that they are aware of their needs and the degree to which the product or service will satisfy them, is to impose upon the salesperson the positive duty of limited paternalism. According to this standard a salesperson is, to a limited degree, "his buyer's keeper."

Consider the following example: A woman takes her car to an auto repair shop and tells the mechanic she needs a new muffler and exhaust pipes because her car makes too much noise. While examining the car, the mechanic concludes that the excessive noise occurs because there is a hole in the tail pipe. The mechanic was told to replace the exhaust pipes and the muffler. He has three options: (1) replace the exhaust pipes and the muffler as requested by the car's owner and collect (say) $90.00; (2) talk to the owner, refuse to do as requested since all that is needed is a $20.00 tail pipe; (3) talk to the owner, explain the situation, and let her decide for herself if she really wants to spend $70.00 more than is necessary to fix the car.

When confronted with this situation, many repairmen or auto parts salespersons would choose the first option: collect as much money as possible. This is perfectly legal since the car's owner did authorize complete replacement. Some perhaps would act paternalistically by following the second option: replace the tail pipe for $20.00, but refuse to replace the longer exhaust pipe and the muffler because it is not necessary. But now he has infringed on the owner's right to decide for herself. Perhaps the owner wanted to be absolutely certain that her exhaust system was perfect and would not need work again soon. Maybe she is rich and does not mind spending the extra money. In any case, it is her car, her money, and her decision. Option number three is the best ethical choice and the standard required for professional responsibility: the mechanic has a duty to inform the owner of facts of which she might not be aware since she is not the expert. The choice should be left to the owner.

But consider a different situation: a customer in a store that specializes in stereo equipment is consulting a salesperson about the specifications, quality and prices of various amplifiers. The salesperson is considered an expert on all equipment available for sale in the show room. After some deliberation, the customer tentatively decides he would like to own a Super Max amplifier. But before making the purchase, he asks the salesperson one more question: "Is there anything else I should know about this particular model before giving you the cash?" Now, to the best of her knowledge, the salesperson has accurately communicated the advantages of the amplifier, told him the price — $400, and that this particular unit does meet his needs. However, she also knows that the same model is being sold at an appliance store across the street for only $350! Does our standard require that she tell the buyer about this possible savings? Clearly not. Although the salesperson was aware of the competitor's price, she did not withhold information that only an expert would know. Anyone could easily find out how much the amplifier sold for at the other stores. The knowledge was not part of the technical expertise that marks her as a professional and which the buyer was presumably relying upon. However, if she held back information, relevant to the decision, which a non-expert could not be expected to know, then her behavior would be unethical by our standard.

Nearly all "hard sell" techniques are unethical according to this standard. Many salespersons intentionally keep information from potential buyers. They try to sell the most expensive product a customer will buy without regard to the needs of that person. Granted, some revenue may be lost in the short term from telling customers the bad as well as the good about a product or service, but profits will increase in the long run. Once a salesperson earns a reputation for being "honest" — i.e., ethical, interested in mutual exchange to mutual advantage rather than

exploitation — he will have more satisfied customers, more referrals, and, eventually, greater income from an overall increase in sales. Even where the policy might not profit the salesperson in a specific case, it is a rule which if generally followed would produce the greatest good for the greatest number. Furthermore, it treats the customer the way we ourselves would want to be treated; it is a rule we would agree to even if we didn't know whether we were going to be the salesperson or the customer; finally, it bases sales ethics on widely accepted standards of professionalism. Clearly it is consistent with our ordinary ethical assumptions.

NOTE

Gerald Dworkin: 1971, "Paternalism", in *Morality and Law*, ed. Richard Wasserstrom (Belmont, CA), p. 108.

Limited Paternalism and the Pontius Pilate Plight

Kerry S. Walters

I

Is there a morally acceptable passage between the Charybdis of *caveat emptor* and the Scylla of full-blown paternalism in the salesperson/buyer relationship? If a salesperson intentionally conceals or misrepresents pertinent information about his product or service because he's adopted a cutthroat attitude of "let the buyer beware," he risks ethi-

cal wreckage by deceptively manipulating his client for the sake of profit. But if he refuses to sell a good or service to a particular customer, even though she wants it, because he thinks it will be harmful or at least not useful to her, he hazards foundering on the rocks of paternalistic violation of her autonomy. How, then, can we oblige the marketplace Ulysses to steer a passage which neither exploits his customers, interferes with their freedom of

Journal of Business Ethics 8: 955–962, 1989. © 1989 Kluwer Academic Publishers. Printed in the Netherlands.

choice, nor puts himself out of business? Is there, in short, a prescriptive criterion upon which to ground a professional sales ethic?

In a recent thoughtful article entitled "Paternalism in the Marketplace: Should a Salesman Be His Buyer's Keeper?"[1] Ebejer and Morden suggest a navigational principle they call "limited paternalism." They argue that a sufficient criterion for protecting the autonomy and rights of the customer as well as the interests of the salesperson is for the latter to provide all pertinent information about his product or service and then let the customer make her own decision about whether or not to buy on the basis of that information. This imposes a limited obligation upon the salesperson that neither violates his marketplace interest nor illegitimately interferes with the customer's autonomy . . .

The notion of limited paternalism in the marketplace is attractive. Its most obvious allure is its simplicity. It appeals to common sense because it seems to provide a realizable standard for protecting the customer that does not demand undue sacrifice on the part of the salesperson. But its immediate simplicity, I fear, is also somewhat deceptive. Although sufficiently regulative, perhaps, for very uncomplicated market transactions, it is inadequate for most others. When one fails to recognize the limits of its application and appeals to it as a sufficient condition for *all* ethically acceptable marketplace interactions (as Ebejer and Morden seem to do), one runs the risk of entangling oneself in an ethical quandary I somewhat tongue-twistingly call the "Pontius Pilate Plight." This quandary in its most general form involves the queer claim that an agent's hands are clean if he conforms to the formal prescriptions of a role-specific obligation, even when the agent does something which, although allowed by the obligation, runs counter to his personal moral convictions. In the specific context of limited paternalism, the Pontius Pilate Plight

appears when a salesperson who has personal ethical reservations about selling a particular product or service assumes that his moral duty is discharged and his hands clean if he informs the customer of the reasons for those ethical reservations. If the customer nonetheless buys, no violation of the limited paternalism principle has occurred. And since limited paternalism is a sufficient regulative criterion for proper marketplace relations, conformity to it is all that matters. This line of reasoning, of course, allows a salesperson to perform with impunity an act he otherwise would be forced as a private individual to condemn as unethical or at least morally dubious — which suggests that the immediately attractive simplicity of the limited paternalism principle may in fact be a weakness rather than a strength.

In what follows, I more fully spell out the queer implications of limited paternalism. In doing so, I do not claim that either *caveat emptor* or fullblown paternalism is the better option, but only that the standard of limited paternalism, as it stands, is not a sufficient foundation for a professional sales ethic.

II

Consider the following situation, adapted from Ebejer and Morden: An auto owner takes her car to the repair shop because it's been making too much noise and instructs the mechanic to replace the muffler and exhaust pipes. After examining the car, the mechanic discovers its excessive noise is due to a hole in the tailpipe, and not a faulty muffler system. He then has three options. (1) He can, following his customer's instructions, replace the muffler and exhaust pipes at a relatively high cost to her. (2) He can refuse to do as the customer instructed, since all she really needs is a relatively inexpensive tailpipe. (3) He can talk to the customer, explain that the actually needed repair is less expensive than the one she requested (that is, "disclose fully all relevant information"), and let her make the decision herself of whether to go with the expensive muffler system or the cheaper tailpipe. If the mechanic chooses the first option, he exploits his customer's ignorance for the sake of profit (*caveat emptor*). But if he goes with the second, he violates the owner's right to decide for herself what she wants (paternalism). Ebejer and Morden conclude that the third option (limited paternalism):

> is the best ethical choice and the standard required for professional responsibility: the mechanic has a duty to inform the owner of facts of which she might not be aware since she is not the expert. The choice should be left to the owner.

Within the context of this particular case, I agree that limited paternalism is the fairest and most reasonable of the three options. But there is a transparency to the example which, I would suggest, is somewhat contrived. Real-life situations are often (and perhaps usually) more complex, less cut and dry. Can the principle of limited paternalism satisfactorily resolve them?

For example: Jane owns a convenience store, and one of the products she sells (and sells a lot of) is tobacco. Although selling cigarettes (to non-minors) is perfectly legal, Jane personally has serious ethical reservations about doing so. She has read and reflected upon the latest Surgeon-General's report on tobacco consumption and is intellectually convinced that cigarette smoking is a costly and dangerous habit, not only to the active smoker but, in certain instances, to so-called passive smokers as well. Moreover, she considers self-destructive behavior to be an evil. She is realistic enough to realize that people *will* smoke, regardless of the

sound medical reasons for not doing so and in spite of the clear warnings on cigarette packs themselves. But she nevertheless feels she ought not encourage or contribute to the self-destructive behavior of other people — that is, that she has a moral duty to refrain from helping people harm themselves, even when they do so knowingly. By selling cigarettes in her store, however, she is doing precisely what she as a private individual judges to be unethical. What ought Jane to do?

She has three options. (1) She can continue selling cigarettes, even though doing so violates her personal ethical standards, and uncomfortably try to excuse her actions by adopting a harsh *caveat emptor* attitude. (2) She can discontinue cigarette sales and hang a sign in the window announcing that her convenience store is henceforth smoke-free for the good of her patrons, thereby treating them in an obviously paternalistic manner. Such a recourse will diminish although not cripple her revenues, but it will also clear her conscience. (3) She can act in a limited paternalistic way by continuing to sell cigarettes if customers insist upon them, but only after she apprises all perspective tobacco buyers of the "relevant information." In this context, relevant information will be not only a litany of the medical risks of smoking. It will also include an explanation of why Jane considers tobacco consumption an evil, in addition to why she feels it is unethical to encourage individuals to harm themselves by selling them tobacco. To keep back *any* of this information is to fail to fully protect the consumer from an "uninformed decision that could be detrimental to him."

Now presumably Ebejer and Morden would argue that the third alternative adequately fulfills Jane's ethical responsibility in the salesperson/buyer relationship. She has informed her customers of the relevant information concerning the commodity they want, and then has allowed them to make their own decision. Her hands, consequently, are clean, regardless of whether or not the customers choose to buy. But such a conclusion, it seems to me, is queer, because it exonerates Jane of moral culpability even when she performs an act (the selling of a harmful commodity) she thinks is unethical. Given her personal ethical standards, the only responsible option Jane has is to declare her store smoke-free. But the principle of limited paternalism allows her to perform as a salesperson what she personally deems to be a normatively illegitimate act. By appealing to limited paternalism, in other words, she can ethically do what she regards as unethical. But this, I would contend, is decidedly odd.

Consider a different situation: Peter owns a custom auto supply shop which specializes in expensive and nonessential gadgetry for cars. A young man comes in and asks Peter to overhaul and "soup up" the engine of his automobile as well as ornament the chassis by adding a great deal of chrome and other cosmetic paraphernalia. Peter quotes the young man a price which is extremely high but, given the nature of Peter's services, fair. The young man fills out a credit application which stipulates that, if approved, he will pay Peter $200 per month for one year in exchange for the services and parts.

After reading the application and running a credit check, Peter decides that granting credit to the young man is a reasonable risk — particularly since he can always take possession of the car in case of default. But he also suspects that the young man will dangerously overextend his financial resources if he buys the nonessential services Peter can sell him. When the young man returns to the shop to check on his credit application, Peter asks him a few subtle but well-directed questions which confirm his suspicions. The young man is a car fanatic who sinks every available dime into his obsession. Peter soon realizes that although the young man is quite

likely to meet his credit payments, he will do so only by depriving himself of much more essential commodities. Moreover, Peter personally thinks such a move is foolish, and that he as a private individual ought not encourage persons to sacrifice essentials for luxuries. To do so, in Peter's opinion, would be unethical or at least morally dubious. What should he do?

Like Jane, Peter has three options. (1) He can say to himself: "To hell with it! This kid needs my services like a hole in the head, and if I approve his credit it's almost certainly going to burn him financially. But I'm not in the business of looking out for fools. It's his tail if he wants to go through with the deal. Besides, I sell quality merchandise for a fair price. I'm not cheating him." (*caveat emptor*) (2) Peter can say to himself: "This kid doesn't need any of this junk, but he's too green to know it. He's got a perfectly good car as it is, and if he buys from me he's going to suffer for it, even though I'll probably get my money out of the deal. Since he hasn't got enough sense to know what's good for him, I'll have to protect his interests myself. I'll reject his credit application. Besides, doing so won't harm me. I've got all the business I can handle." (paternalism) (3) Peter can say to the young man: "Listen kid, I want you to think about this. I can give you credit, but I've got to tell you I think you're making a big mistake. You don't really need all this stuff, and if you insist on it you're going to pinch your income in a major way. Besides, I don't feel right about encouraging you to throw your money away like this. It would be irresponsible on my part. Why don't you sleep on it and let me know your final decision in a day or two? Then, if you still want my services, I'll go along with you, even though it's against my better judgment." (limited paternalism)

Now Peter's dilemma is clearly somewhat different from Jane's. Jane has personal moral reservations about selling tobacco, even if her customers want it, because she thinks it a bad commodity. Peter has no personal qualms with what he's selling, but only with selling it to a particular customer — the young man — who wants it. Although Peter recognizes that his goods and services are nonessential (and perhaps even frivolous) luxuries, he sees no ethical malfeasance in providing them to customers who can afford them without undue suffering. But the young man, in Peter's estimation, is not such a customer. Consequently, to sell to him would violate Peter's personal moral standards.

Once again, however, Ebejer and Morden's limited paternalism principle would absolve Peter of moral culpability because, within the context of the marketplace, it claims to be a sufficient regulative principle. But this means that once again the principle leads to an odd state of affairs: by appealing to it, Peter can with impunity perform an act as a salesperson that he as a private individual considers to be unethical. He can, in short, acquiesce to what he considers to be an immoral course of action without being accused of a breach of duty. And this line of reasoning is queer.

III

. . . Is the Pontius Pilate Plight simply a fancy label for old-fashioned hypocrisy? Perhaps, but I suspect not. The nature of the dilemma is much more subtle. Hypocrisy necessarily involves mendacity — the deliberate intention on the part of the hypocrite to deceive others about his convictions or lifestyle. But Peter and Jane, in conforming their actions to the limited paternalism principle, are necessarily open with their customers about their personal moral qualms. If there is any dishonesty at work here, it is more akin to self-deception, insofar as Peter and Jane confus-

edly suppose themselves innocent of moral failing if they confess their ethical reservations about a commodity to the customer. If he still freely decides to buy, notwithstanding their disclosures, Peter and Jane feel themselves absolved of culpability. Obviously, however, this is a species of ethical buck-passing. If I think it evil to sell a product or service to a customer but do so anyway, even though I've apprised him of the reasons for my opinion, I can hardly claim clean hands by arguing that I at least was honest with him and let him freely choose for himself. Yet the principle of limited paternalism, as it stands, allows for just this response.

IV

I do not wish to claim that the limited paternalism principle is so problematic that it in no way can serve as a coordinate to guide a salesperson through the straits of *caveat emptor* and fullblown paternalism. I suspect it is one of the necessary conditions for any competent sales ethic. But I have argued, contra Ebejer and Morden, that it is inadequate as a sufficient condition — unless, of course, one is comfortable with quandaries such as the Pontius Pilate Plight. I, for one, am not.

How, then, can a salesperson steer a safe passage when dealing with customers? I would suggest the following regulative criteria, which are individually necessary and jointly (although minimally) sufficient.

Condition One. Following Ebejer and Morden, a salesperson is professionally obliged to disclose to customers all relevant information about the commodity or service under consideration which will enable the customer to make an informed decision about whether or not to buy. This duty is the role-specific one of limited paternalism. "Relevant information," as I have reformulated Ebejer and Morden's position, includes the salesperson's ethical reservations about a particular commodity or service under conditions dealt with below in Condition Three.

Condition Two. But the salesperson, like anyone else, has certain ethical obligations that extend beyond role-specific or professional ones. They are what might be called private or nonprofessional responsibilities. Clearly the set of role-specific duties will not be identical to the set of non-professional responsibilities, but the two should be compatible. Role-specific duties, in short, should never preempt the private individual's sense of personal responsibility, regardless of what standard or model his personal code is founded upon. A salesperson, then, is never justified in selling a commodity or service, even if doing so does not violate his professional responsibilities, if the commodity or service is one about which he has serious and reflective ethical qualms. Consequently, it is illegitimate to assume one's hands are clean if one informs the customer of one's personal ethical reservations about a commodity or service and then lets the customer "freely decide" whether or not to buy. The best that can be said about a salesperson who makes this move is that he has been honest with his customer. But mere honesty in this case is not enough, precisely because the salesperson has failed in his responsibilities as a private individual by willingly (albeit honestly) selling a product he personally feels is reprehensible. The salesperson who thus sacrifices his personal integrity can, I suppose, appeal to one of two "justifications." He can simply admit he doesn't give a damn about selling bad commodities. But this is *caveat emptor* at its cynical worst. Or he can try to assuage his conscience by assuring himself that the bad commodity wasn't sold duplicitously. But this, of course, lands him squarely in the Pontius Pilate Plight.

Condition Three. Normatively-laden judgments and actions *überhaupt* have their own Scylla and Charybidis upon which they may founder. On the one hand, they can be unbendingly rigid, insisting on a dogmatic and lock-step fidelity to ironbound rules and principles. On the other, they may succumb to the opposite temptation of falling into the night in which all cows are black quagmire of *laissez-faire* tolerance for any course of action. Given the complexity of interpersonal relations, neither strategy is optimally desirable. The one, in its inflexible conformity to rules, runs the risk of sacrificing personal and situational factors for abstract principles. The other, given its inflexible refusal to acknowledge any objective evaluative criteria, sacrifices normative consistency for the sake of unchallengeable subjective preference.

In order to avoid these two unhappy extremes in the context of a sales ethic, a salesperson's decision about whether or not to provide commodities or services she personally suspects are harmful should be scrupulously reflective. She must realize that there are certain issues over which reasonable people can reasonably disagree. By reasonable disagreement I obviously do not mean one generated by either an honest ignorance of the available facts or a bigoted and self-interested denial of them. Instead, I mean a disagreement in judgment which results when the pertinent data about a particular commodity or service are either ambiguous or incomplete, or when the evidence for making a positive or negative decision is too equally weighted to allow for a conclusive adjudication.

Consider, for example, the following case: Suzanne is a greengrocer, and apples are among the different fruits and vegetables she regularly sells. She is aware of the current controversy over the use of the preservative alar on different kinds of produce, especially apples. She has read and reflected on the reports which claim alar is a carcinogenic as well as those that deny the claim. She has carefully weighed the evidence for both conclusions (statistical correlations, longitudinal studies, possible self-interest on the parts of research reports from either side of the debate, and so on). After conscientiously appraising the arguments on both sides, she concludes that the jury is still out on whether or not alar-treated apples are harmful. Still, being the health conscious person she is, she decides it would be imprudent to ignore the possibility that alar is a powerful carcinogen. Consequently, she decides to quit eating apples she knows are alar-treated. Moreover, she also decides she will not serve alar-treated apples to house guests or her children in the future. Instead, she will substitute organically grown fruit, which she realizes is more costly. She is perfectly aware, however, that such a course of action represents a personal judgment call on her part and that, given the absence of persuasive evidence one way or the other about the toxic effects of alar, it is possible for reasonable people to reasonably disagree about the issue. What ought she to do at her produce store?

One option is for her to adopt an attitude of *caveat emptor* and simply continue selling alar-treated apples to her customers. But such a course of action is irresponsible, since she recognizes there's at least the possibility that alar is harmful. That's precisely why she's quit eating produce treated with it herself (or serving them to others at her home). Or she can discontinue stocking alar-treated apples, and commence selling only organically grown ones. This decision, of course, means that she must raise the price of her apples — for her customer's own good — thereby imposing an added financial burden upon them as well as, conceivably, upon herself (since her escalated prices may drive away a certain number of customers). But this course of action is too precipitantly paternalistic, since

Suzanne herself admits that the debate over alar is inconclusive. Consequently, it seems illegitimate for Suzanne either to totally disregard her personal reservations about alar or to dogmatically canonize them to the extent of adopting fullblown ethical paternalism.

In a case like this, I would argue that Suzanne's best course of action is to adopt the strategy of limited paternalism as I have reformulated it in this discussion. Moreover, I believe she can do so without falling into the Pontius Pilate Plight. She can, for instance, post notices which summarize the inconclusive differences of opinion over alar's toxicity; she can make an effort to tell her customers that they ought to carefully reflect upon the available data before they buy her inorganically grown apples, as well as the fact that she's personally decided to forego eating them for the time being; and she can offer her customers a choice between normally priced alar-treated apples and more expensive organic ones.

Such a course of action breeds no Pontius Pilate clash between her professional obligations and her personal ethical convictions precisely because she *is not convinced* that the selling of alar-treated produce is unethical. She reflectively and in good faith has come to the conclusion that the matter is still debatable. Given this absence of fully persuasive evidence one way or another, she sees she has neither a right not an obligation to impose her personal decision upon customers. She recognizes that a refusal on her part to sell alar-treated apples to customers who want them and who are cognizant of the alar controversy is to interfere unwarrantedly with their autonomy. She also realizes that such an action irrationally contradicts her own conclusion that, in the absence of further data, the alar debate is one which allows for rational difference of opinion and judgment calls. She, after an appraisal of the controversy, has decided to "play it safe." But she recognizes that other individuals, looking at the same body of evidence, can just as legitimately and reflectively decide to take a chance.

The point of Condition Three, then, is this. Role-specific and non-professional duties, following the second condition, should not be compartmentalized in such a way as to entangle a salesperson in the Pontius Pilate Plight. But neither should a salesperson dogmatically canonize what are merely personal judgment calls into uncontestable evaluations. This is simply to acknowledge that even though personal and professional ethical sensibilities should not be contradictory, they are not by that token identical. There is no con-

tradiction in selling commodities or services whose value a salesperson has decided is presently indeterminate, even if she personally opts not to use them herself, so long as she apprises customers of both sets of competing evidence.

NOTE

1. Ebejer, J. M. and M. J. Morden: 1988, 'Paternalism in the Market-place: Should a Salesman Be His Buyer's Keeper?', *Journal of Business Ethics* **7**, 337–339. [This volume, pp. 463–65.]

Manipulative Advertising

Tom L. Beauchamp

Lake Jewelers closed after being in business in Detroit for 36 years. Arthur Lake, president of the local Chamber of Commerce, was not as yet financially imperilled. But he said his business was gradually being ruined by his competitors' misleading advertisements. Lake cited, in particular, "phony discounting," in which retailers present fake percentage markdowns from "suggested retail prices" that are imaginary or artificially inflated. Advertisements depict prices as bargains (50 to 78 percent off), when in fact the prices are comparatively high. Lake said that customers are "duped into thinking" they receive bargains, and that "ethical" merchants find it extremely difficult to compete against such advertisements.[1]

In this paper, I assess a range of criticisms that, like this one, accuse advertisers of ma-

nipulating customers into purchases based on incorrect or inconclusive information. I am concerned exclusively with manipulations that limit free and informed action, especially in the food and alcoholic-beverage industries and in advertising by banks, savings and loans, and brokerage houses. I begin with the rudiments of a theory of influence and manipulation, and then return to advertising.

THE CONTINUUM OF INFLUENCES

To determine whether advertising diminishes free choice, we need to examine how external influences affect free choice. The antithesis of being free is being controlled by an alien influence that deprives one of self-direction. I use terms such as "freedom" and "free to act" to refer specifically to the absence of controlling external influences or constraints.

Coercion is a frequently analyzed form of controlling influence, but coercion does not exhaust the forms of controlling influence. It lies at one end of a continuum of influence. It is at the end that eliminates freedom and entirely compromises free choice. At the other end of the continuum are forms of influence such as (rational) persuasion. Other points on the continuum include indoctrination, seduction, and the like. At one end of the continuum are completely *controlling* influences; at the other end, wholly *noncontrolling* influences in no way undermine a person's free choice.

Three broad categories or classes of influence are spread across this continuum: coercion, manipulation, and persuasion. (1) Coercive influences are always controlling influences; (2) manipulative influences are sometimes controlling influences; and (3) persuasive influences are never controlling influences. Many choices are not substantially free, although we commonly think of them as free. These include actions under powerful family and religious influences, purchases made under partial ignorance of the quality of the merchandise, and deference to an authoritative physician's judgment. Many actions fall short of ideal free action because of a lack of understanding or control by another person. But the central question is whether actions are sufficiently or adequately free, not whether they are ideally or wholly free.

FROM COERCION TO PERSUASION

I begin with definitions of coercion, manipulation, and persuasion that express their differences.

First, *coercion* occurs if one party deliberately and successfully uses force or a credible threat of unwanted, avoidable, and serious harm in order to compel a particular response from another person. No matter how attractive or overwhelming an offer, coercion is not involved unless a threatening sanction is presented. Advertisements directed at a starving population that "offer" food and medical attention in return for marketable blood, constitute a threat and not a mere offer, and so are coercive. But such circumstances are extremely rare in advertising, and thus the problem of "coercive advertising" is a contrived issue that we need not address.

Second, *persuasion* is a deliberate and successful attempt by one person to encourage another to freely accept beliefs, attitudes, values, or actions through appeals to reason. The first person offers what he or she believes to be good reasons for accepting the desired perspective. In paradigmatic cases of persuasion, these good reasons are conveyed through structured verbal facts or argument. However, good reasons can also be expressed through nonverbal communication such as visual evidence. "Rational" persuasion is sometimes distinguished from "nonrational" persuasion, but I will consider only rational persuasion. ("Nonrational" persuasion is a form of manipulation, as defined below.)

The Kellogg Co., which has been attacked for its child-oriented advertisements of pre-sweetened, ready-to-eat cereals, presents an example of self-proclaimed persuasive advertising. Executive Vice President William E. LaMothe once testified before the Senate Select Committee on Nutrition and Human Needs that Kellogg has adopted the following approach to advertising its products: "Our company is very conscious of the fact that social responsibilities go hand-in-hand with business responsibilities. The steps that we are taking to contribute to the improvement of the understanding of the need for a complete and adequate breakfast reflect this consciousness." Any company acting on the principle that advertising should "contribute to the improvement of the understanding" and using bona fide informational appeals to convince viewers to eat healthier breakfasts is employing a policy of persuasion.[2]

The essence of rational persuasion is inducing change by convincing a person through the merit of the reasons put forward.[3] However, "the merit of the reasons" is a tricky notion. Judgments about the credibility and expertise of a person who advances an argument affect our acceptance of a message no less than the premises and the soundness of the argument used. Does persuasion under these conditions occur? Acceding to an argument simply because one likes the person who presents the argument — as in Pepsi's television ads using famous entertainment stars — or finds the person physically attractive — as in typical magazine advertising for Virginia Slims — can be distinguished from accepting an argument because the person is an expert and therefore likely to be correct. The same arguments are often more persuasive if the reasons are presented by a professional rather than by an inexperienced amateur. Authoritative judgment often rationally persuades although fully developed persuasive arguments are not presented.

It is sometimes difficult to determine from the description of an attempt to influence whether the influence is a case of persuasion or a case of manipulation. The central question is not what is done, said, or suggested, but how or through what psychological processes the person responded to and was affected by the influence. Advertising can persuade some persons while misleading others who receive the same message. For example, an FTC staff report concerning children's television noted the following about children six years and under:

(1) They place indiscriminate trust in televised advertising messages; (2) they do not under-

stand the persuasive bias in television advertising; and (3) the techniques, focus and themes used in child-oriented television advertising enhance the appeal of the advertising message and the advertised product. Consequently, young children do not possess the cognitive ability to evaluate adequately child-oriented television advertising.[4]

Although children under six cannot understand the intent of a commercial message, the report argues, children over six often can. Children under six are manipulated, whereas some over six are persuaded. Many questions remain unanswered about the depth and manner of television advertising's influence on both children and adults. For example, there are questions about the effects of television advertising, about the ability of persons to process cognitively the advertising information, about the ability of various persons to discriminate between the content of the program and the commercial, and about the ability of persons to resist appeals even if they understand them to be commercial in nature.

There are also questions about what counts as a good reason, or even a reason at all. Suppose an advertiser believes that the reasons used in an ad are bad reasons, but knows that the persons at whom the advertisement is directed believe they are good reasons. Is this an attempt at persuasion by giving good reasons, or an attempt at manipulation by motivating purchases for bad reasons? Whether anyone except the consumer believes the reason to be a good reason sometimes seems irrelevant. For example, an advertiser may believe it is absurd to buy a soap because it smells good when the wrapper is opened, but if people value the soap for this reason, then the soap's attractive aroma seems to be a good reason to promote the product. Similarly, if a mother believes falsely that a tasty snack food will make her baby healthier, can this be a good reason? As the ads become more deceptive or harmful, we are more likely to abstain from calling them "good reasons." Our criteria of "good reasons" will be governed by a broader conception of legitimate and illegitimate influence.

Consumer protection groups and sometimes government officials focus on the consumers' *response* to advertising and on its human effects, rather than on the *intention* of those who create the advertising. By contrast, those who defend controversial advertising focus more on the intentions of advertising agencies and manufacturers in marketing a product — namely, on the intent to sell a "good product." These different emphases exhibit further complications, because an advertisement created with good intentions nonetheless can be misleading or nonrationally controlling.

MANIPULATION

I move now from coercion and persuasion to the central class of problematic influences. Manipulation is a broad category that includes any successful attempt to elicit a desired response from another person by noncoercively modifying choices available to that person or by nonpersuasively altering another person's perceptions of available choices. A variety of concepts explain this portion of the continuum between coercion and persuasion. Current literature mentions incentives, strong offers, indoctrination, propaganda, emotional pressure, irrational persuasion, temptation, seduction, and deception. I am using the single word *manipulation* to cover all parts of this vast territory.

The major difference between informational manipulation and persuasion is that the former involves deception used to influence a person's choice or action, whereas persuasion is not based on deception. In being influenced by information, persuasion

is an attempt to get one to believe what is correct, sound, or backed by good reasons. Manipulation is an attempt to induce one to believe what is not correct, unsound, or not backed by good reasons.

We should, however, be cautious in using words like "misleading" and "deceptive," which have both subjective and objective connotations. People are often misled by their own bizarre inferences or by their lack of concentration. A presentation is not necessarily misleading because it is misunderstood or because it leads persons to believe what is false. The goal of eliminating all misleading subjective interpretation is a noble ideal, but too demanding as a standard for public advertising.

MANIPULATION IN ADVERTISING

This account of manipulation and the continuum of influence applies to many forms of advertising. I shall discuss advertising for banks, foods, alcoholic beverages, and cigarettes.

Bank Advertising. Banks regularly advertise for new accounts, but some of these advertisements are manipulative, not persuasive. The advertisements I examine are all for fixed-term deposits that pay more than one rate over the term. Banks advertise a high, short-duration rate of interest in very large type, while a lower rate is noted in far smaller type, as is the fact that the lower rate is effective for a far longer term. Also relegated to the smaller print, if mentioned at all, is any statement of effective annual yield or yield over the course of the account. These advertisements are designed to convey the message to a reader that the significant rate for the thrifty-minded is the one in large type, rather than either the effective annual yield or the underlying, lower rate. The ads also often present the rates as "tax-free" or "tax-exempt," when they are only tax-deferred.

A dramatic form of this kind of advertising occurred when interest rates were higher than they presently are and the competition for Individual Retirement Account (IRA) customers was more intense than it currently is. It became apparent to banks that advertising campaigns were more effective as the rates offered were adjusted to higher levels. The higher advertised rates were purely promotional for short, introductory durations and had little or no benefit on annual yields. For example, the Riggs National Bank in Washington, D.C., which advertises itself as "The Most Important Bank in the Most Important City in the World," started out advertising at 14%, but quickly saw the effects of the trends in advertising higher rates and rocketed up to 25% for a short introductory duration, after which the money was locked in at a far lower rate. Standard Federal started out with 15%, then quickly went to 17% and finally to 25% without otherwise changing its ads. Other banks were not about to lose customers, and they followed suit.

How successfully do these ads work to influence customers to open new accounts? An official of the Riggs Bank interviewed by the *Washington Post* confirmed that the promotional rate brought in a large influx of customers from the start. After Riggs raised the promotional rate from 14% to 25%, three times as many depositors signed up for Riggs IRAs on the days the 25% rate was run than had signed up on the days the 14% rate had been run.[5]

More important than short duration at high rates is the inherent complication and confusion involved in interpreting the split rate in a context in which there are no uniform practices, standardized rates, or conventional expectations. This is not a mere problem of chaos in a shifting industry. It is also beyond the powers of many readers to compute average effective annual yields over the life of the deposit, and yet this computation yields the only material information because withdrawals cannot be made from these accounts without loss of *all* interest — promotional as well as long-term. It is beyond the powers of many readers to make significant comparisons across the different banks. The split rate, the method of compounding, and the term of the deposit make for many complicated calculations, even among those few customers who might figure out how to make the basic computations.

For example, Riggs' 25% promotional, 2-month rate was accompanied by an underlying rate of 10.87% for 28 months, while Chevy Chase Savings and Loan's 2-month 15% promotional rate was accompanied by an underlying rate of 11.5% for 28 months. The *undisclosed* (unadvertised) data were that Chevy Chase had an average annual effective yield of 12.39%, while for Riggs the average annual effective yield was 12.31%.

Food Advertising. Deceptive disclosure is likewise found in food labeling and marketing. In 1990-91, the FDA criticized Ragu and Procter and Gamble for their "fresh" claims on processed, packaged foods, such as pasta sauces.[6] These two cases set a precedent for government regulation for an extensive network of food labeling, which had become deceptive and often baffling. Use of words such as *fat free, cholesterol free, fresh,* and *low sugar* traded on consumer ignorance and led to a war of subtle misrepresentation.

Several problems are involved in such deceptive labeling and corresponding advertising. A consumer with high cholesterol typically buys products with labels stating "cholesterol free." However, these products often contain additional sugars or fats to maintain the flavor, creating further, often hidden or undisclosed health risk. To cite a typical example, in 1990 the FDA forced CPC International, marketer of Mazola Corn Oil, to discontinue claims that Mazola helped reduce cholesterol levels. The FDA objected to this claim because the label failed to acknowledge that the product had a high fat content.[7] Mazola is a good product that has no cholesterol; in this respect its ads were correct. However, no margarine helps *reduce* cholesterol levels, although some margarines present a reduced threat to health by comparison to others. All oils are 100% fat, but some have a healthier fat content than others. This was hardly the message communicated by Mazola.

A similar problem occurs in percentage labeling and advertising. An Oscar Mayer turkey product that advertised itself as "98% fat-free" measured this claim about fat content by weight, not by caloric intake. But of the 12 calories in each super-thin slice of this turkey, approximately 9 of the calories were fat. From this perspective, a critical one for those who seek to reduce the fat content in their diet, 98% fat-free is equivalent to 75% fat-caloric content.

These forms of deception mislead consumers into believing in non-existent health benefits, or at least in misleading claims about them. But these problems are subtle difficulties by comparison to many other advertisements for food products. Health claims in labeling had progressed in late 1991, at the time of the FDA's toughest crackdown, to the point that many manufacturers had concluded that they had to place misleading health claims on their label in order to remain competitive. More than one-third of all new food products on the market in 1991 made a claim using some health-related message, without specifying what the message meant. The FDA effectively wrote a new set of standards for food labelling in order to stop this manipulation of consumers. The agency gave standardized meanings to terms such as "light," "reduced," "extra light," "low-fat," and "low in cholesterol" in a circumstance in which they were functioning more as buzzwords to attract customers than as truthful claims.[8]

This FDA decision was praised, not condemned, by leading food manufacturers, such as Kraft General Foods. The reason is that nutritious products that are truthfully labeled make for good advertising and solid sales. These products do better in the market when untruthful claims for inferior products are absent. But the other side of this fact is that manipulation of consumer belief is good for sales of inferior products as long as it goes undetected or unchallenged.

Lifestyle Advertising. A third genre of advertising, often used in cigarette and alcohol advertising, is known as lifestyle advertising. These ad campaigns do not focus on the benefits of a product, but rather on a desirable lifestyle associated with the product. Ads aim either to create the association or psychologically reinforce associations that already exist. A typical example is making a link between alcohol consumption and having a good time at parties, on vacations, and the like.

Manipulation occurs when these advertisements successfully reinforce a certain lifestyle, often in people who cannot legally purchase the product. For example, Brown and Williamson Tobacco Corp. attempted to revitalize their Kool cigarette brand through creating the KOOL PENGUIN. This creature with a spiked, Vanilla Ice hairdo, attractive dark glasses, and youthful personality appeared on billboards, in magazines, and in store displays. The penguin did not directly advocate that minors smoke cigarettes, but it did reinforce youthful perceptions that smoking is cool and a bit rebellious. Company spokesperson Patrick Stone claimed that, although the KOOL PENGUIN resembles Saturday morning cartoon characters and child-hero figures, the company made no attempt to sell to minors.[9]

This interpretation is implausible. The Kool figure's appeal is strictly for the young. It invites smoking, and entices a group vulnerable to such appeals. Kool's market share had fallen 4.9% just prior to its ad, which appears to have been created to cover lost ground. Because the adult market was at the time still declining, the only place to recover ground was with youths who either do not smoke or do not have a preferred brand. This strategy has long been used in the cigarette industry, and the controversy surrounding the KOOL PENGUIN is not new. Camel cigarettes, with noticeable success in the underage market, has long used the cartoon camel figure of Joe Camel, whose coolness was expressed through a leather-jacket image. After selectively placing ads in literature read by minors, Camel's brand share among minors escalated from .5% to 32.8%. The ad campaigns appeared to be especially effective in reaching children under 13.[10] The Camel ads led to a suit in 1994–1996 in federal courts for misleading advertising that attempts to lure children (90% of all new smokers) into smoking.[11]

Alcohol advertising presents a similar form of lifestyle advertising that critics claim reinforces underage drinking. Surgeon General Antonia Novella called for all beer and wine advertisers to cease television advertising immediately on grounds of its manipulative effect and health risks. To support this request she cited major breweries' advertising campaigns targeted at audiences under the legal drinking age. The Surgeon General attacked lifestyle advertisements associating alcohol use with beauty, sex, popularity, and good times. Beach scenes, party scenes, and romantic adventures are manipulative in that they reinforce young peoples' perceptions that one needs only to consume a few beers to loosen up, fit in with the crowd, and have a good time.[12]

A similar style of advertising is found in a "fortified dessert wine," Cisco, which has a 20% alcohol content level, although its packaging is noticeably similar to a standard wine cooler — a clear glass container with a wraparound neck label. Most wine coolers have a 4–5% alcohol content. Purchasers, particularly underage drinkers, often do not appreciate Cisco's potency. Marketed under the slogan "Cisco takes you by surprise," it has been documented that Cisco consumption effects include "combativeness, hallucinations, disorientation, [and] loss of motor control and consciousness."[13] When combined with its "cooler style" packaging, Cisco's marketing success and potency led the Surgeon General to declare Cisco "a dangerous fortified wine, and the ultimate 'wine fooler'."[14]

Similarly, the G. Heileman Brewing Company's malt liquor "PowerMaster" brand created an advertising campaign that featured a black male model, with the intent of targeting young, inner-city black men, who consume roughly one-third of all malt liquors.[15] So conspicuous was this advertising that the Bureau of Alcohol, Tobacco, and Firearms prohibited Heileman from further marketing of the product and shortly thereafter required that similar ads be discontinued for malt liquors marketed by Pabst Brewing Co., Stroh Brewing Co., and McKenzie River Co. Three years later the Bureau sharply criticized new ads promoting increased alcohol content in Miller Lite Ice.[16] Each of these advertisements used images and slogans with virtually no cognitive message other than presenting a high alcohol content. For example, the Miller ads showed the slogan "If you get it, get it," together with the alcohol content of the beverage: 5.5% (a 32% increase in alcohol over regular Miller Lite). The sole objective was to entice consumers to purchase the alcohol products.

AN OBJECTION IN DEFENSE OF THE ADVERTISING INDUSTRY

One objection to this analysis of manipulative advertising is that persons of normal maturity, liberty, and resistibility, do make free choices, in which case my criticism of advertising would fail. Can we not expect persons to take care of themselves when hearing an advertisement no less than when shopping in a department store with attractive displays on every counter? Advocates often defend advertising and marketing by a rules-of-the-game model: There are more or less established, well-delineated procedures or moves for marketing a product. The consumer is well acquainted with these rules of the game, and consumers are often in an equal bargaining position.

One can easily become upset about advertising directed at children, and other vulnerable parties, because the ordinary rules of the game are either suspended or violated. The unsuspecting child may be sacrificed to the greed of the toymaker or cookie manufacturer. But is not advertising, placed in a more favorable light, analogous to activities in which we all engage — for example, purchasing a house or bargaining over the price of a rug in an overpriced store?

This defense of advertising overlooks the fact that advertisers manipulate not only the weak and unwary, but persons of normal discernment and resistibility. Advertisers know the art of subtle deception and manipulation. They use attractive rates, enticing images, and a variety of forms of suggestion to hinder or block reasoned choice. Advertising should enable or at least not prevent an informed choice about purchase of the product or service. It should be persuasive in presentation, not manipulative. Rules of acceptable advertising therefore should encompass more than the mere creation of a market. If persons are misled in the attempt to make an intelligent choice or are enticed into the choice by deception, the advertising has an enormous burden of justification — no matter the target population or the implicit rules of the game.

When implicit rules of games are inadequate, as they are at the present time in advertising, external standards are needed to challenge the presuppositions that underlie the rules. If assumptions in the rules permit inessential and less nutritious products to be advertised to children and adults alike as essential or highly nutritious, and when merchants like Arthur Lake, with whom we began, are driven out of business by "competitive" advertising, we know that some assumptions about the rights of advertisers need to be defended by good reasons.

My proposal, then, is that a simple moral rule be adopted: Advertisements should be persuasive and should be judged morally inappropriate and socially unacceptable when they are manipulative.

NOTES

1. Walter B. Smith, "For Lake, Jewelry Has Lost Its Glitter," *The Detroit News* (December 9, 1982), p. 3B.

2. William E. LaMothe, "Testimony," in Part 5 — TV Advertising of Food to Children, Hearings before the Senate Select Committee on Nutrition and Human Needs, 93rd Congress, 1st Session, 1973, p. 258. By contrast, see the later development in which the state of Texas sued Kellogg for manipulative advertising. See Jennifer Lawrence, "Texas Notches a Win over Kellogg" (regarding Heartwise Cereal), *Advertising Age* 62 (April 8, 1991), p. 6.

3. See Stanley I. Benn, "Freedom and Persuasion," *Australasian Journal of Philosophy* 45 (December 1967): 265.

4. *FTC Final Staff Report and Recommendation in the Matter of Children's Advertising*, 43 Fed. Reg. 17967, TRR No. 215-60, (1981), p. 3.

5. L. Ross, "IRA Jungle Grows More Dense as Tax Time Draws Near," *Washington Post* (March 19, 1984), Business Section, p. 34; Mary W. Walsh, "Banks' Policies on Figuring and Advertising Deposit Interest Make Picking Rates Hard," *Wall Street Journal*, October 8, 1984, Sec. 2, p. 33.

6. Laurie Freeman and Julie Liesse, "FDA Starts Getting Tough on Good Labeling," *Advertising Age* 61 (September 10, 1990), p. 87; "FDA Puts Squeeze on P&G Over Citrus Hill Label-

ing," *Wall Street Journal,* Thursday, April 25, 1991, pp. B1, B4.

7. Steven W. Colford and Judann Dagnoli, "FDA Readies Second Strike," *Advertising Age,* May 13, 1991, pp. 1, 46.

8. FDA, "Food Labeling Regulations: Information Sheet," November 6, 1991 (Washington: DHHS, Public Health Service). For a criticism of FDA rules, see John E. Calfee, "Worried about Your Health? FDA Isn't," *Wall Street Journal,* September 12, 1994, p. A16.

9. Paul Farhi, "Kool's Penguin Draws Health Officials' Heat," *The Washington Post,* October 23, 1991, pp. C1, C7.

10. See Chad Rubel, "Research Fuels Debate about Cigarettes, Kids," *Marketing News* 29, July 17, 1995, p. 10.

11. Paul M. Barrett, "Supreme Court Gives Green Light to Suit Against Tobacco Concern's Cartoon Ads" (on *R. J. Reynolds Tobacco Co. vs. Mangini*), *Wall Street Journal,* November 29, 1994, p. A24; Steven W. Colford, "Joe Camel Heads for Showdown in California Court," *Advertising Age* 65, December 5, 1994, p. 16; Claude R. Martin, "Ethical Advertising Re-search Standards: Three Case Studies," *Journal of Advertising* 23 (September 1994): 17–29; Gary Levin, Poll: Camel Ads Are Effective with Kids," *Advertising Age* 63 (April 27, 1992), p. 12.

12. Paul Farhi, "Novello Urges Tough Curbs on Liquor Ads," *The Washington Post,* November 5, 1991, pp. D1, D8.

13. National Council on Alcoholism and Drug Dependence, *NCADD Demands Removal of Cisco from Market,* NCADD press release, September 13, 1990.

14. Public statement of Antonia C. Novello, M.D., M.P.H., U.S. Surgeon General, Press Conference, January 9, 1991.

15. Courtland Milloy, "Race, Beer Don't Mix," *The Washington Post,* July 9, 1991, p. B3.

16. Suein L. Hwang, "Miller Brewing Gets Heat for New Ice Beer Ads," *Wall Street Journal,* October 12, 1994, p. B1. Steven W. Colford and Ira Teinowitz, "Malt Liquor Power Failure," *Advertising Age* 62, July 1, 1991, p. 1. See also Eben Shapiro, "Molson Ice Ads Raise Hackles of Regulators," *Wall Street Journal,* February 25, 1994, p. B1.

Marketing to Inner-City Blacks: PowerMaster and Moral Responsibility

George G. Brenkert

I. INTRODUCTION

The nature and extent of marketers' moral obligations is a matter of considerable debate. This is particularly the case when those who are targeted by marketers live in disadvantaged circumstances and suffer various problems disproportionately with other members of the same society. An interesting opportunity to explore this difficult area of marketing ethics is presented by Heileman Brewing Company's failed effort to market PowerMaster, a malt liquor, to inner-city blacks. The story of PowerMaster is relatively simple and short. Its ethical dimensions are much more complicated.

In the following, I wish to consider the moral aspects of this case within the context of a market society such as the U.S. which permits the forms of advertising it presently does. To do so, I first briefly evaluate three kinds of objections made to the marketing of PowerMaster. I contend that none of these objections taken by itself clearly justifies the criticism leveled at Heileman. Heileman might reasonably claim that it was fulfilling

Excerpted from a paper to be published by *Business Ethics Quarterly.* Copyright © 1996 by George G. Brenkert. Reprinted by permission of the author.

its economic, social and moral responsibilities in the same manner as were other brewers and marketers. Accordingly, I argue that only if we look to the collective effects of all marketers of malt liquor to the inner-city can we identify morally defensible grounds for the complaints against marketing campaigns such as that of PowerMaster. The upshot of this argument is that marketers must recognize not only their individual moral responsibilities to those they target, but also a collective responsibility of all marketers for those market segments they jointly target. It is on this basis that Heileman's marketing of PowerMaster may be faulted. This result is noteworthy in that it introduces a new kind of moral consideration which has rarely been considered in discussions of corporate moral responsibilities.

II. HEILEMAN AND POWERMASTER

G. Heileman Brewing Co. is a Wisconsin brewer which produces a number of beers and malt liquors, including Colt Dry, Colt 45, and Mickey's. In the early 1990s, competition amongst such brewers was increasingly intense. In January 1991, Heileman was facing such economic difficulties that it filed for protection from creditors under Chapter 11 of the U.S. Bankruptcy Code (Horovitz, 1991b, D1). To improve its financial situation, Heileman sought to market, beginning in June 1991, a new malt liquor called "PowerMaster." At that time there was considerable growth in the "up-strength malt liquor category." In fact, "this higher-alcohol segment of the business [had] been growing at an explosive 25% to 30% a year" (Freedman, 1991a: B1). To attempt to capitalize on this market segment, Heileman produced PowerMaster, a malt liquor that contained 5.9% alcohol, 31% more alcohol than Heileman's top-selling Colt 45 (4.5% alcohol). Reportedly, when introduced only one other malt

liquor (St. Ides) offered such a powerful malt as PowerMaster (Freedman, 1991a: B1).

Further, since malt liquor had become "the drink of choice among many in the inner city," Heileman focused a significant amount of its marketing efforts on inner-city blacks. Heileman's ad campaign played to this group with posters and billboards using black male models. Advertisements assured consumers that PowerMaster was "Bold Not Harsh." Hugh Nelson, Heileman's marketing director, was reported to have claimed that "the company's research . . . shows that consumers will opt for PowerMaster not on basis of its alcohol content but because of its flavor. The higher alcohol content gives PowerMaster a 'bold not nasty' taste . . ." (Freedman, 1991a: B4).

In response, a wide variety of individuals and groups protested against Heileman's actions. Critics claimed that both advertisements and the name "PowerMaster" suggested the alcoholic strength of the drink and the "buzz" that those who consumed it could get. Surgeon General Antonia Novello criticized the PowerMaster marketing scheme as "insensitive" (Milloy, 1991: B3). Reports in *The Wall Street Journal* spoke of community activists and alcohol critics branding Heileman's marketing campaign as "socially irresponsible" (Freedman, 1991b: B1). "Twenty-one consumer and health groups, including the Center for Science in the Public Interest, also publicly called for Heileman to halt the marketing of PowerMaster and for BATF to limit the alcohol content of malt liquor" (Colford and Teinowitz, 1991: 29). A reporter for the *L.A. Times* wrote that "at issue is growing resentment by blacks and other minorities who feel that they are being unfairly targeted — if not exploited — by marketers of beer, liquor and tobacco products" (Horovitz, 1991: D6). Another reporter for the same paper claimed that "[a]nti-alcohol activists contend that alcoholic beverage manufacturers are taking advantage of minority groups and exacerbating inner-city problems by targeting them with high-powered blends" (Lacey, 1992: A32). And Reverend Calvin Butts of the Abyssinian Baptist Church in New York's Harlem said that "this [Heileman] is obviously a company that has no sense of moral or social responsibility" (Freedman, 1991a: B1).

Though the Bureau of Alcohol, Tobacco and Firearms (BATF) initially approved the use of "PowerMaster" as the name for the new malt liquor, in light of the above protests it "reacted by enforcing a beer law that prohibits labels 'considered to be statements of alcoholic content'" (Milloy, 1991: B3). It insisted that the word "Power" be removed from the "PowerMaster" name (Freedman, 1991b: B1). As a consequence of the actions of the BATF and the preceding complaints, Heileman decided not to market PowerMaster.

III. THE OBJECTIONS

The PowerMaster marketing campaign evoked three distinct kinds of moral objections:

First, because its advertisements drew upon images and themes related to power and boldness, they were criticized as promoting satisfactions only artificially and distortedly associated with the real needs of those targeted. As such, the PowerMaster marketing campaign was charged with fostering a form of moral illusion.

Second, Heileman was said to lack concern for the harm likely to be caused by its product. Blacks suffer disproportionately from cirrhosis of the liver and other liver diseases brought on by alcohol. In addition, alcohol-related social problems such as violence and crime are also prominent in the inner-city. Accordingly, Heileman was attacked for its lack of moral sensitivity.

Third, Heileman was accused of taking unfair advantage of those in the inner-city whom they had targeted. Inner-city blacks were said to be especially vulnerable, due to their life circumstances, to advertisements and promotions formulated in terms of power, self-assertion and sexual success. Hence, to target them in the manner they did with a product such as PowerMaster was a form of exploitation. In short, questions of justice were raised.

It is important not only for corporations such as Heileman but also for others concerned with such marketing practices to determine whether these objections show that the PowerMaster marketing program was morally unjustified. The economic losses in failed marketing efforts such as PowerMaster are considerable. In addition, if the above objections are justified, the moral losses are also significant.

The first objection maintained that by emphasizing power Heileman was, in effect, offering a cruel substitute for a real lack in the lives of inner-city blacks. PowerMaster's slogan, "Bold not Harsh," was said to project an image of potency. "The brewers' shrewd marketing," one critic maintained, "has turned malt liquor into an element of machismo" (Lacey, 1992: A1). George Hacker, Director of the National Coalition to Prevent Impaired Driving, commented that "the real irony of marketing PowerMaster to inner-city blacks is that this population is among the most lacking in power in this society" (Freedman, 1991a, B1).

This kind of criticism has been made against many forms of advertising. The linking of one's product with power, fame, and success not to mention sex is nothing new in advertising. Most all those targeted by marketers lack (or at least want) those goods or values associated with the products being promoted. Further, other malt liquor marketing campaigns had referred to power. For example, another malt liquor, Olde English "800," claimed that "It's the Power." The Schlitz Red Bull was associated with the phrase "The Real Power" (Colford and Tenowitz, 1991: 1). Nevertheless, they were not singled out for attack or boycott as PowerMaster was.

Accordingly, however objectionable it may be for marketers to link a product with something which its potential customers (significantly) lack and which the product can only symbolically or indirectly satisfy, this feature of the PowerMaster marketing campaign does not uniquely explain or justify the complaints that were raised against the marketing of PowerMaster. In short, this objection appears far too general in scope to justify the particular attention given PowerMaster. Heileman could not have reasonably concluded, on its basis, that it was being particularly morally irresponsible. It was simply doing what others had done and for which they had not been boycotted or against which such an outcry had not been raised. It is difficult to see how Heileman could have concluded that it was preparing a marketing program that would generate the social and moral protest it did, simply from an examination of its own plan or the similar individual marketing programs of other brewers.

The second objection was that the marketers of PowerMaster showed an especial lack of sensitivity in that a malt liquor with the potency of PowerMaster would likely cause additional harm to inner-city blacks. According to various reports, "alcoholism and other alcohol-related diseases extract a disproportionate toll on blacks. A 1978 study by the National Institute on Alcohol Abuse and Alcoholism found that black men between the ages of 25 and 44 are 10 times more likely than the general population to have cirrhosis of the liver" (*N.Y. Times*, 1991). *Fortune* reported that "The Department of Health and Human Services last spring re-

leased figures showing a decline in life expectancy for blacks for the fourth straight year — down to 69.2 years, vs. 75.6 years for whites. Although much of the drop is attributable to homicide and AIDS, blacks also suffer higher instances of . . . alcohol-related illnesses than whites" (*Fortune*, 1991: 100). Further, due to the combined use of alcohol and cigarettes, blacks suffer cancer of the esophagus at a disproportional rate than the rest of the population. Similarly, assuming that black women would drink PowerMaster, it is relevant that the impact of alcohol use in the inner-city is also manifested in an increased infant mortality rate and by new born children with fetal alcohol syndrome (*The Workbook*, 1991: 18). Finally, a malt liquor with a high percentage of alcohol was expected to have additional harmful effects on the levels of social ills, such as violence, crime, and spousal abuse. As such, PowerMaster would be further destructive of the social fabric of the inner-city.

Under these circumstances, the second objection maintained, anyone who marketed a product which would further increase these harms was being morally obtuse to the problems inner-city blacks suffer. Accordingly, Heileman's PowerMaster marketing campaign was an instance of such moral insensitivity.

Nevertheless, this objection does not seem clearly applicable when pointed simply at PowerMaster. Surely inner-city blacks are adults and should be allowed, as such, to make their own choices, even if those choices harm themselves, so long as they are not deceived or coerced when making those choices and they do not harm others. Since neither deception nor coercion were involved in PowerMaster's marketing campaign, it is an unacceptable form of moral paternalism to deny them what they might otherwise wish to choose.

Further, those who raised the above complaints were not those who would have drunk

PowerMaster, but leaders of various associations both within and outside the inner-city concerned with alcohol abuse and consumption. This was not a consumer-led protest. Reports of the outcry over PowerMaster contain no objections from those whom Heileman had targeted. No evidence was presented that these individuals would have found Power-Master unsatisfactory. Argument is needed, for example, that these individuals had (or should have had) over-riding interests in healthy livers. Obviously there are many people (black as well as white) who claim that their interests are better fulfilled by drinking rather than abstinence.

Finally, argument is also needed to show that this increase in alcoholic content would have any significant effects on the targeted group. It might be that any noteworthy effects would be limited because the increased alcoholic content would prove undesirable to those targeted since they would become intoxicated too quickly. "Overly rapid intoxication undercuts sales volume and annoys consumers," *The Wall Street Journal* reported (Freedman, 1991a: B1). Supposedly this consequence led one malt brewer to lower the alcoholic content of its product (Freedman, 1991a: B1). Furthermore, malt liquor is hardly the strongest alcohol which blacks (or others) drink. Reportedly, "blacks buy more than half the cognac sold in the United States" (*The Workbook*, 1991: 18). Cheap forms of wine and hard liquor are readily available. Thus, it is far from obvious what significant effects Power-Master alone would have in the inner-city.

One possible response to the preceding replies brings us to the third objection. This response is that, though inner-city blacks might not be deceived or coerced into drinking PowerMaster, they were particularly vulnerable to the marketing campaign which Heileman proposed. Because of this, Heileman's marketing campaign (wittingly or unwittingly) would take unfair advantage of inner-city blacks.

Little, if any attempt, has been made to defend or to explore this charge. I suggest that there are at least three ways in which inner-city blacks — or anyone else, for that matter — might be said to be specially vulnerable.

A person would be cognitively vulnerable if he or she lacked certain levels of ability to cognitively process information or to be aware that certain information was being withheld or manipulated in deceptive ways. Thus, if people were not able to process information about the effects of malt liquor on themselves or on their society in ways in which others could, they would be cognitively vulnerable.

A person would be motivationally vulnerable if he or she could not resist ordinary temptations and/or enticements due to his or her own individual characteristics. Thus, if people were unable, as normal individuals are, to resist various advertisements and marketing ploys, they would be motivationally vulnerable.

And people would be socially vulnerable when their social situation renders them significantly less able than others to resist various enticements. For example, due to the poverty within which they live, they might have developed various needs or attitudes which rendered them less able to resist various marketing programs.

Nevertheless, none of these forms of vulnerability was explored or defended as the basis of the unfair advantage which the PowerMaster marketers were said to seek. And indeed it is difficult to see what account could be given which would explain how the use of the name "PowerMaster," and billboards with a black model, a bottle of PowerMaster and the slogan "Bold Not Harsh" would be enough to subvert the decision making or motivational capacities of inner-city blacks. To the extent that they are adults and not under the care or protection of other individuals or agencies due to the state of their cognitive or motivational abilities, there is a prima facie case that they are not so vulnerable. Accordingly, the vulnerability objection raises the legitimate concern that some form of unjustified moral paternalism lurks behind it.

In short, if we consider simply the individual marketing program of PowerMaster, it is difficult to see that the three preceding objections justified the outcry against Heileman. Heileman was seeking to satisfy its customers. As noted above, none of the reported complaints came from them. Heileman was also seeking to enhance its own bottom line. But in doing so it was not engaged in fraud, deception or coercion. The marketing of PowerMaster was not like other morally objectionable individual marketing programs which have used factually deceptive advertisements (e.g., some past shaving commercials), taken advantage of the target group's special vulnerabilities (e.g., certain television advertisements to children who are cognitively vulnerable), or led to unusual harm for the group targeted (e.g., Nestlé's infant formula promotions to Third World Mothers). Black inner-city residents are not obviously cognitively vulnerable and are not, in the use of malt liquor, uniformly faced with a single significant problem such as Third World Mothers are (viz., the care of their infants). As such, it is mistaken to think that PowerMaster's marketing campaign was morally offensive or objectionable in ways in which other such campaigns have been. From this perspective, then, it appears that Heileman could be said to be fulfilling its individual corporate responsibilities.

IV. ASSOCIATED GROUPS AND COLLECTIVE RESPONSIBILITY

So long as we remain simply at the level of the individual marketing campaign of PowerMaster, it is doubtful that we can grasp the basis upon which the complaints against PowerMaster might be justified. To do so, we must look to the social level and the collection of marketing programs of which PowerMaster was simply one part. By pushing on the bounds within which other marketers had remained, PowerMaster was merely the spark which ignited a great deal of resentment which stemmed more generally from the group of malt liquor marketers coming into the inner-city from outside, aggressively marketing products which disproportionately harmed those in the inner-city (both those who consume the product and others), and creating marketing campaigns that took advantage of their vulnerabilities.

As such, this case might better be understood as one involving the collective responsibility of the group of marketers who target inner-city blacks rather than simply the individual responsibility of this or that marketer. By "collective responsibility" I refer to the responsibility which attaches to a group (or collective), rather than to the individual members of the group, even though it is only through the joint action (or inaction) of group members that a particular collective action or consequence results. The objections of the critics could then more plausibly be recast in the form that the *collection* of the marketer's campaigns was consuming or wasting public health or welfare understood in a twofold sense: first, as the lack of illness, violence, and crime, and, second, as the presence of a sense of individual self that is based on the genuine gratification of real needs. When the individual marketers of a group (e.g., of brewers) engage in their own individual marketing campaigns they may not necessarily cause significant harms — or if they do create harm, the customers may have willingly accepted certain levels of individual risk of harm. However, their efforts may collectively result in significant harms not consciously assumed by anyone.

Similarly, though the individual marketing efforts may not be significant enough to expose the vulnerabilities of individuals composing their market segment, their marketing efforts may collectively create a climate within which the vulnerabilities of those targeted may play a role in the collective effect of those marketing campaigns. Thus, it is not the presence of this or that billboard from PowerMaster which may be objectionable so much as the large total number of billboards in the inner-city which advertise alcohol and to which PowerMaster contributed. For example, it has been reported that "in Baltimore, 76 percent of the billboards located in low-income neighborhoods advertise alcohol and cigarettes; in middle and upper-income neighborhoods it is 20 percent" (*The Workbook*, 1991: 18). This "saturation advertising" may have an effect different from the effect of any single advertisement. Similarly, it is not PowerMaster's presence on the market as such, which raises moral questions. Rather, it is that alcohol marketers particularly target a group which not only buys ". . . more than half the cognac sold in the United States and . . . consume[s] more than one-third of all malt liquor . . ." (*The Workbook*, 1991: 18), but also disproportionately suffers health problems associated with alcohol. The connection between the amount of alcohol consumed and the alcohol related health problems is hardly coincidental. Further, if the level of alcohol consumption is significantly related to conditions of poverty and racism, and the consequent vulnerabilities people living in these conditions may suffer, then targeting such individuals may also be an instance of attempting to take unfair advantage of them.

Now to make this case, it must be allowed that individual persons are not the only ones capable of being responsible for the effects of their actions. A variety of arguments have been given, for example, that corporations can be morally responsible for their actions. These arguments need not be recited here since even if they were successful, as I think

some of them are, the marketers who target inner-city blacks do not themselves constitute a corporation. Hence, a different kind of argument is needed.

Can there be subjects of responsibility other than individuals and corporations? Virginia Held has argued that under certain conditions random collections of individuals can be held morally responsible. She has argued that when it would be obvious to the reasonable person what a random collection of individuals ought to do and when the expected outcome of such an action is clearly favorable, then that random collection can be held morally responsible (Held, 1970: 476).

However, again the marketers of malt liquor to inner city blacks do not seem to fit this argument since they are not simply a random collection of individuals. According to Held, a random collection of individuals ". . . is a set of persons distinguishable by some characteristics from the set of all persons, but lacking a decision method for taking action that is distinguishable from such decisions methods, if there are any, as are possessed by all persons" (Held, 1970: 471). The examples she gives, "passengers on a train" and "pedestrians on a sidewalk," fit this definition but are also compatible with a stronger definition of a group of individuals than the one she offers. For example, her definition would include collections of individuals with no temporal, spatial or teleological connection. Clearly marketers of malt liquor to inner-city blacks constitute a group or collection of individuals in a stronger sense than Held's random collection of individuals.

Consequently, I shall speak of a group such as the marketers who target inner-city blacks as an associated group. Such groups are not corporations. Nor are they simply random collections of individuals (in Held's sense). They are groups in a weaker sense than corporations, but a stronger sense than a random collections of individuals. I shall argue that such groups may also be the subject of moral responsibility. This view is based upon the following characteristics of such groups.

First, an associated group is constituted by agents, whether they be corporate or personal, who share certain characteristics related to a common set of activities in which they engage. Thus, the marketers who target inner-city blacks share the characteristic that they (and no one else) target this particular market segment with malt-liquor. They engage in competition with each other to sell their malt-liquor according to the rules of the (relatively) free market. Though they themselves do not occupy some single spatial location, the focus of their activities, the ends they seek, and their temporal relatedness (i.e., marketing to the inner-city in the same time period) are clearly sufficient to constitute them as a group.

Second, though such associated groups do not have a formal decision-making structure which unites them, Stanley Bates has reminded us that "there are other group decision methods, [that] . . . are not formal . . ." (Bates, 1971:345). For example, the brewers presently at issue might engage in various forms of implicit bargaining. These informal and implicit group decision methods may involve unstructured discussions of topics of mutual interest, individual group member monitoring of the expectations and intuitions of other group members, and recognition of mutual understandings that may serve to coordinate the expectations of group members (cf. Schelling, 1963). Further, brewers in the United States have created the Beer Institute, which is their Washington-based trade group, one of whose main purposes is to protect "the market environment allowing for brewers to sell beer profitably, free from what the group views as unfair burdens imposed by government bodies."[1] The Beer Institute provides its members with a forum within which they may meet annually, engage in workshops, discuss issues of mutual concern, agree on which issues will be lobbied before Congress on their behalf and may voluntarily adopt an advertising code to guide their activities. Such informal decision-making methods amongst these brewers and suppliers are means whereby group decisions can be made.

Third, members of associated groups can be said to have other morally relevant characteristics which foster a group "solidarity" and thereby also unify them as a group capable of moral responsibility (cf. Feinberg, 1974: 234). These characteristics take three different forms. a) Members of the group share a community of interests. For example, they all wish to sell their products to inner-city blacks. They all seek to operate with minimal restrictions from the government on their marketing activities within the inner-city. They all are attempting to develop popular malt liquors. They all strive to keep the costs of their operations as low as possible. b) Further, they are joined by bonds of sentiment linked with their valuing of independent action and successfully selling their products. Though they may try to outcompete each other, they may also respect their competitors when they perform well in the marketplace. c) Finally, they can be said to share a common lot in that actions by one brewer that bring public condemnation upon that brewer may also extend public attention and condemnation to the other brewers as well — as happened in the PowerMaster case. Similarly, regulations imposed on one typically also affect the others. Thus, heavy regulation tends to reduce all their profits, whereas light regulation tends to have the opposite effect.

The unity or solidarity constituted by the preceding characteristics among the various marketers would be openly manifested, for example, if the government were to try to deny them all access to the inner-city market segment. In such a circumstance, they would openly resist, take the government to court, and protest with united voice against the injustice done to them, both individually and as a group. In this sense, there is (at the least) a latent sense of solidarity among such marketers (cf. May, 1987: 37). When they act, then each acts in solidarity with the others and each does those things which accord with the kinds of actions fellow group members are inclined to take. All this may occur without the need for votes being taken or explicit directions given among the various brewers (cf. May, 1987:40).

Fourth, associated groups like inner-city marketers can investigate the harms or benefits that their products and marketing programs jointly do to those who are targeted. They can also study the overall effects of their own individual efforts. They could do so both as individual businesses and as a group. In the latter case, the Beer Institute might undertake such studies. Similarly, these marketers might jointly commission some other organization to study these effects. In short, they are capable both as individual businesses and as a group, of receiving notice as to the effects of their individual and collective actions. In short, communication amongst the group members is possible.

Finally, associated groups can modify their activities. They are not simply inevitably or necessarily trapped into acting certain ways. For example, the inner-city malt liquor marketers might voluntarily reduce the number of billboards they use within the inner-city. They might not advertise in certain settings or in certain forms of media. They might not use certain appeals, e.g., touting the high alcoholic content of their products. As such, they could take actions to prevent the harms or injustices of which they are accused. At present brewers subscribe to an advertising code of ethics which the Beer Institute makes available and has recently updated. The Beer

Institute might even lobby the government on behalf of this group for certain limitations on marketing programs so as to eliminate moral objections raised against such marketing programs.

The preceding indicates that this group can act: it has set up the Beer Institute; it may react with unanimity against new regulations; it may defend the actions of its members; it may investigate the effects its group members have on those market segments which they have targeted. It does not act as a group in marketing particular malt liquors. The law prevents such collective actions. However, marketing malt liquor to particular groups is an action which this group may approve or disapprove. The group lobbies Congress on behalf of its members' interests. The group has organized itself such that through development and support of the Beer Institute its interests are protected. There is no reason, then, that such a group may not also be morally responsible for the overall consequences of its members' marketing.

Does the preceding argument suggest that the group of marketers would run afoul of concerns about restraint of trade? The above argument need not imply that inner-city marketers are always a group capable of moral action and responsibility — only that under certain circumstances it could be. Hence, the above argument does not suggest that this group constitutes anything like a cartel. In addition, the above argument does not suggest that marketers agree on pricing formulas, on reserving certain distributional areas for this or that marketer, or similar actions which would constitute classic forms of restraint of trade. Further, the preceding argument leaves open what mechanisms might be legally used whereby these moral responsibilities are discharged. It might be that individual marketers voluntarily agree to such actions as they presently do with their advertising code. On the other hand, they might collectively appeal to the government to approve certain general conditions such that the playing field within which they compete would be altered to alleviate moral objections to their marketing campaigns, but would remain relatively level in comparison with their situations prior to the imposition of such conditions.

If the preceding is correct, then given the assumption that basic items of public welfare (e.g., health, safety, decision-making abilities, etc.) ought not to be harmed, two important conclusions follow regarding the marketing of malt liquor to inner-city blacks.

First, malt liquor marketers have a collective responsibility to monitor the effects of their activities and to ensure that they jointly do not unnecessarily cause harm to those they target or trade on their vulnerabilities. Assuming that malt liquor does harm inner-city blacks and that the marketing programs through which malt liquor is sold to this market segment play some significant causal role in creating this harm, then they have an obligation to alter their marketing to inner-city blacks in such a way that the vulnerabilities of inner-city blacks are not exploited and that unnecessary harm does not come to them.

Second, where the collective consequences of individual marketing efforts create the harms claimed for alcohol among inner-city blacks, and marketers as a group do not discharge the preceding collective responsibility, then there is a need for some agency outside those individual marketers to oversee or regulate their actions. Obviously, one form this may take is that of an industry or professional oversight committee; another form might be that of government intervention.

V. IMPLICATIONS AND CONCLUSION

The implications of this social approach to the PowerMaster case are significant:

First, marketers cannot simply look at their own individual marketing campaigns to judge their moral level. Instead, they must also look at their campaign within the context of all the marketing campaigns which target the market segment at which they are aiming. This accords with Garrett Hardin's suggestion that "the morality of an act is a function of the state of the system at the time it is performed" (Hardin, 1968: 1245; emphasis omitted). It is possible that marketers could fulfill their individual responsibilities but not their collective responsibilities.

Second, when the products targeted at particular market segments cause consumers to suffer disproportionately in comparison with other comparable market segments, marketers must determine the role which their products and marketing programs play in this situation. If they play a contributory role, they should (both individually and as a group) consider measures to reduce the harm produced. One means of doing this is to voluntarily restrict or modify their appeals to that market segment. In the present case, industry organizations such as The Beer Institute might play a leading role in identifying problems and recommending countermeasures. Otherwise when harm occurs disproportionately to a market segment, or members of that segment are especially vulnerable, outside oversight and regulation may be appropriate.

Third, marketers have a joint or collective responsibility to the entire market segment they target, not simply for the effects of their own products and marketing campaigns, but more generally for the effects of the combined marketing which is being done to that segment. The protests against PowerMaster are best understood against the background of this collective responsibility.

Thus, when we think of responsibility in the market we must look beyond simply the responsibility of individual agents (be they personal or corporate). We must look to the responsibility of groups of persons as well as groups of corporations. Such responsibility is not personal or individual, but collective. Examination of the case of PowerMaster helps us to see this.

Accordingly, the preceding analysis helps to explain both why PowerMaster was attacked as it was and also why it seemed simply to be doing what other marketers had previously done. Further, it helps us to understand the circumstances under which the above objections against marketing malt liquor to inner-city blacks might be justified. However, much more analysis of this form of collective harm and the vulnerability which is said to characterize inner-city blacks needs to be undertaken.

Finally, it should be emphasized that this paper advocates recognition of a new subject of moral responsibility in the market. Heretofore, moral responsibility has been attributed to individuals and corporations. Random collections of individuals have little applicability in business ethics. However the concept of associated groups and their collective responsibility has not been previously explored. It adds a new dimension to talk about responsibility within current discussions in business ethics.

NOTE

1. "The Beer Institute," *Encyclopedia of Associations*, Carolyn A. Fischer and Carol A. Schwartz (eds.), vol. 1 (New York: Gale Research Inc., 1995), p. 27.

BIBLIOGRAPHY

Bates, Stanley (1971), "The Responsibility of 'Random Collections'," *Ethics*, 81, 343–349.

Benn, Stanley I. (1967), "Freedom and Persuasion," *The Australasian Journal of Philosophy*, 45, 259–275.

Brown, Jesse W. (1992), "Marketing Exploitation," *Business and Society Review*, Issue 83 (Fall), p. 17.

Colford, Steven W. and Teinowitz, Ira (1991), "Malt liquor 'power' failure," *Advertising Age*, July 1, pp. 1, 29.

Farhi, Paul (1991), "Surgeon General Hits New Malt Liquor's Name, Ads," *Washington Post*, June 26, pp. A1, A4.

Feinberg, Joel (1974), "Collective Responsibility," in *Doing & Deserving* Princeton: Princeton University Press, pp. 222–251.

Fortune (1991), "Selling Sin to Blacks," October 21, p. 100.

Freedman, Alix (1991a), "Potent, New Heileman Malt is Brewing Fierce Industry and Social Criticism," *Wall Street Journal*, June 17, pp. B1, B4.

——— (1991b), "Heileman, Under Pressure, Scuttles PowerMaster Malt," *Wall Street Journal*, July 5, pp. B1, B3.

Hardin, Garrett (1968), "The Tragedy of the Commons," *Science*, 162, 1243–1248.

Held, Virginia (1970), "Can a Random Collection of Individuals Be Morally Responsible?," *The Journal of Philosophy*, 67, 471–481.

Horovitz, Bruce (1991), "Brewer Faces Boycott Over Marketing of Potent Malt Liquor," *L. A. Times*, June 25, pp. D1, D6.

Lacey, Marc (1992), "Marketing of Malt Liquor Fuels Debate," *L. A. Times*, December 15, pp. A32, A34.

May, Larry (1987), *The Morality of Groups* Notre Dame: University of Notre Dame Press.

Milloy, Courland (1991), "Race, Beer Don't Mix," *The Washington Post*, July 9, p. B3.

New York Times, The (1991), "The Threat of Power Master," July 1, p. A12.

Schelling, Thomas (1963), *The Strategy of Conflict* New York: Oxford University Press.

Teinowitz, Ira and Colford, Steven W. (1991), "Targeting Woes in PowerMaster Wake," *Advertising Age*, July 8, 1991, p. 35.

"The Beer Institute," *Encyclopedia of Associations* (1995), Carolyn A. Fischer and Carol A. Schwartz (eds.), vol. 1, New York: Gale Research Inc.

Workbook, The (1991), "Marketing Booze to Blacks," Spring, 16, 18–19.

Zimmerman, Michael J. (1985), "Sharing Responsibility," *American Philosophical Quarterly*, 22, 115–122.

Corporate Policy and Ethics
of Competitor Intelligence Gathering

Lynn Sharp Paine

. . . The purpose of this paper is to highlight the need for management to address the ethics of competitor intelligence gathering. Recent developments in the business environment have generated increasing interest in competitor intelligence, information that helps managers understand their competitors. Although information about rival firms has always been a valued and sought after commodity, competitor intelligence gathering has only recently begun to be systematized and legitimated as a business function. While understanding the competition is an important part of running a business, there are ethical limits on the types of competitor information that may be acquired; on the methods that may be employed to acquire it; and on the purposes for which it may be used. To date, however, few managers or management educators have addressed the ethics of intelligence gathering.

This paper will focus primarily on methods of acquiring competitor information. Separating legitimate from illegitimate approaches to information acquisition is, in practice, the central ethical issue for intelligence-gathering specialists. . . .

GROWTH OF COMPETITOR INTELLIGENCE GATHERING

Evidence of the growth of interest in competitor intelligence is abundant. A 1985 study which looked at the intelligence-gathering budgets of twenty-five Fortune 500 companies found that all had increased substantially over the preceding five-year period.[1] Five years earlier, one-third of the companies had not had intelligence-gathering departments at all. Respondents to a 1986 study of 50 firms anticipated a dramatic increase in their intelligence-gathering budgets and almost all foresaw rapid growth in the staff assigned to intelligence gathering over the succeeding five-year period.[2] The findings of a recent Conference Board study of more than 300 U.S. firms were similar. Nearly all respondents said that monitoring competitors' activities is important and more than two-thirds expect their monitoring efforts to increase.[3] . . .

THE DARKER SIDE

There is, however, a darker side to the growth of intelligence gathering. It is reflected in the use of ethically questionable techniques for collecting information, the increase in trade secret litigation and information crimes, and the increase in the resources devoted to corporate security. One expert on trade secret law estimates that court rulings on theft and misappropriation of information have increased four-fold over the past decade to more than 200 a year and that the actual problem of information misappropriation is at least ten times as large.[4] Another reports a surge in information crimes.[5] The

Journal of Business Ethics 10 (199):423–436. © 1991 Kluwer Academic Publishers. Reprinted by permission of Kluwer Academic Publishers.

American Society for Industrial Security, which includes both outside consultants and in-house security groups, was reported in 1986 to have 24,000 members and to be gaining 5000 new members a year.[6] . . .

The increase in information litigation cannot be explained solely by increasingly complex and costly technology. The increase also reflects the growing use of questionable techniques to gain access to ordinary business information generated by or about competing firms. The use of these techniques may evidence a general decline in ethical standards or a decline in resourcefulness and creativity. It may also be a by-product of increased competition and the competitor orientation of current thinking about business strategy. . . .

QUESTIONABLE METHODS OF ACQUIRING INTELLIGENCE

While surveys have examined people's willingness to engage in specific questionable practices, and at least one author has provided a list of ethical and unethical intelligence-gathering techniques, the ethical principles at issue in this area have not generally been made explicit. However, a review of studies of questionable practices, judicial opinions, news reports, popular articles, and the writings of intelligence-gathering experts, reveals that the most prevalent methods of questionable intelligence gathering fall into three broad ethical categories:

1. those involving deceit or some form of misrepresentation;
2. those involving attempts to influence the judgment of persons entrusted with confidential information, particularly the offering of inducements to reveal information; and
3. those involving covert or unconsented-to surveillance.

Norms prohibiting practices in these categories appear to be weaker than norms prohibiting theft of documents and other tangible property, a fourth category of ethically problematic intelligence gathering.

In contrast to intelligence gathering which relies on information that firms have disclosed to public authorities or to the general public or which is available through open and above-board inquiry, questionable techniques are generally employed to obtain information which the firm has not disclosed, is not obligated to disclose, and probably would not be willing to disclose publicly. But most of these techniques would be objectionable — whatever type of information they elicited — because they offend common standards of morality calling for honesty, respect for relationships of trust and confidence, and respect for privacy. While stating these principles does not resolve difficult and disputed questions concerning their interpretation and application, some of which are discussed below, understanding the principles can contribute to clearer thinking about the factors distinguishing legitimate from illegitimate practice.

Several indicators point to the use of techniques that violate or call into question these principles.

Misrepresentation

Opinion research indicates that many employees say their companies condone, and they themselves approve of, the use of various forms of misrepresentation to gather competitor intelligence.[7] For example, 45.9% of the respondents to a questionnaire administered to 451 participants in seminars on intelligence gathering approved of getting information by posing as a graduate student working on a thesis.[8] A striking 85.6% of the respondents believe their competitors would use this method of intelligence gathering. . . .

The use of misrepresentation can take many forms: conducting phony job interviews,[9] hiring students to gather intelligence under the guise of doing academic work, posing as a potential joint venturer, supplier or customer. The prevalence of phony interviews has led at least one marketing manager to remind his people that "a job interview may be a total sham, a way to get intelligence."[10] The victims of deceit may be rival firms, themselves, their suppliers and customers, or other parties with access to valuable information.

In a recently litigated case, a marketing manager and his firm were found liable for damages incurred by a competitor that had revealed confidential information to the manager and another employee when they posed as a potential customer.[11] The marketing manager, whose branch office was failing to meet his own quotas, arranged to have a new hire who had not yet joined the firm pose as a potential customer for the competitor's software. The manager attended the software presentation as a friend and consultant of the supposed customer, but without identifying himself or his employer. As a result of the misrepresentation, the pair were given a detailed demonstration of the software, in-depth answers to their questions, and access to the competitor's sales manual. They made unauthorized copies of critical information in the manual and successfully developed a competitive software program within a short period of time. In testimony reported in the court's opinion, the marketing manager referred to himself as a "scoundrel," but explained that market pressures had led him to this tactic.

Improper Influence

A second category of questionable techniques centers on attempting to influence potential informants in ways that undermine their judgment or sense of obligation to protect confidentiality or to act in their employer's best interests. Frequently, the attempt involves offering inducements or the possibility of certain advantages to those who may be able to provide valuable information. In its crudest form, this technique is bribery, the offering of something of value in exchange for the breach of a fiduciary duty. In the recent Pentagon scandals, consultants to defense contractors offered large sums of money to government officials in exchange for revealing information they were as fiduciaries legally obliged to protect. In more subtle cases not involving legal obligations of confidentiality, the inducement may work to compromise the potential informant's judgment. The source may decide to reveal information which is not strictly speaking, confidential, but whose revelation is contrary to the employer's interests.

The inducement to disclose need not be cash; it may be a better job. The hiring of a rival's employee to gain access to confidential information appears to be a widely used and approved intelligence-gathering technique. Surveys conducted in 1974, 1976, and 1988 all found that many executives would use the practice.[12] Fifty-one percent of the smaller companies and 37% of the larger ones surveyed in 1974 said they expected employees hired from competitors to contribute all they knew to the new job, including the competitor's trade secrets.[13] And the Conference Board found that nearly half the respondents to its 1988 survey regard former employees of competitors as a very or fairly important source of information.[14] About half the executives responding to the 1976 study said they would try to hire a rival's employee to learn about an important scientific discovery that could substantially reduce profits during the coming year.[15]

In 1988, *Advertising Age* asked its readers whether it was ethical to hire an account supervisor from a competitor in order to gain information about the competitor's client. Seventy-three percent of the 157 professionals responding — advertisers, agency personnel, media people, consultants, and "others" — said the practice was ethical.[16] The Center for Communications posed the same hypothetical to professors and students of marketing. Fifty-nine percent of the 626 students responding said the practice was ethical, and 70% said they would do it.[17]

The hiring of employees with access to valuable competitor information has been the subject of numerous recent lawsuits and threatened lawsuits. When Wendy's International decided to substitute Coke products for Pepsi products in its restaurants, Pepsi threatened to sue Coke for pirating executives to gain information about Pepsi's contract and programs with Wendy's and for tampering with contractual relationships.[18] Similar issues have arisen in litigation between Johns-Manville and Guardian Industries,[19] Avis and Hertz,[20] and AT&T and MCI.[21] . . .

These techniques are ethically problematic because they involve attempts to undermine relationships of trust and confidence. In many cases, the information-seeker deliberately creates a conflict of interest in the hope that self-interest will overcome the potential informant's sense of obligation to protect his employer's confidential information or to act on his behalf. One must assume that the offering of valuable inducements reflects the fact, or at least the information-seeker's belief, that the information is not publicly available and can only be acquired, or can be acquired more cheaply, by attempting to induce a breach of confidence or to otherwise influence the judgment of those acting on behalf of the rival firm.

Part of the effectiveness of these inducements is explained by employees' uncertainty about what information may and may not be disclosed. While most firms treat some information as freely available to the public and other information as strictly confidential, there is a great deal of information that could be quite valuable to a competitor and whose confidentiality status is ambiguous in the minds of many employees, suppliers, and customers. For example, a firm may regard certain information shared with a supplier as confidential while the supplier sees it as public knowledge. The annals of trade secret litigation contain many examples of this sort of discrepancy. Indeed, there may be in-house discrepancies about what information is confidential and what may be revealed. The use of disclosure incentives in these cases may be the decisive influence tipping the potential informant's judgment in the direction of disclosure.

Ethical judgments about particular intelligence-gathering practices in this category are complicated by these same uncertainties. Still, legitimate questions about the scope of employees' obligations of confidentiality do not remove the moral difficulty that attaches to offering inducements deliberately intended to undermine a person's judgment or sense of obligation.

Covert Surveillance

Covert surveillance, another category of ethically problematic intelligence gathering, includes electronic espionage as well as other unconsented-to forms of observation such as eavesdropping and aerial photography. This category, perhaps the most difficult to define, raises questions about the legitimate scope of corporate privacy. When covert surveillance involves trespass or theft of tangible property, there is a convenient legal label for condemning it. But when it involves eavesdropping in public places or observation from afar using sophisticated technology, the wrong is most readily described as a violation of corporate privacy. Although the prevailing view is that corporations have no legal right to privacy, the idea persists that businesses and their employees should be able to assume they will not be observed or listened to in certain situations.

The techniques of covert surveillance are varied. They range from planting a spy in a competitor's operation — a technique which also involves deception and perhaps inducing actual employees to violate duties of confidentiality — to strategic eavesdropping in the bar and grill favored by a competitor's employees.[22] A widely discussed case of covert surveillance which resulted in an award of damages for the target company involved aerial photography of an unfinished manufacturing plant.[23] Clever gadgets of various types are available to assist covert observation: binoculars that hear conversations up to five blocks away, a spray that exposes the content of envelopes, a gadget that can read computer screens some two blocks away by picking up radio waves emitted by the machine.[24] Inspecting the competition's trash is another type of unconsented-to surveillance that has received attention in the press and has been litigated in at least one case.[25]

Covert observation, like misrepresentation and improper influence, is yet another way to obtain information which a rival does not wish to divulge. Ethical assessments of various forms of undisclosed observation may be controversial since privacy expectations are quite variable, as are judgments about the legitimacy of those expectations.

Covert observation in or from public places is especially problematic. For example, it may be possible to ascertain the volume of product that competitors are shipping by observing from public property the number of tractor-trailers leaving the plant's loading bays and by noting the size of the product in relation to the size of the trailers.[26] Opinions vary about the legitimacy of this practice. One might say that the firm has consented to observation by not putting a fence around the property. And yet, just as it is unseemly to peer through an open window into the neighbors' living room while walking down the sidewalk, we may think observation an invasion of the firm's privacy. . . .

Unsolicited Intelligence

The questions raised by covert surveillance are closely related to those raised by the receipt of unsolicited information. Disgruntled former employees of rival firms have been known to offer highly confidential technical information as well as more general information to competitors. Two recently litigated cases involved disputes about valuable information acquired as a result of a rival's mistake. In one case, a coded customer list was inadvertently left in the memory of a computer which was purchased at an auction by a competitor. The rival gained access to the codeword from an unwitting computer operator.[27] In another case, a dealer list was accidentally left in the store of a dealer who later became a competitor.[28]

There is no question of deceit or improper influence in these cases. The ethical question centers on whether unsolicited or inadvertently revealed information should be respected as private to the competitor. If intelligence gathering is governed by respect for the competitors' voluntary disclosure decisions, then information acquired through accident or mistake, or a former employee's breach of fiduciary duty, should not be examined and utilized. Indeed, this is the view reflected in the Uniform Trade Secrets Act.[29] Some courts and commentators, however, have taken the position that privacy is forfeited if information is accidentally revealed.[30]

The forfeiture view has some plausibility when disclosure is the result of a rival firm's carelessness. It is not unreasonable to expect a firm to suffer some loss if it acts carelessly. The view has less merit, however, when a third party, such as a supplier, inadvertently discloses a rival's valuable information. Still, in a survey discussed earlier, nearly half the marketing professionals questioned said it would be ethical to use information acquired as a result of a supplier's mistake.[31] In the survey vignette, a marketing professional is accidentally given slides prepared for a direct competitor's final presentation in a competition in which both are participating. Having examined the slides before returning them to the embarrassed employee of the slide supply house, the marketer must decide whether to use the information to alter his presentation to attack the competitor's recommended strategy. . . .

THE DEARTH OF CORPORATE GUIDANCE

Despite the growing importance of intelligence gathering and the occurrence of unethical and questionable practices, top management has not yet faced the issue squarely. Only a handful of corporations offer employees practical guidance on intelligence gathering in their codes of conduct or ethics policies. While codes of conduct are not the only, or even the most important, index of a corporation's ethical standards, they do provide some indication of ethical issues thought by the code's authors to merit attention. . . .

As a practical matter, the risks of litigation and legal liability can best be minimized by avoiding intelligence-gathering activities in the ethically problematic categories discussed above: misrepresentation, improper influence, unconsented-to surveillance, and theft. Admittedly, the threat of legal reprisal for engaging in these practices may be minimal in certain situations. Victims of unethical practices may not know they are being targeted, or they may lack evidence to prove their case in a court of law. Moreover, the law does not provide a remedy for every violation of ethics. If the victim of misrepresentation is not individually harmed, for example, he will have no legal recourse against the intelligence gatherer. And even if substantially harmed, the victim may have no remedy if the information acquired does not qualify as a trade secret or if the target firm has not taken adequate steps to protect the information in question.

From a management perspective, however, it is quite impractical to instruct employees to fine-tune their use of questionable practices on the basis of the legal risk in particular situations. Not only is it difficult to undertake an objective assessment of legal risk when under everyday performance pressures, but the legal risk of using unethical practices depends on consequences which are difficult, if not impossible, to anticipate in advance: the kind of information that will be obtained, the use to which it will be put, the harm that the target will suffer, the adequacy of the target's security measures, the likelihood of discovery, and the evidentiary strength of the target's case. What is known in advance is that certain types of practices, namely, those involving misrepresentation, theft, improper influence, and covert surveillance, can provide the necessary foundation for legal liability. Even from the narrow perspective of legal costs, there is a good case for instructing employees to avoid questionable practices altogether rather than attempt to assess the fine points of legal risk.

INCREASING SECURITY NEEDS

More costly, perhaps, than the litigation and liability risks involved in the use of questionable practices are the increased security needs these practices generate over the long term. Every user of unethical practices must recognize his contribution to a general climate of distrust and suspicion. Insofar as individuals are more likely to engage in unethical conduct when they believe their rivals are doing so, unethical intelligence gathering contributes further to the general deterioration of ethical expectations. As the recent growth of interest in information security illustrates, declining ethical expectations translate into intensified programs for self-protection.

Firms that expect to be subjected to intelligence gathering through covert surveillance, deceit, and various forms of improper influence — especially when legal recourse is unavailable or uncertain — will take steps to protect themselves. They will tighten information security by building walls, installing security systems, purchasing sophisticated counter-intelligence technology, and instituting management techniques to reduce the risks of information leakage. Although some degree of self-protection is necessary and desirable, security can become a dominant consideration and a drain on resources.

Besides their out-of-pocket cost, security activities often introduce operational inefficiencies and stifle creativity. Avoiding the use of the telephone and restricting access to information to employees who demonstrate a "need to know" impose obvious impediments to the exchange of information vital to cooperation within the firm. When researchers, for instance, are denied information about the projects they are working on and about how their work relates to the work of others, they are cut off from stimuli to creativity and useful innovation.

Employee morale and public confidence may also be at stake. Information systems designed to insure that employees do not know enough to hurt the firm if they depart, like the dissemination of information on a "need to know" basis, proceed from a premise of

distrust which can undermine employee morale. Even more clearly, information protection programs encourage an attitude of distrust toward outsiders. Employees are trained to be suspicious of public inquiries and to be wary of talking to or cooperating with outsiders who do not have security clearances. Over-restrictions on public access to information and excessive corporate secrecy generate public suspicion and hostility.

Although questionable intelligence-gathering practices may offer short-term advantages, they contribute, over the longer term, to a climate of distrust and the need for costly expenditures to tighten information security. These expenditures represent a diversion of management resources from more productive activities. Moreover, it is doubtful that firms can effectively protect their own valuable information if they encourage or tolerate loose ethical standards in acquiring competitor information. As the 1985 Hallcrest Report on private security in America concluded from studies of employee theft, "[E]ffective proprietary security programs . . . must emanate from a . . . strong sense of organizational ethics in all levels of the organization.[32] . . .

CONCLUSION

Managers who remain silent or fail to incorporate their "official" ethics policies into day-to-day management practice run the risk that they, their employees, and their firms will be involved in costly litigation over questionable intelligence-gathering tactics. More important, they jeopardize their own information security and run the risk of contributing further to the increasing demand for information protection. This demand represents a costly diversion of resources from the positive and creative aspects of doing business, a drag on innovation, and an impediment to good public relations. By supporting a competitive system which respects the principles of common morality and the right of rivals not to divulge certain information, management supports its own vitality and the vitality of the competitive system.

NOTES

1. Information Data Search, Inc.: 1986, *Corporate Intelligence Gathering, 1985 and 1986 Surveys* (Cambridge, Massachusetts), p. 24.

2. *Id.* at p. 6.

3. Sutton, H.: 1988, *Competitive Intelligence*, Conference Board Report No. 913 (The Conference Board, Inc., New York), pp. 6–7.

4. Roger Milgrim, author of 12 *Business Organizations*, Milgrim on Trade Secrets (1988), quoted in "Information Thieves Are Now Corporate Enemy No. 1," *Business Week* (May 5, 1986), p. 120.

5. The surge in information crimes is noted by Donn B. Parker of SRI International as reported in "Information Thieves," *Ibid.*

6. Haas, A. D.: 1986, "Corporate Cloak and Dagger," *Amtrak Express* (October/November), pp. 19–20.

7. Cohen, W., and Czepiec, H.: 1988, "The Role of Ethics in Gathering Corporate Intelligence," *Journal of Business Ethics* 7, pp. 199–203.

8. *Id.* at 200–201.

9. Flax, S.: 1984, "How to Snoop On Your Competitors," *Fortune* (May 14), p. 31.

10. Sutton, *Competitive Intelligence*, at p. 15.

11. *Continental Data Systems, Inc. v. Exxon Corporation*, 638 F. Supp. 432 (E.D. Pa. 1986).

12. Wall, "What the Competition is Doing," at pp. 32–34; Brenner, S. N., and Molander, A.: 1977 "Is the Ethics of Business Changing?" *Harvard Business Review* (January–February), p. 57; "Industry Ethics Are Alive," *Advertising Age* (April 18, 1988), p. 88.

13. Wall, "What the Competition is Doing," at p. 38.

14. Sutton, *Competitive Intelligence*, at p. 19.

15. Brenner and Molander, "Is the Ethics of Business Changing?" at p. 57.

16. "Industry Ethics Are Alive."

17. The results noted here are available from the Center for Communications, a nonprofit educational organization located in New York, New York.

18. "Pepsi to Sue Coke Over Wendy's," *Washington Post* (November 13, 1986), p. E1.

19. *Johns-Manville Corp. v. Guardian Industries Corp.*, 586 F. Supp. 1034, 1075 (E.D. Mich. 1983), aff'd, 770 F.2d 178 (Fed. Cir. 1985).

20. Lewin, "Putting a Lid on Corporate Secrets."

21. "Information Thieves," at pp. 122–123.

22. Both practices are described in Flax, "How to Snoop on Your Competitors," at pp. 28, 32.

23. *E.I. duPont deNemours v. Christopher*, 431 F. 2d. 1012 (5th Cir. 1970), cert. denied, 400 U.S. 1024 (1971).

24. "New Ways to Battle Corporate Spooks," *Fortune* (November 7, 1988), p. 72.

25. *Tennant Co. v. Advance Machine Co.*, 355 N.W. 2d 720.

26. Discussed in Flax, "How to Snoop on Your Competitors," at p. 33.

27. *Defiance Button Mach. Co. v. C & C Metal Products*, 759 F. 2d 1053 (2d Cir. 1985).

28. *Fisher Stoves, Inc. v. All Nighter Stove Works*, 626 F. 2d 193 (1st Cir. 1980).

29. *Uniform Trade Secrets Act With 1985 Amendments*, sec. 1 (2) (ii) (c), in *Uniform Laws Annotated*, vol. 14 (1980 with 1988 Pocket Part).

30. *Fisher Stoves; Defiance Button. See also Kewanee Oil Co. v. Bicron Corp.*, 416 U.S. 470, 476 (1973).

31. "Industry Ethics Are Alive."

32. Cunningham, W. C., and H. Taylor: 1985, *Private Security and Police in America*, The Hallcrest Report (Portland, Oregon: The Chancellor Press), p. 41.

Irving A. Backman v. Polaroid Corporation

United States Court of Appeals (First Circuit)

This is a class action brought by Irving A. Backman on behalf of himself and all other persons who purchased shares of stock of defendant Polaroid Corporation on the open market between January 11 and February 22, 1979, allegedly misled by defendant's conduct that violated Section 10(b) of the Securities Exchange Act of 1934 and Rule 10b-5 of the regulations promulgated thereunder. Suit was filed in June 1979. . . . The improprieties asserted, both in the complaint and in plaintiffs' opening to the jury, as responsible for plaintiffs' purchasing shares before a substantial drop in the market, were defendant's failure to disclose unfavorable facts about its new product, Polavision, an instant movie camera. Following trial on liability, the jury found for plaintiffs. . . . On appeal, a divided panel . . . granted a new trial. On this rehearing en banc we reverse and order judgment for defendant. . . .

In their amended complaint plaintiffs alleged that defendant failed to disclose that Polavision, introduced in the spring, had been unprofitable throughout 1978, and would continue so, significantly, at least through 1979; that it had been excessively inventoried and had suffered lagging sales; that little, if any, information had been made public; that defendant knew that this undisclosed information was material to investors, and that major investment research firms had publicly projected defendant's earnings based on assumptions defendant knew were contrary to the true facts, all of which non-disclosure was in violation of the securities laws.

Secondly, plaintiffs re-alleged the above, and added that over the years defendant had advertised that it was a growth company, and that, through its successes, the investment community had come to consider it the best of the growth companies, and that its failing to make the above disclosures operated as a fraud and deceit on the investing public, was a "fraud on the market," and constituted an unlawful manipulation thereof. . . .

However, mere market interest is no basis for imposing liability. We said [in a former case] the materiality of the information claimed not to have been disclosed . . . is not enough to make out a sustainable claim of securities fraud. Even if information is material, there is no liability under Rule 10b-5 unless there is a duty to disclose it.

A duty to disclose "does not arise from the mere possession of non-public information." . . .

In a twelve day trial [the plaintiffs] precisely followed their opening, alleging, simply, nondisclosure of material information. As summarized in their final argument,

> Polaroid . . . violated the federal securities laws which require full disclosure so that people who purchase and sell securities do so on a fair playing field; that people have the same information and people can make their investment decisions based on having all of the information and having truthful information. . . . [Y]ou have to find that Polaroid had adverse information, that information was material — i.e., that it was important — and that Polaroid knowingly and deliberately withheld it. *And that's all we're asking you to do here.* (Emphasis supplied.)

910 F. 2d 10 (1st Cir. 1990).

The summation was not an inadvertence, but was in accord with plaintiffs's own testimony.

Q. Now, Mr. Backman, in this action you are not claiming, are you, that the financial information put out by Polaroid was in any way false and misleading, are you?
A. I think you'll have to refer to the complaint. I believe the failure to disclose is just as improper as providing false information. And I believe the essence of my suit deals with the failure to disclose. . . . I do claim it was false and misleading because the failure to disclose is just as misleading a (sic) improper disclosure.

This, of course, is not so, "Silence, absent a duty to disclose, is not misleading under Rule 10b-5." . . .

We have gone into this at length, not so much to show the emptiness of plaintiff's first claim — agreed to by the full panel — but to accent our finding that there had been no falsity or misleading by defendant in any respect. In eight years of preparation and twelve days of trial, the words misrepresentation and misleading never crossed plaintiffs' lips. . . .

It appeared that Dr. Edwin H. Land, the founder and at all times president or C.E.O. of Polaroid, had added to his invention of the world-famous instant still camera another exceptional invention — an instant movie camera, Polavision. It appeared throughout the case, however, that Polavision's sales appeal did not correspond with the quality of the invention. Launched in early 1978 with great fanfare, the estimates for fall, to which production had been geared, proved to be substantially excessive. As a result, in late October, Eumig, the Austrian manufacturer, having earlier been told to increase production, was instructed to reduce by 20,000. In mid-November Eumig was told to take out another 90,000 sets, and to halt production. Plaintiffs' panel brief, quoting the fortuitous

language of Eumig's cable acknowledgment, "to now finally stop production entirely," gives the impression that the halt was intended to be permanent. Conveniently, from plaintiffs' standpoint, dots in the quotation replace the subsequent sentence, "Steps have been taken to ensure a quick new start-up of production on a reduced scale." This omission aids plaintiffs in their recitation, the regrettable incorrectness of which we will come to, that "management knew that Polavision was a commercial failure." Thereafter, fourth quarter internal figures, not publicly released, confirmed that the original Polavision estimates (also not released) had been substantially excessive.

The next event was a newspaper release published on January 9, 1979, that Rowland Foundation, a charitable trust established by Dr. and Mrs. Land, was to sell 300,000 shares of Polaroid, in part for funds for a new project, and in part to diversify its portfolio. Defendant participated in the preparation of the release, but not in the action itself. It is not claimed that the release was in any way untrue. Plaintiffs' claim is misleading because additional information should then have been given the public. The sale was consummated on January 11. . . .

On February 22, 1979, immediately following the annual meeting, defendant announced further facts about Polavision's lack of success, and the market fell, shortly, by some 20%. . . .

Plaintiffs' brief now finds assisted misrepresentation because "Polaroid featured Polavision on the cover," plaintiffs point out that after President McCune "announced record worldwide sales and earnings for both the third quarter and the first nine months of 1978, . . . Mr. McCune noted that the Company's worldwide manufacturing facilities continue to operate at close to maximum capacity," whereas, in fact, Polavision's contract supplier, Eumig, was told, shortly before the report, to hold up on 20,000 units. We note, first, that the statement, taken as a whole, was true; it expressly recognized an absence of totality. Of more specific importance, it flagged, on three of its three and half pages of text, that Polavision's effect on earnings was negative. . . . With this emphasized three times, we ask did this report mislead investors to buy stock because Polavision was doing so well?

Plaintiffs quote *Roeder,* 814 F.2d at 26, that even a voluntary disclosure of information that a reasonable investor would consider material must be "complete and accurate." This, however, does not mean that by revealing one fact about a product, one must reveal all others, that, too, would be interesting, market-wise, but means only such others, if any, that are needed so that what was revealed would not be "so incomplete as to mislead." . . . Disclosing that Polavision was being sold below cost was not misleading by reason of not saying how much below. Nor was it misleading not to report the number of sales, or that they were below expectations. . . .

We come, next, to the January 9 Rowland Foundation sale release. There was nothing untrue or misleading in the release itself, but plaintiffs say, with support from the panel opinion, that it should have contained additional information in order to keep the November report from being misleading. . . .

Obviously, if a disclosure is in fact misleading when made, and the speaker thereafter learns of this, there is a duty to correct it. . . . In special circumstances, a statement, correct at the time, may have a forward intent and connotation upon which parties may be expected to rely. If this is a clear meaning, and there is a change, correction, more exactly, further disclosure, may be called for. . . . Fear that statements of historical fact might be claimed to fall within it, could inhibit disclosures altogether. And what is the limit? In the present case if the shoe were on the other

foot, and defendant could have, and had, announced continued Polavision profits, for how long would it have been under a duty of disclosure if the tide turned? Plaintiffs' contention that it would be a jury question is scarcely reassuring. . . .

After indicating reluctance to accept plaintiffs' contention that the Third Quarter Report was misleading when made, the panel opinion, in holding that it could be found misleading in light of later developments, said as follows.

> [E]ven if the optimistic Third Quarter Report was not misleading at the time of its issuance, there is sufficient evidence to support a jury's determination that the report's relatively brief mention of Polavision difficulties *became* misleading in light of the subsequent information acquired by Polaroid indicating the seriousness of Polavision's problems. This subsequent information included . . . Polaroid's decision to . . . stop Polavision production by its Austrian manufacturer, Eumig, *and its instruction to its Austrian supplier to keep this production cutback secret.* We feel that a reasonable jury could conclude that this subsequent information rendered the Third Quarter Report's brief mention of Polavision expenses misleading, triggering a duty to disclose on the part of Polaroid. (Emphasis in orig.)

At the time of the Rowland sale, while selling the stock had absolutely nothing to do with Polaroid's financial health. . . . some might find it less than forthcoming for the press release not to have at least mentioned Polavision's difficulties so that the investing public could assess for themselves the reasons behind the sale.

That this was an improper mix was made conspicuous by plaintiffs' oral argument.

> [W]e've cited the specific passages of Mr. McCune's testimony in our brief, where Mr. McCune testified that the expression, "continued to reflect substantial expenses" was intended to convey that that condition would continue in

the future. . . . What we're saying is that a jury could find that this statement, even if it wasn't misleading when issued, became misleading because of the forward-looking nature.

This is a failure to recognize that what Mr. McCune said was a single, simple, statement, that substantial expenses had made Polavision's earnings negative. Though the panel opinion characterized it as "relatively brief," it was precisely correct, initially. Even if for-ward-looking, it remained precisely correct thereafter. . . . In arguing that the statement did not "remain true," plaintiffs' brief, unabashedly, points solely to matters outside the scope of the initial disclosure, in no way making it incorrect or misleading, originally, or later.

The shell in plaintiffs' gun at trial . . . are all percussion cap and no powder. . . . Plaintiffs have no case.

Federal Trade Commission v. Colgate-Palmolive Co., et al.

Supreme Court of the United States

The basic question before us is whether it is a deceptive trade practice, prohibited by § 5 of the Federal Trade Commission Act, to represent falsely that a televised test, experiment, or demonstration provides a viewer with visual proof of a product claim, regardless of whether the product claim is itself true. The case arises out of an attempt by respondent Colgate-Palmolive Company to prove to the television public that its shaving cream, "Rapid Shave," outshaves them all. Respondent Ted Bates & Company, Inc., an advertising agency, prepared for Colgate three one-minute commercials designed to show that Rapid Shave could soften even the toughness of sandpaper. Each of the commercials contained the same "sandpaper test." The announcer informed the audience that, "To prove RAPID SHAVE'S supermoisturizing power, we put it right from the can onto this tough, dry sandpaper. It was apply . . . soak . . . and off in a stroke." While the announcer was speaking, Rapid Shave was applied to a substance that appeared to be sandpaper, and immediately thereafter a razor was shown shaving the substance clean.

The Federal Trade Commission issued a complaint against respondents Colgate and Bates charging that the commercials were false and deceptive. The evidence before the hearing examiner disclosed that sandpaper of the type depicted in the commercials could not be shaved immediately following the application of Rapid Shave, but required a substantial soaking period of approximately 80 minutes. The evidence also showed that the substance resembling sandpaper was in fact a simulated prop, or "mockup," made of plexiglass to which sand had been applied. However, the examiner found that Rapid Shave could shave sandpaper, even though not in the short time represented by the commercials, and that if real sandpaper had been used in the commercials the inadequacies of television transmission would have made it appear to viewers to be nothing more than

---

380 U.S. 374 (1964), 85 S. Ct. 1035, 13 L. Ed. 2nd 904. Opinion by Chief Justice Earl Warren.

plain, colored paper. The examiner dismissed the complaint because neither misrepresentation — concerning the actual moistening time or the identity of the shaved substance — was in his opinion a material one that would mislead the public.

The Commission, in an opinion dated December 29, 1961, reversed the hearing examiner. It found that since Rapid Shave could not shave sandpaper within the time depicted in the commercials, respondents had misrepresented the product's moisturizing power. Moreover, the Commission found that the undisclosed use of a plexiglass substitute for sandpaper was an additional material misrepresentation that was a deceptive act separate and distinct from the misrepresentation concerning Rapid Shave's underlying qualities. Even if the sandpaper could be shaved just as depicted in the commercials, the Commission found that viewers had been misled into believing they had seen it done with their own eyes. As a result of these findings the Commission entered a cease-and-desist order against the respondents.

An appeal was taken to the Court of Appeals for the First Circuit which rendered an opinion on November 20, 1962. That court sustained the Commission's conclusion that respondents had misrepresented the qualities of Rapid Shave, but it would not accept the Commission's order forbidding the future use of undisclosed simulations in television commercials. It set aside the Commission's order and directed that a new order be entered. On May 7, 1963, the Commission, over the protest of respondents, issued a new order narrowing and clarifying its original order to comply with the court's mandate. The Court of Appeals again found unsatisfactory that portion of the order dealing with simulated props and refused to enforce it. We granted certiorari, 377 U.S. 942, to consider this aspect of the case and do not have before us any question concerning the mis-

representation that Rapid Shave could shave sandpaper immediately after application, that being conceded. . . .

We are not concerned in this case with the clear misrepresentation in the commercials concerning the speed with which Rapid Shave could shave sandpaper, since the Court of Appeals upheld the Commission's finding on that matter and the respondents have not challenged the finding here. We granted certiorari to consider the Commission's conclusion that even if an advertiser has himself conducted a test, experiment or demonstration which he honestly believes will prove a certain product claim, he may not convey to television viewers the false impression that they are seeing the test, experiment or demonstration for themselves, when they are not because of the undisclosed use of mock-ups.

We accept the commission's determination that the commercials involved in this case contained three representations to the public: (1) that sandpaper could be shaved by Rapid Shave; (2) that an experiment had been conducted which verified this claim; and (3) that the viewer was seeing this experiment for himself. Respondents admit that the first two representations were made, but deny that the third was. The Commission, however, found to the contrary, and, since this is a matter of fact resting on an inference that could reasonably be drawn from the commercials themselves, the Commission's finding should be sustained. For the purposes of our review, we can assume that the first two representations were true; the focus of our consideration is on the third, which was clearly false. The parties agree that § 5 prohibits the intentional misrepresentation of any fact which would constitute a material factor in a purchaser's decision whether to buy. They differ, however, in their conception of what "facts" constitute a "material factor" in a purchaser's decision to buy. Respondents submit, in effect, that the only material facts are those which deal with the substantive qualities of a product.[1] The Commission, on the other hand, submits that the misrepresentation of *any* fact so long as it materially induces a purchaser's decision to buy is a deception prohibited by § 5.

The Commission's interpretation of what is a deceptive practice seems more in line with the decided cases than that of respondents. This Court said in *Federal Trade Comm'n v. Algoma Lumber Co.,* 291 U.S. 67, 78: "[T]he public is entitled to get what it chooses, though the choice may be dictated by caprice or by fashion or perhaps by ignorance." It has long been considered a deceptive practice to state falsely that a product ordinarily sells for an inflated price but that it is being offered at a special reduced price, even if the offered price represents the actual value of the product and the purchaser is receiving his money's worth.[2] Applying respondents' arguments to these cases, it would appear that so long as buyers paid no more than the product was actually worth and the product contained the qualities advertised, the misstatement of an inflated original price was immaterial.

It had also been held a violation of § 5 for a seller to misrepresent to the public that he is in a certain line of business, even though the misstatement in no way affects the qualities of the product. As was said in *Federal Trade Comm'n v. Royal Milling Co.,* 288 U.S. 212, 216:

> If consumers or dealers prefer to purchase a given article because it was made by a particular manufacturer or class of manufacturers, they have a right to do so, and this right cannot be satisfied by imposing upon them an exactly similar article, or one equally as good, but having a different origin.

The courts of appeals have applied this reasoning to the merchandising of reprocessed products that are as good as new, without a disclosure that they are in fact reprocessed. And it has also been held that it is a deceptive practice to misappropriate the trade name of another.

Respondents claim that all these cases are irrelevant to our decision because they involve misrepresentations related to the product itself and not merely to the manner in which an advertising message is communicated. This distinction misses the mark for two reasons. In the first place, the present case is not concerned with a mode of communication, but with a misrepresentation that viewers have objective proof of a seller's product claim over and above the seller's word. Secondly, all of the above cases, like the present case, deal with methods designed to get a consumer to purchase a product, not with whether the product, when purchased, will perform up to expectations. We find an especially strong similarity between the present case and those cases in which a seller induces the public to purchase an arguably good product by misrepresenting his line of business, by concealing the fact that the product is reprocessed, or by misappropriating another's trademark. In each the seller has used a misrepresentation to break down what he regards to be an annoying or irrational habit of the buying public — the preference for particular manufacturers or known brands regardless of a product's actual qualities, the prejudice against reprocessed goods, and the desire for verification of a product claim. In each case the seller reasons that when the habit is broken the buyer will be satisfied with the performance of the product he receives. Yet, a misrepresentation has been used to break the habit and, as was stated in *Algoma Lumber,* a misrepresentation for such an end is not permitted.

We need not limit ourselves to the cases already mentioned because there are other situations which also illustrate the correctness of the Commission's finding in the present case. It is generally accepted that it is a deceptive practice to state falsely that a product has received a testimonial from a respected source. In addition, the Commission has consistently acted to prevent sellers from falsely stating that their product claims have been "certified." We find these situations to be indistinguishable from the present case. We can assume that in each the underlying product claim is true and in each the seller actually conducted an experiment sufficient to prove to himself the truth of the claim. But in each the seller has told the public that it could rely on something other than his word concerning both the truth of the claim and the validity of his experiment. We find it an immaterial difference that in one case the viewer is told to rely on the word of a celebrity or authority he respects, in another on the word of a testing agency, and in the present case on his own perception of an undisclosed simulation.

Respondents again insist that the present case is not like any of the above, but is more like a case in which a celebrity or independent testing agency has in fact submitted a written verification of an experiment actually observed, but, because of the inability of the camera to transmit accurately an impression of the paper on which the testimonial is written, the seller reproduces it on another substance so that it can be seen by the viewing audience. This analogy ignores the finding of the Commission that in the present case the seller misrepresented to the public that it was being given objective proof of a product claim. In respondents' hypothetical the objective proof of the product claim that is offered, the word of the celebrity or agency that the experiment was actually conducted, does exist; while in the case before us the objective proof offered, the viewer's own perception of an actual experiment, does not exist. Thus, in respondents' hypothetical, un-

like the present case, the use of the undisclosed mock-up does not conflict with the seller's claim that there is objective proof.

We agree with the Commission, therefore, that the undisclosed use of plexiglass in the present commercials was a material deceptive practice independent and separate from the other misrepresentation found. . . .

We turn our attention now to the order issued by the Commission. . . . The Court of Appeals has criticized the reference in the Commission's order to "test, experiment or demonstration" as not capable of practical interpretation. It could find no difference between the Rapid Shave commercial and a commercial which extolled the goodness of ice cream while giving viewers a picture of a scoop of mashed potatoes appearing to be ice cream. We do not understand this difficulty. In the ice cream case the mashed potato prop is not being used for additional proof of the product claim, while the purpose of the Rapid Shave commercial is to give the viewer objective proof of the claims made. If in the ice cream hypothetical the focus of the commercial becomes the undisclosed potato prop and the viewer is invited, explicitly or by implication, to see for himself the truth of the claims about the ice cream's rich texture and full color, and perhaps compare it to a "rival product," then the commercial has become similar to the one now before us. Clearly, however, a commercial which depicts happy actors delightedly eating ice cream that is in fact mashed potatoes or drinking a product appearing to be coffee but which is in fact some other substance is not covered by the present order.

The crucial terms of the present order — "test, experiment or demonstration . . . represented . . . as actual proof of a claim" — are as specific as the circumstances will permit. If respondents in their subsequent commercials attempt to come as close to the line of misrepresentation as the Commission's order permits, they may without specifically intending to do so cross into the area proscribed by this order. However, it does not seem "unfair to require that one who deliberately goes perilously close to an area of proscribed conduct shall take the risk that he may cross the line," *Boyce Motor Lines, Inc. v. United States,* 342 U.S. 337, 340. In commercials where the emphasis is on the seller's word, and not on the viewer's own perception, the respondents need not fear that an undisclosed use of props is prohibited by the present order. On the other hand, when the commercial not only makes a claim, but also invites the viewer to rely on his own perception for demonstrative proof of the claim, the respondents will be aware that the use of undisclosed props in strategic places might be a material deception. We believe that respondents will have no difficulty applying the Commission's order to the vast majority of their contemplated future commercials. If, however, a situation arises in which respondents are sincerely unable to determine whether a proposed course of action would violate the present order, they can, by complying with the Commission's rules, oblige the Commission to give them definitive advice as to whether their proposed action, if pursued, would constitute compliance with the order.

NOTES

1. Brief for Respondent Colgate, p. 16: "What [the buyer] is interested in is whether the actual product he buys will look and perform the way it appeared on his television set."
2. *Federal Trade Comm'n v. Standard Education Society,* 302 U.S. 112, 115–117, *Kalwajtys v. Federal Trade Comm'n.* 237 F.2d 654, 656 (C. A. 7th Cir 1956), cert. denied, 352 U.S. 1025.

CASE 1.   *Food Labels and Artful Sales*

Packaged foods in supermarkets contain a list of the ingredients on the package as well as other information. Much of that information is required by law. However, research has indicated that what is said or not said on the label has an important effect on the sales of the product.

In 1983, the Kellogg Company changed the names of two of its cereals from Sugar Frosted Flakes and Sugar Smacks to Frosted Flakes and Honey Smacks, respectively. At about the same time C.W. Post changed the name of its cereal Super Sugar Crisp to Super Golden Crisp. Market research had shown that some consumers reacted negatively to the word *sugar*. However, the sugar and sweetener content of the cereal continued to be at least 50 percent of the caloric intake.

Market research has also shown that some consumers react *positively* to the word *granola*. Granola bars saw retail sales grow 290 percent from 1980 through 1985 — the fastest growing segment of the candy bar market. Granola bars were first introduced into the market as health food products, and the ingredients were fashioned for consumers concerned about nutrition. However, many complained that they tasted like cardboard. Manufacturers then changed the products by adding peanut butter, chocolate chips, marshmallows, and sugar. Although the bars gradually became more like candy bars than

---

This case was written by Norman E. Bowie and Tom L. Beauchamp.

granola in their nutritional value and sugar content, they are slightly more nutritious than conventional candy bars. They have a higher fiber content, slightly less fat, and a higher percentage of complex carbohydrates. Advertising has continued to present the product with a healthful image, strengthening the public's association of the term *granola* with such concepts as "health food" and "healthy." Quaker Oats, General Mills, and Hershey Foods emphasize the "wholesomeness" and "goodness" of their granola bars in their advertising. In order to compete, conventional candy bar companies such as M&M/Mars have begun to advertise their products as healthy snacks.

The amount of sugar is not the only concern of consumers. Also important is the amount of complex carbohydrates, protein, and vitamins a food contains, as well as its fat content, sodium content, and calories. Although this information is printed on the label, the numbers found there are a function of serving size and are often presented in a way difficult for many persons to interpret. The consumer's information is specified in protein content, calories, and the like *per serving*, but the larger the serving size, the higher the numbers are likely to be. Reducing the serving size lowers the number of calories and the amount of sodium. Companies have therefore begun describing as a "serving" an amount that is much less than most people ordinarily serve themselves.

Around 1982, the Campbell's Soup Company reduced its serving size from ten ounces to eight ounces. A can of Campbell's soup that once had held two servings now held two and one-half servings. As a result, the calorie and sodium levels per serving fell. The Campbell Soup Company said that "people are eating less" and "most bowls hold eight ounces."

Questions

1. Are such marketing practices by candy, cereal, and soup companies manipulative? Deceptive?

2. Should companies be permitted to change the name, contents, or serving size without changing the product or the amount of the product?

3. The term *sugar-free* literally means "free of sucrose." Since many people purchase sugar-free foods to assist them with weight loss, should a standard be required so that "sugar-free" means "free of any high-calorie sweetener"?

4. Flexi-labeling permits wording such as "contains one or more of the following." Hence, the statement that a product "contains sunflower oil, coconut oil, and/or palm oil" is legally permitted. However, sunflower seed oil is a polyunsaturated fat, whereas the other two are saturated fats. Since polyunsaturated fats are more healthy, should flexi-labeling be prohibited?

CASE 2. *The Conventions of Lying on Wall Street*

Salomon Brothers, Inc., is one of forty firms authorized to purchase U.S. Treasury notes from the U.S. government for resale to private investors. These notes are sold periodically at Treasury auctions. Before each auction, a firm receives "buy" orders from customers. The firm then tries to buy securities at the lowest possible price. The government places some restrictions on the bidding. First, a firm may purchase no more than 35 percent of the notes offered at a given auction for its portfolio. Second, if a firm holds large orders from an investor, it can buy bonds directly for that customer, and these bonds are *not* included in the 35 percent limit. If a firm is unable to purchase enough securities to fill the orders from its customers, the firm must then buy from competing firms at a higher rate than the auction rate.

In July 1991, Salomon Brothers, Inc., confessed to illegally purchasing U.S. Treasury notes on three separate occasions. They exploited the system in two ways. First, at the December, February, and May auctions, Salomon used customers' names to submit false bids. That is, they ordered bonds for customers who had *not* placed orders and did not know their names were being used. After the auction, Salomon added these bonds to its own portfolio. On a second occasion, Salomon worked with a customer to purchase a large quantity of bonds in the customer's name. Salomon then bought back a portion of the bonds, effectively making a net purchase from the auction greater than 35 percent. Using this strategy, Salomon purchased 46 percent of Treasury notes sold on one occasion and 57 percent of the securities sold on another occasion.

Treasury auctions are also affected by the prevalent practice of sharing information. Current and former traders at several prominent Wall Street investment banks admit they regularly have shared "secrets" about the size and price of their bids at government auctions. This collusion to create a low bidding strategy results in firms paying less to the federal government. Consequently, the government makes less money to finance debt, causing an increase in taxes and interest rates.

This collusion is further complicated by strategies of deception. Lying has been tolerated and indeed has been expected for many years as part of the competition for trading. "It is part of the playing field. It's ingrained in the way the Street operates," one industry executive says, "I've stood out there on that trading floor and they lie to each other (before the auctions). That's part of the game. It was an exception when traders actually told the truth to each other about their bidding strategy." He adds, "They lie through their teeth to each other. You want to catch the [other] guy in an awkward position and pick him off."

In a report to the U.S. Congress, the Federal Home Mortgage Company claimed that two-thirds of Wall Street firms that it regularly deals with have lied to the agency to increase the chances of buying as many of the agency's securities as possible. Such deceit is so pervasive and routine on Wall Street that it has come to be regarded as the preferred and accepted way of doing business — the "standard of practice," as some put it. The common practice of submitting inflated orders has come under scrutiny from securities firms

---

This case was prepared by Tom L. Beauchamp and revised by Jeff Greene.

and the Federal Trade Commission, but the practice is so pervasive that it cannot be easily remedied. A small group of dealers holds purchasing power on the market and has long operated with financial success and with no serious challenges to its mode of operation.

One bond market specialist says, "I'm not condoning it or excusing it or saying it didn't go to an extreme . . . but people forget that the markets which are under the spotlight are part of that kind of distribution activity which for centuries has [been] associated with a fair amount of caveat emptor and puffery." The traditions of bluffing, deception, and puffery have created an environment in which every player in the "game" expects deception as the condition for playing.

Questions

1. Is Wall Street actually a "game," and can these allegations and expectations be applied equally to every participant?
2. Should the FTC ignore deceit and collusion on Wall Street since it is ingrained in the system? Why or why not?
3. Does Wall Street have a valid standard of practice for disclosing information?

CASE 3. *Green Advertising*

In a recent environmental study, 83 percent of respondents said they prefer buying environmentally safe products, and 37 percent claimed they would pay up to 15 percent more for environmentally safe packaging. These findings present the marketer with a tangible incentive. The practice of so-called green promotion and advertising is an attempt to use corporate publicity to create a message of corporate initiative in creating a healthier, improved natural environment. In a typical example, in 1990 Japan's Kirin Beer launched its "Earth Beer" to be marketed worldwide with a picture of the earth on a green label. Promotionally, Kirin claimed that the product was "earth friendly." However, this beer was not produced or packaged differently from Kirin's original products or the products of other beer manufacturers. Kirin has not been the only company to try to fill the consumer's desire for environmentally friendly products. In 1988 only 2.8% of all new products touted an environmental advantage, but this number jumped to 13.0% in 1993 and 10.5% in 1994.

The rise of green promotion poses this question: are companies taking action to improve the environment, or is it purely publicity? Friends of the Earth President Brent Blackwelder claims that, in many cases, green advertising is not warranted by the conduct of the corporation. For example, he claims that DuPont is not a conscientious protector of the environment, although it uses green advertising. Blackwelder contends that "it's morally reprehensible to portray this type of image [in advertising] when they have this type of track record."

The background of his position on DuPont is as follows. In September 1991, DuPont launched a television ad campaign featuring barking sea lions, jumping dol-

This case was prepared by Katy Cancro and revised by Jeff Greene, using articles in *Advertising Age* in May, June, and September 1991, a Reuters report in *The Washington Post*, August 28, 1991, and *The Journal of Advertising*, Summer 1995, special issue.

phins, and other animals enjoying fresh, unpolluted seas. The ad strongly implied that DuPont was making major changes to protect the environment. A Friends of the Earth report, by contrast, claimed that DuPont had the highest ratio of pollution to profit (14 percent) and that the company paid nearly $1 million monthly from 1989 to June 1991 in fines for environmental infractions. The report also noted that after the devastating 1990 Exxon tanker accident, DuPont's oil-marketing subsidiary promoted its plans to build two new double-hulled tankers to prevent oil spills as a unique environmental strategy. However, since one out of every six crude oil tankers was already double hulled, DuPont's "change" was not a new initiative.

In response to these claims, DuPont issued a public statement that said, "It seems to be a rehash of several of DuPont's most serious environmental challenges — all of which we are working diligently to resolve." DuPont also noted that it had begun working on several new projects to benefit the environment. For example, DuPont had begun developing a chemical to reduce ozone-depleting fluorocarbons and had initiated a buyback of fluorocarbon-producing products in an effort to preserve the ozone layer.

The Federal Trade Commission held public hearings in the summer of 1991 to investigate claims of deceptive green advertising. The following year, in July 1992, the commission issued *Guides for the Use of Environmental Marketing Claims*. The publication attempted to prevent some of the bogus claims that companies were making about their products and to assist the consumer in identifying products that really are making a difference in improving the environment.

Questions

1. Is environmental advertising sometimes no more than a new form of deceptive advertising? What makes it deceptive, if it is?

2. Does green advertising damage the consumer, or is it a harmless method of developing the reputation of the corporation?

3. To what extent should companies be held responsible for demonstrating a track record of environmental preservation that corresponds to its green advertising?

4. Should green advertising be federally regulated?

CASE 4.   *Computer Math for Car Loans*

It is not unusual for automobile dealers to offer customers a financing plan to facilitate a new car purchase. These dealers often say that a customer can borrow money at a stated rate of interest, deposit it in a bank at a lower rate, and come out ahead. To sell this idea, dealers are using an Automatic Data Processing (ADP) computer software program that computes the amount of interest the customer will pay on a car loan and the amount the customer will earn on the same sum deposited in a certificate of deposit or savings account for the same length of time. The presentation to the customer is that the interest

---

This case was prepared by Katy Cancro and Tom L. Beauchamp from interviews with automobile dealers and by reference to "Computer Car-Loan Math Doesn't Add Up," by Albert B. Crenshaw (*Washington Post*, August 31, 1991, p. C1); and "Firm, FTC Settle Charges on Claims in Auto Financing," by Gilbert Fuchsberg (*Wall Street Journal*, August 31, 1991, p. 3).

earned on the deposit will usually exceed the amount paid on the loan, even if the loan rate is considerably higher.

Here is a typical example used in the presentation. A customer borrows $6,469.31 for 36 months at 13 percent interest. He or she will pay $1,417.22 in interest over the three years, a figure based on a declining balance as he or she pays off the loan; the total to be paid is $7,882.52 in both principal and interest. By borrowing the money, the customer is able to leave his or her $6,469.31 in a bank account at 7.5 percent interest. In the account, the customer will earn $1,650.60 in 36 months, for a total balance of $8,119.91. From this presentation, it appears that the customer would save $233.39 by borrowing the money and leaving cash in the bank.

The Federal Trade Commission claims that although this software is mathematically correct, it presents an incomplete and misleading picture to the customer. It is impossible to save money by borrowing at a higher interest rate than that which one earns from an investment. To return to the example, one cannot borrow money at 13 percent interest, earn 7.5 percent on savings, and come out ahead. The ADP software does calculate the correct interest rate, but it calculates these rates with two different methods. It does not take into account repayment of the loan principal with the amount of interest generated from the savings account. As a customer repays the loan in monthly increments, the interest he or she earns on the savings decreases; over 36 months of withdrawals, the actual interest on the remaining balance in the account would be far less than $1,417.22. Therefore, interest on the savings account will be lower than the interest paid to the dealer when the car owner withdraws money to pay off the car.

Studies suggest that the average consumer does not have the ability to identify this discrepancy and to recalculate the actual amount of money he or she will spend on the car, taking into account the decrease in cash in the bank. As a result, consumers may make financially unsound decisions and incur a net financial loss.

For this reason the FTC sought and consummated an agreement with Automatic Data Processing that would alter the software provided to automobile dealers. ADP is prohibited by this agreement from continuing to represent the value of financing as it had; ADP agreed to delete the charts shown on the screen to customers. However, the company refused to admit that the software was actually misleading or defective, and the FTC did not require such an acknowledgment. In response to FTC claims, Arthur Weinbach, senior vice president of ADP, contended that many other software programs on the market "basically do the same thing. It's been a standard industry practice."

Mr. Weinbach appears to be correct. Moreover, automobile dealers were not required by the FTC agreement to stop using their own sales approaches or charts to augment the ADP software. Many automobile dealers have continued to use the same approach even though they lack on-screen charts to show to customers. There is no regulation prohibiting automobile dealers from presenting information in this manner, and it has become standard practice to do so. As they have done even before the ADP software, dealers continue to lead consumers to believe that they can save money by financing a car.

Questions

1. Has the FTC in any way helped the consumer? Should the consumer be helped?
2. Is ADP merely providing dealers with a more graphic presentation of what they say anyway? Is ADP guilty of consumer deception, or is it a legitimate "buyer beware" situation?

CASE 5.   *Marketing the Giant Quart*

Your company sells its products only in the state of New Wyoming, where state law does not prohibit marketing your cola in "giant quarts." A quart is a standard measure, so a giant quart is the same size as an ordinary quart. A survey conducted by your firm indicates that 40 percent of cola buyers think that a giant quart is larger than a regular quart.

Questions

1. Would it be deceptive marketing to call your bottle a giant quart?

2. Does it make any difference in the ethics of marketing as to what percentage of cola buyers think that a giant quart is larger than a regular quart?

3. Suppose a firm sold a half gallon of soda for $.99. In ads, the half-gallon size was called the giant size. The firm finds it necessary to increase the price of soda to $1.09. With the new price comes a new name — the giant economy size. Is the use of the new name deceptive?

4. Should there be a standard according to product for large, extra large, giant, and family sizes? Why?

Suggested Supplementary Readings

ALLMON, DEAN E., and JAMES GRANT. "Real Estate Sales Agents and the Code of Ethics." *Journal of Business Ethics* 9 (October 1990).

ALWITT, LINDA F., and ANDREW A. MITCHELL, eds. *Psychological Processes and Advertising Effects: Theory, Research, and Applications.* Hillsdale, NJ: Lawrence Erlbaum Associates, Publishers, 1985.

BEAUCHAMP, TOM L. *Case Studies in Business, Society, and Ethics.* 3rd ed. Englewood Cliffs, NJ: Prentice-Hall, 1993. Chap 2.

BELLIZZI, JOSEPH, and ROBERT HITE. "Supervising Unethical Salesforce Behavior." *Journal of Marketing* 53 (April 1989).

BROCKWAY, GEORGE. "Limited Paternalism and the Salesperson: A Reconsideration." *Journal of Business Ethics* 12 (April 1993): 275–80.

Business and Professional Ethics Journal 3 (Spring–Summer 1984). The entire issue is devoted to ethical issues in advertising.

CAMENISCH, PAUL. "Marketing Ethics." *Journal of Business Ethics* 10 (April 1991).

COHEN, WILLIAM, and HELENA CZEPIEC. "The Role of Ethics in Gathering Corporate Intelligence." *Journal of Business Ethics* 7 (March 1988): 199–203.

CRISP, ROGER. "Persuasive Advertising, Autonomy, and the Creation of Desire." *Journal of Business Ethics* 6 (1987): 413–18.

DABHOLKAR, PRATIBHA A., and JAMES J. KELLARIS. "Toward Understanding Marketing Students' Ethical Judgement of Controversial Personal Selling Practices." *Journal of Business Research* 24 (June 1992): 313–29.

DE CONICK, J. B., and D. J. GOOD. "Perceptual Differences of Sales Practitioners and Students Concerning Ethical Behavior." *Journal of Business Ethics* 8 (September 1989) 667–76.

FULD, LEONARD M. *The New Competitor Intelligence: The Complete Resource for Finding, Analyzing, and Using Information about Your Competitors.* New York: John Wiley & Sons, Inc., 1995.

HALLAQ, JOHN H., and KIRK STEINHORST. "Business Intelligence Methods — How Ethical." *Journal of Business Ethics* 13 (October 1994): 787–94.

HARE, R. M. "Commentary on Beauchamp's 'Manipulative Advertising'." *Business Professional Ethics Journal* 3 (Spring–Summer 1984): 23–28.

HITE, ROBERT E., and others. "A Content Analysis of Ethical Policy Statements Regarding Marketing Activities." *Journal of Business Ethics* 7 (October 1988).

HOLLEY, DAVID M. "A Moral Evaluation of Sales Practices." *Business and professional Ethics Journal* 5 (1986): 3–21.

HUNT, SHELBY D., and LAWRENCE CHONKO. "Ethical Problems of Advertising Agency Executives." *Journal of Advertising* 16 (1987).

JONES, GARY E. "Lying and Intentions." *Journal of Business Ethics* 5 (August 1986): 347–49.

KAUFMANN, PATRICK J., N. CRAIG SMITH, and GWENDOLYN K. ORTMEYER. "Deception in Retailer High-Low Pricing: A 'Rule of Reason' Approach." *Journal of Retailing* 70 (Summer 1994): 115–38.

KING, CAROLE. "It's Time to Disclose Commissions." *National Underwriter* 94 (November 19, 1990).

LACZNICK, GENE R., and PATRICK E. MURPHY, eds. *Marketing Ethics.* Lexington, MA: Lexington Books, 1985.

LEISER, B. "The Ethics of Advertising." In *Ethics, Free Enterprise, and Public Policy,* edited by Richard DeGeorge and Joseph Pichler. New York: Oxford University Press, 1978.

MACHAN, TIBOR R. "Advertising: The Whole or Only Some of the Truth?" *Public Affairs Quarterly* 1 (October 1987): 59–71.

OAKES, G. "The Sales Process and the Paradoxes of Trust." *Journal of Business Ethics* 9 (August 1990): 671–79.

PERKINS, ANNE G. "Advertising: The Costs of Deception." *Harvard Business Review* 72 (May–June 1994): 10–11.

PETERSON, ROBIN T. "Physical Environment Television Advertisement Themes." *Journal of Business Ethics* 10 (March 1991).

PRESCOTT, JOHN E. *Advances in Competitive Intelligence.* Vienna, VA: Society of Competitor Intelligence Professionals, 1989.

QUINN, JOHN F. "Moral Theory and Defective Tobacco Advertising and Warnings." *Journal of Business Ethics* 8 (November 1989).

SCHULTZ, NORMAN O., ALLISON B. COLLINS, and MICHAEL MCCULLOCH. "The Ethics of Business Intelligence." *Journal of Business Ethics* 13 (April 1994): 305–14.

SMITH, N. CRAIG, and JOHN A. QUELCH. *Ethics in Marketing Management.* Homewood, IL: Irwin, 1992.

SULLIVAN, ROGER J. "A Response to 'Is Business Bluffing Ethical?'" *Business and Professional Ethics Journal* 3 (Winter 1984).

WILLIAMS, GERALD J. *Ethics in Modern Management.* New York: Quorum Books, 1992.

Chapter Eight

— • —

Ethical Issues
in International Business

Perhaps the most important development in business in the past decade has been the recognition that markets are now international. Every U.S. firm realizes that competitors for its market share could come from any corner of the globe. Even fairly small regional firms now attempt to market their products internationally. Any firm concerned with its survival must adopt an international perspective.

Of course there is much more to the awareness of international issues than the development of international markets. International travel is becoming more prevalent, and many more people from abroad are visiting the United States. In addition, many problems that affect one country have an impact on other nations. For example, the disaster at the Soviet nuclear power plant in Chernobyl illustrated that pollution respects no national boundaries.

The subject of ethical issues in international business has no shortage of topics. Bribery is a common problem, as is the marketing of pesticides and the obligations of wealthy economies to so-called lesser developed countries. Before we can address these specific issues with much authority, an overarching problem needs to be addressed. There is a wide variety of opinion on what is acceptable conduct in international business, and a general skepticism prevails that questions whether there are any universal norms for ethical business practice. Since opinions on whether U.S. companies should bribe when conducting business in certain foreign countries depend in part on whether one believes there is a universal norm that bribery is unethical, the issue of international business norms needs to be addressed at the outset.

ARE THERE INTERNATIONAL NORMS
OF BUSINESS PRACTICE?

A U.S. company involved in business abroad must face the question, "When in Rome, should it behave as the Romans do?" This question arises not only for U.S. firms doing business abroad but for non-U.S. firms doing business in the United

States. One is tempted to answer the question as follows: When operating abroad, a firm should always obey the law of the host country. But this answer is inadequate on a number of grounds. First, many differences in business practices between the home country (where the firm is headquartered) and host country are not matters governed by host country law. As noted in Chapter 5, employment at will is both legal and widely practiced in the United States. In Japan employment at will is not the customary business practice. When Japanese auto companies built auto assembly plants in the United States, the executives of these companies could not have looked to U.S. law to instruct them as to whether they should adopt the U.S. employment-at-will practice. Under U.S. law, employment at will is legally permitted, but it is not legally required. Second, it is immoral for a company to obey an unjust law. The most that can be said is that corporations should obey the law of the host country as long as the law does not require the corporation to violate a universal moral norm.

How should a corporation behave when business norms of the host country differ from those of the home country and when host country law is silent concerning how business must behave? The multinational firm has at least four options: (1) Follow the norms of its home country because that is the patriotic thing to do; (2) follow the norms of the host country to show proper respect for the host country's culture; (3) follow whichever norm is most profitable; (4) follow whichever norm is morally best. (Note that these four alternatives are not all mutually exclusive; for example, following the fourth option might require following the second one as well.)

There may be no one appropriate course of action for a multinational business to take. In highly developed industrialized countries, option 3 seems to be a permissible course of action. One might think that choosing option 3 would require following option 2 as well because the most profitable way to conduct business is to follow the practices of the host country. However, Japanese companies operating in the United States have consistently not followed U.S. norms (option 2). Rather, Japanese companies have imported traditional Japanese management practices into the United States.[1] The results have been mixed, but on balance Japanese businesses operating in the United States that obey Japanese management principles are equal or superior in profitability to competing U.S. firms. One U.S. Honda plant that is operated on Japanese management principles is even more productive than comparable Honda plants in Japan. The importing of Japanese management practices with respect to employees into the United States has not created any appreciable resentment from U.S. citizens.

In his article, Iwao Taka provides the religious and philosophical basis for business ethics in Japan. As a result, certain practices that would be morally questionable in our culture are seen as morally appropriate or even required in Japanese culture. Consider the keiretsu system which is so often criticized in the United States as being anticompetitive and hence unfair. In a keiretsu system the capital for each firm is supplied by the banks in that firm's keiretsu, and the firm uses a limited number of suppliers from that firm's keiretsu. The fact that a supplier outside the keiretsu could provide a product at a cheaper price is not normally a decisive criterion. Since foreign (non-Japanese) firms are not members of any Japanese keiretsu, they have an especially difficult time breaking into the Japanese market. However, as Taka points out, the special treatment given keiretsu members is consistent with what Taka calls the Concentric Circles view of ethical obligations. One's ethical obligations are greatest to those close to you, e.g., family, and are least to those most different from you, e.g., foreigners. As Taka says, this ethical point of view rests in turn on Confucianism which permits "people to treat others in proportion to the intimacy of their relations."

Understanding Japanese ethics also explains some of the criticisms that the Japanese level against American business practice. They believe that American firms are short-sighted, focusing only on the short term, that American executives are paid too highly, and that American companies lay off workers too quickly.

On the other hand, Taka realizes that Japan's ethical system is also subject to criticism. Japan should take its obligations to non-Japanese more seriously, even if foreigners are in the outermost circle. Japan also has been criticized for discriminating against women and for driving workers too hard so that some literally die from overwork (karoshi).

This discussion illustrates the importance of establishing the existence and content of international moral norms for business. In his article, Norman Bowie contends that any appeals to justify home country practices over host country practices or vice versa require an appeal to international moral norms. Bowie appeals to three considerations on behalf of international moral norms. First, widespread agreement already exists among nations, as illustrated by the large number of countries that are signatories to the United Nations Declaration of Universal Human Rights and by the existence of numerous international treaties establishing norms of business practice. Second, certain moral norms must be endorsed by each society if society is to exist at all. Corporations ought to accept the moral norms that make society, and hence business practice itself, possible. Third, certain moral norms are required if business practice is to function at all. Bowie uses Kantian arguments to show that business requires a moral norm that corporations keep their contracts. However, similar arguments could be based on utilitarian considerations. If certain moral rules or traits such as truth telling or honesty give a multinational corporation a competitive advantage, then eventually these moral norms or traits will be adopted by all multinationals because those that do not will not survive.

Thomas Donaldson argues that multinationals have a moral duty to honor fundamental rights. Donaldson proposes a threefold test that any rights claim must pass if it is to be considered a fundamental right. He proposes a list of ten such fundamental rights such as the right to own property, the right to physical security, and the rights to subsistence and a minimal education. A morally responsible multinational must honor the rights of the people in host countries. Does that mean that a company has an unlimited obligation to feed the poor and provide education? Donaldson argues that honoring fundamental rights imposes no such obligation, and he distinguishes three ways that rights can be infringed: (1) A person or corporation can take action to deprive people of their rights; (2) a person or corporation can fail to protect people from having their rights violated; and (3) a person or corporation can fail to aid people in achieving their rights. Donaldson argues that the duties of multinationals are limited. Multinationals do not have a duty to aid people in achieving their rights, nor do they have an unlimited duty to provide food and education. However, multinationals do have a duty to avoid depriving people of any of their fundamental rights. In the case of six fundamental rights, multinationals have an additional duty to help people from being deprived of their fundamental rights. The reader is invited to see how persuasive Donaldson's analysis is and how many conflicts between home and host country practices Donaldson's analysis can resolve. Sometimes it might be difficult to distinguish failing to aid (which is permitted) from failing to protect (which for six of the fundamental rights is not permitted). Conflicts also exist between home and host country business practices that the rights portion of Donaldson's theory may not resolve.

Moreover, the existence of universal moral norms or fundamental human rights does not mean that business practice need be the same in all countries even when there are significant differences in the economic development of countries. Neither does it mean that a multinational from a highly industrialized society has the same moral obligations when it does business in a poor country that the local businesses have. These points are convincingly argued by Richard De George, who considers what business ethics amounts to in Russia and Eastern Europe. Although De George believes that there are universal norms of business ethics, he also argues that in a country that lacks adequate property rights, that is plagued by corruption, and that has inadequate law enforcement, local business firms are permitted to deviate from some of the requirements of normal ethical business practice, for example, the paying of bribes for legitimate services. However, the fact that Russians are permitted to bribe does not mean that American or Japanese firms doing business in Russia are morally permitted to bribe. After all, a U.S. or Japanese multinational has alternative means to get the services it needs.

THE REGULATION OF INTERNATIONAL BUSINESS

At first one might think that international business cannot be regulated. After all, Ian Maitland's arguments against self-regulation in Chapter Three would apply with even greater force in the international arena. Secondly, there is no true international government. The authority of the United Nations is severely limited, especially its authority over business.

However, some regulation of international business is conducted by national governments. Do the laws of the United States protect U.S. citizens when they work for U.S. companies abroad? Rulings of the Supreme Court indicate that they do when Congress specifically indicates that they do. Whether Congress actually intended the protection of Title VII of the Civil Rights Act of 1964 to apply to U.S. citizens working abroad for a U.S. company was the subject in 1991 of U.S. Supreme Court case *Boureslan v. Aramco* (reprinted in part in the Legal Perspectives section of this chapter). When the Court ruled that Congress had not explicitly included citizens working for U.S. companies abroad, Congress was forced quickly to amend the law so that they could be included.

What about the rights of foreigners who are injured abroad by U.S. corporations? Do they have any rights to relief in American courts? Normally they do not under the doctrine of *forum non conveniens* (it is not the convenient forum). It makes more practical sense for foreigners to seek relief in the country where the injury took place. But, in *Dow Chemical Company and Shell Oil Company v. Domingo Castro Alfaro et. al.,* the Supreme Court of Texas disagrees. The reasoning of the Court is presented in the Legal Perspectives section of this chapter.

Perhaps the most controversial instance of the U.S. government's regulation of business practice abroad is the attempt to prevent American business people from paying bribes to government officials in order to secure business. In 1977 Congress passed the Foreign Corrupt Practices Act (FCPA), which made it illegal for U.S. companies to pay bribes in order to do business abroad. Several highly publicized incidents led to the passage of the act, but the most prominent was the resignation of Japanese Premier Tanaka in 1974 after being indicted for accepting $1.7 million in bribes from the Lockheed Corporation.

Before discussing the FCPA, a distinction should be made among facilitating payments, extortion, and bribery. These distinctions are important because the FCPA permitted facilitating payments by exempting customs agents and bureaucrats whose jobs were essentially ministerial and clerical and it permitted payments in cases of genuine extortion. The chief difference between bribery and extortion is who does the initiating of the act. A corporation pays a bribe when it offers to pay or provide favors to a person or persons of trust to influence the latters' judgment or conduct. A corporation pays extortion money when it yields to a demand for money in order to have accomplished what it has a legal right to have accomplished without the payment. The difference between extortion and a facilitating payment is often one of degree.

These distinctions are important because discussion and criticism of the FCPA often confuses these activities. For example, the major criticism of the act was that the FCPA made it difficult to do business abroad and put U.S. firms at a competitive disadvantage. Stories of government officials or employees of corporations who demand payment to unload perishables or get a telephone installed are used to attack the FCPA, but such payments are not bribes under the act and hence are permitted. These payments are considered to be facilitating payments.

Business leaders have argued that the FCPA has put U.S. firms at a competitive disadvantage and that U.S. export business has been hurt as a result. There is also a belief that U.S. companies are less likely to offer bribes. There is empirical evidence against these beliefs. For example, a study by Kate Gillespie showed that U.S. export business in the Middle East had not been lost.[2] Her analysis was based on data showing the share of U.S. exports of the total exports to the countries in the region from 1970–1982. The sole exception was Iran, and the explanation for the loss there had nothing to do with the FCPA. She also showed that from 1975 to 1979, U.S. corporations were nearly twice as often involved in financial scandals in the Middle East as were the multinationals of other countries, even though the U.S. share of the exports to these countries was never more than 20 percent. Gillespie did not distinguish cases of bribery from cases of extortion, so the data might show that U.S. companies were more likely to pay extortion money than other multinationals. In any case, a picture that paints the U.S. companies as moral heroes and their foreign competitors as bribers is not accurate. A recent analysis showed that most U.S. firms did not consider the FCPA a major impediment to obtaining markets abroad.[3]

Yet another criticism of the FCPA was that it was an example of moral imperialism in which the United States was forcing its moral views on the rest of the world. This argument is fallacious for at least three reasons. First, the FCPA did not force other countries or the multinationals of other countries to follow U.S. morality. It simply required U.S. companies to follow U.S. moral norms with respect to bribery when doing business abroad. Second, as seen in the discussion of pesticides, good reasons often dictate that U.S. companies should adopt U.S. standards rather than those of host countries. Third, the belief that bribery is an unethical business practice is not unique to the United States. Nearly all countries believe that bribery is wrong. The practice of bribery may vary among countries, but the belief that bribery is wrong is universal — or nearly so. Evidence for this claim can be found in the public reaction when it is exposed. Throughout the world there is moral outrage when bribery is discovered. The bribe taker is morally disgraced and is sometimes sent to prison. Recall that Japanese Premier Tanaka resigned in disgrace when it was discovered that he was a bribe taker. This reaction is hardly to be expected in a country where bribery is morally permitted.

Despite these empirical and moral arguments, FCPA critics were sufficiently influential to have the FCPA amended in 1988. Those favoring the amendments believe that the law still outlaws bribery but is less disadvantageous to U.S. multinationals. Critics of the amendments believe that the FCPA has been gutted. Bartley A. Brennan in his article provides a detailed analysis of the 1988 amendments and refers to them as the "death" of a law. Despite Brennan's arguments, some American firms believe the FCPA still has real teeth.[4]

Since there is no world government and since business practice differs throughout the world, in this age of internationalization of business some common standards for business practice are imperative. This need is particularly acute in light of the criticisms against multinationals launched by representatives of the lesser developed countries. Many informed commentators fear a growing split between the "haves" in the northern hemisphere and the "have nots" in the southern hemisphere. In addition, government officials in many countries are growing concerned about the ability of multinationals to subvert government economic activities. For example, multinationals can often use overseas operations to avoid taxes. Generally, government officials complain that multinationals use their economic power to gain favorable legislation or consideration at the expense of the public good. Although this complaint is most commonly made in lesser developed countries, it has been made in nearly every country. A few years ago, some U.S. officials contended that the Federal Reserve kept interest rates up so that the Japanese would not move their investment funds elsewhere and create a credit crunch. Some negotiated codes for the international conduct of business might lessen the number and intensity of the conflicts.

The advantages for domestic industry-wide codes discussed in Chapter 2 apply equally well for international industry-wide codes. Unfortunately the disadvantages of codes are even more acute in the international arena. Since a truly international code must apply to a number of different cultures, the drafters try to make code provisions general enough so that the codes win acceptance. As a result, however, international codes tend to be too general to implement in specific situations. Since most multinationals are from highly industrialized countries and since many of the criticisms of multinationals are from host countries that are underdeveloped countries, the latter advocate strict enforcement procedures with penalties for violation. The representatives of the developed countries resist such penalties, and disputes become political, contentious, and ultimately intractable. This inability to reach agreement has already occurred at meetings of the United Nations Conference on Trade and Development.

Despite great difficulties in negotiating international codes, the benefits justify the effort. International codes can take a number of forms. One of the more interesting codes emanating from the business community itself is the Caux Round Table Principles for Business. These principles, which are included in this chapter, originated as the Minnesota principles because they were developed by the Minnesota Center for Corporate Responsibility. These principles were based on the stakeholder philosophy discussed in detail in Chapter 2. Ryuzaburo Kaku, then Chairman of Canon, Inc., thought the Minnesota Principles had much in common with the Japanese concept of *kyosei* (roughly translated as "living together in harmony"). After the kyosei concept was incorporated into the principles, they were endorsed by a number of business leaders from Europe, Japan, and the United States who were meeting in Caux, Switzerland, in 1993. Efforts are now under way to increase the endorsements worldwide. In 1995 the principles were introduced to the Chinese, who are considering them. The attempt to have the principles endorsed worldwide is an extraordinary effort at international business self-regulation.

Other efforts at regulating international business are being undertaken by the U.N. and by regional governments. Several codes regulating international business are already working their way through the United Nations, but progress is often excruciatingly slow. For example, the United Nations Code of Conduct in Transnational Corporations has been under discussion since 1972. Other codes are more regional in nature and thus agreement is often quicker. Some of the agreements of the European Economic Community provide good models e.g. the "Guidelines for Multinational Enterprises" adopted by the Organization of Economic Cooperation and Development (OECD). Still another possibility for the development of international codes are self-regulatory codes developed by the industries in the different countries themselves. With respect to exporting hazardous products, guidelines have been adopted by the international pharmaceutical associations and the International Group of National Associations of Agrochemical Producers. As the United Nations or groups of sovereign states establish codes of conduct governing international business practice, one would predict a corresponding increase in the development of selfregulatory codes. The 1990s should be a fertile time of the development of international codes of business practice.

In his article, William Frederick examines six international codes of business practice to see if he can identify any common themes. He identifies a number of common themes such as the way multinationals should treat corporate stakeholders as well as guidelines on political payments and basic human rights. Having identified these common themes, Frederick wonders how this commonality arose. Some of it is based on shared experiences. As business becomes international, people become more knowledgeable about cultural differences in business practice and more aware of the difficulties these differences can create. Given the advantageous nature of international business, there is an incentive to resolve the difficulties those different business practices present. Common norms are then negotiated.

Interestingly, Frederick also appeals to Kantian norms, which seem to have a universal claim to validity. We are thus back at our starting point. Are there international norms of business conduct? Yes, but opinions might differ concerning how they arose. Some have argued that there are norms that are valid across cultures and that all or nearly all cultures recognize them. Others would argue that the utilitarian advantages of international business require that nations develop such norms in order to overcome the difficulties that different business practices create. On this view, the nations cannot afford not to have universal norms for business.

NOTES

1. For example, see "The Difference Japanese Management Makes," *Business Week,* July 14, 1986, pp. 47–50.
2. Kate Gillespie, "Middle East Response to the Foreign Corrupt Practices Act," *California Management Review* 29 (Summer 1987): 9–30.
3. "A World of Greased Palms," *Business Week,* November 6, 1995, 36–38.
4. "Greasing Wheels: How U.S. Concerns Compete in Countries Where Bribes Flourish," *Wall Street Journal,* September 29, 1995.

The Moral Obligations
of Multinational Corporations

Norman Bowie

Now that business ethics is a fashionable topic, it is only natural that the behavior of multinational corporations should come under scrutiny. Indeed, in the past few decades multinationals have allegedly violated a number of fundamental moral obligations. Some of these violations have received great attention in the press.

Lockheed violated an obligation against bribery. Nestlé violated an obligation not to harm consumers when it aggressively and deceptively marketed infant formula to uneducated poor women in Third World countries. Union Carbide violated either an obligation to provide a safe environment or to properly supervise its Indian employees.

Other violations have received less attention. After the Environmental Protection Agency prohibited the use of the pesticide DBCP, the American Vanguard Corporation continued to manufacture and export the product in Third World countries. U.S. cigarette companies are now aggressively marketing their products abroad. Such actions have been criticized because they seem to treat the safety of foreigners as less important than the safety of U.S. citizens. Other charges involve the violation of the autonomy of sovereign governments. Companies such as Firestone and United Fruit have been accused of making countries dependent on one crop, while Union Miniere and ITT were accused of attempting to overthrow governments.[1]

The charges of immoral conduct constitute a startling array of cases where multinationals are alleged to have failed to live up to their moral obligations. However, the charges are of several distinct types. Some have also been brought against purely domestic U.S. firms — for example, issues involving a safe working environment or safe products. Other charges are unique to multinationals — the charge that a multinational values the safety of a foreigner less than the safety of a home country resident. Still others are charges that companies try to justify behavior in other countries that is clearly wrong in the United States, for example, the bribing of government officials.

In this essay, I will focus on the question of whether U.S. multinationals should follow the moral rules of the United States or the moral rules of the host countries (the countries where the U.S. multinationals do business). A popular way of raising this issue is to ask whether U.S. multinationals should follow the advice "When in Rome, do as the Romans do." In discussing that issue I will argue that U.S. multinationals would be morally required to follow that advice if the theory of ethical relativism were true. On the other hand, if ethical universalism is true, there will be times when the advice would be morally inappropriate. In a later section, I will argue that ethical relativism is morally suspect. Finally, I will argue that the ethics of the market provide some universal moral norms for the conduct of multinationals. Before turning to these questions, however, I will show briefly that many of the traditional topics dis-

From Norman Bowie, "The Moral Obligations of Multinational Corporations," *Problems of International Justice* (edited by Steven Luper-Foy), 1988. Reprinted by permission of the author.

cussed under the rubric of the obligations of multinationals fall under standard issues of business ethics.

OBLIGATIONS OF MULTINATIONALS THAT APPLY TO ANY BUSINESS

As Milton Friedman and his followers constantly remind us, the purpose of a corporation is to make money for the stockholders — some say to maximize profits for the stockholders. According to this view, multinationals have the same fundamental purpose as national corporations. However, in recent years, Friedman's theory has been severely criticized. On what moral grounds can the interests of the stockholders be given priority over all the other stakeholders?[2] For a variety of reasons, business ethicists are nearly unanimous in saying that no such moral grounds can be given. Hence, business executives have moral obligations to all their stakeholders. Assuming that Friedman's critics are correct, what follows concerning the obligations of multinationals?

Can the multinationals pursue profit at the expense of the other corporate stakeholders? No; the multinational firm, just like the national firm, is obligated to consider all its stakeholders. In that respect there is nothing distinctive about the moral obligations of a multinational firm. However, fulfilling its obligations is much more complicated than for a national firm. A multinational usually has many more stakeholders. It has all the classes of stakeholders a U.S. company has but multiplied by the number of countries in which the company operates.[3]

It also may be more difficult for the multinational to take the morally correct action. For example, one of the appealing features of a multinational is that it can move resources from one country to another in order

to maximize profits. Resources are moved in order to take advantage of more favorable labor rates, tax laws, or currency rates. Of course, the pursuit of such tactics makes it more difficult to honor the obligation to consider the interests of all stakeholders. Nonetheless, the increased difficulty does not change the nature of the obligation; multinationals, like nationals, are required to consider the interests of all corporate stakeholders.

Should a multinational close a U.S. plant and open a plant in Mexico in order to take advantage of cheap labor? That question is no different in principle from this one: Should a national firm close a plant in Michigan and open a plant in South Carolina in order to take advantage of the more favorable labor climate in South Carolina? The same moral considerations that yield a decision in the latter case yield a similar decision in the former. (Only if the interests of Mexican workers were less morally significant than were the interests of U.S. workers could any differentiation be made.)

These examples can be generalized to apply to any attempt by a multinational to take advantage of discrepancies between the home country and the host country in order to pursue a profit. Any attempt to do so without considering the interests of all the stakeholders is immoral. National firms and multinational firms share the same basic obligations. If I am right here, there is nothing distinctive about the many problems faced by multinationals, and much of the discussion of the obligations of multinationals can be carried on within the framework of traditional business ethics.

DISTINCTIVE OBLIGATIONS

Certain obligations of multinationals do become distinctive where the morality of the host country (any country where the multinational has subsidiaries) differs from or contradicts the morality of the home country (the country where the multinational was legally created). The multinational faces a modern version of the "When in Rome, should you do as the Romans do?" question. That question is the focus of this essay.

On occasion, the "when in Rome" question has an easy answer. In many situations the answer to the question is yes. When in Rome a multinational is obligated to do as the Romans do. Because the circumstances Romans face are different from the circumstances Texans face, it is often appropriate to follow Roman moral judgments because it is entirely possible that Romans and Texans use the same moral principles, but apply those principles differently.

This analysis also works the other way. Just because a certain kind of behavior is right in the United States does not mean that it is right somewhere else. Selling infant formula in the United States is morally permissible in most circumstances, but, I would argue, it is not morally permissible in most circumstances to sell infant formula in Third World countries. U.S. water is safe to drink.

Many moral dilemmas disappear when the factual circumstances that differentiate two cultures are taken into account. It is important to note, however, that this judgment is made because we believe that the divergent practices conform to some general moral principle. The makers of infant formula can sell their product in an advanced country but not in a Third World country because the guiding principle is that we cannot impose avoidable harm on an innocent third party. Selling infant formula in underdeveloped countries would often violate that common fundamental principle; selling the formula in developed countries usually would not.

This situation should be contrasted with cases where the home and the host country have different *moral* principles. Consider different moral principles for the testing of new drugs. Both countries face the following dilemma. If there are fairly lax standards, the drug may have very bad side effects, and if it is introduced too quickly, then many persons who take the drug are likely to be harmed — perhaps fatally. On the other hand, if a country has very strict standards and a long testing period, the number of harmful side effect cases will be less, but a number of people who could have benefited from benign drugs will have perished because they did not survive the long testing period. Where is the trade-off between saving victims of a disease and protecting persons from possible harmful side effects? To bring this problem home, consider a proposed cure for cancer or for AIDS. Two different countries could set different safety standards such that plausible moral arguments could be made for each. In such cases, it is morally permissible to sell a drug abroad that could not yet be sold in the United States.

If all cases were like this one, it would always be morally permissible to do as the Romans do. But alas, all cases are not like this one. Suppose a country totally ignores the problem of side effects and has no safety standards at all. That country "solves" the trade-off problem by ignoring the interests of those who might develop side effects. Wouldn't that country be wrong, and wouldn't a multinational be obligated not to market a drug in that country even if the country permitted it?

If the example seems farfetched, consider countries that are so desperately poor or corrupt that they will permit companies to manufacture and market products that are known to be dangerous. This is precisely the charge that was made against American Vanguard when it exported the pesticide DBCP. Aren't multinationals obligated to stay out even if they are permitted?

That question leads directly to the question of whether multinationals always should do in Rome as the Romans do. To sort through that issue, Figure 1 may be useful. Thus far, I have focused on I and IIA. The remainder of the essay considers the range of ethical problems found in IIB.

In IIB4, the multinational has an obligation to follow the moral principles of the host country because on the issue at hand those of the host country are justified while those of the home country are not. Although Americans may believe that there are few such obligations because their moral principles are far more likely to be justified, it is not hard to think of a contrary case. Suppose it is a moral obligation in a host country that no corporation fire someone without due cause. In other words, in the host country employ-

ment at will is morally forbidden. Although I shall not argue for it here, I think the employment-at-will doctrine cannot stand up to moral scrutiny. Hence, in this case, multinationals are obligated to follow the moral principle of the host country. Except for economic reasons (falling demand for one's product), a multinational is morally obligated not to fire an employee without just cause.

In IIB3, if the moral principles with respect to a given issue are not justified, then the multinational is under no moral obligation to follow them (except in the weak sense where the multinational is under a legal obligation and hence under a moral obligation to obey the law). Actually, IIB3 can be

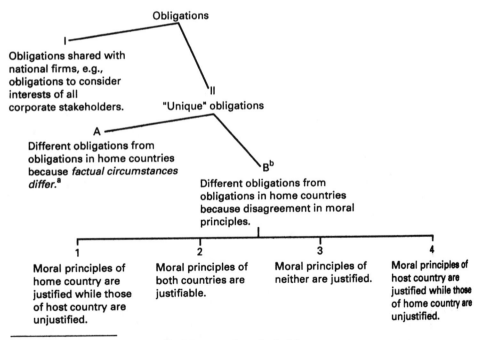

a In my view, different obligations still conform to universal principles.
b It is assumed that the different moral principles referred to here and below refer to the same moral issue. It is also stipulated that "unjustified" in IIB1 and IIB4 means that the unjustified principles are in conflict with the canons of justification in ethics.

FIGURE 1. Obligations of Multinationals

further subdivided into cases where the moral principles are not justified and where the moral principles cannot be justified. Theocratic states with moral principles based on revelation but not in contradiction with rationally justified moral principles are examples of the former. When the "moral" principles based on revelation are in contradiction with rationally justified moral principles, we have an example of the latter. In this latter case, a multinational is obligated not to follow the moral principles of the host country. In these cases, when in Rome, multinationals are not to do as the Romans do.

In Case IIB2, multinationals may do in Rome as the Romans do. In this case, the moral principles of the host country are justified.

Finally, in case IIB1, the multinational is obligated not to follow the moral principles of the host country. In these cases, the principles of the host country are contrary to the canons of ethics.

In summary, then, U.S. multinationals are obligated to do as the Romans do in IIB4, are permitted to do as the Romans do in IIB2 and in IIB3 where the moral principles of the Romans are consistent with what morality would justify. U.S. multinationals are obligated *not* to do as the Romans do in IIB1 and IIB3 where the moral principles of the Romans are inconsistent with what morality would justify.

Notice, however, that the entire analysis assumes there is some means of justifying ethical principles independent of the fact that a society believes they are justified. Otherwise, for example, I could not say that the moral principles of a home country are not justified while those of the host country are. But who is to say whether the moral principles of a country are justified or when they run counter to universal morality. Besides, perhaps there is no universal morality. What then?

RELATIVISM

Cultural relativism is the doctrine that what is right or wrong, good or bad, depends on one's culture. If the Irish consider abortion to be morally wrong, abortion *is* morally wrong in Ireland. If the Swedes do not consider abortion to be morally wrong, then abortion *is not* morally wrong in Sweden. There is no universal principle to which the Swedes and the Irish can appeal that determines whether abortion really is wrong or not.

If a person is a cultural relativist, then the implications for our discussion may seem quite clear. A corporation has an obligation to follow the moral principles of the host country. When one is in Rome, one is obligated to do as the Romans do. On our chart, IIB1, IIB3, and IIB4 have no referents. There are no members of those classes just as there are no members of the class of unicorns.

The officers and managers of many multinationals often speak and act as if cultural relativism were true. Who are we, they argue, to impose our moral standards on the rest of the world? For example, the U.S. Foreign Corrupt Practices Act, which prohibits the payment of unrecorded bribes to foreign governments or officials, has come under intense attack. After all, if the payment of bribes is morally acceptable in country X, why should we impose our moral views about bribery on that country. Besides, if U.S. multinationals do not bribe, German and Japanese multinationals will — or so the argument goes. Former president Jimmy Carter's attempt to include a country's record on violating or not violating fundamental human rights when making foreign policy decisions came under the same kind of criticism. Who is the United States to impose its moral values on others?

This relativistic way of thinking has always been prominent in the thinking of many social scientists. After all, discoveries by anthropologists, sociologists, and psychologists have documented the diversity of moral beliefs and punctured some of the pseudo-justifications that had been given for the superiority of white Western male ways of thinking. Philosophers, by and large, welcomed the corrections to prejudicial moral thinking, but, nonetheless, found the doctrine of cultural relativism seriously flawed.

Recently, however, the situation in philosophy has taken a surprising turn. A number of prominent philosophers have either seemed to embrace cultural relativism or have been forced by the "critics" to admit that their own philosophical positions may be consistent with it. Three examples should make the point.

In 1971, John Rawls published his monumental work *A Theory of Justice*. In that work, Rawls intended to develop a procedure (the original position) that would provide principles for a just society. Although these principles might be implemented in different ways by different societies, Rawls seemed to think that *any* just society would conform to these principles. In part, Rawls held this view because he believed the original position provided a universal justification for the principles of justice the original position produced. Early critics charged that the assumptions behind the original position were individualistic, liberal, Western, and democratic. The original position was biased in favor of individualistic Western democracies; it did not provide a universal method of justification. In a 1985 article in *Philosophy and Public Affairs*, Rawls admitted that his critics were right.

> In particular justice as fairness is framed to apply to what I call the basic structure of a modern constitutional democracy. . . . Whether justice as fairness can be extended to a general political conception for different kinds of societies existing under different historical and social conditions or whether it can be extended

> to a general moral conception . . . are altogether separate questions. I avoid prejudging these larger questions one way or the other.[4]

Another highly influential book in ethics, Alasdair MacIntyre's *After Virtue*, argued that the recent emphasis by ethicists on utilitarianism and deontology was seriously skewed. MacIntyre argued that a full moral theory must give a central place to the virtues. His own account was rich in description of the place of virtue in various societies. . . . However, MacIntyre's critics pointed out that what was considered a virtue in one society was frequently not considered a virtue in another — indeed one culture's virtue might be another culture's vice. MacIntyre now concedes that his earlier attempts to avoid these relativistic implications have largely failed.[5]

In theory, a cultural relativist could have two responses to CEOs of multinationals who wanted to know whether their personnel should behave, when in Rome, as the Romans do. Given that the morality of one culture cannot be shown to be superior to the morality of another, the personnel should follow the moral principles of the host country. Such an attitude of tolerance is the traditional response of most relativists.

But another response is possible. Even though the morality of one culture cannot objectively be shown to be superior to the morality of another, rather than embrace tolerance, once could simply assert the superiority of one's own culture. This is the approach taken by Richard Rorty, who has written extensively on the pretensions to objectivity in philosophy. In his 1984 article "Solidarity or Objectivity," he points out that the objectivist tries to create a dilemma for any subjectivist position. The dilemma is that

> either we attach a special privilege to our own community, or we pretend an impossible tolerance for every other group. I have been argu-

ing that we pragmatists should grasp the ethnocentric horn of this dilemma. We should say that we must, in practice, privilege our own group, even though there can be no noncircular justification for doing so.... We Western liberal intellectuals should accept the fact that we have to start from where we are, and that this means that there are lots of views which we simply cannot take seriously.[6]

But how would Rorty's quotation strike the CEO of a U.S. multinational? In this case, the personnel of a multinational should *not* follow the moral principles of the host country unless they are consistent with U.S. principles. But what would this mean in terms of business practice? Given that in U.S. culture, the capitalist Friedmanite principle — maximize profits! — is the cultural norm, a U.S. multinational with a plant in South Africa would not refuse to follow the rules of apartheid or pull out. It would locate in South Africa and conform to local custom so long as it could make a profit.

Although I argued earlier that the classical view of profit maximization is seriously flawed, I did not do so from Rorty's ethnocentric position. I assumed an objective universal moral standpoint, as have those who have criticized the classical view. If Rorty's theory is correct, there is no transcultural objective perspective; because the classical view is a central principle in U.S. business and legal culture, I assume Rorty would have to accept it.

Hence, whether we are cultural relativists or ethnocentrists, some disconcerting implications seem to follow.

1. A corporation has no obligation to follow the Sullivan principles[7] in South Africa.
2. A corporation that wants to do business with the Arabs has no moral obligation to refuse participation in a boycott against Israel as a condition for doing business with the Arabs.
3. A corporation has no obligation to refrain from doing business with a state that is in systematic violation of human rights.

If these implications do follow, there seems to be something wrong with the position that entails them. Even Ronald Reagan has forbidden U.S. firms from doing business with Libya. Some set of criteria is needed for indicating when multinationals are permitted to follow the moral principles of the host country and when multinationals are forbidden to follow host-country principles. What is also needed are some principles that tell U.S. multinationals when they have an obligation to refrain from doing business either *with* a foreign (host) government or *in* a host country. However, unless cultural relativism is false, these principles will never be forthcoming.

THE ADEQUACY OF CULTURAL RELATIVISM

Although our primary concern is the obligations of multinationals, some considerations of the adequacy of cultural relativism must be made before we can speak meaningfully about the obligations of multinationals. As a starting point, I adopt a strategy used by Derek Parfit to undermine the doctrine of prudentialism.[8] Consider a continuum with three positions:

Individual Relativism	Cultural Relativism	Universalism

Individual relativism is the view that what is right or wrong, good or bad, depends on the feelings or attitudes of the individual. If an individual believes abortion is wrong, then abortion is wrong for that individual. If another individual believes abortion is not wrong, then abortion is not wrong for that individual. There is no valid cultural norm that will tell us which individual is objectively right.

The strategy is to show that any argument the cultural relativist uses against universalism can also be used by the individual relativist against cultural relativism. Similarly, any argument the cultural relativist uses against the individual relativist can be used by the universalist against the cultural relativist. As Parfit would say, the cultural relativist is constantly fighting a war on two fronts.

In this discussion, one example of this strategy will have to suffice. First, against an individual relativist, a cultural relativist would often argue that if individual relativism were the prevailing view, a stable society would be impossible. Arguments from Thomas Hobbes or decision theory would prove the point. If individual relativism were the prevailing norm, life would be "nasty, brutish, and short."

But in the present world, any arguments that appeal to social stability will have to be applied universally. In the atomic age and in an age where terrorism is an acceptable form of political activity, the stability problems that afflict individual relativism equally afflict cultural relativism. If the necessity for social stability is a good argument for a cultural relativist to use against an individual relativist, it is an equally good argument for a universalist to use against a cultural relativist.

This brief argument has not refuted relativism. It has only shown that if the stability argument works for the cultural relativist against the individual relativist, the argument also works for the universalist against the cultural relativist. Moreover, to accept the argument this far is only to show that some universal moral norms are required for stable relationships. The argument itself does not provide those universal moral norms. Multinational CEOs are likely to accept the argument thus far, however, because multinationals need a stable international environment if they are to make a profit in the long run. As any adviser for any multinational will verify,

one of the chief factors affecting an investment decision in a foreign country is the political stability both of that individual country and of the region surrounding it. An unstable country or region is highly inimical to the conduct of international business.

THE MORAL MINIMUM FOR SOCIETY

Thus far we have established that multinational business requires stability and that commonly accepted moral rules are necessary for stability. But what specifically are these moral rules? To answer that question I will appeal to conceptual arguments that will assist in providing answers.

One argument that is especially effective against the charge of moral imperialism develops the point that some universal standards of conduct already have been accepted by all parties. Despite appearances to the contrary, a great deal of morality has already been internationalized either explicitly through treaty, through membership in the U.N., or implicitly through language and conduct. . . .

Note the following: The word *democracy* or *democratic* has become an honorific term. Nearly all national states claim they are democracies — people's democracies, worker democracies, but democracies nonetheless. The August 4, 1986, *Newsweek* carried a story about repression and the denial of civil rights in Chile. The president of Chile responded to his critics by calling his dictatorship a "democratic government with authority." I have yet to come across a state that brags it is not a democracy and has no intention of being one. (Some nations do indicate they do not want to be a democracy like the United States.) Hence, there is no moral imperialism involved in saying that host countries should be democracies. The controversy involves the question, What must a government be like to be properly characterized as a democracy?

A notion of shared values can be of assistance here as well. There is a whole range of behavior, such as torture, murder of the innocent, and racism, that nearly all agree is wrong. A nation-state accused of torture does not respond by saying that a condemnation of torture is just a matter of subjective morality. The state's leaders do not respond by saying, "We think torture is right, but you do not." Rather, the standard response is to deny that any torture took place. If the evidence of torture is too strong, a finger will be pointed either at the victim or at the morally outraged country. "They do it, too." In this case the guilt is spread to all. Even the Nazis denied that genocide took place. What is important is that *no* state replies there is nothing wrong with genocide or torture. Hence, the head of a multinational need have no fear of cultural imperialism when she or he takes a stand in favor of democracy and against torture and genocide.

This conceptual argument is buttressed by another. Suppose an anthropologist discovers a large populated South Pacific island. How many tribes are on the island? Part of the answer to that question will be determined by observing if such acts as killing and murder are permitted and if they are permitted, against whom are they permitted? If they are not permitted, that counts as evidence that there is only one tribe. If people on the northern half of the island permit stealing directed against southerners but do not permit northerners to steal from one another, that provides evidence that there are at least two tribes. What often distinguishes one society from another is the fact that society A does not permit murder, lying, and stealing against members of A — society A could not permit that and still be a society — but society A does permit that kind of behavior against society B. What this strategy shows is that one of the criteria for having a society is that there be a shared morality among the individuals that make up the society.

What follows from this is that there are certain basic rules that must be followed in each society — for example, do not lie; do not commit murder. There is a moral minimum in the sense that if these specific moral rules are not generally followed, then there will not be a society at all. These moral rules are universal, but they are not practiced universally. That is, members of society A agree that they should not lie to each other, but they think it is okay to lie to the members of other societies. Such moral rules are not relative; they simply are not practiced universally.

However, multinational corporations are obligated to follow these moral rules. Because the multinational is practicing business in the society and because these moral norms are necessary for the existence of the society, the multinational has an obligation to support those norms. Otherwise, multinationals would be in the position of benefiting from doing business with the society while at the same time engaging in activity that undermines the society. Such conduct would be unjust.

THE MORALITY OF THE MARKETPLACE

Given that the norms constituting a moral minimum are likely to be few in number, it can be argued that the argument thus far has achieved something — that is, multinationals are obligated to follow the moral norms required for the existence of a society. But the argument has not achieved very much — that is, most issues surrounding multinationals do not involve alleged violations of these norms.

Perhaps a stronger argument can be found by making explicit the morality of the marketplace. That there is an implicit morality of the market is a point that is often ignored by most economists and many businesspersons.

Although economists and businesspersons assume that people are basically self-interested, they must also assume that persons involved in business transactions will honor their contracts. In most economic exchanges, the transfer of product for money is not simultaneous. You deliver and I pay or vice versa. As the economist Kenneth Boulding put it: "without an integrative framework, exchange itself cannot develop, because exchange, even in its most primitive forms, involves trust and credibility."[9]

Philosophers would recognize an implicit Kantianism in Boulding's remarks. Kant tried to show that a contemplated action would be immoral if a world in which the contemplated act was universally practiced was self-defeating. For example, lying and cheating would fail Kant's tests. Kant's point is implicitly recognized by the business community when corporate officials despair of the immoral practices of corporations and denounce executives engaging in shady practices as undermining the business enterprise itself.

Consider what John Rawls says about contracts:

> Such ventures are often hard to initiate and to maintain. This is especially evident in the case of covenants, that is, in those instances where one person is to perform before the other. For this person may believe that the second party will not do his part, and therefore the scheme never gets going.... Now in these situations there may be no way of assuring the party who is to perform first except by giving him a promise, that is, by putting oneself under an obligation to carry through later. Only in this way can the scheme be made secure so that both can gain from the benefits of their cooperation.[10]

Rawls's remarks apply to all contracts. Hence, if the moral norms of a host country permitted practices that undermined contracts, a multinational ought not to follow them. Business practice based on such norms could not pass Kant's test.

In fact, one can push Kant's analysis and contend that business practice generally requires the adoption of a minimum standard of justice. In the United States, a person who participates in business practice and engages in the practice of giving bribes or kickbacks is behaving unjustly. Why? Because the person is receiving the benefits of the rules against such activities without supporting the rules personally. This is an example of what John Rawls calls freeloading. A freeloader is one who accepts the benefits without paying any of the costs.

> In everyday life an individual, if he is so inclined, can sometimes win even greater benefits for himself by taking advantage of the cooperative efforts of others. Sufficiently many persons may be doing their share so that when special circumstances allow him not to contribute (perhaps his omission will not be found out), he gets the best of both worlds.... We cannot preserve a sense of justice and all that this implies while at the same time holding ourselves ready to act unjustly should doing so promise some personal advantage.[11]

This argument does not show that if bribery really is an accepted moral practice in country X, that moral practice is wrong. What it does show is that practices in country X that permit freeloading are wrong and if bribery can be construed as freeloading, then it is wrong. In most countries I think it can be shown that bribery is freeloading, but I shall not make that argument here.

The implications of this analysis for multinationals are broad and important. If activities that are permitted in other countries violate the morality of the marketplace — for example, undermine contracts or involve freeloading on the rules of the market — they nonetheless are morally prohibited to multinationals that operate there. Such multinationals are obligated to follow the moral norms of the market. Contrary behavior is inconsistent and ultimately self-defeating.

Our analysis here has rather startling implications. If the moral norms of a host country are in violation of the moral norms of the marketplace, then the multinational is obligated to follow the norms of the marketplace. Systematic violation of marketplace norms would be self-defeating. Moreover, whenever a multinational establishes businesses in a number of different countries, the multinational provides something approaching a universal morality — the morality of the marketplace itself. If Romans are to do business with the Japanese, then whether in Rome or Tokyo, there is a morality to which members of the business community in both Rome and Tokyo must subscribe — even if the Japanese and Romans differ on other issues of morality.

THE DEFENSE OF MARKETPLACE MORALITY

Up to this point I have argued that multinationals are obligated to follow the moral minimum and the morality of the marketplace. But what justifies the morality of the marketplace? Unless the marketplace morality can be justified, I am stuck in Rorty's ethnocentrism. I can start only where I am, and there are simply a lot of views I cannot take seriously. If a CEO of a U.S. multinational should adopt such an ethnocentric position, she or

he would be accused of cultural imperialism. The claim of objectivity remains the central issue for determining the obligations of multinationals.

One possible argument is that capitalism supports democratic institutions. For example, Milton Friedman argues in *Capitalism and Freedom* that capitalism institutionally promotes political freedom.

> Economic arrangements play a dual role in the promotion of a free society. On the one hand freedom in economic arrangements ... is an end in itself. In the second place economic freedom is also an indispensable means toward the achievement of political freedom. ...
>
> No one who buys bread knows whether the wheat from which it is made was grown by a Communist or a Republican, by a constitutionalist or a Fascist, or for that matter by a Negro or a white. This illustrates how an impersonal market separates economic activities from political views and protects men from being discriminated against in their economic activities for reasons that are irrelevant to their productivity — whether these reasons are associated with their views or their color.[12]

Friedman also points out that freedom of speech is more meaningful so long as alternative opportunities for employment exist. However, these alternatives are impossible if the government owns and operates the means of production. In a private diversified economic community someone has a better chance to publish views that are contrary to the views of a given editor, the government, or even a majority of the public. Usually one can find some audience that is interested. Moreover, even publishers who disagree might still publish. Fear of competition often overcomes the distaste for certain ideas.

Indeed, one of the arguments for morally permitting multinationals to operate in nondemocratic countries is an extension of Friedman's point. Capitalism is allegedly a catalyst for democratic reform. If capitalism promotes democracy, then a moral argument can be made to justify capitalist investment in repressive regimes because investment will serve the moral end of making the government less repressive. This is precisely the argument that many have used to justify U.S. investment in South Africa. Indeed, the South African situation can serve as an interesting case study. The point of the Sullivan principles is to provide moral guidelines so that a company may be morally justified in having plants in South Africa without becoming part of the system of exploitation. The Sullivan principles also prevent profit-seeking corporations from morally justifying immoral behavior. No company can passively do as the South Africans do and then claim that its presence will bring about a more democratic, less racist regime. After all, if it is plausible to argue that capitalism can help create a democracy, it seems equally plausible to argue that a totalitarian regime may corrupt capitalism. The Sullivan principles help keep multinationals with South African facilities morally honest.

Moreover, the morality of the Sullivan principles depends on an empirical claim that profit-seeking corporations behaving in accordance with marketplace morality and acknowledging universally recognized human rights will in fact help transform totalitarian or repressive regimes into more democratic, more humane regimes. If that transformation does not take place within a reasonable amount of time, the moral justification for having facilities in that country disappears. Leon Sullivan recognized that point when he set May 31, 1987, as the deadline for reform of the South African government. When that reform was not forthcoming, he insisted that U.S. companies suspend operations in South Africa. . . .

What about the issue of human rights? Can multinationals ignore that question? No, they cannot. Part of what it means to be a democracy is that respect be shown for fundamental human rights. The only justification for a multinational's doing business with a regime that violates human rights is the claim that in so doing, the country's human rights record will improve. Again, business activity under that justification will have to be judged on results.

Even if the "contribution to democracy argument" is not convincing, there is another argument on behalf of the morality of the marketplace. On the assumption that a multinational business agreement is a voluntary exchange, the morality of the marketplace is voluntarily accepted. Economic prosperity seems to be highly desired by all countries. Given that multinational business is a device for achieving prosperity, participating countries voluntarily accept the morality of the market.

CONCLUSION

I have argued that on occasion multinationals have obligations that would require them *not* to do in Rome as the Romans do — for example, in those cases where Roman practice is in violation of marketplace morality. I have also provided arguments on behalf of marketplace morality, although those arguments require that businesses have obligations to pull out of oppressive countries if there is little hope of reform.

But the appeal to the morality of the marketplace has an added benefit. What often is forgotten by business is that the market is not a morally neutral, well-oiled machine; rather, it is embedded in morality and depends upon the acceptance of morality for its success. Ultimately, the obligations of multinationals, whether in Rome, Tokyo, or Washington, are the obligations required by the market. If corporations live up to those obligations, and if capitalism really could advance the cause of democracy and human rights throughout the world, then the morally responsible multinational could be a force for social justice. However, I regret to say that I am discussing a goal and a hope rather than a reality.

NOTES

I wish to thank Steven Luper-Foy for his helpful comments on an earlier version of this essay.

1. See "There's No Love Lost Between Multinational Companies and the Third World," *Business and Society Review* (Autumn 1974).

2. For the purpose of this discussion, a stakeholder is a member of a group without whose support the organization would cease to exist. The traditional list of stakeholders includes stockholders, employees, customers, suppliers, lenders, and the local community where plants or facilities are located.

3. Of course, one large U.S. company with 10 plants in 10 different states has more classes of stakeholders than 1 U.S. company with 1 U.S. plant and 1 foreign subsidiary.

4. John Rawls, "Justice as Fairness: Political Not Metaphysical," *Philosophy and Public Affairs* 14, no. 3 (Summer 1985):224–226. Also see John Rawls, *A Theory of Justice* (Cambridge, Mass.: Harvard University Press, 1971).

5. The most explicit charge of relativism is made by Robert Wachbroit, "A Genealogy of Virtues," *Yale Law Journal* 92, no. 3 (January 1983):476–564. For Alasdair MacIntyre's discussion, see "Postscript to the Second Edition" in *After Virtue*, 2nd ed. (Notre Dame: University of Notre Dame, 1984) and his Eastern Division American Philosophical Associa-

tion Presidential Address, "Relativism, Power and Philosophy" in *Proceedings and Addresses of the American Philosophical Association* 59, no. 1 (September 1985):5–22. Also see Michael Walzer, *Spheres of Justice* (New York: Basic Books, 1983).

6. Richard Rorty, "Solidarity or Objectivity," in *Post-Analytic Philosophy*, John Rajchman and Cornel West, eds. (New York: Columbia University Press, 1985), pp. 12–13.

7. The Sullivan code affirms the following principles: (1) that there be nonsegregation of the races in all eating, comfort, and work facilities; (2) that equal and fair employment practices be instituted for all employees; (3) that all employees doing equal or comparable work for the same period of time receive equal pay; (4) that training programs be developed and implemented that will prepare substantial numbers of blacks and other nonwhites for supervisory, administrative, technical, and clerical jobs; (5) that the number of blacks and other nonwhites in management and supervisory positions be increased; and (6) that the quality of employees' lives outside the work environment be improved — this includes housing, transportation, schooling, recreation, and health facilities.

8. See Derek Parfit, *Reasons and Persons* (New York: Oxford University Press, 1986), pp. 126–127.

9. Kenneth E. Boulding, "The Basis of Value Judgments in Economics," in *Human Values and Economic Policy*, Sidney Hook, ed. (New York: New York University Press, 1967), p. 68.

10. John Rawls, *A Theory of Justice* (Cambridge, Mass.: Harvard University Press, 1971), p. 569.

11. Ibid., p. 497.

12. Milton Friedman, *Capitalism and Freedom* (Chicago: University of Chicago Press, 1962), pp. 8, 21.

Fundamental Rights
and Multinational Duties

Thomas Donaldson

RIGHTS

Rights establish minimum levels of morally acceptable behavior. One well-known definition of a "right" construes it as a "trump" over a collective good, which is to say that the assertion of one's right to something, such as free speech, takes precedence over all but the most compelling collective goals, and overrides, for example, the state's interest in civil harmony or moral consensus.[1]

Rights are at the rock bottom of modern moral deliberation: Maurice Cranston writes that the litmus test for whether something is a right or not is whether it protects something of "paramount importance."[2] If I have a right to physical security, then you should, at a minimum, refrain from depriving me of physical security (at least without a rights-regarding and overriding reason). It would be nice, of course, if you did more: if you treated me charitably and with love. But you must *at a minimum* respect my rights. Hence, it will help to conceive the problem of assigning minimal responsibilities to multinational corporations through the question, "What specific rights should multinationals respect?"

Notice that the flip side of a right typically is a duty.[3] This, in part, is what gives aptness to Joel Feinberg's well-known definition of a right as a "justified entitlement *to* something *from* someone."[4] It is the "from someone" part of the definition that reflects the assumption of a duty, for without a correlative obligation that attaches to some moral agent or group of agents, a right is weakened — if not beyond the status of a right entirely, then significantly. If we cannot say that a multinational corporation has a duty to keep the levels of arsenic low in the workplace, then the worker's right not to be poisoned means little.

Often, duties fall upon more than one class of moral agent. Consider, for example, the furor over the dumping of toxic waste in West Africa by multinational corporations. During 1988, virtually every country from Morocco to the Congo on Africa's west coast received offers from companies seeking cheap sites for dumping waste.[5] In preceding years, the United States and Europe had become enormously expensive for dumping, in large part because of the costly safety measures mandated by U.S. and European governments. In February of 1988, officials in Guinea-Bissau, one of the world's poorest nations, agreed to bury 15 million tons of toxic wastes from European tanneries and pharmaceutical companies. The companies agreed to pay about 120 million dollars, which is only slightly less than the country's entire gross national product. And in Nigeria in 1987, five European ships unloaded toxic waste containing dangerous poisons such as polychlorinated biphenyls, or PCBs. Workers wearing thongs and shorts unloaded the barrels for $2.50 a day, and placed them in a dirt lot in a residential area in the town of Kiko. They were not told about the contents of the barrels.[6]

Who bears responsibility for protecting the workers' and inhabitants' rights to safety in such instances? It would be wrong to place it entirely upon a single group of agents such as the governments of West African nations. As it happens, the toxic waste dumped in Nigeria entered under an import permit for "nonexplosive, nonradioactive and non-self-combusting chemicals." But the permit turned out to be a loophole; Nigeria had not meant to accept the waste and demanded its removal once word about its presence filtered into official channels. The example reveals the difficulty many developing countries have in formulating the sophisticated language and regulatory procedures necessary to control high-technology hazards. It seems reasonable in such instances, then, to place the responsibility not upon a single class of agents, but upon a broad collection of them, including governments, corporate executives, host country companies and officials, and international organizations. The responsibility for not violating the rights of people living in West Africa to be free from the dangers of toxic waste, then, potentially falls upon every agent whose actions might harm, or contribute to harming, West African inhabitants. Nor is one agent's responsibility always mitigated when another "accepts" responsibility. To take a specific instance, corporate responsibility may not be eliminated if a West African government explicitly agrees to accept toxic waste. There is always the possibility — said to be a reality by some critics — that corrupt government officials will agree to accept and handle waste that threatens safety in order to fatten their own Swiss bank accounts.

In wrestling with the problem of which rights deserve international standing, James Nickel recommends that rights that possess international scope be viewed as occupying an intermediary zone between abstract moral principles such as liberty or fairness on the one hand, and national specifications of rights on the other.[7] International rights must be more specific than abstract principles if they are to facilitate practical application, but less specific than the entries on lists of rights whose duties fall on national governments if they are to preserve cosmopolitan relevance. . . .

As a first approximation, then, let us interpret a multinational's obligations by asking which *international rights* it should respect. We understand international rights to be the sort of moral precepts that lie in a zone between abstract moral principles and national rights specifications. Multinationals, we shall assume, should respect the international rights of those whom they affect, especially when those rights are of the most fundamental sort. . . .

[Donaldson then proposes three conditions that any purported rights claim must pass if it imposes a valid duty on a corporation. Ed.]

1. The right must protect something of very great importance.
2. The right must be subject to substantial and recurrent threats.
3. The obligations or burdens imposed by the right must satisfy a fairness-affordability test.

Let us further stipulate more precisely for our own purposes what shall be meant by the fairness — affordability test in condition number 3. The affordability part of the test implies that for a proposed right to qualify as a genuine right, all moral agents (including nation-states, individuals, and corporations) must be able under ordinary circumstances, and after receiving any share of charitable help due them, to assume the various burdens and duties that fairly fall upon them in honoring the right. "Affordable" here implies literally being *capable of paying for;* it does not imply that something is necessarily unaffordable because paying for it would constitute an inefficient use of funds, or would necessitate trading off other more valuable economic goods.

This use of the term "affordability" means that — at least under unusual circumstances — honoring a right may be a fundamental moral duty for a given multinational even when the result is financial loss to the particular firm. For example, it would be "affordable" in the present sense for multinational corporations to employ older workers and to refuse to hire eight-year-old children as full-time, permanent laborers, and hence doing so would be mandatory even in the unusual situation where a particular firm's paying the higher salaries necessary to hire older laborers would result in financial losses. By the same logic, it would probably not be "affordable" for either multinational corporations or nation-states around the world to guarantee kidney dialysis for all citizens who need it. This sense of the term also implies that any act of forbearance (of a kind involved in not violating a right directly) is "affordable" for any moral agent.[8] To put the last point another way, I can always "afford" to let you exercise your right to vote, no matter how much money it might cost me.

Turning to the "fairness" side of the test, the extent to which it is "fair" to distribute burdens associated with a given right in a certain manner will be controversial. We assume, however, that for any right to qualify as a genuine right, some "fair" arrangement for sharing the duties and costs among the various agents who must honor the right exists, and that such an arrangement makes it possible (although not necessarily probable) for the right to be enjoyed by most people in most instances.

Next, let us stipulate that satisfying all three of the revised conditions qualifies a prospective right as what we shall call a "fundamental international right," and, in turn,

as a right that must be respected by the three major types of international actors: individuals, nation-states, and corporations. This definition does not mean that individuals, nation-states, and corporations must "respect" the rights in precisely the same manner. That is, it does not entail that the correlative duties flowing from the rights are the same for each type of actor. It entails only that each such actor must "respect" fundamental international rights in some manner, and that they possess some duties, however minimal, in consequence. . . .

FUNDAMENTAL INTERNATIONAL RIGHTS

We are now prepared to identify some of the items that should appear on a list of fundamental international rights, as well as to lay the groundwork for interpreting their application to multinational corporations. . . .

Though probably not complete, the following list contains items that appear to satisfy the three conditions and hence to qualify as fundamental international rights:

1. The right to freedom of physical movement
2. The right to ownership of property
3. The right to freedom from torture
4. The right to a fair trial
5. The right to nondiscriminatory treatment (freedom from discrimination on the basis of such characteristics as race or sex.)
6. The right to physical security
7. The right to freedom of speech and association
8. The right to minimal education
9. The right to political participation
10. The right to subsistence

This is a minimal list. Some will wish to add entries such as the right to employment, to social security, or to a certain standard of living. . . . Disputes also may arise about the wording or overlapping features of some rights: for example, is not the right to freedom from torture included in the right to physical security, at least when the latter is properly interpreted? We shall not attempt to resolve such controversies here. Rather, the list as presented aims to suggest, albeit incompletely, a description of a *minimal* set of rights and to serve as a beginning consensus for evaluating international conduct. If I am correct, many would wish to add entries, but few would wish to subtract them. . . .

Because by definition the list contains items that all three major classes of international actors must respect, the next task is to spell out the correlative duties that fall upon our targeted group of international actors, namely, multinational corporations.

This task requires putting the "fairness-affordability" condition to a second, and different, use. This condition was first used as one of the three criteria generating the original list of fundamental rights. There it demanded satisfaction of a fairness-affordability threshold for each potential respecter of a right. For example, if the burdens imposed by a given right are not fair (in relation to other bona fide obligations and burdens) or affordable for nation-states, individuals, and corporations, then presumably the prospective right would not qualify as a fundamental international right.

In its second use, the "fairness-affordability" condition goes beyond the judgment *that* a certain fairness-affordability threshold has been crossed to the determination of *what* the proper duties are for multinational corporations in relation to a given right. In its second use, in other words, the condition's notions of fairness and affordability are invoked to help determine *which* obligations properly fall upon corporations, in contrast to individuals and nation-states. The condition can help determine the correlative du-

ties that attach to multinational corporations in their honoring of fundamental international rights.

As we look over the list of fundamental rights, it is noteworthy that except for a few isolated instances multinational corporations have probably succeeded in fulfilling their duty not to *actively deprive* persons of their enjoyment of the rights at issue. But correlative duties involve more than failing to actively deprive people of the enjoyment of their rights. Henry Shue, for example, notes that three types of correlative duties are possible for any right: (1) to avoid depriving; (2) to help protect from deprivation; and (3) to aid the deprived.[9]

While it is obvious that the honoring of rights clearly imposes duties of the first kind, to avoid depriving directly, it is less obvious, but frequently true, that honoring them involves acts or omissions that help prevent the deprivation of rights. If I receive a note from Murder, Incorporated, and it looks like it means business, my right to security is clearly threatened. If a third party has relevant information which if revealed to the police would help protect my right, it is not a valid excuse for the third party to say that it is Murder, Incorporated, and not the third party, who wishes to kill me. Hence, honoring rights sometimes involves not only duties to *avoid depriving*, but to *help protect from deprivation* as well. Many critics of multinationals, interestingly enough, have faulted them not for the failure to avoid depriving, but for the failure to take reasonable protective steps.

The duties associated with rights often include ones from the third category, that of *aiding the deprived*, as when a government is bound to honor the right of its citizens to adequate nutrition by distributing food in the wake of a famine or natural disaster, or when the same government in the defense of political liberty is required to demand that an employer reinstate or compensate an employee fired for voting for a particular candidate in a government election.

Nonetheless, the honoring of at least some of the ten fundamental rights by multinational corporations requires only the adoption of the first class of correlative duties, that is, only the duty to avoid depriving. The correlative duties for corporations associated with some rights do not extend to protecting from deprivation or to aiding the deprived, because of the "fairness-affordability" condition discussed earlier. . . .

It would be unfair, not to mention unreasonable, to hold corporations to the same standards of charity and love as human individuals. Nor can they be held to the same standards to which we hold civil governments for enhancing social welfare — since many governments are formally dedicated to enhancing the welfare of, and actively preserving the liberties of, their citizens. The profit-making corporation, in contrast, is designed to achieve an economic mission and as a moral actor possesses an exceedingly narrow personality. It is an undemocratic institution, furthermore, which is ill-suited to the broader task of distributing society's goods in accordance with a conception of general welfare. The corporation is an economic animal; . . . although its responsibilities extend beyond maximizing return on investment for shareholders, they are informed directly by its economic mission. . . .

[T]he application of the "fairness-affordability" criterion . . . impl[ies] that duties of the third class, to aid the deprived, do not fall upon for-profit corporations except, of course, in instances in which a corporation itself has done the depriving. Barring highly unusual circumstances, . . . whatever duties corporations may have to aid the deprived are "maximal," not "minimal," duties. They are duties whose performance is not required as a condition of honoring fundamental rights or of preserving the corporation's moral right to exist. . . .

The same, however, is not true of the second class of duties, to protect from deprivation. These duties, like those in the third class, are also usually the province of government, but it sometimes happens that the rights to which they correlate are ones whose protection is a direct outcome of ordinary corporate activities. For example, the duties associated with protecting a worker from the physical threats of other workers may fall not only upon the local police, but also to some extent upon the employer. These duties, in turn, are properly viewed as correlative duties of the right — in this instance, the workers' right — to personal security. This will become clearer in a moment when we discuss the correlative duties of specific rights.

The following table lists correlative duties that reflect the second-stage application of the "fairness-affordability" condition to the earlier list of fundamental international rights. It indicates which rights do, and which do not, impose correlative duties of the three various kinds upon multinational corporations.

A word of caution should be issued for interpreting the table: the first type of correlative obligation, not depriving directly, is broader than might be supposed at first. It includes *cooperative* as well as individual actions. Thus, if a company has personnel policies that inhibit freedom of movement, or if a multinational corporation operating in South Africa cooperates with the government's restrictions on pass laws, then those companies may be said to actively deprive persons of their right to freedom of movement, despite the fact that actions of other agents (in this example, the South African government) may be essential in effecting the deprivation.[10]

Still, the list asserts that at least six of the ten fundamental rights impose correlative duties upon corporations of the second kind, that is, to protect from deprivation. What fol-

Correlative Corporate Duties

	Minimal Correlative Duties of Multinational Corporations		
Fundamental Rights	*To Avoid Depriving*	*To Help Protect From Deprivation*	*To Aid the Deprived*
Freedom of physical movement	X		
Ownership of property	X		
Freedom from torture	X		
Fair trial	X		
Nondiscriminatory treatment	X	X	
Physical security	X	X	
Freedom of speech and association	X	X	
Minimal education	X	X	
Political participation	X	X	
Subsistence	X	X	

lows is a brief set of commentaries discussing sample applications of each of those six rights from the perspective of such correlative duties.

SAMPLE APPLICATIONS

Discrimination

The obligation to protect a person from deprivation of the right to freedom from discrimination properly falls upon corporations as well as governments insofar as everyday corporate activities directly affect compliance with that right. Because employees and prospective employees possess the moral right not to be discriminated against on the basis of race, sex, caste, class, or family affiliation, it follows that multinational corporations have an obligation not only to refrain from discrimination, but in some instances to protect the right to nondiscriminatory treatment by establishing appropriate procedures. This may require, for example, offering notice to prospective employees about the company's policy of nondiscriminatory hiring, or

educating lower-level managers about the need to reward or penalize on the basis of performance rather than irrelevant criteria.

Physical Security

The right to physical security similarly entails duties of protection. If a Japanese multinational corporation operating in Nigeria hires shop workers to run metal lathes in an assembly factory, but fails to provide them with protective goggles, then the corporation has failed to honor the workers' moral right to physical security (no matter what the local law might decree). Injuries from such a failure would be the moral responsibility of the Japanese multinational despite the fact that the company could not be said to have inflicted the injuries directly.

Free Speech and Association

In the same vein, the duty to protect from deprivation the right of free speech and association finds application in the ongoing corporate obligation not to bar the creation of labor unions. Corporations are not obliged on the basis of human rights to encourage or welcome labor unions; indeed they may oppose them using all morally acceptable means at their disposal. But neither are they morally permitted to destroy them or prevent their emergence through coercive tactics; for to do so would violate their workers' international right to association. The corporation's duty to protect from deprivation the right to association, in turn, includes refraining from lobbying host governments for restrictions that would violate the right in question, and perhaps even to protesting host government measures that do violate it. The twin phenomena of commercial concentration and the globalization of business, both associated with the rise of the multinational, have tended to weaken the bargaining power of labor. Some doubt that labor is sharing as fully as it once did from the cyclical gains of industrial productivity. This gives special significance to the right of free speech and association.

Minimal Education

The correlative duty to protect the right of education may be illustrated through the very example used to open this essay: the prevalence of child labor in developing countries. A multinational in Central America is not entitled to hire an eight-year-old for fulltime, permanent work because, among other reasons, doing so blocks the child's ability to receive a minimally sufficient education. What counts as a "minimally sufficient" education may be debated, and it seems likely, moreover, that the specification of the right to a certain level of education depends at least in part upon the level of economic resources available in a given country; nevertheless, it is reasonable to assume that any action by a cor-

poration which has the effect of obstructing the development of a child's ability to read or write would be proscribed on the basis of rights.

Political Participation

Clearly in some instances corporations have failed to honor the correlative duty of protecting from deprivation the right to political participation. Fortunately, the most blatant examples of direct deprivation are becoming so rare as to be nonexistent. I am referring to cases in which companies directly aid in overthrowing democratic regimes, as when United Fruit Company allegedly contributed to overthrowing a democratically elected regime in Guatemala during the 1950s.

A few corporations continue indirectly to threaten this right by failing to protect it from deprivation, however. Some persist, for example, in supporting military dictatorships in countries in which democratic sentiment is growing, and others have blatantly bribed publicly elected officials with large sums of money. Perhaps the most famous example of the latter occurred in 1972 when the prime minister of Japan was bribed with 7 million dollars by the Lockheed Corporation to secure a lucrative Tri-Star Jet contract. Here, the complaint from the perspective of this right is not against bribes or "sensitive payments" in general, but to bribes in contexts where they serve to undermine a democratic system in which publicly elected officials hold a position of public trust.

Even the buying and owning of major segments of a foreign country's land and industry has been criticized in this regard. As Brian Barry has remarked, "The paranoia created in Britain and the United States by land purchases by foreigners (especially Arabs, it seems) should serve to make it understandable that the citizenry of a country might be unhappy with a state of affairs in which the most important natural resources are in foreign ownership." At what point would Americans regard their democratic control threatened by foreign ownership of U.S. industry and resources? At 20 percent ownership? At 40 percent? At 60 percent? At 80 percent? The answer is debatable, yet there seems to be some point beyond which the right to national self-determination, and national democratic control, is violated by foreign ownership of property.[11]

Subsistence

Corporations also have duties to protect from deprivation the right to subsistence. Consider the following scenario: a number of square miles of land in an underdeveloped country has been used for many years to grow beans. Further, the bulk of the land is owned, as it has been for centuries, by two wealthy landowners. Poorer members of the community work the land and receive a portion of the crop, a portion barely sufficient to satisfy nutritional needs. Next, imagine that a multinational corporation offers the two wealthy owners a handsome sum for the land, because it plans to grow coffee for export. Now *if* — and this, admittedly, is a critical "if " — the corporation has reason to *know* that a significant number of people in the community will suffer malnutrition as a result, that is, if it has convincing reasons to believe that either those people will not be hired by the company or will not be paid sufficiently if they are hired, or that if forced to migrate to the city they will receive less than subsistence wages (wages inadequate to provide food and shelter), then the multinational may be said to have failed in its correlative duty to protect individuals from the deprivation of the right to subsistence. This is true despite the fact

that the corporation would never have stooped to take food from workers' mouths, and despite the fact that the malnourished will, in Samuel Coleridge's words, "die so slowly that none call it murder."

Disagreements: The Relevance of . . . Culture

The foregoing commentaries obviously are not intended to complete the project of specifying the correlative duties associated with fundamental international rights; they only begin it. Furthermore, . . . it may be that some of the fundamental rights on our list would not be embraced, at least as formulated here, by cultures different from ours. Would, for example, the Fulanis, a nomadic cattle culture in Nigeria, subscribe to this list with the same eagerness as the citizens of Brooklyn, New York? What list would they draw up if given the chance? And could we, or should we, try to convince them that our list is preferable? Would such a dialogue even make sense?[12]

I want to acknowledge that rights may vary in priority and style of expression from one cultural group to another. Yet . . . I maintain that the list itself is applicable to peoples even when those peoples would fail to compose an identical list. Clearly the Fulanis do not have to *accept* the ten rights in question for it to constitute a valid means of judging their culture. If the Fulanis treat women unfairly and unequally, then at least one fundamental international right remains unfulfilled in their culture, and their culture is so much the worse as a result. . . .

The Drug Lord Problem

One of the most difficult aspects of the proposed rights list concerns the fairness-affordability condition, a problem we can see more clearly by reflecting on what might be called the "drug lord" problem.[13] Imagine that an unfortunate country has a weak government and is run by various drug lords (not, it appears, a hypothetical case). These drug lords threaten the physical security of various citizens and torture others. The government — the country — cannot afford to mount the required police or military actions that would bring these drug lords into moral line. Or, perhaps, this could be done but only by imposing terrible burdens on certain segments of the society which would be unfair to others. Does it follow that members of that society do not have the fundamental international right not to be tortured and to physical security? Surely they do, even if the country cannot afford to guarantee them. But if that is the case, what about the fairness-affordability criterion?

Let us begin by noting the "affordability" part of the fairness-affordability condition does imply some upper limit for the use of resources in the securing of a fundamental international right (for example, at the present moment in history, kidney dialysis cannot be a fundamental international right). With this established, the crucial question becomes *how* to draw the upper limit. The argument advanced in this essay commits us to draw that limit as determined by a number of criteria, two of which have special relevance for the present issue: first, compatibility with other, already recognized, international rights; and second, the level of importance of the interest, moral or otherwise, being protected by the right, that is, the first of the three conditions. In terms of the compatibility criterion, we remember that the duties imposed by any right must be compatible with other moral duties. Hence, a *prima facie* limit may be drawn on the certification of a prospective right corresponding to the point at which other bona fide international rights are violated. As for the importance of the

right, trade-offs among members of a class of prospective rights will be made by reference to the relative importance of the interest being protected by the right. The right not to be tortured protects a more fundamental interest than, say, the right to an aesthetically pleasing environment.

This provides a two-tiered solution for the drug lord problem. At the first tier, we note that the right of people not to be tortured by the drug lords (despite the unaffordability of properly policing the drug lords) implies that people, and especially the drug lords, have a duty not to torture. Here the solution is simple. The argument of this essay establishes a fundamental international right not to be tortured, and it is a right that binds all parties to the duty of forbearance in torturing others. For on the first application of the fairness-affordability condition, that is, when we are considering simply the issue of which fundamental international rights exist, we are only concerned about affordability in relation to *any* of the three classes of correlative duties. Here we look to determine only whether duties of *any* of the three classes of duties are fair and affordable, where "affordable" means literally capable of paying for. And with respect to the issue of affordability, clearly the drug lords, just as every other moral agent, can "afford" to refrain from actively depriving persons of their right not to be tortured. They can afford to refrain from torturing. (Earlier in this essay, the fairness-affordability condition was interpreted to imply that any act of forbearance, of a kind involved in not violating a right directly, is "affordable" for any moral agent.) It follows that people clearly have the fundamental international right not to be tortured, which imposes at least one class of duties upon all international actors, namely the duty of forbearance.

At the second tier, on the other hand, we are concerned with whether the right not to be tortured includes a duty of the government to mount an effective prevention system against torture. Here the fairness-affordability criterion is used in a second application, which helps establish the specific kinds of correlative duties associated with the already-acknowledged-to-exist right not to be tortured. Surely all nation-states can "afford" under ordinary circumstances to shoulder duties of the second and third categories of helping prevent deprivation and of aiding the deprived, although the specific extent of those duties may be further affected by considerations of fairness and affordability. For example, in the instance described in the drug lord problem, it seems questionable that all countries could "afford" to *succeed* completely in preventing torture, and hence the duty to help prevent torture presupposed by a fundamental international right to freedom from torture probably cannot be construed to demand complete success. Nonetheless, a fairly high level of success in preventing torture is probably demanded by virtue of international rights since, as noted earlier, the ordinary protection of civil and political rights, such as the right not to be tortured, carries a negative rather than positive economic cost. We know that the economic cost of allowing the erosion of rights to physical security and fair trial — as an empirical matter of fact — exceeds the cost of maintaining them.

What the list of rights and correlative corporate duties establishes is that multinational corporations frequently do have obligations derived from rights when such obligations extend beyond simply abstaining from depriving directly to actively protecting from deprivation. It implies, in other words, that the relevant factors for analyzing a difficult issue, such as hunger or high-technology agriculture, include not only the degree of factual correlation existing between multinational policy and hunger, but also the recognition

of the existence of a right to subsistence along with a specification of the corporate correlative duties entailed.

I have argued that the ten rights identified in this essay constitute minimal and bedrock moral considerations for multinational corporations operating abroad. Though the list may be incomplete, the human claims that it honors, and the interests those claims represent, are globally relevant. The existence of fundamental international rights implies that no corporation can wholly neglect considerations of racism, hunger, political oppression, or freedom through appeal to its "commercial" mission. These rights are, rather, moral considerations for every international moral agent, although, as we have seen, different moral agents possess different correlative obligations. The specification of the precise correlative duties associated with such rights for corporations is an ongoing task that this chapter has left incomplete. Yet the existence of the rights themselves, including the imposition of duties upon corporations to protect — as well as to refrain from directly violating — such rights, seems beyond reasonable doubt.

NOTES

1. Ronald Dworkin, *Taking Rights Seriously* (Cambridge, Mass.: Harvard University Press, 1977). For other standard definitions of rights see James W. Nickel, *Making Sense of Human Rights: Philosophical Reflections on the Universal Declaration of Human Rights* (Berkeley: University of California Press, 1987), especially chapter 2; Joel Feinberg, "Duties, Rights and Claims," *American Philosophical Quarterly* 3 (1966): 137–44. See also Joel Feinberg, "The Nature and Value of Rights," *Journal of Value Inquiry* 4 (1970): 243–57; Wesley N. Hohfeld, *Fundamental Legal Conceptions* (New Haven, Conn.: Yale University Press, 1964); and H. J. McCloskey, "Rights — Some Conceptual Is-

sues," *Australasian Journal of Philosophy* 54 (1976): 99–115.

2. Maurice Cranston, *What Are Human Rights?* (New York: Tamlinger, 1973), p. 67.

3. H. J. McCloskey, for example, understands a right as a positive entitlement that need not specify who bears the responsibility for satisfying that entitlement. McCloskey, "Rights — Some Conceptual Issues," p. 99.

4. Feinberg, "Duties, Rights and Claims"; see also Feinberg, "The Nature and Value of Rights," pp. 243–57.

5. James Brooke, "Waste Dumpers Turning to West Africa," *New York Times,* July 17, 1988, p. 1, 7.

6. Ibid. Nigeria and other countries have struck back, often by imposing strict rules against the acceptance of toxic waste. For example, in Nigeria officials now warn that anyone caught importing toxic waste will face the firing squad. p. 7.

7. James W. Nickel, *Making Sense of Human Rights,* pp. 107–8.

8. I am indebted to Lynn Sharp Paine who, in critiquing an earlier draft of this essay, made me see the need for a clearer definition of the "fairness — affordability" criterion.

9. Henry Shue, *Basic Rights: Subsistence, Affluence and U.S. Foreign Policy* (Princeton, N.J.: Princeton University Press, 1980) p. 57.

10. I am indebted to Edwin Hartman for establishing this point. Hartman has suggested that this warrants establishing a fourth significant kind of duty, i.e., "avoiding helping to deprive." For a more detailed account of this interesting suggestion, see Edwin Hartman, "Comment on Donaldson's 'Rights in the Global Market,'" in Edward Freeman, ed., *Business Ethics: The State of the Art* (New York: Oxford University Press, 1991, pp. 163–72).

11. Brian Barry, "Humanity and Justice in Global Perspective," in J. Roland Pennock and John W. Chapman, eds., *Ethics, Economics, and the Law: Nomos Vol. XXIV* (New York: New York University Press, 1982), pp. 219–52. Companies are also charged with undermining local governments, and hence infringing on basic rights, through sophisticated tax evasion schemes. Especially when companies buy from their own subsidiaries, they can establish prices that have little connection to existing market values. This, in turn, means that profits can be shifted from high-tax to low-tax countries with the result that poor nations can be deprived of their rightful share.

12. Both for raising these questions, and in helping me formulate answers, I am indebted to William Frederick.

13. I am indebted to George Brenkert for suggesting and formulating the "drug lord" problem.

International Business Ethics: Russia and Eastern Europe

Richard T. De George

An American firm hires Russian scientists for $40 a month, which is above the average wage of the Russian worker but well below what their work is worth to the company. Although the American firm is willing to pay more, the Russian scientists do not want to earn too much more than their colleagues and are content to be able to continue their research. Both the American firm and the Russian scientists benefit. The American firm is accused by Americans of exploitation.

A truck full of toxic waste crosses the border from Germany into Poland and in a Polish border town dumps its hot load into a

From Richard DeGeorge, "International Business Ethics: Russia and Eastern Europe," *Social Responsibility: Business, Journalism, Law, and Medicine,* 19 (1993), pp. 5–23. Used by permission.

large, unprotected landfill. The German company has solved its problem of disposing of toxic waste. A group of Polish entrepreneurs has found a way of getting hard currency. What each side does is not against the law. The town's inhabitants, and probably others downstream, will eventually bear the cost.

A small Russian entrepreneur tries to set up a small plumbing business. He finds that all pipe and other supplies are allocated to big industries and that the only way he can get any at all is through bribes. He defends his paying these as being necessary and de facto the way business is done.

A former East German professor, who has lived in his apartment for forty years, is evicted when the building is privatized by the manager and sold to a West-German buyer who raises the rent beyond the professor's means.

These are just a few samples of the ethical issues that form part of daily life in Russia and Eastern Europe as they go through the torturous and unprecedented journey from socialist ownership and a centralized command economy to private ownership and a market economy. Marx claimed that the initial accumulation of capital was a result of plunder and theft of a variety of kinds and that capitalism was based on exploitation of the workers. Many in the former socialist countries seem to believe that this is in fact the situation they now face and that the system they are attempting to adopt is the system of capitalism as described by Marx.

In discussing business ethics in Russia and Eastern Europe I shall do three things. First, I shall present an overview of both the business and the ethical climate in these countries. Second, I shall investigate issues of business ethics for and from the point of view of the citizens of these countries. Third, I shall ask, given these two foundations, what are the

obligations of foreign firms — especially American firms — that wish to operate in these countries.

I. THE BUSINESS AND ETHICAL CLIMATE OF PRIVATIZATION

Following the October Revolution in 1917, Lenin and his followers started a new society governed by Marxist principles. The newly established Soviet Union entered unchartered waters as it moved from an early capitalist country to socialism. No country had done what this fledgling country did: seize the private instruments of production — all land, all buildings, all firms and business enterprises, large and small — and convert them to state property. There was no compensation given, no ethical qualms entertained. The exploiters and expropriators held their wealth and position unjustly and had no ethical or legal claim to them under the new rules. In theory, the move from capitalism to socialism was easy. The state simply had to nationalize what previously had been private without thought of weighing owner's rights, competing claims, or other similar considerations. Nonetheless, the years of War Communism following the revolution were an economic disaster. This led Lenin to introduce the New Economic Policy, which permitted some small free enterprise and which allowed the peasants to sell some of their produce on the open market. Stalin put an end to that policy and forcibly collectivized the farms, killing millions of kulaks in the process. The period from 1917 to 1933 can be considered the fifteen years it took to change over from a capitalist economy to a socialist one, and the change involved enormous hardships for the people and cost many lives.

The change from a socialist to a free market economy in the former Soviet Union and in Eastern Europe is unprecedented as well. It is even more difficult and complicated than the change in the other direction. And it cannot be understood or appreciated without our being aware of the socialist background out of which these countries are moving.

I shall touch on only three aspects: the ethical and social background, the development of free enterprises, and the privatization of industry.

A) Government control in the USSR and in the socialist countries of Eastern Europe was ubiquitous. The state or government was the owner of all the means of production, including all the land. Housing was state owned, just as was industry. The government was the sole employer, and it in turn provided highly subsidized housing, free education, free medical care, old age pensions. The standard of living was not very high and productivity was correlatively low. There were laws, but there was no real rule of law. Nonetheless, the state provided security. Government control was total, and hence other sources of control were minimal. In 1961 the Communist Party issued a Moral Code of the Builders of Communism, which listed the norms that were to guide Soviet citizens. The norms were collective. Conscience was not something private to be respected but something social to be molded. Any notion of internal norms was undermined by a view of ethics that was external and in the service of the state.

One result was that the vast majority of the population ignored the official morality. They learned how to get around official rules whenever possible. There was little in the way of a work ethic. The standard joke was, "We pretend to work, and the State pretends to pay us." And there was also little in the way of a shared public ethic. People still valued their families and friends, but the values of the

state were never successfully inculcated into the people. Except for those who privately nurtured religious values, the moral fabric of the country was seriously weakened. The old morality had been undermined and the new morality was ineffective. Falsehood was expected from the government and from the Communist Party, and people became immune to Party propaganda. For over seventy years the Soviet Union had preached Marxism-Leninism, and most of those alive today in the former Soviet republics have never known any other approach to history, society, or economics. They think in Marxist terms, and they learned about the West and capitalism from their Marxist texts, which tended to vilify both.

The overthrow of the Communist regime was a protest against the domination by the Party and its control. It was not a fight for capitalism or free enterprise. And how much of socialism the people want to give up is still an open question. The problems are many. Having overthrown communism and repudiated the former system, they are left with little in the way of a system under which to operate. Socialist laws have not yet been effectively replaced by other laws, and the question of which laws to adopt is a continuing topic of debate. With the legal system under revision, the police and the courts are less and less effective — and not free of corruption. As the traditional background institutions that lend stability to a society disintegrate, there is more and more need for morality to function as a source of social order; but there is little public morality left to play that essential role.

The ordinary worker — who has little, who earns an average of 5,000 rubles a month (less than $10 at the May 1993 rate of exchange), and whose savings have disappeared with rampant inflation — considers anyone able to succeed under these circumstances as being crooked: they must be a former communist official or a bureaucrat who is taking advantage of his or her past position; or a member of the "mafia," criminally amassing wealth; or an entrepreneur exploiting others.

This is the social background for the development of free enterprise and for privatization.

B) The development of small entrepreneurs has been officially both encouraged and hampered. It has been encouraged because it is clear that one of the failures of the old system, which relied exclusively on centralized control, was simply not effective. Hence, some of those presently in charge realize, at least in theory, the need for entrepreneurs to develop small businesses and for decentralization to replace the former command economy.

The difficulty is that the former state structures of distribution are for the most part still in place. Large factories and enterprises are still the dominant economic reality, and sources of supplies are still geared toward those enterprises. The result is that small businesses have a very difficult time receiving the wherewithal to conduct their business. If goods are earmarked for the large factories and are not available to the small entrepreneur, the latter effectively cannot operate. The only way they can operate, given the skewed — and, they claim, unfair — allocation system, is by getting what they can where, when, and how they can. In practice, this most often means paying bribes to those who have access to the needed materials — whether they are managers in factories willing to sell what has been allocated to them, or shippers and middle men who divert shipments to the small business for a fee, or black market and other people who steal what they can sell.

The climate for the entrepreneur is very volatile. The laws are constantly changing. The tax rates and rules are similarly in a state

of flux. The status of ownership of whatever property they have is uncertain. In addition, there is a growing crime rate, with extortion not uncommon, and there are reports of a Russian mafia becoming more and more powerful.[1] Dmitri Rozanov, a Russian entrepreneur, says, "Without paying off the local powers-that-be, it's almost impossible to stay in business,"[2] — a view that is echoed by most Russian business persons.

C) The status of privatization is equally unsettled. Privatization has been described as the state's selling enterprises worth nothing to people who have nothing. A major difficulty in the present situation is the amassing of industrial capital. The people have savings that amount to only about 4% of the estimated value of state enterprises. Clearly they cannot buy them. But under socialism they were said to be the owners of the means of production: hence they should not have to buy them because they already own them. One problem is that simply owning the factories, shops, stores does no good if they are not productive, and most of them need an influx of money to retool and modernize. A second problem is great confusion about who owns former state property and who has the right to privatize it.

What is the ethically right, the just, the fair way to privatize state property? When Britain privatized its state-owned industries it did so according to established rules. It was clear who owned the industries, who had a right to sell them, and who would get the proceeds. In the former Soviet Union and Eastern Europe none of this is the case. It is not clear who owns what (since in theory everyone owned everything), who has the right to sell anything, and who should get the proceeds. Issues of fairness and justice arise as competing, conflicting, incompatible claims, with no mechanism for dispute resolution in place and a sense of urgency to make the transition quickly, before reactionary forces can turn the clock back to state ownership. Yelena Kotova, former director of Moscow's privatization, says, "Moral notions are essentially inappropriate, because it's a cruel process."[3]

Privatization is proceeding in a number of different ways — none of which is wholly fair to all. In Czechoslovakia and Russia the government has issued vouchers that may be used to purchase shares in firms of the individual's choosing. In October 1992, the Russian government issued vouchers of 10,000 rubles each and expected to make available all small and medium enterprises and about 5,000 large enterprises in 1993.[4] The vouchers may be sold or the stock one buys may be traded, although capital markets are just now being organized and are still rudimentary. The vouchers were originally worth $40 at the current rate of exchange; by February 1993 they were worth $17 and were selling for half that on the commodities exchange.[5] . . . The voucher system sounds like a good solution, since everyone in theory owned everything. But one can hardly expect the ordinary Russian citizen to believe that his or her share of the nation's wealth was, at best, $40.

A second form of privatization, followed to a large extent in Poland, consists of turning a factory or enterprise over to the workers. But some of the enterprises were favored under the state system and are productive while others were not. Is it fair to treat them all the same? Is it fair for a worker who has been at a plant for two years to get the same share as one who has been there for twenty years? And is it fair to turn over a non-productive factory to workers who have no prospects of making it productive? What of those who were in the service sector, like teachers? In some cases, managers have taken the initiative and sold the enterprise, sometimes to themselves at ridiculously low prices, sometimes to foreign investors and others who had available cash — again often at ridiculously low prices.

Some firms are being privatized by government auction. Poland has used this method, among others. This provides immediate revenue, but it works only for productive enterprises and has been criticized for turning factories over to foreigners. In an attempt to overcome the former problem, Poland is restructuring and intends to sell whole industries rather than just the strongest companies.[6]

A fourth form of privatization is the selling off of the assets of a company piecemeal to whomever will buy the pieces. This has even been done by military units, which are selling off their arms and even in some instances their tanks to whoever is willing to buy them.[7] . . .

Other forms of privatization include: the state's organizing holding companies (which in fact tend to resemble state-owned enterprises) to help the transition; or, as in Hungary, the selling of individual firms through the State Property Agency to investors who ask to buy them; or allowing companies to go private on their own. Each method has advantages and disadvantages, and from an ethical point of view each raises problems. In Russia, if enterprises were simply turned over to the workers, 70% of the population would be left out.[8]

The situation in East Germany and Poland is further complicated because the new regimes are recognizing the legal claims of former owners on property that the state confiscated from them or their families immediately after World War II.

The result is a condition of great confusion and uncertainty. The state is ineffective in its new role. Market forces are not yet in place. The transition period has led to high unemployment and the closing of many factories that simply cannot compete. They were able to sell shoddy goods in the former command economy but not in an economy where goods are available from the West. The social services formerly provided by the state are no longer readily available. The status of apartments and housing is often in dispute, and ownership is not clear. Do the apartments belong to the occupants, to the city, to the state? Who is responsible for their upkeep and repair?

It is within this system that I now turn to the question of business ethics, to consider it first from the point of view of the local entrepreneur and then from the point of view of the foreigner.

II. BUSINESS ETHICS AND RUSSIAN ENTREPRENEURS

What can we say of business ethics from the Russian point of view? The first answer is that it is a perceived problem, at least by some. In June 1993 the Academy of National Economy of the Russian Federation Graduate School of International Business sponsored an international conference on "Business Ethics in New Russia." What a conference can do is certainly minimal, and bears on the insignificant. But it is an indication of the realization on the part of at least some that a move to free enterprise is possible only if it is accompanied by a set of background institutions — laws, enforceable contracts, social understandings, accepted business practices, and acceptability by the general population, which is where ethics enters. Ethics provides the legitimation for the system of business, and it provides both the glue that keeps it together and the oil that allows it to function. Without basic trust, no contracts will be signed, no goods delivered. Markets rely on information, and hence truth becomes a value. Property is central, and hence respect for property is essential. . . .

The issue of ethics in a corrupt system is a difficult one. The claim that in order to operate as a small entrepreneur one must pay bribes and buy supplies where and when one finds them, without questioning their source, is probably correct. Let us suppose that it is. Is one ethically allowed to operate one's business this way? The obvious answer is No, if there is any alternative. But if the allocation system is itself unfair and corrupt, if government bureaucrats get their share of payments and ignore or condone the diverting of goods based on bribes, can the small entrepreneur be held to a standard of ethical behavior proper in a less corrupt environment? To hold one to that standard is, in effect, to preclude one's being a private entrepreneur and to leave all enterprise to the criminal element.

The tax laws keep changing, and no standard method of bookkeeping is in place. In some cases no bookkeeping is required.

Under the circumstances, basic fundamental ethical norms still apply. Extortion, physical harm and threats, robbery, lying, producing defective goods, dumping toxic wastes, all remain unethical — whether or not they are effectively policed. The outright stealing of goods by some of the managers, who receive materials and immediately ship and sell them abroad for below their market value, is unethical by any standard.

But in the given circumstances I believe that some practices that would be clearly wrong, for instance, in the United States, may be ethically justified for people in those circumstances. When, for example, might the paving of bribes to receive legitimate supplies necessary for one's business be allowed? One justifiable answer is that they are justifiable when they are not bribes but part of the cost of doing business. Bribes are payments made to receive special advantage at the expense of others under some orderly system of entitlements. Absent an orderly system of entitlements, and absent the special advantage and the harm done to others, we are no longer describing what is generally thought of as bribery. We have a disorderly system in which goods are not rationally allocated, either by the market or by the government, and in which there is no fair market price. The price of goods is determined by supply and demand in a rough sense. But if all private entrepreneurs are in the same system, and if goods are available to all only through the payment of fees beyond those listed on an invoice (if there is one), then that is the way, and the cost, of doing business. The payments do not undermine a free market but in this case are part of a developing one.

A kind of utilitarian argument might also be mounted according to which both society as a whole and consumers benefit from private entrepreneurs taking the risks of private business and providing goods and services under the present inefficient and chaotic system. Both the entrepreneurs and society will benefit more than if such businesses were not carried on, leaving people without goods and services, and all enterprise to criminal initiatives.

This justification is clearly conditional and temporary. As the system becomes organized and regularized, the status of such payments changes and becomes disruptive rather than productive, unethical rather than justifiable. Moreover, at best this line of reasoning justifies those who are forced to pay what we shall continue to call bribes. It does not justify the actions of government officials who demand bribes, or of police who require bribes to not enforce what law there is. These actions are part of the problem and can in no way be considered a waystation toward the solution.

Similarly, it is difficult for the small entrepreneur to know what his taxes are when the government, for all intents and purposes, does not know and is unable to provide adequate information or to police any rules it does establish. In such a situation, is failure to pay one's taxes unethical? While it is unethical to avoid paying one's fair taxes in an ordinary system, one can hardly call the present Russian situation a system in any functional sense. Hence the small entrepreneur can plausibly follow whatever rules there are that are most favorable to him — possibly even delaying paying where it is not clearly illegal to delay.

The appropriate generalization in these conditions is that more cannot be asked of those in business than the situation warrants. General ethical demands must be placed in context, and in the Russian context the conclusions one comes to, from an ethical point of view, diverge from the conclusions one would come to in a normal situation. That is true primarily because of the lack of any stable or just background institutions.

At the present time it is difficult to know what "just" or "fair" mean in a great many instances having to do with property — because property is a bundle of rights relative to a system of rights. What constitutes property in the United States is a function of our laws that grant property rights and provide a system under which property can be legitimately transferred. Under the Soviet system, private property was not allowed and the system of rights that developed was significantly different from the system of property in the United States. What was fair or just, as well as what was possible under the two systems, differed. But under which system are Russia and the countries of Eastern Europe now, and which notions of property and justice apply? The problem is that no clear system has yet emerged in any of these countries.

This fact makes the problems of privatization and of developing private enterprises very difficult to judge from the point of view of fairness or justice. If what constitutes property, and what is fair with respect to its transfer or control, are a function of a system, then absent a clear system there is no clear answer to the question. The practical difficulty is that privatization is taking place before any coherent system has been put in place. In some ways, then, business ethics requires a background system within which to operate.

This does not mean that there are no norms common to all systems. As we have already seen, both the ordinary citizen and outside observers appropriately condemn violence, outright robbery, the misuse of political or police power for private gain, and the like.

This leads to my third consideration: how should foreign — for instance, American — firms, act in this environment?

III. MULTINATIONALS IN RUSSIA AND EASTERN EUROPE

I have already claimed that the basic norms of respecting life, honoring agreements and contracts, and telling the truth are basic to any society and economic system. The norms are not universally adhered to; but that is consistent with the necessity for basic norms to exist. If basic norms are breached in any significant numbers, the very possibility of social life and hence of doing business is undermined.

Nor does the fact that some moral issues are dependent on the background institutions of a society mean that when in Rome one should do as the Romans do. In the first place, what the Romans do may be unethical and unjustifiable in itself. If some society practices slavery and protects it by law, that does not mean that American companies are ethically allowed to similarly practice slavery in that country. In South Africa under the apartheid laws, American companies could not morally abide by those laws and enforce apartheid within their operations. This led to the Sullivan principles, which precluded firms from following the apartheid laws and yet allowed them to operate in the country in

the hope that they could weaken apartheid from within. After ten years, Leon Sullivan, who had proposed the principles in the first place, declared the experiment a failure and maintained that following his principles no longer could provide justification for continued operation in South Africa.

Although American companies are not required to do business in Eastern Europe and Russia exactly as they do in the United States, they are also not allowed to ignore moral norms, even if these are neither enacted into law nor effectively enforced in the host country. The situation of the multinational that can choose whether to operate in these countries, and the conditions under which it will operate, is different from the situation of native entrepreneurs. The latter's choices are much more restricted if they choose to set up a business.

The example of MacDonald's is a case in point. When MacDonald's first started operating in Moscow, it made provision to receive almost all of its supplies from foreign sources because of the unreliability of Soviet sources. Slowly, as it found reliable local suppliers, it switched from foreign to local sources. This option would not be open to local entrepreneurs. But even though the policy was possible for MacDonalds, it is clear that American firms cannot justify bribery and illegality by arguing that because this is the way business is done in Russia, it is the only way our firm can do business there.

Does this not imply a double standard, since I gave a limited defense of local entrepreneurs working within the system? The answer is No. The reason is that the situation of the local entrepreneur and of the American multinational is very different. One can plausibly argue that the local entrepreneur has no choice but to operate within a corrupt system or not to operate at all. The American multinational, on the other hand, has a very real option of not operating there at all, while continuing to operate everywhere else that it already does. Second, the multinational does not need to engage in bribery. It has available hard currency, which is in such great demand that, if anything, it needs to give some attention to the fact that it can skew the allocation of resources to the serious disadvantage of local firms. If bribes are demanded, an American company can and should point to the American Foreign Corrupt Practices Act as an added reason precluding its paying bribes to public officials. If bribes are actually necessary to conduct business, the American company can protest through official governmental and intergovernmental channels; it can use the media to expose the demands; and it can band together with other American companies similarly situated to jointly refuse to pay such demands. In short, an American company has a wide variety of options available that are not available to the local entrepreneur. Therefore, the multinationals have no justification for engaging in such practices.

The multinational in the given context, because of the strength of its position, has a positive obligation to set an example of ethics in business and to encourage the development of background institutions conducive to stability and to business practices that benefit the society as a whole. As an outside interest entering the country for the company's benefit, it should not be exploitive or seek its own good to the disadvantage of the local population. To do otherwise is the carpetbagger syndrome, exploitive and unethical, even if legal.

Of the stories with which we began, clearly the Western firm that transported its toxic waste to Poland and knew it would be dumped in unprotected landfills acted unethically, even though not yet illegally. It took advantage of the need of the people for hard currency and collaborated with a group of private entrepreneurs willing, for their own profit, to endanger a considerable number of people. Even if the town as a whole had consented to the deal and shared in the proceeds, the Western company would have been taking advantage of them. There are some deals, such as selling oneself into slavery, that are not allowable, even if done with the apparent consent of the disadvantaged party. Using one's backyard for toxic wastes indicates either desperation or lack of appreciation of the consequences of one's act; in any case, it shows flagrant disregard for those who will be adversely affected without their consent.

What of the American firm that hired Russian scientists for $40 a month — as both AT&T and Corning have done? AT&T Bell Laboratories signed a one year agreement with the General Physics Institute of the Russian Academy of Sciences in Moscow, hiring about 100 of the Institute's 1200 scientists and researchers. Corning hired 115 scientists and technicians at Vavilov State Optical Institute in St. Petersburg, which has several thousand scientists.[9] Are the American firms guilty of exploiting the scientists by paying them $480 a year, while a comparable top scientist in the U.S. working, say, in fiber optics could command an annual salary of about $70,000? Despite appearances, the answer is No. In these cases the wages were set by the Russian scientists, who know they could get more but who did not want to be paid too much more than their Russian counterparts. Since $40 a month is well above the average Russian worker's wage, it is sufficient to live at a standard common to large numbers of people in that society. The labor is not forced, and the wage is set by the workers, who have the Russian right to patents on whatever they develop. Hence there is no exploitation in this case. There is rather a mutually satisfactory and ethically justifiable arrangement.

The issues of wages is a difficult one for American companies in many countries abroad. If they pay the going wage — which by American standards seems pitifully low — they are accused by Americans of exploiting the local workers. If they pay well above the going wage, they are accused by local companies of stealing away their best workers and of attempting to drive wages up so as to put them out of business. No matter what the going wage, an American multinational can and should pay at least wages that are sufficient for the worker to live at a standard of living considered acceptable in that country, providing that it is at least sufficient for the worker to live in accordance with general norms of human dignity. These guidelines are admittedly vague, and they are necessarily so because there is no one just wage. Above a certain minimum necessary for decent living conditions, the amount of which varies from country to country, the market can ethically be allowed to operate. What is ethically demanded everywhere is respect for the human rights of workers, which means not only adequate wages but fair treatment and relatively safe and sanitary working conditions.

What of the West German who buys the Berlin apartment building? I have already indicated that in Russia and in some other East European countries it is not clear to whom such property belongs. Nor is it clear how to decide what is a fair way to privatize. No one can legitimately sell what does not belong to him. The difficulty facing an outside buyer is to determine that what he is buying legitimately belongs to the seller, that the title the buyer receives will be legally recognized, and that the attached rights will be upheld and enforced.

In the German case, the buyer knows that German law applies. The fact that long-time residents of the apartment building could not pay the new rent and were forced to leave is an unfortunate consequence of privatization. The buyer, the seller, or the government might try to alleviate the residents'

plight by helping them relocate. But that is an ethical ideal and not an ethical requirement. In itself the transaction is not unethical. It differs from the toxic dumping case because of the difference in the harm done and foreseen in the two cases. Had the building existed prior to World War II, and had it been nationalized by the East Germans, the former owner might have some claim on it. What the claim amounts to and how such claims are to be adjudicated is presently being decided by German courts. Had the apartments been given to the tenants, as the state has done in many cases in Russia, the situation would obviously be different. The fact that persons who had important positions under the Communist regime and had correspondingly favorable housing are now being forced to relocate to more modest housing does not seem unjust, on the face of it. The German laws are adequate to handle difficult cases of homelessness and eviction rights. This case — as opposed to somewhat similar cases in other East European countries that were not able to adopt wholesale a preexisting system of laws — shows the pain many in Eastern Europe are suffering in the period of transition. . . .

What general conclusions can we draw?

The first is that international business ethics is not and cannot be the imposition of American business ethics — whatever one means by that — on all nations. Ethics is one of the restraints on business, and in each country it operates in conjunction with a host of other restraints, demands, and expectations. As we have noted in passing, the system of law, the view of property, the standard of living, and the customs and traditions of the people are all important considerations. This does not imply ethical relativism, or the view that whatever any society says is ethical is in fact ethical — as the cases of slavery and apartheid show. But it does imply that norms appropriately vary in their application, and that one should be cautious of overgeneralization based exclusively on American experience.

A second conclusion has to do with American multinationals. A company that wishes to act with integrity must have its own values to which it adheres. If a company changes its values from country to country, and if the norms it follows are determined exclusively by the enforced local laws, it is questionably a company of integrity. I have suggested that, given the conditions of Eastern Europe and Russia, American companies, and companies from other industrially developed countries, have a special obligation not to abuse the special advantages they have vis-à-vis these countries. They are ethically precluded from exploitation, from cooperating with criminal elements (whether as suppliers or as go-betweens), from paying bribes, and from violating the human rights of workers or consumers — whether or not any of this is precluded by enforced laws.

A third conclusion has to do with international business ethics in general. Business ethics is itself a fairly recent subject of study. It developed in the United States in the 1970s and has grown since then. It has spread to various countries in Europe and more recently to centers in Japan, Brazil, Australia, and elsewhere. But although business is clearly global, there is still a great deal of confusion among both academicians and business people about international or global business ethics: what it means and how it can be implemented. The most significant difference between business ethics in the United States and on a global level is the absence on the global level of what can be called background institutions: laws, agreements, understandings, traditions, and the like. The need worldwide is to adopt agreements, understandings, and rules that make mutually advantageous trade possible and that keep the playing field of competition level.

I suggest that these background institutions should not be established by the imposition of American standards on the world, but that they should be the result of negotiation between all affected parties. Only if all those seriously affected agree to the justice of those institutions will they be stable and perform the function that comparable background institutions play in most developed countries.

Russia and some East European countries are now in a state of economic and social chaos. In such a situation ethics is needed, but even more important are ethically justifiable structures — laws and procedures. The development of such structures is a precondition for any full-fledged consideration of business ethics in Russia and Eastern Europe in the foreseeable future.

NOTES

1. See Stephen Handelman, "Inside Russia's Gangster Economy." *The New York Times Magazine,* January 24, 1993, 12 ff.
2. Cynthia Scharf, "The Wild, Wild East: Everyone's a Capitalist in Russia Today and Nobody Knows the Rules," *Business Ethics,* vol. 6, No. 6, (Nov./Dec. 1992), 21.
3. "Russians Privatize by Looting State Goods," *The Washington Post,* May 17, 1992, A1.
4. "Citizens of Russia To Be Given Share of State's Wealth," *The New York Times,* October 1, 1992, A1, A10.
5. *Christian Science Monitor,* February 10, 1993, 3.
6. "In East Europe, There's More Than One Capitalist Road," *Chicago Tribune,* October 25, 1992, Sec. 7, 1.
7. "Selling Off Big Red," *Newsweek,* March 1, 1993, 50–51; "Russians Privatize by Looting State Goods," *The Washington Post,* May 17, 1992, A1.
8. "Russia's Big Enterprises Privatize, With Communists at the Ready," *Christian Science Monitor,* February 10, 1993, 3.
9. "Russian Scientists for A.T.&T. and Corning," *The New York Times,* May 27, 1992, D1.

Business Ethics: A Japanese View

Iwao Taka

I. TWO NORMATIVE ENVIRONMENTS — RELIGIOUS DIMENSION

In order to evaluate the traditional ethical standards of the Japanese business community, it is necessary to describe the Japanese cultural context or background. When it comes to cultural or ethical background, we can classify Japanese conscious and unconscious beliefs into a "religious dimension" and a "social dimension," in that Japanese culture cannot be understood well in terms of only one of the two dimensions. While the former is closely combined with a metaphysical concept or an idea of human salvation, the latter is based on how Japanese observe or conceive their social environment. Stated otherwise, while the former is "ideal-oriented," the latter is "real-oriented."

First, the religious dimension. This dimension supplies a variety of concrete norms of behavior to the Japanese in relation to the ultimate reality. As a consequence, I shall call this dimension the "normative environment."

By this I mean the environment in which most events and things acquire their own meanings pertaining to something beyond the tangible or secular world. Following this definition, there are mainly two influential normative environments in Japan: the "transcendental normative environment" and the "group normative environment."

1. Transcendental Normative Environment

One of the famous Japanese didactic poems says, "Although there are many paths at the foot of a mountain, they all lead us in the direction of the same moon seen at the top of the mountain." This poem gives us an ontological equivalent of "variety equals one." To put it in another way, though there are innumerable phenomena in this tangible world, each individual phenomenon has its own "numen" (soul, spirit, reason-d'être, or spiritual energy), and its numen is ultimately connected with the unique numen of the universe. In Japanese, this ultimate reality is often called "natural life force," "great life force of the universe," "*michi*" (path of righteousness), "*ri*" (justice), "*ho*" (dharma, laws), and the like.

"Transcendentalism" is the philosophy that every phenomenon is an expression of the great life force and is ultimately connected with the numen of the universe. It follows that the environment where various concrete norms come to exist may be called the "transcendental normative environment." What is more, the set of these norms is simply called "transcendental logic."

In this transcendental environment, everyone has an equal personal numen. This idea has been philosophically supported or strengthened by Confucianism and Buddhism. That is to say, in the case of neo-Confucianism, people are assumed to have a

From Iwao Taka, "Business Ethics: A Japanese View" from *Business Ethics Quarterly* 4:1, (1994). Used with permission.

microcosm within themselves, and are considered condensed expressions of the universe (macrocosm). Their inner universe is expected to be able to connect with the outer universe.

In the case of Buddhism, every living creature is said to have an equal Buddhahood, a Buddhahood which is very similar with the idea of numen and microcosm. Buddhism has long taught, "Although there are differences among living creatures, there is no difference among human beings. What makes human beings different is only their name."

In addition, however, under the transcendental normative environment, not only individuals but also jobs, positions, organizations, rituals, and other events and things incorporate their own "numina." Needless to say, these numina are also expected to be associated with the numen of the universe.

Deities of Shintoism, Buddhism, and the Japanese new religions, which have long been considered objects of worship, are often called the "great life force of the universe," or regarded as expressions of that force. In this respect, the life force can be sacred and religious. On the other hand, however, many Japanese people have unconsciously accepted this way of thinking without belonging to any specific religious sect. In this case, it is rather secular, non-religous, and atheistic. Whether it is holy or secular, the significant feature of Japan is that this transcendental normative environment has been influential and has been shared by Japanese people.

2. Meaning of Work
in the Transcendental Environment

Inasmuch as Japanese people live in such a normative environment, the meaning of work for them becomes unique. That is to say, work is understood to be a self-expression of the great life force. Work is believed to have its own numen so that work is one of the ways to reach something beyond the secular world or the ultimate reality. Accordingly, Japanese people unconsciously and sometimes consciously try to unify themselves with the great life force by concentrating on their own work.

This propensity can be found vividly in the Japanese tendency to view seemingly trivial activities — such as arranging flowers, making tea, practicing martial arts, or studying calligraphy — as ideal ways to complete their personality (or the ideal ways to go beyond the tangible world). Becoming an expert in a field is likely to be thought of as reaching the stage of *kami* (a godlike state). Whatever job people take, if they reach the *kami* stage or even if they make a strong effort to reach it, they will be respected by others.

M. Imai has concluded that whereas Western managers place priority on innovation, Japanese managers and workers put emphasis on *Kaizen* (continuous improvement of products, of ways to work, and of decision-making processes). While innovation can be done intermittently only by a mere handful of elites in a society, *Kaizen* can be carried on continuously by almost every person.

> Technological breakthroughs in the West are generally thought to take a Ph.D., but there are only three Ph.D.s on the engineering staff at one of Japan's most successfully innovative companies — Honda Motor. One is founder Soichiro Honda, whose Ph.D. is an honorary degree, and the other two are no longer active within the company. At Honda, technological improvement does not seem to require a Ph.D.[1]

The transcendental normative environment has contributed to the formation of this Japanese propensity to place emphasis on *Kaizen*. Work has been an important path for Japanese people to reach the numen of the universe. Thus, they dislike skimping on their work, and instead love to improve their products, ways of working, or the decision-making processes. These Japanese attitudes are closely linked with the work ethics in the transcendental normative environment. Kyogoku describes this as follows:

> In marked contrast with an occidental behavioral principle of "Pray to God, and work!" at the cloister, in Japan, "Work, that is a prayer!" became a principle. In this context, devotion of one's time and energy to work, concentration on work to such a degree that one is absorbed in the improvement of work without sparing oneself, and perfectionism of "a demon for work," became institutional traditions of Japan.[2]

In this way, the transcendental environment has supplied many hard workers to the Japanese labor market, providing an ethical basis for "diligence." Nonetheless, it has not created extremely individualistic people who pursue only their own short-term interests. Because they have hoped for job security and life security in the secular world, they have subjectively tried to coordinate their behavior so as to keep harmonious relations with others in the group. Within this subjective coordination, and having the long-term perspective in mind, they pursue their own purposes.

3. Group Normative Environment

The second or group normative environment necessarily derives from this transcendental normative environment, insofar as the latter gives special raisons d'être not only to individuals and their work, but also to their groups. As a result of the transcendental environment, every group holds its own numen. The group acquires this *raison d'être*, as long as it guarantees the life of its members and helps them fulfill their potentials.

But once a group acquires its *raison d'être*, it insists upon its survival. An environment in which norms regarding the existence and prosperity of the group appear and affect its members is called the "group normative environment," and the set of the norms in this environment is called "group logic."

In Japan, the typical groups have been: *ie* (family), *mura* (local community), and *kuni* (nation). After World War II, although the influence of *ie* and *kuni* on their members has been radically weakened, one cannot completely ignore their influence. *Mura* has also lost much power over its members, but *kaisha* (business organization) has taken over many functions of *mura*, in addition to some functions of *ie*. These groups are assumed to have their own numen: *ie* holds the souls of one's ancestors, *mura* relates to a *genius loci* (tutelary deity), *kaisha* keeps its corporate tradition (or culture), and *kuni* has Imperial Ancestors' soul. . . .

Groupism and a group-oriented propensity, which have often been pointed out as Japanese characteristics, stem from this group normative environment.

II. THE ETHICAL DILEMMA OF LIVING BETWEEN TWO ENVIRONMENTS

Japanese often face an ethical dilemma arising from the fact that they live simultaneously in the two different influential normative environments. In the transcendental environment, groups and individuals are regarded as equal numina and equal expressions of the great life force. In the group environment, however, a group (and its representatives) is considered to be superior to its ordinary members, mainly because while the group is expected to be able to connect with the numen of the universe in a direct way, the members are not related to the force in the same way. The only way for the members to connect with the life force is through the activities of their group.

Depending on which normative environment is more relevant in a given context, the group stands either above or on an equal footing with its members. Generally speaking, as long as harmonious human relations within a group can be maintained, discretion is allowed to individuals. In this situation, the transcendental logic is dominant.

But once an individual begins asking for much more discretion than the group can allow, or the group starts requiring of individuals much more selfless devotion than they are willing to give, ethical tension arises between the two environments. In most cases, the members are expected to follow the requirements of the group, justified by the group logic. . . .

The assertion or gesture by a group leader to persuade subordinate members to follow, is called *tatemae* (formal rule). *Tatemae* chiefly arises from the need of the group to adapt itself to its external environment. In order to adjust itself, the group asks its members to accept changes necessary for the group's survival. In this moment, the group insists upon *tatemae*. On the other hand, the assertion or gesture by the members to refuse *tatemae,* is called *honne* (real motive). *Honne* mainly comes from a desire to let the subordinates' numen express itself in a free way.

Usually, a serious confrontation between *tatemae* and *honne* is avoided, because both the leader and subordinates dislike face-to-face discussions or antagonistic relations. Stated otherwise, the members (the leader and the subordinates) tend to give great weight to harmonious relations within the group. Because of this, the leader might change his or her expectation toward the subordinates, or the subordinates might refrain from pursuing their direct self-interest. In either case, the final decision-maker is un-

likely to identify whose assertion was adopted, or who was right in the decision-making, since an emphasis on who was correct or right in the group often disturbs its harmony.

Simply described, this ambiguous decision-making is done in the following way. The group lets the subordinates confirm a priority of group-centeredness, and requires their selfless devotion. This requirement is generally accepted without reserve in the group normative environment. But if the subordinate individuals do not really want to follow the group orders, they "make a wry face," "look displeased," "become sulky," or the like, instead of revealing their opinions clearly. These attitudes are fundamentally different from formal decision-making procedures. In this case, taking efficiency and the harmonious relation of the group into consideration, the group "gives up compelling," "relaxes discipline," or "allows *amae*" of the subordinates.

If the failure to follow the norms endangers the survival of the group, the leader repeatedly asks the members to follow the order. In this case, at first, the leader says, "I really understand your feeling," in order to show that he or she truly sympathizes with the members. And then he or she adds, "This is not for the sake of me, but for the sake of our group." Such persuasion tends to be accepted, because almost everybody implicitly believes that the group has its own numen and the group survival will bring benefits to all of them in the long run. . . .

III. ETHICS OF CONCENTRIC CIRCLES — SOCIAL DIMENSION

Due to human bounded cognitive rationality or cultural heritage, Japanese moral agents, whether individuals or corporations, tend to conceptualize the social environment in a centrifugal order similar to a water ring. Although there are many individuals, groups, and organizations which taken together constitute the overall social environment, the Japanese are likely to categorize them into four concentric circles: family, fellows, Japan, and the world. On the basis of this way of thinking, Japanese people and organizations are likely to attribute different ethics or moral practices to each circle. Let us look at the concentric circles of individuals and of corporations respectively.

* * *

1. The Concentric Circles of Corporations

Just as individuals understand their social environment as concentric circles, so groups such as corporations have a similar tendency to characterize their environment. For the sake of simplicity, I shall classify the corporate environment into four circles: quasi-family, fellows, Japan, and the world.

First, corporations have a quasi-family circle. Of course, though corporations do not have any blood relationships, they might still have closely related business partners. For example, parent, sister, or affiliated companies can be those partners. "Vertical *keiretsu*" (Vertically integrated industrial groups like Toyota, Hitachi, or Matsushita groups) might be a typical example of the quasi-family circle. In this circle we find something similar to the parent-child relationship.

The main corporate members (about 20 to 30 companies in each group) of "horizontal *keiretsu*" (industrial groups such as Mitsubishi, Mitsui, Sumitomo, Dai Ichi Kangyo, Fuyo, and Sanwa groups) might be viewed as quasi-family members. Nonetheless, most of the cross-shareholding corporations in the horizontal *keiretsu* should be placed in the second circle, because their relations are less intimate than commonly understood.

In the second circle, each corporation has its own main bank, fellow traders, distant affiliated firms, employees, steady customers, and the like. If the corporation or its executives belong to some outside associations like *Nihon Jidousha Kogyo Kai* (Japanese Auto Manufactures Association), *Doyukai* (Japan Association of Corporate Executives), *Keidanren* (Japan Federation of Economic Organizations), etc., the other members of such outside associations might constitute part of the second circle of the corporation. And if the corporation is influential enough to affect Japanese politics or administration, the Japanese governmental agencies or ministries, and political parties might constitute part of this circle.

Recognition within the fellow circle requires that there must be a balance between benefits and debts in the long run. On account of this, if a corporation does not offer enough benefits to counterbalance its debts to others in this circle, the corporation will be expelled from the circle, being criticized for neither understanding nor appreciating the benefits given it by others. On the other hand, if the corporation can successfully balance benefits and debts or keep the balance in the black, it will preferentially receive many favorable opportunities from other companies or interest groups. For these reasons, every corporation worries about the balance sheet of benefits and debts in the fellow circle.

This way of recognizing the business context is closely related to original Confucianism, in that Confucianism allows people to treat others in proportion to the intimacy of their relations. Unlike Christianity, Confucianism does not encourage people to love one another equally. It rather inspires people to love or treat others differentially on the grounds that, if people try to treat everybody equally in a social context, they will often face various conflicts among interests. This does not mean that Confucianism asserts that people should deny love to unacquainted people. The main point of this idea is that, although people have to treat all others as human beings, they should love intensely those with whom they are most intimate; those who cannot love this way cannot love strangers either. I can call this "the differential principle" in Confucianism. Influenced or justified by this differential principle, Japanese corporations also classify their business environment in this way.

In the Japan circle, the fellow circle ethics is substantially replaced by "the principle of free competition." Competitors, unrelated-corporations, ordinary stockholders, consumers, (for ordinary corporations, the Japanese government constitutes part of this circle) and so forth, all fall within this circle. Yet almost all corporations in this circle know well that the long-term reciprocal ethics is extremely important in constructing and maintaining their business relations, because of their similar cultural background. This point makes the third circle different from the world circle.

In the fourth or world circle, corporations positively follow "the principle of free competition," subject to the judicial system, with less worrying about their traditional reputations. Roughly speaking, the behavioral imperatives for corporations turn out to be producing or supplying high quality and low price products, dominating much more market share, and using the law to resolve serious contractual problems.

As in the case of the individuals, the world circle is conceived as a relatively chaotic sphere causing corporate attitudes to become contradictory. On the one hand, Japanese corporations tend to exclude foreign counterparts that do not understand the extant Japanese business practices, hoping to maintain the normative order of its own business community. Notwithstanding these closing attitudes, on the other hand, they yearn after

foreign technologies, know-how, products, and services which are expected to help corporations to be successful and competitive in the Japanese and world market. In particular, western technologies have long been objects of admiration for Japanese companies. This tendency vividly shows their global attitudes.

2. Dynamics of the Concentric Circles

Now that I have roughly described the static relations among the concentric circles (of individuals and of corporations), I need to show the dynamic relations among these circles, that is to say, how these circles are interrelated. . . . In order to describe these complicated relations in a parsimonious light, I shall limit my discussion to the relations between the members of an "ideal big Japanese corporation" and its business environment. By a "big Japanese corporation," I mean the "idealized very influential organization" in an industry that places priority on the interests of employees, and holds a long-term strategic perspective. By "operation base" in this context, I mean the place where the members can relax, charge their energy, and develop action programs to be applied to the business environment. Whether the corporation can be such a base or not heavily depends on its members' abilities with respect to human relations: their ability to sympathize or understand other members' feelings, their ability to put themselves in the others' position, their ability to internalize other members' expectations toward them, and the like.

It has been said that in Japanese corporations, many people have such abilities. For instance, E. Hamaguchi has called people with these abilities "the contextuals" in contrast with "the individuals."

An "individual" is not a simple unit or element of a society, but a positive and subjective member. This so-called "individual-centered model of man" is the typical human model of the western society.

This model, however, is clearly different from the Japanese model. The Japanese human model is a "being between people" or an internalized being in its relations. This can be called "the contextual" in contrast with the individual.[3]

To be sure, these abilities have also positively contributed to the performance of Japanese corporations. The corporations have not rigidly divided work into pieces and distributed them to each employee so as to clarify the responsibilities each has to take. The corporations have rather let employees work together so that the contextual members make up for the deficiencies of one another allowing the quality of products and efficiency of performance to be surprisingly improved.

On the contrary, the business environment as a "battlefield" is reckoned to be a strenuous sphere, where "the law of the jungle" is the dominant ethical principle. In the market, the principle of free competition replaces the ethics expected in an operation base (quasi-family and fellow circles). What is more, this principle of free competition is justified by the transcendental logic, because, as I have described earlier, in the transcendental environment, work is one of the most important "ways" or "paths" to reach something sacred or the ultimate reality. In this way, "the principle of free competition" in the battlefield and "the transcendental logic" are coincidentally combined to encourage people to work hard, an encouragement which results in survival and the development of the corporation.

Wealth, power, market share, competitive advantage, or other results acquired in this business context become important scales to measure the degree of the members' efforts to proceed on the "path" to the ultimate

stage. And based on these scales, contributors are praised within the operation base, namely in a corporation, in an industrial group, or in Japan.

For example, the Japanese government, administrative agencies, or ministries have so far endorsed the efforts of corporations under the present *Tenno* system (the Emperor System of Japan). The decoration and the Order of Precedence at the Imperial Court have been given to corporate executives who have contributed to the development of the Japanese economy.

Theoretically speaking, it is very hard to compare the performance of various corporations in different industries of a nation, simply because each industry has its own scale or own philosophy to measure performance. In the case of Japan, however, the annual decoration and attendance at the Imperial Court plays the role of a unitary ranking scale, applied to every industry as well as non-business-related fields. Since the Japanese mass-media makes the annual decoration and attendance public, the Japanese people know well who or which corporations are praiseworthy winners.

3. The Group Environment and the Concentric Circles

Now that I have explained both the group normative environment and the concentric circles of corporations, I should make clear the relationship between the group normative environment and the concentric circles. According to the group logic, each group has its own numen and has different social status. For example, even if the R&D unit of corporation A has its own numen, the status of the unit is lower than that of A itself. The status of A is also lower than that of the leading company B in the same industry. The status of B is lower than that of the Japanese government. But if I observe their relations from the viewpoint of concentric circles, these groups can be members of the same fellow circle of corporation C. Namely, the R&D unit of corporation A, company B, and the government can constitute part of the fellow circle of C. Therefore, even if they are in the same fellow circle, it does not mean that all members have equal status in the group normative environment.

For these reasons, reciprocal relations within the fellow circle are varied according to the members' status in the group normative environment. For instance, because, in most cases, the Japanese government is regarded as a powerful agent in the fellow circle of large corporation C, C makes efforts to maintain its good relations with the government and is likely to depend on the government.

The main reason why *gyosei-shido* (administrative guidance) has so far worked well in Japan comes from this dependent trait of the corporation and from the fact that the administrative agencies or ministries have a very important status in the second circle of the large Japanese corporations.

Each Japanese corporation also maintains relations with the business associations such as *Keidanren* and *Doyukai*. Once an authoritative business association declares *tatemae,* the member corporations make efforts to follow the formal rules, even though they might have some doubts about *tatemae,* simply because those associations hold socially or politically higher status in the group normative environment.

IV. JAPANESE RECOGNITION OF THE AMERICAN BUSINESS COMMUNITY

Because Japanese follow the transcendental logic, group logic, and concentric circles' ethics, their way of observing other business societies might appear to be idiosyncratic. And this idiosyncrasy might bring serious misunderstanding to trading partners such as the United States, European industrialized countries, Asian NIEs, and the other developing countries.

Because of this, I would like to clarify how Japanese conceive the American business community: how the American business community is seen in the eyes of the Japanese business people who adopt the two normative logics and the concentric circles' ethics.

1. Job Discrimination and the Transcendental Logic

First, as noted earlier, in the transcendental normative environment, whatever job people take, they are believed to reach the same goal or the same level of human development. Because of this logic, Japanese are unlikely to evaluate others in terms of their "job" (specialty). They would rather evaluate one another in terms of their "attitudes" toward work.

To be concrete, it is not important for Japanese to maintain the principle of the division of labor. Of importance is the process and the result of work. If people cannot attain goals in the existing framework of the division of labor, they are likely to try other alternatives which have not been clearly defined in the existing framework. This kind of positive attitude toward work is highly appreciated in Japan.

On the contrary, a society such as the United States, where jobs are strictly divided, is perceived as not only inefficient but also discriminatory in Japanese eyes. To be sure, this society might hold a belief that the division of labor makes itself efficient or makes it possible for diverse people to utilize their own abilities. The Japanese business community, however, is likely to assume that people's reluctance to help others' work in the same group is based on job discrimination.

In America, in a large retail shop, for instance, often those who sell a heavy consumer product are reluctant to carry it for the customer. They have a specific person, whose job is just to carry goods, do so. If the person is busy with other goods, the salespeople will ask the customer to wait until the person is finished carrying the other goods.

Similarly, those who manage a large shop typically do not clean up the street in front of their shop. They let a janitor do so. Even if they find garbage there, when the janitor has not come yet, they are likely to wait for the janitor. This kind of attitude of salespeople or managers is regarded as inefficient and discriminatory by Japanese.

2. Employees' Interest and the Group Logic

Second, in the group normative environment, the group is believed to hold its own numen and expected to guarantee the members' life. That is to say, a corporation is thought to exist for its employees rather than for its shareholders.

Because of this logic, the Japanese business community ethically questions American general attitudes toward the company where many accept the ideas that 1) a company is owned by its shareholders, 2) executives should lay off the employees whenever the layoff brings benefits to the shareholders, 3) executives should buy other companies and sell part of their own company whenever such a strategy brings benefits to the shareholders, etc.

Of course, even in Japan, shareholders are legal owners of a company so that the shareholders might use their legal power to change the company in a favorable way for themselves. Therefore, many Japanese corpo-

rations have invented a legitimate way to exclude the legal rights of shareholders, i.e. "cross-shareholding." This is the practice in which a corporation allows trusted companies to hold its own shares, and in return the corporation holds their shares. By holding shares of one another and refraining from appealing to the shareholders' rights, they make it possible to manage the companies for the sake of the employees.[4] Because this cross-shareholding is based on mutual acceptance, any attempts to break this corporate consortium from the outside, whether Japanese or foreigners, are often stymied by the consortium of the member corporations.

For example, in April 1989, Boone Company, controlled by T. Boone Pickens, bought a 20 percent stake in Koito Manufacturing, Japanese auto parts maker. In 1990, Pickens increased it to 25 percent, becoming Koito's largest single shareholder.[5] But because Pickens asked for seats on Koito's board for himself as well as three Boone Company associates, and requested an increase in Koito's annual dividend, he was labeled as a "greenmailer" in the Japanese business community. As a result, the other consortium members cooperatively protected Koito from the Pickens' attack.[6] . . .

In addition, the layoff of employees and the high salaries of American executives are also regarded as unethical by the Japanese business community. . . . In Japan, when executives face serious difficulties, they first reduce their own benefits, then dividends and other costs, and, after that, employees' salary or wage. If the situation is extremely hard to overcome with these measures, they sell assets and only as a last resort do they lay off workers. Even in this case, the executives often find and offer new job opportunities for those who are laid off, taking care of their family's life.

Because of this, Japanese executives criticize the American business climate in which only salaries of executives keep rising, even while they lay off employees (especially in the 1980s). This criticism is also based on the Japanese group normative logic.

3. Claims Against the Japanese Market and the Concentric Circles' Ethics

As I have noted above, because of the framework of concentric circles, especially of the ethics of the fellow circle, foreign corporations often face difficulties entering the Japanese market. Although Japanese admit that the market is very hard to enter, a majority of them believe that it is still possible to accomplish entry.

Even if the Japanese market has many business-related practices such as semi-annual gifts, entertainment, cross-shareholding, "triangular relationship" among business, bureaucracy, and the Liberal Democratic Party, the long-term relationship is formed mainly through a series of business transactions.

That is to say, the most important factor in doing business is whether suppliers can respond to the assemblers' requests for quality, cost, the date of delivery, and the like, or on how producers can respond to the retailers' or wholesalers' expectations. . . .

Foreign corporations might claim that because they are located outside Japan, they cannot enter even the Japan circle. On this claim, the Japanese business community is likely to insist that if they understand the "long-term reciprocal ethics," they can enter the Japan circle; and what is more, might be fellows of Japanese influential corporations. As I have described, what makes the Japan circle different from the world circle is that people in the Japan circle know well the importance of this ethics. In fact, successfully enjoying the Japanese market are foreign corporations such as IBM, Johnson & Johnson,

McDonald, Apple, and General Mills which have understood well this ethics.

In this respect, realistically, the Japanese business community interprets the criticism by the American counterpart of the Japanese market as unfair and unethical. To put it differently, Japanese believe that if foreign corporations understand the long-term ethics, they will easily be real members of the Japanese business community.

V. ETHICAL ISSUES OF THE JAPANESE BUSINESS COMMUNITY

I have shown how Japanese people conceive the American business society and its business-related practices from the viewpoint of the two normative environments and the concentric circles. Yet this does not mean that the Japanese business community has no ethical problems. On the contrary, there are many issues it has to solve. What are the ethical issues of the Japanese business community? . . .

1. Discrimination and the Transcendental Logic

I will shed light on the organizational issues (opening the Japanese organizations) from the prime value of transcendental logic. The prime value here is "everybody has an equal microcosm." Whether men or women, Japanese or foreigners, hard workers or non-hard workers, everybody has to be treated equally as a person. When I observe the organizational phenomena from the viewpoint of this value, there are at least the following two discriminatory issues.

First, the transcendental logic has worked favorably only for male society. That is, in this normative environment, Japanese women have been expected to actualize their potentials through their household tasks. Those tasks have been regarded as their path toward the goal. Of course, insofar as women voluntarily agree with this thinking, there seems to be no ethical problem. And in fact, a majority of women have accepted this way of living to date. Nonetheless, now that an increasing number of women work at companies and hope to get beyond such chores as making tea to more challenging jobs, the Japanese corporations have no longer been allowed to treat women unequally.

Second, the transcendental normative logic itself has often been used to accuse certain workers of laziness. As far as a worker voluntarily strives to fulfill his or her own potential according to the transcendental logic, this presents no ethical problems. Nevertheless, once a person begins to apply the logic to others and evaluate them in terms of their performance, the transcendental logic easily becomes the basis for severe accusations against certain workers.

For example, even if a man really wants to change his job or company, his relatives, colleagues, or acquaintances are unlikely to let him do so, because they unconsciously believe that any job or any company can lead him to the same high stage of human development, if he makes efforts to reach it. Put in a different way, it is believed that despite the differences between the jobs or companies, he can attain the same purpose in either. On account of this, many Japanese say, "once you have decided and started something by yourself, you should not give up until reaching your goal." This is likely to end up justifying a teaching that "enough is as good as a feast."

If the person does not follow this teaching, thereby refusing overtime or transfers, he will jeopardize his promotion and be alienated from his colleagues and bosses, since he is not regarded as a praiseworthy diligent worker. Even if he is making efforts to fulfill his potential in work-unrelated fields, he is not highly appreciated, simply because what he is doing is not related to the company's work.

Analyzing those practices from the viewpoint of the prime value (everybody has equal microcosm), I cannot help concluding that the Japanese business community should alter its organizational climate.

2. Employees' Dependency and the Group Logic

In the group normative environment, groups are regarded as having a higher status than their individual members. Because the members are inclined to take this hierarchical order for granted, they come to be dependent on the groups. And their groups also come to be dependent on the next higher groups. This dependency of the agents, whether of individuals or groups, brings the following two problems into the Japanese business community. Because of the dependent trait, 1) the individual members of the group refrain from expressing their opinions about ethical issues, and 2) they tend to obey the organizational orders, even if they disagree with them. The first tendency is related to decision-making, while the second affects policy-implementation. . . .

One of the typical examples which show this tendency of members to waive their basic rights is *karoshi* (death caused by overwork). In 1991, the Japanese Labor Ministry awarded 33 claims for *karoshi*. Since it is very hard to prove a direct and quantifiable link between overwork and death, this number is not large enough to clarify the actual working condition, but is certainly large enough to show that there is a possibility of turning the group logic into unconditional obedience.

This corporate climate not only jeopardizes the employees' right to life, but also hampers the healthy human development of the individual members. Because of this, the Japanese business community has to alter this group-centered climate into a democratic ground on which the individuals can express their opinions more frankly than before.

3. Exclusiveness of the Concentric Circles

The Japanese conceptualization of the social environment in a centrifugal framework is closely connected with Confucianism (the differential principle): it allows people to treat others in proportion to the intimacy of their relationships. As I touched upon before, however, the main point of this principle is not that people should deny love to strangers, but rather that those who cannot love their most intimate relatives intensely are surely incapable of loving strangers. Stated otherwise, even if the way to achieve a goal is to love differentially, the goal itself is to love everybody. Therefore, "to love everybody" should be regarded as the prime value of the concentric circles' ethics.

If I look at the Japanese market (opening the Japanese market) from the viewpoint of this prime value, there appear to be at least the following two issues. 1) The Japanese business community has to make an effort to help foreigners understand the concept of long-term reciprocal ethics. This effort will bring moral agents of the world circle into the Japan circle. 2) The Japanese community has to give business opportunities to as many newcomers as possible. This effort will bring the newcomers into the fellow circles.

The first issue is how to transfer foreign corporations from the world circle to the Japan circle. . . . This "fairness" implies that they treat foreign companies the same as they treat other Japanese firms. To put it differently, the concept of "fairness" encourages

the Japanese corporations to apply the same ethical standard to all companies.

Although this is a very important point of "fairness," there is a more crucial problem involved in opening the market. That is how to let newcomers know what the rules are and how the Japanese business community applies the rules. As mentioned before, for the purpose of constructing and maintaining business relationships with a Japanese company (a core company), a foreign firm has to be a fellow of the company. In this fellow circle, every fellow makes efforts to balance benefits and debts with the core company in material and spiritual terms in the long run, since making a long-term balance is the most important ethics. Yet balancing them is too complicated to be attained for the foreign corporation, as long as benefits and debts are rather subjective concepts.

For example, in Japan, if company A trusts the executive of company B and helps B, when B is in the midst of serious financial difficulties, then B will give the most preferential trade status to A after overcoming its difficulties. B will rarely change this policy, even if B finishes repaying its monetary debts to A. Moreover, even if A's products are relatively expensive, as long as the price is not extraordinarily unreasonable, B will continue to purchase A's output. If A's products are not sophisticated enough to meet B's standard, B will often help A to improve A's products in various ways.

If A's help is understood only as financial aid, this close relationship between A and B will not appear reasonable. In Japan, in most cases, B is deeply impressed by the fact that A has trusted B (even if B is in serious difficulties) so that B continues to repay its spiritual debts to A as long as possible. Yet if B were to change this policy soon after repaying the borrowed capital to A, and if it began buying the same but cheaper products from company C, not only A but also other corporations which have been aware of this process from the beginning will regard B as an untrustworthy company in their business community.

"Fairness" in a Japanese sense might involve asking foreign companies to follow the former way of doing business. Nonetheless, foreign companies, especially Americans, do not understand "fairness" this way. Their understanding is rather similar to the latter behavior of B: switching from A to C. This difference of understanding "fairness" between Americans and Japanese undoubtedly causes a series of accusations against each other.

The Japanese business community should not let this happen over and over again. If the community takes the prime value seriously, as the first duty, it has to explain the long-term reciprocal ethics to foreign counterparts in an understandable way. This effort will help the foreigners enter the Japan circle.

But even if they can enter the Japan circle successfully, there still remains another problem. That is how those foreigners, which have been already in the Japan circle, enter the fellow circles of influential Japanese corporations. This is related to the second issue of opening the Japanese market.

Even when foreign companies understand and adopt long-term reciprocal ethics, they might not be able to enter those fellow circles, if they rarely have the chance to show their competitive products or services to the influential corporations. On account of this, as an ethical responsibility, the Japanese corporations should have "access channels" through which every newcomer can equally approach.

To be sure, the "mutual trust" found in the fellow circle should not be blamed for everything. But if the trust-based business relation is tightly combined among a few influential corporations, it tends to exclude newcomers. As long as such a relation is not against the Japanese Antimonopoly Law, it is safe to say that efforts to maintain the relationship are

not problematic, because most of the corporations do so according to their free will. Despite that, if I look at the exclusive tendency of a fellow circle like that of the Japanese distribution system, I cannot help saying that the trust-based relation is a critical obstacle for newcomers.

If the Japanese business community follows the prime value (to love everybody) of the concentric circles' ethics, it has to make an effort to remove the obstacles to entry. One of the ideal ways to do so is to give newcomers more competitive bids than before. Of course, it is not obligatory for Japanese corporations to accept every bidder as a fellow after the tender. If a bidder is not qualified as an ideal business partner in terms of its products or services, Japanese corporations do not need to start transactions with the bidder. But as a minimum ethical requirement, Japanese corporations should have access channels through which every newcomer can equally approach them. . . .

NOTES

1. M. Imai, *Kaizen* (New York: McGraw-Hill Publishing Company, 1986), p. 34.
2. Kyogoku, *Nihon no Seiji* (Politics of Japan) (Tokyo: Tokyo University Press, 1983) pp. 182–83.
3. E. Hamaguchi, *"Nihon Rashisa" no Saihakken (Rediscovery of Japaneseness)* (Tokyo; Kodansha, 1988), pp. 66–67.
4. This practice was basically formed for a purpose of defending Japanese industries from foreign threats. But at the same time, Japanese people thought this threat might destroy the employee-centered management. T. Tsuruta, *Sengo Nihon no Sangyo Seisaku (Industrial Policies of Post-War Japan)* (Nihon Keizai Shinbunsha, 1982), pp. 121–30.
5. W. C. Kester, *Japanese Takeovers: The Global Contest for Corporate Control* (Cambridge: Harvard Business School Press, 1991), pp. 258–59.
6. *Mainichi Daily News* (May 15, 1990).

The Foreign Corrupt Practices Act Amendments of 1988: "Death" of a Law

Bartley A. Brennan

The Members of Congress who authored this elimination of the antibribery law chose the perfect vehicle. They needed a big bill that would be handled by a myriad of committees so they could bury the few fatal lines that killed the Foreign Corrupt Practices Act deep in this forest of hundreds of thousands of words. They needed a controversial bill that would concentrate the debate on a series of economic matters that shook and divided the country and distracted the press from the death knell to antiforeign bribery law. What an opportunity to slip through a bribery repealer. The authors of the provision fully understood the gutting provision could not stand by itself. Even in a moderately complex bill the amendment would be vulnerable. But pushed by one of the many committees developing the details of this king size trade bill that was furiously contested by Congress and the President, the press and public could hardly be expected to notice the death of the Foreign Corrupt Practices Act.[1]

INTRODUCTION

An extraordinary eight year effort by some members of Congress and some business lobbyists to amend the Foreign Corrupt Practices Act of 1977 (FCPA or Act) culminated on August 23, 1988, with the enactment of the Omnibus Trade and Competitiveness Act of 1988 (Trade Act). The 1988 FCPA Amend-

ments are only six pages in this approximately four hundred page piece of legislation whose goals only indirectly, at best, were to amend the FCPA. Those seeking to amend the FCPA had, over an eight-year period, failed to obtain passage of such amendments when they were introduced as separate bills. Furthermore, the Trade Act itself was once vetoed by the President and was passed as a result of a series of compromises worked out in a Trade Bill Conference Committee. It is therefore not surprising that proponents of the FCPA, such as Senator Proxmire, have charged those who have been successful in amending the Act with seeking to "gut" the law.

This Article analyzes the major changes that the 1988 Amendments made to the accounting and antibribery sections of the 1977 FCPA. Throughout the discussion particular attention will be given to the way in which the 1988 Amendments address the problems created by the 1977 Act. These problems are identified in a 1981 report issued by the General Accounting Office, which conducted a survey of U.S. corporations. This Article concludes that the 1988 Amendments severely undercut the original objectives of the 1977 Act.

In reviewing the 1988 Amendments to the FCPA, it should be remembered why the 1977 Act was enacted. In the period from 1974 to 1976, approximately 435 corporations voluntarily disclosed to the Securities

From Bartley A. Brennan, "The Foreign Corrupt Practices Act Amendments of 1988: 'Death' of a Law," *North Carolina Journal of International Law & Commerce Regulation*, volume 15 (1990), pp. 229–47. Reprinted by permission of publisher and author.

and Exchange Commission (SEC) that they had made improper or questionable payments to foreign officials or members of foreign political parties. Such bribery led to the downfall of governments and officials in Japan, the Netherlands, and Korea. By weakening its statute against bribery, the United States does not present itself as a good political and economic model for other nations to follow. This message is especially inappropriate at a time when the Soviet Union and several Eastern European nations are evolving toward economies based on the U.S. model. . . .

THE ANTIBRIBERY PROVISIONS OF THE FCPA

The 1977 Antibribery Provisions

In addition to the accounting provisions of the 1977 FCPA which mandated disclosure of questionable or illegal payments, Congress also provided antibribery provisions which prohibited the bribery of any foreign official. Under this section, not all payments were prohibited. Instead, only those payments that were driven by corrupt intentions, those made to influence certain persons to commit or fail to perform certain acts, and those made for the purpose of retaining business were prohibited.

Corporate and government officials, as well as academicians and lawyers, criticized the bribery sections of the 1977 FCPA for vaguely defining what constituted compliance. Some commentators suggested that this vagueness forced U.S. corporations to forego business opportunities abroad for fear of violating the FCPA and incurring its stiff criminal sanctions. The GAO Report found that of "the 30% of our respondents who reported that the Act had caused a decrease in their overseas business, approximately 70% rated

the clarity of at least one of the antibribery provisions as inadequate or very inadequate." The major ambiguities to the antibribery provisions noted by the respondents FCPA were the following:

(1) the degree of responsibility a company has for the actions of the foreign agents;
(2) the definition of the term "foreign official";
(3) whether a payment is a bribe (illegal under the FCPA) or a "facilitating payment" (legal under the FCPA); and
(4) the dual jurisdiction of the SEC and Department of Justice.

The 1988 Amendments to the Antibribery Provisions

The 1988 Amendments change the antibribery provisions of the 1977 FCPA in seven areas.

Corrupt Payments. The 1988 Amendments attempt to clarify the definition of what type of payments are prohibited. The Amendments change this definition in two respects. First, payments under the 1977 FCPA were prohibited if their purpose was to influence "*any act or decision of such foreign official in his official capacity, including a decision to fail to perform his official functions.*"[2] The 1988 Amendments alter this provision to forbid payments or offers to pay foreign officials for the purpose of "*influencing any act or decision of such foreign official in his official capacity, or inducing such foreign official to do or omit to do any act in violation of the lawful duty of such official.*"[3] Thus, it would seem at first glance that the language was changed in order to bring the FCPA into compliance with U.S. bribery laws. However, as one commentator has noted, the conferees failed because our domestic bribery statute forbids *all* corrupt payments intended to influence official functions, while the FCPA, as amended, increases the number of already existing categories of facilitating or "grease" payments.

Second, under the 1977 FCPA, payments were only illegal if made "in order to assist such issuer in obtaining or retaining business. . . ."[4] Some confusion arose as to whether lobbying fell within the definition of "retaining business." Although the Conference Committee rejected a proposed amendment that would have broadened the definition of "retaining business," the Conference Report does attempt to clarify the provision. It states that the conferees:

> wish to make clear that the reference to corrupt payments for "retaining business" in present law is not limited to the renewal of contracts or other business, but also included a prohibition against corrupt payments relating to the execution or performance of contracts or the carrying out of existing business, such as a payment to a foreign official for the purpose of obtaining more favorable tax treatment. . . . The term should not, however, be construed so broadly as to include lobbying or other normal representations to government officials.[5]

The Conference Report as noted here sought on one hand to broaden the scope of prohibited payments beyond the purpose of "retaining business" but also to liberalize its interpretation so as not to include lobbying or normal representations. These conflicting objectives may have unfortunate repercussions in light of the expansion of categories of lawfully permitted facilitating or "grease" payments discussed below.

The "Reason to Know" Standard for Third Party Payments. In addition to prohibiting payments directly to "foreign officials," the 1977 FCPA also prohibited corporate entities or officers from giving anything of value to "any person, while knowing or having reason to know that all or a portion of such money or thing of value will be offered directly or indirectly" to various persons. These payments are referred to as third party payments.

Almost fifty percent of the respondents surveyed by the GAO found the "reason to know" language either "very inadequate" or "marginally inadequate." Lawyers and legal scholars argued that a "reason to know" standard increased the potential liability of a company and its officers for the acts of foreign agents or more closely affiliated third parties even if the company was unable to monitor or control their conduct. Several recurring questions were asked. What does "reason to know" mean? Is "reason to know" something less than full actual knowledge? If so, how much less, and should it be used in prosecution of criminal conduct? Those favoring the language as it stood under the FCPA pointed out that "reason to know" language existed in twenty-nine provisions of other federal laws. An analysis of these provisions, however, showed that thirteen of the twenty-nine provisions were civil or administrative statutes as contrasted with the FCPA, a criminal statute that provided for up to five years imprisonment. The remaining provisions fell into areas relating to federal safety standards or other types of regulatory procedures. Furthermore, similar "reason to know" language is included in eight provisions of the criminal code which has been replaced by the Federal Criminal Code Revisions.

Perhaps the most significant problem was that no precedents existed interpreting the "reason to know" language of the 1977 FCPA. In addition, because both the Department of Justice and the SEC had joint enforcement authority, a question was raised as to whether the agencies had the same interpretation of the "reason to know" language.

The 1988 Amendments delete the "reason to know" language and apply a "knowing" standard, which is defined as follows:

(A) A person's state of mind is "knowing" with respect to conduct, a circumstance, or a result
if —
   (i) such person is aware that such person is
engaging in such conduct, that such circumstance exists, or that such result is
substantially certain to occur; or
  (ii) such person has a firm belief that such
circumstance exists or that such result is
substantially certain to occur.
(B) When knowledge of the existence of a particular circumstance is required for an offense,
such knowledge is established if a person is
aware of a high probability of the existence of
such circumstance, unless the person actually
believes that such circumstance does not
exist. . . . [6]

The "reason to know" standard has been
replaced by a standard that is more difficult
for prosecutors to meet. The Conference Report made it clear that "simple negligence"
or "mere foolishness" was insufficient for
criminal liability. However, the Committee
also stated that management will be held liable for "conscious disregard," "willful blind-
ness," or "deliberate ignorance." In other
words a "head in the sand" state of mind approach by management will not be tolerated.
Citing several federal cases the Conference
Report noted that the knowledge requirement is not equivalent to recklessness. It requires "an awareness of a high probability of
the existence of the circumstance." The Conference Report goes on to state that the
FCPA covers circumstances where any "reasonable person would have realized the existence of the circumstance or result" and the
defendant "consciously chose not to ask
about what he had reason to believe he
would discover." Courts are instructed to use
a mix of subjective and objective standards to
determine the level of knowledge based on
this test.

It would appear that the only circumstance
from which a company must now protect itself is the intentional disregarding of some

mix of subjective and objective signals that illegal payments were made by an agent or employee to a third party. It is not clear at this
point what the signals are. As one commentator has pointed out, the Conference Report
does not cite any cases which "suggest liability
where the consequences of the factual knowledge possessed by the defendant result in future conduct prohibited by the statute," yet
the language of the statute imposes liability
in cases where there is an awareness or belief
"such result is substantially certain to occur."
It would seem clear that the language substituted for the "reason to know" standard may
in fact prevent serious prosecution of violators of the FCPA.

Facilitating Payments. The Amendments
change the exemption for facilitating or
"grease" payments. These payments are not
made to obtain or retain business but merely
to expedite a business activity in which the
ministerial level employee is already employed. An example is the payment of thirty
dollars to a customs official to move paper-
work along so that a shipment of nondurable
goods can be unloaded quickly. Many foreign
governments permit such facilitating payments even though they are illegal in the
United States and several other countries.

Under the 1977 FCPA, facilitating payments were allowed in several ways. The 1977
FCPA defined "foreign official" as any officer
or employee of a foreign government or one
of its departments, agencies, or instrumentalities. This definition expressly excluded any
employee whose duties were "essentially ministerial or clerical." Corporate officials frequently complained that this language was
unclear. Are employees of a publicly held nationalized corporation considered "foreign
officials?" Is an official, or member of that official's family residing in a foreign country,
who is also involved in the private sector a
"foreign official?" How should the law treat

individuals who simultaneously hold positions in both government and business? Can an excluded "ministerial or clerical" employee be paid a "facilitating payment" to use his influence to induce a "foreign official" to act, as long as the clerical employee does not pay the official from funds received from a U.S. corporation?

As stated above, the 1977 FCPA also proscribed only "corrupt" payments. The legislative history of the FCPA defined a corrupt payment as one made "to induce the recipient to misuse his official position in order to wrongfully direct business to the payor or his client" and requires an "evil motive or purpose." Because ministerial employees were excluded from the definition of foreign official, it is clear the FCPA was not intended to proscribe grease or facilitating payments. Moreover, social gifts or routine expenditures for marketing products were lawful. However, consistent complaints about enforcement officials' interpretation led to requests for a congressional clarification of the statute.

Despite the apparently clear legislative intent that facilitating payments to ministerial or clerical employees not be proscribed, thirty-eight percent of those responding to the GAO questionnaire rated the clarity of the provisions inadequate. The dilemma raised was that a large corrupt payment to an official with "ministerial" duties might *not* be prohibited while a small payment to expedite customs papers may be prohibited if made to a senior "official." Furthermore, middle-level employees of U.S. corporations did not fully understand what constituted a facilitating payment. The decision to make such a payment would often have to be made quickly because hesitation might cause a delay in transportation or unloading of goods.

The 1988 Amendments now allow payments to *any* foreign official if they are facilitating or expediting payments for the

purposes of expediting or securing the performance of a routine governmental action. "Routine governmental action" is defined as follows:

an action which is ordinarily and commonly performed by a foreign official in:
(i) obtaining permit[s], licenses, or other official documents to qualify a person to do business in a foreign country;
(ii) processing governmental papers such as visas and work order[s];
(iii) providing police protection, mail pick up and delivery, or scheduling inspections associated with contract performance or inspections related to transit of goods across country;
(iv) providing phone service, power and water supply, loading and unloading cargo, or protecting perishable products or commodities from deterioration; or
(v) actions of a similar nature.

Payments can now be made to *any* foreign official, not just ministerial or clerical persons, as long as they fall within the five categories. This substantially changes the intent of the 1977 FCPA as well as the breadth of the exception. The 1977 FCPA facilitating payments language was directed at the type of foreign official (ministerial or clerical), while 1988 amendments are directed at the type of duties to be performed. The "actions of a similar nature" language greatly expands the types of activities that may be allowed as "grease" or facilitating payments.

Affirmative Defenses. In addition to expanding the "grease" payment exceptions for criminal prosecution, the 1988 Amendments also provide for two affirmative defenses for those accused of violating the FCPA. First, it is now an affirmative defense if a payment to a foreign official is lawful "under the written laws" of the foreign country. The Conference Report makes it clear "that the absence of written laws in a foreign official's country would not by itself be sufficient to satisfy this defense." Also, in interpreting what is lawful under written law, the conference committee members state that "normal rules of legal construction should apply."

This defense was added in response to complaints that U.S. companies were losing business because actions forbidden by the 1977 FCPA were permitted in foreign countries and undertaken by foreign competitors. A related problem was the lack of uniformity among nations regarding the propriety of facilitating payments. While a foreign agent might legally receive such a payment under the law of his or her country, the U.S. corporation making the payment might be violating the FCPA.

A study by Dr. John Graham of the University of Southern California, which reviewed all available empirical data, concluded that:

> (a) During the 1978–1980 period, the FCPA had no negative effect on export performance of American industry. No differences in U.S. markets shown were discovered in nations where the FCPA was reported to be a trade disincentive both in terms of total trade with each country as well as for sales in individual product categories.
>
> (b) During the 1977 statute, U.S. trade with bribe-prone countries has actually outpaced our trade with non-bribe-prone ones.[7]

Dr. Graham further concluded that the FCPA has not hurt the competitive position of U.S. industry. In fact, Dr. Graham's study provides support for the proposition that improper foreign payments are at least unnecessary. He suggests, therefore, that management should question payments to foreign firms on economic as well as ethical grounds.

Another complaint was that the FCPA sought to export U.S. morality. However, David D. Newsome has argued that the corrupt association of a U.S. company and a foreign official carries political implications for both actors which do not concern other for-

eign multinational corporations. He notes that "American businessmen often ask, 'Why us?' Why should America's multinationals be singled out for restrictions when all around them their competitors operate without such restrictions?"[8] Mr. Newsome concludes that the answer lies in the unique position which U.S. corporations have in world business ventures, coupled with their role in domestic affairs of foreign nations. He states that "[o]ur companies cannot escape the fact that their activities will never be totally detached from local sensitivities relating to United States intervention of any sort in the internal affairs of another country."[9] Thus, from both an economic and a moral viewpoint, this new affirmative defense seems unnecessary and unwise.

The second affirmative defense established by the Amendments allows payments to be made for "reasonable and bona fide expenditures." Examples include travel and lodging expenses incurred by or on behalf of a foreign official, party, party official, or candidate that are "directly related to (A) the promotion, demonstration or explanation of products or services; or (B) the execution or performance of a contract with a foreign government or agency thereof." In general, this second affirmative defense codifies the procedure followed by the Justice Department under the 1977 FCPA.

Repeal of the "Eckhardt Amendment." The "Eckhardt Amendment," which was included in the 1977 Act, prevented the prosecution of employees or agents of an issuer or U.S. corporation unless the concern itself was found to have violated the FCPA. The 1988 Amendments delete the language that prevented such prosecution.

Congressman Eckhardt originally proposed such language to prevent senior management of companies from using agents or employees as "scapegoats." Also, the legislative history indicates that the sponsors of the 1977 Act were concerned that agents or employees might not have the resources to defend themselves against charges of violations of the FCPA. The 1988 Amendments now open the door for the "scapegoat" scenario. Therefore, it is now important that individual employees and agents retain their own counsel when any possibility exists of a violation of the FCPA under the "knowing" standard. The repeal of the "Eckhardt Amendment" may create a difficult working environment for employees or agents and their employers or principals. . . .

CONCLUSION

The 1988 Amendments to the FCPA seek to redefine legally and ethically acceptable conduct for U.S. concerns doing business in foreign nations. Those who espouse an efficiency view that the "right to export" is best for the nation have succeeded in "gutting" the FCPA after an eight-year struggle. In the meantime, those who have been concerned about the legal and ethical conduct of U.S. companies doing business abroad have lost the battle to maintain the standards established by the 1977 FCPA. Scientifically sound studies (as opposed to anecdotal comments) indicated that the 1977 FCPA was at most a minor disincentive to export expansion, with other variables being far more important.[10] Moreover, the 1988 Amendments send the wrong signals to U.S. and foreign business communities at a time when new markets are opening in Eastern Europe. If we as a nation wish to encourage the adoption of an economic model based on competition for those who have experienced the poverty of a command model, bribery, under the guise of "fa-cilitating payments," we will only give ammunition to those in Eastern Europe and elsewhere who are opposed to reform. While the proponents of the 1988 Amendments have won in the short run, a return to pre-FCPA (1977) conduct by domestic concerns doing business abroad will lead to more stringent legislation in the long term.

NOTES

1. 134 Cong. Rec. S 8528 (daily ed. June 24, 1988) (statement of Sen. Proxmire).
2. 15 U.S.C. § 78dd-2(a)(1)(A) (1982) (emphasis added).
3. *Id.* § 78dd-1(a)(1)(A)(i) (1988) (emphasis added).
4. *Id.* § 78dd-1(a) (1982).
5. H.R. Conf. Rep. No. 576, 100th Cong., 2d Sess., 134 Cong. Rec. H 1863, H 2116 (daily ed. Apr. 20, 1988), *reprinted in* 1988 U.S. Code Cong. & Admin. News 1949, at 918.
6. 15 U.S.C. § 78dd-1(f)(2)(A), (B) (1988).
7. Graham, *Foreign Corrupt Practices: A Manager's Guide,* 18 COLUM. J. WORLD BUS. 89 (1983).
8. *See* Foreign Corrupt Practices Act — Oversight: Hearings Before the Subcomm. on Telecommunications, Consumer Protection, and Finance of the Comm. on Energy and Commerce, House of Representatives, 97th Cong. 1st & 2d Sess. 176 (1981 & 1982), at 391 (statement of D. Newsome).
9. *See id.* at 391–92.
10. *Id.; see* Sternitzke, *The Great American Competitive Disadvantage: Fact or Fiction,* 10 J. INT'L BUS. STUD 25, 32–35 (1979). Sternitzke concludes that "over the last decade the lagging long run growth of American exports has been due mainly to the loss of competitiveness of American manufacturing goods in affluent markets, and has been attributable only incidentally to commodity structure or mix of American exports." *See* Graham, *Foreign Corrupt Practices: A Manager's Guide,* 18 COLUM J. WORLD BUS. 89 (1983).

The Moral Authority of Transnational Corporate Codes

William C. Frederick

Moral guidelines for corporations may be found embedded in several multilateral compacts adopted by governments since the end of the Second World War. Taken as a whole, these normative guides comprise a framework for identifying the essential moral behaviors expected of multinational corporations. Corporate actions that transgress these principles are understood to be *de facto,* and in some cases *de jure,* unethical and immoral. This set of normative prescriptions and proscriptions embodies a moral authority that transcends national boundaries and societal differences, thereby invoking or manifesting a universal or transcultural standard of corporate ethical behavior. Although this remarkable development has not run its full course and therefore is not yet all-embracing, it is well enough along for its main outlines to be evident and its central normative significance to be clear.

LANDMARK MULTILATERAL COMPACTS

The four decades between 1948 and 1988 have been remarkable for the proliferation of intergovernmental agreements, compacts, accords, and declarations that have been intended to put on the public record various sets of principles regulating the activities of governments, groups, and individuals. The core concerns of these compacts have ranged from military security to economic and social development, from the protection of national sovereignty to specifying acceptable actions by multinational enterprises, from condemnations of genocide and slavery to the regulation of capital flows and the transfer of technology, from the political rights of women to the movements of refugees and stateless persons, and many others too numerous to list here. They reflect the many kinds of problems and issues that have confronted governments in the last half of the 20th century (United Nations, 1983).

This paper focuses on six of these intergovernmental compacts, which by their nature, purpose, and comprehensiveness might well be considered to be the most generic or archetypal of such agreements. Collectively they proclaim the basic outlines of a transcultural corporate ethic. This ethic effectively lays down specific guidelines for the formulation of multinational corporate policies and practices. These six compacts and their respective dates of promulgation are:

- The United Nations Universal Declaration of Human Rights (1948) [Abbreviated as UDHR]
- The European Convention on Human Rights (1950) [ECHR]
- The Helsinki Final Act (1975) [Helsinki]
- The OECD Guidelines for Multinational Enterprises (1976) [OECD]
- The International Labor Office Tripartite Declaration of Principles Concerning Multinational Enterprises and Social Policy (1977) [ILO]
- The United Nations Code of Conduct on Transnational Corporations (Not yet completed

From William C. Frederick, "The Moral Authority of Transnational Corporate Codes," *Journal of Business Ethics* 10 (1991). Reprinted by permission of Kluwer Academic Publishers.

nor promulgated but originating in 1972.) [TNC Code]

The first two compacts are clearly normative in focus and intention, emphasizing human rights, but they are not addressed specifically to multinational enterprises. The principle emphasis of the Helsinki Final Act is the national and political security of the signatory governments, although this accord and its successor protocols carry strong messages concerning human rights and environmental protections, which do concern business operations. The last three compacts are aimed primarily and explicitly at the practices of multinational enterprises across a wide range of issues and problems. While three of the six accords issue primarily from European-North American governments, the other three represent the view of a much wider, even global, range of governments.

NORMATIVE CORPORATE GUIDELINES

By careful reading of these six intergovernmental compacts, one can derive a set of explicitly normative guides for the policies, decisions, and operations of multinational corporations. These guidelines refer to normal business operations, as well as more fundamental responsibilities regarding basic human rights.

Employment Practices and Policies

- MNCs should not contravene the manpower policies of host nations. [ILO]
- MNCs should respect the right of employees to join trade unions and to bargain collectively. [ILO; OECD; UDHR]
- MNCs should develop nondiscriminatory employment policies and promote equal job opportunities. [ILO; OECD; UDHR]

- MNCs should provide equal pay for equal work. [ILO; UDHR]
- MNCs should give advance notice of changes in operations, especially plant closings, and mitigate the adverse effects of these changes. [ILO; OECD]
- MNCs should provide favorable work conditions, limited working hours, holidays with pay, and protection against unemployment. [UDHR]
- MNCs should promote job stability and job security, avoiding arbitrary dismissals and providing severance pay for those unemployed. [ILO; UDHR]
- MNCs should respect local host-country job standards and upgrade the local labor force through training. [ILO; OECD]
- MNCs should adopt adequate health and safety standards for employees and grant them the right to know about job-related health hazards. [ILO]
- MNCs should, minimally, pay basic living wages to employees. [ILO; UDHR]
- MNCs' operations should benefit lower-income groups of the host nation. [ILO]
- MNCs should balance job opportunities, work conditions, job training, and living conditions among migrant workers and host-country nationals. [Helsinki]

Consumer Protection

- MNCs should respect host-country laws and policies regarding the protection of consumers. [OECD; TNC Code]
- MNCs should safeguard the health and safety of consumers by various disclosures, safe packaging, proper labelling, and accurate advertising. [TNC Code]

Environmental Protection

- MNCs should respect host-country laws, goals, and priorities concerning protection of the environment. [OECD; TNC Code; Helsinki]
- MNCs should preserve ecological balance, protect the environment, adopt preventive measures to avoid environmental harm, and rehabilitate environments damaged by operations. [OECD; TNC Code; Helsinki]

- MNCs should disclose likely environmental harms and minimize risks of accidents that could cause environmental damage. [OECD; TNC Code]
- MNCs should promote the development of international environmental standards. [TNC Code; Helsinki]
- MNCs should control specific operations that contribute to pollution of air, water, and soils. [Helsinki]
- MNCs should develop and use technology that can monitor, protect, and enhance the environment. [OECD; Helsinki]

Political Payments and Involvement

- MNCs should not pay bribes nor make improper payments to public officials. [OECD; TNC Code]
- MNCs should avoid improper or illegal involvement or interference in the internal politics of host countries. [OECD; TNC Code]
- MNCs should not interfere in intergovernmental relations. [TNC Code]

Basic Human Rights and Fundamental Freedoms

- MNCs should respect the rights of all persons to life, liberty, security of person, and privacy. [UDHR; ECHR; Helsinki; ILO; TNC Code]

- MNCs should respect the rights of all persons to equal protection of the law, work, choice of job, just and favorable work conditions, and protection against unemployment and discrimination. [UDHR; Helsinki; ILO; TNC Code]
- MNCs should respect all persons' freedom of thought, conscience, religion, opinion and expression, communication, peaceful assembly and association, and movement and residence within each state. [UDHR; ECHR; Helsinki; ILO; TNC Code]
- MNCs should promote a standard of living to support the health and well-being of workers and their families. [UDHR; Helsinki; ILO; TNC Code]
- MNCs should promote special care and assistance to motherhood and childhood. [UDHR; Helsinki; ILO; TNC Code]

These guidelines should be viewed as a *collective* phenomenon since all of them do not appear in each of the six compacts. Table 1 reveals that the OECD compact and the proposed TNC CODE provide the most comprehensive coverage of the guideline categories. The relative lack of guidelines in the ECHR compact may be attributable to the considerable membership overlap with the Organization for Economic Cooperation and Develop-

TABLE 1.   Number of MNC Normative Guidelines by Category for Six Multilateral Compacts

	UDHR	ECHR	HELSINKI	OECD	ILO	TNC CODE	TOTAL
Employment Practices	6	—	—	4	10	—*	20
Consumer Protection	—	—	—	1	—	2	3
Environmental Protection	—	—	5	4	—	4	13
Political Activity	—	—	—	2	—	3	5
Human Rights (re: work)	5	2	5	—	5	5	22
TOTAL	11	2	10	11	15	14	63

*It is expected, but is not a foregone certainty, that the Transnational Corporate Code of Conduct will incorporate into its provisions regarding employment practices the bulk and central meaning of those set forth in the ILO Tripartite Declaration. Hence, their omission in this Table should not be construed to mean that they have been ignored or overlooked by the drafters of the TNC Code.

ment whose members subscribe to the OECD standards for multinationals. Human rights and employment conditions are clearly the leading guideline categories, while consumer protection and corporate political activity appear infrequently. Table 1 suggests that the respective compacts have "specialized" in different types of normative issues involving corporate practices, the most obvious example being the ILO's emphasis on employment issues. The argument of this paper is that the collective weight of the guidelines is more important than the absence of some of them from specific international agreements. Clearly their inclusion across the board would strengthen the case for a global normative system intended to guide corporate practices.

These normative guidelines have direct implications for a wide range of *specific* corporate programs and policies. They include policies regarding childcare, minimum wages, hours of work, employee training and education, adequate housing and health care, pollution control efforts, advertising and marketing activities, severance pay, privacy of employees and consumers, information concerning on-the-job hazards, and, especially for those companies with operations in South Africa, such additional matters as the place of residence and free movement of employees. Quite clearly, the guidelines are not intended to be, nor do they act as, mere rhetoric. Nor do they deal with peripheral matters. They have direct applicability to many of the *central* operations and policies of multinational enterprises.

THE NORMATIVE SOURCES OF THE GUIDELINES

These guides for the practices and policies of multinational companies seem to rest upon and be justified by four normative orienta-

tions. Given sets of the guidelines can be tied directly to one or more of these moral sources.

National sovereignty is one such source. All six compacts invoke the inviolability of national sovereignty. In acting on the compacts' principles, each nation is to take care not to infringe on the sovereignty of its neighbors. Hence, preservation of a nation's integrity and self-interest appears to be one of the moral foundations on which such multilateral accords rest. Multinational enterprises are urged to respect the aims, goals, and directions of a host-country's economic and social development and its cultural and historical traditions. Companies' plans and goals should not contravene these components of a nation's being and sovereignty. Nor should they interfere in the internal political affairs of host countries through improper political activities, political bribes, or questionable payments of any kind made to political candidates or public officials.

Society equity is another normative basis underlying some of the specific corporate guidelines. Pay scales are to be established in ways that will insure equity between men and women, racial and ethnic groups, professional and occupational groups, host-country nationals and parent-country expatriates, indigenous employees and migrant workers, and those well-off and those least-advantaged. The same equity principle is advocated for job opportunities, job training, treatment of the unemployed, and the provision of other work-related benefits and services.

Market integrity is yet another source of moral authority and justification for some of the guidelines identified above, as well as for a large number of other guidelines specified in other agreements that are not treated here which have to do with restrictive business practices, the transnational flow of capital investments, the repatriation of profits, the rights of ownership, and similar matters.

Among the normative corporate guidelines listed earlier, those tinged with the notion of market integrity include restrictions on political payments and bribes that might inject non-market considerations into business transactions, a recognition of private collective bargaining (rather than government mandates) as a preferred technique for establishing pay scales, working conditions, and benefits for employees, and some (but not all) of the consumer protections sought in the accords.

By far the most fundamental, comprehensive, widely acknowledged, and pervasive source of moral authority for the corporate guidelines is *human rights and fundamental freedoms.* This concept is given eloquent expression in the UN Universal Declaration of Human Rights. It is then picked up and adopted by the framers of four of the other five accords analyzed in this paper. Only the OECD Guidelines for Multinational Enterprises fail to invoke the specific language or the basic meaning of human rights and fundamental freedoms as the normative principle on which these accords are erected, although the OECD Guidelines incorporate some of these rights and freedoms as specific duties and obligations of multinationals. As previously noted, a number of OECD members are signatories to the European Convention on Human Rights, thereby subscribing to the basic principles of the Universal Declaration of Human Rights.

Essentially, the Declaration of Human Rights proclaims the existence of a whole host of human rights and freedoms, saying that they are inherent in the human condition. "All human beings are born free and equal in dignity and rights." "Equal and inalienable rights" are possessed by "all members of the human family" who also manifest an "inherent dignity." Other language speaks of "fundamental human rights," "the dignity and worth of the human person," "the equal

rights of men and women," and "fundamental freedoms." These rights and freedoms exist "without distinction of any kind." They are understood as a common possession of humankind, not dependent on membership in any particular group, organization, nation, or society.

This invocation of human rights, as a philosophical principle, owes much to Immanuel Kant. In effect, the Declaration of Human Rights posits the Kantian person as the fundament of moral authority. The human person is said to possess an inherent worth and dignity, as well as inalienable and equal rights and freedoms. This being true of all human beings, correlative duties and obligations are thereby imposed on everyone to respect and not to interfere with the rights of others. No one person is warranted in using another as a means to promote one's own ends and purposes, absent a freely-given informed consent. Hence, a deceptively simple algorithm based on rights and duties sets the stage for the specification of normative rules of conduct for governments, groups, individuals, and — for present purposes — multinational enterprises.[1]

As powerful and compelling as the human rights principle is, it does compete with the other three normative sources — national sovereignty, social equity, and market integrity. This means that human rights are conditioned by political, social, and economic values. Rights do not stand alone or outside the normal range of human institutions, diverse as those institutions are around the globe and from society to society. The nation remains a sacred repository of group allegiance and fierce loyalty, an institution whose leaders at times are fully capable of depriving their own citizens and others of fundamental rights. Witness South Africa's apartheid system, China's brutal suppression of the student-led democracy movement, and the totalitarian excesses of Romania's communist leaders. In all three cases, the state and nation were invoked as ultimate criteria justifying the denial of human rights.

Moreover, societies everywhere erect systems of social status and class, instilling notions of "just claims" and insisting that most people should "know their place." For example, women around the globe find their rights and their life opportunities restricted by male-dominated economic and political systems. The same can be said of the widest variety of ethnic, religious, and racial groups throughout the world, whose fundamental rights and freedoms are often sacrificed on the altar of "social equity" as defined by dominant and competing groups.

Few economic institutions in modern times have appealed more powerfully than markets, whether directed by decentralized economic actors or by centralized states. Those who safeguard the integrity of markets, including officials responsible for high-level governmental or corporate policies, frequently accept the "market necessity" of closing a plant, shifting operations to lower-wage areas, or "busting" a trade union — all in the alleged interest of "allowing the market to work" or "enhancing national and corporate productivity." Doing so may deprive employees of jobs, living wages, retirement security, and other workplace rights.

Hence, in these several ways, rights everywhere are hedged in by such political, social, and economic features of human society. The behavioral guidelines for multinational corporations seem to have been woven, not from a single philosophic principle but by a blending of normative threads. At the pattern's center stand human rights and fundamental freedoms, for in the international compacts reference is found most frequently to this normative marker. But the strands of national sovereignty, social equity, and market integrity are woven into the overall pattern, coloring and giving form to the expression of human rights. Thus are human rights conditioned by societal factors.

One important trait is responsible for the normative dominance of the human rights principle. The human rights spoken of in the Universal Declaration of Human Rights are transcultural. As a principle, human rights span and disregard cultural and national boundaries, class systems, ethnic groupings, economic levels, and other human arrangements which for a variety of reasons differentiate between individuals and groups. Human rights are just that — human. They inhere in *all* humans, regardless of imposed societal classifications and exclusions. They can be defined, disregarded, or violated but they cannot be eradicated.

A transcultural character cannot be claimed for the other three normative sources. National sovereignty is by definition bound to and expressive of the nation. If "nation" is understood to embrace, not only the nation-state but also identification with and allegiance to an ethnic grouping, then it might be more accurate to speak of "socio-ethnicity" as the kind of sovereignty whose protection is sought. In any event, neither "nation-state" nor "socio-ethnic group" is or can be transcultural.

Similarly, social equity meanings rarely if ever span cultural boundaries, in spite of Marxist class theory to the contrary or even the mightiest efforts of Third World nations to see and organize themselves as the world's exploited underclass. That they *are* a global underclass, mistreated, and denied many opportunities by their more prosperous neighbors has not yet bound them together into a solid bloc that could be called transcultural.

Market integrity remains tied firmly to nation-states, even as regional interstate markets such as the European Common Market and the Andean Common Market emerge. Economic systems based on the market principle bear the marks of their national parent's political and ideological institutions. The relatively freer markets that have emerged during the 1980s in the Soviet Union, Eastern Europe, and China are heavily conditioned by the prevailing governmental philosophies of the respective countries, and their operation is not permitted to contravene the perceived needs of the state. The same may be said of markets in the United States, as one observes the ideological swings that accompany successive presidential administrations, legislative elections, and judicial decisions. United States government-imposed commercial sanctions against South Africa, the Soviet Union, Poland, Cuba, Nicaragua, Libya, and other nations reveal the nation-bound character of market operations.

Except for the human rights principle, all other normative sources that undergird the multinational corporate guidelines are thus culture bound, unable to break out of their respective societal contexts. By contrast, human rights are seen to be transcultural. They are the glue or the linchpin that holds the entire normative system together in a coherent international whole. While conditioned by desires for national (or socio-ethnic) sovereignty, social equity, and market integrity — thus finding their operational meaning within a societal context — human rights express attitudes, yearnings, and beliefs common to all humankind. In that sense, they form the core of a global system whose normative aim is to regulate the practices of multinational corporations.

This rights-based normative system finds justification in two ways. One is through deontological obligations implicit in human rights. Here, the philosopher speaks to us. The other justification is more directly operational, taking the form of lessons learned from human experience about the formation and sustenance of human values. These lessons are taught by social scientists. Each of these rationales calls for further elaboration.

RATIONALE I: DEONTOLOGICAL NORMS

The normative corporate guidelines may be seen as extensions and manifestations of broad deontological, i.e., duty-based, principles of human conduct. These principles provide a philosophic basis for defining the duties and obligations of multinational enterprises.

The concurring governments, in the several compacts mentioned here, are saying to multinational enterprises:

- Because your employees have rights to work, to security, to freedom of association, to healthful and safe work conditions, to a pay scale that sustains them and their families at a dignified level of subsistence, to privacy, and to be free from discrimination at work, the managers of multinational corporations incur duties and obligations to respect such rights, to promote them where and when possible, and to avoid taking actions that would deny these rights to the corporation's employees and other stakeholders.

- Because humans and their communities have rights to security, to health, and to the opportunity to develop themselves to their fullest potentials, corporations have an obligation to avoid harming the ecological balance on which human community life and health depend and a positive duty to promote environmental conditions conducive to the pursuit and protection of human rights.

- Because consumers have rights to safe and effective products and to know the quality and traits of the products and services they need to sustain life, companies are obligated, i.e., they have a duty, to offer such products for sale under conditions that permit a free, uncoerced choice for the consumer.

- Because human beings can lay claim to a set of human rights and fundamental freedoms enumerated in the Universal Declaration of Human

Rights, multinational corporations are duty-bound to promote, protect, and preserve those rights and freedoms and to avoid trampling on them through corporate operations. The corporations' Kantian duty is implied in the Kantian rights held by all.

A moral imperative is thus imposed on corporations. The source of this deontological imperative is the rights and freedoms that inhere in all human persons. The corporation is bound, by this moral logic, to respect all persons within the purview of its decisions, policies, and actions. In some such fashion as this, the Universal Declaration of Human Rights serves as the deontological fount, the moral fundament, that defines a corporation's basic duties and obligations toward others. The Declaration's moral principles have been extended to many if not most of the multilateral compacts of the past 40 years, many of whose specific provisions take the form of normative guides for corporate actions across a large range of issues. So goes the moral logic of the accords and compacts.

This philosophic position is compelling and convincing. However, the case for a transcultural corporate ethic need not rest on philosophical arguments alone, or, more positively, the deontological position can be considerably enriched and strengthened by considering the role of human experience as a creator of human values.

RATIONALE II: EXPERIENCE-BASED VALUES

Respect for persons, respect for community integrity, respect for ecological balance, and respect for tested human experience in many spheres of life can be understood both deontologically and as adaptive human value orientations. As value phenomena, they are compatible with the needs and experiences of the world's peoples in a technological era. The need to proclaim many of the rights that appear in the Universal Declaration of Human Rights grew directly out of the gross violations of human rights during the pre-war and war periods of the 1930s and 1940s. Those experiences inspired most of the world's governments to take collective action, in the form of a proclamation, to define an acceptable number of such rights and to urge all to nourish and safeguard them.

Since that time, societies around the globe have felt the bite and seen the promise of technology spawned and applied by multinational corporations and governments. They have experienced the benefits, and have often borne the costs, of business operations undertaken without much regard for environmental, human, and community interests. These experiences have been as compelling, if not as traumatic, as those of the pre-war and war years when human rights were trampled. They have generated widespread agreement and belief in a network of experienced-based values that sustain the lives of individuals, their communities, and their societies. It is these values that have found their way into the several multilateral compacts and accords discussed here. Corporations are urged, not just to tend to their deontological duties but also to support, and not to override, the values that have been found through experience to undergird human flourishing.

Speaking of the role played by experience in formulating value standards, sociologist Robin Williams (1979: 22, 45) reminds us that

... values are learned. This means that they are developed through some kind of experience. ... Similar repeated and pervasive experiences are often characteristic of large numbers of persons similarly situated in society; such experiences are described, discussed, and appraised by the persons involved. The communication of common appraisals eventually builds value standards, which often become widely accepted across many social and cultural boundaries. . . .

> . . . value orientations, repeatedly experienced and reformulated by large numbers of persons over extended periods, will eventually become intellectualized as components of a comprehensive world view.

The gathering together of such experience-derived values concerning the human condition has produced "a comprehensive world view" of what is thought to be morally acceptable behavior by multinational enterprises. The specific "components" of that world view are the normative corporate guidelines described earlier. Humankind is speaking here, making known the basic, minimum, socially acceptable conditions for the conduct of economic enterprise. It is a voice that speaks the language of philosophically inspired rights and duties, as well as the language of a social-scientific conception of experienced-based, adaptive human values. The outcome in both cases is movement toward a transcultural corporate ethic, which is manifested in the six multilateral compacts or codes of conduct discussed here.

Another observer (Dilloway, 1986a: 427) reveals the transcultural moral potential of such international accords:

> The final justification, therefore, for a code of rights is, first, that it defines the conditions in which human potential can develop peacefully in an interdependent milieu; and, second, that such a code, whether for the individual or for interstate relations, offers the *only* frame of common ideas that can span the diversity of cultures, religions, living standards, and political and economic systems to create a common nexus of humane practice for an emergent world community.

This view is echoed by Richard Falk (1980:67, 108):

> To think of human rights in the world as a whole . . . is itself a reflection of the emergence, however weakly, of a planetary perspective based on the notion that persons . . . warrant our normative attention.

Nor is there any reason to restrict this "frame of common ideas" — this morality of the commons — to multinational enterprises alone. It would apply with equal force to domestic and multinational companies. Where nations have been able to identify and agree upon common ethical principles and common values that reflect the experience of even the most diverse cultures, a moral minimum has been established. It remains within the power of some governments and their citizens and businesses to exceed this minimum, while other governments' powers may be insufficiently dedicated to meet even the minimum moral standards. But this minimum — the international common morality, the "common nexus of humane practice," the planetary perspective — stands as a benchmark to be striven for. While it exists, no corporation, domestic or multinational, can legitimately claim the right to operate without referring its policies and practices to this basic moral standard, this morality of the commons that has been writ large upon the global scene.

RESERVATIONS AND QUALIFICATIONS

Four objections might be raised to the derivation of these normative corporate guidelines. . . . [The first and second objections have been omitted. Eds.]

A third difficulty arises when arguing that normative corporate guidelines form the core of a transcultural corporate ethic. The guidelines are not subscribed to by all governments, and even some of the signatory governments may override or ignore them in some circumstances. Thus, it may be charged that the guidelines fall considerably short of representing a universal world view of what multinational corporations should do. Three of the accords are clearly a product of North American-European concerns and issues, while at least one other, the ILO Tripartite Declaration, tends to express the views of employee representatives from industrial nations. Only the UN Universal Declaration of Human Rights and the UN Code of Conduct for Transnational Corporations speak with a more or less global voice, and the last of these two accords has not yet actually come into existence.

This sceptical view is compelling and must be accepted as true. The world is not yet at a point where it can claim to have formulated or projected a set of normative corporate guidelines that are universally or globally accepted and observed. Very real difficulties and genuine controversies have accompanied efforts to forge multilateral compacts that are acceptable to all parties. As noted earlier, the general absence of effective legal enforcement mechanisms weakens these intergovernmental efforts. Sharp differences between multinationals and trade unions have been prominent (Rowan and Campbell, 1983). The sometimes muted struggle between Third World nations and their richer industrial neighbors is always there as a background factor conditioning negotiations. Social ethnicity and diverse religious affiliations become stumbling blocks to consensus. Geopolitical rivalry and *real politik* frequently frustrate the best efforts to reach multilateral accord. Such obstacles are seen by many to be the essence of the international scene, putting the creation of a universal code of conduct beyond reach (Feld, 1980; Waldman, 1980; Wallace, 1982; Windsor and Preston, 1988).

However, a modicum of hope may exist in the very *process* of trying to achieve consensus, prickly as it often is. If nations can agree on procedural rules for determining a fair distribution of the benefits and costs of joining with others in multilateral compacts, more international collaboration might be forthcoming (Windsor and Preston, 1988). The outcome might then be a gradual lessening of substantive differences and a drawing together of the negotiating parties. Robin Williams (1979: 30) explains how this process works:

> . . . opposition of interests and struggles among individuals and collectiveness within a continuing polity and societal system actually can contribute to the establishment and elaboration of generalized values and symbols. . . . If successive contests and conflicts are then successfully resolved without repudiation of the values which legitimate the conflict-resolving process or mechanisms, the more highly generalized values will come more and more to be regarded as axiomatic or unchallengable. Although the specific social implications of the general value principle will be changed through successive occasions, nevertheless, all parties come to have a stake in maintaining the complex value referent as a resource for the future.

This process-based outcome is also thought to be a factor by the UN Centre on Transnational Corporations (United Nations, 1988: 361):

> . . . certain substantive principles are known and relatively undisputed in practice . . . there exists today a large body of authoritative material — agreements, declarations, statements, etc. — on the issues at hand. They are not all

identical, of course, ... but there is also considerable coincidence of views.

... Even where binding legal obligations are not created, legitimate expectations may be established as to the application of corresponding standards within reasonable bounds.

It it worth remembering that corporations remain remarkably attuned to public perceptions of their images and reputations, displaying an often surprising sensitivity to public criticism of their policies and actions. The reasons are frequently self protective, rather than stemming from altruistic or socially responsible motives. Even so, the hovering presence and repeated expression of moral principles seemingly accepted by large public blocs and their governments may influence corporate behavior toward voluntary compliance with these normative standards.

A fourth difficulty is that the normative guidelines are obviously an incomplete set of moral instructions to enterprises. They do not cover many important matters and issues related to multinational corporate operations. None of the five categories shown in Table 1 contains an exhaustive list of all possible issues and needed guidelines. One can easily identify other categories and types of issues relevant to multinational business that apparently have not found their way into this particular group of compacts. . . .

The argument of this paper does not require that all possible issues be included nor that all parties accept all of the provisions of the compacts. It is not claimed that we are witnessing more than the bare beginnings of a globally oriented system of normative principles governing corporate behavior. The only claim being made is that the general outlines of such a system are now discernible and partially operational.

LESSONS FOR POLICY MAKERS

Those who set policies, whether for public or private institutions, can find some important lessons in these multinational codes of conduct.

The most compelling lesson is that highly diverse governments and societies have been able to reach a workable consensus about some core normative directives for multinational enterprises. That should send a strong message to corporate leaders everywhere that the world's peoples, speaking through their governments, are capable of setting standards intended to guide corporate practices and policies into morally desirable channels. As noted, there continues to be much disagreement among governments about many of these issues, but failure to agree on everything should not be allowed to cloak an achieved consensus on many other issues.

Wise corporate leaders will be able to interpret this consensus as a framework of public expectations on which the policies of their own companies can be based. Global stakeholders have set out their positions on a large range of problems and issues that matter to them. In effect, corporations are being offered an opportunity to match their own operations to these public expectations. The best ones will do so. The others may wish they had if, in failing to heed the normative messages, they encounter rising hostility and increased governmental intervention in their affairs. . . .

Acting to promote this normative consensus can be encouraged if policy makers understand both the philosophic roots and the experienced-based values from which these international agreements draw their meaning and strength. The philosophic concept of the human person that one finds in these multilateral compacts, and the human and humane values that grow out of shared global experiences, are no mere passing fancy of a planetary people. Building policy on these twin foundations will bring government and business into alignment with the deep structure of human aspirations.

BEYOND MULTINATIONALS: THE CULTURE OF ETHICS

The transcultural corporate ethic described here is only one part of a much more comprehensive, universal moral order whose shadowy outlines are only partially apparent. This broader "culture of ethics" includes all of those fundamental values and moral orientations that have been proven through long experience to contribute to the sustenance and flourishing of human persons within their communities (Frederick, 1986). It will be important, and increasingly apparent, that all economic enterprises, public and private, domestic and multinational, are bound to acknowledge the moral force of this culture of ethics and to shape their policies and practices accordingly. This "moral dimension" of economic analysis and corporate decision making can no longer be set aside or treated as a peripheral matter (Etzioni, 1988). As human societies are drawn ever closer together by electronic and other technologies, and as they face the multiple threats posed by the unwise and heedless use of these devices, it will become ever more necessary to reach agreement on the core values and ethical principles that permit a humane life to be lived by all. Such planetary agreement is now visible, though yet feeble in its rudiments. This broadscale culture of ethics draws upon many societal, religious, and philosophical sources. It is a great chorus of human voices, human aspirations, and human experiences, arising out of societal and cultural and individual diversity, that expresses the collective normative needs of a global people.

NOTE

1. The algorithm is "deceptively simple" by seeming to overlook the enormous volume of argumentation, qualifications, and exceptions to Kant's views that has been produced by succeeding generations of philosophers. Extended discussion of theories of human rights may be found in Shue (1980) and Nickel (1987). Thomas Donaldson (1989) has developed a far more sophisticated view of ethical algorithms than the one offered here, and I am indebted to him for both the concept and the phrase itself.

REFERENCES

Dilloway, A. J.: 1986a. "Human Rights and Peace," in Ervin Laszlo and Jong Youl Yoo (eds.), *World Encyclopedia of Peace*, vol. 1 (Pergamon Press, Oxford), p. 427.

———: 1986b, "International Bill of Rights," in Ervin Laszlo and Jong Youl Yoo (eds.), *World Encyclopedia of Peace*, vol. 1 (Pergamon Press, Oxford), pp. 458–9.

Donaldson, Thomas: 1989, *The Ethics of International Business* (Oxford University Press, New York).

Etzioni, Amitai: 1988, *The Moral Dimension: Toward a New Economics* (Free Press, New York).

Falk, Richard: 1980, "Theoretical Foundations of Human Rights," in Paula Newberg (ed.): *The Politics of Human Rights* (New York University Press, New York).

Feld, Werner J.: 1980, *Multinational Corporations and U.N. Politics: The Quest for Codes of Conduct* (Pergamon Press, New York).

Frederick, William C.: 1986, "Toward CSR3: Why Ethical Analysis Is Indispensable and Unavoidable in Corporate Affairs," *California Management Review* **28**(3), 126–41.

Nickel, James W.: 1987, *Making Sense of Human Rights: Philosophical Reflections on the Universal*

Declaration of Human Rights (University of California Press, Berkeley).

Rowan, Richard L., and Duncan C. Campbell: 1983, "The Attempt to Regulate Industrial Relations through International Codes of Conduct," *Columbia Journal of World Business* **18**(2), 64–72.

Shue, Henry, 1980, *Basic Rights: Subsistence, Affluence, and U.S. Foreign Policy* (Princeton University Press, Princeton, N.J.).

United Nations: 1983, *Human Rights: A Compilation of International Instruments* (United Nations, New York).

———: 1988, *Transnational Corporations in World Development: Trends and Prospects* (United Nations, New York).

Waldman, Raymond J.: 1980, *Regulating International Business through Codes of Conduct* (American Enterprise Institute, Washington, D.C.).

Wallace, Cynthia Day: 1982, *Legal Control of the Multinational Enterprise: National Regulatory Techniques and the Prospects for International Controls* (Martinus Nijhoff, The Hague).

Williams, Robin: 1979, 'Change and Stability in Values and Value Systems', in Milton Rokeach, *Understanding Human Values* (Free Press, New York).

Windsor, Duane, and Lee E. Preston: 1988, "Corporate Governance, Social Policy and Social Performance in the Multinational Corporation," in Lee E. Preston (ed.), *Research in Corporate Social Performance and Policy*, vol. 10 (JAI Press, Greenwich, Conn.).

Caux Round Table, Principles for Business

INTRODUCTION

The Caux Round Table believes that the world business community should play an important role in improving economic and social conditions. As a statement of aspirations, this document aims to express a world standard against which business behavior can be measured. We seek to begin a process that identifies shared values, reconciles differing values, and thereby develops a shared perspective on business behavior acceptable to and honored by all.

These principles are rooted in two basic ethical ideals: *kyosei* and human dignity. The Japanese concept of *kyosei* means living and working together for the common good — enabling cooperation and mutual prosperity to coexist with healthy and fair competition. "Human dignity" refers to the sacredness or value of each person as an end, not simply as a means to the fulfillment of others' purposes or even majority prescription.

The General Principles in Section 2 seek to clarify the spirit of *kyosei* and "human dignity," while the specific Stakeholder Principles in Section 3 are concerned with their practical application.

In its language and form, the document owes a substantial debt to *The Minnesota Prin-*

ciples, a statement of business behavior developed by the Minnesota Center for Corporate Responsibility. The Center hosted and chaired the drafting committee, which included Japanese, European, and U.S. representatives.

Business behavior can affect relationships among nations and the prosperity and well-being of us all. Business is often the first contact between nations and, by the way in which it causes social and economic changes, has a significant impact on the level of fear or confidence felt by people worldwide. Members of the Caux Round Table place their first emphasis on putting one's own house in order, and on seeking to establish what is right rather than who is right.

SECTION 1. PREAMBLE

The mobility of employment, capital, products and technology is making business increasingly global in its transactions and its effects.

Laws and market forces are necessary but insufficient guides for conduct.

Responsibility for the policies and actions of business and respect for the dignity and interests of its stakeholders are fundamental.

Shared values, including a commitment to shared prosperity, are as important for a global community as for communities of smaller scale.

For these reasons, and because business can be a powerful agent of positive social change, we offer the following principles as a foundation for dialogue and action by business leaders in search of business responsibility. In so doing, we affirm the necessity for moral values in business decision making. Without them, stable business relationships and a sustainable world community are impossible.

SECTION 2. GENERAL PRINCIPLES

Principle 1. The Responsibilities of Businesses: Beyond Shareholders Toward Stakeholders

The value of a business to society is the wealth and employment it creates and the marketable products and services it provides to consumers at a reasonable price commensurate with quality. To create such value, a business must maintain its own economic health and viability, but survival is not a sufficient goal.

Businesses have a role to play in improving the lives of all their customers, employees, and shareholders by sharing with them the wealth they have created. Suppliers and competitors as well should expect businesses to honor their obligations in a spirit of honesty and fairness. As responsible citizens of the local, national, regional and global communities in which they operate, businesses share a part in shaping the future of those communities.

Principle 2. The Economic and Social Impact of Business: Toward Innovation, Justice and World Community

Businesses established in foreign countries to develop, produce or sell should also contribute to the social advancement of those countries by creating productive employment and helping to raise the purchasing power of their citizens. Businesses also should contribute to human rights, education, welfare, and vitalization of the countries in which they operate.

Businesses should contribute to economic and social development not only in the countries in which they operate, but also in the world community at large, through effective and prudent use of resources, free and fair competition, and emphasis upon innovation in technology, production methods, marketing and communications.

Principle 3. Business Behavior: Beyond the Letter of Law Toward a Spirit of Trust

While accepting the legitimacy of trade secrets, businesses should recognize that sincerity, candor, truthfulness, the keeping of promises, and transparency contribute not only to their own credibility and stability but also to the smoothness and efficiency of business transactions, particularly on the international level.

Principle 4. Respect for Rules

To avoid trade frictions and to promote freer trade, equal conditions for competition, and fair and equitable treatment for all participants, businesses should respect international and domestic rules. In addition, they should recognize that some behavior, although legal, may still have adverse consequences.

Principle 5. Support for Multilateral Trade

Businesses should support the multilateral trade systems of the GATT/World Trade Organization and similar international agreements. They should cooperate in efforts to promote the progressive and judicious liberalization of trade and to relax those domestic measures that unreasonably hinder global commerce, while giving due respect to national policy objectives.

Principle 6. Respect for the Environment

A business should protect and, where possible, improve the environment, promote sustainable development, and prevent the wasteful use of natural resources.

Principle 7. Avoidance of Illicit Operations

A business should not participate in or condone bribery, money laundering, or other corrupt practices: indeed, it should seek cooperation with others to eliminate them. It should not trade in arms or other materials used for terrorist activities, drug traffic or other organized crime.

SECTION 3. STAKEHOLDER PRINCIPLES

Customers

We believe in treating all customers with dignity, irrespective of whether they purchase our products and services directly from us or otherwise acquire them in the market. We therefore have a responsibility to:

- provide our customers with the highest quality products and services consistent with their requirements;
- treat our customers fairly in all aspects of our business transactions, including a high level of service and remedies for their dissatisfaction;
- make every effort to ensure that the health and safety of our customers, as well as the quality of their environment, will be sustained or enhanced by our products and services;
- assure respect for human dignity in products offered, marketing, and advertising; and
- respect the integrity of the culture of our customers.

Employees

We believe in the dignity of every employee and in taking employee interests seriously. We therefore have a responsibility to:

- provide jobs and compensation that improve workers' living conditions;

- provide working conditions that respect each employee's health and dignity;
- be honest in communications with employees and open in sharing information, limited only by legal and competitive constraints;
- listen to and, where possible, act on employee suggestions, ideas, requests and complaints;
- engage in good faith negotiations when conflict arises;
- avoid discriminatory practices and guarantee equal treatment and opportunity in areas such as gender, age, race and religion;
- promote in the business itself the employment of differently abled people in places of work where they can be genuinely useful;
- protect employees from avoidable injury and illness in the workplace;
- encourage and assist employees in developing relevant and transferable skills and knowledge; and
- be sensitive to the serious unemployment problems frequently associated with business decisions, and work with governments, employee groups, other agencies and each other in addressing these dislocations.

Owners/Investors

We believe in honoring the trust our investors place in us. We therefore have a responsibility to:

- apply professional and diligent management in order to secure a fair and competitive return on our owners' investment;
- disclose relevant information to owners/investors subject only to legal requirements and competitive constraints;
- conserve, protect and increase the owners/investors' assets; and
- respect owners/investors' requests, suggestions, complaints, and formal resolutions.

Suppliers

Our relationship with suppliers and subcontractors must be based on mutual respect. We therefore have a responsibility to:

- seek fairness and truthfulness in all our activities, including pricing, licensing, and rights to sell;
- ensure that our business activities are free from coercion and unnecessary litigation;
- foster long-term stability in the supplier relationship in return for value, quality, competitiveness and reliability;
- share information with suppliers and integrate them into our planning processes;
- pay suppliers on time and in accordance with agreed terms of trade; and
- seek, encourage and prefer suppliers and subcontractors whose employment practices respect human dignity.

Competitors

We believe that fair economic competition is one of the basic requirements for increasing the wealth of nations and ultimately for making possible the just distribution of goods and services. We therefore have a responsibility to:

- foster open markets for trade and investment;
- promote competitive behavior that is socially and environmentally beneficial and demonstrates mutual respect among competitors;
- refrain from either seeking or participating in questionable payments or favors to secure competitive advantages;
- respect both tangible and intellectual property rights; and
- refuse to acquire commercial information by dishonest or unethical means, such as industrial espionage.

Communities

We believe that as global corporate citizens we can contribute to such forces of reform and human rights as are at work in the communities in which we operate. We therefore have a responsibility in those communities to:

- respect human rights and democratic institutions, and promote them wherever practicable;
- recognize government's legitimate obligation to the society at large and support public policies and practices that promote human development through harmonious relations between business and other segments of society;
- collaborate with those forces in the community dedicated to raising standards of health, education, workplace safety and economic well-being;
- promote and stimulate sustainable development and play a leading role in preserving and enhancing the physical environment and conserving the earth's resources;
- support peace, security, diversity and social integration;
- respect the integrity of local cultures; and
- be a good corporate citizen through charitable donations, educational and cultural contributions, and employee participation in community and civic affairs.

Ali Boureslan v. Arabian American Oil Company and Aramco Services Company

Supreme Court of the United States

These cases present the issue whether Title VII applies extraterritorially to regulate the employment practices of United States employers who employ United States citizens abroad. The United States Court of Appeals for the Fifth Circuit held that it does not, and we agree with that conclusion.

Petitioner Boureslan is a naturalized United States citizen who was born in Lebanon. The respondents are two Delaware corporations, Arabian American Oil Company (Aramco), and its subsidiary, Aramco Service Company (ASC). Aramco's principal place of business is Dhahran, Saudia Arabia, and it is licensed to do business in Texas. ASC's principal place of business is Houston, Texas.

In 1979, Boureslan was hired by ASC as a cost engineer in Houston. A year later he was transferred, at his request, to work for Aramco in Saudi Arabia. Boureslan remained with Aramco in Saudi Arabia until he was discharged in 1984. After filing a charge of discrimination with the Equal Employment Opportunity Commission (EEOC), he instituted this suit in the United States District Court for the Southern District of Texas against Aramco and ASC. He sought relief under both state law and Title VII of the Civil Rights Act of 1964, on the ground that he was harassed and ultimately discharged by respondents on account of his race, religion, and national origin.

Respondents filed a motion for summary judgment on the ground that the District Court lacked subject matter jurisdiction over Boureslan's claim because the protections of Title VII do not extend to United States citizens employed abroad by American employers. The District Court agreed, and dismissed

Majority opinion by Chief Justice Rehnquist decided March 26, 1991. Reprinted with permission from *The United States Law Week* Vol. 59, pp. 4226–29 (March 26, 1991). Published by The Bureau of National Affairs, Inc. (800–372–1033).

Boureslan's Title VII claim; it also dismissed his state-law claims for lack of pendent jurisdiction, and entered final judgment in favor of respondents. A panel for the Fifth Circuit affirmed. After vacating the panel's decision and rehearing the case en banc, the court affirmed the District Court's dismissal of Boureslan's complaint. Both Boureslan and the EEOC petitioned for certiorari. We granted both petitions for certiorari to resolve this important issue of statutory interpretation.

Both parties concede, as they must, that Congress has the authority to enforce its laws beyond the territorial boundaries of the United States. Whether Congress has in fact exercised that authority in this case is a matter of statutory construction. It is our task to determine whether Congress intended the protections of Title VII to apply to United States citizens employed by American employers outside of the United States.

It is a long-standing principle of American law "that legislation of Congress, unless a contrary intent appears, is meant to apply only within the territorial jurisdiction of the United States." This "canon of construction . . . is a valid approach whereby unexpressed congressional intent may be ascertained." It serves to protect against unintended clashes between our laws and those of other nations which could result in international discord.

In applying this rule of construction, we look to see whether "language in the [relevant act] gives any indication of a congressional purpose to extend its coverage beyond places over which the United States has sovereignty or has some measure of legislative control." We assume that Congress legislates against the backdrop of the presumption against extraterritoriality. Therefore, unless there is "the affirmative intention of the Congress clearly expressed," we must presume it "is primarily concerned with domestic conditions."

Boureslan and the EEOC contend that the language of Title VII evinces a clearly ex-

pressed intent on behalf of Congress to legislate extraterritorially. They rely principally on two provisions of the statute. First, petitioners argue that the statute's definitions of the jurisdictional terms "employer" and "commerce" are sufficiently broad to include U.S. firms that employ American citizens overseas. Second, they maintain that the statute's "alien exemption" clause necessarily implies that Congress intended to protect American citizens from employment discrimination abroad. Petitioners also contend that we should defer to the EEOC's consistently held position that Title VII applies abroad. We conclude that petitioners' evidence, while not totally lacking in probative value, falls short of demonstrating the affirmative congressional intent required to extend the protections of the Title VII beyond our territorial borders.

Title VII prohibits various discriminatory employment practices based on an individual's race, color, religion, sex, or national origin. An employer is subject to Title VII if it has employed 15 or more employees for a specified period and is "engaged in an industry affecting commerce." An industry affecting commerce is "any activity, business, or industry in commerce or in which a labor dispute would hinder or obstruct commerce or the free flow of commerce and includes any activity or industry 'affecting commerce' within the meaning of the Labor-Management Reporting and Disclosure Act of 1959. "Commerce," in turn, is defined as "trade, traffic, commerce, transportation, transmission, or communication among the several States; or between a State and any place outside thereof; or within the District of Columbia, or a possession of the United States; or between points in the same State but through a point outside thereof."

Petitioners argue that by its plain language, Title VII's "broad jurisdictional language" reveals Congress's intent to extend the statute's protections to employment discrimination anywhere in the world by a U.S. employer who affects trade "between a State and any place outside thereof." More precisely, they assert that since Title VII defines "States" to include States, the District of Columbia, and specified territories, the clause "between a State and any place outside thereof" must be referring to areas beyond the territorial limit of the United States.

Respondents offer several alternative explanations for the statute's expansive language. They contend that the "or between a State and any place outside thereof" clause "provide[s] the jurisdictional nexus required to regulate commerce that is not wholly within a single state, presumably as it affects both interstate and foreign commerce" but not to "regulate conduct exclusively *within* a foreign country." They also argue that since the definitions of the terms "employer," "commerce," and "industry affecting commerce," make no mention of "commerce with foreign nations," Congress cannot be said to have intended that the statute apply overseas. In support of this argument, petitioners point to Title II of the Civil Rights Act of 1964, governing public accommodation, which specifically defines commerce as it applies to foreign nations. Finally, respondents argue that while language present in the first bill considered by the House of Representatives contained the terms "foreign commerce" and "foreign nations," those terms were deleted by the Senate before the Civil Rights Act of 1964 was passed. They conclude that these deletions "[are] inconsistent with the notion of a clearly expressed congressional intent to apply Title VII extraterritorially."

We need not choose between these competing interpretations as we would be required to do in the absence of the presumption against extraterritorial applications discussed above. Each is plausible, but no more persuasive than that. The language relied upon by petitioners — and it is they who must make the affirmative showing — is ambiguous, and does not speak directly to the question presented here. The intent of Congress as to the extraterritorial application of this statute must be deduced by inference from boilerplate language which can be found in any number of congressional acts, none of which have ever been held to apply overseas. *See, e.g.,* Consumer Product Safety Act; Federal Food, Drug, and Cosmetic Act; Transportation Safety Act of 1974; Labor-Management Reporting and Disclosure Act, of 1959; Americans with Disabilities Act of 1990.

Petitioners' reliance on Title VII's jurisdictional provisions also finds no support in our case law; we have repeatedly held that even statutes that contain broad language in their definitions of "commerce" that expressly refer to "*foreign* commerce," do not apply abroad. For example, in *New York Central R. Co.* v. *Chisholm,* (1925), we addressed the extraterritorial application of the Federal Employers Liability Act (FELA). FELA provides that common carriers by railroad while engaging in "interstate or foreign commerce" or commerce between "any of the States or territories and any foreign nation or nations" shall be liable in damages to its employees who suffer injuries resulting from their employment. Despite this broad jurisdictional language, we found that the Act "contains no words which definitely disclose an intention to give it extraterritorial effect" and therefore there was no jurisdiction under FELA for a damages action by a U.S. citizen employed on a U.S. railroad who suffered fatal injuries at a point 30 miles north of the U.S. border into Canada.

Similarly, in *McCulloch* v. *Sociedad Nacional de Marineros de Honduras,* (1963), we addressed whether Congress intended the National Labor Relations Act to apply overseas. Even though the NLRA contained broad language that referred by its terms to foreign commerce, this Court refused to find a congressional intent to apply the statute abroad because there was not "any specific language" in the Act reflecting congressional intent to do so.

The EEOC places great weight on an assertedly similar "broad jurisdictional grant in the Lanham Act" that this Court held applied extraterritorially in *Steele* v. *Bulova Watch Co.,* (1952). In *Steele,* we addressed whether the Lanham Act, designed to prevent deceptive and misleading use of trademarks, applied to acts of a U.S. citizen consummated in Mexico. The Act defined commerce as "all commerce which may lawfully be regulated by Congress." The stated intent of the statute was "to regulate commerce within the control of Congress by making actionable the deceptive and misleading use of marks in such commerce." While recognizing that "the legislation of Congress will not extend beyond the boundaries of the United States unless a contrary legislative intent appears," the Court concluded that in light of the fact that the allegedly unlawful conduct had some effects within the United States, coupled with the Act's "broad jurisdictional grant" and its "sweeping reach into 'all commerce which may lawfully be regulated by Congress,'" the statute was properly interpreted as applying abroad.

The EEOC's attempt to analogize this case to *Steele* is unpersuasive. The Lanham Act by terms applies to "all commerce which may lawfully be regulated by Congress." The Constitution gives Congress the power "[t]o regulate Commerce with foreign Nations, and among the several States, and with the Indian Tribes." Since the Act expressly stated that it applied to the extent of Congress's power over commerce, the Court in *Steele* concluded that Congress intended that the statute apply abroad. By contrast, Title VII's more limited, boilerplate "commerce" language does not

support such an expansive construction of congressional intent. Moreover, unlike the language in the Lanham Act, Title VII's definition of "commerce" was derived expressly from the LMRDA, a statute that this Court had held, prior to the enactment of Title VII, did not apply abroad.

Thus petitioner's argument based on the jurisdictional language of Title VII fails both as a matter of statutory language and of our previous case law. Many acts of Congress are based on the authority of that body to regulate commerce among the several States, and the parts of these acts setting forth the basis for legislative jurisdiction will obviously refer to such commerce in one way or another. If we were to permit possible, or even plausible interpretations of language such as that involved here to override the presumption against extraterritorial application, there would be little left of the presumption.

Petitioners argue that Title VII's "alien exemption provision," "clearly manifests an intention" by Congress to protect U.S. citizens with respect to their employment outside of the United States. The alien exemption provision says that the statute "shall not apply to an employer with respect to the employment of aliens outside any State." Petitioners contend that from this language a negative inference should be drawn that Congress intended Title VII to cover United States *citizens* working abroad for United States employers. There is "[no] other plausible explanation [that] the alien exemption exists," they argue, because "[i]f Congress believed that the statute did not apply extraterritorially, it would have had no reason to include an exemption for a certain category of individuals employed outside the United States." Since "[t]he statute's jurisdictional provisions cannot possibly be read to confer coverage only upon aliens employed outside the United States," petitioners conclude that "Congress could not rationally have enacted an exemption for the employment of aliens abroad if it intended to foreclose *all* potential extraterritorial applications of the statute."

Respondents resist petitioners' interpretation of the alien-exemption provision and assert two alternative *raisons d'etre* for that language. First, they contend that since aliens are included in the statute's definition of employee, and the definition of commerce includes possessions as well as "States," the purpose of the exemption is to provide that employers of aliens in the possessions of the United States are not covered by the statute. Thus, the "outside any State" clause means outside any State, but within the control of the United States. Respondents argue that "[t]his reading of the alien exemption provision is consistent with and supported by the historical development of the provision" because Congress's inclusion of the provision was a direct response to this Court's interpretation of the term "possessions" in the Fair Labor Standards Act in *Vermilya-Brown Co.* v. *Connell* (1948), to include leased bases in foreign nations that were within the control of the United States. They conclude that the alien exemption provision was included "to limit the impact of *Vermilya-Brown* by excluding from coverage employers of aliens in areas under U.S. control that" were not encompassed within Title VII's definition of the term "State."

Second, respondents assert that by negative implication, the exemption "confirm[s] the coverage of aliens in the United States." They contend that this interpretation is consistent with our conclusion in *Espinoza* v. *Farah Mfg. Co.* (1973), that aliens within the United States are protected from discrimination both because Title VII uses the term "individual" rather than "citizen," and because of the alien-exemption provision.

If petitioners are correct that the alien-exemption clause means that the statute applies to employers overseas, we see no way of distinguishing in its application between United States employers and foreign employers. Thus, a French employer of a United States citizen in France would be subject to Title VII — a result at which even petitioners balk. The EEOC assures us that in its view the term "employer" means only "American employer," but there is no such distinction in this statute, and no indication that EEOC in the normal course of its administration had produced a reasoned basis for such a distinction. Without clearer evidence of congressional intent to do so than is contained in the alien-exemption clause, we are unwilling to ascribe to that body a policy which would raise difficult issues of international law by imposing this country's employment-discrimination regime upon foreign corporations operating in foreign commerce. . . .

Similarly, Congress failed to provide any mechanisms for overseas enforcement of Title VII. For instance, the statute's venue provisions, § 2000e–5(f)(3), are ill-suited for extraterritorial application as they provide for venue only in a judicial district in the state where certain matters related to the employer occurred or were located. And the limited investigative authority provided for the EEOC, permitting the Commission only to issue subpoenas for witnesses and documents from "anyplace in the United States or any Territory or possession thereof," § 2000e–9, suggests that Congress did not intend for the statute to apply abroad.

It is also reasonable to conclude that had Congress intended Title VII to apply overseas, it would have addressed the subject of conflicts with foreign laws and procedures. In amending the Age Discrimination in Employment Act of 1967 (ADEA), to apply abroad, Congress specifically addressed potential conflicts with foreign law by providing that it is not unlawful for an employer to take any action prohibited by the ADEA "where such practices involve an employee in a workplace in a foreign country, and compliance with [the ADEA] would cause such employer . . . to violate the laws of the country in which such workplace is located." Title VII, by contrast, fails to address conflicts with the laws of other nations.

Finally, the EEOC, as one of the two federal agencies with primary responsibility for enforcing Title VII, argues that we should defer to its "consistent" construction of Title VII, first formally expressed in a statement issued after oral argument but before the Fifth Circuit's initial decision in this case (Apr. 1989), "to apply to discrimination against American citizens outside the United States." Citing a 1975 letter from the EEOC's General Counsel, 1983 testimony by its Chairman, and a 1985 decision by the Commission, it argues that its consistent administrative interpretations "reinforce" the conclusion that Congress intended Title VII to apply abroad.

In *General Electric Co.* v. *Gilbert* (1976), we addressed the proper deference to be afforded the EEOC's guidelines. Recognizing that "Congress, in enacting Title VII, did not confer upon the EEOC authority to promulgate rules or regulations," we held that the level of deference afforded "will depend upon the thoroughness evident in its consideration, the validity of its reasoning, its consistency with earlier and later pronouncements, and all those factors which give it power to persuade, if lacking power to control.'"

The EEOC's interpretation does not fare well under these standards. As an initial matter, the position taken by the Commission "contradicts the position which [it] had enunciated at an earlier date, closer to the enactment of the governing statute." The Commission's early pronouncements on

the issue supported the conclusion that the statute was limited to domestic application. ("Title VII . . . protects all individuals, both citizen and noncitizens, domiciled or residing in the United States, against discrimination on the basis of race, color, religion, sex, or national origin.") While the Commission later intimated that the statute applied abroad, this position was not expressly reflected in its policy guidelines until some 24 years after the passage of the statute. The EEOC offers no basis in its experience for the change. The EEOC's interpretation of the statute here thus has been neither contemporaneous with its enactment nor consistent since the statute came into law. As discussed above, it also lacks support in the plain language of the statute. While we do not wholly discount the weight to be given to the 1988 guideline, its persuasive value is limited when judged by the standards set forth in *Skidmore*. We are of the view that, even when considered in combination with petitioners' other arguments, the EEOC's interpretation is insufficiently weighty to overcome the presumption against extraterritorial application.

Our conclusion today is buttressed by the fact that "[w]hen it desires to do so, Congress knows how to place the high seas within the jurisdictional reach of a statute." *Argentine Republic* v. *Amerada Hess Shipping Corp.* (1989). Congress's awareness of the need to make a clear statement that a statute applies overseas is amply demonstrated by the numerous occasions on which it has expressly legislated the extraterritorial application of a statute. . . .

Petitioners have failed to present sufficient affirmative evidence that Congress intended Title VII to apply abroad. Accordingly, the judgment of the Court of Appeals is *Affirmed.*

Dow Chemical Company and Shell Oil Company v. Domingo Castro Alfaro et al.

Supreme Court of Texas

Because its analysis and reasoning are correct I join in the majority opinion without reservation. I write separately, however, to respond to the dissenters who mask their inability to agree among themselves with competing rhetoric. In their zeal to implement their own preferred social policy that Texas corporations not be held responsible at home for harm caused abroad, these dissenters refuse to be restrained by either express statutory language or the compelling precedent, previously approved by this very court, holding that forum non conveniens does not apply in Texas. To accomplish the desired social engineering, they must invoke yet another legal fiction with a fancy name to shield alleged wrongdoers, the so-called doctrine of *forum non conveniens*. The refusal of a Texas corporation to confront a Texas judge and jury is to be labelled "inconvenient" when what is really involved is not convenience but connivance to avoid corporate accountability.

The dissenters are insistent that a jury of Texans be denied the opportunity to evaluate the conduct of a Texas corporation concerning decisions it made in Texas because the only ones allegedly hurt are foreigners. Fortunately Texans are not so provincial and narrow-minded as these dissenters presume. Our citizenry recognizes that a wrong does not fade away because its immediate consequences are first felt far away rather than close to home. Never have we been required to forfeit our membership in the human race in order to maintain our proud heritage as citizens of Texas.

The dissenters argue that it is *inconvenient* and *unfair* for farmworkers allegedly suffering permanent physical and mental injuries, including irreversible sterility, to seek redress by suing a multinational corporation in a court three blocks away from its world headquarters and another corporation, which operates in Texas this country's largest chemical plant. Because the "doctrine" they advocate has nothing to do with fairness and convenience and everything to do with immunizing multinational corporations from accountability for their alleged torts causing injury abroad, I write separately.

THE FACTS

Respondents claim that while working on a banana plantation in Costa Rica for Standard Fruit Company, an American subsidiary of Dole Fresh Fruit Company, headquartered in Boca Raton, Florida, they were required to handle dibromochloropropane ["DBCP"], a pesticide allegedly manufactured and furnished to Standard Fruit by Shell Oil Company ["Shell"] and Dow Chemical Company ["Dow"]. The Environmental Protection Agency issued a notice of intent to cancel all food uses of DBCP on September 22, 1977. 42 Fed. Reg. 48026 (1977). It followed with an order suspending registrations of pesti-

786 S.W. 2d 674 (Tex. 1990). Concurring opinion by Judge Doggett.

cides containing DBCP on November 3, 1977. 42 Fed. Reg. 57543 (1977). Before and after the E.P.A.'s ban of DBCP in the United States, Shell and Dow apparently shipped several hundred thousand gallons of the pesticide to Costa Rica for use by Standard Fruit. The Respondents, Domingo Castro Alfaro and other plantation workers, filed suit in a state district court in Houston, Texas, alleging that their handling of DBCP caused them serious personal injuries for which Shell and Dow were liable under the theories of products liability, strict liability and breach of warranty.

Rejecting an initial contest to its authority by Shell and Dow, the trial court found that it had jurisdiction under Tex. Civ. Prac. & Rem. Code Ann. § 71.031 (Vernon 1986), but dismissed the cause on the grounds of forum non conveniens. The court of appeals reversed and remanded, holding that Section 71.031 provides a foreign plaintiff with an absolute right to maintain a death or personal injury cause of action in Texas without being subject to forum non conveniens dismissal. 751 S.W.2d 208. Shell and Dow have asked this court to reverse the judgment of the court of appeals and affirm the trial court's dismissal.

Shell Oil Company is a multinational corporation with its world headquarters in Houston, Texas. Dow Chemical Company, though headquartered in Midland, Michigan, conducts extensive operations from its Dow Chemical USA building located in Houston. Dow operates this country's largest chemical manufacturing plant within 60 miles of Houston in Freeport, Texas. The district court where this lawsuit was filed is three blocks away from Shell's world headquarters, One Shell Plaza in downtown Houston.

Shell has stipulated that all of its more than 100,000 documents relating to DBCP are located or will be produced in Houston. Shell's medical and scientific witnesses are in Houston. The majority of Dow's documents and witnesses are located in Michigan, which is far closer to Houston (both in terms of geography and communications linkages) than to Costa Rica. The respondents have agreed to be available in Houston for independent medical examinations, for depositions and for trial. Most of the respondents' treating doctors and co-workers have agreed to testify in Houston. Conversely, Shell and Dow have purportedly refused to make their witnesses available in Costa Rica.

The banana plantation workers allegedly injured by DBCP were employed by an American company on American-owned land and grew Dole bananas for export soley to American tables. The chemical allegedly rendering the workers sterile was researched, formulated, tested, manufactured, labeled and shipped by an American company in the United States to another American company. The decision to manufacture DBCP for distribution and use in the third world was made by these two American companies in their corporate offices in the United States. Yet now Shell and Dow argue that the one part of this equation that should not be American is the legal consequences of their actions.

FORUM NON CONVENIENS — "A COMMON LAW DOCTRINE OUT OF CONTROL"

As a reading of Tex. Civ. Prac. & Rem. Code Ann. § 71.031 (Vernon 1986) makes clear, the doctrine of forum non conveniens has been statutorily abolished in Texas. The decision in *Allen* v. *Bass*, . . . approved by this court, clearly holds that, upon a showing of personal jurisdiction over a defendant, article 4678, now section 71.031 of the Texas Civil Practice & Remedies Code, "opens the courts of this state to citizens of a neighboring state and gives them an absolute right to maintain a transitory action of the present nature and to try their cases in the courts of this state."

Displeased that *Allen* stands in the way of immunizing multinational corporations from suits seeking redress for their torts causing injury abroad, the dissenters doggedly attempt to circumvent this precedent. Unsuccessful with arguments based upon Texas law, they criticize the court for not justifying its result on public policy grounds.

Using the "Doctrine" to Kill the Litigation Altogether

Both as a matter of law and of public policy, the doctrine of forum non conveniens is without justification. The proffered foundations for it are "considerations of fundamental fairness and sensible and effective judicial administration." . . . In fact, the doctrine is favored by multinational defendants because a forum non conveniens dismissal is often outcome-determinative, effectively defeating the claim and denying the plaintiff recovery. . . .

Empirical data available demonstrate that less than four percent of cases dismissed under the doctrine of forum non conveniens ever reach trial in foreign court.[1] A forum non conveniens dismissal usually will end the litigation altogether, effectively excusing any liability of the defendant. The plaintiffs leave the courtroom without having had their case resolved on the merits.

The *Gulf Oil* Factors — Balanced Toward the Defendant

Courts today usually apply forum non conveniens by use of the factors set forth at length in *Gulf Oil Corp. v. Gilbert* . . . Briefly summarized, those factors are (i) the private interests of the litigants (ease and cost of access to documents and witnesses); and (ii) the public interest factors (the interest of the forum state, the burden on the courts, and notions of judicial comity). In the forty-three years in which the courts have grappled with the *Gulf Oil* factors, it has become increasingly apparent that their application fails to promote fairness and convenience. Instead, these factors have been used by defendants to achieve objectives violative of public policy. . . .

The Public Interest Factors. The three public interest factors asserted by Justice Gonzalez may be summarized as (1) whether the interests of the jurisdiction are sufficient to justify entertaining the lawsuit; (2) the potential for docket backlog; and (3) judicial comity. . . .

The next justification offered by the dissenters for invoking the legal fiction of "inconvenience" is that judges will be overworked. Not only will foreigners take our jobs, as we are told in the popular press; now they will have our courts. The xenophobic suggestion that foreigners will take over our courts "forcing our residents to wait in the corridors of our courthouses while foreign causes of action are tried," Gonzalez dissent, 786 S.W.2d at 690, is both misleading and false.

It is the height of deception to suggest that docket backlogs in our state's urban centers are caused by so-called "foreign litigation." This assertion is unsubstantiated empirically both in Texas and in other jurisdictions rejecting forum non conveniens.[2] Ten states, including Texas, have not recognized the doctrine. Within these states, there is no evidence that the docket congestion predicted by the dissenters has actually occurred. The best evidence, of course, comes from Texas itself. Although foreign citizens have enjoyed the statutory right to sue defendants living or doing business here since the 1913 enactment of the predecessor to Section 71.031 of the Texas Civil Practice and Remedies Code, reaffirmed in the 1932 decision in *Allen*,

Texas has not been flooded by foreign causes of action.

Moreover, the United States Supreme Court has indicated that docket congestion "is a wholly inappropriate consideration in virtually every other context." . . . If we begin to refuse to hear lawsuits properly filed in Texas because they are sure to require time, we set a precedent that can be employed to deny Texans access to these same courts.

Nor does forum non conveniens afford a panacea for eradicating congestion:

> Making the place of trial turn on a largely imponderable exercise of judicial discretion is extremely costly. Even the strongest proponents of the most suitable forum approach concede that it is inappropriately time-consuming and wasteful for the parties to have to "litigate in order to determine where they shall litigate." If forum non conveniens outcomes are not predictable, such litigation is bound to occur. . . . In terms of delay, expense, uncertainty, and a fundamental loss of judicial accountability, the most suitable forum version of forum non conveniens clearly costs more than it is worth.

Robertson, *supra,* 103 L.Q.Rev. at 414, 426.

Comity — deference shown to the interests of the foreign forum — is a consideration best achieved by rejecting forum non conveniens. Comity is not achieved when the United States allows its multinational corporations to adhere to a double standard when operating abroad and subsequently refuses to hold them accountable for those actions. As S. Jacob Scherr, Senior Project Attorney for the Natural Resources Defense Counsel, has noted

> There is a sense of outrage on the part of many poor countries where citizens are the most vulnerable to exports of hazardous drugs, pesticides and food products. At the 1977 meeting of the UNEP Governing Council, Dr. J.C. Kiano, the Kenyan minister for water development, warned that developing nations will no longer tolerate being used as dumping grounds

for products that had not been adequately tested "and that their peoples should not be used as guinea pigs for determining the safety of chemicals."

Comment, *U.S. Exports Banned For Domestic Use, But Exported to Third World Countries,* 6 Int'l Tr.L.J. 95, 98 (1980–81) [hereinafter *"U.S. Exports Banned"*].

Comity is best achieved by "avoiding the possibility of 'incurring the wrath and distrust of the Third World as it increasingly recognizes that it is being used as the industrial world's garbage can.'" Note, *Hazardous Exports from a Human Rights Perspective,* 14 Sw.U.L. Rev. 81, 101 (1983) [hereinafter *"Hazardous Exports"*] (quoting Hon. Michael D. Barnes (Representative in Congress representing Maryland)).[3] . . .

PUBLIC POLICY & THE TORT LIABILITY OF MULTINATIONAL CORPORATIONS IN UNITED STATES COURTS

The abolition of forum non conveniens will further important public policy considerations by providing a check on the conduct of multinational corporations (MNCs). *See Economic Approach,* 22 Geo.Wash.J. Int'l L. & Econ. at 241. The misconduct of even a few multinational corporations can affect untold millions around the world.[4] For example, after the United States imposed a domestic ban on the sale of cancer-producing TRIS-treated children's sleepwear, American companies exported approximately 2.4 million pieces to Africa, Asia and South America. A similar pattern occurred when a ban was proposed for baby pacifiers that had been linked to choking deaths in infants. *Hazardous Exports, supra,* 14 Sw.U.L.Rev. at 82. These examples of indifference by some corporations towards children abroad are not unusual.[5]

The allegations against Shell and Dow, if proven true, would not be unique, since production of many chemicals banned for domestic use has thereafter continued for foreign marketing.[6] Professor Thomas McGarity, a respected authority in the field of environmental law, explained:

> During the mid-1970s, the United States Environmental Protection Agency (EPA) began to restrict the use of some pesticides because of their environmental effects, and the Occupational Safety and Health Administration (OSHA) established workplace exposure standards for toxic and hazardous substances in the manufacture of pesticides.... [I]t is clear that many pesticides that have been severely restricted in the United States are used without restriction in many Third World countries, with resulting harm to fieldworkers and the global environment.

McGarity, *Bhopal and the Export of Hazardous Technologies*, 20 Tex.Int'l L.J. 333, 334 (1985) (citations omitted). By 1976, "29 percent, or 161 million pounds of all the pesticides exported by the United States were either unregistered or banned for domestic use." McWilliams, *Tom Sawyer's Apology: A Reevaluation of United States Pesticide Export Policy,* 8 Hastings Int'l & Comp.L.Rev. 61, 61 & n. 4 (1984). It is estimated that these pesticides poison 750,000 people in developing countries each year, of which 22,500 die. *Id.* at 62. Some estimates place the death toll from the "improper marketing of pesticides at 400,000 lives a year." *Id.* at 62 n. 7.

Some United States multinational corporations will undoubtedly continue to endanger human life and the environment with such activities until the economic consequences of these actions are such that it becomes unprofitable to operate in this manner. At present, the tort laws of many third world countries are not yet developed. *An Economic Approach, supra,* 22 Geo. Wash.J.Int'l L. & Econ. at 222–23. Industrialization "is occur-

ring faster than the development of domestic infrastructures necessary to deal with the problems associated with industry." *Exporting Hazardous Industries, supra,* 20 Int'l L. & Pol. at 791. When a court dismisses a case against a United States multinational corporation, it often removes the most effective restraint on corporate misconduct. *See An Economic Approach, supra,* 22 Geo.Wash. J.Int'l L. & Econ. at 241.

The doctrine of forum non conveniens is obsolete in a world in which markets are global and in which ecologists have documented the delicate balance of all life on this planet. The parochial perspective embodied in the doctrine of forum non conveniens enables corporations to evade legal control merely because they are transnational. This perspective ignores the reality that actions of our corporations affecting those abroad will also affect Texans. Although DBCP is banned from use within the United States, it and other similarly banned chemicals have been consumed by Texans eating foods imported from Costa Rica and elsewhere. *See* D. Weir & M. Schapiro, *Circle of Poison* 28–30, 77, 82–83 (1981). In the absence of meaningful tort liability in the United States for their actions, some multinational corporations will continue to operate without adequate regard for the human and environmental costs of their actions. This result cannot be allowed to repeat itself for decades to come.

As a matter of law and of public policy, the doctrine of forum non conveniens should be abolished. Accordingly, I concur....

NOTES

1. Professor David Robertson of the University of Texas School of Law attempted to discover the subsequent history of each reported transnational case dismissed under forum non conveniens from *Gulf Oil v. Gilbert,* 330

U.S. 501, 67 S.Ct. 839, 91 L.Ed. 1055 (1947) to the end of 1984. Data was received on 55 personal injury cases and 30 commercial cases. Of the 55 personal injury cases, only one was actually tried in a foreign court. Only two of the 30 commercial cases reached trial. *See* Robertson, *supra,* at 419.

2. Evidence from the most recent and largest national study ever performed regarding the pace of litigation in urban trial courts suggests that there is no empirical basis for the dissenters' argument that Texas dockets will become clogged without forum non conveniens. The state of Massachusetts recognizes forum non conveniens. *See Minnis v. Peebles,* 24 Mass.App. 467, 510 N.E.2d 289 (1987). Conversely, the state of Louisiana has explicitly not recognized forum non conveniens since 1967. . . . Nevertheless, the study revealed the median filing-to-disposition time for tort cases in Boston to be 953 days; in New Orleans, with no forum non conveniens, the median time for the disposition of tort cases was only 405 days. The study revealed the median disposition time for contract cases in Boston to be 1580 days, as opposed to a mere 271 days in New Orleans where forum non conveniens is not used. J. Goerdt, C. Lomvardias, G. Gallas & B. Mahoney, Examining Court Delay — The Pace of Litigation in 26 Urban Trial Courts, 1987 20, 22 (1989).

3. A senior vice-president of a United States multinational corporation acknowledged that "[t]he realization at corporate headquarters that liability for any [industrial] disaster would be decided in the U.S. courts, more than pressure from Third World governments, has forced companies to tighten safety procedures, upgrade plants, supervise maintenance more closely and educate workers and communities." Wall St. J., Nov. 26, 1985, at 22, col. 4 (quoting Harold Corbett, senior vice-president for environmental affairs at Monsanto Co.).

4. As one commentator observed, U.S. multinational corporations "adhere to a double standard when operating abroad. The lack of stringent environmental regulations and worker safety standards abroad and the relaxed enforcement of such laws in industries using hazardous processes provide little incentive for [multinational corporations] to protect the safety of workers, to obtain liabil-

ity insurance to guard against the hazard of product defects or toxic tort exposure, or to take precautions to minimize pollution to the environment. *This double standard has caused catastrophic damages to the environment and to human lives.*"

Note, *Exporting Hazardous Industries: Should American Standards Apply?,* 20 Int'l L. & Pol. 777, 780–81 (1988) (emphasis added) (footnotes omitted) [hereinafter "*Exporting Hazardous Industries*"]. *See also* Diamond, *The Path of Progress Racks the Third World,* N.Y. Times, Dec. 12, 1984, at B1, col. 1.

5. A subsidiary of Sterling Drug Company advertised Winstrol, a synthetic male hormone severely restricted in the United States since it is associated with a number of side effects that the F.D.A. has called "virtually irreversible", in a Brazilian medical journal, picturing a healthy boy and recommending the drug to combat poor appetite, fatigue and weight loss. *U.S. Exports Banned, supra,* 6 Int'l Tr.L.J. at 96. The same company is said to have marketed Dipyrone, a painkiller causing a fatal blood disease and characterized by the American Medical Association as for use only as "a last resort," as "Novaldin" in the Dominican Republic. "Novaldin" was advertised in the Dominican Republic with pictures of a child smiling about its agreeable taste. *Id.* at 97. "In 1975, thirteen children in Brazil died after coming into contact with a toxic pesticide whose use had been severely restricted in this country." *Hazardous Exports, supra,* 14 Sw.U.L. Rev. at 82.

6. Regarding Leptophos, a powerful and hazardous pesticide that was domestically banned, S. Jacob Scherr stated that "In 1975 alone, Velsicol, a Texas-based corporation exported 3,092,842 pounds of Leptophos to thirty countries. Over half of that was shipped to Egypt, a country with no procedures for pesticide regulation or tolerance setting. In December 1976, the *Washington Post* reported that Leptophos use in Egypt resulted in the death of a number of farmers and illness in rural communities. . . . But despite the accumulation of data on Leptophos' severe neurotoxicity, Velsicol continued to market the product abroad for use on grain and vegetable crops while proclaiming the product's safety."

U.S. Exports Banned, 6 Int'l Tr.L. J. at 96.

CASE 1. *Foreign Assignment*

Sara Strong graduated with an MBA from UCLA four years ago. She immediately took a job in the correspondent bank section of the Security Bank of the American Continent. Sara was assigned to work on issues pertaining to relationships with correspondent banks in Latin America. She rose rapidly in the section and received three good promotions in three years. She consistently got high ratings from her superiors, and she received particularly high marks for her professional demeanor.

In her initial position with the bank, Sara was required to travel to Mexico on several occasions. She was always accompanied by a male colleague even though she generally handled similar business by herself on trips within the United States. During her trips to Mexico she observed that Mexican bankers seemed more aware of her being a woman and were personally solicitous to her, but she didn't discern any major problems. The final decisions on the work that she did were handled by male representatives of the bank stationed in Mexico.

A successful foreign assignment was an important step for those on the "fast track" at the bank. Sara applied for a position in Central or South America and was delighted when she was assigned to the bank's office in Mexico City. The office had about twenty bank employees and was headed by William Vitam. The Mexico City office was seen as a preferred assignment by young executives at the bank.

After a month, Sara began to encounter problems. She found it difficult to be effective in dealing with Mexican bankers — the

clients. They appeared reluctant to accept her authority, and they would often bypass her in important matters. The problem was exacerbated by Vitam's compliance in her being bypassed. When she asked that the clients be referred back to her, Vitam replied, "Of course, that isn't really practical." Vitam made matters worse by patronizing her in front of clients and by referring to her as "my cute assistant" and "our lady banker." Vitam never did this when only Americans were present and in fact treated her professionally and with respect in internal situations.

Sara finally complained to Vitam that he was undermining her authority and effectiveness; she asked him in as positive a manner as possible to help her. Vitam listened carefully to Sara's complaints, then replied, "I'm glad that you brought this up, because I've been meaning to sit down and talk to you about my little game playing in front of the clients. Let me be frank with you. Our clients think you're great, but they just don't understand a woman in authority, and you and I aren't going to be able to change their attitudes overnight. As long as the clients see you as my assistant and deferring to me, they can do business with you. I'm willing to give you as much responsibility as they can handle your having. I *know* you can handle it. But we just have to tread carefully. You and I know that my remarks in front of clients don't mean anything. They're just a way of playing the game Latin style. I know it's frustrating for you, but I really need you to support me on this. It's not going to affect your promotions. You just have to act like it's my responsibil-

This case was prepared by Thomas Dunfee and Diana Robertson, The Wharton School.

ity." Sara replied that she would try to cooperate, but that basically she found her role demeaning.

As time went on, Sara found that the patronizing actions in front of clients bothered her more and more. She spoke to Vitam again, but he was firm in his position and urged her to try to be a little more flexible, even a little more "feminine."

Sara also had a problem with Vitam over policy. The Mexico City office had five younger women who worked as receptionists and secretaries. They were all situated at work stations at the entrance of the office. They were required to wear standard uniforms that were colorful and slightly sexy. Sara protested the requirement that uniforms be worn because (1) they were inconsistent to the image of the banking business and (2) they were demeaning to the women who had to wear them. Vitam just curtly replied that he had received a lot of favorable comments about the uniforms from clients of the bank.

Several months later, Sara had what she thought would be a good opportunity to deal with the problem. Tom Fried, an executive vice president who had been a mentor for her since she arrived at the bank, was coming to Mexico City; she arranged a private conference with him. She described her problems and explained that she was not able to be effective in this environment and that she worried that it would have a negative effect on her chance of promotion within the bank. Fried was very careful in his response. He

spoke of certain "realities" that the bank had to respect, and he urged her to "see it through" even though he could understand how she would feel that things weren't fair.

Sara found herself becoming more aggressive and defensive in her meetings with Vitam and her clients. Several clients asked that other bank personnel handle their transactions. Sara has just received an Average rating, which noted "the beginnings of a negative attitude about the bank and its policies."

Questions

1. What obligations does an international company have to ensure that its employees are not harmed, for instance, by having their chances for advancement limited by the social customs of a host country?

2. What international moral code, if any, is being violated by Security Bank of the American Continent?

3. Has the bank made the correct decision by opting to follow the norms of the host country?

4. What steps can be taken on the part of the internationals and their employees to avoid or resolve situations in which employees are offended or harmed by host country practices?

5. In this situation does morality require respect for Mexican practices, or does it require respect for Sara Strong? Are these incompatible?

CASE 2. *The Nestlé Corporation*

Nestlé Corporation, a large international conglomerate, was attacked by many individuals and groups who claimed that the rising infant mortality rate in third-world nations was due to the aggressive sales promotions of the infant formula companies, which influenced women to switch from traditional breast-feeding methods to the more "modern" idea of bottle feeding. Their primary target was the Nestlé Company of Switzerland, which accounted for 50 percent of third world sales of infant formula.

The declining birthrate in industrialized countries, which began in the 1960s, caused all the infant formula companies concern. They had seen the popularity of formula feeding expand their sales tremendously during and after World War II, but in the 1960s their sales began to diminish as the market became saturated. They viewed the developing and underdeveloped countries as potential sources of new markets to restore declining sales.

As reports began to appear about women in the third world who were abandoning breast feeding, many health professionals became alarmed because of the widespread lack of basic nutritional knowledge and adequate sanitation in the third world, two conditions that were necessary for using infant formula safely. It was estimated that only 29 percent of the rural areas and 72 percent of the urban areas in the third world had potable water for mixing formula or for sanitizing feeding equipment. The lack of sanitation facilities and the absence of clean water would only be remedied with further development. The lack of education in underdeveloped countries often meant that people did not

properly mix formulas or did not follow correct sanitary procedures. Sometimes a poor family would also stretch the formula by adding extra water.

Despite these problems, the infant formula companies mounted aggressive marketing and promotional campaigns in third-world countries. These marketing and promotional practices included extensive mass media advertising, large quantities of free promotional samples to doctors and maternity wards, gifts of equipment, trips and conferences for medical personnel, and the use of company representatives called "milk nurses" whose jobs entailed promoting and explaining formula feeding to new mothers. Billboards and posters prominently displayed pictures of fat, rosy-cheeked babies, subtly suggesting that the healthiest babies were those fed formula.

By 1977, an organization called the Infant Formula Action Coalition (INFACT) had been formed in Minneapolis to address the problem. This organization attempted to create public awareness and economic pressure through a nationwide boycott of all Nestlé products. Nestlé was chosen because it had the largest share of the world market and also because it was based in Switzerland and could not be pressured through shareholder resolutions in the United States. The boycott, which had the support of the National Council of Churches, had little effect on Nestlé's business, but the antiformula movement did get the attention of some very powerful groups.

Despite Nestlé's initial reluctance to go along with an International Code of Breast Feeding and Infant Formula Marketing adopted by the World Health Organization

This case was written by Eugene Buchholz, Loyola University of New Orleans, and is reprinted from *Business Environment and Public Policy* with permission.

in 1981, in March 1982 the company announced that it would observe the code. In a further step, Nestlé set up the Infant Formula Audit Commission, composed of doctors, scientists, and churchpeople under the direction of former Secretary of State Edmund Muskie, to monitor its own conduct.

In general, the industry, responding to recommendations from the International Council of Infant Food Industries (ICIFI) and the World Health Organization, started to demarket its products. *Demarketing* means that efforts to sell a product are reduced or stopped completely because of risks to health or safety and is usually initiated because of management decisions, public pressure, or government regulation. Demarketing is ordinarily carried out in declining markets or markets in which a company can no longer compete successfully, but in the developing countries, demarketing decisions were made for growing markets and contrary to usual business practice.

Questions

1. Should Nestlé have avoided marketing its products in lesser developed countries?
2. Is the Nestlé Corporation morally responsible for the malnutrition that resulted when the formula "was stretched" by adding extra water?
3. Did INFACT act morally in putting economic pressure on Nestlé?
4. Was the development of a voluntary code a good way to resolve the problem? Would another type of code have been a better solution?

Suggested Supplementary Readings

ACQUAAH, KWAMENA. *International Regulation of Transnational Corporations.* New York: Praeger, 1986.

BERLEANT, ARNOLD. "Multinationals and the Problem of Ethical Consistency." *Journal of Business Ethics* 8 (August 1982): 185–95.

BRENKERT, GEORGE C. "Can We Afford International Human Rights?" *Journal of Business Ethics* 11 (July 1992): 515–21.

CARSON, THOMAS L. "Bribery, Extortion, and 'The Foreign Corrupt Practices Act.'" *Philosophy and Public Affairs* 14 (Winter 1985): 66–90.

DE GEORGE, RICHARD. *Competing with Integrity in International Business.* New York: Oxford University Press, 1993.

DOLLINGER, MARC J. "Confucian Ethics and Japanese Management Practices." *Journal of Business Ethics* 7 (August 1988): 575–83.

DONALDSON, THOMAS. *The Ethics of International Business.* New York: Oxford University Press, 1989.

DONALDSON, THOMAS. "The Language of International Corporate Ethics." *Business Ethics Quarterly* 2 (July 1992): 271–81.

ETUK, UDO. "Justice and Self-Interest in Transnational Operations." *Public Affairs Quarterly* 1 (October 1987): 43–58.

FILATOTCHEV, IGOR, KEN STARKEY, and MIKE WRIGHT. "The Ethical Challenge of Management Buy-outs as a form of Privatization in Central and Eastern Europe." *Journal of Business Ethics* 13 (July 1994): 523–32.

GETZ, KATHLEEN. "International Codes of Conduct: An Analysis of Ethical Reasoning." *Journal of Business Ethics* 9 (1990): 567–77.

GILLESPIE, KATE. "Middle East Response to the Foreign Corrupt Practices Act." *California Management Review* 29 (Summer 1987): 9–30.

GREANIAS, GEORGE C., and DUANE WINDSOR. *The Foreign Corrupt Practices Act.* Lexington, MA: Lexington Books, 1982.

GUNDLING, ERNEST. "Ethics and Working with the Japanese: The Entrepreneur and the 'Elite Course.'" *California Management Review* 33 (Spring 1991): 25–39.

HAZERA, ALEJANDRO. "A Comparison of Japanese and U.S. Corporate Financial Accountability." *Business Ethics Quarterly* 5 (July 1995): 479–97.

HOFFMAN, W. MICHAEL, and Others, eds. *Ethics and the Multinational Enterprise.* Washington, DC: University Press of America, 1985.

HUSTED, BRYAN W. "Honor Among Thieves: A Transaction-Cost Interpretation of Corruption in Third World Countries." *Business Ethics Quarterly* 4 (January 1994): 17–27.

JOHNSON, HAROLD L. "Bribery in International Markets: Diagnosis, Clarification, and Remedy." *Journal of Business Ethics* 4 (December 1985): 447–55.

KLINE, JOHN M. *International Codes and Multinational Business: Setting Guidelines for International Business Operations.* New York: Quorum, 1985.

LANE, HENRY W., and DONALD G. SIMPSON. "Bribery in International Business: Whose Problem Is It?" *Journal of Business Ethics* 3 (February 1984): 35–42.

LANGLOIS, CATHERINE C., and BODO B. SCHLEGELMILCH. "Do Corporate Codes of Ethics Reflect National Character? Evidence from Europe and the United States." *Journal of International Business Studies* 21 (Fall 1990): 519–39.

LEVY, ANNE C. "Putting the 'O' Back in EEO: Why Congress Had to Act So Swiftly After the Supreme Court Decision in *Bourselan.*" *Columbia Business Law Review* (1991): 239–68.

PASTIN, MARK, and MICHAEL HOOKER. "Ethics and the Foreign Corrupt Practices Act." *Business Horizons* 23 (December 1980): 43–47.

PRATT, CORNELIUS B. "Multinational Corporate Social Policy Process for Ethical Responsibility in Sub-Saharan Africa." *Journal of Business Ethics* 10 (July 1991): 527–41.

REINGOLD, RUTH N. and PAUL LANSING. "An Ethical Analysis of Japan's Response to the Arab Boycott of Israel." *Business Ethics Quarterly* 4 (July 1994): 335–53.

STEIDLMEIER, PAUL. "The Moral Legitimacy of Intellectual Property Claims: American Business and Developing Country Perspectives." *Journal of Business Ethics* 12 (February 1993): 157–64.

TUBBS, WALTER. "Karoushi: Stress-death and the Meaning of Work." *Journal of Business Ethics* 12 (November 1993): 869–77.

VELASQUEZ, MANUEL. "International Business, Morality, and the Common Good." *Business Ethics Quarterly* 2 (January 1992): 26–40.

WINDSOR, DUANE, and LEE E. PRESTON. "Corporate Governance, Social Policy and Social Performance in the Multinational Corporation." *Research in Corporate Social Performance and Policy* 10 (1988).

Chapter Nine

—— • ——

Social and Economic Justice

Economic disparities among individuals and nations have generated heated controversy over systems for distributing and taxing income and wealth. Some sustained political conflicts in the United States concern the justification of taxes, corporate profits, plant closings, international debt relief, and executive salaries and bonuses.

Several well-reasoned and systematic answers to these and related questions have been advanced, based on a theory of justice — that is, a theory of how social and economic benefits, services, and burdens should be distributed. In Chapter 1 we briefly analyzed some problems of ethical theory and justice. In the present chapter, the major distinctions, principles, and methods of moral argument in theories of justice are treated. The first four articles address the question, "Which general system of social and economic organization is most just?" The later articles address the justice of particular policies and forms of behavior.

THEORIES OF DISTRIBUTIVE JUSTICE

What a person deserves or is entitled to is often decided by specific rules and laws, such as those governing state lotteries, food stamp allocation, health care coverage, admission procedures for universities, and the like. These rules may be evaluated, criticized, and revised by reference to moral principles such as equality of persons, nondiscriminatory treatment, property ownership, protection from harm, compensatory justice, retributive justice, and so forth. The word *justice* is used broadly to cover both these principles and specific rules derived from the same principles, but developed for specific situations.

Economists have sometimes complained about philosophers' approaches to justice, on grounds that a "fair price" or "fair trade" is not a matter of moral fairness: Prices may be low or high, affordable or not affordable, but not fair or unfair. It is simply unfortunate, not unfair, if one cannot afford to pay for something or if another person is paid forty times what you are paid. The basis of this exclusion of price as a consideration of justice is the market-established nature of prices and salaries. To speak of "unfair" prices, trade, or salaries is to express a negative opinion, of course, but these economists reason that from a market perspective any price is fair. Salaries must be treated in the same way.

However, the economist may be missing the philosopher's point. The philosopher is asking whether the market itself is a fair arrangement. If so, what makes it fair? If coercion is used in the market to set prices, is this maneuver unfair, or does it render the market not a free market? If health care and education are distributed nationally or internationally with vast inequality, can high prices on essential items such as health care goods and university tuition be fair? If a multinational company has a monopoly on an essential foodstuff, is there no such thing as a price that is too high? These questions of fairness fall under the topic of distributive justice.

The term *distributive justice* refers to the proper distribution of social benefits and burdens. A theory of distributive justice attempts to establish a connection between the properties or characteristics of persons and the morally correct distribution of benefits and burdens in society. *Egalitarian* theories emphasize equal access to primary goods (see John Rawls's article); *communitarian* theories emphasize group goals, collective control, and participation in communal life, by contrast to liberal political systems that emphasize individual welfare and rights (see Michael Walzer's article); *libertarian* theories emphasize rights to social and economic liberty and deemphasize collective control (see Robert Nozick's essay); and *utilitarian* theories emphasize a mixed use of such criteria resulting in the maximization of both public and individual interests (see Peter Singer's article).

Systematic theories of justice attempt to elaborate how people should be compared and what it means to give people what is due them. Philosophers attempt to achieve the needed precision and specificity by developing material principles of justice, so called because they put material content into a theory of justice. Each material principle of justice identifies a relevant property on the basis of which burdens and benefits should be distributed. The following list includes the major candidates for the position of principles of distributive justice.

1. To each person an equal share
2. To each person according to individual need
3. To each person according to that person's rights
4. To each person according to individual effort
5. To each person according to societal contribution
6. To each person according to merit

A theory of justice might accept more than one of these principles. Some theories accept all six as legitimate. Many societies use several, in the belief that different rules are appropriate to different situations.

In the utilitarian theory, problems of justice are viewed as one part of the larger problem of how to maximize value, and it is easy to see how a utilitarian might use all of these material principles to this end. The ideal distribution of benefits and burdens is simply the one having this maximizing effect. According to utilitarian Peter Singer in his essay in this chapter, a heavy element of political planning and economic redistribution is required to ensure that justice is done. Because utilitarianism was treated in Chapter 1, detailed considerations will be given in this introduction only to egalitarian, libertarian, and communitarian theories.

EGALITARIAN THEORY

Equality in the distribution of social benefits and burdens has a central place in many influential ethical theories. For example, in utilitarianism different people are equal in the value accorded their wants, preferences, and happiness, and in Kantian theories all persons are considered equally worthy and deserving of respect as ends in themselves. Egalitarian theory treats the question of how people should be considered equal in some respects (for example, in their basic political and moral rights and obligations), yet unequal in others (for example, in wealth and social burdens such as taxation).

Radical and Qualified Egalitarianism

In its radical form, egalitarian theory proposes that individual differences are always morally insignificant. Distributions of burdens and benefits in a society are just to the extent that they are equal, and deviations from absolute equality in distribution are unjust. For example, the fact that roughly 20 percent of the wealth in the United States is owned by 5 percent of the population, whereas the poorest 20 percent of the population controls only 5 percent of the wealth, makes U.S. society unjust, no matter how relatively "deserving" the people at both extremes might be.

However, most egalitarian accounts are guardedly formulated, so that persons are not entitled to equal shares of all social benefits and so that individual merit justifies some differences in distribution. Egalitarianism, so qualified, is concerned only with basic equalities among individuals. For example, egalitarians prefer *progressive* tax rates (higher incomes taxed more heavily than lower) rather than *proportional* rates (each unit taxed the same). This preference may seem odd since a proportional rate treats everyone equally. However, qualified egalitarians reason that progressive rates tax the wealthy more and thereby distribute wealth more evenly.

John Rawls's Theory

In recent years a qualified egalitarian theory in the Kantian tradition has enjoyed wide discussion. John Rawls's *A Theory of Justice* maintains that all economic goods and services should be distributed equally except when an unequal distribution would work to everyone's advantage (or at least to the advantage of the worst off in society). Rawls presents this egalitarian theory as a direct challenge to utilitarianism. He argues that social distributions produced by maximizing utility permit violations of basic individual liberties and rights. Being indifferent to the distribution of satisfactions among individuals, utilitarianism permits the infringement of people's rights and liberties in order to produce a proportionately greater utility for all concerned.

Rawls defends a hypothetical social contract procedure that is strongly indebted to what he calls the "Kantian conception of equality." Valid principles of justice are those to which all persons would agree if they could freely and impartially consider the social situation. Impartiality is guaranteed by a conceptual device Rawls calls the "veil of ignorance." Here each person is imagined to be ignorant of all his or her particular characteristics, for example, the person's sex, race, IQ, family background, and special talents or handicaps. Theoretically, this veil of ignorance would prevent the adoption of principles biased toward particular groups of persons.

Rawls argues that under these conditions people would unanimously agree on two fundamental principles of justice. The first requires that each person be permitted the maximum amount of basic liberty compatible with a similar liberty for others. The second stipulates that once this equal basic liberty is assured, inequalities in social primary goods (for example, income, rights, and opportunities) are to be allowed only if they benefit everyone. Rawls considers social institutions to be just if and only if they conform to these principles of the social contract. He rejects radical egalitarianism, arguing that inequalities that render everyone better off by comparison to being equal are desirable.

Rawls formulates what is called the *difference principle*: Inequalities are justifiable only if they maximally enhance the position of the "representative least advantaged" person, that is, a hypothetical individual particularly unfortunate in the distribution of fortuitous characteristics or social advantages. Rawls is unclear about who might qualify under this category, but a worker incapacitated from exposure to asbestos and living in poverty clearly would qualify. Formulated in this way, the difference principle could allow, for instance, extraordinary economic rewards to business entrepreneurs, venture capitalists, and corporate takeover artists if the resulting economic situation were to produce improved job opportunities and working conditions for the least advantaged members of society, or possibly greater benefits for pension funds holding stock for the working class.

The difference principle rests on the moral viewpoint that because inequalities of birth, historical circumstance, and natural endowment are undeserved, persons in a cooperative society should make more equal the unequal situation of its naturally disadvantaged members. This and other Rawlsian ideas are defended in an international context by Thomas Donaldson, who argues that it is unjust to allow the economically least well off in developing countries to be harmed as a result of conditions imposed as part of international loan arrangements.

LIBERTARIAN THEORY

What makes a libertarian theory *libertarian* is the priority given to distinctive procedures or mechanisms for ensuring that liberty rights are recognized in social and economic practice, typically the rules and procedures governing economic acquisition and exchange in capitalist or free-market systems.

Role of Individual Freedom

The libertarian contends that it is a basic violation of justice to ensure equal economic returns in a society. In particular, individuals are seen as having a fundamental right to own and dispense with the products of their labor as they choose, even if the exercise of this right leads to large inequalities of wealth in society. Equality and utility principles, from this perspective, sacrifice basic liberty rights to the larger public interest by exploiting one set of individuals for the benefit of another. The most apparent example is the coercive extraction of financial resources through taxation.

Robert Nozick's Theory

Libertarian theory is defended in this chapter by Robert Nozick, who refers to his social philosophy as an "entitlement theory" of justice. Nozick argues that a theory of justice should work to protect individual rights and should not propound a thesis intended to "pattern" society through arrangements such as those in socialist and (impure) capitalist countries in which governments take pronounced steps to redistribute the wealth.

Nozick's libertarian position rejects all distributional patterns imposed by material principles of justice. He is thus committed to a form of *procedural* justice. That is, for Nozick there is no pattern of just distribution independent of fair procedures of acquisition, transfer, and rectification. This claim has been at the center of controversy over the libertarian account, and competing theories of justice are often reactions to an uncompromising commitment to pure procedural justice. For example, Donaldson's Rawlsian convictions may be interpreted as a response to the libertarian tradition. Also, in the Supreme Court opinion in *Ferguson v. Skrupa,* the Court declares that legislatures, not courts, should decide on the wisdom and utility of economic and social policies such as those affecting minimum wages and poverty. However, many critics believe that this conclusion is a relatively recent position of the Court, contrasting with an older U.S. legal tradition of scrutinizing and rectifying circumstances of social and economic injustice.

COMMUNITARIAN THEORY

Moral and political theories that advocate individual responsibility, free-market exchanges, and limited community control are often called *liberal* theories. "Liberalism," which places the individual at the center of moral and political life, views the state as properly limited in the event of a conflict with individual rights such as freedom of association, expression, and religion. The state's proper role is to protect and enforce basic moral and political rights, often called *civil rights.*

Rising up against liberalism in recent years has been a tide of communitarian theories. Although a diverse lot, communitarian theories share many ideas. They see typical liberal theories such as those of Rawls and Nozick (and even Mill and Singer) as subverting communal life and the obligations and commitments that grow out of that perspective on life. These theorists see persons as *constituted* by communal values and thus as best suited to achieve their good through communal life, not state protections or individual moral and political rights.

Communitarians object to the way Rawlsian liberalism has made justice the first virtue of social institutions and then has patterned those institutions to protect the individual against society. The communitarian believes that justice is a less central virtue of social life, one needed only when communal values have broken down into conflicts of the sort litigated in court. Rather than conceptualizing the state's role as that of enforcer of rights allowing individuals to pursue any course they wish, the communitarian takes the view that the community may rightly be expected to impose on individuals certain conceptions of virtue and the good life.

The sole representative of communitarian theories in this chapter is Michael Walzer, a moderate communitarian not as opposed to liberalism as hard-line communitarians. For him notions of justice are not based on some "rational" or "natural" foundation external to the society. Rather, standards of justice are developed internally as the community evolves. Something has to be "given-as-basic" in every ethical theory, and the communitarian sees everything as deriving from communal values and historical practices. Conventions, traditions, and loyalties therefore play a more prominent role in communitarian theories than they do in the other theories we encounter in this chapter.

Communitarians recognize that people sometimes have good reason to challenge and even reject values accepted by the community. To this end, Walzer argues that a community ethic must be particularly vigilant to avoid "oppressing" minorities. Although an individual has a right to challenge community values, a communitarian will not accept an individual's personal values as either moral or respectable when those values depart from the central, defining moral values of the community.

VISIONS OF JUSTICE BEYOND THE FREE MARKET

Many philosophers argue that a conception of fundamental individual rights more inclusive than Nozick's must be recognized in an adequate theory of justice. Even in strictly economic terms, these writers maintain, Nozick's conception of individual rights is excessively restricted. They challenge the proponents of libertarianism to answer the following questions: Why should we assume that people's economic rights extend only to the acquisition and dispensation of private property according to the free-market rules? Is it not equally plausible to posit more substantive moral rights in the economic sphere — say, rights to health care, decent levels of education, and decent standards of living?

Nozick's ideal is generally agreed to be plausible for free transactions among informed and consenting parties who start as equals in the bargaining process. However, this ideal is rarely the case beyond circumstances of contractual bargaining among equals. Contracts, voting privileges, individual investing in the stock market, and family relationships may involve bluffing, differentials of power and wealth, manipulation, and the like. These factors work systematically to disadvantage vulnerable individuals. Imagine, for example, that over the course of time one group in society gains immense wealth and political influence compared with another group. Even if the *transactions* leading to this imbalance may have been legitimate, the *outcome* is not acceptable. If an individual's bargaining position has been deeply eroded, does he or she have a right to protection from social inequalities that have emerged? If he or she is destined to poverty as a result, is there a legitimate claim of justice, as Rawls proposes?

If people have a right to a minimal level of material means, their rights are violated whenever economic distributions leave some with less than that minimal level. A commitment to individual rights, then, may result in a theory of justice that requires a more activist role for government, even if one starts with free-market or libertarian assumptions. Many philosophers agree with Nozick that economic freedom is a value deserving of respect and protection. They disagree, however, with the claim that the principles and procedures that libertarians advocate protect this basic value.

The Principle of Need

In reaction to these problems, some reject the pure procedural commitments of the libertarian theory and replace them with a principle specifying human need as the relevant respect in which people are to be compared for purposes of determining social and economic justice. Donaldson seems to be a prime example of this approach.

Much turns on how the notion of need is defined and implemented. For purposes of justice, a principle of need would be least controversial if it were restricted to fundamental needs. If malnutrition, bodily injury, and the withholding of certain information involve fundamental harms, we have a fundamental need for nutrition, health care facilities, and education. According to theories based on this material principle, justice places the satisfaction of fundamental human needs above the protection of economic freedoms or rights.

This construal of the principle of need has provided alternatives to libertarian justice. Yet there may be some room for reconciliation between the principle of need and libertarianism. Many advanced industrial countries have the capacity to produce more than is strictly necessary to meet their citizens' fundamental needs. One might argue that *after* everyone's fundamental needs have been satisfied, *then* justice requires no particular pattern of distribution. For example, some current discussions of the right to health care and the right to a job are rooted in the idea of meeting basic medical and economic needs, but only basic needs. In this way, a single unified theory of justice might require the maintenance of certain patterns in the distribution of basic goods (for example, a decent minimum level of income, education, and health care), while allowing the market to determine distributions of goods beyond those that satisfy fundamental needs.

This approach accepts a two-tiered system of access to goods and services: (1) social coverage for basic and catastrophic needs, and (2) private purchase of other goods and services. On the first tier, distribution is based on need, and everyone's basic needs are met by the government. Better services may be made available for purchase in an economic system on the second tier. This proposal seems to present an attractive point of convergence and negotiation for libertarians, communitarians, utilitarians, and egalitarians. It provides a premise of equal access to basic goods, while allowing additional rights to economic freedom. Theories such as utilitarianism and communitarianism may also find the compromise particularly attractive because it serves to minimize public dissatisfaction and to maximize community welfare. The egalitarian finds an opportunity to use an equal access principle, and the libertarian retains free-market production and distribution. However, the system clearly does involve compromise by all parties.

CONCLUSION

Rawls, Nozick, and their utilitarian and communitarian opponents all capture some intuitive convictions about justice, and each theory exhibits strengths as a theory of justice. Rawls's difference principle, for example, describes a widely shared belief about justified inequalities. Nozick's theory makes a strong appeal in the domains of property rights and liberties. Utilitarianism is widely used in the Western nations in the development of public policy, and communitarian theories in some form supply the prevailing model of justice in many nations.

Perhaps, then, there are several equally valid, or at least equally defensible, theories of justice. There could, on this analysis, be libertarian societies, egalitarian societies, utilitarian societies, and communitarian societies, as well as societies based on mixed theories or derivative theories of taxation and redistribution. However, this possibility raises other problems in ethical theory discussed in Chapter 1, in particular, relativism and moral disagreement, and before this conclusion is accepted, the details of the arguments in the selections in this chapter should be carefully assessed.

An Egalitarian Theory of Justice

John Rawls

THE ROLE OF JUSTICE

Justice is the first virtue of social institutions, as truth is of systems of thought. A theory however elegant and economical must be rejected or revised if it is untrue; likewise laws and institutions no matter how efficient and well-arranged must be reformed or abolished if they are unjust. Each person possesses an inviolability founded on justice that even the welfare of society as a whole cannot override. For this reason justice denies that the loss of freedom for some is made right by a greater good shared by others. It does not allow that the sacrifices imposed on a few are outweighed by the larger sum of advantages enjoyed by many. Therefore in a just society the liberties of equal citizenship are taken as settled; the rights secured by justice are not subject to political bargaining or to the calculus of social interests. The only thing that permits us to acquiesce in an erroneous theory is the lack of a better one; analogously, an injustice is tolerable only when it is necessary to avoid an even greater injustice. Being first virtues of human activities, truth and justice are uncompromising.

These propositions seem to express our intuitive conviction of the primary of justice. No doubt they are expressed too strongly. In any event I wish to inquire whether these contentions or others similar to them are sound, and if so how they can be accounted for. To this end it is necessary to work out a theory of justice in the light of which these assertions can be interpreted and assessed. I shall begin by considering the role of the principles of justice. Let us assume, to fix ideas, that a society is a more or less self-sufficient association of persons who in their relations to one another recognize certain rules of conduct as binding and who for the most part act in accordance with them. Suppose further that these rules specify a system of cooperation designed to advance the good of those taking part in it. Then, although a society is a cooperative venture for mutual advantage, it is typically marked by a conflict as well as by an identity of interests. There is an identity of interests since social cooperation makes possible a better life for all than any would have if each were to live solely by his own efforts. There is a conflict of interests since persons are not indifferent as to how the greater benefits produced by their collaboration are distributed, for in order to pursue their ends they each prefer a larger to a lesser share. A set of principles is required for choosing among the various social arrangements which determine this division of advantages and for underwriting an agreement on the proper distributive shares. These principles are the principles of social justice: they provide a way of assigning rights and duties in the basic institutions of society and they define the appropriate distribution of the benefits and burdens of social cooperation. . . .

Excerpted from John Rawls, *A Theory of Justice* (Cambridge, Mass.: Harvard University Press, 1971), pp. 3–4, 11–15, 18–19, 60–62, 64–65, 100–104, 274–277. Reprinted by permission of Oxford University Press and The Belknap Press of Harvard University Press, © 1971 by The President and Fellows of Harvard College.

THE MAIN IDEA OF THE THEORY OF JUSTICE

My aim is to present a conception of justice which generalizes and carries to a higher level of abstraction the familiar theory of the social contract as found, say, in Locke, Rousseau, and Kant. In order to do this we are not to think of the original contract as one to enter a particular society or to set up a particular form of government. Rather, the guiding idea is that the principles of justice for the basic structure of society are the object of the original agreement. They are the principles that free and rational persons concerned to further their own interests would accept in an initial position of equality as defining the fundamental terms of their association. These principles are to regulate all further agreements; they specify the kinds of social cooperation that can be entered into and the forms of government that can be established. This way of regarding the principles of justice I shall call justice as fairness.

Thus we are to imagine that those who engage in social cooperation choose together, in one joint act, the principles which are to assign basic rights and duties and to determine the division of social benefits. Men are to decide in advance how they are to regulate their claims against one another and what is to be the foundation charter of their society. Just as each person must decide by rational reflection what constitutes his good, that is, the system of ends which it is rational for him to pursue, so a group of persons must decide once and for all what is to count among them as just and unjust. The choice which rational men would make in this hypothetical situation of equal liberty, assuming for the present that this choice problem has a solution, determines the principles of justice.

In justice as fairness the original position of equality corresponds to the state of nature in the traditional theory of the social contract. This original position is not, of course, thought of as an actual historical state of affairs, much less as a primitive condition of culture. It is understood as a purely hypothetical situation characterized so as to lead to a certain conception of justice. Among the essential features of this situation is that no one knows his place in society, his class position or social status, nor does any one know his fortune in the distribution of natural assets and abilities, his intelligence, strength, and the like. I shall even assume that the parties do not know their conceptions of the good or their special psychological propensities. The principles of justice are chosen behind a veil of ignorance. This ensures that no one is advantaged or disadvantaged in the choice of principles by the outcome of natural chance or the contingency of social circumstances. Since all are similarly situated and no one is able to design principles to favor his particular condition, the principles of justice are the result of a fair agreement or bargain. For given the circumstances of the original position, the symmetry of everyone's relations to each other, this initial situation is fair between individuals as moral persons, that is, as rational beings with their own ends and capable, I shall assume, of a sense of justice. The original position is, one might say, the appropriate initial status quo, and thus the fundamental agreements reached in it are fair. This explains the propriety of the name "justice as fairness": it conveys the idea that the principles of justice are agreed to in an initial situation that is fair. The name does not mean that the concepts of justice and fairness are the same, any more than the phrase "poetry as metaphor" means that the concepts of poetry and metaphor are the same.

Justice as fairness begins, as I have said, with one of the most general of all choices which persons might make together, namely, with the choice of the first principles of a conception of justice which is to regulate all subsequent criticism and reform of institutions. Then, having chosen a conception of justice, we can suppose that they are to choose a constitution and a legislature to enact laws, and so on, all in accordance with the principles of justice initially agreed upon. Our social situation is just if it is such that by this sequence of hypothetical agreements we would have contracted into the general system of rules which defines it.

. . . It may be observed, however, that once the principles of justice are thought of as arising from an original agreement in a situation of equality, it is an open question whether the principle of utility would be acknowledged. Offhand it hardly seems likely that persons who view themselves as equals, entitled to press their claims upon one another, would agree to a principle which may require lesser life prospects for some simply for the sake of a greater sum of advantages enjoyed by others. Since each desires to protect his interests, his capacity to advance his conception of the good, no one has a reason to acquiesce in an enduring loss for himself in order to bring about a greater net balance of satisfaction. In the absence of strong and lasting benevolent impulses, a rational man would not accept a basic structure merely because it maximized the algebraic sum of advantages irrespective of its permanent effects on his own basic rights and interests. Thus it seems that the principle of utility is incompatible with the conception of social cooperation among equals for mutual advantage. It appears to be inconsistent with the idea of reciprocity implicit in the notion of a well-ordered society. Or, at any rate, so I shall argue.

I shall maintain instead that the persons in the initial situation would choose two rather different principles: the first requires equality in the assignment of basic rights and duties, while the second holds that social and economic inequalities, for example inequalities

of wealth and authority, are just only if they result in compensating benefits for everyone, and in particular for the least advantaged members of society. These principles rule out justifying institutions on the grounds that the hardships of some are offset by a greater good in the aggregate. It may be expedient but it is not just that some should have less in order that others may prosper. But there is no injustice in the greater benefits earned by a few provided that the situation of persons not so fortunate is thereby improved. The intuitive idea is that since everyone's well-being depends upon a scheme of cooperation without which no one could have a satisfactory life, the division of advantages should be such as to draw forth the willing cooperation of everyone taking part in it, including those less well situated. Yet this can be expected only if reasonable terms are proposed. The two principles mentioned seem to be a fair agreement on the basis of which those better endowed, or more fortunate in their social position, neither of which we can be said to deserve, could expect the willing cooperation of others when some workable scheme is a necessary condition of the welfare of all. Once we decide to look for a conception of justice that nullifies the accidents of natural endowment and the contingencies of social circumstance as counters in quest for political and economic advantage, we are led to these principles. They express the result of leaving aside those aspects of the social world that seem arbitrary from a moral point of view. . . .

THE ORIGINAL POSITION AND JUSTIFICATION

. . . The idea here is simply to make vivid to ourselves the restrictions that it seems reasonable to impose on arguments for principles of justice, and therefore on these principles themselves. Thus it seems reasonable and generally acceptable that no one should be advantaged or disadvantaged by natural fortune or social circumstances in the choice of principles. It is also seems widely agreed that it should be impossible to tailor principles to the circumstances of one's own case. We should insure further that particular inclinations and aspirations, and persons' conceptions of their good, do not affect the principles adopted. The aim is to rule out those principles that it would be rational to propose for acceptance, however little the chance of success, only if one knew certain things that are irrelevant from the standpoint of justice. For example, if a man knew that he was wealthy, he might find it rational to advance the principle that various taxes for welfare measures be counted unjust; if he knew that he was poor, he would most likely propose the contrary principle. To represent the desired restrictions one imagines a situation in which everyone is deprived of this sort of information. One excludes the knowledge of those contingencies which sets men at odds and allows them to be guided by their prejudices. In this manner the veil of ignorance is arrived at in a natural way. . . .

TWO PRINCIPLES OF JUSTICE

I shall now state in a provisional form the two principles of justice that I believe would be chosen in the original position. . . .

The first statement of the two principles reads as follows.

> **First:** each person is to have an equal right to the most extensive basic liberty compatible with a similar liberty for others.
> **Second:** social and economic inequalities are to be arranged so that they are both (a) reasonably expected to be to everyone's advantage, and (b) attached to positions and offices open to all. . . . [The Difference Principle]

By way of general comment, these principles primarily apply, as I have said, to the basic structure of society. They are to govern the assignment of rights and duties and to regulate the distribution of social and economic advantages. As their formulation suggests, these principles presuppose that the social structure can be divided into two more or less distinct parts, the first principle applying to the one, the second to the other. They distinguish between those aspects of the social system that define and secure the equal liberties of citizenship and those that specify and establish social and economic inequalities. The basic liberties of citizens are, roughly speaking, political liberty (the right to vote and to be eligible for public office) together with freedom of speech and assembly; liberty of conscience and freedom of thought; freedom of the person along with the right to hold (personal) property; and freedom from arbitrary arrest and seizure as defined by the concept of the rule of law. These liberties are all required to be equal by the first principle, since citizens of a just society are to have the same basic rights.

The second principle applies, in the first approximation, to the distribution of income and wealth and to the design of organizations that make use of differences in authority and responsibility, or chains of command. While the distribution of wealth and income need not be equal, it must be to everyone's advantage, and at the same time, positions of authority and offices of command must be accessible to all. One applies the second principle by holding positions open, and then, subject to this constraint, arranges social and economic inequalities so that everyone benefits.

These principles are to be arranged in a serial order with the first principle prior to the second. This ordering means that a departure from the institutions of equal liberty required by the first principle cannot be justified, or compensated for, by greater social and economic advantages. The distribution of wealth and income, and the hierarchies of authority must be consistent with both the liberties of equal citizenship and equality of opportunity.

It is clear that these principles are rather specific in their content, and their acceptance rests on certain assumptions that I must eventually try to explain and justify. A theory of justice depends upon a theory of society in ways that will become evident as we proceed. For the present, it should be observed that the two principles (and this holds for all formulations) are a special case of a more general conception of justice that can be expressed as follows.

> All social values — liberty and opportunity, income and wealth, and the bases of self-respect — are to be distributed equally unless an unequal distribution of any, or all, of these values is to everyone's advantage.

Injustice, then, is simply inequalities that are not to the benefit of all. Of course, this conception is extremely vague and requires interpretation.

As a first step, suppose that the basic structure of society distributes certain primary goods, that is, things that every rational man is presumed to want. These goods normally have a use whatever a person's rational plan of life. For simplicity, assume that the chief primary goods at the disposition of society are rights and liberties, powers and opportunities, income and wealth. These are the social primary goods. Other primary goods such as health and vigor, intelligence and imagination, are natural goods; although their possession is influenced by the basic structure, they are not so directly under its control. Imagine, then, a hypothetical initial arrangement in which all the social primary goods are equally distributed: everyone has similar rights and duties, and income and

wealth are evenly shared. This state of affairs provides a benchmark for judging improvements. If certain inequalities of wealth and organizational powers would make everyone better off than in this hypothetical starting situation, then they accord with the general conception.

Now it is possible, at least theoretically, that by giving up some of their fundamental liberties men are sufficiently compensated by the resulting social and economic gains. The general conception of justice imposes no restrictions on what sort of inequalities are permissible; it only requires that everyone's position be improved. . . .

Now the second principle insists that each person benefit from permissible inequalities in the basic structure. This means that it must be reasonable for each relevant representative man defined by this structure, when he views it as a going concern, to prefer his prospects with the inequality to his prospects without it. One is not allowed to justify differences in income or organizational powers on the ground that the disadvantages of those in one position are outweighed by the greater advantages of those in another. Much less can infringements of liberty be counterbalanced in this way. Applied to the basic structure, the principle of utility would have us maximize the sum of expectations of representative men (weighted by the number of persons they represent, on the classical view); and this would permit us to compensate for the losses of some by the gains of others. Instead, the two principles require that everyone benefit from economic and social inequalities. . . .

THE TENDENCY TO EQUALITY

I wish to conclude this discussion of the two principles by explaining the sense in which they express an egalitarian conception of justice. Also I should like to forestall the objection to the principle of fair opportunity that it leads to a callous meritocratic society. In order to prepare the way for doing this, I note several aspects of the conception of justice that I have set out.

First we may observe that the difference principle gives some weight to the considerations singled out by the principle of redress. This is the principle that undeserved inequalities call for redress; and since inequalities of birth and natural endowment are undeserved, these inequalities are to be somehow compensated for. Thus the principle holds that in order to treat all persons equally, to provide genuine equality of opportunity, society must give more attention to those with fewer native assets and to those born into the less favorable social positions. The idea is to redress the bias of contingencies in the direction of equality. In pursuit of this principle greater resources might be spent on the education of the less rather than the more intelligent, at least over a certain time of life, say the earlier years of school.

Now the principle of redress has not to my knowledge been proposed as the sole criterion of justice, as the single aim of the social order. It is plausible as most such principles are only as a prima facie principle, one that is to be weighed in the balance with others. For example, we are to weigh it against the principle to improve the average standard of life, or to advance the common good. But whatever other principles we hold, the claims of redress are to be taken into account. It is thought to represent one of the elements in our conception of justice. Now the difference principle is not of course the principle of redress. It does not require society to try to even out handicaps as if all were expected to compete on a fair basis in the same race. But the difference principle would allocate resources in education, say, so as to improve the long-term expectation of the least fa-

vored. If this end is attained by giving more attention to the better endowed, it is permissible; otherwise not. And in making this decision, the value of education should not be assessed only in terms of economic efficiency and social welfare. Equally if not more important is the role of education in enabling a person to enjoy the culture of his society and to take part in its affairs, and in this way to provide for each individual a secure sense of his own worth.

Thus although the difference principle is not the same as that of redress, it does achieve some of the intent of the latter principle. It transforms the aims of the basic structure so that the total scheme of institutions no longer emphasizes social efficiency and technocratic values. . . .

. . . The natural distribution is neither just nor unjust; nor is it unjust that men are born into society at some particular position. These are simply natural facts. What is just and unjust is the way that institutions deal with these facts. Aristocratic and caste societies are unjust because they make these contingencies the ascriptive basis for belonging to more or less enclosed and privileged social classes. The basic structure of these societies incorporates the arbitrariness found in nature. But there is no necessity for men to resign themselves to these contingencies. The social system is not an unchangeable order beyond human control but a pattern of human action. In justice as fairness men agree to share one another's fate. In designing institutions they undertake to avail themselves of the accidents of nature and social circumstance only when doing so is for the common benefit. The two principles are a fair way of meeting the arbitrariness of fortune; and while no doubt imperfect in other ways, the institutions which satisfy these principles are just. . . .

There is a natural inclination to object that those better situated deserve their greater advantages whether or not they are to the benefit of others. At this point it is necessary to be clear about the notion of desert. It is perfectly true that given a just system of cooperation as a scheme of public rules and the expectations set up by it, those who, with the prospect of improving their condition, have done what the system announces that it will reward are entitled to their advantages. In this sense the more fortunate have a claim to their better situation; their claims are legitimate expectations established by social institutions, and the community is obligated to meet them. But this sense of desert presupposes the existence of the cooperative scheme; it is irrelevant to the question whether in the first place the scheme is to be designed in accordance with the difference principle or some other criterion.

Perhaps some will think that the person with greater natural endowments deserves those assets and the superior character that made their development possible. Because he is more worthy in this sense, he deserves the greater advantages that he could achieve with them. This view, however, is surely incorrect. It seems to be one of the fixed points of our considered judgments that no one deserves his place in the distribution of native endowments, any more than one deserves one's initial starting place in society. The assertion that a man deserves the superior character that enables him to make the effort to cultivate his abilities is equally problematic, for his character depends in large part upon fortunate family and social circumstances for which he can claim no credit. The notion of desert seems not to apply to these cases. Thus the more advantaged representative man cannot say that he deserves and therefore has a right to a scheme of cooperation in which he is permitted to acquire benefits in ways that do not contribute to the welfare of others. There is no basis for his making this claim. From the standpoint of common

sense, then, the difference principle appears to be acceptable both to the more advantaged and to the less advantaged individual. . . .

BACKGROUND INSTITUTIONS FOR DISTRIBUTIVE JUSTICE

The main problem of distributive justice is the choice of a social system. The principles of justice apply to the basic structure and regulate how its major institutions are combined into one scheme. Now, as we have seen, the idea of justice as fairness is to use the notion of pure procedural justice to handle the contingencies of particular situations. The social system is to be designed so that the resulting distribution is just however things turn out. To achieve this end it is necessary to get the social and economic process within the surroundings of suitable political and legal institutions. Without an appropriate scheme of these background institutions the outcome of the distributive process will not be just. Background fairness is lacking. I shall give a brief description of these supporting institutions as they might exist in a properly organized democratic state that allows private ownership of capital and natural resources. . . .

In establishing these background institutions the government may be thought of as divided into four branches.[1] Each branch consists of various agencies, or activities thereof, charged with preserving certain social and economic conditions. These divisions do not overlap with the usual organization of government but are to be understood as different functions. The allocation branch, for example, is to keep the price system workably competitive and to prevent the formation of unreasonable market power. Such power does not exist as long as markets cannot be made more competitive consistent with the requirements of efficiency and the facts of geography and the preferences of households. The allocation branch is also charged with identifying and correcting, say by suitable taxes and subsidies and by changes in the definition of property rights, the more obvious departures from efficiency caused by the failure of prices to measure accurately social benefits and costs. To this end suitable taxes and subsidies may be used, or the scope and definition of property rights may be revised. The stabilization branch, on the other hand, strives to bring about reasonably full employment in the sense that those who want work can find it and the free choice of occupation and the deployment of finance are supported by strong effective demand. These two branches together are to maintain the efficiency of the market economy generally.

The social minimum is the responsibility of the transfer branch. . . . The essential idea is that the workings of this branch take needs into account and assign them an appropriate weight with respect to other claims. A competitive price system gives no consideration to needs and therefore it cannot be the sole device of distribution. There must be a division of labor between the parts of the social system in answering to the common sense precepts of justice. Different institutions meet different claims. Competitive markets properly regulated secure free choice of occupation and lead to an efficient use of resources and allocation of commodities to households. They set a weight on the conventional precepts associated with wages and earnings, whereas a transfer branch guarantees a certain level of well-being and honors the claims of need. . . .

It is clear that the justice of distributive shares depends on the background institutions and how they allocate total income, wages and other income plus transfers. There is with reason strong objection to the competitive determination of total income, since this ignores the claims of need and an appropriate standard of life. From the standpoint of

the legislative stage it is rational to insure oneself and one's descendants against these contingencies of the market. Indeed, the difference principle presumably requires this. But once a suitable minimum is provided by transfers, it may be perfectly fair that the rest of total income be settled by the price system, assuming that it is moderately efficient and free from monopolistic restrictions, and unreasonable externalities have been eliminated. Moreover, this way of dealing with the claims of need would appear to be more effective than trying to regulate income by minimum wage standards, and the like. It is better to assign to each branch only such tasks as are compatible with one another. Since the market is not suited to answer the claims of need, these should be met by a separate arrangement. Whether the principles of justice are satisfied, then, turns on whether the total income of the least advantaged (wages plus transfers) is such as to maximize their long-run expectations (consistent with the constraints of equal liberty and fair equality of opportunity).

Finally, there is a distribution branch. Its task is to preserve an approximate justice in distributive shares by means of taxation and the necessary adjustments in the rights of property. Two aspects of this branch may be distinguished. First of all, it imposes a number of inheritance and gift taxes, and sets restrictions on the rights of bequest. The purpose of these levies and regulations is not to raise revenue (release resources to government) but gradually and continually to correct the distribution of wealth and to prevent concentrations of power detrimental to the fair value of political liberty and fair equality of opportunity. For example, the progressive principle might be applied at the beneficiary's end.[2] Doing this would encourage the wide dispersal of property which is a necessary condition, it seems, if the fair value of the equal liberties is to be maintained.

NOTES

1. For the idea of branches of government, see R. A. Musgrave, *The Theory of Public Finance* (New York: McGraw-Hill, 1959), Ch. 1.

2. See Meade, *Efficiency, Equality and the Ownership of Property*, pp. 56f.

The Entitlement Theory

Robert Nozick

The term "distributive justice" is not a neutral one. Hearing the term "distribution," most people presume that some thing or mechanism uses some principle or criterion to give out a supply of things. Into this process of distributing shares some error may have crept. So it is an open question, at least, whether *re*distribution should take place; whether we should do again what has already been done once, though poorly. However, we are not in the position of children who have been given portions of pie by someone who now makes last minute adjustments to rectify careless cutting. There is no *central* distribution, no person or group entitled to control all the resources, jointly deciding how they are to be doled out. What each person gets, he gets from others who give to him in exchange for something, or as a gift. In a free society, diverse persons control different resources, and new holdings arise out of the voluntary exchanges and actions of persons. . . .

The subject of justice in holdings consists of three major topics. The first is the *original acquisition of holdings,* the appropriation of unheld things. This includes the issues of how unheld things may come to be held, the process, or processes, by which unheld things may come to be held, the things that may come to be held by these processes, the extent of what comes to be held by a particular person, and so on. We shall refer to the complicated truth about this topic, which we shall not formulate here, as the principle of justice in acquisition. The second topic concerns the *transfer of holdings* from one person to another. By what processes may a person transfer holdings to another? How may a person acquire a holding from another who holds it? Under this topic come general descriptions of voluntary exchange, and gift and (on the other hand) fraud, as well as reference to particular conventional details fixed upon in a given society. The complicated truth about this subject (with placeholders for conventional details) we shall call the principle of justice in transfer. (And we shall suppose it also includes principles governing how a person may divest himself of a holding, passing it into an unheld state.)

If the world were wholly just, the following inductive definition would exhaustively cover the subject of justice in holdings.

1. A person who acquires a holding in accordance with the principle of justice in acquisition is entitled to that holding.
2. A person who acquires a holding in accordance with the principle of justice in transfer, from someone else entitled to the holding, is entitled to the holding.
3. No one is entitled to a holding except by (repeated) applications of 1 and 2.

The complete principle of distributive justice would say simply that a distribution is just if everyone is entitled to the holdings they possess under the distribution. . . .

Not all actual situations are generated in accordance with the two principles of justice in holdings: the principle of justice in acquisition and the principle of justice in transfer. Some people steal from others, or defraud them, or enslave them, seizing their product and preventing them from living as they choose, or forcibly exclude others from competing in exchanges. None of these are permissible modes of transition from one situation to another. And some persons acquire holdings by means not sanctioned by the principle of justice in acquisition. The existence of past injustice (previous violations of the first two principles of justice in holdings) raises the third major topic under justice in holdings: the rectification of injustice in holdings. If past injustice has shaped present holdings in various ways, some identifiable and some not, what now, if anything, ought to be done to rectify these injustices? . . .

HISTORICAL PRINCIPLES AND END-RESULT PRINCIPLES

The general outlines of the entitlement theory illuminate the nature and defects of other conceptions of distributive justice. The entitlement theory of justice in distribution is *historical*; whether a distribution is just depends upon how it came about. In contrast, *current time-slice principles* of justice hold that the justice of a distribution is determined by how things are distributed (who has what) as judged by some *structural* principle(s) of just distribution. A utilitarian who judges between any two distributions by seeing which has the greater sum of utility and, if the sums tie, applies some fixed equality criterion to choose the more equal distribution, would hold a current time-slice principle of justice. As would someone who had a fixed schedule of trade-offs between the sum of happiness and equality. According to a current time-slice principle, all that needs to be looked at, in judging the justice of a distribution, is who ends up with what; in comparing any two distributions one need look only at the matrix presenting the distributions. No further information need be fed into a principle of justice. It is a consequence of such principles of justice that any two structurally identical distributions are equally just. . . .

Most persons do not accept current time-slice principles as constituting the whole story about distributive shares. They think it relevant in assessing the justice of a situation to consider not only the distribution it embodies, but also how that distribution came about. If some persons are in prison for murder or war crimes, we do not say that to assess the justice of the distribution in the society we must look only at what this person has, and that person has, and that person has, . . . at the current time. We think it relevant to ask whether someone did something so that he deserved to be punished, *deserved* to have a lower share. . . .

PATTERNING

. . . Almost every suggested principle of distributive justice is patterned: to each according to his moral merit, or needs, or marginal product, or how hard he tries, or the weighted sum of the foregoing, and so on. The principle of entitlement we have sketched is *not* patterned. There is no one natural dimension or weighted sum or combination of a small number of natural dimensions that yields the distributions generated in accordance with the principle of entitlement. The set of holdings that results when some persons receive their marginal products, others win at gambling, others receive a share of their mate's income, others receive gifts from foundations, others receive interest on loans, others receive gifts from admirers, others receive returns on investment, others make for themselves much of what they have, others find things, and so on, will not be patterned. . . .

To think that the task of a theory of distributive justice is to fill in the blank in "to each according to his _____" is to be predisposed to search for a pattern; and the separate treatment of "from each according to his _____" treats production and distribution as two separate and independent issues. On an entitlement view these are *not* two separate questions. Whoever makes something, having bought or contracted for all other held resources used in the process (transferring some of his holdings for these cooperating factors), is entitled to it. . . .

So entrenched are maxims of the usual form that perhaps we should present the entitlement conception as a competitor. Ignoring acquisition and rectification, we might say:

> From each according to what he chooses to do, to each according to what he makes for himself (perhaps with the contracted aid of others) and what others choose to do for him and choose to give him of what they've been given previously (under this maxim) and haven't yet expended or transferred.

This, the discerning reader will have noticed, has its defects as a slogan. So as a summary and great simplification (and not as a maxim with any independent meaning) we have:

> *From each as they choose, to each as they are chosen.*

HOW LIBERTY UPSETS PATTERNS

It is not clear how those holding alternative conceptions of distributive justice can reject the entitlement conception of justice in holdings. For suppose a distribution favored by one of these non-entitlement conceptions is realized. Let us suppose it is your favorite one and let us call this distribution D_1; perhaps everyone has an equal share, perhaps shares vary in accordance with some dimension you treasure. Now suppose that Wilt Chamberlain is greatly in demand by basketball teams, being a great gate attraction. (Also suppose contracts run only for a year, with players being free agents). He signs the following sort of contract with a team: In each home game, twenty-five cents from the price of each ticket of admission goes to him. (We ignore the question of whether he is "gouging" the owners, letting them look out for themselves.) The season starts, and people cheerfully attend his team's games; they buy their tickets, each time dropping a separate twenty-five cents of their admission price into a special box with Chamberlain's name on it. They are excited about seeing him play; it is worth the total admission price to them. Let us suppose that in one season one million persons attend his home games, and Wilt Chamberlain winds up with $250,000, a much larger sum than the average income and larger even than anyone else has. Is he entitled to this income? Is this new distribution D_2, unjust? If so, why? There is *no* question about whether each of the people was entitled to the control over the resources they held in D_1; because that was the distribution (your favorite) that (for the purposes of argument) we assumed was acceptable. Each of these persons *chose* to give twenty-five cents of their money to Chamberlain. They could have spent it on going to the movies, or on candy bars, or on copies of *Dissent* magazine, or of *Monthly Review*. But they all, at least one million of them, converged on giving it to Wilt Chamberlain in exchange for watching him play basketball. If D_1 was a just distribution, and people voluntarily moved from it to D_2, transferring parts of their shares they were given under D_1 (what was it for if not to do something with?), isn't D_2 also just? If the people were entitled to dispose of the resources to which they were entitled (under D_1) didn't this include their being entitled to give it to, or exchange it with, Wilt Chamberlain? Can anyone else complain on grounds or justice? Each other person already has his legitimate share under D_1. Under D_1, there is nothing that anyone has that anyone else has a claim of justice against. After someone transfers something to Wilt Chamberlain, third parties *still* have their legitimate shares; *their* shares are not changed. By what process could such a transfer among two persons give a rise to a legitimate claim of distributive justice on a portion of what was transferred, by a third party who had no claim of justice on any holding of the others *before* the transfer? To cut off objections irrelevant here, we might imagine the exchanges occurring in a socialist society, after hours. After playing whatever basketball he does in his daily work, or doing whatever other daily work he does, Wilt Chamberlain decides to put in *overtime* to earn additional money. (First his work quota is set; he works time over that.) Or imagine it is a skilled juggler people like to see, who puts on shows after hours. . . .

The general point illustrated by the Wilt Chamberlain example is that no end-state principle or distributional patterned principle of justice can be continuously realized without continuous interference with peo-

ple's lives. Any favored pattern would be transformed into one unfavored by the principle, by people choosing to act in various ways; for example, by people exchanging goods and services with other people, or giving things to other people, things the transferrers are entitled to under the favored distributional pattern. To maintain a pattern one must either continually interfere to stop people from transferring resources as they wish to, or continually (or periodically) interfere to take from some persons resources that others for some reason chose to transfer to them. . . .

Patterned principles of distributive justice necessitate *re*distributive activities. The likelihood is small that any actual freely-arrived-at set of holdings fits a given pattern; and the likelihood is nil that it will continue to fit the pattern as people exchange and give. From the point of view of an entitlement theory, redistribution is a serious matter indeed, involving, as it does, the violation of people's rights. (An exception is those takings that fall under the principle of the rectification of injustices.) . . .

LOCKE'S THEORY OF ACQUISITION

. . . [Let us] introduce an additional bit of complexity into the structure of the entitlement theory. This is best approached by considering Locke's attempt to specify a principle of justice in acquisition. Locke views property rights in an unowned object as originating through someone's mixing his labor with it. This gives rise to many questions. What are the boundaries of what labor is mixed with? If a private astronaut clears a place on Mars, has he mixed his labor with (so that he comes to own) the whole planet, the whole uninhabited universe, or just a particular plot? Which plot does an act bring under ownership? . . .

Locke's proviso that there be "enough and as good left in common for others" is meant to ensure that the situation of others is not worsened. . . .

. . . I assume that any adequate theory of justice in acquisition will contain a proviso similar to [Locke's]. . . .

I believe that the free operation of a market system will not actually run afoul of the Lockean proviso. . . . If this is correct, the proviso will not . . . provide a significant opportunity for future state action.

Rich and Poor

Peter Singer

One way of making sense of the non-consequentialist view of responsibility is by basing it on a theory of rights of the kind proposed by John Locke or, more recently, Robert Nozick. If everyone has a right to life, and this right is a right *against* others who might threaten my life, but not a right *to* assistance from others when my life is in danger, then we can understand the feeling that we are responsible for acting to kill but not for omitting to save. The former violates the rights of others, the latter does not.

Should we accept such a theory of rights? If we build up our theory of rights by imagining, as Locke and Nozick do, individuals living independently from each other in a 'state of nature', it may seem natural to adopt a conception of rights in which as long as each leaves the other alone, no rights are violated. I might, on this view, quite properly have maintained my independent existence if I had wished to do so. So if I do not make you any worse off than you would have been if I had had nothing at all to do with you, how can I have violated your rights? But why start from such an unhistorical, abstract and ultimately inexplicable idea as an independent individual? We now know that our ancestors were social beings long before they were human beings, and could not have developed the abilities and capacities of human beings if they had not been social beings first. In any case we are not, now, isolated individuals. If we consider people living together in a community, it is less easy to assume that rights must be restricted to rights against interference. We might, instead, adopt the view that taking rights to life seriously is incompatible with standing by and watching people die when one could easily save them. . . .

THE OBLIGATION TO ASSIST

The Argument for an Obligation to Assist

The path from the library at my university to the Humanities lecture theatre passes a shallow ornamental pond. Suppose that on my way to give a lecture I notice that a small child has fallen in and is in danger of drowning. Would anyone deny that I ought to wade in and pull the child out? This will mean get-

From Peter Singer, "Rich and Poor," in *Practical Ethics* (New York: Cambridge University Press, 1979), pp. 166, 168–179. Reprinted with permission of the publisher.

ting my clothes muddy, and either cancelling my lecture or delaying it until I can find something dry to change into; but compared with the avoidable death of a child this is insignificant.

A plausible principle that would support the judgment that I ought to pull the child out is this: if it is in our power to prevent something very bad happening, without thereby sacrificing anything of comparable moral significance, we ought to do it. This principle seems uncontroversial. It will obviously win the assent of consequentialists; but non-consequentialists should accept it too, because the injunction to prevent what is bad applies only when nothing comparably significant is at stake. Thus the principle cannot lead to the kinds of actions of which non-consequentialists strongly disapprove — serious violations of individual rights, injustice, broken promises, and so on. If a non-consequentialist regards any of these as comparable in moral significance to the bad thing that is to be prevented, he will automatically regard the principle as not applying in those cases in which the bad thing can only be prevented by violating rights, doing injustice, breaking promises, or whatever else is at stake. Most non-consequentialists hold that we ought to prevent what is bad and promote what is good. Their dispute with consequentialists lies in their insistence that this is not the sole ultimate ethical principle: that it is *an* ethical principle is not denied by any plausible ethical theory.

Nevertheless the uncontroversial appearance of the principle that we ought to prevent what is bad when we can do so without sacrificing anything of comparable moral significance is deceptive. If it were taken seriously and acted upon, our lives and our world would be fundamentally changed. For the principle applies, not just to rare situations in which one can save a child from a pond, but to the everyday situations in which we can assist those living in absolute poverty. In saying this I assume that absolute poverty, with its hunger and malnutrition, lack of shelter, illiteracy, disease, high infant mortality and low life expectancy, is a bad thing. And I assume that it is within the power of the affluent to reduce absolute poverty, without sacrificing anything of comparable moral significance. If these two assumptions and the principle we have been discussing are correct, we have an obligation to help those in absolute poverty which is no less strong than our obligation to rescue a drowning child from a pond. Not to help would be wrong, whether or not it is intrinsically equivalent to killing. Helping is not, as conventionally thought, a charitable act which it is praiseworthy to do, but not wrong to omit; it is something that everyone ought to do.

This is the argument for an obligation to assist. Set out more formally, it would look like this.

> **First premise**: If we can prevent something bad without sacrificing anything of comparable significance, we ought to do it.
> **Second premise**: Absolute poverty is bad.
> **Third premise**: There is some absolute poverty we can prevent without sacrificing anything of comparable moral significance.
> **Conclusion**: We ought to prevent some absolute poverty.

The first premise is the substantive moral premise on which the argument rests, and I have tried to show that it can be accepted by people who hold a variety of ethical positions.

The second premise is unlikely to be challenged. Absolute poverty is, as [Robert] McNamara put in, 'beneath any reasonable definition of human decency' and it would be hard to find a plausible ethical view which did not regard it as a bad thing.

The third premise is more controversial, even though it is cautiously framed. It claims only that some absolute poverty can be prevented without the sacrifice of anything of comparable moral significance. It thus avoids the objection that any aid I can give is just 'drops in the ocean' for the point is not whether my personal contribution will make any noticeable impression on world poverty as a whole (of course it won't) but whether it will prevent some poverty. This is all the argument needs to sustain its conclusion, since the second premise says that any absolute poverty is bad, and not merely the total amount of absolute poverty. If without sacrificing anything of comparable moral significance we can provide just one family with the means to raise itself out of absolute poverty, the third premise is vindicated.

I have left the notion of moral significance unexamined in order to show that the argument does not depend on any specific values or ethical principles. I think the third premise is true for most people living in industrialized nations, on any defensible view of what is morally significant. Our affluence means that we have income we can dispose of without giving up the basic necessities of life, and we can use this income to reduce absolute poverty. Just how much we will think ourselves obliged to give up will depend on what we consider to be of comparable moral significance to the poverty we could prevent: colour television, stylish clothes, expensive dinners, a sophisticated stereo system, overseas holidays, a (second?) car, a larger house, private schools for our children. . . . For a utilitarian, none of these is likely to be of comparable significance to the reduction of absolute poverty; and those who are not utilitarians surely must, if they subscribe to the principle of universalizability, accept that at least *some* of these things are of far less moral significance than the absolute poverty that could be prevented by the money they cost.

So the third premise seems to be true on any plausible ethical view — although the precise amount of absolute poverty that can be prevented before anything of moral significance is sacrificed will vary according to the ethical view one accepts.

Objections to the Argument

Taking Care of Our Own. Anyone who has worked to increase overseas aid will have come across the argument that we should look after those near us, our families and then the poor in our own country, before we think about poverty in distant places.

No doubt we do instinctively prefer to help those who are close to us. Few could stand by and watch a child drown; many can ignore a famine in Africa. But the question is not what we usually do, but what we ought to do, and it is difficult to see any sound moral justification for the view that distance, or community membership, makes a crucial difference to our obligations.

Consider, for instance, racial affinities. Should whites help poor whites before helping poor blacks? Most of us would reject such a suggestion out of hand, [by appeal to] the principle of equal consideration of interests: people's needs for food has nothing to do with their race, and if blacks need food more than whites, it would be a violation of the principle of equal consideration to give preference to whites.

The same point applies to citizenship or nationhood. Every affluent nation has some relatively poor citizens, but absolute poverty is limited largely to the poor nations. Those living on the streets of Calcutta, or in a drought-stricken region of the Sahel, are experiencing poverty unknown in the West. Under these circumstances it would be wrong to decide that only those fortunate enough to be citizens of our own community will share our abundance.

We feel obligations of kinship more strongly than those of citizenship. Which parents could give away their last bowl of rice if their own children were starving? To do so would seem unnatural, contrary to our nature as biologically evolved beings — although whether it would be wrong is another question altogether. In any case, we are not faced with that situation, but with one in which our own children are well-fed, well-clothed, well-educated, and would now like new bikes, a stereo set, or their own car. In these circumstances any special obligations we might have to our children have been fulfilled, and the needs of strangers make a stronger claim upon us.

The element of truth in the view that we should first take care of our own, lies in the advantage of a recognized system of responsibilities. When families and local communities look after their own poorer members, ties of affection and personal relationships achieve ends that would otherwise require a large, impersonal bureaucracy. Hence it would be absurd to propose that from now on we all regard ourselves as equally responsible for the welfare of everyone in the world; but the argument for an obligation to assist does not propose that. It applies only when some are in absolute poverty, and others can help without sacrificing anything of comparable moral significance. To allow one's own kin to sink into absolute poverty would be to sacrifice something of comparable significance; and before that point had been reached, the breakdown of the system of family and community responsibility would be a factor to weigh the balance in favour of a small degree of preference for family and community. This small degree of preference is, however, decisively outweighed by existing discrepancies in wealth and property.

Property Rights. Do people have a right to private property, a right which contradicts the view that they are under an obligation to give some of their wealth away to those in absolute poverty? According to some theories of rights (for instance, Robert Nozick's) provided one has acquired one's property without the use of unjust means like force and fraud, one may be entitled to enormous wealth while others starve. This individualistic conception of rights is in contrast to other views, like the early Christian doctrine to be found in the works of Thomas Aquinas, which holds that since property exists for the satisfaction of human needs, 'whatever a man has in superabundance is owed, of natural right, to the poor for their sustenance.' A socialist would also, of course, see wealth as belonging to the community rather than the individual, while utilitarians, whether socialist or not, would be prepared to override property rights to prevent great evils.

Does the argument for an obligation to assist others therefore presuppose one of these other theories of property rights, and not an individualistic theory like Nozick's? Not necessarily. A theory of property rights can insist on our *right* to retain wealth without pronouncing on whether the rich *ought* to give to the poor. Nozick, for example, rejects the use of compulsory means like taxation to redistribute income, but suggests that we can achieve the ends we deem morally desirable by voluntary means. So Nozick would reject the claim that rich people have an 'obligation' to give to the poor, in so far as this implies that the poor have a right to our aid, but might accept that giving is something we ought to do and failure to give, though within one's rights, is wrong — for rights is not all there is to ethics.

The argument for an obligation to assist can survive, with only minor modifications, even if we accept an individualistic theory of property rights. In any case, however, I do not think we should accept such a theory. It leaves too much to chance to be an acceptable ethical view. For instance, those whose forefathers happened to inhabit some sandy wastes around the Persian Gulf are now fabulously wealthy, because oil lay under those sands; while those whose forefathers settled on better land south of the Sahara live in absolute poverty, because of drought and bad harvests. Can this distribution be acceptable from an impartial point of view? If we imagine ourselves about to begin life as a citizen of either Kuwait or Chad — but we do not know which — would we accept the principle that citizens of Kuwait are under no obligation to assist people living in Chad?

Population and the Ethics of Triage. Perhaps the most serious objection to the argument that we have an obligation to assist is that since the major cause of absolute poverty is overpopulation, helping those now in poverty will only ensure that yet more people are born to live in poverty in the future.

In its most extreme form, this objection is taken to show that we should adopt a policy of 'triage.' The term comes from medical policies adopted in wartime. With too few doctors to cope with all the casualties, the wounded were divided into three categories: those who would probably survive without medical assistance, those who might survive if they received assistance, but otherwise probably would not, and those who even with medical assistance probably would not survive. Only those in the middle category were given medical assistance. The idea, of course, was to use limited medical resources as effectively as possible. For those in the first category, medical treatment was not strictly necessary; for those in the third category, it was likely to be useless. It has been suggested that we should apply the same policies to countries,

according to their prospects of becoming self-sustaining. We would not aid countries which even without our help will soon be able to feed their populations. We would not aid countries which, even with our help, will not be able to limit their population to a level they can feed. We would aid those countries where our help might make the difference between success and failure in bringing food and population into balance.

Advocates of this theory are understandably reluctant to give a complete list of the countries they would place into the 'hopeless' category; but Bangladesh is often cited as an example. Adopting the policy of triage would, then, mean cutting off assistance to Bangladesh and allowing famine, disease and natural disasters to reduce the population of that country (now around 80 million) to the level at which it can provide adequately for all.

In support of this view Garrett Hardin has offered a metaphor: we in the rich nations are like the occupants of a crowded lifeboat adrift in a sea full of drowning people. If we try to save the drowning by bringing them aboard our boat will be overloaded and we shall all drown. Since it is better that some survive than none, we should leave the others to drown. In the world today, according to Hardin, 'lifeboat ethics' apply. The rich should leave the poor to starve, for otherwise the poor will drag the rich down with them. . . .

Anyone whose initial reaction to triage was not one of repugnance would be an unpleasant sort of person. Yet initial reactions based on strong feelings are not always reliable guides. Advocates of triage are rightly concerned with the long-term consequences of our actions. They say that helping the poor and starving now merely ensures more poor and starving in the future. When our capacity to help is finally unable to cope — as one day it must be — the suffering will be greater than it would be if we stopped helping now. If this is correct, there is nothing we can do to prevent absolute starvation and poverty, in the long run, and so we have no obligation to assist. Nor does it seem reasonable to hold that under these circumstances people have a right to our assistance. If we do accept such a right, irrespective of the consequences, we are saying that, in Hardin's metaphor, we would continue to haul the drowning into our lifeboat until the boat sank and we all drowned.

If triage is to be rejected it must be tackled on its own ground, within the framework of consequentialist ethics. Here it is vulnerable. Any consequentialist ethics must take probability of outcome into account. A course of action that will certainly produce some benefit is to be preferred to an alternative course that may lead to a slightly larger benefit, but is equally likely to result in no benefit at all. Only if the greater magnitude of the uncertain benefit outweighs its uncertainty should we choose it. Better one certain unit of benefit than a 10% chance of 5 units; but better a 50% chance of 3 units than a single certain unit. The same principle applies when are we trying to avoid evils.

The policy of triage involves a certain, very great evil: population control by famine and disease. Tens of millions would die slowly. Hundreds of millions would continue to live in absolute poverty, at the very margin of existence. Against this prospect, advocates of the policy place a possible evil which is greater still: the same process of famine and disease, taking place in, say, fifty years time, when the world's population may be three times its present level, and the number who will die from famine, or struggle on in absolute poverty, will be that much greater. The question is: how probable is this forecast that continued assistance now will lead to greater disasters in the future?

Forecasts of population growth are notoriously fallible, and theories about the factors which affect it remain speculative. One theory, at least as plausible as any other, is that countries pass through a 'demographic transition' as their standard of living rises. When people are very poor and have no access to modern medicine their fertility is high, but population is kept in check by high death rates. The introduction of sanitation, modern medical techniques and other improvements reduces the death rate, but initially has little effect on the birth rate. Then population grows rapidly. Most poor countries are now in this phase. If standards of living continue to rise, however, couples begin to realize that to have the same number of children surviving to maturity as in the past, they do not need to give birth to as many children as their parents did. The need for children to provide economic support in old age diminishes. Improved education and the emancipation and employment of women also reduce the birthrate, and so population growth begins to level off. Most rich nations have reached this stage, and their populations are growing only very slowly.

If this theory is right, there is an alternative to the disasters accepted as inevitable by supports of triage. We can assist poor countries to raise the living standards of the poorest members of their population. We can encourage the governments of these countries to enact land reform measures, improve education, and liberate women from a purely child-bearing role. We can also help other countries to make contraception and sterilization widely available. There is a fair chance that these measures will hasten the onset of the demographic transition and bring population growth down to a manageable level. Success cannot be guaranteed; but the evidence that improved economic security and education reduce population growth is strong enough to make triage ethically unacceptable. We cannot allow millions to die from starvation and disease when there is a reasonable probability that population can be brought under control without such horrors.

Population growth is therefore not a reason against giving overseas aid, although it should make us think about the kind of aid to give. Instead of food handouts, it may be better to give aid that hastens the demographic transition. This may mean agricultural assistance for the rural poor, or assistance with education, or the provision of contraceptive services. Whatever kind of aid proves most effective in specific circumstances, the obligation to assist is not reduced.

One awkward question remains. What should we do about a poor and already overpopulated country which, for religious or nationalistic reasons, restricts the use of contraceptives and refuses to slow its population

growth? Should we nevertheless offer development assistance? Or should we make our offer conditional on effective steps being taken to reduce the birthrate? To the latter course, some would object that putting conditions on aid is an attempt to impose our own ideas on independent sovereign nations. So it is — but is this imposition unjustifiable? If the argument for an obligation to assist is sound, we have an obligation to reduce absolute poverty; but we have no obligation to make sacrifices that, to the best of our knowledge, have no prospect of reducing poverty in the long run. Hence we have no obligation to assist countries whose governments have policies which will make our aid ineffective. This could be very harsh on poor citizens of these countries — for they may have no say in the government's policies — but we will help more people in the long run by using our resources where they are most effective.

Spheres of Justice

Michael Walzer

COMPLEX EQUALITY AND PLURALISM

Distributive justice is a large idea. It draws the entire world of goods within the reach of philosophical reflection. Nothing can be omitted; no feature of our common life can escape scrutiny. Human society is a distributive community. That's not all it is, but it is importantly that: we come together to share, divide, and exchange. We also come together to make the things that are shared, divided, and exchanged; but that very making — work

itself — is distributed among us in a division of labor. My place in the economy, my standing in the political order, my reputation among my fellows, my material holdings: all these come to me from other men and women. It can be said that I have what I have rightly or wrongly, justly or unjustly; but given the range of distributions and the number of participants, such judgments are never easy.

The idea of distributive justice has as much to do with being and doing as with having, as much to do with production as with consumption, as much to do with identity and status as with land, capital, or personal possessions. Different political arrangements enforce, and different ideologies justify, different distributions of membership, power, honor, ritual eminence, divine grace, kinship and love, knowledge, wealth, physical security, work and leisure, rewards and punishments, and a host of goods more narrowly and materially conceived — food, shelter, clothing, transportation, medical care, commodities of every sort, and all the odd things (paintings, rare books, postage stamps) that human beings collect. And this multiplicity of goods is matched by a multiplicity of distributive procedures, agents, and criteria. There are such things as simple distributive systems — slave galleys, monasteries, insane asylums, kindergartens (though each of these, looked at closely, might show unexpected complexities); but no full-fledged human society has ever avoided the multiplicity. We must study it all, the goods and the distributions, in many different times and places.

There is, however, no single point of access to this world of distributive arrangements and ideologies. There has never been a universal medium of exchange. Since the decline of the barter economy, money has been the most common medium. But the old maxim according to which there are some things that money can't buy is not only normatively but also factually true. What should and should not be up for sale is something men and women always have to decide and have decided in many different ways. Throughout history, the market has been one of the most important mechanisms for the distribution of social goods; but it has never been, it nowhere is today, a complete distributive system.

Similarly, there has never been either a single decision point from which all distributions are controlled or a single set of agents making decisions. No state power has ever been so pervasive as to regulate all the patterns of sharing, dividing, and exchanging out of which a society takes shape. Things slip away from the state's grasp; new patterns are worked out — familial networks, black markets, bureaucratic alliances, clandestine political and religious organizations. State officials can tax, conscript, allocate, regulate, appoint, reward, punish, but they cannot capture the full range of goods or substitute themselves for every other agent of distribution. Nor can anyone else do that: there are market coups and cornerings, but there has never been a fully successful distributive conspiracy.

And finally, there has never been a single criterion, or a single set of interconnected criteria, for all distributions. Desert, qualification, birth and blood, friendship, need, free exchange, political loyalty, democratic decision: each has had its place, along with many others, uneasily coexisting, invoked by competing groups, confused with one another.

In the matter of distributive justice, history displays a great variety of arrangements and ideologies. But the first impulse of the philosopher is to resist the displays of history, the world of appearances, and to search for some underlying unity: a short list of basic goods, quickly abstracted to a single good; a single distributive criterion or an interconnected set; and the philosopher himself standing, symbolically at least, at a single decision point. I shall argue that to search for unity is to misunderstand the subject matter of distributive justice. Nevertheless, in some sense the philosophical impulse is unavoidable. Even if we choose pluralism, as I shall do, that choice still requires a coherent defense. There must be principles that justify the choice and set limits to it, for pluralism does not require us to endorse every proposed distributive criterion or to accept every would-be agent. Conceivably, there is a single principle and a single legitimate kind of pluralism. But this would still be a pluralism that encompassed a wide range of distributions. By contrast, the deepest assumption of most of the philosophers who have written about justice, from Plato onward, is that there is one, and only one, distributive system that philosophy can rightly encompass.

Today this system is commonly described as the one that ideally rational men and women would choose if they were forced to choose impartially, knowing nothing of their own situation, barred from making particularist claims, confronting an abstract set of goods.[1] If these constraints on knowing and claiming are suitably shaped, and if the goods are suitably defined, it is probably true that a singular conclusion can be produced. Rational men and women, constrained this way or that, will choose one, and only one, distributive system. But the force of that singular conclusion is not easy to measure. It is surely doubtful that those same men and women, if they were transformed into ordinary people, with a firm sense of their own identity, with their own goods in their hands, caught up in everyday troubles, would reiterate their hypothetical choice or even recognize it as their own. The problem is not, most importantly, with the particularism of interest, which philosophers have always assumed they could safely — that is, uncontroversially — set aside. Ordinary people can do that too, for the sake, say, of the public interest. The greater problem is with the particularism of history, culture, and membership. Even if they are committed to impartiality, the question most likely to arise in the minds of the members of a political community is not, What would rational individuals choose under universalizing conditions of such-and-such a sort? But rather, What would individuals like us choose, who are situated as we are, who share a culture and are determined to go on sharing it? And this is a question that is readily transformed into, What choices have we already made in the course of our common life? What understandings do we (really) share?

Justice is a human construction, and it is doubtful that it can be made in only one way. At any rate, I shall begin by doubting, and more than doubting, this standard philosophical assumption. The questions posed by the theory of distributive justice admit of a range of answers, and there is room within the range for cultural diversity and political choice. It's not only a matter of implementing some singular principle or set of principles in different historical settings. No one would deny that there is a range of morally permissible implementations. I want to argue for more than this: that the principles of justice are themselves pluralistic in form; that different social goods ought to be distributed for different reasons, in accordance with different procedures, by different agents; and that all these differences derive from different understandings of the social goods themselves — the inevitable product of historical and cultural particularism. . . .

MEMBERSHIP AND JUSTICE

The distribution of membership is not pervasively subject to the constraints of justice. Across a considerable range of the decisions that are made, states are simply free to take in strangers (or not) — much as they are free, leaving aside the claims of the needy, to share their wealth with foreign friends, to honor the achievements of foreign artists, scholars, and scientists, to choose their trading partners, and to enter into collective security arrangements with foreign states. But the right to choose an admissions policy is more basic than any of these, for it is not merely a matter of acting in the world, exercising sovereignty, and pursuing national interests. At stake here is the shape of the community that acts in the world, exercises sovereignty, and so on. Admission and exclusion are at the core of communal independence. They suggest the deepest meaning of self-determination. Without them, there could not be *communities of character,* historically stable, ongoing associations of men and women with some special commitment to one another and some special sense of their common life.[2]

But self-determination in the sphere of membership is not absolute. It is a right exercised, most often, by national clubs or families, but it is held in principle by territorial states. Hence it is subject both to internal decisions by the members themselves (*all* the members, including those who hold membership simply by right of place) and to the external principle of mutual aid. Immigration, then, is both a matter of political choice and moral constraint. Naturalization, by contrast, is entirely constrained: every new immigrant, every refugee taken in, every resident and worker must be offered the opportunities of citizenship. If the community is so radically divided that a single citizenship is impossible, then its territory must be divided, too, before the rights of admission and exclusion can be exercised. For these rights are to be exercised only by the community as a whole (even if, in practice, some national majority dominates the decision making) and only with regard to foreigners, not by some members with regard to others. No community can be half-metic, half-citizen and claim that its admissions policies are acts of self-determination or that its politics is democratic.

The determination of aliens and guests by an exclusive band of citizens (or of slaves by masters, or women by men, or blacks by whites, or conquered peoples by their conquerors) is not communal freedom but oppression. The citizens are free, of course, to set up a club, make membership as exclusive as they like, write a constitution, and govern one another. But they can't claim territorial jurisdiction and rule over the people with whom they share the territory. To do this is to act outside their sphere, beyond their rights. It is a form of tyranny. Indeed, the rule of citizens over non-citizens, of members over strangers, is probably the most common form of tyranny in human history. . . .

FREE EXCHANGE

Free exchange is obviously open-ended; it guarantees no particular distributive outcome. At no point in any exchange process plausibly called "free" will it be possible to predict the particular division of social goods that will obtain at some later point.[3] (It may be possible, however, to predict the general structure of the division.) In theory at least, free exchange creates a market within which all goods are convertible into all other goods through the neutral medium of money. There are no dominant goods and no monopolies. Hence the successive divisions that obtain will directly reflect the social meanings of the goods that are divided. For each bargain, trade, sale, and purchase will have been agreed to voluntarily by men and women who know what that meaning is, who are indeed its makers. Every exchange is a revelation of social meaning. By definition, then, no x will ever fall into the hands of someone who possesses y, merely because he possesses y and without regard to what x actually means to some other member of society. The market is radically pluralistic in its operations and its outcomes, infinitely sensitive to the meanings that individuals attach to goods. What possible restraints can be imposed on free exchange, then, in the name of pluralism?

But everyday life in the market, the actual experience of free exchange, is very different from what the theory suggests. Money, supposedly the neutral medium, is in practice a dominant good, and it is monopolized by people who possess a special talent for bargaining and trading — the green thumb of bourgeois society. Then other people demand a redistribution of money and the establishment of the regime of simple equality, and the search begins for some way to sustain that regime. But even if we focus on the first untroubled moment of simple equality — free exchange on the basis of equal shares — we will still need to set limits on what can be exchanged for what. For free exchange leaves distributions entirely in the hands of individuals, and social meanings are not subject, or are not always subject, to the interpretative decisions of individual men and women.

Consider an easy example, the case of political power. We can conceive of political power as a set of goods of varying value, votes, influence, offices, and so on. Any of these can be traded on the market and accumulated by individuals willing to sacrifice other goods. Even if the sacrifices are real, however, the result is a form of tyranny — petty tyranny, given the conditions of simple equality. Because I am willing to do without my hat, I shall vote twice; and you who value the vote less than you value my hat, will not vote at all. I suspect that the result is tyrannical even with regard to the two of us, who have reached a voluntary agreement. . . .

Free exchange is not a general criterion, but we will be able to specify the boundaries within which it operates only through a careful analysis of particular social goods. . . .

THE MARKETPLACE

There is a stronger argument about the sphere of money, the common argument of the defenders of capitalism: that market outcomes matter a great deal because the market, if it is free, gives to each person exactly what he deserves. The market rewards us all in accordance with the contributions we make to one another's well-being.[4] The goods and services we provide are valued by potential consumers in such-and-such a way, and these values are aggregated by the market, which determines the price we receive. And that price is our desert, for it expresses the only worth our goods and services can have, the worth they actually have for other people. But this is to misunderstand the meaning of desert. Unless there are standards of worth independent of what people want (and are willing to buy) at this or that moment in time, there can be no deservingness at all. We would never know what a person deserved until we saw what he had gotten. And that can't be right.

Imagine a novelist who writes what he hopes will be a best seller. He studies his potential audience, designs his book to meet the current fashion. Perhaps he had to violate the canons of his art in order to do that, and perhaps he is a novelist for whom the violation was painful. He has stooped to conquer. Does he now deserve the fruits of his conquest? Does he deserve a conquest that bears fruit? His novel appears, let's say, during a depression when no one has money for books, and very few copies are sold; his reward is small. Has he gotten less than he deserves? (His fellow writers smile at his disappointment; perhaps that's what he deserves.) Years later, in better times, the book is reissued and does well. Has its author become more deserving? Surely desert can't hang on the state of the economy. There is too much luck involved here; talk of desert makes little sense. We would do better to say simply that the writer is entitled to his royalties, large or small.[5] He is like any other entrepreneur; he has bet on the market. It's a chancy business, but he knew that when he made the bet. He has a right to what he gets — after he has paid the costs of communal provision (he lives not only in the market but also in the city). But he can't claim that he has gotten less than he deserves, and it doesn't matter if the rest of us think that he has gotten more. The market doesn't recognize desert. Initiative, enterprise, innovation, hard work, ruthless dealing, reckless gambling, the prostitution of talent: all these are sometimes rewarded, sometimes not.

But the rewards that the market provides, when it provides them, are appropriate to these sorts of effort. The man or woman who builds a better mousetrap, or opens a restaurant and sells delicious blintzes, or does a little teaching on the side, is looking to earn money. And why not? No one would want to feed blintzes to strangers, day after day, merely to win their gratitude. Here in the world of the petty bourgeoisie, it seems only right that an entrepreneur, able to provide timely goods and services, should reap the rewards he had in mind when he went to work.

This is, indeed, a kind of "rightness" that the community may see fit to enclose and restrain. The morality of the bazaar belongs in the bazaar. The market is a zone of the city, not the whole of the city. But it is a great mistake, I think, when people worried about the tyranny of the market seek its entire abolition. It is one thing to clear the Temple of traders, quite another to clear the streets. The latter move would require a radical shift in our understanding of what material things are for and of how we relate to them and to other people through them. But the shift is not accomplished by the abolition; commodity exchange is merely driven underground; or it takes place in state stores, as in parts of Eastern Europe today, drearily and inefficiently.

The liveliness of the open market reflects our sense of the great variety of desirable things; and so long as that is our sense, we have no reason not to relish the liveliness. . . .

THE RELATIVITY AND THE NON-RELATIVITY OF JUSTICE

Justice is relative to social meanings. Indeed, the relativity of justice follows from the classic non-relative definition, giving each person his due, as much as it does from my own proposal, distributing goods for "internal" reasons. These are formal definitions that require, as I have tried to show, historical completion. We cannot say what is due to this person or that one until we know how these people relate to one another through the things they make and distribute. There cannot be a just society until there is a society; and the adjective *just* doesn't determine, it only modifies, the substantive life of the societies it describes. There are an infinite number of possible lives, shaped by an infinite number of possible cultures, religions, political arrangements, geographical conditions, and so on. A given society is just if its substantive life is lived in a certain way — that is, in a way faithful to the shared understandings of the members. . . .

We are (all of us) culture-producing creatures; we make and inhabit meaningful worlds. Since there is no way to rank and order these worlds with regard to their understanding of social goods, we do justice to actual men and women by respecting their particular creations. And they claim justice, and resist tyranny, by insisting on the meaning of social goods among themselves. Justice is rooted in the distinct understandings of places, honors, jobs, things of all sorts, that constitute a shared way of life. To override those understandings is (always) to act unjustly.

Just as one can describe a caste system that meets (internal) standards of justice, so one can describe a capitalist system that does the same thing. But now the description will have to be a great deal more complex, for social meanings are no longer integrated in the same way. It may be the case, as Marx says in the first volume of *Capital,* that the creation and appropriation of surplus value "is peculiar good fortune for the buyer [of labor power], but no injustice at all to the seller."[6] But this is by no means the whole story of justice and injustice in capitalist society. It will also be crucially important whether this surplus value is convertible, whether it purchases special privileges, in the law courts, or in the educational system, or in the spheres of office and politics. Since capitalism develops along with and actually sponsors a considerable differentiation of social goods, no account of buying and selling, no description of free exchange, can possibly settle the question of justice. We will need to learn a great deal about other distributive processes and about their relative autonomy from or integration into the market. The dominance of capital outside the market makes capitalism unjust.

The theory of justice is alert to differences, sensitive to boundaries. It doesn't follow from the theory, however, that societies are more just if they are more differentiated. Justice simply has more scope in such societies, because there are more distinct goods, more distributive principles, more agents, more procedures. And the more scope justice has, the more certain it is that complex equality will be the form that justice takes. Tyranny also has more scope. Viewed from the outside, from our own perspective, the Indian Brahmins look very much like tyrants — and so they will come to be if the understandings on which their high position is based cease to be shared. From the inside, however, things come to them naturally, as it were, by virtue of their ritual purity. They don't need to turn themselves into tyrants in order to enjoy the full range of social goods. Or, when they do turn themselves into tyrants, they merely exploit the advantages they already possess. But when goods are distinct and distributive spheres autonomous, that same enjoyment requires exertion, intrigue, and violence. This is the crucial sign of tyranny: a continual grabbing of things that don't come naturally, an unrelenting struggle to rule outside one's own company. . . .

JUSTICE IN THE TWENTIETH CENTURY

. . . Contemporary forms of egalitarian politics have their origin in the struggle against capitalism and the particular tyranny of money. And surely in the United States today it is the tyranny of money that most clearly invites resistance: property/power rather than power itself. But it is a common argument that without property/power, power itself is too dangerous. State officials will be tyrants, we are told, whenever their power is not balanced by the power of money. It follows, then, that capitalists will be tyrants whenever wealth is not balanced by a strong government. Or, in the alternative metaphor of American political science, political power and wealth must check one another: since armies of ambitious men and women push forward from one side of the boundary, what we require are similar armies pushing forward from the other side. John Kenneth Galbraith developed this metaphor into a theory of "counter-vailing powers."[7] There is also a competing argument according to which freedom is served only if the armies of capitalism are always and everywhere unopposed. But that argument can't be right, for it isn't only equality but freedom, too, that we defend when we block a large number of (the larger number of) possible exchanges. . . .

Money can buy power and influence, as it can buy office, education, honor, and so on, without radically coordinating the various distributive spheres and without eliminating alternative processes and agents. It corrupts distributions without transforming them; and then corrupt distributions coexist with legitimate ones, like prostitution alongside married love. But this is tyranny still, and it can make for harsh forms of domination. And if resistance is less heroic than in totalitarian states, it is hardly less important. . . .

The appropriate arrangements in our own society are those, I think, of a decentralized democratic socialism; a strong welfare state run, in part at least, by local and amateur officials; a constrained market; an open and demystified civil service; independent public schools; the sharing of hard work and free time; the protection of religious and familial life; a system of public honoring and dishonoring free from all considerations of rank or class; workers' control of companies and factories; a politics of parties, movements, meetings, and public debate. But institutions of this sort are of little use unless they are inhabited by men and women who feel at home within them and are prepared to defend them. It may be an argument against complex equality that it requires a strenuous defense — and a defense that begins while equality is still in the making. But this is also an argument against liberty. Eternal vigilance is the price of both.

EQUALITY AND SOCIAL CHANGE

Complex equality might look more secure if we could describe it in terms of the harmony, rather than the autonomy, of spheres. But social meanings and distributions are harmonious only in this respect: that when we see why one good has a certain form and is distributed in a certain way, we also see why another must be different. Precisely because of these differences, however, boundary conflict

is endemic. The principles appropriate to the different spheres are not harmonious with one another; nor are the patterns of conduct and feeling they generate. Welfare systems and markets, offices and families, schools and states are run on different principles: so they should be. The principles must somehow fit together within a single culture; they must be comprehensible across the different companies of men and women. But this doesn't rule out deep strains and odd juxtapositions. Ancient China was ruled by a hereditary divine-right emperor and a meritocratic bureaucracy. One has to tell a complex story to explain that sort of coexistence. A community's culture is the story its members tell so as to make sense of all the different pieces of their social life — and justice is the doctrine that distinguishes the pieces. In any differentiated society, justice will make for harmony only if it first makes for separation. Good fences make just societies.

We never know exactly where to put the fences; they have no natural location. The goods they distinguish are artifacts; as they were made, so they can be remade. Boundaries, then, are vulnerable to shifts in social meaning, and we have no choice but to live with the continual probes and incursions through which these shifts are worked out. Commonly, the shifts are like sea changes, very slow. . . . But the actual boundary revision, when it comes, is likely to come suddenly, as in the creation of a national health service in Britain after the Second World War: one year, doctors were professionals and entrepreneurs; and the next year, they were professionals and public servants. We can map a program of such revisions, based on our current understanding of social goods. We can set ourselves in opposition, as I have done, to the prevailing forms of dominance. But we can't anticipate the deeper changes in consciousness, not in our own community and certainly not in any other.

The social world will one day look different from the way it does today, and distributive justice will take on a different character than it has for us. Eternal vigilance is no guarantee of eternity. . . .

NOTES

1. See John Rawls, *A Theory of Justice* (Cambridge, Mass., 1971): Jürgen Habermas, *Legitimation Crisis,* trans. Thomas McCarthy (Boston, 1975), esp. p. 113; Bruce Ackerman, *Social Justice in the Liberal State* (New Haven, 1980).

2. I have taken the term "communities of character" from Otto Bauer (see *Austro-Marxism* [13], p. 107).

3. Cf. Nozick on "patterning," *Anarchy, State, and Utopia,* pp. 155 ff [this text, Chap 9].

4. See Louis O. Kelso and Mortimer J. Adler, *The Capitalist Manifesto* (New York, 1958), pp. 67–77, for an argument that makes the distribution of wealth on the basis of contribution analogous to the distribution of office on the basis of merit. Economists like Milton Friedman are more cautious, but this is surely the popular ideology of capitalism: success is a deserved reward for "intelligence, resolution, hard work, and a willingness to take risks" (George Gilder, *Wealth and Poverty* [New York, 1981], p. 101).

5. See Robert Nozick's distinction between entitlement and desert, *Anarchy, State, and Utopia* (New York, 1974), pp. 155–60.

6. Karl Marx, *Capital,* ed. Frederick Engels (New York, 1967), p. 194; I have followed the translation and interpretation of Allen W. Wood, "The Marxian Critique of Justice," *Philosophy and Public Affairs* 1 (1972): 263ff.

7. John Kenneth Galbraith, *American Capitalism* (Boston, 1956), chap. 9.

The Ethics of Conditionality in International Debt

Thomas Donaldson

Increasingly, international financial agencies such as the International Monetary Fund (IMF) and the World Bank lend money to developing countries under conditions that aim at economic reforms, a practice dubbed "conditionality." The standard characteristics of conditionality include restrictions on credit from the domestic banking system, currency devaluation, an agreement to liberalize the economy by removing trade restraints and internal economic controls, and the reduction of government deficits.

Let us begin by noting an oddity about such lending. If, as creditor institutions claim, the austerity typically associated with such conditionality is in the interest of the borrowing country, why then does the borrower so often object to it? One would expect a debtor to pay for good advice, not have to be enticed to accept it. This oddity not only draws attention to the fact that lenders and borrowers often disagree about the wisdom of given structural reform programs, but implies that global lenders who structure conditions are responsible for the shape and fairness of those conditions. The conditions imposed are, in the most important sense, *their* conditions. Being fair, in turn, requires a

From Thomas Donaldson, "The Ethics of Conditionality in International Debt," *Millennium: Journal of International Studies* 20, 2, 1991. England.

recognition of the distinction between the interests of those who contract for loans and those who suffer or succeed under their conditions, and while the very poor of a Third World country stand to be harmed or helped dramatically by austerity programs, their interests are seldom material factors in the loan approval process.

I will argue that:

> The economically least well off in a developing country ought not be made worse off, even in the short-to-medium term, as a result of conditions imposed as a part of an international loan arrangement made by an intergovernmental loan agency.

I mean by this that the economically least well off ought not be made worse off as a result of the conditions of the loan relative to the level of welfare they would have achieved without the loan. I shall defend the proposition in two ways: first, by appealing to the moral concept of justice, including Rawlsian constructions of distributive justice and the rights-respecting obligations entailed by the concept of justice; and, second, by appealing to the criterion of consistency in moral analysis. . . .

THE HISTORY OF THE PROBLEM

. . . The IMF has moved from a situation immediately following WW II when its mission was narrowly construed as one of encouraging liberal trade relations and making short term loans to handle balance of payments problems, as its formal charter prescribes, to one where issues of development are taken seriously. Indeed, the IMF has undergone a dramatic shift in its debtor portfolio, and is now frequently the lender of last resort for the developing world.

The reason for the shift lies primarily in the diminished sources of alternative funds.

The shift to a floating currency market in the 1970s and other economic forces spawned credit and balance of payments problems precisely at a time when development funds of the World Bank were becoming scarcer.[1] Into the breach stepped the private banks, who, flush with oil money from the Arab states, by 1980 accounted for 80% of all loans to developing countries, in contrast to only 40% in 1970.[2]

When in 1982 Brazil and Mexico lost their creditworthiness, they and private banks turned to the IMF. The nations did so to obtain desperately needed funds; the banks to establish conditions that would help guarantee repayment of their loans. A global train of national defaults in the 1980s were followed by the imposition of new, creditor-imposed austerity measures. Real interest rates (i.e., interest rates adjusted for inflation) for much of Latin America exceeded 30% during the 1980s, rates at which most economists agree make growth difficult or impossible.[3] Debt repayments, constrained by increasing interest rates as well as austerity, loan-related conditions and worsening terms of trade (especially the lowering commodity prices for a developing country's exports), combined in the 1980s to give Latin America a dismal decade. . . .

Critics complain that because it is easier to cut the prerogatives of the politically weak, austerity programs in Latin America and elsewhere have a disproportionate and negative impact upon the poor.[4] Demand control policies are subject to the obvious objection that when demand is curtailed, the rich and middle class can give up inessentials, while the poor are left to their own resources. There is no doubt that debt puts enormous pressure on governments to cut welfare programs, and when governments fail to meet IMF specified criteria, the Fund is capable of responding quickly.

Criticism of structural adjustment occurs in a context of adjustment programs' growing adherence to free market development strategy. A Fund sponsored study of nine IMF adjustment programs in seven countries[5] revealed that most of the programs contained: "fiscal policies designed to reduce government deficits; monetary and credit policies to restrain domestic credit expansion . . . ; exchange rate policies, combined with domestic pricing policies . . . ; and labor market policies to restrain real wages in the organized sector, and increase the flexibility of wages and labor markets."[6] Structural reform is encouraged through the IMF's Extended Fund Facility. It augments the Fund's old standby arrangements, and allows repayment schedules to be extended to as long as six years (in contrast to the six months-to-a-year format of the standby arrangements) and thus accommodates medium-term, structural reform programs.

During the 1980s the tone of the IMF's response to criticism of austerity programs shifted. In the early 1980s the Fund insisted that issues of distribution were improper objects of its concern, since it dealt with sovereign countries, who were formally responsible for such matters. But recent IMF publications indicate a willingness at least to study distributive issues and to provide the results of its findings to prospective loan recipients. Nevertheless, the Fund has not backed away from its insistence that distributive concerns are ultimately the sole business of the nation state.

The Fund's literature tends to justify austerity programs' impact on the economically least well off in two ways: first, by noting that even short term negative results for the economically least well off, in the context of reasonable economic restructuring, may well bring long-term benefits; and, second, by denying that the short term negative impacts are as severe as critics have claimed. Yet even Fund believers who insist that adjustment programs play a positive role in protecting the long-term interests of the poor, grant that in the short run the poor frequently suffer — and the short term can be devastating.[7]

Let us grant the IMF's denial that short term impact upon the economically least well off is invariably negative. In some countries, for example, small farmers dominate the agricultural scene and are helped by the expanded opportunities brought by either devaluation (in foreign markets) or the removal of price controls. . . . [But] in claiming that the economically least well off of a third world country ought not to suffer, even in the short term as a result of conditions imposed as a part of an international loan arrangement, it is important to specify that this means they ought not be made worse off as a result of the conditions of the loan *relative to the level of welfare they would have achieved without the loan.*

MORAL THEORY

One way of criticizing debt programs is by pointing to their politically destabilizing effects. But this misses the more fundamental moral issue confronting major lending organizations, namely, how do we frame such obligations regardless of political vicissitudes? Also, interestingly enough, recent analysis suggests that the political case against austerity conditions may be overstated. In recent research, Scott Sidell argues that there is no compelling evidence to assert that political instability on average increases in the face of mounting debt and debt conditionality.[8]

Instead, we can find support for the proposition under consideration by appealing to two uniquely moral concepts, namely, that of justice, including distributive justice, and moral consistency.

GENERAL JUSTICE CONSIDERATIONS

We may presume that, at a minimum, any theory of justice will also be a theory which entails that bona fide rights be respected. . . .

Let us use [a] list of fundamental international rights for which I have recently argued, namely:[9]

1. The right to freedom of physical movement
2. The right to ownership of property
3. The right to freedom from torture
4. The right to a fair trial
5. The right to non-discriminatory treatment (i.e., freedom from discrimination on the basis of such characteristics as race or sex.)
6. The right to physical security
7. The right to freedom of speech and association
8. The right to minimal education
9. The right to political participation
10. The right to subsistence

. . . Every right entails a duty, that is, every right entails that other persons and institutions not violate the right. But correlative duties involve more than failing to actively deprive people of the enjoyment of their rights. Shue, for example, notes that three types of correlative duties are possible for any right, namely duties to 1) avoid depriving; 2) help protect from deprivation; and 3) aid the deprived.[10] While it is obvious that the honoring of rights clearly imposes duties of the first kinds, i.e., to avoid depriving directly, it is less obvious, but frequently true, that honoring them involves acts or omissions that help prevent the deprivation of rights. As I have argued elsewhere, multinational corporations have obligations primarily of the first and second kind, while governments have obligations of all three kinds. For example, a multinational corporation has an obligation not to bribe a high government official because it

has an obligation to help protect the right to political participation; and it has an obligation to refrain from hiring eight year old children for permanent, full time labor because it has an obligation to help protect the right to a minimal education. In both instances, the corporation's possible direct denial of the rights to political participation and minimal education is not at issue. What is at issue, rather, is the organization's correlative obligation to protect the rights from deprivation.

Similarly, governmental organizations have a moral obligation frequently to aid the deprived, i.e., the third category of obligation. If citizens are starving to death, most would agree that the local national government is obliged to step in and provide food, at least insofar as it is capable. And if citizens are denied even a minimal education, the government must similarly do what it can to provide one.

The very moral status of an international organization such as the World Bank or the IMF is ambiguous. One might argue that its functions resemble that of private banks to a point where its responsibilities should mirror those of private, not government, institutions. Yet surely this view neglects the obvious fact that these organizations are composed entirely of member nation-states that are themselves government bodies. Hence, in at least one important sense, both bodies are governmental organizations. Space prevents us from undertaking a thoroughgoing discussion of the issue of the moral status of international lending agencies, and, instead, I propose to nuance it by noting that for purposes of assigning moral status, such agencies are partially, but perhaps not wholly, to be understood as government entities. This means that they are at least responsible for shouldering the correlative obligations attaching to rights that are appropriate for private banks (of the first and second kind), and are also responsible for shouldering *some* correlative obligations appropriate to government agencies (of the third kind), although we shall leave unspecified for present purposes what those duties are.

It follows that the IMF and the World Bank have obligations to refrain from directly depriving people of their rights, as well as, in some instances, to help protect such rights from deprivation. In turn, it follows that any loan arrangement which has the effect of depriving or of failing adequately to protect the economically least well off of a given country of their right to subsistence, or their right to a minimal education, is an arrangement that is unjust, and which ought not be undertaken. I follow Henry Shue in defining the right to subsistence as a right to "minimal economic security," entailing, in turn, a right to, e.g., "unpolluted air, unpolluted water, adequate food, adequate clothing, adequate shelter, and minimal preventative public health care."[11] While what counts as a "minimally sufficient" education may be debated, and while it seems likely, moreover, that the specification of the right to a certain level of education will depend at least in part upon the level of economic resources available in a given country, it is reasonable to assume that any action by a corporation which has the effect of, say, blocking the development of a child's ability to read or write will be morally proscribed on the basis of rights.

Hence, we can say that at a minimum the IMF should refuse to engage in an arrangement that will result in conditions in which the economically least well off are unable to possess adequate food, adequate clothing, minimal education, and minimal preventative public health care. This is a simple requirement of justice, and has obvious application to international lending policies. For in many of the poor debtor countries, the economically least well off, if made still worse off, will fall or stay below levels of adequate education and subsistence.

DISTRIBUTIVE JUSTICE CONSIDERATION

The issue of distributive justice is trickier than that of general justice. Distributive justice, a concept which refers to justice in the distribution of goods, may appear to be irrelevant in international contexts. Indeed, it is not uncommon to hear that while justice in the distribution of key goods such as wealth, food, or health care, is an appropriate topic for national contexts, it is not for international contexts. The recent and monumental analysis of distributive justice undertaken by John Rawls[12] explicitly exempts international considerations from the reach of his famous two principles, i.e., (1) that everyone is entitled to maximal liberty, and (2) that inequalities in the distribution of primary goods are unjust unless everyone, including the average person in the worst affected group, stands to benefit. Rawls's reasons for nationalizing distributive justice are tied to his belief that distributive claims can be evaluated meaningfully only against a background scheme of cooperation that yields goods subject to distribution. Since nation-states are customarily the agents that provide the mechanisms necessary for facilitating cooperative arrangements and for pooling and distributing the fruits of such arrangements, and since such mechanisms are conspicuously not provided on the international scale, it seems both idealistic and implausible to speak seriously of distributive justice on an international scale.

Rawls's underlying reasons stem from the notion of the "circumstances of justice" articulated by the English philosopher, David Hume. . . . Hume argued that people usually find themselves in circumstances manifesting four general characteristics which limit the possibility of justice: dependence, moderate scarcity, restrained benevolence, and individual vulnerability. Rawls refers to the circumstances of justice as "the normal conditions under which human cooperation is both possible and necessary," and gives special attention to the condition of dependence and of moderate scarcity, the latter of which he defines as the existence of natural resources "not so abundant that schemes of cooperation become superfluous," nor "conditions so harsh that fruitful ventures must inevitably break down."[13] He explicitly denies that the former characterizes international relations in a way to make the two principles generally relevant, and he may wish to deny in the instance of some third world nations that the latter is applicable.

In the end, however, it seems clear that considerations of distributive justice do apply to international transactions such as lending to poor countries. To begin with, Rawls may be wrong about the scope of his own theory. As Brian Barry often notes, no scheme of cooperation need exist in order to demonstrate the unjustness of allowing toxic air pollution, generated in one country for the benefit of that country, to waft over into the unpolluted atmosphere of a second country.[14] . . .

Hence, one is brought to wonder whether the so-called circumstances of justice are, in truth, necessary either for the meaningful application of such terms as "just" and "unjust," or for the existence of just institutions. For example, it seems at first glance that if people have either an extravagant abundance of material goods, or an extreme scarcity, then issues of justice will not arise. But first impressions may be misleading. Suppose an extravagant abundance of material goods exists; might not questions of justice nonetheless arise over, say, the bestowing of awards in public contests, or in structuring systems of seniority and status? Or, alternatively, suppose that a dramatic scarcity of goods exists. Might not questions of justice arise in determining, say, who should be utterly deprived in order for others to survive?

Yet, even if Rawls were correct in limiting the *general* application of the two principles in the international realm on the grounds of insufficient interdependence, two considerations show that distributive justice is applicable in the specific instance of international loan arrangements. First, the important distribution issues affecting developing countries do not depend on *inter*-national distributive comparisons (distributions *among* nations), but on intra-national comparisons (distributions *within* a nation). Hence Rawls's principles have important application, even when inter-national distributive comparisons are excluded. In saying that the economically least well off of a third world country ought not suffer as a result of a loan arrangement, we are not making a claim about the distribution of resources among all nations of the world, but only about the distribution of a single country's resources.

Second, the mere existence of an international loan arrangement is not only testimony to a cooperative endeavor, but representative of an underlying economic association in which at least the developed and probably also the developing countries benefit. For the developed world to be left without benefit of the commodities and markets provided by the developing countries would certainly be an economic blow. While the relationship may be one of absolute dependence, extreme dependence is not required by the concept of the conditions of justice. And certainly no representative of the IMF has ever suggested that the IMF's activities qualify as *pure* charity, that is, charity of a kind such that the developed nations expect no benefits from virtue of their association. This, in turn, implies a satisfaction of the first condition of justice and the relevance of the concept of distributive justice.

It follows that at least insofar as one accepts Rawls's claim that distributive justice entails the principle that no inequality promoting policy is just if it has the effect of failing to aid the worst off class of person, i.e., the "second principle," then no policy affecting a developing country can be labeled just that makes the economically least well off worse off. Hence, any loan arrangement entered into by the World Bank, the IMF, or any other intergovernmental lending agency which has the effect of increasing the poverty of the very poor in a third world country would fail to satisfy the Rawlsian test of distributive justice.

MORAL CONSISTENCY

The final consideration supporting the proposition under consideration invokes the notion of moral consistency. In particular, I am concerned with the tendency of the international lending agencies to insist on the absolute sovereignty of nation states, especially with respect to the issue of the distributive impact of loan arrangements, and the way such an insistence relates to other accepted policies.

Consider, for example, the widely shared conviction among representatives of global lending agencies that the absence of a European or U.S. style government, including even the absence of a truly democratic government, is insufficient to prohibit such loans and moral grounds. That is, almost every international lending agency agrees that a nation ought not be blacklisted from lending simply for reason of nondemocratic practice. The rationale, sometimes explicit, sometimes implicit, turns on the obvious prospect of benefiting those subject to non-democratic rule even through an arrangement with the rulers themselves. The ruled may benefit even though they did not voluntarily engage in the agreement. . . . The justification of lending to non-democratic regimes presumes that lending agencies can fathom the difference between the interests of the rulers and the ruled, and act accordingly. If so, then there is no reason why they cannot act accordingly also with respect to the issue of distributive justice.

This brings us again to the irony presented at the beginning of the article, namely, why if, as creditor institutions claim, the austerity typically associated with such conditionality is in the interest of the borrowing country, why then does the borrower so often object to it? Again, one would expect a debtor to pay for good advice, not to be enticed to accept it. The answer here, as above, lies in noting that the politicians who contract for loans are not the same persons as those who must suffer or succeed under the loans' conditions, and, as already noted, this distinction is inconsistent with a full reliance on the rationality of decisions made by national governments.

Indeed, the argument that concerns of justice are the exclusive territory of debtor country governments is inconsistent at a still deeper level. Even if we regard international lending arrangements as purely voluntary transactions between consenting parties and leave aside the issue of the contracting rights of governments in contrast to the people they govern, the stipulation of a condition by one party in a proposed voluntary agreement is never regarded as an invasion of the freedom or sovereignty of the other party — since, of course, the other party can voluntarily reject the condition and refuse to engage in the transaction. This is precisely why the loan conditions that are so commonly inserted in international arrangements, i.e., of reducing price controls and inducing monetary restraint, are *not* regarded as a violation of sovereignty. Ordinarily, fiscal policy is regarded as the proper and exclusive province of a sovereign government. The reason why we may not regard the fiscal policy conditions of IMF adjustment agreements to be in violation of national sovereignty is that such conditions are the features of a voluntary statement of reciprocal intent between two sovereign, free agents. But clearly it would be inconsistent to proceed to argue that restrictions on the distributive impact of a given loan arrangement, when set as a condition by an international lending agency to a loan arrangement, violates the national sovereignty of the borrowing country. One cannot have matters both ways.

CONCLUSION

It may be argued that the proposition under consideration *would* be acceptable were it not for the phrase "even in the short to medium term." If the economically least well off must suffer today in order to benefit tomorrow, then how can justice and moral consistency condemn the requisite "medicine"? But this rhetorical question, which poses a hypothetical state of affairs, is misleading, and truth in this instance does not accommodate our hypotheses. First, there is insufficient reason to believe that the economically least well off *must* suffer now in order to achieve their own long term improvement. A social cushion for the poor in austerity programs is an acceptable, much analyzed option. Nor is there any reason to believe that preventing the very poor in the short to medium term from suffering more than they would have in the absence of a loan agreement will shipwreck the future prospects of an adjustment program.

Short term injustice would be more tempting — though even then not justified — if optimistic economic predictions were certain and incorrigible. If we knew for certain that the economically least well off could *only* benefit in the long-term by suffering in the short

term, and that the policies that caused them to suffer would *without question* bring long term benefits, our welfare calculations would be different. Yet, even modern economic theory has not reached the point where it allows epistemological certainty about such propositions in individual cases. We cannot predict with absolute certainty that adjustment programs of a certain kind, whether free market or other, will in a given instance deliver the desired result.

For example, it is doubtful that pricist extremists are right when they say that if only prices could be left to market forces, everything would be fine, and that, in turn, no independent public sector action would be necessary. As Paul Streeten notes, even if prices were allowed to rise to a "natural" level in Tanzania, farmers would not benefit by producing more. In Tanzania, roads are so inadequate that even if farmers produced more in response to higher prices, the crops could not be transported.[15] The problem is one of infrastructure, not prices, and the cooperation of the public authority is essential. . . .

It is also well to remember that justice is not a concept admitting of short-term or long-term qualifications. The logic of the concept of justice does not allow one to trade off justice here for justice there, or to trade off justice now for justice later. If an act or policy is unjust, it must not be undertaken. And it must not be undertaken either now or in the future. . . .

NOTES

1. Irving S. Friedman, "The International Monetary Fund: A Founder's Evaluation," in *The Political Morality of the International Monetary Fund. Ethics and Foreign Policy* (New York: Transaction Books) ed., Robert J. Myers, Vol. 3 (1987), pp. 21–22.
2. Henry B. Schechter, "IMF Conditionality and the International Economy: A U.S. Labor Per-

spective," in *The Political Morality of the International Monetary Fund. Ethics and Foreign Policy* (New York: Transaction Books) ed., Robert J. Myers, Vol. 3 (1987), p. 5.

3. John Williamson, "Reforming the IMF: Different or Better?" in *The Political Morality of the International Monetary Fund. Ethics and Foreign Policy* (New York: Transaction Books) ed., Robert J. Myers, Vol. 3 (1987).

4. Special concern for the poor is evident in the U.S. Catholic Conference Administrative Board in its "Statement on Relieving Third World Debt," *Origins* (October 12, 1989), Vol. 19, 1, 307–314.

5. Chile, the Dominican Republic, Bhana, Kenya, the Philippines, Sri Lanka, and Thailand.

6. Peter Heller, "Fund-Supported Adjustment Programs and the Poor," *Finance & Development* (Washington, The World Bank, December 1988), pp. 2–5. See also the original study, i.e., Peter S. Heller, A. Lans Bovenberg, Thanos Catsambas, *et al*, "The Implications of Fund-Supported Adjustment Programs for Poverty: Experiences in Selected Countries" (Washington: International Monetary Fund, May 1988).

7. Heller, Bovenberg, Catsambas, *et al.*, p. 32.

8. Scott R. Sidell, *The IMF and Third-World Political Instability. Is There a Connection?* (London: The MacMillan Press Ltd., 1988).

9. See especially Thomas Donaldson, *The Ethics of International Business* (New York: Oxford University Press, 1989), chapter 5.

10. Henry Shue, *Basic Rights: Subsistence, Affluence, and U.S. Foreign Policy* (Princeton, N.J.: Princeton University Press, 1980), p. 57.

11. Shue, pp. 20–23.

12. John Rawls, *A Theory of Justice* (Cambridge, Mass.: Harvard University Press, 1971).

13. Ibid., pp. 126–28.

14. Brian Barry, "The Case for a New International Economic Order," in J. Roland Pennock and John W. Chapman, eds., *Ethics, Economics, and the Law: Nomos Vol. XXIV* (New York: New York University Press, 1982).

15. Paul Streeten, "Structural Adjustment: A Survey of the Issues and Options," *World Development,* (Boston University) Vol. 15, No. 12 (Pergamon Journals Ltd., 1987), p. 1474.

William M. Ferguson, Attorney General for the State of Kansas v. Frank C. Skrupa . . . Credit Advisors

Supreme Court of the United States

In this case, . . . we are asked to review the judgment of a three-judge District Court enjoining, as being in violation of the Due Process Clause of the Fourteenth Amendment, a Kansas statute making it a misdemeanor for any person to engage "in the business of debt adjusting" except as an inci-dent to "the lawful practice of law in this state."[1] The statute defines "debt adjusting" as "the making of a contract, express, or implied with a particular debtor whereby the debtor agrees to pay a certain amount of money periodically to the person engaged in the debt adjusting business who shall for a

83 S.Ct. 1028 (1963).

consideration distribute the same among certain specified creditors in accordance with a plan agreed upon."

The complaint, filed by appellee Skrupa doing business as "Credit Advisors," alleged that Skrupa was engaged in the business of "debt adjusting" as defined by the statute, that his business was a "useful and desirable" one, that his business activities were not "inherently immoral or dangerous" or in any way contrary to the public welfare, and that therefore the business could not be "absolutely prohibited" by Kansas. The three-judge court heard evidence by Skrupa tending to show the usefulness and desirability of his business and evidence by the state officials tending to show that "debt adjusting" lends itself to grave abuses against distressed debtors, particularly in the lower income brackets, and that these abuses are of such gravity that a number of States have strictly regulated "debt adjusting" or prohibited it altogether.[2] The court found that Skrupa's business did fall within the Act's proscription and concluded, one judge dissenting, that the Act was prohibitory, not regulatory, but that even if construed in part as regulatory it was an unreasonable regulation of a "lawful business," which the court held amounted to a violation of the Due Process Clause of the Fourteenth Amendment. The court accordingly enjoined enforcement of the statute.[3]

The only case discussed by the court below as support for its invalidation of the statute was *Commonwealth v. Stone*, 191 Pa.Super. 117, 155 A.2d 453 (1959), in which the Superior Court of Pennsylvania struck down a statute almost identical to the Kansas act involved here. In Stone the Pennsylvania court held that the State could regulate, but could not prohibit, a "legitimate" business. Finding debt adjusting, called "budget planning" in the Pennsylvania statute, not to be "against the public interest" and concluding that it could "see no justification for such interference" with this business, the Pennsylvania

court ruled that State's statute to be unconstitutional. In doing so, the Pennsylvania court relied heavily on *Adams v. Tanner*, 244 U.S. 590, 37 S.Ct. 662, 61 L.Ed. 1336 (1917), which held that the Due Process Clause forbids a State to prohibit a business which is "useful" and not "inherently immoral or dangerous to public welfare."

Both the District Court in the present case and the Pennsylvania court in Stone adopted the philosophy of *Adams v. Tanner* and cases like it that it is the province of courts to draw on their own views as to the morality, legitimacy, and usefulness of a particular business in order to decide whether a statute bears too heavily upon that business and by so doing violates due process. Under the system of government created by our Constitution, it is up to legislatures, not courts, to decide on the wisdom and utility of legislation. There was a time when the Due Process Clause was used by this Court to strike down laws which were thought unreasonable, that is, unwise or incompatible with some particular economic or social philosophy. In this manner the Due Process Clause was used, for example, to nullify laws prescribing maximum hours for work in bakeries, *Lochner v. New York*, 198 U.S. 45, 25 S.Ct. 539, 49 L.Ed. 937 (1905), . . . setting minimum wages for women, *Adkins v. Children's Hospital*, 261 U.S. 525, 43 S.Ct. 394, 67 L.Ed. 785 (1923), and fixing the weight of loaves of bread, *Jay Burns Baking Co. v. Bryan*, 264 U.S. 504, 44 S.Ct. 412, 68, L.Ed. 813 (1924). This intrusion by the judiciary into the realm of legislative value judgments was strongly objected to at the time, particularly by Mr. Justice Holmes and Mr. Justice Brandeis. Dissenting from the Court's invalidating a state statute which regulated the resale price of theatre and other tickets, Mr. Justice Holmes said,

"I think the proper course is to recognize that a state Legislature can do whatever it sees fit to do unless it is restrained by some express prohibition in the Constitution of the United States or of the State, and that Courts should be careful not to extend such prohibitions beyond their obvious meaning by reading into them conceptions of public policy that the particular Court may happen to entertain."[4]

And in an earlier case he had emphasized that, "The criterion of constitutionality is not whether we believe the law to be for the public good."[5]

The doctrine that prevailed in Lochner, Coppage, Adkins, Burns, and like cases — that due process authorizes courts to hold laws unconstitutional when they believe the legislature has acted unwisely — has long since been discarded. We have returned to the original constitutional proposition that courts do not substitute their social and economic beliefs for the judgment of legislative bodies, who are elected to pass laws. As this Court stated in a unanimous opinion in 1941, "We are not concerned . . . with the wisdom, need, or appropriateness of the legislation."[6] Legislative bodies have broad scope to experiment with economic problems, and this Court does not sit to "subject the state to an intolerable supervision hostile to the basic principles of our government and wholly beyond the protection which the general clause of the Fourteenth Amendment was intended to secure."[7] It is now settled that States "have power to legislate against what are found to be injurious practices in their internal commercial and business affairs, so long as their laws do not run afoul of some specific federal constitutional prohibition, or of some valid federal law."[8] . . .

We conclude that the Kansas Legislature was free to decide for itself that legislation was needed to deal with the business of debt adjusting. Unquestionably, there are arguments showing that the business of debt adjusting has social utility, but such arguments are properly addressed to the legislature, not to us . . .

Whether the legislature takes for its textbook Adam Smith, Herbert Spencer, Lord Keynes, or some other is no concern of ours.[9] The Kansas debt adjusting statute may be wise or unwise. But relief, if any be needed, lies not with us but with the body constituted to pass laws for the State of Kansas.

Nor is the statute's exception of lawyers a denial of equal protection of the laws to non-lawyers. Statutes create many classifications which do not deny equal protection; it is only "individuous discrimination" which offends the Constitution. The business of debt adjusting gives rise to a relationship of trust in which the debt adjuster will, in a situation of insolvency, be marshalling assets in the manner of a proceeding in bankruptcy. The debt adjuster's client may need advice as to the legality of the various claims against him, remedies existing under state laws governing debtor-creditor relationships, or provisions of the Bankruptcy Act — advice which a non-lawyer cannot lawfully give him. If the State of Kansas wants to limit debt adjusting to lawyers, the Equal Protection Clause does not forbid it. We also find no merit in the contention that the Fourteenth Amendment is violated by the failure of the Kansas statute's title to be as specific as appellee thinks it ought to be under the Kansas Constitution.

Reversed. . . .

NOTES

1. Kan.Gen.Stat. (Supp. 1961) § 21-2464.
2. Twelve other States have outlawed the business of debt adjusting. Fla.Stat.Ann. (1962).
3. *Skrupa v. Sanborn,* 210 F.Supp. 200 (D.C.D. Kan. 1961).
4. *Tyson & Brother, etc. v. Banton,* 273 U.S. 418, 445, 446, 47 S.Ct. 426, 433, 434, 71 L.Ed. 718 (1927) (dissenting opinion). . . .
5. *Adkins v. Children's Hospital,* 261 U.S. 525, 567, 570, 43 S.Ct. 394, 406, 67 L.Ed. 785 (1923) (dissenting opinion). . . .

6. *Olsen v. Nebraska ex rel. Western Reference &
Bond Assn.*, 313 U.S. 236, 246, 61 S.Ct. 862,
865, 85 L.Ed. 1305 (1941). . . .
7. *Sproles v. Binford*, 286 U.S. 374, 388, 52 S.Ct.
581, 585, 76 L.Ed. 1167 (1932). . . .
8. *Lincoln Federal Labor Union, etc. v. Northwestern
Iron & Metal Co.*, 335 U.S. 525, 536, 69 S.Ct.
251, 257, 93 L.Ed. 212 (1949). . . .

9. "The 14th Amendment does not enact Mr.
Herbert Spencer's Social Statics." *Lochner v.
New York*, 198 U.S. 45, 74, 75, 25 S.Ct. 539,
546, 49 L.Ed. 937 (1905) (Holmes, J., dissenting).

CASE 1.   *Baseball Economics*

In December 1981, the Baltimore Orioles hall-of-fame pitcher Jim Palmer gave a newspaper interview in Portland, Oregon. He was highly critical of the system of economic incentives operative in baseball. He argued that money controlled almost all decisions by management and players alike. Many players, he said, "make a lot more money than they should." He argued that the salaries are often determined through "panic" on the part of management, which plans at all cost against a situation in which star players leave and join other teams at increased salary levels. He noted that players make $300,000 to $400,000 in their second year and sign multi-year contracts. This kind of security, he said, leads players to relax and to lose their concentration on skilled performance.

On the same day Palmer gave his interview in Portland, Baseball Commissioner Bowie Kuhn was testifying before a Congressional subcommittee on issues surrounding the costs of cable television. Kuhn described the possible introduction of massive cable television broadcasts of baseball as economically intolerable for the sport. Both gate receipts and network television revenues would decline, he held, and this would be a disaster for a sport already "treading on financial quicksand." Kuhn supported this judgment

with figures to show that only nine of baseball's twenty-six teams had made a profit in the previous year. He argued that the aggregate loss was $25 million. He further contended that cable television would bring competing sporting events into a city without the consent or agreement of anyone in baseball management.

Ted Turner, who owns both Turner Broadcasting System (cable) and the Atlanta Braves baseball team, also testified at the same hearing as Kuhn. "If baseball is in trouble," he said, "it is because they are paying the [superstar] baseball players a million and half dollars a year. . . . There isn't one single example of a proven economic harm from cable television."

Salaries have continued to rise dramatically. A survey of New York Mets' baseball fans in 1992 indicated that most thought the salary figures outrageous and that the money should be more evenly spread across the players. In 1995, fourteen years after Palmer's interview and this testimony before Congress, players' salaries had escalated beyond what Palmer, Kuhn, or Turner could have then imagined. The New York Yankees led the league with a record breaking payroll of $58.1 million. For the 1995 season, the average player's salary was over $1.2 million.

This case was prepared by Tom L. Beauchamp and Jeff Greene, using articles from numerous newspapers and journals.

Frank Thomas of the Chicago White Sox and Ken Griffey, Jr of the Seattle Mariners were both making over $7 million dollars for the season. The Toronto Blue Jays not only were giving $8 million dollars to David Cone, but also were paying Joe Carter $7.5 million for his services. Finally, the Detroit Tigers were paying slugger Cecil Fielder a whopping $9.2 million to lead a team low in the standings and in gate receipts.

With the explosion of salaries it has become harder and harder for the small market teams to compete, because the big players consistently go for big money. However, in 1994 the Montreal Expos proved, at least for that season, that in some cases more than just money matters. Their $18.6 million payroll was the second lowest in the league, yet when the season ended (because of a strike), they were six games ahead of everyone in the National League, including the Atlanta Braves. However, their dream season would be short-lived because they needed approximately $30 million merely to keep the team together, according to fair market value. Since the club could not even come close to the $30 million figure, it was inevitable that they would lose many of their best players; and they did. "I think that the world realizes that our market cannot support that sort of payroll," said Bill Stoneman, Expos' vice president of baseball operations. "We'd like to re-sign all of our players, but we'd like to be in business a year from now."

Montreal's problem is not unique. Pittsburgh had to break up one of the National League's best teams in the 1990s, and San Diego had to dump its best talent just as the club seemed poised to become a serious contender. It now seems clear that if some sort of revenue sharing does not come into effect, the small market teams will not be able to compete on equal terms.

Questions

1. Does a team like the New York Yankees have an obligation to share some of their revenues with other teams that have a weaker economic base?
2. Do Bowie Kuhn's comments reflect a libertarian or a utilitarian theory of justice?
3. If Peter Singer's proposals (in this chapter) were followed, what would be the obligations of major league baseball players to help the poor both within and outside their own country?

CASE 2. *Selling Cyclamates Abroad*

In 1969 the Food and Drug Administration banned cyclamates, a popular sweetening agent, from the U.S. market. The evidence regarding dangers presented by cyclamates was heavily discussed at the time, producing considerable scientific disagreement. What some persons regarded as telling animal studies were regarded by others as inconclusive studies. Nonetheless, by FDA criteria cyclamates presented an unacceptable level of risk to the public.

After the ban was in place, Libby, McNeil, & Libby sold approximately 300,000 cases of cyclamate-sweetened fruit to customers in Germany, Spain, and other countries where cyclamates had not been banned and were still in use. James Nadler, Libby's vice president for international relations, announced

This case was prepared by Tom L. Beauchamp.

the following justification for these sales abroad: "Fortunately the older civilizations of the world are more deliberate about judging momentary fads that are popular in the United States from time to time." (*Wall Street Journal,* February 11, 1971.)

Such sales abroad are common practice in U.S. business when products have been banned in the home country but not in other countries. In some cases involving prescription drugs, the products are not *banned* in the United States but are required to carry strong warnings about negative side effects. If such warnings are not required in other countries, the drugs are shipped from the United States and sold without attached warnings.

This practice is not unilateral. In some cases, drugs and other products banned in a foreign country are exported to the United States by the manufacturers in the country of origin. In effect, this is standard business practice throughout the world.

This practice has been heavily criticized as unjust to consumers, especially when warnings are omitted that could easily be included. Concerning Libby's decision to ship the cyclamates, Robert L. Heilbroner commented as follows: "The momentary fad to which [Vice President Nadler] was referring was the upshot of nineteen years of increasingly alarming laboratory findings concerning the effects of cyclamates on chick embryos — effects that produced grotesque malformations similar to those induced by thalidomide." (*In the Name of Profit,* Doubleday & Co., 1970, p. 12.)

Questions

1. Does Heilbroner seem to be accusing Libby of an injustice? If so, what principle of justice does he think the company violated?
2. Do you think Singer or Nozick would agree with Heilbroner?
3. Assuming that it is standard business practice to do what Libby did, is Libby's announced justification adequate?
4. Is it unjust to market these products abroad without warning labels?

CASE 3. *Cocaine at the Fortune-500 Level*

Roberto, a pure libertarian in moral and political philosophy, is deeply impressed by his reading of Robert Nozick's account of justice. He lives in Los Angeles and teaches philosophy at a local university. Roberto is also a frequent user of cocaine, which he enjoys immensely and provides to friends at parties. Neither he nor any of his close friends is addicted. Over the years Roberto has become tired of teaching philosophy and now has an opportunity, through old friends who live in Peru, to become a middleman in the cocaine business. Although he is disturbed about the effects cocaine has on some persons, he has never witnessed these effects firsthand. He is giving his friends' business offer serious consideration.

Roberto's research has told him the following: Selling cocaine is a $29 billion plus industry. Although he is interested primarily in a Peruvian connection, his research has shown conclusively that the Colombian cartel

This case was prepared by Tom L. Beauchamp and updated by Jeff Greene, based on accounts in *The Wall Street Journal* and *The Economist.*

alone is large enough to place it among the Fortune 500 corporations. Between 0.75 and 1.1 million jobs in Colombia, Bolivia, and Peru combined are in the cocaine industry — over 5 percent of the entire work force in these countries. These figures are roughly comparable to the dollar and workforce figures for the diamond industry throughout the world.

Peruvian President Alan Garcia once described cocaine as Latin America's "only successful multinational." It can be and has been analyzed in traditional business categories, with its own entrepreneurs, chemists, laboratories, employment agencies, small organizations, distribution systems, market giants, growth phases, and so forth. Cocaine's profit margins have narrowed in some markets, while expanding in others. It often seeks new markets in order to expand its product line. For example, in the mid-1980s "crack" — a potent form of smoked cocaine — was moved heavily into new markets in Europe. Between the mid-1960s and the early-1990s the demand for cocaine grew dramatically because of successful supply and marketing. Middlemen in Miami and Los Angeles were established to increase already abundant profits. Heavy investments were made in airplanes, efficient modes of production, training managers, and regular schedules of distribution. In the late 1980s there was a downturn in cocaine consumption after the deaths of two prominent athletes. In the early 1990s the market recovered slightly before again slipping in the mid-1990s. However, cocaine remains an enormously powerful industry in many countries.

Roberto sees the cocaine industry as not being subject to taxes, tariffs, or government regulations other than those pertaining to its illegality. It is a pure form of the free market in which supply and demand control transactions. This fact about the business appeals to Roberto, as it seems perfectly suited to his libertarian views. He is well aware that there are severe problems of coercion and violence in some parts of the industry, but he is quite certain that the wealthy clientele whom he would supply in Los Angeles would neither abuse the drug nor redistribute it to others who might be harmed. Roberto is confident that his Peruvian associates are honorable and that he can escape problems of violence, coercion, and abusive marketing. However, he has just read a newspaper story that Cocaine-use emergencies — especially those involving cocaine-induced heart attacks — have tripled in the last five years. It is only this fact that has given him pause before deciding to enter the cocaine business. He views these health emergencies as unfortunate but not unfair outcomes of the business. Therefore, it is his humanity and not his theory of justice that gives him pause.

Questions

1. Would a libertarian — as Roberto thinks — say that the cocaine business is not unfair so long as no coercion is involved and the system is a pure function of supply and demand?
2. Does justice demand that cocaine be outlawed, or is this not a matter of justice at all? Are questions of justice even meaningful when the activity is beyond the boundaries of law?
3. Is the distinction Roberto draws between what is unfortunate and what is unfair relevant to a decision about whether an activity is just?

CASE 4. *Covering the Costs of Health Care*

Medicare and Medicaid were passed into law in the United States to provide coverage for health care costs in populations that could not afford adequate coverage, especially the elderly, poor, and disabled. Then, as now, health care technology produced by major corporations was rapidly being developed and costs were skyrocketing. In 1994, $140 billion was spent on Medicare. Current trends show little letup in this explosion of costs. In 1994 Medicare and Medicaid comprised 16.4% of the total federal budget. By the year 2003 this figure is expected to balloon to approximately 26.4%. Total national expenditures on health care costs in the United States for 1994 were 14% of the Gross Domestic Product. For U.S. corporations and individuals, health care has become a burdensome expense.

With over 37.4 million Americans uninsured, health care costs have been under intense study by many politicians and agencies. In an effort to limit future increases in physician costs, the Omnibus Budget Reconciliation Act of 1989 created a Medicare Fee Schedule that affected 34.7 million U.S. citizens. This schedule attempts to redistribute payments across specialties in medicine and geographic areas of the country. The legislation called for this restructuring to be phased in over a five-year period from 1992 to 1996. In passing the legislation, members of Congress agreed that Medicare's former payment policies fueled unacceptable increases in expenditure for health care services. Neither the old legislation nor the new covers the kind of catastrophic illness that can wipe out a family's assets and put a family in lifetime debt.

It has been demonstrated that there is substantial variation across the United States in payment rates for services. Urban, specialist, and in-patient services are typically much higher than rural, generalist, and ambulatory services. Surgeons make more money than those in other specialties. It has been widely agreed that these differentials are independent of quality of services, depending more on urban location, the high costs of specialists, and the like. A large supply of physicians in a single location does not stimulate competition and drive prices down; instead, higher fees for physician services tend to be the norm. Social scientists who have studied the changes made in the Omnibus Budget Reconciliation Act of 1989 predict that large redistributions of Medicare payments among specialties will occur, thus changing longstanding patterns in physicians' salaries.

When Bill Clinton came into office, he promised major reforms in the health care system. The Clinton plan, headed by first lady Hillary Clinton, attempted to steer the nation towards serious health care reform. The idea was to eliminate waste and inflated prices, and to give health care access to all — so called universal access. However, with many of the economic consequences falling on the business community, the Clinton plan met strong criticism. Private interests spent over $300 million and Republicans fought hard to kill the bill, and they succeeded.

Many believed that the Clinton plan did not adequately handle the primary reason for continued increases in health care costs, namely advances in technology that push the growth of costs in the health care industry much higher than costs in the rest of the

---

This case was prepared by Tom L. Beauchamp and Jeff Greene.

economy. Consider a typical case, involving a man named Toney Kincard. For ten years he was tortured by over six hundred seizures a week. Kincard was unable to carry on a conversation, eat dinner with his family, or even shower unsupervised. Despite thousands of dollars spent in drug therapy, he lost both his job and his driver's license. In 1989 he became the second person to try a new product, the Vogus Nerve Stimulator. Since his $50,000 outlay to receive this product, he has been seizure-free and says, "The stimulator was the best thing that happened to my life. It was worth everything it cost."

There is little doubt that such expensive technology is invaluable for improving the lives of many people. However, these products will continue to drive up the price of health care for everyone. If antibiotics had never been discovered, many people would die of pneumonia; now they receive antibiotics and then will die later of a costlier disease. Another example is the discovery in 1980 of the drug cyclosporine, which prevents the body's immune system from rejecting organ transplants. In 1980 the number of liver transplants totaled 15; however, with the help of cyclosporine, this figure jumped to 3,056 in 1992, at a minimum price of $200,000 per transplant. Experts believe that advances in molecular biology and genetic therapy, among many other technologies, will continue to propel the cost of health care in the future. Unless access to high-cost, life-extending technology is rationed, health care costs will continue to increase rapidly.

Questions

1. Is a nation obligated to provide quality health care for the elderly who otherwise could afford no care? Is the obligation unrelated to the ability to pay?

2. Should health care be distributed purely on a free-market basis? Should everyone have access to even the highest priced procedures?

3. Is Medicare justifiable on either utilitarian or egalitarian premises of justice?

4. Would a communitarian approve of Medicare even if he or she did not think the system comprehensive enough? Are libertarians and communitarians necessarily in opposition on the question of state-supported systems of health care coverage?

5. Is it better to extend one person's life a few months at the cost of $200,000 or to spend the money on preventive health care measures such as immunization shots?

Suggested Supplementary Readings

Concepts and Principles of Justice

BEAUCHAMP, TOM L., *Philosophical Ethics.* 2nd ed. New York: McGraw-Hill, 1991. Chaps. 8–9.

BENN, STANLEY I. "Justice." In Vol. 4 of *Encyclopedia of Philosophy,* edited by Paul Edwards. New York: Macmillan and Free Press, 1967.

CAMPBELL, TOM. *Justice.* London: Macmillan, 1988.

FEINBERG, JOEL. "Justice and Personal Desert." In *Nomos 6: Justice,* edited by Carl J. Friedrich and John W. Chapman. New York: Atherton Press, 1963.

KIPNIS, KENNETH, and DIANA T. MEYERS. *Economic Justice.* Totowa, N.J.: Rowman and Allanheld, 1985.

KYMLICKA, WILL, ed. *Justice in Political Philosophy: Schools of Thought in Politics.* 2 vols. Ashgate, Brookfield, 1992.

Egalitarian Theories

BARRY, BRIAN. *Theories of Justice.* Berkeley: University of California Press, 1989.

CHRISTMAN, JOHN P. *The Myth of Property: Toward an Egalitarian Theory of Ownership.* New York: Oxford University Press, 1994.

DANIELS, NORMAN, ed. *Reading Rawls: Critical Studies of a Theory of Justice.* New York: Basic Books, 1975.

POGGE, THOMAS W. "An Egalitarian Law of Peoples." *Philosophy and Public Affairs* 23 (Summer 1994): 195–224.

POGGE, THOMAS W. *Realizing Rawls.* Ithaca, NY: Cornell University Press, 1991.

RAWLS, JOHN. *Justice as Fairness: A Guided Tour.* Cambridge, MA: Harvard University, 1989; unpublished monograph.

RAWLS, JOHN. "Reply to Alexander and Musgrave." *Quarterly Journal of Economics* 88 (1974): 633–55.

Libertarian Theories

FRIEDMAN, MILTON. *Capitalism and Freedom.* Chicago: University of Chicago Press, 1962.

HAYEK, FRIEDRICH. *Individualism and Economic Order.* Chicago: University of Chicago Press, 1948.

HAYEK, FRIEDRICH. *The Mirage of Social Justice. Vol. 2, Law, Legislation, and Liberty.* Chicago: University of Chicago Press, 1976.

MACK, ERIC. "Liberty and Justice." In *Justice and Economic Distribution,* edited by John Arthur and William Shaw. Englewood Cliffs, NJ: Prentice Hall, 1978.

NAGEL, THOMAS. "Libertarianism Without Foundations." *Yale Law Journal* 85 (1975).

Utilitarian Theories

FREY, R. G., ed. *Utility and Rights.* Minneapolis: University of Minnesota Press, 1984.

GOLDMAN, ALAN H. "Business Ethics: Profits, Utilities, and Moral Rights." *Philosophy and Public Affairs* 9 (1980): 260–86.

GRIFFIN, JAMES. *Well-Being: Its Meaning, Measurement, and Importance.* Oxford, England: Clarendon Press, 1986.

HARDIN, RUSSELL. *Morality within the Limits of Reason.* Chicago: University of Chicago Press, 1988.

POSNER, RICHARD A. *The Economics of Justice.* 2nd ed. Cambridge, MA: Harvard University Press, 1983.

SEN, AMARTYA, and BERNARD WILLIAMS, eds. *Utilitariansim and Beyond.* Cambridge, England: Cambridge University Press, 1982.

Communitarian Theories

AVINERI, SHLOMO, and AVNER DE-SHALIT, eds., *Communitarianism and Individualism.* Oxford: Oxford University Press, 1992.

BUCHANAN, ALLEN. "Assessing the Communitarian Critique of Liberalism." *Ethics* 99 (1989).

FREEDEN, MICHAEL. "Human Rights and Welfare: A Communitarian View." *Ethics* 100 (1990).

GUTMANN, AMY. "Communitarian Critics of Liberalism." *Philosophy and Public Affairs* 14 (1985).

KYMLICKA, WILL. *Liberalism, Community, and Culture.* Oxford, England: Clarendon Press, 1989.

MACINTYRE, ALASDAIR. *Whose Justice? Which Rationality?* Notre Dame, IN: Notre Dame University Press, 1988.

RASMUSSEN, DAVID, ed. *Universalism vs. Communitarianism: Contemporary Debates in Ethics.* Cambridge, MA: MIT Press, 1990.

ROSENBLUM, NANCY L. ed. *Liberalism and the Moral Life.* Cambridge, MA: Harvard University Press, 1989.

SANDEL, MICHAEL J. "Democrats and Community." *The New Republic* (February 22, 1988).

WALLACH, JOHN R. "Liberals, Communitarians, and the Tasks of Political Theory." *Political Theory* 15 (1987).

WALZER, MICHAEL. "The Communitarian Critique of Liberalism." *Political Theory* 18 (1990).

Issues in International Markets, Plant Closings, and Social Policy

BOWIE, NORMAN. "Fair Markets." *Journal of Business Ethics* 7 (1988).

BUCHANAN, ALLEN. *Ethics, Efficiency and the Market.* Totowa, NJ: Rowman and Allanheld, 1985.

COPP, DAVID. "The Right to an Adequate Standard of Living: Justice, Autonomy, and the Basic Needs." *Social Philosophy and Policy* 9 (Winter 1992): 231–61.

EHRENBERG, RONALD G., and GEORGE H. JAKUBSON. "Why Warn? Plant Closing Legislation." *Regulation* 13 (Summer 1990).

KINIKI, ANGELO, and others. "Socially Responsible Plant Closings." *Personnel Administrator* 32 (June 1987).

KOVACH, KENNETH A., and PETER E. MILLSPAUGH. "Plant Closings." *Business Horizons* 30 (March-April 1987).

LIPPKE, RICHARD L. "Justice and Insider Trading." *Journal of Applied Philosophy* 10 (1993): 215–26.

LUPER-FOY, STEVEN. "Justice and Natural Resources." *Environmental Values* 1 (Spring 1992): 47–64.

LUPER-FOY, STEVEN. *Problems of International Justice.* Boulder, CO: Westview Press, 1988.

MILLSPAUGH, PETER E. "Plant Closing Ethics Root in American Law." *Journal of Business Ethics* 9 (August 1990).

"Note: Resurrecting Economic Rights: The Doctrine of Economic Due Process Reconsidered." *Harvard Law Review* 103 (1990).

NOWLIN, WILLIAM A., and GEORGE M. SULLIVAN. "The Plant Closing Law: Worker Protection or Government Interference?" *Industrial Management* 31 (November–December 1989).

PRATT, CORNELIUS B. "Multinational Corporate Social Policy Process for Ethical Responsibility in Sub-Saharan Africa." *Journal of Business Ethics* 10 (July 1991): 527–41.

SPINELLO, RICHARD A. "Ethics, Pricing and the Pharmaceutical Industry." *Journal of Business Ethics* 11 (August 1992): 617–26.

STEINER, HILLEL. "Three Just Taxes." In *Arguing for Basic Income,* edited by Philippe Van Parijs. New York: Verso, 1992.